FAR FC

2015

**FEDERAL AVIATION REGULATIONS
FOR FLIGHT CREW**

Rules for Part 121 and 135 Operators, Career Aviators, and Fractional Ownership Programs

U.S. Department of Transportation
From Titles 14 and 49 of the Code of Federal Regulations

Updated and Published by

asa

Aviation Supplies & Academics, Inc.
Newcastle, Washington

FAR Flight Crew
(Federal Aviation Regulations for Flight Crew)
2015 Edition

Aviation Supplies & Academics, Inc.
7005 132nd Place SE
Newcastle, Washington 98059-3153

© 2014 Aviation Supplies & Academics, Inc.

This publication contains current regulations as of June 11, 2014.
None of the material in this publication supersedes any documents,
procedures, or regulations issued by the Federal Aviation Administration.

Visit the FAA's website to review changes to the regulations:
http://www.faa.gov/regulations_policies/faa_regulations/

Visit ASA's website to sign-up for free FAR/AIM Update subscription service:
http://www.asa2fly.com/farupdate

ASA does not claim copyright on any material published herein that was
taken from United States government sources.

ASA-15-FAR-FC
ISBN 978-1-61954-149-8

Printed in the United States of America
2015   2014   9   8   7   6   5   4   3   2   1

Stay informed of aviation industry happenings	**Website** www.asa2fly.com **Updates** www.asa2fly.com/farupdate **Twitter** www.twitter.com/asa2fly **Facebook** www.facebook.com/asa2fly

Introduction
2015 FAR/AIM • FAR for Flight Crew • FAR for AMT

ASA has been supplying the standard reference of the industry, the FAR/AIM Series, for three decades. The 2015 series continues to provide information directly from the Federal Aviation Regulations and the *Aeronautical Information Manual*. Each regulation Part is preceded by a table of contents. Changes since last year's printing are identified on Page v and in the table of contents for each regulation Part (in bold and marked with an asterisk), as well as within the text for quick reference (changed text is indicated with a bold line in the margin). In the AIM, changes are explained in lists at the beginning, and with bold lines in the margins. It is recommended you familiarize yourself with all the changes to identify those that affect your aviation activities.

Changes affecting the regulations can take place daily; the AIM changes every 6 months. ASA tracks all changes and offers you two options for free **Updates**:

- Updates are posted on the ASA website that you can download for free—go to **www.asa2fly.com/farupdate**
- You may sign up on our website for ASA's free service to have Update notices automatically emailed to you

Visit the FAA website at **www.faa.gov** to review Advisory Circulars (AC), Notices of Proposed Rulemaking (NPRM), current regulations, FSDO contact details, and FAA Orders and publications. Pilots operating internationally should be familiar with Customs and Border Patrol regulations, which can be found at **www.cbp.gov**.

Although ASA is not a government agency, and we do not write the regulations or the AIM, we do work closely with the FAA. Questions or concerns can be forwarded to our attention, and we will in turn pass the comments on to the FAA. They are interested in user-feedback and your comments could foster improvements in the regulations which affect the entire industry.

FAR/AIM Comments
Aviation Supplies & Academics, Inc.
7005 132nd Place SE
Newcastle, Washington 98059

Internet www.asa2fly.com
Fax 425.235.0128
Email asa@asa2fly.com

What's Changed Since Last Year?

Changes since last year's printing of the book are noted in the table of contents of each Part with an asterisk and bold title:

Example:

> ***61.5 Certificates and ratings issued under this part.**

The updated text within the context of the regulation is indicated by a bold line in the margin:

> | **(a)** The following certificates are issued under this part to an applicant who satisfactorily accomplishes the training and certification requirements for the certificate sought:
> | (1) Pilot certificates—
> | (i) Student pilot.
> | (ii) Sport pilot.
> | (iii) Recreational pilot.
> | (iv) Private pilot.
> | (v) Commercial pilot.
> | (vi) Airline transport pilot.
> | (2) Flight instructor certificates.
> | (3) Ground instructor certificates.

How to Identify the Currency of the Regulations

In each Part following the Table of Contents is a Source, with the date of origin for that regulation.

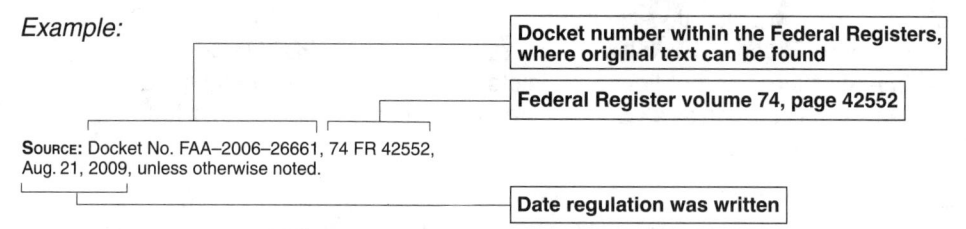

Example:

SOURCE: Docket No. FAA–2006–26661, 74 FR 42552, Aug. 21, 2009, unless otherwise noted.

- Docket number within the Federal Registers, where original text can be found
- Federal Register volume 74, page 42552
- Date regulation was written

If a change has taken place since the original Regulation was written, it is noted at the end of the regulation.

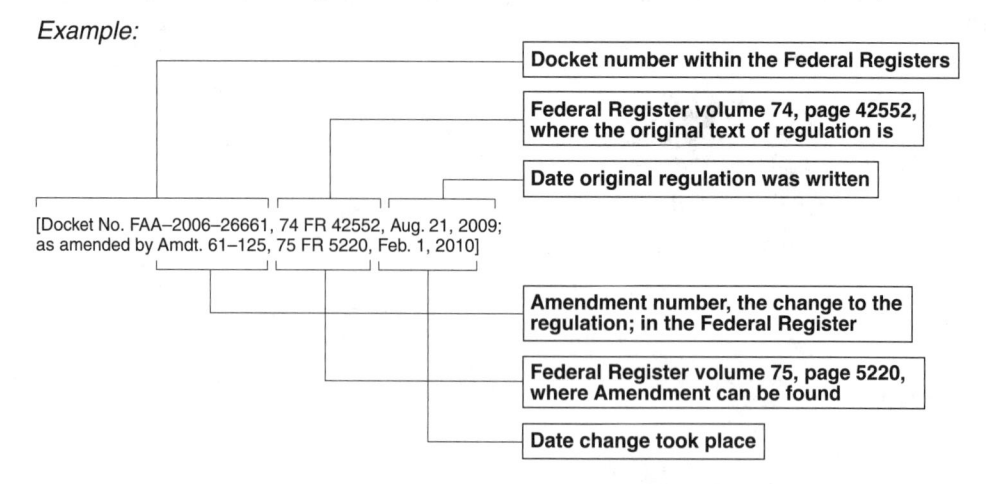

Example:

[Docket No. FAA–2006–26661, 74 FR 42552, Aug. 21, 2009; as amended by Amdt. 61–125, 75 FR 5220, Feb. 1, 2010]

- Docket number within the Federal Registers
- Federal Register volume 74, page 42552, where the original text of regulation is
- Date original regulation was written
- Amendment number, the change to the regulation; in the Federal Register
- Federal Register volume 75, page 5220, where Amendment can be found
- Date change took place

iv   ASA

Summary of Major Changes
Since the 2014 Book was Published

14 CFR

Parts 61, 121, 135, 141, and 142 ("HR 5900 rule change")
- New certification and qualification requirements for pilots in air carrier operations and airline transport pilot (ATP) certificates.

Part 117, 121
- The FAA is correcting the final flightcrew member duty and rest rule published on January 4, 2012.

Part 120, 135
- This final rule implements or modifies operational procedures, equipment requirements, pilot testing, alternate airports, and weather minimums associated with helicopter air ambulance, commercial helicopter, and general aviation helicopter operations.

Part 121
- Corrections to the operating regulations for flight data recorder recording rates in three different appendices.
- This final rule revises the training requirements for pilots in air carrier operations by emphasizing the development of pilots' manual handling skills and adding safety-critical tasks such as recovery from stall and upset.
- This action amends the FAA's rules for permitting use of portable oxygen concentrator (POC) devices on board aircraft, provided certain conditions in the SFAR are met.
- This final rule will prohibit flightcrew members in operations under part 121 from using a personal wireless communications device or laptop computer for personal use while at their duty station on the flight deck while the aircraft is being operated.

Part 121, 135
- The FAA is correcting a final rule which unintentionally required a pilot serving as a second in command in part 135 commuter operations to have an airline transport pilot certificate and an aircraft type rating, and a pilot in command in part 135 commuter operations to have 1,000 hours of air carrier experience.
- This rulemaking amends and harmonizes minimum altitudes for use of autopilots for transport category airplanes. It also enables the operational use of advanced autopilot and navigation systems by incorporating the capabilities of current and future autopilots, flight guidance systems, and GNSS guidance systems while protecting the continued use of legacy systems at current autopilot minimum use altitudes.

49 CFR

Part 175
- This final rule corrects editorial errors and amends certain requirements in response to administrative appeals submitted by persons affected by certain rules published in the Federal Register.

Note: Changes affecting the regulations can take place daily. ASA tracks all changes and posts them on the ASA website so you always have the most current information. To view the rules currently in effect and to have Update notices automatically emailed to you, visit: **www.asa2fly.com/farupdate**

Pilot's Bill of Rights

The following legislative excerpt was signed into law by the U.S. Congress. It is law pertinent to the aviation industry that is outside the usual placement of Title 14 or 49 Code of Federal Regulations, but is included here since it has a direct effect on all pilots. Current congressional bills can be found **http://www.govtrack.us/congress/bills/**.

Public Law 112–153
112th Congress

An Act

To amend title 49, United States Code, to provide rights for pilots, and for other purposes.

Be it enacted by the Senate and House of Representatives of the United States of America in Congress assembled,

SECTION 1. SHORT TITLE.

This Act may be cited as the "Pilot's Bill of Rights".

SEC. 2. FEDERAL AVIATION ADMINISTRATION ENFORCEMENT PROCEEDINGS AND ELIMINATION OF DEFERENCE.

(a) IN GENERAL.—Any proceeding conducted under subpart C, D, or F of part 821 of title 49, Code of Federal Regulations, relating to denial, amendment, modification, suspension, or revocation of an airman certificate, shall be conducted, to the extent practicable, in accordance with the Federal Rules of Civil Procedure and the Federal Rules of Evidence.

(b) ACCESS TO INFORMATION.—

(1) IN GENERAL.—Except as provided under paragraph (3), the Administrator of the Federal Aviation Administration (referred to in this section as the "Administrator") shall provide timely, written notification to an individual who is the subject of an investigation relating to the approval, denial, suspension, modification, or revocation of an airman certificate under chapter 447 of title 49, United States Code.

(2) INFORMATION REQUIRED.—The notification required under paragraph (1) shall inform the individual—

(A) of the nature of the investigation;

(B) that an oral or written response to a Letter of Investigation from the Administrator is not required;

(C) that no action or adverse inference can be taken against the individual for declining to respond to a Letter of Investigation from the Administrator;

(D) that any response to a Letter of Investigation from the Administrator or to an inquiry made by a representative of the Administrator by the individual may be used as evidence against the individual;

(E) that the releasable portions of the Administrator's investigative report will be available to the individual; and

(F) that the individual is entitled to access or otherwise obtain air traffic data described in paragraph (4).

(3) EXCEPTION.—The Administrator may delay timely notification under paragraph (1) if the Administrator determines that such notification may threaten the integrity of the investigation.

(4) ACCESS TO AIR TRAFFIC DATA.—

(A) FAA AIR TRAFFIC DATA.—The Administrator shall provide an individual described in paragraph (1) with timely access to any air traffic data in the possession of the Federal Aviation Administration that would facilitate the individual's ability to productively participate in a proceeding relating to an investigation described in such paragraph.

(B) AIR TRAFFIC DATA DEFINED.—As used in subparagraph (A), the term "air traffic data" includes—

(i) relevant air traffic communication tapes;
(ii) radar information;
(iii) air traffic controller statements;
(iv) flight data;
(v) investigative reports; and
(vi) any other air traffic or flight data in the Federal Aviation Administration's possession that would facilitate the individual's ability to productively participate in the proceeding.

(C) GOVERNMENT CONTRACTOR AIR TRAFFIC DATA.—

(i) IN GENERAL.—Any individual described in paragraph (1) is entitled to obtain any air traffic data that would facilitate the individual's ability to productively participate in a proceeding relating to an investigation described in such paragraph from a government contractor that provides operational services to the Federal Aviation Administration, including control towers and flight service stations.

(ii) REQUIRED INFORMATION FROM INDIVIDUAL.—The individual may obtain the information described in clause (i) by submitting a request to the Administrator that—

(I) describes the facility at which such information is located; and
(II) identifies the date on which such information was generated.

(iii) PROVISION OF INFORMATION TO INDIVIDUAL.—If the Administrator receives a request under this subparagraph, the Administrator shall—

(I) request the contractor to provide the requested information; and
(II) upon receiving such information, transmitting the information to the requesting individual in a timely manner.

(5) TIMING.—Except when the Administrator determines that an emergency exists under section 44709(c)(2) or 46105(c), the Administrator may not proceed against an individual that is the subject of an investigation described in paragraph (1) during the 30-day period beginning on the date on which the air traffic data required under paragraph (4) is made available to the individual.

(c) AMENDMENTS TO TITLE 49.—

(1) AIRMAN CERTIFICATES.—Section 44703(d)(2) of title 49, United States Code, is amended by striking "but is bound by all validly adopted interpretations of laws and regulations the Administrator carries out unless the Board finds an interpretation is arbitrary, capricious, or otherwise not according to law".

(2) AMENDMENTS, MODIFICATIONS, SUSPENSIONS, AND REVOCATIONS OF CERTIFICATES.—Section 44709(d)(3) of such title is amended by striking "but is bound by all validly adopted interpretations of laws and regulations the Administrator carries out and of written agency policy guidance available to the public related to sanctions to be imposed under this section unless the Board finds an interpretation is arbitrary, capricious, or otherwise not according to law".

(3) REVOCATION OF AIRMAN CERTIFICATES FOR CONTROLLED SUBSTANCE VIOLATIONS.—Section 44710(d)(1) of such title is amended by striking "but shall be bound by all validly adopted interpretations of laws and regulations the Administrator carries out and of written agency policy guidance available to the public related to sanctions to be imposed under this section unless the Board finds an interpretation is arbitrary, capricious, or otherwise not according to law".

(d) APPEAL FROM CERTIFICATE ACTIONS.—

(1) IN GENERAL.—Upon a decision by the National Transportation Safety Board upholding an order or a final decision by the Administrator denying an airman certificate under section 44703(d) of title 49, United States Code, or imposing a punitive civil action or an emergency order of revocation under subsections (d) and (e) of section 44709 of such title, an individual substantially affected by an order of the Board may, at the individual's election, file an appeal in the United States district court in which the individual resides or in which the action in question occurred, or in the United States District Court for the District of Columbia. If the individual substantially affected by an order of the Board elects not to file an appeal in a United States district court, the individual may file an appeal in an appropriate United States court of appeals.

(2) EMERGENCY ORDER PENDING JUDICIAL REVIEW.—Subsequent to a decision by the Board to uphold an Administrator's emergency order under section 44709(e)(2) of title 49, United States Code, and absent a stay of the enforcement of that order by the Board, the emergency order of amendment, modification, suspension, or revocation of a certificate shall remain in effect, pending the exhaustion of an appeal to a Federal district court as provided in this Act.

(e) STANDARD OF REVIEW.—

(1) IN GENERAL.—In an appeal filed under subsection (d) in a United States district court, the district court shall give full independent review of a denial, suspension, or revocation ordered by the Administrator, including substantive independent and expedited review of any decision by the Administrator to make such order effective immediately.

(2) EVIDENCE.—A United States district court's review under paragraph (1) shall include in evidence any record of the proceeding before the Administrator and any record of the proceeding before the National Transportation Safety Board, including hearing testimony, transcripts, exhibits, decisions, and briefs submitted by the parties.

SEC. 3. NOTICES TO AIRMEN.

(a) IN GENERAL.—

(1) DEFINITION.—In this section, the term "NOTAM" means Notices to Airmen.

(2) IMPROVEMENTS.—Not later than 180 days after the date of the enactment of this Act, the Administrator of the Federal Aviation Administration shall begin a Notice to Airmen Improvement Program (in this section referred to as the "NOTAM Improvement Program")—

(A) to improve the system of providing airmen with pertinent and timely information regarding the national airspace system;

(B) to archive, in a public central location, all NOTAMs, including the original content and form of the notices, the original date of publication, and any amendments to such notices with the date of each amendment; and

(C) to apply filters so that pilots can prioritize critical flight safety information from other airspace system information.

(b) GOALS OF PROGRAM.—The goals of the NOTAM Improvement Program are—

(1) to decrease the overwhelming volume of NOTAMs an airman receives when retrieving airman information prior to a flight in the national airspace system;

(2) make the NOTAMs more specific and relevant to the airman's route and in a format that is more useable to the airman;

(3) to provide a full set of NOTAM results in addition to specific information requested by airmen;

(4) to provide a document that is easily searchable; and

(5) to provide a filtering mechanism similar to that provided by the Department of Defense Notices to Airmen.

(c) ADVICE FROM PRIVATE SECTOR GROUPS.—The Administrator shall establish a NOTAM Improvement Panel, which shall be comprised of representatives of relevant nonprofit and not-for-profit general aviation pilot groups, to advise the Administrator in carrying out the goals of the NOTAM Improvement Program under this section.

(d) PHASE-IN AND COMPLETION.—The improvements required by this section shall be phased in as quickly as practicable and shall be completed not later than the date that is 1 year after the date of the enactment of this Act.

SEC. 4. MEDICAL CERTIFICATION.

(a) ASSESSMENT.—

(1) IN GENERAL.—Not later than 180 days after the date of the enactment of this Act, the Comptroller General of the United States shall initiate an assessment of the Federal Aviation Administration's medical certification process and the associated medical standards and forms.

(2) REPORT.—The Comptroller General shall submit a report to Congress based on the assessment required under paragraph (1) that examines—

(A) revisions to the medical application form that would provide greater clarity and guidance to applicants;

(B) the alignment of medical qualification policies with present-day qualified medical judgment and practices, as applied to an individual's medically relevant circumstances; and

(C) steps that could be taken to promote the public's understanding of the medical requirements that determine an airman's medical certificate eligibility.

(b) GOALS OF THE FEDERAL AVIATION ADMINISTRATION'S MEDICAL CERTIFICATION PROCESS.—The goals of the Federal Aviation Administration's medical certification process are—

(1) to provide questions in the medical application form that—

(A) are appropriate without being overly broad;

(B) are subject to a minimum amount of misinterpretation and mistaken responses;

(C) allow for consistent treatment and responses during the medical application process; and

(D) avoid unnecessary allegations that an individual has intentionally falsified answers on the form;

(2) to provide questions that elicit information that is relevant to making a determination of an individual's medical qualifications within the standards identified in the Administrator's regulations;

(3) to give medical standards greater meaning by ensuring the information requested aligns with present-day medical judgment and practices; and

(4) to ensure that—

(A) the application of such medical standards provides an appropriate and fair evaluation of an individual's qualifications; and

(B) the individual understands the basis for determining medical qualifications.

(c) ADVICE FROM PRIVATE SECTOR GROUPS.—The Administrator shall establish a panel, which shall be comprised of representatives of relevant nonprofit and not-for-profit general aviation pilot groups, aviation medical examiners, and other qualified medical experts, to advise the Administrator in carrying out the goals of the assessment required under this section.

(d) FEDERAL AVIATION ADMINISTRATION RESPONSE.—Not later than 1 year after the issuance of the report by the Comptroller General pursuant to subsection (a)(2), the Administrator shall take appropriate actions to respond to such report.

Approved August 3, 2012.

LEGISLATIVE HISTORY—S. 1335:
CONGRESSIONAL RECORD, Vol. 158 (2012):
    June 29, considered and passed Senate.
    July 23, considered and passed House.

FAR Parts Listed in Titles 14 and 49 of the Code of Federal Regulations

Location Key
ALL ....Published in ASA's *FAR/AIM, FAR-FC,* and *FAR-AMT* books
FAR/AIM.........*FAR/AIM* combination book
FAR-FC ....*FAR for Flight Crew* book
FAR-AMT........*FAR for Aviation Maintenance Technician* book
FAA................Available at www.faa.gov

14 CFR Aeronautics and Space
Part Title   Location

Subchapter A—Definitions
1   Definitions and abbreviations.. ALL
3   General requirements ....FAR-AMT

Subchapter B—Procedural Rules
11   General rulemaking procedures .... FAA
13   Investigative and enforcement procedures...FAR-AMT
14   Rules implementing the Equal Access to Justice Act of 1980......................... FAA
15   Administrative claims under Federal Tort Claims Act.................................... FAA
16   Rules of practice for Federally-assisted airport enforcement proceedings...... FAA
17   Procedures for protests and contract disputes... FAA

Subchapter C—Aircraft
21   Certification procedures for products and parts ....FAR-AMT
23   Airworthiness standards: Normal, utility, acrobatic,
       and commuter category airplanes ....FAR-AMT
25   Airworthiness standards: Transport category airplanes................................ FAA
26   Continued airworthiness and safety improvements for
       transport category airplanes ....FAR-AMT
27   Airworthiness standards: Normal category rotorcraft..............................FAR-AMT
29   Airworthiness standards: Transport category rotorcraft................................ FAA
31   Airworthiness standards: Manned free balloons .... FAA
33   Airworthiness standards: Aircraft engines...FAR-AMT
34   Fuel venting and exhaust emission requirements
       for turbine engine powered airplanes ....FAR-AMT
35   Airworthiness standards: Propellers..FAR-AMT
36   Noise standards: Aircraft type and airworthiness certification........................ FAA
39   Airworthiness directives..FAR-AMT
43   Maintenance, preventive maintenance,
       rebuilding, and alteration... FAR/AIM, FAR-AMT
45   Identification and registration marking...FAR-AMT
47   Aircraft registration...FAR-AMT
49   Recording of aircraft titles and security documents .... FAA
50-59 *[Reserved]*

Subchapter D—Airmen

60	Flight simulation training device initial and continuing qualification and use	FAA
61	Certification: Pilots, flight instructors, and ground instructors	FAR/AIM
63	Certification: Flight crewmembers other than pilots	FAR-FC
65	Certification: Airmen other than flight crewmembers	FAR-AMT, FAR-FC
67	Medical standards and certification	FAR/AIM

Subchapter E—Airspace

71	Designation of class A, B, C, D, and E airspace areas; air traffic service routes; and reporting points	FAR/AIM
73	Special use airspace	FAR/AIM
75	[Reserved]	
77	Safe, efficient use, and preservation of the navigable airspace	FAA

Subchapter F—Air Traffic and General Operating Rules

91	General operating and flight rules	ALL (FAR-FC Subpart K only)
93	Special air traffic rules	FAA
95	IFR altitudes	FAA
97	Standard instrument procedures	FAR/AIM
99	Security control of air traffic	FAA
101	Moored balloons, kites, amateur rockets and unmanned free balloons	FAA
103	Ultralight vehicles	FAR/AIM
105	Parachute operations	FAR/AIM
106-109	[Reserved]	

Subchapter G—Air Carriers and Operators for Compensation or Hire: Certification and Operations

110	General requirements	ALL
111-116	[Reserved]	
117	Flight and duty limitations and rest requirements: Flightcrew members	FAR/AIM, FAR-FC
118	[Reserved]	
119	Certification: Air carriers and commercial operators	ALL
120	Drug and alcohol testing program	FAR-FC
121	Operating requirements: Domestic, flag, and supplemental operations	FAR-FC, FAR-AMT (Subparts J, L, Z, AA, DD)
125	Certification and operations: Airplanes having a seating capacity of 20 or more passengers or a maximum payload capacity of 6,000 pounds or more; and rules governing persons on board such aircraft	FAR-AMT
129	Operations: Foreign air carriers and foreign operators of U.S.-registered aircraft engaged in common carriage	FAA
133	Rotorcraft external-load operations	FAA
135	Operating requirements: Commuter and on-demand operations and rules governing persons on board such aircraft	ALL
136	Commercial air tours and national parks air tour management	FAR/AIM
137	Agricultural aircraft operations	FAR/AIM
139	Certification of airports	FAA

Subchapter H—Schools and Other Certificated Agencies

140	*[Reserved]*	
141	Pilot schools	FAR/AIM
142	Training centers	FAR/AIM
143	*[Reserved]*	
145	Repair stations	FAR-AMT
147	Aviation maintenance technician schools	FAR-AMT

Subchapter I—Airports

150	Airport noise compatibility planning	FAA
151	Federal aid to airports	FAA
152	Airport aid program	FAA
153	Airport operations	FAA
155	Release of airport property from surplus property disposal restrictions	FAA
156	State block grant pilot program	FAA
157	Notice of construction, alteration, activation, and deactivation of airports	FAA
158	Passenger facility charges (PFCs)	FAA
161	Notice and approval of airport noise and access restrictions	FAA
169	Expenditure of Federal funds for nonmilitary airports or air navigation facilities thereon	FAA

Subchapter J—Navigational Facilities

170	Establishment and discontinuance criteria for air traffic control services and navigational facilities	FAA
171	Non-Federal navigation facilities	FAA

Subchapter K—Administrative Regulations

183	Representatives of the Administrator	FAR-AMT
185	Testimony by employees and production of records in legal proceedings, and service of legal process and pleadings	FAA
187	Fees	FAA
189	Use of Federal Aviation Administration communications system	FAA
193	Protection of voluntarily submitted information	FAA

Subchapters L through M *[Reserved]*

Subchapter N—War Risk Insurance

198	Aviation insurance	FAA
199	*[Reserved]*	

49 CFR Transportation

Subtitle B—Other Regulations Pertaining to Transportation

175	Hazardous materials: Carriage by aircraft	FAR-FC
830	Notification and reporting of aircraft accidents or incidents and overdue aircraft, and preservation of aircraft wreckage, mail, cargo, and records	FAR/AIM
1544	Aircraft operator security: Air carriers and commercial operators	FAR-FC
1552	Flight schools	FAR/AIM

Pilots operating internationally should be familiar with Customs and Border Patrol regulations, which can be found at **www.cbp.gov**.

FAR for Flight Crew Contents

Federal Aviation Regulations (from Titles 14 and 49 Code of Federal Regulations)

Part 1 *Page*
Definitions and Abbreviations.. 1

Part 63
Certification: Flight Crewmembers Other Than Pilots....................................15

Part 65
Certification: Airmen Other Than Flight Crewmembers................................ 33

Part 91
General Operating and Flight Rules: Subpart K 55

Part 110
General Requirements 91

Part 117
Flight and Duty Limitations and Rest Requirements: Flightcrew Members .. 95

Part 119
Certification: Air Carriers and Commercial Operators 103

Part 120
Drug and Alcohol Testing Program 119

Part 121
Operating Requirements: Domestic, Flag, & Supplemental Operations......145

Part 135
Operating Requirements: Commuter and On Demand Operations 367

Part 175 (49 CFR)
Hazardous Materials: Carriage By Aircraft.. 485

Part 1544 (49 CFR)
Aircraft Operator Security: Air Carriers and Commercial Operators............ 505

FAR Index 527

PART 1
DEFINITIONS AND ABBREVIATIONS

Sec.
1.1 General definitions.
1.2 Abbreviations and symbols.
1.3 Rules of construction.

Authority: 49 U.S.C. 106(g), 40113, 44701.

§1.1 General definitions.

As used in Subchapters A through K of this chapter, unless the context requires otherwise:

Administrator means the Federal Aviation Administrator or any person to whom he has delegated his authority in the matter concerned.

Aerodynamic coefficients means nondimensional coefficients for aerodynamic forces and moments.

Air carrier means a person who undertakes directly by lease, or other arrangement, to engage in air transportation.

Air commerce means interstate, overseas, or foreign air commerce or the transportation of mail by aircraft or any operation or navigation of aircraft within the limits of any Federal airway or any operation or navigation of aircraft which directly affects, or which may endanger safety in, interstate, overseas, or foreign air commerce.

Aircraft means a device that is used or intended to be used for flight in the air.

Aircraft engine means an engine that is used or intended to be used for propelling aircraft. It includes turbosuperchargers, appurtenances, and accessories necessary for its functioning, but does not include propellers.

Airframe means the fuselage, booms, nacelles, cowlings, fairings, airfoil surfaces (including rotors but excluding propellers and rotating airfoils of engines), and landing gear of an aircraft and their accessories and controls.

Airplane means an engine-driven fixed-wing aircraft heavier than air, that is supported in flight by the dynamic reaction of the air against its wings.

Airport means an area of land or water that is used or intended to be used for the landing and takeoff of aircraft, and includes its buildings and facilities, if any.

Airship means an engine-driven lighter-than-air aircraft that can be steered.

Air traffic means aircraft operating in the air or on an airport surface, exclusive of loading ramps and parking areas.

Air traffic clearance means an authorization by air traffic control, for the purpose of preventing collision between known aircraft, for an aircraft to proceed under specified traffic conditions within controlled airspace.

Air traffic control means a service operated by appropriate authority to promote the safe, orderly, and expeditious flow of air traffic.

Air Traffic Service (ATS) route is a specified route designated for channeling the flow of traffic as necessary for the provision of air traffic services. The term "ATS route" refers to a variety of airways, including jet routes, area navigation (RNAV) routes, and arrival and departure routes. An ATS route is defined by route specifications, which may include:

(1) An ATS route designator;
(2) The path to or from significant points;
(3) Distance between significant points;
(4) Reporting requirements; and
(5) The lowest safe altitude determined by the appropriate authority.

Air transportation means interstate, overseas, or foreign air transportation or the transportation of mail by aircraft.

Alert Area. An alert area is established to inform pilots of a specific area wherein a high volume of pilot training or an unusual type of aeronautical activity is conducted.

Alternate airport means an airport at which an aircraft may land if a landing at the intended airport becomes inadvisable.

Altitude engine means a reciprocating aircraft engine having a rated takeoff power that is producible from sea level to an established higher altitude.

Amateur rocket means an unmanned rocket that:

(1) Is propelled by a motor or motors having a combined total impulse of 889,600 Newton-seconds (200,000 pound-seconds) or less; and
(2) Cannot reach an altitude greater than 150 kilometers (93.2 statute miles) above the earth's surface.

Appliance means any instrument, mechanism, equipment, part, apparatus, appurtenance, or accessory, including communications equipment, that is used or intended to be used in operating or controlling an aircraft in flight, is installed in or attached to the aircraft, and is not part of an airframe, engine, or propeller.

Approved, unless used with reference to another person, means approved by the FAA or any person to whom the FAA has delegated its authority in the matter concerned, or approved under the provisions of a bilateral agreement between the United States and a foreign country or jurisdiction.

ASA   1

Area navigation (RNAV) is a method of navigation that permits aircraft operations on any desired flight path.

Area navigation (RNAV) route is an ATS route based on RNAV that can be used by suitably equipped aircraft.

Armed Forces means the Army, Navy, Air Force, Marine Corps, and Coast Guard, including their regular and reserve components and members serving without component status.

Autorotation means a rotorcraft flight condition in which the lifting rotor is driven entirely by action of the air when the rotorcraft is in motion.

Auxiliary rotor means a rotor that serves either to counteract the effect of the main rotor torque on a rotorcraft or to maneuver the rotorcraft about one or more of its three principal axes.

Balloon means a lighter-than-air aircraft that is not engine driven, and that sustains flight through the use of either gas buoyancy or an airborne heater.

Brake horsepower means the power delivered at the propeller shaft (main drive or main output) of an aircraft engine.

Calibrated airspeed means the indicated airspeed of an aircraft, corrected for position and instrument error. Calibrated airspeed is equal to true airspeed in standard atmosphere at sea level.

Canard means the forward wing of a canard configuration and may be a fixed, movable, or variable geometry surface, with or without control surfaces.

Canard configuration means a configuration in which the span of the forward wing is substantially less than that of the main wing.

Category:

(1) As used with respect to the certification, ratings, privileges, and limitations of airmen, means a broad classification of aircraft. Examples include: airplane; rotorcraft; glider; and lighter-than-air; and

(2) As used with respect to the certification of aircraft, means a grouping of aircraft based upon intended use or operating limitations. Examples include: transport, normal, utility, acrobatic, limited, restricted, and provisional.

Category A, with respect to transport category rotorcraft, means multiengine rotorcraft designed with engine and system isolation features specified in Part 29 and utilizing scheduled takeoff and landing operations under a critical engine failure concept which assures adequate designated surface area and adequate performance capability for continued safe flight in the event of engine failure.

Category B, with respect to transport category rotorcraft, means single-engine or multiengine rotorcraft which do not fully meet all Category A standards. Category B rotorcraft have no guaranteed stay-up ability in the event of engine failure and unscheduled landing is assumed.

Category II operations, with respect to the operation of aircraft, means a straight-in ILS approach to the runway of an airport under a Category II ILS instrument approach procedure issued by the Administrator or other appropriate authority.

Category III operations, with respect to the operation of aircraft, means an ILS approach to, and landing on, the runway of an airport using a Category III ILS instrument approach procedure issued by the Administrator or other appropriate authority.

Ceiling means the height above the earth's surface of the lowest layer of clouds or obscuring phenomena that is reported as "broken," "overcast," or "obscuration," and not classified as "thin" or "partial."

Civil aircraft means aircraft other than public aircraft.

Class:

(1) As used with respect to the certification, ratings, privileges, and limitations of airmen, means a classification of aircraft within a category having similar operating characteristics. Examples include: single engine; multiengine; land; water; gyroplane; helicopter; airship; and free balloon; and

(2) As used with respect to the certification of aircraft, means a broad grouping of aircraft having similar characteristics of propulsion, flight, or landing. Examples include: airplane; rotorcraft; glider; balloon; landplane; and seaplane.

Clearway means:

(1) For turbine engine powered airplanes certificated after August 29, 1959, an area beyond the runway, not less than 500 feet wide, centrally located about the extended centerline of the runway, and under the control of the airport authorities. The clearway is expressed in terms of a clearway plane, extending from the end of the runway with an upward slope not exceeding 1.25 percent, above which no object nor any terrain protrudes. However, threshold lights may protrude above the plane if their height above the end of the runway is 26 inches or less and if they are located to each side of the runway.

(2) For turbine engine powered airplanes certificated after September 30, 1958, but before August 30, 1959, an area beyond the takeoff runway extending no less than 300 feet on either side of the extended centerline of the runway, at an elevation no higher than the elevation of the end of the runway, clear of all fixed obstacles, and under the control of the airport authorities.

Part 1: Definitions and Abbreviations §1.1

Climbout speed, with respect to rotorcraft, means a referenced airspeed which results in a flight path clear of the height-velocity envelope during initial climbout.

Commercial operator means a person who, for compensation or hire, engages in the carriage by aircraft in air commerce of persons or property, other than as an air carrier or foreign air carrier or under the authority of Part 375 of this title. Where it is doubtful that an operation is for "compensation or hire", the test applied is whether the carriage by air is merely incidental to the person's other business or is, in itself, a major enterprise for profit.

Configuration, Maintenance, and Procedures (CMP) document means a document approved by the FAA that contains minimum configuration, operating, and maintenance requirements, hardware life-limits, and Master Minimum Equipment List (MMEL) constraints necessary for an airplane-engine combination to meet ETOPS type design approval requirements.

Consensus standard means, for the purpose of certificating light-sport aircraft, an industry-developed consensus standard that applies to aircraft design, production, and airworthiness. It includes, but is not limited to, standards for aircraft design and performance, required equipment, manufacturer quality assurance systems, production acceptance test procedures, operating instructions, maintenance and inspection procedures, identification and recording of major repairs and major alterations, and continued airworthiness.

Controlled airspace means an airspace of defined dimensions within which air traffic control service is provided to IFR flights and to VFR flights in accordance with the airspace classification.

NOTE—Controlled airspace is a generic term that covers Class A, Class B, Class C, Class D, and Class E airspace.

Controlled Firing Area. A controlled firing area is established to contain activities, which if not conducted in a controlled environment, would be hazardous to nonparticipating aircraft.

Crewmember means a person assigned to perform duty in an aircraft during flight time.

Critical altitude means the maximum altitude at which, in standard atmosphere, it is possible to maintain, at a specified rotational speed, a specified power or a specified manifold pressure. Unless otherwise stated, the critical altitude is the maximum altitude at which it is possible to maintain, at the maximum continuous rotational speed, one of the following:

(1) The maximum continuous power, in the case of engines for which this power rating is the same at sea level and at the rated altitude.

(2) The maximum continuous rated manifold pressure, in the case of engines, the maximum continuous power of which is governed by a constant manifold pressure.

Critical engine means the engine whose failure would most adversely affect the performance or handling qualities of an aircraft.

Decision altitude (DA) is a specified altitude in an instrument approach procedure at which the pilot must decide whether to initiate an immediate missed approach if the pilot does not see the required visual reference, or to continue the approach. Decision altitude is expressed in feet above mean sea level.

Decision height (DH) is a specified height above the ground in an instrument approach procedure at which the pilot must decide whether to initiate an immediate missed approach if the pilot does not see the required visual reference, or to continue the approach. Decision height is expressed in feet above ground level.

Early ETOPS means ETOPS type design approval obtained without gaining non-ETOPS service experience on the candidate airplane-engine combination certified for ETOPS.

Enhanced flight visibility (EFV) means the average forward horizontal distance, from the cockpit of an aircraft in flight, at which prominent topographical objects may be clearly distinguished and identified by day or night by a pilot using an enhanced flight vision system.

Enhanced flight vision system (EFVS) means an electronic means to provide a display of the forward external scene topography (the natural or manmade features of a place or region especially in a way to show their relative positions and elevation) through the use of imaging sensors, such as a forward looking infrared, millimeter wave radiometry, millimeter wave radar, low light level image intensifying.

Equivalent airspeed means the calibrated airspeed of an aircraft corrected for adiabatic compressible flow for the particular altitude. Equivalent airspeed is equal to calibrated airspeed in standard atmosphere at sea level.

ASA

ETOPS Significant System means an airplane system, including the propulsion system, the failure or malfunctioning of which could adversely affect the safety of an ETOPS flight, or the continued safe flight and landing of an airplane during an ETOPS diversion. Each ETOPS significant system is either an ETOPS group 1 significant system or an ETOPS group 2 significant system.

(1) An ETOPS group 1 Significant System—

(i) Has fail-safe characteristics directly linked to the degree of redundancy provided by the number of engines on the airplane.

(ii) Is a system, the failure or malfunction of which could result in an IFSD, loss of thrust control, or other power loss.

(iii) Contributes significantly to the safety of an ETOPS diversion by providing additional redundancy for any system power source lost as a result of an inoperative engine.

(iv) Is essential for prolonged operation of an airplane at engine inoperative altitudes.

(2) An ETOPS group 2 significant system is an ETOPS significant system that is not an ETOPS group 1 significant system.

Extended Operations (ETOPS) means an airplane flight operation, other than an all-cargo operation in an airplane with more than two engines, during which a portion of the flight is conducted beyond a time threshold identified in part 121 or part 135 of this chapter that is determined using an approved one-engine-inoperative cruise speed under standard atmospheric conditions in still air.

Extended over-water operation means—

(1) With respect to aircraft other than helicopters, an operation over water at a horizontal distance of more than 50 nautical miles from the nearest shoreline; and

(2) With respect to helicopters, an operation over water at a horizontal distance of more than 50 nautical miles from the nearest shoreline and more than 50 nautical miles from an off-shore heliport structure.

External load means a load that is carried, or extends, outside of the aircraft fuselage.

External-load attaching means the structural components used to attach an external load to an aircraft, including external-load containers, the backup structure at the attachment points, and any quick-release device used to jettison the external load.

Final approach fix (FAF) defines the beginning of the final approach segment and the point where final segment descent may begin.

Final takeoff speed means the speed of the airplane that exists at the end of the takeoff path in the en route configuration with one engine inoperative.

Fireproof—

(1) With respect to materials and parts used to confine fire in a designated fire zone, means the capacity to withstand at least as well as steel in dimensions appropriate for the purpose for which they are used, the heat produced when there is a severe fire of extended duration in that zone; and

(2) With respect to other materials and parts, means the capacity to withstand the heat associated with fire at least as well as steel in dimensions appropriate for the purpose for which they are used.

Fire resistant—

(1) With respect to sheet or structural members means the capacity to withstand the heat associated with fire at least as well as aluminum alloy in dimensions appropriate for the purpose for which they are used; and

(2) With respect to fluid-carrying lines, fluid system parts, wiring, air ducts, fittings, and powerplant controls, means the capacity to perform the intended functions under the heat and other conditions likely to occur when there is a fire at the place concerned.

Flame resistant means not susceptible to combustion to the point of propagating a flame, beyond safe limits, after the ignition source is removed.

Flammable, with respect to a fluid or gas, means susceptible to igniting readily or to exploding.

Flap extended speed means the highest speed permissible with wing flaps in a prescribed extended position.

Flash resistant means not susceptible to burning violently when ignited.

Flight crewmember means a pilot, flight engineer, or flight navigator assigned to duty in an aircraft during flight time.

Flight level means a level of constant atmospheric pressure related to a reference datum of 29.92 inches of mercury. Each is stated in three digits that represent hundreds of feet. For example, flight level 250 represents a barometric altimeter indication of 25,000 feet; flight level 255, an indication of 25,500 feet.

Flight plan means specified information, relating to the intended flight of an aircraft, that is filed orally or in writing with air traffic control.

Flight simulation training device (FSTD) means a flight simulator or a flight training device.

Flight time means:

(1) Pilot time that commences when an aircraft moves under its own power for the purpose of flight and ends when the aircraft comes to rest after landing; or

(2) For a glider without self-launch capability, pilot times that commences when the glider is towed for the purpose of flight and ends when the glider comes to rest after landing.

Part 1: Definitions and Abbreviations §1.1

Flight training device (FTD) means a replica of aircraft instruments, equipment, panels, and controls in an open flight deck area or an enclosed aircraft cockpit replica. It includes the equipment and computer programs necessary to represent aircraft (or set of aircraft) operations in ground and flight conditions having the full range of capabilities of the systems installed in the device as described in part 60 of this chapter and the qualification performance standard (QPS) for a specific FTD qualification level.

Flight visibility means the average forward horizontal distance, from the cockpit of an aircraft in flight, at which prominent unlighted objects may be seen and identified by day and prominent lighted objects may be seen and identified by night.

Foreign air carrier means any person other than a citizen of the United States, who undertakes directly, by lease or other arrangement, to engage in air transportation.

Foreign air commerce means the carriage by aircraft of persons or property for compensation or hire, or the carriage of mail by aircraft, or the operation or navigation of aircraft in the conduct or furtherance of a business or vocation, in commerce between a place in the United States and any place outside thereof; whether such commerce moves wholly by aircraft or partly by aircraft and partly by other forms of transportation.

Foreign air transportation means the carriage by aircraft of persons or property as a common carrier for compensation or hire, or the carriage of mail by aircraft, in commerce between a place in the United States and any place outside of the United States, whether that commerce moves wholly by aircraft or partly by aircraft and partly by other forms of transportation.

Forward wing means a forward lifting surface of a canard configuration or tandem-wing configuration airplane. The surface may be a fixed, movable, or variable geometry surface, with or without control surfaces.

Full flight simulator (FFS) means a replica of a specific type; or make, model, and series aircraft cockpit. It includes the assemblage of equipment and computer programs necessary to represent aircraft operations in ground and flight conditions, a visual system providing an out-of-the-cockpit view, a system that provides cues at least equivalent to those of a three-degree-of-freedom motion system, and has the full range of capabilities of the systems installed in the device as described in part 60 of this chapter and the qualification performance standards (QPS) for a specific FFS qualification level.

Glider means a heavier-than-air aircraft, that is supported in flight by the dynamic reaction of the air against its lifting surfaces and whose free flight does not depend principally on an engine.

Go-around power or thrust setting means the maximum allowable in-flight power or thrust setting identified in the performance data.

Ground visibility means prevailing horizontal visibility near the earth's surface as reported by the United States National Weather Service or an accredited observer.

Gyrodyne means a rotorcraft whose rotors are normally engine-driven for takeoff, hovering, and landing, and for forward flight through part of its speed range, and whose means of propulsion, consisting usually of conventional propellers, is independent of the rotor system.

Gyroplane means a rotorcraft whose rotors are not engine-driven, except for initial starting, but are made to rotate by action of the air when the rotorcraft is moving; and whose means of propulsion, consisting usually of conventional propellers, is independent of the rotor system.

Helicopter means a rotorcraft that, for its horizontal motion, depends principally on its engine-driven rotors.

Heliport means an area of land, water, or structure used or intended to be used for the landing and takeoff of helicopters.

Idle thrust means the jet thrust obtained with the engine power control level set at the stop for the least thrust position at which it can be placed.

IFR conditions means weather conditions below the minimum for flight under visual flight rules.

IFR over-the-top, with respect to the operation of aircraft, means the operation of an aircraft over-the-top on an IFR flight plan when cleared by air traffic control to maintain "VFR conditions" or "VFR conditions on top".

Indicated airspeed means the speed of an aircraft as shown on its pitot static airspeed indicator calibrated to reflect standard atmosphere adiabatic compressible flow at sea level uncorrected for airspeed system errors.

In-flight shutdown (IFSD) means, for ETOPS only, when an engine ceases to function (when the airplane is airborne) and is shutdown, whether self induced, flightcrew initiated or caused by an external influence. The FAA considers IFSD for all causes: for example, flameout, internal failure, flightcrew initiated shutdown, foreign object ingestion, icing, inability to obtain or control desired thrust or power, and cycling of the start control, however briefly, even if the engine operates normally for the remainder of the flight. This definition excludes the airborne cessation of the functioning of an engine when immediately followed by an automatic engine relight and when an engine does not achieve desired thrust or power but is not shutdown.

Instrument means a device using an internal mechanism to show visually or aurally the attitude, altitude, or operation of an aircraft or aircraft part. It includes electronic devices for automatically controlling an aircraft in flight.

Instrument approach procedure (IAP) is a series of predetermined maneuvers by reference to flight instruments with specified protection from obstacles and assurance of navigation signal reception capability. It begins from the initial approach fix, or where applicable, from the beginning of a defined arrival route to a point:

(1) From which a landing can be completed; or

(2) If a landing is not completed, to a position at which holding or en route obstacle clearance criteria apply.

Interstate air commerce means the carriage by aircraft of persons or property for compensation or hire, or the carriage of mail by aircraft, or the operation or navigation of aircraft in the conduct or furtherance of a business or vocation, in commerce between a place in any State of the United States, or the District of Columbia, and a place in any other State of the United States, or the District of Columbia; or between places in the same State of the United States through the airspace over any place outside thereof; or between places in the same territory or possession of the United States, or the District of Columbia.

Interstate air transportation means the carriage by aircraft of persons or property as a common carrier for compensation or hire, or the carriage of mail by aircraft in commerce:

(1) Between a place in a State or the District of Columbia and another place in another State or the District of Columbia;

(2) Between places in the same State through the airspace over any place outside that State; or

(3) Between places in the same possession of the United States;

Whether that commerce moves wholly by aircraft of partly by aircraft and partly by other forms of transportation.

Intrastate air transportation means the carriage of persons or property as a common carrier for compensation or hire, by turbojet-powered aircraft capable of carrying thirty or more persons, wholly within the same State of the United States.

Kite means a framework, covered with paper, cloth, metal, or other material, intended to be flown at the end of a rope or cable, and having as its only support the force of the wind moving past its surfaces.

Landing gear extended speed means the maximum speed at which an aircraft can be safely flown with the landing gear extended.

Landing gear operating speed means the maximum speed at which the landing gear can be safely extended or retracted.

Large aircraft means aircraft of more than 12,500 pounds, maximum certificated takeoff weight.

Lighter-than-air aircraft means aircraft that can rise and remain suspended by using contained gas weighing less than the air that is displaced by the gas.

Light-sport aircraft means an aircraft, other than a helicopter or powered-lift that, since its original certification, has continued to meet the following:

(1) A maximum takeoff weight of not more than—

(i) 1,320 pounds (600 kilograms) for aircraft not intended for operation on water; or

(ii) 1,430 pounds (650 kilograms) for an aircraft intended for operation on water.

(2) A maximum airspeed in level flight with maximum continuous power (V_H) of not more than 120 knots CAS under standard atmospheric conditions at sea level.

(3) A maximum never-exceed speed (V_{NE}) of not more than 120 knots CAS for a glider.

(4) A maximum stalling speed or minimum steady flight speed without the use of lift-enhancing devices (V_{S1}) of not more than 45 knots CAS at the aircraft's maximum certificated takeoff weight and most critical center of gravity.

(5) A maximum seating capacity of no more than two persons, including the pilot.

(6) A single, reciprocating engine, if powered.

(7) A fixed or ground-adjustable propeller if a powered aircraft other than a powered glider.

(8) A fixed or feathering propeller system if a powered glider.

(9) A fixed-pitch, semi-rigid, teetering, two-blade rotor system, if a gyroplane.

(10) A nonpressurized cabin, if equipped with a cabin.

(11) Fixed landing gear, except for an aircraft intended for operation on water or a glider.

(12) Fixed or retractable landing gear, or a hull, for an aircraft intended for operation on water.

(13) Fixed or retractable landing gear for a glider.

Load factor means the ratio of a specified load to the total weight of the aircraft. The specified load is expressed in terms of any of the following: aerodynamic forces, inertia forces, or ground or water reactions.

Long-range communication system (LRCS). A system that uses satellite relay, data link, high frequency, or another approved communication system which extends beyond line of sight.

Long-range navigation system (LRNS). An electronic navigation unit that is approved for use under instrument flight rules as a primary means of navigation, and has at least one source of navigational input, such as inertial navigation system, global positioning system, Omega/very low frequency, or Loran C.

Part 1: Definitions and Abbreviations §1.1

Mach number means the ratio of true airspeed to the speed of sound.

Main rotor means the rotor that supplies the principal lift to a rotorcraft.

Maintenance means inspection, overhaul, repair, preservation, and the replacement of parts, but excludes preventive maintenance.

Major alteration means an alteration not listed in the aircraft, aircraft engine, or propeller specifications—

(1) That might appreciably affect weight, balance, structural strength, performance, powerplant operation, flight characteristics, or other qualities affecting airworthiness; or

(2) That is not done according to accepted practices or cannot be done by elementary operations.

Major repair means a repair:

(1) That, if improperly done, might appreciably affect weight, balance, structural strength, performance, powerplant operation, flight characteristics, or other qualities affecting airworthiness; or

(2) That is not done according to accepted practices or cannot be done by elementary operations.

Manifold pressure means absolute pressure as measured at the appropriate point in the induction system and usually expressed in inches of mercury.

Maximum engine overtorque, as it applies to turbopropeller and turboshaft engines incorporating free power turbines for all ratings except one engine inoperative (OEI) ratings of two minutes or less, means the maximum torque of the free power turbine rotor assembly, the inadvertent occurrence of which, for periods of up to 20 seconds, will not require rejection of the engine from service, or any maintenance action other than to correct the cause.

Maximum speed for stability characteristics, V_{FC}/M_{FC} means a speed that may not be less than a speed midway between maximum operating limit speed (V_{MO}/M_{MO}) and demonstrated flight diving speed (V_{DF}/M_{DF}), except that, for altitudes where the Mach number is the limiting factor, M_{FC} need not exceed the Mach number at which effective speed warning occurs.

Medical certificate means acceptable evidence of physical fitness on a form prescribed by the Administrator.

Military operations area. A military operations area (MOA) is airspace established outside Class A airspace to separate or segregate certain nonhazardous military activities from IFR Traffic and to identify for VFR traffic where theses activities are conducted.

Minimum descent altitude (MDA) is the lowest altitude specified in an instrument approach procedure, expressed in feet above mean sea level, to which descent is authorized on final approach or during circle-to-land maneuvering until the pilot sees the required visual references for the heliport or runway of intended landing.

Minor alteration means an alteration other than a major alteration.

Minor repair means a repair other than a major repair.

National defense airspace means airspace established by a regulation prescribed, or an order issued under, 49 U.S.C. 40103(b)(3).

Navigable airspace means airspace at and above the minimum flight altitudes prescribed by or under this chapter, including airspace needed for safe takeoff and landing.

Night means the time between the end of evening civil twilight and the beginning of morning civil twilight, as published in the Air Almanac, converted to local time.

Nonprecision approach procedure means a standard instrument approach procedure in which no electronic glide slope is provided.

Operate, with respect to aircraft, means use, cause to use or authorize to use aircraft, for the purpose (except as provided in §91.13 of this chapter) of air navigation including the piloting of aircraft, with or without the right of legal control (as owner, lessee, or otherwise).

Operational control, with respect to a flight, means the exercise of authority over initiating, conducting or terminating a flight.

Overseas air commerce means the carriage by aircraft of persons or property for compensation or hire, or the carriage of mail by aircraft, or the operation or navigation of aircraft in the conduct or furtherance of a business or vocation, in commerce between a place in any State of the United States, or the District of Columbia, and any place in a territory or possession of the United States; or between a place in a territory or possession of the United States, and a place in any other territory or possession of the United States.

Overseas air transportation means the carriage by aircraft of persons or property as a common carrier for compensation or hire, or the carriage of mail by aircraft, in commerce:

(1) Between a place in a State or the District of Columbia and a place in a possession of the United States; or

(2) Between a place in a possession of the United States and a place in another possession of the United States; whether that commerce moves wholly by aircraft or partly by aircraft and partly by other forms of transportation.

Over-the-top means above the layer of clouds or other obscuring phenomena forming the ceiling.

Parachute means a device used or intended to be used to retard the fall of a body or object through the air.

Person means an individual, firm, partnership, corporation, company, association, joint-stock association, or governmental entity. It includes a trustee, receiver, assignee, or similar representative of any of them.

Pilotage means navigation by visual reference to landmarks.

Pilot in command means the person who:

(1) Has final authority and responsibility for the operation and safety of the flight;

(2) Has been designated as pilot in command before or during the flight; and

(3) Holds the appropriate category, class, and type rating, if appropriate, for the conduct of the flight.

Pitch setting means the propeller blade setting as determined by the blade angle measured in a manner, and at a radius, specified by the instruction manual for the propeller.

Positive control means control of all air traffic, within designated airspace, by air traffic control.

Powered-lift means a heavier-than-air aircraft capable of vertical takeoff, vertical landing, and low speed flight that depends principally on engine-driven lift devices or engine thrust for lift during these flight regimes and on nonrotating airfoil(s) for lift during horizontal flight.

Powered parachute means a powered aircraft comprised of a flexible or semi-rigid wing connected to a fuselage so that the wing is not in position for flight until the aircraft is in motion. The fuselage of a powered parachute contains the aircraft engine, a seat for each occupant and is attached to the aircraft's landing gear.

Precision approach procedure means a standard instrument approach procedure in which an electronic glide slope is provided, such as ILS and PAR.

Preventive maintenance means simple or minor preservation operations and the replacement of small standard parts not involving complex assembly operations.

Prohibited area. A prohibited area is airspace designated under part 73 within which no person may operate an aircraft without the permission of the using agency.

Propeller means a device for propelling an aircraft that has blades on an engine-driven shaft and that, when rotated, produces by its action on the air, a thrust approximately perpendicular to its plane of rotation. It includes control components normally supplied by its manufacturer, but does not include main and auxiliary rotors or rotating airfoils of engines.

Public aircraft means any of the following aircraft when not being used for a commercial purpose or to carry an individual other than a crewmember or qualified non-crewmember:

(1) An aircraft used only for the United States Government; an aircraft owned by the Government and operated by any person for purposes related to crew training, equipment development, or demonstration; an aircraft owned and operated by the government of a State, the District of Columbia, or a territory or possession of the United States or a political subdivision of one of these governments; or an aircraft exclusively leased for at least 90 continuous days by the government of a State, the District of Columbia, or a territory or possession of the United States or a political subdivision of one of these governments.

(i) For the sole purpose of determining public aircraft status, commercial purposes means the transportation of persons or property for compensation or hire, but does not include the operation of an aircraft by the armed forces for reimbursement when that reimbursement is required by any Federal statute, regulation, or directive, in effect on November 1, 1999, or by one government on behalf of another government under a cost reimbursement agreement if the government on whose behalf the operation is conducted certifies to the Administrator of the Federal Aviation Administration that the operation is necessary to respond to a significant and imminent threat to life or property (including natural resources) and that no service by a private operator is reasonably available to meet the threat.

(ii) For the sole purpose of determining public aircraft status, governmental function means an activity undertaken by a government, such as national defense, intelligence missions, firefighting, search and rescue, law enforcement (including transport of prisoners, detainees, and illegal aliens), aeronautical research, or biological or geological resource management.

(iii) For the sole purpose of determining public aircraft status, qualified non-crewmember means an individual, other than a member of the crew, aboard an aircraft operated by the armed forces or an intelligence agency of the United States Government, or whose presence is required to perform, or is associated with the performance of, a governmental function.

(2) An aircraft owned or operated by the armed forces or chartered to provide transportation to the armed forces if—

(i) The aircraft is operated in accordance with title 10 of the United States Code;

(ii) The aircraft is operated in the performance of a governmental function under title 14, 31, 32, or 50 of the United States Code and the aircraft is not used for commercial purposes; or

Part 1: Definitions and Abbreviations §1.1

(iii) The aircraft is chartered to provide transportation to the armed forces and the Secretary of Defense (or the Secretary of the department in which the Coast Guard is operating) designates the operation of the aircraft as being required in the national interest.

(3) An aircraft owned or operated by the National Guard of a State, the District of Columbia, or any territory or possession of the United States, and that meets the criteria of paragraph (2) of this definition, qualifies as a public aircraft only to the extent that it is operated under the direct control of the Department of Defense.

Rated continuous OEI power, with respect to rotorcraft turbine engines, means the approved brake horsepower developed under static conditions at specified altitudes and temperatures within the operating limitations established for the engine under part 33 of this chapter, and limited in use to the time required to complete the flight after the failure or shutdown of one engine of a multiengine rotorcraft.

Rated maximum continuous augmented thrust, with respect to turbojet engine type certification, means the approved jet thrust that is developed statically or in flight, in standard atmosphere at a specified altitude, with fluid injection or with the burning of fuel in a separate combustion chamber, within the engine operating limitations established under Part 33 of this chapter, and approved for unrestricted periods of use.

Rated maximum continuous power, with respect to reciprocating, turbopropeller, and turboshaft engines, means the approved brake horsepower that is developed statically or in flight, in standard atmosphere at a specified altitude, within the engine operating limitations established under Part 33, and approved for unrestricted periods of use.

Rated maximum continuous thrust, with respect to turbojet engine type certification, means the approved jet thrust that is developed statically or in flight, in standard atmosphere at a specified altitude, without fluid injection and without the burning of fuel in a separate combustion chamber, within the engine operating limitations established under Part 33 of this chapter, and approved for unrestricted periods of use.

Rated takeoff augmented thrust, with respect to turbojet engine type certification, means the approved jet thrust that is developed statically under standard sea level conditions, with fluid injection or with the burning of fuel in a separate combustion chamber, within the engine operating limitations established under Part 33 of this chapter, and limited in use to periods of not over 5 minutes for takeoff operation.

Rated takeoff power, with respect to reciprocating, turbopropeller, and turboshaft engine type certification, means the approved brake horsepower that is developed statically under standard sea level conditions, within the engine operating limitations established under Part 33, and limited in use to periods of not over 5 minutes for takeoff operation.

Rated takeoff thrust, with respect to turbojet engine type certification, means the approved jet thrust that is developed statically under standard sea level conditions, without fluid injection and without the burning of fuel in a separate combustion chamber, within the engine operating limitations established under Part 33 of this chapter, and limited in use to periods of not over 5 minutes for takeoff operation.

Rated 30-minute OEI power, with respect to rotorcraft turbine engines, means the approved brake horsepower developed under static conditions at specified altitudes and temperatures within the operating limitations established for the engine under part 33 of this chapter, and limited in use to one period of use no longer than 30 minutes after the failure or shutdown of one engine of a multiengine rotorcraft.

Rated 30-second OEI power, with respect to rotorcraft turbine engines, means the approved brake horsepower developed under static conditions at specified altitudes and temperatures within the operating limitations established for the engine under part 33 of this chapter, for continuation of one flight operation after the failure or shutdown of one engine in multiengine rotorcraft, for up to three periods of use no longer than 30 seconds each in any one flight, and followed by mandatory inspection and prescribed maintenance action.

Rated 2-minute OEI power, with respect to rotorcraft turbine engines, means the approved brake horsepower developed under static conditions at specified altitudes and temperatures within the operating limitations established for the engine under part 33 of this chapter, for continuation of one flight operation after the failure or shutdown of one engine in multiengine rotorcraft, for up to three periods of use no longer than 2 minutes each in any one flight, and followed by mandatory inspection and prescribed maintenance action.

Rated 2½-minute OEI power, with respect to rotorcraft turbine engines, means the approved brake horsepower developed under static conditions at specified altitudes and temperatures within the operating limitations established for the engine under part 33 of this chapter for periods of use no longer than 2-1/2 minutes each after the failure or shutdown of one engine of a multiengine rotorcraft.

Rating means a statement that, as a part of a certificate, sets forth special conditions, privileges, or limitations.

Reference landing speed means the speed of the airplane, in a specified landing configuration, at the point where it descends through the 50 foot height in the determination of the landing distance.

Reporting point means a geographical location in relation to which the position of an aircraft is reported.

Restricted area. A restricted area is airspace designated under Part 73 within which the flight of aircraft, while not wholly prohibited, is subject to restriction.

Rocket means an aircraft propelled by ejected expanding gases generated in the engine from self-contained propellants and not dependent on the intake of outside substances. It includes any part which becomes separated during the operation.

Rotorcraft means a heavier-than-air aircraft that depends principally for its support in flight on the lift generated by one or more rotors.

Rotorcraft-load combination means the combination of a rotorcraft and an external-load, including the external-load attaching means. Rotorcraft-load combinations are designated as Class A, Class B, Class C, and Class D, as follows:

(1) Class A rotorcraft-load combination means one in which the external load cannot move freely, cannot be jettisoned, and does not extend below the landing gear.

(2) Class B rotorcraft-load combination means one in which the external load is jettisonable and is lifted free of land or water during the rotorcraft operation.

(3) Class C rotorcraft-load combination means one in which the external load is jettisonable and remains in contact with land or water during the rotorcraft operation.

(4) Class D rotorcraft-load combination means one in which the external-load is other than a Class A, B, or C and has been specifically approved by the Administrator for that operation.

Route segment is a portion of a route bounded on each end by a fix or navigation aid (NAVAID).

Sea level engine means a reciprocating aircraft engine having a rated takeoff power that is producible only at sea level.

Second in command means a pilot who is designated to be second in command of an aircraft during flight time.

Show, unless the context otherwise requires, means to show to the satisfaction of the Administrator.

Small aircraft means aircraft of 12,500 pounds or less, maximum certificated takeoff weight.

Special VFR conditions mean meteorological conditions that are less than those required for basic VFR flight in controlled airspace and in which some aircraft are permitted flight under visual flight rules.

Special VFR operations means aircraft operating in accordance with clearances within controlled airspace in meteorological conditions less than the basic VFR weather minima. Such operations must be requested by the pilot and approved by ATC.

Standard atmosphere means the atmosphere defined in U.S. Standard Atmosphere, 1962 (Geopotential altitude tables).

Stopway means an area beyond the takeoff runway, no less wide than the runway and centered upon the extended centerline of the runway, able to support the airplane during an aborted takeoff, without causing structural damage to the airplane, and designated by the airport authorities for use in decelerating the airplane during an aborted takeoff.

Suitable RNAV system is an RNAV system that meets the required performance established for a type of operation, e.g. IFR; and is suitable for operation over the route to be flown in terms of any performance criteria (including accuracy) established by the air navigation service provider for certain routes (e.g. oceanic, ATS routes, and IAPs). An RNAV system's suitability is dependent upon the availability of ground and/or satellite navigation aids that are needed to meet any route performance criteria that may be prescribed in route specifications to navigate the aircraft along the route to be flown. Information on suitable RNAV systems is published in FAA guidance material.

Synthetic vision means a computer-generated image of the external scene topography from the perspective of the flight deck that is derived from aircraft attitude, high-precision navigation solution, and database of terrain, obstacles and relevant cultural features.

Synthetic vision system means an electronic means to display a synthetic vision image of the external scene topography to the flight crew.

Takeoff power:

(1) With respect to reciprocating engines, means the brake horsepower that is developed under standard sea level conditions, and under the maximum conditions of crankshaft rotational speed and engine manifold pressure approved for the normal takeoff, and limited in continuous use to the period of time shown in the approved engine specification; and

Part 1: Definitions and Abbreviations §1.1

(2) With respect to turbine engines, means the brake horsepower that is developed under static conditions at a specified altitude and atmospheric temperature, and under the maximum conditions of rotor shaft rotational speed and gas temperature approved for the normal takeoff, and limited in continuous use to the period of time shown in the approved engine specification.

Takeoff safety speed means a referenced airspeed obtained after lift-off at which the required one-engine-inoperative climb performance can be achieved.

Takeoff thrust, with respect to turbine engines, means the jet thrust that is developed under static conditions at a specific altitude and atmospheric temperature under the maximum conditions of rotorshaft rotational speed and gas temperature approved for the normal takeoff, and limited in continuous use to the period of time shown in the approved engine specification.

Tandem wing configuration means a configuration having two wings of similar span, mounted in tandem.

TCAS I means a TCAS that utilizes interrogations of, and replies from, airborne radar beacon transponders and provides traffic advisories to the pilot.

TCAS II means a TCAS that utilizes interrogations of, and replies from airborne radar beacon transponders and provides traffic advisories and resolution advisories in the vertical plane.

TCAS III means a TCAS that utilizes interrogation of, and replies from, airborne radar beacon transponders and provides traffic advisories and resolution advisories in the vertical and horizontal planes to the pilot.

Time in service, with respect to maintenance time records, means the time from the moment an aircraft leaves the surface of the earth until it touches it at the next point of landing.

True airspeed means the airspeed of an aircraft relative to undisturbed air. True airspeed is equal to equivalent airspeed multiplied by $(\rho 0/\rho)^{1/2}$.

Traffic pattern means the traffic flow that is prescribed for aircraft landing at, taxiing on, or taking off from, an airport.

Type:
(1) As used with respect to the certification, ratings, privileges, and limitations of airmen, means a specific make and basic model of aircraft, including modifications thereto that do not change its handling or flight characteristics. Examples include: DC-7, 1049, and F-27; and

(2) As used with respect to the certification of aircraft, means those aircraft which are similar in design. Examples include: DC-7 and DC-7C; 1049G and 1049H; and F-27 and F-27F.

(3) As used with respect to the certification of aircraft engines means those engines which are similar in design. For example, JT8D and JT8D-7 are engines of the same type, and JT9D-3A and JT9D-7 are engines of the same type.

United States, in a geographical sense, means (1) the States, the District of Columbia, Puerto Rico, and the possessions, including the territorial waters, and (2) the airspace of those areas.

United States air carrier means a citizen of the United States who undertakes directly by lease, or other arrangement, to engage in air transportation.

VFR over-the-top, with respect to the operation of aircraft, means the operation of an aircraft over-the-top under VFR when it is not being operated on an IFR flight plan.

Warning area. A warning area is airspace of defined dimensions, extending from 3 nautical miles outward from the coast of the United States, that contains activity that may be hazardous to nonparticipating aircraft. The purpose of such warning areas is to warn nonparticipating pilots of the potential danger. A warning area may be located over domestic or international waters or both.

Weight-shift-control aircraft means a powered aircraft with a framed pivoting wing and a fuselage controllable only in pitch and roll by the pilot's ability to change the aircraft's center of gravity with respect to the wing. Flight control of the aircraft depends on the wing's ability to flexibly deform rather than the use of control surfaces.

Winglet or tip fin means an out-of-plane surface extending from a lifting surface. The surface may or may not have control surfaces.

Editorial note: For Federal Register citations affecting §1.1, see the List of CFR Sections Affected, which appears in the Finding Aids section of the printed volume and at www.fdsys.gov

§1.2 Abbreviations and symbols.

In Subchapters A through K of this chapter:

AFM means airplane flight manual.
AGL means above ground level.
ALS means approach light system.
APU means auxiliary power unit.
ASR means airport surveillance radar.
ATC means air traffic control.
ATS means Air Traffic Service.
CAMP means continuous airworthiness maintenance program.
CAS means calibrated airspeed.
CAT II means Category II.
CHDO means an FAA Flight Standards certificate holding district office.
CONSOL or *CONSOLAN* means a kind of low or medium frequency long range navigational aid.
CMP means configuration, maintenance, and procedures.
DH means decision height.
DME means distance measuring equipment compatible with TACAN.
EAS means equivalent airspeed.
EFVS means enhanced flight vision system.
Equi-Time Point means a point on the route of flight where the flight time, considering wind, to each of two selected airports is equal.
ETOPS means extended operations.
EWIS, as defined by §25.1701 of this chapter, means electrical wiring interconnection system.
FAA means Federal Aviation Administration.
FFS means full flight simulator.
FM means fan marker.
FSTD means flight simulation training device.
FTD means flight training device.
GS means glide slope.
HIRL means high-intensity runway light system.
IAS means indicated airspeed.
ICAO means International Civil Aviation Organization.
IFR means instrument flight rules.
IFSD means in-flight shutdown.
ILS means instrument landing system.
IM means ILS inner marker.
INT means intersection.
LDA means localizer-type directional aid.
LFR means low-frequency radio range.
LMM means compass locator at middle marker.
LOC means ILS localizer.
LOM means compass locator at outer marker.
M means mach number.
MAA means maximum authorized IFR altitude.
MALS means medium intensity approach light system.
MALSR means medium intensity approach light system with runway alignment indicator lights.
MCA means minimum crossing altitude.
MDA means minimum descent altitude.
MEA means minimum en route IFR altitude.
MEL means minimum equipment list.
MM means ILS middle marker.
MOCA means minimum obstruction clearance altitude.
MRA means minimum reception altitude.
MSL means mean sea level.
NDB (ADF) means nondirectional beacon (automatic direction finder).
NM means nautical mile.
NOPAC means North Pacific area of operation.
NOPT means no procedure turn required.
OEI means one engine inoperative.
OM means ILS outer marker.
OPSPECS means operations specifications.
PACOTS means Pacific Organized Track System.
PAR means precision approach radar.
PMA means parts manufacturer approval.
PTRS means Performance Tracking and Reporting System.
RAIL means runway alignment indicator light system.
RBN means radio beacon.
RCLM means runway centerline marking.
RCLS means runway centerline light system.
REIL means runway end identification lights.
RFFS means rescue and firefighting services.
RNAV means area navigation.
RR means low or medium frequency radio range station.
RVR means runway visual range as measured in the touchdown zone area.

Part 1: Definitions and Abbreviations §1.2

SALS means short approach light system.

SATCOM means satellite communications.

SSALS means simplified short approach light system.

SSALSR means simplified short approach light system with runway alignment indicator lights.

TACAN means ultra-high frequency tactical air navigational aid.

TAS means true airspeed.

TCAS means a traffic alert and collision avoidance system.

TDZL means touchdown zone lights.

TSO means technical standard order.

TVOR means very high frequency terminal omnirange station.

V_A means design maneuvering speed.

V_B means design speed for maximum gust intensity.

V_C means design cruising speed.

V_D means design diving speed.

V_{DF}/M_{DF} means demonstrated flight diving speed.

V_{EF} means the speed at which the critical engine is assumed to fail during takeoff.

V_F means design flap speed.

V_{FC}/M_{FC} means maximum speed for stability characteristics.

V_{FE} means maximum flap extended speed.

V_{FTO} means final takeoff speed.

V_H means maximum speed in level flight with maximum continuous power.

V_{LE} means maximum landing gear extended speed.

V_{LO} means maximum landing gear operating speed.

V_{LOF} means lift-off speed.

V_{MC} means minimum control speed with the critical engine inoperative.

V_{MO}/M_{MO} means maximum operating limit speed.

V_{MU} means minimum unstick speed.

V_{NE} means never-exceed speed.

V_{NO} means maximum structural cruising speed.

V_R means rotation speed.

V_{REF} means reference landing speed.

V_S means the stalling speed or the minimum steady flight speed at which the airplane is controllable.

V_{S0} means the stalling speed or the minimum steady flight speed in the landing configuration.

V_{S1} means the stalling speed or the minimum steady flight speed obtained in a specific configuration.

V_{SR} means reference stall speed.

V_{SR0} means reference stall speed in the landing configuration.

V_{SR1} means reference stall speed in a specific configuration.

V_{SW} means speed at which onset of natural or artificial stall warning occurs.

V_{TOSS} means takeoff safety speed for Category A rotorcraft.

V_X means speed for best angle of climb.

V_Y means speed for best rate of climb.

V_1 means the maximum speed in the takeoff at which the pilot must take the first action (e.g., apply brakes, reduce thrust, deploy speed brakes) to stop the airplane within the accelerate-stop distance. V_1 also means the minimum speed in the takeoff, following a failure of the critical engine at V_{EF}, at which the pilot can continue the takeoff and achieve the required height above the takeoff surface within the takeoff distance.

V_2 means takeoff safety speed.

V_{2min} means minimum takeoff safety speed.

VFR means visual flight rules.

VHF means very high frequency.

VOR means very high frequency omnirange station.

VORTAC means collocated VOR and TACAN.

[Docket No. 1150, 27 FR 4590, May 15, 1962; as amended by Amdt. 1–48, 63 FR 8318, Feb. 18, 1998; Amdt. 1–49, 67 FR 70825, Nov. 26, 2002; Amdt. 1–52, 69 FR 1639, Jan. 9, 2004; Amdt. 1–54, 71 FR 63426, Oct. 30, 2006; Amdt. 1–55, 72 FR 1872, Jan. 16, 2007; Amdt. 1–57, 72 FR 31677, June 7, 2007; Amdt. 1–60, 72 FR 63404, Nov. 8, 2007; Amdt. 1–64, 74 FR 53384, Oct. 16, 2009]

§1.3 Rules of construction.

(a) In Subchapters A through K of this chapter, unless the context requires otherwise:

(1) Words importing the singular include the plural;

(2) Words importing the plural include the singular; and

(3) Words importing the masculine gender include the feminine.

(b) In Subchapters A through K of this chapter, the word:

(1) "Shall" is used in an imperative sense;

(2) "May" is used in a permissive sense to state authority or permission to do the act prescribed, and the words "no person may * * *" or "a person may not * * *" mean that no person is required, authorized, or permitted to do the act prescribed; and

(3) "Includes" means "includes but is not limited to".

[Docket No. 1150, 27 FR 4590, May 15, 1962; as amended by Amdt. 1–10, 31 FR 5055, March 29, 1966]

PART 63
CERTIFICATION: FLIGHT CREWMEMBERS OTHER THAN PILOTS

Special Federal Aviation Regulation
SFAR No. 100-2

Subpart A—General

Sec.
63.1 Applicability.
63.2 Certification of foreign flight crewmembers other than pilots.
63.3 Certificates and ratings required.
63.11 Application and issue.
63.12 Offenses involving alcohol or drugs.
63.12a Refusal to submit to an alcohol test or to furnish test results.
63.12b [Reserved]
63.13 Temporary certificate.
63.14 Security disqualification.
63.15 Duration of certificates.
63.15a [Reserved]
63.16 Change of name; replacement of lost or destroyed certificate.
63.17 Tests: General procedure.
63.18 Written tests: Cheating or other unauthorized conduct.
63.19 Operations during physical deficiency.
63.20 Applications, certificates, logbooks, reports, and records; falsification, reproduction, or alteration.
63.21 Change of address.
63.23 Special purpose flight engineer and flight navigator certificates: Operation of U.S.-registered civil airplanes leased by a person not a U.S. citizen.

Subpart B—Flight Engineers

63.31 Eligibility requirements; general.
63.33 Aircraft ratings.
63.35 Knowledge requirements.
63.37 Aeronautical experience requirements.
63.39 Skill requirements.
63.41 Retesting after failure.
63.42 Flight engineer certificate issued on basis of a foreign flight engineer license.
63.43 Flight engineer courses.

Subpart C—Flight Navigators

63.51 Eligibility requirements; general.
63.53 Knowledge requirements.
63.55 Experience requirements.
63.57 Skill requirements.
63.59 Retesting after failure.
63.61 Flight navigator courses.

Appendix A to Part 63—Test Requirements For Flight Navigator Certificate
Appendix B to Part 63—Flight Navigator Training Course Requirements
Appendix C to Part 63—Flight Engineer Training Course Requirements

Authority: 49 U.S.C. 106(g), 40113, 44701–44703, 44707, 44709–44711, 45102–45103, 45301–45302.

Special Federal Aviation Regulation

SFAR No. 100-2 to Part 63
Relief for U.S. Military and Civilian Personnel Who are Assigned Outside the United States in Support of U.S. Armed Forces Operations

1. Applicability. Flight Standards District Offices are authorized to accept from an eligible person, as described in paragraph 2 of this SFAR, the following:

(a) An expired flight instructor certificate to show eligibility for renewal of a flight instructor certificate under §61.197, or an expired written test report to show eligibility under part 61 to take a practical test;

(b) An expired written test report to show eligibility under §§63.33 and 63.57 to take a practical test; and

(c) An expired written test report to show eligibility to take a practical test required under part 65 or an expired inspection authorization to show eligibility for renewal under §65.93.

2. Eligibility. A person is eligible for the relief described in paragraph 1 of this SFAR if:

(a) The person served in a U.S. military or civilian capacity outside the United States in support of the U.S. Armed Forces' operation during some period of time from September 11, 2001, to termination of SFAR 100–2;

(b) The person's flight instructor certificate, airman written test report, or inspection authorization expired some time between September 11, 2001, and 6 calendar months after returning to the United States or termination of SFAR 100–2, whichever is earlier; and

(c) The person complies with §61.197 or §65.93 of this chapter, as appropriate, or completes the appropriate practical test within 6 calendar months after returning to the United States, or upon termination of SFAR 100–2, whichever is earlier.

3. *Required documents.* The person must send the Airman Certificate and/or Rating Application (FAA Form 8710–1) to the appropriate Flight Standards District Office. The person must include with the application one of the following documents, which must show the date of assignment outside the United States and the date of return to the United States:

(a) An official U.S. Government notification of personnel action, or equivalent document, showing the person was a civilian on official duty for the U.S. Government outside the United States and was assigned to a U.S. Armed Forces' operation some time between September 11, 2001, to termination of SFAR 100–2;

(b) Military orders showing the person was assigned to duty outside the United States and was assigned to a U.S. Armed Forces' operation some time between September 11, 2001, to termination of SFAR 100–2; or

(c) A letter from the person's military commander or civilian supervisor providing the dates during which the person served outside the United States and was assigned to a U.S. Armed Forces' operation some time between September 11, 2001, to termination of SFAR 100–2.

4. *Expiration date.* This Special Federal Aviation Regulation No. 100–2 is effective until further notice.

[Docket No. FAA–2009–0923, SFAR No. 100–2, 75 FR 9766, March 4, 2010]

Subpart A—General

Source: Docket No. 1179, 27 FR 7969, Aug. 10, 1962, unless otherwise noted.

§63.1 Applicability.

This part prescribes the requirements for issuing flight engineer and flight navigator certificates and the general operating rules for holders of those certificates.

§63.2 Certification of foreign flight crewmembers other than pilots.

A person who is neither a United States citizen nor a resident alien is issued a certificate under this part (other than under §63.23 or §63.42) outside the United States only when the Administrator finds that the certificate is needed for the operation of a U.S.-registered civil aircraft.

(Secs. 313, 601, 602, Federal Aviation Act of 1958; as amended (49 U.S.C. 1354, 1421, and 1422); sec. 6(c), Department of Transportation Act (49 U.S.C. 1655(c)); Title V, Independent Offices Appropriations Act of 1952 (31 U.S.C. 483(a)); sec. 28, International Air Transportation Competition Act of 1979 (49 U.S.C. 1159(b)))

[Docket No. 22052, 47 FR 35693, Aug. 18, 1982]

§63.3 Certificates and ratings required.

(a) No person may act as a flight engineer of a civil aircraft of U.S. registry unless he has in his personal possession a current flight engineer certificate with appropriate ratings issued to him under this part and a second-class (or higher) medical certificate issued to him under part 67 of this chapter within the preceding 12 months. However, when the aircraft is operated within a foreign country, a current flight engineer certificate issued by the country in which the aircraft is operated, with evidence of current medical qualification for that certificate, may be used. Also, in the case of a flight engineer certificate issued under §63.42, evidence of current medical qualification accepted for the issue of that certificate is used in place of a medical certificate.

(b) No person may act as a flight navigator of a civil aircraft of U.S. registry unless he has in his personal possession a current flight navigator certificate issued to him under this part and a second-class (or higher) medical certificate issued to him under part 67 of this chapter within the preceding 12 months. However, when the aircraft is operated within a foreign country, a current flight navigator certificate issued by the country in which the aircraft is operated, with evidence of current medical qualification for that certificate, may be used.

(c) Each person who holds a flight engineer or flight navigator certificate, or medical certificate, shall present either or both for inspection upon the request of the Administrator or an authorized representative of the National Transportation Safety Board, or of any Federal, State, or local law enforcement officer.

(Secs. 3, 6, 9, 80 Stat. 931, 49 U.S.C. 1652, 1655, 1657)

[Docket No. 1179, 27 FR 7969, Aug. 10, 1962; as amended by Amdt. 63–1, 27 FR 10410, Oct. 25, 1962; Amdt. 63–3, 30 FR 14559, Nov. 23, 1965; Amdt. 63–7, 31 FR 13523, Oct. 20, 1966; Docket No. 8084, 32 FR 5769, April 11, 1967; Amdt. 63–9, 33 FR 18613, Dec. 17, 1968; Amdt. 63–11, 35 FR 5320, March 31, 1970]

§63.11 Application and issue.

(a) An application for a certificate and appropriate class rating, or for an additional rating, under this part must be made on a form and in a manner prescribed by the Administrator. Each person who applies for airmen certification services to be administered outside the United States for any certificate or rating issued under this part must show evidence that the fee prescribed in appendix A of part 187 of this chapter has been paid.

(b) An applicant who meets the requirements of this part is entitled to an appropriate certificate and appropriate class ratings.

(c) Unless authorized by the Administrator, a person whose flight engineer certificate is suspended may not apply for any rating to be added to that certificate during the period of suspension.

(d) Unless the order of revocation provides otherwise, a person whose flight engineer or flight navigator certificate is revoked may not apply for the same kind of certificate for 1 year after the date of revocation.

(Secs. 313, 601, 602, Federal Aviation Act of 1958; as amended (49 U.S.C. 1354, 1421, and 1422); sec. 6(c), Department of Transportation Act (49 U.S.C. 1655(c)); Title V, Independent Offices Appropriations Act of 1952 (31 U.S.C. 483(a)); sec. 28, International Air Transportation Competition Act of 1979 (49 U.S.C. 1159(b)))

[Docket No. 1179, 27 FR 7969, Aug. 10, 1962; as amended by Amdt. 63–3, 30 FR 14559, Nov. 23, 1965; Amdt. 63–7, 31 FR 13523, Oct. 20, 1966; Amdt. 63–22, 47 FR 35693, Aug. 16, 1982; Amdt. 63–35, 72 FR 18558, April 12, 2007]

§63.12 Offenses involving alcohol or drugs.

(a) A conviction for the violation of any Federal or state statute relating to the growing, processing, manufacture, sale, disposition, possession, transportation, or importation of narcotic drugs, marihuana, or depressant or stimulant drugs or substances is grounds for—

(1) Denial of an application for any certificate or rating issued under this part for a period of up to 1 year after the date of final conviction; or

(2) Suspension or revocation of any certificate or rating issued under this part.

(b) The commission of an act prohibited by §91.17(a) or §91.19(a) of this chapter is grounds for—

(1) Denial of an application for a certificate or rating issued under this part for a period of up to 1 year after the date of that act; or

(2) Suspension or revocation of any certificate or rating issued under this part.

[Docket No. 21956, 50 FR 15379, April 17, 1985; as amended by Amdt. 63–27, 54 FR 34330, Aug. 18, 1989]

§63.12a Refusal to submit to an alcohol test or to furnish test results.

A refusal to submit to a test to indicate the percentage by weight of alcohol in the blood, when requested by a law enforcement officer in accordance with §91.11(c) of this chapter, or a refusal to furnish or authorize the release of the test results when requested by the Administrator in accordance with §91.17 (c) or (d) of this chapter, is grounds for—

(a) Denial of an application for any certificate or rating issued under this part for a period of up to 1 year after the date of that refusal; or

(b) Suspension or revocation of any certificate or rating issued under this part.

[Docket No. 21956, 51 FR 1229, Jan. 9, 1986; as amended by Amdt. 63–27, 54 FR 34330, Aug. 18, 1989]

§63.12b [Reserved]

§63.13 Temporary certificate.

A certificate effective for a period of not more than 120 days may be issued to a qualified applicant, pending review of his application and supplementary documents and the issue of the certificate for which he applied.

[Docket No. 1179, 27 FR 7969, Aug. 10, 1962; as amended by Amdt. 63–19, 43 FR 22639, May 25, 1978]

§63.14 Security disqualification.

(a) *Eligibility standard.* No person is eligible to hold a certificate, rating, or authorization issued under this part when the Transportation Security Administration (TSA) has notified the FAA in writing that the person poses a security threat.

(b) *Effect of the issuance by the TSA of an Initial Notification of Threat Assessment.*

(1) The FAA will hold in abeyance pending the outcome of the TSA's final threat assessment review an application for any certificate, rating, or authorization under this part by any person who has been issued an Initial Notification of Threat Assessment by the TSA.

(2) The FAA will suspend any certificate, rating, or authorization issued under this part after the TSA issues to the holder an Initial Notification of Threat Assessment.

(c) *Effect of the issuance by the TSA of a Final Notification of Threat Assessment.*

(1) The FAA will deny an application for any certificate, rating, or authorization under this part to any person who has been issued a Final Notification of Threat Assessment.

(2) The FAA will revoke any certificate, rating, or authorization issued under this part after the TSA has issued to the holder a Final Notification of Threat Assessment.

[Docket No. FAA–2003–14293, 68 FR 3774, Jan. 24, 2003]

§63.15 Duration of certificates.

(a) Except as provided in §63.23 and paragraph (b) of this section, a certificate or rating issued under this part is effective until it is surrendered, suspended, or revoked.

(b) A flight engineer certificate (with any amendment thereto) issued under §63.42 expires at the end of the 24th month after the month in which the certificate was issued or renewed. However, the holder may exercise the privileges of that certificate only while the foreign flight engineer license on which that certificate is based is effective.

(c) Any certificate issued under this part ceases to be effective if it is surrendered, suspended, or revoked. The holder of any certificate issued under this part that is suspended or revoked shall, upon the Administrator's request, return it to the Administrator.

(d) Except for temporary certificate issued under §63.13, the holder of a paper certificate issued under this part may not exercise the privileges of that certificate after March 31, 2013.

(Sec. 6, 80 Stat. 937, 49 U.S.C. 1655; secs. 313, 601, 602, Federal Aviation Act of 1958; as amended (49 U.S.C. 1354, 1421, and 1422); sec. 6(c), Department of Transportation Act (49 U.S.C. 1655(c)); Title V, Independent Offices Appropriations Act of 1952 (31 U.S.C. 483(a)); sec. 28, International Air Transportation Competition Act of 1979 (49 U.S.C. 1159(b)))

[Docket No. 8846, 33 FR 18613, Dec. 17, 1968; as amended by Amdt. 63–22, 47 FR 35693, Aug. 16, 1982; Amdt. 63–36, 73 FR 10668, Feb. 28, 2008]

§63.15a [Reserved]

§63.16 Change of name; replacement of lost or destroyed certificate.

(a) An application for a change of name on a certificate issued under this part must be accompanied by the applicant's current certificate and the marriage license, court order, or other document verifying the change. The documents are returned to the applicant after inspection.

(b) An application for a replacement of a lost or destroyed certificate is made by letter to the Department of Transportation, Federal Aviation Administration, Airman Certification Branch, Post Office Box 25082, Oklahoma City, OK 73125. The letter must—

(1) Contain the name in which the certificate was issued, the permanent mailing address (including zip code), social security number (if any), and date and place of birth of the certificate holder, and any available information regarding the grade, number, and date of issue of the certificate, and the ratings on it; and

(2) Be accompanied by a check or money order for $2, payable to the Federal Aviation Administration.

(c) An application for a replacement of a lost or destroyed medical certificate is made by letter to the Department of Transportation, Federal Aviation Administration, Civil Aeromedical Institute, Aeromedical Certification Branch, Post Office Box 25082, Oklahoma City, OK 73125, accompanied by a check or money order for $2.00.

(d) A person whose certificate issued under this part or medical certificate, or both, has been lost may obtain a telegram from the Federal Aviation Administration confirming that it was issued. The telegram may be carried as a certificate for a period not to exceed 60 days pending his receiving a duplicate under paragraph (b) or (c) of this section, unless he has been notified that the certificate has been suspended or revoked. The request for such a telegram may be made by prepaid telegram, stating the date upon which a duplicate certificate was requested, or including the request for a duplicate and a money order for the necessary amount. The request for a telegraphic certificate should be sent to the office prescribed in paragraph (b) or (c) of this section, as appropriate. However, a request for both at the same time should be sent to the office prescribed in paragraph (b) of this section.

[Docket No. 7258, 31 FR 13523, Oct. 20, 1966; as amended by Docket No. 8084, 32 FR 5769, April 11, 1967; Amdt. 63–12, 35 FR 14075, Sept. 4, 1970; Amdt. 63–13, 36 FR 28654, Feb. 11, 1971]

§63.17 Tests: General procedure.

(a) Tests prescribed by or under this part are given at times and places, and by persons, designated by the Administrator.

(b) The minimum passing grade for each test is 70 percent.

§63.18 Written tests: Cheating or other unauthorized conduct.

(a) Except as authorized by the Administrator, no person may—

(1) Copy, or intentionally remove, a written test under this part;

(2) Give to another, or receive from another, any part or copy of that test;

(3) Give help on that test to, or receive help on that test from, any person during the period that test is being given;

(4) Take any part of that test in behalf of another person;

(5) Use any material or aid during the period that test is being given; or

(6) Intentionally cause, assist, or participate in any act prohibited by this paragraph.

(b) No person who commits an act prohibited by paragraph (a) of this section is eligible for any airman or ground instructor certificate or rating under this chapter for a period of 1 year after the date of that act. In addition, the commission of that act is a basis for suspending or revoking any airman or ground instructor certificate or rating held by that person.

[Docket No. 4086, 30 FR 2196, Feb. 18, 1965]

§63.19 Operations during physical deficiency.

No person may serve as a flight engineer or flight navigator during a period of known physical deficiency, or increase in physical deficiency, that would make him unable to meet the physical requirements for his current medical certificate.

§63.20 Applications, certificates, logbooks, reports, and records; falsification, reproduction, or alteration.

(a) No person may make or cause to be made—

(1) Any fraudulent or intentionally false statement on any application for a certificate or rating under this part;

(2) Any fraudulent or intentionally false entry in any logbook, record, or report that is required to be kept, made, or used, to show compliance with any requirement for any certificate or rating under this part;

(3) Any reproduction, for fraudulent purpose, of any certificate or rating under this part; or

(4) Any alteration of any certificate or rating under this part.

(b) The commission by any person of an act prohibited under paragraph (a) of this section is a basis for suspending or revoking any airman or ground instructor certificate or rating held by that person.

[Docket No. 4086, 30 FR 2196, Feb. 18, 1965]

§63.21 Change of address.

Within 30 days after any change in his permanent mailing address, the holder of a certificate issued under this part shall notify the Department of Transportation, Federal Aviation Administration, Airman Certification Branch, Post Office Box 25082, Oklahoma City, OK 73125, in writing, of his new address.

[Docket No. 10536, 35 FR 14075, Sept. 4, 1970]

§63.23 Special purpose flight engineer and flight navigator certificates: Operation of U.S.-registered civil airplanes leased by a person not a U.S. citizen.

(a) *General.* The holder of a current foreign flight engineer or flight navigator certificate, license, or authorization issued by a foreign contracting State to the Convention on International Civil Aviation, who meets the requirements of this section, may hold a special purpose flight engineer or flight navigator certificate, as appropriate, authorizing the holder to perform flight engineer or flight navigator duties on a civil airplane of U.S. registry, leased to a person not a citizen of the United States, carrying persons or property for compensation or hire. Special purpose flight engineer and flight navigator certificates are issued under this section only for airplane types that can have a maximum passenger seating configuration, excluding any flight crewmember seat, of more than 30 seats or a maximum payload capacity (as defined in §135.2(e) of this chapter) of more than 7,500 pounds.

(b) *Eligibility.* To be eligible for the issuance, or renewal, of a certificate under this section, an applicant must present the following to the Administrator:

(1) A current foreign flight engineer or flight navigator certificate, license, or authorization issued by the aeronautical authority of a foreign contracting State to the Convention on International Civil Aviation or a facsimile acceptable to the Administrator. The certificate or license must authorize the applicant to perform the flight engineer or flight navigator duties to be authorized by a certificate issued under this section on the same airplane type as the leased airplane.

(2) A current certification by the lessee of the airplane—

(i) Stating that the applicant is employed by the lessee;

(ii) Specifying the airplane type on which the applicant will perform flight engineer or flight navigator duties; and

(iii) Stating that the applicant has received ground and flight instruction which qualifies the applicant to perform the duties to be assigned on the airplane.

(3) Documentation showing that the applicant currently meets the medical standards for the foreign flight engineer or flight navigator certificate, license, or authorization required by paragraph (b)(1) of this section, except that a U.S. medical certificate issued under part 67 of this chapter is not evidence that the applicant meets those standards unless the State which issued the applicant's foreign flight engineer or flight navigator certificate, license, or authorization accepts a U.S. medical certificate as evidence of medical fitness for a flight engineer or flight navigator certificate, license, or authorization.

(c) *Privileges.* The holder of a special purpose flight engineer or flight navigator certificate issued under this section may exercise the same privileges as those shown on the certificate, license, or authorization specified in paragraph (b)(1) of this section, subject to the limitations specified in this section.

(d) *Limitations.* Each certificate issued under this section is subject to the following limitations:

(1) It is valid only—

(i) For flights between foreign countries and for flights in foreign air commerce;

(ii) While it and the certificate, license, or authorization required by paragraph (b)(1) of this section are in the certificate holder's personal possession and are current;

(iii) While the certificate holder is employed by the person to whom the airplane described in the certification required by paragraph (b)(2) of this section is leased;

(iv) While the certificate holder is performing flight engineer or flight navigator duties on the U.S.-registered civil airplane described in the certification required by paragraph (b)(2) of this section; and

(v) While the medical documentation required by paragraph (b)(3) of this section is in the certificate holder's personal possession and is currently valid.

(2) Each certificate issued under this section contains the following:

(i) The name of the person to whom the U.S.-registered civil airplane is leased.

(ii) The type of airplane.

(iii) The limitation: "Issued under, and subject to, §63.23 of the Federal Aviation Regulations."

(iv) The limitation: "Subject to the privileges and limitations shown on the holder's foreign flight (engineer or navigator) certificate, license, or authorization."

(3) Any additional limitations placed on the certificate which the Administrator considers necessary.

(e) *Termination.* Each special purpose flight engineer or flight navigator certificate issued under this section terminates—

(1) When the lease agreement for the airplane described in the certification required by paragraph (b)(2) of this section terminates;

(2) When the foreign flight engineer or flight navigator certificate, license, or authorization, or the medical documentation required by paragraph (b) of this section is suspended, revoked, or no longer valid; or

(3) After 24 months after the month in which the special purpose flight engineer or flight navigator certificate was issued.

(f) *Surrender of certificate.* The certificate holder shall surrender the special purpose flight engineer or flight navigator certificate to the Administrator within 7 days after the date it terminates.

(g) *Renewal.* The certificate holder may have the certificate renewed by complying with the requirements of paragraph (b) of this section at the time of application for renewal.

(Secs. 313(a), 601, and 602, Federal Aviation Act of 1958; as amended (49 U.S.C. 1354(a), 1421, and 1422); sec. 6(c), Department of Transportation Act (49 U.S.C. 1655(c)))

[Docket No. 19300, 45 FR 5672, Jan. 24, 1980]

Subpart B— Flight Engineers

Authority: Secs. 313(a), 601, and 602, Federal Aviation Act of 1958; 49 U.S.C. 1354, 1421, 1422.

Source: Docket No. 6458, 30 FR 14559, Nov. 23, 1965, unless otherwise noted.

§63.31 Eligibility requirements; general.

To be eligible for a flight engineer certificate, a person must—

(a) Be at least 21 years of age;

(b) Be able to read, speak, and understand the English language, or have an appropriate limitation placed on his flight engineer certificate;

(c) Hold at least a second-class medical certificate issued under part 67 of this chapter within the 12 months before the date he applies, or other evidence of medical qualification accepted for the issue of a flight engineer certificate under §63.42; and

(d) Comply with the requirements of this subpart that apply to the rating he seeks.

(Sec. 6, 80 Stat. 937, 49 U.S.C. 1655)

[Docket No. 6458, 30 FR 14559, Nov. 23, 1965; as amended by Amdt. 63–9, 33 FR 18614, Dec. 17, 1968]

§63.33 Aircraft ratings.

(a) The aircraft class ratings to be placed on flight engineer certificates are—

(1) Reciprocating engine powered;

(2) Turbopropeller powered; and

(3) Turbojet powered.

(b) To be eligible for an additional aircraft class rating after his flight engineer certificate with a class rating is issued to him, an applicant must pass the written test that is appropriate to the class of airplane for which an additional rating is sought, and—

(1) Pass the flight test for that class of aircraft; or

(2) Satisfactorily complete an approved flight engineer training program that is appropriate to the additional class rating sought.

§63.35 Knowledge requirements.

(a) An applicant for a flight engineer certificate must pass a written test on the following:

(1) The regulations of this chapter that apply to the duties of a flight engineer.

(2) The theory of flight and aerodynamics.

(3) Basic meteorology with respect to engine operations.

(4) Center of gravity computations.

(b) An applicant for the original or additional issue of a flight engineer class rating must pass a written test for that airplane class on the following:

(1) Preflight.

(2) Airplane equipment.
(3) Airplane systems.
(4) Airplane loading.
(5) Airplane procedures and engine operations with respect to limitations.
(6) Normal operating procedures.
(7) Emergency procedures.
(8) Mathematical computation of engine operations and fuel consumption.

(c) Before taking the written tests prescribed in paragraphs (a) and (b) of this section, an applicant for a flight engineer certificate must present satisfactory evidence of having completed one of the experience requirements of §63.37. However, he may take the written tests before acquiring the flight training required by §63.37.

(d) An applicant for a flight engineer certificate or rating must have passed the written tests required by paragraphs (a) and (b) of this section since the beginning of the 24th calendar month before the month in which the flight is taken. However, this limitation does not apply to an applicant for a flight engineer certificate or rating if—
(1) The applicant—
(i) Within the period ending 24 calendar months after the month in which the applicant passed the written test, is employed as a flight crewmember or mechanic by a U.S. air carrier or commercial operator operating either under part 121 or as a commuter air carrier under part 135 (as defined in part 298 of this title) and is employed by such a certificate holder at the time of the flight test;
(ii) If employed as a flight crewmember, has completed initial training, and, if appropriate, transition or upgrade training; and
(iii) Meets the recurrent training requirements of the applicable part or, for mechanics, meets the recency of experience requirements of part 65; or
(2) Within the period ending 24 calendar months after the month in which the applicant passed the written test, the applicant participated in a flight engineer or maintenance training program of a U.S. scheduled military air transportation service and is currently participating in that program.

(e) An air carrier or commercial operator with an approved training program under part 121 of this chapter may, when authorized by the Administrator, provide as part of that program a written test that it may administer to satisfy the test required for an additional rating under paragraph (b) of this section.

(Sec. 6, 80 Stat. 937, 49 U.S.C. 1655; Secs. 313(a), 601 through 605 of the Federal Aviation Act of 1958 (49 U.S.C. 1354(a), 1421 through 1425); sec. 6(c), Department of Transportation Act (49 U.S.C. 1655(c)); and 14 CFR 11.49)

[Docket No. 1179, 27 FR 7969, Aug. 10, 1962; as amended by Amdt. 63-17, 40 FR 32830, Aug. 5, 1975; Amdt. 63-21, 47 FR 13316, March 29, 1982]

§63.37 Aeronautical experience requirements.

(a) Except as otherwise specified therein, the flight time used to satisfy the aeronautical experience requirements of paragraph (b) of this section must have been obtained on an airplane—
(1) On which a flight engineer is required by this chapter; or
(2) That has at least three engines that are rated at least 800 horsepower each or the equivalent in turbine-powered engines.

(b) An applicant for a flight engineer certificate with a class rating must present, for the class rating sought, satisfactory evidence of one of the following:
(1) At least 3 years of diversified practical experience in aircraft and aircraft engine maintenance (of which at least 1 year was in maintaining multiengine aircraft with engines rated at least 800 horsepower each, or the equivalent in turbine engine powered aircraft), and at least 5 hours of flight training in the duties of a flight engineer.
(2) Graduation from at least a 2-year specialized aeronautical training course in maintaining aircraft and aircraft engines (of which at least 6 calendar months were in maintaining multiengine aircraft with engines rated at least 800 horsepower each or the equivalent in turbine engine powered aircraft), and at least 5 hours of flight training in the duties of a flight engineer.
(3) A degree in aeronautical, electrical, or mechanical engineering from a recognized college, university, or engineering school; at least 6 calendar months of practical experience in maintaining multiengine aircraft with engines rated at least 800 horsepower each, or the equivalent in turbine engine powered aircraft; and at least 5 hours of flight training in the duties of a flight engineer.
(4) At least a commercial pilot certificate with an instrument rating and at least 5 hours of flight training in the duties of a flight engineer.
(5) At least 200 hours of flight time in a transport category airplane (or in a military airplane with at least two engines and at least equivalent weight and horsepower) as pilot in command or second in command performing the functions of a pilot in command under the supervision of a pilot in command.
(6) At least 100 hours of flight time as a flight engineer.
(7) Within the 90-day period before he applies, successful completion of an approved flight engineer ground and flight course of instruction as provided in Appendix C of this part.

(Sec. 6, 80 Stat. 937, 49 U.S.C. 1655)

[Docket No. 6458, 30 FR 14559, Nov. 23, 1965; as amended by Amdt. 63-5, 31 FR 9047, July 1, 1966; Amdt. 63-17, 40 FR 32830, Aug. 5, 1975]

§63.39 Skill requirements.

(a) An applicant for a flight engineer certificate with a class rating must pass a practical test on the duties of a flight engineer in the class of airplane for which a rating is sought. The test may only be given on an airplane specified in §63.37(a).

(b) The applicant must—

(1) Show that he can satisfactorily perform preflight inspection, servicing, starting, pretakeoff, and postlanding procedures;

(2) In flight, show that he can satisfactorily perform the normal duties and procedures relating to the airplane, airplane engines, propellers (if appropriate), systems, and appliances; and

(3) In flight, in an airplane simulator, or in an approved flight engineer training device, show that he can satisfactorily perform emergency duties and procedures and recognize and take appropriate action for malfunctions of the airplane, engines, propellers (if appropriate), systems and appliances.

§63.41 Retesting after failure.

An applicant for a flight engineer certificate who fails a written test or practical test for that certificate may apply for retesting—

(a) After 30 days after the date he failed that test; or

(b) After he has received additional practice or instruction (flight, synthetic trainer, or ground training, or any combination thereof) that is necessary, in the opinion of the Administrator or the applicant's instructor (if the Administrator has authorized him to determine the additional instruction necessary) to prepare the applicant for retesting.

§63.42 Flight engineer certificate issued on basis of a foreign flight engineer license.

(a) *Certificates issued.* The holder of a current foreign flight engineer license issued by a contracting State to the Convention on International Civil Aviation, who meets the requirements of this section, may have a flight engineer certificate issued to him for the operation of civil aircraft of U.S. registry. Each flight engineer certificate issued under this section specifies the number and State of issuance of the foreign flight engineer license on which it is based. If the holder of the certificate cannot read, speak, or understand the English language, the Administrator may place any limitation on the certificate that he considers necessary for safety.

(b) *Medical standards and certification.* An applicant must submit evidence that he currently meets the medical standards for the foreign flight engineer license on which the application for a certificate under this section is based. A current medical certificate issued under part 67 of this chapter will be excepted as evidence that the applicant meets those standards. However, a medical certificate issued under part 67 of this chapter is not evidence that the applicant meets those standards outside the United States unless the State that issued the applicant's foreign flight engineer license also accepts that medical certificate as evidence of the applicant's physical fitness for his foreign flight engineer license.

(c) *Ratings issued.* Aircraft class ratings listed on the applicant's foreign flight engineer license, in addition to any issued to him after testing under the provisions of this part, are placed on the applicant's flight engineer certificate. An applicant without an aircraft class rating on his foreign flight engineer license may be issued a class rating if he shows that he currently meets the requirements for exercising the privileges of his foreign flight engineer license on that class of aircraft.

(d) *Privileges and limitations.* The holder of a flight engineer certificate issued under this section may act as a flight engineer of a civil aircraft of U.S. registry subject to the limitations of this part and any additional limitations placed on his certificate by the Administrator. He is subject to these limitations while he is acting as a flight engineer of the aircraft within or outside the United States. However, he may not act as flight engineer or in any other capacity as a required flight crewmember, of a civil aircraft of U.S. registry that is carrying persons or property for compensation or hire.

(e) *Renewal of certificate and ratings.* The holder of a certificate issued under this section may have that certificate and the ratings placed thereon renewed if, at the time of application for renewal, the foreign flight engineer license on which that certificate is based is in effect. Application for the renewal of the certificate and ratings thereon must be made before the expiration of the certificate.

(Sec. 6, 80 Stat. 937, 49 U.S.C. 1655)

[Docket No. 8846, 33 FR 18614, Dec. 17, 1968; as amended by Amdt. 63–20, 45 FR 5673, Jan. 24, 1980]

§63.43 Flight engineer courses.

An applicant for approval of a flight engineer course must submit a letter to the Administrator requesting approval, and must also submit three copies of each course outline, a description of the facilities and equipment, and a list of the instructors and their qualifications. An air carrier or commercial operator with an approved flight engineer training course under part 121 of this chapter may apply for approval of a training course under this part by letter without submitting the additional information required by this paragraph. Minimum requirements for obtaining approval of a flight engineer course are set forth in Appendix C of this part.

Subpart C— Flight Navigators

Authority: Secs. 313(a), 314, 601, and 607; 49 U.S.C. 1354(a), 1355, 1421, and 1427.

Source: Docket No. 1179, 27 FR 7970, Aug. 10, 1962, unless otherwise noted.

§63.51 Eligibility requirements; general.

To be eligible for a flight navigator certificate, a person must—

(a) Be at least 21 years of age;
(b) Be able to read, write, speak, and understand the English language;
(c) Hold at least a second-class medical certificate issued under part 67 of this chapter within the 12 months before the date he applies; and
(d) Comply with §§63.53, 63.55, and 63.57.

§63.53 Knowledge requirements.

(a) An applicant for a flight navigator certificate must pass a written test on—
(1) The regulations of this chapter that apply to the duties of a flight navigator;
(2) The fundamentals of flight navigation, including flight planning and cruise control;
(3) Practical meteorology, including analysis of weather maps, weather reports, and weather forecasts; and weather sequence abbreviations, symbols, and nomenclature;
(4) The types of air navigation facilities and procedures in general use;
(5) Calibrating and using air navigation instruments;
(6) Navigation by dead reckoning;
(7) Navigation by celestial means;
(8) Navigation by radio aids;
(9) Pilotage and map reading; and
(10) Interpretation of navigation aid identification signals.

(b) A report of the test is mailed to the applicant. A passing grade is evidence, for a period of 24 months after the test, that the applicant has complied with this section.

[Docket No. 1179, 27 FR 7970, Aug. 10 1962; as amended by Amdt. 63–19, 43 FR 22639, May 25, 1978]

§63.55 Experience requirements.

(a) An applicant for a flight navigator certificate must be a graduate of a flight navigator course approved by the Administrator or present satisfactory documentary evidence of—
(1) Satisfactory determination of his position in flight at least 25 times by night by celestial observations and at least 25 times by day by celestial observations in conjunction with other aids; and
(2) At least 200 hours of satisfactory flight navigation including celestial and radio navigation and dead reckoning.

A pilot who has logged 500 hours of cross-country flight time, of which at least 100 hours were at night, may be credited with not more than 100 hours for the purposes of paragraph (a)(2) of this section.

(b) Flight time used exclusively for practicing long-range navigation methods, with emphasis on celestial navigation and dead reckoning, is considered to be satisfactory navigation experience for the purposes of paragraph (a) of this section. It must be substantiated by a logbook, by records of an armed force or a certificated air carrier, or by a letter signed by a certificated flight navigator and attached to the application.

§63.57 Skill requirements.

(a) An applicant for a flight navigator certificate must pass a practical test in navigating aircraft by—
(1) Dead reckoning;
(2) Celestial means; and
(3) Radio aids to navigation.

(b) An applicant must pass the written test prescribed by §63.53 before taking the test under this section. However, if a delay in taking the test under this section would inconvenience the applicant or an air carrier, he may take it before he receives the result of the written test, or after he has failed the written test.

(c) The test requirements for this section are set forth in Appendix A of this part.

[Docket No. 1179, 27 FR 7970, Aug. 10, 1962; as amended by Amdt. 63–19, 43 FR 22639, May 25, 1978]

§63.59 Retesting after failure.

(a) An applicant for a flight navigator certificate who fails a written or practical test for that certificate may apply for retesting—
(1) After 30 days after the date he failed that test; or
(2) Before the 30 days have expired if the applicant presents a signed statement from a certificated flight navigator, certificated ground instructor, or any other qualified person approved by the Administrator, certifying that person has given the applicant additional instruction in each of the subjects failed and that person considers the applicant ready for retesting.

(b) A statement from a certificated flight navigator, or from an operations official of an approved navigator course, is acceptable, for the purposes of paragraph (a)(2) of this section, for the written test and for the flight test. A statement from a person approved by the Administrator is acceptable for the written tests. A statement from a supervising or check navigator with the United

States Armed Forces is acceptable for the written test and for the practical test.

(c) If the applicant failed the flight test, the additional instruction must have been administered in flight.

[Docket No. 1179, 27 FR 7970, Aug. 10, 1962; as amended by Amdt. 63–19, 43 FR 22640, May 25, 1978]

§63.61 Flight navigator courses.

An applicant for approval of a flight navigator course must submit a letter to the Administrator requesting approval, and must also submit three copies of the course outline, a description of his facilities and equipment, and a list of the instructors and their qualifications. Requirements for the course are set forth in Appendix B to this part.

APPENDIX A TO PART 63
TEST REQUIREMENTS FOR FLIGHT NAVIGATOR CERTIFICATE

(a) *Demonstration of skill.* An applicant will be required to pass practical tests on the prescribed subjects. These tests may be given by FAA inspectors and designated flight navigator examiners.

(b) *The examination.* The practical examination consists of a ground test and a flight test as itemized on the examination check sheet. Each item must be completed satisfactorily in order for the applicant to obtain a passing grade. Items 5, 6, 7 of the ground test may be completed orally, and items 17, 22, 23, 34, 36, 37, 38, and 39 of the flight test may be completed by an oral examination when a lack of ground facilities or navigation equipment makes such procedure necessary. In these cases a notation to that effect shall be made in the "Remarks" space on the check sheet.

(c) *Examination procedure.*

(1) An applicant will provide an aircraft in which celestial observations can be taken in all directions. Minimum equipment shall include a table for plotting, a drift meter or absolute altimeter, an instrument for taking visual bearings, and a radio direction finder.

(2) More than one flight may be used to complete the flight test and any type of flight pattern may be used. The test will be conducted chiefly over water whenever practicable, and without regard to radio range legs or radials. If the test is conducted chiefly over land, a chart should be used which shows very little or no topographical and aeronautical data. The total flight time will cover a period of at least four hours. Only one applicant may be examined at one time, and no applicant may perform other than navigator duties during the examination.

(3) When the test is conducted with an aircraft belonging to an air carrier, the navigation procedures should conform with those set forth in the carrier's operations manual. Items of the flight test which are not performed during the routine navigation of the flight will be completed by oral examination after the flight or at times during flight which the applicant indicates may be used for tests on those items. Since in-flight weather conditions, the reliability of the weather forecast, and the stability of the aircraft will have considerable effect on an applicant's performance, good judgment must be used by the agent or examiner in evaluating the tests.

(d) *Ground test.* For the ground test, in the order of the numbered items on the examination check sheet, an applicant will be required to:

(1) Identify without a star identifier, at least six navigational stars and all planets available for navigation at the time of the examination and explain the method of identification.

(2) Identify two additional stars with a star identifier or sky diagrams and explain identification procedure.

(3) Precompute a time-altitude curve for a period of about 20 minutes and take 10 single observations of a celestial body which is rising or setting rapidly. The intervals between observations should be at least one minute. Mark each observation on the graph to show accuracy. All observations, after corrections, shall plot within 8 minutes of arc from the time-altitude curve, and the average error shall not exceed 5 minutes of arc.

(4) Take and plot one 3-star fix and 3 LOPs of the sun. Plotted fix or an average of LOPs must fall within 5 miles of the actual position of the observer.

(5) Demonstrate or explain the compensation and swinging of a liquid-type magnetic compass.

(6) Demonstrate or explain a method of aligning one type of drift meter.

(7) Demonstrate or explain a method of aligning an astro-compass or periscopic sextant.

(e) *Flight test.* For the flight test, in the order of the numbered items on the examination check sheet, an applicant will be required to:

(1) Demonstrate his ability to read weather symbols and interpret synoptic surface and upper air weather maps with particular emphasis being placed on winds.

(2) Prepare a flight plan by zones from the forecast winds or pressure data of an upper air chart and the operator's data.

(3) Compute from the operator's data the predicted fuel consumption for each zone of the flight, including the alternate.

(4) Determine the point-of-no-return for the flight with all engines running and the equitime point with one engine inoperative. Graphical methods which are part of the company's oper-

Part 63: Certification: Flight Crewmembers   **Appendix A to Part 63**

ations manual may be used for these computations.

(5) Prepare a cruise control (howgozit) chart from the operator's data.

(6) Enter actual fuel consumed on the cruise control chart and interpret the variations of the actual curve from the predicted curve.

(7) Check the presence on board and operating condition of all navigation equipment. Normally a check list will be used. This check will include a time tick or chronometer comparison. Any lack of thoroughness during this check will justify this item being graded unsatisfactory.

(8) Locate emergency equipment, such as, the nearest fire extinguisher, life preserver, life rafts, exits, axe, first aid kits, etc.

(9) Recite the navigator's duties and stations during emergencies for the type of aircraft used for the test.

(10) Demonstrate the proper use of a flux gate compass or gyrosyn compass (when available), with special emphasis on the caging methods and the location of switches, circuit breakers, and fuses. If these compasses are not part of the aircraft's equipment, an oral examination will be given.

(11) Be accurate and use good judgment when setting and altering headings. Erroneous application of variation, deviation, or drift correction, or incorrect measurement of course on the chart will be graded as unsatisfactory.

(12) Demonstrate or explain the use of characteristics of various chart projections used in long-range air navigation, including the plotting of courses and bearings, and the measuring of distances.

(13) Demonstrate ability to identify designated landmarks by the use of a sectional or WAC chart.

(14) Use a computer with facility and accuracy for the computation of winds, drift correction and drift angles, ground speeds, ETAs, fuel loads, etc.

(15) Determine track, ground speed, and wind by the double drift method. When a drift meter is not part of the aircraft's equipment, an oral examination on the use of the drift meter and a double drift problem shall be completed.

(16) Determine ground speed and wind by the timing method with a drift meter. When a drift meter is not part of the aircraft's equipment, an oral examination on the procedure and a problem shall be completed.

(17) Demonstrate the use of air plot for determining wind between fixes and for plotting pressure lines of position when using pressure and absolute altimeter comparisons.

(18) Give ETAs to well defined check points at least once each hour after the second hour of flight. The average error shall not be more than 5 percent of the intervening time intervals, and the maximum error of any one ETA shall not be more than 10 percent.

(19) Demonstrate knowledge and use of D/F equipment and radio facility information. Grading on this item will be based largely on the applicant's selection of those radio aids which will be of most value to his navigation, the manner with which he uses equipment, including filter box controls, and the precision with which he reads bearings. The aircraft's compass heading and all compass corrections must be considered for each bearing.

(20) Use care in tuning to radio stations to insure maximum reception of signal and check for interference signals. Receiver will be checked to ascertain that antenna and BFO (Voice-CW) switches are in correct positions.

(21) Identify at least three radio stations using International Morse code only for identification. The agent or examiner will tune in these stations so that the applicant will have no knowledge of the direction, distance, or frequency of the stations.

(22) Take at least one radio bearing by manual use of the loop. The agent or examiner will check the applicant's bearing by taking a manual bearing on the same station immediately after the applicant.

(23) Show the use of good judgment in evaluating radio bearings, and explain why certain bearings may be of doubtful value.

(24) Determine and apply correctly the correction required to be made to radio bearings before plotting them on a Mercator chart, and demonstrate the ability to plot bearings accurately on charts of the Mercator and Lambert conformal projections.

(25) Compute the compass heading, ETA, and fuel remaining if it is assumed that the flight would be diverted to an alternate airport at a time specified by the agent or examiner.

(26) Check the counter scales of a Loran receiver for accuracy, and explain the basic (face) adjustments which affect tuning and counter alignment. A guide sheet may be used for this test.

(27) Demonstrate a knowledge of the basic principle of Loran and the ability to tune a Loran receiver, to match signals, to read time differences, to plot Loran LOPs, and to identify and use sky waves.

(28) Take and plot bearings from a consol station and explain the precautions which must be taken when tuning a radio receiver for consol signals. Also, discuss those conditions which affect the reliability of consol bearings.

(29) Demonstrate the ability to properly operate and read an absolute altimeter.

ASA

Appendix A to Part 63   **Federal Aviation Regulations**

(30) Determine the "D" factors for a series of compared readings of an absolute altimeter and a pressure altimeter.

(31) Determine drift angle or lateral displacement from the true headingline by application of Bellamy's formula or a variation thereof.

(32) Interpret the altimeter comparison data with respect to the pressure system found at flight level. From this data evaluate the accuracy of the prognostic weather map used for flight planning and apply this analysis to the navigation of the flight.

(33) Interpret single LOPs for most probable position, and show how a series of single LOPs of the same body may be used to indicate the probable track and ground speed. Also, show how a series of single LOPs (celestial or radio) from the same celestial body or radio station may be used to determine position when the change of azimuth or bearing is 30° or more between observations.

(34) Select one of the celestial LOPs used during the flight and explain how to make a single line of position approach to a point selected by the agent or examiner, giving headings, times, and ETAs.

(35) Demonstrate the proper use of an astrocompass or periscopic sextant for taking bearings.

(36) Determine compass deviation as soon as possible after reaching cruising altitude and whenever there is a change of compass heading of 15° or more.

(37) Take celestial fixes at hourly intervals when conditions permit. The accuracy of these fixes shall be checked by means of a Loran, radio, or visual fix whenever practicable. After allowing for the probable error of a Loran, radio, or visual fix, a celestial fix under favorable conditions should plot within 10 miles of the actual position.

(38) Select celestial bodies for observation, when possible, whose azimuths will differ by approximately 120° for a 3-body fix and will differ by approximately 90° for a 2-body fix. The altitudes of the selected bodies should be between 25° and 75° whenever practicable.

(39) Have POMAR and any other required reports ready for transmission at time of schedule, and be able to inform the pilot in command promptly with regard to the aircraft's position and progress in comparison with the flight plan.

(40) Keep a log with sufficient legible entries to provide a record from which the flight could be retraced.

(41) Note significant weather changes which might influence the drift or ground speed of the aircraft, such as, temperature, "D" factors, frontal conditions, turbulence, etc.

(42) Determine the wind between fixes as a regular practice.

(43) Estimate the time required and average ground speed during a letdown, under conditions specified by the pilot in command.

(44) Work with sufficient speed to determine the aircraft's position hourly by celestial means and also make all other observations and records pertinent to the navigation. The applicant should be able to take the observation, compute, and plot a celestial LOP within a time limit of 8 minutes; take and plot a Loran LOP within a time limit of 3 minutes for ground waves and 4 minutes for sky waves; observe the absolute and pressure altimeters and compute the drift or lateral displacement within a time limit of 3 minutes.

(45) Be accurate in reading instruments and making computations. Errors which are made and corrected without affecting the navigation will be disregarded unless they cause considerable loss of time.

An uncorrected error in computation (including reading instruments and books) which will affect the reported position more than 25 miles, the heading more than 3°, or any ETA more than 15 minutes will cause this item to be graded unsatisfactory.

(46) Be alert to changing weather or other conditions during flight which might affect the navigation. An applicant should not fail to take celestial observations just prior to encountering a broken or overcast sky condition; and he should not fail to take a bearing on a radio station, which operates at scheduled intervals and which would be a valuable aid to the navigation.

(47) Show a logical choice and sequence in using the various navigation methods according to time and accuracy, and check the positions determined by one method against positions determined by other methods.

(48) Use a logical sequence in performing the various duties of a navigator and plan work according to a schedule. The more important duties should not be neglected for others of less importance.

26   ASA

APPENDIX B TO PART 63
FLIGHT NAVIGATOR
TRAINING COURSE REQUIREMENTS

(a) *Training course outline—*

(1) *Format.* The ground course outline and the flight course outline shall be combined in one looseleaf binder and shall include a table of contents, divided into two parts—ground course and flight course. Each part of the table of contents must contain a list of the major subjects, together with hours allotted to each subject and the total classroom and flight hours.

(2) *Ground course outline.*

(i) It is not mandatory that a course outline have the subject headings arranged exactly as listed in this paragraph. Any arrangement of general headings and subheadings will be satisfactory provided all the subject material listed here is included and the acceptable minimum number of hours is assigned to each subject. Each general subject shall be broken down into detail showing items to be covered.

(ii) If any agency desires to include additional subjects in the ground training curriculum, such as international law, flight hygiene, or others which are not required, the hours allotted these additional subjects may not be included in the minimum classroom hours.

(iii) The following subjects with classroom hours are considered the minimum coverage for a ground training course for flight navigators:

Subject	Classroom hours
Federal Aviation Regulations To include Parts 63, 91, and 121 of this chapter.	5

Meteorology
To include:
  Basic weather principles
  Temperature
  Pressure
  Winds
  Moisture in the atmosphere
  Stability
  Clouds
  Hazards
  Air masses
  Front weather
  Fog
  Thunderstorms
  Icing
  World weather and climate
  Weather maps and weather reports
  Forecasting
	40

International Morse code: Ability to receive code groups of letters and numerals at a speed of eight words per minute	

Navigation instruments
(exclusive of radio and radar)
To include:
  Compasses
  Pressure altimeters
  Airspeed indicators
  Driftmeters
  Bearing indicators
  Aircraft octants
  Instrument calibration and alignment
	20

Charts and pilotage
To include:
  Chart projections
  Chart symbols
  Principles of pilotage
	15

Dead Reckoning
To include:
  Air plot
  Ground plot
  Calculation of ETA
  Vector analysis
  Use of computer
  Search
	30

Absolute altimeter with: Applications
To include:
  Principles of construction
  Operating instructions
  Use of Bellamy's formula
  Flight planning with single drift correction
	15

Radio and long-range navigational aids
To include:
  Principles of radio transmission and reception
  Radio aids to navigation
  Government publications
  Airborne D/F equipment
  Errors of radio bearings
  Quadrantal correction
  Plotting radio bearings
  ICAO Q code for direction finding
  Loran
  Consol
	35

Celestial navigation
To include:
  The solar system
  The celestial sphere
  The astronomical triangle
  Theory of lines of position
  Use of the Air Almanac
  Time and its applications
  Navigation tables
  Precomputation
  Celestial line of position approach
  Star identification
  Corrections to celestial observations
	150

Flight planning and cruise control
To include:
  The flight plan
  Fuel consumption charts
  Methods of cruise control
  Flight progress chart
  Point-of-no-return
  Equitime point
	25

Long-range flight problems	15
Total (exclusive of final examinations)	350

Appendix B to Part 63   **Federal Aviation Regulations**

(3) *Flight course outline.*

(i) A minimum of 150 hours of supervised flight training shall be given, of which at least 50 hours of flight training must be given at night, and celestial navigation must be used during flights which total at least 125 hours.

(ii) A maximum of 50 hours of the required flight training may be obtained in acceptable types of synthetic flight navigator training devices.

(iii) Flights should be at least four hours in length and should be conducted off civil airways. Some training on long-range flights is desirable, but is not required. There is no limit to the number of students that may be trained on one flight, but at least one astrodome or one periscopic sextant mounting must be provided for each group of four students.

(iv) Training must be given in dead reckoning, pilotage, radio navigation, celestial navigation, and the use of the absolute altimeter.

(b) *Equipment.*

(1) Classroom equipment shall include one table at least 24" x 32" in dimensions for each student.

(2) Aircraft suitable for the flight training must be available to the approved course operator to insure that the flight training may be completed without undue delay.

The approved course operator may contract or obtain written agreements with aircraft operators for the use of suitable aircraft. A copy of the contract or written agreement with an aircraft operator shall be attached to each of the three copies of the course outline submitted for approval. In all cases, the approved course operator is responsible for the nature and quality of instruction given during flight.

(c) *Instructors.*

(1) Sufficient classroom instructors must be available to prevent an excessive ratio of students to instructors. Any ratio in excess of 20 to 1 will be considered unsatisfactory.

(2) At least one ground instructor must hold a valid flight navigator certificate, and be utilized to coordinate instruction of ground school subjects.

(3) Each instructor who conducts flight training must hold a valid flight navigator certificate.

(d) *Revision of training course.*

(1) Requests for revisions to course outlines, facilities, and equipment shall follow procedures for original approval of the course. Revisions should be submitted in such form that an entire page or pages of the approved outline can be removed and replaced by the revisions.

(2) The list of instructors may be revised at any time without request for approval, provided the minimum requirement of paragraph (e) of this section is maintained.

(e) *Credit for previous training and experience.*

(1) Credit may be granted by an operator to students for previous training and experience which is provable and comparable to portions of the approved curriculum. When granting such credit, the approved course operator should be fully cognizant of the fact that he is responsible for the proficiency of his graduates in accordance with subdivision (i) of paragraph (3) of this section.

(2) Where advanced credit is allowed, the operator shall evaluate the student's previous training and experience in accordance with the normal practices of accredited technical schools. Before credit is given for any ground school subject or portion thereof, the student must pass an appropriate examination given by the operator. The results of the examination, the basis for credit allowance, and the hours credited shall be incorporated as a part of the student's records.

(3) Credit up to a maximum of 50 hours toward the flight training requirement may be given to pilots who have logged at least 500 hours while a member of a flight crew which required a certificated flight navigator or the Armed Forces equivalent. A similar credit may also be given to a licensed deck officer of the Maritime Service who has served as such for at least one year on ocean-going vessels. One-half of the flight time credited under the terms of this paragraph may be applied toward the 50 hours of flight training required at night.

(f) *Students records and reports.* Approval of a course shall not be continued in effect unless the course operator keeps an accurate record of each student, including a chronological log of all instruction, subjects covered and course examinations and grades, and unless he prepares and transmits to the local Flight Standards District Office not later than January 31 of each year, a report containing the following information for the previous calendar year:

(1) The names of all students graduated, together with their school grades for ground and flight subjects.

(2) The names of all students failed or dropped, together with their school grades and reasons for dropping.

(g) *Quality of instruction.* Approval of a course shall not be continued in effect unless at least 80 percent of the students who apply within 90 days after graduation are able to qualify on the first attempt for certification as flight navigators.

(h) *Statement of graduation.* Each student who successfully completes an approved flight navigator course shall be given a statement of graduation.

(i) *Inspections.* Approved course operations will be inspected by authorized representatives of the Administrator as often as deemed necessary to insure that instruction is maintained at the required standards, but the period between inspections shall not exceed 12 months.

(j) *Change of ownership, name, or location—*

(1) *Change of ownership.* Approval of a flight navigator course shall not be continued in effect after the course has changed ownership. The new owner must obtain a new approval by following the procedure prescribed for original approval.

(2) *Change in name.* An approved course changed in name but not changed in ownership shall remain valid if the change is reported by the approved course operator to the local Flight Standards District Office. A letter of approval under the new name will be issued by the regional office.

(3) *Change in location.* An approved course shall remain in effect even though the approved course operator changes location if the change is reported without delay by the operator to the local Flight Standards District Office, which will inspect the facilities to be used. If they are found to be adequate, a letter of approval showing the new location will be issued by the regional office.

(k) *Cancellation of approval.*

(1) Failure to meet or maintain any of the requirements set forth in this section for the approval or operation of an approved flight navigator course shall be considered sufficient reason for cancellation of the approval.

(2) If an operator should desire voluntary cancellation of his approved course, he should submit the effective letter of approval and a written request for cancellation to the Administrator through the local Flight Standards District Office.

(l) *Duration.* The authority to operate an approved flight navigator course shall expire 24 months after the last day of the month of issuance.

(m) *Renewal.* Application for renewal of authority to operate an approved flight navigator course may be made by letter to the local Flight Standards District Office at any time within 60 days before to the expiration date. Renewal of approval will depend upon the course operator meeting the current conditions for approval and having a satisfactory record as an operator.

[Docket No. 1179, 27 FR 7970, Aug. 10, 1962; as amended by Amdt. 63–6, 31 FR 9211, July 6, 1966; Amdt. 63–28, 54 FR 39291, Sept. 25, 1989]

APPENDIX C TO PART 63
FLIGHT ENGINEER TRAINING COURSE REQUIREMENTS

(a) *Training course outline—*

(1) *Format.* The ground course outline and the flight course outline are independent. Each must be contained in a looseleaf binder to include a table of contents. If an applicant desires approval of both a ground school course and a flight school course, they must be combined in one looseleaf binder that includes a separate table of contents for each course. Separate course outlines are required for each type of airplane.

(2) *Ground course outline.*

(i) It is not mandatory that the subject headings be arranged exactly as listed in this paragraph. Any arrangement of subjects is satisfactory if all the subject material listed here is included and at least the minimum programmed hours are assigned to each subject. Each general subject must be broken down into detail showing the items to be covered.

(ii) If any course operator desires to include additional subjects in the ground course curriculum, such as international law, flight hygiene, or others that are not required, the hours allotted these additional subjects may not be included in the minimum programmed classroom hours.

(iii) The following subjects and classroom hours are the minimum programmed coverage for the initial approval of a ground training course for flight engineers. Subsequent to initial approval of a ground training course an applicant may apply to the Administrator for a reduction in the programmed hours. Approval of a reduction in the approved programmed hours is based on improved training effectiveness due to improvements in methods, training aids, quality of instruction, or any combination thereof.

Appendix C to Part 63   Federal Aviation Regulations

Subject	Classroom hours
Federal Aviation Regulations	10
To include the regulations of this chapter that apply to flight engineers	
Theory of Flight and Aerodynamics	10
Airplane Familiarization	90
To include as appropriate: Specifications Construction features Flight controls Hydraulic systems Pneumatic systems Electrical systems Anti-icing and de-icing systems Pressurization and air-conditioning systems Vacuum systems Pitot static systems Instrument systems Fuel and oil systems Emergency equipment	
Engine Familiarization	45
To include as appropriate: Specifications Construction features Lubrication Ignition Carburetor and induction, supercharging and fuel control systems Accessories Propellers Instrumentation Emergency equipment	
Normal Operations (Ground and Flight)	50
To include as appropriate: Servicing methods and procedures Operation of all the airplane systems Operation of all the engine systems Loading and center of gravity computations Cruise control (normal, long range, maximum endurance) Power and fuel computation Meteorology as applicable to engine operation	
Emergency Operations	80
To include as appropriate: Landing gear, brakes, flaps, speed brakes, and leading edge devices Pressurization and air-conditioning Portable fire extinguishers Fuselage fire and smoke control Loss of electrical power Engine fire control Engine shut-down and restart Oxygen	
Total (exclusive of final tests)	235

The above subjects, except Theory of Flight and Aerodynamics, and Regulations must apply to the same type of airplane in which the student flight engineer is to receive flight training.

(3) *Flight Course Outline.*

(i) The flight training curriculum must include at least 10 hours of flight instruction in an airplane specified in §63.37(a). The flight time required for the practical test may not be credited as part of the required flight instruction.

(ii) All of the flight training must be given in the same type airplane.

(iii) As appropriate to the airplane type, the following subjects must be taught in the flight training course:

Subject

Normal duties, procedures and operations
To include as appropriate:
 Airplane preflight.
 Engine starting, power checks, pretakeoff, postlanding and shut-down procedures.
 Power control.
  Temperature control.
  Engine operation analysis.
  Operation of all systems.
  Fuel management.
  Logbook entries.
  Pressurization and air conditioning.

Recognition and correction of in-flight malfunctions
To include:
 Analysis of abnormal engine operation.
 Analysis of abnormal operation of all systems.
 Corrective action.

Emergency operations in flight
To include as appropriate:
 Engine fire control.
 Fuselage fire control.
 Smoke control.
 Loss of power or pressure in each system.
 Engine overspeed.
 Fuel dumping.
 Landing gear, spoilers, speed brakes, and flap extension and retraction.
 Engine shut-down and restart.
 Use of oxygen.

(iv) If the Administrator finds a simulator or flight engineer training device to accurately reproduce the design, function, and control characteristics, as pertaining to the duties and responsibilities of a flight engineer on the type of airplane to be flown, the flight training time may be reduced by a ratio of 1 hour of flight time to 2 hours of airplane simulator time, or 3 hours of flight engineer training device time, as the case may be, subject to the following limitations:

(a) Except as provided in subdivision (b) of this paragraph, the required flight instruction time in an airplane may not be less than 5 hours.

(b) As to a flight engineer student holding at least a commercial pilot certificate with an instrument rating, airplane simulator or a combination of airplane simulator and flight engineer training device time may be submitted for up to all 10 hours of the required flight instruction time in an airplane. However, not more than 15 hours of flight engineer training device time may be substituted for flight instruction time.

(v) To obtain credit for flight training time, airplane simulator time, or flight engineer training device time, the student must occupy the flight engineer station and operate the controls.

(b) Classroom equipment. Classroom equipment should consist of systems and procedural training devices, satisfactory to the Administrator, that duplicate the operation of the systems of the airplane in which the student is to receive his flight training.

(c) Contracts or agreements.

(1) An approved flight engineer course operator may contract with other persons to obtain suitable airplanes, airplane simulators, or other training devices or equipment.

(2) An operator who is approved to conduct both the flight engineer ground course and the flight engineer flight course may contract with others to conduct one course or the other in its entirety but may not contract with others to conduct both courses for the same airplane type.

(3) An operator who has approval to conduct a flight engineer ground course or flight course for a type of airplane, but not both courses, may not contract with another person to conduct that course in whole or in part.

(4) An operator who contracts with another to conduct a flight engineer course may not authorize or permit the course to be conducted in whole or in part by a third person.

(5) In all cases, the course operator who is approved to operate the course is responsible for the nature and quality of the instruction given.

(6) A copy of each contract authorized under this paragraph must be attached to each of the 3 copies of the course outline submitted for approval.

(d) Instructors.

(1) Only certificated flight engineers may give the flight instruction required by this appendix in an airplane, simulator, or flight engineer training device.

(2) There must be a sufficient number of qualified instructors available to prevent an excess ratio of students to instructors.

(e) Revisions.

(1) Requests for revisions of the course outlines, facilities or equipment must follow the procedures for original approval of the course. Revisions must be submitted in such form that an entire page or pages of the approved outline can be removed and replaced by the revisions.

(2) The list of instructors may be revised at any time without request for approval, if the requirements of paragraph (d) of this appendix are maintained.

(f) Ground school credits.

(1) Credit may be granted a student in the ground school course by the course operator for comparable previous training or experience that the student can show by written evidence: however, the course operator must still meet the quality of instruction as described in paragraph (h) of this appendix.

(2) Before credit for previous training or experience may be given, the student must pass a test given by the course operator on the subject for which the credit is to be given. The course operator shall incorporate results of the test, the basis for credit allowance, and the hours credited as part of the student's records.

(g) Records and reports.

(1) The course operator must maintain, for at least two years after a student graduates, fails, or drops from a course, a record of the student's training, including a chronological log of the subject course, attendance examinations, and grades.

(2) Except as provided in paragraph (3) of this section, the course operator must submit to the Administrator, not later than January 31 of each year, a report for the previous calendar year's training, to include:

(i) Name, enrollment and graduation date of each student;

(ii) Ground school hours and grades of each student;

(iii) Flight, airplane simulator, flight engineer training device hours, and grades of each student; and

(iv) Names of students failed or dropped, together with their school grades and reasons for dropping.

(3) Upon request, the Administrator may waive the reporting requirements of paragraph (2) of this section for an approved flight engineer course that is part of an approved training course under subpart N of part 121 of this chapter.

(h) Quality of instruction.

(1) Approval of a ground course is discontinued whenever less than 80 percent of the students pass the FAA written test on the first attempt.

(2) Approval of a flight course is discontinued whenever less than 80 percent of the students pass the FAA practical test on the first attempt.

(3) Notwithstanding paragraphs (1) and (2) of this section, approval of a ground or flight course may be continued when the Administrator finds—

(i) That the failure rate was based on less than a representative number of students; or

(ii) That the course operator has taken satisfactory means to improve the effectiveness of the training.

(i) Time limitation. Each student must apply for the written test and the flight test within 90 days after completing the ground school course.

(j) Statement of course completion.

(1) The course operator shall give to each student who successfully completes an approved flight engineer ground school training course, and passes the FAA written test, a statement of successful completion of the course that indicates the date of training, the type of airplane on which the ground course training was based, and the number of hours received in the ground school course.

(2) The course operator shall give each student who successfully completes an approved flight engineer flight course, and passed the FAA practical test, a statement of successful completion of the flight course that indicates the dates of the training, the type of airplane used in the flight course, and the number of hours received in the flight course.

(3) A course operator who is approved to conduct both the ground course and the flight course may include both courses in a single statement of course completion if the provisions of paragraphs (1) and (2) of this section are included.

(4) The requirements of this paragraph do not apply to an air carrier or commercial operator with an approved training course under part 121 of this chapter providing the student receives a flight engineer certificate upon completion of that course.

(k) Inspections. Each course operator shall allow the Administrator at any time or place, to make any inspection necessary to ensure that the quality and effectiveness of the instruction are maintained at the required standards.

(l) Change of ownership, name, or location.

(1) Approval of a flight engineer ground course or flight course is discontinued if the ownership of the course changes. The new owner must obtain a new approval by following the procedure prescribed for original approval.

(2) Approval of a flight engineer ground course or flight course does not terminate upon a change in the name of the course that is reported to the Administrator within 30 days. The Administrator issues a new letter of approval, using the new name, upon receipt of notice within that time.

(3) Approval of a flight engineer ground course or flight course does not terminate upon a change in location of the course that is reported to the Administrator within 30 days. The Administrator issues a new letter of approval, showing the new location, upon receipt of notice within that time, if he finds the new facilities to be adequate.

(m) Cancellation of approval.

(1) Failure to meet or maintain any of the requirements of this appendix for the approval of a flight engineer ground course or flight course is reason for cancellation of the approval.

(2) If a course operator desires to voluntarily terminate the course, he should notify the Administrator in writing and return the last letter of approval.

(n) Duration. Except for a course operated as part of an approved training course under subpart N of part 121 of this chapter, the approval to operate a flight engineer ground course or flight course terminates 24 months after the last day of the month of issue.

(o) Renewal.

(1) Renewal of approval to operate a flight engineer ground course or flight course is conditioned upon the course operator's meeting the requirements of this appendix.

(2) Application for renewal may be made to the Administrator at any time after 60 days before the termination date.

(p) Course operator approvals. An applicant for approval of a flight engineer ground course, or flight course, or both, must meet all of the requirements of this appendix concerning application, approval, and continuing approval of that course or courses.

(q) Practical test eligibility. An applicant for a flight engineer certificate and class rating under the provisions of §63.37(b)(6) is not eligible to take the practical test unless he has successfully completed an approved flight engineer ground school course in the same type of airplane for which he has completed an approved flight engineer flight course.

[Docket No. 6458, 30 FR 14560, Nov. 23, 1965; as amended by Amdt. 63–15, 37 FR 9758, May 17, 1972]

14 CFR • Subchapter D—Airmen

PART 65
CERTIFICATION: AIRMEN OTHER THAN FLIGHT CREWMEMBERS

Special Federal Aviation Regulations
SFAR No. 100–2 [Note]
SFAR No. 103

Subpart A—General
Sec.
65.1 Applicability.
65.3 Certification of foreign airmen other than flight crewmembers.
65.11 Application and issue.
65.12 Offenses involving alcohol or drugs.
65.13 Temporary certificate.
65.14 Security disqualification.
65.15 Duration of certificates.
65.16 Change of name: Replacement of lost or destroyed certificate.
65.17 Tests: General procedure.
65.18 Written tests: Cheating or other unauthorized conduct.
65.19 Retesting after failure.
65.20 Applications, certificates, logbooks reports, and records: Falsification, reproduction, or alteration.
65.21 Change of address.
65.23 [Reserved]

Subpart B—Air Traffic Control Tower Operators
65.31 Required certificates, and rating or qualification.
65.33 Eligibility requirements: General.
65.35 Knowledge requirements.
65.37 Skill requirements: Operating positions.
65.39 Practical experience requirements: Facility rating.
65.41 Skill requirements: Facility ratings.
65.43 Rating privileges and exchange.
65.45 Performance of duties.
65.46 [Reserved]
65.46a [Reserved]
65.46b [Reserved]
65.47 Maximum hours.
65.49 General operating rules.
65.50 Currency requirements.

Subpart C—Aircraft Dispatchers
65.51 Certificate required.
65.53 Eligibility requirements: General.
65.55 Knowledge requirements.
65.57 Experience or training requirements.
65.59 Skill requirements.
65.61 Aircraft dispatcher certification courses: Content and minimum hours.
65.63 Aircraft dispatcher certification courses: Application, duration, and other general requirements.
65.65 Aircraft dispatcher certification courses: Training facilities.
65.67 Aircraft dispatcher certification courses: Personnel.
65.70 Aircraft dispatcher certification courses: Records.

Subpart D—Mechanics
65.71 Eligibility requirements: General.
65.73 Ratings.
65.75 Knowledge requirements.
65.77 Experience requirements.
65.79 Skill requirements.
65.80 Certificated aviation maintenance technician school students.
65.81 General privileges and limitations.
65.83 Recent experience requirements.
65.85 Airframe rating; additional privileges.
65.87 Powerplant rating; additional privileges.
65.89 Display of certificate.
65.91 Inspection authorization.
65.92 Inspection authorization: Duration.
65.93 Inspection authorization: Renewal.
65.95 Inspection authorization: Privileges and limitations.

Subpart E—Repairmen
65.101 Eligibility requirements: General.
65.103 Repairman certificate: Privileges and limitations.
65.104 Repairman certificate—experimental aircraft builder—Eligibility, privileges and limitations.
65.105 Display of certificate.
65.107 Repairman certificate (light-sport aircraft): Eligibility, privileges, and limits.

Subpart F—Parachute Riggers
65.111 Certificate required.
65.113 Eligibility requirements: General.
65.115 Senior parachute rigger certificate: Experience, knowledge, and skill requirements.
65.117 Military riggers or former military riggers: Special certification rule.
65.119 Master parachute rigger certificate: Experience, knowledge, and skill requirements.
65.121 Type ratings.
65.123 Additional type ratings: Requirements.
65.125 Certificates: Privileges.

65.127 Facilities and equipment.
65.129 Performance standards.
65.131 Records.
65.133 Seal.

Appendix A to Part 65—Aircraft Dispatcher Courses

Authority: 49 U.S.C. 106(g). 40113, 44701–44703, 44707, 44709–44711, 45102–45103, 45301–45302.

Source: Docket No. 1179, 27 FR 7973, Aug. 10, 1962, unless otherwise noted.

SPECIAL FEDERAL AVIATION REGULATIONS

SFAR No. 100–2 to Part 65
RELIEF FOR U.S. MILITARY AND CIVILIAN PERSONNEL WHO ARE ASSIGNED OUTSIDE THE UNITED STATES IN SUPPORT OF U.S. ARMED FORCES OPERATIONS

Editorial Note: For the text of SFAR No. 100–2, see Part 63 in this book.

SFAR No. 103 to Part 65
PROCESS FOR REQUESTING WAIVER OF MANDATORY SEPARATION AGE FOR A FEDERAL AVIATION ADMINISTRATION AIR TRAFFIC CONTROL SPECIALIST IN FLIGHT SERVICE STATIONS, ENROUTE OR TERMINAL FACILITIES, AND THE DAVID J. HURLEY AIR TRAFFIC CONTROL SYSTEM COMMAND CENTER

1. To whom does this SFAR apply? This Special Federal Aviation Regulation (SFAR) applies to you if you are an air traffic control specialist (ATCS) employed by the FAA in flight service stations, enroute facilities, terminal facilities, or at the David J. Hurley Air Traffic Control System Command Center who wishes to obtain a waiver of the mandatory separation age as provided by 5 U.S.C. section 8335(a).

2. When must I file for a waiver? No earlier than the beginning of the twelfth month before, but no later than the beginning of the sixth month before, the month in which you turn 56, your official chain-of-command must receive your written request asking for a waiver of mandatory separation.

3. What if I do not file a request before six months before the month in which I turn 56? If your official chain-of-command does not receive your written request for a waiver of mandatory separation before the beginning of the sixth month before the month in which you turn 56, your request will be denied.

4. How will the FAA determine if my request meets the filing time requirements of this SFAR?
a. We consider your request to be filed in a timely manner under this SFAR if your official chain-of-command receives it or it is postmarked:
   i. After 12 a.m. on the first day of the twelfth month before the month in which you turn 56; and
   ii. Before 12 a.m. of the first day of the sixth month before the month in which you turn 56.
b. If you file your request by mail and the postmark is not legible, we will consider it to comply with paragraph a.2 of this section if we receive it by 12 p.m. of the fifth day of the sixth month before the month in which you turn 56.
c. If the last day of the time period specified in paragraph a.2 or paragraph b falls on a Saturday, Sunday, or Federal holiday, we will consider the time period to end at 12 p.m. of the next business day.

5. Where must I file my request for waiver and what must it include?
a. You must file your request for waiver of mandatory separation in writing with the Air Traffic Manager in flight service stations, enroute facilities, terminal facilities, or the David J. Hurley Air Traffic Control System Command Center in which you are employed.
b. Your request for waiver must include all of the following:
   i. Your name.
   ii. Your current facility.
   iii. Your starting date at the facility.
   iv. A list of positions at the facility that you are certified in and how many hours it took to achieve certification at the facility.
   v. Your area of specialty at the facility.
   vi. Your shift schedule.
   vii. [Reserved]
   viii. A list of all facilities where you have worked as a certified professional controller (CPC) including facility level and dates at each facility;
   ix. Evidence of your exceptional skills and experience as a controller; and
   x. Your signature.

6. How will my waiver request be reviewed?
a. Upon receipt of your request for waiver, the Air Traffic Manager of your facility will make a written recommendation that the Administrator either approve or deny your request. If the manager recommends approval of your request, he or she will certify in writing the accuracy of the information you provided as evidence of your exceptional skills and experience as a controller.
b. The Air Traffic Manager will then forward the written recommendation with a copy of your re-

quest to the senior executive manager in the Air Traffic Manager's regional chain-of-command.

c. The senior executive manager in the regional chain-of-command will make a written recommendation that the Administrator either approve or deny your request. If the senior executive manager recommends approval of your request, he or she will certify in writing the accuracy of the information you have provided as evidence of exceptional skills and experience.

d. The senior executive manager in the regional chain-of-command will then forward his or her recommendation with a copy of your request to the appropriate Vice President at FAA Headquarters. Depending on the facility in which you are employed, the request will be forwarded to either the Vice President for Flight Services, the Vice President for Enroute and Oceanic Services, the Vice President for Terminal Services or the Vice President for Systems Operations. For example, if you work at a flight service station at the time that you request a waiver, the request will be forwarded to the Vice President for Flight Services.

e. The appropriate Vice President will review your request and make a written recommendation that the Administrator either approve or deny your request, which will be forwarded to the Administrator.

f. The Administrator will issue the final decision on your request.

7. If I am granted a waiver, when will it expire?

a. Waivers will be granted for a period of one year.

b. No later than 90-days prior to expiration of a waiver, you may request that the waiver be extended using the same process identified in section 6.

c. If you timely request an extension of the waiver and it is denied, you will receive a 60-day advance notice of your separation date simultaneously with notification of the denial.

d. If you do not request an extension of the waiver granted, you will receive a 60-day advance notice of your separation date.

e. Action to separate you from your covered position becomes effective on the last day of the month in which the 60-day notice expires.

8. *Under what circumstances may my waiver be terminated?*

a. The FAA/DOT may terminate your waiver under the following circumstances:
 i. The needs of the FAA; or
 ii. If you are identified as a primary contributor to an operational error/deviation or runway incursion.

b. If the waiver is terminated for either of the reasons identified in paragraph 1 of this section, the air traffic control specialist will receive a 60-day advance notice.

c. Action to separate you from your covered position becomes effective on the last day of the month in which the 60-day notice expires.

9. *Appeal of denial or termination of waiver request:* The denial or termination of a waiver of mandatory separation request is neither appealable nor grievable.

[Docket No. FAA–2004–17334; SFAR No. 103, 70 FR 1636, Jan. 7, 2005; as amended by 71 FR 10607, March 2, 2006; Amdt. 65–55, 76 FR 12, Jan. 3, 2011]

Subpart A—General

§65.1 Applicability.

This part prescribes the requirements for issuing the following certificates and associated ratings and the general operating rules for the holders of those certificates and ratings:

(a) Air-traffic control-tower operators.
(b) Aircraft dispatchers.
(c) Mechanics.
(d) Repairmen.
(e) Parachute riggers.

§65.3 Certification of foreign airmen other than flight crewmembers.

A person who is neither a U.S. citizen nor a resident alien is issued a certificate under subpart D of this part, outside the United States, only when the Administrator finds that the certificate is needed for the operation or continued airworthiness of a U.S.-registered civil aircraft.

[Docket 65–28, 47 FR 35693, Aug. 16, 1982]

§65.11 Application and issue.

(a) Application for a certificate and appropriate class rating, or for an additional rating, under this part must be made on a form and in a manner prescribed by the Administrator. Each person who applies for airmen certification services to be administered outside the United States or for any certificate or rating issued under this part must show evidence that the fee prescribed in appendix A of part 187 of this chapter has been paid.

(b) An applicant who meets the requirements of this part is entitled to an appropriate certificate and rating.

(c) Unless authorized by the Administrator, a person whose air traffic control tower operator, mechanic, or parachute rigger certificate is suspended may not apply for any rating to be added to that certificate during the period of suspension.

(d) Unless the order of revocation provides otherwise—

(1) A person whose air traffic control tower operator, aircraft dispatcher, or parachute rigger certificate is revoked may not apply for the same kind

of certificate for 1 year after the date of revocation; and

(2) A person whose mechanic or repairman certificate is revoked may not apply for either of those kinds of certificates for 1 year after the date of revocation.

[Docket No. 1179, 27 FR 7973, Aug. 10, 1962; as amended by Amdt. 65–9, 31 FR 13524, Oct. 20, 1966; Amdt. 65–28, 47 FR 35693, Aug. 16, 1982; Amdt. 65–49, 72 FR 18559, April 12, 2007]

§65.12 Offenses involving alcohol or drugs.

(a) A conviction for the violation of any Federal or state statute relating to the growing, processing, manufacture, sale, disposition, possession, transportation, or importation of narcotic drugs, marihuana, or depressant or stimulant drugs or substances is grounds for—

(1) Denial of an application for any certificate or rating issued under this part for a period of up to 1 year after the date of final conviction; or

(2) Suspension or revocation of any certificate or rating issued under this part.

(b) The commission of an act prohibited by §91.19(a) of this chapter is grounds for—

(1) Denial of an application for a certificate or rating issued under this part for a period of up to 1 year after the date of that act; or

(2) Suspension or revocation of any certificate or rating issued under this part.

[Docket No. 21956, 50 FR 15379, Apr. 17, 1985; as amended by Amdt. 65–34, 54 FR 34330, Aug. 18, 1989]

§65.13 Temporary certificate.

A certificate and ratings effective for a period of not more than 120 days may be issued to a qualified applicant, pending review of his application and supplementary documents and the issue of the certificate and ratings for which he applied.

[Docket No. 1179, 27 FR 7973, Aug. 10, 1962; as amended by Amdt. 65–23, 43 FR 22640, May 25, 1978]

§65.14 Security disqualification.

(a) *Eligibility standard.* No person is eligible to hold a certificate, rating, or authorization issued under this part when the Transportation Security Administration (TSA) has notified the FAA in writing that the person poses a security threat.

(b) *Effect of the issuance by the TSA of an Initial Notification of Threat Assessment.*

(1) The FAA will hold in abeyance pending the outcome of the TSA's final threat assessment review an application for any certificate, rating, or authorization under this part by any person who has been issued an Initial Notification of Threat Assessment by the TSA.

(2) The FAA will suspend any certificate, rating, or authorization issued under this part after the TSA issues to the holder an Initial Notification of Threat Assessment.

(c) *Effect of the issuance by the TSA of a Final Notification of Threat Assessment.*

(1) The FAA will deny an application for any certificate, rating, or authorization under this part to any person who has been issued a Final Notification of Threat Assessment.

(2) The FAA will revoke any certificate, rating, or authorization issued under this part after the TSA has issued to the holder a Final Notification of Threat Assessment.

[Docket No. FAA–2003–14293, 68 FR 3775, Jan. 24, 2003]

§65.15 Duration of certificates.

(a) Except for repairman certificates, a certificate or rating issued under this part is effective until it is surrendered, suspended, or revoked.

(b) Unless it is sooner surrendered, suspended, or revoked, a repairman certificate is effective until the holder is relieved from the duties for which the holder was employed and certificated.

(c) The holder of a certificate issued under this part that is suspended, revoked, or no longer effective shall return it to the Administrator.

(d) Except for temporary certificates issued under §65.13, the holder of a paper certificate issued under this part may not exercise the privileges of that certificate after March 31, 2013.

[Docket No. 22052, 47 FR 35693, Aug. 16, 1982; as amended by Amdt. 65–51, 73 FR 10668, Feb. 28, 2008]

§65.16 Change of name: Replacement of lost or destroyed certificate.

(a) An application for a change of name on a certificate issued under this part must be accompanied by the applicant's current certificate and the marriage license, court order, or other document verifying the change. The documents are returned to the applicant after inspection.

(b) An application for a replacement of a lost or destroyed certificate is made by letter to the Department of Transportation, Federal Aviation Administration, Airman Certification Branch, Post Office Box 25082, Oklahoma City, OK 73125. The letter must—

(1) Contain the name in which the certificate was issued, the permanent mailing address (including zip code), social security number (if any), and date and place of birth of the certificate holder, and any available information regarding the grade, number, and date of issue of the certificate, and the ratings on it; and

(2) Be accompanied by a check or money order for $2, payable to the Federal Aviation Administration.

Part 65: Certification: Other Than Crewmembers §65.21

(c) An application for a replacement of a lost or destroyed medical certificate is made by letter to the Department of Transportation, Federal Aviation Administration, Aerospace Medical Certification Division, Post Office Box 26200, Oklahoma City, OK 73125, accompanied by a check or money order for $2.00.

(d) A person whose certificate issued under this part or medical certificate, or both, has been lost may obtain a telegram from the FAA confirming that it was issued. The telegram may be carried as a certificate for a period not to exceed 60 days pending his receiving a duplicate certificate under paragraph (b) or (c) of this section, unless he has been notified that the certificate has been suspended or revoked. The request for such a telegram may be made by prepaid telegram, stating the date upon which a duplicate certificate was requested, and including the request for a duplicate and a money order for the necessary amount. The request for a telegraphic certificate should be sent to the office prescribed in paragraph (b) or (c) of this section, as appropriate. However, a request for both at the same time should be sent to the office prescribed in paragraph (b) of this section.

[Docket No. 7258, 31 FR 13524, Oct. 20, 1966; as amended by Docket No. 8084, 32 FR 5769, Apr. 11, 1967; Amdt. 65–16, 35 FR 14075, Sept. 4, 1970; Amdt. 65–17, 36 FR 2865, Feb. 11, 1971; Amdt. 65–52, 73 FR 43065, July 24, 2008]

§65.17 Tests: General procedure.

(a) Tests prescribed by or under this part are given at times and places, and by persons, designated by the Administrator.

(b) The minimum passing grade for each test is 70 percent.

§65.18 Written tests: Cheating or other unauthorized conduct.

(a) Except as authorized by the Administrator, no person may—

(1) Copy, or intentionally remove, a written test under this part;

(2) Give to another, or receive from another, any part or copy of that test;

(3) Give help on that test to, or receive help on that test from, any person during the period that test is being given;

(4) Take any part of that test in behalf of another person;

(5) Use any material or aid during the period that test is being given; or

(6) Intentionally cause, assist, or participate in any act prohibited by this paragraph.

(b) No person who commits an act prohibited by paragraph (a) of this section is eligible for any airman or ground instructor certificate or rating under this chapter for a period of 1 year after the date of that act. In addition, the commission of that act is a basis for suspending or revoking any airman or ground instructor certificate or rating held by that person.

[Docket No. 4086, 30 FR 2196, Feb. 18, 1965]

§65.19 Retesting after failure.

An applicant for a written, oral, or practical test for a certificate and rating, or for an additional rating under this part, may apply for retesting—

(a) After 30 days after the date the applicant failed the test; or

(b) Before the 30 days have expired if the applicant presents a signed statement from an airman holding the certificate and rating sought by the applicant, certifying that the airman has given the applicant additional instruction in each of the subjects failed and that the airman considers the applicant ready for retesting.

[Docket No. 16383, 43 FR 22640, May 25, 1978]

§65.20 Applications, certificates, logbooks, reports, and records: Falsification, reproduction, or alteration.

(a) No person may make or cause to be made—

(1) Any fraudulent or intentionally false statement on any application for a certificate or rating under this part;

(2) Any fraudulent or intentionally false entry in any logbook, record, or report that is required to be kept, made, or used, to show compliance with any requirement for any certificate or rating under this part;

(3) Any reproduction, for fraudulent purpose, of any certificate or rating under this part; or

(4) Any alteration of any certificate or rating under this part.

(b) The commission by any person of an act prohibited under paragraph (a) of this section is a basis for suspending or revoking any airman or ground instructor certificate or rating held by that person.

[Docket No. 4086, 30 FR 2196, Feb. 18, 1965]

§65.21 Change of address.

Within 30 days after any change in his permanent mailing address, the holder of a certificate issued under this part shall notify the Department of Transportation, Federal Aviation Administration, Airman Certification Branch, Post Office Box 25082, Oklahoma City, OK 73125, in writing, of his new address.

[Docket No. 10536, 35 FR 14075, Sept. 4, 1970]

§65.23 [Reserved]

Subpart B—Air Traffic Control Tower Operators

Source: Docket No. 10193, 35 FR 12326, Aug. 1, 1970, unless otherwise noted.

§65.31 Required certificates, and rating or qualification.

No person may act as an air traffic control tower operator at an air traffic control tower in connection with civil aircraft unless he—

(a) Holds an air traffic control tower operator certificate issued to him under this subpart;

(b) Holds a facility rating for that control tower issued to him under this subpart, or has qualified for the operating position at which he acts and is under the supervision of the holder of a facility rating for that control tower; and

For the purpose of this subpart, *operating position* means an air traffic control function performed within or directly associated with the control tower;

(c) Except for a person employed by the FAA or employed by, or on active duty with, the Department of the Air Force, Army, or Navy or the Coast Guard, holds at least a second-class medical certificate issued under part 67 of this chapter.

[Docket No. 10193, 35 FR 12326, Aug. 1, 1970; as amended by Amdt. 65–25, 45 FR 18911, March 24, 1980; Amdt. 65–31, 52 FR 17518, May 8, 1987]

§65.33 Eligibility requirements: General.

To be eligible for an air traffic control tower operator certificate a person must—

(a) Be at least 18 years of age;

(b) Be of good moral character;

(c) Be able to read, write, and understand the English language and speak it without accent or impediment of speech that would interfere with two-way radio conversation;

(d) Except for a person employed by the FAA or employed by, or on active duty with, the Department of the Air Force, Army, or Navy or the Coast Guard, hold at least a second-class medical certificate issued under part 67 of this chapter within the 12 months before the date application is made; and

(e) Comply with §65.35.

[Docket No. 10193, 35 FR 12326, Aug. 1, 1970; as amended by Amdt. 65–25, 45 FR 18911, March 24, 1980; Amdt. 65–31, 52 FR 17518, May 8, 1987]

§65.35 Knowledge requirements.

Each applicant for an air traffic control tower operator certificate must pass a written test on—

(a) The flight rules in part 91 of this chapter:

(b) Airport traffic control procedures, and this subpart:

(c) En route traffic control procedures;

(d) Communications operating procedures;

(e) Flight assistance service;

(f) Air navigation, and aids to air navigation; and

(g) Aviation weather.

§65.37 Skill requirements: Operating positions.

No person may act as an air traffic control tower operator at any operating position unless he has passed a practical test on—

(a) Control tower equipment and its use;

(b) Weather reporting procedures and use of reports;

(c) Notices to Airmen, and use of the Airman's Information Manual;

(d) Use of operational forms;

(e) Performance of noncontrol operational duties; and

(f) Each of the following procedures that is applicable to that operating position and is required by the person performing the examination:

(1) The airport, including rules, equipment, runways, taxiways, and obstructions.

(2) The terrain features, visual check-points, and obstructions within the lateral boundaries of the surface areas of Class B, Class C, Class D, or Class E airspace designated for the airport.

(3) Traffic patterns and associated procedures for use of preferential runways and noise abatement.

(4) Operational agreements.

(5) The center, alternate airports, and those airways, routes, reporting points, and air navigation aids used for terminal air traffic control.

(6) Search and rescue procedures.

(7) Terminal air traffic control procedures and phraseology.

(8) Holding procedures, prescribed instrument approach, and departure procedures.

(9) Radar alignment and technical operation.

(10) The application of the prescribed radar and nonradar separation standard, as appropriate.

[Docket No. 10193, 35 FR 12326, Aug. 1, 1991; as amended by Amdt. 65–36, 56 FR 65653, Dec. 17, 1991]

§65.39 Practical experience requirements: Facility rating.

Each applicant for a facility rating at any air traffic control tower must have satisfactorily served—

(a) As an air traffic control tower operator at that control tower without a facility rating for at least 6 months; or

(b) As an air traffic control tower operator with a facility rating at a different control tower for at least 6 months before the date he applies for the rating.

However, an applicant who is a member of an Armed Force of the United States meets the requirements of this section if he has satisfactorily served as an air traffic control tower operator for at least 6 months.

[Docket No. 1179, 27 FR 7973, Aug. 10, 1962; as amended by Amdt. 65–19, 36 FR 21280, Nov. 5, 1971]

§65.41 Skill requirements: Facility ratings.

Each applicant for a facility rating at an air traffic control tower must have passed a practical test on each item listed in §65.37 of this part that is applicable to each operating position at the control tower at which the rating is sought.

§65.43 Rating privileges and exchange.

(a) The holder of a senior rating on August 31, 1970, may at any time after that date exchange his rating for a facility rating at the same air traffic control tower. However, if he does not do so before August 31, 1971, he may not thereafter exercise the privileges of his senior rating at the control tower concerned until he makes the exchange.

(b) The holder of a junior rating on August 31, 1970, may not control air traffic, at any operating position at the control tower concerned, until he has met the applicable requirements of §65.37 of this part. However, before meeting those requirements he may control air traffic under the supervision, where required, of an operator with a senior rating (or facility rating) in accordance with §65.41 of this part in effect before August 31, 1970.

§65.45 Performance of duties.

(a) An air traffic control tower operator shall perform his duties in accordance with the limitations on his certificate and the procedures and practices prescribed in air traffic control manuals of the FAA, to provide for the safe, orderly, and expeditious flow of air traffic.

(b) An operator with a facility rating may control traffic at any operating position at the control tower at which he holds a facility rating. However, he may not issue an air traffic clearance for IFR flight without authorization from the appropriate facility exercising IFR control at that location.

(c) An operator who does not hold a facility rating for a particular control tower may act at each operating position for which he has qualified, under the supervision of an operator holding a facility rating for that control tower.

[Docket No. 10193, 35 FR 12326, Aug. 1, 1970; as amended by Amdt. 65–16, 35 FR 14075, Sept. 4, 1970]

§65.46 [Reserved]

§65.46a [Reserved]

§65.46b [Reserved]

§65.47 Maximum hours.

Except in an emergency, a certificated air traffic control tower operator must be relieved of all duties for at least 24 consecutive hours at least once during each 7 consecutive days. Such an operator may not serve or be required to serve—

(a) For more than 10 consecutive hours; or

(b) For more than 10 hours during a period of 24 consecutive hours, unless he has had a rest period of at least 8 hours at or before the end of the 10 hours of duty.

§65.49 General operating rules.

(a) Except for a person employed by the FAA or employed by, or on active duty with, the Department of the Air Force, Army, or Navy, or the Coast Guard, no person may act as an air traffic control tower operator under a certificate issued to him or her under this part unless he or she has in his or her personal possession an appropriate current medical certificate issued under part 67 of this chapter.

(b) Each person holding an air traffic control tower operator certificate shall keep it readily available when performing duties in an air traffic control tower, and shall present that certificate or his medical certificate or both for inspection upon the request of the Administrator or an authorized representative of the National Transportation Safety Board, or of any Federal, State, or local law enforcement officer.

(c) A certificated air traffic control tower operator who does not hold a facility rating for a particular control tower may not act at any operating position at the control tower concerned unless there is maintained at that control tower, readily available to persons named in paragraph (b) of this section, a current record of the operating positions at which he has qualified.

(d) An air traffic control tower operator may not perform duties under his certificate during any period of known physical deficiency that would make him unable to meet the physical requirements for his current medical certificate. However, if the deficiency is temporary, he may perform duties that are not affected by it whenever another certificated and qualified operator is present and on duty.

(e) A certificated air traffic control tower operator may not control air traffic with equipment that the Administrator has found to be inadequate.

(f) The holder of an air traffic control tower operator certificate, or an applicant for one, shall, upon the reasonable request of the Administrator, cooperate fully in any test that is made of him.

[Docket No. 1179, 27 FR 7973, Aug. 10, 1962; as amended by Amdt. 65–31, 52 FR 17519, May 8, 1987]

§65.50 Currency requirements.

The holder of an air traffic control tower operator certificate may not perform any duties under that certificate unless—

(a) He has served for at least three of the preceding 6 months as an air traffic control tower operator at the control tower to which his facility rating applies, or at the operating positions for which he has qualified; or

(b) He has shown that he meets the requirements for his certificate and facility rating at the control tower concerned, or for operating at positions for which he has previously qualified.

Subpart C— Aircraft Dispatchers

Source: Docket No. FAA–1998–4553, 64 FR 68923, Dec. 8, 1999, unless otherwise noted.

§65.51 Certificate required.

(a) No person may act as an aircraft dispatcher (exercising responsibility with the pilot in command in the operational control of a flight) in connection with any civil aircraft in air commerce unless that person has in his or her personal possession an aircraft dispatcher certificate issued under this subpart.

(b) Each person who holds an aircraft dispatcher certificate must present it for inspection upon the request of the Administrator or an authorized representative of the National Transportation Safety Board, or of any Federal, State, or local law enforcement officer.

§65.53 Eligibility requirements: General.

(a) To be eligible to take the aircraft dispatcher knowledge test, a person must be at least 21 years of age.

(b) To be eligible for an aircraft dispatcher certificate, a person must—

(1) Be at least 23 years of age;

(2) Be able to read, speak, write, and understand the English language;

(3) Pass the required knowledge test prescribed by §65.55 of this part;

(4) Pass the required practical test prescribed by §65.59 of this part; and

(5) Comply with the requirements of §65.57 of this part.

§65.55 Knowledge requirements.

(a) A person who applies for an aircraft dispatcher certificate must pass a knowledge test on the following aeronautical knowledge areas:

(1) Applicable Federal Aviation Regulations of this chapter that relate to airline transport pilot privileges, limitations, and flight operations;

(2) Meteorology, including knowledge of and effects of fronts, frontal characteristics, cloud formations, icing, and upper-air data;

(3) General system of weather and NOTAM collection, dissemination, interpretation, and use;

(4) Interpretation and use of weather charts, maps, forecasts, sequence reports, abbreviations, and symbols;

(5) National Weather Service functions as they pertain to operations in the National Airspace System;

(6) Windshear and microburst awareness, identification, and avoidance;

(7) Principles of air navigation under instrument meteorological conditions in the National Airspace System;

(8) Air traffic control procedures and pilot responsibilities as they relate to enroute operations, terminal area and radar operations, and instrument departure and approach procedures;

(9) Aircraft loading, weight and balance, use of charts, graphs, tables, formulas, and computations, and their effect on aircraft performance;

(10) Aerodynamics relating to an aircraft's flight characteristics and performance in normal and abnormal flight regimes;

(11) Human factors;

(12) Aeronautical decision making and judgment; and

(13) Crew resource management, including crew communication and coordination.

(b) The applicant must present documentary evidence satisfactory to the administrator of having passed an aircraft dispatcher knowledge test within the preceding 24 calendar months.

§65.57 Experience or training requirements.

An applicant for an aircraft dispatcher certificate must present documentary evidence satisfactory to the Administrator that he or she has the experience prescribed in paragraph (a) of this section or has accomplished the training described in paragraph (b) of this section as follows:

(a) A total of at least 2 years experience in the 3 years before the date of application, in any one or in any combination of the following areas:

(1) In military aircraft operations as a—
(i) Pilot;
(ii) Flight navigator; or
(iii) Meteorologist.

(2) In aircraft operations conducted under part 121 of this chapter as—
(i) An assistant in dispatching air carrier aircraft, under the direct supervision of a dispatcher certificated under this subpart;
(ii) A pilot;
(iii) A flight engineer; or
(iv) A meteorologist.
(3) In aircraft operations as—
(i) An Air Traffic Controller; or
(ii) A Flight Service Specialist.
(4) In aircraft operations, performing other duties that the Administrator finds provide equivalent experience.
(b) A statement of graduation issued or revalidated in accordance with §65.70(b) of this part, showing that the person has successfully completed an approved aircraft dispatcher course.

§65.59 Skill requirements.

An applicant for an aircraft dispatcher certificate must pass a practical test given by the Administrator, with respect to any one type of large aircraft used in air carrier operations. The practical test must be based on the aircraft dispatcher practical test standards, as published by the FAA, on the items outlined in appendix A of this part.

§65.61 Aircraft dispatcher certification courses: Content and minimum hours.

(a) An approved aircraft dispatcher certification course must:
(1) Provide instruction in the areas of knowledge and topics listed in appendix A of this part;
(2) Include a minimum of 200 hours of instruction.
(b) An applicant for approval of an aircraft dispatcher course must submit an outline that describes the major topics and subtopics to be covered and the number of hours proposed for each.
(c) Additional subject headings for an aircraft dispatcher certification course may also be included, however the hours proposed for any subjects not listed in appendix A of this part must be in addition to the minimum 200 course hours required in paragraph (a) of this section.
(d) For the purpose of completing an approved course, a student may substitute previous experience or training for a portion of the minimum 200 hours of training. The course operator determines the number of hours of credit based on an evaluation of the experience or training to determine if it is comparable to portions of the approved course curriculum. The credit allowed, including the total hours and the basis for it, must be placed in the student's record required by §65.70(a) of this part.

§65.63 Aircraft dispatcher certification courses: Application, duration, and other general requirements.

(a) *Application.* Application for original approval of an aircraft dispatcher certification course or the renewal of approval of an aircraft dispatcher certification course under this part must be:
(1) Made in writing to the Administrator;
(2) Accompanied by two copies of the course outline required under §65.61(b) of this part, for which approval is sought;
(3) Accompanied by a description of the equipment and facilities to be used; and
(4) Accompanied by a list of the instructors and their qualifications.
(b) *Duration.* Unless withdrawn or canceled, an approval of an aircraft dispatcher certification course of study expires:
(1) On the last day of the 24th month from the month the approval was issued; or
(2) Except as provided in paragraph (f) of this section, on the date that any change in ownership of the school occurs.
(c) *Renewal.* Application for renewal of an approved aircraft dispatcher certification course must be made within 30 days preceding the month the approval expires, provided the course operator meets the following requirements:
(1) At least 80 percent of the graduates from that aircraft dispatcher certification course, who applied for the practical test required by §65.59 of this part, passed the practical test on their first attempt; and
(2) The aircraft dispatcher certification course continues to meet the requirements of this subpart for course approval.
(d) *Course revisions.* Requests for approval of a revision of the course outline, facilities, or equipment must be in accordance with paragraph (a) of this section. Proposed revisions of the course outline or the description of facilities and equipment must be submitted in a format that will allow an entire page or pages of the approved outline or description to be removed and replaced by any approved revision. The list of instructors may be revised at any time without request for approval, provided the minimum requirements of §65.67 of this part are maintained and the Administrator is notified in writing.
(e) *Withdrawal or cancellation of approval.* Failure to continue to meet the requirements of this subpart for the approval or operation of an approved aircraft dispatcher certification course is grounds for withdrawal of approval of the course. A course operator may request cancellation of course approval by a letter to the Administrator. The operator must forward any records to the FAA as requested by the Administrator.

(f) Change in ownership. A change in ownership of a part 65, appendix A-approved course does not terminate that aircraft dispatcher certification course approval if, within 10 days after the date that any change in ownership of the school occurs:

(1) Application is made for an appropriate amendment to the approval; and

(2) No change in the facilities, personnel, or approved aircraft dispatcher certification course is involved.

(g) Change in name or location. A change in name or location of an approved aircraft dispatcher certification course does not invalidate the approval if, within 10 days after the date that any change in name or location occurs, the course operator of the part 65, appendix A-approved course notifies the Administrator, in writing, of the change.

§65.65 Aircraft dispatcher certification courses: Training facilities.

An applicant for approval of authority to operate an aircraft dispatcher course of study must have facilities, equipment, and materials adequate to provide each student the theoretical and practical aspects of aircraft dispatching. Each room, training booth, or other space used for instructional purposes must be temperature controlled, lighted, and ventilated to conform to local building, sanitation, and health codes. In addition, the training facility must be so located that the students in that facility are not distracted by the instruction conducted in other rooms.

§65.67 Aircraft dispatcher certification courses: Personnel.

(a) Each applicant for an aircraft dispatcher certification course must meet the following personnel requirements:

(1) Each applicant must have adequate personnel, including one instructor who holds an aircraft dispatcher certificate and is available to coordinate all training course instruction.

(2) Each applicant must not exceed a ratio of 25 students for one instructor.

(b) The instructor who teaches the practical dispatch applications area of the appendix A course must hold an aircraft dispatchers certificate.

§65.70 Aircraft dispatcher certification courses: Records.

(a) The operator of an aircraft dispatcher course must maintain a record for each student, including a chronological log of all instructors, subjects covered, and course examinations and results. The record must be retained for at least 3 years after graduation. The course operator also must prepare, for its records, and transmit to the Administrator not later than January 31 of each year, a report containing the following information for the previous year:

(1) The names of all students who graduated, together with the results of their aircraft dispatcher certification courses.

(2) The names of all the students who failed or withdrew, together with the results of their aircraft dispatcher certification courses or the reasons for their withdrawal.

(b) Each student who successfully completes the approved aircraft dispatcher certification course must be given a written statement of graduation, which is valid for 90 days. After 90 days, the course operator may revalidate the graduation certificate for an additional 90 days if the course operator determines that the student remains proficient in the subject areas listed in appendix A of this part.

Subpart D—Mechanics

§65.71 Eligibility requirements: General.

(a) To be eligible for a mechanic certificate and associated ratings, a person must—

(1) Be at least 18 years of age;

(2) Be able to read, write, speak, and understand the English language, or in the case of an applicant who does not meet this requirement and who is employed outside of the United States by a U.S. air carrier, have his certificate endorsed "Valid only outside the United States";

(3) Have passed all of the prescribed tests within a period of 24 months; and

(4) Comply with the sections of this subpart that apply to the rating he seeks.

(b) A certificated mechanic who applies for an additional rating must meet the requirements of §65.77 and, within a period of 24 months, pass the tests prescribed by §§65.75 and 65.79 for the additional rating sought.

[Docket No. 1179, 27 FR 7973, Aug. 10, 1962; as amended by Amdt. 65-6, 31 FR 5950, April 19, 1966]

§65.73 Ratings.

(a) The following ratings are issued under this subpart:

(1) Airframe.

(2) Powerplant.

(b) A mechanic certificate with an aircraft or aircraft engine rating, or both, that was issued before, and was valid on, June 15, 1952, is equal to a mechanic certificate with an airframe or powerplant rating, or both, as the case may be, and may be exchanged for such a corresponding certificate and rating or ratings.

§65.75 Knowledge requirements.

(a) Each applicant for a mechanic certificate or rating must, after meeting the applicable experience requirements of §65.77, pass a written test covering the construction and maintenance of aircraft appropriate to the rating he seeks, the regulations in this subpart, and the applicable provisions of parts 43 and 91 of this chapter. The basic principles covering the installation and maintenance of propellers are included in the powerplant test.

(b) The applicant must pass each section of the test before applying for the oral and practical tests prescribed by §65.79. A report of the written test is sent to the applicant.

[Docket No. 1179, 27 FR 7973, Aug. 10, 1962; as amended by Amdt. 65–1, 27 FR 10410, Oct. 25, 1962; Amdt. 65–6, 31 FR 5950, April 19, 1966]

§65.77 Experience requirements.

Each applicant for a mechanic certificate or rating must present either an appropriate graduation certificate or certificate of completion from a certificated aviation maintenance technician school or documentary evidence, satisfactory to the Administrator, of—

(a) At least 18 months of practical experience with the procedures, practices, materials, tools, machine tools, and equipment generally used in constructing, maintaining, or altering airframes, or powerplants appropriate to the rating sought; or

(b) At least 30 months of practical experience concurrently performing the duties appropriate to both the airframe and powerplant ratings.

[Docket No. 1179, 27 FR 7973, Aug. 10, 1962; as amended by Amdt. 65–14, 35 FR, 5533, April 3, 1970]

§65.79 Skill requirements.

Each applicant for a mechanic certificate or rating must pass an oral and a practical test on the rating he seeks. The tests cover the applicant's basic skill in performing practical projects on the subjects covered by the written test for that rating. An applicant for a powerplant rating must show his ability to make satisfactory minor repairs to, and minor alterations of, propellers.

§65.80 Certificated aviation maintenance technician school students.

Whenever an aviation maintenance technician school certificated under part 147 of this chapter shows to an FAA inspector that any of its students has made satisfactory progress at the school and is prepared to take the oral and practical tests prescribed by §65.79, that student may take those tests during the final subjects of his training in the approved curriculum, before he meets the applicable experience requirements of §65.77 and before he passes each section of the written test prescribed by §65.75.

[Docket No. 1179, 27 FR, 7973, Aug. 10, 1962; as amended by Amdt. 65–14, 35 FR, 5533, April 3, 1970]

§65.81 General privileges and limitations.

(a) A certificated mechanic may perform or supervise the maintenance, preventive maintenance or alteration of an aircraft or appliance, or a part thereof, for which he is rated (but excluding major repairs to, and major alterations of, propellers, and any repair to, or alteration of, instruments), and may perform additional duties in accordance with §§65.85, 65.87, and 65.95. However, he may not supervise the maintenance, preventive maintenance, or alteration of, or approve and return to service, any aircraft or appliance, or part thereof, for which he is rated unless he has satisfactorily performed the work concerned at an earlier date. If he has not so performed that work at an earlier date, he may show his ability to do it by performing it to the satisfaction of the Administrator or under the direct supervision of a certificated and appropriately rated mechanic, or a certificated repairman, who has had previous experience in the specific operation concerned.

(b) A certificated mechanic may not exercise the privileges of his certificate and rating unless he understands the current instructions of the manufacturer, and the maintenance manuals, for the specific operation concerned.

[Docket No. 1179, 27 FR 7973, Aug. 10, 1962; as amended by Amdt. 65–2, 29 FR 5451, April 23, 1964; Amdt. 65–26, 45 FR 46737, July 10, 1980]

§65.83 Recent experience requirements.

A certificated mechanic may not exercise the privileges of his certificate and rating unless, within the preceding 24 months—

(a) The Administrator has found that he is able to do that work; or

(b) He has, for at least 6 months—

(1) Served as a mechanic under his certificate and rating;

(2) Technically supervised other mechanics;

(3) Supervised, in an executive capacity, the maintenance or alteration of aircraft; or

(4) Been engaged in any combination of paragraph (b) (1), (2), or (3) of this section.

§65.85 Airframe rating; additional privileges.

(a) Except as provided in paragraph (b) of this section, a certificated mechanic with an airframe rating may approve and return to service an airframe, or any related part or appliance, after he has performed, supervised, or inspected its maintenance or alteration (excluding major repairs and major alterations). In addition, he may perform the 100-hour inspection required by part 91 of this chapter on an airframe, or any related part or appliance, and approve and return it to service.

(b) A certificated mechanic with an airframe rating can approve and return to service an airframe, or any related part or appliance, of an aircraft with a special airworthiness certificate in the light-sport category after performing and inspecting a major repair or major alteration for products that are not produced under an FAA approval provided the work was performed in accordance with instructions developed by the manufacturer or a person acceptable to the FAA.

[Docket No. 1179, 27 FR 7973, Aug. 10, 1962; as amended by Amdt. 65–10, 32 FR 5770, April 11, 1967; Amdt. 65–45, 69 FR 44879, July 27, 2004]

§65.87 Powerplant rating; additional privileges.

(a) Except as provided in paragraph (b) of this section, a certificated mechanic with a powerplant rating may approve and return to service a powerplant or propeller or any related part or appliance, after he has performed, supervised, or inspected its maintenance or alteration (excluding major repairs and major alterations). In addition, he may perform the 100-hour inspection required by part 91 of this chapter on a powerplant or propeller, or any part thereof, and approve and return it to service.

(b) A certificated mechanic with a powerplant rating can approve and return to service a powerplant or propeller, or any related part or appliance, of an aircraft with a special airworthiness certificate in the light-sport category after performing and inspecting a major repair or major alteration for products that are not produced under an FAA approval, provided the work was performed in accordance with instructions developed by the manufacturer or a person acceptable to the FAA.

[Docket No. 1179, 27 FR 7973, Aug. 10, 1962; as amended by Amdt. 65–10, 32 FR 5770, April 11, 1967; Amdt. 65–45, 69 FR 44879, July 27, 2004]

§65.89 Display of certificate.

Each person who holds a mechanic certificate shall keep it within the immediate area where he normally exercises the privileges of the certificate and shall present it for inspection upon the request of the Administrator or an authorized representative of the National Transportation Safety Board, or of any Federal, State, or local law enforcement officer.

[Docket No. 7258, 31 FR 13524, Oct. 20, 1966; as amended by Docket No. 8084, 32 FR 5769, April 11, 1967]

§65.91 Inspection authorization.

(a) An application for an inspection authorization is made on a form and in a manner prescribed by the Administrator.

(b) An applicant who meets the requirements of this section is entitled to an inspection authorization.

(c) To be eligible for an inspection authorization, an applicant must—

(1) Hold a currently effective mechanic certificate with both an airframe rating and a powerplant rating, each of which is currently effective and has been in effect for a total of at least 3 years;

(2) Have been actively engaged, for at least the 2-year period before the date he applies, in maintaining aircraft certificated and maintained in accordance with this chapter;

(3) Have a fixed base of operations at which he may be located in person or by telephone during a normal working week but it need not be the place where he will exercise his inspection authority;

(4) Have available to him the equipment, facilities, and inspection data necessary to properly inspect airframes, powerplants, propellers, or any related part or appliance; and

(5) Pass a written test on his ability to inspect according to safety standards for returning aircraft to service after major repairs and major alterations and annual and progressive inspections performed under part 43 of this chapter.

An applicant who fails the test prescribed in paragraph (c)(5) of this section may not apply for retesting until at least 90 days after the date he failed the test.

[Docket No. 1179, 27 FR 7973, Aug. 10, 1962; as amended by Amdt. 65–5, 31 FR 3337, March 3, 1966; Amdt. 65–22, 42 FR 46279, Sept. 15, 1977; Amdt. 65–30, 50 FR 15700, April 19, 1985]

§65.92 Inspection authorization: Duration.

(a) Each inspection authorization expires on March 31 of each odd-numbered year. However, the holder may exercise the privileges of that authorization only while he holds a currently effective mechanic certificate with both a currently effective airframe rating and a currently effective powerplant rating.

(b) An inspection authorization ceases to be effective whenever any of the following occurs:

Part 65: Certification: Other Than Crewmembers §65.95

(1) The authorization is surrendered, suspended, or revoked.

(2) The holder no longer has a fixed base of operation.

(3) The holder no longer has the equipment, facilities, and inspection data required by §65.91(c) (3) and (4) for issuance of his authorization.

(c) The holder of an inspection authorization that is suspended or revoked shall, upon the Administrator's request, return it to the Administrator.

[Docket No. 12537, 42 FR 46279, Sept. 15, 1977; as amended by Amdt. 65–50, 72 FR 4404, Jan. 30, 2007]

§65.93 Inspection authorization: Renewal.

(a) To be eligible for renewal of an inspection authorization for a 2-year period an applicant must present evidence during the month of March of each odd-numbered year, at an FAA Flight Standards District Office or an International Field Office, that the applicant still meets the requirements of §65.91(c) (1) through (4). In addition, during the time the applicant held the inspection authorization, the applicant must show completion of one of the activities in §65.93(a) (1) through (5) below by March 31 of the first year of the 2-year inspection authorization period, and completion of one of the five activities during the second year of the 2-year period:

(1) Performed at least one annual inspection for each 90 days that the applicant held the current authority; or

(2) Performed at least two major repairs or major alterations for each 90 days that the applicant held the current authority; or

(3) Performed or supervised and approved at least one progressive inspection in accordance with standards prescribed by the Administrator; or

(4) Attended and successfully completed a refresher course, acceptable to the Administrator, of not less than 8 hours of instruction; or

(5) Passed an oral test by an FAA inspector to determine that the applicant's knowledge of applicable regulations and standards is current.

(b) The holder of an inspection authorization that has been in effect:

(1) for less than 90 days before the expiration date need not comply with paragraphs (a)(1) through (5) of this section.

(2) for less than 90 days before March 31 of an even-numbered year need not comply with paragraphs (a)(1) through (5) of this section for the first year of the 2-year inspection authorization period.

(c) An inspection authorization holder who does not complete one of the activities set forth in §65.93(a) (1) through (5) of this section by March 31 of the first year of the 2-year inspection authorization period may not exercise inspection authorization privileges after March 31 of the first year. The inspection authorization holder may resume exercising inspection authorization privileges after passing an oral test from an FAA inspector to determine that the applicant's knowledge of the applicable regulations and standards is current. An inspection authorization holder who passes this oral test is deemed to have completed the requirements of §65.93(a) (1) through (5) by March 31 of the first year.

[Docket No. FAA–2007–27108, 72 FR 4404, Jan. 30, 2007]

§65.95 Inspection authorization: Privileges and limitations.

(a) The holder of an inspection authorization may—

(1) Inspect and approve for return to service any aircraft or related part or appliance (except any aircraft maintained in accordance with a continuous airworthiness program under part 121 of this chapter) after a major repair or major alteration to it in accordance with part 43 [New] of this chapter, if the work was done in accordance with technical data approved by the Administrator; and

(2) Perform an annual, or perform or supervise a progressive inspection according to §§43.13 and 43.15 of this chapter.

(b) When he exercises the privileges of an inspection authorization the holder shall keep it available for inspection by the aircraft owner, the mechanic submitting the aircraft, repair, or alteration for approval (if any), and shall present it upon the request of the Administrator or an authorized representative of the National Transportation Safety Board, or of any Federal, State, or local law enforcement officer.

(c) If the holder of an inspection authorization changes his fixed base of operation, he may not exercise the privileges of the authorization until he has notified the FAA Flight Standards District Office or International Field Office for the area in which the new base is located, in writing, of the change.

[Docket No. 1179, 27 FR 7973, Aug. 10, 1962; as amended by Amdt. 65–2, 29 FR 5451, April 23, 1964; Amdt. 65–4, 30 FR 3638, March 14, 1965; Amdt. 65–5, 31 FR 3337, March 3, 1966; Amdt. 65–9, 31 FR 13524, Oct. 20, 1966; 32 FR 5769, April 11, 1967; Amdt. 65–35, 54 FR 39292, Sept. 25, 1989; Amdt. 65–41, 66 FR 21066, April 27, 2001]

Subpart E—Repairmen

§65.101 Eligibility requirements: General.

(a) To be eligible for a repairman certificate a person must—
(1) Be at least 18 years of age;
(2) Be specially qualified to perform maintenance on aircraft or components thereof, appropriate to the job for which he is employed;
(3) Be employed for a specific job requiring those special qualifications by a certificated repair station, or by a certificated commercial operator or certificated air carrier, that is required by its operating certificate or approved operations specifications to provide a continuous airworthiness maintenance program according to its maintenance manuals;
(4) Be recommended for certification by his employer, to the satisfaction of the Administrator, as able to satisfactorily maintain aircraft or components, appropriate to the job for which he is employed;
(5) Have either—
(i) At least 18 months of practical experience in the procedures, practices, inspection methods, materials, tools, machine tools, and equipment generally used in the maintenance duties of the specific job for which the person is to be employed and certificated; or
(ii) Completed formal training that is acceptable to the Administrator and is specifically designed to qualify the applicant for the job on which the applicant is to be employed; and
(6) Be able to read, write, speak, and understand the English language, or, in the case of an applicant who does not meet this requirement and who is employed outside the United States by a certificated repair station, a certificated U.S. commercial operator, or a certificated U.S. air carrier, described in paragraph (a)(3) of this section, have this certificate endorsed "Valid only outside the United States."

(b) This section does not apply to the issuance of a repairman certificate (experimental aircraft builder) under §65.104 or to a repairman certificate (light-sport aircraft) under §65.107.

[Docket No. 1179, 27 FR 7973, Aug. 10, 1962; as amended by Amdt. 65–11, 32 FR 13506, Sept. 27, 1967; Amdt. 65–24, 44 FR 46781, Aug. 9, 1979; Amdt. 65–27, 47 FR 13316, March 29, 1982; Amdt. 65–45, 69 FR 44879, July 27, 2004; 72 FR 7739, Feb. 20, 2007]

§65.103 Repairman certificate: Privileges and limitations.

(a) A certificated repairman may perform or supervise the maintenance, preventive maintenance, or alteration of aircraft or aircraft components appropriate to the job for which the repairman was employed and certificated, but only in connection with duties for the certificate holder by whom the repairman was employed and recommended.

(b) A certificated repairman may not perform or supervise duties under the repairman certificate unless the repairman understands the current instructions of the certificate holder by whom the repairman is employed and the manufacturer's instructions for continued airworthiness relating to the specific operations concerned.

(c) This section does not apply to the holder of a repairman certificate (light-sport aircraft) while that repairman is performing work under that certificate.

[Docket No. 18241, 45 FR 46738, July 10, 1980; as amended by Amdt. 65–45, 69 FR 44879, July 27, 2004]

§65.104 Repairman certificate— experimental aircraft builder— Eligibility, privileges and limitations.

(a) To be eligible for a repairman certificate (experimental aircraft builder), an individual must—
(1) Be at least 18 years of age;
(2) Be the primary builder of the aircraft to which the privileges of the certificate are applicable;
(3) Show to the satisfaction of the Administrator that the individual has the requisite skill to determine whether the aircraft is in a condition for safe operations; and
(4) Be a citizen of the United States or an individual citizen of a foreign country who has lawfully been admitted for permanent residence in the United States.

(b) The holder of a repairman certificate (experimental aircraft builder) may perform condition inspections on the aircraft constructed by the holder in accordance with the operating limitations of that aircraft.

(c) Section 65.103 does not apply to the holder of a repairman certificate (experimental aircraft builder) while performing under that certificate.

[Docket No. 18739, 44 FR 46781, Aug. 9, 1979]

§65.105 Display of certificate.

Each person who holds a repairman certificate shall keep it within the immediate area where he normally exercises the privileges of the certificate and shall present it for inspection upon the request of the Administrator or an authorized representative of the National Transportation Safety Board, or of any Federal, State, or local law enforcement officer.

[Docket No. 7258, 31 FR 13524, Oct. 20, 1966; as amended by Docket No. 8084, 32 FR 5769, April 11, 1967]

§65.107 Repairman certificate (light-sport aircraft): Eligibility, privileges, and limits.

(a) Use the following table to determine your eligibility for a repairman certificate (light-sport aircraft) and appropriate rating:

To be eligible for...	You must...
(1) A repairman certificate (light-sport aircraft),	(i) Be at least 18 years old, (ii) Be able to read, speak, write, and understand English. If for medical reasons you cannot meet one of these requirements, the FAA may place limits on your repairman certificate necessary to safely perform the actions authorized by the certificate and rating, (iii) Demonstrate the requisite skill to determine whether a light-sport aircraft is in a condition for safe operation, and (iv) Be a citizen of the United States, or a citizen of a foreign country who has been lawfully admitted for permanent residence in the United States.
(2) A repairman certificate (light-sport aircraft) with an inspection rating,	(i) Meet the requirements of paragraph (a)(1) of this section, and (ii) Complete a 16-hour training course acceptable to the FAA on inspecting the particular class of experimental light-sport aircraft for which you intend to exercise the privileges of this rating.
(3) A repairman certificate (light-sport aircraft) with a maintenance rating,	(i) Meet the requirements of paragraph (a)(1) of this section, and (ii) Complete a training course acceptable to the FAA on maintaining the particular class of light-sport aircraft for which you intend to exercise the privileges of this rating. The training course must, at a minimum, provide the following number of hours of instruction: (A) For airplane class privileges—120-hours, (B) For weight-shift control aircraft class privileges—104 hours, (C) For powered parachute class privileges—104 hours, (D) For lighter than air class privileges—80 hours, (E) For glider class privileges—80 hours.

(b) The holder of a repairman certificate (light-sport aircraft) with an inspection rating may perform the annual condition inspection on a light-sport aircraft:

(1) That is owned by the holder;

(2) That has been issued an experimental certificate for operating a light-sport aircraft under §21.191 (i) of this chapter; and

(3) That is in the same class of light-sport aircraft for which the holder has completed the training specified in paragraph (a)(2)(ii) of this section.

(c) The holder of a repairman certificate (light-sport aircraft) with a maintenance rating may—

(1) Approve and return to service an aircraft that has been issued a special airworthiness certificate in the light-sport category under §21.190 of this chapter, or any part thereof, after performing or inspecting maintenance (to include the annual condition inspection and the 100-hour inspection required by §91.327 of this chapter), preventive maintenance, or an alteration (excluding a major repair or a major alteration on a product produced under an FAA approval);

(2) Perform the annual condition inspection on a light-sport aircraft that has been issued an experimental certificate for operating a light-sport aircraft under §21.191(i) of this chapter; and

(3) Only perform maintenance, preventive maintenance, and an alteration on a light-sport aircraft that is in the same class of light-sport aircraft for which the holder has completed the training specified in paragraph (a)(3)(ii) of this section. Before performing a major repair, the holder must complete additional training acceptable to the FAA and appropriate to the repair performed.

(d) The holder of a repairman certificate (light-sport aircraft) with a maintenance rating may not approve for return to service any aircraft or part thereof unless that person has previously performed the work concerned satisfactorily. If that person has not previously performed that work, the person may show the ability to do the work by performing it to the satisfaction of the FAA, or by performing it under the direct supervision of a certificated and appropriately rated mechanic, or a certificated repairman, who has had previous experience in the specific operation concerned. The repairman may not exercise the privileges of the certificate unless the repairman understands the current instructions of the manufacturer and the maintenance manuals for the specific operation concerned.

[Docket No. FAA–2001–11133, 69 FR 44879, July 27, 2004]

Subpart F— Parachute Riggers

§65.111 Certificate required.

(a) No person may pack, maintain, or alter any personnel-carrying parachute intended for emergency use in connection with civil aircraft of the United States (including the reserve parachute of a dual parachute system to be used for intentional parachute jumping) unless that person holds an appropriate current certificate and type rating issued under this subpart and complies with §§65.127 through 65.133.

(b) No person may pack any main parachute of a dual-parachute system to be used for intentional parachute jumping in connection with civil aircraft of the United States unless that person—

(1) Has an appropriate current certificate issued under this subpart;

(2) Is under the supervision of a current certificated parachute rigger;

(3) Is the person making the next parachute jump with that parachute in accordance with §105.43(a) of this chapter; or

(4) Is the parachutist in command making the next parachute jump with that parachute in a tandem parachute operation conducted under §105.45(b)(1) of this chapter.

(c) No person may maintain or alter any main parachute of a dual-parachute system to be used for intentional parachute jumping in connection with civil aircraft of the United States unless that person—

(1) Has an appropriate current certificate issued under this subpart; or

(2) Is under the supervision of a current certificated parachute rigger.

(d) Each person who holds a parachute rigger certificate shall present it for inspection upon the request of the Administrator or an authorized representative of the National Transportation Safety Board, or of any Federal, State, or local law enforcement officer.

(e) The following parachute rigger certificates are issued under this part:

(1) Senior parachute rigger.
(2) Master parachute rigger.

(f) Sections 65.127 through 65.133 do not apply to parachutes packed, maintained, or altered for the use of the armed forces.

[Docket No. 1179, 27 FR 7973, Aug. 10, 1962; as amended by Amdt. 65–9, 31 FR 13524, Oct. 20, 1966; 32 FR 5769, April 11, 1967; Amdt. 65–42, 66 FR 23553, May 9, 2001; Amdt. 65–54, 75 FR 31285, June 3, 2010]

§65.113 Eligibility requirements: General.

(a) To be eligible for a parachute rigger certificate, a person must—

(1) Be at least 18 years of age;

(2) Be able to read, write, speak, and understand the English language, or, in the case of a citizen of Puerto Rico, or a person who is employed outside of the United States by a U.S. air carrier, and who does not meet this requirement, be issued a certificate that is valid only in Puerto Rico or while he is employed outside of the United States by that air carrier, as the case may be; and

(3) Comply with the sections of this subpart that apply to the certificate and type rating he seeks.

(b) Except for a master parachute rigger certificate, a parachute rigger certificate that was issued before, and was valid on, October 31, 1962, is equal to a senior parachute rigger certificate, and may be exchanged for such a corresponding certificate.

§65.115 Senior parachute rigger certificate: Experience, knowledge, and skill requirements.

Except as provided in §65.117, an applicant for a senior parachute rigger certificate must—

(a) Present evidence satisfactory to the Administrator that he has packed at least 20 parachutes of each type for which he seeks a rating, in accordance with the manufacturer's instructions and under the supervision of a certificated parachute rigger holding a rating for that type or a person holding an appropriate military rating;

(b) Pass a written test, with respect to parachutes in common use, on—

(1) Their construction, packing, and maintenance;
(2) The manufacturer's instructions;
(3) The regulations of this subpart; and

(c) Pass an oral and practical test showing his ability to pack and maintain at least one type of parachute in common use, appropriate to the type rating he seeks.

[Docket No. 10468, 37 FR 13251, July 6, 1972]

§65.117 Military riggers or former military riggers: Special certification rule.

In place of the procedure in §65.115, an applicant for a senior parachute rigger certificate is entitled to it if he passes a written test on the regulations of this subpart and presents satisfactory documentary evidence that he—

(a) Is a member or civilian employee of an Armed Force of the United States, is a civilian employee of a regular armed force of a foreign country, or has, within the 12 months before he applies, been honorably discharged or released from any status covered by this paragraph;

(b) Is serving, or has served within the 12 months before he applies, as a parachute rigger for such an Armed Force; and

(c) Has the experience required by §65.115(a).

§65.119 Master parachute rigger certificate: Experience, knowledge, and skill requirements.

An applicant for a master parachute rigger certificate must meet the following requirements:

(a) Present evidence satisfactory to the Administrator that he has had at least 3 years of experience as a parachute rigger and has satisfactorily packed at least 100 parachutes of each of two types in common use, in accordance with the manufacturer's instructions—

(1) While a certificated and appropriately rated senior parachute rigger; or

(2) While under the supervision of a certificated and appropriately rated parachute rigger or a person holding appropriate military ratings.

An applicant may combine experience specified in paragraphs (a) (1) and (2) of this section to meet the requirements of this paragraph.

(b) If the applicant is not the holder of a senior parachute rigger certificate, pass a written test, with respect to parachutes in common use, on—

(1) Their construction, packing, and maintenance;

(2) The manufacturer's instructions; and

(3) The regulations of this subpart.

(c) Pass an oral and practical test showing his ability to pack and maintain two types of parachutes in common use, appropriate to the type ratings he seeks.

[Docket No. 10468, 37 FR 13252, July 6, 1972]

§65.121 Type ratings.

(a) The following type ratings are issued under this subpart:

(1) Seat.
(2) Back.
(3) Chest.
(4) Lap.

(b) The holder of a senior parachute rigger certificate who qualifies for a master parachute rigger certificate is entitled to have placed on his master parachute rigger certificate the ratings that were on his senior parachute rigger certificate.

§65.123 Additional type ratings: Requirements.

A certificated parachute rigger who applies for an additional type rating must—

(a) Present evidence satisfactory to the Administrator that he has packed at least 20 parachutes of the type for which he seeks a rating, in accordance with the manufacturer's instructions and under the supervision of a certificated parachute rigger holding a rating for that type or a person holding an appropriate military rating; and

(b) Pass a practical test, to the satisfaction of the Administrator, showing his ability to pack and maintain the type of parachute for which he seeks a rating.

[Docket No. 1179, 27 FR 7973, Aug. 10, 1962; as amended by Amdt. 65–20, 37 FR 13251, July 6, 1972]

§65.125 Certificates: Privileges.

(a) A certificated senior parachute rigger may—

(1) Pack or maintain (except for major repair) any type of parachute for which he is rated; and

(2) Supervise other persons in packing any type of parachute for which that person is rated in accordance with §105.43(a) or §105.45(b)(1) of this chapter.

(b) A certificated master parachute rigger may—

(1) Pack, maintain, or alter any type of parachute for which he is rated; and

(2) Supervise other persons in packing, maintaining, or altering any type of parachute for which the certificated parachute rigger is rated in accordance with §105.43(a) or §105.45(b)(1) of this chapter.

(c) A certificated parachute rigger need not comply with §§65.127 through 65.133 (relating to facilities, equipment, performance standards, records, recent experience, and seal) in packing, maintaining, or altering (if authorized) the main parachute of a dual parachute pack to be used for intentional jumping.

[Docket No. 1179, 27 FR 7973, Aug. 10, 1962; as amended by Amdt. 65–20, 37 FR 13252, July 6, 1972; Amdt. 65–42, 66 FR 23553, May 9, 2001]

§65.127 Facilities and equipment.

No certificated parachute rigger may exercise the privileges of his certificate unless he has at least the following facilities and equipment available to him:

(a) A smooth top table at least three feet wide by 40 feet long.

(b) Suitable housing that is adequately heated, lighted, and ventilated for drying and airing parachutes.

(c) Enough packing tools and other equipment to pack and maintain the types of parachutes that he services.

(d) Adequate housing facilities to perform his duties and to protect his tools and equipment.

[Docket No. 1179, 27 FR 7973, Aug. 10, 1962; as amended by Amdt. 65–27, 47 FR 13316, March 29, 1982]

§65.129 Performance standards.

No certificated parachute rigger may—

(a) Pack, maintain, or alter any parachute unless he is rated for that type;

(b) Pack a parachute that is not safe for emergency use;

(c) Pack a parachute that has not been thoroughly dried and aired;

(d) Alter a parachute in a manner that is not specifically authorized by the Administrator or the manufacturer;

(e) Pack, maintain, or alter a parachute in any manner that deviates from procedures approved by the Administrator or the manufacturer of the parachute; or

(f) Exercise the privileges of his certificate and type rating unless he understands the current manufacturer's instructions for the operation involved and has—

(1) Performed duties under his certificate for at least 90 days within the preceding 12 months; or

(2) Shown the Administrator that he is able to perform those duties.

§65.131 Records.

(a) Each certificated parachute rigger shall keep a record of the packing, maintenance, and alteration of parachutes performed or supervised by him. He shall keep in that record, with respect to each parachute worked on, a statement of—

(1) Its type and make;

(2) Its serial number;

(3) The name and address of its owner;

(4) The kind and extent of the work performed;

(5) The date when and place where the work was performed; and

(6) The results of any drop tests made with it.

(b) Each person who makes a record under paragraph (a) of this section shall keep it for at least 2 years after the date it is made.

(c) Each certificated parachute rigger who packs a parachute shall write, on the parachute packing record attached to the parachute, the date and place of the packing and a notation of any defects he finds on inspection. He shall sign that record with his name and the number of his certificate.

§65.133 Seal.

Each certificated parachute rigger must have a seal with an identifying mark prescribed by the Administrator, and a seal press. After packing a parachute he shall seal the pack with his seal in accordance with the manufacturer's recommendation for that type of parachute.

APPENDIX A TO PART 65
AIRCRAFT DISPATCHER COURSES

Source: Docket No. FAA–1998–4553, 64 FR 68925, Dec. 8, 1999, unless otherwise noted.

Overview

This appendix sets forth the areas of knowledge necessary to perform dispatcher functions. The items listed below indicate the minimum set of topics that must be covered in a training course for aircraft dispatcher certification. The order of coverage is at the discretion of the approved school. For the latest technological advancements refer to the Practical Test Standards as published by the FAA.

I. Regulations

　A. Subpart C of this part;
　B. Parts 1, 25, 61, 71, 91, 121, 139, and 175, of this chapter;
　C. 49 CFR part 830;
　D. General Operating Manual.

II. Meteorology

　A. Basic Weather Studies
　(1) The earth's motion and its effects on weather.
　(2) Analysis of the following regional weather types, characteristics, and structures, or combinations thereof:
　(a) Maritime.
　(b) Continental.
　(c) Polar.
　(d) Tropical.
　(3) Analysis of the following local weather types, characteristics, and structures or combinations thereof:

Part 65: Certification: Other Than Crewmembers   **Appendix A to Part 65**

(a) Coastal.
(b) Mountainous.
(c) Island.
(d) Plains.
(4) The following characteristics of the atmosphere:
(a) Layers.
(b) Composition.
(c) Global Wind Patterns.
(d) Ozone.
(5) Pressure:
(a) Units of Measure.
(b) Weather Systems Characteristics.
(c) Temperature Effects on Pressure.
(d) Altimeters.
(e) Pressure Gradient Force.
(f) Pressure Pattern Flying Weather.
(6) Wind:
(a) Major Wind Systems and Coriolis Force.
(b) Jetstreams and their Characteristics.
(c) Local Wind and Related Terms.
(7) States of Matter:
(a) Solids, Liquid, and Gases.
(b) Causes of change of state.
(8) Clouds:
(a) Composition, Formation, and Dissipation.
(b) Types and Associated Precipitation.
(c) Use of Cloud Knowledge in Forecasting.
(9) Fog:
(a) Causes, Formation, and Dissipation.
(b) Types.
(10) Ice:
(a) Causes, Formation, and Dissipation.
(b) Types.
(11) Stability/Instability:
(a) Temperature Lapse Rate, Convection.
(b) Adiabatic Processes.
(c) Lifting Processes.
(d) Divergence.
(e) Convergence.
(12) Turbulence:
(a) Jetstream Associated.
(b) Pressure Pattern Recognition.
(c) Low Level Windshear.
(d) Mountain Waves.
(e) Thunderstorms.
(f) Clear Air Turbulence.
(13) Airmasses:
(a) Classification and Characteristics.
(b) Source Regions.
(c) Use of Airmass Knowledge in Forecasting.
(14) Fronts:
(a) Structure and Characteristics, Both Vertical and Horizontal.
(b) Frontal Types.
(c) Frontal Weather Flying.

(15) Theory of Storm Systems:
(a) Thunderstorms.
(b) Tornadoes.
(c) Hurricanes and Typhoons.
(d) Microbursts.
(e) Causes, Formation, and Dissipation.
B. Weather, Analysis, and Forecasts
(1) Observations:
(a) Surface Observations.
(i) Observations made by certified weather observer.
(ii) Automated Weather Observations.
(b) Terminal Forecasts.
(c) Significant En route Reports and Forecasts.
(i) Pilot Reports.
(ii) Area Forecasts.
(iii) Sigmets, Airmets.
(iv) Center Weather Advisories.
(d) Weather Imagery.
(i) Surface Analysis.
(ii) Weather Depiction.
(iii) Significant Weather Prognosis.
(iv) Winds and Temperature Aloft.
(v) Tropopause Chart.
(vi) Composite Moisture Stability Chart.
(vii) Surface Weather Prognostic Chart.
(viii) Radar Meteorology.
(ix) Satellite Meteorology.
(x) Other charts as applicable.
(e) Meteorological Information Data Collection Systems.
(2) Data Collection, Analysis, and Forecast Facilities.
(3) Service Outlets Providing Aviation Weather Products.
C. Weather Related Aircraft Hazards
(1) Crosswinds and Gusts.
(2) Contaminated Runways.
(3) Restrictions to Surface Visibility.
(4) Turbulence and Windshear.
(5) Icing.
(6) Thunderstorms and Microburst.
(7) Volcanic Ash.

III. Navigation
A. Study of the Earth
(1) Time reference and location (0 Longitude, UTC).
(2) Definitions.
(3) Projections.
(4) Charts.
B. Chart Reading, Application, and Use.
C. National Airspace Plan.
D. Navigation Systems.
E. Airborne Navigation Instruments.
F. Instrument Approach Procedures.

(1) Transition Procedures.
(2) Precision Approach Procedures.
(3) Non-precision Approach Procedures.
(4) Minimums and the relationship to weather.
G. Special Navigation and Operations.
(1) North Atlantic.
(2) Pacific.
(3) Global Differences.

IV. Aircraft
A. Aircraft Flight Manual.
B. Systems Overview.
(1) Flight controls.
(2) Hydraulics.
(3) Electrical.
(4) Air Conditioning and Pressurization.
(5) Ice and Rain protection.
(6) Avionics, Communication, and Navigation.
(7) Powerplants and Auxiliary Power Units.
(8) Emergency and Abnormal Procedures.
(9) Fuel Systems and Sources.
C. Minimum Equipment List/Configuration Deviation List (MEL/CDL) and Applications.
D. Performance.
(1) Aircraft in general.
(2) Principles of flight:
(a) Group one aircraft.
(b) Group two aircraft.
(3) Aircraft Limitations.
(4) Weight and Balance.
(5) Flight instrument errors.
(6) Aircraft performance:
(a) Take-off performance.
(b) En route performance.
(c) Landing performance.

V. Communications
A. Regulatory requirements.
B. Communication Protocol.
C. Voice and Data Communications.
D. Notice to Airmen (NOTAMs).
E. Aeronautical Publications.
F. Abnormal Procedures.

VI. Air Traffic Control
A. Responsibilities.
B. Facilities and Equipment.
C. Airspace classification and route structure.
D. Flight Plans.
(1) Domestic.
(2) International.
E. Separation Minimums.
F. Priority Handling.
G. Holding Procedures.
H. Traffic Management.

VII. Emergency and Abnormal Procedures
A. Security measures on the ground.
B. Security measures in the air.
C. FAA responsibility and services.
D. Collection and dissemination of information on overdue or missing aircraft.
E. Means of declaring an emergency.
F. Responsibility for declaring an emergency.
G. Required reporting of an emergency.
H. NTSB reporting requirements.

VIII. Practical Dispatch Applications
A. Human Factors.
(1) Decisionmaking:
(a) Situation Assessment.
(b) Generation and Evaluation of Alternatives.
(i) Tradeoffs and Prioritization.
(ii) Contingency Planning.
(c) Support Tools and Technologies.
(2) Human Error:
(a) Causes.
(i) Individual and Organizational Factors.
(ii) Technology-Induced Error.
(b) Prevention.
(c) Detection and Recovery.
(3) Teamwork:
(a) Communication and Information Exchange.
(b) Cooperative and Distributed Problem-Solving.
(c) Resource Management.
(i) Air Traffic Control (ATC) activities and workload.
(ii) Flightcrew activities and workload.
(iii) Maintenance activities and workload.
(iv) Operations Control Staff activities and workload.
B. Applied Dispatching.
(1) Briefing techniques, Dispatcher, Pilot.
(2) Preflight:
(a) Safety.
(b) Weather Analysis.
(i) Satellite imagery.
(ii) Upper and lower altitude charts.
(iii) Significant en route reports and forecasts.
(iv) Surface charts.
(v) Surface observations.
(vi) Terminal forecasts and orientation to Enhanced Weather Information System (EWINS).
(c) NOTAMs and airport conditions.
(d) Crew.
(i) Qualifications.
(ii) Limitations.
(e) Aircraft.
(i) Systems.
(ii) Navigation instruments and avionics systems.
(iii) Flight instruments.
(iv) Operations manuals and MEL/CDL.
(v) Performance and limitations.
(f) Flight Planning.
(i) Route of flight.

1. Standard Instrument Departures and Standard Terminal Arrival Routes.
2. En route charts.
3. Operational altitude.
4. Departure and arrival charts.
(ii) Minimum departure fuel.
1. Climb.
2. Cruise.
3. Descent.
(g) Weight and balance.
(h) Economics of flight overview (Performance, Fuel Tankering).
(i) Decision to operate the flight.
(j) ATC flight plan filing.
(k) Flight documentation.
(i) Flight plan.
(ii) Dispatch release.
(3) Authorize flight departure with concurrence of pilot in command.
(4) In-flight operational control:
(a) Current situational awareness.
(b) Information exchange.
(c) Amend original flight release as required.
(5) Post-Flight:
(a) Arrival verification.
(b) Weather debrief.
(c) Flight irregularity reports as required.

PART 91
GENERAL OPERATING AND FLIGHT RULES

**Subpart K—
Fractional Ownership Operations**

91.1001 Applicability.
91.1002 Compliance date.
91.1003 Management contract between owner and program manager.
91.1005 Prohibitions and limitations.
91.1007 Flights conducted under part 121 or part 135 of this chapter.

OPERATIONAL CONTROL

91.1009 Clarification of operational control.
91.1011 Operational control responsibilities and delegation.
91.1013 Operational control briefing and acknowledgment.

PROGRAM MANAGEMENT

91.1014 Issuing or denying management specifications.
91.1015 Management specifications.
91.1017 Amending program manager's management specifications.
91.1019 Conducting tests and inspections.
91.1021 Internal safety reporting and incident/accident response.
91.1023 Program operating manual requirements.
91.1025 Program operating manual contents.
91.1027 Recordkeeping.
91.1029 Flight scheduling and locating requirements.
91.1031 Pilot in command or second in command: Designation required.
91.1033 Operating information required.
91.1035 Passenger awareness.
91.1037 Large transport category airplanes: Turbine engine powered; Limitations; Destination and alternate airports.
91.1039 IFR takeoff, approach and landing minimums.
91.1041 Aircraft proving and validation tests.
91.1043 [Reserved]
91.1045 Additional equipment requirements.
91.1047 Drug and alcohol misuse education program.
91.1049 Personnel.
91.1050 Employment of former FAA employees.
91.1051 Pilot safety background check.
91.1053 Crewmember experience.
91.1055 Pilot operating limitations and pairing requirement.
91.1057 Flight, duty and rest time requirements: All crewmembers.
91.1059 Flight time limitations and rest requirements: One or two pilot crews.
91.1061 Augmented flight crews.
91.1062 Duty periods and rest requirements: Flight attendants.
91.1063 Testing and training: Applicability and terms used.
91.1065 Initial and recurrent pilot testing requirements.
91.1067 Initial and recurrent flight attendant crewmember testing requirements.
91.1069 Flight crew: Instrument proficiency check requirements.
91.1071 Crewmember: Tests and checks, grace provisions, training to accepted standards.
91.1073 Training program: General.
91.1075 Training program: Special rules.
91.1077 Training program and revision: Initial and final approval.
91.1079 Training program: Curriculum.
91.1081 Crewmember training requirements.
91.1083 Crewmember emergency training.
91.1085 Hazardous materials recognition training.
91.1087 Approval of aircraft simulators and other training devices.
91.1089 Qualifications: Check pilots (aircraft) and check pilots (simulator).
91.1091 Qualifications: Flight instructors (aircraft) and flight instructors (simulator).
91.1093 Initial and transition training and checking: Check pilots (aircraft), check pilots (simulator).
91.1095 Initial and transition training and checking: Flight instructors (aircraft), flight instructors (simulator).
91.1097 Pilot and flight attendant crewmember training programs.
91.1099 Crewmember initial and recurrent training requirements.
91.1101 Pilots: Initial, transition, and upgrade ground training.
91.1103 Pilots: Initial, transition, upgrade, requalification, and differences flight training.
91.1105 Flight attendants: Initial and transition ground training.
→ 91.1107 Recurrent training.
91.1109 Aircraft maintenance: Inspection program.
91.1111 Maintenance training.
91.1113 Maintenance recordkeeping.
91.1115 Inoperable instruments and equipment.

§91.1001   Federal Aviation Regulations

91.1411   Continuous airworthiness maintenance program use by fractional ownership program manager.
91.1413   CAMP: Responsibility for airworthiness.
91.1415   CAMP: Mechanical reliability reports.
91.1417   CAMP: Mechanical interruption summary report.
91.1423   CAMP: Maintenance organization.
91.1425   CAMP: Maintenance, preventive maintenance, and alteration programs.
91.1427   CAMP: Manual requirements.
91.1429   CAMP: Required inspection personnel.
91.1431   CAMP: Continuing analysis and surveillance.
91.1433   CAMP: Maintenance and preventive maintenance training program.
91.1435   CAMP: Certificate requirements.
91.1437   CAMP: Authority to perform and approve maintenance.
91.1439   CAMP: Maintenance recording requirements.
91.1441   CAMP: Transfer of maintenance records.
91.1443   CAMP: Airworthiness release or aircraft maintenance log entry.

Subpart K—Fractional Ownership Operations

Source: Docket No. FAA–2001–10047, 68 FR 54561, Sept. 17, 2003 unless otherwise noted.

§91.1001 Applicability.

(a) This subpart prescribes rules, in addition to those prescribed in other subparts of this part, that apply to fractional owners and fractional ownership program managers governing—

(1) The provision of program management services in a fractional ownership program;

(2) The operation of a fractional ownership program aircraft in a fractional ownership program; and

(3) The operation of a program aircraft included in a fractional ownership program managed by an affiliate of the manager of the program to which the owner belongs.

(b) As used in this part—

(1) *Affiliate of a program manager* means a manager that, directly, or indirectly, through one or more intermediaries, controls, is controlled by, or is under common control with, another program manager. The holding of at least forty percent (40 percent) of the equity and forty percent (40 percent) of the voting power of an entity will be presumed to constitute control for purposes of determining an affiliation under this subpart.

(2) A *dry-lease aircraft exchange* means an arrangement, documented by the written program agreements, under which the program aircraft are available, on an as needed basis without crew, to each fractional owner.

(3) A *fractional owner* or *owner* means an individual or entity that possesses a minimum fractional ownership interest in a program aircraft and that has entered into the applicable program agreements; provided, however, that in the case of the flight operations described in paragraph (b)(6)(ii) of this section, and solely for purposes of requirements pertaining to those flight operations, the fractional owner operating the aircraft will be deemed to be a fractional owner in the program managed by the affiliate.

(4) A *fractional ownership interest* means the ownership of an interest or holding of a multi-year leasehold interest and/or a multi-year leasehold interest that is convertible into an ownership interest in a program aircraft.

(5) A *fractional ownership program* or *program* means any system of aircraft ownership and exchange that consists of all of the following elements:

(i) The provision for fractional ownership program management services by a single fractional ownership program manager on behalf of the fractional owners.

(ii) Two or more airworthy aircraft.

(iii) One or more fractional owners per program aircraft, with at least one program aircraft having more than one owner.

(iv) Possession of at least a minimum fractional ownership interest in one or more program aircraft by each fractional owner.

(v) A dry-lease aircraft exchange arrangement among all of the fractional owners.

(vi) Multi-year program agreements covering the fractional ownership, fractional ownership program management services, and dry-lease aircraft exchange aspects of the program.

(6) A *fractional ownership program aircraft* or *program aircraft* means:

(i) An aircraft in which a fractional owner has a minimal fractional ownership interest and that has been included in the dry-lease aircraft exchange pursuant to the program agreements, or

(ii) In the case of a fractional owner from one program operating an aircraft in a different fractional ownership program managed by an affiliate of the operating owner's program manager, the aircraft being operated by the fractional owner, so long as the aircraft is:

(A) Included in the fractional ownership program managed by the affiliate of the operating owner's program manager, and

(B) Included in the operating owner's program's dry-lease aircraft exchange pursuant to the program agreements of the operating owner's program.

(iii) An aircraft owned in whole or in part by the program manager that has been included in the dry-lease aircraft exchange and is used to supplement program operations.

(7) A *Fractional Ownership Program Flight* or *Program Flight* means a flight under this subpart when one or more passengers or property designated by a fractional owner are on board the aircraft.

(8) *Fractional ownership program management services* or *program management services* mean administrative and aviation support services furnished in accordance with the applicable requirements of this subpart or provided by the program manager on behalf of the fractional owners, including, but not limited to, the—

(i) Establishment and implementation of program safety guidelines;

(ii) Employment, furnishing, or contracting of pilots and other crewmembers;

(iii) Training and qualification of pilots and other crewmembers and personnel;

(iv) Scheduling and coordination of the program aircraft and crews;

(v) Maintenance of program aircraft;

(vi) Satisfaction of recordkeeping requirements;

(vii) Development and use of a program operations manual and procedures; and

(viii) Application for and maintenance of management specifications and other authorizations and approvals.

(9) A *fractional ownership program manager* or *program manager* means the entity that offers fractional ownership program management services to fractional owners, and is designated in the multi-year program agreements referenced in paragraph (b)(1)(v) of this section to fulfill the requirements of this chapter applicable to the manager of the program containing the aircraft being flown. When a fractional owner is operating an aircraft in a fractional ownership program managed by an affiliate of the owner's program manager, the references in this subpart to the flight-related responsibilities of the program manager apply, with respect to that particular flight, to the affiliate of the owner's program manager rather than to the owner's program manager.

(10) A *minimum fractional ownership interest* means—

(i) A fractional ownership interest equal to, or greater than, one-sixteenth (1/16) of at least one subsonic, fixed-wing or powered-lift program aircraft; or

(ii) A fractional ownership interest equal to, or greater than, one-thirty-second (1/32) of at least one rotorcraft program aircraft.

(c) The rules in this subpart that refer to a fractional owner or a fractional ownership program manager also apply to any person who engages in an operation governed by this subpart without the management specifications required by this subpart.

§91.1002 Compliance date.

No person that conducted flights before November 17, 2003 under a program that meets the definition of fractional ownership program in §91.1001 may conduct such flights after February 17, 2005 unless it has obtained management specifications under this subpart.

[Docket No. FAA–2001–10047, 68 FR 54561, Sept. 17, 2003; as amended by Amdt. 91–274, 69 FR 74413, Dec. 14, 2004]

§91.1003 Management contract between owner and program manager.

Each owner must have a contract with the program manager that—

(a) Requires the program manager to ensure that the program conforms to all applicable requirements of this chapter.

(b) Provides the owner the right to inspect and to audit, or have a designee of the owner inspect and audit, the records of the program manager pertaining to the operational safety of the program and those records required to show compliance with the management specifications and all applicable regulations. These records include, but are not limited to, the management specifications, authorizations, approvals, manuals, log books, and maintenance records maintained by the program manager.

(c) Designates the program manager as the owner's agent to receive service of notices pertaining to the program that the FAA seeks to provide to owners and authorizes the FAA to send such notices to the program manager in its capacity as the agent of the owner for such service.

(d) Acknowledges the FAA's right to contact the owner directly if the Administrator determines that direct contact is necessary.

§91.1005 Prohibitions and limitations.

(a) Except as provided in §91.321 or §91.501, no owner may carry persons or property for compensation or hire on a program flight.

(b) During the term of the multi-year program agreements under which a fractional owner has obtained a minimum fractional ownership interest in a program aircraft, the flight hours used during that term by the owner on program aircraft must not exceed the total hours associated with the fractional owner's share of ownership.

(c) No person may sell or lease an aircraft interest in a fractional ownership program that is smaller than that prescribed in the definition of "minimum fractional ownership interest" in §91.1001(b)(10) unless flights associated with that interest are operated under part 121 or 135 of this chapter and are conducted by an air carrier or commercial operator certificated under part 119 of this chapter.

§91.1007 Flights conducted under part 121 or part 135 of this chapter.

(a) Except as provided in §91.501(b), when a nonprogram aircraft is used to substitute for a program flight, the flight must be operated in compliance with part 121 or part 135 of this chapter, as applicable.

(b) A program manager who holds a certificate under part 119 of this chapter may conduct a flight for the use of a fractional owner under part 121 or part 135 of this chapter if the aircraft is listed on that certificate holder's operations specifications for part 121 or part 135, as applicable.

(c) The fractional owner must be informed when a flight is being conducted as a program flight or is being conducted under part 121 or part 135 of this chapter.

OPERATIONAL CONTROL

§91.1009 Clarification of operational control.

(a) An owner is in operational control of a program flight when the owner—

(1) Has the rights and is subject to the limitations set forth in §§91.1003 through 91.1013;

(2) Has directed that a program aircraft carry passengers or property designated by that owner; and

(3) The aircraft is carrying those passengers or property.

(b) An owner is not in operational control of a flight in the following circumstances:

(1) A program aircraft is used for a flight for administrative purposes such as demonstration, positioning, ferrying, maintenance, or crew training, and no passengers or property designated by such owner are being carried; or

(2) The aircraft being used for the flight is being operated under part 121 or 135 of this chapter.

§91.1011 Operational control responsibilities and delegation.

(a) Each owner in operational control of a program flight is ultimately responsible for safe operations and for complying with all applicable requirements of this chapter, including those related to airworthiness and operations in connection with the flight. Each owner may delegate some or all of the performance of the tasks associated with carrying out this responsibility to the program manager, and may rely on the program manager for aviation expertise and program management services. When the owner delegates performance of tasks to the program manager or relies on the program manager's expertise, the owner and the program manager are jointly and individually responsible for compliance.

(b) The management specifications, authorizations, and approvals required by this subpart are issued to, and in the sole name of, the program manager on behalf of the fractional owners collectively. The management specifications, authorizations, and approvals will not be affected by any change in ownership of a program aircraft, as long as the aircraft remains a program aircraft in the identified program.

§91.1013 Operational control briefing and acknowledgment.

(a) Upon the signing of an initial program management services contract, or a renewal or extension of a program management services contract, the program manager must brief the fractional owner on the owner's operational control responsibilities, and the owner must review and sign an acknowledgment of these operational control responsibilities. The acknowledgment must be included with the program management services contract. The acknowledgment must define when a fractional owner is in operational control and the owner's responsibilities and liabilities under the program. These include:

(1) Responsibility for compliance with the management specifications and all applicable regulations.

(2) Enforcement actions for any noncompliance.

(3) Liability risk in the event of a flight-related occurrence that causes personal injury or property damage.

(b) The fractional owner's signature on the acknowledgment will serve as the owner's affirmation that the owner has read, understands, and accepts the operational control responsibilities described in the acknowledgment.

(c) Each program manager must ensure that the fractional owner or owner's representatives have access to the acknowledgments for such owner's program aircraft. Each program manager must ensure that the FAA has access to the acknowledgments for all program aircraft.

PROGRAM MANAGEMENT

§91.1014 Issuing or denying management specifications.

(a) A person applying to the Administrator for management specifications under this subpart must submit an application—

(1) In a form and manner prescribed by the Administrator; and

(2) Containing any information the Administrator requires the applicant to submit.

(b) Management specifications will be issued to the program manager on behalf of the fractional owners if, after investigation, the Administrator finds that the applicant:

(1) Meets the applicable requirements of this subpart; and

(2) Is properly and adequately equipped in accordance with the requirements of this chapter and is able to conduct safe operations under appropriate provisions of part 91 of this chapter and management specifications issued under this subpart.

(c) An application for management specifications will be denied if the Administrator finds that the applicant is not properly or adequately equipped or is not able to conduct safe operations under this part.

§91.1015 Management specifications.

(a) Each person conducting operations under this subpart or furnishing fractional ownership program management services to fractional owners must do so in accordance with management specifications issued by the Administrator to the fractional ownership program manager under this subpart. Management specifications must include:

(1) The current list of all fractional owners and types of aircraft, registration markings and serial numbers;

(2) The authorizations, limitations, and certain procedures under which these operations are to be conducted;

(3) Certain other procedures under which each class and size of aircraft is to be operated;

(4) Authorization for an inspection program approved under §91.1109, including the type of aircraft, the registration markings and serial numbers of each aircraft to be operated under the program. No person may conduct any program flight using any aircraft not listed.

(5) Time limitations, or standards for determining time limitations, for overhauls, inspections, and checks for airframes, engines, propellers, rotors, appliances, and emergency equipment of aircraft.

(6) The specific location of the program manager's principal base of operations and, if different, the address that will serve as the primary point of contact for correspondence between the FAA and the program manager and the name and mailing address of the program manager's agent for service;

(7) Other business names the program manager may use;

(8) Authorization for the method of controlling weight and balance of aircraft;

(9) Any authorized deviation and exemption granted from any requirement of this chapter; and

(10) Any other information the Administrator determines is necessary.

(b) The program manager may keep the current list of all fractional owners required by paragraph (a)(1) of this section at its principal base of operation or other location approved by the Administrator and referenced in its management specifications. Each program manager shall make this list of owners available for inspection by the Administrator.

(c) Management specifications issued under this subpart are effective unless—

(1) The management specifications are amended as provided in §91.1017; or

(2) The Administrator suspends or revokes the management specifications.

(d) At least 30 days before it proposes to establish or change the location of its principal base of operations, its main operations base, or its main maintenance base, a program manager must provide written notification to the Flight Standards District Office that issued the program manager's management specifications.

(e) Each program manager must maintain a complete and separate set of its management specifications at its principal base of operations, or at a place approved by the Administrator, and must make its management specifications available for inspection by the Administrator and the fractional owner(s) to whom the program manager furnishes its services for review and audit.

(f) Each program manager must insert pertinent excerpts of its management specifications, or references thereto, in its program manual and must—

(1) Clearly identify each such excerpt as a part of its management specifications; and

(2) State that compliance with each management specifications requirement is mandatory.

(g) Each program manager must keep each of its employees and other persons who perform duties material to its operations informed of the provisions of its management specifications that apply to that employee's or person's duties and responsibilities.

§91.1017 Amending program manager's management specifications.

(a) The Administrator may amend any management specifications issued under this subpart if—

(1) The Administrator determines that safety and the public interest require the amendment of any management specifications; or

(2) The program manager applies for the amendment of any management specifications, and the Administrator determines that safety and the public interest allows the amendment.

(b) Except as provided in paragraph (e) of this section, when the Administrator initiates an amendment of a program manager's management specifications, the following procedure applies:

(1) The Flight Standards District Office that issued the program manager's management specifications will notify the program manager in writing of the proposed amendment.

(2) The Flight Standards District Office that issued the program manager's management specifications will set a reasonable period (but not less than 7 days) within which the program manager may submit written information, views, and arguments on the amendment.

(3) After considering all material presented, the Flight Standards District Office that issued the program manager's management specifications will notify the program manager of—

(i) The adoption of the proposed amendment,

(ii) The partial adoption of the proposed amendment, or

(iii) The withdrawal of the proposed amendment.

(4) If the Flight Standards District Office that issued the program manager's management specifications issues an amendment of the management specifications, it becomes effective not less than 30 days after the program manager receives notice of it unless—

(i) The Flight Standards District Office that issued the program manager's management specifications finds under paragraph (e) of this section that there is an emergency requiring immediate action with respect to safety; or

(ii) The program manager petitions for reconsideration of the amendment under paragraph (d) of this section.

(c) When the program manager applies for an amendment to its management specifications, the following procedure applies:

(1) The program manager must file an application to amend its management specifications—

(i) At least 90 days before the date proposed by the applicant for the amendment to become effective, unless a shorter time is approved, in cases such as mergers, acquisitions of operational assets that require an additional showing of safety (for example, proving tests or validation tests), and resumption of operations following a suspension of operations as a result of bankruptcy actions.

(ii) At least 15 days before the date proposed by the applicant for the amendment to become effective in all other cases.

(2) The application must be submitted to the Flight Standards District Office that issued the program manager's management specifications in a form and manner prescribed by the Administrator.

(3) After considering all material presented, the Flight Standards District Office that issued the program manager's management specifications will notify the program manager of—

(i) The adoption of the applied for amendment;

(ii) The partial adoption of the applied for amendment; or

(iii) The denial of the applied for amendment. The program manager may petition for reconsideration of a denial under paragraph (d) of this section.

(4) If the Flight Standards District Office that issued the program manager's management specifications approves the amendment, following coordination with the program manager regarding its implementation, the amendment is effective on the date the Administrator approves it.

(d) When a program manager seeks reconsideration of a decision of the Flight Standards District Office that issued the program manager's management specifications concerning amendment of management specifications, the following procedure applies:

(1) The program manager must petition for reconsideration of that decision within 30 days of the date that the program manager receives a notice of denial of the amendment of its management specifications, or of the date it receives notice of an FAA-initiated amendment of its management specifications, whichever circumstance applies.

(2) The program manager must address its petition to the Director, Flight Standards Service.

(3) A petition for reconsideration, if filed within the 30-day period, suspends the effectiveness of any amendment issued by the Flight Standards District Office that issued the program manager's management specifications unless that District Office has found, under paragraph (e) of this section, that an emergency exists requiring immediate action with respect to safety.

(4) If a petition for reconsideration is not filed within 30 days, the procedures of paragraph (c) of this section apply.

(e) If the Flight Standards District Office that issued the program manager's management specifications finds that an emergency exists requiring immediate action with respect to safety that makes the procedures set out in this section impracticable or contrary to the public interest—

(1) The Flight Standards District Office amends the management specifications and makes the amendment effective on the day the program manager receives notice of it; and

(2) In the notice to the program manager, the Flight Standards District Office will articulate the reasons for its finding that an emergency exists requiring immediate action with respect to safety or that makes it impracticable or contrary to the public interest to stay the effectiveness of the amendment.

§91.1019 Conducting tests and inspections.

(a) At any time or place, the Administrator may conduct an inspection or test, other than an en route inspection, to determine whether a program manager under this subpart is complying with title 49 of the United States Code, applicable regulations, and the program manager's management specifications.

(b) The program manager must—

(1) Make available to the Administrator at the program manager's principal base of operations, or at a place approved by the Administrator, the program manager's management specifications; and

(2) Allow the Administrator to make any test or inspection, other than an en route inspection, to determine compliance respecting any matter stated in paragraph (a) of this section.

(c) Each employee of, or person used by, the program manager who is responsible for maintaining the program manager's records required by or necessary to demonstrate compliance with this subpart must make those records available to the Administrator.

(d) The Administrator may determine a program manager's continued eligibility to hold its management specifications on any grounds listed in paragraph (a) of this section, or any other appropriate grounds.

(e) Failure by any program manager to make available to the Administrator upon request, the management specifications, or any required record, document, or report is grounds for suspension of all or any part of the program manager's management specifications.

§91.1021 Internal safety reporting and incident/accident response.

(a) Each program manager must establish an internal anonymous safety reporting procedure that fosters an environment of safety without any potential for retribution for filing the report.

(b) Each program manager must establish procedures to respond to an aviation incident/accident.

§91.1023 Program operating manual requirements.

(a) Each program manager must prepare and keep current a program operating manual setting forth procedures and policies acceptable to the Administrator. The program manager's management, flight, ground, and maintenance personnel must use this manual to conduct operations under this subpart. However, the Administrator may authorize a deviation from this paragraph if the Administrator finds that, because of the limited size of the operation, part of the manual is not necessary for guidance of management, flight, ground, or maintenance personnel.

(b) Each program manager must maintain at least one copy of the manual at its principal base of operations.

(c) No manual may be contrary to any applicable U.S. regulations, foreign regulations applicable to the program flights in foreign countries, or the program manager's management specifications.

(d) The program manager must make a copy of the manual, or appropriate portions of the manual (and changes and additions), available to its maintenance and ground operations personnel and must furnish the manual to—

(1) Its crewmembers; and

(2) Representatives of the Administrator assigned to the program manager.

(e) Each employee of the program manager to whom a manual or appropriate portions of it are furnished under paragraph (d)(1) of this section must keep it up-to-date with the changes and additions furnished to them.

(f) Except as provided in paragraph (h) of this section, the appropriate parts of the manual must be carried on each aircraft when away from the principal operations base. The appropriate parts must be available for use by ground or flight personnel.

(g) For the purpose of complying with paragraph (d) of this section, a program manager may furnish the persons listed therein with all or part of its manual in printed form or other form, acceptable to the Administrator, that is retrievable in the English language. If the program manager furnishes all or part of the manual in other than printed form, it must ensure there is a compatible reading device available to those persons that provides a legible image of the maintenance information and instructions, or a system that is able to retrieve the maintenance information and instructions in the English language.

(h) If a program manager conducts aircraft inspections or maintenance at specified facilities where the approved aircraft inspection program is available, the program manager is not required to ensure that the approved aircraft inspection program is carried aboard the aircraft en route to those facilities.

(i) Program managers that are also certificated to operate under part 121 or 135 of this chapter may be authorized to use the operating manual required by those parts to meet the manual requirements of subpart K, provided:

(1) The policies and procedures are consistent for both operations, or

(2) When policies and procedures are different, the applicable policies and procedures are identified and used.

§91.1025 Program operating manual contents.

Each program operating manual must have the date of the last revision on each revised page. Unless otherwise authorized by the Administrator, the manual must include the following:

(a) Procedures for ensuring compliance with aircraft weight and balance limitations;

(b) Copies of the program manager's management specifications or appropriate extracted information, including area of operations authorized, category and class of aircraft authorized, crew complements, and types of operations authorized;

(c) Procedures for complying with accident notification requirements;

(d) Procedures for ensuring that the pilot in command knows that required airworthiness inspections have been made and that the aircraft has been approved for return to service in compliance with applicable maintenance requirements;

(e) Procedures for reporting and recording mechanical irregularities that come to the attention of the pilot in command before, during, and after completion of a flight;

(f) Procedures to be followed by the pilot in command for determining that mechanical irregularities or defects reported for previous flights have been corrected or that correction of certain mechanical irregularities or defects have been deferred;

(g) Procedures to be followed by the pilot in command to obtain maintenance, preventive maintenance, and servicing of the aircraft at a place where previous arrangements have not been made by the program manager or owner, when the pilot is authorized to so act for the operator;

(h) Procedures under §91.213 for the release of, and continuation of flight if any item of equipment required for the particular type of operation becomes inoperative or unserviceable en route;

(i) Procedures for refueling aircraft, eliminating fuel contamination, protecting from fire (including electrostatic protection), and supervising and protecting passengers during refueling;

(j) Procedures to be followed by the pilot in command in the briefing under §91.1035.

(k) Procedures for ensuring compliance with emergency procedures, including a list of the functions assigned each category of required crewmembers in connection with an emergency and emergency evacuation duties;

(l) The approved aircraft inspection program, when applicable;

(m) Procedures for the evacuation of persons who may need the assistance of another person to move expeditiously to an exit if an emergency occurs;

(n) Procedures for performance planning that take into account take off, landing and en route conditions;

(o) An approved Destination Airport Analysis, when required by §91.1037(c), that includes the following elements, supported by aircraft performance data supplied by the aircraft manufacturer for the appropriate runway conditions—

(1) Pilot qualifications and experience;

(2) Aircraft performance data to include normal, abnormal and emergency procedures as supplied by the aircraft manufacturer;

(3) Airport facilities and topography;

(4) Runway conditions (including contamination);

(5) Airport or area weather reporting;

(6) Appropriate additional runway safety margins, if required;

(7) Airplane inoperative equipment;

(8) Environmental conditions; and

(9) Other criteria that affect aircraft performance.

(p) A suitable system (which may include a coded or electronic system) that provides for preservation and retrieval of maintenance recordkeeping information required by §91.1113 in a manner acceptable to the Administrator that provides—

(1) A description (or reference to date acceptable to the Administrator) of the work performed:

(2) The name of the person performing the work if the work is performed by a person outside the organization of the program manager; and

(3) The name or other positive identification of the individual approving the work.

(q) Flight locating and scheduling procedures; and

(r) Other procedures and policy instructions regarding program operations that are issued by the program manager or required by the Administrator.

§91.1027 Recordkeeping.

(a) Each program manager must keep at its principal base of operations or at other places approved by the Administrator, and must make available for inspection by the Administrator all of the following:

(1) The program manager's management specifications.

(2) A current list of the aircraft used or available for use in operations under this subpart, the operations for which each is equipped (for example, MNPS, RNP5/10, RVSM.).

(3) An individual record of each pilot used in operations under this subpart, including the following information:

(i) The full name of the pilot.

(ii) The pilot certificate (by type and number) and ratings that the pilot holds.

(iii) The pilot's aeronautical experience in sufficient detail to determine the pilot's qualifications to pilot aircraft in operations under this subpart.

(iv) The pilot's current duties and the date of the pilot's assignment to those duties.

(v) The effective date and class of the medical certificate that the pilot holds.

(vi) The date and result of each of the initial and recurrent competency tests and proficiency checks required by this subpart and the type of aircraft flown during that test or check.

(vii) The pilot's flight time in sufficient detail to determine compliance with the flight time limitations of this subpart.

(viii) The pilot's check pilot authorization, if any.

(ix) Any action taken concerning the pilot's release from employment for physical or professional disqualification; and

(x) The date of the satisfactory completion of initial, transition, upgrade, and differences training and each recurrent training phase required by this subpart.

(4) An individual record for each flight attendant used in operations under this subpart, including the following information:

(i) The full name of the flight attendant, and

(ii) The date and result of training required by §91.1063, as applicable.

(5) A current list of all fractional owners and associated aircraft. This list or a reference to its location must be included in the management specifications and should be of sufficient detail to determine the minimum fractional ownership interest of each aircraft.

(b) Each program manager must keep each record required by paragraph (a)(2) of this section for at least 6 months, and must keep each record required by paragraphs (a)(3) and (a)(4) of this section for at least 12 months. When an employee is no longer employed or affiliated with the program manager or fractional owner, each record required by paragraphs (a)(3) and (a)(4) of this section must be retained for at least 12 months.

(c) Each program manager is responsible for the preparation and accuracy of a load manifest in duplicate containing information concerning the loading of the aircraft. The manifest must be prepared before each takeoff and must include—

(1) The number of passengers;

(2) The total weight of the loaded aircraft;

(3) The maximum allowable takeoff weight for that flight;

(4) The center of gravity limits;

(5) The center of gravity of the loaded aircraft, except that the actual center of gravity need not be computed if the aircraft is loaded according to a loading schedule or other approved method that ensures that the center of gravity of the loaded aircraft is within approved limits. In those cases, an entry must be made on the manifest indicating that the center of gravity is within limits according to a loading schedule or other approved method;

(6) The registration number of the aircraft or flight number;

(7) The origin and destination; and

(8) Identification of crewmembers and their crew position assignments.

(d) The pilot in command of the aircraft for which a load manifest must be prepared must carry a copy of the completed load manifest in the aircraft to its destination. The program manager must keep copies of completed load manifest for at least 30 days at its principal operations base, or at another location used by it and approved by the Administrator.

(e) Each program manager is responsible for providing a written document that states the name of the entity having operational control on that flight and the part of this chapter under which the flight is operated. The pilot in command of the aircraft must carry a copy of the document in the aircraft to its destination. The program manager must keep a copy of the document for at least 30 days at its principal operations base, or at another location used by it and approved by the Administrator.

(f) Records may be kept either in paper or other form acceptable to the Administrator.

(g) Program managers that are also certificated to operate under part 121 or 135 of this chapter may satisfy the recordkeeping requirements of this section and of §91.1113 with records maintained to fulfill equivalent obligations under part 121 or 135 of this chapter.

§91.1029 Flight scheduling and locating requirements.

(a) Each program manager must establish and use an adequate system to schedule and release program aircraft.

(b) Except as provided in paragraph (d) of this section, each program manager must have adequate procedures established for locating each flight, for which a flight plan is not filed, that—

(1) Provide the program manager with at least the information required to be included in a VFR flight plan;

(2) Provide for timely notification of an FAA facility or search and rescue facility, if an aircraft is overdue or missing; and

(3) Provide the program manager with the location, date, and estimated time for reestablishing radio or telephone communications, if the flight will operate in an area where communications cannot be maintained.

(c) Flight locating information must be retained at the program manager's principal base of operations, or at other places designated by the program manager in the flight locating procedures, until the completion of the flight.

(d) The flight locating requirements of paragraph (b) of this section do not apply to a flight for which an FAA flight plan has been filed and the flight plan is canceled within 25 nautical miles of the destination airport.

§91.1031 Pilot in command or second in command: Designation required.

(a) Each program manager must designate a—

(1) Pilot in command for each program flight; and

(2) Second in command for each program flight requiring two pilots.

(b) The pilot in command, as designated by the program manager, must remain the pilot in command at all times during that flight.

§91.1033 Operating information required.

(a) Each program manager must, for all program operations, provide the following materials, in current and appropriate form, accessible to the pilot at the pilot station, and the pilot must use them—

(1) A cockpit checklist;

(2) For multiengine aircraft or for aircraft with retractable landing gear, an emergency cockpit checklist containing the procedures required by paragraph (c) of this section, as appropriate;

(3) At least one set of pertinent aeronautical charts; and

(4) For IFR operations, at least one set of pertinent navigational en route, terminal area, and instrument approach procedure charts.

(b) Each cockpit checklist required by paragraph (a)(1) of this section must contain the following procedures:

(1) Before starting engines;
(2) Before takeoff;
(3) Cruise;
(4) Before landing;
(5) After landing; and
(6) Stopping engines.

(c) Each emergency cockpit checklist required by paragraph (a)(2) of this section must contain the following procedures, as appropriate:

(1) Emergency operation of fuel, hydraulic, electrical, and mechanical systems.

(2) Emergency operation of instruments and controls.

(3) Engine inoperative procedures.

(4) Any other emergency procedures necessary for safety.

§91.1035 Passenger awareness.

(a) Prior to each takeoff, the pilot in command of an aircraft carrying passengers on a program flight must ensure that all passengers have been orally briefed on—

(1) *Smoking:* Each passenger must be briefed on when, where, and under what conditions smoking is prohibited. This briefing must include a statement, as appropriate, that the regulations require passenger compliance with lighted passenger information signs and no smoking placards, prohibit smoking in lavatories, and require compliance with crewmember instructions with regard to these items;

(2) *Use of safety belts, shoulder harnesses, and child restraint systems:* Each passenger must be briefed on when, where and under what conditions it is necessary to have his or her safety belt and, if installed, his or her shoulder harness fastened about him or her, and if a child is being transported, the appropriate use of child restraint systems, if available. This briefing must include a statement, as appropriate, that the regulations require passenger compliance with the lighted passenger information sign and/or crewmember instructions with regard to these items;

(3) The placement of seat backs in an upright position before takeoff and landing;

(4) Location and means for opening the passenger entry door and emergency exits;

(5) Location of survival equipment;

(6) Ditching procedures and the use of flotation equipment required under §91.509 for a flight over water;

(7) The normal and emergency use of oxygen installed in the aircraft; and

(8) Location and operation of fire extinguishers.

(b) Prior to each takeoff, the pilot in command of an aircraft carrying passengers on a program flight must ensure that each person who may need the assistance of another person to move expeditiously to an exit if an emergency occurs and that person's attendant, if any, has received a briefing as to the procedures to be followed if an evacuation occurs. This paragraph does not apply to a person who has been given a briefing before a previous leg of that flight in the same aircraft.

(c) Prior to each takeoff, the pilot in command must advise the passengers of the name of the entity in operational control of the flight.

(d) The oral briefings required by paragraphs (a), (b), and (c) of this section must be given by the pilot in command or another crewmember.

(e) The oral briefing required by paragraph (a) of this section may be delivered by means of an approved recording playback device that is audible to each passenger under normal noise levels.

(f) The oral briefing required by paragraph (a) of this section must be supplemented by printed cards that must be carried in the aircraft in locations convenient for the use of each passenger. The cards must—

(1) Be appropriate for the aircraft on which they are to be used;

(2) Contain a diagram of, and method of operating, the emergency exits; and

(3) Contain other instructions necessary for the use of emergency equipment on board the aircraft.

§91.1037 Large transport category airplanes: Turbine engine powered; Limitations; Destination and alternate airports.

(a) No program manager or any other person may permit a turbine engine powered large transport category airplane on a program flight to take off that airplane at a weight that (allowing for normal consumption of fuel and oil in flight to the destination or alternate airport) the weight of the airplane on arrival would exceed the landing weight in the Airplane Flight Manual for the elevation of the destination or alternate airport and the ambient temperature expected at the time of landing.

(b) Except as provided in paragraph (c) of this section, no program manager or any other person may permit a turbine engine powered large transport category airplane on a program flight to take off that airplane unless its weight on arrival, allowing for normal consumption of fuel and oil in flight (in accordance with the landing distance in the Airplane Flight Manual for the elevation of the destination airport and the wind conditions expected there at the time of landing), would allow a full stop landing at the intended destination airport within 60 percent of the effective length of each runway described below from a point 50 feet above the intersection of the obstruction clearance plane and the runway. For the purpose of determining the allowable landing weight at the destination airport, the following is assumed:

(1) The airplane is landed on the most favorable runway and in the most favorable direction, in still air.

(2) The airplane is landed on the most suitable runway considering the probable wind velocity and direction and the ground handling characteristics of that airplane, and considering other conditions such as landing aids and terrain.

(c) A program manager or other person flying a turbine engine powered large transport category airplane on a program flight may permit that airplane to take off at a weight in excess of that allowed by paragraph (b) of this section if all of the following conditions exist:

(1) The operation is conducted in accordance with an approved Destination Airport Analysis in that person's program operating manual that contains the elements listed in §91.1025(o).

(2) The airplane's weight on arrival, allowing for normal consumption of fuel and oil in flight (in accordance with the landing distance in the Airplane Flight Manual for the elevation of the destination airport and the wind conditions expected there at the time of landing), would allow a full stop landing at the intended destination airport within 80 percent of the effective length of each runway described below from a point 50 feet above the intersection of the obstruction clearance plane and the runway. For the purpose of determining the allowable landing weight at the destination airport, the following is assumed:

(i) The airplane is landed on the most favorable runway and in the most favorable direction, in still air.

(ii) The airplane is landed on the most suitable runway considering the probable wind velocity and direction and the ground handling characteristics of that airplane, and considering other conditions such as landing aids and terrain.

(3) The operation is authorized by management specifications.

(d) No program manager or other person may select an airport as an alternate airport for a turbine engine powered large transport category airplane unless (based on the assumptions in paragraph (b) of this section) that airplane, at the weight expected at the time of arrival, can be brought to a full stop landing within 80 percent of the effective length of the runway from a point 50 feet above the intersection of the obstruction clearance plane and the runway.

(e) Unless, based on a showing of actual operating landing techniques on wet runways, a shorter landing distance (but never less than that required by paragraph (b) or (c) of this section) has been approved for a specific type and model airplane and included in the Airplane Flight Manual, no person may take off a turbojet airplane when the appropriate weather reports or forecasts, or any combination of them, indicate that the runways at the destination or alternate airport may be wet or slippery at the estimated time of arrival unless the effective runway length at the destination airport is at least 115 percent of the runway length required under paragraph (b) or (c) of this section.

§91.1039 IFR takeoff, approach and landing minimums.

(a) No pilot on a program aircraft operating a program flight may begin an instrument approach procedure to an airport unless—

(1) Either that airport or the alternate airport has a weather reporting facility operated by the U.S. National Weather Service, a source approved by the U.S. National Weather Service, or a source approved by the Administrator; and

(2) The latest weather report issued by the weather reporting facility includes a current local altimeter setting for the destination airport. If no local altimeter setting is available at the destination airport, the pilot must obtain the current local altimeter setting from a source provided by the facility designated on the approach chart for the destination airport.

(b) For flight planning purposes, if the destination airport does not have a weather reporting facility described in paragraph (a)(1) of this section, the pilot must designate as an alternate an airport that has a weather reporting facility meeting that criteria.

(c) The MDA or Decision Altitude and visibility landing minimums prescribed in part 97 of this chapter or in the program manager's management specifications are increased by 100 feet and 1/2 mile respectively, but not to exceed the ceiling and visibility minimums for that airport when used as an alternate airport, for each pilot in command of a turbine-powered aircraft who has not served at least 100 hours as pilot in command in that type of aircraft.

(d) No person may take off an aircraft under IFR from an airport where weather conditions are at or above takeoff minimums but are below authorized IFR landing minimums unless there is an alternate airport within one hour's flying time (at normal cruising speed, in still air) of the airport of departure.

(e) Each pilot making an IFR takeoff or approach and landing at an airport must comply with applicable instrument approach procedures and take off and landing weather minimums prescribed by the authority having jurisdiction over the airport. In addition, no pilot may, at that airport take off when the visibility is less than 600 feet.

§91.1041 Aircraft proving and validation tests.

(a) No program manager may permit the operation of an aircraft, other than a turbojet aircraft, for which two pilots are required by the type certification requirements of this chapter for operations under VFR, if it has not previously proved such an aircraft in operations under this part in at least 25 hours of proving tests acceptable to the Administrator including—

(1) Five hours of night time, if night flights are to be authorized;

(2) Five instrument approach procedures under simulated or actual conditions, if IFR flights are to be authorized; and

(3) Entry into a representative number of en route airports as determined by the Administrator.

(b) No program manager may permit the operation of a turbojet airplane if it has not previously proved a turbojet airplane in operations under this part in at least 25 hours of proving tests acceptable to the Administrator including—

(1) Five hours of night time, if night flights are to be authorized;

(2) Five instrument approach procedures under simulated or actual conditions, if IFR flights are to be authorized; and

(3) Entry into a representative number of en route airports as determined by the Administrator.

(c) No program manager may carry passengers in an aircraft during proving tests, except those needed to make the tests and those designated by the Administrator to observe the tests. However, pilot flight training may be conducted during the proving tests.

(d) Validation testing is required to determine that a program manager is capable of conducting operations safely and in compliance with applicable regulatory standards. Validation tests are required for the following authorizations:

(1) The addition of an aircraft for which two pilots are required for operations under VFR or a turbojet airplane, if that aircraft or an aircraft of the same make or similar design has not been previously proved or validated in operations under this part.

(2) Operations outside U.S. airspace.

(3) Class II navigation authorizations.

(4) Special performance or operational authorizations.

(e) Validation tests must be accomplished by test methods acceptable to the Administrator. Actual flights may not be required when an applicant can demonstrate competence and compliance with appropriate regulations without conducting a flight.

(f) Proving tests and validation tests may be conducted simultaneously when appropriate.

(g) The Administrator may authorize deviations from this section if the Administrator finds that special circumstances make full compliance with this section unnecessary.

§91.1043 [Reserved]

§91.1045 Additional equipment requirements.

No person may operate a program aircraft on a program flight unless the aircraft is equipped with the following—

(a) Airplanes having a passenger-seat configuration of more than 30 seats or a payload capacity of more than 7,500 pounds:

(1) A cockpit voice recorder as required by §121.359 of this chapter as applicable to the aircraft specified in that section.

(2) A flight recorder as required by §121.343 or §121.344 of this chapter as applicable to the aircraft specified in that section.

(3) A terrain awareness and warning system as required by §121.354 of this chapter as applicable to the aircraft specified in that section.

(4) A traffic alert and collision avoidance system as required by §121.356 of this chapter as applicable to the aircraft specified in that section.

(5) Airborne weather radar as required by §121.357 of this chapter, as applicable to the aircraft specified in that section.

(b) Airplanes having a passenger-seat configuration of 30 seats or fewer, excluding each crewmember, and a payload capacity of 7,500 pounds or less, and any rotorcraft (as applicable):

(1) A cockpit voice recorder as required by §135.151 of this chapter as applicable to the aircraft specified in that section.

(2) A flight recorder as required by §135.152 of this chapter as applicable to the aircraft specified in that section.

(3) A terrain awareness and warning system as required by §135.154 of this chapter as applicable to the aircraft specified in that section.

(4) A traffic alert and collision avoidance system as required by §135.180 of this chapter as applicable to the aircraft specified in that section.

(5) As applicable to the aircraft specified in that section, either:

(i) Airborne thunderstorm detection equipment as required by §135.173 of this chapter; or

(ii) Airborne weather radar as required by §135.175 of this chapter.

§91.1047 Drug and alcohol misuse education program.

(a) Each program manager must provide each direct employee performing flight crewmember, flight attendant, flight instructor, or aircraft maintenance duties with drug and alcohol misuse education.

(b) No program manager may use any contract employee to perform flight crewmember, flight attendant, flight instructor, or aircraft maintenance duties for the program manager unless that contract employee has been provided with drug and alcohol misuse education.

(c) Program managers must disclose to their owners and prospective owners the existence of a company drug and alcohol misuse testing program. If the program manager has implemented a company testing program, the program manager's disclosure must include the following:

(1) Information on the substances that they test for, for example, alcohol and a list of the drugs;

(2) The categories of employees tested, the types of tests, for example, pre-employment, random, reasonable cause/suspicion, post accident, return to duty and follow-up; and

(3) The degree to which the program manager's company testing program is comparable to the federally mandated drug and alcohol testing program required under part 120 of this chapter regarding the information in paragraphs (c)(1) and (c)(2) of this section.

(d) If a program aircraft is operated on a program flight into an airport at which no maintenance personnel are available that are subject to the requirements of paragraphs (a) or (b) of this section and emergency maintenance is required, the program manager may use persons not meeting the requirements of paragraphs (a) or (b) of this section to provide such emergency maintenance under both of the following conditions:

(1) The program manager must notify the Drug Abatement Program Division, AAM-800, 800 Independence Avenue, SW, Washington, DC 20591 in writing within 10 days after being provided emergency maintenance in accordance with this paragraph. The program manager must retain copies of all such written notifications for two years.

(2) The aircraft must be reinspected by maintenance personnel who meet the requirements of paragraph (a) or (b) of this section when the aircraft is next at an airport where such maintenance personnel are available.

(e) For purposes of this section, emergency maintenance means maintenance that—

(1) Is not scheduled, and

(2) Is made necessary by an aircraft condition not discovered prior to the departure for that location.

(f) Notwithstanding paragraphs (a) and (b) of this section, drug and alcohol misuse education conducted under an FAA-approved drug and alcohol misuse prevention program may be used to satisfy these requirements.

[Docket No. FAA–2001–10047, 68 FR 54561, Sept. 17, 2003; as amended by Amdt. 91–307, 74 FR 22653, May 14, 2009]

§91.1049 Personnel.

(a) Each program manager and each fractional owner must use in program operations on program aircraft flight crews meeting §91.1053 criteria and qualified under the appropriate regulations. The program manager must provide oversight of those crews.

(b) Each program manager must employ (either directly or by contract) an adequate number of pilots per program aircraft. Flight crew staffing must be determined based on the following factors, at a minimum:

(1) Number of program aircraft.
(2) Program manager flight, duty, and rest time considerations, and in all cases within the limits set forth in §§91.1057 through 91.1061.
(3) Vacations.
(4) Operational efficiencies.
(5) Training.
(6) Single pilot operations, if authorized by deviation under paragraph (d) of this section.

(c) Each program manager must publish pilot and flight attendant duty schedules sufficiently in advance to follow the flight, duty, and rest time limits in §§91.1057 through 91.1061 in program operations.

(d) Unless otherwise authorized by the Administrator, when any program aircraft is flown in program operations with passengers onboard, the crew must consist of at least two qualified pilots employed or contracted by the program manager or the fractional owner.

(e) The program manager must ensure that trained and qualified scheduling or flight release personnel are on duty to schedule and release program aircraft during all hours that such aircraft are available for program operations.

§91.1050 Employment of former FAA employees.

(a) Except as specified in paragraph (c) of this section, no fractional owner or fractional ownership program manager may knowingly employ or make a contractual arrangement which permits an individual to act as an agent or representative of the fractional owner or fractional ownership program manager in any matter before the Federal Aviation Administration if the individual, in the preceding 2 years—

(1) Served as, or was directly responsible for the oversight of, a Flight Standards Service aviation safety inspector; and
(2) Had direct responsibility to inspect, or oversee the inspection of, the operations of the fractional owner or fractional ownership program manager.

(b) For the purpose of this section, an individual shall be considered to be acting as an agent or representative of a fractional owner or fractional ownership program manager in a matter before the agency if the individual makes any written or oral communication on behalf of the fractional owner or fractional ownership program manager to the agency (or any of its officers or employees) in connection with a particular matter, whether or not involving a specific party and without regard to whether the individual has participated in, or had responsibility for, the particular matter while serving as a Flight Standards Service aviation safety inspector.

(c) The provisions of this section do not prohibit a fractional owner or fractional ownership program manager from knowingly employing or making a contractual arrangement which permits an individual to act as an agent or representative of the fractional owner or fractional ownership program manager in any matter before the Federal Aviation Administration if the individual was employed by the fractional owner or fractional ownership program manager before October 21, 2011.

[Docket No. FAA–2008–1154, 76 FR 52235, Aug. 22, 2011]

§91.1051 Pilot safety background check.

Within 90 days of an individual beginning service as a pilot, the program manager must request the following information:

(a) FAA records pertaining to—
(1) Current pilot certificates and associated type ratings.
(2) Current medical certificates.
(3) Summaries of legal enforcement actions resulting in a finding by the Administrator of a violation.

(b) Records from all previous employers during the five years preceding the date of the employment application where the applicant worked as a pilot. If any of these firms are in bankruptcy, the records must be requested from the trustees in bankruptcy for those employees. If the previous employer is no longer in business, a documented good faith effort must be made to obtain the records. Records from previous employers must include, as applicable—

(1) Crew member records.

Part 91: General Operating and Flight Rules §91.1055

(2) Drug testing—collection, testing, and rehabilitation records pertaining to the individual.

(3) Alcohol misuse prevention program records pertaining to the individual.

(4) The applicant's individual record that includes certifications, ratings, aeronautical experience, effective date and class of the medical certificate.

§91.1053 Crewmember experience.

(a) No program manager or owner may use any person, nor may any person serve, as a pilot in command or second in command of a program aircraft, or as a flight attendant on a program aircraft, in program operations under this subpart unless that person has met the applicable requirements of part 61 of this chapter and has the following experience and ratings:

(1) Total flight time for all pilots:

(i) Pilot in command—A minimum of 1,500 hours.

(ii) Second in command—A minimum of 500 hours.

(2) For multi-engine turbine-powered fixed-wing and powered-lift aircraft, the following FAA certification and ratings requirements:

(i) Pilot in command—Airline transport pilot and applicable type ratings.

(ii) Second in command—Commercial pilot and instrument ratings.

(iii) Flight attendant (if required or used)— Appropriately trained personnel.

(3) For all other aircraft, the following FAA certification and rating requirements:

(i) Pilot in command—Commercial pilot and instrument ratings.

(ii) Second in command—Commercial pilot and instrument ratings.

(iii) Flight attendant (if required or used)— Appropriately trained personnel.

(b) The Administrator may authorize deviations from paragraph (a)(1) of this section if the Flight Standards District Office that issued the program manager's management specifications finds that the crewmember has comparable experience, and can effectively perform the functions associated with the position in accordance with the requirements of this chapter. Grants of deviation under this paragraph may be granted after consideration of the size and scope of the operation, the qualifications of the intended personnel and the circumstances set forth in §91.1055(b)(1) through (3). The Administrator may, at any time, terminate any grant of deviation authority issued under this paragraph.

§91.1055 Pilot operating limitations and pairing requirement.

(a) If the second in command of a fixed-wing program aircraft has fewer than 100 hours of flight time as second in command flying in the aircraft make and model and, if a type rating is required, in the type aircraft being flown, and the pilot in command is not an appropriately qualified check pilot, the pilot in command shall make all takeoffs and landings in any of the following situations:

(1) Landings at the destination airport when a Destination Airport Analysis is required by §91.1037(c); and

(2) In any of the following conditions:

(i) The prevailing visibility for the airport is at or below 3/4 mile.

(ii) The runway visual range for the runway to be used is at or below 4,000 feet.

(iii) The runway to be used has water, snow, slush, ice or similar contamination that may adversely affect aircraft performance.

(iv) The braking action on the runway to be used is reported to be less than "good."

(v) The crosswind component for the runway to be used is in excess of 15 knots.

(vi) Windshear is reported in the vicinity of the airport.

(vii) Any other condition in which the pilot in command determines it to be prudent to exercise the pilot in command's authority.

(b) No program manager may release a program flight under this subpart unless, for that aircraft make or model and, if a type rating is required, for that type aircraft, either the pilot in command or the second in command has at least 75 hours of flight time, either as pilot in command or second in command. The Administrator may, upon application by the program manager, authorize deviations from the requirements of this paragraph by an appropriate amendment to the management specifications in any of the following circumstances:

(1) A newly authorized program manager does not employ any pilots who meet the minimum requirements of this paragraph.

(2) An existing program manager adds to its fleet a new category and class aircraft not used before in its operation.

(3) An existing program manager establishes a new base to which it assigns pilots who will be required to become qualified on the aircraft operated from that base.

(c) No person may be assigned in the capacity of pilot in command in a program operation to more than two aircraft types that require a separate type rating.

ASA 69

§91.1057 Flight, duty and rest time requirements: All crewmembers.

(a) For purposes of this subpart—

Augmented flight crew means at least three pilots.

Calendar day means the period of elapsed time, using Coordinated Universal Time or local time that begins at midnight and ends 24 hours later at the next midnight.

Duty period means the period of elapsed time between reporting for an assignment involving flight time and release from that assignment by the program manager. All time between these two points is part of the duty period, even if flight time is interrupted by nonflight-related duties. The time is calculated using either Coordinated Universal Time or local time to reflect the total elapsed time.

Extension of flight time means an increase in the flight time because of circumstances beyond the control of the program manager or flight crewmember (such as adverse weather) that are not known at the time of departure and that prevent the flightcrew from reaching the destination within the planned flight time.

Flight attendant means an individual, other than a flight crewmember, who is assigned by the program manager, in accordance with the required minimum crew complement under the program manager's management specifications or in addition to that minimum complement, to duty in an aircraft during flight time and whose duties include but are not necessarily limited to cabin-safety-related responsibilities.

Multi-time zone flight means an easterly or westerly flight or multiple flights in one direction in the same duty period that results in a time zone difference of 5 or more hours and is conducted in a geographic area that is south of 60 degrees north latitude and north of 60 degrees south latitude.

Reserve status means that status in which a flight crewmember, by arrangement with the program manager: Holds himself or herself fit to fly to the extent that this is within the control of the flight crewmember; remains within a reasonable response time of the aircraft as agreed between the flight crewmember and the program manager; and maintains a ready means whereby the flight crewmember may be contacted by the program manager. Reserve status is not part of any duty period or rest period.

Rest period means a period of time required pursuant to this subpart that is free of all responsibility for work or duty prior to the commencement of, or following completion of, a duty period, and during which the flight crewmember or flight attendant cannot be required to receive contact from the program manager. A rest period does not include any time during which the program manager imposes on a flight crewmember or flight attendant any duty or restraint, including any actual work or present responsibility for work should the occasion arise.

Standby means that portion of a duty period during which a flight crewmember is subject to the control of the program manager and holds himself or herself in a condition of readiness to undertake a flight. Standby is not part of any rest period.

(b) A program manager may assign a crewmember and a crewmember may accept an assignment for flight time only when the applicable requirements of this section and §§91.1059–91.1062 are met.

(c) No program manager may assign any crewmember to any duty during any required rest period.

(d) Time spent in transportation, not local in character, that a program manager requires of a crewmember and provides to transport the crewmember to an airport at which he or she is to serve on a flight as a crewmember, or from an airport at which he or she was relieved from duty to return to his or her home station, is not considered part of a rest period.

(e) A flight crewmember may continue a flight assignment if the flight to which he or she is assigned would normally terminate within the flight time limitations, but because of circumstances beyond the control of the program manager or flight crewmember (such as adverse weather conditions), is not at the time of departure expected to reach its destination within the planned flight time. The extension of flight time under this paragraph may not exceed the maximum time limits set forth in §91.1059.

(f) Each flight assignment must provide for at least 10 consecutive hours of rest during the 24-hour period that precedes the completion time of the assignment.

(g) The program manager must provide each crewmember at least 13 rest periods of at least 24 consecutive hours each in each calendar quarter.

(h) A flight crewmember may decline a flight assignment if, in the flight crewmember's determination, to do so would not be consistent with the standard of safe operation required under this subpart, this part, and applicable provisions of this title.

(i) Any rest period required by this subpart may occur concurrently with any other rest period.

(j) If authorized by the Administrator, a program manager may use the applicable unscheduled flight time limitations, duty period limitations, and rest requirements of part 121 or part 135 of this chapter instead of the flight time limitations, duty period limitations, and rest requirements of this subpart.

Part 91: General Operating and Flight Rules §91.1062

§91.1059 Flight time limitations and rest requirements: One or two pilot crews.

(a) No program manager may assign any flight crewmember, and no flight crewmember may accept an assignment, for flight time as a member of a one- or two-pilot crew if that crewmember's total flight time in all commercial flying will exceed—

(1) 500 hours in any calendar quarter;
(2) 800 hours in any two consecutive calendar quarters;
(3) 1,400 hours in any calendar year.

(b) Except as provided in paragraph (c) of this section, during any 24 consecutive hours the total flight time of the assigned flight, when added to any commercial flying by that flight crewmember, may not exceed—

(1) 8 hours for a flight crew consisting of one pilot; or
(2) 10 hours for a flight crew consisting of two pilots qualified under this subpart for the operation being conducted.

(c) No program manager may assign any flight crewmember, and no flight crewmember may accept an assignment, if that crewmember's flight time or duty period will exceed, or rest time will be less than—

	Normal duty	Extension of flight time
(1) Minimum Rest Immediately Before Duty	10 hours	10 hours
(2) Duty Period	Up to 14 hours	Up to 14 hours
(3) Flight Time For 1 Pilot	Up to 8 hours	Exceeding 8 hours up to 9 hours
(4) Flight Time For 2 Pilots	Up to 10 hours	Exceeding 10 hours up to 12 hours
(5) Minimum After Duty Rest	10 hours	12 hours
(6) Minimum After Duty Rest Period for Multi-Time Zone Flights	14 hours	18 hours

§91.1061 Augmented flight crews.

(a) No program manager may assign any flight crewmember, and no flight crewmember may accept an assignment, for flight time as a member of an augmented crew if that crewmember's total flight time in all commercial flying will exceed—

(1) 500 hours in any calendar quarter;
(2) 800 hours in any two consecutive calendar quarters;
(3) 1,400 hours in any calendar year.

(b) No program manager may assign any pilot to an augmented crew, unless the program manager ensures:

(1) Adequate sleeping facilities are installed on the aircraft for the pilots.
(2) No more than 8 hours of flight deck duty is accrued in any 24 consecutive hours.
(3) For a three-pilot crew, the crew must consist of at least the following:

(i) A pilot in command (PIC) who meets the applicable flight crewmember requirements of this subpart and §61.57 of this chapter.
(ii) A PIC qualified pilot who meets the applicable flight crewmember requirements of this subpart and §61.57(c) and (d) of this chapter.
(iii) A second in command (SIC) who meets the SIC qualifications of this subpart. For flight under IFR, that person must also meet the recent instrument experience requirements of part 61 of this chapter.

(4) For a four-pilot crew, at least three pilots who meet the conditions of paragraph (b)(3) of this section, plus a fourth pilot who meets the SIC qualifications of this subpart. For flight under IFR, that person must also meet the recent instrument experience requirements of part 61 of this chapter.

(c) No program manager may assign any flight crewmember, and no flight crewmember may accept an assignment, if that crewmember's flight time or duty period will exceed, or rest time will be less than—

	3-Pilot Crew	4-Pilot Crew
(1) Minimum Rest Immediately Before Duty	10 hours	10 hours
(2) Duty Period	Up to 16 hours	Up to 18 hours
(3) Flight Time	Up to 12 hours	Up to 16 hours
(4) Minimum After Duty Rest	12 hours	18 hours
(5) Minimum After Duty Rest Period for Multi-Time Zone Flights	18 hours	24 hours

§91.1062 Duty periods and rest requirements: Flight attendants.

(a) Except as provided in paragraph (b) of this section, a program manager may assign a duty period to a flight attendant only when the assignment meets the applicable duty period limitations and rest requirements of this paragraph.

(1) Except as provided in paragraphs (a)(4), (a)(5), and (a)(6) of this section, no program manager may assign a flight attendant to a scheduled duty period of more than 14 hours.

(2) Except as provided in paragraph (a)(3) of this section, a flight attendant scheduled to a duty period of 14 hours or less as provided under paragraph (a)(1) of this section must be given a

§91.1062

scheduled rest period of at least 9 consecutive hours. This rest period must occur between the completion of the scheduled duty period and the commencement of the subsequent duty period.

(3) The rest period required under paragraph (a)(2) of this section may be scheduled or reduced to 8 consecutive hours if the flight attendant is provided a subsequent rest period of at least 10 consecutive hours; this subsequent rest period must be scheduled to begin no later than 24 hours after the beginning of the reduced rest period and must occur between the completion of the scheduled duty period and the commencement of the subsequent duty period.

(4) A program manager may assign a flight attendant to a scheduled duty period of more than 14 hours, but no more than 16 hours, if the program manager has assigned to the flight or flights in that duty period at least one flight attendant in addition to the minimum flight attendant complement required for the flight or flights in that duty period under the program manager's management specifications.

(5) A program manager may assign a flight attendant to a scheduled duty period of more than 16 hours, but no more than 18 hours, if the program manager has assigned to the flight or flights in that duty period at least two flight attendants in addition to the minimum flight attendant complement required for the flight or flights in that duty period under the program manager's management specifications.

(6) A program manager may assign a flight attendant to a scheduled duty period of more than 18 hours, but no more than 20 hours, if the scheduled duty period includes one or more flights that land or take off outside the 48 contiguous states and the District of Columbia, and if the program manager has assigned to the flight or flights in that duty period at least three flight attendants in addition to the minimum flight attendant complement required for the flight or flights in that duty period under the program manager's management specifications.

(7) Except as provided in paragraph (a)(8) of this section, a flight attendant scheduled to a duty period of more than 14 hours but no more than 20 hours, as provided in paragraphs (a)(4), (a)(5), and (a)(6) of this section, must be given a scheduled rest period of at least 12 consecutive hours. This rest period must occur between the completion of the scheduled duty period and the commencement of the subsequent duty period.

(8) The rest period required under paragraph (a)(7) of this section may be scheduled or reduced to 10 consecutive hours if the flight attendant is provided a subsequent rest period of at least 14 consecutive hours; this subsequent rest period must be scheduled to begin no later than 24 hours after the beginning of the reduced rest

Federal Aviation Regulations

period and must occur between the completion of the scheduled duty period and the commencement of the subsequent duty period.

(9) Notwithstanding paragraphs (a)(4), (a)(5), and (a)(6) of this section, if a program manager elects to reduce the rest period to 10 hours as authorized by paragraph (a)(8) of this section, the program manager may not schedule a flight attendant for a duty period of more than 14 hours during the 24-hour period commencing after the beginning of the reduced rest period.

(b) Notwithstanding paragraph (a) of this section, a program manager may apply the flight crewmember flight time and duty limitations and rest requirements of this part to flight attendants for all operations conducted under this part provided that the program manager establishes written procedures that—

(1) Apply to all flight attendants used in the program manager's operation;

(2) Include the flight crewmember rest and duty requirements of §§91.1057, 91.1059, and 91.1061, as appropriate to the operation being conducted, except that rest facilities on board the aircraft are not required;

(3) Include provisions to add one flight attendant to the minimum flight attendant complement for each flight crewmember who is in excess of the minimum number required in the aircraft type certificate data sheet and who is assigned to the aircraft under the provisions of §91.1061; and

(4) Are approved by the Administrator and described or referenced in the program manager's management specifications.

§91.1063 Testing and training: Applicability and terms used.

(a) Sections 91.1065 through 91.1107:

(1) Prescribe the tests and checks required for pilots and flight attendant crewmembers and for the approval of check pilots in operations under this subpart;

(2) Prescribe the requirements for establishing and maintaining an approved training program for crewmembers, check pilots and instructors, and other operations personnel employed or used by the program manager in program operations;

(3) Prescribe the requirements for the qualification, approval and use of aircraft simulators and flight training devices in the conduct of an approved training program; and

(4) Permits training center personnel authorized under part 142 of this chapter who meet the requirements of §91.1075 to conduct training, testing and checking under contract or other arrangements to those persons subject to the requirements of this subpart.

(b) If authorized by the Administrator, a program manager may comply with the applicable

Part 91: General Operating and Flight Rules §91.1065

training and testing sections of subparts N and O of part 121 of this chapter instead of §§91.1065 through 91.1107, except for the operating experience requirements of §121.434 of this chapter.

(c) If authorized by the Administrator, a program manager may comply with the applicable training and testing sections of subparts G and H of part 135 of this chapter instead of §§91.1065 through 91.1107, except for the operating experience requirements of §135.244 of this chapter.

(d) For the purposes of this subpart, the following terms and definitions apply:

(1) *Initial training.* The training required for crewmembers who have not qualified and served in the same capacity on an aircraft.

(2) *Transition training.* The training required for crewmembers who have qualified and served in the same capacity on another aircraft.

(3) *Upgrade training.* The training required for crewmembers who have qualified and served as second in command on a particular aircraft type, before they serve as pilot in command on that aircraft.

(4) *Differences training.* The training required for crewmembers who have qualified and served on a particular type aircraft, when the Administrator finds differences training is necessary before a crewmember serves in the same capacity on a particular variation of that aircraft.

(5) *Recurrent training.* The training required for crewmembers to remain adequately trained and currently proficient for each aircraft crewmember position, and type of operation in which the crewmember serves.

(6) *In flight.* The maneuvers, procedures, or functions that will be conducted in the aircraft.

(7) *Training center.* An organization governed by the applicable requirements of part 142 of this chapter that conducts training, testing, and checking under contract or other arrangement to program managers subject to the requirements of this subpart.

(8) *Requalification training.* The training required for crewmembers previously trained and qualified, but who have become unqualified because of not having met within the required period any of the following:

(I) Recurrent crewmember training requirements of §91.1107.

(ii) Instrument proficiency check requirements of §91.1069.

(iii) Testing requirements of §91.1065.

(iv) Recurrent flight attendant testing requirements of §91.1067.

§91.1065 Initial and recurrent pilot testing requirements.

(a) No program manager or owner may use a pilot, nor may any person serve as a pilot, unless, since the beginning of the 12th month before that service, that pilot has passed either a written or oral test (or a combination), given by the Administrator or an authorized check pilot, on that pilot's knowledge in the following areas—

(1) The appropriate provisions of parts 61 and 91 of this chapter and the management specifications and the operating manual of the program manager;

(2) For each type of aircraft to be flown by the pilot, the aircraft powerplant, major components and systems, major appliances, performance and operating limitations, standard and emergency operating procedures, and the contents of the accepted operating manual or equivalent, as applicable;

(3) For each type of aircraft to be flown by the pilot, the method of determining compliance with weight and balance limitations for takeoff, landing and en route operations;

(4) Navigation and use of air navigation aids appropriate to the operation or pilot authorization, including, when applicable, instrument approach facilities and procedures;

(5) Air traffic control procedures, including IFR procedures when applicable;

(6) Meteorology in general, including the principles of frontal systems, icing, fog, thunderstorms, and windshear, and, if appropriate for the operation of the program manager, high altitude weather;

(7) Procedures for—

(i) Recognizing and avoiding severe weather situations;

(ii) Escaping from severe weather situations, in case of inadvertent encounters, including low-altitude windshear (except that rotorcraft aircraft pilots are not required to be tested on escaping from low-altitude windshear); and

(iii) Operating in or near thunderstorms (including best penetration altitudes), turbulent air (including clear air turbulence), icing, hail, and other potentially hazardous meteorological conditions; and

(8) New equipment, procedures, or techniques, as appropriate.

(b) No program manager or owner may use a pilot, nor may any person serve as a pilot, in any aircraft unless, since the beginning of the 12th month before that service, that pilot has passed a competency check given by the Administrator or an authorized check pilot in that class of aircraft, if single-engine aircraft other than turbojet, or that type of aircraft, if rotorcraft, multiengine aircraft, or turbojet airplane, to determine the

ASA 73

pilot's competence in practical skills and techniques in that aircraft or class of aircraft. The extent of the competency check will be determined by the Administrator or authorized check pilot conducting the competency check. The competency check may include any of the maneuvers and procedures currently required for the original issuance of the particular pilot certificate required for the operations authorized and appropriate to the category, class and type of aircraft involved. For the purposes of this paragraph, type, as to an airplane, means any one of a group of airplanes determined by the Administrator to have a similar means of propulsion, the same manufacturer, and no significantly different handling or flight characteristics. For the purposes of this paragraph, type, as to a rotorcraft, means a basic make and model.

(c) The instrument proficiency check required by §91.1069 may be substituted for the competency check required by this section for the type of aircraft used in the check.

(d) For the purpose of this subpart, competent performance of a procedure or maneuver by a person to be used as a pilot requires that the pilot be the obvious master of the aircraft, with the successful outcome of the maneuver never in doubt.

(e) The Administrator or authorized check pilot certifies the competency of each pilot who passes the knowledge or flight check in the program manager's pilot records.

(f) All or portions of a required competency check may be given in an aircraft simulator or other appropriate training device, if approved by the Administrator.

§91.1067 Initial and recurrent flight attendant crewmember testing requirements.

No program manager or owner may use a flight attendant crewmember, nor may any person serve as a flight attendant crewmember unless, since the beginning of the 12th month before that service, the program manager has determined by appropriate initial and recurrent testing that the person is knowledgeable and competent in the following areas as appropriate to assigned duties and responsibilities—

(a) Authority of the pilot in command;

(b) Passenger handling, including procedures to be followed in handling deranged persons or other persons whose conduct might jeopardize safety;

(c) Crewmember assignments, functions, and responsibilities during ditching and evacuation of persons who may need the assistance of another person to move expeditiously to an exit in an emergency;

(d) Briefing of passengers;

(e) Location and operation of portable fire extinguishers and other items of emergency equipment;

(f) Proper use of cabin equipment and controls;

(g) Location and operation of passenger oxygen equipment;

(h) Location and operation of all normal and emergency exits, including evacuation slides and escape ropes; and

(i) Seating of persons who may need assistance of another person to move rapidly to an exit in an emergency as prescribed by the program manager's operations manual.

§91.1069 Flight crew: Instrument proficiency check requirements.

(a) No program manager or owner may use a pilot, nor may any person serve, as a pilot in command of an aircraft under IFR unless, since the beginning of the 6th month before that service, that pilot has passed an instrument proficiency check under this section administered by the Administrator or an authorized check pilot.

(b) No program manager or owner may use a pilot, nor may any person serve, as a second command pilot of an aircraft under IFR unless, since the beginning of the 12th month before that service, that pilot has passed an instrument proficiency check under this section administered by the Administrator or an authorized check pilot.

(c) No pilot may use any type of precision instrument approach procedure under IFR unless, since the beginning of the 6th month before that use, the pilot satisfactorily demonstrated that type of approach procedure. No pilot may use any type of nonprecision approach procedure under IFR unless, since the beginning of the 6th month before that use, the pilot has satisfactorily demonstrated either that type of approach procedure or any other two different types of nonprecision approach procedures. The instrument approach procedure or procedures must include at least one straight-in approach, one circling approach, and one missed approach. Each type of approach procedure demonstrated must be conducted to published minimums for that procedure.

(d) The instrument proficiency checks required by paragraphs (a) and (b) of this section consists of either an oral or written equipment test (or a combination) and a flight check under simulated or actual IFR conditions. The equipment test includes questions on emergency procedures, engine operation, fuel and lubrication systems, power settings, stall speeds, best engine-out speed, propeller and supercharger operations, and hydraulic, mechanical, and electrical systems, as appropriate. The flight check includes navigation by instruments, recovery from simulated emergencies, and standard instrument approaches involving navigational facilities which that pilot is to be authorized to use.

(e) Each pilot taking the instrument proficiency check must show that standard of competence required by §91.1065(d).

(1) The instrument proficiency check must—

(i) For a pilot in command of an aircraft requiring that the PIC hold an airline transport pilot certificate, include the procedures and maneuvers for an airline transport pilot certificate in the particular type of aircraft, if appropriate; and

(ii) For a pilot in command of a rotorcraft or a second in command of any aircraft requiring that the SIC hold a commercial pilot certificate include the procedures and maneuvers for a commercial pilot certificate with an instrument rating and, if required, for the appropriate type rating.

(2) The instrument proficiency check must be given by an authorized check pilot or by the Administrator.

(f) If the pilot is assigned to pilot only one type of aircraft, that pilot must take the instrument proficiency check required by paragraph (a) of this section in that type of aircraft.

(g) If the pilot in command is assigned to pilot more than one type of aircraft, that pilot must take the instrument proficiency check required by paragraph (a) of this section in each type of aircraft to which that pilot is assigned, in rotation, but not more than one flight check during each period described in paragraph (a) of this section.

(h) If the pilot in command is assigned to pilot both single-engine and multiengine aircraft, that pilot must initially take the instrument proficiency check required by paragraph (a) of this section in a multiengine aircraft, and each succeeding check alternately in single-engine and multiengine aircraft, but not more than one flight check during each period described in paragraph (a) of this section.

(i) All or portions of a required flight check may be given in an aircraft simulator or other appropriate training device, if approved by the Administrator.

§91.1071 Crewmember: Tests and checks, grace provisions, training to accepted standards.

(a) If a crewmember who is required to take a test or a flight check under this subpart, completes the test or flight check in the month before or after the month in which it is required, that crewmember is considered to have completed the test or check in the month in which it is required.

(b) If a pilot being checked under this subpart fails any of the required maneuvers, the person giving the check may give additional training to the pilot during the course of the check. In addition to repeating the maneuvers failed, the person giving the check may require the pilot being checked to repeat any other maneuvers that are necessary to determine the pilot's proficiency. If the pilot being checked is unable to demonstrate satisfactory performance to the person conducting the check, the program manager may not use the pilot, nor may the pilot serve, as a flight crewmember in operations under this subpart until the pilot has satisfactorily completed the check. If a pilot who demonstrates unsatisfactory performance is employed as a pilot for a certificate holder operating under part 121, 125, or 135 of this chapter, he or she must notify that certificate holder of the unsatisfactory performance.

§91.1073 Training program: General.

(a) Each program manager must have a training program and must:

(1) Establish, obtain the appropriate initial and final approval of, and provide a training program that meets this subpart and that ensures that each crewmember, including each flight attendant if the program manager uses a flight attendant crewmember, flight instructor, check pilot, and each person assigned duties for the carriage and handling of hazardous materials (as defined in 49 CFR 171.8) is adequately trained to perform these assigned duties.

(2) Provide adequate ground and flight training facilities and properly qualified ground instructors for the training required by this subpart.

(3) Provide and keep current for each aircraft type used and, if applicable, the particular variations within the aircraft type, appropriate training material, examinations, forms, instructions, and procedures for use in conducting the training and checks required by this subpart.

(4) Provide enough flight instructors, check pilots, and simulator instructors to conduct required flight training and flight checks, and simulator training courses allowed under this subpart.

(b) Whenever a crewmember who is required to take recurrent training under this subpart completes the training in the month before, or the month after, the month in which that training is required, the crewmember is considered to have completed it in the month in which it was required.

(c) Each instructor, supervisor, or check pilot who is responsible for a particular ground training subject, segment of flight training, course of training, flight check, or competence check under this subpart must certify as to the proficiency and knowledge of the crewmember, flight instructor, or check pilot concerned upon completion of that training or check. That certification must be made a part of the crewmember's record. When the certification required by this paragraph is made by an entry in a computerized recordkeeping system, the certifying instructor, supervisor, or check pilot, must be identified with that entry. However, the signature of the certifying instructor, supervisor, or check pilot is not required for computerized entries.

(d) Training subjects that apply to more than one aircraft or crewmember position and that have been satisfactorily completed during previous training while employed by the program manager for another aircraft or another crewmember position, need not be repeated during subsequent training other than recurrent training.

(e) Aircraft simulators and other training devices may be used in the program manager's training program if approved by the Administrator.

(f) Each program manager is responsible for establishing safe and efficient crew management practices for all phases of flight in program operations including crew resource management training for all crewmembers used in program operations.

(g) If an aircraft simulator has been approved by the Administrator for use in the program manager's training program, the program manager must ensure that each pilot annually completes at least one flight training session in an approved simulator for at least one program aircraft. The training session may be the flight training portion of any of the pilot training or check requirements of this subpart, including the initial, transition, upgrade, requalification, differences, or recurrent training, or the accomplishment of a competency check or instrument proficiency check. If there is no approved simulator for that aircraft type in operation, then all flight training and checking must be accomplished in the aircraft.

§91.1075 Training program: Special rules.

Other than the program manager, only the following are eligible under this subpart to conduct training, testing, and checking under contract or other arrangement to those persons subject to the requirements of this subpart.

(a) Another program manager operating under this subpart;

(b) A training center certificated under part 142 of this chapter to conduct training, testing, and checking required by this subpart if the training center—

(1) Holds applicable training specifications issued under part 142 of this chapter;

(2) Has facilities, training equipment, and courseware meeting the applicable requirements of part 142 of this chapter;

(3) Has approved curriculums, curriculum segments, and portions of curriculum segments applicable for use in training courses required by this subpart; and

(4) Has sufficient instructors and check pilots qualified under the applicable requirements of §§91.1089 through 91.1095 to conduct training, testing, and checking to persons subject to the requirements of this subpart.

(c) A part 119 certificate holder operating under part 121 or part 135 of this chapter.

(d) As authorized by the Administrator, a training center that is not certificated under part 142 of this chapter.

§91.1077 Training program and revision: Initial and final approval.

(a) To obtain initial and final approval of a training program, or a revision to an approved training program, each program manager must submit to the Administrator—

(1) An outline of the proposed or revised curriculum, that provides enough information for a preliminary evaluation of the proposed training program or revision; and

(2) Additional relevant information that may be requested by the Administrator.

(b) If the proposed training program or revision complies with this subpart, the Administrator grants initial approval in writing after which the program manager may conduct the training under that program. The Administrator then evaluates the effectiveness of the training program and advises the program manager of deficiencies, if any, that must be corrected.

(c) The Administrator grants final approval of the proposed training program or revision if the program manager shows that the training conducted under the initial approval in paragraph (b) of this section ensures that each person who successfully completes the training is adequately trained to perform that person's assigned duties.

(d) Whenever the Administrator finds that revisions are necessary for the continued adequacy of a training program that has been granted final approval, the program manager must, after notification by the Administrator, make any changes in the program that are found necessary by the Administrator. Within 30 days after the program manager receives the notice, it may file a petition to reconsider the notice with the Administrator. The filing of a petition to reconsider stays the notice pending a decision by the Administrator. However, if the Administrator finds that there is an emergency that requires immediate action in the interest of safety, the Administrator may, upon a statement of the reasons, require a change effective without stay.

§91.1079 Training program: Curriculum.

(a) Each program manager must prepare and keep current a written training program curriculum for each type of aircraft for each crewmember required for that type aircraft. The curriculum must include ground and flight training required by this subpart.

(b) Each training program curriculum must include the following:

(1) A list of principal ground training subjects, including emergency training subjects, that are provided.

(2) A list of all the training devices, mock-ups, systems trainers, procedures trainers, or other training aids that the program manager will use.

(3) Detailed descriptions or pictorial displays of the approved normal, abnormal, and emergency maneuvers, procedures and functions that will be performed during each flight training phase or flight check, indicating those maneuvers, procedures and functions that are to be performed during the inflight portions of flight training and flight checks.

§91.1081 Crewmember training requirements.

(a) Each program manager must include in its training program the following initial and transition ground training as appropriate to the particular assignment of the crewmember:

(1) Basic indoctrination ground training for newly hired crewmembers including instruction in at least the—

(i) Duties and responsibilities of crewmembers as applicable;

(ii) Appropriate provisions of this chapter;

(iii) Contents of the program manager's management specifications (not required for flight attendants); and

(iv) Appropriate portions of the program manager's operating manual.

(2) The initial and transition ground training in §§91.1101 and 91.1105, as applicable.

(3) Emergency training in §91.1083.

(b) Each training program must provide the initial and transition flight training in §91.1103, as applicable.

(c) Each training program must provide recurrent ground and flight training as provided in §91.1107.

(d) Upgrade training in §§91.1101 and 91.1103 for a particular type aircraft may be included in the training program for crewmembers who have qualified and served as second in command on that aircraft.

(e) In addition to initial, transition, upgrade and recurrent training, each training program must provide ground and flight training, instruction, and practice necessary to ensure that each crewmember—

(1) Remains adequately trained and currently proficient for each aircraft, crewmember position, and type of operation in which the crewmember serves; and

(2) Qualifies in new equipment, facilities, procedures, and techniques, including modifications to aircraft.

§91.1083 Crewmember emergency training.

(a) Each training program must provide emergency training under this section for each aircraft type, model, and configuration, each crewmember, and each kind of operation conducted, as appropriate for each crewmember and the program manager.

(b) Emergency training must provide the following:

(1) Instruction in emergency assignments and procedures, including coordination among crewmembers.

(2) Individual instruction in the location, function, and operation of emergency equipment including—

(i) Equipment used in ditching and evacuation;

(ii) First aid equipment and its proper use; and

(iii) Portable fire extinguishers, with emphasis on the type of extinguisher to be used on different classes of fires.

(3) Instruction in the handling of emergency situations including—

(i) Rapid decompression;

(ii) Fire in flight or on the surface and smoke control procedures with emphasis on electrical equipment and related circuit breakers found in cabin areas;

(iii) Ditching and evacuation;

(iv) Illness, injury, or other abnormal situations involving passengers or crewmembers; and

(v) Hijacking and other unusual situations.

(4) Review and discussion of previous aircraft accidents and incidents involving actual emergency situations.

(c) Each crewmember must perform at least the following emergency drills, using the proper emergency equipment and procedures, unless the Administrator finds that, for a particular drill, the crewmember can be adequately trained by demonstration:

(1) Ditching, if applicable.

(2) Emergency evacuation.

(3) Fire extinguishing and smoke control.

(4) Operation and use of emergency exits, including deployment and use of evacuation slides, if applicable.

(5) Use of crew and passenger oxygen.

(6) Removal of life rafts from the aircraft, inflation of the life rafts, use of lifelines, and boarding of passengers and crew, if applicable.

(7) Donning and inflation of life vests and the use of other individual flotation devices, if applicable.

(d) Crewmembers who serve in operations above 25,000 feet must receive instruction in the following:

(1) Respiration.
(2) Hypoxia.
(3) Duration of consciousness without supplemental oxygen at altitude.
(4) Gas expansion.
(5) Gas bubble formation.
(6) Physical phenomena and incidents of decompression.

§91.1085 Hazardous materials recognition training.

No program manager may use any person to perform, and no person may perform, any assigned duties and responsibilities for the handling or carriage of hazardous materials (as defined in 49 CFR 171.8), unless that person has received training in the recognition of hazardous materials.

§91.1087 Approval of aircraft simulators and other training devices.

(a) Training courses using aircraft simulators and other training devices may be included in the program manager's training program if approved by the Administrator.

(b) Each aircraft simulator and other training device that is used in a training course or in checks required under this subpart must meet the following requirements:

(1) It must be specifically approved for—
 (i) The program manager; and
 (ii) The particular maneuver, procedure, or crewmember function involved.
(2) It must maintain the performance, functional, and other characteristics that are required for approval.
(3) Additionally, for aircraft simulators, it must be—
 (i) Approved for the type aircraft and, if applicable, the particular variation within type for which the training or check is being conducted; and
 (ii) Modified to conform with any modification to the aircraft being simulated that changes the performance, functional, or other characteristics required for approval.

(c) A particular aircraft simulator or other training device may be used by more than one program manager.

(d) In granting initial and final approval of training programs or revisions to them, the Administrator considers the training devices, methods, and procedures listed in the program manager's curriculum under §91.1079.

§91.1089 Qualifications: Check pilots (aircraft) and check pilots (simulator).

(a) For the purposes of this section and §91.1093:

(1) A check pilot (aircraft) is a person who is qualified to conduct flight checks in an aircraft, in a flight simulator, or in a flight training device for a particular type aircraft.

(2) A check pilot (simulator) is a person who is qualified to conduct flight checks, but only in a flight simulator, in a flight training device, or both, for a particular type aircraft.

(3) Check pilots (aircraft) and check pilots (simulator) are those check pilots who perform the functions described in §91.1073(a)(4) and (c).

(b) No program manager may use a person, nor may any person serve as a check pilot (aircraft) in a training program established under this subpart unless, with respect to the aircraft type involved, that person—

(1) Holds the pilot certificates and ratings required to serve as a pilot in command in operations under this subpart;

(2) Has satisfactorily completed the training phases for the aircraft, including recurrent training, that are required to serve as a pilot in command in operations under this subpart;

(3) Has satisfactorily completed the proficiency or competency checks that are required to serve as a pilot in command in operations under this subpart;

(4) Has satisfactorily completed the applicable training requirements of §91.1093;

(5) Holds at least a Class III medical certificate unless serving as a required crewmember, in which case holds a Class I or Class II medical certificate as appropriate; and

(6) Has been approved by the Administrator for the check pilot duties involved.

(c) No program manager may use a person, nor may any person serve as a check pilot (simulator) in a training program established under this subpart unless, with respect to the aircraft type involved, that person meets the provisions of paragraph (b) of this section, or—

(1) Holds the applicable pilot certificates and ratings, except medical certificate, required to serve as a pilot in command in operations under this subpart;

(2) Has satisfactorily completed the appropriate training phases for the aircraft, including recurrent training, that are required to serve as a pilot in command in operations under this subpart;

(3) Has satisfactorily completed the appropriate proficiency or competency checks that are required to serve as a pilot in command in operations under this subpart;

(4) Has satisfactorily completed the applicable training requirements of §91.1093; and

(5) Has been approved by the Administrator for the check pilot (simulator) duties involved.

(d) Completion of the requirements in paragraphs (b)(2), (3), and (4) or (c)(2), (3), and (4) of this section, as applicable, must be entered in the individual's training record maintained by the program manager.

(e) A check pilot who does not hold an appropriate medical certificate may function as a check pilot (simulator), but may not serve as a flightcrew member in operations under this subpart.

(f) A check pilot (simulator) must accomplish the following—

(1) Fly at least two flight segments as a required crewmember for the type, class, or category aircraft involved within the 12-month period preceding the performance of any check pilot duty in a flight simulator; or

(2) Before performing any check pilot duty in a flight simulator, satisfactorily complete an approved line-observation program within the period prescribed by that program.

(g) The flight segments or line-observation program required in paragraph (f) of this section are considered to be completed in the month required if completed in the month before or the month after the month in which they are due.

§91.1091 Qualifications: Flight instructors (aircraft) and flight instructors (simulator).

(a) For the purposes of this section and §91.1095:

(1) A flight instructor (aircraft) is a person who is qualified to instruct in an aircraft, in a flight simulator, or in a flight training device for a particular type, class, or category aircraft.

(2) A flight instructor (simulator) is a person who is qualified to instruct in a flight simulator, in a flight training device, or in both, for a particular type, class, or category aircraft.

(3) Flight instructors (aircraft) and flight instructors (simulator) are those instructors who perform the functions described in §91.1073(a)(4) and (c).

(b) No program manager may use a person, nor may any person serve as a flight instructor (aircraft) in a training program established under this subpart unless, with respect to the type, class, or category aircraft involved, that person—

(1) Holds the pilot certificates and ratings required to serve as a pilot in command in operations under this subpart or part 121 or 135 of this chapter;

(2) Has satisfactorily completed the training phases for the aircraft, including recurrent training, that are required to serve as a pilot in command in operations under this subpart;

(3) Has satisfactorily completed the proficiency or competency checks that are required to serve as a pilot in command in operations under this subpart;

(4) Has satisfactorily completed the applicable training requirements of §91.1095; and

(5) Holds at least a Class III medical certificate.

(c) No program manager may use a person, nor may any person serve as a flight instructor (simulator) in a training program established under this subpart, unless, with respect to the type, class, or category aircraft involved, that person meets the provisions of paragraph (b) of this section, or—

(1) Holds the pilot certificates and ratings, except medical certificate, required to serve as a pilot in command in operations under this subpart or part 121 or 135 of this chapter;

(2) Has satisfactorily completed the appropriate training phases for the aircraft, including recurrent training, that are required to serve as a pilot in command in operations under this subpart;

(3) Has satisfactorily completed the appropriate proficiency or competency checks that are required to serve as a pilot in command in operations under this subpart; and

(4) Has satisfactorily completed the applicable training requirements of §91.1095.

(d) Completion of the requirements in paragraphs (b)(2), (3), and (4) or (c)(2), (3), and (4) of this section, as applicable, must be entered in the individual's training record maintained by the program manager.

(e) A pilot who does not hold a medical certificate may function as a flight instructor in an aircraft if functioning as a non-required crewmember, but may not serve as a flightcrew member in operations under this subpart.

(f) A flight instructor (simulator) must accomplish the following—

(1) Fly at least two flight segments as a required crewmember for the type, class, or category aircraft involved within the 12-month period preceding the performance of any flight instructor duty in a flight simulator; or

(2) Satisfactorily complete an approved line-observation program within the period prescribed by that program proceding the performance of any flight instructor duty in a flight simulator.

(g) The flight segments or line-observation program required in paragraph (f) of this section are considered completed in the month required if completed in the month before, or in the month after, the month in which they are due.

[Docket No. FAA–2001–10047, 68 FR 54561, Sept. 17, 2003; as amended by Amdt. 91–322, 76 FR 31823, June 2, 2011]

§91.1093 Initial and transition training and checking: Check pilots (aircraft), check pilots (simulator).

(a) No program manager may use a person nor may any person serve as a check pilot unless—

(1) That person has satisfactorily completed initial or transition check pilot training; and

(2) Within the preceding 24 months, that person satisfactorily conducts a proficiency or competency check under the observation of an FAA inspector or an aircrew designated examiner employed by the program manager. The observation check may be accomplished in part or in full in an aircraft, in a flight simulator, or in a flight training device.

(b) The observation check required by paragraph (a)(2) of this section is considered to have been completed in the month required if completed in the month before or the month after the month in which it is due.

(c) The initial ground training for check pilots must include the following:

(1) Check pilot duties, functions, and responsibilities.

(2) The applicable provisions of the Code of Federal Regulations and the program manager's policies and procedures.

(3) The applicable methods, procedures, and techniques for conducting the required checks.

(4) Proper evaluation of student performance including the detection of—

(i) Improper and insufficient training; and

(ii) Personal characteristics of an applicant that could adversely affect safety.

(5) The corrective action in the case of unsatisfactory checks.

(6) The approved methods, procedures, and limitations for performing the required normal, abnormal, and emergency procedures in the aircraft.

(d) The transition ground training for a check pilot must include the approved methods, procedures, and limitations for performing the required normal, abnormal, and emergency procedures applicable to the aircraft to which the check pilot is in transition.

(e) The initial and transition flight training for a check pilot (aircraft) must include the following—

(1) The safety measures for emergency situations that are likely to develop during a check;

(2) The potential results of improper, untimely, or nonexecution of safety measures during a check;

(3) Training and practice in conducting flight checks from the left and right pilot seats in the required normal, abnormal, and emergency procedures to ensure competence to conduct the pilot flight checks required by this subpart; and

(4) The safety measures to be taken from either pilot seat for emergency situations that are likely to develop during checking.

(f) The requirements of paragraph (e) of this section may be accomplished in full or in part in flight, in a flight simulator, or in a flight training device, as appropriate.

(g) The initial and transition flight training for a check pilot (simulator) must include the following:

(1) Training and practice in conducting flight checks in the required normal, abnormal, and emergency procedures to ensure competence to conduct the flight checks required by this subpart. This training and practice must be accomplished in a flight simulator or in a flight training device.

(2) Training in the operation of flight simulators, flight training devices, or both, to ensure competence to conduct the flight checks required by this subpart.

§91.1095 Initial and transition training and checking: Flight instructors (aircraft), flight instructors (simulator).

(a) No program manager may use a person nor may any person serve as a flight instructor unless—

(1) That person has satisfactorily completed initial or transition flight instructor training; and

(2) Within the preceding 24 months, that person satisfactorily conducts instruction under the observation of an FAA inspector, a program manager check pilot, or an aircrew designated examiner employed by the program manager. The observation check may be accomplished in part or in full in an aircraft, in a flight simulator, or in a flight training device.

(b) The observation check required by paragraph (a)(2) of this section is considered to have been completed in the month required if completed in the month before, or the month after, the month in which it is due.

(c) The initial ground training for flight instructors must include the following:

(1) Flight instructor duties, functions, and responsibilities.

(2) The applicable Code of Federal Regulations and the program manager's policies and procedures.

(3) The applicable methods, procedures, and techniques for conducting flight instruction.

(4) Proper evaluation of student performance including the detection of—

(i) Improper and insufficient training; and

(ii) Personal characteristics of an applicant that could adversely affect safety.

(5) The corrective action in the case of unsatisfactory training progress.

(6) The approved methods, procedures, and limitations for performing the required normal,

Part 91: General Operating and Flight Rules §91.1101

abnormal, and emergency procedures in the aircraft.

(7) Except for holders of a flight instructor certificate—

(i) The fundamental principles of the teaching-learning process;

(ii) Teaching methods and procedures; and

(iii) The instructor-student relationship.

(d) The transition ground training for flight instructors must include the approved methods, procedures, and limitations for performing the required normal, abnormal, and emergency procedures applicable to the type, class, or category aircraft to which the flight instructor is in transition.

(e) The initial and transition flight training for flight instructors (aircraft) must include the following—

(1) The safety measures for emergency situations that are likely to develop during instruction;

(2) The potential results of improper or untimely safety measures during instruction;

(3) Training and practice from the left and right pilot seats in the required normal, abnormal, and emergency maneuvers to ensure competence to conduct the flight instruction required by this subpart; and

(4) The safety measures to be taken from either the left or right pilot seat for emergency situations that are likely to develop during instruction.

(f) The requirements of paragraph (e) of this section may be accomplished in full or in part in flight, in a flight simulator, or in a flight training device, as appropriate.

(g) The initial and transition flight training for a flight instructor (simulator) must include the following:

(1) Training and practice in the required normal, abnormal, and emergency procedures to ensure competence to conduct the flight instruction required by this subpart. These maneuvers and procedures must be accomplished in full or in part in a flight simulator or in a flight training device.

(2) Training in the operation of flight simulators, flight training devices, or both, to ensure competence to conduct the flight instruction required by this subpart.

§91.1097 Pilot and flight attendant crewmember training programs.

(a) Each program manager must establish and maintain an approved pilot training program, and each program manager who uses a flight attendant crewmember must establish and maintain an approved flight attendant training program, that is appropriate to the operations to which each pilot and flight attendant is to be assigned, and will ensure that they are adequately trained to meet the applicable knowledge and practical testing requirements of §§91.1065 through 91.1071.

(b) Each program manager required to have a training program by paragraph (a) of this section must include in that program ground and flight training curriculums for—

(1) Initial training;

(2) Transition training;

(3) Upgrade training;

(4) Differences training;

(5) Recurrent training; and

(6) Requalification training.

(c) Each program manager must provide current and appropriate study materials for use by each required pilot and flight attendant.

(d) The program manager must furnish copies of the pilot and flight attendant crewmember training program, and all changes and additions, to the assigned representative of the Administrator. If the program manager uses training facilities of other persons, a copy of those training programs or appropriate portions used for those facilities must also be furnished. Curricula that follow FAA published curricula may be cited by reference in the copy of the training program furnished to the representative of the Administrator and need not be furnished with the program.

§91.1099 Crewmember initial and recurrent training requirements.

No program manager may use a person, nor may any person serve, as a crewmember in operations under this subpart unless that crewmember has completed the appropriate initial or recurrent training phase of the training program appropriate to the type of operation in which the crewmember is to serve since the beginning of the 12th month before that service.

§91.1101 Pilots: Initial, transition, and upgrade ground training.

Initial, transition, and upgrade ground training for pilots must include instruction in at least the following, as applicable to their duties:

(a) General subjects—

(1) The program manager's flight locating procedures;

(2) Principles and methods for determining weight and balance, and runway limitations for takeoff and landing;

(3) Enough meteorology to ensure a practical knowledge of weather phenomena, including the principles of frontal systems, icing, fog, thunderstorms, windshear and, if appropriate, high altitude weather situations;

(4) Air traffic control systems, procedures, and phraseology;

(5) Navigation and the use of navigational aids, including instrument approach procedures;

ASA 81

(6) Normal and emergency communication procedures;

(7) Visual cues before and during descent below Decision Altitude or MDA; and

(8) Other instructions necessary to ensure the pilot's competence.

(b) For each aircraft type—

(1) A general description;

(2) Performance characteristics;

(3) Engines and propellers;

(4) Major components;

(5) Major aircraft systems (that is, flight controls, electrical, and hydraulic), other systems, as appropriate, principles of normal, abnormal, and emergency operations, appropriate procedures and limitations;

(6) Knowledge and procedures for—

(i) Recognizing and avoiding severe weather situations;

(ii) Escaping from severe weather situations, in case of inadvertent encounters, including low-altitude windshear (except that rotorcraft pilots are not required to be trained in escaping from low-altitude windshear);

(iii) Operating in or near thunderstorms (including best penetration altitudes), turbulent air (including clear air turbulence), inflight icing, hail, and other potentially hazardous meteorological conditions; and

(iv) Operating airplanes during ground icing conditions, (that is, any time conditions are such that frost, ice, or snow may reasonably be expected to adhere to the aircraft), if the program manager expects to authorize takeoffs in ground icing conditions, including:

(A) The use of holdover times when using deicing/anti-icing fluids;

(B) Airplane deicing/anti-icing procedures, including inspection and check procedures and responsibilities;

(C) Communications;

(D) Airplane surface contamination (that is, adherence of frost, ice, or snow) and critical area identification, and knowledge of how contamination adversely affects airplane performance and flight characteristics;

(E) Types and characteristics of deicing/anti-icing fluids, if used by the program manager;

(F) Cold weather preflight inspection procedures;

(G) Techniques for recognizing contamination on the airplane;

(7) Operating limitations;

(8) Fuel consumption and cruise control;

(9) Flight planning;

(10) Each normal and emergency procedure; and

(11) The approved Aircraft Flight Manual or equivalent.

§91.1103 Pilots: Initial, transition, upgrade, requalification, and differences flight training.

(a) Initial, transition, upgrade, requalification, and differences training for pilots must include flight and practice in each of the maneuvers and procedures contained in each of the curriculums that are a part of the approved training program.

(b) The maneuvers and procedures required by paragraph (a) of this section must be performed in flight, except to the extent that certain maneuvers and procedures may be performed in an aircraft simulator, or an appropriate training device, as allowed by this subpart.

(c) If the program manager's approved training program includes a course of training using an aircraft simulator or other training device, each pilot must successfully complete—

(1) Training and practice in the simulator or training device in at least the maneuvers and procedures in this subpart that are capable of being performed in the aircraft simulator or training device; and

(2) A flight check in the aircraft or a check in the simulator or training device to the level of proficiency of a pilot in command or second in command, as applicable, in at least the maneuvers and procedures that are capable of being performed in an aircraft simulator or training device.

§91.1105 Flight attendants: Initial and transition ground training.

Initial and transition ground training for flight attendants must include instruction in at least the following—

(a) General subjects—

(1) The authority of the pilot in command; and

(2) Passenger handling, including procedures to be followed in handling deranged persons or other persons whose conduct might jeopardize safety.

(b) For each aircraft type—

(1) A general description of the aircraft emphasizing physical characteristics that may have a bearing on ditching, evacuation, and inflight emergency procedures and on other related duties;

(2) The use of both the public address system and the means of communicating with other flight crewmembers, including emergency means in the case of attempted hijacking or other unusual situations; and

(3) Proper use of electrical galley equipment and the controls for cabin heat and ventilation.

§91.1107 Recurrent training.

(a) Each program manager must ensure that each crewmember receives recurrent training and is adequately trained and currently proficient for the type aircraft and crewmember position involved.

(b) Recurrent ground training for crewmembers must include at least the following:

(1) A quiz or other review to determine the crewmember's knowledge of the aircraft and crewmember position involved.

(2) Instruction as necessary in the subjects required for initial ground training by this subpart, as appropriate, including low-altitude windshear training and training on operating during ground icing conditions, as prescribed in §91.1097 and described in §91.1101, and emergency training.

(c) Recurrent flight training for pilots must include, at least, flight training in the maneuvers or procedures in this subpart, except that satisfactory completion of the check required by §91.1065 within the preceding 12 months may be substituted for recurrent flight training.

§91.1109 Aircraft maintenance: Inspection program.

Each program manager must establish an aircraft inspection program for each make and model program aircraft and ensure each aircraft is inspected in accordance with that inspection program.

(a) The inspection program must be in writing and include at least the following information:

(1) Instructions and procedures for the conduct of inspections for the particular make and model aircraft, including necessary tests and checks. The instructions and procedures must set forth in detail the parts and areas of the airframe, engines, propellers, rotors, and appliances, including survival and emergency equipment required to be inspected.

(2) A schedule for performing the inspections that must be accomplished under the inspection program expressed in terms of the time in service, calendar time, number of system operations, or any combination thereof.

(3) The name and address of the person responsible for scheduling the inspections required by the inspection program. A copy of the inspection program must be made available to the person performing inspections on the aircraft and, upon request, to the Administrator.

(b) Each person desiring to establish or change an approved inspection program under this section must submit the inspection program for approval to the Flight Standards District Office that issued the program manager's management specifications. The inspection program must be derived from one of the following programs:

(1) An inspection program currently recommended by the manufacturer of the aircraft, aircraft engines, propellers, appliances, and survival and emergency equipment;

(2) An inspection program that is part of a continuous airworthiness maintenance program currently in use by a person holding an air carrier or operating certificate issued under part 119 of this chapter and operating that make and model aircraft under part 121 or 135 of this chapter;

(3) An aircraft inspection program approved under §135.419 of this chapter and currently in use under part 135 of this chapter by a person holding a certificate issued under part 119 of this chapter; or

(4) An airplane inspection program approved under §125.247 of this chapter and currently in use under part 125 of this chapter.

(5) An inspection program that is part of the program manager's continuous airworthiness maintenance program under §§91.1411 through 91.1443.

(c) The Administrator may require revision of the inspection program approved under this section in accordance with the provisions of §91.415.

§91.1111 Maintenance training.

The program manager must ensure that all employees who are responsible for maintenance related to program aircraft undergo appropriate initial and annual recurrent training and are competent to perform those duties.

§91.1113 Maintenance recordkeeping.

Each fractional ownership program manager must keep (using the system specified in the manual required in §91.1025) the records specified in §91.417(a) for the periods specified in §91.417(b).

§91.1115 Inoperable instruments and equipment.

(a) No person may take off an aircraft with inoperable instruments or equipment installed unless the following conditions are met:

(1) An approved Minimum Equipment List exists for that aircraft.

(2) The program manager has been issued management specifications authorizing operations in accordance with an approved Minimum Equipment List. The flight crew must have direct access at all times prior to flight to all of the information contained in the approved Minimum Equipment List through printed or other means approved by the Administrator in the program manager's management specifications. An approved Minimum Equipment List, as authorized by the management specifications, constitutes an

§91.1411

approved change to the type design without requiring recertification.

(3) The approved Minimum Equipment List must:

(i) Be prepared in accordance with the limitations specified in paragraph (b) of this section.

(ii) Provide for the operation of the aircraft with certain instruments and equipment in an inoperable condition.

(4) Records identifying the inoperable instruments and equipment and the information required by (a)(3)(ii) of this section must be available to the pilot.

(5) The aircraft is operated under all applicable conditions and limitations contained in the Minimum Equipment List and the management specifications authorizing use of the Minimum Equipment List.

(b) The following instruments and equipment may not be included in the Minimum Equipment List:

(1) Instruments and equipment that are either specifically or otherwise required by the airworthiness requirements under which the airplane is type certificated and that are essential for safe operations under all operating conditions.

(2) Instruments and equipment required by an airworthiness directive to be in operable condition unless the airworthiness directive provides otherwise.

(3) Instruments and equipment required for specific operations by this part.

(c) Notwithstanding paragraphs (b)(1) and (b)(3) of this section, an aircraft with inoperable instruments or equipment may be operated under a special flight permit under §§21.197 and 21.199 of this chapter.

(d) A person authorized to use an approved Minimum Equipment List issued for a specific aircraft under part 121, 125, or 135 of this chapter must use that Minimum Equipment List to comply with this section.

§91.1411 Continuous airworthiness maintenance program use by fractional ownership program manager.

Fractional ownership program aircraft may be maintained under a continuous airworthiness maintenance program (CAMP) under §§91.1413 through 91.1443. Any program manager who elects to maintain the program aircraft using a continuous airworthiness maintenance program must comply with §§91.1413 through 91.1443.

§91.1413 CAMP:
Responsibility for airworthiness.

(a) For aircraft maintained in accordance with a Continuous Airworthiness Maintenance Program, each program manager is primarily responsible for the following:

(1) Maintaining the airworthiness of the program aircraft, including airframes, aircraft engines, propellers, rotors, appliances, and parts.

(2) Maintaining its aircraft in accordance with the requirements of this chapter.

(3) Repairing defects that occur between regularly scheduled maintenance required under part 43 of this chapter.

(b) Each program manager who maintains program aircraft under a CAMP must—

(1) Employ a Director of Maintenance or equivalent position. The Director of Maintenance must be a certificated mechanic with airframe and powerplant ratings who has responsibility for the maintenance program on all program aircraft maintained under a continuous airworthiness maintenance program. This person cannot also act as Chief Inspector.

(2) Employ a Chief Inspector or equivalent position. The Chief Inspector must be a certificated mechanic with airframe and powerplant ratings who has overall responsibility for inspection aspects of the CAMP. This person cannot also act as Director of Maintenance.

(3) Have the personnel to perform the maintenance of program aircraft, including airframes, aircraft engines, propellers, rotors, appliances, emergency equipment and parts, under its manual and this chapter; or make arrangements with another person for the performance of maintenance. However, the program manager must ensure that any maintenance, preventive maintenance, or alteration that is performed by another person is performed under the program manager's operating manual and this chapter.

§91.1415 CAMP:
Mechanical reliability reports.

(a) Each program manager who maintains program aircraft under a CAMP must report the occurrence or detection of each failure, malfunction, or defect in an aircraft concerning—

(1) Fires during flight and whether the related fire-warning system functioned properly;

(2) Fires during flight not protected by related fire-warning system;

(3) False fire-warning during flight;

(4) An exhaust system that causes damage during flight to the engine, adjacent structure, equipment, or components;

Part 91: General Operating and Flight Rules §91.1417

(5) An aircraft component that causes accumulation or circulation of smoke, vapor, or toxic or noxious fumes in the crew compartment or passenger cabin during flight;
(6) Engine shutdown during flight because of flameout;
(7) Engine shutdown during flight when external damage to the engine or aircraft structure occurs;
(8) Engine shutdown during flight because of foreign object ingestion or icing;
(9) Shutdown of more than one engine during flight;
(10) A propeller feathering system or ability of the system to control overspeed during flight;
(11) A fuel or fuel-dumping system that affects fuel flow or causes hazardous leakage during flight;
(12) An unwanted landing gear extension or retraction or opening or closing of landing gear doors during flight;
(13) Brake system components that result in loss of brake actuating force when the aircraft is in motion on the ground;
(14) Aircraft structure that requires major repair;
(15) Cracks, permanent deformation, or corrosion of aircraft structures, if more than the maximum acceptable to the manufacturer or the FAA; and
(16) Aircraft components or systems that result in taking emergency actions during flight (except action to shut down an engine).

(b) For the purpose of this section, *during flight* means the period from the moment the aircraft leaves the surface of the earth on takeoff until it touches down on landing.

(c) In addition to the reports required by paragraph (a) of this section, each program manager must report any other failure, malfunction, or defect in an aircraft that occurs or is detected at any time if, in the manager's opinion, the failure, malfunction, or defect has endangered or may endanger the safe operation of the aircraft.

(d) Each program manager must send each report required by this section, in writing, covering each 24-hour period beginning at 0900 hours local time of each day and ending at 0900 hours local time on the next day to the Flight Standards District Office that issued the program manager's management specifications. Each report of occurrences during a 24-hour period must be mailed or transmitted to that office within the next 72 hours. However, a report that is due on Saturday or Sunday may be mailed or transmitted on the following Monday and one that is due on a holiday may be mailed or transmitted on the next workday. For aircraft operated in areas where mail is not collected, reports may be mailed or transmitted within 72 hours after the aircraft returns to a point where the mail is collected.

(e) The program manager must transmit the reports required by this section on a form and in a manner prescribed by the Administrator, and must include as much of the following as is available:
(1) The type and identification number of the aircraft.
(2) The name of the program manager.
(3) The date.
(4) The nature of the failure, malfunction, or defect.
(5) Identification of the part and system involved, including available information pertaining to type designation of the major component and time since last overhaul, if known.
(6) Apparent cause of the failure, malfunction or defect (for example, wear, crack, design deficiency, or personnel error).
(7) Other pertinent information necessary for more complete identification, determination of seriousness, or corrective action.

(f) A program manager that is also the holder of a type certificate (including a supplemental type certificate), a Parts Manufacturer Approval, or a Technical Standard Order Authorization, or that is the licensee of a type certificate need not report a failure, malfunction, or defect under this section if the failure, malfunction, or defect has been reported by it under §21.3 of this chapter or under the accident reporting provisions of part 830 of the regulations of the National Transportation Safety Board.

(g) No person may withhold a report required by this section even when not all information required by this section is available.

(h) When the program manager receives additional information, including information from the manufacturer or other agency, concerning a report required by this section, the program manager must expeditiously submit it as a supplement to the first report and reference the date and place of submission of the first report.

§91.1417 CAMP: Mechanical interruption summary report.

Each program manager who maintains program aircraft under a CAMP must mail or deliver, before the end of the 10th day of the following month, a summary report of the following occurrences in multiengine aircraft for the preceding month to the Flight Standards District Office that issued the management specifications:

(a) Each interruption to a flight, unscheduled change of aircraft en route, or unscheduled stop or diversion from a route, caused by known or suspected mechanical difficulties or malfunctions that are not required to be reported under §91.1415.

ASA 85

(b) The number of propeller featherings in flight, listed by type of propeller and engine and aircraft on which it was installed. Propeller featherings for training, demonstration, or flight check purposes need not be reported.

§91.1423 CAMP: Maintenance organization.

(a) Each program manager who maintains program aircraft under a CAMP that has its personnel perform any of its maintenance (other than required inspections), preventive maintenance, or alterations, and each person with whom it arranges for the performance of that work, must have an organization adequate to perform the work.

(b) Each program manager who has personnel perform any inspections required by the program manager's manual under §91.1427(b)(2) or (3), (in this subpart referred to as required inspections), and each person with whom the program manager arranges for the performance of that work, must have an organization adequate to perform that work.

(c) Each person performing required inspections in addition to other maintenance, preventive maintenance, or alterations, must organize the performance of those functions so as to separate the required inspection functions from the other maintenance, preventive maintenance, or alteration functions. The separation must be below the level of administrative control at which overall responsibility for the required inspection functions and other maintenance, preventive maintenance, or alterations is exercised.

§91.1425 CAMP: Maintenance, preventive maintenance, and alteration programs.

Each program manager who maintains program aircraft under a CAMP must have an inspection program and a program covering other maintenance, preventive maintenance, or alterations that ensures that—

(a) Maintenance, preventive maintenance, or alterations performed by its personnel, or by other persons, are performed under the program manager's manual;

(b) Competent personnel and adequate facilities and equipment are provided for the proper performance of maintenance, preventive maintenance, or alterations; and

(c) Each aircraft released to service is airworthy and has been properly maintained for operation under this part.

§91.1427 CAMP: Manual requirements.

(a) Each program manager who maintains program aircraft under a CAMP must put in the operating manual the chart or description of the program manager's organization required by §91.1423 and a list of persons with whom it has arranged for the performance of any of its required inspections, and other maintenance, preventive maintenance, or alterations, including a general description of that work.

(b) Each program manager must put in the operating manual the programs required by §91.1425 that must be followed in performing maintenance, preventive maintenance, or alterations of that program manager's aircraft, including airframes, aircraft engines, propellers, rotors, appliances, emergency equipment, and parts, and must include at least the following:

(1) The method of performing routine and non-routine maintenance (other than required inspections), preventive maintenance, or alterations.

(2) A designation of the items of maintenance and alteration that must be inspected (required inspections) including at least those that could result in a failure, malfunction, or defect endangering the safe operation of the aircraft, if not performed properly or if improper parts or materials are used.

(3) The method of performing required inspections and a designation by occupational title of personnel authorized to perform each required inspection.

(4) Procedures for the reinspection of work performed under previous required inspection findings (buy-back procedures).

(5) Procedures, standards, and limits necessary for required inspections and acceptance or rejection of the items required to be inspected and for periodic inspection and calibration of precision tools, measuring devices, and test equipment.

(6) Procedures to ensure that all required inspections are performed.

(7) Instructions to prevent any person who performs any item of work from performing any required inspection of that work.

(8) Instructions and procedures to prevent any decision of an inspector regarding any required inspection from being countermanded by persons other than supervisory personnel of the inspection unit, or a person at the level of administrative control that has overall responsibility for the management of both the required inspection functions and the other maintenance, preventive maintenance, or alterations functions.

(9) Procedures to ensure that maintenance (including required inspections), preventive main-

tenance, or alterations that are not completed because of work interruptions are properly completed before the aircraft is released to service.

(c) Each program manager must put in the manual a suitable system (which may include an electronic or coded system) that provides for the retention of the following information—

(1) A description (or reference to data acceptable to the Administrator) of the work performed;

(2) The name of the person performing the work if the work is performed by a person outside the organization of the program manager; and

(3) The name or other positive identification of the individual approving the work.

(d) For the purposes of this part, the program manager must prepare that part of its manual containing maintenance information and instructions, in whole or in part, in a format acceptable to the Administrator, that is retrievable in the English language.

§91.1429 CAMP: Required inspection personnel.

(a) No person who maintains an aircraft under a CAMP may use any person to perform required inspections unless the person performing the inspection is appropriately certificated, properly trained, qualified, and authorized to do so.

(b) No person may allow any person to perform a required inspection unless, at the time the work was performed, the person performing that inspection is under the supervision and control of the chief inspector.

(c) No person may perform a required inspection if that person performed the item of work required to be inspected.

(d) Each program manager must maintain, or must ensure that each person with whom it arranges to perform required inspections maintains, a current listing of persons who have been trained, qualified, and authorized to conduct required inspections. The persons must be identified by name, occupational title, and the inspections that they are authorized to perform. The program manager (or person with whom it arranges to perform its required inspections) must give written information to each person so authorized, describing the extent of that person's responsibilities, authorities, and inspectional limitations. The list must be made available for inspection by the Administrator upon request.

§91.1431 CAMP: Continuing analysis and surveillance.

(a) Each program manager who maintains program aircraft under a CAMP must establish and maintain a system for the continuing analysis and surveillance of the performance and effectiveness of its inspection program and the program covering other maintenance, preventive maintenance, and alterations and for the correction of any deficiency in those programs, regardless of whether those programs are carried out by employees of the program manager or by another person.

(b) Whenever the Administrator finds that the programs described in paragraph (a) of this section does not contain adequate procedures and standards to meet this part, the program manager must, after notification by the Administrator, make changes in those programs requested by the Administrator.

(c) A program manager may petition the Administrator to reconsider the notice to make a change in a program. The petition must be filed with the Director, Flight Standards Service, within 30 days after the program manager receives the notice. Except in the case of an emergency requiring immediate action in the interest of safety, the filing of the petition stays the notice pending a decision by the Administrator.

§91.1433 CAMP: Maintenance and preventive maintenance training program.

Each program manager who maintains program aircraft under a CAMP or a person performing maintenance or preventive maintenance functions for it must have a training program to ensure that each person (including inspection personnel) who determines the adequacy of work done is fully informed about procedures and techniques and new equipment in use and is competent to perform that person's duties.

§91.1435 CAMP:
Certificate requirements.

(a) Except for maintenance, preventive maintenance, alterations, and required inspections performed by repair stations located outside the United States certificated under the provisions of part 145 of this chapter, each person who is directly in charge of maintenance, preventive maintenance, or alterations for a CAMP, and each person performing required inspections for a CAMP must hold an appropriate airman certificate.

(b) For the purpose of this section, a person "directly in charge" is each person assigned to a position in which that person is responsible for the work of a shop or station that performs maintenance, preventive maintenance, alterations, or other functions affecting airworthiness. A person who is directly in charge need not physically observe and direct each worker constantly but must be available for consultation and decision on matters requiring instruction or decision from higher authority than that of the person performing the work.

§91.1437 CAMP:
Authority to perform and approve maintenance.

A program manager who maintains program aircraft under a CAMP may employ maintenance personnel, or make arrangements with other persons to perform maintenance and preventive maintenance as provided in its maintenance manual. Unless properly certificated, the program manager may not perform or approve maintenance for return to service.

§91.1439 CAMP:
Maintenance recording requirements.

(a) Each program manager who maintains program aircraft under a CAMP must keep (using the system specified in the manual required in §91.1427) the following records for the periods specified in paragraph (b) of this section:

(1) All the records necessary to show that all requirements for the issuance of an airworthiness release under §91.1443 have been met.

(2) Records containing the following information:

(i) The total time in service of the airframe, engine, propeller, and rotor.

(ii) The current status of life-limited parts of each airframe, engine, propeller, rotor, and appliance.

(iii) The time since last overhaul of each item installed on the aircraft that are required to be overhauled on a specified time basis.

(iv) The identification of the current inspection status of the aircraft, including the time since the last inspections required by the inspection program under which the aircraft and its appliances are maintained.

(v) The current status of applicable airworthiness directives, including the date and methods of compliance, and, if the airworthiness directive involves recurring action, the time and date when the next action is required.

(vi) A list of current major alterations and repairs to each airframe, engine, propeller, rotor, and appliance.

(b) Each program manager must retain the records required to be kept by this section for the following periods:

(1) Except for the records of the last complete overhaul of each airframe, engine, propeller, rotor, and appliance the records specified in paragraph (a)(1) of this section must be retained until the work is repeated or superseded by other work or for one year after the work is performed.

(2) The records of the last complete overhaul of each airframe, engine, propeller, rotor, and appliance must be retained until the work is superseded by work of equivalent scope and detail.

(3) The records specified in paragraph (a)(2) of this section must be retained as specified unless transferred with the aircraft at the time the aircraft is sold.

(c) The program manager must make all maintenance records required to be kept by this section available for inspection by the Administrator or any representative of the National Transportation Safety Board.

§91.1441 CAMP:
Transfer of maintenance records.

When a U.S.-registered fractional ownership program aircraft maintained under a CAMP is removed from the list of program aircraft in the management specifications, the program manager must transfer to the purchaser, at the time of the sale, the following records of that aircraft, in plain language form or in coded form that provides for the preservation and retrieval of information in a manner acceptable to the Administrator:

(a) The records specified in §91.1439(a)(2).

(b) The records specified in §91.1439(a)(1) that are not included in the records covered by paragraph (a) of this section, except that the purchaser may allow the program manager to keep physical custody of such records. However, custody of records by the program manager does not relieve the purchaser of its responsibility under §91.1439(c) to make the records available for inspection by the Administrator or any representative of the National Transportation Safety Board.

§91.1443 CAMP: Airworthiness release or aircraft maintenance log entry.

(a) No program aircraft maintained under a CAMP may be operated after maintenance, preventive maintenance, or alterations are performed unless qualified, certificated personnel employed by the program manager prepare, or cause the person with whom the program manager arranges for the performance of the maintenance, preventive maintenance, or alterations, to prepare—

(1) An airworthiness release; or

(2) An appropriate entry in the aircraft maintenance log.

(b) The airworthiness release or log entry required by paragraph (a) of this section must—

(1) Be prepared in accordance with the procedure in the program manager's manual;

(2) Include a certification that—

(i) The work was performed in accordance with the requirements of the program manager's manual;

(ii) All items required to be inspected were inspected by an authorized person who determined that the work was satisfactorily completed;

(iii) No known condition exists that would make the aircraft unairworthy;

(iv) So far as the work performed is concerned, the aircraft is in condition for safe operation; and

(3) Be signed by an authorized certificated mechanic.

(c) Notwithstanding paragraph (b)(3) of this section, after maintenance, preventive maintenance, or alterations performed by a repair station certificated under the provisions of part 145 of this chapter, the approval for return to service or log entry required by paragraph (a) of this section may be signed by a person authorized by that repair station.

(d) Instead of restating each of the conditions of the certification required by paragraph (b) of this section, the program manager may state in its manual that the signature of an authorized certificated mechanic or repairman constitutes that certification.

14 CFR • Subchapter G—Air Carriers and Operators for Compensation or Hire: Certification and Operations

PART 110
GENERAL REQUIREMENTS

110.1 Applicability.
110.2 Definitions.

Authority: 49 U.S.C. 106(g), 1153, 40101, 40102, 40103, 40113, 44105, 44106, 44111, 44701-44717, 44722, 44901, 44903, 44904, 44906, 44912, 44914, 44936, 44938, 46103, 46105.

Source: Docket No. FAA–2009–0140, 76 FR 7486, Feb. 10, 2011, unless otherwise noted.

§110.1 Applicability.

This part governs all operations conducted under subchapter G of this chapter.

§110.2 Definitions

For the purpose of this subchapter, the term—

All-cargo operation means any operation for compensation or hire that is other than a passenger-carrying operation or, if passengers are carried, they are only those specified in §121.583(a) or §135.85 of this chapter.

Certificate-holding district office means the Flight Standards District Office that has responsibility for administering the certificate and is charged with the overall inspection of the certificate holder's operations.

Commercial air tour means a flight conducted for compensation or hire in an airplane or helicopter where a purpose of the flight is sightseeing. The FAA may consider the following factors in determining whether a flight is a commercial air tour:

(1) Whether there was a holding out to the public of willingness to conduct a sightseeing flight for compensation or hire;

(2) Whether the person offering the flight provided a narrative that referred to areas or points of interest on the surface below the route of the flight;

(3) The area of operation;

(4) How often the person offering the flight conducts such flights;

(5) The route of flight;

(6) The inclusion of sightseeing flights as part of any travel arrangement package;

(7) Whether the flight in question would have been canceled based on poor visibility of the surface below the route of the flight; and

(8) Any other factors that the FAA considers appropriate.

Commuter operation means any scheduled operation conducted by any person operating one of the following types of aircraft with a frequency of operations of at least five round trips per week on at least one route between two or more points according to the published flight schedules:

(1) Airplanes, other than turbojet-powered airplanes, having a maximum passenger-seat configuration of 9 seats or less, excluding each crewmember seat, and a maximum payload capacity of 7,500 pounds or less; or

(2) Rotorcraft.

Direct air carrier means a person who provides or offers to provide air transportation and who has control over the operational functions performed in providing that transportation.

DOD commercial air carrier evaluator means a qualified Air Mobility Command, Survey and Analysis Office cockpit evaluator performing the duties specified in Public Law 99-661 when the evaluator is flying on an air carrier that is contracted or pursuing a contract with the U.S. Department of Defense (DOD).

Domestic operation means any scheduled operation conducted by any person operating any airplane described in paragraph (1) of this definition at locations described in paragraph (2) of this definition:

(1) Airplanes:

(i) Turbojet-powered airplanes;

(ii) Airplanes having a passenger-seat configuration of more than 9 passenger seats, excluding each crewmember seat; or

(iii) Airplanes having a payload capacity of more than 7,500 pounds.

(2) Locations:

(i) Between any points within the 48 contiguous States of the United States or the District of Columbia; or

(ii) Operations solely within the 48 contiguous States of the United States or the District of Columbia; or

(iii) Operations entirely within any State, territory, or possession of the United States; or

(iv) When specifically authorized by the Administrator, operations between any point within the 48 contiguous States of the United States or the District of Columbia and any specifically authorized point located outside the 48 contiguous States of the United States or the District of Columbia.

Empty weight means the weight of the airframe, engines, propellers, rotors, and fixed equipment. Empty weight excludes the weight of the crew and payload, but includes the weight of all fixed ballast, unusable fuel supply, undrainable oil, total quantity of engine coolant, and total quantity of hydraulic fluid.

§110.2

Flag operation means any scheduled operation conducted by any person operating any airplane described in paragraph (1) of this definition at the locations described in paragraph (2) of this definition:

(1) Airplanes:

(i) Turbojet-powered airplanes;

(ii) Airplanes having a passenger-seat configuration of more than 9 passenger seats, excluding each crewmember seat; or

(iii) Airplanes having a payload capacity of more than 7,500 pounds.

(2) Locations:

(i) Between any point within the State of Alaska or the State of Hawaii or any territory or possession of the United States and any point outside the State of Alaska or the State of Hawaii or any territory or possession of the United States, respectively; or

(ii) Between any point within the 48 contiguous States of the United States or the District of Columbia and any point outside the 48 contiguous States of the United States and the District of Columbia.

(iii) Between any point outside the U.S. and another point outside the U.S.

Justifiable aircraft equipment means any equipment necessary for the operation of the aircraft. It does not include equipment or ballast specifically installed, permanently or otherwise, for the purpose of altering the empty weight of an aircraft to meet the maximum payload capacity.

Kind of operation means one of the various operations a certificate holder is authorized to conduct, as specified in its operations specifications, i.e., domestic, flag, supplemental, commuter, or on-demand operations.

Maximum payload capacity means:

(1) For an aircraft for which a maximum zero fuel weight is prescribed in FAA technical specifications, the maximum zero fuel weight, less empty weight, less all justifiable aircraft equipment, and less the operating load (consisting of minimum flightcrew, foods and beverages, and supplies and equipment related to foods and beverages, but not including disposable fuel or oil).

(2) For all other aircraft, the maximum certificated takeoff weight of an aircraft, less the empty weight, less all justifiable aircraft equipment, and less the operating load (consisting of minimum fuel load, oil, and flightcrew). The allowance for the weight of the crew, oil, and fuel is as follows:

(i) Crew—for each crewmember required by the Federal Aviation Regulations—

(A) For male flightcrew members—180 pounds.

(B) For female flightcrew members—140 pounds.

(C) For male flight attendants—180 pounds.

(D) For female flight attendants—130 pounds.

(E) For flight attendants not identified by gender—140 pounds.

(ii) Oil—350 pounds or the oil capacity as specified on the Type Certificate Data Sheet.

(iii) Fuel—the minimum weight of fuel required by the applicable Federal Aviation Regulations for a flight between domestic points 174 nautical miles apart under VFR weather conditions that does not involve extended overwater operations.

Maximum zero fuel weight means the maximum permissible weight of an aircraft with no disposable fuel or oil. The zero fuel weight figure may be found in either the aircraft type certificate data sheet, the approved Aircraft Flight Manual, or both.

Noncommon carriage means an aircraft operation for compensation or hire that does not involve a holding out to others.

On-demand operation means any operation for compensation or hire that is one of the following:

(1) Passenger-carrying operations conducted as a public charter under part 380 of this chapter or any operations in which the departure time, departure location, and arrival location are specifically negotiated with the customer or the customer's representative that are any of the following types of operations:

(i) Common carriage operations conducted with airplanes, including turbojet-powered airplanes, having a passenger-seat configuration of 30 seats or fewer, excluding each crewmember seat, and a payload capacity of 7,500 pounds or less, except that operations using a specific airplane that is also used in domestic or flag operations and that is so listed in the operations specifications as required by §119.49(a)(4) of this chapter for those operations are considered supplemental operations;

(ii) Noncommon or private carriage operations conducted with airplanes having a passenger-seat configuration of less than 20 seats, excluding each crewmember seat, and a payload capacity of less than 6,000 pounds; or

(iii) Any rotorcraft operation.

(2) Scheduled passenger-carrying operations conducted with one of the following types of aircraft with a frequency of operations of less than five round trips per week on at least one route between two or more points according to the published flight schedules:

(i) Airplanes, other than turbojet powered airplanes, having a maximum passenger-seat configuration of 9 seats or less, excluding each crewmember seat, and a maximum payload capacity of 7,500 pounds or less; or

(ii) Rotorcraft.

(3) All-cargo operations conducted with airplanes having a payload capacity of 7,500 pounds or less, or with rotorcraft.

Part 110: General Requirements §110.2

Passenger-carrying operation means any aircraft operation carrying any person, unless the only persons on the aircraft are those identified in §§121.583(a) or 135.85 of this chapter, as applicable. An aircraft used in a passenger-carrying operation may also carry cargo or mail in addition to passengers.

Principal base of operations means the primary operating location of a certificate holder as established by the certificate holder.

Provisional airport means an airport approved by the Administrator for use by a certificate holder for the purpose of providing service to a community when the regular airport used by the certificate holder is not available.

Regular airport means an airport used by a certificate holder in scheduled operations and listed in its operations specifications.

Scheduled operation means any common carriage passenger-carrying operation for compensation or hire conducted by an air carrier or commercial operator for which the certificate holder or its representative offers in advance the departure location, departure time, and arrival location. It does not include any passenger-carrying operation that is conducted as a public charter operation under part 380 of this chapter.

Supplemental operation means any common carriage operation for compensation or hire conducted with any airplane described in paragraph (1) of this definition that is a type of operation described in paragraph (2) of this definition:

(1) Airplanes:

(i) Airplanes having a passenger-seat configuration of more than 30 seats, excluding each crewmember seat;

(ii) Airplanes having a payload capacity of more than 7,500 pounds; or

(iii) Each propeller-powered airplane having a passenger-seat configuration of more than 9 seats and less than 31 seats, excluding each crewmember seat, that is also used in domestic or flag operations and that is so listed in the operations specifications as required by §119.49(a)(4) of this chapter for those operations; or

(iv) Each turbojet powered airplane having a passenger seat configuration of 1 or more and less than 31 seats, excluding each crewmember seat, that is also used in domestic or flag operations and that is so listed in the operations specifications as required by §119.49(a)(4) of this chapter for those operations.

(2) Types of operation:

(i) Operations for which the departure time, departure location, and arrival location are specifically negotiated with the customer or the customer's representative;

(ii) All-cargo operations; or

(iii) Passenger-carrying public charter operations conducted under part 380 of this chapter.

Wet lease means any leasing arrangement whereby a person agrees to provide an entire aircraft and at least one crewmember. A wet lease does not include a code-sharing arrangement.

When common carriage is not involved or operations not involving common carriage means any of the following:

(1) Noncommon carriage.

(2) Operations in which persons or cargo are transported without compensation or hire.

(3) Operations not involving the transportation of persons or cargo.

(4) Private carriage.

Years in service means the calendar time elapsed since an aircraft was issued its first U.S. or first foreign airworthiness certificate.

14 CFR • Subchapter G—Air Carriers and Operators for Compensation or Hire: Certification and Operations

PART 117

FLIGHT AND DUTY LIMITATIONS AND REST REQUIREMENTS: FLIGHTCREW MEMBERS

117.1 Applicability.
*117.3 **Definitions.**
117.5 Fitness for duty.
117.7 Fatigue risk management system.
117.9 Fatigue education and awareness training program.
*117.11 **Flight time limitation.**
117.13 Flight duty period: Unaugmented operations.
117.15 Flight duty period: Split duty.
117.17 Flight duty period: Augmented flightcrew.
*117.19 **Flight duty period extensions.**
117.21 Reserve status.
*117.23 **Cumulative limitations.**
117.25 Rest period.
117.27 Consecutive nighttime operations.
*117.29 **Emergency and government sponsored operations.**
Table A to Part 117—Maximum Flight Time Limits for Unaugmented Operations
Table B to Part 117—Flight Duty Period: Unaugmented Operations
Table C to Part 117—Flight Duty Period: Augmented Operations

Authority: 49 U.S.C. 106(g), 40113, 40119, 44101, 44701–44702, 44705, 44709–44711, 44713, 44716–44717, 44722, 46901, 44903–44904, 44912, 46105.

Source: Docket No. FAA–2009–1093, 77 FR 398, Jan. 4, 2012, as amended by Amdt. 117–1A, 77 FR 28764, May 16, 2012; Amdt. 117–1 correction, 78 FR 8361, Feb. 6, 2013; Amdt. 117–1 correction, 78 FR 11090, Feb. 15, 2013; Amdt. 117–1 correction, 78 FR 69288, Nov. 19, 2013, unless otherwise noted.

§117.1 Applicability.

(a) This part prescribes flight and duty limitations and rest requirements for all flightcrew members and certificate holders conducting passenger operations under part 121 of this chapter.

(b) This part applies to all operations directed by part 121 certificate holders under part 91, other than subpart K, of this chapter if any segment is conducted as a domestic passenger, flag passenger, or supplemental passenger operation.

(c) This part applies to all flightcrew members when participating in an operation under part 91, other than subpart K of this chapter, on behalf of the part 121 certificate holder if any flight segment is conducted as a domestic passenger, flag passenger, or supplemental passenger operation

(d) Notwithstanding paragraphs (a), (b) and (c) of this section, a certificate holder may conduct under part 117 its part 121 operations pursuant to 121.470, 121.480, or 121.500.

§117.3 Definitions.

In addition to the definitions in §§1.1 and 110.2 of this chapter, the following definitions apply to this part. In the event there is a conflict in definitions, the definitions in this part control for purposes of the flight and duty limitations and rest requirements of this part.

Acclimated means a condition in which a flightcrew member has been in a theater for 72 hours or has been given at least 36 consecutive hours free from duty.

Airport/standby reserve means a defined duty period during which a flightcrew member is required by a certificate holder to be at an airport for a possible assignment.

Augmented flightcrew means a flightcrew that has more than the minimum number of flightcrew members required by the airplane type certificate to operate the aircraft to allow a flightcrew member to be replaced by another qualified flightcrew member for in-flight rest.

Calendar day means a 24-hour period from 0000 through 2359 using Coordinated Universal Time or local time.

Certificate holder means a person who holds or is required to hold an air carrier certificate or operating certificate issued under part 119 of this chapter.

Deadhead transportation means transportation of a flightcrew member as a passenger or non-operating flightcrew member, by any mode of transportation, as required by a certificate holder, excluding transportation to or from a suitable accommodation. All time spent in deadhead transportation is duty and is not rest. For purposes of determining the maximum flight duty period in Table B of this part, deadhead transportation is not considered a flight segment.

Duty means any task that a flightcrew member performs as required by the certificate holder, including but not limited to flight duty period, flight duty, pre- and post-flight duties, administrative work, training, deadhead transportation, aircraft positioning on the ground, aircraft loading, and aircraft servicing.

Fatigue means a physiological state of reduced mental or physical performance capability

§117.3   Federal Aviation Regulations

resulting from lack of sleep or increased physical activity that can reduce a flightcrew member's alertness and ability to safely operate an aircraft or perform safety-related duties.

Fatigue risk management system (FRMS) means a management system for a certificate holder to use to mitigate the effects of fatigue in its particular operations. It is a data-driven process and a systematic method used to continuously monitor and manage safety risks associated with fatigue-related error.

Fit for duty means physiologically and mentally prepared and capable of performing assigned duties at the highest degree of safety.

Flight duty period (FDP) means a period that begins when a flightcrew member is required to report for duty with the intention of conducting a flight, a series of flights, or positioning or ferrying flights, and ends when the aircraft is parked after the last flight and there is no intention for further aircraft movement by the same flightcrew member. A flight duty period includes the duties performed by the flightcrew member on behalf of the certificate holder that occur before a flight segment or between flight segments without a required intervening rest period. Examples of tasks that are part of the flight duty period include deadhead transportation, training conducted in an aircraft or flight simulator, and airport/standby reserve, if the above tasks occur before a flight segment or between flight segments without an intervening required rest period.

Home base means the location designated by a certificate holder where a flightcrew member normally begins and ends his or her duty periods.

Lineholder means a flightcrew member who has an assigned flight duty period and is not acting as a reserve flightcrew member.

Long-call reserve means that, prior to beginning the rest period required by §117.25, the flightcrew member is notified by the certificate holder to report for a flight duty period following the completion of the rest period.

Physiological night's rest means 10 hours of rest that encompasses the hours of 0100 and 0700 at the flightcrew member's home base, unless the individual has acclimated to a different theater. If the flightcrew member has acclimated to a different theater, the rest must encompass the hours of 0100 and 0700 at the acclimated location.

Report time means the time that the certificate holder requires a flightcrew member to report for an assignment.

Reserve availability period means a duty period during which a certificate holder requires a flightcrew member on short call reserve to be available to receive an assignment for a flight duty period.

Reserve flightcrew member means a flightcrew member who a certificate holder requires to be available to receive an assignment for duty.

Rest facility means a bunk or seat accommodation installed in an aircraft that provides a flightcrew member with a sleep opportunity.

(1) *Class 1 rest facility* means a bunk or other surface that allows for a flat sleeping position and is located separate from both the flight deck and passenger cabin in an area that is temperature-controlled, allows the flightcrew member to control light, and provides isolation from noise and disturbance.

(2) *Class 2 rest facility* means a seat in an aircraft cabin that allows for a flat or near flat sleeping position; is separated from passengers by a minimum of a curtain to provide darkness and some sound mitigation; and is reasonably free from disturbance by passengers or flightcrew members.

(3) *Class 3 rest facility* means a seat in an aircraft cabin or flight deck that reclines at least 40 degrees and provides leg and foot support.

Rest period means a continuous period determined prospectively during which the flightcrew member is free from all restraint by the certificate holder, including freedom from present responsibility for work should the occasion arise.

Scheduled means to appoint, assign, or designate for a fixed time.

Short-call reserve means a period of time in which a flightcrew member is assigned to a reserve availability period.

Split duty means a flight duty period that has a scheduled break in duty that is less than a required rest period.

Suitable accommodation means a temperature-controlled facility with sound mitigation and the ability to control light that provides a flightcrew member with the ability to sleep either in a bed, bunk or in a chair that allows for flat or near flat sleeping position. Suitable accommodation only applies to ground facilities and does not apply to aircraft onboard rest facilities.

Theater means a geographical area in which the distance between the flightcrew member's flight duty period departure point and arrival point differs by no more than 60 degrees longitude.

Unforeseen operational circumstance means an unplanned event of insufficient duration to allow for adjustments to schedules, including unforecast weather, equipment malfunction, or air traffic delay that is not reasonably expected.

Window of circadian low means a period of maximum sleepiness that occurs between 0200 and 0559 during a physiological night.

[Docket No. FAA–2009–1093, 77 FR 398, Jan. 4, 2012, as amended by Amdt. 117–1A, 77 FR 28764, May 16, 2012; Amdt. 117–1, 78 FR 69288, Nov. 19, 2013]

§117.5 Fitness for duty.

(a) Each flightcrew member must report for any flight duty period rested and prepared to perform his or her assigned duties.

(b) No certificate holder may assign and no flightcrew member may accept assignment to a flight duty period if the flightcrew member has reported for a flight duty period too fatigued to safely perform his or her assigned duties.

(c) No certificate holder may permit a flightcrew member to continue a flight duty period if the flightcrew member has reported him or herself too fatigued to continue the assigned flight duty period.

(d) As part of the dispatch or flight release, as applicable, each flightcrew member must affirmatively state he or she is fit for duty prior to commencing flight.

§117.7 Fatigue risk management system.

(a) No certificate holder may exceed any provision of this part unless approved by the FAA under a Fatigue Risk Management System that provides at least an equivalent level of safety against fatigue-related accidents or incidents as the other provisions of this part.

(b) The Fatigue Risk Management System must include:

(1) A fatigue risk management policy.

(2) An education and awareness training program.

(3) A fatigue reporting system.

(4) A system for monitoring flightcrew fatigue.

(5) An incident reporting process.

(6) A performance evaluation.

§117.9 Fatigue education and awareness training program.

(a) Each certificate holder must develop and implement an education and awareness training program, approved by the Administrator. This program must provide annual education and awareness training to all employees of the certificate holder responsible for administering the provisions of this rule including flightcrew members, dispatchers, individuals directly involved in the scheduling of flightcrew members, individuals directly involved in operational control, and any employee providing direct management oversight of those areas.

(b) The fatigue education and awareness training program must be designed to increase awareness of:

(1) Fatigue;

(2) The effects of fatigue on pilots; and

(3) Fatigue countermeasures

(c) (1) Each certificate holder must update its fatigue education and awareness training program every two years and submit the update to the Administrator for review and acceptance.

(2) Not later than 12 months after the date of submission of the fatigue education and awareness training program required by (c)(1) of this section, the Administrator shall review and accept or reject the update. If the Administrator rejects an update, the Administrator shall provide suggested modifications for resubmission of the update.

§117.11 Flight time limitation.

(a) No certificate holder may schedule and no flightcrew member may accept an assignment or continue an assigned flight duty period if the total flight time:

(1) Will exceed the limits specified in Table A of this part if the operation is conducted with the minimum required flightcrew.

(2) Will exceed 13 hours if the operation is conducted with a 3-pilot flightcrew.

(3) Will exceed 17 hours if the operation is conducted with a 4-pilot flightcrew.

(b) If unforeseen operational circumstances arise after takeoff that are beyond the certificate holder's control, a flightcrew member may exceed the maximum flight time specified in paragraph (a) of this section and the cumulative flight time limits in 117.23(b) to the extent necessary to safely land the aircraft at the next destination airport or alternate, as appropriate.

(c) Each certificate holder must report to the Administrator within 10 days any flight time that exceeded the maximum flight time limits permitted by this section or §117.23(b). The report must contain a description of the extended flight time limitation and the circumstances surrounding the need for the extension.

[Docket No. FAA–2009–1093, 77 FR 398, Jan. 4, 2012, as amended by Amdt. 117–1, 78 FR 8362, Feb. 6, 2013; Amdt. 117–1, 78 FR 69288, Nov. 19, 2013]

§117.13 Flight duty period: Unaugmented operations.

(a) Except as provided for in §117.15, no certificate holder may assign and no flightcrew member may accept an assignment for an unaugmented flight operation if the scheduled flight duty period will exceed the limits in Table B of this part.

(b) If the flightcrew member is not acclimated:

(1) The maximum flight duty period in Table B of this part is reduced by 30 minutes.

(2) The applicable flight duty period is based on the local time at the theater in which the flightcrew member was last acclimated.

§117.15 Flight duty period: Split duty.

For an unaugmented operation only, if a flightcrew member is provided with a rest opportunity (an opportunity to sleep) in a suitable accommodation during his or her flight duty period, the time that the flightcrew member spends in the suitable accommodation is not part of that flightcrew member's flight duty period if all of the following conditions are met:

(a) The rest opportunity is provided between the hours of 22:00 and 05:00 local time.

(b) The time spent in the suitable accommodation is at least 3 hours, measured from the time that the flightcrew member reaches the suitable accommodation.

(c) The rest opportunity is scheduled before the beginning of the flight duty period in which that rest opportunity is taken.

(d) The rest opportunity that the flightcrew member is actually provided may not be less than the rest opportunity that was scheduled.

(e) The rest opportunity is not provided until the first segment of the flight duty period has been completed.

(f) The combined time of the flight duty period and the rest opportunity provided in this section does not exceed 14 hours.

§117.17 Flight duty period: Augmented flightcrew.

(a) For flight operations conducted with an acclimated augmented flightcrew, no certificate holder may assign and no flightcrew member may accept an assignment if the scheduled flight duty period will exceed the limits specified in Table C of this part.

(b) If the flightcrew member is not acclimated:

(1) The maximum flight duty period in Table C of this part is reduced by 30 minutes.

(2) The applicable flight duty period is based on the local time at the theater in which the flightcrew member was last acclimated.

(c) No certificate holder may assign and no flightcrew member may accept an assignment under this section unless during the flight duty period:

(1) Two consecutive hours in the second half of the flight duty period are available for in-flight rest for the pilot flying the aircraft during landing.

(2) Ninety consecutive minutes are available for in-flight rest for the pilot performing monitoring duties during landing.

(d) No certificate holder may assign and no flightcrew member may accept an assignment involving more than three flight segments under this section.

(e) At all times during flight, at least one flightcrew member qualified in accordance with §121.543(b)(3)(i) of this chapter must be at the flight controls.

§117.19 Flight duty period extensions.

(a) For augmented and unaugmented operations, if unforeseen operational circumstances arise prior to takeoff:

(1) The pilot in command and the certificate holder may extend the maximum flight duty period permitted in Tables B or C of this part up to 2 hours. The pilot in command and the certificate holder may also extend the maximum combined flight duty period and reserve availability period limits specified in §117.21(c)(3) and (4) of this part up to 2 hours.

(2) An extension in the flight duty period under paragraph (a)(1) of this section of more than 30 minutes may occur only once prior to receiving a rest period described in §117.25(b).

(3) A flight duty period cannot be extended under paragraph (a)(1) of this section if it causes a flightcrew member to exceed the cumulative flight duty period limits specified in 117.23(c).

(4) Each certificate holder must report to the Administrator within 10 days any flight duty period that exceeded the maximum flight duty period permitted in Tables B or C of this part by more than 30 minutes. The report must contain the following:

(i) A description of the extended flight duty period and the circumstances surrounding the need for the extension; and

(ii) If the circumstances giving rise to the extension were within the certificate holder's control, the corrective action(s) that the certificate holder intends to take to minimize the need for future extensions.

(5) Each certificate holder must implement the corrective action(s) reported in paragraph (a)(4) of this section within 30 days from the date of the extended flight duty period.

(b) For augmented and unaugmented operations, if unforeseen operational circumstances arise after takeoff:

(1) The pilot in command and the certificate holder may extend maximum flight duty periods specified in Tables B or C of this part to the extent necessary to safely land the aircraft at the next destination airport or alternate airport, as appropriate.

(2) An extension of the flight duty period under paragraph (b)(1) of this section of more than 30 minutes may occur only once prior to receiving a rest period described in §117.25(b).

(3) An extension taken under paragraph (b) of this section may exceed the cumulative flight duty period limits specified in 117.23(c).

(4) Each certificate holder must report to the Administrator within 10 days any flight duty period that either exceeded the cumulative flight duty periods specified in §117.23(c), or exceeded the maximum flight duty period limits permitted by Tables B or C of this part by more than 30

Part 117: Duty Limitations and Rest Requirements: Flightcrew §117.25

minutes. The report must contain a description of the circumstances surrounding the affected flight duty period.

[Docket No. FAA–2009–1093, 77 FR 398, Jan. 4, 2012, as amended by Amdt. 117–1A, 77 FR 28764, May 16, 2012; Amdt. 117–1, 78 FR 8362, Feb. 6, 2013; Amdt. 117–1, 78 FR 69288, Nov. 19, 2013]

§117.21 Reserve status.

(a) Unless specifically designated as airport/standby or short-call reserve by the certificate holder, all reserve is considered long-call reserve.

(b) Any reserve that meets the definition of airport/standby reserve must be designated as airport/standby reserve. For airport/standby reserve, all time spent in a reserve status is part of the flightcrew member's flight duty period.

(c) For short call reserve,

(1) The reserve availability period may not exceed 14 hours.

(2) For a flightcrew member who has completed a reserve availability period, no certificate holder may schedule and no flightcrew member may accept an assignment of a reserve availability period unless the flightcrew member receives the required rest in §117.25(e).

(3) For an unaugmented operation, the total number of hours a flightcrew member may spend in a flight duty period and a reserve availability period may not exceed the lesser of the maximum applicable flight duty period in Table B of this part plus 4 hours, or 16 hours, as measured from the beginning of the reserve availability period.

(4) For an augmented operation, the total number of hours a flightcrew member may spend in a flight duty period and a reserve availability period may not exceed the flight duty period in Table C of this part plus 4 hours, as measured from the beginning of the reserve availability period.

(d) For long call reserve, if a certificate holder contacts a flightcrew member to assign him or her to a flight duty period that will begin before and operate into the flightcrew member's window of circadian low, the flightcrew member must receive a 12 hour notice of report time from the certificate holder.

(e) A certificate holder may shift a reserve flightcrew member's reserve status from long-call to short-call only if the flightcrew member receives a rest period as provided in §117.25(e).

§117.23 Cumulative limitations.

(a) The limitations of this section include all flying by flightcrew members on behalf of any certificate holder or 91K Program Manager during the applicable periods.

(b) No certificate holder may schedule and no flightcrew member may accept an assignment if the flightcrew member's total flight time will exceed the following:

(1) 100 hours in any 672 consecutive hours or

(2) 1,000 hours in any 365 consecutive calendar day period.

(c) No certificate holder may schedule and no flightcrew member may accept an assignment if the flightcrew member's total Flight Duty Period will exceed:

(1) 60 flight duty period hours in any 168 consecutive hours or

(2) 190 flight duty period hours in any 672 consecutive hours.

[Docket No. FAA–2009–1093, 77 FR 398, Jan. 4, 2012, as amended by Amdt. 117–1A, 77 FR 28764, May 16, 2012; Amdt. 117–1, 78 FR 69288, Nov. 19, 2013]

§117.25 Rest period.

(a) No certificate holder may assign and no flightcrew member may accept assignment to any reserve or duty with the certificate holder during any required rest period.

(b) Before beginning any reserve or flight duty period a flightcrew member must be given at least 30 consecutive hours free from all duty within the past 168 consecutive hour period.

(c) If a flightcrew member operating in a new theater has received 36 consecutive hours of rest, that flightcrew member is acclimated and the rest period meets the requirements of paragraph (b) of this section.

(d) A flightcrew member must be given a minimum of 56 consecutive hours rest upon return to home base if the flightcrew member: (1) Travels more than 60° longitude during a flight duty period or a series of flight duty period, and (2) is away from home base for more than 168 consecutive hours during this travel. The 56 hours of rest specified in this section must encompass three physiological nights' rest based on local time.

(e) No certificate holder may schedule and no flightcrew member may accept an assignment for any reserve or flight duty period unless the flightcrew member is given a rest period of at least 10 consecutive hours immediately before beginning the reserve or flight duty period measured from the time the flightcrew member is released from duty. The 10 hour rest period must provide the flightcrew member with a minimum of 8 uninterrupted hours of sleep opportunity.

(f) If a flightcrew member determines that a rest period under paragraph (e) of this section will not provide eight uninterrupted hours of sleep opportunity, the flightcrew member must notify the certificate holder. The flightcrew member cannot report for the assigned flight duty period until he or she receives a rest period specified in paragraph (e) of this section.

(g) If a flightcrew member engaged in deadhead transportation exceeds the applicable flight duty period in Table B of this part, the flightcrew member must be given a rest period equal to the length of the deadhead transportation but not less than the required rest in paragraph (e) of this section before beginning a flight duty period.

[Docket No. FAA–2009–1093, 77 FR 398, Jan. 4, 2012, as amended by Amdt. 117–1A, 77 FR 28764, May 16, 2012; Amdt. 117–1, 78 FR 8362, Feb. 6, 2013]

§117.27 Consecutive nighttime operations.

A certificate holder may schedule and a flightcrew member may accept up to five consecutive flight duty periods that infringe on the window of circadian low if the certificate holder provides the flightcrew member with an opportunity to rest in a suitable accommodation during each of the consecutive nighttime flight duty periods. The rest opportunity must be at least 2 hours, measured from the time that the flightcrew member reaches the suitable accommodation, and must comply with the conditions specified in §117.15(a), (c), (d), and (e). Otherwise, no certificate holder may schedule and no flightcrew member may accept more than three consecutive flight duty periods that infringe on the window of circadian low. For purposes of this section, any split duty rest that is provided in accordance with §117.15 counts as part of a flight duty period.

§117.29 Emergency and government sponsored operations.

(a) This section applies to operations conducted pursuant to contracts with the U.S. Government and operations conducted pursuant to a deviation under §119.57 of this chapter that cannot otherwise be conducted under this part because of circumstances that could prevent flightcrew members from being relieved by another crew or safely provided with the rest required under §117.25 at the end of the applicable flight duty period.

(b) The pilot-in-command may determine that the maximum applicable flight duty period, flight time, and/or combined flight duty period and reserve availability period limits must be exceeded to the extent necessary to allow the flightcrew to fly to the closest destination where they can safely be relieved from duty by another flightcrew or can receive the requisite amount of rest prior to commencing their next flight duty period.

(c) A flight duty period may not be extended for an operation conducted pursuant to a contract with the U.S. Government if it causes a flightcrew member to exceed the cumulative flight time limits in §117.23(b) and the cumulative flight duty period limits in §117.23(c).

(d) The flightcrew shall be given a rest period immediately after reaching the destination described in paragraph (b) of this section equal to the length of the actual flight duty period or 24 hours, whichever is less.

(e) Each certificate holder must report within 10 days:

(1) Any flight duty period that exceeded the maximum flight duty period permitted in Tables B or C of this part, as applicable, by more than 30 minutes;

(2) Any flight time that exceeded the maximum flight time limits permitted in Table A of this part and §117.11, as applicable; and

(3) Any flight duty period or flight time that exceeded the cumulative limits specified in §117.23.

(f) The report must contain the following:

(1) A description of the extended flight duty period and flight time limitation, and the circumstances surrounding the need for the extension; and

(2) If the circumstances giving rise to the extension(s) were within the certificate holder's control, the corrective action(s) that the certificate holder intends to take to minimize the need for future extensions.

(g) Each certificate holder must implement the corrective action(s) reported pursuant to paragraph (f)(2) of this section within 30 days from the date of the extended flight duty period and/or the extended flight time.

[Docket No. FAA–2009–1093, 77 FR 398, Jan. 4, 2012, as amended by Amdt. 117–1A, 77 FR 28764, May 16, 2012; Amdt. 117–1, 78 FR 8362, Feb. 6, 2013; Amdt. 117–1, 78 FR 69288, Nov. 19, 2013]

Part 117: Duty Limitations and Rest Requirements: Flightcrew §117.29

TABLE A TO PART 117—MAXIMUM FLIGHT TIME LIMITS FOR UNAUGMENTED OPERATIONS TABLE

Time of report (acclimated)	Maximum flight time (hours)
0000-0459	8
0500-1959	9
2000-2359	8

TABLE B TO PART 117—FLIGHT DUTY PERIOD: UNAUGMENTED OPERATIONS

Scheduled time of start (acclimated time)	Maximum flight duty period (hours) for lineholders based on number of flight segments						
	1	2	3	4	5	6	7+
0000-0359	9	9	9	9	9	9	9
0400-0459	10	10	10	10	9	9	9
0500-0559	12	12	12	12	11.5	11	10.5
0600-0659	13	13	12	12	11.5	11	10.5
0700-1159	14	14	13	13	12.5	12	11.5
1200-1259	13	13	13	13	12.5	12	11.5
1300-1659	12	12	12	12	11.5	11	10.5
1700-2159	12	12	11	11	10	9	9
2200-2259	11	11	10	10	9	9	9
2300-2359	10	10	10	9	9	9	9

TABLE C TO PART 117—FLIGHT DUTY PERIOD: AUGMENTED OPERATIONS

Scheduled time of start (acclimated time)	Maximum flight duty period (hours) based on rest facility and number of pilots					
	Class 1 rest facility		Class 2 rest facility		Class 3 rest facility	
	3 pilots	4 pilots	3 pilots	4 pilots	3 pilots	4 pilots
0000-0559	15	17	14	15.5	13	13.5
0600-0659	16	18.5	15	16.5	14	14.5
0700-1259	17	19	16.5	18	15	15.5
1300-1659	16	18.5	15	16.5	14	14.5
1700-2359	15	17	14	15.5	13	13.5

14 CFR • Subchapter G—Air Carriers and Operators for
Compensation or Hire: Certification and Operations

PART 119

CERTIFICATION: AIR CARRIERS AND COMMERCIAL OPERATORS

Subpart A—General

Sec.
119.1 Applicability.
119.3 [Reserved]
119.5 Certifications, authorizations, and prohibitions.
119.7 Operations specifications.
119.9 Use of business names.

Subpart B—Applicability of Operating Requirements to Different Kinds of Operations Under Parts 121, 125, and 135 of this Chapter

119.21 Commercial operators engaged in intrastate common carriage and direct air carriers.
119.23 Operators engaged in passenger-carrying operations, cargo operations, or both with airplanes when common carriage is not involved.
119.25 Rotorcraft operations: Direct air carriers and commercial operators.

Subpart C—Certification, Operations Specifications, and Certain Other Requirements for Operations Conducted Under Part 121 or Part 135 of this Chapter

119.31 Applicability.
119.33 General requirements.
119.35 Certificate application requirements for all operators.
119.36 Additional certificate application requirements for commercial operators.
119.37 Contents of an Air Carrier Certificate or Operating Certificate.
119.39 Issuing or denying a certificate.
119.41 Amending a certificate.
119.43 Certificate holder's duty to maintain operations specifications.
119.45 [Reserved]
119.47 Maintaining a principal base of operations, main operations base, and main maintenance base; change of address.
119.49 Contents of operations specifications.
119.51 Amending operations specifications.
119.53 Wet leasing of aircraft and other arrangements for transportation by air.
119.55 Obtaining deviation authority to perform operations under a U.S. military contract.
119.57 Obtaining deviation authority to perform an emergency operation.
119.59 Conducting tests and inspections.
119.61 Duration and surrender of certificate and operations specifications.
119.63 Recency of operation.
119.65 Management personnel required for operations conducted under part 121 of this chapter.
119.67 Management personnel: Qualifications for operations conducted under part 121 of this chapter.
119.69 Management personnel required for operations conducted under part 135 of this chapter.
119.71 Management personnel: Qualifications for operations conducted under part 135 of this chapter.
119.73 Employment of former FAA employees.

Authority: 49 U.S.C. 106(g), 1153, 40101, 40102, 40103, 40113, 44105, 44106, 44111, 44701–44717, 44722, 44901, 44903, 44904, 44906, 44912, 44914, 44936, 44938, 46103, 46105.

Source: Docket No. 28154, 60 FR 65913, Dec. 20, 1995, unless otherwise noted.

Subpart A—General

§119.1 Applicability.

(a) This part applies to each person operating or intending to operate civil aircraft—

(1) As an air carrier or commercial operator, or both, in air commerce or

(2) When common carriage is not involved, in operations of U.S.-registered civil airplanes with a seat configuration of 20 or more passengers, or a maximum payload capacity of 6,000 pounds or more.

(b) This part prescribes—

(1) The types of air operator certificates issued by the Federal Aviation Administration, including air carrier certificates and operating certificates;

(2) The certification requirements an operator must meet in order to obtain and hold a certificate authorizing operations under part 121, 125, or 135 of this chapter and operations specifications for each kind of operation to be conducted and each class and size of aircraft to be operated under part 121 or 135 of this chapter;

(3) The requirements an operator must meet to conduct operations under part 121, 125, or 135 of this chapter and in operating each class and size of aircraft authorized in its operations specifications;

(4) Requirements affecting wet leasing of aircraft and other arrangements for transportation by air;

(5) Requirements for obtaining deviation authority to perform operations under a military contract and obtaining deviation authority to perform an emergency operation; and

(6) Requirements for management personnel for operations conducted under part 121 or part 135 of this chapter.

(c) Persons subject to this part must comply with the other requirements of this chapter, except where those requirements are modified by or where additional requirements are imposed by part 119, 121, 125, or 135 of this chapter.

(d) This part does not govern operations conducted under part 91, subpart K (when common carriage is not involved) nor does it govern operations conducted under part 129, 133, 137, or 139 of this chapter.

(e) Except for operations when common carriage is not involved conducted with airplanes having a passenger-seat configuration of 20 seats or more, excluding any required crewmember seat, or a payload capacity of 6,000 pounds or more, this part does not apply to—

(1) Student instruction;

(2) Nonstop Commercial Air Tours conducted after September 11, 2007, in an airplane or helicopter having a standard airworthiness certificate and passenger-seat configuration of 30 seats or fewer and a maximum payload capacity of 7,500 pounds or less that begin and end at the same airport, and are conducted within a 25-statute mile radius of that airport, in compliance with the Letter of Authorization issued under §91.147 of this chapter. For nonstop Commercial Air Tours conducted in accordance with part 136, subpart B of this chapter, National Parks Air Tour Management, the requirements of part 119 of this chapter apply unless excepted in §136.37(g)(2). For Nonstop Commercial Air Tours conducted in the vicinity of the Grand Canyon National Park, Arizona, the requirements of SFAR 50–2, part 93, subpart U, and part 119 of this chapter, as applicable, apply.

(3) Ferry or training flights;

(4) Aerial work operations, including—

(i) Crop dusting, seeding, spraying, and bird chasing;

(ii) Banner towing;

(iii) Aerial photography or survey;

(iv) Fire fighting;

(v) Helicopter operations in construction or repair work (but it does apply to transportation to and from the site of operations); and

(vi) Powerline or pipeline patrol;

(5) Sightseeing flights conducted in hot air balloons;

(6) Nonstop flights conducted within a 25-statute-mile radius of the airport of takeoff carrying persons or objects for the purpose of conducting intentional parachute operations.

(7) Helicopter flights conducted within a 25 statute mile radius of the airport of takeoff if—

(i) Not more than two passengers are carried in the helicopter in addition to the required flightcrew;

(ii) Each flight is made under day VFR conditions;

(iii) The helicopter used is certificated in the standard category and complies with the 100-hour inspection requirements of part 91 of this chapter;

(iv) The operator notifies the FAA Flight Standards District Office responsible for the geographic area concerned at least 72 hours before each flight and furnishes any essential information that the office requests;

(v) The number of flights does not exceed a total of six in any calendar year;

(vi) Each flight has been approved by the Administrator; and

(vii) Cargo is not carried in or on the helicopter;

(8) Operations conducted under part 133 of this chapter or 375 of this title;

(9) Emergency mail service conducted under 49 U.S.C. 41906; or

(10) Operations conducted under the provisions of §91.321 of this chapter.

[Docket No. 28154, 60 FR 65913, Dec. 20, 1995; as amended by Amdt. 119–4, 66 FR 23557, May 9, 2001; Amdt. 119–5, 67 FR 9554, March 1, 2002; Amdt. 119–7, 68 FR 54584, Sept. 17, 2003; 72 FR 6911, Feb. 13, 2007]

§119.3 [Reserved]

§119.5 Certifications, authorizations, and prohibitions.

(a) A person authorized by the Administrator to conduct operations as a direct air carrier will be issued an Air Carrier Certificate.

(b) A person who is not authorized to conduct direct air carrier operations, but who is authorized by the Administrator to conduct operations as a U.S. commercial operator, will be issued an Operating Certificate.

(c) A person who is not authorized to conduct direct air carrier operations, but who is authorized by the Administrator to conduct operations when common carriage is not involved as an operator of U.S.-registered civil airplanes with a seat configuration of 20 or more passengers, or a maximum payload capacity of 6,000 pounds or more, will be issued an Operating Certificate.

(d) A person authorized to engage in common carriage under part 121 or part 135 of this chapter, or both, shall be issued only one certificate authorizing such common carriage, regardless of the kind of operation or the class or size of aircraft to be operated.

(e) A person authorized to engage in noncommon or private carriage under part 125 or part 135 of this chapter, or both, shall be issued only one certificate authorizing such carriage, regardless of the kind of operation or the class or size of aircraft to be operated.

(f) A person conducting operations under more than one paragraph of §§119.21, 119.23, or 119.25 shall conduct those operations in compliance with—

(1) The requirements specified in each paragraph of those sections for the kind of operation conducted under that paragraph; and

(2) The appropriate authorizations, limitations, and procedures specified in the operations specifications for each kind of operation.

(g) No person may operate as a direct air carrier or as a commercial operator without, or in violation of, an appropriate certificate and appropriate operations specifications. No person may operate as a direct air carrier or as a commercial operator in violation of any deviation or exemption authority, if issued to that person or that person's representative.

(h) A person holding an Operating Certificate authorizing noncommon or private carriage operations shall not conduct any operations in common carriage. A person holding an Air Carrier Certificate or Operating Certificate authorizing common carriage operations shall not conduct any operations in noncommon carriage.

(i) No person may operate as a direct air carrier without holding appropriate economic authority from the Department of Transportation.

(j) A certificate holder under this part may not operate aircraft under part 121 or part 135 of this chapter in a geographical area unless its operations specifications specifically authorize the certificate holder to operate in that area.

(k) No person may advertise or otherwise offer to perform an operation subject to this part unless that person is authorized by the Federal Aviation Administration to conduct that operation.

(l) No person may operate an aircraft under this part, part 121 of this chapter, or part 135 of this chapter in violation of an air carrier operating certificate, operating certificate, or appropriate operations specifications issued under this part.

[Docket No. 28154, 60 FR 65913, Dec. 20, 1995; as amended by Amdt. 119–3, 62 FR 13253, March 19, 1997]

§119.7 Operations specifications.

(a) Each certificate holder's operations specifications must contain—

(1) The authorizations, limitations, and certain procedures under which each kind of operation, if applicable, is to be conducted; and

(2) Certain other procedures under which each class and size of aircraft is to be operated.

(b) Except for operations specifications paragraphs identifying authorized kinds of operations, operations specifications are not a part of a certificate.

§119.9 Use of business names.

(a) A certificate holder under this part may not operate an aircraft under part 121 or part 135 of this chapter using a business name other than a business name appearing in the certificate holder's operations specifications.

(b) No person may operate an aircraft under part 121 or part 135 of this chapter unless the name of the certificate holder who is operating the aircraft, or the air carrier or operating certificate number of the certificate holder who is operating the aircraft, is legibly displayed on the aircraft and is clearly visible and readable from the outside of the aircraft to a person standing on the ground at any time except during flight time. The means of displaying the name on the aircraft and its readability must be acceptable to the Administrator.

[Docket No. 28154, 60 FR 65913, Dec. 20, 1995; as amended by Amdt. 119–3, 62 FR 13253, March 19, 1997]

Subpart B—
Applicability of Operating Requirements to Different Kinds of Operations Under Parts 121, 125, and 135 of this Chapter

§119.21 Commercial operators engaged in intrastate common carriage and direct air carriers.

(a) Each person who conducts airplane operations as a commercial operator engaged in intrastate common carriage of persons or property for compensation or hire in air commerce, or as a direct air carrier, shall comply with the certification and operations specifications requirements in subpart C of this part, and shall conduct its:

(1) Domestic operations in accordance with the applicable requirements of part 121 of this chapter, and shall be issued operations specifications for those operations in accordance with those requirements. However, based on a show-

ing of safety in air commerce, the Administrator may permit persons who conduct domestic operations between any point located within any of the following Alaskan islands and any point in the State of Alaska to comply with the requirements applicable to flag operations contained in subpart U of part 121 of this chapter:

(i) The Aleutian Islands.
(ii) The Pribilof Islands.
(iii) The Shumagin Islands.

(2) Flag operations in accordance with the applicable requirements of part 121 of this chapter, and shall be issued operations specifications for those operations in accordance with those requirements.

(3) Supplemental operations in accordance with the applicable requirements of part 121 of this chapter, and shall be issued operations specifications for those operations in accordance with those requirements. However, based on a determination of safety in air commerce, the Administrator may authorize or require those operations to be conducted under paragraph (a)(1) or (a)(2) of this section.

(4) Commuter operations in accordance with the applicable requirements of part 135 of this chapter, and shall be issued operations specifications for those operations in accordance with those requirements.

(5) On-demand operations in accordance with the applicable requirements of part 135 of this chapter, and shall be issued operations specifications for those operations in accordance with those requirements.

(b) Persons who are subject to the requirements of paragraph (a)(4) of this section may conduct those operations in accordance with the requirements of paragraph (a)(1) or (a)(2) of this section, provided they obtain authorization from the Administrator.

(c) Persons who are subject to the requirements of paragraph (a)(5) of this section may conduct those operations in accordance with the requirements of paragraph (a)(3) of this section, provided they obtain authorization from the Administrator.

[Docket No. 28154, 60 FR 65913, Dec. 20, 1995; as amended by Amdt. 119–2, 61 FR 30433, June 14, 1996; Amdt. 119–3, 62 FR 13254, March 19, 1997; Amdt. 119–13, 75 FR 26645, May 12, 2010]

§119.23 Operators engaged in passenger-carrying operations, cargo operations, or both with airplanes when common carriage is not involved.

(a) Each person who conducts operations when common carriage is not involved with airplanes having a passenger-seat configuration of 20 seats or more, excluding each crewmember seat, or a payload capacity of 6,000 pounds or more, shall, unless deviation authority is issued—

(1) Comply with the certification and operations specifications requirements of part 125 of this chapter;

(2) Conduct its operations with those airplanes in accordance with the requirements of part 125 of this chapter; and

(3) Be issued operations specifications in accordance with those requirements.

(b) Each person who conducts noncommon carriage (except as provided in §91.501(b) of this chapter) or private carriage operations for compensation or hire with airplanes having a passenger-seat configuration of less than 20 seats, excluding each crewmember seat, and a payload capacity of less than 6,000 pounds shall—

(1) Comply with the certification and operations specifications requirements in subpart C of this part;

(2) Conduct those operations in accordance with the requirements of part 135 of this chapter, except for those requirements applicable only to commuter operations; and

(3) Be issued operations specifications in accordance with those requirements.

[Docket No. 28154, 60 FR 65913, Dec. 20, 1995; as amended by Amdt. 119–2, 61 FR 30434, June 14, 1996]

§119.25 Rotorcraft operations: Direct air carriers and commercial operators.

Each person who conducts rotorcraft operations for compensation or hire must comply with the certification and operations specifications requirements of Subpart C of this part, and shall conduct its:

(a) Commuter operations in accordance with the applicable requirements of part 135 of this chapter, and shall be issued operations specifications for those operations in accordance with those requirements.

(b) On-demand operations in accordance with the applicable requirements of part 135 of this chapter, and shall be issued operations specifications for those operations in accordance with those requirements.

Subpart C—
Certification, Operations Specifications, and Certain Other Requirements for Operations Conducted Under Part 121 or Part 135 of this Chapter

§119.31 Applicability.

This subpart sets out certification requirements and prescribes the content of operations specifications and certain other requirements for operations conducted under part 121 or part 135 of this chapter.

§119.33 General requirements.

(a) A person may not operate as a direct air carrier unless that person—
 (1) Is a citizen of the United States;
 (2) Obtains an Air Carrier Certificate; and
 (3) Obtains operations specifications that prescribe the authorizations, limitations, and procedures under which each kind of operation must be conducted.

(b) A person other than a direct air carrier may not conduct any commercial passenger or cargo aircraft operation for compensation or hire under part 121 or part 135 of this chapter unless that person—
 (1) Is a citizen of the United States;
 (2) Obtains an Operating Certificate; and
 (3) Obtains operations specifications that prescribe the authorizations, limitations, and procedures under which each kind of operation must be conducted.

(c) Each applicant for a certificate under this part and each applicant for operations specifications authorizing a new kind of operation that is subject to §121.163 or §135.145 of this chapter shall conduct proving tests as authorized by the Administrator during the application process for authority to conduct operations under part 121 or part 135 of this chapter. All proving tests must be conducted in a manner acceptable to the Administrator. All proving tests must be conducted under the appropriate operating and maintenance requirements of part 121 or 135 of this chapter that would apply if the applicant were fully certificated. The Administrator will issue a letter of authorization to each person stating the various authorities under which the proving tests shall be conducted.

[Docket No. 28154, 60 FR 65913, Dec. 20, 1995; as amended by Amdt. 119–2, 61 FR 30434, June 14, 1996]

§119.35 Certificate application requirements for all operators.

(a) A person applying to the Administrator for an Air Carrier Certificate or Operating Certificate under this part (applicant) must submit an application—
 (1) In a form and manner prescribed by the Administrator; and
 (2) Containing any information the Administrator requires the applicant to submit.

(b) Each applicant must submit the application to the Administrator at least 90 days before the date of intended operation.

[Docket No. 28154, 62 FR 13254, March 19, 1997; as amended by Amdt. 119–3, 62 FR 15570, April 1, 1997]

§119.36 Additional certificate application requirements for commercial operators.

(a) Each applicant for the original issue of an operating certificate for the purpose of conducting intrastate common carriage operations under part 121 or part 135 of this chapter must submit an application in a form and manner prescribed by the Administrator to the Flight Standards District Office in whose area the applicant proposes to establish or has established his or her principal base of operations.

(b) Each application submitted under paragraph (a) of this section must contain a signed statement showing the following:
 (1) For corporate applicants:
  (i) The name and address of each stockholder who owns 5 percent or more of the total voting stock of the corporation, and if that stockholder is not the sole beneficial owner of the stock, the name and address of each beneficial owner. An individual is considered to own the stock owned, directly or indirectly, by or for his or her spouse, children, grandchildren, or parents.
  (ii) The name and address of each director and each officer and each person employed or who will be employed in a management position described in §§119.65 and 119.69, as applicable.
  (iii) The name and address of each person directly or indirectly controlling or controlled by the applicant and each person under direct or indirect control with the applicant.
 (2) For non-corporate applicants:
  (i) The name and address of each person having a financial interest therein and the nature and extent of that interest.
  (ii) The name and address of each person employed or who will be employed in a management position described in §§119.65 and 119.69, as applicable.

(c) In addition, each applicant for the original issue of an operating certificate under paragraph

(a) of this section must submit with the application a signed statement showing—

(1) The nature and scope of its intended operation, including the name and address of each person, if any, with whom the applicant has a contract to provide services as a commercial operator and the scope, nature, date, and duration of each of those contracts; and

(2) For applicants intending to conduct operations under part 121 of this chapter, the financial information listed in paragraph (e) of this section.

(d) Each applicant for, or holder of, a certificate issued under paragraph (a) of this section, shall notify the Administrator within 10 days after—

(1) A change in any of the persons, or the names and addresses of any of the persons, submitted to the Administrator under paragraph (b)(1) or (b)(2) of this section; or

(2) For applicants intending to conduct operations under part 121 of this chapter, a change in the financial information submitted to the Administrator under paragraph (e) of this section that occurs while the application for the issue is pending before the FAA and that would make the applicant's financial situation substantially less favorable than originally reported.

(e) Each applicant for the original issue of an operating certificate under paragraph (a) of this section who intends to conduct operations under part 121 of this chapter must submit the following financial information:

(1) A balance sheet that shows assets, liabilities, and net worth, as of a date not more than 60 days before the date of application.

(2) An itemization of liabilities more than 60 days past due on the balance sheet date, if any, showing each creditor's name and address, a description of the liability, and the amount and due date of the liability.

(3) An itemization of claims in litigation, if any, against the applicant as of the date of application showing each claimant's name and address and a description and the amount of the claim.

(4) A detailed projection of the proposed operation covering 6 complete months after the month in which the certificate is expected to be issued including—

(i) Estimated amount and source of both operating and nonoperating revenue, including identification of its existing and anticipated income producing contracts and estimated revenue per mile or hour of operation by aircraft type;

(ii) Estimated amount of operating and nonoperating expenses by expense objective classification; and

(iii) Estimated net profit or loss for the period.

(5) An estimate of the cash that will be needed for the proposed operations during the first 6 months after the month in which the certificate is expected to be issued, including—

(i) Acquisition of property and equipment (explain);

(ii) Retirement of debt (explain);

(iii) Additional working capital (explain);

(iv) Operating losses other than depreciation and amortization (explain); and

(v) Other (explain).

(6) An estimate of the cash that will be available during the first 6 months after the month in which the certificate is expected to be issued, from—

(i) Sale of property or flight equipment (explain);

(ii) New debt (explain);

(iii) New equity (explain);

(iv) Working capital reduction (explain);

(v) Operations (profits) (explain);

(vi) Depreciation and amortization (explain); and

(vii) Other (explain).

(7) A schedule of insurance coverage in effect on the balance sheet date showing insurance companies; policy numbers; types, amounts, and period of coverage; and special conditions, exclusions, and limitations.

(8) Any other financial information that the Administrator requires to enable him or her to determine that the applicant has sufficient financial resources to conduct his or her operations with the degree of safety required in the public interest.

(f) Each financial statement containing financial information required by paragraph (e) of this section must be based on accounts prepared and maintained on an accrual basis in accordance with generally accepted accounting principles applied on a consistent basis, and must contain the name and address of the applicant's public accounting firm, if any. Information submitted must be signed by an officer, owner, or partner of the applicant or certificate holder.

[Docket No. 28154, 62 FR 133254, March 19, 1999; as amended by Amdt. 119–3, 62 FR 15570, April 1, 1997]

§119.37 Contents of an Air Carrier Certificate or Operating Certificate.

The Air Carrier Certificate or Operating Certificate includes—

(a) The certificate holder's name;

(b) The location of the certificate holder's principal base of operations;

(c) The certificate number;

(d) The certificate's effective date; and

(e) The name or the designator of the certificate-holding district office.

§119.39 Issuing or denying a certificate.

(a) An applicant may be issued an Air Carrier Certificate or Operating Certificate if, after investigation, the Administrator finds that the applicant—

(1) Meets the applicable requirements of this part;

(2) Holds the economic authority applicable to the kinds of operations to be conducted, issued by the Department of Transportation, if required; and

(3) Is properly and adequately equipped in accordance with the requirements of this chapter and is able to conduct a safe operation under appropriate provisions of part 121 or part 135 of this chapter and operations specifications issued under this part.

(b) An application for a certificate may be denied if the Administrator finds that—

(1) The applicant is not properly or adequately equipped or is not able to conduct safe operations under this subchapter;

(2) The applicant previously held an Air Carrier Certificate or Operating Certificate which was revoked;

(3) The applicant intends to or fills a key management position listed in §119.65(a) or §119.69(a), as applicable, with an individual who exercised control over or who held the same or a similar position with a certificate holder whose certificate was revoked, or is in the process of being revoked, and that individual materially contributed to the circumstances causing revocation or causing the revocation process;

(4) An individual who will have control over or have a substantial ownership interest in the applicant had the same or similar control or interest in a certificate holder whose certificate was revoked, or is in the process of being revoked, and that individual materially contributed to the circumstances causing revocation or causing the revocation process; or

(5) In the case of an applicant for an Operating Certificate for intrastate common carriage, that for financial reasons the applicant is not able to conduct a safe operation.

§119.41 Amending a certificate.

(a) The Administrator may amend any certificate issued under this part if—

(1) The Administrator determines, under 49 U.S.C. 44709 and part 13 of this chapter, that safety in air commerce and the public interest requires the amendment; or

(2) The certificate holder applies for the amendment and the certificate-holding district office determines that safety in air commerce and the public interest allows the amendment.

(b) When the Administrator proposes to issue an order amending, suspending, or revoking all or part of any certificate, the procedure in §13.19 of this chapter applies.

(c) When the certificate holder applies for an amendment of its certificate, the following procedure applies:

(1) The certificate holder must file an application to amend its certificate with the certificate-holding district office at least 15 days before the date proposed by the applicant for the amendment to become effective, unless the administrator approves filing within a shorter period; and

(2) The application must be submitted to the certificate-holding district office in the form and manner prescribed by the Administrator.

(d) When a certificate holder seeks reconsideration of a decision from the certificate-holding district office concerning amendments of a certificate, the following procedure applies:

(1) The petition for reconsideration must be made within 30 days after the certificate holder receives the notice of denial; and

(2) The certificate holder must petition for reconsideration to the Director, Flight Standards Service.

§119.43 Certificate holder's duty to maintain operations specifications.

(a) Each certificate holder shall maintain a complete and separate set of its operations specifications at its principal base of operations.

(b) Each certificate holder shall insert pertinent excerpts of its operations specifications, or references thereto, in its manual and shall—

(1) Clearly identify each such excerpt as a part of its operations specifications; and

(2) State that compliance with each operations specifications requirement is mandatory.

(c) Each certificate holder shall keep each of its employees and other persons used in its operations informed of the provisions of its operations specifications that apply to that employee's or person's duties and responsibilities.

§119.45 [Reserved]

§119.47 Maintaining a principal base of operations, main operations base, and main maintenance base; change of address.

(a) Each certificate holder must maintain a principal base of operations. Each certificate holder may also establish a main operations base and a main maintenance base which may be located at either the same location as the principal base of operations or at separate locations.

(b) At least 30 days before it proposes to establish or change the location of its principal base of operations, its main operations base, or its main maintenance base, a certificate holder must provide written notification to its certificate-holding district office.

§119.49 Contents of operations specifications.

(a) Each certificate holder conducting domestic, flag, or commuter operations must obtain operations specifications containing all of the following:

(1) The specific location of the certificate holder's principal base of operations and, if different, the address that shall serve as the primary point of contact for correspondence between the FAA and the certificate holder and the name and mailing address of the certificate holder's agent for service.

(2) Other business names under which the certificate holder may operate.

(3) Reference to the economic authority issued by the Department of Transportation, if required.

(4) Type of aircraft, registration markings, and serial numbers of each aircraft authorized for use, each regular and alternate airport to be used in scheduled operations, and, except for commuter operations, each provisional and refueling airport.

(i) Subject to the approval of the Administrator with regard to form and content, the certificate holder may incorporate by reference the items listed in paragraph (a)(4) of this section into the certificate holder's operations specifications by maintaining a current listing of those items and by referring to the specific list in the applicable paragraph of the operations specifications.

(ii) The certificate holder may not conduct any operation using any aircraft or airport not listed.

(5) Kinds of operations authorized.

(6) Authorization and limitations for routes and areas of operations.

(7) Airport limitations.

(8) Time limitations, or standards for determining time limitations, for overhauling, inspecting, and checking airframes, engines, propellers, rotors, appliances, and emergency equipment.

(9) Authorization for the method of controlling weight and balance of aircraft.

(10) Interline equipment interchange requirements, if relevant.

(11) Aircraft wet lease information required by §119.21(a)(c).

(12) Any authorized deviation and exemption granted from any requirement of this chapter.

(13) An authorization permitting, or a prohibition against, accepting, handling, and transporting materials regulated as hazardous materials in transport under 49 CFR parts 171 through 180.

(14) Any other item the Administrator determines is necessary.

(b) Each certificate holder conducting supplemental operations must obtain operations specifications containing all of the following:

(1) The specific location of the certificate holder's principal base of operations, and, if different, the address that shall serve as the primary point of contact for correspondence between the FAA and the certificate holder and the name and mailing address of the certificate holder's agent for service.

(2) Other business names under which the certificate holder may operate.

(3) Reference to the economic authority issued by the Department of Transportation, if required.

(4) Type of aircraft, registration markings, and serial number of each aircraft authorized for use.

(i) Subject to the approval of the Administrator with regard to form and content, the certificate holder may incorporate by reference the items listed in paragraph (b)(4) of this section into the certificate holder's operations specifications by maintaining a current listing of those items and by referring to the specific list in the applicable paragraph of the operations specifications.

(ii) The certificate holder may not conduct any operation using any aircraft not listed.

(5) Kinds of operations authorized.

(6) Authorization and limitations for routes and areas of operations.

(7) Special airport authorizations and limitations.

(8) Time limitations, or standards for determining time limitations, for overhauling, inspecting, and checking airframes, engines, propellers, appliances, and emergency equipment.

(9) Authorization for the method of controlling weight and balance of aircraft.

(10) Aircraft wet lease information required by §119.53(c).

(11) Any authorization or requirement to conduct supplemental operations as provided by §119.21(a)(3).

(12) Any authorized deviation or exemption from any requirement of this chapter.

(13) An authorization permitting, or a prohibition against, accepting, handling, and transporting materials regulated as hazardous materials in transport under 49 CFR parts 171 through 180.

(14) Any other item the Administrator determines is necessary.

(c) Each certificate holder conducting on-demand operations must obtain operations specifications containing all of the following:

(1) The specific location of the certificate holder's principal base of operations, and if different, the address that shall serve as the primary point of contact for correspondence between the FAA and the name and mailing address of the certificate holder's agent for service.

(2) Other business names under which the certificate holder may operate.
(3) Reference to the economic authority issued by the Department of Transportation, if required.
(4) Kind and area of operations authorized.
(5) Category and class of aircraft that may be used in those operations.
(6) Type of aircraft, registration markings, and serial number of each aircraft that is subject to an airworthiness maintenance program required by §135.411(a)(2) of this chapter.
(i) Subject to the approval of the Administrator with regard to form and content, the certificate holder may incorporate by reference the items listed in paragraph (c)(6) of this section into the certificate holder's operations specifications by maintaining a current listing of those items and by referring to the specific list in the applicable paragraph of the operations specifications.
(ii) The certificate holder may not conduct any operation using any aircraft not listed.
(7) Registration markings of each aircraft that is to be inspected under an approved aircraft inspection program under §135.419 of this chapter.
(8) Time limitations or standards for determining time limitations, for overhauls, inspections, and checks for airframes, engines, propellers, rotors, appliances, and emergency equipment of aircraft that are subject to an airworthiness maintenance program required by §135.411(a)(2) of this chapter.
(9) Additional maintenance items required by the Administrator under §135.421 of this chapter.
(10) Aircraft wet lease information required by §119.53(c).
(11) Any authorized deviation or exemption from any requirement of this chapter.
(12) An authorization permitting, or a prohibition against, accepting, handling, and transporting materials regulated as hazardous materials in transport under 49 CFR parts 171 through 180.
(13) Any other item the Administrator determines is necessary.

[Docket No. 28154, 60 FR 65913, Dec. 20, 1995; as amended by Amdt. 119–10, 70 FR 58823, Oct. 7, 2005; Amdt. 119–13, 75 FR 26645, May 12, 2010]

§119.51 Amending operations specifications.

(a) The Administrator may amend any operations specifications issued under this part if—
(1) The Administrator determines that safety in air commerce and the public interest require the amendment; or
(2) The certificate holder applies for the amendment, and the Administrator determines that safety in air commerce and the public interest allows the amendment.

(b) Except as provided in paragraph (e) of this section, when the Administrator initiates an amendment to a certificate holder's operations specifications, the following procedure applies:
(1) The certificate-holding district office notifies the certificate holder in writing of the proposed amendment.
(2) The certificate-holding district office sets a reasonable period (but not less than 7 days) within which the certificate holder may submit written information, views, and arguments on the amendment.
(3) After considering all material presented, the certificate-holding district office notifies the certificate holder of—
(i) The adoption of the proposed amendment;
(ii) The partial adoption of the proposed amendment; or
(iii) The withdrawal of the proposed amendment.
(4) If the certificate-holding district office issues an amendment to the operations specifications, it becomes effective not less than 30 days after the certificate holder receives notice of it unless—
(i) The certificate-holding district office finds under paragraph (e) of this section that there is an emergency requiring immediate action with respect to safety in air commerce; or
(ii) The certificate holder petitions for reconsideration of the amendment under paragraph (d) of this section.

(c) When the certificate holder applies for an amendment to its operations specifications, the following procedure applies:
(1) The certificate holder must file an application to amend its operations specifications—
(i) At least 90 days before the date proposed by the applicant for the amendment to become effective, unless a shorter time is approved, in cases of mergers; acquisitions of airline operational assets that require an additional showing of safety (e.g., proving tests); changes in the kind of operation as defined in §110.2; resumption of operations following a suspension of operations as a result of bankruptcy actions; or the initial introduction of aircraft not before proven for use in air carrier or commercial operator operations.
(ii) At least 15 days before the date proposed by the applicant for the amendment to become effective in all other cases.
(2) The application must be submitted to the certificate-holding district office in a form and manner prescribed by the Administrator.
(3) After considering all material presented, the certificate-holding district office notifies the certificate holder of—
(i) The adoption of the applied for amendment;
(ii) The partial adoption of the applied for amendment; or

(iii) The denial of the applied for amendment. The certificate holder may petition for reconsideration of a denial under paragraph (d) of this section.

(4) If the certificate-holding district office approves the amendment, following coordination with the certificate holder regarding its implementation, the amendment is effective on the date the Administrator approves it.

(d) When a certificate holder seeks reconsideration of a decision from the certificate-holding district office concerning the amendment of operations specifications, the following procedure applies:

(1) The certificate holder must petition for reconsideration of that decision within 30 days of the date that the certificate holder receives a notice of denial of the amendment to its operations specifications, or of the date it receives notice of an FAA-initiated amendment to its operations specifications, whichever circumstance applies.

(2) The certificate holder must address its petition to the Director, Flight Standards Service.

(3) A petition for reconsideration, if filed within the 30-day period, suspends the effectiveness of any amendment issued by the certificate-holding district office unless the certificate-holding district office has found, under paragraph (e) of this section, that an emergency exists requiring immediate action with respect to safety in air transportation or air commerce.

(4) If a petition for reconsideration is not filed within 30 days, the procedures of paragraph (c) of this section apply.

(e) If the certificate-holding district office finds that an emergency exists requiring immediate action with respect to safety in air commerce or air transportation that makes the procedures set out in this section impracticable or contrary to the public interest:

(1) The certificate-holding district office amends the operations specifications and makes the amendment effective on the day the certificate holder receives notice of it.

(2) In the notice to the certificate holder, the certificate-holding district office articulates the reasons for its finding that an emergency exists requiring immediate action with respect to safety in air transportation or air commerce or that makes it impracticable or contrary to the public interest to stay the effectiveness of the amendment.

§119.53 Wet leasing of aircraft and other arrangements for transportation by air.

(a) Unless otherwise authorized by the Administrator, prior to conducting operations involving a wet lease, each certificate holder under this part authorized to conduct common carriage operations under this subchapter shall provide the Administrator with a copy of the wet lease to be executed which would lease the aircraft to any other person engaged in common carriage operations under this subchapter, including foreign air carriers, or to any other foreign person engaged in common carriage wholly outside the United States.

(b) No certificate holder under this part may wet lease from a foreign air carrier or any other foreign person or any person not authorized to engage in common carriage.

(c) Upon receiving a copy of a wet lease, the Administrator determines which party to the agreement has operational control of the aircraft and issues amendments to the operations specifications of each party to the agreement, as needed. The lessor must provide the following information to be incorporated into the operations specifications of both parties, as needed.

(1) The names of the parties to the agreement and the duration thereof.

(2) The nationality and registration markings of each aircraft involved in the agreement.

(3) The kind of operation (e.g., domestic, flag, supplemental, commuter, or on-demand).

(4) The airports or areas of operation.

(5) A statement specifying the party deemed to have operational control and the times, airports, or areas under which such operational control is exercised.

(d) In making the determination of paragraph (c) of this section, the Administrator will consider the following:

(1) Crewmembers and training.

(2) Airworthiness and performance of maintenance.

(3) Dispatch.

(4) Servicing the aircraft.

(5) Scheduling.

(6) Any other factor the Administrator considers relevant.

(e) Other arrangements for transportation by air: Except as provided in paragraph (f) of this section, a certificate holder under this part operating under part 121 or 135 of this chapter may not conduct any operation for another certificate holder under this part or a foreign air carrier under part 129 of this chapter or a foreign person engaged in common carriage wholly outside the United States unless it holds applicable Department of Transportation economic authority, if required, and is authorized under its operations specifications to conduct the same kinds of operations (as defined in §110.2). The certificate holder conducting the substitute operation must conduct that operation in accordance with the same operations authority held by the certificate holder arranging for the substitute operation. These substitute operations must be conducted between airports for which the substitute certificate holder holds authority for scheduled operations or within areas of operations for which the substitute certificate holder has authority for supplemental or on-demand operations.

(f) A certificate holder under this part may, if authorized by the Department of Transportation under §380.3 of this title and the Administrator in the case of interstate commuter, interstate domestic, and flag operations, or the Administrator in the case of scheduled intrastate common carriage operations, conduct one or more flights for passengers who are stranded because of the cancellation of their scheduled flights. These flights must be conducted under the rules of part 121 or part 135 of this chapter applicable to supplemental or on-demand operations.

§119.55 Obtaining deviation authority to perform operations under a U.S. military contract.

(a) The Administrator may authorize a certificate holder that is authorized to conduct supplemental or on-demand operations to deviate from the applicable requirements of this part, part 117, part 121, or part 135 of this chapter in order to perform operations under a U.S. military contract.

(b) A certificate holder that has a contract with the U.S. Department of Defense's Air Mobility Command (AMC) must submit a request for deviation authority to AMC. AMC will review the requests, then forward the carriers' consolidated requests, along with AMC's recommendations, to the FAA for review and action.

(c) The Administrator may authorize a deviation to perform operations under a U.S. military contract under the following conditions—

(1) The Department of Defense certifies to the Administrator that the operation is essential to the national defense;

(2) The Department of Defense further certifies that the certificate holder cannot perform the operation without deviation authority;

(3) The certificate holder will perform the operation under a contract or subcontract for the benefit of a U.S. armed service; and

(4) The Administrator finds that the deviation is based on grounds other than economic advantage either to the certificate holder or to the United States.

(d) In the case where the Administrator authorizes a deviation under this section, the Administrator will issue an appropriate amendment to the certificate holder's operations specifications.

(e) The Administrator may, at any time, terminate any grant of deviation authority issued under this section.

[Docket No. 28154, 60 FR 65913, Dec. 20, 1995; as amended by Amdt. 119-16, 77 FR 402, Jan. 4, 2012; Amdt. 119-16A, 77 FR 28763, May 16, 2012]

§119.57 Obtaining deviation authority to perform an emergency operation.

(a) In emergency conditions, the Administrator may authorize deviations if—

(1) Those conditions necessitate the transportation of persons or supplies for the protection of life or property; and

(2) The Administrator finds that a deviation is necessary for the expeditious conduct of the operations.

(b) When the Administrator authorizes deviations for operations under emergency conditions—

(1) The Administrator will issue an appropriate amendment to the certificate holder's operations specifications; or

(2) If the nature of the emergency does not permit timely amendment of the operations specifications—

(i) The Administrator may authorize the deviation orally; and

(ii) The certificate holder shall provide documentation describing the nature of the emergency to the certificate-holding district office within 24 hours after completing the operation.

§119.59 Conducting tests and inspections.

(a) At any time or place, the Administrator may conduct an inspection or test to determine whether a certificate holder under this part is complying with title 49 of the United States Code, applicable regulations, the certificate, or the certificate holder's operations specifications.

(b) The certificate holder must—

(1) Make available to the Administrator at the certificate holder's principal base of operations—

(i) The certificate holder's Air Carrier Certificate or the certificate holder's Operating Certificate and the certificate holder's operations specifications; and

(ii) A current listing that will include the location and persons responsible for each record, document, and report required to be kept by the certificate holder under title 49 of the United States Code applicable to the operation of the certificate holder.

(2) Allow the Administrator to make any test or inspection to determine compliance respecting any matter stated in paragraph (a) of this section.

(c) Each employee of, or person used by, the certificate holder who is responsible for maintaining the certificate holder's records must make those records available to the Administrator.

(d) The Administrator may determine a certificate holder's continued eligibility to hold its certificate and/or operations specifications on any grounds listed in paragraph (a) of this section, or any other appropriate grounds.

(e) Failure by any certificate holder to make available to the Administrator upon request, the certificate, operations specifications, or any required record, document, or report is grounds for suspension of all or any part of the certificate holder's certificate and operations specifications.

(f) In the case of operators conducting intrastate common carriage operations, these inspections and tests include inspections and tests of financial books and records.

§119.61 Duration and surrender of certificate and operations specifications.

(a) An Air Carrier Certificate or Operating Certificate issued under this part is effective until—

(1) The certificate holder surrenders it to the Administrator; or

(2) The Administrator suspends, revokes, or otherwise terminates the certificate.

(b) Operations specifications issued under this part, part 121, or part 135 of this chapter are effective unless—

(1) The Administrator suspends, revokes, or otherwise terminates the certificate;

(2) The operations specifications are amended as provided in §119.51;

(3) The certificate holder does not conduct a kind of operation for more than the time specified in §119.63 and fails to follow the procedures of §119.63 upon resuming that kind of operation; or

(4) The Administrator suspends or revokes the operations specifications for a kind of operation.

(c) Within 30 days after a certificate holder terminates operations under part 135 of this chapter, the operating certificate and operations specifications must be surrendered by the certificate holder to the certificate-holding district office.

§119.63 Recency of operation.

(a) Except as provided in paragraph (b) of this section, no certificate holder may conduct a kind of operation for which it holds authority in its operations specifications unless the certificate holder has conducted that kind of operation within the preceding number of consecutive calendar days specified in this paragraph:

(1) For domestic, flag, or commuter operations—30 days.

(2) For supplemental or on-demand operations—90 days, except that if the certificate holder has authority to conduct domestic, flag, or commuter operations, and has conducted domestic, flag or commuter operations within the previous 30 days, this paragraph does not apply.

(b) If a certificate holder does not conduct a kind of operation for which it is authorized in its operations specifications within the number of calendar days specified in paragraph (a) of this section, it shall not conduct such kind of operation unless—

(1) It advises the Administrator at least 5 consecutive calendar days before resumption of that kind of operation; and

(2) It makes itself available and accessible during the 5 consecutive calendar day period in the event that the FAA decides to conduct a full inspection reexamination to determine whether the certificate holder remains properly and adequately equipped and able to conduct a safe operation.

[Docket No. 28154, 60 FR 65913, Dec. 20, 1995; as amended by Amdt. 119–2, 61 FR 30434, June 14, 1996]

§119.65 Management personnel required for operations conducted under part 121 of this chapter.

(a) Each certificate holder must have sufficient qualified management and technical personnel to ensure the highest degree of safety in its operations. The certificate holder must have qualified personnel serving full-time in the following or equivalent positions:

(1) Director of Safety.
(2) Director of Operations.
(3) Chief Pilot.
(4) Director of Maintenance.
(5) Chief Inspector.

(b) The Administrator may approve positions or numbers of positions other than those listed in paragraph (a) of this section for a particular operation if the certificate holder shows that it can perform the operation with the highest degree of safety under the direction of fewer or different categories of management personnel due to—

(1) The kind of operation involved;
(2) The number and type of airplanes used; and
(3) The area of operations.

(c) The title of the positions required under paragraph (a) of this section or the title and number of equivalent positions approved under paragraph (b) of this section shall be set forth in the certificate holder's operations specifications.

(d) The individuals who serve in the positions required or approved under paragraph (a) or (b)

of this section and anyone in a position to exercise control over operations conducted under the operating certificate must—
(1) Be qualified through training, experience, and expertise;
(2) To the extent of their responsibilities, have a full understanding of the following materials with respect to the certificate holder's operation—
(i) Aviation safety standards and safe operating practices;
(ii) 14 CFR Chapter I (Federal Aviation Regulations);
(iii) The certificate holder's operations specifications;
(iv) All appropriate maintenance and airworthiness requirements of this chapter (e.g., parts 1, 21, 23, 25, 43, 45, 47, 65, 91, and 121 of this chapter); and
(v) The manual required by §121.133 of this chapter; and
(3) Discharge their duties to meet applicable legal requirements and to maintain safe operations.
(e) Each certificate holder must:
(1) State in the general policy provisions of the manual required by §121.133 of this chapter, the duties, responsibilities, and authority of personnel required under paragraph (a) of this section;
(2) List in the manual the names and business addresses of the individuals assigned to those positions; and
(3) Notify the certificate-holding district office within 10 days of any change in personnel or any vacancy in any position listed.

§119.67 Management personnel: Qualifications for operations conducted under part 121 of this chapter.

(a) To serve as Director of Operations under §119.65(a) a person must—
(1) Hold an airline transport pilot certificate;
(2) Have at least 3 years supervisory or managerial experience within the last 6 years in a position that exercised operational control over any operations conducted with large airplanes under part 121 or part 135 of this chapter, or if the certificate holder uses only small airplanes in its operations, the experience may be obtained in large or small airplanes; and
(3) In the case of a person becoming a Director of Operations—
(i) For the first time ever, have at least 3 years experience, within the past 6 years, as pilot in command of a large airplane operated under part 121 or part 135 of this chapter, if the certificate holder operates large airplanes. If the certificate holder uses only small airplanes in its operation, the experience may be obtained in either large or small airplanes.
(ii) In the case of a person with previous experience as a Director of Operations, have at least 3 years experience as pilot in command of a large airplane operated under part 121 or part 135 of this chapter, if the certificate holder operates large airplanes. If the certificate holder uses only small airplanes in its operation, the experience may be obtained in either large or small airplanes.

(b) To serve as Chief Pilot under §119.65(a) a person must hold an airline transport pilot certificate with appropriate ratings for at least one of the airplanes used in the certificate holder's operation and:
(1) In the case of a person becoming a Chief Pilot for the first time ever, have at least 3 years experience, within the past 6 years, as pilot in command of a large airplane operated under part 121 or part 135 of this chapter, if the certificate holder operates large airplanes. If the certificate holder uses only small airplanes in its operation, the experience may be obtained in either large or small airplanes.
(2) In the case of a person with previous experience as a Chief Pilot, have at least 3 years experience, as pilot in command of a large airplane operated under part 121 or part 135 of this chapter, if the certificate holder operates large airplanes. If the certificate holder uses only small airplanes in its operation, the experience may be obtained in either large or small airplanes.

(c) To serve as Director of Maintenance under §119.65(a) a person must—
(1) Hold a mechanic certificate with airframe and powerplant ratings;
(2) Have 1 year of experience in a position responsible for returning airplanes to service;
(3) Have at least 1 year of experience in a supervisory capacity under either paragraph (c)(4)(i) or (c)(4)(ii) of this section maintaining the same category and class of airplane as the certificate holder uses; and
(4) Have 3 years experience within the past 6 years in one or a combination of the following—
(i) Maintaining large airplanes with 10 or more passenger seats, including at the time of appointment as Director of Maintenance, experience in maintaining the same category and class of airplane as the certificate holder uses; or
(ii) Repairing airplanes in a certificated airframe repair station that is rated to maintain airplanes in the same category and class of airplane as the certificate holder uses.

(d) To serve as Chief Inspector under §119.65(a) a person must—
(1) Hold a mechanic certificate with both airframe and powerplant ratings, and have held these ratings for at least 3 years;

§119.69

(2) Have at least 3 years of maintenance experience on different types of large airplanes with 10 or more passenger seats with an air carrier or certificated repair station, 1 year of which must have been as maintenance inspector; and

(3) Have at least 1 year of experience in a supervisory capacity maintaining the same category and class of aircraft as the certificate holder uses.

(e) A certificate holder may request a deviation to employ a person who does not meet the appropriate airman experience, managerial experience, or supervisory experience requirements of this section if the Manager of the Air Transportation Division, AFS–200, or the Manager of the Aircraft Maintenance Division, AFS–300, as appropriate, finds that the person has comparable experience, and can effectively perform the functions associated with the position in accordance with the requirements of this chapter and the procedures outlined in the certificate holder's manual. Grants of deviation under this paragraph may be granted after consideration of the size and scope of the operation and the qualifications of the intended personnel. The Administrator may, at any time, terminate any grant of deviation authority issued under this paragraph.

[Docket No. 28154, 60 FR 65913, Dec. 20, 1995; as amended by Amdt. 119–2, 61 FR 30434, June 14, 1996; Amdt. 119–3, 62 FR 13255, March 19, 1997]

§119.69 Management personnel required for operations conducted under part 135 of this chapter.

(a) Each certificate holder must have sufficient qualified management and technical personnel to ensure the safety of its operations. Except for a certificate holder using only one pilot in its operations, the certificate holder must have qualified personnel serving in the following or equivalent positions:

(1) Director of Operations.
(2) Chief Pilot.
(3) Director of Maintenance.

(b) The Administrator may approve positions or numbers of positions other than those listed in paragraph (a) of this section for a particular operation if the certificate holder shows that it can perform the operation with the highest degree of safety under the direction of fewer or different categories of management personnel due to—

(1) The kind of operation involved;
(2) The number and type of aircraft used; and
(3) The area of operations.

(c) The title of the positions required under paragraph (a) of this section or the title and number of equivalent positions approved under paragraph (b) of this section shall be set forth in the certificate holder's operations specifications.

(d) The individuals who serve in the positions required or approved under paragraph (a) or (b) of this section and anyone in a position to exercise control over operations conducted under the operating certificate must—

(1) Be qualified through training, experience, and expertise;

(2) To the extent of their responsibilities, have a full understanding of the following material with respect to the certificate holder's operation—

(i) Aviation safety standards and safe operating practices;

(ii) 14 CFR Chapter I (Federal Aviation Regulations);

(iii) The certificate holder's operations specifications;

(iv) All appropriate maintenance and airworthiness requirements of this chapter (e.g., parts 1, 21, 23, 25, 43, 45, 47, 65, 91, and 135 of this chapter); and

(v) The manual required by §135.21 of this chapter; and

(3) Discharge their duties to meet applicable legal requirements and to maintain safe operations.

(e) Each certificate holder must—

(1) State in the general policy provisions of the manual required by §135.21 of this chapter, the duties, responsibilities, and authority of personnel required or approved under paragraph (a) or (b), respectively, of this section;

(2) List in the manual the names and business addresses of the individuals assigned to those positions; and

(3) Notify the certificate-holding district office within 10 days of any change in personnel or any vacancy in any position listed.

§119.71 Management personnel: Qualifications for operations conducted under part 135 of this chapter.

(a) To serve as Director of Operations under §119.69(a) for a certificate holder conducting any operations for which the pilot in command is required to hold an airline transport pilot certificate a person must hold an airline transport pilot certificate and either:

(1) Have at least 3 years supervisory or managerial experience within the last 6 years in a position that exercised operational control over any operations conducted under part 121 or part 135 of this chapter; or

(2) In the case of a person becoming Director of Operations—

(i) For the first time ever, have at least 3 years experience, within the past 6 years, as pilot in command of an aircraft operated under part 121 or part 135 of this chapter.

(ii) In the case of a person with previous experience as a Director of Operations, have at least 3 years experience, as pilot in command of an aircraft operated under part 121 or part 135 of this chapter.

(b) To serve as Director of Operations under §119.69(a) for a certificate holder that only conducts operations for which the pilot in command is required to hold a commercial pilot certificate, a person must hold at least a commercial pilot certificate. If an instrument rating is required for any pilot in command for that certificate holder, the Director of Operations must also hold an instrument rating. In addition, the Director of Operations must either—

(1) Have at least 3 years supervisory or managerial experience within the last 6 years in a position that exercised operational control over any operations conducted under part 121 or part 135 of this chapter; or

(2) In the case of a person becoming Director of Operations—

(i) For the first time ever, have at least 3 years experience, within the past 6 years, as pilot in command of an aircraft operated under part 121 or part 135 of this chapter.

(ii) In the case of a person with previous experience as a Director of Operations, have at least 3 years experience as pilot in command of an aircraft operated under part 121 or part 135 of this chapter.

(c) To serve as Chief Pilot under §119.69(a) for a certificate holder conducting any operation for which the pilot in command is required to hold an airline transport pilot certificate a person must hold an airline transport pilot certificate with appropriate ratings and be qualified to serve as pilot in command in at least one aircraft used in the certificate holder's operation and:

(1) In the case of a person becoming a Chief Pilot for the first time ever, have at least 3 years experience, within the past 6 years, as pilot in command of an aircraft operated under part 121 or part 135 of this chapter.

(2) In the case of a person with previous experience as a Chief Pilot, have at least 3 years experience as pilot in command of an aircraft operated under part 121 or part 135 of this chapter.

(d) To serve as Chief Pilot under §119.69(a) for a certificate holder that only conducts operations for which the pilot in command is required to hold a commercial pilot certificate, a person must hold at least a commercial pilot certificate. If an instrument rating is required for any pilot in command for that certificate holder, the Chief Pilot must also hold an instrument rating. The Chief Pilot must be qualified to serve as pilot in command in at least one aircraft used in the certificate holder's operation. In addition, the Chief Pilot must:

(1) In the case of a person becoming a Chief Pilot for the first time ever, have at least 3 years experience, within the past 6 years, as pilot in command of an aircraft operated under part 121 or part 135 of this chapter.

(2) In the case of a person with previous experience as a Chief Pilot, have at least 3 years experience as pilot in command of an aircraft operated under part 121 or part 135 of this chapter.

(e) To serve as Director of Maintenance under §119.69(a) a person must hold a mechanic certificate with airframe and powerplant ratings and either:

(1) Have 3 years of experience within the past 6 years maintaining aircraft as a certificated mechanic, including, at the time of appointment as Director of Maintenance, experience in maintaining the same category and class of aircraft as the certificate holder uses; or

(2) Have 3 years of experience within the past 6 years repairing aircraft in a certificated airframe repair station, including 1 year in the capacity of approving aircraft for return to service.

(f) A certificate holder may request a deviation to employ a person who does not meet the appropriate airmen experience requirements, managerial experience requirements, or supervisory experience requirements of this section if the Manager of the Air Transportation Division, AFS–200, or the Manager of the Aircraft Maintenance Division, AFS–300, as appropriate, find that the person has comparable experience, and can effectively perform the functions associated with the position in accordance with the requirements of this chapter and the procedures outlined in the certificate holder's manual. Grants of deviation under this paragraph may be granted after consideration of the size and scope of the operation and the qualifications of the intended personnel. The Administrator may, at any time, terminate any grant of deviation authority issued under this paragraph.

[Docket No. 28154, 60 FR 65913, Dec. 20, 1995; as amended by Amdt. 119–3, 62 FR 13255, March 19, 1997; Amdt. 119–12, 72 FR 54816, Sept. 27, 2007]

§119.73 Employment of former FAA employees.

(a) Except as specified in paragraph (c) of this section, no certificate holder conducting operations under part 121 or 135 of this chapter may knowingly employ or make a contractual arrangement which permits an individual to act as an agent or representative of the certificate holder in any matter before the Federal Aviation Administration if the individual, in the preceding 2 years—

(1) Served as, or was directly responsible for the oversight of, a Flight Standards Service aviation safety inspector; and

(2) Had direct responsibility to inspect, or oversee the inspection of, the operations of the certificate holder.

(b) For the purpose of this section, an individual shall be considered to be acting as an agent or representative of a certificate holder in a matter before the agency if the individual makes any written or oral communication on behalf of the certificate holder to the agency (or any of its officers or employees) in connection with a particular matter, whether or not involving a specific party and without regard to whether the individual has participated in, or had responsibility for, the particular matter while serving as a Flight Standards Service aviation safety inspector.

(c) The provisions of this section do not prohibit a certificate holder from knowingly employing or making a contractual arrangement which permits an individual to act as an agent or representative of the certificate holder in any matter before the Federal Aviation Administration if the individual was employed by the certificate holder before October 21, 2011.

[Docket No. FAA–2008–1154, 76 FR 52235, Aug. 22, 2011]

14 CFR • Subchapter G—Air Carriers and Operators for Compensation or Hire: Certification and Operations

PART 120
DRUG AND ALCOHOL TESTING PROGRAM

Subpart A—General

Sec.
120.1 Applicability.
120.3 Purpose.
120.5 Procedures.
120.7 Definitions.

Subpart B—Individuals Certificated Under Parts 61, 63, and 65

120.11 Refusal to submit to a drug or alcohol test by a Part 61 certificate holder.
120.13 Refusal to submit to a drug or alcohol test by a Part 63 certificate holder.
120.15 Refusal to submit to a drug or alcohol test by a Part 65 certificate holder.

Subpart C—Air Traffic Controllers

120.17 Use of prohibited drugs.
120.19 Misuse of alcohol.
120.21 Testing for alcohol.

Subpart D—Part 119 Certificate Holders Authorized To Conduct Operations Under Part 121 or Part 135 or Operators Under §91.147 of This Chapter and Safety-Sensitive Employees

120.31 Prohibited drugs.
120.33 Use of prohibited drugs.
120.35 Testing for prohibited drugs.
120.37 Misuse of alcohol.
120.39 Testing for alcohol.

Subpart E—Drug Testing Program Requirements

120.101 Scope.
120.103 General.
*120.105 **Employees who must be tested.**
120.107 Substances for which testing must be conducted.
120.109 Types of drug testing required.
120.111 Administrative and other matters.
120.113 Medical Review Officer, Substance Abuse Professional, and employer responsibilities.
*120.115 **Employee Assistance Program (EAP).**
*120.117 **Implementing a drug testing program.**
120.119 Annual reports.
120.121 Preemption.
120.123 Drug testing outside the territory of the United States.
120.125 Waivers from 49 CFR 40.21.

Subpart F—Alcohol Testing Program Requirements

120.201 Scope.
120.203 General.
120.205 Preemption of State and local laws.
120.207 Other requirements imposed by employers.
120.209 Requirement for notice.
120.211 Applicable Federal regulations.
120.213 Falsification.
*120.215 **Covered employees.**
120.217 Tests required.
120.219 Handling of test results, record retention, and confidentiality.
*120.221 **Consequences for employees engaging in alcohol-related conduct.**
120.223 Alcohol misuse information, training, and substance abuse professionals.
*120.225 **How to implement an alcohol testing program.**
120.227 Employees located outside the U.S.

Authority: 49 U.S.C. 106(f), 106(g), 40101–40103, 40113, 40120, 41706, 41721, 44106, 44701, 44702, 44703, 44709, 44710, 44711, 45101–45105, 46105, 46306.

Source: Docket No. FAA–2008–0937, 74 FR 22653, May 14, 2009, unless otherwise noted.

Subpart A—General

§120.1 Applicability.

This part applies to the following persons:

(a) All air carriers and operators certificated under part 119 of this chapter authorized to conduct operations under part 121 or part 135 of this chapter, all air traffic control facilities not operated by the FAA or by or under contract to the U.S. military; and all operators as defined in 14 CFR 91.147.

(b) All individuals who perform, either directly or by contract, a safety-sensitive function listed in subpart E or subpart F of this part.

(c) All part 145 certificate holders who perform safety-sensitive functions and elect to implement a drug and alcohol testing program under this part.

(d) All contractors who elect to implement a drug and alcohol testing program under this part.

§120.3 Purpose.

The purpose of this part is to establish a program designed to help prevent accidents and injuries resulting from the use of prohibited drugs or the misuse of alcohol by employees who perform safety-sensitive functions in aviation.

§120.5 Procedures.

Each employer having a drug and alcohol testing program under this part must ensure that all drug and alcohol testing conducted pursuant to this part complies with the procedures set forth in 49 CFR part 40.

§120.7 Definitions.

For the purposes of this part, the following definitions apply:

(a) *Accident* means an occurrence associated with the operation of an aircraft which takes place between the time any individual boards the aircraft with the intention of flight and all such individuals have disembarked, and in which any individual suffers death or serious injury, or in which the aircraft receives substantial damage.

(b) *Alcohol* means the intoxicating agent in beverage alcohol, ethyl alcohol, or other low molecular weight alcohols, including methyl or isopropyl alcohol.

(c) *Alcohol concentration (or content)* means the alcohol in a volume of breath expressed in terms of grams of alcohol per 210 liters of breath as indicated by an evidential breath test under subpart F of this part.

(d) *Alcohol use* means the consumption of any beverage, mixture, or preparation, including any medication, containing alcohol.

(e) *Contractor* is an individual or company that performs a safety-sensitive function by contract for an employer or another contractor.

(f) *Covered employee* means an individual who performs, either directly or by contract, a safety-sensitive function listed in §§120.105 and 120.215 for an employer (as defined in paragraph (i) of this section). For purposes of pre-employment testing only, the term "covered employee" includes an individual applying to perform a safety-sensitive function.

(g) *DOT agency* means an agency (or "operating administration") of the United States Department of Transportation administering regulations requiring drug and alcohol testing (14 CFR parts 61, 65, 121, and 135; 46 CFR part 16; 49 CFR parts 199, 219, and 382) in accordance with 49 CFR part 40.

(h) *Employee* is an individual who is hired, either directly or by contract, to perform a safety-sensitive function for an employer, as defined in paragraph (i) of this section. An employee is also an individual who transfers into a position to perform a safety-sensitive function for an employer.

(i) *Employer* is a part 119 certificate holder with authority to operate under parts 121 and/or 135 of this chapter, an operator as defined in §91.147 of this chapter, or an air traffic control facility not operated by the FAA or by or under contract to the U.S. Military. An employer may use a contract employee who is not included under that employer's FAA-mandated drug and alcohol testing program to perform a safety-sensitive function only if that contract employee is included under the contractor's FAA-mandated drug and alcohol testing program and is performing a safety-sensitive function on behalf of that contractor (i.e., within the scope of employment with the contractor.)

(j) *Hire* means retaining an individual for a safety-sensitive function as a paid employee, as a volunteer, or through barter or other form of compensation.

(k) *Performing (a safety-sensitive function):* an employee is considered to be performing a safety-sensitive function during any period in which he or she is actually performing, ready to perform, or immediately available to perform such function.

(l) *Positive rate for random drug testing* means the number of verified positive results for random drug tests conducted under subpart E of this part, plus the number of refusals of random drug tests required by subpart E of this part, divided by the total number of random drug test results (i.e., positives, negatives, and refusals) under subpart E of this part.

(m) *Prohibited drug* means marijuana, cocaine, opiates, phencyclidine (PCP), and amphetamines, as specified in 49 CFR 40.85.

(n) Refusal to submit to alcohol test means that a covered employee has engaged in conduct including but not limited to that described in 49 CFR 40.261, or has failed to remain readily available for post-accident testing as required by subpart F of this part.

(o) Refusal to submit to drug test means that an employee engages in conduct including but not limited to that described in 49 CFR 40.191.

(p) Safety-sensitive function means a function listed in §§120.105 and 120.215.

(q) Verified negative drug test result means a drug test result from an HHS-certified laboratory that has undergone review by an MRO and has been determined by the MRO to be a negative result.

(r) Verified positive drug test result means a drug test result from an HHS-certified laboratory that has undergone review by an MRO and has been determined by the MRO to be a positive result.

(s) Violation rate for random alcohol testing means the number of 0.04, and above, random alcohol confirmation test results conducted under subpart F of this part, plus the number of refusals of random alcohol tests required by subpart F of this part, divided by the total number of random alcohol screening tests (including refusals) conducted under subpart F of this part.

[Docket No. FAA–2008–0937, 74 FR 22653, May 14, 2009; as amended by Amdt. 120–0A, 75 FR 3153, Jan. 20, 2010]

Subpart B— Individuals Certificated Under Parts 61, 63, and 65

§120.11 Refusal to submit to a drug or alcohol test by a Part 61 certificate holder.

(a) This section applies to all individuals who hold a certificate under part 61 of this chapter and who are subject to drug and alcohol testing under this part.

(b) Refusal by the holder of a certificate issued under part 61 of this chapter to take a drug or alcohol test required under the provisions of this part is grounds for:

(1) Denial of an application for any certificate, rating, or authorization issued under part 61 of this chapter for a period of up to 1 year after the date of such refusal; and

(2) Suspension or revocation of any certificate, rating, or authorization issued under part 61 of this chapter.

§120.13 Refusal to submit to a drug or alcohol test by a Part 63 certificate holder.

(a) This section applies to all individuals who hold a certificate under part 63 of this chapter and who are subject to drug and alcohol testing under this part.

(b) Refusal by the holder of a certificate issued under part 63 of this chapter to take a drug or alcohol test required under the provisions of this part is grounds for:

(1) Denial of an application for any certificate or rating issued under part 63 of this chapter for a period of up to 1 year after the date of such refusal; and

(2) Suspension or revocation of any certificate or rating issued under part 63 of this chapter.

[Docket No. FAA–2008–0937, 74 FR 22653, May 14, 2009; as amended by Amdt. 120–0A, 75 FR 3153, Jan. 20, 2010]

§120.15 Refusal to submit to a drug or alcohol test by a Part 65 certificate holder.

(a) This section applies to all individuals who hold a certificate under part 65 of this chapter and who are subject to drug and alcohol testing under this part.

(b) Refusal by the holder of a certificate issued under part 65 of this chapter to take a drug or alcohol test required under the provisions of this part is grounds for:

(1) Denial of an application for any certificate or rating issued under part 65 of this chapter for a period of up to 1 year after the date of such refusal; and

(2) Suspension or revocation of any certificate or rating issued under part 65 of this chapter.

[Docket No. FAA–2008–0937, 74 FR 22653, May 14, 2009; as amended by Amdt. 120–0A, 75 FR 3153, Jan. 20, 2010]

Subpart C— Air Traffic Controllers

§120.17 Use of prohibited drugs.

(a) Each employer shall provide each employee performing a function listed in subpart E of this part, and his or her supervisor, with the training specified in that subpart. No employer may use any contractor to perform an air traffic control function unless that contractor provides each of its employees performing that function for the employer, and his or her supervisor, with the training specified in subpart E of this part.

(b) No employer may knowingly use any individual to perform, nor may any individual perform for an employer, either directly or by contract, any air traffic control function while that individual has a prohibited drug, as defined in this part, in his or her system.

(c) No employer shall knowingly use any individual to perform, nor may any individual perform for an employer, either directly or by contract, any air traffic control function if the individual has a verified positive drug test result on, or has refused to submit to, a drug test required by subpart E of this part and the individual has not met the requirements of subpart E of this part for returning to the performance of safety-sensitive duties.

(d) Each employer shall test each of its employees who perform any air traffic control function in accordance with subpart E of this part. No employer may use any contractor to perform any air traffic control function unless that contractor tests each employee performing such a function for the employer in accordance with subpart E of this part.

[Docket No. FAA–2008–0937, 74 FR 22653, May 14, 2009; as amended by Amdt. 120–0A, 75 FR 3153, Jan. 20, 2010]

§120.19 Misuse of alcohol.

(a) This section applies to covered employees who perform air traffic control duties directly or by contract for an employer that is an air traffic control facility not operated by the FAA or the U.S. military.

(b) *Alcohol concentration.* No covered employee shall report for duty or remain on duty requiring the performance of safety-sensitive functions while having an alcohol concentration of 0.04 or greater. No employer having actual knowledge that an employee has an alcohol concentration of 0.04 or greater shall permit the employee to perform or continue to perform safety-sensitive functions.

(c) *On-duty use.* No covered employee shall use alcohol while performing safety-sensitive functions. No employer having actual knowledge that a covered employee is using alcohol while performing safety-sensitive functions shall permit the employee to perform or continue to perform safety-sensitive functions.

(d) *Pre-duty use.* No covered employee shall perform air traffic control duties within 8 hours after using alcohol. No employer having actual knowledge that such an employee has used alcohol within 8 hours shall permit the employee to perform or continue to perform air traffic control duties.

(e) *Use following an accident.* No covered employee who has actual knowledge of an accident involving an aircraft for which he or she performed a safety-sensitive function at or near the time of the accident shall use alcohol for 8 hours following the accident, unless he or she has been given a post-accident test under subpart F of this part or the employer has determined that the employee's performance could not have contributed to the accident.

(f) *Refusal to submit to a required alcohol test.* A covered employee may not refuse to submit to any alcohol test required under subpart F of this part. An employer may not permit an employee who refuses to submit to such a test to perform or continue to perform safety-sensitive functions.

§120.21 Testing for alcohol.

(a) Each air traffic control facility not operated by the FAA or the U.S. military must establish an alcohol testing program in accordance with the provisions of subpart F of this part.

(b) No employer shall use any individual who meets the definition of covered employee in subpart A of this part to perform a safety-sensitive function listed in subpart F of this part unless that individual is subject to testing for alcohol misuse in accordance with the provisions of that subpart.

Subpart D— Part 119 Certificate Holders Authorized To Conduct Operations under Part 121 or Part 135 or Operators Under §91.147 of This Chapter and Safety-Sensitive Employees

§120.31 Prohibited drugs.

(a) Each certificate holder or operator shall provide each employee performing a function listed in subpart E of this part, and his or her supervisor, with the training specified in that subpart.

(b) No certificate holder or operator may use any contractor to perform a function listed in subpart E of this part unless that contractor provides each of its employees performing that function for the certificate holder or operator, and his or her supervisor, with the training specified in that subpart.

§120.33 Use of prohibited drugs.

(a) This section applies to individuals who perform a function listed in subpart E of this part for a certificate holder or operator. For the purpose of this section, an individual who performs such a function pursuant to a contract with the certificate holder or the operator is considered to be performing that function for the certificate holder or the operator.

(b) No certificate holder or operator may knowingly use any individual to perform, nor may any individual perform for a certificate holder or an operator, either directly or by contract, any function listed in subpart E of this part while that individual has a prohibited drug, as defined in this part, in his or her system.

(c) No certificate holder or operator shall knowingly use any individual to perform, nor shall any individual perform for a certificate holder or operator, either directly or by contract, any safety-sensitive function if that individual has a verified positive drug test result on, or has refused to submit to, a drug test required by subpart E of this part and the individual has not met the requirements of that subpart for returning to the performance of safety-sensitive duties.

[Docket No. FAA–2008–0937, 74 FR 22653, May 14, 2009; as amended by Amdt. 120–0A, 75 FR 3153, Jan. 20, 2010]

§120.35 Testing for prohibited drugs.

(a) Each certificate holder or operator shall test each of its employees who perform a function listed in subpart E of this part in accordance with that subpart.

(b) Except as provided in paragraph (c) of this section, no certificate holder or operator may use any contractor to perform a function listed in subpart E of this part unless that contractor tests each employee performing such a function for the certificate holder or operator in accordance with that subpart.

(c) If a certificate holder conducts an on-demand operation into an airport at which no maintenance providers are available that are subject to the requirements of subpart E of this part and emergency maintenance is required, the certificate holder may use individuals not meeting the requirements of paragraph (b) of this section to provide such emergency maintenance under both of the following conditions:

(1) The certificate holder must give written notification of the emergency maintenance to the Drug Abatement Program Division, AAM-800, 800 Independence Avenue, SW., Washington, DC 20591, within 10 days after being provided same in accordance with this paragraph. A certificate holder must retain copies of all such written notifications for two years.

(2) The aircraft must be reinspected by maintenance personnel who meet the requirements of paragraph (b) of this section when the aircraft is next at an airport where such maintenance personnel are available.

(d) For purposes of this section, emergency maintenance means maintenance that—

(1) Is not scheduled and

(2) Is made necessary by an aircraft condition not discovered prior to the departure for that location.

§120.37 Misuse of alcohol.

(a) *General.* This section applies to covered employees who perform a function listed in subpart F of this part for a certificate holder. For the purpose of this section, an individual who meets the definition of covered employee in subpart F of this part is considered to be performing the function for the certificate holder.

(b) *Alcohol concentration.* No covered employee shall report for duty or remain on duty requiring the performance of safety-sensitive functions while having an alcohol concentration of 0.04 or greater. No certificate holder having actual knowledge that an employee has an alcohol concentration of 0.04 or greater shall permit the employee to perform or continue to perform safety-sensitive functions.

(c) *On-duty use.* No covered employee shall use alcohol while performing safety-sensitive functions. No certificate holder having actual knowledge that a covered employee is using alcohol while performing safety-sensitive functions shall permit the employee to perform or continue to perform safety-sensitive functions.

(d) *Pre-duty use.*

(1) No covered employee shall perform flight crewmember or flight attendant duties within 8 hours after using alcohol. No certificate holder having actual knowledge that such an employee has used alcohol within 8 hours shall permit the employee to perform or continue to perform the specified duties.

(2) No covered employee shall perform safety-sensitive duties other than those specified in paragraph (d)(1) of this section within 4 hours after using alcohol. No certificate holder having actual knowledge that such an employee has used alcohol within 4 hours shall permit the employee to perform or to continue to perform safety-sensitive functions.

(e) *Use following an accident.* No covered employee who has actual knowledge of an accident involving an aircraft for which he or she performed a safety-sensitive function at or near the time of the accident shall use alcohol for 8 hours following the accident, unless he or she has been given a post-accident test under subpart F of this part, or the employer has determined that the employee's performance could not have contributed to the accident.

§120.39

(f) *Refusal to submit to a required alcohol test.* A covered employee must not refuse to submit to any alcohol test required under subpart F of this part. A certificate holder must not permit an employee who refuses to submit to such a test to perform or continue to perform safety-sensitive functions.

§120.39 Testing for alcohol.

(a) Each certificate holder must establish an alcohol testing program in accordance with the provisions of subpart F of this part.

(b) Except as provided in paragraph (c) of this section, no certificate holder or operator may use any individual who meets the definition of covered employee in subpart A of this part to perform a safety-sensitive function listed in that subpart F of this part unless that individual is subject to testing for alcohol misuse in accordance with the provisions of that subpart.

(c) If a certificate holder conducts an on-demand operation into an airport at which no maintenance providers are available that are subject to the requirements of subpart F of this part and emergency maintenance is required, the certificate holder may use individuals not meeting the requirements of paragraph (b) of this section to provide such emergency maintenance under both of the following conditions:

(1) The certificate holder must give written notification of the emergency maintenance to the Drug Abatement Program Division, AAM-800, 800 Independence Avenue, SW., Washington, DC 20591, within 10 days after being provided same in accordance with this paragraph. A certificate holder must retain copies of all such written notifications for two years.

(2) The aircraft must be reinspected by maintenance personnel who meet the requirements of paragraph (b) of this section when the aircraft is next at an airport where such maintenance personnel are available.

(d) For purposes of this section, emergency maintenance means maintenance that—

(1) Is not scheduled and

(2) Is made necessary by an aircraft condition not discovered prior to the departure for that location.

Subpart E—Drug Testing Program Requirements

§120.101 Scope.

This subpart contains the standards and components that must be included in a drug testing program required by this part.

§120.103 General.

(a) *Purpose.* The purpose of this subpart is to establish a program designed to help prevent accidents and injuries resulting from the use of prohibited drugs by employees who perform safety-sensitive functions.

(b) *DOT procedures.*

(1) Each employer shall ensure that drug testing programs conducted pursuant to 14 CFR parts 65, 91, 121, and 135 comply with the requirements of this subpart and the "Procedures for Transportation Workplace Drug Testing Programs" published by the Department of Transportation (DOT) (49 CFR part 40).

(2) An employer may not use or contract with any drug testing laboratory that is not certified by the Department of Health and Human Services (HHS) under the National Laboratory Certification Program.

(c) *Employer responsibility.* As an employer, you are responsible for all actions of your officials, representatives, and service agents in carrying out the requirements of this subpart and 49 CFR part 40.

(d) *Applicable Federal Regulations.* The following applicable regulations appear in 49 CFR or 14 CFR:

(1) 49 CFR Part 40—Procedures for Transportation Workplace Drug Testing Programs

(2) 14 CFR:

(i) §67.107—First-Class Airman Medical Certificate, Mental.

(ii) §67.207—Second-Class Airman Medical Certificate, Mental.

(iii) §67.307—Third-Class Airman Medical Certificate, Mental.

(iv) §91.147—Passenger carrying flight for compensation or hire.

(v) §135.1—Applicability

(e) *Falsification.* No individual may make, or cause to be made, any of the following:

(1) Any fraudulent or intentionally false statement in any application of a drug testing program.

(2) Any fraudulent or intentionally false entry in any record or report that is made, kept, or used to show compliance with this part.

(3) Any reproduction or alteration, for fraudulent purposes, of any report or record required to be kept by this part.

[Docket No. FAA–2008–0937, 74 FR 22653, May 14, 2009; as amended by Amdt. 120–0A, 75 FR 3153, Jan. 20, 2010]

§120.105 Employees who must be tested.

Each employee, including any assistant, helper, or individual in a training status, who performs a safety-sensitive function listed in this section directly or by contract (including by subcontract at any tier) for an employer as defined in this subpart must be subject to drug testing under a drug testing program implemented in accordance with this subpart. This includes full-time, part-time, temporary, and intermittent employees regardless of the degree of supervision. The safety-sensitive functions are:

(a) Flight crewmember duties.
(b) Flight attendant duties.
(c) Flight instruction duties.
(d) Aircraft dispatcher duties.
(e) Aircraft maintenance and preventive maintenance duties.
(f) Ground security coordinator duties.
(g) Aviation screening duties.
(h) Air traffic control duties.
(i) Operations control specialist duties.

[Docket No. FAA–2008–0937, 74 FR 22653, May 14, 2009; as amended by Amdt. 120–2, 79 FR 9973, Feb. 21, 2014]

§120.107 Substances for which testing must be conducted.

Each employer shall test each employee who performs a safety-sensitive function for evidence of marijuana, cocaine, opiates, phencyclidine (PCP), and amphetamines during each test required by §120.109.

§120.109 Types of drug testing required.

Each employer shall conduct the types of testing described in this section in accordance with the procedures set forth in this subpart and the DOT "Procedures for Transportation Workplace Drug Testing Programs" (49 CFR part 40).

(a) *Pre-employment drug testing.*

(1) No employer may hire any individual for a safety-sensitive function listed in §120.105 unless the employer first conducts a pre-employment test and receives a verified negative drug test result for that individual.

(2) No employer may allow an individual to transfer from a nonsafety-sensitive to a safety-sensitive function unless the employer first conducts a pre-employment test and receives a verified negative drug test result for the individual.

(3) Employers must conduct another pre-employment test and receive a verified negative drug test result before hiring or transferring an individual into a safety-sensitive function if more than 180 days elapse between conducting the pre-employment test required by paragraphs (a)(1) or (2) of this section and hiring or transferring the individual into a safety-sensitive function, resulting in that individual being brought under an FAA drug testing program.

(4) If the following criteria are met, an employer is permitted to conduct a pre-employment test, and if such a test is conducted, the employer must receive a negative test result before putting the individual into a safety-sensitive function:

(i) The individual previously performed a safety-sensitive function for the employer and the employer is not required to pre-employment test the individual under paragraphs (a)(1) or (2) of this section before putting the individual to work in a safety-sensitive function;

(ii) The employer removed the individual from the employer's random testing program conducted under this subpart for reasons other than a verified positive test result on an FAA-mandated drug test or a refusal to submit to such testing; and

(iii) The individual will be returning to the performance of a safety-sensitive function.

(5) Before hiring or transferring an individual to a safety-sensitive function, the employer must advise each individual that the individual will be required to undergo pre-employment testing in accordance with this subpart, to determine the presence of marijuana, cocaine, opiates, phencyclidine (PCP), and amphetamines, or a metabolite of those drugs in the individual's system. The employer shall provide this same notification to each individual required by the employer to undergo pre-employment testing under paragraph (a)(4) of this section.

(b) *Random drug testing.*

(1) Except as provided in paragraphs (b)(2) through (b)(4) of this section, the minimum annual percentage rate for random drug testing shall be 50 percent of covered employees.

(2) The Administrator's decision to increase or decrease the minimum annual percentage rate for random drug testing is based on the reported positive rate for the entire industry. All information used for this determination is drawn from the statistical reports required by §120.119. In order to ensure reliability of the data, the Administrator considers the quality and completeness of the reported data, may obtain additional information or reports from employers, and may make appropriate modifications in calculating the industry positive rate. Each year, the Administrator will publish

in the **Federal Register** the minimum annual percentage rate for random drug testing of covered employees. The new minimum annual percentage rate for random drug testing will be applicable starting January 1 of the calendar year following publication.

(3) When the minimum annual percentage rate for random drug testing is 50 percent, the Administrator may lower this rate to 25 percent of all covered employees if the Administrator determines that the data received under the reporting requirements of this subpart for two consecutive calendar years indicate that the reported positive rate is less than 1.0 percent.

(4) When the minimum annual percentage rate for random drug testing is 25 percent, and the data received under the reporting requirements of this subpart for any calendar year indicate that the reported positive rate is equal to or greater than 1.0 percent, the Administrator will increase the minimum annual percentage rate for random drug testing to 50 percent of all covered employees.

(5) The selection of employees for random drug testing shall be made by a scientifically valid method, such as a random-number table or a computer-based random number generator that is matched with employees' Social Security numbers, payroll identification numbers, or other comparable identifying numbers. Under the selection process used, each covered employee shall have an equal chance of being tested each time selections are made.

(6) As an employer, you must select and test a percentage of employees at least equal to the minimum annual percentage rate each year.

(i) As an employer, to determine whether you have met the minimum annual percentage rate, you must divide the number of random testing results for safety-sensitive employees by the average number of safety-sensitive employees eligible for random testing.

(A) To calculate whether you have met the annual minimum percentage rate, count all random positives, random negatives, and random refusals as your "random testing results."

(B) To calculate the average number of safety-sensitive employees eligible for random testing throughout the year, add the total number of safety-sensitive employees eligible for testing during each random testing period for the year and divide that total by the number of random testing periods. Only safety-sensitive employees are to be in an employer's random testing pool, and all safety-sensitive employees must be in the random pool. If you are an employer conducting random testing more often than once per month (e.g., you select daily, weekly, bi-weekly) you do not need to compute this total number of safety-sensitive employees more than on a once per month basis.

(ii) As an employer, you may use a service agent to perform random selections for you, and your safety-sensitive employees may be part of a larger random testing pool of safety-sensitive employees. However, you must ensure that the service agent you use is testing at the appropriate percentage established for your industry and that only safety-sensitive employees are in the random testing pool. For example:

(A) If the service agent has your employees in a random testing pool for your company alone, you must ensure that the testing is conducted at least at the minimum annual percentage rate under this part.

(B) If the service agent has your employees in a random testing pool combined with other FAA-regulated companies, you must ensure that the testing is conducted at least at the minimum annual percentage rate under this part.

(C) If the service agent has your employees in a random testing pool combined with other DOT-regulated companies, you must ensure that the testing is conducted at least at the highest rate required for any DOT-regulated company in the pool.

(7) Each employer shall ensure that random drug tests conducted under this subpart are unannounced and that the dates for administering random tests are spread reasonably throughout the calendar year.

(8) Each employer shall require that each safety-sensitive employee who is notified of selection for random drug testing proceeds to the collection site immediately; provided, however, that if the employee is performing a safety-sensitive function at the time of the notification, the employer shall instead ensure that the employee ceases to perform the safety-sensitive function and proceeds to the collection site as soon as possible.

(9) If a given covered employee is subject to random drug testing under the drug testing rules of more than one DOT agency, the employee shall be subject to random drug testing at the percentage rate established for the calendar year by the DOT agency regulating more than 50 percent of the employee's function.

(10) If an employer is required to conduct random drug testing under the drug testing rules of more than one DOT agency, the employer may—

(i) Establish separate pools for random selection, with each pool containing the covered employees who are subject to testing at the same required rate; or

(ii) Randomly select covered employees for testing at the highest percentage rate established for the calendar year by any DOT agency to which the employer is subject.

(11) An employer required to conduct random drug testing under the anti-drug rules of more than one DOT agency shall provide each such agency access to the employer's records of random drug testing, as determined to be necessary by the agency to ensure the employer's compliance with the rule.

(c) *Post-accident drug testing.* Each employer shall test each employee who performs a safety-sensitive function for the presence of marijuana, cocaine, opiates, phencyclidine (PCP), and amphetamines, or a metabolite of those drugs in the employee's system if that employee's performance either contributed to an accident or can not be completely discounted as a contributing factor to the accident. The employee shall be tested as soon as possible but not later than 32 hours after the accident. The decision not to administer a test under this section must be based on a determination, using the best information available at the time of the determination, that the employee's performance could not have contributed to the accident. The employee shall submit to post-accident testing under this section.

(d) *Drug testing based on reasonable cause.* Each employer must test each employee who performs a safety-sensitive function and who is reasonably suspected of having used a prohibited drug. The decision to test must be based on a reasonable and articulable belief that the employee is using a prohibited drug on the basis of specific contemporaneous physical, behavioral, or performance indicators of probable drug use. At least two of the employee's supervisors, one of whom is trained in detection of the symptoms of possible drug use, must substantiate and concur in the decision to test an employee who is reasonably suspected of drug use; except that in the case of an employer, other than a part 121 certificate holder, who employs 50 or fewer employees who perform safety-sensitive functions, one supervisor who is trained in detection of symptoms of possible drug use must substantiate the decision to test an employee who is reasonably suspected of drug use.

(e) *Return to duty drug testing.* Each employer shall ensure that before an individual is returned to duty to perform a safety-sensitive function after refusing to submit to a drug test required by this subpart or receiving a verified positive drug test result on a test conducted under this subpart the individual shall undergo a return-to-duty drug test. No employer shall allow an individual required to undergo return-to-duty testing to perform a safety-sensitive function unless the employer has received a verified negative drug test result for the individual. The test cannot occur until after the SAP has determined that the employee has successfully complied with the prescribed education and/or treatment.

(f) *Follow-up drug testing.*

(1) Each employer shall implement a reasonable program of unannounced testing of each individual who has been hired to perform or who has been returned to the performance of a safety-sensitive function after refusing to submit to a drug test required by this subpart or receiving a verified positive drug test result on a test conducted under this subpart.

(2) The number and frequency of such testing shall be determined by the employer's Substance Abuse Professional conducted in accordance with the provisions of 49 CFR part 40, but shall consist of at least six tests in the first 12 months following the employee's return to duty.

(3) The employer must direct the employee to undergo testing for alcohol in accordance with subpart F of this part, in addition to drugs, if the Substance Abuse Professional determines that alcohol testing is necessary for the particular employee. Any such alcohol testing shall be conducted in accordance with the provisions of 49 CFR part 40.

(4) Follow-up testing shall not exceed 60 months after the date the individual begins to perform or returns to the performance of a safety-sensitive function. The Substance Abuse Professional may terminate the requirement for follow-up testing at any time after the first six tests have been conducted, if the Substance Abuse Professional determines that such testing is no longer necessary.

§120.111 Administrative and other matters.

(a) *MRO record retention requirements.*

(1) Records concerning drug tests confirmed positive by the laboratory shall be maintained by the MRO for 5 years. Such records include the MRO copies of the custody and control form, medical interviews, documentation of the basis for verifying as negative test results confirmed as positive by the laboratory, any other documentation concerning the MRO's verification process.

(2) Should the employer change MROs for any reason, the employer shall ensure that the former MRO forwards all records maintained pursuant to this rule to the new MRO within ten working days of receiving notice from the employer of the new MRO's name and address.

(3) Any employer obtaining MRO services by contract, including a contract through a C/TPA, shall ensure that the contract includes a record-keeping provision that is consistent with this paragraph, including requirements for transferring records to a new MRO.

(b) *Access to records.* The employer and the MRO shall permit the Administrator or the Administrator's representative to examine records required to be kept under this subpart and 49 CFR part 40. The Administrator or the Administrator's representative may require that all records maintained by the service agent for the employer must be produced at the employer's place of business.

(c) *Release of drug testing information.* An employer shall release information regarding an employee's drug testing results, evaluation, or rehabilitation to a third party in accordance with 49 CFR part 40. Except as required by law, this subpart, or 49 CFR part 40, no employer shall release employee information.

(d) *Refusal to submit to testing.* Each employer must notify the FAA within 2 working days of any employee who holds a certificate issued under part 61, part 63, or part 65 of this chapter who has refused to submit to a drug test required under this subpart. Notification must be sent to: Federal Aviation Administration, Office of Aerospace Medicine, Drug Abatement Division (AAM-800), 800 Independence Avenue, SW., Washington, DC 20591, or by fax to (202) 267-5200.

(e) *Permanent disqualification from service.*

(1) An employee who has verified positive drug test results on two drug tests required by this subpart of this chapter, and conducted after September 19, 1994, is permanently precluded from performing for an employer the safety-sensitive duties the employee performed prior to the second drug test.

(2) An employee who has engaged in prohibited drug use during the performance of a safety-sensitive function after September 19, 1994 is permanently precluded from performing that safety-sensitive function for an employer.

(f) *DOT management information system annual reports.* Copies of any annual reports submitted to the FAA under this subpart must be maintained by the employer for a minimum of 5 years.

§120.113 Medical Review Officer, Substance Abuse Professional, and Employer Responsibilities.

(a) The employer shall designate or appoint a Medical Review Officer (MRO) who shall be qualified in accordance with 49 CFR part 40 and shall perform the functions set forth in 49 CFR part 40 and this subpart. If the employer does not have a qualified individual on staff to serve as MRO, the employer may contract for the provision of MRO services as part of its drug testing program.

(b) *Medical Review Officer (MRO).* The MRO must perform the functions set forth in subpart G of 49 CFR part 40, and subpart E of this part. The MRO shall not delay verification of the primary test result following a request for a split specimen test unless such delay is based on reasons other than the fact that the split specimen test result is pending. If the primary test result is verified as positive, actions required under this rule (e.g., notification to the Federal Air Surgeon, removal from safety-sensitive position) are not stayed during the 72-hour request period or pending receipt of the split specimen test result.

(c) *Substance Abuse Professional (SAP).* The SAP must perform the functions set forth in 49 CFR part 40, subpart O.

(d) Additional Medical Review Officer, Substance Abuse Professional, and Employer Responsibilities Regarding 14 CFR part 67 Airman Medical Certificate Holders.

(1) As part of verifying a confirmed positive test result or refusal to submit to a test, the MRO must ask and the individual must answer whether he or she holds an airman medical certificate issued under 14 CFR part 67 or would be required to hold an airman medical certificate to perform a safety-sensitive function for the employer. If the individual answers in the affirmative to either question, in addition to notifying the employer in accordance with 49 CFR part 40, the MRO must forward to the Federal Air Surgeon, at the address listed in paragraph (d)(5) of this section, the name of the individual, along with identifying information and supporting documentation, within 2 working days after verifying a positive drug test result or refusal to submit to a test.

(2) During the SAP interview required for a verified positive test result or a refusal to submit to a test, the SAP must ask and the individual must answer whether he or she holds or would be required to hold an airman medical certificate issued under 14 CFR part 67 to perform a safety-sensitive function for the employer. If the individual answers in the affirmative, the individual must obtain an airman medical certificate issued by the Federal Air Surgeon dated after the verified positive drug test result date or refusal to test date. After the individual obtains this airman medical certificate, the SAP may recommend to the employer that the individual may be returned to a safety-sensitive position. The receipt of an airman medical certificate does not alter any obligations otherwise required by 49 CFR part 40 or this subpart.

(3) An employer must forward to the Federal Air Surgeon within 2 working days of receipt, copies of all reports provided to the employer by a SAP regarding the following:

(i) An individual who the MRO has reported to the Federal Air Surgeon under §120.113 (d)(1); or

(ii) An individual who the employer has reported to the Federal Air Surgeon under §120.111(d).

(4) The employer must not permit an employee who is required to hold an airman medical certificate under 14 CFR part 67 to perform a safety-sensitive duty to resume that duty until the employee has:

(i) Been issued an airman medical certificate from the Federal Air Surgeon after the date of the verified positive drug test result or refusal to test; and

(ii) Met the return to duty requirements in accordance with 49 CFR part 40.

(5) Reports required under this section shall be forwarded to the Federal Air Surgeon, Federal Aviation Administration, Office of Aerospace Medicine, Attn: Drug Abatement Division (AAM-800), 800 Independence Avenue, SW., Washington, DC 20591.

(6) MROs, SAPs, and employers who send reports to the Federal Air Surgeon must keep a copy of each report for 5 years.

§120.115 Employee Assistance Program (EAP).

(a) The employer shall provide an EAP for employees. The employer may establish the EAP as a part of its internal personnel services or the employer may contract with an entity that will provide EAP services to an employee. Each EAP must include education and training on drug use for employees and training for supervisors making determinations for testing of employees based on reasonable cause.

(b) *EAP education program.*

(1) Each EAP education program must include at least the following elements:

(i) Display and distribution of informational material;

(ii) Display and distribution of a community service hot-line telephone number for employee assistance; and

(iii) Display and distribution of the employer's policy regarding drug use in the workplace.

(2) The employer's policy shall include information regarding the consequences under the rule of using drugs while performing safety-sensitive functions, receiving a verified positive drug test result, or refusing to submit to a drug test required under the rule.

(c) *EAP training program.*

(1) Each employer shall implement a reasonable program of initial training for employees. The employee training program must include at least the following elements:

(i) The effects and consequences of drug use on individual health, safety, and work environment; and

(ii) The manifestations and behavioral cues that may indicate drug use and abuse.

(2) The employer's supervisory personnel who will determine when an employee is subject to testing based on reasonable cause shall receive specific training on specific, contemporaneous physical, behavioral, and performance indicators of probable drug use in addition to the training specified in §120.115(c).

(3) The employer shall ensure that supervisors who will make reasonable cause determinations receive at least 60 minutes of initial training.

(4) The employer shall implement a reasonable recurrent training program for supervisory personnel making reasonable cause determinations during subsequent years.

(5) Documentation of all training given to employees and supervisory personnel must be included in the training program.

(6) The employer shall identify the employee and supervisor EAP training in the employer's drug testing program.

[Docket No. FAA–2008–0937, 74 FR 22653, May 14, 2009; as amended by Amdt. 120–1, 79 FR 42003, July 15, 2013]

§120.117 Implementing a drug testing program.

(a) Each company must meet the requirements of this subpart. Use the following chart to determine whether your company must obtain an Antidrug and Alcohol Misuse Prevention Program Operations Specification or whether you must register with the FAA:

If you are...	You must...
(1) A part 119 certificate holder with authority to operate under parts 121 or 135.	Obtain an Antidrug and Alcohol Misuse Prevention Program Operations Specification by contacting your FAA Principal Operations Inspector.
(2) An operator as defined in §91.147 of this chapter	Obtain a Letter of Authorization by contacting the Flight Standards District Office nearest to your principal place of business.
(3) A part 119 certificate holder with authority to operate under parts 121 or 135 and an operator as defined in §91.147 of this chapter.	Complete the requirements in paragraphs 1 and 2 of this chart and advise the Flight Standards District Office and the Drug Abatement Division that the §91.147 operation will be included under the part 119 testing program. Contact the Drug Abatement Division at FAA, Office of Aerospace Medicine, Drug Abatement Division (AAM-800), 800 Independence Avenue SW., Washington, DC 20591.
(4) An air traffic control facility not operated by the FAA or by or under contract to the U.S. Military.	Register with the FAA, Office of Aerospace Medicine, Drug Abatement Division (AAM-800), 800 Independence Avenue SW., Washington, DC 20591.
(5) A part 145 certificate holder who has your own drug testing program.	Obtain an Antidrug and Alcohol Misuse Prevention Program Operations Specification by contacting your Principal Maintenance Inspector or register with the FAA, Office of Aerospace Medicine, Drug Abatement Division (AAM-800), 800 Independence Avenue SW., Washington, DC 20591, if you opt to conduct your own drug testing program.
(6) A contractor who has your own drug testing program.	Register with the FAA, Office of Aerospace Medicine, Drug Abatement Division (AAM-800), 800 Independence Avenue SW., Washington, DC 20591, if you opt to conduct your own drug testing program.

(b) Use the following chart for implementing a drug testing program if you are applying for a part 119 certificate with authority to operate under parts 121 or 135 of this chapter, if you intend to begin operations as defined in §91.147 of this chapter, or if you intend to begin air traffic control operations (not operated by the FAA or by or under contract to the U.S. Military). Use it to determine whether you need to have an Antidrug and Alcohol Misuse Prevention Program Operations Specification, Letter of Authorization, or Drug and Alcohol Testing Program Registration from the FAA. Your employees who perform safety-sensitive functions must be tested in accordance with this subpart. The chart follows:

If you...	You must...
(1) Apply for a part 119 certificate with authority to operate under parts 121 or 135	(i) Have an Antidrug and Alcohol Misuse Prevention Program Operations Specification, (ii) Implement an FAA drug testing program no later than the date you start operations, and (iii) Meet the requirements of this subpart.
(2) Intend to begin operations as defined in §91.147 of this chapter.	(i) Have a Letter of Authorization, (ii) Implement an FAA drug testing program no later than the date you start operations, and (iii) Meet the requirements of this subpart.
(3) Apply for a part 119 certificate with authority to operate under parts 121 or 135 and intend to begin operations as defined in §91.147 of this chapter.	(i) Have an Antidrug and Alcohol Misuse Prevention Program Operations Specification and a Letter of Authorization, (ii) Implement your combined FAA drug testing program no later than the date you start operations, and (iii) Meet the requirements of this subpart.
(4) Intend to begin air traffic control operations (at an air traffic control facility not operated by the FAA or by or under contract to the U.S. military).	(i) Register with the FAA, Office of Aerospace Medicine, Drug Abatement Division (AAM-800), 800 Independence Avenue SW., Washington, DC 20591 prior to starting operations, (ii) Implement an FAA drug testing program no later than the date you start operations, and (iii) Meet the requirements of this subpart.

Part 120: Drug and Alcohol Testing Program §120.117

(c) If you are an individual or company that intends to provide safety-sensitive services by contract to a part 119 certificate holder with authority to operate under parts 121 and/or 135 of this chapter, an operation as defined in §91.147 of this chapter, or an air traffic control facility not operated by the FAA or by or under contract to the U.S. military, use the following chart to determine what you must do if you opt to have your own drug testing program.

If you...	And you opt to conduct your own drug program, you must...
(1) Are a part 145 certificate holder.	(i) Have an Antidrug and Alcohol Misuse Prevention Program Operations Specification or register with the FAA, Office of Aerospace Medicine, Drug Abatement Division (AAM-800), 800 Independence Avenue, SW., Washington, DC 20591; (ii) Implement an FAA drug testing program no later than the date you start performing safety-sensitive functions for a part 119 certificate holder with authority to operate under parts 121 or 135, or operator as defined in §91.147 of this chapter, and (iii) Meet the requirements of this subpart as if you were an employer.
(2) Are a contractor	(i) Register with the FAA, Office of Aerospace Medicine, Drug Abatement Division (AAM-800), 800 Independence Avenue, SW., Washington, DC 20591; (ii) Implement an FAA drug testing program no later than the date you start performing safety-sensitive functions for a part 119 certificate holder with authority to operate under parts 121 or 135, or operator as defined in §91.147 of this chapter, or an air traffic control facility not operated by the FAA or by or under contract to the U.S. Military, and (iii) Meet the requirements of this subpart as if you were an employer.

(d) *Obtaining an Antidrug and Alcohol Misuse Prevention Program Operations Specification.*

(1) To obtain an Antidrug and Alcohol Misuse Prevention Program Operations Specification, you must contact your FAA Principal Operations Inspector or Principal Maintenance Inspector. Provide him/her with the following information:
(i) Company name.
(ii) Certificate number.
(iii) Telephone number.
(iv) Address where your drug and alcohol testing program records are kept.
(v) Whether you have 50 or more safety-sensitive employees, or 49 or fewer safety-sensitive employees. (Part 119 certificate holders with authority to operate only under part 121 of this chapter are not required to provide this information.)

(2) You must certify on your Antidrug and Alcohol Misuse Prevention Program Operations Specification issued by your FAA Principal Operations Inspector or Principal Maintenance Inspector that you will comply with this part and 49 CFR part 40.

(3) You are required to obtain only one Antidrug and Alcohol Misuse Prevention Program Operations Specification to satisfy this requirement under this part.

(4) You must update the Antidrug and Alcohol Misuse Prevention Program Operations Specification when any changes to the information contained in the Operation Specification occur.

(e) *Register your Drug and Alcohol Testing Program by obtaining a Letter of Authorization from the FAA in accordance with §91.147.*

(1) A drug and alcohol testing program is considered registered when the following information is submitted to the Flight Standards District Office nearest your principal place of business:
(i) Company name.
(ii) Telephone number.
(iii) Address where your drug and alcohol testing program records are kept.
(iv) Type of safety-sensitive functions you or your employees perform (such as flight instruction duties, aircraft dispatcher duties, maintenance or preventive maintenance duties, ground security coordinator duties, aviation screening duties, air traffic control duties).
(v) Whether you have 50 or more covered employees, or 49 or fewer covered employees.
(vi) A signed statement indicating that your company will comply with this part and 49 CFR part 40.

(2) This Letter of Authorization will satisfy the requirements for both your drug testing program under this subpart and your alcohol testing program under subpart F of this part.

(3) Update the Letter of Authorization information as changes occur. Send the updates to the Flight Standards District Office nearest your principal place of business.

(4) If you are a part 119 certificate holder with authority to operate under parts 121 or 135 and intend to begin operations as defined in §91.147

of this chapter, you must also advise the Federal Aviation Administration, Office of Aerospace Medicine, Drug Abatement Division (AAM-800), 800 Independence Avenue SW., Washington, DC 20591.

(f) Obtaining a Drug and Alcohol Testing Program Registration from the FAA.

(1) Except as provided in paragraphs (d) and (e) of this section, to obtain a Drug and Alcohol Testing Program Registration from the FAA, you must submit the following information to the Office of Aerospace Medicine, Drug Abatement Division:

(i) Company name.

(ii) Telephone number.

(iii) Address where your drug and alcohol testing program records are kept.

(iv) Type of safety-sensitive functions you or your employees perform (such as flight instruction duties, aircraft dispatcher duties, maintenance or preventive maintenance duties, ground security coordinator duties, aviation screening duties, air traffic control duties).

(v) Whether you have 50 or more covered employees, or 49 or fewer covered employees.

(vi) A signed statement indicating that: your company will comply with this part and 49 CFR part 40; and you intend to provide safety-sensitive functions by contract (including subcontract at any tier) to a part 119 certificate holder with authority to operate under part 121 or part 135 of this chapter, an operator as defined in §91.147 of this chapter, or an air traffic control facility not operated by the FAA or by or under contract to the U.S. military.

(2) Send this information to the Federal Aviation Administration, Office of Aerospace Medicine, Drug Abatement Division (AAM-800), 800 Independence Avenue SW., Washington, DC 20591.

(3) This Drug and Alcohol Testing Program Registration will satisfy the registration requirements for both your drug testing program under this subpart and your alcohol testing program under subpart F of this part.

(4) Update the registration information as changes occur. Send the updates to the address specified in paragraph (f)(2) of this section.

[Docket No. FAA-2008-0937, 74 FR 22653, May 14, 2009; as amended by Amdt. 120-0A, 75 FR 3154, Jan. 20, 2010; Amdt. 120-1, 78 FR 42003, July 15, 2013]

§120.119 Annual reports.

(a) Annual reports of testing results must be submitted to the FAA by March 15 of the succeeding calendar year for the prior calendar year (January 1 through December 31) in accordance with the following provisions:

(1) Each part 121 certificate holder shall submit an annual report each year.

(2) Each entity conducting a drug testing program under this part, other than a part 121 certificate holder, that has 50 or more employees performing a safety-sensitive function on January 1 of any calendar year shall submit an annual report to the FAA for that calendar year.

(3) The Administrator reserves the right to require that aviation employers not otherwise required to submit annual reports prepare and submit such reports to the FAA. Employers that will be required to submit annual reports under this provision will be notified in writing by the FAA.

(b) As an employer, you must use the Management Information System (MIS) form and instructions as required by 49 CFR part 40 (at 49 CFR 40.26 and appendix H to 49 CFR part 40). You may also use the electronic version of the MIS form provided by DOT. The Administrator may designate means (e.g., electronic program transmitted via the Internet) other than hard-copy, for MIS form submission. For information on where to submit MIS forms and for the electronic version of the form, see:

http://www.faa.gov/about/office_org/headquarters_offices/avs/offices/aam/drug_alcohol

(c) A service agent may prepare the MIS report on behalf of an employer. However, a company official (e.g., Designated Employer Representative as defined in 49 CFR part 40) must certify the accuracy and completeness of the MIS report, no matter who prepares it.

[Docket No. FAA-2008-0937, 74 FR 22653, May 14, 2009; as amended by Amdt. 120-0A, 75 FR 3154, Jan. 20, 2010]

§120.121 Preemption.

(a) The issuance of 14 CFR parts 65, 91, 121, and 135 by the FAA preempts any State or local law, rule, regulation, order, or standard covering the subject matter of 14 CFR parts 65, 91, 121, and 135, including but not limited to, drug testing of aviation personnel performing safety-sensitive functions.

(b) The issuance of 14 CFR parts 65, 91, 121, and 135 does not preempt provisions of state criminal law that impose sanctions for reckless conduct of an individual that leads to actual loss of life, injury, or damage to property whether such provisions apply specifically to aviation employees or generally to the public.

§120.123 Drug testing outside the territory of the United States.

(a) No part of the testing process (including specimen collection, laboratory processing, and MRO actions) shall be conducted outside the territory of the United States.

(1) Each employee who is assigned to perform safety-sensitive functions solely outside the territory of the United States shall be removed from the random testing pool upon the inception of such assignment.

(2) Each covered employee who is removed from the random testing pool under this section shall be returned to the random testing pool when the employee resumes the performance of safety-sensitive functions wholly or partially within the territory of the United States.

(b) The provisions of this subpart shall not apply to any individual who performs a function listed in §120.105 by contract for an employer outside the territory of the United States.

§120.125 Waivers from 49 CFR 40.21.

An employer subject to this part may petition the Drug Abatement Division, Office of Aerospace Medicine, for a waiver allowing the employer to stand down an employee following a report of a laboratory confirmed positive drug test or refusal, pending the outcome of the verification process.

(a) Each petition for a waiver must be in writing and include substantial facts and justification to support the waiver. Each petition must satisfy the substantive requirements for obtaining a waiver, as provided in 49 CFR 40.21.

(b) Each petition for a waiver must be submitted to the Federal Aviation Administration, Office of Aerospace Medicine, Drug Abatement Division (AAM-800), 800 Independence Avenue, SW., Washington, DC 20591.

(c) The Administrator may grant a waiver subject to 49 CFR 40.21(d).

Subpart F—Alcohol Testing Program Requirements

§120.201 Scope.

This subpart contains the standards and components that must be included in an alcohol testing program required by this part.

§120.203 General.

(a) *Purpose.* The purpose of this subpart is to establish programs designed to help prevent accidents and injuries resulting from the misuse of alcohol by employees who perform safety-sensitive functions in aviation.

(b) *Alcohol testing procedures.* Each employer shall ensure that all alcohol testing conducted pursuant to this subpart complies with the procedures set forth in 49 CFR part 40. The provisions of 49 CFR part 40 that address alcohol testing are made applicable to employers by this subpart.

(c) *Employer responsibility.* As an employer, you are responsible for all actions of your officials, representatives, and service agents in carrying out the requirements of the DOT agency regulations.

§120.205 Preemption of State and local laws.

(a) Except as provided in paragraph (a)(2) of this section, these regulations preempt any State or local law, rule, regulation, or order to the extent that:

(1) Compliance with both the State or local requirement and this subpart is not possible; or

(2) Compliance with the State or local requirement is an obstacle to the accomplishment and execution of any requirement in this subpart.

(b) The alcohol testing requirements of this title shall not be construed to preempt provisions of State criminal law that impose sanctions for reckless conduct leading to actual loss of life, injury, or damage to property, whether the provisions apply specifically to transportation employees or employers or to the general public.

§120.207 Other requirements imposed by employers.

Except as expressly provided in these alcohol testing requirements, nothing in this subpart shall be construed to affect the authority of employers, or the rights of employees, with respect to the use or possession of alcohol, including any authority and rights with respect to alcohol testing and rehabilitation.

§120.209 Requirement for notice.

Before performing an alcohol test under this subpart, each employer shall notify a covered employee that the alcohol test is required by this subpart. No employer shall falsely represent that a test is administered under this subpart.

§120.211 Applicable Federal regulations.

The following applicable regulations appear in 49 CFR and 14 CFR:

(a) *49 CFR Part 40*—Procedures for Transportation Workplace Drug Testing Programs

(b) *14 CFR:*

(1) §67.107—First-Class Airman Medical Certificate, Mental.

(2) §67.207—Second-Class Airman Medical Certificate, Mental.
(3) §67.307—Third-Class Airman Medical Certificate, Mental.
(4) §91.147—Passenger carrying flights for compensation or hire.
(5) §135.1—Applicability

[Docket No. FAA–2008–0937, 74 FR 22653, May 14, 2009; as amended by Amdt. 120–0A, 75 FR 3154, Jan. 20, 2010]

§120.213 Falsification.

No individual may make, or cause to be made, any of the following:

(a) Any fraudulent or intentionally false statement in any application of an alcohol testing program.

(b) Any fraudulent or intentionally false entry in any record or report that is made, kept, or used to show compliance with this subpart.

(c) Any reproduction or alteration, for fraudulent purposes, of any report or record required to be kept by this subpart.

§120.215 Covered employees.

(a) Each employee, including any assistant, helper, or individual in a training status, who performs a safety-sensitive function listed in this section directly or by contract (including by subcontract at any tier) for an employer as defined in this subpart must be subject to alcohol testing under an alcohol testing program implemented in accordance with this subpart. This includes full-time, part-time, temporary, and intermittent employees regardless of the degree of supervision. The safety-sensitive functions are:

(1) Flight crewmember duties.
(2) Flight attendant duties.
(3) Flight instruction duties.
(4) Aircraft dispatcher duties.
(5) Aircraft maintenance or preventive maintenance duties.
(6) Ground security coordinator duties.
(7) Aviation screening duties.
(8) Air traffic control duties.
(9) Operations control specialist duties.

(b) Each employer must identify any employee who is subject to the alcohol testing regulations of more than one DOT agency. Prior to conducting any alcohol test on a covered employee subject to the alcohol testing regulations of more than one DOT agency, the employer must determine which DOT agency authorizes or requires the test.

[Docket No. FAA–2008–0937, 74 FR 22653, May 14, 2009; as amended by Amdt. 120–2, 79 FR 9973, Feb. 21, 2014]

§120.217 Tests required.

(a) *Pre-employment alcohol testing.* As an employer, you may, but are not required to, conduct pre-employment alcohol testing under this subpart. If you choose to conduct pre-employment alcohol testing, you must comply with the following requirements:

(1) You must conduct a pre-employment alcohol test before the first performance of safety-sensitive functions by every covered employee (whether a new employee or someone who has transferred to a position involving the performance of safety-sensitive functions).

(2) You must treat all safety-sensitive employees performing safety-sensitive functions the same for the purpose of pre-employment alcohol testing (i.e., you must not test some covered employees and not others).

(3) You must conduct the pre-employment tests after making a contingent offer of employment or transfer, subject to the employee passing the pre-employment alcohol test.

(4) You must conduct all pre-employment alcohol tests using the alcohol testing procedures of 49 CFR part 40.

(5) You must not allow a covered employee to begin performing safety-sensitive functions unless the result of the employee's test indicates an alcohol concentration of less than 0.04. If a pre-employment test result under this paragraph indicates an alcohol concentration of 0.02 or greater but less than 0.04, the provisions of §120.221(f) apply.

(b) *Post-accident alcohol testing.*

(1) As soon as practicable following an accident, each employer shall test each surviving covered employee for alcohol if that employee's performance of a safety-sensitive function either contributed to the accident or cannot be completely discounted as a contributing factor to the accident. The decision not to administer a test under this section shall be based on the employer's determination, using the best available information at the time of the determination, that the covered employee's performance could not have contributed to the accident.

(2) If a test required by this section is not administered within 2 hours following the accident, the employer shall prepare and maintain on file a record stating the reasons the test was not promptly administered. If a test required by this section is not administered within 8 hours following the accident, the employer shall cease attempts to administer an alcohol test and shall prepare and maintain the same record. Records shall be submitted to the FAA upon request of the Administrator or his or her designee.

(3) A covered employee who is subject to post-accident testing shall remain readily available for such testing or may be deemed by the employer

to have refused to submit to testing. Nothing in this section shall be construed to require the delay of necessary medical attention for injured people following an accident or to prohibit a covered employee from leaving the scene of an accident for the period necessary to obtain assistance in responding to the accident or to obtain necessary emergency medical care.

(c) *Random alcohol testing.*

(1) Except as provided in paragraphs (c)(2) through (c)(4) of this section, the minimum annual percentage rate for random alcohol testing will be 25 percent of the covered employees.

(2) The Administrator's decision to increase or decrease the minimum annual percentage rate for random alcohol testing is based on the violation rate for the entire industry. All information used for this determination is drawn from MIS reports required by this subpart. In order to ensure reliability of the data, the Administrator considers the quality and completeness of the reported data, may obtain additional information or reports from employers, and may make appropriate modifications in calculating the industry violation rate. Each year, the Administrator will publish in the **Federal Register** the minimum annual percentage rate for random alcohol testing of covered employees. The new minimum annual percentage rate for random alcohol testing will be applicable starting January 1 of the calendar year following publication.

(3)(i) When the minimum annual percentage rate for random alcohol testing is 25 percent or more, the Administrator may lower this rate to 10 percent of all covered employees if the Administrator determines that the data received under the reporting requirements of this subpart for two consecutive calendar years indicate that the violation rate is less than 0.5 percent.

(ii) When the minimum annual percentage rate for random alcohol testing is 50 percent, the Administrator may lower this rate to 25 percent of all covered employees if the Administrator determines that the data received under the reporting requirements of this subpart for two consecutive calendar years indicate that the violation rate is less than 1.0 percent but equal to or greater than 0.5 percent.

(4)(i) When the minimum annual percentage rate for random alcohol testing is 10 percent, and the data received under the reporting requirements of this subpart for that calendar year indicate that the violation rate is equal to or greater than 0.5 percent but less than 1.0 percent, the Administrator will increase the minimum annual percentage rate for random alcohol testing to 25 percent of all covered employees.

(ii) When the minimum annual percentage rate for random alcohol testing is 25 percent or less, and the data received under the reporting requirements of this subpart for that calendar year indicate that the violation rate is equal to or greater than 1.0 percent, the Administrator will increase the minimum annual percentage rate for random alcohol testing to 50 percent of all covered employees.

(5) The selection of employees for random alcohol testing shall be made by a scientifically valid method, such as a random-number table or a computer-based random number generator that is matched with employees' Social Security numbers, payroll identification numbers, or other comparable identifying numbers. Under the selection process used, each covered employee shall have an equal chance of being tested each time selections are made.

(6) As an employer, you must select and test a percentage of employees at least equal to the minimum annual percentage rate each year.

(i) As an employer, to determine whether you have met the minimum annual percentage rate, you must divide the number of random alcohol screening test results for safety-sensitive employees by the average number of safety-sensitive employees eligible for random testing.

(A) To calculate whether you have met the annual minimum percentage rate, count all random screening test results below 0.02 breath alcohol concentration, random screening test results of 0.02 or greater breath alcohol concentration, and random refusals as your "random alcohol screening test results."

(B) To calculate the average number of safety-sensitive employees eligible for random testing throughout the year, add the total number of safety-sensitive employees eligible for testing during each random testing period for the year and divide that total by the number of random testing periods. Only safety-sensitive employees are to be in an employer's random testing pool, and all safety-sensitive employees must be in the random pool. If you are an employer conducting random testing more often than once per month (e.g., you select daily, weekly, bi-weekly) you do not need to compute this total number of safety-sensitive employees more than on a once per month basis.

(ii) As an employer, you may use a service agent to perform random selections for you, and your safety-sensitive employees may be part of a larger random testing pool of safety-sensitive employees. However, you must ensure that the service agent you use is testing at the appropriate percentage established for your industry and that only safety-sensitive employees are in the random testing pool. For example:

(A) If the service agent has your employees in a random testing pool for your company alone, you must ensure that the testing is conducted at least at the minimum annual percentage rate under this part.

(B) If the service agent has your employees in a random testing pool combined with other FAA-regulated companies, you must ensure that the testing is conducted at least at the minimum annual percentage rate under this part.

(C) If the service agent has your employees in a random testing pool combined with other DOT-regulated companies, you must ensure that the testing is conducted at least at the highest rate required for any DOT-regulated company in the pool.

(7) Each employer shall ensure that random alcohol tests conducted under this subpart are unannounced and that the dates for administering random tests are spread reasonably throughout the calendar year.

(8) Each employer shall require that each covered employee who is notified of selection for random testing proceeds to the testing site immediately; provided, however, that if the employee is performing a safety-sensitive function at the time of the notification, the employer shall instead ensure that the employee ceases to perform the safety-sensitive function and proceeds to the testing site as soon as possible.

(9) A covered employee shall only be randomly tested while the employee is performing safety-sensitive functions; just before the employee is to perform safety-sensitive functions; or just after the employee has ceased performing such functions.

(10) If a given covered employee is subject to random alcohol testing under the alcohol testing rules of more than one DOT agency, the employee shall be subject to random alcohol testing at the percentage rate established for the calendar year by the DOT agency regulating more than 50 percent of the employee's functions.

(11) If an employer is required to conduct random alcohol testing under the alcohol testing rules of more than one DOT agency, the employer may—

(i) Establish separate pools for random selection, with each pool containing the covered employees who are subject to testing at the same required rate; or

(ii) Randomly select such employees for testing at the highest percentage rate established for the calendar year by any DOT agency to which the employer is subject.

(d) *Reasonable suspicion alcohol testing.*

(1) An employer shall require a covered employee to submit to an alcohol test when the employer has reasonable suspicion to believe that the employee has violated the alcohol misuse prohibitions in §§120.19 or 120.37.

(2) The employer's determination that reasonable suspicion exists to require the covered employee to undergo an alcohol test shall be based on specific, contemporaneous, articulable observations concerning the appearance, behavior, speech or body odors of the employee. The required observations shall be made by a supervisor who is trained in detecting the symptoms of alcohol misuse. The supervisor who makes the determination that reasonable suspicion exists shall not conduct the breath alcohol test on that employee.

(3) Alcohol testing is authorized by this section only if the observations required by paragraph (d)(2) of this section are made during, just preceding, or just after the period of the work day that the covered employee is required to be in compliance with this rule. An employee may be directed by the employer to undergo reasonable suspicion testing for alcohol only while the employee is performing safety-sensitive functions; just before the employee is to perform safety-sensitive functions; or just after the employee has ceased performing such functions.

(4)(i) If a test required by this section is not administered within 2 hours following the determination made under paragraph (d)(2) of this section, the employer shall prepare and maintain on file a record stating the reasons the test was not promptly administered. If a test required by this section is not administered within 8 hours following the determination made under paragraph (d)(2) of this section, the employer shall cease attempts to administer an alcohol test and shall state in the record the reasons for not administering the test.

(ii) Notwithstanding the absence of a reasonable suspicion alcohol test under this section, no covered employee shall report for duty or remain on duty requiring the performance of safety-sensitive functions while the employee is under the influence of, or impaired by, alcohol, as shown by the behavioral, speech, or performance indicators of alcohol misuse, nor shall an employer permit the covered employee to perform or continue to perform safety-sensitive functions until:

(A) An alcohol test is administered and the employee's alcohol concentration measures less than 0.02; or

(B) The start of the employee's next regularly scheduled duty period, but not less than 8 hours following the determination made under paragraph (d)(2) of this section that there is reasonable suspicion that the employee has violated the alcohol misuse provisions in §§120.19 or 120.37.

(iii) No employer shall take any action under this subpart against a covered employee based solely on the employee's behavior and appearance in the absence of an alcohol test. This does not prohibit an employer with authority independent of this subpart from taking any action otherwise consistent with law.

Part 120: Drug and Alcohol Testing Program §120.219

(e) *Return-to-duty alcohol testing.* Each employer shall ensure that before a covered employee returns to duty requiring the performance of a safety-sensitive function after engaging in conduct prohibited in §§120.19 or 120.37 the employee shall undergo a return-to-duty alcohol test with a result indicating an alcohol concentration of less than 0.02. The test cannot occur until after the SAP has determined that the employee has successfully complied with the prescribed education and/or treatment.

(f) *Follow-up alcohol testing.*

(1) Each employer shall ensure that the employee who engages in conduct prohibited by §§120.19 or 120.37, is subject to unannounced follow-up alcohol testing as directed by a SAP.

(2) The number and frequency of such testing shall be determined by the employer's SAP, but must consist of at least six tests in the first 12 months following the employee's return to duty.

(3) The employer must direct the employee to undergo testing for drugs in accordance with subpart E of this part, in addition to alcohol, if the SAP determines that drug testing is necessary for the particular employee. Any such drug testing shall be conducted in accordance with the provisions of 49 CFR part 40.

(4) Follow-up testing shall not exceed 60 months after the date the individual begins to perform, or returns to the performance of, a safety-sensitive function. The SAP may terminate the requirement for follow-up testing at any time after the first six tests have been conducted, if the SAP determines that such testing is no longer necessary.

(5) A covered employee shall be tested for alcohol under this section only while the employee is performing safety-sensitive functions, just before the employee is to perform safety-sensitive functions, or just after the employee has ceased performing such functions.

(g) *Retesting of covered employees with an alcohol concentration of 0.02 or greater but less than 0.04.* Each employer shall retest a covered employee to ensure compliance with the provisions of §120.221(f) if the employer chooses to permit the employee to perform a safety-sensitive function within 0 hours following the administration of an alcohol test indicating an alcohol concentration of 0.02 or greater but less than 0.04.

§120.219 Handling of test results, record retention, and confidentiality.

(a) *Retention of records.*

(1) General requirement. In addition to the records required to be maintained under 49 CFR part 40, employers must maintain records required by this subpart in a secure location with controlled access.

(2) Period of retention.

(i) Five years.

(A) Copies of any annual reports submitted to the FAA under this subpart for a minimum of 5 years.

(B) Records of notifications to the Federal Air Surgeon of refusals to submit to testing and violations of the alcohol misuse prohibitions in this chapter by covered employees who hold medical certificates issued under part 67 of this chapter.

(C) Documents presented by a covered employee to dispute the result of an alcohol test administered under this subpart.

(D) Records related to other violations of §§120.19 or 120.37.

(ii) Two years. Records related to the testing process and training required under this subpart.

(A) Documents related to the random selection process.

(B) Documents generated in connection with decisions to administer reasonable suspicion alcohol tests.

(C) Documents generated in connection with decisions on post-accident tests.

(D) Documents verifying existence of a medical explanation of the inability of a covered employee to provide adequate breath for testing.

(E) Materials on alcohol misuse awareness, including a copy of the employer's policy on alcohol misuse.

(F) Documentation of compliance with the requirements of §120.223(a).

(G) Documentation of training provided to supervisors for the purpose of qualifying the supervisors to make a determination concerning the need for alcohol testing based on reasonable suspicion.

(H) Certification that any training conducted under this subpart complies with the requirements for such training.

(b) *Annual reports.*

(1) Annual reports of alcohol testing program results must be submitted to the FAA by March 15 of the succeeding calendar year for the prior calendar year (January 1 through December 31) in accordance with the provisions of paragraphs (b)(1)(i) through (iii) of this section.

(i) Each part 121 certificate holder shall submit an annual report each year.

(ii) Each entity conducting an alcohol testing program under this part, other than a part 121 certificate holder, that has 50 or more employees performing a safety-sensitive function on January 1 of any calendar year shall submit an annual report to the FAA for that calendar year.

(iii) The Administrator reserves the right to require that aviation employers not otherwise required to submit annual reports prepare and submit such reports to the FAA. Employers that will be required to submit annual reports under this provision will be notified in writing by the FAA.

(2) As an employer, you must use the Management Information System (MIS) form and instructions as required by 49 CFR part 40 (at 49 CFR 40.26 and appendix H to 49 CFR part 40). You may also use the electronic version of the MIS form provided by the DOT. The Administrator may designate means (e.g., electronic program transmitted via the Internet) other than hard-copy, for MIS form submission. For information on where to submit MIS forms and for the electronic version of the form, see:

http://www.faa.gov/about/office_org/headquarters_offices/avs/offices/aam/drug_alcohol/

(3) A service agent may prepare the MIS report on behalf of an employer. However, a company official (e.g., Designated Employer Representative as defined in 49 CFR part 40) must certify the accuracy and completeness of the MIS report, no matter who prepares it.

(c) *Access to records and facilities.*

(1) Except as required by law or expressly authorized or required in this subpart, no employer shall release covered employee information that is contained in records required to be maintained under this subpart.

(2) A covered employee is entitled, upon written request, to obtain copies of any records pertaining to the employee's use of alcohol, including any records pertaining to his or her alcohol tests in accordance with 49 CFR part 40. The employer shall promptly provide the records requested by the employee. Access to an employee's records shall not be contingent upon payment for records other than those specifically requested.

(3) Each employer shall permit access to all facilities utilized in complying with the requirements of this subpart to the Secretary of Transportation or any DOT agency with regulatory authority over the employer or any of its covered employees.

§120.221 Consequences for employees engaging in alcohol-related conduct.

(a) *Removal from safety-sensitive function.*

(1) Except as provided in 49 CFR part 40, no covered employee shall perform safety-sensitive functions if the employee has engaged in conduct prohibited by §§120.19 or 120.37, or an alcohol misuse rule of another DOT agency.

(2) No employer shall permit any covered employee to perform safety-sensitive functions if the employer has determined that the employee has violated this section.

(b) *Permanent disqualification from service.*

(1) An employee who violates §§120.19(c) or 120.37(c) is permanently precluded from performing for an employer the safety-sensitive duties the employee performed before such violation.

(2) An employee who engages in alcohol use that violates another alcohol misuse provision of §§120.19 or 120.37, and who had previously engaged in alcohol use that violated the provisions of §§120.19 or 120.37 after becoming subject to such prohibitions, is permanently precluded from performing for an employer the safety-sensitive duties the employee performed before such violation.

(c) *Notice to the Federal Air Surgeon.*

(1) An employer who determines that a covered employee who holds an airman medical certificate issued under part 67 of this chapter has engaged in alcohol use that violated the alcohol misuse provisions of §§120.19 or 120.37 shall notify the Federal Air Surgeon within 2 working days.

(2) Each such employer shall forward to the Federal Air Surgeon a copy of the report of any evaluation performed under the provisions of §120.223(c) within 2 working days of the employer's receipt of the report.

(3) All documents must be sent to the Federal Air Surgeon, Federal Aviation Administration, Office of Aerospace Medicine, Attn: Drug Abatement Division (AAM-800), 800 Independence Avenue, SW., Washington, DC 20591.

(4) No covered employee who is required to hold an airman medical certificate in order to perform a safety-sensitive duty may perform that duty following a violation of this subpart until the covered employee obtains an airman medical certificate issued by the Federal Air Surgeon dated after the alcohol test result or refusal to test date. After the covered employee obtains this airman medical certificate, the SAP may recommend to the employer that the covered employee may be returned to a safety-sensitive position. The receipt of an airman medical certificate does not alter any obligations otherwise required by 49 CFR part 40 or this subpart.

(5) Once the Federal Air Surgeon has recommended under paragraph (c)(4) of this section that the employee be permitted to perform safety-sensitive duties, the employer cannot permit the employee to perform those safety-sensitive duties until the employer has ensured that the employee meets the return to duty requirements in accordance with 49 CFR part 40.

(d) *Notice of refusals.* Each covered employer must notify the FAA within 2 working days of any employee who holds a certificate issued under part 61, part 63, or part 65 of this chapter who has refused to submit to an alcohol test required under this subpart. Notification must be sent to: Federal Aviation Administration, Office of Aerospace Medicine, Drug Abatement Division (AAM-800), 800 Independence Avenue, SW., Washington, DC 20591, or by fax to (202) 267-5200.

(e) *Required evaluation and alcohol testing.* No covered employee who has engaged in conduct prohibited by §§120.19 or 120.37 shall perform safety-sensitive functions unless the employee has met the requirements of 49 CFR part 40. No employer shall permit a covered employee who has engaged in such conduct to perform safety-sensitive functions unless the employee has met the requirements of 49 CFR part 40.

(f) *Other alcohol-related conduct.*

(1) No covered employee tested under this subpart who is found to have an alcohol concentration of 0.02 or greater but less than 0.04 shall perform or continue to perform safety-sensitive functions for an employer, nor shall an employer permit the employee to perform or continue to perform safety-sensitive functions, until:

(i) The employee's alcohol concentration measures less than 0.02; or

(ii) The start of the employee's next regularly scheduled duty period, but not less than 8 hours following administration of the test.

(2) Except as provided in paragraph (f)(1) of this section, no employer shall take any action under this rule against an employee based solely on test results showing an alcohol concentration less than 0.04. This does not prohibit an employer with authority independent of this rule from taking any action otherwise consistent with law.

[Docket No. FAA–2008–0937, 74 FR 22653, May 14, 2009; as amended by Amdt. 120–1, 78 FR 42004, July 15, 2013]

§120.223 Alcohol misuse information, training, and substance abuse professionals.

(a) *Employer obligation to promulgate a policy on the misuse of alcohol.*

(1) *General requirements.* Each employer shall provide educational materials that explain these alcohol testing requirements and the employer's policies and procedures with respect to meeting those requirements.

(i) The employer shall ensure that a copy of these materials is distributed to each covered employee prior to the start of alcohol testing under the employer's FAA-mandated alcohol testing program and to each individual subsequently hired for or transferred to a covered position.

(ii) Each employer shall provide written notice to representatives of employee organizations of the availability of this information.

(2) *Required content.* The materials to be made available to employees shall include detailed discussion of at least the following:

(i) The identity of the individual designated by the employer to answer employee questions about the materials.

(ii) The categories of employees who are subject to the provisions of these alcohol testing requirements.

(iii) Sufficient information about the safety-sensitive functions performed by those employees to make clear what period of the work day the covered employee is required to be in compliance with these alcohol testing requirements.

(iv) Specific information concerning employee conduct that is prohibited by this chapter.

(v) The circumstances under which a covered employee will be tested for alcohol under this subpart.

(vi) The procedures that will be used to test for the presence of alcohol, protect the employee and the integrity of the breath testing process, safeguard the validity of the test results, and ensure that those results are attributed to the correct employee.

(vii) The requirement that a covered employee submit to alcohol tests administered in accordance with this subpart.

(viii) An explanation of what constitutes a refusal to submit to an alcohol test and the attendant consequences.

(ix) The consequences for covered employees found to have violated the prohibitions in this chapter, including the requirement that the employee be removed immediately from performing safety-sensitive functions, and the process in 49 CFR part 40, subpart O.

(x) The consequences for covered employees found to have an alcohol concentration of 0.02 or greater but less than 0.04.

(xi) Information concerning the effects of alcohol misuse on an individual's health, work, and personal life; signs and symptoms of an alcohol problem; available methods of evaluating and resolving problems associated with the misuse of alcohol; and intervening when an alcohol problem is suspected, including confrontation, referral to any available employee assistance program, and/or referral to management.

(xii) *Optional provisions.* The materials supplied to covered employees may also include information on additional employer policies with respect to the use or possession of alcohol, including any consequences for an employee found to have a specified alcohol level, that are based on the employer's authority independent of this subpart. Any such additional policies or consequences must be clearly and obviously described as being based on independent authority.

(b) *Training for supervisors.* Each employer shall ensure that persons designated to determine whether reasonable suspicion exists to require a covered employee to undergo alcohol testing under §120.217(d) of this subpart receive at least 60 minutes of training on the physical,

§120.223

behavioral, speech, and performance indicators of probable alcohol misuse.

(c) *Substance abuse professional (SAP) duties.* The SAP must perform the functions set forth in 49 CFR part 40, subpart O, and this subpart.

§120.225 How to implement an alcohol testing program.

(a) Each company must meet the requirements of this subpart. Use the following chart to determine whether your company must obtain an Antidrug and Alcohol Misuse Prevention Program Operations Specification or whether you must register with the FAA:

If you...	You must...
(1) A part 119 certificate holder with authority to operate under part 121 or 135.	Obtain an Antidrug and Alcohol Misuse Prevention Program Operations Specification by contacting your FAA Principal Operations Inspector.
(2) An operator as defined in §91.147 of this chapter	Obtain a Letter of Authorization by contacting the Flight Standards District Office nearest to your principal place of business.
(3) A part 119 certificate holder with authority to operate under part 121 or 135 and an operator as defined in §91.147 of this chapter.	Complete the requirements in paragraphs 1 and 2 of this chart and advise the Flight Standards District Office and the Drug Abatement Division that the §91.147 operation will be included under the part 119 testing program. Contact the Drug Abatement Division at FAA, Office of Aerospace Medicine, Drug Abatement Division (AAM-800), 800 Independence Avenue SW., Washington, DC 20591.
(4) An air traffic control facility not operated by the FAA or by or under contract to the U.S. Military.	Register with the FAA, Office of Aerospace Medicine, Drug Abatement Division (AAM-800), 800 Independence Avenue SW., Washington, DC 20591.
(5) A part 145 certificate holder who has your own alcohol testing program.	Obtain an Antidrug and Alcohol Misuse Prevention Program Operations Specification by contacting your Principal Maintenance Inspector or register with the FAA, Office of Aerospace Medicine, Drug Abatement Division (AAM-800), 800 Independence Avenue SW., Washington, DC 20591, if you opt to conduct your own drug testing program.
(6) A contractor who has your own alcohol testing program.	Register with the FAA, Office of Aerospace Medicine, Drug Abatement Division (AAM-800), 800 Independence Avenue SW., Washington, DC 20591, if you opt to conduct your own drug testing program.

(b) Use the following chart for implementing an alcohol testing program if you are applying for a part 119 certificate with authority to operate under parts 121 and/or 135 of this chapter, if you intend to begin operations as defined in §91.147 of this chapter, or if you intend to begin operations as defined air traffic control operations (not operated by the FAA or by or under contract to the U.S. Military). Use it to determine whether you need to have an Antidrug and Alcohol Misuse Prevention Program Operations Specification, or whether you need to register with the FAA. Your employees who perform safety-sensitive duties must be tested in accordance with this subpart. The chart follows:

Part 120: Drug and Alcohol Testing Program §120.225

If you...	You must...
(1) Apply for a part 119 certificate with authority to operate under parts 121 or 135	(i) Have an Antidrug and Alcohol Misuse Prevention Program Operations Specification, (ii) Implement an FAA drug testing program no later than the date you start operations, and (iii) Meet the requirements of this subpart.
(2) Intend to begin operations as defined in §91.147 of this chapter.	(i) Have a Letter of Authorization, (ii) Implement an FAA drug testing program no later than the date you start operations, and (iii) Meet the requirements of this subpart.
(3) Apply for a part 119 certificate with authority to operate under parts 121 or 135 and intend to begin operations as defined in §91.147 of this chapter.	(i) Have an Antidrug and Alcohol Misuse Prevention Program Operations Specification and a Letter of Authorization, (ii) Implement your combined FAA drug testing program no later than the date you start operations, and (iii) Meet the requirements of this subpart.
(4) Intend to begin air traffic control operations (at an air traffic control facility not operated by the FAA or by or under contract to the U.S. military).	(i) Register with the FAA, Office of Aerospace Medicine, Drug Abatement Division (AAM-800), 800 Independence Avenue SW., Washington, DC 20591 prior to starting operations, (ii) Implement an FAA drug testing program no later than the date you start operations, and (iii) Meet the requirements of this subpart.

(c) If you are an individual or a company that intends to provide safety-sensitive services by contract to a part 119 certificate holder with authority to operate under parts 121 and/or 135 of this chapter or an operator as defined in §91.147 of this chapter, use the following chart to determine what you must do if you opt to have your own alcohol testing program.

If you...	And you opt to conduct your own Alcohol Testing Program, you must...
(1) Are a part 145 certificate holder.	(i) Have an Antidrug and Alcohol Misuse Prevention Program Operations Specifications or register with the FAA, Office of Aerospace Medicine, Drug Abatement Division (AAM-800), 800 Independence Avenue, SW., Washington, DC 20591, (ii) Implement an FAA alcohol testing program no later than the date you start performing safety-sensitive functions for a part 119 certificate holder with the authority to operate under parts 121 and/or 135, or operator as defined in §91.147 of this chapter, and (iii) Meet the requirements of this subpart as if you were an employer.
(2) Are a contractor	(i) Register with the FAA, Office of Aerospace Medicine, Drug Abatement Division (AAM-800), 800 Independence Avenue, SW., Washington, DC 20591, (ii) Implement an FAA alcohol testing program no later than the date you start performing safety-sensitive functions for a part 119 certificate holder with authority to operate under parts 121 and/or 135, or operator as defined in §91.147 of this chapter, and (iii) Meet the requirements of this subpart as if you were an employer.

(d)(1) To obtain an Antidrug and Alcohol Misuse Prevention Program Operations Specification, you must contact your FAA Principal Operations Inspector or Principal Maintenance Inspector. Provide him/her with the following information:
  (i) Company name.
  (ii) Certificate number.
  (iii) Telephone number.
  (iv) Address where your drug and alcohol testing program records are kept.
  (v) Whether you have 50 or more covered employees, or 49 or fewer covered employees. (Part 119 certificate holders with authority to operate only under part 121 of this chapter are not required to provide this information.)

(2) You must certify on your Antidrug and Alcohol Misuse Prevention Program Operations Specification, issued by your FAA Principal Operations Inspector or Principal Maintenance Inspector, that you will comply with this part and 49 CFR part 40.

(3) You are required to obtain only one Antidrug and Alcohol Misuse Prevention Program Operations Specification to satisfy this requirement under this part.

(4) You must update the Antidrug and Alcohol Misuse Prevention Program Operations Specification when any changes to the information contained in the Operation Specification occur.

(e) *Register your Drug and Alcohol Testing Program by obtaining a Letter of Authorization from the FAA in accordance with §91.147.*

(1) A drug and alcohol testing program is considered registered when the following information is submitted to the Flight Standards District Office nearest your principal place of business:
  (i) Company name.
  (ii) Telephone number.
  (iii) Address where your drug and alcohol testing program records are kept.
  (iv) Type of safety-sensitive functions you or your employees perform (such as flight instruction duties, aircraft dispatcher duties, maintenance or preventive maintenance duties, ground security coordinator duties, aviation screening duties, air traffic control duties).
  (v) Whether you have 50 or more covered employees, or 49 or fewer covered employees.
  (vi) A signed statement indicating that your company will comply with this part and 49 CFR part 40.

(2) This Letter of Authorization will satisfy the requirements for both your drug testing program under subpart E of this part and your alcohol testing program under this subpart.

(3) Update the Letter of Authorization information as changes occur. Send the updates to the Flight Standards District Office nearest your principal place of business.

(4) If you are a part 119 certificate holder with authority to operate under part 121 or part 135 and intend to begin operations as defined in §91.147 of this chapter, you must also advise the Federal Aviation Administration, Office of Aerospace Medicine, Drug Abatement Division (AAM-800), 800 Independence Avenue SW., Washington, DC 20591.

(f) *Obtaining a Drug and Alcohol Testing Program Registration from the FAA.*

(1) Except as provided in paragraphs (d) and (e) of this section, to obtain a Drug and Alcohol Testing Program Registration from the FAA you must submit the following information to the Office of Aerospace Medicine, Drug Abatement Division:
  (i) Company name.
  (ii) Telephone number.
  (iii) Address where your drug and alcohol testing program records are kept.
  (iv) Type of safety-sensitive functions you or your employees perform (such as flight instruction duties, aircraft dispatcher duties, maintenance or preventive maintenance duties, ground security coordinator duties, aviation screening duties, air traffic control duties).
  (v) Whether you have 50 or more covered employees, or 49 or fewer covered employees.
  (vi) A signed statement indicating that: your company will comply with this part and 49 CFR part 40; and you intend to provide safety-sensitive functions by contract (including subcontract at any tier) to a part 119 certificate holder with authority to operate under part 121 or part 135 of this chapter, an operator as defined in §91.147 of this chapter, or an air traffic control facility not operated by the FAA or by or under contract to the U.S. military.

(2) Send this information to the Federal Aviation Administration, Office of Aerospace Medicine, Drug Abatement Division (AAM-800), 800 Independence Avenue SW., Washington, DC 20591.

(3) This Drug and Alcohol Testing Program Registration will satisfy the registration requirements for both your drug testing program under subpart E of this part and your alcohol testing program under this subpart.

(4) Update the registration information as changes occur. Send the updates to the address specified in paragraph (f)(2) of this section.

[Docket No. FAA-2008-0937, 74 FR 22653, May 14, 2009; as amended by Amdt. 120-0A, 75 FR 3154, Jan. 20, 2010; Amdt. 120-1, 78 FR 42005, July 15, 2013]

§120.227 Employees located outside the U.S.

(a) No covered employee shall be tested for alcohol misuse while located outside the territory of the United States.

(1) Each covered employee who is assigned to perform safety-sensitive functions solely outside the territory of the United States shall be removed from the random testing pool upon the inception of such assignment.

(2) Each covered employee who is removed from the random testing pool under this paragraph shall be returned to the random testing pool when the employee resumes the performance of safety-sensitive functions wholly or partially within the territory of the United States.

(b) The provisions of this subpart shall not apply to any person who performs a safety-sensitive function by contract for an employer outside the territory of the United States.

14 CFR • Subchapter G—Air Carriers and Operators for Compensation or Hire: Certification and Operations

PART 121
OPERATING REQUIREMENTS: DOMESTIC, FLAG, AND SUPPLEMENTAL OPERATIONS

SPECIAL FEDERAL AVIATION REGULATIONS
SFAR No. 50–2
SFAR No. 97
*SFAR No. 106

Subpart A—General
Sec.
121.1   Applicability.
121.2   Compliance schedule for operators that transition to Part 121; certain new entrant operators.
121.4   Applicability of rules to unauthorized operators.
121.7   Definitions.
*121.9   Fraud and falsification.
121.11 Rules applicable to operations in a foreign country.
121.15 Carriage of narcotic drugs, marihuana, and depressant or stimulant drugs or substances.

Subpart B—[Reserved]
Certification Rules for Domestic and Flag Air Carriers

Subpart C—[Reserved]
Certification Rules for Supplemental Air Carriers and Commercial Operators

Subpart D—[Reserved]
Rules Governing All Certificate Holders Under This Part

Subpart E—Approval of Routes: Domestic and Flag Operations
121.91 Applicability.
121.93 Route requirements: General.
121.95 Route width.
121.97 Airports: Required data.
121.99 Communications facilities—domestic and flag operations.
121.101 Weather reporting facilities.
121.103 En route navigation facilities.
121.105 Servicing and maintenance facilities.
121.106 ETOPS Alternate Airport: Rescue and firefighting service.
121.107 Dispatch centers.

Subpart F—Approval of Areas and Routes for Supplemental Operations
121.111 Applicability.
121.113 Area and route requirements: General.
121.115 Route width.
121.117 Airports: Required data.
121.119 Weather reporting facilities.
121.121 En route navigation facilities.
121.122 Communications facilities—supplemental operations.
121.123 Servicing maintenance facilities.
121.125 Flight following system.
121.127 Flight following system; requirements.

Subpart G—Manual Requirements
121.131 Applicability.
121.133 Preparation.
121.135 Manual contents.
121.137 Distribution and availability.
121.139 Requirements for manual aboard aircraft: Supplemental operations.
121.141 Airplane flight manual.

Subpart H—Aircraft Requirements
121.151 Applicability.
121.153 Aircraft requirements: General.
121.155 [Reserved]
121.157 Aircraft certification and equipment requirements.
121.159 Single-engine airplanes prohibited.
121.161 Airplane limitations: Type of route.
121.162 ETOPS Type Design Approval Basis.
121.163 Aircraft proving tests.

Subpart I—Airplane Performance Operating Limitations
121.171 Applicability.
121.173 General.
121.175 Airplanes: Reciprocating engine-powered: Weight limitations.
121.177 Airplanes: Reciprocating engine-powered: Takeoff limitations.
121.179 Airplanes: Reciprocating engine-powered: En route limitations: All engines operating.
121.181 Airplanes: Reciprocating engine-powered: En route limitations: One engine inoperative.

121.183	Part 25 airplanes with four or more engines: Reciprocating engine-powered: En route limitations: Two engines inoperative.	121.241	Oil system drains.
		121.243	Engine breather lines.
		121.245	Fire walls.
		121.247	Fire-wall construction.
121.185	Airplanes: Reciprocating engine-powered: Landing limitations: Destination airport.	121.249	Cowling.
		121.251	Engine accessory section diaphragm.
		121.253	Powerplant fire protection.
121.187	Airplanes: Reciprocating engine-powered: Landing limitations: Alternate airport.	121.255	Flammable fluids.
		121.257	Shutoff means.
		121.259	Lines and fittings.
121.189	Airplanes: Turbine engine-powered: Takeoff limitations.	121.261	Vent and drain lines.
		121.263	Fire-extinguishing systems.
121.191	Airplanes: Turbine engine-powered: En route limitations: One engine inoperative.	121.265	Fire-extinguishing agents.
		121.267	Extinguishing agent container pressure relief.
121.193	Airplanes: Turbine engine-powered: En route limitations: Two engines inoperative.	121.269	Extinguishing agent container compartment temperature.
		121.271	Fire-extinguishing system materials.
121.195	Airplanes: Turbine engine-powered: Landing limitations: Destination airports.	121.273	Fire-detector systems.
		121.275	Fire detectors.
		121.277	Protection of other airplane components against fire.
121.197	Airplanes: Turbine engine-powered: Landing limitations: Alternate airports.	121.279	Control of engine rotation.
		121.281	Fuel system independence.
121.198	Cargo service airplanes: Increased zero fuel and landing weights.	121.283	Induction system ice prevention.
		121.285	Carriage of cargo in passenger compartments.
121.199	Nontransport category airplanes: Takeoff limitations.	121.287	Carriage of cargo in cargo compartments.
121.201	Nontransport category airplanes: En route limitations: One engine inoperative.	121.289	Landing gear: Aural warning device.
		121.291	Demonstration of emergency evacuation procedures.
121.203	Nontransport category airplanes: Landing limitations: Destination airport.	121.293	Special airworthiness requirements for nontransport category airplanes type certificated after December 31, 1964.
121.205	Nontransport category airplanes: Landing limitations: Alternate airport.		
		121.295	Location for a suspect device.
121.207	Provisionally certificated airplanes: Operating limitations.		

Subpart J—
Special Airworthiness Requirements

Subpart K—
Instrument and Equipment Requirements

121.211	Applicability.	121.301	Applicability.
121.213	[Reserved]	121.303	Airplane instruments and equipment.
121.215	Cabin interiors.	121.305	Flight and navigational equipment.
121.217	Internal doors.	121.306	Portable electronic devices.
121.219	Ventilation.	121.307	Engine instruments.
121.221	Fire precautions.	121.308	Lavatory fire protection.
121.223	Proof of compliance with §121.221.	121.309	Emergency equipment.
121.225	Propeller deicing fluid.	121.310	Additional emergency equipment.
121.227	Pressure cross-feed arrangements.	*121.311	Seats, safety belts, and shoulder harnesses.
121.229	Location of fuel tanks.	121.312	Materials for compartment interiors.
121.231	Fuel system lines and fittings.	121.313	Miscellaneous equipment.
121.233	Fuel lines and fittings in designated fire zones.	121.314	Cargo and baggage compartments.
		121.315	Cockpit check procedure.
121.235	Fuel valves.	121.316	Fuel tanks.
121.237	Oil lines and fittings in designated fire zones.	121.317	Passenger information requirements, smoking prohibitions, and additional seat belt requirements.
121.239	Oil valves.		
		121.318	Public address system.

Part 121: Air Carriers & Commercial Operators

121.319 Crewmember interphone system.
121.321 Operations in icing.
121.323 Instruments and equipment for operations at night.
121.325 Instruments and equipment for operations under IFR or over-the-top.
121.327 Supplemental oxygen: Reciprocating engine powered airplanes.
121.329 Supplemental oxygen for sustenance: Turbine engine powered airplanes.
121.331 Supplemental oxygen requirements for pressurized cabin airplanes: Reciprocating engine powered airplanes.
121.333 Supplemental oxygen for emergency descent and for first aid; turbine engine powered airplanes with pressurized cabins.
121.335 Equipment standards.
121.337 Protective breathing equipment.
121.339 Emergency equipment for extended over-water operations.
121.340 Emergency flotation means.
121.341 Equipment for operations in icing conditions.
121.342 Pitot heat indication systems.
121.343 Flight data recorders.
121.344 Digital flight data recorders for transport category airplanes.
121.344a Digital flight data recorders for 10–19 seat airplanes.
121.345 Radio equipment.
121.346 Flight data recorders: Filtered data.
121.347 Communication and navigation equipment for operations under VFR over routes navigated by pilotage.
121.349 Communication and navigation equipment for operations under VFR over routes not navigated by pilotage or for operations under IFR or over the top.
121.351 Communication and navigation equipment for extended overwater operations and for certain other operations.
121.353 Emergency equipment for operations over uninhabited terrain areas: Flag, supplemental, and certain domestic operations.
121.354 Terrain awareness and warning system
121.355 Equipment for operations on which specialized means of navigation are used.
121.356 Collision avoidance system.
121.357 Airborne weather radar equipment requirements.
121.358 Low-altitude windshear system equipment requirements.
121.359 Cockpit voice recorders.
121.360 [Reserved]

Subpart L—Maintenance, Preventive Maintenance, and Alterations

121.361 Applicability.
121.363 Responsibility for airworthiness.
121.365 Maintenance, preventive maintenance, and alteration organization.
121.367 Maintenance, preventive maintenance, and alterations programs.
121.368 [Reserved]
121.369 Manual requirements.
121.370 [Reserved]
121.370a [Reserved]
121.371 Required inspection personnel.
121.373 Continuing analysis and surveillance.
121.374 Continuous airworthiness maintenance program (CAMP) for two-engine ETOPS.
121.375 Maintenance and preventive maintenance training program.
121.377 Maintenance and preventive maintenance personnel duty time limitations.
121.378 Certificate requirements.
121.379 Authority to perform and approve maintenance, preventive maintenance, and alterations.
121.380 Maintenance recording requirements.
121.380a Transfer of maintenance records.

Subpart M—Airman and Crewmember Requirements

121.381 Applicability.
121.383 Airman: Limitations on use of services.
121.385 Composition of flight crew.
121.387 Flight engineer.
121.389 Flight navigator and specialized navigation equipment.
121.391 Flight attendants.
*121.392 Personnel identified as flight attendants.
121.393 Crewmember requirements at stops where passengers remain on board.
121.394 Flight attendant requirements during passenger boarding and deplaning.
121.395 Aircraft dispatcher: Domestic and flag operations.
121.397 Emergency and emergency evacuation duties.

Part 121   **Federal Aviation Regulations**

Subpart N—Training Program

- *121.400 Applicability and terms used.
- 121.401 Training program: General.
- 121.402 Training program: Special rules.
- *121.403 Training program: Curriculum.
- 121.404 Compliance dates: Crew and dispatcher resource management training.
- 121.405 Training program and revision: Initial and final approval.
- 121.406 Credit for previous CRM/DRM training.
- *121.407 Training program: Approval of airplane simulators and other training devices.
- *121.408 Training equipment other than flight simulation training devices.
- *121.409 Training courses using airplane simulators and other training devices.
- *121.410 Airline transport pilot certification training program.
- *121.411 Qualifications: Check airmen (airplane) and check airmen (simulator).
- *121.412 Qualifications: Flight instructors (airplane) and flight instructors (simulator).
- *121.413 Initial, transition and recurrent training and checking requirements: Check airmen (airplane), check airmen (simulator).
- *121.414 Initial, transition and recurrent training and checking requirements; flight instructors (airplane), flight instructors (simulator).
- *121.415 Crewmember and dispatcher training program requirements.
- 121.417 Crewmember emergency training.
- *121.418 Differences training and related aircraft differences training.
- *121.419 Pilots and flight engineers: Initial, transition, and upgrade ground training.
- *121.420 [Removed and reserved]
- 121.421 Flight attendants: Initial and transition ground training.
- 121.422 Aircraft dispatchers: Initial and transition ground training.
- *121.423 Pilot: Extended envelope training.
- *121.424 Pilots: Initial, transition and upgrade flight training.
- 121.425 Flight engineers: Initial and transition flight training.
- *121.426 [Removed and reserved]
- *121.427 Recurrent training.
- 121.429 [Reserved]

Subpart O—Crewmember Qualifications

- 121.431 Applicability.
- *121.432 General.
- *121.433 Training required.
- *121.434 Operating experience, operating cycles, and consolidation of knowledge and skills.
- *121.435 [Removed and reserved]
- *121.436 Pilot qualification: Certificates and experience requirements.
- *121.437 [Removed]
- 121.438 Pilot operating limitations and pairing requirements.
- *121.439 Pilot qualification: Recent experience.
- 121.440 Line checks.
- *121.441 Proficiency checks.
- 121.443 Pilot in command qualification: Route and airports.
- 121.445 Pilot in command airport qualification: Special areas and airports.
- 121.447 [Reserved]
- 121.453 Flight engineer qualifications.
- 121.455–121.459 [Reserved]

Subpart P—Aircraft Dispatcher Qualifications and Duty Time

- 121.461 Applicability.
- 121.463 Aircraft dispatcher qualifications.
- 121.465 Aircraft dispatcher duty time limitations: Domestic and flag operations.
- 121.467 Flight attendant duty period limitations and rest requirements: Domestic, flag, and supplemental operations.

Subpart Q—Flight Time Limitations and Rest Requirements: Domestic Operations

- *121.470 Applicability.
- 121.471 Flight time limitations and rest requirements: All flight crewmembers.
- 121.473 Fatigue risk management system.

Subpart R—Flight Time Limitations: Flag Operations

- 121.480 Applicability.
- 121.481 Flight time limitations: One or two pilot crews.
- 121.483 Flight time limitations: Two pilots and one additional flight crewmember.
- 121.485 Flight time limitations: Three or more pilots and an additional flight crewmember.

Part 121: Air Carriers & Commercial Operators

121.487 Flight time limitations: Pilots not regularly assigned.
121.489 Flight time limitations: Other commercial flying.
121.491 Flight time limitations: Deadhead transportation.
121.493 Flight time limitations: Flight engineers and flight navigators.
121.495 Fatigue risk management system.

Subpart S—Flight Time Limitations: Supplemental Operations

121.500 Applicability.
121.503 Flight time limitations: Pilots: airplanes.
121.505 Flight time limitations: Two pilot crews: airplanes.
121.507 Flight time limitations: Three pilot crews: airplanes.
121.509 Flight time limitations: Four pilot crews: airplanes.
121.511 Flight time limitations: Flight engineers: airplanes.
121.513 Flight time limitations: Overseas and international operations: airplanes.
121.515 Flight time limitations: All airmen: airplanes.
121.517 Flight time limitations: Other commercial flying: airplanes.
121.519 Flight time limitations: Deadhead transportation: airplanes.
121.521 Flight time limitations: Crew of two pilots and one additional airman as required.
121.523 Flight time limitations: Crew of three or more pilots and additional airmen as required.
121.525 Flight time limitations: Pilots serving in more than one kind of flight crew.
121.527 Fatigue risk management system.

Subpart T—Flight Operations

121.531 Applicability.
121.533 Responsibility for operational control: Domestic operations.
121.535 Responsibility for operational control: Flag operations.
121.537 Responsibility for operational control: Supplemental operations.
121.538 Aircraft security.
121.539 Operations notices.
121.541 Operations schedules: Domestic and flag operations.
*121.542 Flight crewmember duties.
*121.543 Flight crewmembers at controls.
*121.544 Pilot monitoring.
121.545 Manipulation of controls.
121.547 Admission to flight deck.

121.548 Aviation safety inspector's credentials: Admission to pilot's compartment.
121.548a DOD Commercial Air Carrier Evaluator's Credential.
121.549 Flying equipment.
121.550 Secret Service Agents: Admission to flight deck.
121.551 Restriction or suspension of operation: Domestic and flag operations.
121.553 Restriction or suspension of operation: Supplemental operations.
121.555 Compliance with approved routes and limitations: Domestic and flag operations.
121.557 Emergencies: Domestic and flag operations.
121.559 Emergencies: Supplemental operations.
121.561 Reporting potentially hazardous meteorological conditions and irregularities of ground facilities or navigation aids.
121.563 Reporting mechanical irregularities.
121.565 Engine inoperative: Landing; reporting.
121.567 Instrument approach procedures and IFR landing minimums.
121.569 Equipment interchange: Domestic and flag operations.
121.570 Airplane evacuation capability.
121.571 Briefing passengers before takeoff.
121.573 Briefing passengers: Extended overwater operations.
121.574 Oxygen for medical use by passengers.
121.575 Alcoholic beverages.
121.576 Retention of items of mass in passenger and crew compartments.
121.577 Stowage of food, beverage, and passenger service equipment during airplane movement on the surface, takeoff, and landing.
121.578 Cabin ozone concentration.
*121.579 Minimum altitudes for use of autopilot.
121.580 Prohibition on interference with crewmembers.
121.581 Observer's seat: En route inspections.
121.582 Means to discreetly notify a flightcrew.
121.583 Carriage of persons without compliance with the passenger-carrying requirements of this part and part 117.
121.584 Requirement to view the area outside the flightdeck door.
121.585 Exit seating.
121.586 Authority to refuse transportation.

ASA

Part 121

121.587 Closing and locking of flightcrew compartment door.
121.589 Carry-on baggage.
121.590 Use of certificated land airports in the United States.

Subpart U—Dispatching and Flight Release Rules

121.591 Applicability.
121.593 Dispatching authority: Domestic operations.
121.595 Dispatching authority: Flag operations.
121.597 Flight release authority: Supplemental operations.
121.599 Familiarity with weather conditions.
121.601 Aircraft dispatcher information to pilot in command: Domestic and flag operations.
121.603 Facilities and services: Supplemental operations.
121.605 Airplane equipment.
121.607 Communication and navigation facilities: Domestic and flag operations.
121.609 Communication and navigation facilities: Supplemental operations.
121.611 Dispatch or flight release under VFR.
121.613 Dispatch or flight release under IFR or over the top.
121.615 Dispatch or flight release over water: Flag and supplemental operations.
121.617 Alternate airport for departure.
121.619 Alternate airport for destination: IFR or over-the-top: Domestic operations.
121.621 Alternate airport for destination: Flag operations.
121.623 Alternate airport for destination: IFR or over-the-top: Supplemental operations.
121.624 ETOPS Alternate Airports.
121.625 Alternate airport weather minima.
121.627 Continuing flight in unsafe conditions.
121.628 Inoperable instruments and equipment.
121.629 Operation in icing conditions.
121.631 Original dispatch or flight release, redispatch or amendment of dispatch or flight release.
121.633 Considering time-limited systems in planning ETOPS alternates.
121.635 Dispatch to and from refueling or provisional airports: Domestic and flag operations.
121.637 Takeoffs from unlisted and alternate airports: Domestic and flag operations.
121.639 Fuel supply: All domestic operations.
121.641 Fuel supply: Nonturbine and turbo-propeller-powered airplanes: Flag operations.
121.643 Fuel supply: Nonturbine and turbo-propeller-powered airplanes: supplemental operations.
121.645 Fuel supply: Turbine-engine powered airplanes, other than turbo-propeller: Flag and supplemental operations.
121.646 Enroute fuel supply: Flag and supplemental operations.
121.647 Factors for computing fuel required.
121.649 Takeoff and landing weather minimums: VFR: Domestic operations.
121.651 Takeoff and landing weather minimums: IFR: All certificate holders.
121.652 Landing weather minimums: IFR: All certificate holders.
121.653 [Reserved]
121.655 Applicability of reported weather minimums.
121.657 Flight altitude rules.
121.659 Initial approach altitude: Domestic and supplemental operations.
121.661 Initial approach altitude: Flag operations.
121.663 Responsibility for dispatch release: Domestic and flag operations.
121.665 Load manifest.
121.667 Flight plan: VFR and IFR: Supplemental operations.

Subpart V—Records and Reports

121.681 Applicability.
121.683 Crewmember and dispatcher record.
121.685 Aircraft record: Domestic and flag operations.
121.687 Dispatch release: Flag and domestic operations.
121.689 Flight release form: Supplemental operations.
121.691 [Reserved]
121.693 Load manifest: All certificate holders.
121.695 Disposition of load manifest, dispatch release, and flight plans: Domestic and flag operations.
121.697 Disposition of load manifest, flight release, and flight plans: Supplemental operations.
121.698–121.699 [Reserved]
121.701 Maintenance log: Aircraft.
121.703 Service difficulty reports.
121.705 Mechanical interruption summary report.
121.707 Alteration and repair reports.
121.709 Airworthiness release or aircraft log entry.

Part 121: Air Carriers & Commercial Operators

*121.711 Communication records: Domestic and flag operations.
121.713 Retention of contracts and amendments: Commercial operators who conduct intrastate operations for compensation or hire.

Subpart W—Crewmember Certificate: International

121.721 Applicability.
121.723 Surrender of international crewmember certificate.

Subpart X—Emergency Medical Equipment and Training

121.801 Applicability.
121.803 Emergency medical equipment.
121.805 Crewmember training for in-flight medical events.

Subpart Y—Advanced Qualification Program

121.901 Purpose and eligibility.
121.903 General requirements for Advanced Qualification Programs.
121.905 Confidential commercial information
121.907 Definitions.
121.909 Approval of Advanced Qualification Program.
121.911 Indoctrination curriculum.
121.913 Qualification curriculum.
121.915 Continuing qualification curriculum.
121.917 Other requirements.
121.919 Certification.
121.921 Training devices and simulators.
121.923 Approval of training, qualification, or evaluation by a person who provides training by arrangement.
121.925 Recordkeeping requirements.

Subpart Z—Hazardous Materials Training Program

121.1001 Applicability and definitions.
121.1003 Hazardous materials training: General.
121.1005 Hazardous materials training required.
121.1007 Hazardous materials training records.

Subpart AA—Continued Airworthiness and Safety Improvements

121.1101 Purpose and definition.
121.1103 [Reserved]
121.1105 Aging airplane inspections and records reviews.
121.1107 Repairs assessment for pressurized fuselages.
121.1109 Supplemental inspections.
121.1111 Electrical wiring interconnection systems (EWIS) maintenance program.
121.1113 Fuel tank system maintenance program.
121.1115 Limit of validity.
121.1117 Flammability reduction means.

Subpart BB—[Reserved]

121.1200–121.1399 [Reserved]

Subpart CC—[Reserved]

121.1400–121.1499 [Reserved]

Subpart DD— Special Federal Aviation Regulations

121.1500 SFAR No. 111—Lavatory Oxygen Systems

APPENDICES TO PART 121

Appendix A—First-Aid Kits and Emergency Medical Kits
Appendix B—Aircraft Flight Recorder Specifications
Appendix C—C-46 Nontransport Category Airplanes
Appendix D—Criteria for Demonstration of Emergency Evacuation Procedures Under §121.291
*Appendix E—Flight Training Requirements
*Appendix F—Proficiency Check Requirements
Appendix G—Doppler Radar and Inertial Navigation System (INS): Request for Evaluation; Equipment and Equipment Installation; Training Program; Equipment Accuracy and Reliability; Evaluation Program
*Appendix H—Advanced Simulation
Appendix I—[Reserved]
Appendix J—[Reserved]
Appendix K—Performance Requirements for Certain Turbopropeller Powered Airplanes
Appendix L—Type Certification Regulations Made Previously Effective
*Appendix M—Airplane Flight Recorder Specifications
Appendix N—[Reserved]
Appendix O—Hazardous Materials Training Requirements for Certificate Holders
Appendix P—Requirements for ETOPS and Polar Operations

Authority: 49 U.S.C. 106(f), 106(g), 40113, 40119, 41706, 44101, 44701–44702, 44705, 44709–44711, 44713, 44716–44717, 44722, 44732, 46105; Pub. L. 111–216, 124 Stat. 2348 (49 U.S.C. 44701 note); Pub. L. 112–95, 126 Stat. 62 (49 U.S.C. 44732 note).

SPECIAL FEDERAL AVIATION REGULATIONS

SFAR No. 50–2 TO PART 121

SPECIAL FLIGHT RULES IN THE VICINITY OF THE GRAND CANYON NATIONAL PARK, AZ

1. Applicability. This rule prescribes special operating rules for all persons operating aircraft in the following airspace, designated as the Grand Canyon National Park Special Flight Rules Area:

That airspace extending upward from the surface up to but not including 14,500 feet MSL within an area bounded by a line beginning at lat. 36°09'30" N., long. 114°03'00" W.; northeast to lat. 36°14'00" N., long. 113°09'50" W.; thence northeast along the boundary of the Grand Canyon National Park to lat. 36°24'47" N., long. 112°52'00" W.; to lat. 36°30'30" N., long. 112°36'15" W. to lat. 36°21'30" N., long. 112°00'00" W. to lat. 36°35'30" N., long. 111°53'10" W., to lat. 36°53'00" N., long. 111°36'45" W. to lat. 36°53'00" N., long. 111°33'00" W.; to lat. 36°19'00" N., long. 111°50'50" W.; to lat. 36°17'00" N., long. 111°42'00" W.; to lat. 35°59'30" N., long. 111°42'00" W.; to lat. 35°57'30" N., long. 112°03'55" W.; thence counterclockwise via the 5 statute mile radius of the Grand Canyon Airport airport reference point (lat. 35°57'09" N., long. 112°08'47" W.) to lat. 35°57'30" N., long. 112°14'00" W.; to lat. 35°57'30" N., long. 113°11'00" W.; to lat. 35°42'30" N., long. 113°11'00" W.; to 35°38'30" N.; long. 113°27'30" W.; thence counterclockwise via the 5 statute mile radius of the Peach Springs VORTAC to lat. 35°41'20" N., long. 113°36'00" W.; to lat. 35°55'25" N., long. 113°49'10" W.; to lat. 35°57'45" N., 113°45'20" W.; thence northwest along the park boundary to lat. 36°02'20" N., long. 113°50'15" W.; to 36°00'10" N., long. 113°53'45" W.; thence to the point of beginning.

[Editorial Note: Section 2 omitted by the FAA]

3. Aircraft operations: general. Except in an emergency, no person may operate an aircraft in the Special Flight Rules, Area under VFR on or after September 22, 1988, or under IFR on or after April 6, 1989, unless the operation—

(a) Is conducted in accordance with the following procedures:

Note: The following procedures do not relieve the pilot from see-and-avoid responsibility or compliance with FAR 91.119.

(1) Unless necessary to maintain a safe distance from other aircraft or terrain—

(i) Remain clear of the areas described in Section 4; and

(ii) Remain at or above the following altitudes in each sector of the canyon:

Eastern section from Lees Ferry to North Canyon and North Canyon to Boundary Ridge: as prescribed in Section 5.

Boundary Ridge to Supai Point (Yumtheska Point): 10,000 feet MSL.

Western section from Diamond Creek to the Grant Wash Cliffs: 8,000 feet MSL.

(2) Proceed through the four flight corridors describe in Section 4 at the following altitudes unless otherwise authorized in writing by the Flight Standards District Office:

Northbound
11,500 or
13,500 feet MSL

Southbound
>10,500 or
>12,500 feet MSL

(b) Is authorized in writing by the Flight Standards District Office and is conducted in compliance with the conditions contained in that authorization. Normally authorization will be granted for operation in the areas described in Section 4 or below the altitudes listed in Section 5 only for operations of aircraft necessary for law enforcement, firefighting, emergency medical treatment/evacuation of persons in the vicinity of the Park; for support of Park maintenance or activities; or for aerial access to and maintenance of other property located within the Special Flight Rules Area. Authorization may be issued on a continuing basis.

(c)(1) Prior to November 1, 1988, is conducted in accordance with a specific authorization to operate in that airspace incorporated in the operator's part 135 operations specifications in accordance with the provisions of SFAR 50–1, notwithstanding the provisions of Sections 4 and 5; and

(2) On or after November 1, 1988, is conducted in accordance with a specific authorization to operate in that airspace incorporated in the operated in the operator's operations specifications and approved by the Flight Standards District Office in accordance with the provisions of SFAR 50–2.

(d) Is a search and rescue mission directed by the U.S. Air Force Rescue Coordination Center.

(e) Is conducted within 3 nautical miles of Whitmore Airstrip, Pearce Ferry Airstrip, North Rim Airstrip, Cliff Dwellers Airstrip, or Marble Canyon Airstrip at an altitudes less than 3,000 feet above airport elevation, for the purpose of landing at or taking off from that facility. Or

(f) Is conducted under an IFR clearance and the pilot is acting in accordance with ATC instructions. An IFR flight plan may not be filed on a route or at an altitude that would require operation in an area described in Section 4.

Part 121: Air Carriers & Commercial Operators   **SFAR No. 97 to Part 121**

4. Flight-free zones. Except in an emergency or if otherwise necessary for safety of flight, or unless otherwise authorized by the Flight Standards District Office for a purpose listed in Section 3(b), no person may operate an aircraft in the Special Flight Rules Area within the following areas:

(a) Desert View Flight-Free Zone. Within an area bounded by a line beginning at Lat. 35°59'30" N., Long. 111°46'20" W. to 35°59'30" N., Long. 111°52'45" W.; to Lat. 36°04'50" N., Long. 111°52'00" W.; to Lat. 36°06'00" N., Long. 111°46'20" W.; to the point of origin; but not including the airspace at and above 10,500 feet MSL within 1 mile of the western boundary of the zone. The area between the Desert View and Bright Angel Flight-Free Zones is designated the "Zuni Point Corridor."

(b) Bright Angel Flight-Free Zone. Within an area bounded by a line beginning at Lat. 35°59'30" N., Long. 111°55'30" W.; to Lat. 35°59'30" N., Long. 112°04'00" W.; thence counterclockwise via the 5 statute mile radius of the Grand Canyon Airport point (Lat. 35°57'09" N., Long. 112°08'47" W.) to Lat. 36°01'30" N., Long. 112°11'00" W.; to Lat. 36°06'15" N., Long. 112°12'50" W.; to Lat. 36°14'40" N., Long. 112°08'50" W.; to Lat. 36°14'40" N., Long. 111°57'30" W.; to Lat. 36°12'30" N., Long. 111°53'50" W.; to the point of origin; but not including the airspace at and above 10,500 feet MSL within 1 mile of the eastern boundary between the southern boundary and Lat. 36°04'50" N. or the airspace at and above 10,500 feet MSL within 2 miles of the northwest boundary. The area bounded by the Bright Angel and Shinumo Flight-Free Zones is designated the "Dragon Corridor."

(c) Shinumo Flight-Free Zone. Within an area bounded by a line beginning at Lat. 36°04'00" N., Long. 112°16'40" W.; northwest along the park boundary to a point at Lat. 36°12'47" N., Long. 112°30'53" W.; to Lat. 36°21'15" N., Long. 112°20'20" W.; east along the park boundary to Lat. 36°21'15" N., Long. 112°13'55" W.; to Lat. 36°14'40" N., Long. 112°11'25" W.; to the point of origin. The area between the Thunder River/Toroweap and Shinumo Flight Free Zones is designated the "Fossil Canyon Corridor."

(d) Toroweap/Thunder River Flight-Free Zone. Within an area bounded by a line beginning at Lat. 36°22'45" N., Long. 112°20'35" W.; thence northwest along the boundary of the Grand Canyon National Park to Lat. 36°17'48" N., Long. 113°03'15" W.; to Lat. 36°15'00" N., Long. 113°07'10" W.; to Lat. 36°10'30" N., Long. 113°07'10" W.; thence east along the Colorado River to the confluence of Havasu Canyon (Lat. 36°18'40" N., Long. 112°45'45" W.;) including that area within a 1.5 nautical mile radius of Toroweap Overlook (Lat. 36°12'45" N., Long. 113°03'30" W.); to the point of origin; but not including the following airspace designated as the "Tuckup Corridor": at or above 10,500 feet MSL within 2 nautical miles either side of a line extending between Lat. 36°24'47" N., Long. 112°48'50" W. and Lat. 36°17'10" N., Long. 112°48'50" W.; to the point of origin.

5. Minimum flight altitudes. Except in an emergency or if otherwise necessary for safety of flight, or unless otherwise authorized by the Flight Standards District Office for a purpose listed in Section 3(b), no person may operate an aircraft in the Special Flight Rules Area at an altitude lower than the following:

(a) Eastern section from Lees Ferry to North Canyon: 5,000 feet MSL.

(b) Eastern section from North Canyon to Boundary Ridge: 6,000 feet MSL.

(c) Boundary Ridge to Supai (Yumtheska) Point: 7,500 feet MSL.

(d) Supai Point to Diamond Creek: 6,500 feet MSL.

(e) Western section from Diamond Creek to the Grand Wash Cliffs: 5,000 feet MSL.

[Editorial Note: Sections 6–8 omitted by the FAA]

9. Termination date. Section 1. Applicability, Section 4, Flight-free zones, and Section 5. Minimum flight altitudes, expire on April 19, 2001.

[Docket No. FAA–1999–5926, 66 FR 1003, Jan. 4, 2001; as amended by FAA–2001–9218, 66 FR 16584, March 26, 2001; 72 FR 9846, March 6, 2007]

SFAR No. 97 to Part 121
SPECIAL OPERATING RULES FOR THE CONDUCT OF INSTRUMENT FLIGHT RULES (IFR) AREA NAVIGATION (RNAV) OPERATIONS USING GLOBAL POSITIONING SYSTEMS (GPS) IN ALASKA

Those persons identified in Section 1 may conduct IFR en route RNAV operations in the State of Alaska and its airspace on published air traffic routes using TSO C145a/C146a navigation systems as the only means of IFR navigation. Despite contrary provisions of parts 71, 91, 95, 121, 125, and 135 of this chapter, a person may operate aircraft in accordance with this SFAR if the following requirements are met.

1. Purpose, use, and limitations

a. This SFAR permits TSO C145a/C146a GPS (RNAV) systems to be used for IFR en route operations in the United States airspace over and near Alaska (as set forth in paragraph c of this section) at Special Minimum En Route Altitudes (MEA) that are outside the operational service volume of ground-based navigation aids, if the aircraft operation also meets the requirements of sections 3 and 4 of this SFAR.

SFAR No. 97 to Part 121

b. Certificate holders and part 91 operators may operate aircraft under this SFAR provided that they comply with the requirements of this SFAR.

c. Operations conducted under this SFAR are limited to United States Airspace within and near the State of Alaska as defined in the following area description:
From 62°00'00.000"N, Long. 141°00'00.00"W.;
to Lat. 59°47'54.11"N., Long. 135°28'38.34"W.;
to Lat. 56°00'04.11"N., Long. 130°00'07.80"W.;
to Lat. 54°43'00.00"N., Long. 130°37'00.00"W.;
to Lat. 51°24'00.00"N., Long. 167°49'00.00"W.;
to Lat. 50°08'00.00"N., Long. 176°34'00.00"W.;
to Lat. 45°42'00.00"N., Long. -162°55'00.00"E.;
to Lat. 50°05'00.00"N., Long. -159°00'00.00"E.;
to Lat. 54°00'00.00"N., Long. -169°00'00.00"E.;
to Lat. 60°00 00.00"N., Long. -180°00' 00.00"E;
to Lat. 65°00'00.00"N., Long. 168°58'23.00"W.;
to Lat. 90°00'00.00"N., Long. 00°00'0.00"W.;
to Lat. 62°00'00.000"N, Long. 141°00'00.00"W.

(d) No person may operate an aircraft under IFR during the en route portion of flight below the standard MEA or at the special MEA unless the operation is conducted in accordance with sections 3 and 4 of this SFAR.

2. Definitions and abbreviations

For the purposes of this SFAR, the following definitions and abbreviations apply.

Area navigation (RNAV). RNAV is a method of navigation that permits aircraft operations on any desired flight path.

Area navigation (RNAV) route. RNAV route is a published route based on RNAV that can be used by suitably equipped aircraft.

Certificate holder. A certificate holder means a person holding a certificate issued under part 119 or part 125 of this chapter or holding operations specifications issued under part 129 of this chapter.

Global Navigation Satellite System (GNSS). GNSS is a world-wide position and time determination system that uses satellite ranging signals to determine user location. It encompasses all satellite ranging technologies, including GPS and additional satellites. Components of the GNSS include GPS, the Global Orbiting Navigation Satellite System, and WAAS satellites.

Global Positioning System (GPS). GPS is a satellite-based radio navigational, positioning, and time transfer system. The system provides highly accurate position and velocity information and precise time on a continuous global basis to properly equipped users.

Minimum crossing altitude (MCA). The minimum crossing altitude (MCA) applies to the operation of an aircraft proceeding to a higher minimum en route altitude when crossing specified fixes.

Required navigation system. Required navigation system means navigation equipment that meets the performance requirements of TSO C145a/C146a navigation systems certified for IFR en route operations.

Route segment. Route segment is a portion of a route bounded on each end by a fix or NAVAID.

Special MEA. Special MEA refers to the minimum en route altitudes, using required navigation systems, on published routes outside the operational service volume of ground-based navigation aids and are depicted on the published Low Altitude and High Altitude En Route Charts using the color blue and with the suffix "G." For example, a GPS MEA of 4000 feet MSL would be depicted using the color blue, as 4000G.

Standard MEA. Standard MEA refers to the minimum en route IFR altitude on published routes that uses ground-based navigation aids and are depicted on the published Low Altitude and High Altitude En Route Charts using the color black.

Station referenced. Station referenced refers to radio navigational aids or fixes that are referenced by ground based navigation facilities such as VOR facilities.

Wide Area Augmentation System (WAAS). WAAS is an augmentation to GPS that calculates GPS integrity and correction data on the ground and uses geo-stationary satellites to broadcast GPS integrity and correction data to GPS/WAAS users and to provide ranging signals. It is a safety critical system consisting of a ground network of reference and integrity monitor data processing sites to assess current GPS performance, as well as a space segment that broadcasts that assessment to GNSS users to support en route through precision approach navigation. Users of the system include all aircraft applying the WAAS data and ranging signal.

3. Operational Requirements

To operate an aircraft under this SFAR, the following requirements must be met:

a. Training and qualification for operations and maintenance personnel on required navigation equipment used under this SFAR.

b. Use authorized procedures for normal, abnormal, and emergency situations unique to these operations, including degraded navigation capabilities, and satellite system outages.

c. For certificate holders, training of flight crewmembers and other personnel authorized to exercise operational control on the use of those procedures specified in paragraph b of this section.

d. Part 129 operators must have approval from the State of the operator to conduct operations in accordance with this SFAR.

e. In order to operate under this SFAR, a certificate holder must be authorized in operations specifications.

4. Equipment Requirements

a. The certificate holder must have properly installed, certificated, and functional dual required navigation systems as defined in section 2 of this SFAR for the en route operations covered under this SFAR.

b. When the aircraft is being operated under part 91, the aircraft must be equipped with at least one properly installed, certificated, and functional required navigation system as defined in section 2 of this SFAR for the en route operations covered under this SFAR.

5. Expiration date

This Special Federal Aviation Regulation will remain in effect until rescinded.

[Docket No. FAA–2003–14305, SFAR No. 97; 68 FR 14077, March 21, 2003]

SFAR No. 106 to Part 121
RULES FOR USE OF PORTABLE OXYGEN CONCENTRATOR SYSTEMS ON BOARD AIRCRAFT

1. Applicability. This rule prescribes special operating rules for the use of portable oxygen concentrator units on board civil aircraft. This rule applies to both the aircraft operator and the passenger using the portable oxygen concentrator on board the aircraft.

2. Definitions—For the purposes of this SFAR the following definitions apply: Portable Oxygen Concentrator: means the AirSep FreeStyle, AirSep LifeStyle, AirSep Focus, AirSep Freestyle 5, Delphi RS-00400, DeVilbiss Healthcare iGo, Inogen One, Inogen One G2, Inogen One G3, Inova Labs LifeChoice, Inova Labs LifeChoice Activox, International Biophysics LifeChoice, Invacare XPO2, Invacare Solo2, Oxlife Independence Oxygen Concentrator, Oxus RS-00400, Precision Medical EasyPulse, Respironics EverGo, Respironics SimplyGo, SeQual Eclipse, SeQual eQuinox Oxygen System (model 4000), SeQual Oxywell Oxygen System (model 4000), SeQual SAROS and VBOX Trooper Oxygen Concentrator medical device units as long as those medical device units: (1) Do not contain hazardous materials as determined by the Pipeline and Hazardous Materials Safety Administration; (2) are also regulated by the Food and Drug Administration; and (3) assist a user of medical oxygen under a doctor's care. These units perform by separating oxygen from nitrogen and other gases contained in ambient air and dispensing it in concentrated form to the user.

3. Operating Requirements—

(a) No person may use and no aircraft operator may allow the use of any portable oxygen concentrator device, except the AirSep FreeStyle, AirSep LifeStyle, AirSep Focus, AirSep FreeStyle 5, Delphi RS-00400, DeVilbiss Healthcare iGo, Inogen One, Inogen One G2, Inogen One G3, Inova Labs LifeChoice, Inova Labs LifeChoice Activox, International Biophysics LifeChoice, Invacare XPO2, Invacare Solo2, Oxlife Independence Oxygen Concentrator, Oxus RS-00400, Precision Medical EasyPulse, Respironics EverGo, Respironics SimplyGo, SeQual Eclipse, SeQual eQuinox Oxygen System (model 4000), SeQual Oxywell Oxygen System (model 4000), SeQual SAROS and VBOX Trooper Portable Oxygen Concentrator units. These units may be carried on and used by a passenger on board an aircraft provided the aircraft operator ensures that the following conditions are satisfied:

(1) The device does not cause interference with the electrical, navigation or communication equipment on the aircraft on which the device is to be used;

(2) No smoking or open flame is permitted within 10 feet of any seat row where a person is using a portable oxygen concentrator.

(3) During movement on the surface, takeoff, and landing, the unit must:

(i) Either be stowed under the seat in front of the user, or in another approved stowage location, so that it does not block the aisle way or the entryway into the row; or

(ii) If it is to be operated by the user, be used only at a seat location that does not restrict any passenger's access to, or use of, any required emergency or regular exit, or the aisle(s) in the passenger compartment;

(4) No person using a portable oxygen concentrator is permitted to sit in an exit row;

(5) The pilot in command must be apprised whenever a passenger brings and intends to use a portable oxygen concentrator on board the aircraft and the pilot in command must be informed about the contents of the physician's written statement (as required in Section 3(b)(3) of this SFAR), including the magnitude and nature of the passenger's oxygen needs.

(6) Whenever the pilot in command turns off the "Fasten Seat Belt" sign, or otherwise signifies that permission is granted to move about the passenger cabin, passengers operating their portable oxygen concentrator may continue to operate it while moving about the cabin.

(b) The user of the portable oxygen concentrator must comply with the following conditions to use the device on board the aircraft:

(1) The user must be capable of hearing the unit's alarms, seeing the alarm light indicators, and have the cognitive ability to take the appropriate action in response to the various caution and warning alarms and alarm light indicators, or be travelling with someone who is capable of performing those functions;

(2) The user must ensure that the portable oxygen concentrator is free of oil, grease or other petroleum products and is in good condition free from damage or other signs of excessive wear or abuse;

(3) The user must inform the aircraft operator that he or she intends to use a portable oxygen concentrator on board the aircraft and must allow the crew of the aircraft to review the contents of the physician's statement. The user must have a written statement, to be kept in that person's possession, signed by a licensed physician that:

(i) States whether the user of the device has the physical and cognitive ability to see, hear, and understand the device's aural and visual cautions and warnings and is able, without assistance, to take the appropriate action in response to those cautions and warnings;

(ii) States whether or not oxygen use is medically necessary for all or a portion of the duration of the trip; and

(iii) Specifies the maximum oxygen flow rate corresponding to the pressure in the cabin of the aircraft under normal operating conditions.

(4) Only lotions or salves that are oxygen approved may be used by persons using the portable oxygen concentrator device;

(5) The user, whose physician statement specifies the duration of oxygen use, must obtain from the aircraft operator, or by other means, the duration of the planned flight. The user must carry on the flight a sufficient number of batteries to power the device for the duration of the oxygen use specified in the user's physician statement, including a conservative estimate of any unanticipated delays; and

(6) The user must ensure that all portable oxygen concentrator batteries carried onboard the aircraft in carry-on baggage are protected from short circuit and are packaged in a manner that protects them from physical damage. Batteries protected from short circuit include: (1) Those designed with recessed battery terminals; or (2) those packaged so that the battery terminals do not contact metal objects (including the battery terminals of other batteries). When a battery-powered oxygen concentrator is carried onboard aircraft as carry-on baggage and is not intended to be used during the flight, the battery must be removed and packaged separately unless the concentrator contains at least two effective protective features to prevent accidental operation during transport.

4. Expiration Date. This SFAR No. 106 will remain in effect until further notice.

[Docket No. FAA–2004–18596, SFAR No. 106, 70 FR 40164, July 12, 2005; as amended by SFAR 106, 71 FR 53956, Sept. 12, 2006; Docket No. FAA–2008–1227, SFAR 106, 74 FR 2354, Jan. 15, 2009; Docket No. FAA–2009–0767, SFAR 106, 75 FR 742, Jan. 6, 2010; Docket No. FAA–2009–1059, SFAR 106, 75 FR 39632, July 12, 2010; Amdt. 121–358, 77 FR 4220, Jan. 27, 2012; Amdt. 121–361, 77 FR 63221, Oct. 16, 2012; Amdt. 121–367, 79 FR 6081, Feb. 3, 2014]

Subpart A—General

§121.1 Applicability.

This part prescribes rules governing—

(a) The domestic, flag, and supplemental operations of each person who holds or is required to hold an Air Carrier Certificate or Operating Certificate under part 119 of this chapter.

(b) Each person employed or used by a certificate holder conducting operations under this part including maintenance, preventive maintenance, and alteration of aircraft.

(c) Each person who applies for provisional approval of an Advanced Qualification Program curriculum, curriculum segment, or portion of a curriculum segment under Subpart Y of Part 121 of this chapter, and each person employed or used by an air carrier or commercial operator under this part to perform training, qualification, or evaluation functions under an Advanced Qualification Program under Subpart Y of Part 121 of this chapter.

(d) Nonstop Commercial Air Tours conducted for compensation or hire in accordance with §119.1(e)(2) of this chapter must comply with drug and alcohol requirements in §§121.455, 121.457, 121.458 and 121.459, and with the provisions of part 136, subpart A of this chapter by September 11, 2007. An operator who does not hold an air carrier certificate or an operating certificate is permitted to use a person who is otherwise authorized to perform aircraft maintenance or preventive maintenance duties and who is not subject to anti-drug and alcohol misuse prevention programs to perform—

(1) Aircraft maintenance or preventive maintenance on the operator's aircraft if the operator would otherwise be required to transport the aircraft more than 50 nautical miles further than the repair point closest to the operator's principal base of operations to obtain these services; or

(2) Emergency repairs on the operator's aircraft if the aircraft cannot be safely operated to a location where an employee subject to FAA-approved programs can perform the repairs.

(e) Each person who is on board an aircraft being operated under this part.

(f) Each person who is an applicant for an Air Carrier Certificate or an Operating Certificate under part 119 of this chapter, when conducting proving tests.

(g) This part also establishes requirements for operators to take actions to support the continued airworthiness of each airplane.

[Docket No. 28154, 60 FR 65925, Dec. 20, 1995; as amended by Amdt. 121–313, 70 FR 54815, Sept. 16, 2005; Amdt. 121–328, 72 FR 6912, Feb. 13, 2007; Amdt. 121–336, 72 FR 63411, Nov. 8, 2007]

§121.2 Compliance schedule for operators that transition to Part 121; certain new entrant operators.

(a) *Applicability:* This section applies to the following:

(1) Each certificate holder that was issued an air carrier or operating certificate and operations specifications under the requirements of part 135 of this chapter or under SFAR No. 38–2 of 14 CFR part 121 before January 19, 1996, and that conducts scheduled passenger-carrying operations with:

(i) Nontransport category turbopropeller powered airplanes type certificated after December 31, 1964, that have a passenger seat configuration of 10–19 seats;

(ii) Transport category turbopropeller powered airplanes that have a passenger seat configuration of 20–30 seats; or

(iii) Turbojet engine powered airplanes having a passenger seat configuration of 1–30 seats.

(2) Each person who, after January 19, 1996, applies for or obtains an initial air carrier or operating certificate and operations specifications to conduct scheduled passenger-carrying operations in the kinds of airplanes described in paragraphs (a)(1)(i), (a)(1)(ii), or paragraph (a)(1)(iii) of this section.

(b) *Obtaining operations specifications.* A certificate holder described in paragraph (a)(1) of this section may not, after March 20, 1997, operate an airplane described in paragraphs (a)(1)(i), (a)(1)(ii), or (a)(1)(iii) of this section in scheduled passenger-carrying operations, unless it obtains operations specifications to conduct its scheduled operations under this part on or before March 20, 1997.

(c) *Regular or accelerated compliance.* Except as provided in paragraphs (d), (e), and (i) of this section, each certificate holder described in paragraphs (a)(1) of this section shall comply with each applicable requirement of this part on and after March 20, 1997, or on and after the date on which the certificate holder is issued operations specifications under this part, whichever occurs first. Except as provided in paragraphs (d) and (e) of this section, each person described in paragraph (a)(2) of this section shall comply with each applicable requirement of this part on and after the date on which that person is issued a certificate and operations specifications under this part.

(d) *Delayed compliance dates.* Unless paragraph (e) of this section specifies an earlier compliance date, no certificate holder that is covered by paragraph (a) of this section may operate an airplane in 14 CFR part 121 operations on or after a date listed in this paragraph unless that airplane meets the applicable requirement of this paragraph (d):

(1) *Nontransport category turbopropeller powered airplanes type certificated after December 31, 1964, that have a passenger seat configuration of 10–19 seats.* No certificate holder may operate under this part an airplane that is described in paragraph (a)(1)(i) of this section on or after a date listed in paragraph (d)(1) of this section unless that airplane meets the applicable requirement listed in this paragraph (d)(1) of this section:

(i) December 20, 1997:

(A) Section 121.289, Landing gear aural warning.

(B) Section 121.308, Lavatory fire protection.

(C) Section 121.310(e), Emergency exit handle illumination.

(D) Section 121.337(b)(8), Protective breathing equipment.

(E) Section 121.340, Emergency flotation means.

(ii) December 20, 1999: Section 121.342, Pitot heat indication system.

(iii) December 20, 2010:

(A) For airplanes described in §121.157(f), the Airplane Performance Operating Limitations in §§121.189 through 121.197.

(B) Section 121.161(b), Ditching approval.

(C) Section 121.305(j), Third attitude indicator.

(D) Section 121.312(c), Passenger seat cushion flammability.

(iv) March 12, 1999: Section 121.310(b)(1), Interior emergency exit locating sign.

(2) *Transport category turbopropeller powered airplanes that have a passenger seat configuration of 20–30 seats.* No certificate holder may operate under this part an airplane that is described in paragraph (a)(1)(ii) of this section on or after a date listed in paragraph (d)(2) of this section unless that airplane meets the applicable requirement listed in paragraph (d)(2) of this section:

(i) December 20, 1997:

(A) Section 121.308, Lavatory fire protection.

(B) Section 121.337(b)(8) and (9), Protective breathing equipment.

(C) Section 121.340, Emergency flotation means.

(ii) December 20, 2010: §121.305(j), third attitude indicator.

(e) *Newly manufactured airplanes.* No certificate holder that is described in paragraph (a) of this section may operate under this part an airplane manufactured on or after a date listed in this paragraph unless that airplane meets the applicable requirement listed in this paragraph (e).

(1) For nontransport category turbopropeller powered airplanes type certificated after Decem-

ber 31, 1964, that have a passenger seat configuration of 10–19 seats:

(i) Manufactured on or after March 20, 1997:

(A) Section 121.305(j), Third attitude indicator.

(B) Section 121.311(f), Safety belts and shoulder harnesses.

(ii) Manufactured on or after December 20, 1997: Section 121.317(a), Fasten seat belt light.

(iii) Manufactured on or after December 20, 1999: Section 121.293, Takeoff warning system.

(iv) Manufactured on or after March 12, 1999: Section 121.310(b)(1), Interior emergency exit locating sign.

(2) For transport category turbopropeller powered airplanes that have a passenger seat configuration of 20–30 seats manufactured on or after March 20, 1997: Section 121.305(j), Third attitude indicator.

(f) *New type certification requirements.* No person may operate an airplane for which the application for a type certificate was filed after March 29, 1995, in 14 CFR part 121 operations unless that airplane is type certificated under part 25 of this chapter.

(g) *Transition plan.* Before March 19, 1996, each certificate holder described in paragraph (a)(1) of this section must submit to the FAA a transition plan (containing a calendar of events) for moving from conducting its scheduled operations under the commuter requirements of part 135 of this chapter to the requirements for domestic or flag operations under this part. Each transition plan must contain details on the following:

(1) Plans for obtaining new operations specifications authorizing domestic or flag operations;

(2) Plans for being in compliance with the applicable requirements of this part on or before March 20, 1997; and

(3) Plans for complying with the compliance date schedules contained in paragraphs (d) and (e) of this section.

(h) *Continuing requirements.* A certificate holder described in paragraph (a) of this section shall comply with the applicable airplane operating and equipment requirements of part 135 of this chapter for the airplanes described in paragraph (a)(1) of this section, until the airplane meets the specific compliance dates in paragraphs (d) and (e) of this section.

(i) Any training or qualification obtained by a crewmember under part 135 of this chapter before March 20, 1997, is entitled to credit under this part for the purpose of meeting the requirements of this part, as determined by the Administrator. Records kept by a certificate holder under part 135 of this chapter before March 20, 1997, can be annotated with the approval of the Administrator, to reflect crewmember training and qualification credited toward part 121 requirements.

[Docket No. 28154, 60 FR 65925, Dec. 20, 1995; as amended by Amdt. 121–253, 61 FR 2609, Jan. 26, 1996; Amdt. 121–256, 61 FR 30434, June 14, 1996; Amdt. 121–262, 62 FR 13256, March 19, 1997; Amdt. 121–344, 74 FR 34234, July 15, 2009]

§121.4 Applicability of rules to unauthorized operators.

The rules in this part which refer to a person certificated under Part 119 of this chapter apply also to any person who engages in an operation governed by this part without the appropriate certificate and operations specifications required by Part 119 of this chapter.

[Docket No. 11675, 37 FR 20937, Oct. 5, 1972; as amended by Amdt. 121–251, 60 FR 65926, Dec. 20, 1995]

§121.7 Definitions.

The following definitions apply to those sections of part 121 that apply to ETOPS:

Adequate Airport means an airport that an airplane operator may list with approval from the FAA because that airport meets the landing limitations of §121.197 and is either—

(1) An airport that meets the requirements of part 139, subpart D of this chapter, excluding those that apply to aircraft rescue and firefighting service, or

(2) A military airport that is active and operational.

ETOPS Alternate Airport means an adequate airport listed in the certificate holder's operations specifications that is designated in a dispatch or flight release for use in the event of a diversion during ETOPS. This definition applies to flight planning and does not in any way limit the authority of the pilot-in-command during flight.

ETOPS Area of Operation means one of the following areas:

(1) For turbine-engine-powered airplanes with two engines, an area beyond 60 minutes from an adequate airport, computed using a one-engine-inoperative cruise speed under standard conditions in still air.

(2) For turbine-engine-powered passenger-carrying airplanes with more than two engines, an area beyond 180 minutes from an adequate airport, computed using a one-engine-inoperative cruise speed under standard conditions in still air.

ETOPS Entry Point means the first point on the route of an ETOPS flight, determined using a one-engine-inoperative cruise speed under standard conditions in still air, that is—

(1) More than 60 minutes from an adequate airport for airplanes with two engines;

(2) More than 180 minutes from an adequate airport for passenger-carrying airplanes with more than two engines.

ETOPS Qualified Person means a person, performing maintenance for the certificate holder, who has satisfactorily completed the certificate holder's ETOPS training program.

Maximum Diversion Time means, for the purposes of ETOPS route planning, the longest diversion time authorized for a flight under the operator's ETOPS authority. It is calculated under standard conditions in still air at a one-engine-inoperative cruise speed.

North Pacific Area of Operation means Pacific Ocean areas north of 40°N latitudes including NOPAC ATS routes, and published PACOTS tracks between Japan and North America.

North Polar Area means the entire area north of 78°N latitude.

One-engine-inoperative–Cruise Speed means a speed within the certified operating limits of the airplane that is specified by the certificate holder and approved by the FAA for—

(1) Calculating required fuel reserves needed to account for an inoperative engine; or

(2) Determining whether an ETOPS alternate is within the maximum diversion time authorized for an ETOPS flight.

South Polar Area means the entire area South of 60°S latitude.

[Docket No. FAA–2002–6717, 72 FR 1878, Jan. 16, 2007]

§121.9 Fraud and falsification.

(a) No person may make, or cause to be made, any of the following:

(1) A fraudulent or intentionally false statement in any application or any amendment thereto, or in any other record or test result required by this part.

(2) A fraudulent or intentionally false statement in, or a known omission from, any record or report that is kept, made, or used to show compliance with this part, or to exercise any privileges under this chapter.

(b) The commission by any person of any act prohibited under paragraph (a) of this section is a basis for any one or any combination of the following:

(1) A civil penalty.

(2) Suspension or revocation of any certificate held by that person that was issued under this chapter.

(3) The denial of an application for any approval under this part.

(4) The removal of any approval under this part.

[Docket No. FAA–2008–0677, 78 FR 67836, Nov. 12, 2013]

§121.11 Rules applicable to operations in a foreign country.

Each certificate holder shall, while operating an airplane within a foreign country, comply with the air traffic rules of the country concerned and the local airport rules, except where any rule of this part is more restrictive and may be followed without violating the rules of that country.

[Docket No. 16383, 43 FR 22641, May 25, 1978]

§121.15 Carriage of narcotic drugs, marihuana, and depressant or stimulant drugs or substances.

If a certificate holder operating under this part permits any aircraft owned or leased by that holder to be engaged in any operation that the certificate holder knows to be in violation of §91.19(a) of this chapter, that operation is a basis for suspending or revoking the certificate.

[Docket No. 28154, 60 FR 65926, Dec. 20, 1995]

Subpart B—[Reserved]
Certification Rules for Domestic and Flag Air Carriers

Subpart C—[Reserved]
Certification Rules for Supplemental Air Carriers and Commercial Operators

Subpart D—[Reserved]
Rules Governing All Certificate Holders Under This Part

Subpart E—Approval of Routes: Domestic and Flag Operations

Source: Docket No. 6258, 29 FR 19194, December 31, 1964, unless otherwise noted.

§121.91 Applicability.

This subpart prescribes rules for obtaining approval of routes by certificate holders conducting domestic or flag operations.

[Docket No. 28154, 61 FR 2610, Jan. 26, 1996]

§121.93 Route requirements: General.

(a) Each certificate holder conducting domestic or flag operations seeking a route approval must show—

(1) That it is able to conduct satisfactorily scheduled operations between each regular, pro-

visional, and refueling airport over that route or route segment; and

(2) That the facilities and services required by §§121.97 through 121.107 are available and adequate for the proposed operation.

The Administrator approves a route outside of controlled airspace if he determines that traffic density is such that an adequate level of safety can be assured.

(b) Paragraph (a) of this section does not require actual flight over a route or route segment if the certificate holder shows that the flight is not essential to safety, considering the availability and adequacy of airports, lighting, maintenance, communication, navigation, fueling, ground, and airplane radio facilities, and the ability of the personnel to be used in the proposed operation.

[Docket No. 6258, 29 FR 19194, Dec. 31, 1964; as amended by Amdt. 121–3, 30 FR 3638, March 19, 1965; Amdt. 121–253, 61 FR 2610, Jan. 26, 1996]

§121.95 Route width.

(a) Approved routes and route segments over U.S. Federal airways or foreign airways (and advisory routes in the case of certificate holders conducting flag operations) have a width equal to the designated width of those airways or routes. Whenever the Administrator finds it necessary to determine the width of other approved routes, he considers the following:

(1) Terrain clearance.
(2) Minimum en route altitudes.
(3) Ground and airborne navigation aids.
(4) Air traffic density.
(5) ATC procedures.

(b) Any route widths of other approved routes determined by the Administrator are specified in the certificate holder's operations specifications.

[Docket No. 6258, 29 FR 19194, Dec. 31, 1964; as amended by Amdt. 121–253, 61 FR 2610, Jan. 26, 1996]

§121.97 Airports: Required data.

(a) Each certificate holder conducting domestic or flag operations must show that each route it submits for approval has enough airports that are properly equipped and adequate for the proposed operation, considering such items as size, surface, obstructions, facilities, public protection, lighting, navigational and communications aids, and ATC.

(b) Each certificate holder conducting domestic or flag operations must show that it has an approved system for obtaining, maintaining, and distributing to appropriate personnel current aeronautical data for each airport it uses to ensure a safe operation at that airport. The aeronautical data must include the following:

(1) Airports.
(i) Facilities.
(ii) Public protection. After February 15, 2008, for ETOPS beyond 180 minutes or operations in the North Polar area and South Polar area, this includes facilities at each airport or in the immediate area sufficient to protect the passengers from the elements and to see to their welfare.
(iii) Navigational and communications aids.
(iv) Construction affecting takeoff, landing, or ground operations.
(v) Air traffic facilities.
(2) Runways, clearways and stopways.
(i) Dimensions.
(ii) Surface.
(iii) Marking and lighting systems.
(iv) Elevation and gradient.
(3) Displaced thresholds.
(i) Location.
(ii) Dimensions.
(iii) Takeoff or landing or both.
(4) Obstacles.
(i) Those affecting takeoff and landing performance computations in accordance with Subpart I of this part.
(ii) Controlling obstacles.
(5) Instrument flight procedures.
(i) Departure procedure.
(ii) Approach procedure.
(iii) Missed approach procedure.
(6) Special information.
(i) Runway visual range measurement equipment.
(ii) Prevailing winds under low visibility conditions.

(c) If the certificate-holding district office charged with the overall inspection of the certificate holder's operations finds that revisions are necessary for the continued adequacy of the certificate holder's system for collection, dissemination, and usage of aeronautical data that has been granted approval, the certificate holder shall, after notification by the certificate-holding district office, make those revisions in the system. Within 30 days after the certificate holder receives such notice, the certificate holder may file a petition to reconsider the notice with the Director, Flight Standards Service. This filing of a petition to reconsider stays the notice pending a decision by the Director, Flight Standards Service. However, if the certificate-holding district office finds that there is an emergency that requires immediate action in the interest of safety in air transportation, the Director, Flight Standards Service may, upon statement of the reasons, require a change effective without stay.

[Docket No. 6258, 29 FR 19194, Dec. 31, 1964; as amended by Amdt. 121–162, 45 FR 46738, July 10, 1980; Amdt. 121–207, 54 FR 39293, Sept. 25, 1989; Amdt. 121–253, 61 FR 2610, Jan. 26, 1996; Amdt. 121–329, 72 FR 1878, Jan. 16, 2007]

§121.99 Communications facilities—domestic and flag operations.

(a) Each certificate holder conducting domestic or flag operations must show that a two-way communication system, or other means of communication approved by the FAA certificate holding district office, is available over the entire route. The communications may be direct links or via an approved communication link that will provide reliable and rapid communications under normal operating conditions between each airplane and the appropriate dispatch office, and between each airplane and the appropriate air traffic control unit.

(b) Except in an emergency, for all flag and domestic kinds of operations, the communications systems between each airplane and the dispatch office must be independent of any system operated by the United States.

(c) Each certificate holder conducting flag operations must provide voice communications for ETOPS where voice communication facilities are available. In determining whether facilities are available, the certificate holder must consider potential routes and altitudes needed for diversion to ETOPS Alternate Airports. Where facilities are not available or are of such poor quality that voice communication is not possible, another communication system must be substituted.

(d) Except as provided in paragraph (e) of this section, after February 15, 2008 for ETOPS beyond 180 minutes, each certificate holder conducting flag operations must have a second communication system in addition to that required by paragraph (c) of this section. That system must be able to provide immediate satellite-based voice communications of landline-telephone fidelity. The system must be able to communicate between the flight crew and air traffic services, and the flight crew and the certificate holder. In determining whether such communications are available, the certificate holder must consider potential routes and altitudes needed for diversion to ETOPS Alternate Airports. Where immediate, satellite-based voice communications are not available, or are of such poor quality that voice communication is not possible, another communication system must be substituted.

(e) Operators of two-engine turbine-powered airplanes with 207 minute ETOPS approval in the North Pacific Area of Operation must comply with the requirements of paragraph (d) of this section as of February 15, 2007.

[Docket No. 28154, 62 FR 13256, March 19, 1997; as amended by Amdt. 121–329, 72 FR 1878, Jan. 16, 2007; Amdt. 121–333, 72 FR 31680, June 7, 2007]

§121.101 Weather reporting facilities.

(a) Each certificate holder conducting domestic or flag operations must show that enough weather reporting services are available along each route to ensure weather reports and forecasts necessary for the operation.

(b) Except as provided in paragraph (d) of this section, no certificate holder conducting domestic or flag operations may use any weather report to control flight unless—

(1) For operations within the 48 contiguous States and the District of Columbia, it was prepared by the U.S. National Weather Service or a source approved by the U.S. National Weather Service; or

(2) For operations conducted outside the 48 contiguous States and the District of Columbia, it was prepared by a source approved by the Administrator.

(c) Each certificate holder conducting domestic or flag operations that uses forecasts to control flight movements shall use forecasts prepared from weather reports specified in paragraph (b) of this section and from any source approved under its system adopted pursuant to paragraph (d) of this section.

(d) Each certificate holder conducting domestic or flag operations shall adopt and put into use an approved system for obtaining forecasts and reports of adverse weather phenomena, such as clear air turbulence, thunderstorms, and low altitude wind shear, that may affect safety of flight on each route to be flown and at each airport to be used.

[Docket No. 6258, 29 FR 19194, Dec. 31, 1964; as amended by Amdt. 121–27, 36 FR 13911, July 28, 1971; Amdt. 121–134, 42 FR 27573, May 31, 1977; Amdt. 121–253, 61 FR 2610, Jan. 26, 1996]

§121.103 En route navigation facilities.

(a) Except as provided in paragraph (b) of this section, each certificate holder conducting domestic or flag operations must show, for each proposed route (including to any regular, provisional, refueling or alternate airports), that suitable navigation aids are available to navigate the airplane along the route within the degree of accuracy required for ATC. Navigation aids required for approval of routes outside of controlled airspace are listed in the certificate holder's operations specifications except for those aids required for routes to alternate airports.

(b) Navigation aids are not required for any of the following operations—

(1) Day VFR operations that the certificate holder shows can be conducted safely by pilotage because of the characteristics of the terrain;

§121.105

(2) Night VFR operations on routes that the certificate holder shows have reliably lighted landmarks adequate for safe operation; and

(3) Other operations approved by the certificate holding district office.

[Docket No. FAA–2002–14002, 72 FR 31681, June 7, 2007]

§121.105 Servicing and maintenance facilities.

Each certificate holder conducting domestic or flag operations must show that competent personnel and adequate facilities and equipment (including spare parts, supplies, and materials) are available at such points along the certificate holder's route as are necessary for the proper servicing, maintenance, and preventive maintenance of airplanes and auxiliary equipment.

[Docket No. 28154, 61 FR 2610, Jan. 26, 1996]

§121.106 ETOPS Alternate Airport: Rescue and fire fighting service.

(a) Except as provided in paragraph (b) of this section, the following rescue and fire fighting service (RFFS) must be available at each airport listed as an ETOPS Alternate Airport in a dispatch or flight release.

(1) For ETOPS up to 180 minutes, each designated ETOPS Alternate Airport must have RFFS equivalent to that specified by ICAO as Category 4, or higher.

(2) For ETOPS beyond 180 minutes, each designated ETOPS Alternate Airport must have RFFS equivalent to that specified by ICAO Category 4, or higher. In addition, the aircraft must remain within the ETOPS authorized diversion time from an Adequate Airport that has RFFS equivalent to that specified by ICAO Category 7, or higher.

(b) If the equipment and personnel required in paragraph (a) of this section are not immediately available at an airport, the certificate holder may still list the airport on the dispatch or flight release if the airport's RFFS can be augmented to meet paragraph (a) of this section from local fire fighting assets. A 30-minute response time for augmentation is adequate if the local assets can be notified while the diverting airplane is en route. The augmenting equipment and personnel must be available on arrival of the diverting airplane and must remain as long as the diverting airplane needs RFFS.

[Docket No. FAA–2002–6717, 72 FR 1879, Jan. 16, 2007]

§121.107 Dispatch centers.

Each certificate holder conducting domestic or flag operations must show that it has enough dispatch centers, adequate for the operations to be conducted, that are located at points necessary to ensure proper operational control of each flight.

[Docket No. 28154, 61 FR 2610, Jan. 26, 1996]

Subpart F—Approval of Areas and Routes for Supplemental Operations

Source: Docket No. 6258, 29 FR 19195, December 31, 1964, unless otherwise noted.

§121.111 Applicability.

This subpart prescribes rules for obtaining approval of areas and routes by certificate holders conducting supplemental operations.

[Docket No. 28154, 61 FR 2610, Jan. 26, 1996]

§121.113 Area and route requirements: General.

(a) Each certificate holder conducting supplemental operations seeking route and area approval must show—

(1) That it is able to conduct operations within the United States in accordance with paragraphs (a)(3) and (4) of this section;

(2) That it is able to conduct operations in accordance with the applicable requirements for each area outside the United States for which authorization is requested;

(3) That it is equipped and able to conduct operations over, and use the navigational facilities associated with, the Federal airways, foreign airways, or advisory routes (ADR's) to be used; and

(4) That it will conduct all IFR and night VFR operations over Federal airways, foreign airways, controlled airspace, or advisory routes (ADR's).

(b) Notwithstanding paragraph (a)(4) of this section, the Administrator may approve a route outside of controlled airspace if the certificate holder conducting supplemental operations shows the route is safe for operations and the Administrator finds that traffic density is such that an adequate level of safety can be assured. The certificate holder may not use such a route unless it is approved by the Administrator and is listed in the certificate holder's operations specifications.

[Docket No. 6258, 29 FR 19195, Dec. 31, 1964; as amended by Amdt. 121–253, 61 FR 2610, Jan. 26, 1996]

§121.115 Route width.

(a) Routes and route segments over Federal airways, foreign airways, or advisory routes have a width equal to the designated width of those airways or advisory routes. Whenever the Administrator finds it necessary to determine the width of other routes, he considers the following:
(1) Terrain clearance.
(2) Minimum en route altitudes.
(3) Ground and airborne navigation aids.
(4) Air traffic density.
(5) ATC procedures.

(b) Any route widths of other routes determined by the Administrator are specified in the certificate holder's operations specifications.

[Docket No. 6258, 29 FR 19195, Dec. 31, 1964; as amended by Amdt. 121–253, 61 FR 2610, Jan. 26, 1996]

§121.117 Airports: Required data.

(a) No certificate holder conducting supplemental operations may use any airport unless it is properly equipped and adequate for the proposed operation, considering such items as size, surface, obstructions, facilities, public protection, lighting, navigational and communications aids, and ATC.

(b) Each certificate holder conducting supplemental operations must show that it has an approved system for obtaining, maintaining, and distributing to appropriate personnel current aeronautical data for each airport it uses to ensure a safe operation at that airport. The aeronautical data must include the following:
(1) Airports.
 (i) Facilities.
 (ii) Public protection.
 (iii) Navigational and communications aids.
 (iv) Construction affecting takeoff, landing, or ground operations.
 (v) Air traffic facilities.
(2) Runways, clearways, and stopways.
 (i) Dimensions.
 (ii) Surface.
 (iii) Marking and lighting systems.
 (iv) Elevation and gradient.
(3) Displaced thresholds.
 (i) Location.
 (ii) Dimensions.
 (iii) Takeoff or landing or both.
(4) Obstacles.
 (i) Those affecting takeoff and landing performance computations in accordance with Subpart I of this part.
 (ii) Controlling obstacles.
(5) Instrument flight procedures.
 (i) Departure procedure.
 (ii) Approach procedure.
 (iii) Missed approach procedure.
(6) Special information.

 (i) Runway visual range measurement equipment.
 (ii) Prevailing winds under low visibility conditions.

(c) If the certificate-holding district office charged with the overall inspection of the certificate holder's operations finds that revisions are necessary for the continued adequacy of the certificate holder's system for collection, dissemination, and usage of aeronautical data that has been granted approval, the certificate holder shall, after notification by the certificate-holding district office, make those revisions in the system. Within 30 days after the certificate holder receives such notice, the certificate holder may file a petition to reconsider the notice with the Director, Flight Standards Service. This filing of a petition to reconsider stays the notice pending a decision by the Director, Flight Standards Service. However, if the certificate-holding district office finds that there is an emergency that requires immediate action in the interest of safety in air transportation, the Director, Flight Standards Service may, upon a statement of the reasons, require a change effective without stay.

[Docket No. 6258, 29 FR 19195, Dec. 31, 1964; as amended by Amdt. 121–162, 45 FR 46738, July 10, 1980; Amdt. 121–207, 54 FR 39293, Sept. 25, 1989; Amdt. 121–253, 61 FR 2610, Jan. 26, 1996]

§121.119 Weather reporting facilities.

(a) No certificate holder conducting supplemental operations may use any weather report to control flight unless it was prepared and released by the U.S. National Weather Service or a source approved by the Weather Bureau. For operations outside the U.S., or at U.S. Military airports, where those reports are not available, the certificate holder must show that its weather reports are prepared by a source found satisfactory by the Administrator.

(b) Each certificate holder conducting supplemental operations that uses forecasts to control flight movements shall use forecasts prepared from weather reports specified in paragraph (a) of this section.

[Docket No. 6258, 29 FR 19195, Dec. 31, 1964; as amended by Amdt. 121–76, 36 FR 13911, July 28, 1971; Amdt. 121–253, 61 FR 2611, Jan. 26, 1996]

§121.121 En route navigation facilities.

(a) Except as provided in paragraph (b) of this section, no certificate holder conducting supplemental operations may conduct any operation over a route (including to any destination, refueling or alternate airports) unless suitable navigation aids are available to navigate the airplane along the route within the degree of accuracy required for ATC. Navigation aids required for

§121.122

routes outside of controlled airspace are listed in the certificate holder's operations specifications except for those aids required for routes to alternate airports.

(b) Navigation aids are not required for any of the following operations—

(1) Day VFR operations that the certificate holder shows can be conducted safely by pilotage because of the characteristics of the terrain;

(2) Night VFR operations on routes that the certificate holder shows have reliably lighted landmarks adequate for safe operation; and

(3) Other operations approved by the certificate holding district office.

[Docket No. FAA–2002–14002, 72 FR 31681, June 7, 2007]

§121.122 Communications facilities—supplemental operations.

(a) Each certificate holder conducting supplemental operations other than all-cargo operations in an airplane with more than two engines must show that a two-way radio communication system or other means of communication approved by the FAA is available. It must ensure reliable and rapid communications under normal operating conditions over the entire route (either direct or via approved point-to-point circuits) between each airplane and the certificate holder, and between each airplane and the appropriate air traffic services, except as specified in §121.351(c).

(b) Except as provided in paragraph (d) of this section, each certificate holder conducting supplemental operations other than all-cargo operations in an airplane with more than two engines must provide voice communications for ETOPS where voice communication facilities are available. In determining whether facilities are available, the certificate holder must consider potential routes and altitudes needed for diversion to ETOPS Alternate Airports. Where facilities are not available or are of such poor quality that voice communication is not possible, another communication system must be substituted.

(c) Except as provided in paragraph (d) of this section, for ETOPS beyond 180 minutes each certificate holder conducting supplemental operations other than all-cargo operations in an airplane with more than two engines must have a second communication system in addition to that required by paragraph (b) of this section. That system must be able to provide immediate satellite-based voice communications of landline telephone-fidelity. The system must provide communication capabilities between the flight crew and air traffic services and the flight crew and the certificate holder. In determining whether such communications are available, the certificate holder must consider potential routes and altitudes needed for diversion to ETOPS Alternate Airports. Where immediate, satellite-based voice communications are not available, or are of such poor quality that voice communication is not possible, another communication system must be substituted.

(d) Operators of turbine engine powered airplanes do not need to meet the requirements of paragraphs (b) and (c) of this section until February 15, 2008.

[Docket No. FAA–2002–6717, 72 FR 1879, Jan. 16, 2007]

§121.123 Servicing maintenance facilities.

Each certificate holder conducting supplemental operations must show that competent personnel and adequate facilities and equipment (including spare parts, supplies, and materials) are available for the proper servicing, maintenance, and preventive maintenance of aircraft and auxiliary equipment.

[Docket No. 28154, 61 FR 2611, Jan. 26, 1996]

§121.125 Flight following system.

(a) Each certificate holder conducting supplemental operations must show that it has—

(1) An approved flight following system established in accordance with Subpart U of this part and adequate for the proper monitoring of each flight, considering the operations to be conducted; and

(2) Flight following centers located at those points necessary—

(i) To ensure the proper monitoring of the progress of each flight with respect to its departure at the point of origin and arrival at its destination, including intermediate stops and diversions therefrom, and maintenance or mechanical delays encountered at those points or stops; and

(ii) To ensure that the pilot in command is provided with all information necessary for the safety of the flight.

(b) A certificate holder conducting supplemental operations may arrange to have flight following facilities provided by persons other than its employees, but in such a case the certificate holder continues to be primarily responsible for operational control of each flight.

(c) A flight following system need not provide for in-flight monitoring by a flight following center.

(d) The certificate holder's operations specifications specify the flight following system it is authorized to use and the location of the centers.

[Docket No. 6258, 29 FR 19195, Dec. 31, 1964; as amended by Amdt. 121–253, 61 FR 2611, Jan. 26, 1996]

§121.127 Flight following system; requirements.

(a) Each certificate holder conducting supplemental operations using a flight following system must show that—

(1) The system has adequate facilities and personnel to provide the information necessary for the initiation and safe conduct of each flight to—

(i) The flight crew of each aircraft; and

(ii) The persons designated by the certificate holder to perform the function of operational control of the aircraft; and

(2) The system has a means of communication by private or available public facilities (such as telephone, telegraph, or radio) to monitor the progress of each flight with respect to its departure at the point of origin and arrival at its destination, including intermediate stops and diversions therefrom, and maintenance or mechanical delays encountered at those points or stops.

(b) The certificate holder conducting supplemental operations must show that the personnel specified in paragraph (a) of this section, and those it designates to perform the function of operational control of the aircraft, are able to perform their required duties.

[Docket No. 6258, 29 FR 19195, Dec. 31, 1964; as amended by Amdt. 121–253, 61 FR 2611, Jan. 26, 1996]

Subpart G— Manual Requirements

§121.131 Applicability.

This subpart prescribes requirements for preparing and maintaining manuals by all certificate holders.

[Docket No. 6258, 29 FR 19196, Dec. 31, 1964]

§121.133 Preparation.

(a) Each certificate holder shall prepare and keep current a manual for the use and guidance of flight, ground operations, and management personnel in conducting its operations.

(b) For the purpose of this subpart, the certificate holder may prepare that part of the manual containing maintenance information and instructions, in whole or in part, in printed form or other form acceptable to the Administrator.

[Docket No. 28154, 60 FR 65926, Dec. 20, 1995]

§121.135 Manual contents.

(a) Each manual required by §121.133 must—

(1) Include instructions and information necessary to allow the personnel concerned to perform their duties and responsibilities with a high degree of safety;

(2) Be in a form that is easy to revise;

(3) Have the date of last revision on each page concerned; and

(4) Not be contrary to any applicable Federal regulation and, in the case of a flag or supplemental operation, any applicable foreign regulation, or the certificate holder's operations specifications or operating certificate.

(b) The manual may be in two or more separate parts, containing together all of the following information, but each part must contain that part of the information that is appropriate for each group of personnel:

(1) General policies.

(2) Duties and responsibilities of each crewmember, appropriate members of the ground organization, and management personnel.

(3) Reference to appropriate Federal Aviation Regulations.

(4) Flight dispatching and operational control, including procedures for coordinated dispatch or flight control or flight following procedures, as applicable.

(5) En route flight, navigation, and communication procedures, including procedures for the dispatch or release or continuance of flight if any item of equipment required for the particular type of operation becomes inoperative or unserviceable en route.

(6) For domestic or flag operations, appropriate information from the en route operations specifications, including for each approved route the types of airplanes authorized, the type of operation such as VFR, IFR, day, night, etc., and any other pertinent information.

(7) For supplemental operations, appropriate information from the operations specifications, including the area of operations authorized, the types of airplanes authorized, the type of operation such as VFR, IFR, day, night, etc., and any other pertinent information.

(8) Appropriate information from the airport operations specifications, including for each airport—

(i) Its location (domestic and flag operations only);

(ii) Its designation (regular, alternate, provisional, etc.) (domestic and flag operations only);

(iii) The types of airplanes authorized (domestic and flag operations only);

(iv) Instrument approach procedures;

(v) Landing and takeoff minimums; and

(vi) Any other pertinent information.

(9) Takeoff, en route, and landing weight limitations.

(10) For ETOPS, airplane performance data to support all phases of these operations.

(11) Procedures for familiarizing passengers with the use of emergency equipment, during flight.

(12) Emergency equipment and procedures.

§121.135

(13) The method of designating succession of command of flight crewmembers.

(14) Procedures for determining the usability of landing and takeoff areas, and for disseminating pertinent information thereon to operations personnel.

(15) Procedures for operating in periods of ice, hail, thunderstorms, turbulence, or any potentially hazardous meteorological condition.

(16) Each training program curriculum required by §121.403.

(17) Instructions and procedures for maintenance, preventive maintenance, and servicing.

(18) Time limitations, or standards for determining time limitations, for overhauls, inspections, and checks of airframes, engines, propellers, appliances and emergency equipment.

(19) Procedures for refueling aircraft, eliminating fuel contamination, protection from fire (including electrostatic protection), and supervising and protecting passengers during refueling.

(20) Airworthiness inspections, including instructions covering procedures, standards, responsibilities, and authority of inspection personnel.

(21) Methods and procedures for maintaining the aircraft weight and center of gravity within approved limits.

(22) Where applicable, pilot and dispatcher route and airport qualification procedures.

(23) Accident notification procedures.

(24) After February 15, 2008, for passenger flag operations and for those supplemental operations that are not all-cargo operations outside the 48 contiguous States and Alaska,

(i) For ETOPS greater than 180 minutes a specific passenger recovery plan for each ETOPS Alternate Airport used in those operations, and

(ii) For operations in the North Polar Area and South Polar Area a specific passenger recovery plan for each diversion airport used in those operations.

(25)(i) Procedures and information, as described in paragraph (b)(25)(ii) of this section, to assist each crewmember and person performing or directly supervising the following job functions involving items for transport on an aircraft:

(A) Acceptance;
(B) Rejection;
(C) Handling;
(D) Storage incidental to transport;
(E) Packaging of company material; or
(F) Loading.

(ii) Ensure that the procedures and information described in this paragraph are sufficient to assist the person in identifying packages that are marked or labeled as containing hazardous materials or that show signs of containing undeclared hazardous materials. The procedures and information must include:

(A) Procedures for rejecting packages that do not conform to the Hazardous Materials Regulations in 49 CFR parts 171 through 180 or that appear to contain undeclared hazardous materials;

(B) Procedures for complying with the hazardous materials incident reporting requirements of 49 CFR 171.15 and 171.16 and discrepancy reporting requirements of 49 CFR 175.31

(C) The certificate holder's hazmat policies and whether the certificate holder is authorized to carry, or is prohibited from carrying, hazardous materials; and

(D) If the certificate holder's operations specifications permit the transport of hazardous materials, procedures and information to ensure the following:

(1) That packages containing hazardous materials are properly offered and accepted in compliance with 49 CFR parts 171 through 180;

(2) That packages containing hazardous materials are properly handled, stored, packaged, loaded, and carried on board an aircraft in compliance with 49 CFR parts 171 through 180;

(3) That the requirements for Notice to the Pilot in Command (49 CFR 175.33) are complied with; and

(4) That aircraft replacement parts, consumable materials or other items regulated by 49 CFR parts 171 through 180 are properly handled, packaged, and transported.

(26) Other information or instructions relating to safety.

(c) Each certificate holder shall maintain at least one complete copy of the manual at its principal base of operations.

[Docket No. 6258, 29 FR 19196, Dec. 31, 1964; as amended by Amdt. 121–104, 38 FR 14915, June 7, 1973; Amdt. 121–106, 38 FR 22377, Aug. 20, 1973; Amdt. 121–143, 43 FR 22641, May 25, 1978; Amdt. 121–162, 45 FR 46739, July 10, 1980; Amdt. 121–251, 60 FR 65926, Dec. 20, 1995; Amdt. 121–250, 60 FR 65948, Dec. 20, 1995; Amdt. 121–316, 70 FR 58823, Oct. 7, 2005; Amdt. 121–329, 72 FR 1879, Jan. 16, 2007]

§121.137 Distribution and availability.

(a) Each certificate holder shall furnish copies of the manual required by §121.133 (and the changes and additions thereto) or appropriate parts of the manual to—

(1) Its appropriate ground operations and maintenance personnel;

(2) Crewmembers; and

(3) Representatives of the Administrator assigned to it.

(b) Each person to whom a manual or appropriate parts of it are furnished under paragraph (a) of this section shall keep it up-to-date with the changes and additions furnished to that person and shall have the manual or appropriate parts of it accessible when performing assigned duties.

(c) For the purpose of complying with paragraph (a) of this section, a certificate holder may furnish the persons listed therein the maintenance part of the manual in printed form or other form, acceptable to the Administrator, that is retrievable in the English language.

[Docket No. 6258, 29 FR 19196, Dec. 31, 1964; as amended by Amdt. 121–71, 35 FR 17176, Nov. 7, 1970; Amdt. 121–162, 45 FR 46739, July 10, 1980; Amdt. 121–262, 62 FR 13256, March 19, 1997]

§121.139 Requirements for manual aboard aircraft: Supplemental operations.

(a) Except as provided in paragraph (b) of this section, each certificate holder conducting supplemental operations shall carry appropriate parts of the manual on each airplane when away from the principal base of operations. The appropriate parts must be available for use by ground or flight personnel. If the certificate holder carries aboard an airplane all or any portion of the maintenance part of its manual in other than printed form, it must carry a compatible reading device that produces a legible image of the maintenance information and instructions or a system that is able to retrieve the maintenance information and instructions in the English language.

(b) If a certificate holder conducting supplemental operations is able to perform all scheduled maintenance at specified stations where it keeps maintenance parts of the manual, it does not have to carry those parts of the manual aboard the aircraft en route to those stations.

[Docket No. 6258, 29 FR 19196, Dec. 31, 1964; as amended by Amdt. 121–71, 35 FR 17176, Nov. 7, 1970; Amdt. 121–253, 61 FR 2611, Jan. 26, 1996; Amdt. 121–262, 62 FR 13256, March 19, 1997; Amdt. 121–262, 62 FR 15570, April 1, 1997]

§121.141 Airplane flight manual.

(a) Each certificate holder shall keep a current approved airplane flight manual for each type of airplane that it operates except for nontransport category airplanes certificated before January 1, 1965.

(b) In each airplane required to have an airplane flight manual in paragraph (a) of this section, the certificate holder shall carry either the manual required by §121.133, if it contains the information required for the applicable flight manual and this information is clearly identified as flight manual requirements, or an approved Airplane Manual. If the certificate holder elects to carry the manual required by §121.133, the certificate holder may revise the operating procedures sections and modify the presentation of performance data from the applicable flight manual if the revised operating procedures and modified performance date presentation are—

(1) Approved by the Administrator; and

(2) Clearly identified as airplane flight manual requirements.

[Docket No. 28154, 60 FR 65927, Dec. 20, 1995]

Subpart H— Aircraft Requirements

Source: Docket No. 6258, 29 FR 19197, December 31, 1964, unless otherwise noted.

§121.151 Applicability.

This subpart prescribes aircraft requirements for all certificate holders.

§121.153 Aircraft requirements: General.

(a) Except as provided in paragraph (c) of this section, no certificate holder may operate an aircraft unless that aircraft—

(1) Is registered as a civil aircraft of the United States and carries an appropriate current airworthiness certificate issued under this chapter; and

(2) Is in an airworthy condition and meets the applicable airworthiness requirements of this chapter, including those relating to identification and equipment.

(b) A certificate holder may use an approved weight and balance control system based on average, assumed, or estimated weight to comply with applicable airworthiness requirements and operating limitations.

(c) A certificate holder may operate in common carriage, and for the carriage of mail, a civil aircraft which is leased or chartered to it without crew and is registered in a country which is a party to the Convention on International Civil Aviation if—

(1) The aircraft carries an appropriate airworthiness certificate issued by the country of registration and meets the registration and identification requirements of that country;

(2) The aircraft is of a type design which is approved under a U.S. type certificate and complies with all of the requirements of this chapter (14 CFR Chapter 1) that would be applicable to that aircraft were it registered in the United States, including the requirements which must be met for issuance of a U.S. standard airworthiness certificate (including type design conformity, condition for safe operation, and the noise, fuel venting, and engine emission requirements of this chapter), except that a U.S. registration certificate and a U.S. standard airworthiness certificate will not be issued for the aircraft;

(3) The aircraft is operated by U.S.-certificated airmen employed by the certificate holder; and

§121.157

(4) The certificate holder files a copy of the aircraft lease or charter agreement with the FAA Aircraft Registry, Department of Transportation, 6400 South MacArthur Boulevard, Oklahoma City, OK (Mailing address: P.O. Box 25504, Oklahoma City, OK 73125).

[Docket No. 6258, 29 FR 19197, Dec. 31, 1964; as amended by Amdt. 121–165, 45 FR 68649, Oct. 16, 1980]

§121.155 [Reserved]

§121.157 Aircraft certification and equipment requirements.

(a) *Airplanes certificated before July 1, 1942.* No certificate holder may operate an airplane that was type certificated before July 1, 1942, unless—

(1) That airplane meets the requirements of §121.173(c), or

(2) That airplane and all other airplanes of the same or related type operated by that certificate holder meet the performance requirements of sections 4a.737-T through 4a.750-T of the Civil Air Regulations as in effect on January 31, 1965; or §§25.45 through 25.75 and §121.173 (a), (b), (d), and (e) of this title.

(b) *Airplanes certificated after June 30, 1942.* Except as provided in paragraphs (c), (d), (e), and (f) of this section, no certificate holder may operate an airplane that was type certificated after June 30, 1942, unless it is certificated as a transport category airplane and meets the requirements of §121.173(a), (b), (d), and (e).

(c) *C–46 type airplanes: passenger-carrying operations.* No certificate holder may operate a C–46 airplane in passenger-carrying operations unless that airplane is operated in accordance with the operating limitations for transport category airplanes and meets the requirements of paragraph (b) of this section or meets the requirements of part 4b, as in effect July 20, 1950, and the requirements of §121.173(a), (b), (d) and (e), except that—

(1) The requirements of sections 4b.0 through 4b.19 as in effect May 18, 1954, must be complied with;

(2) The birdproof windshield requirements of section 4b.352 need not be complied with;

(3) The provisions of sections 4b.480 through 4b.490 (except sections 4b.484(a)(1) and 4b.487(e)), as in effect May 16, 1953, must be complied with; and

(4) The provisions of paragraph 4b.484(a)(1), as in effect July 20, 1950, must be complied with.

In determining the takeoff path in accordance with section 4b.116 and the one-engine inoperative climb in accordance with section 4b.120 (a) and (b), the propeller of the inoperative engine may be assumed to be feathered if the airplane is equipped with either an approved means for automatically indicating when the particular engine has failed or an approved means for automatically feathering the propeller of the inoperative engine. The Administrator may authorize deviations from compliance with the requirements of sections 4b.130 through 4b.190 and Subparts C, D, E, and F of part 4b (as designated in this paragraph) if he finds that (considering the effect of design changes) compliance is extremely difficult to accomplish and that service experience with the C–46 airplane justifies the deviation.

(d) *C–46 type airplanes: cargo operations.* No certificate holder may use a nontransport category C–46 type airplane in cargo operations unless—

(1) It is certificated at a maximum gross weight that is not greater than 48,000 pounds;

(2) It meets the requirements of §§121.199 through 121.205 using the performance data in Appendix C to this part;

(3) Before each flight, each engine contains at least 25 gallons of oil; and

(4) After December 31, 1964—

(i) It is powered by a type and model engine as set forth in Appendix C of this part, when certificated at a maximum gross takeoff weight greater than 45,000 pounds; and

(ii) It complies with the special airworthiness requirement set forth in §§121.213 through 121.287 of this part or in Appendix C of this part.

(e) *Commuter category airplanes.* Except as provided in paragraph (f) of this section, no certificate holder may operate under this part a nontransport category airplane type certificated after December 31, 1964, and before March 30, 1995, unless it meets the applicable requirements of §121.173(a), (b), (d), and (e) and was type certificated in the commuter category.

(f) *Other nontransport category airplanes.* No certificate holder may operate under this part a nontransport category airplane type certificated after December 31, 1964, unless it meets the applicable requirements of §121.173(a), (b), (d), and (e), was manufactured before March 20, 1997, and meets one of the following:

(1) Until December 20, 2010:

(i) The airplane was type certificated in the normal category before July 1, 1970, and meets special conditions issued by the Administrator for airplanes intended for use in operations under part 135 of this chapter.

(ii) The airplane was type certificated in the normal category before July 19, 1970, and meets the additional airworthiness standards in SFAR No. 23, 14 CFR part 23.

(iii) The airplane was type certificated in the normal category and meets the additional airworthiness standards in Appendix A of part 135 of this chapter.

Part 121: Air Carriers & Commercial Operators   §121.162

(iv) The airplane was type certificated in the normal category and complies with either section 1.(a) or 1.(b) of SFAR No. 41 of 14 CFR part 21.

(2) The airplane was type certificated in the normal category, meets the additional requirements described in paragraphs (f)(1)(i) through (f)(1)(iv) of this section, and meets the performance requirements in Appendix K of this part.

(g) Certain newly manufactured airplanes. No certificate holder may operate an airplane under this part that was type certificated as described in paragraphs (f)(1)(i) through (f)(1)(iv) of this section and that was manufactured after March 20, 1997, unless it meets the performance requirements in Appendix K of this part.

(h) Newly type certificated airplanes. No person may operate under this part an airplane for which the application for a type certificate is submitted after March 29, 1995, unless the airplane is type certificated under part 25 of this chapter.

[Docket No. 6258, 29 FR 19197, Dec. 31, 1964; as amended by Amdt. 121–251, 60 FR 65927, Dec. 20, 1995; Amdt. 121–256, 61 FR 30434, June 14, 1996]

§121.159 Single-engine airplanes prohibited.

No certificate holder may operate a single-engine airplane under this part.

[Docket No. 28154, 60 FR 65927, Dec. 20, 1995]

§121.161 Airplane limitations: Type of route.

(a) Except as provided in paragraph (e) of this section, unless approved by the Administrator in accordance with Appendix P of this part and authorized in the certificate holder's operations specifications, no certificate holder may operate a turbine-engine-powered airplane over a route that contains a point—

(1) Farther than a flying time from an Adequate Airport (at a one-engine-inoperative cruise speed under standard conditions in still air) of 60 minutes for a two-engine airplane or 180 minutes for a passenger-carrying airplane with more than two engines;

(2) Within the North Polar Area; or

(3) Within the South Polar Area.

(b) Except as provided in paragraph (c) of this section, no certificate holder may operate a land airplane (other than a DC-3, C-46, CV-240, CV-340, CV-440, CV-580, CV-600, CV-640, or Martin 404) in an extended overwater operation unless it is certificated or approved as adequate for ditching under the ditching provisions of part 25 of this chapter.

(c) Until December 20, 2010, a certificate holder may operate, in an extended overwater operation, a nontransport category land airplane type certificated after December 31, 1964, that was not certificated or approved as adequate for ditching under the ditching provisions of part 25 of this chapter.

(d) Unless authorized by the Administrator based on the character of the terrain, the kind of operation, or the performance of the airplane to be used, no certificate holder may operate a reciprocating-engine-powered airplane over a route that contains a point farther than 60 minutes flying time (at a one-engine-inoperative cruise speed under standard conditions in still air) from an Adequate Airport.

(e) Operators of turbine-engine powered airplanes with more than two engines do not need to meet the requirements of paragraph (a)(1) of this section until February 15, 2008.

[Docket No. 7329, 31 FR 13078, Oct. 8, 1966; as amended by Amdt. 121–162, 45 FR 46739, July 10, 1980; Amdt. 121–251, 60 FR 65927, Dec. 20, 1995; Amdt. 121–329, 72 FR 1879, Jan. 16, 2007]

§121.162 ETOPS Type Design Approval Basis.

Except for a passenger-carrying airplane with more than two engines manufactured prior to February 17, 2015 and except for a two-engine airplane that, when used in ETOPS, is only used for ETOPS of 75 minutes or less, no certificate holder may conduct ETOPS unless the airplane has been type design approved for ETOPS and each airplane used in ETOPS complies with its CMP document as follows:

(a) For a two-engine airplane, that is of the same model airplane–engine combination that received FAA approval for ETOPS up to 180 minutes prior to February 15, 2007, the CMP document for that model airplane–engine combination in effect on February 14, 2007.

(b) For a two-engine airplane, that is not of the same model airplane–engine combination that received FAA approval for ETOPS up to 180 minutes before February 15, 2007, the CMP document for that new model airplane–engine combination issued in accordance with §25.3(b)(1) of this chapter.

(c) For a two-engine airplane approved for ETOPS beyond 180 minutes, the CMP document for that model airplane–engine combination issued in accordance with §25.3(b)(2) of this chapter.

(d) For an airplane with more than 2 engines manufactured on or after February 17, 2015, the CMP document for that model airplane–engine combination issued in accordance with §25.3(c) of this chapter.

[Docket No. FAA–2002–6717, 72 FR 1879, Jan. 16, 2007]

§121.163 Aircraft proving tests.

(a) *Initial airplane proving tests.* No person may operate an airplane not before proven for use in a kind of operation under this part or part 135 of this chapter unless an airplane of that type has had, in addition to the airplane certification tests, at least 100 hours of proving tests acceptable to the Administrator, including a representative number of flights into en route airports. The requirement for at least 100 hours of proving tests may be reduced by the Administrator if the Administrator determines that a satisfactory level of proficiency has been demonstrated to justify the reduction. At least 10 hours of proving flights must be flown at night; these tests are irreducible.

(b) *Proving tests for kinds of operations.* Unless otherwise authorized by the Administrator, for each type of airplane, a certificate holder must conduct at least 50 hours of proving tests acceptable to the Administrator for each kind of operation it intends to conduct, including a representative number of flights into en route airports.

(c) *Proving tests for materially altered airplanes.* Unless otherwise authorized by the Administrator, for each type of airplane that is materially altered in design, a certificate holder must conduct at least 50 hours of proving tests acceptable to the Administrator for each kind of operation it intends to conduct with that airplane, including a representative number of flights into en route airports.

(d) *Definition of materially altered.* For the purposes of paragraph (c) of this section, a type of airplane is considered to be materially altered in design if the alteration includes—

(1) The installation of powerplants other than those of a type similar to those with which it is certificated; or

(2) Alterations to the aircraft or its components that materially affect flight characteristics.

(e) No certificate holder may carry passengers in an aircraft during proving tests, except for those needed to make the test and those designated by the Administrator. However, it may carry mail, express, or other cargo, when approved.

[Docket No. 6258, 29 FR 19197, Dec. 31, 1964; as amended by Amdt. 121–42, 33 FR 10330, July 19, 1968; 34 FR 13468, Aug. 21, 1969; Amdt. 121–162, 45 FR 46739, July 10, 1980; Amdt. 121–251, 60 FR 65927, Dec. 20, 1995]

Subpart I— Airplane Performance Operating Limitations

Source: Docket No. 6258, 29 FR 19198, December 31, 1964; 30 FR 130, Jan. 7, 1965, unless otherwise noted.

§121.171 Applicability.

(a) This subpart prescribes airplane performance operating limitations for all certificate holders.

(b) For purposes of this part, *effective length of the runway for landing* means the distance from the point at which the obstruction clearance plane associated with the approach end of the runway intersects the centerline of the runway to the far end thereof.

(c) For the purposes of this subpart, *obstruction clearance plane* means a plane sloping upward from the runway at a slope of 1:20 to the horizontal, and tangent to or clearing all obstructions within a specified area surrounding the runway as shown in a profile view of that area. In the plan view, the centerline of the specified area coincides with the centerline of the runway, beginning at the point where the obstruction clearance plane intersects the centerline of the runway and proceeding to a point at least 1,500 feet from the beginning point. Thereafter the centerline coincides with the takeoff path over the ground for the runway (in the case of takeoffs) or with the instrument approach counterpart (for landings), or, where the applicable one of these paths has not been established, it proceeds consistent with turns of at least 4,000 foot radius until a point is reached beyond which the obstruction clearance plane clears all obstructions. This area extends laterally 200 feet on each side of the centerline at the point where the obstruction clearance plane intersects the runway and continues at this width to the end of the runway; then it increases uniformly to 500 feet on each side of the centerline at a point 1,500 feet from the intersection of the obstruction clearance plane with the runway; thereafter it extends laterally 500 feet on each side of the centerline.

[Docket No. 6258, 29 FR 19198, Dec. 31, 1964; as amended by Amdt. 121–132, 41 FR 55475, Dec. 20, 1976]

§121.173 General.

(a) Except as provided in paragraph (c) of this section, each certificate holder operating a reciprocating-engine-powered airplane shall comply with §§121.175 through 121.187.

(b) Except as provided in paragraph (c) of this section, each certificate holder operating a turbine-engine-powered airplane shall comply with the applicable provisions of §§121.189 through 121.197, except that when it operates—

Part 121: Air Carriers & Commercial Operators §121.177

(1) A turbo-propeller-powered airplane type certificated after August 29, 1959, but previously type certificated with the same number of reciprocating engines, the certificate holder may comply with §§121.175 through 121.187; or

(2) Until December 20, 2010, a turbo-propeller-powered airplane described in §121.157(f), the certificate holder may comply with the applicable performance requirements of Appendix K of this part.

(c) Each certificate holder operating a large nontransport category airplane type certificated before January 1, 1965, shall comply with §§121.199 through 121.205 and any determination of compliance must be based only on approved performance data.

(d) The performance data in the Airplane Flight Manual applies in determining compliance with §§121.175 through 121.197. Where conditions are different from those on which the performance data is based, compliance is determined by interpolation or by computing the effects of changes in the specific variables if the results of the interpolation or computations are substantially as accurate as the results of direct tests.

(e) Except as provided in paragraph (c) of this section, no person may take off a reciprocating-engine-powered airplane at a weight that is more than the allowable weight for the runway being used (determined under the runway takeoff limitations of the operating rules of 14 CFR part 121, Subpart I) after taking into account the temperature operating correction factors in the applicable Airplane Flight Manual.

(f) The Administrator may authorize in the operations specifications deviations from the requirements in the subpart if special circumstances make a literal observance of a requirement unnecessary for safety.

(g) The ten-mile width specified in §§121.179 through 121.183 may be reduced to five miles, for not more than 20 miles, when operating VFR or where navigation facilities furnish reliable and accurate identification of high ground and obstructions located outside of five miles, but within ten miles, on each side of the intended track.

[Docket No. 6258, 29 FR 19198, Dec. 31, 1964; as amended by Amdt. 121–251, 60 FR 65920, Dec. 20, 1995]

§121.175 Airplanes: Reciprocating engine-powered: Weight limitations.

(a) No person may take off a reciprocating engine powered airplane from an airport located at an elevation outside of the range for which maximum takeoff weights have been determined for that airplane.

(b) No person may take off a reciprocating engine powered airplane for an airport of intended destination that is located at an elevation outside of the range for which maximum landing weights have been determined for that airplane.

(c) No person may specify, or have specified, an alternate airport that is located at an elevation outside of the range for which maximum landing weights have been determined for the reciprocating engine powered airplane concerned.

(d) No person may take off a reciprocating engine powered airplane at a weight more than the maximum authorized takeoff weight for the elevation of the airport.

(e) No person may take off a reciprocating engine powered airplane if its weight on arrival at the airport of destination will be more than the maximum authorized landing weight for the elevation of that airport, allowing for normal consumption of fuel and oil en route.

(f) This section does not apply to large nontransport category airplanes operated under §121.173(c).

[Docket No. 6258, 29 FR 19195, Dec. 31, 1964; as amended by Amdt. 121–251, 60 FR 65928, Dec. 20, 1995]

§121.177 Airplanes: Reciprocating engine-powered: Takeoff limitations.

(a) No person operating a reciprocating engine powered airplane may takeoff that airplane unless it is possible—

(1) To stop the airplane safely on the runway, as shown by the accelerate stop distance data, at any time during takeoff until reaching critical-engine failure speed;

(2) If the critical engine fails at any time after the airplane reaches critical-engine failure speed V_1, to continue the takeoff and reach a height of 50 feet, as indicated by the takeoff path data, before passing over the end of the runway; and

(3) To clear all obstacles either by at least 50 feet vertically (as shown by the takeoff path data) or 200 feet horizontally within the airport boundaries and 300 feet horizontally beyond the boundaries, without banking before reaching a height of 50 feet (as shown by the takeoff path data) and thereafter without banking more than 15 degrees.

(b) In applying this section, corrections must be made for the effective runway gradient. To allow for wind effect, takeoff data based on still air may be corrected by taking into account not more than 50 percent of any reported headwind component and not less than 150 percent of any reported tailwind component.

(c) This section does not apply to large nontransport category airplanes operated under §121.173(c).

[Docket No. 6258, 29 FR 19198, Dec. 31, 1964; as amended by Amdt. 121–159, 45 FR 41593, June 19, 1980; Amdt. 121–251, 60 FR 65928, Dec. 20, 1995]

§121.179 Airplanes: Reciprocating engine-powered: En route limitations: All engines operating.

(a) No person operating a reciprocating engine powered airplane may take off that airplane at a weight, allowing for normal consumption of fuel and oil, that does not allow a rate of climb (in feet per minute), with all engines operating, of at least 6.90 V_{S0} (that is, the number of feet per minute is obtained by multiplying the number of knots by 6.90) at an altitude of at least 1,000 feet above the highest ground or obstruction within ten miles of each side of the intended track.

(b) This section does not apply to airplanes certificated under part 4a of the Civil Air Regulations.

(c) This section does not apply to large non-transport category airplanes operated under §121.173(c).

[Docket No. 6258, 29 FR 19195, Dec. 31, 1964; as amended by Amdt. 121–251, 60 FR 65928, Dec. 20, 1995]

§121.181 Airplanes: Reciprocating engine-powered: En route limitations: One engine inoperative.

(a) Except as provided in paragraph (b) of this section, no person operating a reciprocating engine powered airplane may take off that airplane at a weight, allowing for normal consumption of fuel and oil, that does not allow a rate of climb (in feet per minute), with one engine inoperative, of at least

$$(0.079 - 0.106/N) V_{S0}^2$$

(where N is the number of engines installed and V_{S0} is expressed in knots) at an altitude of at least 1,000 feet above the highest ground or obstruction within 10 miles of each side of the intended track. However, for the purposes of this paragraph the rate of climb for airplanes certificated under part 4a of the Civil Air Regulations is 0.026 V_{S0}^2.

(b) In place of the requirements of paragraph (a) of this section, a person may, under an approved procedure, operate a reciprocating engine powered airplane, at an all-engines-operating altitude that allows the airplane to continue, after an engine failure, to an alternate airport where a landing can be made in accordance with §121.187, allowing for normal consumption of fuel and oil. After the assumed failure, the flight path must clear the ground and any obstruction within five miles on each side of the intended track by at least 2,000 feet.

(c) If an approved procedure under paragraph (b) of this section is used, the certificate holder shall comply with the following:

(1) The rate of climb (as prescribed in the Airplane Flight Manual for the appropriate weight and altitude) used in calculating the airplane's flight path shall be diminished by an amount, in feet per minute, equal to

$$(0.079 - 0.106/N) V_{S0}^2$$

(when N is the number of engines installed and V_{S0} is expressed in knots) for airplanes certificated under part 25 of this chapter and by 0.026 V_{S0}^2 for airplanes certificated under part 4a of the Civil Air Regulations.

(2) The all-engines-operating altitude shall be sufficient so that in the event the critical engine becomes inoperative at any point along the route, the flight will be able to proceed to a predetermined alternate airport by use of this procedure. In determining the takeoff weight, the airplane is assumed to pass over the critical obstruction following engine failure at a point no closer to the critical obstruction than the nearest approved radio navigational fix, unless the Administrator approves a procedure established on a different basis upon finding that adequate operational safeguards exist.

(3) The airplane must meet the provisions of paragraph (a) of this section at 1,000 feet above the airport used as an alternate in this procedure.

(4) The procedure must include an approved method of accounting for winds and temperatures that would otherwise adversely affect the flight path.

(5) In complying with this procedure fuel jettisoning is allowed if the certificate holder shows that it has an adequate training program, that proper instructions are given to the flight crew, and all other precautions are taken to insure a safe procedure.

(6) The certificate holder shall specify in the dispatch or flight release an alternate airport that meets the requirements of §121.625.

(d) This section does not apply to large non-transport category airplanes operated under §121.173(c).

[Docket No. 6258, 29 FR 19198, Dec. 31, 1964; as amended by Amdt. 121–251, 60 FR 65928, Dec. 20, 1995]

§121.183 Part 25 airplanes with four or more engines: Reciprocating engine-powered: En route limitations: Two engines inoperative.

(a) No person may operate an airplane certificated under part 25 and having four or more engines unless—

(1) There is no place along the intended track that is more than 90 minutes (with all engines operating at cruising power) from an airport that meets the requirements of §121.187; or

(2) It is operated at a weight allowing the airplane, with the two critical engines inoperative, to climb at 0.013 V_{S0}^2 feet per minute (that is, the number of feet per minute is obtained by multiply-

ing the number of knots squared by 0.013) at an altitude of 1,000 feet above the highest ground or obstruction within 10 miles on each side of the intended track, or at an altitude of 5,000 feet, whichever is higher.

(b) For the purposes of paragraph (a)(2) of this section, it is assumed that—

(1) The two engines fail at the point that is most critical with respect to the takeoff weight;

(2) Consumption of fuel and oil is normal with all engines operating up to the point where the two engines fail and with two engines operating beyond that point;

(3) Where the engines are assumed to fail at an altitude above the prescribed minimum altitude, compliance with the prescribed rate of climb at the prescribed minimum altitude need not be shown during the descent from the cruising altitude to the prescribed minimum altitude, if those requirements can be met once the prescribed minimum altitude is reached, and assuming descent to be along a net flight path and the rate of descent to be 0.013 V_{S0}^2 greater than the rate in the approved performance data; and

(4) If fuel jettisoning is provided, the airplane's weight at the point where the two engines fail is considered to be not less than that which would include enough fuel to proceed to an airport meeting the requirements of §121.187 and to arrive at an altitude of at least 1,000 feet directly over that airport.

[Docket No. 6258, 29 FR 19198, Dec. 31, 1964; as amended by Amdt. 121–251, 60 FR 65928, Dec. 20, 1995]

§121.185 Airplanes: Reciprocating engine-powered: Landing limitations: Destination airport.

(a) Except as provided in paragraph (b) of this section no person operating a reciprocating engine powered airplane may take off that airplane, unless its weight on arrival, allowing for normal consumption of fuel and oil in flight, would allow a full stop landing at the intended destination within 60 percent of the effective length of each runway described below from a point 50 feet directly above the intersection of the obstruction clearance plane and the runway. For the purposes of determining the allowable landing weight at the destination airport the following is assumed:

(1) The airplane is landed on the most favorable runway and in the most favorable direction in still air.

(2) The airplane is landed on the most suitable runway considering the probable wind velocity and direction (forecast for the expected time of arrival), the ground handling characteristics of the type of airplane, and other conditions such as landing aids and terrain, and allowing for the effect of the landing path and roll of not more than 50 percent of the headwind component or not less than 150 percent of the tailwind component.

(b) An airplane that would be prohibited from being taken off because it could not meet the requirements of paragraph (a)(2) of this section may be taken off if an alternate airport is specified that meets all of the requirements of this section except that the airplane can accomplish a full stop landing within 70 percent of the effective length of the runway.

(c) This section does not apply to large non-transport category airplanes operated under §121.173(c).

[Docket No. 6258, 29 FR 19198, Dec. 31, 1964; as amended by Amdt. 121–251, 60 FR 65928, Dec. 20, 1995]

§121.187 Airplanes: Reciprocating-engine-powered: Landing limitations: Alternate airport.

(a) No person may list an airport as an alternate airport in a dispatch or flight release unless the airplane (at the weight anticipated at the time of arrival at the airport), based on the assumptions in §121.185, can be brought to a full stop landing, within 70 percent of the effective length of the runway.

(b) This section does not apply to large non-transport category airplanes operated under §121.173(c).

[Docket No. 6258, 29 FR 19198, Dec. 31, 1964; as amended by Amdt. 121–251, 60 FR 65928, Dec. 20, 1995]

§121.189 Airplanes: Turbine engine-powered: Takeoff limitations.

(a) No person operating a turbine engine powered airplane may take off that airplane at a weight greater than that listed in the Airplane Flight Manual for the elevation of the airport and for the ambient temperature existing at takeoff.

(b) No person operating a turbine engine powered airplane certificated after August 26, 1957, but before August 30, 1959 (SR422, 422A), may take off that airplane at a weight greater than that listed in the Airplane Flight Manual for the minimum distances required for takeoff. In the case of an airplane certificated after September 30, 1958 (SR422A, 422B), the takeoff distance may include a clearway distance but the clearway distance included may not be greater than 1/2 of the takeoff run.

(c) No person operating a turbine engine powered airplane certificated after August 29, 1959 (SR422B), may take off that airplane at a weight greater than that listed in the Airplane Flight Manual at which compliance with the following may be shown:

(1) The accelerate-stop distance must not exceed the length of the runway plus the length of any stopway.

§121.189

(2) The takeoff distance must not exceed the length of the runway plus the length of any clearway except that the length of any clearway included must not be greater than one-half the length of the runway.

(3) The takeoff run must not be greater than the length of the runway.

(d) No person operating a turbine engine powered airplane may take off that airplane at a weight greater than that listed in the Airplane Flight Manual—

(1) In the case of an airplane certificated after August 26, 1957, but before October 1, 1958 (SR422), that allows a takeoff path that clears all obstacles either by at least (35+0.01D) feet vertically (D is the distance along the intended flight path from the end of the runway in feet), or by at least 200 feet horizontally within the airport boundaries and by at least 300 feet horizontally after passing the boundaries; or

(2) In the case of an airplane certificated after September 30, 1958 (SR 422A, 422B), that allows a net takeoff flight path that clears all obstacles either by a height of at least 35 feet vertically, or by at least 200 feet horizontally within the airport boundaries and by at least 300 feet horizontally after passing the boundaries.

(e) In determining maximum weights, minimum distances, and flight paths under paragraphs (a) through (d) of this section, correction must be made for the runway to be used, the elevation of the airport, the effective runway gradient, the ambient temperature and wind component at the time of takeoff, and, if operating limitations exist for the minimum distances required for takeoff from wet runways, the runway surface condition (dry or wet). Wet runway distances associated with grooved or porous friction course runways, if provided in the Airplane Flight Manual, may be used only for runways that are grooved or treated with a porous friction course (PFC) overlay, and that the operator determines are designed, constructed, and maintained in a manner acceptable to the Administrator.

(f) For the purposes of this section, it is assumed that the airplane is not banked before reaching a height of 50 feet, as shown by the takeoff path or net takeoff flight path data (as appropriate) in the Airplane Flight Manual, and thereafter that the maximum bank is not more than 15 degrees.

(g) For the purposes of this section the terms, *takeoff distance, takeoff run, net takeoff flight path* and *takeoff path* have the same meanings as set forth in the rules under which the airplane was certificated.

[Docket No. 6258, 29 FR 19197, Dec. 31, 1964; as amended by Amdt. 121–268, 63 FR 8321, Feb. 18, 1998]

§121.191 Airplanes: Turbine engine-powered: En route limitations: One engine inoperative.

(a) No person operating a turbine engine powered airplane may take off that airplane at a weight, allowing for normal consumption of fuel and oil, that is greater than that which (under the approved, one engine inoperative, en route net flight path data in the Airplane Flight Manual for that airplane) will allow compliance with paragraph (a)(1) or (2) of this section, based on the ambient temperatures expected en route:

(1) There is a positive slope at an altitude of at least 1,000 feet above all terrain and obstructions within five statute miles on each side of the intended track, and, in addition, if that airplane was certificated after August 29, 1959 (SR 422B) there is a positive slope at 1,500 feet above the airport where the airplane is assumed to land after an engine fails.

(2) The net flight path allows the airplane to continue flight from the cruising altitude to an airport where a landing can be made under §121.197, clearing all terrain and obstructions within five statute miles of the intended track by at least 2,000 feet vertically and with a positive slope at 1,000 feet above the airport where the airplane lands after an engine fails, or, if that airplane was certificated after September 30, 1958 (SR 422A, 422B), with a positive slope at 1,500 feet above the airport where the airplane lands after an engine fails.

(b) For the purposes of paragraph (a)(2) of this section, it is assumed that—

(1) The engine fails at the most critical point en route;

(2) The airplane passes over the critical obstruction, after engine failure at a point that is no closer to the obstruction than the nearest approved radio navigation fix, unless the Administrator authorizes a different procedure based on adequate operational safeguards;

(3) An approved method is used to allow for adverse winds;

(4) Fuel jettisoning will be allowed if the certificate holder shows that the crew is properly instructed, that the training program is adequate, and that all other precautions are taken to insure a safe procedure;

(5) The alternate airport is specified in the dispatch or flight release and meets the prescribed weather minimums; and

(6) The consumption of fuel and oil after engine failure is the same as the consumption that is allowed for in the approved net flight path data in the Airplane Flight Manual.

[Docket No. 6258, 29 FR 19198, Dec. 31, 1964; 30 FR 130, Jan. 7, 1965; as amended by Amdt. 121–143, 43 FR 22641, May 25, 1978]

§121.193 Airplanes: Turbine engine-powered: En route limitations: Two engines inoperative.

(a) *Airplanes certificated after August 26, 1957, but before October 1, 1958* (SR 422). No person may operate a turbine engine powered airplane along an intended route unless he complies with either of the following:

(1) There is no place along the intended track that is more than 90 minutes (with all engines operating at cruising power) from an airport that meets the requirements of §121.197.

(2) Its weight, according to the two-engine-inoperative, en route, net flight path data in the Airplane Flight Manual, allows the airplane to fly from the point where the two engines are assumed to fail simultaneously to an airport that meets the requirements of §121.197, with a net flight path (considering the ambient temperature anticipated along the track) having a positive slope at an altitude of at least 1,000 feet above all terrain and obstructions within five miles on each side of the intended track, or at an altitude of 5,000 feet, whichever is higher.

For the purposes of paragraph (a)(2) of this section, it is assumed that the two engines fail at the most critical point en route, that if fuel jettisoning is provided, the airplane's weight at the point where the engines fail includes enough fuel to continue to the airport and to arrive at an altitude of at least 1,000 feet directly over the airport, and that the fuel and oil consumption after engine failure is the same as the consumption allowed for in the net flight path data in the Airplane Flight Manual.

(b) *Aircraft certificated after September 30, 1958, but before August 30, 1959* (SR 422A). No person may operate a turbine engine powered airplane along an intended route unless he complies with either of the following:

(1) There is no place along the intended track that is more than 90 minutes (with all engines operating at cruising power) from an airport that meets the requirements of §121.197.

(2) Its weight, according to the two-engine-inoperative, en route, net flight path data in the Airplane Flight Manual, allows the airplane to fly from the point where the two engines are assumed to fail simultaneously to an airport that meets the requirements of §121.197, with a net flight path (considering the ambient temperatures anticipated along the track) having a positive slope at an altitude of at least 1,000 feet above all terrain and obstructions within 5 miles on each side of the intended track, or at an altitude of 2,000 feet, whichever is higher.

For the purposes of paragraph (b)(2) of this section, it is assumed that the two engines fail at the most critical point en route, that the airplane's weight at the point where the engines fail includes enough fuel to continue to the airport, to arrive at an altitude of at least 1,500 feet directly over the airport, and thereafter to fly for 15 minutes at cruise power or thrust, or both, and that the consumption of fuel and oil after engine failure is the same as the consumption allowed for in the net flight path data in the Airplane Flight Manual.

(c) *Aircraft certificated after August 29, 1959* (SR 422B). No person may operate a turbine engine powered airplane along an intended route unless he complies with either of the following:

(1) There is no place along the intended track that is more than 90 minutes (with all engines operating at cruising power) from an airport that meets the requirements of §121.197.

(2) Its weight, according to the two-engine inoperative, en route, net flight path data in the Airplane Flight Manual, allows the airplane to fly from the point where the two engines are assumed to fail simultaneously to an airport that meets the requirements of §121.197, with the net flight path (considering the ambient temperatures anticipated along the track) clearing vertically by at least 2,000 feet all terrain and obstructions within five statute miles (4.34 nautical miles) on each side of the intended track. For the purposes of this subparagraph, it is assumed that—

(i) The two engines fail at the most critical point en route;

(ii) The net flight path has a positive slope at 1,500 feet above the airport where the landing is assumed to be made after the engines fail;

(iii) Fuel jettisoning will be approved if the certificate holder shows that the crew is properly instructed, that the training program is adequate, and that all other precautions are taken to ensure a safe procedure;

(iv) The airplane's weight at the point where the two engines are assumed to fail provides enough fuel to continue to the airport, to arrive at an altitude of at least 1,500 feet directly over the airport, and thereafter to fly for 15 minutes at cruise power or thrust, or both; and

(v) The consumption of fuel and oil after the engine failure is the same as the consumption that is allowed for in the net flight path data in the Airplane Flight Manual.

§121.195 Airplanes: Turbine engine-powered: Landing limitations: Destination airports.

(a) No person operating a turbine engine powered airplane may take off that airplane at such a weight that (allowing for normal consumption of fuel and oil in flight to the destination or alternate airport) the weight of the airplane on arrival would exceed the landing weight set forth in the Airplane Flight Manual for the elevation of the destination

§121.195

or alternate airport and the ambient temperature anticipated at the time of landing.

(b) Except as provided in paragraph (c), (d), or (e) of this section, no person operating a turbine engine powered airplane may take off that airplane unless its weight on arrival, allowing for normal consumption of fuel and oil in flight (in accordance with the landing distance set forth in the Airplane Flight Manual for the elevation of the destination airport and the wind conditions anticipated there at the time of landing), would allow a full stop landing at the intended destination airport within 60 percent of the effective length of each runway described below from a point 50 feet above the intersection of the obstruction clearance plane and the runway. For the purpose of determining the allowable landing weight at the destination airport the following is assumed:

(1) The airplane is landed on the most favorable runway and in the most favorable direction, in still air.

(2) The airplane is landed on the most suitable runway considering the probable wind velocity and direction and the ground handling characteristics of the airplane, and considering other conditions such as landing aids and terrain.

(c) A turbopropeller powered airplane that would be prohibited from being taken off because it could not meet the requirements of paragraph (b)(2) of this section, may be taken off if an alternate airport is specified that meets all the requirements of this section except that the airplane can accomplish a full stop landing within 70 percent of the effective length of the runway.

(d) Unless, based on a showing of actual operating landing techniques on wet runways, a shorter landing distance (but never less than that required by paragraph (b) of this section) has been approved for a specific type and model airplane and included in the Airplane Flight Manual, no person may takeoff a turbojet powered airplane when the appropriate weather reports and forecasts, or a combination thereof, indicate that the runways at the destination airport may be wet or slippery at the estimated time of arrival unless the effective runway length at the destination airport is at least 115 percent of the runway length required under paragraph (b) of this section.

(e) A turbojet powered airplane that would be prohibited from being taken off because it could not meet the requirements of paragraph (b)(2) of this section may be taken off if an alternate airport is specified that meets all the requirements of paragraph (b) of this section.

[Docket No. 6258, 29 FR 19198, Dec. 31, 1964; as amended by Amdt. 121–9, 30 FR 8572, July 7, 1965]

§121.197 Airplanes: Turbine engine-powered: Landing limitations: Alternate airports.

No person may list an airport as an alternate airport in a dispatch or flight release for a turbine engine powered airplane unless (based on the assumptions in §121.195(b)) that airplane at the weight anticipated at the time of arrival can be brought to a full stop landing within 70 percent of the effective length of the runway for turbopropeller powered airplanes and 60 percent of the effective length of the runway for turbojet powered airplanes, from a point 50 feet above the intersection of the obstruction clearance plane and the runway. In the case of an alternate airport for departure, as provided in §121.617, allowance may be made for fuel jettisoning in addition to normal consumption of fuel and oil when determining the weight anticipated at the time of arrival.

[Docket No. 6258, 29 FR 19198, Dec. 31, 1964; as amended by Amdt. 121–9, 30 FR 8572, July 7, 1965; Amdt. 121–179, 47 FR 33390, Aug. 2, 1982]

§121.198 Cargo service airplanes: Increased zero fuel and landing weights.

(a) Notwithstanding the applicable structural provisions of the airworthiness regulations but subject to paragraphs (b) through (g) of this section, a certificate holder may operate (for cargo service only) any of the following airplanes (certificated under part 4b of the Civil Air Regulations effective before March 13, 1956) at increased zero fuel and landing weights—

(1) DC–6A, DC–6B, DC–7B, and DC–7C; and

(2) L1049B, C, D, E, F, G, and H, and the L1649A when modified in accordance with supplemental type certificate SA 4–1402.

(b) The zero fuel weight (maximum weight of the airplane with no disposable fuel and oil) and the structural landing weight may be increased beyond the maximum approved in full compliance with applicable regulations only if the Administrator finds that—

(1) The increase is not likely to reduce seriously the structural strength;

(2) The probability of sudden fatigue failure is not noticeably increased;

(3) The flutter, deformation, and vibration characteristics do not fall below those required by applicable regulations; and

(4) All other applicable weight limitations will be met.

(c) No zero fuel weight may be increased by more than five percent, and the increase in the structural landing weight may not exceed the amount, in pounds, of the increase in zero fuel weight.

(d) Each airplane must be inspected in accordance with the approved special inspection procedures, for operations at increased weights, established and issued by the manufacturer of the type of airplane.

(e) Each airplane operated under this section must be operated in accordance with the passenger-carrying performance operating limitations prescribed in this part.

(f) The Airplane Flight Manual for each airplane operated under this section must be appropriately revised to include the operating limitations and information needed for operation at the increased weights.

(g) Except as provided for the carrying of persons under §121.583 each airplane operated at an increased weight under this section must, before it is used in passenger service, be inspected under the special inspection procedures for return to passenger service established and issued by the manufacturer and approved by the Administrator.

§121.199 Nontransport category airplanes: Takeoff limitations.

(a) No person operating a nontransport category airplane may take off that airplane at a weight greater than the weight that would allow the airplane to be brought to a safe stop within the effective length of the runway, from any point during the takeoff before reaching 105 percent of minimum control speed (the minimum speed at which an airplane can be safely controlled in flight after an engine becomes inoperative) or 115 percent of the power off stalling speed in the takeoff configuration, whichever is greater.

(b) For the purposes of this section—

(1) It may be assumed that takeoff power is used on all engines during the acceleration;

(2) Not more than 50 percent of the reported headwind component, or not less than 150 percent of the reported tailwind component, may be taken into account;

(3) The average runway gradient (the difference between the elevations of the endpoints of the runway divided by the total length) must be considered if it is more than one-half of 1 percent;

(4) It is assumed that the airplane is operating in standard atmosphere; and

(5) The *effective length of the runway* for takeoff means the distance from the end of the runway at which the takeoff is started to a point at which the obstruction clearance plane associated with the other end of the runway intersects the runway centerline.

[Docket No. 6258, 29 FR 19198, Dec. 31, 1964; as amended by Amdt. 121–132, 41 FR 55475, Dec. 20, 1976]

§121.201 Nontransport category airplanes: En route limitations: One engine inoperative.

(a) Except as provided in paragraph (b) of this section, no person operating a nontransport category airplane may take off that airplane at a weight that does not allow a rate of climb of at least 50 feet a minute, with the critical engine inoperative, at an altitude of at least 1,000 feet above the highest obstruction within five miles on each side of the intended track, or 5,000 feet, whichever is higher.

(b) Notwithstanding paragraph (a) of this section, if the Administrator finds that safe operations are not impaired, a person may operate the airplane at an altitude that allows the airplane, in case of engine failure, to clear all obstructions within 5 miles on each side of the intended track by 1,000 feet. If this procedure is used, the rate of descent for the appropriate weight and altitude is assumed to be 50 feet a minute greater than the rate in the approved performance data. Before approving such a procedure, the Administrator considers the following for the route, route segment, or area concerned:

(1) The reliability of wind and weather forecasting.

(2) The location and kinds of navigation aids.

(3) The prevailing weather conditions, particularly the frequency and amount of turbulence normally encountered.

(4) Terrain features.

(5) Air traffic control problems.

(6) Any other operational factors that affect the operation.

(c) For the purposes of this section, it is assumed that—

(1) The critical engine is inoperative;

(2) The propeller of the inoperative engine is in the minimum drag position;

(3) The wing flaps and landing gear are in the most favorable position;

(4) The operating engines are operating at the maximum continuous power available;

(5) The airplane is operating in standard atmosphere; and

(6) The weight of the airplane is progressively reduced by the anticipated consumption of fuel and oil.

§121.203 Nontransport category airplanes: Landing limitations: Destination airport.

(a) No person operating a nontransport category airplane may take off that airplane at a weight that—

(1) Allowing for anticipated consumption of fuel and oil, is greater than the weight that would allow a full stop landing within 60 percent of the ef-

fective length of the most suitable runway at the destination airport; and

(2) Is greater than the weight allowable if the landing is to be made on the runway—

(i) With the greatest effective length in still air; and

(ii) Required by the probable wind, taking into account not more than 50 percent of the headwind component or not less than 150 percent of the tailwind component.

(b) For the purposes of this section, it is assumed that—

(1) The airplane passes directly over the intersection of the obstruction clearance plane and the runway at a height of 50 feet in a steady gliding approach at a true indicated airspeed of at least 1.3 V_{SO};

(2) The landing does not require exceptional pilot skill; and

(3) The airplane is operating in standard atmosphere.

§121.205 Nontransport category airplanes: Landing limitations: Alternate airport.

No person may list an airport as an alternate airport in a dispatch or flight release for a nontransport category airplane unless that airplane (at the weight anticipated at the time of arrival) based on the assumptions contained in §121.203, can be brought to a full stop landing within 70 percent of the effective length of the runway.

§121.207 Provisionally certificated airplanes: Operating limitations.

In addition to the limitations in §91.317 of this chapter, the following limitations apply to the operation of provisionally certificated airplanes by certificate holders:

(a) In addition to crewmembers, each certificate holder may carry on such an airplane only those persons who are listed in §121.547(c) or who are specifically authorized by both the certificate holder and the Administrator.

(b) Each certificate holder shall keep a log of each flight conducted under this section and shall keep accurate and complete records of each inspection made and all maintenance performed on the airplane. The certificate holder shall make the log and records made under this section available to the manufacturer and the Administrator.

[Docket No. 28154, 61 FR 2611, Jan. 26, 1996]

Subpart J— Special Airworthiness Requirements

Source: Docket No. 6258, 29 FR 19202, December 31, 1964, unless otherwise noted.

§121.211 Applicability.

(a) This subpart prescribes special airworthiness requirements applicable to certificate holders as stated in paragraphs (b) through (e) of this section.

(b) Except as provided in paragraph (d) of this section, each airplane type certificated under Aero Bulletin 7A or part 04 of the Civil Air Regulations in effect before November 1, 1946 must meet the special airworthiness requirements in §§121.215 through 121.283.

(c) Each certificate holder must comply with the requirements of §§121.285 through 121.291.

(d) If the Administrator determines that, for a particular model of airplane used in cargo service, literal compliance with any requirement under paragraph (b) of this section would be extremely difficult and that compliance would not contribute materially to the objective sought, he may require compliance only with those requirements that are necessary to accomplish the basic objectives of this part.

(e) No person may operate under this part a nontransport category airplane type certificated after December 31, 1964, unless the airplane meets the special airworthiness requirements in §121.293.

[Docket No. 28154, 60 FR 65928, Dec. 20, 1995]

§121.213 [Reserved]

§121.215 Cabin interiors.

(a) Except as provided in §121.312, each compartment used by the crew or passengers must meet the requirements of this section.

(b) Materials must be at least flash resistant.

(c) The wall and ceiling linings and the covering of upholstering, floors, and furnishings must be flame resistant.

(d) Each compartment where smoking is to be allowed must be equipped with self-contained ash trays that are completely removable and other compartments must be placarded against smoking.

(e) Each receptacle for used towels, papers, and wastes must be of fire-resistant material and must have a cover or other means of containing possible fires started in the receptacles.

[Docket No. 6258, 29 FR 19202, Dec. 31, 1964; as amended by Amdt. 121–84, 37 FR 3974, Feb. 24, 1972]

§121.217 Internal doors.

In any case where internal doors are equipped with louvres or other ventilating means, there must be a means convenient to the crew for closing the flow of air through the door when necessary.

§121.219 Ventilation.

Each passenger or crew compartment must be suitably ventilated. Carbon monoxide concentration may not be more than one part in 20,000 parts of air, and fuel fumes may not be present. In any case where partitions between compartments have louvres or other means allowing air to flow between compartments, there must be a means convenient to the crew for closing the flow of air through the partitions, when necessary.

§121.221 Fire precautions.

(a) Each compartment must be designed so that, when used for storing cargo or baggage, it meets the following requirements:

(1) No compartment may include controls, wiring, lines, equipment, or accessories that would upon damage or failure, affect the safe operation of the airplane unless the item is adequately shielded, isolated, or otherwise protected so that it cannot be damaged by movement of cargo in the compartment and so that damage to or failure of the item would not create a fire hazard in the compartment.

(2) Cargo or baggage may not interfere with the functioning of the fire-protective features of the compartment.

(3) Materials used in the construction of the compartments, including tie-down equipment, must be at least flame resistant.

(4) Each compartment must include provisions for safeguarding against fires according to the classifications set forth in paragraphs (b) through (f) of this section.

(b) *Class A.* Cargo and baggage compartments are classified in the "A" category if—

(1) A fire therein would be readily discernible to a member of the crew while at his station; and

(2) All parts of the compartment are easily accessible in flight.

There must be a hand fire extinguisher available for each Class A compartment.

(c) *Class B.* Cargo and baggage compartments are classified in the "B" category if enough access is provided while in flight to enable a member of the crew to effectively reach all of the compartment and its contents with a hand fire extinguisher and the compartment is so designed that, when the access provisions are being used, no hazardous amount of smoke, flames, or extinguishing agent enters any compartment occupied by the crew or passengers. Each Class B compartment must comply with the following:

(1) It must have a separate approved smoke or fire detector system to give warning at the pilot or flight engineer station.

(2) There must be a hand fire extinguisher available for the compartment.

(3) It must be lined with fire-resistant material, except that additional service lining of flame-resistant material may be used.

(d) *Class C.* Cargo and baggage compartments are classified in the "C" category if they do not conform with the requirements for the "A," "B," "D," or "E" categories. Each Class C compartment must comply with the following:

(1) It must have a separate approved smoke or fire detector system to give warning at the pilot or flight engineer station.

(2) It must have an approved built-in fire-extinguishing system controlled from the pilot or flight engineer station.

(3) It must be designed to exclude hazardous quantities of smoke, flames, or extinguishing agents from entering into any compartment occupied by the crew or passengers.

(4) It must have ventilation and draft controlled so that the extinguishing agent provided can control any fire that may start in the compartment.

(5) It must be lined with fire-resistant material, except that additional service lining of flame-resistant material may be used.

(e) *Class D.* Cargo and baggage compartments are classified in the "D" category if they are so designed and constructed that a fire occurring therein will be completely confined without endangering the safety of the airplane or the occupants. Each Class D compartment must comply with the following:

(1) It must have a means to exclude hazardous quantities of smoke, flames, or noxious gases from entering any compartment occupied by the crew or passengers.

(2) Ventilation and drafts must be controlled within each compartment so that any fire likely to occur in the compartment will not progress beyond safe limits.

(3) It must be completely lined with fire-resistant material.

(4) Consideration must be given to the effect of heat within the compartment on adjacent critical parts of the airplane.

(f) *Class E.* On airplanes used for the carriage of cargo only, the cabin area may be classified as a Class "E" compartment. Each Class E compartment must comply with the following:

(1) It must be completely lined with fire-resistant material.

(2) It must have a separate system of an approved type smoke or fire detector to give warning at the pilot or flight engineer station.

(3) It must have a means to shut off the ventilating air flow to or within the compartment and the controls for that means must be accessible to the flight crew in the crew compartment.

(4) It must have a means to exclude hazardous quantities of smoke, flames, or noxious gases from entering the flight crew compartment.

(5) Required crew emergency exits must be accessible under all cargo loading conditions.

§121.223 Proof of compliance with §121.221.

Compliance with those provisions of §121.221 that refer to compartment accessibility, the entry of hazardous quantities of smoke or extinguishing agent into compartments occupied by the crew or passengers, and the dissipation of the extinguishing agent in Class "C" compartments must be shown by tests in flight. During these tests it must be shown that no inadvertent operation of smoke or fire detectors in other compartments within the airplane would occur as a result of fire contained in any one compartment, either during the time it is being extinguished, or thereafter, unless the extinguishing system floods those compartments simultaneously.

§121.225 Propeller deicing fluid.

If combustible fluid is used for propeller deicing, the certificate holder must comply with §121.255.

§121.227 Pressure cross-feed arrangements.

(a) Pressure cross-feed lines may not pass through parts of the airplane used for carrying persons or cargo unless—

(1) There is a means to allow crewmembers to shut off the supply of fuel to these lines; or

(2) The lines are enclosed in a fuel and fume-proof enclosure that is ventilated and drained to the exterior of the airplane.

However, such an enclosure need not be used if those lines incorporate no fittings on or within the personnel or cargo areas and are suitably routed or protected to prevent accidental damage.

(b) Lines that can be isolated from the rest of the fuel system by valves at each end must incorporate provisions for relieving excessive pressures that may result from exposure of the isolated line to high temperatures.

§121.229 Location of fuel tanks.

(a) Fuel tanks must be located in accordance with §121.255.

(b) No part of the engine nacelle skin that lies immediately behind a major air outlet from the engine compartment may be used as the wall of an integral tank.

(c) Fuel tanks must be isolated from personnel compartments by means of fume- and fuel-proof enclosures.

§121.231 Fuel system lines and fittings.

(a) Fuel lines must be installed and supported so as to prevent excessive vibration and so as to be adequate to withstand loads due to fuel pressure and accelerated flight conditions.

(b) Lines connected to components of the airplanes between which there may be relative motion must incorporate provisions for flexibility.

(c) Flexible connections in lines that may be under pressure and subject to axial loading must use flexible hose assemblies rather than hose clamp connections.

(d) Flexible hose must be of an acceptable type or proven suitable for the particular application.

§121.233 Fuel lines and fittings in designated fire zones.

Fuel lines and fittings in each designated fire zone must comply with §121.259.

§121.235 Fuel valves.

Each fuel valve must—

(a) Comply with §121.257;

(b) Have positive stops or suitable index provisions in the "on" and "off" positions; and

(c) Be supported so that loads resulting from its operation or from accelerated flight conditions are not transmitted to the lines connected to the valve.

§121.237 Oil lines and fittings in designated fire zones.

Oil line and fittings in each designated fire zone must comply with §121.259.

§121.239 Oil valves.

(a) Each oil valve must—

(1) Comply with §121.257;

(2) Have positive stops or suitable index provisions in the "on" and "off" positions; and

(3) Be supported so that loads resulting from its operation or from accelerated flight conditions are not transmitted to the lines attached to the valve.

(b) The closing of an oil shutoff means must not prevent feathering the propeller, unless equivalent safety provisions are incorporated.

§121.241 Oil system drains.

Accessible drains incorporating either a manual or automatic means for positive locking in the closed position, must be provided to allow safe drainage of the entire oil system.

§121.243 Engine breather lines.

(a) Engine breather lines must be so arranged that condensed water vapor that may freeze and obstruct the line cannot accumulate at any point.

(b) Engine breathers must discharge in a location that does not constitute a fire hazard in case foaming occurs and so that oil emitted from the line does not impinge upon the pilots' windshield.

(c) Engine breathers may not discharge into the engine air induction system.

§121.245 Fire walls.

Each engine, auxiliary power unit, fuel-burning heater, or other item of combustion equipment that is intended for operation in flight must be isolated from the rest of the airplane by means of firewalls or shrouds, or by other equivalent means.

§121.247 Fire-wall construction.

Each fire wall and shroud must—

(a) Be so made that no hazardous quantity of air, fluids, or flame can pass from the engine compartment to other parts of the airplane;

(b) Have all openings in the fire wall or shroud sealed with close-fitting fire-proof grommets, bushings, or firewall fittings;

(c) Be made of fireproof material; and

(d) Be protected against corrosion.

§121.249 Cowling.

(a) Cowling must be made and supported so as to resist the vibration inertia, and air loads to which it may be normally subjected.

(b) Provisions must be made to allow rapid and complete drainage of the cowling in normal ground and flight attitudes. Drains must not discharge in locations constituting a fire hazard. Parts of the cowling that are subjected to high temperatures because they are near exhaust system parts or because of exhaust gas impingement must be made of fireproof material. Unless otherwise specified in these regulations all other parts of the cowling must be made of material that is at least fire resistant.

§121.251 Engine accessory section diaphragm.

Unless equivalent protection can be shown by other means, a diaphragm that complies with §121.247 must be provided on air-cooled engines to isolate the engine power section and all parts of the exhaust system from the engine accessory compartment.

§121.253 Powerplant fire protection.

(a) Designated fire zones must be protected from fire by compliance with §§121.255 through 121.261.

(b) Designated fire zones are—

(1) Engine accessory sections;

(2) Installations where no isolation is provided between the engine and accessory compartment; and

(3) Areas that contain auxiliary power units, fuel-burning heaters, and other combustion equipment.

§121.255 Flammable fluids.

(a) No tanks or reservoirs that are a part of a system containing flammable fluids or gases may be located in designated fire zones, except where the fluid contained, the design of the system, the materials used in the tank, the shutoff means, and the connections, lines, and controls provide equivalent safety.

(b) At least one-half inch of clear airspace must be provided between any tank or reservoir and a firewall or shroud isolating a designated fire zone.

§121.257 Shutoff means.

(a) Each engine must have a means for shutting off or otherwise preventing hazardous amounts of fuel, oil, deicer, and other flammable fluids from flowing into, within, or through any designated fire zone. However, means need not be provided to shut off flow in lines that are an integral part of an engine.

(b) The shutoff means must allow an emergency operating sequence that is compatible with the emergency operation of other equipment, such as feathering the propeller, to facilitate rapid and effective control of fires.

(c) Shutoff means must be located outside of designated fire zones, unless equivalent safety is provided, and it must be shown that no hazardous amount of flammable fluid will drain into any designated fire zone after a shut off.

(d) Adequate provisions must be made to guard against inadvertent operation of the shutoff means and to make it possible for the crew to reopen the shutoff means after it has been closed.

§121.259 Lines and fittings.

(a) Each line, and its fittings, that is located in a designated fire zone, if it carries flammable fluids or gases under pressure, or is attached directly to the engine, or is subject to relative motion between components (except lines and fittings forming an integral part of the engine), must be flexible and fire-resistant with fire-resistant, factory-fixed, detachable, or other approved fire-resistant ends.

(b) Lines and fittings that are not subject to pressure or to relative motion between components must be of fire-resistant materials.

§121.261 Vent and drain lines.

All vent and drain lines and their fittings, that are located in a designated fire zone must, if they carry flammable fluids or gases, comply with §121.259, if the Administrator finds that the rupture or breakage of any vent or drain line may result in a fire hazard.

§121.263 Fire-extinguishing systems.

(a) Unless the certificate holder shows that equivalent protection against destruction of the airplane in case of fire is provided by the use of fireproof materials in the nacelle and other components that would be subjected to flame, fire-extinguishing systems must be provided to serve all designated fire zones.

(b) Materials in the fire-extinguishing system must not react chemically with the extinguishing agent so as to be a hazard.

§121.265 Fire-extinguishing agents.

Only methyl bromide, carbon dioxide, or another agent that has been shown to provide equivalent extinguishing action may be used as a fire-extinguishing agent. If methyl bromide or any other toxic extinguishing agent is used, provisions must be made to prevent harmful concentrations of fluid or fluid vapors from entering any personnel compartment either because of leakage during normal operation of the airplane or because of discharging the fire extinguisher on the ground or in flight when there is a defect in the extinguishing system. If a methyl bromide system is used, the containers must be charged with dry agent and sealed by the fire-extinguisher manufacturer or some other person using satisfactory recharging equipment. If carbon dioxide is used, it must not be possible to discharge enough gas into the personnel compartments to create a danger of suffocating the occupants.

§121.267 Extinguishing agent container pressure relief.

Extinguishing agent containers must be provided with a pressure relief to prevent bursting of the container because of excessive internal pressures. The discharge line from the relief connection must terminate outside the airplane in a place convenient for inspection on the ground. An indicator must be provided at the discharge end of the line to provide a visual indication when the container has discharged.

§121.269 Extinguishing agent container compartment temperature.

Precautions must be taken to insure that the extinguishing agent containers are installed in places where reasonable temperatures can be maintained for effective use of the extinguishing system.

§121.271 Fire-extinguishing system materials.

(a) Except as provided in paragraph (b) of this section, each component of a fire-extinguishing system that is in a designated fire zone must be made of fireproof materials.

(b) Connections that are subject to relative motion between components of the airplane must be made of flexible materials that are at least fire-resistant and be located so as to minimize the probability of failure.

§121.273 Fire-detector systems.

Enough quick-acting fire detectors must be provided in each designated fire zone to assure the detection of any fire that may occur in that zone.

§121.275 Fire detectors.

Fire detectors must be made and installed in a manner that assures their ability to resist, without failure, all vibration, inertia, and other loads to which they may be normally subjected. Fire detectors must be unaffected by exposure to fumes, oil, water, or other fluids that may be present.

§121.277 Protection of other airplane components against fire.

(a) Except as provided in paragraph (b) of this section, all airplane surfaces aft of the nacelles in the area of one nacelle diameter on both sides of the nacelle centerline must be made of material that is at least fire resistant.

(b) Paragraph (a) of this section does not apply to tail surfaces lying behind nacelles unless the dimensional configuration of the airplane is such that the tail surfaces could be affected readily by heat, flames, or sparks emanating from a designated fire zone or from the engine compartment of any nacelle.

§121.279 Control of engine rotation.

(a) Except as provided in paragraph (b) of this section, each airplane must have a means of individually stopping and restarting the rotation of any engine in flight.

(b) In the case of turbine engine installations, a means of stopping the rotation need be provided only if the Administrator finds that rotation could jeopardize the safety of the airplane.

§121.281 Fuel system independence.

(a) Each airplane fuel system must be arranged so that the failure of any one component does not result in the irrecoverable loss of power of more than one engine.

(b) A separate fuel tank need not be provided for each engine if the certificate holder shows that the fuel system incorporates features that provide equivalent safety.

§121.283 Induction system ice prevention.

A means for preventing the malfunctioning of each engine due to ice accumulation in the engine air induction system must be provided for each airplane.

§121.285 Carriage of cargo in passenger compartments.

(a) Except as provided in paragraph (b), (c), or (d) or this section, no certificate holder may carry cargo in the passenger compartment of an airplane.

(b) Cargo may be carried anywhere in the passenger compartment if it is carried in an approved cargo bin that meets the following requirements:

(1) The bin must withstand the load factors and emergency landing conditions applicable to the passenger seats of the airplane in which the bin is installed, multiplied by a factor of 1.15, using the combined weight of the bin and the maximum weight of cargo that may be carried in the bin.

(2) The maximum weight of cargo that the bin is approved to carry and any instructions necessary to insure proper weight distribution within the bin must be conspicuously marked on the bin.

(3) The bin may not impose any load on the floor or other structure of the airplane that exceeds the load limitations of that structure.

(4) The bin must be attached to the seat tracks or to the floor structure of the airplane, and its attachment must withstand the load factors and emergency landing conditions applicable to the passenger seats of the airplane in which the bin is installed, multiplied by either the factor 1.15 or the seat attachment factor specified for the airplane, whichever is greater, using the combined weight of the bin and the maximum weight of cargo that may be carried in the bin.

(5) The bin may not be installed in a position that restricts access to or use of any required emergency exit, or of the aisle in the passenger compartment.

(6) The bin must be fully enclosed and made of material that is at least flame resistant.

(7) Suitable safeguards must be provided within the bin to prevent the cargo from shifting under emergency landing conditions.

(8) The bin may not be installed in a position that obscures any passenger's view of the "seat belt" sign "no smoking" sign, or any required exit sign, unless an auxiliary sign or other approved means for proper notification of the passenger is provided.

(c) Cargo may be carried aft of a bulkhead or divider in any passenger compartment provided the cargo is restrained to the load factors in §25.561(b)(3) and is loaded as follows:

(1) It is properly secured by a safety belt or other tiedown having enough strength to eliminate the possibility of shifting under all normally anticipated flight and ground conditions.

(2) It is packaged or covered in a manner to avoid possible injury to passengers and passenger compartment occupants.

(3) It does not impose any load on seats or the floor structure that exceeds the load limitation for those components.

(4) Its location does not restrict access to or use of any required emergency or regular exit, or of the aisle in the passenger compartment.

(5) Its location does not obscure any passenger's view of the "seat belt" sign, "no smoking" sign, or required exit sign, unless an auxiliary sign or other approved means for proper notification of the passenger is provided.

(d) Cargo, including carry-on baggage, may be carried anywhere in the passenger compartment of a nontransport category airplane type certificated after December 31, 1964, if it is carried in an approved cargo rack, bin, or compartment installed in or on the airplane, if it is secured by an approved means, or if it is carried in accordance with each of the following:

(1) For cargo, it is properly secured by a safety belt or other tie-down having enough strength to eliminate the possibility of shifting under all normally anticipated flight and ground conditions, or for carry-on baggage, it is restrained so as to prevent its movement during air turbulence.

(2) It is packaged or covered to avoid possible injury to occupants.

(3) It does not impose any load on seats or in the floor structure that exceeds the load limitation for those components.

(4) It is not located in a position that obstructs the access to, or use of, any required emergency or regular exit, or the use of the aisle between the crew and the passenger compartment, or is located in a position that obscures any passenger's view of the "seat belt" sign, "no smoking" sign or placard, or any required exit sign, unless an auxiliary sign or other approved means for proper notification of the passengers is provided.

(5) It is not carried directly above seated occupants.

(6) It is stowed in compliance with this section for takeoff and landing.

(7) For cargo-only operations, paragraph (d)(4) of this section does not apply if the cargo is loaded so that at least one emergency or regular exit is available to provide all occupants of the airplane a means of unobstructed exit from the airplane if an emergency occurs.

[Docket No. 6258, 29 FR 19202, Dec. 31, 1964; as amended by Amdt. 121–179, 47 FR 33390, Aug. 2, 1982; Amdt. 121–251, 60 FR 65928, Dec. 20, 1995]

§121.287 Carriage of cargo in cargo compartments.

When cargo is carried in cargo compartments that are designed to require the physical entry of a crewmember to extinguish any fire that may occur during flight, the cargo must be loaded so as to allow a crewmember to effectively reach all parts of the compartment with the contents of a hand fire extinguisher.

§121.289 Landing gear: Aural warning device.

(a) Except for airplanes that comply with the requirements of §25.729 of this chapter on or after January 6, 1992, each airplane must have a landing gear aural warning device that functions continuously under the following conditions:

(1) For airplanes with an established approach wing-flap position, whenever the wing flaps are extended beyond the maximum certificated approach climb configuration position in the Airplane Flight Manual and the landing gear is not fully extended and locked.

(2) For airplanes without an established approach climb wing-flap position, whenever the wing flaps are extended beyond the position at which landing gear extension is normally performed and the landing gear is not fully extended and locked.

(b) The warning system required by paragraph (a) of this section—

(1) May not have a manual shutoff;

(2) Must be in addition to the throttle-actuated device installed under the type certification airworthiness requirements; and

(3) May utilize any part of the throttle-actuated system including the aural warning device.

(c) The flap position sensing unit may be installed at any suitable place in the airplane.

[Docket No. 6258, 29 FR 19202, Dec. 31, 1964; as amended by Amdt. 121–3, 30 FR 3638, March 19, 1965; Amdt. 121–130, 41 FR 47229, Oct. 28, 1976; Amdt. 121–227, 56 FR 63762, Dec. 5, 1991; Amdt. 121–251, 60 FR 65929, Dec. 20, 1995]

§121.291 Demonstration of emergency evacuation procedures.

(a) Except as provided in paragraph (a)(1) of this section, each certificate holder must conduct an actual demonstration of emergency evacuation procedures in accordance with paragraph (a) of Appendix D to this part to show that each type and model of airplane with a seating capacity of more than 44 passengers to be used in its passenger-carrying operations allows the evacuation of the full capacity, including crewmembers, in 90 seconds or less.

(1) An actual demonstration need not be conducted if that airplane type and model has been shown to be in compliance with this paragraph in effect on or after October 24, 1967, or, if during type certification, with §25.803 of this chapter in effect on or after December 1, 1978.

(2) Any actual demonstration conducted after September 27, 1993, must be in accordance with paragraph (a) of Appendix D to this part in effect on or after that date or with §25.803 in effect on or after that date.

(b) Each certificate holder conducting operations with airplanes with a seating capacity of more than 44 passengers must conduct a partial demonstration of emergency evacuation procedures in accordance with paragraph (c) of this section upon:

(1) Initial introduction of a type and model of airplane into passenger-carrying operation;

(2) Changing the number, location, or emergency evacuation duties or procedures of flight attendants who are required by §121.391; or

(3) Changing the number, location, type of emergency exits, or type of opening mechanism on emergency exits available for evacuation.

(c) In conducting the partial demonstration required by paragraph (b) of this section, each certificate holder must:

(1) Demonstrate the effectiveness of its crewmember emergency training and evacuation procedures by conducting a demonstration, not requiring passengers and observed by the Administrator, in which the flight attendants for that type and model of airplane, using that operator's line operating procedures, open 50 percent of the required floor-level emergency exits and 50 percent of the required non-floor-level emergency exits whose opening by a flight attendant is defined as an emergency evacuation duty under §121.397, and deploy 50 percent of the exit slides. The exits and slides will be selected by the administrator and must be ready for use within 15 seconds;

(2) Apply for and obtain approval from the certificate-holding district office before conducting the demonstration;

(3) Use flight attendants in this demonstration who have been selected at random by the Administrator, have completed the certificate holder's FAA-approved training program for the type and model of airplane, and have passed a written or practical examination on the emergency equipment and procedures; and

(4) Apply for and obtain approval from the certificate-holding district office before commencing operations with this type and model airplane.

(d) Each certificate holder operating or proposing to operate one or more landplanes in extended overwater operations, or otherwise required to have certain equipment under §121.339, must show, by simulated ditching conducted in accordance with paragraph (b) of Appendix D to this part, that it has the ability to efficiently carry out its ditching procedures. For certificate holders subject to §121.2(a)(1), this paragraph applies only when a new type or model airplane is introduced into the certificate holder's operations after January 19, 1996.

(e) For a type and model airplane for which the simulated ditching specified in paragraph (d) has been conducted by a part 121 certificate holder, the requirements of paragraphs (b)(2), (b)(4), and (b)(5) of Appendix D to this part are complied with if each life raft is removed from stowage, one life raft is launched and inflated (or one slide life raft is inflated) and crewmembers assigned to the inflated life raft display and describe the use of each item of required emergency equipment. The life raft or slide life raft to be inflated will be selected by the Administrator.

[Docket No. 21269, 46 FR 61453, Dec. 17, 1981; as amended by Amdt. 121–233, 58 FR 45230, Aug. 26, 1993; Amdt. 121–251, 60 FR 65929, Dec. 20, 1995; Amdt. 121–307, 69 FR 67499, Nov. 17, 2004]

§121.293 Special airworthiness requirements for nontransport category airplanes type certificated after December 31, 1964.

No certificate holder may operate a nontransport category airplane manufactured after December 20, 1999, unless the airplane contains a takeoff warning system that meets the requirements of 14 CFR 25.703. However, the takeoff warning system does not have to cover any device for which it has been demonstrated that takeoff with that device in the most adverse position would not create a hazardous condition.

[Docket No. 28154, 60 FR 65929, Dec. 20, 1995]

§121.295 Location for a suspect device.

After November 28, 2009, all airplanes with a maximum certificated passenger seating capacity of more than 60 persons must have a location where a suspected explosive or incendiary device found in flight can be placed to minimize the risk to the airplane.

[Docket No. FAA–2006–26722, 73 FR 63880, Oct. 28, 2008]

Subpart K— Instrument and Equipment Requirements

Source: Docket No. 6258, 29 FR 19205, December 31, 1964, unless otherwise noted.

§121.301 Applicability.

This subpart prescribes instrument and equipment requirements for all certificate holders.

§121.303 Airplane instruments and equipment.

(a) Unless otherwise specified, the instrument and equipment requirements of this subpart apply to all operations under this part.

(b) Instruments and equipment required by §§121.305 through 121.359 and 121.803 must be approved and installed in accordance with the airworthiness requirements applicable to them.

(c) Each airspeed indicator must be calibrated in knots, and each airspeed limitation and item of related information in the Airplane Flight Manual and pertinent placards must be expressed in knots.

(d) Except as provided in §§121.627(b) and 121.628, no person may take off any airplane unless the following instruments and equipment are in operable condition:

(1) Instruments and equipment required to comply with airworthiness requirements under which the airplane is type certificated as required by §§121.213 through 121.283 and 121.289.

(2) Instruments and equipment specified in §§121.305 through 121.321, 121.359, 121.360, and 121.803 for all operations, and the instruments and equipment specified in §§121.323 through 121.351 for the kind of operation indicated, wherever these items are not already required by paragraph (d)(1) of this section.

[Docket No. 6258, 29 FR 19202, Dec. 31, 1964; as amended by Amdt. 121–44, 33 FR 14406, Sept. 25, 1968; Amdt. 121–65, 35 FR 12709, Aug. 11, 1970; Amdt. 121–114, 39 FR 44440, Dec. 24, 1974; Amdt. 121–126, 40 FR 55314, Nov. 28, 1975; Amdt. 121–222, 56 FR 12310, March 22, 1991; Amdt. 121–253, 61 FR, Jan. 26, 1996; Amdt. 121–281, 66 FR 19043, April 12, 2001]

§121.305 Flight and navigational equipment.

No person may operate an airplane unless it is equipped with the following flight and navigational instruments and equipment:

(a) An airspeed indicating system with heated pitot tube or equivalent means for preventing malfunctioning due to icing.

(b) A sensitive altimeter.

(c) A sweep-second hand clock (or approved equivalent).

(d) A free-air temperature indicator.

(e) A gyroscopic bank and pitch indicator (artificial horizon).

(f) A gyroscopic rate-of-turn indicator combined with an integral slip-skid indicator (turn-and-bank indicator) except that only a slip-skid indicator is required when a third attitude instrument system usable through flight attitudes of 360° of pitch and roll is installed in accordance with paragraph (k) of this section.

(g) A gyroscopic direction indicator (directional gyro or equivalent).

(h) A magnetic compass.

(i) A vertical speed indicator (rate-of-climb indicator).

(j) On the airplane described in this paragraph, in addition to two gyroscopic bank and pitch indicators (artificial horizons) for use at the pilot stations, a third such instrument is installed in accordance with paragraph (k) of this section:

(1) On each turbojet powered airplane.

(2) On each turbopropeller powered airplane having a passenger-seat configuration of more than 30 seats, excluding each crewmember seat, or a payload capacity of more than 7,500 pounds.

(3) On each turbopropeller powered airplane having a passenger-seat configuration of 30 seats or fewer, excluding each crewmember seat, and a payload capacity of 7,500 pounds or less that is manufactured on or after March 20, 1997.

(4) After December 20, 2010, on each turbopropeller powered airplane having a passenger seat configuration of 10–30 seats and a payload capacity of 7,500 pounds or less that was manufactured before March 20, 1997.

(k) When required by paragraph (j) of this section, a third gyroscopic bank-and-pitch indicator (artificial horizon) that:

(1) Is powered from a source independent of the electrical generating system;

(2) Continues reliable operation for a minimum of 30 minutes after total failure of the electrical generating system;

(3) Operates independently of any other attitude indicating system;

(4) Is operative without selection after total failure of the electrical generating system;

(5) Is located on the instrument panel in a position acceptable to the Administrator that will make it plainly visible to and usable by each pilot at his or her station; and

(6) Is appropriately lighted during all phases of operation.

[Docket No. 6258, 29 FR 19205, Dec. 31, 1964; as amended by Amdt. 121–57, 35 FR 304, Jan. 8, 1970; Amdt. 121–60, 35 FR 7108, May 6, 1970; Amdt. 121–81, 36 FR 23050, Dec. 3, 1971; Amdt. 121–130, 41 FR 47229, Oct. 28, 1976; Amdt. 121–230, 58 FR 12158, March 3, 1993; Amdt. 121–251, 60 FR 65929, Dec. 20, 1995; Amdt. 121–262, 62 FR 13256, March 19, 1997]

§121.306 Portable electronic devices.

(a) Except as provided in paragraph (b) of this section, no person may operate, nor may any operator or pilot in command of an aircraft allow the operation of, any portable electronic device on any U.S.-registered civil aircraft operating under this part.

(b) Paragraph (a) of this section does not apply to—

(1) Portable voice recorders;

(2) Hearing aids;

(3) Heart pacemakers;

(4) Electric shavers; or

(5) Any other portable electronic device that the part 119 certificate holder has determined will not cause interference with the navigation or communication system of the aircraft on which it is to be used.

(c) The determination required by paragraph (b)(5) of this section shall be made by that part 119 certificate holder operating the particular device to be used.

[Docket No. 6258, 29 FR 19205, Dec. 31, 1964; as amended by Amdt. 121–270, 64 FR 1080, Jan. 7, 1999]

§121.307 Engine instruments.

Unless the Administrator allows or requires different instrumentation for turbine engine powered airplanes to provide equivalent safety, no person may conduct any operation under this part without the following engine instruments:

(a) A carburetor air temperature indicator for each engine.

(b) A cylinder head temperature indicator for each air-cooled engine.

(c) A fuel pressure indicator for each engine.

(d) A fuel flowmeter or fuel mixture indicator for each engine not equipped with an automatic altitude mixture control.

(e) A means for indicating fuel quantity in each fuel tank to be used.

(f) A manifold pressure indicator for each engine.

(g) An oil pressure indicator for each engine.

(h) An oil quantity indicator for each oil tank when a transfer or separate oil reserve supply is used.

(i) An oil-in temperature indicator for each engine.

(j) A tachometer for each engine.

(k) An independent fuel pressure warning device for each engine or a master warning device for all engines with a means for isolating the individual warning circuits from the master warning device.

(l) A device for each reversible propeller, to indicate to the pilot when the propeller is in reverse pitch, that complies with the following:

(1) The device may be actuated at any point in the reversing cycle between the normal low pitch stop position and full reverse pitch, but it may not give an indication at or above the normal low pitch stop position.

(2) The source of indication must be actuated by the propeller blade angle or be directly responsive to it.

§121.308 Lavatory fire protection.

(a) Except as provided in paragraphs (c) and (d) of this section, no person may operate a passenger-carrying airplane unless each lavatory in the airplane is equipped with a smoke detector system or equivalent that provides a warning light in the cockpit or provides a warning light or audio warning in the passenger cabin which would be readily detected by a flight attendant, taking into consideration the positioning of flight attendants throughout the passenger compartment during various phases of flight.

(b) Except as provided in paragraph (c) of this section, no person may operate a passenger-carrying airplane unless each lavatory in the airplane is equipped with a built-in fire extinguisher for each disposal receptacle for towels, paper, or waste located within the lavatory. The built-in fire extinguisher must be designed to discharge automatically into each disposal receptacle upon occurrence of a fire in the receptacle.

(c) Until December 22, 1997, a certificate holder described in §121.2(a)(1) or (2) may operate an airplane with a passenger seat configuration of 30 or fewer seats that does not comply with the smoke detector system requirements described in paragraph (a) of this section and the fire extinguisher requirements described in paragraph (b) of this section.

(d) After December 22, 1997, no person may operate a nontransport category airplane type certificated after December 31, 1964, with a passenger seat configuration of 10–19 seats unless that airplane complies with the smoke detector system requirements described in paragraph (a) of this section, except that the smoke detector system or equivalent must provide a warning light in the cockpit or an audio warning that would be readily detected by the flightcrew.

[Docket No. 28154, 60 FR 65929, Dec. 20, 1995]

§121.309 Emergency equipment.

(a) *General:* No person may operate an airplane unless it is equipped with the emergency equipment listed in this section and in §121.310.

(b) Each item of emergency and flotation equipment listed in this section and in §§121.310, 121.339, and 121.340—

(1) Must be inspected regularly in accordance with inspection periods established in the operations specifications to ensure its condition for continued serviceability and immediate readiness to perform its intended emergency purposes;

(2) Must be readily accessible to the crew and, with regard to equipment located in the passenger compartment, to passengers;

(3) Must be clearly identified and clearly marked to indicate its method of operation; and

(4) When carried in a compartment or container, must be carried in a compartment or container marked as to contents and the compartment or container, or the item itself, must be marked as to date of last inspection.

(c) *Hand fire extinguishers for crew, passenger, cargo, and galley compartments.* Hand fire extinguishers of an approved type must be provided for use in crew, passenger, cargo and galley compartments in accordance with the following:

(1) The type and quantity of extinguishing agent must be suitable for the kinds of fires likely to occur in the compartment where the extinguisher is intended to be used and, for passenger compartments, must be designed to minimize the hazard of toxic gas concentrations.

(2) *Cargo compartments.* At least one hand fire extinguisher must be conveniently located for use in each Class E cargo compartment that is accessible to crew members during flight.

(3) *Galley compartments.* At least one hand fire extinguisher must be conveniently located for use in each galley located in a compartment other than a passenger, cargo or crew compartment.

(4) *Flightcrew compartment.* At least one hand fire extinguisher must be conveniently located on the flight deck for use by the flightcrew.

(5) *Passenger compartments.* Hand fire extinguishers for use in passenger compartments must be conveniently located and, when two or more are required, uniformly distributed throughout each compartment. Hand fire extinguishers shall be provided in passenger compartments as follows:

§121.309

(i) For airplanes having passenger seats accommodating more than 6 but fewer than 31 passengers, at least one.

(ii) For airplanes having passenger seats accommodating more than 30 but fewer than 61 passengers, at least two.

(iii) For airplanes having passenger seats accommodating more than 60 passengers, there must be at least the following number of hand fire extinguishers:

Minimum Number of Hand Fire Extinguishers

Passenger seating accommodations:

61 through 200	3
201 through 300	4
301 through 400	5
401 through 500	6
501 through 600	7
601 or more	8

(6) Notwithstanding the requirement for uniform distribution of hand fire extinguishers as prescribed in paragraph (c)(5) of this section, for those cases where a galley is located in a passenger compartment, at least one hand fire extinguisher must be conveniently located and easily accessible for use in the galley.

(7) At least two of the required hand fire extinguisher installed in passenger-carrying airplanes must contain Halon 1211 (bromochlorofluoromethane) or equivalent as the extinguishing agent. At least one hand fire extinguisher in the passenger compartment must contain Halon 1211 or equivalent.

(d) Reserved.

(e) *Crash ax.* Except for nontransport category airplanes type certificated after December 31, 1964, each airplane must be equipped with a crash ax.

(f) *Megaphones.* Each passenger-carrying airplane must have a portable battery-powered megaphone or megaphones readily accessible to the crewmembers assigned to direct emergency evacuation, installed as follows:

(1) One megaphone on each airplane with a seating capacity of more than 60 and less than 100 passengers, at the most rearward location in the passenger cabin where it would be readily accessible to a normal flight attendant seat. However, the Administrator may grant a deviation from the requirements of this subparagraph if he finds that a different location would be more useful for evacuation of persons during an emergency.

(2) Two megaphones in the passenger cabin on each airplane with a seating capacity of more than 99 passengers, one installed at the forward end and the other at the most rearward location where it would be readily accessible to a normal flight attendant seat.

[Docket No. 6258, 29 FR 19205, Dec. 31, 1964; as amended by Amdt. 121–30, 32 FR 13267, Sept. 20, 1967; Amdt. 121–48, 34 FR 11489, July 11, 1969; Amdt. 121–106, 38 FR 22377, Aug. 20, 1973; Amdt. 121–185, 50 FR 12733, March 29, 1985; 50 FR 14373, April 12, 1985; Amdt. 121–188, 51 FR 1223, Jan. 9, 1986; Amdt. 121–230, 57 FR 42672, Sept. 15, 1992; Amdt. 121–242, 59 FR 52642, Oct. 18, 1994; Amdt. 121–242, 59 FR 55208, Nov. 4, 1994; Amdt. 121–251, 60 FR 65930, Dec. 20, 1995; Amdt. 121–281, 66 FR 19043, April 12, 2001]

§121.310 Additional emergency equipment.

(a) *Means for emergency evacuation.* Each passenger-carrying landplane emergency exit (other than over-the-wing) that is more than 6 feet from the ground with the airplane on the ground and the landing gear extended, must have an approved means to assist the occupants in descending to the ground. The assisting means for a floor-level emergency exit must meet the requirements of §25.809(f)(1) of this chapter in effect on April 30, 1972, except that, for any airplane for which the application for the type certificate was filed after that date, it must meet the requirements under which the airplane was type certificated. An assisting means that deploys automatically must be armed during taxiing, takeoffs, and landings. However, if the Administrator finds that the design of the exit makes compliance impractical, he may grant a deviation from the requirement of automatic deployment if the assisting means automatically erects upon deployment and, with respect to required emergency exits, if an emergency evacuation demonstration is conducted in accordance with §121.291(a). This paragraph does not apply to the rear window emergency exit of DC-3 airplanes operated with less than 36 occupants, including crewmembers and less than five exits authorized for passenger use.

(b) *Interior emergency exit marking.* The following must be complied with for each passenger-carrying airplane:

(1) Each passenger emergency exit, its means of access, and its means of opening must be conspicuously marked. The identity and location of each passenger emergency exit must be recognizable from a distance equal to the width of the cabin. The location of each passenger emergency exit must be indicated by a sign visible to occupants approaching along the main passenger aisle. There must be a locating sign—

(i) Above the aisle near each over-the-wing passenger emergency exit, or at another ceiling location if it is more practical because of low headroom;

(ii) Next to each floor level passenger emergency exit, except that one sign may serve two such exits if they both can be seen readily from that sign; and

Part 121: Air Carriers & Commercial Operators §121.310

(iii) On each bulkhead or divider that prevents fore and aft vision along the passenger cabin, to indicate emergency exits beyond and obscured by it, except that if this is not possible the sign may be placed at another appropriate location.

(2) Each passenger emergency exit marking and each locating sign must meet the following:

(i) Except as provided in paragraph (b)(2)(iii) of this section, for an airplane for which the application for the type certificate was filed prior to May 1, 1972, each passenger emergency exit marking and each locating sign must be manufactured to meet the requirements of §25.812(b) of this chapter in effect on April 30, 1972. On these airplanes, no sign may continue to be used if its luminescence (brightness) decreases to below 100 microlamberts. The colors may be reversed if it increases the emergency illumination of the passenger compartment. However, the Administrator may authorize deviation from the 2-inch background requirements if he finds that special circumstances exist that make compliance impractical and that the proposed deviation provides an equivalent level of safety.

(ii) For a transport category airplane for which the application for the type certificate was filed on or after May 1, 1972, each passenger emergency exit marking and each locating sign must be manufactured to meet the interior emergency exit marking requirements under which the airplane was type certificated. On these airplanes, no sign may continue to be used if its luminescence (brightness) decreases to below 250 microlamberts.

(iii) For a nontransport category turbopropeller powered airplane type certificated after December 31, 1964, each passenger emergency exit marking and each locating sign must be manufactured to meet the requirements of §23.811(b) of this chapter. On these airplanes, no sign may continue to be used if its luminescence (brightness) decreases to below 100 microlamberts.

(c) Lighting for interior emergency exit markings. Except for nontransport category airplanes type certificated after December 31, 1964, each passenger-carrying airplane must have an emergency lighting system, independent of the main lighting system. However, sources of general cabin illumination may be common to both the emergency and the main lighting systems if the power supply to the emergency lighting system is independent of the power supply to the main lighting system. The emergency lighting system must—

(1) Illuminate each passenger exit marking and locating sign;

(2) Provide enough general lighting in the passenger cabin so that the average illumination when measured at 40-inch intervals at seat armrest height, on the centerline of the main passenger aisle, is at least 0.05 foot-candles; and

(3) For airplanes type certificated after January 1, 1958, after November 26, 1986, include floor proximity emergency escape path marking which meets the requirements of §25.812(e) of this chapter in effect on November 26, 1984.

(d) Emergency light operation. Except for lights forming part of emergency lighting subsystems provided in compliance with §25.812(h) of this chapter (as prescribed in paragraph (h) of this section) that serve no more than one assist means, are independent of the airplane's main emergency lighting systems, and are automatically activated when the assist means is deployed, each light required by paragraphs (c) and (h) of this section must comply with the following:

(1) Each light must—

(i) Be operable manually both from the flightcrew station and, for airplanes on which a flight attendant is required, from a point in the passenger compartment that is readily accessible to a normal flight attendant seat;

(ii) Have a means to prevent inadvertent operation of the manual controls; and

(iii) When armed or turned on at either station, remain lighted or become lighted upon interruption of the airplane's normal electric power.

(2) Each light must be armed or turned on during taxiing, takeoff, and landing. In showing compliance with this paragraph a transverse vertical separation of the fuselage need not be considered.

(3) Each light must provide the required level of illumination for at least 10 minutes at the critical ambient conditions after emergency landing.

(4) Each light must have a cockpit control device that has an "on," "off," and "armed" position.

(e) Emergency exit operating handles.

(1) For a passenger-carrying airplane for which the application for the type certificate was filed prior to May 1, 1972, the location of each passenger emergency exit operating handle, and instructions for opening the exit, must be shown by a marking on or near the exit that is readable from a distance of 30 inches. In addition, for each Type I and Type II emergency exit with a locking mechanism released by rotary motion of the handle, the instructions for opening must be shown by—

(i) A red arrow with a shaft at least three-fourths inch wide and a head twice the width of the shaft, extending along at least 70° of arc at a radius approximately equal to three-fourths of the handle length; and

(ii) The word "open" in red letters 1 inch high placed horizontally near the head of the arrow.

(2) For a passenger-carrying airplane for which the application for the type certificate was filed on or after May 1, 1972, the location of each passenger emergency exit operating handle and in-

structions for opening the exit must be shown in accordance with the requirements under which the airplane was type certificated. On these airplanes, no operating handle or operating handle cover may continue to be used if its luminescence (brightness) decreases to below 100 microlamberts.

(f) *Emergency exit access.* Access to emergency exits must be provided as follows for each passenger-carrying transport category airplane:

(1) Each passage way between individual passenger areas, or leading to a Type I or Type II emergency exit, must be unobstructed and at least 20 inches wide.

(2) For each Type I or Type II emergency exit equipped with an assist means, there must be enough space next to the exit to allow a crewmember to assist in the evacuation of passengers without reducing the unobstructed width of the passageway below that required in paragraph (f)(1) of this section. In addition, all airplanes manufactured on or after November 26, 2008 must comply with the provisions of §25.813(b)(1), (b)(2), (b)(3) and (b)(4) in effect on November 26, 2004. However, a deviation from this requirement may be authorized for an airplane certificated under the provisions of part 4b of the Civil Air Regulations in effect before December 20, 1951, if the Administrator finds that special circumstances exist that provide an equivalent level of safety.

(3) There must be access from the main aisle to each Type III and Type IV exit. The access from the aisle to these exits must not be obstructed by seats, berths, or other protrusions in a manner that would reduce the effectiveness of the exit. In addition—

(i) For an airplane for which the application for the type certificate was filed prior to May 1, 1972, the access must meet the requirements of §25.813(c) of this chapter in effect on April 30, 1972; and

(ii) For an airplane for which the application for the type certificate was filed on or after May 1, 1972, the access must meet the emergency exit access requirements under which the airplane was type certificated; except that,

(iii) After December 3, 1992, the access for an airplane type certificated after January 1, 1958, must meet the requirements of §25.813(c) of this chapter, effective June 3, 1992.

(iv) Contrary provisions of this section notwithstanding, the Manager of the Transport Airplane Directorate, Aircraft Certification Service, Federal Aviation Administration, may authorize deviation from the requirements of paragraph (f)(3)(iii) of this section if it is determined that special circumstances make compliance impractical. Such special circumstances include, but are not limited to, the following conditions when they preclude achieving compliance with §25.813(c)(1)(i) or (ii) without a reduction in the total number of passenger seats: emergency exits located in close proximity to each other; fixed installations such as lavatories, galleys, etc.; permanently mounted bulkheads; an insufficient number of rows ahead of or behind the exit to enable compliance without a reduction in the seat row pitch of more than one inch; or an insufficient number of such rows to enable compliance without a reduction in the seat row pitch to less than 30 inches. A request for such grant of deviation must include credible reasons as to why literal compliance with §25.813(c)(1)(i) or (ii) is impractical and a description of the steps taken to achieve a level of safety as close to that intended by §25.813(c)(1)(i) or (ii) as is practical.

(v) The Manager of the Transport Airplane Directorate, Aircraft Certification Service, Federal Aviation Administration, may also authorize a compliance date later than December 3, 1992, if it is determined that special circumstances make compliance by that date impractical. A request for such grant of deviation must outline the airplanes for which compliance will be achieved by December 3, 1992, and include a proposed schedule for incremental compliance of the remaining airplanes in the operator's fleet. In addition, the request must include credible reasons why compliance cannot be achieved earlier.

(4) If it is necessary to pass through a passageway between passenger compartments to reach any required emergency exit from any seat in the passenger cabin, the passageway must not be obstructed. However, curtains may be used if they allow free entry through the passageway.

(5) No door may be installed in any partition between passenger compartments.

(6) No person may operate an airplane manufactured after November 27, 2006, that incorporates a door installed between any passenger seat occupiable for takeoff and landing and any passenger emergency exit, such that the door crosses any egress path (including aisles, crossaisles and passageways).

(7) If it is necessary to pass through a doorway separating any seat (except those seats on the flightdeck), occupiable for takeoff and landing, from an emergency exit, the door must have a means to latch it in the open position, and the door must be latched open during each takeoff and landing. The latching means must be able to withstand the loads imposed upon it when the door is subjected to the ultimate inertia forces, relative to the surrounding structure, listed in §25.561(b) of this chapter.

(g) *Exterior exit markings.* Each passenger emergency exit and the means of opening that exit from the outside must be marked on the outside of the airplane. There must be a 2-inch colored band outlining each passenger emergency exit on the side of the fuselage. Each outside marking, including the band, must be readily distinguishable from the surrounding fuselage area by contrast in color. The markings must comply with the following:

(1) If the reflectance of the darker color is 15 percent or less, the reflectance of the lighter color must be at least 45 percent.

(2) If the reflectance of the darker color is greater than 15 percent, at least a 30 percent difference between its reflectance and the reflectance of the lighter color must be provided.

(3) Exits that are not in the side of the fuselage must have the external means of opening and applicable instructions marked conspicuously in red or, if red is inconspicuous against the background color, in bright chrome yellow and, when the opening means for such an exit is located on only one side of the fuselage, a conspicuous marking to that effect must be provided on the other side. Reflectance is the ratio of the luminous flux reflected by a body to the luminous flux it receives.

(h) *Exterior emergency lighting and escape route.*

(1) Except for nontransport category airplanes certificated after December 31, 1964, each passenger-carrying airplane must be equipped with exterior lighting that meets the following requirements:

(i) For an airplane for which the application for the type certificate was filed prior to May 1, 1972, the requirements of §25.812(f) and (g) of this chapter in effect on April 30, 1972.

(ii) For an airplane for which the application for the type certificate was filed on or after May 1, 1972, the exterior emergency lighting requirements under which the airplane was type certificated.

(2) Each passenger-carrying airplane must be equipped with a slip-resistant escape route that meets the following requirements:

(i) For an airplane for which the application for the type certificate was filed prior to May 1, 1972, the requirements of §25.803(e) of this chapter in effect on April 30, 1972.

(ii) For an airplane for which the application for the type certificate was filed on or after May 1, 1972, the slip-resistant escape route requirements under which the airplane was type certificated.

(i) *Floor level exits.* Each floor level door or exit in the side of the fuselage (other than those leading into a cargo or baggage compartment that is not accessible from the passenger cabin) that is 44 or more inches high and 20 or more inches wide, but not wider than 46 inches, each passenger ventral exit (except the ventral exits on M-404 and CV-240 airplanes), and each tail cone exit, must meet the requirements of this section for floor level emergency exits. However, the Administrator may grant a deviation from this paragraph if he finds that circumstances make full compliance impractical and that an acceptable level of safety has been achieved.

(j) *Additional emergency exits.* Approved emergency exits in the passenger compartments that are in excess of the minimum number of required emergency exits must meet all of the applicable provisions of this section except paragraphs (f)(1), (2), and (3) of this section and must be readily accessible.

(k) On each large passenger-carrying turbojet-powered airplane, each ventral exit and tailcone exit must be—

(1) Designed and constructed so that it cannot be opened during flight; and

(2) Marked with a placard readable from a distance of 30 inches and installed at a conspicuous location near the means of opening the exit, stating that the exit has been designed and constructed so that it cannot be opened during flight.

(l) *Emergency exit features.*

(1) Each transport category airplane manufactured after November 26, 2007 must comply with the provisions of §25.809(i) and

(2) After November 26, 2007 each transport category airplane must comply with the provisions of §25.813(b)(6)(ii) in effect on November 26, 2007.

(m) Except for an airplane used in operations under this part on October 16, 1987, and having an emergency exit configuration installed and authorized for operation prior to October 16, 1987, for an airplane that is required to have more than one passenger emergency exit for each side of the fuselage, no passenger emergency exit shall be more than 60 feet from any adjacent passenger emergency exit on the same side of the same deck of the fuselage, as measured parallel to the airplane's longitudinal axis between the nearest exit edges.

(n) *Portable lights.* No person may operate a passenger-carrying airplane unless it is equipped with flashlight stowage provisions accessible from each flight attendant seat.

[Docket No. 2033, 30 FR 3205, March 9, 1965; as amended by Amdt. 121–251, 60 FR 65030, Dec. 20, 1995; Amdt. 121–262, 62 FR 13256, March 19, 1997; Amdt. 121–283, 66 FR 20740, April 25, 2001; Amdt. 121–306, 69 FR 62789, Oct. 27, 2004]

§121.311 Seats, safety belts, and shoulder harnesses.

(a) No person may operate an airplane unless there are available during the takeoff, en route flight, and landing—

(1) An approved seat or berth for each person on board the airplane who has reached his second birthday; and

(2) An approved safety belt for separate use by each person on board the airplane who has reached his second birthday, except that two persons occupying a berth may share one approved safety belt and two persons occupying a multiple lounge or divan seat may share one approved safety belt during en route flight only.

(b) Except as provided in this paragraph, each person on board an airplane operated under this part shall occupy an approved seat or berth with a separate safety belt properly secured about him or her during movement on the surface, takeoff, and landing. A safety belt provided for the occupant of a seat may not be used by more than one person who has reached his or her second birthday. Notwithstanding the preceding requirements, a child may:

(1) Be held by an adult who is occupying an approved seat or berth, provided the child has not reached his or her second birthday and the child does not occupy or use any restraining device; or

(2) Notwithstanding any other requirement of this chapter, occupy an approved child restraint system furnished by the certificate holder or one of the persons described in paragraph (b)(2)(i) of this section, provided:

(i) The child is accompanied by a parent, guardian, or attendant designated by the child's parent or guardian to attend to the safety of the child during the flight;

(ii) Except as provided in paragraph (b)(2)(ii)(D) of this section, the approved child restraint system bears one or more labels as follows:

(A) Seats manufactured to U.S. standards between January 1, 1981 and February 25, 1985, must bear the label: "This child restraint system conforms to all applicable Federal motor vehicle safety standards.";

(B) Seats manufactured to U.S. standards on or after February 26, 1985, must bear two labels:

(1) "This child restraint system conforms to all applicable Federal motor vehicle safety standards;" and

(2) "THIS RESTRAINT IS CERTIFIED FOR USE IN MOTOR VEHICLES AND AIRCRAFT" in red lettering;

(C) Seats that do not qualify under paragraphs (B)(2)(ii)(A) and (b)(2)(ii)(B) of this section must bear a label or markings showing:

(1) That the seat was approved by a foreign government;

(2) That the seat was manufactured under the standards of the United Nations;

(3) That the seat or child restraint device furnished by the certificate holder was approved by the FAA through Type Certificate or Supplemental Type Certificate; or

(4) That the seat or child restraint device furnished by the certificate holder, or one of the persons described in paragraph (b)(2)(i) of this section, was approved by the FAA in accordance with §21.8(d) of this chapter or Technical Standard Order C-100b, or a later version. The child restraint device manufactured by AmSafe, Inc. (CARES, Part No. 4082) and approved by the FAA in accordance with §21.305(d) (2010 ed.) of this chapter may continue to bear a label or markings showing FAA approval in accordance with §21.305(d) (2010 ed.) of this chapter.

(D) Except as provided in §121.311 (b)(2)(ii)(C)(3) and §121.311(b)(2)(ii)(C)(4), booster-type child restraint systems (as defined in Federal Motor Vehicle Safety Standard No. 213 (49 CFR 571.213)), vest- and harness-type child restraint systems, and lap held child restraints are not approved for use in aircraft; and

(iii) The certificate holder complies with the following requirements:

(A) The restraint system must be properly secured to an approved forward-facing seat or berth;

(B) The child must be properly secured in the restraint system and must not exceed the specified weight limit for the restraint system; and

(C) The restraint system must bear the appropriate label(s).

(c) Except as provided in paragraph (c)(3) of this section, the following prohibitions apply to certificate holders:

(1) Except as provided in §121.311 (b)(2)(ii)(C)(3) and §121.311(b)(2)(ii)(C)(4), no certificate holder may permit a child, in an aircraft, to occupy a booster-type child restraint system, a vest-type child restraint system, a harness-type child restraint system, or a lap held child restraint system during take off, landing, and movement on the surface.

(2) Except as required in paragraph (c)(1) of this section, no certificate holder may prohibit a child, if requested by the child's parent, guardian, or designated attendant, from occupying a child restraint system furnished by the child's parent, guardian, or designated attendant provided—

(i) The child holds a ticket for an approved seat or berth or such seat or berth is otherwise made available by the certificate holder for the child's use;

(ii) The requirements of paragraph (b)(2)(i) of this section are met;

(iii) The requirements of paragraph (b)(2)(iii) of this section are met; and

(iv) The child restraint system has one or more of the labels described in paragraphs (b)(2)(ii)(A) through (b)(2)(ii)(C) of this section.

(3) This section does not prohibit the certificate holder from providing child restraint systems authorized by this section or, consistent with safe operating practices, determining the most appropriate passenger seat location for the child restraint system.

Part 121: Air Carriers & Commercial Operators §121.312

(d) Each sideward facing seat must comply with the applicable requirements of §25.785(c) of this chapter.

(e) Except as provided in paragraphs (e)(1) through (e)(3) of this section, no certificate holder may take off or land an airplane unless each passenger seat back is in the upright position.

Each passenger shall comply with instructions given by a crewmember in compliance with this paragraph.

(1) This paragraph does not apply to seat backs placed in other than the upright position in compliance with §121.310(f)(3).

(2) This paragraph does not apply to seats on which cargo or persons who are unable to sit erect for a medical reason are carried in accordance with procedures in the certificate holder's manual if the seat back does not obstruct any passenger's access to the aisle or to any emergency exit.

(3) On airplanes with no flight attendant, the certificate holder may take off or land as long as the flightcrew instructs each passenger to place his or her seat back in the upright position for takeoff and landing.

(f) No person may operate a transport category airplane that was type certificated after January 1, 1958, or a nontransport category airplane manufactured after March 20, 1997, unless it is equipped at each flight deck station with a combined safety belt and shoulder harness that meets the applicable requirements specified in §25.785 of this chapter, effective March 6, 1980, except that—

(1) Shoulder harnesses and combined safety belt and shoulder harnesses that were approved and installed before March 6, 1980, may continue to be used; and

(2) Safety belt and shoulder harness restraint systems may be designed to the inertia load factors established under the certification basis of the airplane.

(g) Each flight attendant must have a seat for takeoff and landing in the passenger compartment that meets the requirements of §25.785 of this chapter, effective March 6, 1980, except that—

(1) Combined safety belt and shoulder harnesses that were approved and installed before March 6, 1980, may continue to be used; and

(2) Safety belt and shoulder harness restraint systems may be designed to the inertia load factors established under the certification basis of the airplane.

(3) The requirements of §25.785(h) do not apply to passenger seats occupied by flight attendants not required by §121.391.

(h) Each occupant of a seat equipped with a shoulder harness or with a combined safety belt and shoulder harness must have the shoulder harness or combined safety belt and shoulder harness properly secured about that occupant during takeoff and landing, except that a shoulder harness that is not combined with a safety belt may be unfastened if the occupant cannot perform the required duties with the shoulder harness fastened.

(i) At each unoccupied seat, the safety belt and shoulder harness, if installed, must be secured so as not to interfere with crewmembers in the performance of their duties or with the rapid egress of occupants in an emergency.

(j) After October 27, 2009, no person may operate a transport category airplane type certificated after January 1, 1958 and manufactured on or after October 27, 2009 in passenger-carrying operations under this part unless all passenger and flight attendant seats on the airplane meet the requirements of §25.562 in effect on or after June 16, 1988.

[Docket No. 7522, 32 FR 13267, Sept. 20, 1967; as amended by Amdt. 121–41, 33 FR 9067, June 20, 1968; Amdt. 121–75, 36 FR 12512, July 1, 1971; Amdt. 121–133, 42 FR 18394, April 7, 1977; Amdt. 121–155, 45 FR 7756, Feb. 4, 1980; Amdt. 121–170, 46 FR 15482, March 5, 1981; Amdt. 121–177, 47 FR 10516, March 11, 1982; Amdt. 121–230, 57 FR 42673, Sept. 15, 1992; Amdt. 121–251, 60 FR 65930, Dec. 20, 1995; Amdt. 121–255, 61 FR 28421, June 4, 1996; Amdt. 121–314, 70 FR 50907, Aug. 26, 2005; Amdt. 121–315, 70 FR 56559, Sept. 27, 2005; Amdt. 121–326, 71 FR 40009, July 14, 2006; Amdt. 121–370, 79 FR 28812, May 20, 2014]

§121.312 Materials for compartment interiors.

(a) *All interior materials; transport category airplanes and nontransport category airplanes type certificated before January 1, 1965.* Except for the materials covered by paragraph (b) of this section, all materials in each compartment of a transport category airplane, or a nontransport category airplane type certificated before January 1, 1965, used by the crewmembers and passengers, must meet the requirements of §25.853 of this chapter in effect as follows, or later amendment thereto:

(1) Airplane with passenger seating capacity of 20 or more.

(i) Manufactured after August 19, 1988, but prior to August 20, 1990. Except as provided in paragraph (a)(3)(ii) of this section, each airplane with a passenger capacity of 20 or more and manufactured after August 19, 1988, but prior to August 20, 1990, must comply with the heat release rate testing provisions of §25.853(d) in effect March 6, 1995 (formerly §25.853(a-1) in effect on August 20, 1986) (see Appendix L of this part), except that the total heat release over the first 2 minutes of sample exposure must not exceed 100 kilowatt minutes per square meter and the peak heat release rate must not exceed 100 kilowatts per square meter.

(ii) Manufactured after August 19, 1990. Each airplane with a passenger capacity of 20 or more and manufactured after August 19, 1990, must comply with the heat release rate and smoke testing provisions of §25.853(d) in effect March 6, 1995 (formerly §25.853(a-1) (see Appendix L of this part) in effect on September 26, 1988).

(2) Substantially complete replacement of the cabin interior on or after May 1, 1972.

(i) Airplane for which the application for type certificate was filed prior to May 1, 1972. Except as provided in paragraph (a)(3)(i) or (a)(3)(ii) of this section, each airplane for which the application for type certificate was filed prior to May 1, 1972, must comply with the provisions of §25.853 in effect on April 30, 1972, regardless of passenger capacity, if there is a substantially complete replacement of the cabin interior after April 30, 1972.

(ii) Airplane for which the application for type certificate was filed on or after May 1, 1972. Except as provided in paragraph (a)(3)(i) or (a)(3)(ii) of this section, each airplane for which the application for type certificate was filed on or after May 1, 1972, must comply with the material requirements under which the airplane was type certificated, regardless of passenger capacity, if there is a substantially complete replacement of the cabin interior on or after that date.

(3) Airplane type certificated after January 1, 1958, with passenger capacity of 20 or more.

(i) Substantially complete replacement of the cabin interior on or after March 6, 1995. Except as provided in paragraph (a)(3)(ii) of this section, each airplane that was type certificated after January 1, 1958, and has a passenger capacity of 20 or more, must comply with the heat release rate testing provisions of §25.853(d) in effect March 6, 1995 (formerly §25.853(a-1) in effect on August 20, 1986) (see Appendix L of this part), if there is a substantially complete replacement of the cabin interior components identified in §25.853(d), on or after that date, except that the total heat release over the first 2 minutes of sample exposure shall not exceed 100 kilowatt-minutes per square meter and the peak heat release rate must not exceed 100 kilowatts per square meter.

(ii) Substantially complete replacement of the cabin interior on or after August 20, 1990. Each airplane that was type certificated after January 1, 1958, and has a passenger capacity of 20 or more, must comply with the heat release rate and smoke testing provisions of §25.853(d) in effect March 6, 1995 (formerly §25.853(a-1) in effect on September 26, 1988) (see Appendix L of this part), if there is a substantially complete replacement of the cabin interior components identified in §25.853(d), on or after August 20, 1990.

(4) Contrary provisions of this section notwithstanding, the Manager of the Transport Airplane Directorate, Aircraft Certification Service, Federal Aviation Administration, may authorize deviation from the requirements of paragraph (a)(1)(i), (a)(1)(ii), (a)(3)(i), or (a)(3)(ii) of this section for specific components of the cabin interior that do not meet applicable flammability and smoke emission requirements, if the determination is made that special circumstances exist that make compliance impractical. Such grants of deviation will be limited to those airplanes manufactured within 1 year after the applicable date specified in this section and those airplanes in which the interior is replaced within 1 year of that date. A request for such grant of deviation must include a thorough and accurate analysis of each component subject to §25.853(a-1), the steps being taken to achieve compliance, and, for the few components for which timely compliance will not be achieved, credible reasons for such noncompliance.

(5) Contrary provisions of this section notwithstanding, galley carts and galley standard containers that do not meet the flammability and smoke emission requirements of §25.853(d) in effect March 6, 1995 (formerly §25.853(a-1)) (see Appendix L of this part) may be used in airplanes that must meet the requirements of paragraphs (a)(1)(i), (a)(1)(ii), (a)(3)(i), or (a)(3)(ii) of this section, provided the galley carts or standard containers were manufactured prior to March 6, 1995.

(b) *Seat cushions.* Seat cushions, except those on flight crewmember seats, in each compartment occupied by crew or passengers, must comply with the requirements pertaining to seat cushions in §25.853(c) effective on November 26, 1984, on each airplane as follows:

(1) Each transport category airplane type certificated after January 1, 1958; and

(2) On or after December 20, 2010, each nontransport category airplane type certificated after December 31, 1964.

(c) *All interior materials; airplanes type certificated in accordance with SFAR No. 41 of 14 CFR part 21.* No person may operate an airplane that conforms to an amended or supplemental type certificate issued in accordance with SFAR No. 41 of 14 CFR part 21 for a maximum certificated takeoff weight in excess of 12,500 pounds unless the airplane meets the compartment interior requirements set forth in §25.853(a) in effect March 6, 1995 (formerly §25.853(a), (b), (b-1), (b-2), and (b-3) of this chapter in effect on September 26, 1978)(see Appendix L of this part).

(d) *All interior materials; other airplanes.* For each material or seat cushion to which a requirement in paragraphs (a), (b), or (c) of this section does not apply, the material and seat cushion in each compartment used by the crewmembers and passengers must meet the applicable requirement under which the airplane was type certificated.

(e) *Thermal/acoustic insulation materials.* For transport category airplanes type certificated after January 1, 1958:

(1) For airplanes manufactured before September 2, 2005, when thermal/acoustic insulation is installed in the fuselage as replacements after September 2, 2005, the insulation must meet the flame propagation requirements of §25.856 of this chapter, effective September 2, 2003, if it is:

(i) Of a blanket construction or
(ii) Installed around air ducting.

(2) For airplanes manufactured after September 2, 2005, thermal/acoustic insulation materials installed in the fuselage must meet the flame propagation requirements of §25.856 of this chapter, effective September 2, 2003.

(3) For airplanes with a passenger capacity of 20 or greater, manufactured after September 2, 2009, thermal/acoustic insulation materials installed in the lower half of the fuselage must meet the flame penetration resistance requirements of §25.856 of this chapter, effective September 2, 2003.

[Docket No. 28154, 60 FR 65930, Dec. 20, 1995; as amended by Amdt. 121–301, 68 FR 45083, July 31, 2003; Amdt. 121–320, 70 FR 77752, Dec. 30, 2005; Amdt. 121–330, 72 FR 1442, Jan. 12, 2007]

§121.313 Miscellaneous equipment.

No person may conduct any operation unless the following equipment is installed in the airplane:

(a) If protective fuses are installed on an airplane, the number of spare fuses approved for that airplane and appropriately described in the certificate holder's manual.

(b) A windshield wiper or equivalent for each pilot station.

(c) A power supply and distribution system that meets the requirements of §§25.1309, 25.1331, 25.1351(a) and (b)(1) through (4), 25.1353, 25.1355, and 25.1431(b) or that is able to produce and distribute the load for the required instruments and equipment, with use of an external power supply if any one power source or component of the power distribution system fails. The use of common elements in the system may be approved if the Administrator finds that they are designed to be reasonably protected against malfunctioning. Engine-driven sources of energy, when used, must be on separate engines.

(d) A means for indicating the adequacy of the power being supplied to required flight instruments.

(e) Two independent static pressure systems, vented to the outside atmospheric pressure so that they will be least affected by air flow variation or moisture or other foreign matter, and installed so as to be airtight except for the vent. When a means is provided for transferring an instrument from its primary operating system to an alternate system, the means must include a positive positioning control and must be marked to indicate clearly which system is being used.

(f) A door between the passenger and pilot compartments (i.e., flightdeck door), with a locking means to prevent passengers from opening it without the pilot's permission, except that non-transport category airplanes certificated after December 31, 1964, are not required to comply with this paragraph. For airplanes equipped with a crew rest area having separate entries from the flightdeck and the passenger compartment, a door with such a locking means must be provided between the crew rest area and the passenger compartment.

(g) A key for each door that separates a passenger compartment from another compartment that has emergency exit provisions. Except for flightdeck doors, a key must be readily available for each crewmember. Except as provided below, no person other than a person who is assigned to perform duty on the flightdeck may have a key to the flightdeck door. Before April 22, 2003, any crewmember may have a key to the flightdeck door but only if the flightdeck door has an internal flightdeck locking device installed, operative, and in use. Such "internal flightdeck locking device" has to be designed so that it can only be unlocked from inside the flightdeck.

(h) A placard on each door that is the means of access to a required passenger emergency exit, to indicate that it must be open during takeoff and landing.

(i) A means for the crew, in an emergency to unlock each door that leads to a compartment that is normally accessible to passengers and that can be locked by passengers.

(j) After April 9, 2003, for airplanes required by paragraph (f) of this section to have a door between the passenger and pilot or crew rest compartments, and for transport category, all-cargo airplanes that have a door installed between the pilot compartment and any other occupied compartment on January 15, 2002;

(1) After April 9, 2003, for airplanes required by paragraph (f) of this section to have a door between the passenger and pilot or crew rest compartments,

(i) Each such door must meet the requirements of §25.795(a)(1) and (2) in effect on January 15, 2002; and

(ii) Each operator must establish methods to enable a flight attendant to enter the pilot compartment in the event that a flightcrew member becomes incapacitated. Any associated signal or confirmation system must be operable by each

§121.314

flightcrew member from that flightcrew member's duty station.

(2) After October 1, 2003, for transport category, all-cargo airplanes that had a door installed between the pilot compartment and any other occupied compartment on or after January 15, 2002, each such door must meet the requirements of §25.795(a)(1) and (2) in effect on January 15, 2002; or the operator must implement a security program approved by the Transportation Security Administration (TSA) for the operation of all airplanes in that operator's fleet.

(k) Except for all-cargo operations as defined in §110.2 of this chapter, for all passenger-carrying airplanes that require a lockable flightdeck door in accordance with paragraph (f) of this section, a means to monitor from the flightdeck side of the door to the area outside the flightdeck door to identify persons requesting entry and to detect suspicious behavior and potential threats.

[Docket No. 6258, 29 FR 19205, Dec. 31, 1964; as amended by Amdt. 121–5, 30 FR 6113, April 30, 1965; Amdt. 121–251, 60 FR 65931, Dec. 20, 1995; Amdt. 121–288, 67 FR 2127, Jan. 15, 2002; Amdt. 121–299, 68 FR 42881, July 18, 2003; Amdt. 121–334, 72 FR 45635, Aug. 15, 2007]

§121.314 Cargo and baggage compartments.

For each transport category airplane type certificated after January 1, 1958:

(a) Each Class C or Class D compartment, as defined in §25.857 of this Chapter in effect on June 16, 1986 (see Appendix L to this part), that is greater than 200 cubic feet in volume must have ceiling and sidewall liner panels which are constructed of:

(1) Glass fiber reinforced resin;

(2) Materials which meet the test requirements of part 25, Appendix F, part III of this chapter; or

(3) In the case of liner installations approved prior to March 20, 1989, aluminum.

(b) For compliance with paragraph (a) of this section, the term "liner" includes any design feature, such as a joint or fastener, which would affect the capability of the liner to safely contain a fire.

(c) After March 19, 2001, each Class D compartment, regardless of volume, must meet the standards of §§25.857(c) and 25.858 of this Chapter for a Class C compartment unless the operation is an all-cargo operation in which case each Class D compartment may meet the standards in §25.857(e) for a Class E compartment.

(d) Reports of conversions and retrofits.

(1) Until such time as all Class D compartments in aircraft operated under this part by the certificate have been converted or retrofitted with appropriate detection and suppression systems, each certificate holder must submit written progress reports to the FAA that contain the information specified below.

(i) The serial number of each airplane listed in the operations specifications issued to the certificate holder for operation under this part in which all Class D compartments have been converted to Class C or Class E compartments;

(ii) The serial number of each airplane listed in the operations specification issued to the certificate holder for operation under this part, in which all Class D compartments have been retrofitted to meet the fire detection and suppression requirements for Class C or the fire detection requirements for Class E; and

(iii) The serial number of each airplane listed in the operations specifications issued to the certificate holder for operation under this part that has at least one Class D compartment that has not been converted or retrofitted.

(2) The written report must be submitted to the Certificate Holding District Office by July 1, 1998, and at each three-month interval thereafter.

[Docket No. 28937, 63 FR 8049, Feb. 17, 1998]

§121.315 Cockpit check procedure.

(a) Each certificate holder shall provide an approved cockpit check procedure for each type of aircraft.

(b) The approved procedures must include each item necessary for flight crewmembers to check for safety before starting engines, taking off, or landing, and in engine and systems emergencies. The procedures must be designed so that a flight crewmember will not need to rely upon his memory for items to be checked.

(c) The approved procedures must be readily usable in the cockpit of each aircraft and the flight crew shall follow them when operating the aircraft.

§121.316 Fuel tanks.

Each turbine powered transport category airplane operated after October 30, 1991, must meet the requirements of §25.963(e) of this chapter in effect on October 30, 1989.

[Docket No. 25614, 54 FR 40354, Sept. 29, 1989]

§121.317 Passenger information requirements, smoking prohibitions, and additional seat belt requirements.

(a) Except as provided in paragraph (l) of this section, no person may operate an airplane unless it is equipped with passenger information signs that meet the requirements of §25.791 of this chapter. Except as provided in paragraph (l) of this section, the signs must be constructed so that the crewmembers can turn them on and off.

(b) Except as provided in paragraph (l) of this section, the "Fasten Seat Belt" sign shall be turned on during any movement on the surface, for each takeoff, for each landing, and at any other time considered necessary by the pilot in command.

(c) No person may operate an airplane on a flight on which smoking is prohibited by part 252 of this title unless either the "No Smoking" passenger information signs are lighted during the entire flight, or one or more "No Smoking" placards meeting the requirements of §25.1541 of this chapter are posted during the entire flight segment. If both the lighted signs and the placards are used, the signs must remain lighted during the entire flight segment.

(d) No person may operate a passenger-carrying airplane under this part unless at least one legible sign or placard that reads "Fasten Seat Belt While Seated" is visible from each passenger seat. These signs or placards need not meet the requirements of paragraph (a) of this section.

(e) No person may operate an airplane unless there is installed in each lavatory a sign or placard that reads: "Federal law provides for a penalty of up to $2,000 for tampering with the smoke detector installed in this lavatory." These signs or placards need not meet the requirements of paragraph (a) of this section.

(f) Each passenger required by §121.311(b) to occupy a seat or berth shall fasten his or her safety belt about him or her and keep it fastened while the "Fasten Seat Belt" sign is lighted.

(g) No person may smoke while a "No Smoking" sign is lighted or while "No Smoking" placards are posted, except as follows:

(1) *Supplemental operations.* The pilot in command of an airplane engaged in a supplemental operation may authorize smoking on the flight deck (if it is physically separated from any passenger compartment), but not in any of the following situations:

(i) During airplane movement on the surface or during takeoff or landing;

(ii) During scheduled passenger-carrying public charter operations conducted under part 380 of this title; or

(iii) During any operation where smoking is prohibited by part 252 of this title or by international agreement.

(2) *Certain intrastate domestic operations.* Except during airplane movement on the surface or during takeoff or landing, a pilot in command of an airplane engaged in a domestic operation may authorize smoking on the flight deck (if it is physically separated from the passenger compartment) if—

(i) Smoking on the flight deck is not otherwise prohibited by part 252 of this title; and

(ii) The flight is conducted entirely within the same State of the United States (a flight from one place in Hawaii to another place in Hawaii through the airspace over a place outside of Hawaii is not entirely within the same State); and

(iii) The airplane is either not turbojet-powered or the airplane is not capable of carrying at least 30 passengers.

(h) No person may smoke in any airplane lavatory.

(i) No person may tamper with, disable, or destroy any smoke detector installed in any airplane lavatory.

(j) On flight segments other than those described in paragraph (c) of this section, the "No Smoking" sign must be turned on during any movement on the surface, for each takeoff, for each landing, and at any other time considered necessary by the pilot in command.

(k) Each passenger shall comply with instructions given him or her by a crewmember regarding compliance with paragraphs (f), (g), (h), and (l) of this section.

(l) A certificate holder may operate a nontransport category airplane type certificated after December 31, 1964, that is manufactured before December 20, 1997, if it is equipped with at least one placard that is legible to each person seated in the cabin that states "Fasten Seat Belt," and if, during any movement on the surface, for each takeoff, for each landing, and at any other time considered necessary by the pilot in command, a crewmember orally instructs the passengers to fasten their seat belts.

[Docket No. 25590, 53 FR 12361, April 13, 1988; as amended by Amdt. 121–196, 53 FR 44182, Nov 2, 1988; Amdt. 121–213, 55 FR 8367, March 7, 1990; Amdt. 121–230, 57 FR 42673, Sept. 15, 1992; Amdt. 121–251, 60 FR 65931, Dec. 20, 1995; Amdt. 121–256, 61 FR 30434, June 14, 1996; Amdt. 121–277, 65 FR 36779, June 9, 2000]

§121.318 Public address system.

No person may operate an airplane with a seating capacity of more than 19 passengers unless it is equipped with a public address system which—

(a) Is capable of operation independent of the crewmember interphone system required by §121.319, except for handsets, headsets, microphones, selector switches, and signaling devices;

(b) Is approved in accordance with §21.305 of this chapter;

(c) Is accessible for immediate use from each of two flight crewmember stations in the pilot compartment;

(d) For each required floor-level passenger emergency exit which has an adjacent flight attendant seat, has a microphone which is readily accessible to the seated flight attendant, except that one microphone may serve more than one exit, provided the proximity of the exits allows unassisted verbal communication between seated flight attendants;

§121.319

(e) Is capable of operation within 10 seconds by a flight attendant at each of those stations in the passenger compartment from which its use is accessible;

(f) Is audible at all passenger seats, lavatories, and flight attendant seats and work stations; and

(g) For transport category airplanes manufactured on or after November 27, 1990, meets the requirements of §25.1423 of this chapter.

[Docket No. 24995, 54 FR 43926, Oct. 27, 1989]

§121.319 Crewmember interphone system.

(a) No person may operate an airplane with a seating capacity of more than 19 passengers unless the airplane is equipped with a crewmember interphone system that:

(1) [Reserved]

(2) Is capable of operation independent of the public address system required by §121.318(a) except for handsets, headsets, microphones, selector switches, and signaling devices; and

(3) Meets the requirements of paragraph (b) of this section.

(b) The crewmember interphone system required by paragraph (a) of this section must be approved in accordance with §21.305 of this chapter and meet the following requirements:

(1) It must provide a means of two-way communication between the pilot compartment and—

  (i) Each passenger compartment; and

  (ii) Each galley located on other than the main passenger deck level.

(2) It must be accessible for immediate use from each of two flight crewmember stations in the pilot compartment;

(3) It must be accessible for use from at least one normal flight attendant station in each passenger compartment;

(4) It must be capable of operation within 10 seconds by a flight attendant at those stations in each passenger compartment from which its use is accessible; and

(5) For large turbojet-powered airplanes:

  (i) It must be accessible for use at enough flight attendant stations so that all floor-level emergency exits (or entryways to those exits in the case of exits located within galleys) in each passenger compartment are observable from one or more of those stations so equipped;

  (ii) It must have an alerting system incorporating aural or visual signals for use by flight crewmembers to alert flight attendants and for use by flight attendants to alert flight crewmembers;

  (iii) The alerting system required by paragraph (b)(5)(ii) of this section must have a means for the recipient of a call to determine whether it is a normal call or an emergency call; and

  (iv) When the airplane is on the ground, it must provide a means of two-way communication between ground personnel and either of at least two flight crewmembers in the pilot compartment. The interphone system station for use by ground personnel must be so located that personnel using the system may avoid visible detection from within the airplane.

[Docket No. 10865, 38 FR 21494, Aug. 9, 1973; as amended by Amdt. 121–121, 40 FR 42186, Sept. 11, 1975; Amdt. 121–149, 43 FR 50602, Oct. 30, 1978; Amdt. 121–178, 47 FR 13316, March 29, 1982; Amdt. 121–253, 61 FR 611, Jan. 26, 1996]

§121.321 Operations in icing.

After October 21, 2013 no person may operate an airplane with a certificated maximum takeoff weight less than 60,000 pounds in conditions conducive to airframe icing unless it complies with this section. As used in this section, the phrase "conditions conducive to airframe icing" means visible moisture at or below a static air temperature of 5°C or a total air temperature of 10°C, unless the approved Airplane Flight Manual provides another definition.

(a) When operating in conditions conducive to airframe icing, compliance must be shown with paragraph (a)(1), or (2), or (3) of this section.

(1) The airplane must be equipped with a certificated primary airframe ice detection system.

  (i) The airframe ice protection system must be activated automatically, or manually by the flightcrew, when the primary ice detection system indicates activation is necessary.

  (ii) When the airframe ice protection system is activated, any other procedures in the Airplane Flight Manual for operating in icing conditions must be initiated.

(2) Visual cues of the first sign of ice formation anywhere on the airplane and a certificated advisory airframe ice detection system must be provided.

  (i) The airframe ice protection system must be activated when any of the visual cues are observed or when the advisory airframe ice detection system indicates activation is necessary; whichever occurs first.

  (ii) When the airframe ice protection system is activated, any other procedures in the Airplane Flight Manual for operating in icing conditions must be initiated.

(3) If the airplane is not equipped to comply with the provisions of paragraph (a)(1) or (2) of this section, then the following apply:

  (i) When operating in conditions conducive to airframe icing, the airframe ice protection system must be activated prior to, and operated during, the following phases of flight:

  (A) Takeoff climb after second segment,

  (B) En route climb,

Part 121: Air Carriers & Commercial Operators §121.327

(C) Go-around climb,
(D) Holding,
(E) Maneuvering for approach and landing, and
(F) Any other operation at approach or holding airspeeds.

(ii) During any other phase of flight, the airframe ice protection system must be activated and operated at the first sign of ice formation anywhere on the airplane, unless the Airplane Flight Manual specifies that the airframe ice protection system should not be used or provides other operational instructions.

(iii) Any additional procedures for operation in conditions conducive to icing specified in the Airplane Flight Manual or in the manual required by §121.133 must be initiated.

(b) If the procedures specified in paragraph (a)(3)(i) of this section are specifically prohibited in the Airplane Flight Manual, compliance must be shown with the requirements of paragraph (a)(1) or (2) of this section.

(c) Procedures necessary for safe operation of the airframe ice protection system must be established and documented in:

(1) The Airplane Flight Manual for airplanes that comply with paragraph (a)(1) or (2) of this section, or

(2) The Airplane Flight Manual or in the manual required by §121.133 for airplanes that comply with paragraph (a)(3) of this section.

(d) Procedures for operation of the airframe ice protection system must include initial activation, operation after initial activation, and deactivation. Procedures for operation after initial activation of the ice protection system must address—

(1) Continuous operation,
(2) Automatic cycling,
(3) Manual cycling if the airplane is equipped with an ice detection system that alerts the flight crew each time the ice protection system must be cycled, or
(4) Manual cycling based on a time interval if the airplane type is not equipped with features necessary to implement (d)(1)–(3) of this section.

(e) System installations used to comply with paragraph (a)(1) or (2) of this section must be approved through an amended or supplemental type certificate in accordance with part 21 of this chapter.

[Docket No. FAA–2009–0675, 76 FR 52249, Aug. 22, 2011; as amended by Amdt. 121–363, 78 FR 15876, March 13, 2013]

§121.323 Instruments and equipment for operations at night.

No person may operate an airplane at night under this part unless it is equipped with the following instruments and equipment in addition to those required by §§121.305 through 121.321 and 121.803:

(a) Position lights.
(b) An anti-collision light.
(c) Two landing lights, except that only one landing light is required for nontransport category airplanes type certificated after December 31, 1964.
(d) Instrument lights providing enough light to make each required instrument, switch, or similar instrument, easily readable and installed so that the direct rays are shielded from the flight crewmembers' eyes and that no objectionable reflections are visible to them. There must be a means of controlling the intensity of illumination unless it is shown that nondimming instrument lights are satisfactory.
(e) An airspeed-indicating system with heated pitot tube or equivalent means for preventing malfunctioning due to icing.
(f) A sensitive altimeter.

[Docket No. 6258, 29 FR 19205, Dec. 31, 1964; as amended by Amdt. 121–251, 60 FR 65932, Dec. 20, 1995; Amdt. 121–281, 66 FR 19043, April 12, 2001]

§121.325 Instruments and equipment for operations under IFR or over-the-top.

No person may operate an airplane under IFR or over-the-top conditions under this part unless it is equipped with the following instruments and equipment, in addition to those required by §§121.305 through 121.321 and 121.803:

(a) An airspeed indicating system with heated pitot tube or equivalent means for preventing malfunctioning due to icing.
(b) A sensitive altimeter.
(c) Instrument lights providing enough light to make each required instrument, switch, or similar instrument, easily readable and so installed that the direct rays are shielded from the flight crewmembers' eyes and that no objectionable reflections are visible to them, and a means of controlling the intensity of illumination unless it is shown that nondimming instrument lights are satisfactory.

[Docket No. 6258, 29 FR 19205, Dec. 31, 1964; as amended by Amdt. 121–281, 66 FR 19043, April 12, 2001]

§121.327 Supplemental oxygen: Reciprocating engine powered airplanes.

(a) *General.* Except where supplemental oxygen is provided in accordance with §121.331, no person may operate an airplane unless supplemental oxygen is furnished and used as set forth in paragraphs (b) and (c) of this section. The amount of supplemental oxygen required for a particular operation is determined on the basis of flight altitudes and flight duration, consistent with

§121.329

the operation procedures established for each operation and route.

(b) *Crewmembers.*

(1) At cabin pressure altitudes above 10,000 feet up to and including 12,000 feet, oxygen must be provided for, and used by, each member of the flight crew on flight deck duty, and must be provided for other crewmembers, for that part of the flight at those altitudes that is of more than 30 minutes duration.

(2) At cabin pressure altitudes above 12,000 feet, oxygen must be provided for, and used by, each member of the flight crew on flight deck duty, and must be provided for other crewmembers, during the entire flight time at those altitudes.

(3) When a flight crewmember is required to use oxygen, he must use it continuously, except when necessary to remove the oxygen mask or other dispenser in connection with his regular duties. Standby crewmembers who are on call or are definitely going to have flight deck duty before completing the flight must be provided with an amount of supplemental oxygen equal to that provided for crewmembers on duty other than on flight deck duty. If a standby crewmember is not on call and will not be on flight deck duty during the remainder of the flight, he is considered to be a passenger for the purposes of supplemental oxygen requirements.

(c) *Passengers.* Each certificate holder shall provide a supply of oxygen, approved for passenger safety, in accordance with the following:

(1) For flights of more than 30 minutes duration at cabin pressure altitudes above 8,000 feet up to and including 14,000 feet, enough oxygen for 30 minutes for 10 percent of the passengers.

(2) For flights at cabin pressure altitudes above 14,000 feet up to and including 15,000 feet, enough oxygen for that part of the flight at those altitudes for 30 percent of the passengers.

(3) For flights at cabin pressure altitudes above 15,000 feet, enough oxygen for each passenger carried during the entire flight at those altitudes.

(d) For the purposes of this subpart *cabin pressure altitude* means the pressure altitude corresponding with the pressure in the cabin of the airplane, and *flight altitude* means the altitude above sea level at which the airplane is operated. For airplanes without pressurized cabins, "cabin pressure altitude" and "flight altitude" mean the same thing.

§121.329 Supplemental oxygen for sustenance: Turbine engine powered airplanes.

(a) *General.* When operating a turbine engine powered airplane, each certificate holder shall equip the airplane with sustaining oxygen and dispensing equipment for use as set forth in this section:

(1) The amount of oxygen provided must be at least the quantity necessary to comply with paragraphs (b) and (c) of this section.

(2) The amount of sustaining and first-aid oxygen required for a particular operation to comply with the rules in this part is determined on the basis of cabin pressure altitudes and flight duration, consistent with the operating procedures established for each operation and route.

(3) The requirements for airplanes with pressurized cabins are determined on the basis of cabin pressure altitude and the assumption that a cabin pressurization failure will occur at the altitude or point of flight that is most critical from the standpoint of oxygen need, and that after the failure the airplane will descend in accordance with the emergency procedures specified in the Airplane Flight Manual, without exceeding its operating limitations, to a flight altitude that will allow successful termination of the flight.

(4) Following the failure, the cabin pressure altitude is considered to be the same as the flight altitude unless it is shown that no probable failure of the cabin or pressurization equipment will result in a cabin pressure altitude equal to the flight altitude. Under those circumstances, the maximum cabin pressure altitude attained may be used as a basis for certification or determination of oxygen supply, or both.

(b) *Crewmembers.* Each certificate holder shall provide a supply of oxygen for crewmembers in accordance with the following:

(1) At cabin pressure altitudes above 10,000 feet, up to and including 12,000 feet, oxygen must be provided for and used by each member of the flight crew on flight deck duty and must be provided for other crewmembers for that part of the flight at those altitudes that is of more than 30 minutes duration.

(2) At cabin pressure altitudes above 12,000 feet, oxygen must be provided for, and used by, each member of the flight crew on flight deck duty, and must be provided for other crewmembers during the entire flight at those altitudes.

(3) When a flight crewmember is required to use oxygen, he must use it continuously except when necessary to remove the oxygen mask or other dispenser in connection with his regular duties. Standby crewmembers who are on call or are definitely going to have flight deck duty before completing the flight must be provided with an amount of supplemental oxygen equal to that provided for crewmembers on duty other than on flight duty. If a standby crewmember is not on call and will not be on flight deck duty during the remainder of the flight, he is considered to be a passenger for the purposes of supplemental oxygen requirements.

Part 121: Air Carriers & Commercial Operators §121.333

(c) *Passengers.* Each certificate holder shall provide a supply of oxygen for passengers in accordance with the following:

(1) For flights at cabin pressure altitudes above 10,000 feet, up to and including 14,000 feet, enough oxygen for that part of the flight at those altitudes that is of more than 30 minutes duration, for 10 percent of the passengers.

(2) For flights at cabin pressure altitudes above 14,000 feet, up to and including 15,000 feet, enough oxygen for that part of the flight at those altitudes for 30 percent of the passengers.

(3) For flights at cabin pressure altitudes above 15,000 feet, enough oxygen for each passenger carried during the entire flight at those altitudes.

§121.331 Supplemental oxygen requirements for pressurized cabin airplanes: Reciprocating engine powered airplanes.

(a) When operating a reciprocating engine powered airplane pressurized cabin, each certificate holder shall equip the airplane to comply with paragraphs (b) through (d) of this section in the event of cabin pressurization failure.

(b) *For crewmembers.* When operating at flight altitudes above 10,000 feet, the certificate holder shall provide enough oxygen for each crewmember for the entire flight at those altitudes and not less than a two-hour supply for each flight crewmember on flight deck duty. The required two hours supply is that quantity of oxygen necessary for a constant rate of descent from the airplane's maximum certificated operating altitude to 10,000 feet in ten minutes and followed by 110 minutes at 10,000 feet. The oxygen required by §121.337 may be considered in determining the supplemental breathing supply required for flight crewmembers on flight deck duty in the event of cabin pressurization failure.

(c) *For passengers.* When operating at flight altitudes above 8,000 feet, the certificate holder shall provide oxygen as follows:

(1) When an airplane is not flown at a flight altitude above flight level 250, enough oxygen for 30 minutes for 10 percent of the passengers, if at any point along the route to be flown the airplane can safely descend to a flight altitude of 14,000 feet or less within four minutes.

(2) If the airplane cannot descend to a flight altitude of 14,000 feet or less within four minutes, the following supply of oxygen must be provided:

(i) For that part of the flight that is more than four minutes duration at flight altitudes above 15,000 feet, the supply required by §121.327(c)(3).

(ii) For that part of the flight at flight altitudes above 14,000 feet, up to and including 15,000 feet, the supply required by §121.327(c)(2).

(iii) For flight at flight altitudes above 8,000 feet up to and including 14,000 feet, enough oxygen for 30 minutes for 10 percent of the passengers.

(3) When an airplane is flown at a flight altitude above flight level 250, enough oxygen for 30 minutes for 10 percent of the passengers for the entire flight (including emergency descent) above 8,000 feet, up to and including 14,000 feet, and to comply with §121.327(c)(2) and (3) for flight above 14,000 feet.

(d) For the purposes of this section it is assumed that the cabin pressurization failure occurs at a time during flight that is critical from the standpoint of oxygen need and that after the failure the airplane will descend, without exceeding its normal operating limitations, to flight altitudes allowing safe flight with respect to terrain clearance.

[Docket No. 6258, 29 FR 19205, Dec. 31, 1964; as amended by Amdt. 121–132, 41 FR 55475, Dec. 20, 1976]

§121.333 Supplemental oxygen for emergency descent and for first aid; turbine engine powered airplanes with pressurized cabins.

(a) *General.* When operating a turbine engine powered airplane with a pressurized cabin, the certificate holder shall furnish oxygen and dispensing equipment to comply with paragraphs (b) through (e) of this section in the event of cabin pressurization failure.

(b) *Crewmembers.* When operating at flight altitudes above 10,000 feet, the certificate holder shall supply enough oxygen to comply with §121.329, but not less than a two-hour supply for each flight crewmember on flight deck duty. The required two hours supply is that quantity of oxygen necessary for a constant rate of descent from the airplane's maximum certificated operating altitude to 10,000 feet in ten minutes and followed by 110 minutes at 10,000 feet. The oxygen required in the event of cabin pressurization failure by §121.337 may be included in determining the supply required for flight crewmembers on flight deck duty.

(c) *Use of oxygen masks by flight crewmembers.*

(1) When operating at flight altitudes above flight level 250, each flight crewmember on flight deck duty must be provided with an oxygen mask so designed that it can be rapidly placed on his face from its ready position, properly secured, sealed, and supplying oxygen upon demand; and so designed that after being placed on the face it does not prevent immediate communication between the flight crewmember and other crewmembers over the airplane intercommunication system. When it is not being used at flight

§121.333

altitudes above flight level 250, the oxygen mask must be kept in condition for ready use and located so as to be within the immediate reach of the flight crewmember while at his duty station.

(2) When operating at flight altitudes above flight level 250, one pilot at the controls of the airplane shall at all times wear and use an oxygen mask secured, sealed, and supplying oxygen, in accordance with the following:

(i) The one pilot need not wear and use an oxygen mask at or below the following flight levels if each flight crewmember on flight deck duty has a quick-donning type of oxygen mask that the certificate holder has shown can be placed on the face from its ready position, properly secured, sealed, and supplying oxygen upon demand, with one hand and within five seconds:

(A) For airplanes having a passenger seat configuration of more than 30 seats, excluding any required crewmember seat, or a payload capacity of more than 7,500 pounds, at or below flight level 410.

(B) For airplanes having a passenger seat configuration of less than 31 seats, excluding any required crewmember seat, and a payload capacity of 7,500 pounds or less, at or below flight level 350.

(ii) Whenever a quick-donning type of oxygen mask is to be used under this section, the certificate holder must also show that the mask can be put on without disturbing eye glasses and without delaying the flight crewmember from proceeding with his assigned emergency duties. The oxygen mask after being put on must not prevent immediate communication between the flight crewmember and other crewmembers over the airplane intercommunication system.

(3) Notwithstanding paragraph (c)(2) of this section, if for any reason at any time it is necessary for one pilot to leave his station at the controls of the airplane when operating at flight altitudes above flight level 250, the remaining pilot at the controls must put on and use his oxygen mask until the other pilot has returned to his duty station.

(4) Before the takeoff of a flight, each flight crewmember must personally preflight his oxygen equipment to insure that the oxygen mask is functioning, fitted properly, and connected to appropriate supply terminals, and that the oxygen supply and pressure are adequate for use.

(d) *Use of portable oxygen equipment by cabin attendants.* After November 28, 2005 each mask used for portable oxygen equipment must be connected to its oxygen supply. Above flight level 250, one of the following is required:

(1) Each attendant must carry portable oxygen equipment with a 15 minute supply of oxygen; or

(2) There must be sufficient portable oxygen equipment (including masks and spare outlets) distributed throughout the cabin so that such equipment is immediately available to each attendant, regardless of their location in the cabin; or

(3) There are sufficient spare outlets and masks distributed throughout the cabin to ensure immediate availability of oxygen to each cabin attendant, regardless of their location in the cabin.

(e) *Passenger cabin occupants.* When the airplane is operating at flight altitudes above 10,000 feet, the following supply of oxygen must be provided for the use of passenger cabin occupants:

(1) When an airplane certificated to operate at flight altitudes up to and including flight level 250, can at any point along the route to be flown, descend safely to a flight altitude of 14,000 feet or less within four minutes, oxygen must be available at the rate prescribed by this part for a 30-minute period for at least 10 percent of the passenger cabin occupants.

(2) When an airplane is operated at flight altitudes up to and including flight level 250 and cannot descend safely to a flight altitude of 14,000 feet within four minutes, or when an airplane is operated at flight altitudes above flight level 250, oxygen must be available at the rate prescribed by this part for not less than 10 percent of the passenger cabin occupants for the entire flight after cabin depressurization, at cabin pressure altitudes above 10,000 feet up to and including 14,000 feet and, as applicable, to allow compliance with §121.329(c)(2) and (3), except that there must be not less than a 10-minute supply for the passenger cabin occupants.

(3) For first-aid treatment of occupants who for physiological reasons might require undiluted oxygen following descent from cabin pressure altitudes above flight level 250, a supply of oxygen in accordance with the requirements of §25.1443(d) must be provided for two percent of the occupants for the entire flight after cabin depressurization at cabin pressure altitudes above 8,000 feet, but in no case to less than one person. An appropriate number of acceptable dispensing units, but in no case less than two, must be provided, with a means for the cabin attendants to use this supply.

(f) *Passenger briefing.* Before flight is conducted above flight level 250, a crewmember must instruct the passengers on the necessity of using oxygen in the event of cabin depressurization and must point out to them the location and demonstrate the use of the oxygen-dispensing equipment.

[Docket No. 6258, 29 FR 19205, Dec. 31, 1964; as amended by Amdt. 121–11, 30 FR 12466, Sept. 30, 1965; Amdt. 121–132, 41 FR 55475, Dec. 20, 1976; Amdt. 121–262, 62 FR 13256, March 19, 1997; Amdt. 121–262, 62 FR 15570, April 1, 1997; Amdt. 121–306, 69 FR 62789, Oct. 27, 2004; Amdt. 121–317, 70 FR 68333,

Nov. 10, 2005; Amdt. 121–322, 71 FR 1688, Jan. 11, 2006]

§121.335 Equipment standards.

(a) *Reciprocating engine powered airplanes.* The oxygen apparatus, the minimum rates of oxygen flow, and the supply of oxygen necessary to comply with §121.327 must meet the standards established in section 4b.651 of the Civil Air Regulations as in effect on July 20, 1950, except that if the certificate holder shows full compliance with those standards to be impracticable, the Administrator may authorize any change in those standards that he finds will provide an equivalent level of safety.

(b) *Turbine engine powered airplanes.* The oxygen apparatus, the minimum rate of oxygen flow, and the supply of oxygen necessary to comply with §§121.329 and 121.333 must meet the standards established in section 4b.651 of the Civil Air Regulations as in effect on September 1, 1958, except that if the certificate holder shows full compliance with those standards to be impracticable, the Administrator may authorize any changes in those standards that he finds will provide an equivalent level of safety.

§121.337 Protective breathing equipment.

(a) The certificate holder shall furnish approved protective breathing equipment (PBE) meeting the equipment, breathing gas, and communication requirements contained in paragraph (b) of this section.

(b) *Pressurized and nonpressurized cabin airplanes.* Except as provided in paragraph (f) of this section, no person may operate an airplane unless protective breathing equipment meeting the requirements of this section is provided as follows:

(1) *General.* The equipment must protect the flightcrew from the effects of smoke, carbon dioxide or other harmful gases or an oxygen deficient environment caused by other than an airplane depressurization while on flight deck duty and must protect crewmembers from the above effects while combatting fires on board the airplane.

(2) The equipment must be inspected regularly in accordance with inspection guidelines and the inspection periods established by the equipment manufacturer to ensure its condition for continued serviceability and immediate readiness to perform its intended emergency purposes. The inspection periods may be changed upon a showing by the certificate holder that the changes would provide an equivalent level of safety.

(3) That part of the equipment protecting the eyes must not impair the wearer's vision to the extent that a crewmember's duties cannot be accomplished and must allow corrective glasses to be worn without impairment of vision or loss of the protection required by paragraph (b)(1) of this section.

(4) The equipment, while in use, must allow the flightcrew to communicate using the airplane radio equipment and to communicate by interphone with each other while at their assigned duty stations. The equipment, while in use, must also allow crewmember interphone communications between each of two flight crewmember stations in the pilot compartment and at least one normal flight attendant station in each passenger compartment.

(5) The equipment, while in use, must allow any crewmember to use the airplane interphone system at any of the flight attendant stations referred to in paragraph (b)(4) of this section.

(6) The equipment may also be used to meet the supplemental oxygen requirements of this part provided it meets the oxygen equipment standards of §121.335 of this part.

(7) Protective breathing gas duration and supply system equipment requirements are as follows:

(i) The equipment must supply breathing gas for 15 minutes at a pressure altitude of 8,000 feet for the following:

(A) Flight crewmembers while performing flight deck duties; and

(B) Crewmembers while combatting an in-flight fire.

(ii) The breathing gas system must be free from hazards in itself, in its method of operation, and in its effect upon other components.

(iii) For breathing gas systems other than chemical oxygen generators, there must be a means to allow the crew to readily determine, during the equipment preflight described in paragraph (c) of this section, that the gas supply is fully charged.

(iv) For each chemical oxygen generator, the supply system equipment must meet the requirements of §25.1450(b) and (c) of this chapter.

(8) *Smoke and fume protection.* Protective breathing equipment with a fixed or portable breathing gas supply meeting the requirements of this section must be conveniently located on the flight deck and be easily accessible for immediate use by each required flight crewmember at his or her assigned duty station.

(9) *Fire combatting.* Except for nontransport category airplanes type certificated after December 31, 1964, protective breathing equipment with a portable breathing gas supply meeting the requirements of this section must be easily accessible and conveniently located for immediate use by crewmembers in combatting fires as follows:

(i) One PBE is required for each hand fire extinguisher located for use in a galley other than a galley located in a passenger, cargo, or crew compartment.

(ii) One on the flight deck, except that the Administrator may authorize another location for this PBE if special circumstances exist that make compliance impractical and the proposed deviation would provide an equivalent level of safety.

(iii) In each passenger compartment, one for each hand fire extinguisher required by §121.309 of this part, to be located within 3 feet of each required hand fire extinguisher, except that the Administrator may authorize a deviation allowing locations of PBE more than 3 feet from required hand fire extinguisher locations if special circumstances exist that make compliance impractical and if the proposed deviation provides an equivalent level of safety.

(c) *Equipment preflight.*

(1) Before each flight, each item of PBE at flight crewmember duty stations must be checked by the flight crewmember who will use the equipment to ensure that the equipment—

(i) For other than chemical oxygen generator systems, is functioning, is serviceable, fits properly (unless a universal-fit type), and is connected to supply terminals and that the breathing gas supply and pressure are adequate for use; and

(ii) For chemical oxygen generator systems, is serviceable and fits properly (unless a universal-fit type).

(2) Each item of PBE located at other than a flight crewmember duty station must be checked by a designated crewmember to ensure that each is properly stowed and serviceable, and, for other than chemical oxygen generator systems, the breathing gas supply is fully charged. Each certificate holder, in its operations manual, must designate at least one crewmember to perform those checks before he or she takes off in that airplane for his or her first flight of the day.

[Docket No. 24792, 52 FR 20957, June 3, 1987; as amended by Amdt. 121–204, 54 FR 22271, May 22, 1989; Amdt. 121–212, 55 FR 5551, Feb. 15, 1990; Amdt. 121–218, 55 FR 31565, Aug. 2, 1990; Amdt. 121–230, 57 FR 42674, Sept. 15, 1992; Amdt. 121–251, 60 FR 65932, Dec. 20, 1995; Amdt. 121–261, 61 FR 43921, Aug. 26, 1996; Amdt. 121–261, 61 FR 57585, Nov. 7, 1996]

§121.339 Emergency equipment for extended over-water operations.

(a) Except where the Administrator, by amending the operations specifications of the certificate holder, requires the carriage of all or any specific items of the equipment listed below for any over-water operation, or upon application of the certificate holder, the Administrator allows deviation for a particular extended overwater operation, no person may operate an airplane in extended over-water operations without having on the airplane the following equipment:

(1) A life preserver equipped with an approved survivor locator light, for each occupant of the airplane.

(2) Enough life rafts (each equipped with an approved survivor locator light) of a rated capacity and buoyancy to accommodate the occupants of the airplane. Unless excess rafts of enough capacity are provided, the buoyancy and seating capacity beyond the rated capacity of the rafts must accommodate all occupants of the airplane in the event of a loss of one raft of the largest rated capacity.

(3) At least one pyrotechnic signaling device for each life raft.

(4) An approved survival type emergency locator transmitter. Batteries used in this transmitter must be replaced (or recharged, if the battery is rechargeable) when the transmitter has been in use for more than 1 cumulative hour, or when 50 percent of their useful life (or for rechargeable batteries, 50 percent of their useful life of charge) has expired, as established by the transmitter manufacturer under its approval. The new expiration date for replacing (or recharging) the battery must be legibly marked on the outside of the transmitter. The battery useful life (or useful life of charge) requirements of this paragraph do not apply to batteries (such as water-activated batteries) that are essentially unaffected during probable storage intervals.

(b) The required life rafts, life preservers, and survival type emergency locator transmitter must be easily accessible in the event of a ditching without appreciable time for preparatory procedures. This equipment must be installed in conspicuously marked, approved locations.

(c) A survival kit, appropriately equipped for the route to be flown, must be attached to each required life raft.

[Docket No. 6258, 29 FR 19205, Dec. 31, 1964; as amended by Amdt. 121–53, 34 FR 15244, Sept. 30, 1969; Amdt. 121–79, 36 FR 18724, Sept. 21, 1971; Amdt. 121–93, 37 FR 14294, June 19, 1972; Amdt. 121–106, 38 FR 22378, Aug. 20, 1973; Amdt. 121–149, 43 FR 50603, Oct. 30, 1978; Amdt. 121–158, 45 FR 38348, June 9, 1980; Amdt. 121–239, 59 FR 32057, June 21, 1994]

§121.340 Emergency flotation means.

(a) Except as provided in paragraph (b) of this section, no person may operate an airplane in any overwater operation unless it is equipped with life preservers in accordance with §121.339(a)(1) or with an approved flotation means for each occupant. This means must be within easy reach of each seated occupant and must be readily removable from the airplane.

(b) Upon application by the air carrier or commercial operator, the Administrator may approve the operation of an airplane over water without the life preservers or flotation means required by paragraph (a) of this section, if the air carrier or commercial operator shows that the water over which the airplane is to be operated is not of such size and depth that life preservers or flotation means would be required for the survival of its occupants in the event the flight terminates in that water.

[Docket No. 6713, 31 FR 1147, Jan. 28, 1966; as amended by Amdt. 121–25, 32 FR 3223, Feb. 24, 1967; Amdt. 121–251, 60 FR 65932, Dec. 20, 1995]

§121.341 Equipment for operations in icing conditions.

(a) Except as permitted in paragraph (c)(2) of this section, unless an airplane is type certificated under the transport category airworthiness requirements relating to ice protection, or unless an airplane is a non-transport category airplane type certificated after December 31, 1964, that has the ice protection provisions that meet section 34 of Appendix A of part 135 of this chapter, no person may operate an airplane in icing conditions unless it is equipped with means for the prevention or removal of ice on windshields, wings, empennage, propellers, and other parts of the airplane where ice formation will adversely affect the safety of the airplane.

(b) No person may operate an airplane in icing conditions at night unless means are provided for illuminating or otherwise determining the formation of ice on the parts of the wings that are critical from the standpoint of ice accumulation. Any illuminating that is used must be of a type that will not cause glare or reflection that would handicap crewmembers in the performance of their duties.

(c) Non-transport category airplanes type certificated after December 31, 1964. Except for an airplane that has ice protection provisions that meet section 34 of Appendix A of part 135 of this chapter, or those for transport category airplane type certification, no person may operate—

(1) Under IFR into known or forecast light or moderate icing conditions;

(2) Under VFR into known light or moderate icing conditions; unless the airplane has functioning deicing anti-icing equipment protecting each propeller, windshield, wing, stabilizing or control surface, and each airspeed, altimeter, rate of climb, or flight attitude instrument system; or

(3) Into known or forecast severe icing conditions.

(d) If current weather reports and briefing information relied upon by the pilot in command indicate that the forecast icing condition that would otherwise prohibit the flight will not be encountered during the flight because of changed weather conditions since the forecast, the restrictions in paragraph (c) of this section based on forecast conditions do not apply.

[Docket No. 6258, 29 FR 18205, Dec. 31, 1964; as amended by Amdt. 121–251, 60 FR 65932, Dec. 20, 1995]

§121.342 Pitot heat indication systems.

No person may operate a transport category airplane or, after December 20, 1999, a non-transport category airplane type certificated after December 31, 1964, that is equipped with a flight instrument pitot heating system unless the airplane is also equipped with an operable pitot heat indication system that complies §25.1326 of this chapter in effect on April 12, 1978.

[Docket No. 28154, 60 FR 65932, Dec. 20, 1995]

§121.343 Flight data recorders.

(a) Except as provided in paragraphs (b), (c), (d), (e), and (f) of this section, no person may operate a large airplane that is certificated for operations above 25,000 feet altitude or is turbine-engine powered unless it is equipped with one or more approved flight recorders that record data from which the following may be determined within the ranges, accuracies, and recording intervals specified in Appendix B of this part:

(1) Time;
(2) Altitude;
(3) Airspeed;
(4) Vertical acceleration;
(5) Heading; and
(6) Time of each radio transmission either to or from air traffic control.

(b) No person may operate a large airplane type certificated up to and including September 30, 1969, for operations above 25,000 feet altitude, or a turbine-engine powered airplane certificated before the same date, unless it is equipped before May 26, 1989 with one or more approved flight recorders that utilize a digital method of recording and storing data and a method of readily retrieving that data from the storage medium. The following information must be able to be determined within the ranges, accuracies, and recording intervals specified in Appendix B of this part:

(1) Time;
(2) Altitude;
(3) Airspeed;
(4) Vertical acceleration;
(5) Heading; and
(6) Time of each radio transmission either to or from air traffic control.

(c) Except as provided in paragraph (l) of this section, no person may operate an airplane specified in paragraph (b) of this section unless it is equipped, before May 26, 1995, with one or more approved flight recorders that utilize a digital method of recording and storing data and a method of readily retrieving that data from the storage medium. The following information must

§121.343

be able to be determined within the ranges, accuracies and recording intervals specified in Appendix B of this part:
(1) Time;
(2) Altitude;
(3) Airspeed;
(4) Vertical acceleration;
(5) Heading;
(6) Time of each radio transmission either to or from air traffic control;
(7) Pitch attitude;
(8) Roll attitude;
(9) Longitudinal acceleration;
(10) Control column or pitch control surface position; and
(11) Thrust of each engine.

(d) No person may operate an airplane specified in paragraph (b) of this section that is manufactured after May 26, 1989, as well as airplanes specified in paragraph (a) of this section that have been type certificated after September 30, 1969, unless it is equipped with one or more approved flight recorders that utilize a digital method of recording and storing data and a method of readily retrieving that data from the storage medium. The following information must be able to be determined within the ranges, accuracies, and recording intervals specified in Appendix B of this part:
(1) Time;
(2) Altitude;
(3) Airspeed;
(4) Vertical acceleration;
(5) Heading;
(6) Time of each radio transmission either to or from air traffic control;
(7) Pitch attitude;
(8) Roll attitude;
(9) Longitudinal acceleration;
(10) Pitch trim position;
(11) Control column or pitch control surface position;
(12) Control wheel or lateral control surface position;
(13) Rudder pedal or yaw control surface position;
(14) Thrust of each engine;
(15) Position of each thrust reverser;
(16) Trailing edge flap or cockpit flap control position; and
(17) Leading edge flap or cockpit flap control position.

For the purpose of this section, *manufactured* means the point in time at which the airplane inspection acceptance records reflect that the airplane is complete and meets the FAA-approved type design data.

(e) After October 11, 1991, no person may operate a large airplane equipped with a digital data bus and ARINC 717 digital flight data acquisition unit (DFDAU) or equivalent unless it is equipped with one or more approved flight recorders that utilize a digital method of recording and storing data and a method of readily retrieving that data from the storage medium. Any parameters specified in Appendix B of this part that are available on the digital data bus must be recorded within the ranges, accuracies, resolutions, and sampling intervals specified.

(f) After October 11, 1991, no person may operate an airplane specified in paragraph (b) of this section that is manufactured after October 11, 1991, nor an airplane specified in paragraph (a) of this section that has been type certificated after September 30, 1969, and manufactured after October 11, 1991, unless it is equipped with one or more flight recorders that utilize a digital method of recording and storing data and a method of readily retrieving that data from the storage medium. The parameters specified in Appendix B of this part must be recorded within the ranges, accuracies, resolutions, and sampling intervals specified.

(g) Whenever a flight recorder required by this section is installed, it must be operated continuously from the instant the airplane begins the takeoff roll until it has completed the landing roll at an airport.

(h) Except as provided in paragraph (i) of this section, and except for recorded data erased as authorized in this paragraph, each certificate holder shall keep the recorded data prescribed in paragraph (a), (b), (c), or (d) of this section, as appropriate, until the airplane has been operated for at least 25 hours of the operating time specified in §121.359(a). A total of 1 hour of recorded data may be erased for the purpose of testing the flight recorder or the flight recorder system. Any erasure made in accordance with this paragraph must be of the oldest recorded data accumulated at the time of testing. Except as provided in paragraph (i) of this section, no record need be kept more than 60 days.

(i) In the event of an accident or occurrence that requires immediate notification of the National Transportation Safety Board under part 830 of its regulations and that results in termination of the flight, the certificate holder shall remove the recording media from the airplane and keep the recorded data required by paragraph (a), (b), (c), or (d) of this section, as appropriate, for at least 60 days or for a longer period upon the request of the Board or the Administrator.

(j) Each flight recorder required by this section must be installed in accordance with the requirements of §25.1459 of this chapter in effect on August 31, 1977. The correlation required by §25.1459(c) of this chapter need be established only on one airplane of any group of airplanes—

Part 121: Air Carriers & Commercial Operators §121.344

(1) That are of the same type;
(2) On which the model flight recorder and its installation are the same; and
(3) On which there is no difference in the type design with respect to the installation of those first pilot's instruments associated with the flight recorder. The most recent instrument calibration, including the recording medium from which this calibration is derived, and the recorder correlation must be retained by the certificate holder.

(k) Each flight recorder required by this section that records the data specified in paragraph (a), (b), (c), or (d) of this section, as appropriate, must have an approved device to assist in locating that recorder under water.

(l) No person may operate an airplane specified in paragraph (b) of this section that meets the Stage 2 noise levels of part 36 of this chapter and is subject to §91.801(c) of this chapter unless it is equipped with one or more approved flight data recorders that utilize a digital method of recording and storing data and a method of readily retrieving that data from the storage medium. The information specified in paragraphs (c)(1) through (c)(11) of this section must be able to be determined within the ranges, accuracies and recording intervals specified in Appendix B of this part. In addition—

(1) This flight data recorder must be installed at the next heavy maintenance check after May 26, 1994, but no later than May 26, 1995. A heavy maintenance check is considered to be any time an aircraft is scheduled to be out of service for 4 or more days.

(2) By June 23, 1994, each carrier must submit to the FAA Flight Standards Service, Air Transportation Division (AFS-200), documentation listing those airplanes covered under this paragraph and evidence that it has ordered a sufficient number of flight data recorders to meet the May 26, 1995, compliance date for all aircraft on that list.

(3) After May 26, 1994, any aircraft that is modified to meet Stage 3 noise levels must have the flight data recorder described in paragraph (c) of this section installed before operating under this part.

(m) After August 20, 2001, this section applies only to the airplane models listed in §121.344(l)(2). All other airplanes must comply with the requirements of §121.344, as applicable.

[Docket No. 24418, 52 FR 9636, March 25, 1987; as amended by Amdt. 121–197, 53 FR 26147, July 11, 1988; Amdt. 121–238, 59 FR 26900, May 24, 1994; Amdt. 121–338, 73 FR 12565, March 7, 2008]

§121.344 Digital flight data recorders for transport category airplanes.

(a) Except as provided in paragraph (l) of this section, no person may operate under this part a turbine-engine-powered transport category airplane unless it is equipped with one or more approved flight recorders that use a digital method of recording and storing data and a method of readily retrieving that data from the storage medium. The operational parameters required to be recorded by digital flight data recorders required by this section are as follows: the phrase "when an information source is installed" following a parameter indicates that recording of that parameter is not intended to require a change in installed equipment:

(1) Time;
(2) Pressure altitude;
(3) Indicated airspeed;
(4) Heading—primary flight crew reference (if selectable, record discrete, true or magnetic);
(5) Normal acceleration (Vertical);
(6) Pitch attitude;
(7) Roll attitude;
(8) Manual radio transmitter keying, or CVR/DFDR synchronization reference;
(9) Thrust/power of each engine—primary flight crew reference;
(10) Autopilot engagement status;
(11) Longitudinal acceleration;
(12) Pitch control input;
(13) Lateral control input;
(14) Rudder pedal input;
(15) Primary pitch control surface position;
(16) Primary lateral control surface position;
(17) Primary yaw control surface position;
(18) Lateral acceleration;
(19) Pitch trim surface position or parameters of paragraph (a)(82) of this section if currently recorded;
(20) Trailing edge flap or cockpit flap control selection (except when parameters of paragraph (a)(85) of this section apply);
(21) Leading edge flap or cockpit flap control selection (except when parameters of paragraph (a)(86) of this section apply);
(22) Each Thrust reverser position (or equivalent for propeller airplane);
(23) Ground spoiler position or speed brake selection (except when parameters of paragraph (a)(87) of this section apply);
(24) Outside or total air temperature;
(25) Automatic Flight Control System (AFCS) modes and engagement status, including autothrottle;
(26) Radio altitude (when an information source is installed);
(27) Localizer deviation, MLS Azimuth;
(28) Glideslope deviation, MLS Elevation;

§121.344   **Federal Aviation Regulations**

(29) Marker beacon passage;
(30) Master warning;
(31) Air/ground sensor (primary airplane system reference nose or main gear);
(32) Angle of attack (when information source is installed);
(33) Hydraulic pressure low (each system);
(34) Ground speed (when an information source is installed);
(35) Ground proximity warning system;
(36) Landing gear position or landing gear cockpit control selection;
(37) Drift angle (when an information source is installed);
(38) Wind speed and direction (when an information source is installed);
(39) Latitude and longitude (when an information source is installed);
(40) Stick shaker/pusher (when an information source is installed);
(41) Windshear (when an information source is installed);
(42) Throttle/power lever position;
(43) Additional engine parameters (as designated in Appendix M of this part);
(44) Traffic alert and collision avoidance system;
(45) DME 1 and 2 distances;
(46) Nav 1 and 2 selected frequency;
(47) Selected barometric setting (when an information source is installed);
(48) Selected altitude (when an information source is installed);
(49) Selected speed (when an information source is installed);
(50) Selected mach (when an information source is installed);
(51) Selected vertical speed (when an information source is installed);
(52) Selected heading (when an information source is installed);
(53) Selected flight path (when an information source is installed);
(54) Selected decision height (when an information source is installed);
(55) EFIS display format;
(56) Multi-function/engine/alerts display format;
(57) Thrust command (when an information source is installed);
(58) Thrust target (when an information source is installed);
(59) Fuel quantity in CG trim tank (when an information source is installed);
(60) Primary Navigation System Reference;
(61) Icing (when an information source is installed);
(62) Engine warning each engine vibration (when an information source is installed);

(63) Engine warning each engine over temp. (when an information source is installed);
(64) Engine warning each engine oil pressure low (when an information source is installed);
(65) Engine warning each engine over speed (when an information source is installed);
(66) Yaw trim surface position;
(67) Roll trim surface position;
(68) Brake pressure (selected system);
(69) Brake pedal application (left and right);
(70) Yaw or sideslip angle (when an information source is installed);
(71) Engine bleed valve position (when an information source is installed);
(72) De-icing or anti-icing system selection (when an information source is installed);
(73) Computed center of gravity (when an information source is installed);
(74) AC electrical bus status;
(75) DC electrical bus status;
(76) APU bleed valve position (when an information source is installed);
(77) Hydraulic pressure (each system);
(78) Loss of cabin pressure;
(79) Computer failure;
(80) Heads-up display (when an information source is installed);
(81) Para-visual display (when an information source is installed);
(82) Cockpit trim control input position—pitch;
(83) Cockpit trim control input position—roll;
(84) Cockpit trim control input position—yaw;
(85) Trailing edge flap and cockpit flap control position;
(86) Leading edge flap and cockpit flap control position;
(87) Ground spoiler position and speed brake selection;
(88) All cockpit flight control input forces (control wheel, control column, rudder pedal);
(89) Yaw damper status;
(90) Yaw damper command; and
(91) Standby rudder valve status.

(b) For all turbine-engine powered transport category airplanes manufactured on or before October 11, 1991, by August 20, 2001.

(1) For airplanes not equipped as of July 16, 1996, with a flight data acquisition unit (FDAU), the parameters listed in paragraphs (a)(1) through (a)(18) of this section must be recorded within the ranges and accuracies specified in Appendix B of this part, and—

(i) For airplanes with more than two engines, the parameter described in paragraph (a)(18) is not required unless sufficient capacity is available on the existing recorder to record that parameter;

(ii) Parameters listed in paragraphs (a)(12) through (a)(17) each may be recorded from a single source.

(2) For airplanes that were equipped as of July 16, 1996, with a flight data acquisition unit (FDAU), the parameters listed in paragraphs (a)(1) through (a)(22) of this section must be recorded within the ranges, accuracies, and recording intervals specified in Appendix M of this part. Parameters listed in paragraphs (a)(12) through (a)(17) each may be recorded from a single source.

(3) The approved flight recorder required by this section must be installed at the earliest time practicable, but no later than the next heavy maintenance check after August 18, 1999 and no later than August 20, 2001. A heavy maintenance check is considered to be any time an airplane is scheduled to be out of service for 4 or more days and is scheduled to include access to major structural components.

(c) For all turbine-engine powered transport category airplanes manufactured on or before October 11, 1991—

(1) That were equipped as of July 16, 1996, with one or more digital data bus(es) and an ARINC 717 digital flight data acquisition unit (DFDAU) or equivalent, the parameters specified in paragraphs (a)(1) through (a)(22) of this section must be recorded within the ranges, accuracies, resolutions, and sampling intervals specified in Appendix M of this part by August 20, 2001. Parameters listed in paragraphs (a)(12) through (a)(14) each may be recorded from a single source.

(2) Commensurate with the capacity of the recording system (DFDAU or equivalent and the DFDR), all additional parameters for which information sources are installed and which are connected to the recording system must be recorded within the ranges, accuracies, resolutions, and sampling intervals specified in Appendix M of this part by August 20, 2001.

(3) That were subject to §121.343(e) of this part, all conditions of §121.343(e) must continue to be met until compliance with paragraph (c)(1) of this section is accomplished.

(d) For all turbine-engine-powered transport category airplanes that were manufactured after October 11, 1991—

(1) The parameters listed in paragraph (a)(1) through (a)(34) of this section must be recorded within the ranges, accuracies, and recording intervals specified in Appendix M of this part by August 20, 2001. Parameters listed in paragraphs (a)(12) through (a)(14) each may be recorded from a single source.

(2) Commensurate with the capacity of the recording system, all additional parameters for which information sources are installed and which are connected to the recording system must be recorded within the ranges, accuracies, resolutions, and sampling intervals specified in Appendix M of this part by August 20, 2001.

(e) For all turbine-engine-powered transport category airplanes that are manufactured after August 18, 2000—

(1) The parameters listed in paragraph (a)(1) through (57) of this section must be recorded within the ranges, accuracies, resolutions, and recording intervals specified in Appendix M of this part.

(2) Commensurate with the capacity of the recording system, all additional parameters for which information sources are installed and which are connected to the recording system, must be recorded within the ranges, accuracies, resolutions, and sampling intervals specified in Appendix M of this part.

(3) In addition to the requirements of paragraphs (e)(1) and (e)(2) of this section, all Boeing 737 model airplanes must also comply with the requirements of paragraph (n) of this section, as applicable.

(f) For all turbine-engine-powered transport category airplanes manufactured after August 19, 2002—

(1) The parameters listed in paragraphs (a)(1) through (a)(88) of this section must be recorded within the ranges, accuracies, resolutions, and recording intervals specified in appendix M to this part.

(2) In addition to the requirements of paragraphs (f)(1) of this section, all Boeing 737 model airplanes must also comply with the requirements of paragraph (n) of this section.

(g) Whenever a flight data recorder required by this section is installed, it must be operated continuously from the instant the airplane begins its takeoff roll until it has completed its landing roll.

(h) Except as provided in paragraph (i) of this section, and except for recorded data erased as authorized in this paragraph, each certificate holder shall keep the recorded data prescribed by this section, as appropriate, until the airplane has been operated for at least 25 hours of the operating time specified in §121.359(a) of this part. A total of 1 hour of recorded data may be erased for the purpose of testing the flight recorder or the flight recorder system. Any erasure made in accordance with this paragraph must be of the oldest recorded data accumulated at the time of testing. Except as provided in paragraph (i) of this section, no record need be kept more than 60 days.

(i) In the event of an accident or occurrence that requires immediate notification of the National Transportation Safety Board under 49 CFR 830 of its regulations and that results in termination of the flight, the certificate holder shall remove the recorder from the airplane and keep the recorder data prescribed by this section, as appropriate, for at least 60 days or for a longer period upon the request of the Board or the Administrator.

§121.344

(j) Each flight data recorder system required by this section must be installed in accordance with the requirements of §25.1459(a) (except paragraphs (a)(3)(ii) and (a)(7)), (b), (d) and (e) of this chapter. A correlation must be established between the values recorded by the flight data recorder and the corresponding values being measured. The correlation must contain a sufficient number of correlation points to accurately establish the conversion from the recorded values to engineering units or discrete state over the full operating range of the parameter. Except for airplanes having separate altitude and airspeed sensors that are an integral part of the flight data recorder system, a single correlation may be established for any group of airplanes—

(1) That are of the same type;

(2) On which the flight recorder system and its installation are the same; and

(3) On which there is no difference in the type design with respect to the installation of those sensors associated with the flight data recorder system. Documentation sufficient to convert recorded data into the engineering units and discrete values specified in the applicable appendix must be maintained by the certificate holder.

(k) Each flight data recorder required by this section must have an approved device to assist in locating that recorder under water.

(l) The following airplanes that were manufactured before August 18, 1997 need not comply with this section, but must continue to comply with applicable paragraphs of §121.343 of this chapter, as appropriate:

(1) Airplanes that meet the State 2 noise levels of part 36 of this chapter and are subject to §91.801(c) of this chapter, until January 1, 2000. On and after January 1, 2000, any Stage 2 airplane otherwise allowed to be operated under Part 91 of this chapter must comply with the applicable flight data recorder requirements of this section for that airplane.

(2) British Aerospace 1-11, General Dynamics Convair 580, General Dynamics Convair 600, General Dynamics Convair 640, deHavilland Aircraft Company Ltd. DHC-7, Fairchild Industries FH 227, Fokker F-27 (except Mark 50), F-28 Mark 1000 and Mark 4000, Gulfstream Aerospace G-159, Jetstream 4100 Series, Lockheed Aircraft Corporation Electra 10-A, Lockheed Aircraft Corporation Electra 10-B, Lockheed Aircraft Corporation Electra 10-E, Lockheed Aircraft Corporation Electra L-188, Lockheed Martin Model 382 (L-100) Hercules, Maryland Air Industries, Inc. F27, Mitsubishi Heavy Industries, Ltd. YS-11, Short Bros. Limited SD3-30, Short Bros. Limited SD3-60.

(m) All aircraft subject to the requirements of this section that are manufactured on or after April 7, 2010, must have a digital flight data recorder installed that also—

(1) Meets the requirements of §§25.1459(a)(3), (a)(7), and (a)(8) of this chapter; and

(2) Retains the 25 hours of recorded information required in paragraph (h) of this section using a recorder that meets the standards of TSO–C124a, or later revision.

(n) In addition to all other applicable requirements of this section, all Boeing 737 model airplanes manufactured after August 18, 2000 must record the parameters listed in paragraphs (a)(88) through (a)(91) of this section within the ranges, accuracies, resolutions, and recording intervals specified in Appendix M to this part. Compliance with this paragraph is required no later than February 2, 2011.

[Docket No. 28109, 62 FR 38378, July 17, 1997; as amended by Amdt. 121–266, 62 FR 48135, Sept. 12, 1997; Amdt. 121–299, 68 FR 42936, July 18, 2003; Amdt. 121–299, 68 FR 50069, Aug. 20, 2003; Amdt. 121–338, 73 FR 12565, March 7, 2008; Amdt. 121–342, 73 FR 73178, Dec. 2, 2008; Amdt. 121–338, 74 FR 32800, July 9, 2009]

§121.344a Digital flight data recorders for 10–19 seat airplanes.

(a) Except as provided in paragraph (f) of this section, no person may operate under this part a turbine-engine-powered airplane having a passenger seating configuration, excluding any required crewmember seat, of 10 to 19 seats, that was brought onto the U.S. register after, or was registered outside the United States and added to the operator's U.S. operations specifications after, October 11, 1991, unless it is equipped with one or more approved flight recorders that use a digital method of recording and storing data and a method of readily retrieving that data from the storage medium. On or before August 20, 2001, airplanes brought onto the U.S. register after October 11, 1991, must comply with either the requirements in this section or the applicable paragraphs in §135.152 of this chapter. In addition, by August 20, 2001:

(1) The parameters listed in §§121.344(a)(1) through 121.344(a)(18) of this part must be recorded with the ranges, accuracies, and resolutions specified in Appendix B of part 135 of this chapter, except that—

(i) Either the parameter listed in §121.344 (a)(12) or (a)(15) of this part must be recorded; either the parameters listed in §121.344(a)(13) or (a)(16) of this part must be recorded; and either the parameter listed in §121.344(a)(14) or (a)(17) of this part must be recorded.

(ii) For airplanes with more than two engines, the parameter described in §121.344(a)(18) of this part must also be recorded if sufficient capacity is available on the existing recorder to record that parameter;

(iii) Parameters listed in §§121.344(a)(12) through 121.344(a)(17) of this part each may be recorded from a single source;

(iv) Any parameter for which no value is contained in Appendix B of part 135 of this chapter must be recorded within the ranges, accuracies, and resolutions specified in Appendix M of this part.

(2) Commensurate with the capacity of the recording system (FDAU or equivalent and the DFDR), the parameters listed in §§121.344(a)(19) through 121.344(a)(22) of this part also must be recorded within the ranges, accuracies, resolutions, and recording intervals specified in Appendix B of part 135 of this chapter.

(3) The approved flight recorder required by this section must be installed as soon as practicable, but no later than the next heavy maintenance check or equivalent after August 18, 1999. A heavy maintenance check is considered to be any time an airplane is scheduled to be out of service for 4 more days and is scheduled to include access to major structural components.

(b) For a turbine-engine-powered airplanes having a passenger seating configuration, excluding any required crewmember seat, of 10 to 19 seats, that are manufactured after August 18, 2000.

(1) The parameters listed in §§121.344(a)(1) through 121.344(a)(57) of this part, must be recorded within the ranges, accuracies, resolutions, and recording intervals specified in Appendix M of this part.

(2) Commensurate with the capacity of the recording system, all additional parameters listed in §121.344(a) of this part for which information sources are installed and which are connected to the recording system, must be recorded within the ranges, accuracies, resolutions, and sampling intervals specified in Appendix M of this part by August 20, 2001.

(c) For all turbine-engine-powered airplanes having a passenger seating configuration, excluding any required crewmember seats, of 10 to 19 seats, that are manufactured after August 19, 2002, the parameters listed in §121.344(a)(1) through (a)(88) of this part must be recorded within the ranges, accuracies, resolutions, and recording intervals specified in Appendix M of this part.

(d) Each flight data recorder system required by this section must be installed in accordance with the requirements of §23.1459(a) (except paragraphs (a)(3)(ii) and (6)), (b), (d) and (e) of this chapter. A correlation must be established between the values recorded by the flight data recorder and the corresponding values being measured. The correlation must contain a sufficient number of correlation points to accurately establish the conversion from the recorded values to engineering units or discrete state over the full operating range of the parameter. A single correlation may be established for any group of airplanes—

(1) That are of the same type;

(2) On which the flight recorder system and its installation are the same; and

(3) On which there is no difference in the type design with respect to the installation of those sensors associated with the flight data recorder system. Correlation documentation must be maintained by the certificate holder.

(e) All airplanes subject to this section are also subject to the requirements and exceptions stated in §121.344(g) through (k) and §121.346.

(f) For airplanes that were manufactured before August 18, 1997, the following airplane types need not comply with this section, but must continue to comply with applicable paragraphs of §135.152 of this chapter, as appropriate: Beech Aircraft-99 Series, Beech Aircraft 1300, Beech Aircraft 1900C, Construcciones Aeronauticas, S.A. (CASA) C-212, deHavilland DHC-6, Dornier 228, HS-748, Embraer EMB 110, Jetstream 3101, Jetstream 3201, Fairchild Aircraft SA-226, Fairchild Metro SA-227.

(g) All airplanes subject to the requirements of this section that are manufactured on or after April 7, 2010, must have a digital flight data recorder installed that also—

(1) Meets the requirements in §23.1459(a)(3), (a)(6), and (a)(7) or §25.1459(a)(3), (a)(7), and (a)(8) of this chapter, as applicable; and

(2) Retains the 25 hours of recorded information required in §121.344(g) using a recorder that meets the standards of TSO-C124a, or later revision.

[Docket No. 28109, 62 FR 38380, July 17, 1997; as amended by Amdt. 121–266, 62 FR 48135, Sept. 12, 1997; Amdt. 121–266, 62 FR 65202, Dec. 11, 1997; Amdt. 121–299, 68 FR 42936, July 18, 2003; Amdt. 121–338, 73 FR 12566, March 7, 2008; Amdt. 121–338, 74 FR 32801, July 9, 2009; Amdt. 121–347, 75 FR 7356, Feb. 19, 2010]

§121.345 Radio equipment.

(a) No person may operate an airplane unless it is equipped with radio equipment required for the kind of operation being conducted.

(b) Where two independent (separate and complete) radio systems are required by §§121.347 and 121.349, each system must have an independent antenna installation except that, where rigidly supported nonwire antennas or other antenna installations of equivalent reliability are used, only one antenna is required.

§121.346

(c) ATC transponder equipment installed within the time periods indicated below must meet the performance and environmental requirements of the following TSO's:

(1) *Through January 1, 1992:*

(i) Any class of TSO–C74b or any class of TSO–C74c as appropriate, provided that the equipment was manufactured before January 1, 1990; or

(ii) The appropriate class of TSO–C112 (Mode S).

(2) *After January 1, 1992:* The appropriate class of TSO–C112 (Mode S). For purposes of paragraph (c)(2) of this section, "installation" does not include—

(i) Temporary installation of TSO–C74b or TSO–C74c substitute equipment, as appropriate, during maintenance of the permanent equipment;

(ii) Reinstallation of equipment after temporary removal for maintenance; or

(iii) For fleet operations, installation of equipment in a fleet aircraft after removal of the equipment for maintenance from another aircraft in the same operator's fleet.

[Docket No. 6258, 29 FR 19205, Dec. 31, 1964; as amended by Amdt. 121–101, 37 FR 28499, Dec. 27, 1972; Amdt. 121–190, 52 FR 3391, Feb. 3, 1987]

§121.346 Flight data recorders: Filtered data.

(a) A flight data signal is filtered when an original sensor signal has been changed in any way, other than changes necessary to:

(1) Accomplish analog to digital conversion of the signal;

(2) Format a digital signal to be DFDR compatible; or

(3) Eliminate a high frequency component of a signal that is outside the operational bandwidth of the sensor.

(b) An original sensor signal for any flight recorder parameter required to be recorded under §121.344 may be filtered only if the recorded signal value continues to meet the requirements of Appendix B or M of this part, as applicable.

(c) For a parameter described in §121.344(a)(12) through (17), (42), or (88), or the corresponding parameter in Appendix B of this part, if the recorded signal value is filtered and does not meet the requirements of Appendix B or M of this part, as applicable, the certificate holder must:

(1) Remove the filtering and ensure that the recorded signal value meets the requirements of Appendix B or M of this part, as applicable; or

(2) Demonstrate by test and analysis that the original sensor signal value can be reconstructed from the recorded data. This demonstration requires that:

(i) The FAA determine that the procedure and the test results submitted by the certificate holder as its compliance with paragraph (c)(2) of this section are repeatable; and

(ii) The certificate holder maintains documentation of the procedure required to reconstruct the original sensor signal value. This documentation is also subject to the requirements of §121.344(i).

(d) *Compliance.* Compliance is required as follows:

(1) No later than October 20, 2011, each operator must determine, for each airplane on its operations specifications, whether the airplane's DFDR system is filtering any of the parameters listed in paragraph (c) of this section. The operator must create a record of this determination for each airplane it operates, and maintain it as part of the correlation documentation required by §121.344(j)(3) of this part.

(2) For airplanes that are not filtering any listed parameter, no further action is required unless the airplane's DFDR system is modified in a manner that would cause it to meet the definition of filtering on any listed parameter.

(3) For airplanes found to be filtering a parameter listed in paragraph (c) of this section, the operator must either:

(i) No later than April 21, 2014, remove the filtering; or

(ii) No later than April 22, 2013, submit the necessary procedure and test results required by paragraph (c)(2) of this section.

(4) After April 21, 2014, no aircraft flight data recording system may filter any parameter listed in paragraph (c) of this section that does not meet the requirements of Appendix B or M of this part, unless the certificate holder possesses test and analysis procedures and the test results that have been approved by the FAA. All records of tests, analysis and procedures used to comply with this section must be maintained as part of the correlation documentation required by §121.344(j)(3) of this part.

[Docket No. FAA–2006–26135, 75 FR 7356, Feb. 19, 2010]

§121.347 Communication and navigation equipment for operations under VFR over routes navigated by pilotage.

(a) No person may operate an airplane under VFR over routes that can be navigated by pilotage unless the airplane is equipped with the radio communication equipment necessary under normal operating conditions to fulfill the following:

(1) Communicate with at least one appropriate station from any point on the route;

(2) Communicate with appropriate air traffic control facilities from any point within Class B, Class C, or Class D airspace, or within a Class E surface area designated for an airport in which flights are intended; and

(3) Receive meteorological information from any point en route by either of two independent systems. One of the means provided to comply with this subparagraph may be used to comply with paragraphs (a)(1) and (2) of this section.

(b) No person may operate an airplane at night under VFR over routes that can be navigated by pilotage unless that airplane is equipped with—

(1) Radio communication equipment necessary under normal operating conditions to fulfill the functions specified in paragraph (a) of this section; and

(2) Navigation equipment suitable for the route to be flown.

[Docket No. 6258, 29 FR 19205, Dec. 30, 1964; as amended by Amdt. 121–226, 56 FR 65663, Dec. 17, 1991; Amdt. 121–333, 72 FR 31681, June 7, 2007]

§121.349 Communication and navigation equipment for operations under VFR over routes not navigated by pilotage or for operations under IFR or over the top.

(a) *Navigation equipment requirements—General.* No person may conduct operations under VFR over routes that cannot be navigated by pilotage, or operations conducted under IFR or over the top, unless—

(1) The en route navigation aids necessary for navigating the airplane along the route (e.g., ATS routes, arrival and departure routes, and instrument approach procedures, including missed approach procedures if a missed approach routing is specified in the procedure) are available and suitable for use by the aircraft navigation systems required by this section;

(2) The airplane used in those operations is equipped with at least—

(i) Except as provided in paragraph (c) of this section, two approved independent navigation systems suitable for navigating the airplane along the route to be flown within the degree of accuracy required for ATC;

(ii) One marker beacon receiver providing visual and aural signals; and

(iii) One ILS receiver; and

(3) Any RNAV system used to meet the navigation equipment requirements of this section is authorized in the certificate holder's operations specifications.

(b) *Communication equipment requirements.* No person may operate an airplane under VFR over routes that cannot be navigated by pilotage, and no person may operate an airplane under IFR or over the top, unless the airplane is equipped with—

(1) At least two independent communication systems necessary under normal operating conditions to fulfill the functions specified in §121.347 (a); and

(2) At least one of the communication systems required by paragraph (b)(1) of this section must have two-way voice communication capability.

(c) *Use of a single independent navigation system for operations under VFR over routes that cannot be navigated by pilotage, or operations conducted under IFR or over the top.* Notwithstanding the requirements of paragraph (a)(2)(i) of this section, the airplane may be equipped with a single independent navigation system suitable for navigating the airplane along the route to be flown within the degree of accuracy required for ATC if:

(1) It can be shown that the airplane is equipped with at least one other independent navigation system suitable, in the event of loss of the navigation capability of the single independent navigation system permitted by this paragraph at any point along the route, for proceeding safely to a suitable airport and completing an instrument approach; and

(2) The airplane has sufficient fuel so that the flight may proceed safely to a suitable airport by use of the remaining navigation system, and complete an instrument approach and land.

(d) *Use of VOR navigation equipment.* If VOR navigation equipment is used to comply with paragraph (a) or (c) of this section, no person may operate an airplane unless it is equipped with at least one approved DME or suitable RNAV system.

(e) *Additional communication system equipment requirements for operators subject to §121.2.* In addition to the requirements in paragraph (b) of this section, no person may operate an airplane having a passenger seat configuration of 10 to 30 seats, excluding each crewmember seat, and a maximum payload capacity of 7,500 pounds or less, under IFR, over the top, or in extended over-water operations unless it is equipped with at least—

(1) Two microphones; and

(2) Two headsets, or one headset and one speaker.

[Docket No. FAA–2002–14002, 72 FR 31681, June 7, 2007]

§121.351 Communication and navigation equipment for extended overwater operations and for certain other operations.

(a) Except as provided in paragraph (c) of this section, no person may conduct an extended over-water operation unless the airplane is equipped with at least two independent long-range navigation systems and at least two independent long-range communication systems necessary under normal operating conditions to fulfill the following functions—

(1) Communicate with at least one appropriate station from any point on the route;

(2) Receive meteorological information from any point on the route by either of two independent communication systems. One of the communication systems used to comply with this paragraph may be used to comply with paragraphs (a)(1) and (a)(3) of this section; and

(3) At least one of the communication systems must have two-way voice communication capability.

(b) No certificate holder conducting a flag or supplemental operation or a domestic operation within the State of Alaska may conduct an operation without the equipment specified in paragraph (a) of this section, if the Administrator finds that equipment to be necessary for search and rescue operations because of the nature of the terrain to be flown over.

(c) Notwithstanding the requirements of paragraph (a) of this section, installation and use of a single LRNS and a single LRCS may be authorized by the Administrator and approved in the certificate holder's operations specifications for operations and routes in certain geographic areas. The following are among the operational factors the Administrator may consider in granting an authorization:

(1) The ability of the flightcrew to navigate the airplane along the route within the degree of accuracy required for ATC,

(2) The length of the route being flown, and

(3) The duration of the very high frequency communications gap.

[Docket No. 6258, 29 FR 19205, Dec. 31, 1964; as amended by Amdt. 121–253, 61 FR, Jan. 26, 1996; Amdt. 121–254, 61 FR, Feb. 26, 1996; Amdt. 121–333, 72 FR 31682, June 7, 2007]

§121.353 Emergency equipment for operations over uninhabited terrain areas: Flag, supplemental and certain domestic operations.

Unless the airplane has the following equipment, no person may conduct a flag or supplemental operation or a domestic operation within the States of Alaska or Hawaii over an uninhabited area or any other area that (in its operations specifications) the Administrator specifies required equipment for search and rescue in case of an emergency:

(a) Suitable pyrotechnic signaling devices.

(b) An approved survival type emergency locator transmitter. Batteries used in this transmitter must be replaced (or recharged, if the battery is rechargeable) when the transmitter has been in use for more than 1 cumulative hour, or when 50 percent of their useful life (or for rechargeable batteries, 50 percent of their useful life of charge) has expired, as established by the transmitter manufacturer under its approval. The new expiration date for replacing (or recharging) the battery must be legibly marked on the outside of the transmitter. The battery useful life (or useful life of charge) requirements of this paragraph do not apply to batteries (such as water-activated batteries) that are essentially unaffected during probable storage intervals.

(c) Enough survival kits, appropriately equipped for the route to be flown for the number of occupants of the airplane.

[Docket No. 6258, 29 FR 19205, Dec. 31, 1964; as amended by Amdt. 121–79, 36 FR 18724, Sept. 21, 1971; Amdt. 121–106, 38 FR 22378 Aug. 20, 1973; Amdt. 121–158, 45 FR 38348, June 9, 1980; Amdt. 121–239, 59 FR 32057, June 21, 1994; Amdt. 121–251, 60 FR 65932, Dec. 20, 1995]

§121.354 Terrain awareness and warning system.

(a) *Airplanes manufactured after March 29, 2002.* No person may operate a turbine-powered airplane unless that airplane is equipped with an approved terrain awareness and warning system that meets the requirements for Class A equipment in Technical Standard Order (TSO)–C151. The airplane must also include an approved terrain situational awareness display.

(b) *Airplanes manufactured on or before March 29, 2002.* No person may operate a turbine-powered airplane after March 29, 2005, unless that airplane is equipped with an approved terrain awareness and warning system that meets the requirements for Class A equipment in Technical Standard Order (TSO)–C151. The airplane must also include an approved terrain situational awareness display.

Part 121: Air Carriers & Commercial Operators §121.356

(Approved by the Office of Management and Budget under control number 2120-0631)

(c) Airplane Flight Manual. The Airplane Flight Manual shall contain appropriate procedures for—

(1) The use of the terrain awareness and warning system; and

(2) Proper flight crew reaction in response to the terrain awareness and warning system audio and visual warnings.

[Docket No. 29312, 65 FR 16755, March 29, 2000]

§121.355 Equipment for operations on which specialized means of navigation are used.

(a) No certificate holder may conduct an operation—

(1) Using Doppler Radar or an Inertial Navigation System outside the 48 contiguous States and the District of Columbia, unless such systems have been approved in accordance with Appendix G to this part; or

(2) Using Doppler Radar or an Inertial Navigation System within the 48 contiguous States and the District of Columbia, or any other specialized means of navigation, unless it shows that an adequate airborne system is provided for the specialized navigation authorized for the particular operation.

(b) Notwithstanding paragraph (a) of this section, Doppler Radar and Inertial Navigation Systems, and the training programs, maintenance programs, relevant operations manual material, and minimum equipment lists prepared in accordance therewith, approved before April 29, 1972, are not required to be approved in accordance with that paragraph.

[Docket No. 10204, 37 FR 6464, March 30, 1972]

§121.356 Collision avoidance system.

Effective January 1, 2005, any airplane you operate under this part must be equipped and operated according to the following table:

Collision Avoidance Systems

If you operate any—	Then you must operate that airplane with
(a) Turbine-powered airplane of more than 33,000 pounds maximum certificated takeoff weight.	(1) An appropriate class of Mode S transponder that meets Technical Standard Order (TSO) C-112, or a later version, and one of the following approved units: (i) TCAS II that meets TSO C-119b (version 7.0), or takeoff weight a later version. (ii) TCAS II that meets TSO C-119a (version 6.04A Enhanced) that was installed in that airplane before May 1, 2003. If that TCAS II version 6.04A Enhanced no longer can be repaired to TSO C-119a standards, it must be replaced with a TCAS II that meets TSO C-119b (version 7.0), or a later version. (iii) A collision avoidance system equivalent to TSO C-119b (version 7.0), or a later version, capable of coordinating with units that meet TSO C-119a (version 6.04A Enhanced), or a later version.
(b) Passenger or combination cargo/passenger (combi) airplane that has a passenger seat configuration of 10-30 seats.	(1) TCAS I that meets TSO C-118, or a later version, or (2) A collision avoidance system equivalent to has a TSO C-118, or a later version, or (3) A collision avoidance system and Mode S transponder that meet paragraph (a)(1) of this section.
(c) Piston-powered airplane of more 33,000 pounds maximum certificated takeoff weight.	(1) TCAS I that meets TSO C-118, or a later version, or (2) A collision avoidance system equivalent to maximum TSO C-118, or a later version, or (3) A collision avoidance system and Mode S transponder that meet paragraph (a)(1) of this section.

[Docket No. FAA–2001–10910, 68 FR 15902, April 1, 2003]

§121.357 Airborne weather radar equipment requirements.

(a) No person may operate any transport category airplane (except C-46 type airplanes) or a nontransport category airplane certificated after December 31, 1964, unless approved airborne weather radar equipment has been installed in the airplane.

(b) [Reserved]

(c) Each person operating an airplane required to have approved airborne weather radar equipment installed shall, when using it under this part, operate it in accordance with the following:

(1) *Dispatch.* No person may dispatch an airplane (or begin the flight of an airplane in the case of a certificate holder that does not use a dispatch system) under IFR or night VFR conditions when current weather reports indicate that thunderstorms, or other potentially hazardous weather conditions that can be detected with airborne weather radar, may reasonably be expected along the route to be flown, unless the airborne weather radar equipment is in satisfactory operating condition.

(2) If the airborne weather radar becomes inoperative en route, the airplane must be operated in accordance with the approved instructions and procedures specified in the operations manual for such an event.

(d) This section does not apply to airplanes used solely within the State of Hawaii or within the State of Alaska and that part of Canada west of longitude 130 degrees W, between latitude 70 degrees N, and latitude 53 degrees N, or during any training, test, or ferry flight.

(e) Notwithstanding any other provision of this chapter, an alternate electrical power supply is not required for airborne weather radar equipment.

[Docket No. 6258, 29 FR 19205, Dec. 31, 1964; as amended by Amdt. 121–18, 31 FR 5825, April 15, 1966; Amdt. 121–130, 41 FR 47229, Oct. 28, 1976; Amdt. 121–251, 60 FR 65932, Dec. 20, 1995]

§121.358 Low-altitude windshear system equipment requirements.

(a) *Airplanes manufactured after January 2, 1991.* No person may operate a turbine-powered airplane manufactured after January 2, 1991, unless it is equipped with either an approved airborne windshear warning and flight guidance system, an approved airborne detection and avoidance system, or an approved combination of these systems.

(b) *Airplanes manufactured before January 3, 1991.* Except as provided in paragraph (c) of this section, after January 2, 1991, no person may operate a turbine-powered airplane manufactured before January 3, 1991 unless it meets one of the following requirements as applicable.

(1) The makes/models/series listed below must be equipped with either an approved airborne windshear warning and flight guidance system, an approved airborne detection and avoidance system, or an approved combination of these systems:

(i) A–300—600;
(ii) A–310—all series;
(iii) A–320—all series;
(iv) B–737—300, 400, and 500 series;
(v) B–747—400;
(vi) B–757—all series;
(vii) B–767—all series;
(viii) F–100—all series;
(ix) MD–11—all series; and
(x) MD–80 series equipped with an EFIS and Honeywell–970 digital flight guidance computer.

(2) All other turbine-powered airplanes not listed above must be equipped with as a minimum requirement, an approved airborne windshear warning system. These airplanes may be equipped with an approved airborne windshear detection and avoidance system, or an approved combination of these systems.

(c) *Extension of the compliance date.* A certificate holder may obtain an extension of the compliance date in paragraph (b) of this section if it obtains FAA approval of a retrofit schedule. To obtain approval of a retrofit schedule and show continued compliance with that schedule, a certificate holder must do the following:

(1) Submit a request for approval of a retrofit schedule by June 1, 1990, to the Flight Standards Division Manager in the region of the certificate holding district office.

(2) Show that all of the certificate holder's airplanes required to be equipped in accordance with this section will be equipped by the final compliance date established for TCAS II retrofit.

(3) Comply with its retrofit schedule and submit status reports containing information acceptable to the Administrator. The initial report must be submitted by January 2, 1991, and subsequent reports must be submitted every six months thereafter until completion of the schedule. The reports must be submitted to the certificate holder's assigned Principal Avionics Inspector.

(d) *Definitions.* For the purposes of this section the following definitions apply—

(1) *Turbine-powered airplane* includes, e.g., turbofan-, turbojet-, propfan-, and ultra-high bypass fan-powered airplanes. The definition specifically excludes turbopropeller-powered airplanes.

(2) An airplane is considered manufactured on the date the inspection acceptance records reflect that the airplane is complete and meets the FAA Approved Type Design data.

[Docket No. 25954, 55 FR 13242, April 9, 1990]

§121.359 Cockpit voice recorders.

(a) No certificate holder may operate a large turbine engine powered airplane or a large pressurized airplane with four reciprocating engines unless an approved cockpit voice recorder is installed in that airplane and is operated continuously from the start of the use of the checklist (before starting engines for the purpose of flight), to completion of the final checklist at the termination of the flight.

(b) [Reserved]

(c) The cockpit voice recorder required by paragraph (a) of this section must meet the following application standards:

(1) The requirements of part 25 of this chapter in affect on August 31, 1977.

(2) After September 1, 1980, each recorder container must—

(i) Be either bright orange or bright yellow;

(ii) Have reflective tape affixed to the external surface to facilitate its location under water; and

(iii) Have an approved underwater locating device on or adjacent to the container which is secured in such a manner that they are not likely to be separated during crash impact, unless the cockpit voice recorder, and the flight recorder required by §121.343, are installed adjacent to each other in such a manner that they are not likely to be separated during crash impact.

(d) No person may operate a multiengine, turbine-powered airplane having a passenger seat configuration of 10–19 seats unless it is equipped with an approved cockpit voice recorder that:

(1) Is installed in compliance with §23.1457(a)(1) and (2), (b), (c), (d)(1)(i), (2) and (3), (e), (f), and (g); or §25.1457(a)(1) and (2), (b), (c), (d)(1)(i), (2) and (3), (e), (f), and (g) of this chapter, as applicable; and

(2) Is operated continuously from the use of the checklist before the flight to completion of the final checklist at the end of the flight.

(e) No person may operate a multiengine, turbine-powered airplane having a passenger seat configuration of 20 to 30 seats unless it is equipped with an approved cockpit voice recorder that—

(1) Is installed in accordance with the requirements of §23.1457 (except paragraphs (a)(6), (d)(1)(ii), (4), and (5)) or §25.1457 (except paragraphs (a)(6), (d)(1)(ii), (4), and (5)) of this chapter, as applicable; and

(2) Is operated continuously from the use of the checklist before the flight to completion of the final checklist at the end of the flight.

(f) In complying with this section, an approved cockpit voice recorder having an erasure feature may be used, so that at any time during the operation of the recorder, information recorded more than 30 minutes earlier may be erased or otherwise obliterated.

(g) For those aircraft equipped to record the uninterrupted audio signals received by a boom or a mask microphone, the flight crewmembers are required to use the boom microphone below 18,000 feet mean sea level. No person may operate a large turbine engine powered airplane or a large pressurized airplane with four reciprocating engines manufactured after October 11, 1991, or on which a cockpit voice recorder has been installed after October 11, 1991, unless it is equipped to record the uninterrupted audio signal received by a boom or mask microphone in accordance with §25.1457(c)(5) of this chapter.

(h) In the event of an accident or occurrence requiring immediate notification of the National Transportation Safety Board under part 830 of its regulations, which results in the termination of the flight, the certificate holder shall keep the recorded information for at least 60 days or, if requested by the Administrator or the Board, for a longer period. Information obtained from the record is used to assist in determining the cause of accidents or occurrences in connection with investigations under part 830. The Administrator does not use the record in any civil penalty or certificate action.

(i) By April 7, 2012, all turbine engine-powered airplanes subject to this section that are manufactured before April 7, 2010, must have a cockpit voice recorder installed that also—

(1) Meets the requirements of §23.1457(d)(6) or §25.1457(d)(6) of this chapter, as applicable;

(2) Retains at least the last 2 hours of recorded information using a recorder that meets the standards of TSO-C123a, or later revision; and

(3) Is operated continuously from the use of the checklist before the flight to completion of the final checklist at the end of the flight.

(4) If transport category, meets the requirements in §25.1457(a)(3), (a)(4), and (a)(5) of this chapter.

(j) All turbine engine-powered airplanes subject to this section that are manufactured on or after April 7, 2010, must have a cockpit voice recorder installed that also—

(1) Is installed in accordance with the requirements of §23.1457 (except for paragraph (a)(6)) or §25.1457 (except for paragraph (a)(6)) of this chapter, as applicable;

(2) Retains at least the last 2 hours of recorded information using a recorder that meets the standards of TSO-C123a, or later revision; and

(3) Is operated continuously from the use of the checklist before the flight to completion of the final checklist at the end of the flight.

(4) For all airplanes manufactured on or after December 6, 2010, also meets the requirements of §23.1457(a)(6) or §25.1457(a)(6) of this chapter, as applicable.

(k) All airplanes required by this part to have a cockpit voice recorder and a flight data recorder, that install datalink communication equipment on or after December 6, 2010, must record all datalink messages as required by the certification rule applicable to the airplane.

[Docket No. 6258, 29 FR 19205, Dec. 31, 1964; as amended by Amdt. 121–20, 31 FR 8912, June 28, 1966; Amdt. 121–23, 31 FR 15192, Dec. 3, 1966; Amdt. 121–32, 32 FR 13914, Oct. 6, 1967; Amdt. 121–130, 41 FR 47229, Oct. 28, 1976; Amdt. 121–135, 42 FR 36973, July 18, 1977; Amdt. 121–143, 43 FR 22642, May 25, 1978; Amdt. 121–197, 53 FR 26147, July 11, 1988; Amdt. 121–251, 60 FR 65933, Dec. 20, 1995; Amdt. 121–338, 73 FR 12566, March 7, 2008; Amdt. 121–338, 74 FR 32801, July 9, 2009; Amdt. 121–349, 75 FR 17046, April 5, 2010]

§121.360 [Reserved]

Subpart L—Maintenance, Preventive Maintenance, and Alterations

Source: Docket No. 6258, 29 FR 19210, Dec. 31, 1964, unless otherwise noted.

§121.361 Applicability.

(a) Except as provided by paragraph (b) of this section, this subpart prescribes requirements for maintenance, preventive maintenance, and alterations for all certificate holders.

(b) The Administrator may amend a certificate holder's operations specifications to permit deviation from those provisions of this subpart that would prevent the return to service and use of airframe components, powerplants, appliances, and spare parts thereof because those items have been maintained, altered, or inspected by persons employed outside the United States who do not hold U.S. airman certificates. Each certificate holder who uses parts under this deviation must provide for surveillance of facilities and practices to assure that all work performed on these parts is accomplished in accordance with the certificate holder's manual.

[Docket No. 8754, 33 FR 14406, Sept. 25, 1968]

§121.363 Responsibility for airworthiness.

(a) Each certificate holder is primarily responsible for—

(1) The airworthiness of its aircraft, including airframes, aircraft engines, propellers, appliances, and parts thereof; and

(2) The performance of the maintenance, preventive maintenance, and alteration of its aircraft, including airframes, aircraft engines, propellers, appliances, emergency equipment, and parts thereof, in accordance with its manual and the regulations of this chapter.

(b) A certificate holder may make arrangements with another person for the performance of any maintenance, preventive maintenance, or alterations. However, this does not relieve the certificate holder of the responsibility specified in paragraph (a) of this section.

[Docket No. 6258, 29 FR 19210, Dec. 31, 1964; as amended by Amdt. 121–106, 38 FR 22378, Aug. 20, 1973]

§121.365 Maintenance, preventive maintenance, and alteration organization.

(a) Each certificate holder that performs any of its maintenance (other than required inspections), preventive maintenance, or alterations, and each person with whom it arranges for the performance of that work must have an organization adequate to perform the work.

(b) Each certificate holder that performs any inspections required by its manual in accordance with §121.369(b)(2) or (3) (in this subpart referred to as required inspections) and each person with whom it arranges for the performance of that work must have an organization adequate to perform that work.

(c) Each person performing required inspections in addition to other maintenance, preventive maintenance, or alterations, shall organize the performance of those functions so as to separate the required inspection functions from the other maintenance, preventive maintenance, and alteration functions. The separation shall be below the level of administrative control at which overall responsibility for the required inspection functions and other maintenance, preventive maintenance, and alteration functions are exercised.

[Docket No. 6258, 29 FR 19210, Dec. 31, 1964; as amended by Amdt. 121–3, 30 FR 3639, March 19, 1965]

§121.367 Maintenance, preventive maintenance, and alterations programs.

Each certificate holder shall have an inspection program and a program covering other maintenance, preventive maintenance, and alterations that ensures that—

(a) Maintenance, preventive maintenance, and alterations performed by it, or by other persons, are performed in accordance with the certificate holder's manual;

(b) Competent personnel and adequate facilities and equipment are provided for the proper performance of maintenance, preventive maintenance, and alterations; and

(c) Each aircraft released to service is airworthy and has been properly maintained for operation under this part.

[Docket No. 6258, 29 FR 19210, Dec. 31, 1964; as amended by Amdt. 121–100, 37 FR 28053, Dec. 20, 1972]

§121.368 [Reserved]

§121.369 Manual requirements.

(a) The certificate holder shall put in its manual a chart or description of the certificate holder's organization required by §121.365 and a list of persons with whom it has arranged for the performance of any of its required inspections, other maintenance, preventive maintenance, or alterations, including a general description of that work.

(b) The certificate holder's manual must contain the programs required by §121.367 that must be followed in performing maintenance, preventive maintenance, and alterations of that certificate holder's airplanes, including airframes, aircraft engines, propellers, appliances, emergency equipment, and parts thereof, and must include at least the following:

(1) The method of performing routine and non-routine maintenance (other than required inspections), preventive maintenance, and alterations.

(2) A designation of the items of maintenance and alteration that must be inspected (required inspections), including at least those that could result in a failure, malfunction, or defect endangering the safe operation of the aircraft, if not performed properly or if improper parts or materials are used.

(3) The method of performing required inspections and a designation by occupational title of personnel authorized to perform each required inspection.

(4) Procedures for the reinspection of work performed pursuant to previous required inspection findings (buy-back procedures).

(5) Procedures, standards, and limits necessary for required inspections and acceptance or rejection of the items required to be inspected and for periodic inspection and calibration of precision tools, measuring devices, and test equipment.

(6) Procedures to ensure that all required inspections are performed.

(7) Instructions to prevent any person who performs any item of work from performing any required inspection of that work.

(8) Instructions and procedures to prevent any decision of an inspector, regarding any required inspection from being countermanded by persons other than supervisory personnel of the inspection unit, or a person at that level of administrative control that has overall responsibility for the management of both the required inspection functions and the other maintenance, preventive maintenance, and alterations functions.

(9) Procedures to ensure that required inspections, other maintenance, preventive maintenance, and alterations that are not completed as a result of shift changes or similar work interruptions are properly completed before the aircraft is released to service.

(c) The certificate holder must set forth in its manual a suitable system (which may include a coded system) that provides for preservation and retrieval of information in a manner acceptable to the Administrator and that provides—

(1) A description (or reference to data acceptable to the Administrator) of the work performed;

(2) The name of the person performing the work if the work is performed by a person outside the organization of the certificate holder; and

(3) The name or other positive identification of the individual approving the work.

[Docket No. 6258, 29 FR 19210, Dec. 31, 1964; as amended by Amdt. 121–94, 37 FR 15983, Aug. 9, 1972; Amdt. 121–106, 38 FR 22378, Aug. 20, 1973]

§121.370 [Reserved]

§121.370a [Reserved]

§121.371 Required inspection personnel.

(a) No person may use any person to perform required inspections unless the person performing the inspection is appropriately certificated, properly trained, qualified, and authorized to do so.

(b) No person may allow any person to perform a required inspection unless, at that time, the person performing that inspection is under the supervision and control of an inspection unit.

(c) No person may perform a required inspection if he performed the item of work required to be inspected.

(d) Each certificate holder shall maintain, or shall determine that each person with whom it arranges to perform its required inspections maintains, a current listing of persons who have been trained, qualified, and authorized to conduct required inspections. The persons must be identified by name, occupational title, and the inspections that they are authorized to perform. The certificate holder (or person with whom it arranges to perform its required inspections) shall give written information to each person so authorized describing the extent of his responsibilities, authorities, and inspectional limitations. The list shall be made available for inspection by the Administrator upon request.

§121.373 Continuing analysis and surveillance.

(a) Each certificate holder shall establish and maintain a system for the continuing analysis and surveillance of the performance and effectiveness of its inspection program and the program covering other maintenance, preventive maintenance, and alterations and for the correction of any deficiency in those programs, regardless of whether those programs are carried out by the certificate holder or by another person.

(b) Whenever the Administrator finds that either or both of the programs described in paragraph (a) of this section does not contain adequate procedures and standards to meet the requirements of this part, the certificate holder shall, after notification by the Administrator, make any changes in those programs that are necessary to meet those requirements.

(c) A certificate holder may petition the Administrator to reconsider the notice to make a change in a program. The petition must be filed with the FAA certificate-holding district office charged with the overall inspection of the certificate holder's operations within 30 days after the certificate holder receives the notice. Except in the case of an emergency requiring immediate action in the interest of safety, the filing of the petition stays the notice pending a decision by the Administrator.

[Docket No. 6258, 29 FR 19210, Dec. 31, 1964; as amended by Amdt. 121–207, 54 FR 39293, Sept. 25, 1989; Amdt. 121–253, 61 FR, Jan. 26, 1996]

§121.374 Continuous airworthiness maintenance program (CAMP) for two-engine ETOPS.

In order to conduct an ETOPS flight using a two-engine airplane, each certificate holder must develop and comply with the ETOPS continuous airworthiness maintenance program, as authorized in the certificate holder's operations specifications, for each airplane–engine combination used in ETOPS. The certificate holder must develop this ETOPS CAMP by supplementing the manufacturer's maintenance program or the CAMP currently approved for the certificate holder. This ETOPS CAMP must include the following elements:

(a) *ETOPS maintenance document.* The certificate holder must have an ETOPS maintenance document for use by each person involved in ETOPS.

(1) The document must—
(i) List each ETOPS significant system;
(ii) Refer to or include all of the ETOPS maintenance elements in this section;
(iii) Refer to or include all supportive programs and procedures;
(iv) Refer to or include all duties and responsibilities, and
(v) Clearly state where referenced material is located in the certificate holder's document system.

(b) *ETOPS pre-departure service check.* Except as provided in Appendix P of this part, the certificate holder must develop a pre-departure check tailored to their specific operation.

(1) The certificate holder must complete a pre-departure service check immediately before each ETOPS flight.

(2) At a minimum, this check must—
(i) Verify the condition of all ETOPS Significant Systems;
(ii) Verify the overall status of the airplane by reviewing applicable maintenance records; and
(iii) Include an interior and exterior inspection to include a determination of engine and APU oil levels and consumption rates.

(3) An appropriately trained maintenance person, who is ETOPS qualified, must accomplish and certify by signature ETOPS specific tasks. Before an ETOPS flight may commence, an ETOPS pre-departure service check (PDSC) Signatory Person, who has been authorized by the certificate holder, must certify by signature, that the ETOPS PDSC has been completed.

(4) For the purposes of this paragraph (b) only, the following definitions apply:

(i) *ETOPS qualified person:* A person is ETOPS qualified when that person satisfactorily completes the operator's ETOPS training program and is authorized by the certificate holder.

(ii) *ETOPS PDSC Signatory Person:* A person is an ETOPS PDSC Signatory Person when that person is ETOPS qualified and that person:

(A) When certifying the completion of the ETOPS PDSC in the United States:

(1) Works for an operator authorized to engage in part 121 operation or works for a part 145 repair station; and

(2) Holds a U.S. Mechanic's Certificate with airframe and powerplant ratings.

(B) When certifying the completion of the ETOPS PDSC outside of the U.S. holds a certificate in accordance with §43.17(c)(1) of this chapter; or

(C) When certifying the completion of the ETOPS PDSC outside the U.S. holds the certificates needed or has the requisite experience or training to return aircraft to service on behalf of an ETOPS maintenance entity.

(iii) *ETOPS maintenance entity:* An entity authorized to perform ETOPS maintenance and complete ETOPS PDSC and that entity is:

(A) Certificated to engage in part 121 operations;

(B) Repair station certificated under part 145 of this chapter; or

(C) Entity authorized pursuant to §43.17(c)(2) of this chapter.

(c) *Limitations on dual maintenance.*

(1) Except as specified in paragraph (c)(2), the certificate holder may not perform scheduled or unscheduled dual maintenance during the same maintenance visit on the same or a substantially

similar ETOPS Significant System listed in the ETOPS maintenance document, if the improper maintenance could result in the failure of an ETOPS Significant System.

(2) In the event dual maintenance as defined in paragraph (c)(1) of this section cannot be avoided, the certificate holder may perform maintenance provided:

(i) The maintenance action on each affected ETOPS Significant System is performed by a different technician, or

(ii) The maintenance action on each affected ETOPS Significant System is performed by the same technician under the direct supervision of a second qualified individual; and

(iii) For either paragraph (c)(2)(i) or (ii) of this section, a qualified individual conducts a ground verification test and any inflight verification test required under the program developed pursuant to paragraph (d) of this section.

(d) *Verification program.* The certificate holder must develop and maintain a program for the resolution of discrepancies that will ensure the effectiveness of maintenance actions taken on ETOPS Significant Systems. The verification program must identify potential problems and verify satisfactory corrective action. The verification program must include ground verification and inflight verification policy and procedures. The certificate holder must establish procedures to indicate clearly who is going to initiate the verification action and what action is necessary. The verification action may be performed on an ETOPS revenue flight provided the verification action is documented as satisfactorily completed upon reaching the ETOPS Entry Point.

(e) *Task identification.* The certificate holder must identify all ETOPS-specific tasks. An appropriately trained mechanic who is ETOPS qualified must accomplish and certify by signature that the ETOPS-specific task has been completed.

(f) *Centralized maintenance control procedures.* The certificate holder must develop and maintain procedures for centralized maintenance control for ETOPS.

(g) *Parts control program.* The certificate holder must develop an ETOPS parts control program to ensure the proper identification of parts used to maintain the configuration of airplanes used in ETOPS.

(h) *Reliability program.* The certificate holder must have an ETOPS reliability program. This program must be the certificate holder's existing reliability program or its Continuing Analysis and Surveillance System (CASS) supplemented for ETOPS. This program must be event-oriented and include procedures to report the events listed below, as follows:

(1) The certificate holder must report the following events within 96 hours of the occurrence to its certificate holding district office (CHDO):

(i) IFSDs, except planned IFSDs performed for flight training.

(ii) Diversions and turnbacks for failures, malfunctions, or defects associated with any airplane or engine system.

(iii) Uncommanded power or thrust changes or surges.

(iv) Inability to control the engine or obtain desired power or thrust.

(v) Inadvertent fuel loss or unavailability, or uncorrectable fuel imbalance in flight.

(vi) Failures, malfunctions or defects associated with ETOPS Significant Systems.

(vii) Any event that would jeopardize the safe flight and landing of the airplane on an ETOPS flight.

(2) The certificate holder must investigate the cause of each event listed in paragraph (h)(1) of this section and submit findings and a description of corrective action to its CHDO. The report must include the information specified in §121.703(e). The corrective action must be acceptable to its CHDO.

(i) *Propulsion system monitoring.*

(1) If the IFSD rate (computed on a 12-month rolling average) for an engine installed as part of an airplane–engine combination exceeds the following values, the certificate holder must do a comprehensive review of its operations to identify any common cause effects and systemic errors. The IFSD rate must be computed using all engines of that type in the certificate holder's entire fleet of airplanes approved for ETOPS.

(i) A rate of 0.05 per 1,000 engine hours for ETOPS up to and including 120 minutes.

(ii) A rate of 0.03 per 1,000 engine hours for ETOPS beyond 120-minutes up to and including 207 minutes in the North Pacific Area of Operation and up to and including 180 minutes elsewhere.

(iii) A rate of 0.02 per 1,000 engine hours for ETOPS beyond 207 minutes in the North Pacific Area of Operation and beyond 180 minutes elsewhere.

(2) Within 30 days of exceeding the rates above, the certificate holder must submit a report of investigation and any necessary corrective action taken to its CHDO.

(j) *Engine condition monitoring.*

(1) The certificate holder must have an engine condition monitoring program to detect deterioration at an early stage and to allow for corrective action before safe operation is affected.

(2) This program must describe the parameters to be monitored, the method of data collection, the method of analyzing data, and the process for taking corrective action.

(3) The program must ensure that engine-limit margins are maintained so that a prolonged engine-inoperative diversion may be conducted at approved power levels and in all expected environmental conditions without exceeding approved engine limits. This includes approved limits for items such as rotor speeds and exhaust gas temperatures.

(k) *Oil-consumption monitoring.* The certificate holder must have an engine oil consumption monitoring program to ensure that there is enough oil to complete each ETOPS flight. APU oil consumption must be included if an APU is required for ETOPS. The operator's oil consumption limit may not exceed the manufacturer's recommendation. Monitoring must be continuous and include oil added at each ETOPS departure point. The program must compare the amount of oil added at each ETOPS departure point with the running average consumption to identify sudden increases.

(l) *APU in-flight start program.* If the airplane type certificate requires an APU but does not require the APU to run during the ETOPS portion of the flight, the certificate holder must develop and maintain a program acceptable to the FAA for cold soak in-flight start-and-run reliability.

(m) *Maintenance training.* For each airplane–engine combination, the certificate holder must develop a maintenance training program that provides training adequate to support ETOPS. It must include ETOPS specific training for all persons involved in ETOPS maintenance that focuses on the special nature of ETOPS. This training must be in addition to the operator's maintenance training program used to qualify individuals to perform work on specific airplanes and engines.

(n) *Configuration, maintenance, and procedures (CMP) document.* If an airplane–engine combination has a CMP document, the certificate holder must use a system that ensures compliance with the applicable FAA-approved document.

(o) *Procedural changes.* Each substantial change to the maintenance or training procedures that were used to qualify the certificate holder for ETOPS, must be submitted to the CHDO for review. The certificate holder cannot implement a change until its CHDO notifies the certificate holder that the review is complete.

[Docket No. FAA–2002–6717, 72 FR 1880, Jan. 16, 2007; as amended by Amdt. 121–329, 72 FR 7348, Feb. 15, 2007; Amdt. 121–329, 72 FR 26541, May 10, 2007; Amdt. 121–339, 73 FR 33881, June 16, 2008]

§121.375 Maintenance and preventive maintenance training program.

Each certificate holder or person performing maintenance or preventive maintenance functions for it shall have a training program to ensure that each person (including inspection personnel) who determines the adequacy of work done is fully informed about procedures and techniques and new equipment in use and is competent to perform his duties.

§121.377 Maintenance and preventive maintenance personnel duty time limitations.

Within the United States, each certificate holder (or person performing maintenance or preventive maintenance functions for it) shall relieve each person performing maintenance or preventive maintenance from duty for a period of at least 24 consecutive hours during any seven consecutive days, or the equivalent thereof within any one calendar month.

§121.378 Certificate requirements.

(a) Except for maintenance, preventive maintenance, alterations, and required inspections performed by a certificated repair station that is located outside the United States, each person who is directly in charge of maintenance, preventive maintenance, or alterations, and each person performing required inspections must hold an appropriate airman certificate.

(b) For the purposes of this section, a person *directly in charge* is each person assigned to a position in which he is responsible for the work of a shop or station that performs maintenance, preventive maintenance, alterations, or other functions affecting aircraft airworthiness. A person who is *directly in charge* need not physically observe and direct each worker constantly but must be available for consultation and decision on matters requiring instruction or decision from higher authority than that of the persons performing the work.

[Docket No. 6258, 29 FR 19210, Dec. 31, 1964; as amended by Amdt. 121–21, 31 FR 10618, Aug. 9, 1966; Amdt. 121–286, 66 FR 41116, Aug. 6, 2001]

§121.379 Authority to perform and approve maintenance, preventive maintenance, and alterations.

(a) A certificate holder may perform, or it may make arrangements with other persons to perform, maintenance, preventive maintenance, and alterations as provided in its continuous airworthiness maintenance program and its maintenance manual. In addition, a certificate holder may perform these functions for another certificate holder as provided in the continuous airworthiness maintenance program and maintenance manual of the other certificate holder.

(b) A certificate holder may approve any aircraft, airframe, aircraft engine, propeller, or appliance for return to service after maintenance, preventive maintenance, or alterations that are performed under paragraph (a) of this section. However, in the case of a major repair or major alteration, the work must have been done in accordance with technical data approved by the Administrator.

[Docket No. 10289, 35 FR 16793, Oct. 30, 1970]

§121.380 Maintenance recording requirements.

(a) Each certificate holder shall keep (using the system specified in the manual required in §121.369) the following records for the periods specified in paragraph (c) of this section:

(1) All the records necessary to show that all requirements for the issuance of an airworthiness release under §121.709 have been met.

(2) Records containing the following information:

(i) The total time in service of the airframe.

(ii) Except as provided in paragraph (b) of this section, the total time in service of each engine and propeller.

(iii) The current status of life-limited parts of each airframe, engine, propeller, and appliance.

(iv) The time since last overhaul of all items installed on the aircraft which are required to be overhauled on a specified time basis.

(v) The identification of the current inspection status of the aircraft, including the times since the last inspections required by the inspection program under which the aircraft and its appliances are maintained.

(vi) The current status of applicable airworthiness directives, including the date and methods of compliance, and, if the airworthiness directive involves recurring action, the time and date when the next action is required.

(vii) A list of current major alterations to each airframe, engine, propeller, and appliance.

(b) A certificate holder need not record the total time in service of an engine or propeller on a transport category cargo airplane, a transport category airplane that has a passenger seat configuration of more than 30 seats, or a nontransport category airplane type certificated before January 1, 1958, until the following, whichever occurs first:

(1) March 20, 1997; or

(2) The date of the first overhaul of the engine or propeller, as applicable, after January 19, 1996.

(c) Each certificate holder shall retain the records required to be kept by this section for the following periods:

(1) Except for the records of the last complete overhaul of each airframe, engine, propeller, and appliance, the records specified in paragraph (a)(1) of this section shall be retained until the work is repeated or superseded by other work or for one year after the work is performed.

(2) The records of the last complete overhaul of each airframe, engine, propeller, and appliance shall be retained until the work is superseded by work of equivalent scope and detail.

(3) The records specified in paragraph (a)(2) of this section shall be retained and transferred with the aircraft at the time the aircraft is sold.

(d) The certificate holder shall make all maintenance records required to be kept by this section available for inspection by the Administrator or any authorized representative of the National Transportation Safety Board (NTSB).

[Docket No. 10658, 37 FR 15983, Aug. 9, 1972; as amended by Amdt. 121–251, 60 FR 65933, Dec. 20, 1995; Amdt. 121–321, 71 FR 536, Jan. 4, 2006]

§121.380a Transfer of maintenance records.

Each certificate holder who sells a U.S. registered aircraft shall transfer to the purchaser, at the time of sale, the following records of that aircraft, in plain language form or in coded form at the election of the purchaser, if the coded form provides for the preservation and retrieval of information in a manner acceptable to the Administrator:

(a) The record specified in §121.380(a)(2).

(b) The records specified in §121.380(a)(1) which are not included in the records covered by paragraph (a) of this section, except that the purchaser may permit the seller to keep physical custody of such records. However, custody of records in the seller does not relieve the purchaser of his responsibility under §121.380(c) to make the records available for inspection by the Administrator or any authorized representative of the National Transportation Safety Board (NTSB).

[Docket No. 10658, 37 FR 15984, Aug. 9, 1972]

Subpart M—Airman and Crewmember Requirements

Source: Docket No. 6258, 29 FR 19212, December 31, 1964, unless otherwise noted.

§121.381 Applicability.

This subpart prescribes airman and crewmember requirements for all certificate holders.

§121.383 Airman: Limitations on use of services.

(a) No certificate holder may use any person as an airman nor may any person serve as an airman unless that person—

(1) Holds an appropriate current airman certificate issued by the FAA;

(2) Has any required appropriate current airman and medical certificates in his possession while engaged in operations under this part; and

(3) Is otherwise qualified for the operation for which he is to be used.

(b) Each airman covered by paragraph (a)(2) of this section shall present either or both certificates for inspection upon the request of the Administrator.

(c) [Reserved]

(d) No certificate holder may:

(1) Use the services of any person as a pilot on an airplane engaged in operations under this part if that person has reached his or her 65th birthday.

(2) Use the services of any person as a pilot in command in operations under this part between the United States and another country, or in operations between other countries, if that person has reached his or her 60th birthday unless there is another pilot in the flight deck crew who has not yet attained 60 years of age.

(e) No pilot may:

(1) Serve as a pilot in operations under this part if that person has reached his or her 65th birthday.

(2) Serve as a pilot in command in operations under this part between the United States and another country, or in operations between other countries, if that person has reached his or her 60th birthday unless there is another pilot in the flight deck crew who has not yet attained 60 years of age.

[Docket No. 6258, 29 FR 19212, Dec. 31, 1964; as amended by Amdt. 121–144, 43 FR 22646, May 25, 1978; Amdt. 121–344, 74 FR 34234, July 15, 2009]

§121.385 Composition of flight crew.

(a) No certificate holder may operate an airplane with less than the minimum flight crew in the airworthiness certificate or the airplane Flight Manual approved for that type airplane and required by this part for the kind of operation being conducted.

(b) In any case in which this part requires the performance of two or more functions for which an airman certificate is necessary, that requirement is not satisfied by the performance of multiple functions at the same time by one airman.

(c) The minimum pilot crew is two pilots and the certificate holder shall designate one pilot as pilot in command and the other second in command.

(d) On each flight requiring a flight engineer at least one flight crewmember, other than the flight engineer, must be qualified to provide emergency performance of the flight engineer's functions for the safe completion of the flight if the flight engineer becomes ill or is otherwise incapacitated. A pilot need not hold a flight engineer's certificate to perform the flight engineer's functions in such a situation.

[Docket No. 6258, 29 FR 19212, Dec. 31, 1964; as amended by Amdt. 121–178, 47 FR 13316, March 29, 1982; Amdt. 121–253, 61 FR, Jan. 26, 1996; Amdt. 121–256, 61 FR 30434, June 14, 1996]

§121.387 Flight engineer.

No certificate holder may operate an airplane for which a type certificate was issued before January 2, 1964, having a maximum certificated takeoff weight of more than 80,000 pounds without a flight crewmember holding a current flight engineer certificate. For each airplane type certificated after January 1, 1964, the requirement for a flight engineer is determined under the type certification requirements of §25.1523.

[Docket No. 5025, 30 FR 6067, April 29, 1965]

§121.389 Flight navigator and specialized navigation equipment.

(a) No certificate holder may operate an airplane outside the 48 contiguous States and the District of Columbia, when its position cannot be reliably fixed for a period of more than 1 hour, without—

(1) A flight crewmember who holds a current flight navigator certificate; or

(2) Specialized means of navigation approved in accordance with §121.355 which enables a reliable determination to be made of the position of the airplane by each pilot seated at his duty station.

(b) Notwithstanding paragraph (a) of this section, the Administrator may also require a flight navigator or special navigation equipment, or both, when specialized means of navigation are necessary for 1 hour or less. In making this determination, the Administrator considers—

(1) The speed of the airplane;
(2) Normal weather conditions en route;
(3) Extent of air traffic control;
(4) Traffic congestion;
(5) Area of navigational radio coverage at destination;
(6) Fuel requirements;
(7) Fuel available for return to point of departure or alternates;
(8) Predication of flight upon operation beyond the point of no return; and
(9) Any other factors he determines are relevant in the interest of safety.

(c) Operations where a flight navigator or special navigation equipment, or both, are required are specified in the operations specifications of the air carrier or commercial operator.

[Docket No. 10204, 37 FR 6464, March 30, 1972; as amended by Amdt. 121–178, 47 FR 13316, March 29, 1982]

§121.391 Flight attendants.

(a) Except as specified in §121.393 and §121.394, each certificate holder must provide at least the following flight attendants on board each passenger-carrying airplane when passengers are on board:

(1) For airplanes having a maximum payload capacity of more than 7,500 pounds and having a seating capacity of more than 9 but less than 51 passengers—one flight attendant.

(2) For airplanes having a maximum payload capacity of 7,500 pounds or less and having a seating capacity of more than 19 but less than 51 passengers—one flight attendant.

(3) For airplanes having a seating capacity of more than 50 but less than 101 passengers—two flight attendants.

(4) For airplanes having a seating capacity of more than 100 passengers—two flight attendants plus one additional flight attendant for each unit (or part of a unit) of 50 passenger seats above a seating capacity of 100 passengers.

(b) If, in conducting the emergency evacuation demonstration required under §121.291(a) or (b), the certificate holder used more flight attendants than is required under paragraph (a) of this section for the maximum seating capacity of the airplane used in the demonstration, he may not, thereafter, take off that airplane—

(1) In its maximum seating capacity configuration with fewer flight attendants than the number used during the emergency evacuation demonstration; or

(2) In any reduced seating capacity configuration with fewer flight attendants than the number required by paragraph (a) of this section for that seating capacity plus the number of flight attendants used during the emergency evacuation demonstration that were in excess of those required under paragraph (a) of this section.

(c) The number of flight attendants approved under paragraphs (a) and (b) of this section are set forth in the certificate holder's operations specifications.

(d) During takeoff and landing, flight attendants required by this section shall be located as near as practicable to required floor level exists and shall be uniformly distributed throughout the airplane in order to provide the most effective egress of passengers in event of an emergency evacuation. During taxi, flight attendants required by this section must remain at their duty stations with safety belts and shoulder harnesses fastened except to perform duties related to the safety of the airplane and its occupants.

[Docket No. 2033, 30 FR 3206, March 9, 1965; as amended by Amdt. 121–30, 32 FR 13268, Sept. 20, 1967; Amdt. 121–46, 34 FR 5545, March 22, 1969; Amdt. 121–84, 37 FR 3975, Feb. 24, 1972; Amdt. 121–88, 37 FR 5606, March 17, 1972; Amdt. 121–159, 45 FR 41593, June 19, 1980; Amdt. 121–176, 46 FR 61454, Dec. 17, 1981; Amdt. 121–180, 47 FR 56463, Dec. 16, 1982; Amdt. 121–251, 60 FR 65933, Dec. 20, 1995; Amdt. 121–350, 75 FR 68198, Nov. 5, 2010]

§121.392 Personnel identified as flight attendants.

(a) Any person identified by the certificate holder as a flight attendant on an aircraft in operations under this part must be trained and qualified in accordance with subparts N and O of this part. This includes:

(1) Flight attendants provided by the certificate holder in excess of the number required by §121.391(a); and

(2) Flight attendants provided by the certificate holder when flight attendants are not required by §121.391(a).

(b) A qualifying flight attendant who is receiving operating experience on an aircraft in operations under subpart O of this part must be identified to passengers as a qualifying flight attendant.

[Docket No. FAA–2008–0677, 78 FR 67836, Nov. 12, 2013]

§121.393 Crewmember requirements at stops where passengers remain on board.

At stops where passengers remain on board, the certificate holder must meet the following requirements:

(a) On each airplane for which a flight attendant is not required by §121.391(a), the certificate holder must ensure that a person who is qualified in the emergency evacuation procedures for the airplane, as required in §121.417, and who is identified to the passengers, remains:

(1) On board the airplane; or

(2) Nearby the airplane, in a position to adequately monitor passenger safety, and:

(i) The airplane engines are shut down; and

(ii) At least one floor level exit remains open to provide for the deplaning of passengers.

(b) On each airplane for which flight attendants are required by §121.391(a), but the number of flight attendants remaining on board is fewer than required by §121.391(a), the certificate holder must meet the following requirements:

(1) The certificate holder shall ensure that:

(i) The airplane engines are shut down;

(ii) At least one floor level exit remains open to provide for the deplaning of passengers; and

(iii) The number of flight attendants on board is at least half the number required by §121.391(a), rounded down to the next lower number in the case of fractions, but never fewer than one.

(2) The certificate holder may substitute for the required flight attendants other persons qualified in the emergency evacuation procedures for that aircraft as required in §121.417, if these persons are identified to the passengers.

(3) If only one flight attendant or other qualified person is on board during a stop, that flight attendant or other qualified person shall be located in accordance with the certificate holder's FAA-approved operating procedures. If more than one flight attendant or other qualified person is on board, the flight attendants or other qualified persons shall be spaced throughout the cabin to provide the most effective assistance for the evacuation in case of an emergency.

[Docket No. 28154, 60 FR 65934, Dec. 20, 1995]

§121.394 Flight attendant requirements during passenger boarding and deplaning.

(a) During passenger boarding, on each airplane for which more than one flight attendant is required by §121.391, the certificate holder may:

(1) Reduce the number of required flight attendants by one, provided that:

(i) The flight attendant that leaves the aircraft remains within the immediate vicinity of the door through which passengers are boarding;

(ii) The flight attendant that leaves the aircraft only conducts safety duties related to the flight being boarded;

(iii) The airplane engines are shut down; and

(iv) At least one floor level exit remains open to provide for passenger egress; or

(2) Substitute a pilot or flight engineer employed by the certificate holder and trained and qualified on that type airplane for one flight attendant, provided the certificate holder—

(i) Describes in the manual required by §121.133:

(A) The necessary functions to be performed by the substitute pilot or flight engineer in an emergency, to include a situation requiring an emergency evacuation. The certificate holder must show those functions are realistic, can be practically accomplished, and will meet any reasonably anticipated emergency; and

(B) How other regulatory functions performed by a flight attendant will be accomplished by the substitute pilot or flight engineer on the airplane.

(ii) Ensures that the following requirements are met:

(A) The substitute pilot or flight engineer is not assigned to operate the flight for which that person is substituting for a required flight attendant.

(B) The substitute pilot or flight engineer is trained in all assigned flight attendant duties regarding passenger handling.

(C) The substitute pilot or flight engineer meets the emergency training requirements for flight attendants in evacuation management and evacuation commands, as appropriate, and frequency of performance drills regarding operation of exits in the normal and emergency modes on that type aircraft.

(D) The substitute pilot or flight engineer is in possession of all items required for duty.

(E) The substitute pilot or flight engineer is located in the passenger cabin.

(F) The substitute pilot or flight engineer is identified to the passengers.

(G) The substitution of a pilot or flight engineer for a required flight attendant does not interfere with the safe operation of the flight.

(H) The airplane engines are shut down.

(I) At least one floor-level exit remains open to provide for passenger egress.

(b) During passenger deplaning, on each airplane for which more than one flight attendant is required by §121.391, the certificate holder may reduce the number of flight attendants required by that paragraph provided:

(1) The airplane engines are shut down;

(2) At least one floor level exit remains open to provide for passenger egress; and

(3) The number of flight attendants on board is at least half the number required by §121.391,

rounded down to the next lower number in the case of fractions, but never fewer than one.

(c) If only one flight attendant is on the airplane during passenger boarding or deplaning, that flight attendant must be located in accordance with the certificate holder's FAA-approved operating procedures. If more than one flight attendant is on the airplane during passenger boarding or deplaning, the flight attendants must be evenly distributed throughout the airplane cabin, in the vicinity of the floor-level exits, to provide the most effective assistance in the event of an emergency.

(d) The time spent by any crewmember conducting passenger boarding or deplaning duties is considered duty time.

[Docket No. FAA–2009–0022, 75 FR 68198, Nov. 5, 2010]

§121.395 Aircraft dispatcher: Domestic and flag operations.

Each certificate holder conducting domestic or flag operations shall provide enough qualified aircraft dispatchers at each dispatch center to ensure proper operational control of each flight.

[Docket No. 28154, 61 FR 2611, Jan. 26, 1996]

§121.397 Emergency and emergency evacuation duties.

(a) Each certificate holder shall, for each type and model of airplane, assigned to each category of required crewmember, as appropriate, the necessary functions to be performed in an emergency or a situation requiring emergency evacuation. The certificate holder shall show those functions are realistic, can be practically accomplished, and will meet any reasonably anticipated emergency including the possible incapacitation of individual crewmembers or their inability to reach the passenger cabin because of shifting cargo in combination cargo-passenger airplanes.

(b) The certificate holder shall describe in its manual the functions of each category of required crewmembers under paragraph (a) of this section.

[Docket No. 2033, 30 FR 3206, March 9, 1965; as amended by Amdt. 121–7, 30 FR 6727, May 18, 1965]

Subpart N— Training Program

Source: Docket No. 9509, 35 FR 90, January 3, 1970, unless otherwise noted.

§121.400 Applicability and terms used.

(a) This subpart prescribes the requirements applicable to each certificate holder for establishing and maintaining a training program for crewmembers, aircraft dispatchers, and other operations personnel, and for the approval and use of training devices in the conduct of the program.

(b) For the purpose of this subpart, airplane groups are as follows:

(1) *Group I.* Propeller driven, including—
(i) Reciprocating powered; and
(ii) Turbopropeller powered.
(2) *Group II.* Turbojet powered.

(c) For the purpose of this subpart, the following terms and definitions apply:

(1) *Initial training.* The training required for crewmembers and dispatchers who have not qualified and served in the same capacity on another airplane of the same group.

(2) *Transition training.* The training required for crewmembers and dispatchers who have qualified and served in the same capacity on another airplane of the same group.

(3) *Upgrade training.* The training required for crewmembers who have qualified and served as second in command or flight engineer on a particular airplane type, before they serve as pilot in command or second in command, respectively, on that airplane.

(4) *Differences training.* The training required for crewmembers and dispatchers who have qualified and served on a particular type airplane, when the Administrator finds differences training is necessary before a crewmember serves in the same capacity on a particular variation of that airplane.

(5) *Programmed hours.* The hours of training prescribed in this subpart which may be reduced by the Administrator upon a showing by the certificate holder that circumstances justify a lesser amount.

(6) *Inflight.* Refers to maneuvers, procedures, or functions that must be conducted in the airplane.

(7) *Training center.* An organization governed by the applicable requirements of part 142 of this chapter that provides training, testing, and checking under contract or other arrangement to certificate holders subject to the requirements of this part.

(8) *Requalification training.* The training required for crewmembers previously trained and qualified, but who have become unqualified due to not having met within the required period the recurrent training requirements of §121.427 or the proficiency check requirements of §121.441.

(9) *Related aircraft.* Any two or more aircraft of the same make with either the same or different type certificates that have been demonstrated and determined by the Administrator to have commonality to the extent that credit between those aircraft may be applied for flightcrew member training, checking, recent experience, operating experience, operating cycles, and line operat-

ing flight time for consolidation of knowledge and skills.

(10) *Related aircraft differences training.* The flightcrew member training required for aircraft with different type certificates that have been designated as related by the Administrator.

(11) *Base aircraft.* An aircraft identified by a certificate holder for use as a reference to compare differences with another aircraft.

[Docket No. 9509, 35 FR 90, Jan. 3, 1970; 35 FR 2819, Feb. 11, 1970; as amended by Amdt. 121–104, 38 FR 14915, June 7, 1973; Amdt. 121–259, 61 FR 34560, July 2, 1996; Amdt. 121–366, 78 FR 67836, Nov. 12, 2013]

§121.401 Training program: General.

(a) Each certificate holder shall:

(1) Establish and implement a training program that satisfies the requirements of this subpart and appendices E and F of this part and that ensures that each crewmember, aircraft dispatcher, flight instructor and check airman is adequately trained to perform his or her assigned duties. Prior to implementation, the certificate holder must obtain initial and final FAA approval of the training program.

(2) Provide adequate ground and flight training facilities and properly qualified ground instructors for the training required by this subpart;

(3) Provide and keep current with respect to each airplane type and, if applicable, the particular variations within that airplane type, appropriate training material, examinations, forms, instructions, and procedures for use in conducting the training and checks required by this part; and

(4) Provide enough flight instructors, simulator instructors, and approved check airmen to conduct required flight training and flight checks, and simulator training courses permitted under this part.

(b) Whenever a crewmember or aircraft dispatcher who is required to take recurrent training, a flight check, or a competence check, takes the check or completes the training in the calendar month before or after the calendar month in which that training or check is required, he is considered to have taken or completed it in the calendar month in which it was required.

(c) Each instructor, supervisor, or check airman who is responsible for a particular ground training subject, segment of flight training, course of training, flight check, or competence check under this part shall certify as to the proficiency and knowledge of the crewmember, aircraft dispatcher, flight instructor, or check airman concerned upon completion of that training or check. That certification shall be made a part of the crewmember's or dispatcher's record. When the certification required by this paragraph is made by an entry in a computerized recordkeeping system, the certifying instructor, supervisor, or check airman must be identified with that entry. However, the signature of the certifying instructor, supervisor, or check airman is not required for computerized entries.

(d) Training subjects that are applicable to more than one airplane or crewmember position and that have been satisfactorily completed in connection with prior training for another airplane or another crewmember position, need not be repeated during subsequent training other than recurrent training.

(e) A person who progresses successfully through flight training, is recommended by his instructor or a check airman, and successfully completes the appropriate flight check for a check airman or the Administrator, need not complete the programmed hours of flight training for the particular airplane. However, whenever the Administrator finds that 20 percent of the flight checks given at a particular training base during the previous 6 months under this paragraph are unsuccessful, this paragraph may not be used by the certificate holder at that base until the Administrator finds that the effectiveness of the flight training there has improved.

In the case of a certificate holder using a course of training permitted in §121.409(c), the Administrator may require the programmed hours of in-flight training in whole or in part, until he finds the effectiveness of the flight training has improved as provided in paragraph (e) of this section.

[Docket No. 9509, 35 FR 90, Jan. 3, 1970; as amended by Amdt. 121–104, 38 FR 14915, June 7, 1973; Amdt. 121–108, 38 FR 35446, Dec. 28, 1973; Amdt. 121–143, 43 FR 22642, May 25, 1978; Amdt. 121–316, 70 FR 58823, Oct. 7, 2005]

§121.402 Training program: Special rules.

(a) Other than the certificate holder, only another certificate holder certificated under this part or a flight training center certificated under part 142 of this chapter is eligible under this subpart to provide flight training, testing, and checking under contract or other arrangement to those persons subject to the requirements of this subpart.

(b) A certificate holder may contract with, or otherwise arrange to use the services of, a training center certificated under part 142 of this chapter to provide training, testing, and checking required by this part only if the training center—

(1) Holds applicable training specifications issued under part 142 of this chapter;

(2) Has facilities, training equipment, and courseware meeting the applicable requirements of part 142 of this chapter;

(3) Has approved curriculums, curriculum segments, and portions of curriculum segments applicable for use in training courses required by this subpart; and

(4) Has sufficient instructor and check airmen qualified under the applicable requirements of §§121.411 or 121.413 to provide training, testing, and checking to persons subject to the requirements of this subpart.

[Docket No. 26933, 61 FR 34560, July 2, 1996; as amended by Amdt. 121–263, 62 FR 13791, March 21, 1997]

§121.403 Training program: Curriculum.

(a) Each certificate holder must prepare and keep current a written training program curriculum for each type of airplane with respect to dispatchers and each crewmember required for that type airplane. The curriculum must include ground and flight training required by this subpart.

(b) Each training program curriculum must include:

(1) A list of principal ground training subjects, including emergency training subjects, that are provided.

(2) A list of all the training device mockups, systems trainers, procedures trainers, or other training aids that the certificate holder will use. No later than March 12, 2019, a list of all the training equipment approved under §121.408 as well as other training aids that the certificate holder will use.

(3) Detailed descriptions or pictorial displays of the approved normal, abnormal, and emergency maneuvers, procedures and functions that will be performed during each flight training phase or flight check, indicating those maneuvers, procedures and functions that are to be performed during the inflight portions of flight training and flight checks.

(4) A list of airplane simulators or other training devices approved under §121.407, including approvals for particular maneuvers, procedures, or functions.

(5) The programmed hours of training that will be applied to each phase of training.

(6) A copy of each statement issued by the Administrator under §121.405(d) for reduction of programmed hours of training.

[Docket No. 9509, 35 FR 90, Jan. 3, 1970; as amended by Amdt. 121–366, 78 FR 67836, Nov. 12, 2013]

§121.404 Compliance dates: Crew and dispatcher resource management training.

After March 19, 1998, no certificate holder may use a person as a flight crewmember, and after March 19, 1999, no certificate holder may use a person as a flight attendant or aircraft dispatcher unless that person has completed approved crew resource management (CRM) or dispatcher resource management (DRM) initial training, as applicable, with that certificate holder or with another certificate holder.

[Docket No. 28154, 61 FR 30435, June 14, 1996]

§121.405 Training program and revision: Initial and final approval.

(a) To obtain initial and final approval of a training program, or a revision to an approved training program, each certificate holder must submit to the Administrator—

(1) An outline of the proposed program or revision, including an outline of the proposed or revised curriculum, that provides enough information for a preliminary evaluation of the proposed training program or revised training program; and

(2) Additional relevant information as may be requested by the Administrator.

(b) If the proposed training program or revision complies with this subpart the Administrator grants initial approval in writing after which the certificate holder may conduct the training in accordance with that program. The Administrator then evaluates the effectiveness of the training program and advises the certificate holder of deficiencies, if any, that must be corrected.

(c) The Administrator grants final approval of the training program or revision if the certificate holder shows that the training conducted under the initial approval set forth in paragraph (b) of this section ensures that each person that successfully completes the training is adequately trained to perform his assigned duties.

(d) In granting initial and final approval of training programs or revisions, including reductions in programmed hours specified in this subpart, the Administrator considers the training aids, devices, methods, and procedures listed in the certificate holder's curriculum as set forth in §121.403 that increase the quality and effectiveness of the teaching-learning process.

If approval of reduced programmed hours of training is granted, the Administrator provides the certificate holder with a statement of the basis for the approval.

(e) Whenever the Administrator finds that revisions are necessary for the continued adequacy of a training program that has been granted final approval, the certificate holder shall, after notification by the Administrator, make any changes in the program that are found necessary by the Administrator. Within 30 days after the certificate holder receives such notice, it may file a petition to reconsider the notice with the certificate-holding district office. The filing of a petition to reconsider stays the notice pending a decision by the Administrator. However, if the Administrator finds

§121.406

that there is an emergency that requires immediate action in the interest of safety in air transportation, he may, upon a statement of the reasons, require a change effective without stay.

(f) Each certificate holder described in §135.3(b) and (c) of this chapter must include the material required by §121.403 in the manual required by §135.21 of this chapter.

(g) The Administrator may grant a deviation to certificate holders described in §135.3(b) and (c) of this chapter to allow reduced programmed hours of ground training required by §121.419 if it is found that a reduction is warranted based on the certificate holder's operations and the complexity of the make, model, and series of the aircraft used.

[Docket No. 9509, 35 FR 90, Jan. 3, 1970; as amended by Amdt. 121–207, 54 FR 39293, Sept. 25, 1989; Amdt. 121–250, 60 FR 65948, Dec. 20, 1995; Amdt. 121–253, 61 FR 2612, Jan. 26, 1996]

§121.406 Credit for previous CRM/DRM training.

(a) For flightcrew members, the Administrator may credit CRM training received before March 19, 1998, toward all or part of the initial ground CRM training required by §121.419.

(b) For flight attendants, the Administrator may credit CRM training received before March 19, 1999, toward all or part of the initial ground CRM training required by §121.421.

(c) For aircraft dispatchers, the Administrator may credit CRM training received before March 19, 1999, toward all or part of the initial ground CRM training required by §121.422.

(d) In granting credit for initial ground CRM or DRM training, the Administrator considers training aids, devices, methods, and procedures used by the certificate holder in a voluntary CRM or DRM program or in an AQP program that effectively meets the quality of an approved CRM or DRM initial ground training program under section 121.419, 121.421, or 121.422 as appropriate.

[Docket No. 27993, 60 FR 65949, Dec. 20, 1995; as amended by Amdt. 121–256, 61 FR 30435, June 14, 1996]

§121.407 Training program: Approval of airplane simulators and other training devices.

(a) Each airplane simulator and other training device used to satisfy a training requirement of this part in an approved training program, must meet all of the following requirements:

(1) Be specifically approved by the Administrator for—

(i) Use in the certificate holder's approved training program;

(ii) The type airplane and, if applicable, the particular variation within type, for which the training or check is being conducted; and

(iii) The particular maneuver, procedure, or flightcrew member function involved.

(2) Maintain the performance, function, and other characteristics that are required for qualification in accordance with part 60 of this chapter or a previously qualified device, as permitted in accordance with §60.17 of this chapter.

(3) Be modified in accordance with part 60 of this chapter to conform with any modification to the airplane being simulated that results in changes to performance, function, or other characteristics required for qualification.

(4) Be given a daily functional preflight check before being used.

(5) Have a daily discrepancy log kept with each discrepancy entered in that log by the appropriate instructor or check airman at the end of each training or check flight.

(b) A particular airplane simulator or other training device may be approved for use by more than one certificate holder.

(c) An airplane simulator may be used instead of the airplane to satisfy the in-flight requirements of §§121.439 and 121.441 and Appendices E and F of this part, if the simulator—

(1) Is approved under this section and meets the appropriate simulator requirements of Appendix H of this part; and

(2) Is used as part of an approved program that meets the training requirements of §121.424(a) and (c) and Appendix H of this part.

(d) An airplane simulator approved under this section must be used instead of the airplane to satisfy the pilot flight training requirements prescribed in the certificate holder's approved low-altitude windshear flight training program set forth in §121.409(d) of this part.

(e) An airplane simulator approved under this section must be used instead of the airplane to satisfy the pilot flight training requirements prescribed in the extended envelope training set forth in §121.423 of this part. Compliance with this paragraph is required no later than March 12, 2019.

[Docket No. 9509, 35 FR 90, Jan. 3, 1970; as amended by Amdt. 121–161, 45 FR 44183, June 30, 1980; Amdt. 121–199, 53 FR 37696, Sept. 27, 1988; Amdt. 121–366, 78 FR 67836, Nov. 12, 2013]

§121.408 Training equipment other than flight simulation training devices.

(a) The Administrator must approve training equipment used in a training program approved under this part and that functionally replicates aircraft equipment for the certificate holder and the crewmember duty or procedure. Training equip-

Part 121: Air Carriers & Commercial Operators §121.409

ment does not include FSTDs qualified under part 60 of this chapter.

(b) The certificate holder must demonstrate that the training equipment described in paragraph (a) of this section, used to meet the training requirements of this subpart, meets all of the following:

(1) The form, fit, function, and weight, as appropriate, of the aircraft equipment.

(2) Replicates the normal operation (and abnormal and emergency operation, if appropriate) of the aircraft equipment including the following:

(i) The required force, actions and travel of the aircraft equipment.

(ii) Variations in aircraft equipment operated by the certificate holder, if applicable.

(3) Replicates the operation of the aircraft equipment under adverse conditions, if appropriate.

(c) Training equipment must be modified to ensure that it maintains the performance and function of the aircraft type or aircraft equipment replicated.

(d) All training equipment must have a record of discrepancies. The documenting system must be readily available for review by each instructor, check airman or supervisor, prior to conducting training or checking with that equipment.

(1) Each instructor, check airman or supervisor conducting training or checking, and each person conducting an inspection of the equipment who discovers a discrepancy, including any missing, malfunctioning or inoperative components, must record a description of that discrepancy and the date that the discrepancy was identified.

(2) All corrections to discrepancies must be recorded when the corrections are made. This record must include the date of the correction.

(3) A record of a discrepancy must be maintained for at least 60 days.

(e) No person may use, allow the use of, or offer the use of training equipment with a missing, malfunctioning, or inoperative component to meet the crewmember training or checking requirements of this chapter for tasks that require the use of the correctly operating component.

(f) Compliance with this section is required no later than March 12, 2019.

[Docket No. FAA–2008–0677, 78 FR 67837, Nov. 12, 2013]

§121.409 Training courses using airplane simulators and other training devices.

(a) Training courses utilizing airplane simulators and other training devices may be included in the certificate holder's approved training program for use as provided in this section.

(b) Except for the airline transport pilot certification training program approved to satisfy the requirements of §61.156 of this chapter, a course of training in an airplane simulator may be included for use as provided in §121.441 if that course—

(1) Provides at least 4 hours of training at the pilot controls of an airplane simulator as well as a proper briefing before and after the training.

(2) Provides training in at least the following:

(i) The procedures and maneuvers set forth in appendix F to this part; or

(ii) Line-oriented flight training (LOFT) that—

(A) Before March 12, 2019,

(1) Utilizes a complete flight crew;

(2) Includes at least the maneuvers and procedures (abnormal and emergency) that may be expected in line operations; and

(3) Is representative of the flight segment appropriate to the operations being conducted by the certificate holder.

(B) Beginning on March 12, 2019—

(1) Utilizes a complete flight crew;

(2) Includes at least the maneuvers and procedures (abnormal and emergency) that may be expected in line operations;

(3) Includes scenario-based or maneuver-based stall prevention training before, during or after the LOFT scenario for each pilot;

(4) Is representative of two flight segments appropriate to the operations being conducted by the certificate holder; and

(5) Provides an opportunity to demonstrate workload management and pilot monitoring skills.

(3) Is given by an instructor who meets the applicable requirements of §121.412.

The satisfactory completion of the course of training must be certified by either the Administrator or a qualified check airman.

(c) The programmed hours of flight training set forth in this subpart do not apply if the training program for the airplane type includes—

(1) A course of pilot training in an airplane simulator as provided in §121.424(d); or

(2) A course of flight engineer training in an airplane simulator or other training device as provided in §121.425(c).

(d) Each certificate holder required to comply with §121.358 of this part must use an approved simulator for each airplane type in each of its pilot training courses that provides training in at least the procedures and maneuvers set forth in the certificate holder's approved low-altitude windshear flight training program. The approved low-altitude windshear flight training, if applicable, must be included in each of the pilot flight training courses prescribed in §§121.409(b), 121.418, 121.424, and 121.427 of this part.

[Docket No. 9509, 35 FR 90, Jan. 3, 1970; as amended by Amdt. 121–130, 41 FR 47229, Oct. 28, 1976; Amdt.

§121.410

121–144, 43 FR 22646, May 25, 1978; Amdt. 121–199, 53 FR 37696, Sept. 27, 1988; Amdt. 121–264, 62 FR 23120, April 28, 1997; Amdt. 121–365, 78 FR 42377, July 15, 2013; Amdt. 121–366, 78 FR 67837, Nov. 12, 2013]

§121.410 Airline transport pilot certification training program.

(a) A certificate holder may obtain approval to establish and implement a training program to satisfy the requirements of §61.156 of this chapter. The training program must be separate from the air carrier training program required by this part.

(b) No certificate holder may use a person nor may any person serve as an instructor in a training program approved to meet the requirements of §61.156 of this chapter unless the instructor:

(1) Holds an airline transport pilot certificate with an airplane category multiengine class rating;

(2) Has at least 2 years of experience as a pilot in command in operations conducted under §91.1053(a)(2)(i) or §135.243(a)(1) of this chapter, or as a pilot in command or second in command in any operation conducted under this part;

(3) Except for the holder of a flight instructor certificate, receives initial training on the following topics:

(i) The fundamental principles of the learning process;

(ii) Elements of effective teaching, instruction methods, and techniques;

(iii) Instructor duties, privileges, responsibilities, and limitations;

(iv) Training policies and procedures; and

(v) Evaluation.

(4) If providing training in a flight simulation training device, hold an aircraft type rating for the aircraft represented by the flight simulation training device utilized in the training program and have received training within the preceding 12 months from the certificate holder on:

(i) Proper operation of flight simulator and flight training device controls and systems;

(ii) Proper operation of environmental and fault panels;

(iii) Data and motion limitations of simulation;

(iv) Minimum equipment requirements for each curriculum; and

(v) The maneuvers that will be demonstrated in the flight simulation training device.

(c) A certificate holder may not issue a graduation certificate to a student unless that student has completed all the curriculum requirements of the course.

(d) A certificate holder must conduct evaluations to ensure that training techniques, procedures, and standards are acceptable to the Administrator.

[Docket No. FAA–2010–0100, 78 FR 42377, July 15, 2013]

§121.411 Qualifications: Check airmen (airplane) and check airmen (simulator).

(a) For the purposes of this section and §121.413:

(1) A check airman (airplane) is a person who is qualified, and permitted, to conduct flight checks or instruction in an airplane, in a flight simulator, or in a flight training device for a particular type airplane.

(2) A check airman (simulator) is a person who is qualified to conduct flight checks or instruction, but only in a flight simulator or in a flight training device for a particular type airplane.

(3) Check airmen (airplane) and check airmen (simulator) are those check airmen who perform the functions described in §121.401(a)(4).

(b) No certificate holder may use a person, nor may any person serve as a check airman (airplane) in a training program established under this subpart unless, with respect to the airplane type involved, that person—

(1) Holds the airman certificates and ratings required to serve as a pilot in command or flight engineer, as applicable, in operations under this part;

(2) Has satisfactorily completed the appropriate training phases for the airplane, including recurrent training, that are required to serve as a pilot in command or flight engineer, as applicable, in operations under this part;

(3) Has satisfactorily completed the appropriate proficiency or flight checks that are required to serve as a pilot in command or flight engineer, as applicable, in operations under this part;

(4) Has satisfactorily completed the applicable training requirements of §121.413 including inflight training and practice for initial and transition training;

(5) Holds at least a Class III medical certificate unless serving as a required crewmember, in which case holds a Class I or Class II medical certificate as appropriate;

(6) Has satisfied the recency of experience requirements of §121.439 of this part, as applicable; and

(7) Has been approved by the Administrator for the check airman duties involved.

(c) No certificate holder may use a person nor may any person serve as a check airman (simulator) in a training program established under this subpart unless, with respect to the airplane type involved, that person meets the provisions of paragraph (b) of this section, or—

(1) Holds the airman certificates and ratings, except medical certificate, required to serve as a pilot in command or a flight engineer, as applicable, in operations under this part;
(2) Has satisfactorily completed the appropriate training phases for the airplane, including recurrent training, that are required to serve as a pilot in command or flight engineer, as applicable, in operations under this part;
(3) Has satisfactorily completed the appropriate proficiency or flight checks that are required to serve as a pilot in command or flight engineer, as applicable, in operations under this part;
(4) Has satisfactorily completed the applicable training requirements of §121.413; and
(5) Has been approved by the Administrator for the check airman (simulator) duties involved.

(d) Completion of the requirements in paragraphs (b)(2), (3), and (4) or (c)(2), (3), and (4) of this section, as applicable, shall be entered in the individual's training record maintained by the certificate holder.

(e) Check airmen who have reached their 65th birthday or who do not hold an appropriate medical certificate may function as check airmen, but may not serve as pilot flightcrew members in operations under this part.

(f) A check airman (simulator) must accomplish the following—
(1) Fly at least two flight segments as a required crewmember for the type airplane involved within the 12-month period preceding the performance of any check airman duty in a flight simulator; or
(2) Satisfactorily complete an approved line-observation program within the period prescribed by that program and that must precede the performance of any check airman duty in a flight simulator.

(g) The flight segments or line-observation program required in paragraph (f) of this section are considered to be completed in the month required if completed in the calendar month before or in the calendar month after the month in which it is due.

[Docket No. 28471, 61 FR 30741, June 17, 1996; as amended by Amdt. 121–344, 74 FR 34235, July 15, 2009; Amdt. 121–366, 78 FR 67837, Nov. 12, 2013]

§121.412 Qualifications: Flight instructors (airplane) and flight instructors (simulator).

(a) For the purposes of this section and §121.414:
(1) A flight instructor (airplane) is a person who is qualified to instruct in an airplane, in a flight simulator, or in a flight training device for a particular type airplane.
(2) A flight instructor (simulator) is a person who is qualified to instruct, but only in a flight simulator, in a flight training device, or both, for a particular type airplane.
(3) Flight instructors (airplane) and flight instructors (simulator) are those instructors who perform the functions described in §121.401(a)(4).

(b) No certificate holder may use a person nor may any person serve as a flight instructor (airplane) in a training program established under this subpart unless, with respect to the airplane type involved, that person—
(1) Holds the airman certificates and rating required to serve as a pilot in command or flight engineer, as applicable, in operations under this part;
(2) Has satisfactorily completed the appropriate training phases for the airplane, including recurrent training, that are required to serve as a pilot in command or flight engineer, as applicable, in operations under this part;
(3) Has satisfactorily completed the appropriate proficiency or flight checks that are required to serve as a pilot in command or flight engineer, as applicable, in operations under this part;
(4) Has satisfactorily completed the applicable training requirements of §121.414, including inflight training and practice for initial and transition training;
(5) Holds at least a Class III medical certificate unless serving as a required crewmember, in which case holds a Class I or a Class II medical certificate as appropriate; and
(6) Has satisfied the recency of experience requirements of §121.439 of this part, as applicable.

(c) No certificate holder may use a person, nor may any person serve as a flight instructor (simulator) in a training program established under this subpart, unless, with respect to the airplane type involved, that person meets the provisions of paragraph (b) of this section, or—
(1) Holds the airman certificates and ratings, except medical certificate, required to serve as a pilot in command or flight engineer, as applicable, in operations under this part;
(2) Has satisfactorily completed the appropriate training phases for the airplane, including recurrent training, that are required to serve as a pilot in command or flight engineer, as applicable, in operations under this part;
(3) Has satisfactorily completed the appropriate proficiency or flight checks that are required to serve as a pilot in command or flight engineer, as applicable, in operations under this part; and
(4) Has satisfactorily completed the applicable training requirements of §121.414.

(d) Completion of the requirements in paragraphs (b)(2), (3), and (4) or (c)(2), (3), and (4) of this section as applicable shall be entered in

§121.413

the individual's training record maintained by the certificate holder.

(e) Flight instructors who have reached their 65th birthday or who do not hold an appropriate medical certificate may function as flight instructors, but may not serve as pilot flightcrew members in operations under this part.

(f) A flight instructor (simulator) must accomplish the following—

(1) Fly at least two flight segments as a required crewmember for the type of airplane within the 12-month period preceding the performance of any flight instructor duty in a flight simulator (and must hold a Class I or Class II medical certificate as appropriate); or

(2) Satisfactorily complete an approved line-observation program within the period prescribed by that program preceding the performance of any flight instructor duty in a flight simulator.

(g) The flight segments or line-observation program required in paragraph (f) of this section is considered completed in the month required if completed in the calendar month before, or the calendar month after the month in which it is due.

[Docket No. 28471, 61 FR 30742, June 17, 1996; as amended by Amdt. 121–257, 62 FR 3739, Jan. 24, 1997; Amdt. 121–264, 62 FR 23120, April 28, 1997; Amdt. 121–344, 74 FR 34235, July 15, 2009; Amdt. 121–355, 76 FR 35104, June 16, 2011; Amdt. 121–366, 78 FR 67837, Nov. 12, 2013]

§121.413 Initial, transition and recurrent training and checking requirements: Check airmen (airplane), check airmen (simulator).

(a) No certificate holder may use a person nor may any person serve as a check airman unless—

(1) That person has satisfactorily completed initial or transition check airman training; and

(2) Within the preceding 24 calendar months that person satisfactorily conducts a check or supervises operating experience under the observation of an FAA inspector or an aircrew designated examiner employed by the operator. The observation check may be accomplished in part or in full in an airplane, in a flight simulator, or in a flight training device.

(b) The observation check required by paragraph (a)(2) of this section is considered to have been completed in the month required if completed in the calendar month before, or the calendar month after, the month in which it is due.

(c) The initial ground training for check airmen must include the following:

(1) Check airman duties, functions, and responsibilities.

(2) The applicable Code of Federal Regulations and the certificate holder's policies and procedures.

(3) The appropriate methods, procedures, and techniques for conducting the required checks.

(4) Proper evaluation of student performance including the detection of—

(i) Improper and insufficient training; and

(ii) Personal characteristics of an applicant that could adversely affect safety.

(5) The appropriate corrective action in the case of unsatisfactory checks.

(6) The approved methods, procedures, and limitations for performing the required normal, abnormal, and emergency procedures in the airplane.

(7) For check airmen who conduct training or checking in a flight simulator or a flight training device, the following subjects specific to the device(s) for the airplane type:

(i) Proper operation of the controls and systems;

(ii) Proper operation of environmental and fault panels;

(iii) Data and motion limitations of simulation; and

(iv) The minimum airplane simulator equipment required by this part or part 60 of this chapter, for each maneuver and procedure completed in a flight simulator or a flight training device.

(d) The transition ground training for check airmen must include the following:

(1) The approved methods, procedures, and limitations for performing the required normal, abnormal, and emergency procedures applicable to the airplane to which the check airman is transitioning.

(2) For check airmen who conduct training or checking in a flight simulator or a flight training device, the following subjects specific to the device(s) for the airplane type to which the check airman is transitioning:

(i) Proper operation of the controls and systems;

(ii) Proper operation of environmental and fault panels;

(iii) Data and motion limitations of simulation; and

(iv) The minimum airplane simulator equipment required by this part or part 60 of this chapter, for each maneuver and procedure completed in a flight simulator or a flight training device.

(e) The initial and transition flight training for check airmen (airplane) must include the following:

(1) The safety measures for emergency situations that are likely to develop during a check.

(2) The potential results of improper, untimely, or non-execution of safety measures during a check.

(3) For pilot check airman (airplane)—

(i) Training and practice in conducting flight checks from the left and right pilot seats in the required normal, abnormal, and emergency procedures to ensure competence to conduct the pilot flight checks required by this part; and

(ii) The safety measures to be taken from either pilot seat for emergency situations that are likely to develop during a check.

(4) For flight engineer check airmen (airplane), training to ensure competence to perform assigned duties.

(f) The requirements of paragraph (e) of this section may be accomplished in full or in part in flight, in a flight simulator, or in a flight training device, as appropriate.

(g) The initial and transition flight training for check airmen who conduct training or checking in a flight simulator or a flight training device must include the following:

(1) Training and practice in conducting flight checks in the required normal, abnormal, and emergency procedures to ensure competence to conduct the flight checks required by this part. This training and practice must be accomplished in a flight simulator or in a flight training device.

(2) Training in the operation of flight simulators or flight training devices, or both, to ensure competence to conduct the flight checks required by this part.

(h) Recurrent ground training for check airmen who conduct training or checking in a flight simulator or a flight training device must be completed every 12 calendar months and must include the subjects required in paragraph (c)(7) of this section.

(i) Compliance with paragraphs (c)(7), (d)(2), and (h) of this section is required no later than March 12, 2019.

[Docket No. 28471, 61 FR 30783, June 17, 1996; as amended by Amdt. 121–257, 62 FR 3739, Jan. 24, 1997; Amdt. 121–264, 62 FR 23120, April 28, 1997; Amdt. 121–366, 78 FR 67838, Nov. 12, 2013]

§121.414 Initial, transition and recurrent training and checking requirements: flight instructors (airplane), flight instructors (simulator).

(a) No certificate holder may use a person nor may any person serve as a flight instructor unless—

(1) That person has satisfactorily completed initial or transition flight instructor training; and

(2) Within the preceding 24 calendar months, that person satisfactorily conducts instruction under the observation of an FAA inspector, an operator check airman, or an aircrew designated examiner employed by the operator. The observation check may be accomplished in part or in full in an airplane, in a flight simulator, or in a flight training device.

(b) The observation check required by paragraph (a)(2) of this section is considered to have been completed in the month required if completed in the calendar month before, or the calendar month after, the month in which it is due.

(c) The initial ground training for flight instructors must include the following:

(1) Flight instructor duties, functions, and responsibilities.

(2) The applicable Code of Federal Regulations and the certificate holder's policies and procedures.

(3) The appropriate methods, procedures, and techniques for conducting flight instruction.

(4) Proper evaluation of student performance including the detection of—

(i) Improper and insufficient training; and

(ii) Personal characteristics of an applicant that could adversely affect safety.

(5) The corrective action in the case of unsatisfactory training progress.

(6) The approved methods, procedures, and limitations for performing the required normal, abnormal, and emergency procedures in the airplane.

(7) Except for holders of a flight instructor certificate—

(i) The fundamental principles of the teaching-learning process;

(ii) Teaching methods and procedures; and

(iii) The instructor-student relationship.

(8) For flight instructors who conduct training in a flight simulator or a flight training device, the following subjects specific to the device(s) for the airplane type:

(i) Proper operation of the controls and systems;

(ii) Proper operation of environmental and fault panels;

(iii) Data and motion limitations of simulation; and

(iv) The minimum airplane simulator equipment required by this part or part 60 of this chapter, for each maneuver and procedure completed in a flight simulator or a flight training device.

(d) The transition ground training for flight instructors must include the following:

(1) The approved methods, procedures, and limitations for performing the required normal, abnormal, and emergency procedures applicable to the airplane to which the flight instructor is transitioning.

(2) For flight instructors who conduct training in a flight simulator or a flight training device, the following subjects specific to the device(s) for the airplane type to which the flight instructor is transitioning:

(i) Proper operation of the controls and systems;

(ii) Proper operation of environmental and fault panels;

§121.414

(iii) Data and motion limitations of simulation; and

(iv) The minimum airplane simulator equipment required by this part or part 60 of this chapter, for each maneuver and procedure completed in a flight simulator or a flight training device.

(e) The initial and transition flight training for flight instructors (airplane) must include the following:

(1) The safety measures for emergency situations that are likely to develop during instruction.

(2) The potential results of improper, untimely, or non-execution of safety measures during instruction.

(3) For pilot flight instructor (airplane)—

(i) In-flight training and practice in conducting flight instruction from the left and right pilot seats in the required normal, abnormal, and emergency procedures to ensure competence as an instructor; and

(ii) The safety measures to be taken from either pilot seat for emergency situations that are likely to develop during instruction.

(4) For flight engineer instructors (airplane), in-flight training to ensure competence to perform assigned duties.

(f) The requirements of paragraph (e) of this section may be accomplished in full or in part in flight, in a flight simulator, or in a flight training device, as appropriate.

(g) The initial and transition flight training for flight instructors who conduct training in a flight simulator or a flight training device must include the following:

(1) Training and practice in the required normal, abnormal, and emergency procedures to ensure competence to conduct the flight instruction required by this part. This training and practice must be accomplished in full or in part in a flight simulator or in a flight training device.

(2) Training in the operation of flight simulators or flight training devices, or both, to ensure competence to conduct the flight instruction required by this part.

(h) Recurrent flight instructor ground training for flight instructors who conduct training in a flight simulator or a flight training device must be completed every 12 calendar months and must include the subjects required in paragraph (c)(8) of this section.

(i) Compliance with paragraphs (c)(8), (d)(2), and (h) of this section is required no later than March 12, 2019.

[Docket No. 28471, 61 FR 30743, June 17, 1996; as amended by Amdt. 121–257, 62 FR 3739, Jan. 24, 1997; Amdt. 121–366, 78 FR 67838, Nov. 12, 2013]

§121.415 Crewmember and dispatcher training program requirements.

(a) Each training program must provide the following ground training as appropriate to the particular assignment of the crewmember or dispatcher:

(1) Basic indoctrination ground training for newly hired crewmembers or dispatchers including 40 programmed hours of instruction, unless reduced under §121.405 or as specified in §121.401(d), in at least the following—

(i) Duties and responsibilities of crewmembers or dispatchers, as applicable;

(ii) Appropriate provisions of the Federal Aviation Regulations;

(iii) Contents of the certificate holder's operating certificate and operations specifications (not required for flight attendants); and

(iv) Appropriate portions of the certificate holder's operating manual.

(2) The initial and transition ground training specified in §§121.419, 121.421 and 121.422, as applicable.

(3) For crewmembers, emergency training as specified in §§121.417 and 121.805.

(4) After February 15, 2008, training for crewmembers and dispatchers in their roles and responsibilities in the certificate holder's passenger recovery plan, if applicable.

(b) Each training program must provide the flight training specified in §§121.424 through 121.425, as applicable.

(c) Each training program must provide recurrent ground and flight training as provided in §121.427.

(d) Each training program must provide the differences training specified in §121.418(a) if the Administrator finds that, due to differences between airplanes of the same type operated by the certificate holder, additional training is necessary to insure that each crewmember and dispatcher is adequately trained to perform their assigned duties.

(e) Upgrade training as specified in §§121.419 and 121.424 for a particular type airplane may be included in the training program for crewmembers who have qualified and served as second in command pilot or flight engineer on that airplane.

(f) Particular subjects, maneuvers, procedures, or parts thereof specified in §§121.419, 121.421, 121.422, 121.424, and 121.425 for transition or upgrade training, as applicable, may be omitted, or the programmed hours of ground instruction or inflight training may be reduced, as provided in §121.405.

(g) In addition to initial, transition, upgrade, recurrent and differences training, each training program must also provide ground and flight training, instruction, and practice as necessary to insure that each crewmember and dispatcher—

(1) Remains adequately trained and currently proficient with respect to each airplane, crewmember position, and type of operation in which he serves; and

(2) Qualifies in new equipment, facilities, procedures, and techniques, including modifications to airplanes.

(h) Each training program must include a process to provide for the regular analysis of individual pilot performance to identify pilots with performance deficiencies during training and checking and multiple failures during checking.

(i) Each training program must include methods for remedial training and tracking of pilots identified in the analysis performed in accordance with paragraph (h) of this section.

(j) Compliance with paragraphs (h) and (i) of this section is required no later than March 12, 2019.

[Docket No. 9509, 35 FR 90, Jan. 3, 1970; as amended by Amdt. 121–130, 41 FR 47229, Oct. 28, 1976; Amdt. 121–281, 66 FR 19043, April 12, 2001; Amdt. 121–329, 72 FR 1881, Jan. 16, 2007; Amdt. 121–366, 78 FR 67839, Nov. 12, 2013]

§121.417 Crewmember emergency training.

(a) Each training program must provide the emergency training set forth in this section with respect to each airplane type, model, and configuration, each required crewmember, and each kind of operation conducted, insofar as appropriate for each crewmember and the certificate holder.

(b) Emergency training must provide the following:

(1) Instruction in emergency assignments and procedures, including coordination among crewmembers.

(2) Individual instruction in the location, function, and operation of emergency equipment including—

(i) Equipment used in ditching and evacuation;
(ii) [Reserved]
(iii) Portable fire extinguishers, with emphasis on type of extinguisher to be used on different classes of fires; and
(iv) Emergency exits in the emergency mode with the evacuation slide/raft pack attached (if applicable), with training emphasis on the operation of the exits under adverse conditions.

(3) Instruction in the handling of emergency situations including—

(i) Rapid decompression;
(ii) Fire in flight or on the surface, and smoke control procedures with emphasis on electrical equipment and related circuit breakers found in cabin areas including all galleys, service centers, lifts, lavatories and movie screens;

(iii) Ditching and other evacuation, including the evacuation of persons and their attendants, if any, who may need the assistance of another person to move expeditiously to an exit in the event of an emergency.
(iv) [Reserved]
(v) Hijacking and other unusual situations.

(4) Review and discussion of previous aircraft accidents and incidents pertaining to actual emergency situations.

(c) Each crewmember must accomplish the following emergency training during the specified training periods, using those items of installed emergency equipment for each type of airplane in which he or she is to serve (Alternate recurrent training required by §121.433(c) of this part may be accomplished by approved pictorial presentation or demonstration):

(1) One-time emergency drill requirements to be accomplished during initial training. Each crewmember must perform—

(i) At least one approved protective breathing equipment (PBE) drill in which the crewmember combats an actual or simulated fire using at least one type of installed hand fire extinguisher or approved fire extinguisher that is appropriate for the type of actual fire or simulated fire to be fought while using the type of installed PBE required by §121.337 or approved PBE simulation device as defined by paragraph (d) of this section for combatting fires aboard airplanes;

(ii) At least one approved firefighting drill in which the crewmember combats an actual fire using at least one type of installed hand fire extinguisher or approved fire extinguisher that is appropriate for the type of fire to be fought. This firefighting drill is not required if the crewmember performs the PBE drill of paragraph (c)(1)(i) by combating an actual fire; and

(iii) An emergency evacuation drill with each person egressing the airplane or approved training device using at least one type of installed emergency evacuation slide. The crewmember may either observe the airplane exits being opened in the emergency mode and the associated exit slide/raft pack being deployed and inflated, or perform the tasks resulting in the accomplishment of these actions.

(2) Additional emergency drill requirements to be accomplished during initial training and once each 24 calendar months during recurrent training. Each crewmember must—

(i) Perform the following emergency drills and operate the following equipment:

(A) Each type of emergency exit in the normal and emergency modes, including the actions and forces required in the deployment of the emergency evacuation slides;

(B) Each type of installed hand fire extinguisher;

§121.417

(C) Each type of emergency oxygen system to include protective breathing equipment;
(D) Donning, use, and inflation of individual flotation means, if applicable; and
(E) Ditching, if applicable, including but not limited to, as appropriate:
(1) Cockpit preparation and procedures;
(2) Crew coordination;
(3) Passenger briefing and cabin preparation;
(4) Donning and inflation of life preservers;
(5) Use of life-lines; and
(6) Boarding of passengers and crew into raft or a slide/raft pack.
(ii) Observe the following drills:
(A) Removal from the airplane (or training device) and inflation of each type of life raft, if applicable;
(B) Transfer of each type of slide/raft pack from one door to another;
(C) Deployment, inflation, and detachment from the airplane (or training device) of each type of slide/raft pack; and
(D) Emergency evacuation including the use of a slide.

(d) After September 1, 1993, no crewmember may serve in operations under this part unless that crewmember has performed the PBE drill and the firefighting drill described by paragraphs (c)(1)(i) and (c)(1)(ii) of this section, as part of a one-time training requirement of paragraphs (c)(1) or (c)(2) of this section as appropriate. Any crewmember who performs the PBE drill and the firefighting drill prescribed in paragraphs (c)(1)(i) and (c)(1)(ii) of this section after May 26, 1987, is deemed to be in compliance with this regulation upon presentation of information or documentation, in a form and manner acceptable to the Director, Flight Standards Service, showing that the appropriate drills have been accomplished.

(e) Crewmembers who serve in operations above 25,000 feet must receive instruction in the following:
(1) Respiration.
(2) Hypoxia.
(3) Duration of consciousness without supplemental oxygen at altitude.
(4) Gas expansion.
(5) Gas bubble formation.
(6) Physical phenomena and incidents of decompression.

(f) For the purposes of this section the following definitions apply:
(1) *Actual fire* means an ignited combustible material, in controlled conditions, of sufficient magnitude and duration to accomplish the training objectives outlined in paragraphs (c)(1)(i) and (c)(1)(ii) of this section.
(2) *Approved fire extinguisher* means a training device that has been approved by the Administrator for use in meeting the training requirements of Part 121.417(c).
(3) *Approved PBE simulation device* means a training device that has been approved by the Administrator for use in meeting the training requirements of Part 121.417(c).
(4) *Combats,* in this context, means to properly fight an actual or simulated fire using an appropriate type of fire extinguisher until that fire is extinguished.
(5) *Observe* means to watch without participating actively in the drill.
(6) *PBE drill* means an emergency drill in which a crewmember demonstrates the proper use of protective breathing equipment while fighting an actual or simulated fire.
(7) *Perform* means to satisfactorily accomplish a prescribed emergency drill using established procedures that stress the skill of the persons involved in the drill.
(8) *Simulated fire* means an artificial duplication of smoke or flame used to create various aircraft firefighting scenarios, such as lavatory, galley oven, and aircraft seat fires.

[Docket No. 9509, 35 FR 90, Jan. 3, 1970; as amended by Amdt. 121–281, 66 FR 19043, April 12, 2001]

§121.418 Differences training and related aircraft differences training.

(a) *Differences training.*
(1) Differences training for crewmembers and dispatchers must consist of at least the following as applicable to their assigned duties and responsibilities:
(i) Instruction in each appropriate subject or part thereof required for initial ground training in the airplane unless the Administrator finds that particular subjects are not necessary.
(ii) Flight training in each appropriate maneuver or procedure required for initial flight training in the airplane unless the Administrator finds that particular maneuvers or procedures are not necessary.
(iii) The number of programmed hours of ground and flight training determined by the Administrator to be necessary for the airplane, the operation, and the crewmember or aircraft dispatcher involved.
(2) Differences training for all variations of a particular type airplane may be included in initial, transition, upgrade, and recurrent training for the airplane.

(b) *Related aircraft differences training.*
(1) In order to seek approval of related aircraft differences training for flightcrew members, a certificate holder must submit a request for related aircraft designation to the Administrator, and obtain approval of that request.

(2) If the Administrator determines under paragraph (b)(1) of this section that a certificate holder is operating related aircraft, the certificate holder may submit to the Administrator a request for approval of a training program that includes related aircraft differences training.

(3) A request for approval of a training program that includes related aircraft differences training must include at least the following:

(i) Each appropriate subject required for the ground training for the related aircraft.

(ii) Each appropriate maneuver or procedure required for the flight training and crewmember emergency training for the related aircraft.

(iii) The number of programmed hours of ground training, flight training and crewmember emergency training necessary based on review of the related aircraft and the duty position.

(c) *Approved related aircraft differences training.* Approved related aircraft differences training for flightcrew members may be included in initial, transition, upgrade and recurrent training for the base aircraft. If the certificate holder's approved training program includes related aircraft differences training in accordance with paragraph (b) of this section, the training required by §§121.419, 121.424, 121.425, and 121.427, as applicable to flightcrew members, may be modified for the related aircraft.

[Docket No. 9509, 35 FR 90, Jan. 3, 1970; as amended by Amdt. 121–366, 78 67839, Nov. 12, 2013]

§121.419 Pilots and flight engineers: Initial, transition, and upgrade ground training.

(a) Except as provided in paragraph (b) of this section, initial, transition, and upgrade ground training for pilots and flight engineers must include instruction in at least the following as applicable to their assigned duties:

(1) General subjects—

(i) The certificate holder's dispatch or flight release procedures;

(ii) Principles and methods for determining weight and balance, and runway limitations for takeoff and landing;

(iii) Enough meteorology to insure a practical knowledge of weather phenomena, including the principles of frontal systems, icing, fog, thunderstorms, and high altitude weather situations;

(iv) Air traffic control systems, procedures, and phraseology;

(v) Navigation and the use of navigation aids, including instrument approach procedures;

(vi) Normal and emergency communication procedures;

(vii) Visual cues prior to and during descent below DA/DH or MDA;

(viii) Approved crew resource management initial training; and

(ix) Other instructions as necessary to ensure pilot and flight engineer competence.

(2) For each airplane type—

(i) A general description;

(ii) Performance characteristics;

(iii) Engines and propellers;

(iv) Major components;

(v) Major airplane systems (e.g., flight controls, electrical, hydraulic); other systems as appropriate; principles of normal, abnormal, and emergency operations; appropriate procedures and limitations;

(vi) Procedures for—

(A) Recognizing and avoiding severe weather situations;

(B) Escaping from severe weather situations, in case of inadvertent encounters, including low-altitude windshear, and

(C) Operating in or near thunderstorms (including best penetrating altitudes), turbulent air (including clear air turbulence), icing, hail, and other potentially hazardous meteorological conditions;

(vii) Operating limitations;

(viii) Fuel consumption and cruise control;

(ix) Flight planning;

(x) Each normal and emergency procedure;

(xi) For pilots, stall prevention and recovery in clean configuration, takeoff and maneuvering configuration, and landing configuration.

(xii) For pilots, upset prevention and recovery; and

(xiii) The approved Airplane Flight Manual.

(b) Initial ground training for pilots who have completed the airline transport pilot certification training program in §61.156 must include instruction in at least the following as applicable to their assigned duties:

(1) Ground training specific to the certificate holder's—

(i) Dispatch or flight release procedures;

(ii) Method for determining weight and balance and runway limitations for takeoff and landing;

(iii) Meteorology hazards applicable to the certificate holder's areas of operation;

(iv) Approved departure, arrival, and approach procedures;

(v) Normal and emergency communication procedures; and

(vi) Approved crew resource management training.

(2) The training required by paragraph (a)(2) of this section for the airplane type.

(c) Initial ground training for pilots and flight engineers must consist of at least the following programmed hours of instruction in the required subjects specified in paragraph (a) of this section and in §121.415(a) unless reduced under §121.405:

(1) Group I airplanes—

§121.421

(i) Reciprocating powered, 64 hours; and
(ii) Turbopropeller powered, 80 hours.
(2) Group II airplanes, 120 hours.

(d) Initial ground training for pilots who have completed the airline transport pilot certification training program in §61.156 must consist of at least the following programmed hours of instruction in the required subjects specified in paragraph (b) of this section and in §121.415(a) unless reduced under §121.405:
(1) Group I airplanes—
(i) Reciprocating powered, 54 hours; and
(ii) Turbopropeller powered, 70 hours.
(2) Group II airplanes, 110 hours.

(e) *Compliance and pilot programmed hours.*
(1) Compliance with the requirements identified in paragraphs (a)(2)(xi) and (a)(2)(xii) of this section is required no later than March 12, 2019.
(2) Beginning March 12, 2019, initial programmed hours applicable to pilots as specified in paragraphs (c) and (d) of this section must include 2 additional hours.

[Docket No. 9509, 35 FR 90, Jan. 3, 1970; as amended by Amdt. 121–199, 53 FR 37696, Sept. 27, 1988; Amdt. 121–250, 60 FR 65949, Dec. 20, 1995; Amdt. 121–250, 61 FR, Jan. 29, 1996; Amdt. 121–333, 72 FR 31682, June 7, 2007; Amdt. 121–365, 78 FR 42377, July 15, 2013; Amdt. 121–366, 78 FR 67839, Nov. 12, 2013]

§121.420 [Removed and reserved]

[Amdt. 121–366, 78 FR 67839, Nov. 12, 2013]

§121.421 Flight attendants:
Initial and transition ground training.

(a) Initial and transition ground training for flight attendants must include instruction in at least the following:
(1) General subjects—
(i) The authority of the pilot in command;
(ii) Passenger handling, including the procedures to be followed in the case of deranged persons or other persons whose conduct might jeopardize safety; and
(iii) Approved crew resource management initial training.
(2) For each airplane type—
(i) A general description of the airplane emphasizing physical characteristics that may have a bearing on ditching, evacuation, and inflight emergency procedures and on other related duties;
(ii) The use of both the public address system and the means of communicating with other flight crewmembers, including emergency means in the case of attempted hijacking or other unusual situations; and
(iii) Proper use of electrical galley equipment and the controls for cabin heat and ventilation.

(b) Initial and transition ground training for flight attendants must include a competence check to determine ability to perform assigned duties and responsibilities.

(c) Initial ground training for flight attendants must consist of at least the following programmed hours of instruction in the subjects specified in paragraph (a) of this section and in §121.415(a) unless reduced under §121.405.
(1) Group I airplanes—
(i) Reciprocating powered, 8 hours; and
(ii) Turbopropeller powered, 8 hours.
(2) Group II airplanes, 16 hours.

[Docket No. 9509, 35 FR 90, Jan. 3, 1970; as amended by Amdt. 121–250, 60 FR 65949, Dec. 20, 1995]

§121.422 Aircraft dispatchers:
Initial and transition ground training.

(a) Initial and transition ground training for aircraft dispatchers must include instruction in at least the following:
(1) General subjects—
(i) Use of communications systems including the characteristics of those systems and the appropriate normal and emergency procedures;
(ii) Meteorology, including various types of meteorological information and forecasts, interpretation of weather data (including forecasting of en route and terminal temperatures and other weather conditions), frontal systems, wind conditions, and use of actual and prognostic weather charts for various altitudes;
(iii) The NOTAM system;
(iv) Navigational aids and publications;
(v) Joint dispatcher-pilot responsibilities;
(vi) Characteristics of appropriate airports;
(vii) Prevailing weather phenomena and the available sources of weather information;
(viii) Air traffic control and instrument approach procedures; and
(ix) Approved dispatcher resource management (DRM) initial training.
(2) For each airplane—
(i) A general description of the airplane emphasizing operating and performance characteristics, navigation equipment, instrument approach and communication equipment, emergency equipment and procedures, and other subjects having a bearing on dispatcher duties and responsibilities;
(ii) Flight operation procedures including procedures specified in §121.419(a)(2)(vi);
(iii) Weight and balance computations;
(iv) Basic airplane performance dispatch requirements and procedures;
(v) Flight planning including track selection, flight time analysis, and fuel requirements; and
(vi) Emergency procedures.

(3) Emergency procedures must be emphasized, including the alerting of proper governmental, company, and private agencies during emergencies to give maximum help to an airplane in distress.

(b) Initial and transition ground training for aircraft dispatchers must include a competence check given by an appropriate supervisor or ground instructor that demonstrates knowledge and ability with the subjects set forth in paragraph (a) of this section.

(c) Initial ground training for aircraft dispatchers must consist of at least the following programmed hours of instruction in the subjects specified in paragraph (a) of this section and in §121.415(a) unless reduced under §121.405:
 (1) Group I airplanes—
 (i) Reciprocating powered, 30 hours; and
 (ii) Turbopropeller powered, 40 hours.
 (2) Group II airplanes, 40 hours.

[Docket No. 9509, 35 FR 90, Jan. 3, 1970; as amended by Amdt. 121–250, 60 FR 65949, Dec. 20, 1995]

§121.423 Pilot: Extended envelope training.

(a) Each certificate holder must include in its approved training program, the extended envelope training set forth in this section with respect to each airplane type for each pilot. The extended envelope training required by this section must be performed in a Level C or higher full flight simulator, approved by the Administrator in accordance with §121.407 of this part.

(b) Extended envelope training must include the following maneuvers and procedures:
 (1) Manually controlled slow flight;
 (2) Manually controlled loss of reliable airspeed;
 (3) Manually controlled instrument departure and arrival;
 (4) Upset recovery maneuvers; and
 (5) Recovery from bounced landing.

(c) Extended envelope training must include instructor-guided hands on experience of recovery from full stall and stick pusher activation, if equipped.

(d) Recurrent training: Within 24 calendar months preceding service as a pilot, each person must satisfactorily complete the extended envelope training described in paragraphs (b)(1) through (4) and (c) of this section. Within 36 calendar months preceding service as a pilot, each person must satisfactorily complete the extended envelope training described in paragraph (b)(5) of this section.

(e) Deviation from use of Level C or higher full flight simulator:

(1) A certificate holder may submit a request to the Administrator for approval of a deviation from the requirements of paragraph (a) of this section to conduct the extended envelope training using an alternative method to meet the learning objectives of this section.

(2) A request for deviation from paragraph (a) of this section must include the following information:
 (i) A simulator availability assessment, including hours by specific simulator and location of the simulator, and a simulator shortfall analysis that includes the training that cannot be completed in a Level C or higher full flight simulator; and
 (ii) Alternative methods for achieving the learning objectives of this section.

(3) A certificate holder may request an extension of a deviation issued under this section.

(4) Deviations or extensions to deviations will be issued for a period not to exceed 12 months.

(f) Compliance with this section is required no later than March 12, 2019. For the recurrent training required in paragraph (d) of this section, each pilot qualified to serve as second in command or pilot in command in operations under this part on March 12, 2019 must complete the recurrent extended envelope training within 12 calendar months after March 12, 2019.

[Docket No. FAA–2008–0677, 78 FR 67839, Nov. 12, 2013]

§121.424 Pilots: Initial, transition, and upgrade flight training.

(a) Initial, transition, and upgrade training for pilots must include the following:
 (1) Flight training and practice in the maneuvers and procedures set forth in the certificate holder's approved low-altitude windshear flight training program and in appendix E to this part, as applicable; and
 (2) Extended envelope training set forth in §121.423.

(b) The training required by paragraph (a) of this section must be performed inflight except—
 (1) That windshear maneuvers and procedures must be performed in a simulator in which the maneuvers and procedures are specifically authorized to be accomplished;
 (2) That the extended envelope training required by §121.423 must be performed in a Level C or higher full flight simulator unless the Administrator has issued to the certificate holder a deviation in accordance with §121.423(e); and
 (3) To the extent that certain other maneuvers and procedures may be performed in an airplane simulator, an appropriate training device, or a static airplane as permitted in Appendix E to this part.

(c) Except as permitted in paragraph (d) of this section, the initial flight training required by paragraph (a)(1) of this section must include at least the following programmed hours of inflight training and practice unless reduced under §121.405;

(1) *Group I airplanes—*

(i) *Reciprocating powered.* Pilot in command, 10 hours; second in command, 6 hours; and

(ii) *Turbopropeller powered.* Pilot in command, 15 hours; second in command, 7 hours.

(2) *Group II airplanes.* Pilot in command, 20 hours; second in command, 10 hours.

(d) If the certificate holder's approved training program includes a course of training utilizing an airplane simulator under §121.409(c) and (d) of this part, each pilot must successfully complete—

(1) With respect to §121.409(c) of this part—

(i) Training and practice in the simulator in at least all of the maneuvers and procedures set forth in Appendix E to this part for initial flight training that are capable of being performed in an airplane simulator without a visual system; and

(ii) A flight check in the simulator or the airplane to the level of proficiency of a pilot in command or second in command, as applicable, in at least the maneuvers and procedures set forth in Appendix F to this part that are capable of being performed in an airplane simulator without a visual system.

(2) With respect to §121.409(d) of this part, training and practice in at least the maneuvers and procedures set forth in the certificate holder's approved low-altitude windshear flight training program that are capable of being performed in an airplane simulator in which the maneuvers and procedures are specifically authorized.

(e) Compliance with paragraphs (a)(2) and (b)(2) of this section is required no later than March 12, 2019.

[Docket No. 9509, 35 FR 90, Jan. 3, 1970; as amended by Amdt. 121–199, 53 FR 37697, Sept. 27, 1988; Amdt. 121–366, 78 FR 67840, Nov. 12, 2013]

§121.425 Flight engineers: Initial and transition flight training.

(a) Initial and transition flight training for flight engineers must include at least the following:

(1) Training and practice in procedures related to the carrying out of flight engineer duties and functions. This training and practice may be accomplished either inflight, in an airplane simulator, or in a training device.

(2) A flight check that includes—

(i) Preflight inspection;

(ii) Inflight performance of assigned duties accomplished from the flight engineer station during taxi, runup, takeoff, climb, cruise, descent, approach, and landing;

(iii) Accomplishment of other functions, such as fuel management and preparation of fuel consumption records, and normal and emergency or alternate operation of all airplane flight systems, performed either inflight, in an airplane simulator, or in a training device.

Flight engineers possessing a commercial pilot certificate with an instrument, category and class rating, or pilots already qualified as second in command and reverting to flight engineer, may complete the entire flight check in an approved airplane simulator.

(b) Except as permitted in paragraph (c) of this section, the initial flight training required by paragraph (a) of this section must include at least the same number of programmed hours of flight training and practice that are specified for a second in command pilot under §121.424(c) unless reduced under §121.405.

(c) If the certificate holder's approved training program includes a course of training utilizing an airplane simulator or other training device under §121.409(c), each flight engineer must successfully complete in the simulator or other training device—

(1) Training and practice in at least all of the assigned duties, procedures, and functions required by paragraph (a) of this section; and

(2) A flight check to a flight engineer level of proficiency in the assigned duties, procedures, and functions.

[Docket No. 9509, Amdt. 121–55, 35 FR 90, Jan. 3, 1970; as amended by Amdt. 121–144, 43 FR 22647, May 25, 1978]

§121.426 [Removed and reserved]

[Amdt. 121–366, 78 FR 67840, Nov. 12, 2013]

§121.427 Recurrent training.

(a) Recurrent training must ensure that each crew member or dispatcher is adequately trained and currently proficient with respect to the type airplane (including differences training, if applicable) and crewmember position involved.

(b) Recurrent ground training for crewmembers and dispatchers must include at least the following:

(1) A quiz or other review to determine the state of the crewmember's or dispatcher's knowledge with respect to the airplane and position involved.

(2) Instruction as necessary in the subjects required for initial ground training by §§121.415(a) and 121.805, as appropriate, including emergency training (not required for aircraft dispatchers).

(3) For flight attendants and dispatchers, a competence check as required by §§121.421(b) and 121.422(b), respectively.

(4) CRM and DRM training. For flightcrew members, CRM training or portions thereof may be accomplished during an approved simulator line operational flight training (LOFT) session. The recurrent CRM or DRM training requirements do not apply until a person has completed the applicable initial CRM or DRM training required by §§121.419, 121.421, or 121.422

(c) Recurrent ground training for crewmembers and dispatchers must consist of at least the following programmed hours unless reduced under §121.405:

(1) For pilots and flight engineers—
(i) Group I, reciprocating powered airplanes, 16 hours;
(ii) Group I turbopropeller powered airplanes, 20 hours; and
(iii) Group II airplanes, 25 hours.
(2) For flight attendants—
(i) Group I reciprocating powered airplanes, 4 hours;
(ii) Group I turbopropeller powered airplanes, 5 hours; and
(iii) Group II airplanes, 12 hours.
(3) For aircraft dispatchers—
(i) Group I reciprocating powered airplanes, 8 hours;
(ii) Group I turbopropeller powered airplanes, 10 hours; and
(iii) Group II airplanes, 20 hours.

(d) Recurrent flight training for flightcrew members must include at least the following:
(1) For pilots—
(i) Extended envelope training as required by §121.423 of this part; and
(ii) Flight training in an approved simulator in maneuvers and procedures set forth in the certificate holder's approved low-altitude windshear flight training program and flight training in maneuvers and procedures set forth in appendix F to this part, or in a flight training program approved by the Administrator, except as follows—
(A) The number of programmed inflight hours is not specified; and
(B) Satisfactory completion of a proficiency check may be substituted for recurrent flight training as permitted in §121.433(c) and (e) of this part.

(2) For flight engineers, flight training as provided by §121.425(a) except as follows—
(i) The specified number of inflight hours is not required; and
(ii) The flight check, other than the preflight inspection, may be conducted in an airplane simulator or other training device. The preflight inspection may be conducted in an airplane, or by using an approved pictorial means that realistically portrays the location and detail or preflight inspection items and provides for the portrayal of abnormal conditions. Satisfactory completion of an approved line-oriented simulator training program may be substituted for the flight check.

(e) Compliance and pilot programmed hours:
(1) Compliance with the requirements identified in paragraphs (d)(1)(i) of this section is required no later than March 12, 2019.
(2) After March 12, 2019, recurrent programmed hours applicable to pilots as specified in paragraph (c)(1) of this section must include 30 additional minutes.

[Docket No. 9509, 35 FR 90, Jan. 30, 1970; as amended by Amdt. 121–80, 36 FR 19362, Oct. 5, 1971; Amdt. 121–144, 43 FR 22647, May 25, 1978; Amdt. 121–199, 53 FR 37697, Sept. 27, 1988; Amdt. 121–250, 60 FR 65949, Dec. 20, 1995; Amdt. 121–281, 66 FR 19043, April 12, 2001; Amdt. 121–366, 78 FR 67840, Nov. 12, 2013]

§121.429 [Reserved]

Subpart O—Crewmember Qualifications

§121.431 Applicability.

(a) This subpart:
(1) Prescribes crewmember qualifications for all certificate holders except where otherwise specified. The qualification requirements of this subpart also apply to each certificate holder that conducts commuter operations under part 135 of this chapter with airplanes for which two pilots are required by the aircraft type certification rules of this chapter. The Administrator may authorize any other certificate holder that conducts operations under part 135 of this chapter to comply with the training and qualification requirements of this subpart instead of Subparts E, G, and H of part 135 of this chapter, except that these certificate holders may choose to comply with the operating experience requirements of §135.344 of this chapter, instead of the requirements of §121.434 of this chapter; and
(2) Permits training center personnel authorized under part 142 of this chapter who meet the requirements of §§121.411 through 121.414 to provide training, testing, and checking under contract or other arrangement to those persons subject to the requirements of this subpart.

(b) For the purpose of this subpart, the airplane groups and terms and definitions prescribed in §121.400 and the following definitions apply:

Consolidation is the process by which a person through practice and practical experience increases proficiency in newly acquired knowledge and skills.

Line operating flight time is flight time performed in operations under this part.

Operating cycle is a complete flight segment consisting of a takeoff, climb, enroute portion, descent, and a landing.

[Docket No. 10171, 36 FR 12284, June 30, 1971; as amended by Amdt. 121–248, 60 FR 20869, April 27, 1995; Amdt. 121–250, 60 FR 65949, Dec. 20, 1995; Amdt. 121–256, 61 FR 30435, June 14, 1996; Amdt. 121–259, 61 FR 34561, July 2, 1996; Amdt. 121–263, 62 FR 13791, March 21, 1997]

§121.432 General.

(a) Except in the case of operating experience under §121.434, a pilot who serves as second in command of an operation that requires three or more pilots must be fully qualified to act as pilot in command of that operation.

(b) No certificate holder may conduct a check or any training in operations under this part, except for the following checks and training required by this part or the certificate holder:

(1) Line checks for pilots.

(2) Flight engineer checks (except for emergency procedures), if the person being checked is qualified and current in accordance with §121.453(a).

(3) Flight attendant training and competence checks.

(c) Except for pilot line checks and flight engineer flight checks, the person being trained or checked may not be used as a required crewmember.

[Docket No. 9509, 35 FR 95, Jan. 3, 1970; as amended by Amdt. 121–130, 41 FR 47229, Oct. 28, 1976; Amdt. 121–366, 78 FR 67840, Nov. 12, 2013]

§121.433 Training required.

(a) *Initial training.* No certificate holder may use any person nor may any person serve as a required crewmember on an airplane unless that person has satisfactorily completed, in a training program approved under Subpart N of this part, initial ground and flight training for that type airplane and for the particular crewmember position, except as follows:

(1) Crewmembers who have qualified and served as a crewmember on another type airplane of the same group may serve in the same crewmember capacity upon completion of transition training as provided in §121.415.

(2) Crewmembers who have qualified and served as second in command or flight engineer on a particular type airplane may serve as pilot in command or second in command, respectively, upon completion of upgrade training for that airplane as provided in §121.415.

(b) *Differences training.* No certificate holder may use any person nor may any person serve as a required crewmember on an airplane of a type for which differences training is included in the certificate holder's approved training program unless that person has satisfactorily completed, with respect to both the crewmember position and the particular variation of the airplane in which the person serves, either initial or transition ground and flight training, or differences training, as provided in §121.415.

(c) *Recurrent training.*

(1) No certificate holder may use any person nor may any person serve as a required crewmember on an airplane unless, within the preceding 12 calendar months—

(i) For flight crewmembers, the person has satisfactorily completed recurrent ground and flight training for that airplane and crewmember position and a flight check as applicable;

(ii) For flight attendants and dispatchers, the person has satisfactorily completed recurrent ground training and a competence check; and

(iii) In addition, for pilots in command the person has satisfactorily completed, within the preceding 6 calendar months, recurrent flight training in addition to the recurrent flight training required in paragraph (c)(1)(i) of this section, in an airplane in which the person serves as pilot in command in operations under this part.

(2) For pilots, a proficiency check as provided in §121.441 of this part may be substituted for the recurrent flight training required by this paragraph and the approved simulator course of training under §121.409(b) of this part may be substituted for alternate periods of recurrent flight training required in that airplane, except as provided in paragraphs (d) and (e) of this section.

(d) For each airplane in which a pilot serves as pilot in command, the person must satisfactorily complete either recurrent flight training or a proficiency check within the preceding 12 calendar months. The requirement in this paragraph expires on March 12, 2019. After that date, the requirement in §121.441(a)(1)(ii) of this part applies.

(e) Notwithstanding paragraphs (c)(2) and (d) of this section, a proficiency check as provided in §121.441 of this part may not be substituted for the extended envelope training required by §121.423 or training in those maneuvers and procedures set forth in a certificate holder's approved low-altitude windshear flight training program when that program is included in a recurrent flight training course as required by §121.409(d) of this part.

[Docket No. 9509, 35 FR 95, Jan. 3, 1970; as amended by Amdt. 121–91, 37 FR 10729, May 27, 1972; Amdt. 121–199, 53 FR 37697, Sept. 27, 1988; Amdt. 121–366, 78 FR 67840, Nov. 12, 2013]

§121.434 Operating experience, operating cycles, and consolidation of knowledge and skills.

(a) No certificate holder may use a person nor may any person serve as a required crewmember of an airplane unless the person has satisfactorily completed, on that type airplane and in that crewmember position, the operating experience, operating cycles, and the line operating flight time for consolidation of knowledge and skills, required by this section, except as follows:

(1) Crewmembers other than pilots in command may serve as provided herein for the purpose of meeting the requirements of this section.

(2) Pilots who are meeting the pilot in command requirements may serve as second in command.

(3) Separate operating experience, operating cycles, and line operating flight time for consolidation of knowledge and skills are not required for variations within the same type airplane.

(4) Deviation based upon designation of related aircraft in accordance with §121.418(b).

(i) The Administrator may authorize a deviation from the operating experience, operating cycles, and line operating flight time for consolidation of knowledge and skills required by this section based upon a designation of related aircraft in accordance with §121.418(b) of this part and a determination that the certificate holder can demonstrate an equivalent level of safety.

(ii) A request for deviation from the operating experience, operating cycles, and line operating flight time for consolidation of knowledge and skills required by this section based upon a designation of related aircraft must be submitted to the Administrator. The request must include the following:

(A) Identification of aircraft operated by the certificate holder designated as related aircraft.

(B) Hours of operating experience and number of operating cycles necessary based on review of the related aircraft, the operation, and the duty position.

(C) Consolidation hours necessary based on review of the related aircraft, the operation, and the duty position.

(iii) The administrator may, at any time, terminate a grant of deviation authority issued under this paragraph (a)(4).

(b) In acquiring the operating experience, operating cycles, and line operating flight time for consolidation of knowledge and skills, crewmembers must comply with the following:

(1) In the case of a flight crewmember, the person must hold the appropriate certificates and ratings for the crewmember position and the airplane, except that a pilot who is meeting the pilot in command requirements must hold the appropriate certificates and ratings for a pilot in command in the airplane.

(2) The operating experience, operating cycles, and line operating flight time for consolidation of knowledge and skills must be acquired after satisfactory completion of the appropriate ground and flight training for the particular airplane type and crewmember position.

(3) The experience must be acquired in flight during operations under this part. However, in the case of an aircraft not previously used by the certificate holder in operations under this part, operating experience acquired in the aircraft during proving flights or ferry flights may be used to meet this requirement.

(c) Pilot crewmembers must acquire operating experience and operating cycles as follows:

(1) A pilot in command must—

(i) Perform the duties of a pilot in command under the supervision of a check pilot; and

(ii) In addition, if a qualifying pilot in command is completing initial or upgrade training specified in §121.424, be observed in the performance of prescribed duties by an FAA inspector during at least one flight leg which includes a takeoff and landing. During the time that a qualifying pilot in command is acquiring the operating experience in paragraphs (c)(1) (i) and (ii) of this section, a check pilot who is also serving as the pilot in command must occupy a pilot station. However, in the case of a transitioning pilot in command the check pilot serving as pilot in command may occupy the observer's seat, if the transitioning pilot has made at least two takeoffs and landings in the type airplane used, and has satisfactorily demonstrated to the check pilot that he is qualified to perform the duties of a pilot in command of that type of airplane.

(2) A second in command pilot must perform the duties of a second in command under the supervision of an appropriately qualified check pilot.

(3) The hours of operating experience and operating cycles for all pilots are as follows:

(i) For initial training, 15 hours in Group I reciprocating powered airplanes, 20 hours in Group I turbopropeller powered airplanes, and 25 hours in Group II airplanes. Operating experience in both airplane groups must include at least 4 operating cycles (at least 2 as the pilot flying the airplane).

(ii) For transition training, except as provided in paragraph (c)(3)(iii) of this section, 10 hours in Group I reciprocating powered airplanes, 12 hours in Group I turbopropeller powered airplanes, 25 hours for pilots in command in Group II airplanes, and 15 hours for second in command pilots in Group II airplanes. Operating experience in both airplane groups must include at least 4 operating cycles (at least 2 as the pilot flying the airplane).

(iii) In the case of transition training where the certificate holder's approved training program includes a course of training in an airplane simulator under §121.409(c), each pilot in command must comply with the requirements prescribed in paragraph (c)(3)(i) of this section for initial training.

(d) A flight engineer must perform the duties of a flight engineer under the supervision of a check airman or a qualified flight engineer for at least the following number of hours:

(1) Group I reciprocating powered airplanes, 8 hours.

(2) Group I turbopropeller powered airplanes, 10 hours.

(3) Group II airplanes, 12 hours.

(e) A flight attendant must, for at least 5 hours, perform the assigned duties of a flight attendant under the supervision of a flight attendant supervisor qualified under this part who personally observes the performance of these duties. However, operating experience is not required for a flight attendant who has previously acquired such experience on any large passenger carrying airplane of the same group, if the certificate holder shows that the flight attendant has received sufficient ground training for the airplane in which the flight attendant is to serve. Flight attendants receiving operating experience may not be assigned as a required crewmember. Flight attendants who have satisfactorily completed training time acquired in an approved training program conducted in a full-scale (except for length) cabin training device of the type airplane in which they are to serve may substitute this time for 50 percent of the hours required by this paragraph.

(f) Flight crewmembers may substitute one additional takeoff and landing for each hour of flight to meet the operating experience requirements of this section, up to a maximum reduction of 50% of flight hours, except those in Group II initial training, and second in command pilots in Group II transition training.

(g) Except as provided in paragraph (h) of this section, pilot in command and second in command crewmembers must each acquire at least 100 hours of line operating flight time for consolidation of knowledge and skills (including operating experience required under paragraph (c) of this section) within 120 days after the satisfactory completion of:

(1) Any part of the flight maneuvers and procedures portion of either an airline transport pilot certificate with type rating practical test or an additional type rating practical test, or

(2) A §121.441 proficiency check.

(h) The following exceptions apply to the consolidation requirement of paragraph (g) of this section:

(1) Pilots who have qualified and served as pilot in command or second in command on a particular type airplane in operations under this part before August 25, 1995 are not required to complete line operating flight time for consolidation of knowledge and skills.

(2) Pilots who have completed the line operating flight time requirement for consolidation of knowledge and skills while serving as second in command on a particular type airplane in operations under this part after August 25, 1995 are not required to repeat the line operating flight time before serving as pilot in command on the same type airplane.

(3) If, before completing the required 100 hours of line operating flight time, a pilot serves as pilot in another airplane type operated by the certificate holder, the pilot may not serve as a pilot in the airplane for which the pilot has newly qualified unless the pilot satisfactorily completes refresher training as provided in the certificate holder's approved training program and that training is conducted by an appropriately qualified instructor or check pilot.

(4) If the required 100 hours of line operating flight time are not completed within 120 days, the certificate holder may extend the 120-day period to no more than 150 days if—

(i) The pilot continues to meet all other applicable requirements of Subpart O of this part; and

(ii) On or before the 120th day the pilot satisfactorily completes refresher training conducted by an appropriately qualified instructor or check pilot as provided in the certificate holder's approved training program, or a check pilot determines that the pilot has retained an adequate level of proficiency after observing that pilot in a supervised line operating flight.

(5) The Administrator, upon application by the certificate holder, may authorize deviations from the requirements of paragraph (g) of this section, by an appropriate amendment to the operations specifications, to the extent warranted by any of the following circumstances:

(i) A newly certificated certificate holder does not employ any pilots who meet the minimum requirements of paragraph (g) of this section.

(ii) An existing certificate holder adds to its fleet an airplane type not before proven for use in its operations.

(iii) A certificate holder establishes a new domicile to which it assigns pilots who will be required to become qualified on the airplanes operated from that domicile.

(i) Notwithstanding the reductions in programmed hours permitted under §§121.405 and 121.409 of subpart N of this part, the hours of operating experience for crewmembers are not subject to reduction other than as provided in accordance with a deviation authorized under paragraph (a) of this section or as provided in paragraphs (e) and (f) of this section.

[Docket No. 9509, 35 FR 95, Jan. 3, 1970; as amended by Amdt. 121–74, 36 FR 12284, June 30, 1971; Amdt. 121–91, 37 FR 10729, May 27, 1972; Amdt. 121–140, 43 FR 9599, March 9, 1978; Amdt. 121–144, 43 FR 22647, May 25, 1978; Amdt. 121–159, 45 FR 41593, June 19, 1980; Amdt. 121–248, 60 FR 20870, April 27, 1995; Amdt. 121–366, 78 FR 67840, Nov. 12, 2013]

§121.435 [Removed and reserved]

[Docket No. FAA–2010–0100, 78 FR 42378, July 15, 2013; as amended by Amdt. 121–366, 78 FR 67841, Nov. 12, 2013]

§121.436 Pilot qualification: Certificates and experience requirements.

(a) No certificate holder may use nor may any pilot act as pilot in command of an aircraft (or as second in command of an aircraft in a flag or supplemental operation that requires three or more pilots) unless the pilot:

(1) Holds an airline transport pilot certificate not subject to the limitations in §61.167 of this chapter;

(2) Holds an appropriate aircraft type rating for the aircraft being flown; and

(3) If serving as pilot in command in part 121 operations, has 1,000 hours as second in command in operations under this part, pilot in command in operations under §91.1053(a)(2)(i) of this chapter, pilot in command in operations under §135.243(a)(1) of this chapter, or any combination thereof. For those pilots who are employed as pilot in command in part 121 operations on July 31, 2013, compliance with the requirements of this paragraph (a)(3) is not required.

(b) No certificate holder may use nor may any pilot act as second in command unless the pilot holds an airline transport pilot certificate and an appropriate aircraft type rating for the aircraft being flown. A second-in-command type rating obtained under §61.55 does not satisfy the requirements of this section.

(c) For the purpose of satisfying the flight hour requirement in paragraph (a)(3) of this section, a pilot may credit 500 hours of military flight time obtained as pilot in command of a multiengine turbinepowered, fixed-wing airplane in an operation requiring more than one pilot.

(d) Compliance with the requirements of this section is required by August 1, 2013. However, for those pilots who are employed as second in command in part 121 operations on July 31, 2013, compliance with the type rating requirement in paragraph (b) of this section is not required until January 1, 2016.

[Docket No. FAA–2010–0100, 78 FR 42378, July 15, 2013; as amended by Amdt. 121–365A, 78 FR 77574, Dec. 24, 2013]

§121.437 [Removed]

[Docket No. 6258, 29 FR 19215, Dec. 31, 1964; as amended by Amdt. 121–148, 43 FR 46235, Oct. 5, 1978; 44 FR 25202, April 30, 1979; Amdt. 121–207, 54 FR 39293, Sept. 25, 1989; Amdt. 121–253, 61 FR 2612, Jan. 26, 1996; Amdt. 121–262, 62 FR 13257, March 19, 1997; Amdt. 121–365, 78 FR 42378, July 15, 2013]

§121.438 Pilot operating limitations and pairing requirements.

(a) If the second in command has fewer than 100 hours of flight time as second in command in operations under this part in the type airplane being flown, and the pilot in command is not an appropriately qualified check pilot, the pilot in command must make all takeoffs and landings in the following situations:

(1) At special airports designated by the Administrator or at special airports designated by the certificate holder; and

(2) In any of the following conditions:

(i) The prevailing visibility value in the latest weather report for the airport is at or below 3/4 mile.

(ii) The runway visual range for the runway to be used is at or below 4,000 feet.

(iii) The runway to be used has water, snow, slush or similar conditions that may adversely affect airplane performance.

(iv) The braking action on the runway to be used is reported to be less than "good."

(v) The crosswind component for the runway to be used is in excess of 15 knots.

(vi) Windshear is reported in the vicinity of the airport.

(vii) Any other condition in which the PIC determines it to be prudent to exercise the PIC's prerogative.

(b) No person may conduct operations under this part unless, for that type airplane, either the pilot in command or the second in command has at least 75 hours of line operating flight time, either as pilot in command or second in command. The Administrator may, upon application by the certificate holder, authorize deviations from the requirements of this paragraph (b) by an appropriate amendment to the operations specifications in any of the following circumstances:

(1) A newly certificated certificate holder does not employ any pilots who meet the minimum requirements of this paragraph.

(2) An existing certificate holder adds to its fleet a type airplane not before proven for use in its operations.

(3) An existing certificate holder establishes a new domicile to which it assigns pilots who will be required to become qualified on the airplanes operated from that domicile.

[Docket No. 27210, 60 FR 20870, April 27, 1995]

§121.439 Pilot qualification: Recent experience.

(a) No certificate holder may use any person nor may any person serve as a required pilot flight crewmember, unless within the preceding 90 days, that person has made at least three takeoffs and landings in the type airplane in which that person is to serve. The takeoffs and landings required by this paragraph may be performed in a visual simulator approved under §121.407 to include takeoff and landing maneuvers. In addition, any person who fails to make the three required takeoffs and landings within any consecutive 90-day period must reestablish recency of experience as provided in paragraph (b) of this section.

(b) In addition to meeting all applicable training and checking requirements of this part, a required pilot flight crewmember who has not met the requirements of paragraph (a) of this section must reestablish recency of experience as follows:

(1) Under the supervision of a check airman, make at least three takeoffs and landings in the type airplane in which that person is to serve or in an advanced simulator or visual simulator. When a visual simulator is used, the requirements of paragraph (c) of this section must be met.

(2) The takeoffs and landings required in paragraph (b)(1) of this section must include—

(i) At least one takeoff with a simulated failure of the most critical powerplant;

(ii) At least one landing from an ILS approach to the lowest ILS minimum authorized for the certificate holder; and

(iii) At least one landing to a full stop.

(c) A required pilot flight crewmember who performs the maneuvers prescribed in paragraph (b) of this section in a visual simulator must—

(1) Have previously logged 100 hours of flight time in the same type airplane in which he is to serve;

(2) Be observed on the first two landings made in operations under this part by an approved check airman who acts as pilot in command and occupies a pilot seat. The landings must be made in weather minimums that are not less than those contained in the certificate holder's operations specifications for Category I Operations, and must be made within 45 days following completion of simulator training.

(d) When using a simulator to accomplish any of the requirements of paragraph (a) or (b) of this section, each required flight crewmember position must be occupied by an appropriately qualified person and the simulator must be operated as if in a normal in-flight environment without use of the repositioning features of the simulator.

(e) A check airman who observes the takeoffs and landings prescribed in paragraphs (b)(1) and (c) of this section shall certify that the person being observed is proficient and qualified to perform flight duty in operations under this part and may require any additional maneuvers that are determined necessary to make this certifying statement.

(f) Deviation authority based upon designation of related aircraft in accordance with §121.418(b).

(1) The Administrator may authorize a deviation from the requirements of paragraph (a) of this section based upon a designation of related aircraft in accordance with §121.418(b) of this part and a determination that the certificate holder can demonstrate an equivalent level of safety.

(2) A request for deviation from paragraph (a) of this section must be submitted to the Administrator. The request must include the following:

(i) Identification of aircraft operated by the certificate holder designated as related aircraft.

(ii) The number of takeoffs, landings, maneuvers, and procedures necessary to maintain or reestablish recency based on review of the related aircraft, the operation, and the duty position.

(3) The administrator may, at any time, terminate a grant of deviation authority issued under this paragraph (f).

[Docket No. 16383, 43 FR 22648, May 25, 1978; as amended by Amdt. 121–148, 43 FR 46235, Oct. 5, 1978; Amdt. 121–179, 47 FR 33390, Aug. 2, 1982; Amdt. 121–366, 78 FR 67841, Nov. 12, 2013]

§121.440 Line checks.

(a) No certificate holder may use any person nor may any person serve as pilot in command of an airplane unless, within the preceding 12 calendar months, that person has passed a line check in which he satisfactorily performs the duties and responsibilities of a pilot in command in one of the types of airplanes he is to fly.

(b) A pilot in command line check for domestic and flag operations must—

(1) Be given by a pilot check airman who is currently qualified on both the route and the airplane; and

(2) Consist of at least one flight over a typical part of the certificate holder's route, or over a foreign or Federal airway, or over a direct route.

(c) A pilot in command line check for supplemental operations must—

(1) Be given by a pilot check airman who is currently qualified on the airplane; and

(2) Consist of at least one flight over a part of a Federal airway, foreign airway, or advisory route over which the pilot may be assigned.

[Docket No. 9509, 35 FR 96, Jan. 3, 1970; as amended by Amdt. 121–143, 43 FR 22642, May 25, 1978; Amdt. 121–253, 61 FR 2612, Jan. 26, 1996; Amdt. 121–344, 74 FR 34235, July 15, 2009; Amdt. 121–359, 77 FR 34785, June 12, 2012]

§121.441 Proficiency checks.

(a) No certificate holder may use any person nor may any person serve as a required pilot flight crewmember unless that person has satisfactorily completed either a proficiency check, or an approved simulator course of training under §121.409, as follows:

(1) For a pilot in command—
(i) Before March 12, 2019,
(A) A proficiency check within the preceding 12 calendar months and,
(B) In addition, within the preceding 6 calendar months, either a proficiency check or the approved simulator course of training.
(ii) Beginning on March 12, 2019,
(A) A proficiency check within the preceding 12 calendar months in the aircraft type in which the person is to serve and,
(B) In addition, within the preceding 6 calendar months, either a proficiency check or the approved simulator course of training.
(2) For all other pilots—
(i) Within the preceding 24 calendar months either a proficiency check or the line-oriented simulator training course under §121.409; and
(ii) Within the preceding 12 calendar months, either a proficiency check or any simulator training course under §121.409.

(b) Except as provided in paragraphs (c) and (d) of this section, a proficiency check must meet the following requirements:
(1) It must include at least the procedures and maneuvers set forth in Appendix F to this part unless otherwise specifically provided in that appendix.
(2) It must be given by the Administrator or a pilot check airman.

(c) An approved airplane simulator or other appropriate training device may be used in the conduct of a proficiency check as provided in Appendix F to this part.

(d) A person giving a proficiency check may, in his discretion, waive any of the maneuvers or procedures for which a specific waiver authority is set forth in Appendix F to this part if—
(1) The Administrator has not specifically required the particular maneuver or procedure to be performed;
(2) The pilot being checked is, at the time of the check, employed by a certificate holder as a pilot; and
(3) The pilot being checked is currently qualified for operations under this part in the particular type airplane and flight crewmember position or has, within the preceding six calendar months, satisfactorily completed an approved training program for the particular type airplane.

(e) If the pilot being checked fails any of the required maneuvers, the person giving the proficiency check may give additional training to the pilot during the course of the proficiency check. In addition to repeating the maneuvers failed, the person giving the proficiency check may require the pilot being checked to repeat any other maneuvers he finds are necessary to determine the pilot's proficiency. If the pilot being checked is unable to demonstrate satisfactory performance to the person conducting the check, the certificate holder may not use him nor may he serve in operations under this part until he has satisfactorily completed a proficiency check.

However, the entire proficiency check (other than the initial second-in-command proficiency check) required by this section may be conducted in an approved visual simulator if the pilot being checked accomplishes at least two landings in the appropriate airplane during a line check or other check conducted by a pilot check airman (a pilot-in-command may observe and certify the satisfactory accomplishment of these landings by a second-in-command). If a pilot proficiency check is conducted in accordance with this paragraph, the next required proficiency check for that pilot must be conducted in the same manner, or in accordance with Appendix F of this part, or a course of training in an airplane visual simulator under §121.409 may be substituted therefor.

(f) Deviation authority based upon designation of related aircraft in accordance with §121.418(b) of this part.
(1) The Administrator may authorize a deviation from the proficiency check requirements of paragraphs (a) and (b)(1) of this section based upon a designation of related aircraft in accordance with §121.418(b) of this part and a determination that the certificate holder can demonstrate an equivalent level of safety.
(2) A request for deviation from paragraphs (a) and (b)(1) of this section must be submitted to the Administrator. The request must include the following:
(i) Identification of aircraft operated by the certificate holder designated as related aircraft.
(ii) For recurrent proficiency checks, the frequency of the related aircraft proficiency check and the maneuvers and procedures to be included in the related aircraft proficiency check based on review of the related aircraft, the operation, and the duty position.
(iii) For qualification proficiency checks, the maneuvers and procedures to be included in the related aircraft proficiency check based on review of the related aircraft, the operation, and the duty position.
(3) The administrator may, at any time, terminate a grant of deviation authority issued under this paragraph (f).

[Docket No. 9509, 35 FR 96, Jan. 3, 1970; as amended by Amdt. 121–103, 38 FR 12203, May 10, 1973, Amdt.

121–108, 38 FR 35446, Dec. 28, 1973; Amdt. 121–144, 43 FR 22648, May 25, 1978; Amdt. 121–263, 62 FR 13791, March 21, 1997; Amdt. 121–366, 78 FR 67841, Nov. 12, 2013]

§121.443 Pilot in command qualification: Route and airports.

(a) Each certificate holder shall provide a system acceptable to the Administrator for disseminating the information required by paragraph (b) of this section to the pilot in command and appropriate flight operation personnel. The system must also provide an acceptable means for showing compliance with §121.445.

(b) No certificate holder may use any person, nor may any person serve, as pilot in command unless the certificate holder has provided that person current information concerning the following subjects pertinent to the areas over which that person is to serve, and to each airport and terminal area into which that person is to operate, and ensures that person has adequate knowledge of, and the ability to use, the information:

(1) Weather characteristics appropriate to the season.
(2) Navigation facilities.
(3) Communication procedures, including airport visual aids.
(4) Kinds of terrain and obstructions.
(5) Minimum safe flight levels.
(6) En route and terminal area arrival and departure procedures, holding procedures and authorized instrument approach procedures for the airports involved.
(7) Congested areas and physical layout of each airport in the terminal area in which the pilot will operate.
(8) Notices to Airmen.

[Docket No. 17897, 45 FR 41594, June 19, 1980; as amended by Amdt. 121–159, 45 FR 43154, June 26, 1980]

§121.445 Pilot in command airport qualification: Special areas and airports.

(a) The Administrator may determine that certain airports (due to items such as surrounding terrain, obstructions, or complex approach or departure procedures) are special airports requiring special airport qualifications and that certain areas or routes, or both, require a special type of navigation qualification.

(b) Except as provided in paragraph (c) of this section, no certificate holder may use any person, nor may any person serve, as pilot in command to or from an airport determined to require special airport qualifications unless, within the preceding 12 calendar months:

(1) The pilot in command or second in command has made an entry to that airport (including a takeoff and landing) while serving as a pilot flight crewmember; or

(2) The pilot in command has qualified by using pictorial means acceptable to the Administrator for that airport.

(c) Paragraph (b) of this section does not apply when an entry to that airport (including a takeoff or a landing) is being made if the ceiling at that airport is at least 1,000 feet above the lowest MEA or MOCA, or initial approach altitude prescribed for the instrument approach procedure for that airport, and the visibility at that airport is at least 3 miles.

(d) No certificate holder may use any person, nor may any person serve, as pilot in command between terminals over a route or area that requires a special type of navigation qualification unless, within the preceding 12 calendar months, that person has demonstrated qualification on the applicable navigation system in a manner acceptable to the Administrator, by one of the following methods:

(1) By flying over a route or area as pilot in command using the applicable special type of navigation system.
(2) By flying over a route or area as pilot in command under the supervision of a check airman using the special type of navigation system.
(3) By completing the training program requirements of Appendix G of this part.

[Docket No. 17897, 45 FR 41594, June 19, 1980]

§121.447 [Reserved]

§121.453 Flight engineer qualifications.

(a) No certificate holder may use any person nor may any person serve as a flight engineer on an airplane unless, within the preceding 6 calendar months, he has had at least 50 hours of flight time as a flight engineer on that type airplane or the certificate holder or the Administrator has checked him on that type airplane and determined that he is familiar and competent with all essential current information and operating procedures.

(b) A flight check given in accordance with §121.425(a)(2) satisfies the requirements of paragraph (a) of this section.

[Docket No. 9509, 35 FR 96, Jan. 3, 1970]

§121.455–121.459 [Reserved]

Subpart P—Aircraft Dispatcher Qualifications and Duty Time

Limitations: Domestic and Flag Operations; Flight Attendant Duty Period Limitations and Rest Requirements: Domestic, Flag, and Supplemental Operations

§121.461 Applicability.

This subpart prescribes—

(a) Qualifications and duty time limitations for aircraft dispatchers for certificate holders conducting domestic flag operations; and

(b) Duty period limitations and rest requirements for flight attendants used by certificate holders conducting domestic, flag, or supplemental operations.

[Docket No. 28154, 61 FR 2612, Jan. 26, 1996]

§121.463 Aircraft dispatcher qualifications.

(a) No certificate holder conducting domestic or flag operations may use any person, nor may any person serve, as an aircraft dispatcher for a particular airplane group unless that person has, with respect to an airplane of that group, satisfactorily completed the following:

(1) Initial dispatcher training, except that a person who has satisfactorily completed such training for another type airplane of the same group need only complete the appropriate transition training.

(2) Operating familiarization consisting of at least 5 hours observing operations under this part from the flight deck or, for airplanes without an observer seat on the flight deck, from a forward passenger seat with headset or speaker. This requirement may be reduced to a minimum of 2-1/2 hours by the substitution of one additional takeoff and landing for an hour of flight. A person may serve as an aircraft dispatcher without meeting the requirement of this paragraph (a) for 90 days after initial introduction of the airplane into operations under this part.

(b) No certificate holder conducting domestic or flag operations may use any person, nor may any person serve, as an aircraft dispatcher for a particular type airplane unless that person has, with respect to that airplane, satisfactorily completed differences training, if applicable.

(c) No certificate holder conducting domestic or flag operations may use any person, nor may any person serve, as an aircraft dispatcher unless within the preceding 12 calendar months the aircraft dispatcher has satisfactorily completed operating familiarization consisting of at least 5 hours observing operations under this part, in one of the types of airplanes in each group to be dispatched. This observation shall be made from the flight deck or, for airplanes without an observer seat on the flight deck, from a forward passenger seat with headset or speaker. The requirement of paragraph (a) of this section may be reduced to a minimum of 2-1/2 hours by the substitution of one additional takeoff and landing for an hour of flight. The requirement of this paragraph may be satisfied by observation of 5 hours of simulator training for each airplane group in one of the simulators approved under §121.407 for the group. However, if the requirement of paragraph (a) is met by the use of a simulator, no reduction in hours is permitted.

(d) No certificate holder conducting domestic or flag operations may use any person, nor may any person serve as an aircraft dispatcher to dispatch airplanes in operations under this part unless the certificate holder has determined that he is familiar with all essential operating procedures for that segment of the operation over which he exercises dispatch jurisdiction. However, a dispatcher who is qualified to dispatch airplanes through one segment of an operation may dispatch airplanes through other segments of the operation after coordinating with dispatchers who are qualified to dispatch airplanes through those other segments.

(e) For the purposes of this section, the airplane groups, terms, and definitions in §121.400 apply.

[Docket No. 7325, 37 FR 5607, March 17, 1972; as amended by Amdt. 121–251, 60 FR 65934, Dec. 20, 1995]

§121.465 Aircraft dispatcher duty time limitations: Domestic and flag operations.

(a) Each certificate holder conducting domestic or flag operations shall establish the daily duty period for a dispatcher so that it begins at a time that allows him or her to become thoroughly familiar with existing and anticipated weather conditions along the route before he or she dispatches any airplane. He or she shall remain on duty until each airplane dispatched by him or her has completed its flight, or has gone beyond his or her jurisdiction, or until he or she is relieved by another qualified dispatcher.

(b) Except in cases where circumstances or emergency conditions beyond the control of the certificate holder require otherwise—

(1) No certificate holder conducting domestic or flag operations may schedule a dispatcher for more than 10 consecutive hours of duty;

§121.467   **Federal Aviation Regulations**

(2) If a dispatcher is scheduled for more than 10 hours of duty in 24 consecutive hours, the certificate holder shall provide him or her a rest period of at least eight hours at or before the end of 10 hours of duty.

(3) Each dispatcher must be relieved of all duty with the certificate holder for at least 24 consecutive hours during any seven consecutive days or the equivalent thereof within any calendar month.

(c) Notwithstanding paragraphs (a) and (b) of this section, a certificate holder conducting flag operations may, if authorized by the Administrator, schedule an aircraft dispatcher at a duty station outside of the 48 contiguous States and the District of Columbia, for more than 10 consecutive hours of duty in a 24-hour period if that aircraft dispatcher is relieved of all duty with the certificate holder for at least eight hours during each 24-hour period.

[Docket No. 28154, 61 FR 2612, Jan. 26, 1996]

§121.467 Flight attendant duty period limitations and rest requirements: Domestic, flag, and supplemental operations.

(a) For purposes of this section—

Calendar day means the period of elapsed time, using Coordinated Universal Time or local time, that begins at midnight and ends 24 hours later at the next midnight.

Duty period means the period of elapsed time between reporting for an assignment involving flight time and release from that assignment by the certificate holder conducting domestic, flag, or supplemental operations. The time is calculated using either Coordinated Universal Time or local time to reflect the total elapsed time.

Flight attendant means an individual, other than a flight crewmember, who is assigned by a certificate holder conducting domestic, flag, or supplemental operations, in accordance with the required minimum crew complement under the certificate holder's operations specification or in addition to that minimum complement, to duty in an aircraft during flight time and whose duties include but are not necessarily limited to cabin-safety-related responsibilities.

Rest period means the period free of all restraint or duty for a certificate holder conducting domestic, flag, or supplemental operations and free of all responsibility for work or duty should the occasion arise.

(b) Except as provided in paragraph (c) of this section, a certificate holder conducting domestic, flag, or supplemental operations may assign a duty period to a flight attendant only when the applicable duty period limitations and rest requirements of this paragraph are met.

(1) Except as provided in paragraphs (b)(4), (b)(5), and (b)(6) of this section, no certificate holder conducting domestic, flag, or supplemental operations may assign a flight attendant to a scheduled duty period of more than 14 hours.

(2) Except as provided in paragraph (b)(3) of this section, a flight attendant scheduled to a duty period of 14 hours or less as provided under paragraph (b)(1) of this section must be given a scheduled rest period of at least 9 consecutive hours. This rest period must occur between the completion of the scheduled duty period and the commencement of the subsequent duty period.

(3) The rest period required under paragraph (b)(2) of this section may be scheduled or reduced to 8 consecutive hours if the flight attendant is provided a subsequent rest period of at least 10 consecutive hours; this subsequent rest period must be scheduled to begin no later than 24 hours after the beginning of the reduced rest period and must occur between the completion of the scheduled duty period and the commencement of the subsequent duty period.

(4) A certificate holder conducting domestic, flag, or supplemental operations may assign a flight attendant to a scheduled duty period of more than 14 hours, but no more than 16 hours, if the certificate holder has assigned to the flight or flights in that duty period at least one flight attendant in addition to the minimum flight attendant complement required for the flight or flights in that duty period under the certificate holder's operations specifications.

(5) A certificate holder conducting domestic, flag, or supplemental operations may assign a flight attendant to a scheduled duty period of more than 16 hours, but no more than 18 hours, if the certificate holder has assigned to the flight or flights in that duty period at least two flight attendants in addition to the minimum flight attendant complement required for the flight or flights in that duty period under the certificate holder's operations specifications.

(6) A certificate holder conducting domestic, flag, or supplemental operations may assign a flight attendant to a scheduled duty period of more than 18 hours, but no more than 20 hours, if the scheduled duty period includes one or more flights that land or take off outside the 48 contiguous states and the District of Columbia, and if the certificate holder has assigned to the flight or flights in that duty period at least three flight attendants in addition to the minimum flight attendant complement required for the flight or flights in that duty period under the domestic certificate holder's operations specifications.

(7) Except as provided in paragraph (b)(8) of this section, a flight attendant scheduled to a duty

Part 121: Air Carriers & Commercial Operators §121.467

period of more than 14 hours but no more than 20 hours, as provided in paragraphs (b)(4), (b)(5), and (b)(6) of this section, must be given a scheduled rest period of at least 12 consecutive hours. This rest period must occur between the completion of the scheduled duty period and the commencement of the subsequent duty period.

(8) The rest period required under paragraph (b)(7) of this section may be scheduled or reduced to 10 consecutive hours if the flight attendant is provided a subsequent rest period of at least 14 consecutive hours; this subsequent rest period must be scheduled to begin no later than 24 hours after the beginning of the reduced rest period and must occur between the completion of the scheduled duty period and the commencement of the subsequent duty period.

(9) Notwithstanding paragraphs (b)(4), (b)(5), and (b)(6) of this section, if a certificate holder conducting domestic, flag, or supplemental operations elects to reduce the rest period to 10 hours as authorized by paragraph (b)(8) of this section, the certificate holder may not schedule a flight attendant for a duty period of more than 14 hours during the 24-hour period commencing after the beginning of the reduced rest period.

(10) No certificate holder conducting domestic, flag, or supplemental operations may assign a flight attendant any duty period with the certificate holder unless the flight attendant has had at least the minimum rest required under this section.

(11) No certificate holder conducting domestic, flag, or supplemental operations may assign a flight attendant to perform any duty with the certificate holder during any required rest period.

(12) Time spent in transportation, not local in character, that a certificate holder conducting domestic, flag, or supplemental operations requires of a flight attendant and provides to transport the flight attendant to an airport at which that flight attendant is to serve on a flight as a crewmember, or from an airport at which the flight attendant was relieved from duty to return to the flight attendant's home station, is not considered part of a rest period.

(13) Each certificate holder conducting domestic, flag, or supplemental operations must relieve each flight attendant engaged in air transportation and each commercial operator must relieve each flight attendant engaged in air commerce from all further duty for at least 24 consecutive hours during any 7 consecutive calendar days.

(14) A flight attendant is not considered to be scheduled for duty in excess of duty period limitations if the flights to which the flight attendant is assigned are scheduled and normally terminate within the limitations but due to circumstances beyond the control of the certificate holder conducting domestic, flag, or supplemental operations (such as adverse weather conditions) are not at the time of departure expected to reach their destination within the scheduled time.

(c) Notwithstanding paragraph (b) of this section, a certificate holder conducting domestic, flag, or supplemental operations may apply the flightcrew member flight time and duty limitations and rest requirements of part 117 of this chapter to flight attendants for all operations conducted under this part provided that—

(1) The certificate holder establishes written procedures that—

(i) Apply to all flight attendants used in the certificate holder's operation;

(ii) Include the flightcrew member requirements contained in part 117, as appropriate to the operation being conducted, except that rest facilities on board the aircraft are not required;

(iii) Include provisions to add one flight attendant to the minimum flight attendant complement for each flightcrew member who is in excess of the minimum number required in the aircraft type certificate data sheet and who is assigned to the aircraft under the provisions of part 117, as applicable, of this part;

(iv) Are approved by the Administrator and are described or referenced in the certificate holder's operations specifications; and

(2) Whenever the Administrator finds that revisions are necessary for the continued adequacy of the written procedures that are required by paragraph (c)(1) of this section and that had been granted final approval, the certificate holder must, after notification by the Administrator, make any changes in the procedures that are found necessary by the Administrator. Within 30 days after the certificate holder receives such notice, it may file a petition to reconsider the notice with the certificate-holding district office. The filing of a petition to reconsider stays the notice, pending decision by the Administrator. However, if the Administrator finds that an emergency requires immediate action in the interest of safety, the Administrator may, upon a statement of the reasons, require a change effective without stay.

[Docket No. 27229, 59 FR 42991, August 19, 1994; as amended by Amdt. 121-253, 61 FR 2612, Jan. 26, 1996; Amdt. 121-357, 77 FR 402, Jan. 4, 2012; Amdt. 121-357A, 77 FR 28764, May 16, 2012]

Subpart Q—
Flight Time Limitations and Rest Requirements: Domestic Operations

Source: Docket No. 23634, 50 FR 29319, July 18, 1985, unless otherwise noted.

§121.470 Applicability.

This subpart prescribes flight time limitations and rest requirements for domestic all-cargo operations, except that:

(a) Certificate holders conducting operations with airplanes having a passenger seat configuration of 30 seats or fewer, excluding each crewmember seat, and a payload capacity of 7,500 pounds or less, may comply with the applicable requirements of §§135.261 through 135.273 of this chapter.

(b) Certificate holders conducting scheduled operations entirely within the States of Alaska or Hawaii with airplanes having a passenger seat configuration of more than 30 seats, excluding each crewmember seat, or a payload capacity of more than 7,500 pounds, may comply with the requirements of this subpart or subpart R of this part for those operations.

(c) A certificate holder may apply the flightcrew member flight time and duty limitations and requirements of part 117 of this chapter. A certificate holder may choose to apply part 117 to its—

(1) Cargo operations conducted under contract to a U.S. government agency;

(2) All-cargo operations not conducted under contract to a U.S. Government agency;

(3) A certificate holder may elect to treat operations in paragraphs (c)(1) and (c)(2) of this section differently but, once having decided to conduct those operations under part 117, may not segregate those operations between this subpart and part 117.

[Docket No. 28154, 60 FR 65934, Dec. 20, 1995; as amended by Amdt. 121–357, 77 FR 402, Jan. 4, 2012; Amdt. 121–357A, 77 FR 28764, May 16, 2012; Amdt. 121–357, 78 FR 69288, Nov. 19, 2013]

§121.471 Flight time limitations and rest requirements: All flight crewmembers.

(a) No certificate holder conducting domestic operations may schedule any flight crewmember and no flight crewmember may accept an assignment for flight time in scheduled air transportation or in other commercial flying if that crewmember's total flight time in all commercial flying will exceed—

(1) 1,000 hours in any calendar year;
(2) 100 hours in any calendar month;
(3) 30 hours in any 7 consecutive days;
(4) 8 hours between required rest periods.

(b) Except as provided in paragraph (c) of this section, no certificate holder conducting domestic operations may schedule a flight crewmember and no flight crewmember may accept an assignment for flight time during the 24 consecutive hours preceding the scheduled completion of any flight segment without a scheduled rest period during that 24 hours of at least the following:

(1) 9 consecutive hours of rest for less than 8 hours of scheduled flight time.

(2) 10 consecutive hours of rest for 8 or more but less than 9 hours of scheduled flight time.

(3) 11 consecutive hours of rest for 9 or more hours of scheduled flight time.

(c) An certificate holder may schedule a flight crewmember for less than the rest required in paragraph (b) of this section or may reduce a scheduled rest under the following conditions:

(1) A rest required under paragraph (b)(1) of this section may be scheduled for or reduced to a minimum of 8 hours if the flight crewmember is given a rest period of at least 10 hours that must begin no later than 24 hours after the commencement of the reduced rest period.

(2) A rest required under paragraph (b)(2) of this section may be scheduled for or reduced to a minimum of 8 hours if the flight crewmember is given a rest period of at least 11 hours that must begin no later than 24 hours after the commencement of the reduced rest period.

(3) A rest required under paragraph (b)(3) of this section may be scheduled for or reduced to a minimum of 9 hours if the flight crewmember is given a rest period of at least 12 hours that must begin no later than 24 hours after the commencement of the reduced rest period.

(4) No certificate holder may assign, nor may any flight crewmember perform any flight time with the certificate holder unless the flight crewmember has had at least the minimum rest required under this paragraph.

(d) Each certificate holder conducting domestic operations shall relieve each flight crewmember engaged in scheduled air transportation from all further duty for at least 24 consecutive hours during any 7 consecutive days.

(e) No certificate holder conducting domestic operations may assign any flight crewmember and no flight crewmember may accept assignment to any duty with the air carrier during any required rest period.

(f) Time spent in transportation, not local in character, that an certificate holder requires of a flight crewmember and provides to transport the crewmember to an airport at which he is to serve on a flight as a crewmember, or from an airport at which he was relieved from duty to return to his home station, is not considered part of a rest period.

(g) A flight crewmember is not considered to be scheduled for flight time in excess of flight time limitations if the flights to which he is assigned are scheduled and normally terminate within the limitations, but due to circumstances beyond the control of the certificate holder (such as adverse weather conditions), are not at the time of departure expected to reach their destination within the scheduled time.

[Docket No. 23634, 50 FR 29319, July 18, 1985; as amended by Amdt. 121–253, 61 FR 2612, Jan. 26, 1996]

§121.473 Fatigue risk management system.

(a) No certificate holder may exceed any provision of this subpart unless approved by the FAA under a Fatigue Risk Management System.

(b) The Fatigue Risk Management System must include:

(1) A fatigue risk management policy.
(2) An education and awareness training program.
(3) A fatigue reporting system.
(4) A system for monitoring flightcrew fatigue.
(5) An incident reporting process.
(6) A performance evaluation.

[Docket No. FAA–2009–1093, 77 FR 403, Jan. 4, 2012; Amdt. 121–357A, 77 FR 28764, May 16, 2012]

Subpart R—
Flight Time Limitations:
Flag Operations

Source: Docket No. 6258, 29 FR 19217, Dec. 31, 1964; 30 FR 3639, March 19, 1965, unless otherwise noted.

§121.480 Applicability.

This subpart prescribes flight time limitations and rest requirements for flag all-cargo operations, except that:

(a) Certificate holders conducting operations with airplanes having a passenger seat configuration of 30 seats or fewer, excluding each crewmember seat, and a payload capacity of 7,500 pounds or less, may comply with the applicable requirements of §§135.261 through 135.273 of this chapter.

(b) A certificate holder may apply the flightcrew member flight time and duty limitations and requirements of part 117 of this chapter. A certificate holder may choose to apply part 117 to its—

(1) All-cargo operations conducted under contract to a U.S. government agency.
(2) All-cargo operations not conducted under contract to a U.S. Government agency,

(3) A certificate holder may elect to treat operations in paragraphs (b)(1) and (b)(2) of this section differently but, once having decided to conduct those operations under part 117, may not segregate those operations between this subpart and part 117.

[Docket No. 28154, 60 FR 65934, Dec. 20, 1995; as amended by Amdt. 121–357, 77 FR 403, Jan. 4, 2012; Amdt. 121–357A, 77 FR 28764, May 16, 2012]

§121.481 Flight time limitations: One or two pilot crews.

(a) A certificate holder conducting flag operations may schedule a pilot to fly in an airplane that has a crew of one or two pilots for eight hours or less during any 24 consecutive hours without a rest period during these eight hours.

(b) If a certificate holder conducting flag operations schedules a pilot to fly more than eight hours during any 24 consecutive hours, it shall give him an intervening rest period, at or before the end of eight scheduled hours of flight duty. This rest period must be at least twice the number of hours flown since the preceding rest period, but not less than eight hours. The certificate holder shall relieve that pilot of all duty with it during that rest period.

(c) Each pilot who has flown more than eight hours during 24 consecutive hours must be given at least 18 hours of rest before being assigned to any duty with the certificate holder.

(d) No pilot may fly more than 32 hours during any seven consecutive days, and each pilot must be relieved from all duty for at least 24 consecutive hours at least once during any seven consecutive days.

(e) No pilot may fly as a member of a crew more than 100 hours during any one calendar month.

(f) No pilot may fly as a member of a crew more than 1,000 hours during any 12-calendar-month period.

[Docket No. 6258, 29 FR 19217, Dec. 31, 1964; as amended by Amdt. 121–253, 61 FR 2612, Jan. 26, 1996]

§121.483 Flight time limitations: Two pilots and one additional flight crewmember.

(a) No certificate holder conducting flag operations may schedule a pilot to fly, in an airplane that has a crew of two pilots and at least one additional flight crewmember, for a total of more than 12 hours during any 24 consecutive hours.

(b) If a pilot has flown 20 or more hours during any 48 consecutive hours or 24 or more hours during any 72 consecutive hours, he must be given at least 18 hours of rest before being assigned to any duty with the air carrier. In any case,

§121.485

he must be given at least 24 consecutive hours of rest during any seven consecutive days.

(c) No pilot may fly as a flight crewmember more than—

(1) 120 hours during any 30 consecutive days;
(2) 300 hours during any 90 consecutive days; or
(3) 1,000 hours during any 12-calendar-month period.

[Docket No. 6258, 29 FR 19217, Dec. 31, 1964; as amended by Amdt. 121–253, 61 FR 2612, Jan. 26, 1996]

§121.485 Flight time limitations: Three or more pilots and an additional flight crewmember.

(a) Each certificate holder conducting flag operations shall schedule its flight hours to provide adequate rest periods on the ground for each pilot who is away from his base and who is a pilot on an airplane that has a crew of three or more pilots and an additional flight crewmember. It shall also provide adequate sleeping quarters on the airplane whenever a pilot is scheduled to fly more than 12 hours during any 24 consecutive hours.

(b) The certificate holder conducting flag operations shall give each pilot, upon return to his base from any flight or series of flights, a rest period that is at least twice the total number of hours he flew since the last rest period at his base. During the rest period required by this paragraph, the air carrier may not require him to perform any duty for it. If the required rest period is more than seven days, that part of the rest period in excess of seven days may be given at any time before the pilot is again scheduled for flight duty on any route.

(c) No pilot may fly as a flight crewmember more than—

(1) 350 hours during any 90 consecutive days; or
(2) 1,000 hours during any 12-calendar-month period.

[Docket No. 6258, 29 FR 19217, Dec. 31, 1964; as amended by Amdt. 121–253, 61 FR 2612, Jan. 26, 1996]

§121.487 Flight time limitations: Pilots not regularly assigned.

(a) Except as provided in paragraphs (b) through (e) of this section, a pilot who is not regularly assigned as a flight crewmember for an entire calendar month under §121.483 or 121.485 may not fly more than 100 hours in any 30 consecutive days.

(b) The monthly flight time limitations for a pilot who is scheduled for duty aloft for more than 20 hours in two-pilot crews in any calendar month, or whose assignment in such a crew is interrupted more than once in that calendar month by assignment to a crew consisting of two or more pilots and an additional flight crewmember, are those set forth in §121.481.

(c) Except for a pilot covered by paragraph (b) of this section, the monthly and quarterly flight time limitations for a pilot who is scheduled for duty aloft for more than 20 hours in two-pilot and additional flight crewmember crews in any calendar month, or whose assignment in such a crew is interrupted more than once in that calendar month by assignment to a crew consisting of three pilots and additional flight crewmember, are those set forth in §121.483.

(d) The quarterly flight time limitations for a pilot to whom paragraphs (b) and (c) of this section do not apply and who is scheduled for duty aloft for a total of not more than 20 hours within any calendar month in two-pilot crews (with or without additional flight crewmembers) are those set forth in §121.485.

(e) The monthly and quarterly flight time limitations for a pilot assigned to each of two-pilot, two-pilot and additional flight crewmember, and three-pilot and additional flight crewmember crews in a given calendar month, and who is not subject to paragraph (b), (c), or (d) of this section, are those set forth in §121.483.

[Docket No. 6258, 29 FR 19217, Dec. 31, 1964; as amended by Amdt. 121–3, 30 FR 3639, March 19, 1965; Amdt. 121–137, 42 FR 43973, Sept. 1, 1977]

§121.489 Flight time limitations: Other commercial flying.

No pilot that is employed as a pilot by a certificate holder conducting flag operations may do any other commercial flying if that commercial flying plus his flying in air transportation will exceed any flight time limitation in this part.

[Docket No. 28154, 61 FR 2612, Jan. 26, 1996]

§121.491 Flight time limitations: Deadhead transportation.

Time spent in deadhead transportation to or from duty assignment is not considered to be a part of a rest period.

§121.493 Flight time limitations: Flight engineers and flight navigators.

(a) In any operation in which one flight engineer or flight navigator is required, the flight time limitations in §121.483 apply to that flight engineer or flight navigator.

(b) In any operation in which more than one flight engineer or flight navigator is required, the flight time limitations in §121.485 apply to those flight engineers or flight navigators.

§121.495 Fatigue risk management system.

(a) No certificate holder may exceed any provision of this subpart unless approved by the FAA under a Fatigue Risk Management System.

(b) The Fatigue Risk Management System must include:

(1) A fatigue risk management policy.
(2) An education and awareness training program.
(3) A fatigue reporting system.
(4) A system for monitoring flightcrew fatigue.
(5) An incident reporting process.
(6) A performance evaluation.

[Docket No. FAA–2009–1093, 77 FR 403, Jan. 4, 2012; Amdt. 121–357A, 77 FR 28764, May 16, 2012]

Subpart S— Flight Time Limitations: Supplemental Operations

Source: Docket No. 6258, 29 FR 19218, Dec. 31, 1964; 30 FR 3639, March 19, 1965, unless otherwise noted.

§121.500 Applicability.

This subpart prescribes flight time limitations and rest requirements for supplemental all-cargo operations, except that:

(a) Certificate holders conducting operations with airplanes having a passenger seat configuration of 30 seats or fewer, excluding each crewmember seat, and a payload capacity of 7,500 pound or less, may comply with the applicable requirements of §§135.261 through 135.273 of this chapter.

(b) A certificate holder may apply the flightcrew member flight time and duty limitations and requirements of part 117 of this chapter. A certificate holder may choose to apply part 117 to its—

(1) All-cargo operations conducted under contract to a U.S. Government agency.
(2) All-cargo operations not conducted under contract to a U.S. Government agency,
(3) A certificate holder may elect to treat operations in paragraphs (b)(1) and (b)(2) of this section differently but, once having decided to conduct those operations under part 117, may not segregate those operations between this subpart and part 117.

[Docket No. 28154, 60 FR 65934, Dec. 20, 1995; as amended by Amdt. 121–357, 77 FR 403, Jan. 4, 2012; Amdt. 121–357A, 77 FR 28764, May 16, 2012]

§121.503 Flight time limitations: Pilots: airplanes.

(a) A certificate holder conducting supplemental operations may schedule a pilot to fly in an airplane for eight hours or less during any 24 consecutive hours without a rest period during those eight hours.

(b) Each pilot who has flown more than eight hours during any 24 consecutive hours must be given at least 16 hours of rest before being assigned to any duty with the certificate holder.

(c) Each certificate holder conducting supplemental operations shall relieve each pilot from all duty for at least 24 consecutive hours at least once during any seven consecutive days.

(d) No pilot may fly as a crewmember in air transportation more than 100 hours during any 30 consecutive days.

(e) No pilot may fly as a crewmember in air transportation more than 1,000 hours during any calendar year.

(f) Notwithstanding paragraph (a) of this section, the certificate holder may, in conducting a transcontinental nonstop flight, schedule a flight crewmember for more than eight but not more than 10 hours of continuous duty aloft without an intervening rest period, if—

(1) The flight is in an airplane with a pressurization system that is operative at the beginning of the flight;
(2) The flight crew consists of at least two pilots and a flight engineer; and
(3) The certificate holder uses, in conducting the operation, an air/ground communication service that is independent of systems operated by the United States, and a dispatch organization, both of which are approved by the Administrator as adequate to serve the terminal points concerned.

[Docket No. 6258, 29 FR 19218, Dec. 31, 1964; as amended by Amdt. 121–253, 61 FR 2613, Jan. 26, 1996]

§121.505 Flight time limitations: Two pilot crews: airplanes.

(a) If a certificate holder conducting supplemental operations schedules a pilot to fly more than eight hours during any 24 consecutive hours, it shall give him an intervening rest period at or before the end of eight scheduled hours of flight duty. This rest period must be at least twice the number of hours flown since the preceding rest period, but not less than eight hours. The certificate holder conducting supplemental operations shall relieve that pilot of all duty with it during that rest period.

(b) No pilot of an airplane that has a crew of two pilots may be on duty for more than 16 hours during any 24 consecutive hours.

[Docket No. 6258, 29 FR 19218, Dec. 31, 1964; as amended by Amdt. 121–253, 61 FR 2613, Jan. 26, 1996]

§121.507 Flight time limitations: Three pilot crews: Airplanes.

(a) No certificate holder conducting supplemental operations may schedule a pilot—

(1) For flight deck duty in an airplane that has a crew of three pilots for more than eight hours in any 24 consecutive hours; or

(2) To be aloft in an airplane that has a crew of three pilot for more than 12 hours in any 24 consecutive hours.

(b) No pilot of an airplane that has a crew of three pilots may be on duty for more than 18 hours in any 24 consecutive hours.

[Docket No. 6258, 29 FR 19218, Dec. 31, 1964; as amended by Amdt. 121–253, 61 FR 2613, Jan. 26, 1996]

§121.509 Flight time limitations: Four pilot crews: airplanes.

(a) No certificate holder conducting supplemental operations may schedule a pilot—

(1) For flight deck duty in an airplane that has a crew of four pilots for more than eight hours in any 24 consecutive hours; or

(2) To be aloft in an airplane that has a crew of four pilots for more than 16 hours in any 24 consecutive hours.

(b) No pilot of an airplane that has a crew of four pilots may be on duty for more than 20 hours in any 24 consecutive hours.

[Docket No. 6258, 29 FR 19218, Dec. 31, 1964; as amended by Amdt. 121–253, 61 FR 2613, Jan. 26, 1996]

§121.511 Flight time limitations: Flight engineers: airplanes.

(a) In any operation in which one flight engineer is serving the flight time limitations in §§121.503 and 121.505 apply to that flight engineer.

(b) In any operation in which more than one flight engineer is serving and the flight crew contains more than two pilots the flight time limitations in §121.509 apply in place of those in §121.505.

§121.513 Flight time limitations: Overseas and international operations: airplanes.

In place of the flight time limitations in §§121.503 through 121.511, a certificate holder conducting supplemental operations may elect to comply with the flight time limitations of §§121.515 and 121.521 through 121.525 for operations conducted—

(a) Between a place in the 48 contiguous States and the District of Columbia, or Alaska, and any place outside thereof;

(b) Between any two places outside the 48 contiguous States, the District of Columbia, and Alaska; or

(c) Between two places within the State of Alaska or the State of Hawaii.

[Docket No. 6258, 29 FR 19218, Dec. 31, 1964; as amended by Amdt. 121–253, 61 FR 2613, Jan. 26, 1996]

§121.515 Flight time limitations: All airmen: airplanes.

No airman may be aloft as a flight crewmember more than 1,000 hours in any 12-calendar-month period.

§121.517 Flight time limitations: Other commercial flying: airplanes.

No airman who is employed by a certificate holder conducting supplemental operations may do any other commercial flying, if that commercial flying plus his flying in operations under this part will exceed any flight time limitation in this part.

[Docket No. 28154, 61 FR 2613, Jan. 26, 1996]

§121.519 Flight time limitations: Deadhead transportation: Airplanes.

Time spent by an airman in deadhead transportation to or from a duty assignment is not considered to be part of any rest period.

§121.521 Flight time limitations: Crew of two pilots and one additional airman as required.

(a) No certificate holder conducting supplemental operations may schedule an airman to be aloft as a member of the flight crew in an airplane that has a crew of two pilots and at least one additional flight crewmember for more than 12 hours during any 24 consecutive hours.

(b) If an airman has been aloft as a member of a flight crew for 20 or more hours during any 48 consecutive hours or 24 or more hours during any 72 consecutive hours, he must be given at least 18 hours of rest before being assigned to any duty with the certificate holder. In any case, he must be relieved of all duty for at least 24 consecutive hours during any seven consecutive days.

(c) No airman may be aloft as a flight crewmember more than—

(1) 120 hours during any 30 consecutive days; or

(2) 300 hours during any 90 consecutive days.

[Docket No. 6258, 29 FR 19218, Dec. 31, 1964; as amended by Amdt. 121–17, 31 FR 1147, Jan. 28, 1966; Amdt. 121–253, 61 FR 2613, Jan. 26, 1996]

§121.523 Flight time limitations: Crew of three or more pilots and additional airmen as required.

(a) No certificate holder conducting supplemental operations may schedule an airman for flight deck duty as a flight engineer, or navigator in a crew of three or more pilots and additional airmen for a total of more than 12 hours during any 24 consecutive hours.

(b) Each certificate holder conducting supplemental operations shall schedule its flight hours to provide adequate rest periods on the ground for each airman who is away from his principal operations base. It shall also provide adequate sleeping quarters on the airplane whenever an airman is scheduled to be aloft as a flight crewmember for more than 12 hours during any 24 consecutive hours.

(c) No certificate holder conducting supplemental operations may schedule any flight crewmember to be on continuous duty for more than 30 hours. Such a crewmember is considered to be on continuous duty from the time he reports for duty until the time he is released from duty for a rest period of at least 10 hours on the ground. If a flight crewmember is on continuous duty for more than 24 hours (whether scheduled or not) duty any scheduled duty period, he must be given at least 16 hours for rest on the ground after completing the last flight scheduled for that scheduled duty period before being assigned any further flight duty.

(d) If a flight crewmember is required to engage in deadhead transportation for more than four hours before beginning flight duty, one half of the time spent in deadhead transportation must be treated as duty time for the purpose of complying with duty time limitations, unless he is given at least 10 hours of rest on the ground before being assigned to flight duty.

(e) Each certificate holder conducting supplemental operations shall give each airman, upon return to his operations base from any flight or series of flights, a rest period that is at least twice the total number of hours he was aloft as a flight crewmember since the last rest period at his base, before assigning him to any further duty. If the required rest period is more than seven days, that part of the rest period that is more than seven days may be given at any time before the pilot is again scheduled for flight duty.

(f) No airman may be aloft as a flight crewmember for more than 350 hours in any 90 consecutive days.

[Docket No. 6258, 29 FR 19218, Dec. 31, 1964; as amended by Amdt. 121–253, 61 FR 2613, Jan. 26, 1996]

§121.525 Flight time limitations: Pilots serving in more than one kind of flight crew.

(a) This section applies to each pilot assigned during any 30 consecutive days to more than one type of flight crew.

(b) The flight time limitations for a pilot who is scheduled for duty aloft for more than 20 hours in two-pilot crews in 30 consecutive days, or whose assignment in such a crew is interrupted more than once in any 30 consecutive days by assignment to a crew of two or more pilots and an additional flight crewmember, are those listed in §§121.503 through 121.509, as appropriate.

(c) Except for a pilot covered by paragraph (b) of this section, the flight time limitations for a pilot scheduled for duty aloft for more than 20 hours in two-pilot and additional flight crewmember crews in 30 consecutive days or whose assignment in such a crew is interrupted more than once in any 30 consecutive days by assignment to a crew consisting of three pilots and an additional flight crewmember, are those set forth in §121.521.

(d) The flight time limitations for a pilot to whom paragraphs (b) and (c) of this section do not apply, and who is scheduled for duty aloft for a total of not more than 20 hours within 30 consecutive days in two-pilot crews (with or without additional flight crewmembers) are those set forth in §121.523.

(e) The flight time limitations for a pilot assigned to each of two-pilot, two-pilot and additional flight crewmember, and three-pilot and additional flight crewmember crews in 30 consecutive days, and who is not subject to paragraph (b), (c), or (d) of this section, are those listed in §121.523.

§121.527 Fatigue risk management system.

(a) No certificate holder may exceed any provision of this subpart unless approved by the FAA under a Fatigue Risk Management System.

(b) The Fatigue Risk Management System must include:

(1) A fatigue risk management policy.
(2) An education and awareness training program.
(3) A fatigue reporting system.
(4) A system for monitoring flightcrew fatigue.
(5) An incident reporting process.
(6) A performance evaluation.

[Docket No. FAA–2009–1093, 77 FR 403, Jan. 4, 2012; Amdt. 121–357A, 77 FR 28764, May 16, 2012]

Subpart T— Flight Operations

Source: Docket No. 6258, 29 FR 19219, December 31, 1964, unless otherwise noted.

§121.531 Applicability.

This subpart prescribes requirements for flight operations applicable to all certificate holders, except where otherwise specified.

§121.533 Responsibility for operational control: Domestic operations.

(a) Each certificate holder conducting domestic operations is responsible for operational control.

(b) The pilot in command and the aircraft dispatcher are jointly responsible for the preflight planning, delay, and dispatch release of a flight in compliance with this chapter and operations specifications.

(c) The aircraft dispatcher is responsible for—

(1) Monitoring the progress of each flight;

(2) Issuing necessary information for the safety of the flight; and

(3) Canceling or redispatching a flight if, in his opinion or the opinion of the pilot in command, the flight cannot operate or continue to operate safely as planned or released.

(d) Each pilot in command of an aircraft is, during flight time, in command of the aircraft and crew and is responsible for the safety of the passengers, crewmembers, cargo, and airplane.

(e) Each pilot in command has full control and authority in the operation of the aircraft, without limitation, over other crewmembers and their duties during flight time, whether or not he holds valid certificates authorizing him to perform the duties of those crewmembers.

[Docket No. 6258, 29 FR 19219, Dec. 31, 1964; as amended by Amdt. 121–253, 61 FR 2613, Jan. 26, 1996]

§121.535 Responsibility for operational control: Flag operations.

(a) Each certificate holder conducting flag operations is responsible for operational control.

(b) The pilot in command and the aircraft dispatcher are jointly responsible for the preflight planning, delay, and dispatch release of a flight in compliance with this chapter and operations specifications.

(c) The aircraft dispatcher is responsible for—

(1) Monitoring the progress of each flight;

(2) Issuing necessary instructions and information for the safety of the flight; and

(3) Canceling or redispatching a flight if, in his opinion or the opinion of the pilot in command, the flight cannot operate or continue to operate safely as planned or released.

(d) Each pilot in command of an aircraft is, during flight time, in command of the aircraft and crew and is responsible for the safety of the passengers, crewmembers, cargo, and airplane.

(e) Each pilot in command has full control and authority in the operation of the aircraft, without limitation, over other crewmembers and their duties during flight time, whether or not he holds valid certificates authorizing him to perform the duties of those crewmembers.

(f) No pilot may operate an aircraft in a careless or reckless manner so as to endanger life or property.

[Docket No. 6258, 29 FR 19219, Dec. 31, 1964; as amended by Amdt. 121–253, 61 FR 2613, Jan. 26, 1996]

§121.537 Responsibility for operational control: Supplemental operations.

(a) Each certificate holder conducting supplemental operations—

(1) Is responsible for operational control; and

(2) Shall list each person authorized by it to exercise operational control in its operator's manual.

(b) The pilot in command and the director of operations are jointly responsible for the initiation, continuation, diversion, and termination of a flight in compliance with this chapter and the operations specifications. The director of operations may delegate the functions for the initiation, continuation, diversion, and termination of a flight but he may not delegate the responsibility for those functions.

(c) The director of operations is responsible for canceling, diverting, or delaying a flight if in his opinion or the opinion of the pilot in command the flight cannot operate or continue to operate safely as planned or released. The director of operations is responsible for assuring that each flight is monitored with respect to at least the following:

(1) Departure of the flight from the place of origin and arrival at the place of destination, including intermediate stops and any diversions therefrom.

(2) Maintenance and mechanical delays encountered at places of origin and destination and intermediate stops.

(3) Any known conditions that may adversely affect the safety of flight.

(d) Each pilot in command of an aircraft is, during flight time, in command of the aircraft and crew and is responsible for the safety of the passengers, crewmembers, cargo, and aircraft. The pilot in command has full control and authority in the operation of the aircraft, without limitation, over other crewmembers and their duties during flight time, whether or not he holds valid certificates authorizing him to perform the duties of those crewmembers.

(e) Each pilot in command of an aircraft is responsible for the preflight planning and the operation of the flight in compliance with this chapter and the operations specifications.

(f) No pilot may operate an aircraft, in a careless or reckless manner, so as to endanger life or property.

[Docket No. 6258, 29 FR 19219, Dec. 31, 1964; as amended by Amdt. 121–253, 61 FR 2613, Jan. 26, 1996]

§121.538 Aircraft security.

Certificate holders conducting operations under this part must comply with the applicable security requirements in 49 CFR chapter XII.

[Docket No. TSA–2002–11602, 67 FR 8350, Feb. 22, 2002]

§121.539 Operations notices.

Each certificate holder shall notify its appropriate operations personnel of each change in equipment and operating procedures, including each known change in the use of navigation aids, airports, air traffic control procedures and regulations, local airport traffic control rules, and known hazards to flight, including icing and other potentially hazardous meteorological conditions and irregularities in ground and navigation facilities.

§121.541 Operations schedules: Domestic and flag operations.

In establishing flight operations schedules, each certificate holder conducting domestic or flag operations shall allow enough time for the proper servicing of aircraft at intermediate stops, and shall consider the prevailing winds en route and the cruising speed of the type of aircraft used. This cruising speed may not be more than that resulting from the specified cruising output of the engines.

[Docket No. 28154, 61 FR 2613, Jan. 26, 1996]

§121.542 Flight crewmember duties.

(a) No certificate holder shall require, nor may any flight crewmember perform, any duties during a critical phase of flight except those duties required for the safe operation of the aircraft. Duties such as company required calls made for such nonsafety related purposes as ordering galley supplies and confirming passenger connections, announcements made to passengers promoting the air carrier or pointing out sights of interest, and filling out company payroll and related records are not required for the safe operation of the aircraft.

(b) No flight crewmember may engage in, nor may any pilot in command permit, any activity during a critical phase of flight which could distract any flight crewmember from the performance of his or her duties or which could interfere in any way with the proper conduct of those duties. Activities such as eating meals, engaging in nonessential conversations within the cockpit and nonessential communications between the cabin and cockpit crews, and reading publications not related to the proper conduct of the flight are not required for the safe operation of the aircraft.

(c) For the purposes of this section, critical phases of flight includes all ground operations involving taxi, takeoff and landing, and all other flight operations conducted below 10,000 feet, except cruise flight.

Note: Taxi is defined as "movement of an airplane under its own power on the surface of an airport."

(d) During all flight time as defined in 14 CFR §1.1, no flight crewmember may use, nor may any pilot in command permit the use of, a personal wireless communications device (as defined in 49 U.S.C. 44732(d)) or laptop computer while at a flight crewmember duty station unless the purpose is directly related to operation of the aircraft, or for emergency, safety-related, or employment-related communications, in accordance with air carrier procedures approved by the Administrator.

[Docket No. 20661, 46 FR 5502, Jan. 19, 1981; as amended by Amdt. 121–369, 79 FR 8263, Feb. 12, 2014]

§121.543 Flight crewmembers at controls.

(a) Except as provided in paragraph (b) of this section, each required flight crewmember on flight deck duty must remain at the assigned duty station with seat belt fastened while the aircraft is taking off or landing, and while it is en route.

(b) A required flight crewmember may leave the assigned duty station—

(1) If the crewmember's absence is necessary for the performance of duties in connection with the operation of the aircraft;

(2) If the crewmember's absence is in connection with physiological needs; or

(3) If the crewmember is taking a rest period, and relief is provided—

(i) In the case of the assigned pilot in command during the en route cruise portion of the flight, by a pilot who holds an airline transport pilot certificate not subject to the limitations in §61.167 of this chapter and an appropriate type rating, is currently qualified as pilot in command or second in command, and is qualified as pilot in command of that aircraft during the en route cruise portion of the flight. A second in command qualified to act as a pilot in command en route need not have completed the following pilot in command requirements: The 6-month recurrent flight training required by §121.433(c)(1)(iii); the operating experience required by §121.434; the

§121.544

takeoffs and landings required by §121.439; the line check required by §121.440; and the 6-month proficiency check or simulator training required by §121.441(a)(1); and

(ii) In the case of the assigned second in command, by a pilot qualified to act as second in command of that aircraft during en route operations. However, the relief pilot need not meet the recent experience requirements of §121.439(b).

[Docket No. 16383, 43 FR 22648, May 25, 1978; as amended by Amdt. 121–179, 47 FR 33390, Aug. 2, 1982; Amdt. 121–365, 78 FR 42378, July 15, 2013]

§121.544 Pilot monitoring.

Each pilot who is seated at the pilot controls of the aircraft, while not flying the aircraft, must accomplish pilot monitoring duties as appropriate in accordance with the certificate holder's procedures contained in the manual required by §121.133 of this part. Compliance with this section is required no later than March 12, 2019.

[Docket No. FAA–2008–0677, 78 FR 67841, Nov. 12, 2013

§121.545 Manipulation of controls.

No pilot in command may allow any person to manipulate the controls of an aircraft during flight nor may any person manipulate the controls during flight unless that person is—

(a) A qualified pilot of the certificate holder operating that aircraft.

(b) An authorized pilot safety representative of the Administrator or of the National Transportation Safety Board who has the permission of the pilot in command, is qualified in the aircraft, and is checking flight operations; or

(c) A pilot of another certificate holder who has the permission of the pilot in command, is qualified in the aircraft, and is authorized by the certificate holder operating the aircraft.

[Docket No. 6258, 29 FR 19220, Dec. 31, 1964; as amended by Docket No. 8084, 32 FR 5769, April 11, 1967; Amdt. 121–144, 43 FR 22648, May 25, 1978]

§121.547 Admission to flight deck.

(a) No person may admit any person to the flight deck of an aircraft unless the person being admitted is—

(1) A crewmember;

(2) An FAA air carrier inspector, a DOD commercial air carrier evaluator, or an authorized representative of the National Transportation Safety Board, who is performing official duties;

(3) Any person who—

(i) Has permission of the pilot in command, an appropriate management official of the part 119 certificate holder, and the Administrator; and

(ii) Is an employee of—

(A) The United States, or

(B) A part 119 certificate holder and whose duties are such that admission to the flightdeck is necessary or advantageous for safe operation; or

(C) An aeronautical enterprise certificated by the Administrator and whose duties are such that admission to the flightdeck is necessary or advantageous for safe operation.

(4) Any person who has the permission of the pilot in command, an appropriate management official of the part 119 certificate holder and the Administrator. Paragraph (a)(2) of this section does not limit the emergency authority of the pilot in command to exclude any person from the flightdeck in the interests of safety.

(b) For the purposes of paragraph (a)(3) of this section, employees of the United States who deal responsibly with matters relating to safety and employees of the certificate holder whose efficiency would be increased by familiarity with flight conditions, may be admitted by the certificate holder. However, the certificate holder may not admit employees of traffic, sales, or other departments that are not directly related to flight operations, unless they are eligible under paragraph (a)(4) of this section.

(c) No person may admit any person to the flight deck unless there is a seat available for his use in the passenger compartment, except—

(1) An FAA air carrier inspector, a DOD commercial air carrier evaluator, or an authorized representative of the Administrator or National Transportation Safety Board who is checking or observing flight operations;

(2) An air traffic controller who is authorized by the Administrator to observe ATC procedures;

(3) A certificated airman employed by the certificate holder whose duties require an airman certificate;

(4) A certificated airman employed by another part 119 certificate holder whose duties with that part 119 certificate holder require an airman certificate and who is authorized by the part 119 certificate holder operating the aircraft to make specific trips over a route;

(5) An employee of the part 119 certificate holder operating the aircraft whose duty is directly related to the conduct or planning of flight operations or the in-flight monitoring of aircraft equipment or operating procedures, if his presence on the flightdeck is necessary to perform his duties and he has been authorized in writing by a responsible supervisor, listed in the Operations Manual as having that authority; and

(6) A technical representative of the manufacturer of the aircraft or its components whose duties are directly related to the in-flight monitoring of aircraft equipment or operating procedures, if his presence on the flightdeck is necessary to perform his duties and he has been authorized in writing by the Administrator and by a responsible

supervisor of the operations department of the part 119 certificate holder, listed in the Operations Manual as having that authority.

[Docket No. 6258, 29 FR 19220, Dec. 31, 1964; as amended by Docket No. 8084, 32 FR 5769, April 11, 1967; Amdt. 121–253, 61 FR 2613, Jan. 26, 1996; Amdt. 121–288, 67 FR 2127, Jan. 15, 2002; Amdt. 121–298, 68 FR 41217, July 10, 2003]

§121.548 Aviation safety inspector's credentials: Admission to pilot's compartment.

Whenever, in performing the duties of conducting an inspection, an inspector of the Federal Aviation Administration presents form FAA 110A, "Aviation Safety Inspector's Credential," to the pilot in command of an aircraft operated by a certificate holder, the inspector must be given free and uninterrupted access to the pilot's compartment of that aircraft.

[Docket No. 28154, 61 FR 3613, Jan. 26, 1996]

§121.548a DOD Commercial Air Carrier Evaluator's Credential.

Whenever, in performing the duties of conducting an evaluation, a DOD commercial air carrier evaluator presents S&A Form 110B, "DOD Commercial Air Carrier Evaluator's Credential," to the pilot in command of an airplane operated by the certificate holder, the evaluator must be given free and uninterrupted access to the pilot's compartment of that airplane.

[Docket No. FAA–2003–15571, 68 FR 41217, July 10, 2003]

§121.549 Flying equipment.

(a) The pilot in command shall ensure that appropriate aeronautical charts containing adequate information concerning navigation aids and instrument approach procedures are aboard the aircraft for each flight.

(b) Each crewmember shall, on each flight, have readily available for his use a flashlight that is in good working order.

§121.550 Secret Service Agents: Admission to flight deck.

Whenever an Agent of the Secret Service who is assigned the duty of protecting a person aboard an aircraft operated by a certificate holder considers it necessary in the performance of his duty to ride on the flight deck of the aircraft, he must, upon request and presentation of his Secret Service credentials to the pilot in command of the aircraft, be admitted to the flight deck and permitted to occupy an observer seat thereon.

[Docket No. 9031, 35 FR 12061, July 28, 1970; as amended by Amdt. 121–253, 61 FR 2613, Jan. 26, 1996]

§121.551 Restriction or suspension of operation: Domestic and flag operations.

When a certificate holder conducting domestic or flag operations knows of conditions, including airport and runway conditions, that are a hazard to safe operations, it shall restrict or suspend operations until those conditions are corrected.

[Docket No. 28154, 61 FR 2613, Jan. 26, 1996]

§121.553 Restriction or suspension of operation: Supplemental operations.

When a certificate holder conducting supplemental operations or pilot in command knows of conditions, including airport and runway conditions, that are a hazard to safe operations, the certificate holder or pilot in command, as the case may be, shall restrict or suspend operations until those conditions are corrected.

[Docket No. 28154, 61 FR 2613, Jan. 26, 1996]

§121.555 Compliance with approved routes and limitations: Domestic and flag operations.

No pilot may operate an airplane in scheduled air transportation—

(a) Over any route or route segment unless it is specified in the certificate holder's operations specifications; or

(b) Other than in accordance with the limitations in the operations specifications.

[Docket No. 6258, 29 FR 19219, Dec. 31, 1964; as amended by Amdt. 121–253, 61 FR 2614, Jan. 26, 1996]

§121.557 Emergencies: Domestic and flag operations.

(a) In an emergency situation that requires immediate decision and action the pilot in command may take any action that he considers necessary under the circumstances. In such a case he may deviate from prescribed operations procedures and methods, weather minimums, and this chapter, to the extent required in the interests of safety.

(b) In an emergency situation arising during flight that requires immediate decision and action by an aircraft dispatcher, and that is known to him, the aircraft dispatcher shall advise the pilot in command of the emergency, shall ascertain the decision of the pilot in command, and shall have the decision recorded. If the aircraft dispatcher cannot communicate with the pilot, he shall declare an emergency and take any action that he considers necessary under the circumstances.

(c) Whenever a pilot in command or dispatcher exercises emergency authority, he shall keep the appropriate ATC facility and dispatch centers fully informed of the progress of the flight. The person declaring the emergency shall send a written report of any deviation through the certificate holder's operations manager, to the Administrator. A dispatcher shall send his report within 10 days after the date of the emergency, and a pilot in command shall send his report within 10 days after returning to his home base.

[Docket No. 6258, 29 FR 19219, Dec. 31, 1964; as amended by Amdt. 121–253, 61 FR 2614, Jan. 26, 1996]

§121.559 Emergencies: Supplemental operations.

(a) In an emergency situation that requires immediate decision and action, the pilot in command may take any action that he considers necessary under the circumstances. In such a case, he may deviate from prescribed operations, procedures and methods, weather minimums, and this chapter, to the extent required in the interests of safety.

(b) In an emergency situation arising during flight that requires immediate decision and action by appropriate management personnel in the case of operations conducted with a flight following service and which is known to them, those personnel shall advise the pilot in command of the emergency, shall ascertain the decision of the pilot in command, and shall have the decision recorded. If they cannot communicate with the pilot, they shall declare an emergency and take any action that they consider necessary under the circumstances.

(c) Whenever emergency authority is exercised, the pilot in command or the appropriate management personnel shall keep the appropriate communication facility fully informed of the progress of the flight. The person declaring the emergency shall send a written report of any deviation, through the certificate holder's director of operations, to the Administrator within 10 days after the flight is completed or, in the case of operations outside the United States, upon return to the home base.

[Docket No. 6258, 29 FR 19219, Dec. 31, 1964; as amended by Amdt. 121–253, 61 FR 2614, Jan. 26, 1996; Amdt. 121–333, 72 FR 31682, June 7, 2007]

§121.561 Reporting potentially hazardous meteorological conditions and irregularities of ground facilities or navigation aids.

(a) Whenever he encounters a meteorological condition or an irregularity in a ground facility or navigation aid, in flight, the knowledge of which he considers essential to the safety of other flights, the pilot in command shall notify an appropriate ground station as soon as practicable.

(b) The ground radio station that is notified under paragraph (a) of this section shall report the information to the agency directly responsible for operating the facility.

[Docket No. 17897, 45 FR 41594, June 19, 1980; as amended by Amdt. 121–333, 72 FR 31682, June 7, 2007]

§121.563 Reporting mechanical irregularities.

The pilot in command shall ensure that all mechanical irregularities occurring during flight time are entered in the maintenance log of the airplane at the end of that flight time. Before each flight the pilot in command shall ascertain the status of each irregularity entered in the log at the end of the preceding flight.

[Docket No. 17897, 45 FR 41594, June 19, 1980; as amended by Amdt. 121–179, 47 FR 33390, Aug. 2, 1982]

§121.565 Engine inoperative: Landing; reporting.

(a) Except as provided in paragraph (b) of this section, whenever an airplane engine fails or whenever an engine is shutdown to prevent possible damage, the pilot in command must land the airplane at the nearest suitable airport, in point of time, at which a safe landing can be made.

(b) If not more than one engine of an airplane that has three or more engines fails or is shut down to prevent possible damage, the pilot-in-command may proceed to an airport that the pilot selects if, after considering the following, the pilot makes a reasonable decision that proceeding to that airport is as safe as landing at the nearest suitable airport:

(1) The nature of the malfunction and the possible mechanical difficulties that may occur if flight is continued.

(2) The altitude, weight, and useable fuel at the time that the engine is shutdown.

(3) The weather conditions en route and at possible landing points.

(4) The air traffic congestion.

(5) The kind of terrain.

(6) His familiarity with the airport to be used.

(c) The pilot-in-command must report each engine shutdown in flight to the appropriate communication facility as soon as practicable and must keep that facility fully informed of the progress of the flight.

(d) If the pilot in command lands at an airport other than the nearest suitable airport, in point of time, he or she shall (upon completing the trip) send a written report, in duplicate, to his or her director of operations stating the reasons for determining that the selection of an airport, other than the nearest airport, was as safe a course of action as landing at the nearest suitable airport. The director of operations shall, within 10 days after the pilot returns to his or her home base, send a copy of this report with the director of operation's comments to the certificate-holding district office.

[Docket No. 6258, 29 FR 19219, Dec. 31, 1964; as amended by Amdt. 121–207, 54 FR 39293, Sept. 25, 1989; Amdt. 121–253, 61 FR 2614, Jan. 26, 1996; Amdt. 121–329, 72 FR 1881, Jan. 16, 2007; Amdt. 121–333, 72 FR 31682, June 7, 2007]

§121.567 Instrument approach procedures and IFR landing minimums.

No person may make an instrument approach at an airport except in accordance with IFR weather minimums and instrument approach procedures set forth in the certificate holder's operations specifications.

§121.569 Equipment interchange: Domestic and flag operations.

(a) Before operating under an interchange agreement, each certificate holder conducting domestic or flag operations shall show that—

(1) The procedures for the interchange operation conform with this chapter and with safe operating practices;

(2) Required crewmembers and dispatchers meet approved training requirements for the airplanes and equipment to be used and are familiar with the communications and dispatch procedures to be used;

(3) Maintenance personnel meet training requirements for the airplanes and equipment, and are familiar with the maintenance procedures to be used;

(4) Flight crewmembers and dispatchers meet appropriate route and airport qualifications; and

(5) The airplanes to be operated are essentially similar to the airplanes of the certificate holder with whom the interchange is effected with respect to the arrangement of flight instruments and the arrangement and motion of controls that are critical to safety unless the Administrator determines that the certificate holder has adequate training programs to insure that any potentially hazardous dissimilarities are safely overcome by flight crew familiarization.

(b) Each certificate holder conducting domestic or flag operations shall include the pertinent provisions and procedures involved in the equipment interchange agreement in its manuals.

[Docket No. 6258, 29 FR 19219, Dec. 31, 1964; as amended by Amdt. 121–253, 61 FR 2614, Jan. 26, 1996]

§121.570 Airplane evacuation capability.

(a) No person may cause an airplane carrying passengers to be moved on the surface, take off or land unless each automatically deployable emergency evacuation assisting means installed pursuant to §121.310(a), is ready for evacuation.

(b) Each certificate holder shall ensure that, at all times passengers are on board prior to airplane movement on the surface, at least one floor-level exit provides for the egress of passengers through normal or emergency means.

[Docket No. 26142, 57 FR 42674, Sept. 15, 1992]

§121.571 Briefing passengers before takeoff.

(a) Each certificate holder operating a passenger-carrying airplane shall insure that all passengers are orally briefed by the appropriate crewmember as follows:

(1) Before each takeoff, on each of the following:

(i) *Smoking.* Each passenger shall be briefed on when, where, and under what conditions smoking is prohibited (including, but not limited to, any applicable requirements of part 252 of this title). This briefing shall include a statement that the Federal Aviation Regulations require passenger compliance with the lighted passenger information signs, posted placards, areas designated for safety purposes as no smoking areas, and crewmember instructions with regard to these items. The briefing shall also include a statement that Federal law prohibits tampering with, disabling, or destroying any smoke detector in an airplane lavatory; smoking in lavatories; and, when applicable, smoking in passenger compartments.

(ii) The location of emergency exits.

(iii) The use of safety belts, including instructions on how to fasten and unfasten the safety belts. Each passenger shall be briefed on when, where, and under what conditions the safety belt must be fastened about that passenger. This briefing shall include a statement that the Federal Aviation Regulations require passenger compliance with lighted passenger information signs and crewmember instructions concerning the use of safety belts.

(iv) The location and use of any required emergency flotation means.

(v) On operations that do not use a flight attendant, the following additional information:

(A) The placement of seat backs in an upright position before takeoff and landing.

(B) Location of survival equipment.

(C) If the flight involves operations above 12,000 MSL, the normal and emergency use of oxygen.

(D) Location and operation of fire extinguisher.

(2) After each takeoff, immediately before or immediately after turning the seat belt sign off, an announcement shall be made that passengers should keep their seat belts fastened, while seated, even when the seat belt sign is off.

(3) Except as provided in paragraph (a)(4) of this section, before each takeoff a required crewmember assigned to the flight shall conduct an individual briefing of each person who may need the assistance of another person to move expeditiously to an exit in the event of an emergency. In the briefing the required crewmember shall—

(i) Brief the person and his attendant, if any, on the routes to each appropriate exit and on the most appropriate time to begin moving to an exit in the event of an emergency; and

(ii) Inquire of the person and his attendant, if any, as to the most appropriate manner of assisting the person so as to prevent pain and further injury.

(4) The requirements of paragraph (a)(3) of this section do not apply to a person who has been given a briefing before a previous leg of a flight in the same aircraft when the crewmembers on duty have been advised as to the most appropriate manner of assisting the person so as to prevent pain and further injury.

(b) Each certificate holder must carry on each passenger-carrying airplane, in convenient locations for use of each passenger, printed cards supplementing the oral briefing. Each card must contain information pertinent only to the type and model of airplane used for that flight, including—

(1) Diagrams of, and methods of operating, the emergency exits;

(2) Other instructions necessary for use of emergency equipment; and

(3) No later than June 12, 2005, for Domestic and Flag scheduled passenger-carrying flights, the sentence, "Final assembly of this airplane was completed in [INSERT NAME OF COUNTRY]."

(c) The certificate holder shall describe in its manual the procedure to be followed in the briefing required by paragraph (a) of this section.

[Docket No. 2033, 30 FR 3206, March 9, 1965; as amended by Amdt. 121–30, 32 FR 13268, Sept. 20, 1967; Amdt. 121–84, 37 FR 3975, Feb. 24, 1972; Amdt. 121–133, 42 FR 18394, April 7, 1977; Amdt. 121–144, 43 FR 22648, May 25, 1978; Amdt. 121–146, 43 FR 28403, June 29, 1978; Amdt. 121–196, 53 FR 12362, April 13, 1988; Amdt. 121–230, 57 FR 42674, Sept. 15, 1992; Amdt. 121–251, 60 FR 65935, Dec. 20, 1995; Amdt. 121–312, 69 FR 39294, June 29, 2004; Amdt. 121–312, 70 FR 36020, June 22, 2005]

§121.573 Briefing passengers: Extended overwater operations.

(a) In addition to the oral briefing required by §121.571(a), each certificate holder operating an airplane in extended overwater operations shall ensure that all passengers are orally briefed by the appropriate crewmember on the location and operation of life preservers, liferafts, and other flotation means, including a demonstration of the method of donning and inflating a life preserver.

(b) The certificate holder shall describe in its manual the procedure to be followed in the briefing required by paragraph (a) of this section.

(c) If the airplane proceeds directly over water after takeoff, the briefing required by paragraph (a) of this section must be done before takeoff.

(d) If the airplane does not proceed directly over water after takeoff, no part of the briefing required by paragraph (a) of this section has to be given before takeoff, but the entire briefing must be given before reaching the overwater part of the flight.

[Docket No. 2033, 30 FR 3206, March 9, 1965; as amended by Amdt. 121–144, 43 FR 22648, May 25, 1978; Amdt. 121–146, 43 FR 28403, June 29, 1978]

§121.574 Oxygen for medical use by passengers.

(a) A certificate holder may allow a passenger to carry and operate equipment for the storage, generation, or dispensing of oxygen when the following conditions are met:

(1) The equipment is—

(i) Furnished by the certificate holder;

(ii) Of an approved type or is in conformity with the manufacturing, packaging, marking, labeling, and maintenance requirements of 49 CFR parts 171, 172, and 173, except §173.24(a)(1);

(iii) Maintained by the certificate holder in accordance with an approved maintenance program;

(iv) Free of flammable contaminants on all exterior surfaces;

(v) Capable of providing a minimum mass flow of oxygen to the user of four liters per minute;

(vi) Constructed so that all valves, fittings, and gauges are protected from damage; and

(vii) Appropriately secured.

(2) When the oxygen is stored in the form of a liquid, the equipment has been under the certificate holder's approved maintenance program since its purchase new or since the storage container was last purged.

(3) When the oxygen is stored in the form of a compressed gas as defined in 49 CFR 173.300(a)—

(i) The equipment has been under the certificate holder's approved maintenance program since its purchase new or since the last hydrostatic test of the storage cylinder; and

(ii) The pressure in any oxygen cylinder does not exceed the rated cylinder pressure.

(4) Each person using the equipment has a medical need to use it evidenced by a written statement to be kept in that person's possession, signed by a licensed physician which specifies the maximum quantity of oxygen needed each hour and the maximum flow rate needed for the pressure altitude corresponding to the pressure in

the cabin of the airplane under normal operating conditions. This paragraph does not apply to the carriage of oxygen in an airplane in which the only passengers carried are persons who may have a medical need for oxygen during flight, no more than one relative or other interested person for each of those persons, and medical attendants.

(5) When a physician's statement is required by paragraph (a)(4) of this section, the total quantity of oxygen carried is equal to the maximum quantity of oxygen needed each hour, as specified in the physician's statement, multiplied by the number of hours used to compute the amount of airplane fuel required by this part.

(6) The pilot in command is advised when the equipment is on board, and when it is intended to be used.

(7) The equipment is stowed, and each person using the equipment is seated, so as not to restrict access to or use of any required emergency, or regular exit or of the aisle in the passenger compartment.

(b) No person may, and no certificate holder may allow any person to, smoke within 10 feet of oxygen storage and dispensing equipment carried in accordance with paragraph (a) of this section.

(c) No certificate holder may allow any person to connect or disconnect oxygen dispensing equipment, to or from a gaseous oxygen cylinder while any passenger is aboard the airplane.

(d) The requirements of this section do not apply to the carriage of supplemental or first-aid oxygen and related equipment required by this chapter.

[Docket No. 12169, 39 FR 42677, Dec. 6, 1974; as amended by Amdt. 121–159, 45 FR 41594, June 19, 1980]

§121.575 Alcoholic beverages.

(a) No person may drink any alcoholic beverage aboard an aircraft unless the certificate holder operating the aircraft has served that beverage to him.

(b) No certificate holder may serve any alcoholic beverage to any person aboard any of its aircraft who—

(1) Appears to be intoxicated;

(2) Is escorting a person or being escorted in accordance with 49 CFR 1544.221; or

(3) Has a deadly or dangerous weapon accessible to him while aboard the aircraft in accordance with 49 CFR 1544.219, 1544.221, or 1544.223.

(c) No certificate holder may allow any person to board any of its aircraft if that person appears to be intoxicated.

(d) Each certificate holder shall, within five days after the incident, report to the Administrator the refusal of any person to comply with paragraph (a) of this section, or of any disturbance caused by a person who appears to be intoxicated aboard any of its aircraft.

[Docket No. 6258, 29 FR 19219, Dec. 31, 1964; as amended by Amdt. 121–118, 40 FR 17552, April 21, 1975; Amdt. 121–178, 47 FR 13316, March 29, 1982; Amdt. 121–275, 67 FR 31932, May 10, 2002]

§121.576 Retention of items of mass in passenger and crew compartments.

The certificate holder must provide and use means to prevent each item of galley equipment and each serving cart, when not in use, and each item of crew baggage, which is carried in a passenger or crew compartment from becoming a hazard by shifting under the appropriate load factors corresponding to the emergency landing conditions under which the airplane was type certificated.

[Docket No. 16383, 43 FR 22648, May 25, 1978]

§121.577 Stowage of food, beverage, and passenger service equipment during airplane movement on the surface, takeoff, and landing.

(a) No certificate holder may move an airplane on the surface, take off or land when any food, beverage, or tableware, furnished by the certificate holder is located at any passenger seat.

(b) No certificate holder may move an airplane on the surface, take off, or land unless each food and beverage tray and seat back tray table is secured in its stowed position.

(c) No certificate holder may permit an airplane to move on the surface, takeoff, or land unless each passenger serving cart is secured in its stowed position.

(d) No certificate holder may permit an airplane to move on the surface, takeoff, or land unless each movie screen that extends into an aisle is stowed.

(e) Each passenger shall comply with instructions given by a crewmember with regard to compliance with this section.

[Docket No. 26142, 57 FR 42674, Sept. 15, 1992]

§121.578 Cabin ozone concentration.

(a) For the purpose of this section, the following definitions apply:

(1) *Flight segment* means scheduled nonstop flight time between two airports.

(2) *Sea level equivalent* refers to conditions of 25°C and 760 millimeters of mercury pressure.

(b) Except as provided in paragraphs (d) and (e) of this section, no certificate holder may operate an airplane above the following flight levels unless it is successfully demonstrated to the Administrator that the concentration of ozone inside the cabin will not exceed—

(1) For flight above flight level 320, 0.25 parts per million by volume, sea level equivalent, at any time above that flight level; and

(2) For flight above flight level 270, 0.1 parts per million by volume, sea level equivalent, time-weighted average for each flight segment that exceeds 4 hours and includes flight above that flight level. (For this purpose, the amount of ozone below flight level 180 is considered to be zero.)

(c) Compliance with this section must be shown by analysis or tests, based on either airplane operational procedures and performance limitations or the certificate holder's operations. The analysis or tests must show either of the following:

(1) Atmospheric ozone statistics indicate, with a statistical confidence of at least 84%, that at the altitudes and locations at which the airplane will be operated cabin ozone concentrations will not exceed the limits prescribed by paragraph (b) of this section.

(2) The airplane ventilation system including any ozone control equipment, will maintain cabin ozone concentrations at or below the limits prescribed by paragraph (b) of this section.

(d) A certificate holder may obtain an authorization to deviate from the requirements of paragraph (b) of this section, by an amendment to its operations specifications, if—

(1) It shows that due to circumstances beyond its control or to unreasonable economic burden it cannot comply for a specified period of time; and

(2) It has submitted a plan acceptable to the Administrator to effect compliance to the extent possible.

(e) A certificate holder need not comply with the requirements of paragraph (b) of this section for an aircraft—

(1) When the only persons carried are flight crewmembers and persons listed in §121.583;

(2) If the aircraft is scheduled for retirement before January 1, 1985; or

(3) If the aircraft is scheduled for re-engining under the provisions of Subpart E of part 91, until it is re-engined.

[Docket No. 121-154, 45 FR 3883, Jan. 21, 1980. Redesignated by Amdt. 121-162, 45 FR 46739, July 10, 1980; Amdt. 121-181, 47 FR 58489, Dec. 30, 1982; Amdt. 121-251, 60 FR 65935, Dec. 20, 1995]

§121.579 Minimum altitudes for use of autopilot.

(a) *Definitions.* For purpose of this section—

(1) Altitudes for takeoff/initial climb and go-around/missed approach are defined as above the airport elevation.

(2) Altitudes for enroute operations are defined as above terrain elevation.

(3) Altitudes for approach are defined as above the touchdown zone elevation (TDZE), unless the altitude is specifically in reference to DA (H) or MDA, in which case the altitude is defined by reference to the DA(H) or MDA itself.

(b) *Takeoff and initial climb.* No person may use an autopilot for takeoff or initial climb below the higher of 500 feet or an altitude that is no lower than twice the altitude loss specified in the Airplane Flight Manual (AFM), except as follows—

(1) At a minimum engagement altitude specified in the AFM; or

(2) At an altitude specified by the Administrator, whichever is greater.

(c) *Enroute.* No person may use an autopilot enroute, including climb and descent, below the following—

(1) 500 feet;

(2) At an altitude that is no lower than twice the altitude loss specified in the AFM for an autopilot malfunction in cruise conditions; or

(3) At an altitude specified by the Administrator, whichever is greater.

(d) *Approach.* No person may use an autopilot at an altitude lower than 50 feet below the DA(H) or MDA for the instrument procedure being flown, except as follows—

(1) For autopilots with an AFM specified altitude loss for approach operations—

(i) An altitude no lower than twice the specified altitude loss if higher than 50 feet below the MDA or DA(H);

(ii) An altitude no lower than 50 feet higher than the altitude loss specified in the AFM, when the following conditions are met—

(A) Reported weather conditions are less than the basic VFR weather conditions in §91.155 of this chapter;

(B) Suitable visual references specified in §91.175 of this chapter have been established on the instrument approach procedure; and

(C) The autopilot is coupled and receiving both lateral and vertical path references;

(iii) An altitude no lower than the higher of the altitude loss specified in the AFM or 50 feet above the TDZE, when the following conditions are met—

(A) Reported weather conditions are equal to or better than the basic VFR weather conditions in §91.155 of this chapter; and

(B) The autopilot is coupled and receiving both lateral and vertical path references; or

(iv) A greater altitude specified by the Administrator.

(2) For autopilots with AFM specified approach altitude limitations, the greater of—

(i) The minimum use altitude specified for the coupled approach mode selected;

(ii) 50 feet; or

(iii) An altitude specified by Administrator.

(3) For autopilots with an AFM specified negligible or zero altitude loss for an autopilot approach mode malfunction, the greater of—
(i) 50 feet; or
(ii) An altitude specified by Administrator.

(4) If executing an autopilot coupled go-around or missed approach using a certificated and functioning autopilot in accordance with paragraph (e) in this section.

(e) *Go-Around/Missed Approach.* No person may engage an autopilot during a go-around or missed approach below the minimum engagement altitude specified for takeoff and initial climb in paragraph (b) in this section. An autopilot minimum use altitude does not apply to a go-around/missed approach initiated with an engaged autopilot. Performing a go-around or missed approach with an engaged autopilot must not adversely affect safe obstacle clearance.

(f) *Landing.* Notwithstanding paragraph (d) of this section, autopilot minimum use altitudes do not apply to autopilot operations when an approved automatic landing system mode is being used for landing. Automatic landing systems must be authorized in an operations specification issued to the operator.

[Docket No. 6258, 29 FR 19219, Dec. 31, 1964; as amended by Amdt. 121–13, 30 FR 14781, Nov. 30, 1965; Amdt. 121–33, 32 FR 13912, Oct. 6, 1967; Amdt. 121–130, 41 FR 47229, Oct. 28, 1976; Amdt. 121–206, 54 FR 34331, Aug. 18, 1989; Amdt. 121–265, 62 FR 27922, May 21, 1997; Amdt. 121–333, 72 FR 31682, June 7, 2007; Amdt. 121–368, 79 FR 6086, Feb. 3, 2014]

§121.580 Prohibition on interference with crewmembers.

No person may assault, threaten, intimidate, or interfere with a crewmember in the performance of the crewmember's duties aboard an aircraft being operated under this part.

[Docket No. 6258, 29 FR 19219, Dec. 31, 1964; as amended by Amdt. 121–270, 64 FR 1080, Jan. 7, 1999]

§121.581 Observer's seat: En route inspections.

(a) Except as provided in paragraph (c) of this section, each certificate holder shall make available a seat on the flight deck of each airplane, used by it in air commerce, for occupancy by the Administrator while conducting en route inspections. The location and equipment of the seat, with respect to its suitability for use in conducting en route inspections, is determined by the Administrator.

(b) In each airplane that has more than one observer's seat, in addition to the seats required for the crew complement for which the airplane was certificated, the forward observer's seat or the observer's seat selected by the Administrator must be made available when complying with paragraph (a) of this section.

(c) For any airplane type certificated before December 20, 1995, for not more than 30 passengers that does not have an observer seat on the flightdeck, the certificate holder must provide a forward passenger seat with headset or speaker for occupancy by the Administrator while conducting en route inspections.

[Docket No. 6258, 29 FR 19219, Dec. 31, 1964; as amended by Amdt. 121–144, 43 FR 22648, May 25, 1978; Amdt. 121–251, 60 FR 65935, Dec. 20, 1995; Amdt. 121–288, 67 FR 2128, Jan. 15, 2002]

§121.582 Means to discreetly notify a flightcrew.

Except for all-cargo operations as defined in §110.2 of this chapter, after October 15, 2007, for all passenger-carrying airplanes that require a lockable flightdeck door in accordance with §121.313(f), the certificate holder must have an approved means by which the cabin crew can discreetly notify the flightcrew in the event of suspicious activity or security breaches in the cabin.

[Docket No. FAA–2005–22449, 72 FR 45635, Aug. 15, 2007]

§121.583 Carriage of persons without compliance with the passenger-carrying requirements of this part and part 117.

(a) When authorized by the certificate holder, the following persons, but no others, may be carried aboard an airplane without complying with the passenger-carrying airplane requirements in §§121.309(f), 121.310, 121.391, 121.571, and 121.587; the passenger-carrying operation requirements in part 117 and §§121.157(c) and 121.291; and the requirements pertaining to passengers in §§21.285, 121.313(f), 121.317, 121.547, and 121.573:

(1) A crewmember.
(2) A company employee.
(3) An FAA air carrier inspector, a DOD commercial air carrier evaluator, or an authorized representative of the National Transportation Safety Board, who is performing official duties.
(4) A person necessary for—
(i) The safety of the flight;
(ii) The safe handling of animals;
(iii) The safe handling of hazardous materials whose carriage is governed by regulations in 49 CFR part 175;
(iv) The security of valuable or confidential cargo;
(v) The preservation of fragile or perishable cargo;

§121.583

(vi) Experiments on, or testing of, cargo containers or cargo handling devices;
(vii) The operation of special equipment for loading or unloading cargo; and
(viii) The loading or unloading of outsize cargo.
(5) A person described in paragraph (a)(4) of this section, when traveling to or from his assignment.
(6) A person performing duty as an honor guard accompanying a shipment made by or under the authority of the United States.
(7) A military courier, military route supervisor, military cargo contract coordinator, or a flight crewmember of another military cargo contract air carrier or commercial operator, carried by a military cargo contract air carrier or commercial operator in operations under a military cargo contract, if that carriage is specifically authorized by the appropriate armed forces.
(8) A dependent of an employee of the certificate holder when traveling with the employee on company business to or from outlying stations not served by adequate regular passenger flights.
(b) No certificate holder may operate an airplane carrying a person covered by paragraph (a) of this section unless—
(1) Each person has unobstructed access from his seat to the pilot compartment or to a regular or emergency exit;
(2) The pilot in command has a means of notifying each person when smoking is prohibited and when safety belts must be fastened; and
(3) The airplane has an approved seat with an approved safety belt for each person. The seat must be located so that the occupant is not in any position to interfere with the flight crewmembers performing their duties.
(c) Before each takeoff, each certificate holder operating an airplane carrying persons covered by paragraph (a) of this section shall ensure that all such persons have been orally briefed by the appropriate crewmember on—
(1) Smoking;
(2) The use of seat belts;
(3) The location and operation of emergency exits;
(4) The use of oxygen and emergency oxygen equipment; and
(5) For extended overwater operations, the location of life rafts, and the location and operation of life preservers including a demonstration of the method of donning and inflating a life preserver.
(d) Each certificate holder operating an airplane carrying persons covered by paragraph (a) of this section shall incorporate procedures for the safe carriage of such persons into the certificate holder's operations manual.
(e) The pilot in command may authorize a person covered by paragraph (a) of this section to be admitted to the crew compartment of the airplane.

[Docket No. 10580, 35 FR 14612, Sept. 18, 1970; as amended by Amdt. 121–96, 37 FR 19608, Sept. 21, 1972; Amdt. 121–159, 45 FR 41594, June 19, 1980; Amdt. 121–232, 57 FR 48663, Oct. 27, 1992; Amdt. 121–251, 60 FR 65935, Dec. 20, 1995; Amdt. 121–253, 61 FR 2614, Jan. 26, 1996; Amdt. 121–298, 68 FR 41217, July 10, 2003; Amdt. 121–357, 77 FR 403, Jan. 4, 2012; Amdt. 121–357A, 77 FR 28764, May 16, 2012]

§121.584 Requirement to view the area outside the flightdeck door.

From the time the airplane moves in order to initiate a flight segment through the end of that flight segment, no person may unlock or open the flightdeck door unless:
(a) A person authorized to be on the flightdeck uses an approved audio procedure and an approved visual device to verify that:
(1) The area outside the flightdeck door is secure, and;
(2) If someone outside the flightdeck is seeking to have the flightdeck door opened, that person is not under duress, and;
(b) After the requirements of paragraph (a) of this section have been satisfactorily accomplished, the crewmember in charge on the flightdeck authorizes the door to be unlocked and open.

[Docket No. FAA–2005–22449, 72 FR 45635, Aug. 15, 2007]

§121.585 Exit seating.

(a)(1) Each certificate holder shall determine, to the extent necessary to perform the applicable functions of paragraph (d) of this section, the suitability of each person it permits to occupy an exit seat, in accordance with this section. For the purpose of this section—
(i) *Exit seat* means—
(A) Each seat having direct access to an exit; and,
(B) Each seat in a row of seats through which passengers would have to pass to gain access to an exit, from the first seat inboard of the exit to the first aisle inboard of the exit.
(ii) A *passenger seat having direct access* means a seat from which a passenger can proceed directly to the exit without entering an aisle or passing around an obstruction.
(2) Each certificate holder shall make the passenger exit seating determinations required by this paragraph in a non-discriminatory manner consistent with the requirements of this section, by person designated in the certificate holder's required operations manual.
(3) Each certificate holder shall designate the exit seats for each passenger seating configuration in its fleet in accordance with the definitions in this paragraph and submit those designations for approval as part of the procedures required to

be submitted for approval under paragraphs (n) and (p) of this section.

(b) No certificate holder may seat a person in a seat affected by this section if the certificate holder determines that it is likely that the person would be unable to perform one or more of the applicable functions listed in paragraph (d) of this section because—

(1) The person lacks sufficient mobility, strength, or dexterity in both arms and hands, and both legs:

(i) To reach upward, sideways, and downward to the location of emergency exit and exit-slide operating mechanisms;

(ii) To grasp and push, pull, turn, or otherwise manipulate those mechanisms;

(iii) To push, shove, pull, or otherwise open emergency exits;

(iv) To lift out, hold, deposit on nearby seats, or maneuver over the seatbacks to the next row objects the size and weight of over-wing window exit doors;

(v) To remove obstructions similar in size and weight to over-wing exit doors;

(vi) To reach the emergency exit expeditiously;

(vii) To maintain balance while removing obstructions;

(viii) To exit expeditiously;

(ix) To stabilize an escape slide after deployment; or

(x) To assist others in getting off an escape slide;

(2) The person is less than 15 years of age or lacks the capacity to perform one or more of the applicable functions listed in paragraph (d) of this section without the assistance of an adult companion, parent, or other relative;

(3) The person lacks the ability to read and understand instructions required by this section and related to emergency evacuation provided by the certificate holder in printed or graphic form or the ability to understand oral crew commands.

(4) The person lacks sufficient visual capacity to perform one or more of the applicable functions in paragraph (d) of this section without the assistance of visual aids beyond contact lenses or eyeglasses;

(5) The person lacks sufficient aural capacity to hear and understand instructions shouted by flight attendants, without assistance beyond a hearing aid;

(6) The person lacks the ability adequately to impart information orally to other passengers; or,

(7) The person has:

(i) A condition or responsibilities, such as caring for small children, that might prevent the person from performing one or more of the applicable functions listed in paragraph (d) of this section; or

(ii) A condition that might cause the person harm if he or she performs one or more of the applicable functions listed in paragraph (d) of this section.

(c) Each passenger shall comply with instructions given by a crewmember or other authorized employee of the certificate holder implementing exit seating restrictions established in accordance with this section.

(d) Each certificate holder shall include on passenger information cards, presented in the language in which briefings and oral commands are given by the crew, at each exit seat affected by this section, information that, in the event of an emergency in which a crewmember is not available to assist, a passenger occupying an exit seat may use if called upon to perform the following functions:

(1) Locate the emergency exit;

(2) Recognize the emergency exit opening mechanism;

(3) Comprehend the instructions for operating the emergency exit;

(4) Operate the emergency exit;

(5) Assess whether opening the emergency exit will increase the hazards to which passengers may be exposed;

(6) Follow oral directions and hand signals given by a crewmember;

(7) Stow or secure the emergency exit door so that it will not impede use of the exit;

(8) Assess the condition of an escape slide, activate the slide, and stabilize the slide after deployment to assist others in getting off the slide;

(9) Pass expeditiously through the emergency exit; and

(10) Assess, select, and follow a safe path away from the emergency exit.

(e) Each certificate holder shall include on passenger information cards, at each exit seat—

(1) In the primary language in which emergency commands are given by the crew, the selection criteria set forth in paragraph (b) of this section, and a request that a passenger identify himself or herself to allow reseating if he or she:

(i) Cannot meet the selection criteria set forth in paragraph (b) of this section;

(ii) Has a nondiscernible condition that will prevent him or her from performing the applicable functions listed in paragraph (d) of this section;

(iii) May suffer bodily harm as the result of performing one or more of those functions; or,

(iv) Does not wish to perform those functions.

(2) In each language used by the certificate holder for passenger information cards, a request that a passenger identify himself or herself to allow reseating if he or she lacks the ability to read, speak, or understand the language or the graphic form in which instructions required by this section and related to emergency evacuation are provided by the certificate holder, or the ability to

understand the specified language in which crew commands will be given in an emergency.

(3) May suffer bodily harm as the result of performing one or more of those functions; or,

(4) Does not wish to perform those functions.

A certificate holder shall not require the passenger to disclose his or her reason for needing reseating.

(f) Each certificate holder shall make available for inspection by the public at all passenger loading gates and ticket counters at each airport where it conducts passenger operations, written procedures established for making determinations in regard to exit row seating.

(g) No certificate holder may allow taxi or pushback unless at least one required crewmember has verified that no exit seat is occupied by a person the crewmember determines is likely to be unable to perform the applicable functions listed in paragraph (d) of this section.

(h) Each certificate holder shall include in its passenger briefings a reference to the passenger information cards, required by paragraphs (d) and (e), the selection criteria set forth in paragraph (b), and the functions to be performed, set forth in paragraph (d) of this section.

(i) Each certificate holder shall include in its passenger briefings a request that a passenger identify himself or herself to allow reseating if he or she—

(1) Cannot meet the selection criteria set forth in paragraph (b) of this section;

(2) Has a nondiscernible condition that will prevent him or her from performing the applicable functions listed in paragraph (d) of this section;

(3) May suffer bodily harm as the result of performing one or more of those functions listed in paragraph (d) of this section; or,

(4) Does not wish to perform those functions listed in paragraph (d) of this section.

A certificate holder shall not require the passenger to disclose his or her reason for needing reseating.

(j) [Reserved]

(k) In the event a certificate holder determines in accordance with this section that it is likely that a passenger assigned to an exit row seat would be unable to perform the functions listed in paragraph (d) of this section, or a passenger requests a non-exit seat, the certificate holder shall expeditiously relocate the passenger to a non-exit seat.

(l) In the event of full booking in the non-exit seats and if necessary to accommodate a passenger being relocated from an exit row seat, the certificate holder shall move a passenger who is willing and able to assume the evacuation functions that may be required, to an exit row seat.

(m) A certificate holder may deny transportation to any passenger under this section only because—

(1) The passenger refuses to comply with instructions given by a crewmember or other authorized employee of the certificate holder, implementing exit row seating restrictions established in accordance with this section, or

(2) The only seat that will physically accommodate the person's handicap is an exit seat.

(n) In order to comply with this section certificate holders shall—

(1) Establish procedures that address:

(i) The criteria listed in paragraph (b) of this section;

(ii) The functions listed in paragraph (d) of this section;

(iii) The requirements for airport information, passenger information cards, crewmember verification of appropriate seating in exit seats, passenger briefings, seat assignments, and denial of transportation as set forth in this section;

(iv) How to resolve disputes arising from implementation of this section, including identification of the certificate holder employee on the airport to whom complaints should be addressed for resolution; and,

(2) Submit their procedures for preliminary review and approval to the principal operations inspectors assigned to them at the certificate-holding district office.

(o) Certificate holders shall assign seats prior to boarding consistent with the criteria listed in paragraph (b) and the functions listed in paragraph (d) of this section, to the maximum extent feasible.

(p) The procedures required by paragraph (n) of this section will not become effective until final approval is granted by the Director, Flight Standards Service, Washington, DC. Approval will be based solely upon the safety aspects of the certificate holder's procedures.

[Docket No. 25821, 55 FR 8072, March 6, 1990; as amended by Amdt. 121–232, 57 FR 48663, Oct. 27, 1992; Amdt. 121–253, 61 FR 2614, Jan. 26, 1996]

§121.586 Authority to refuse transportation.

(a) No certificate holder may refuse transportation to a passenger on the basis that, because the passenger may need the assistance of another person to move expeditiously to an exit in the event of an emergency, his transportation would or might be inimical to safety of flight unless—

(1) The certificate holder has established procedures (including reasonable notice requirements) for the carriage of passengers who may need the assistance of another person to move expeditiously to an exit in the event of an emergency; and

(2) At least one of the following conditions exist:

Part 121: Air Carriers & Commercial Operators §121.589

(i) The passenger fails to comply with the notice requirements in the certificate holder's procedures.

(ii) The passenger cannot be carried in accordance with the certificate holder's procedures.

(b) Each certificate holder shall provide the certificate-holding district office with a copy of each procedure it establishes in accordance with paragraph (a)(2) of this section.

(c) Whenever the Administrator finds that revisions in the procedures described in paragraph (a)(2) of this section are necessary in the interest of safety or in the public interest, the certificate holder, after notification by the Administrator, shall make those revisions in its procedures. Within 30 days after the certificate holder receives such notice, it may file a petition to reconsider the notice with the certificate-holding district office. The filing of a petition to reconsider stays the notice pending a decision by the Administrator. However, if the Administrator finds that there is an emergency that requires immediate action in the interest of safety in air commerce, he may, upon a statement of the reasons, require a change effective without stay.

(d) Each certificate holder shall make available to the public at each airport it serves a copy of each procedure it establishes in accordance with paragraph (a)(1) of this section.

[Docket No. 12881, 42 FR 18394, April 7, 1977; as amended by Amdt. 121–174, 46 FR 38051, July 23, 1981; Amdt. 121–207, 54 FR 39293, Sept. 25, 1989; Amdt. 121–253, 61 FR 2614, Jan. 26, 1996]

§121.587 Closing and locking of flightcrew compartment door.

(a) Except as provided in paragraph (b) of this section, a pilot in command of an airplane that has a lockable flightcrew compartment door in accordance with §121.313 and that is carrying passengers shall ensure that the door separating the flightcrew compartment from the passenger compartment is closed and locked at all times when the aircraft is being operated.

(b) The provisions of paragraph (a) of this section do not apply at any time when it is necessary to permit access and egress by persons authorized in accordance with §121.547 and provided the part 119 operator complies with FAA approved procedures regarding the opening, closing and locking of the flightdeck doors.

[Docket No. FAA–2001–11032, 67 FR 2128, Jan. 15, 2002]

§121.589 Carry-on baggage.

(a) No certificate holder may allow the boarding of carry-on baggage on an airplane unless each passenger's baggage has been scanned to control the size and amount carried on board in accordance with an approved carry-on baggage program in its operations specifications. In addition, no passenger may board an airplane if his/her carry-on baggage exceeds the baggage allowance prescribed in the carry-on baggage program in the certificate holder's operations specifications.

(b) No certificate holder may allow all passenger entry doors of an airplane to be closed in preparation for taxi or pushback unless at least one required crewmember has verified that each article of baggage is stowed in accordance with this section and §121.285 (c) and (d).

(c) No certificate holder may allow an airplane to take off or land unless each article of baggage is stowed:

(1) In a suitable closet or baggage or cargo stowage compartment placarded for its maximum weight and providing proper restraint for all baggage or cargo stowed within, and in a manner that does not hinder the possible use of any emergency equipment; or

(2) As provided in §121.285 (c) and (d); or

(3) Under a passenger seat.

(d) Baggage, other than articles of loose clothing, may not be placed in an overhead rack unless that rack is equipped with approved restraining devices or doors.

(e) Each passenger must comply with instructions given by crewmembers regarding compliance with paragraphs (a), (b), (c), (d), and (g) of this section.

(f) Each passenger seat under which baggage is allowed to be stowed shall be fitted with a means to prevent articles of baggage stowed under it from sliding forward. In addition, each aisle seat shall be fitted with a means to prevent articles of baggage stowed under it from sliding sideward into the aisle under crash impacts severe enough to induce the ultimate inertia forces specified in the emergency landing condition regulations under which the airplane was type certificated.

(g) In addition to the methods of stowage in paragraph (c) of this section, flexible travel canes carried by blind individuals may be stowed—

(1) Under any series of connected passenger seats in the same row, if the cane does not protrude into an aisle and if the cane is flat on the floor; or

(2) Between a nonemergency exit window seat and the fuselage, if the cane is flat on the floor; or

(3) Beneath any two nonemergency exit window seats, if the cane is flat on the floor; or

(4) In accordance with any other method approved by the Administrator.

[Docket No. 24996, 52 FR 21476, June 5, 1987; as amended by Amdt. 121–251, 60 FR 65935, Dec. 20, 1995]

§121.590 Use of certificated land airports in the United States.

(a) Except as provided in paragraphs (b) or (c) of this section, or unless authorized by the Administrator under 49 U.S.C. 44706(c), no air carrier and no pilot being used by an air carrier may operate, in the conduct of a domestic type operation, flag type operation, or supplemental type operation, an airplane at a land airport in any State of the United States, the District of Columbia, or any territory or possession of the United States unless that airport is certificated under part 139 of this chapter. Further, after June 9, 2005 for Class I airports and after December 9, 2005 for Class II, III, and IV airports, when an air carrier and a pilot being used by the air carrier are required to operate at an airport certificated under part 139 of this chapter, the air carrier and the pilot may only operate at that airport if the airport is classified under part 139 to serve the type airplane to be operated and the type of operation to be conducted.

(b)(1) An air carrier and a pilot being used by the air carrier in the conduct of a domestic type operation, flag type operation, or supplemental type operation may designate and use as a required alternate airport for departure or destination an airport that is not certificated under part 139 of this chapter.

(2) Until December 9, 2005, an air carrier and a pilot being used by the air carrier in the conduct of domestic type operations and flag type operations, may operate an airplane designed for more than 9 but less than 31 passenger seats, at a land airport, in any State of the United States, the District of Columbia, or any territory or possession of the United States, that does not hold an airport operating certificate issued under part 139 of this chapter, and that serves small air carrier aircraft (as defined under "Air carrier aircraft" and "Class III airport" in §139.5 of this Chapter).

(c) An air carrier and a pilot used by the air carrier in conducting a domestic type operation, flag type operation, or supplemental type operation may operate an airplane at an airport operated by the U.S. Government that is not certificated under part 139 of this chapter, only if that airport meets the equivalent—

(1) Safety standards for airports certificated under part 139 of this chapter; and

(2) Airport classification requirements under part 139 to serve the type airplane to be operated and the type of operation to be conducted.

(d) An air carrier, a commercial operator, and a pilot being used by the air carrier or the commercial operator—when conducting a passenger-carrying airplane operation under this part that is not a domestic type operation, a flag type operation, or a supplemental type operation—may operate at a land airport not certificated under part 139 of this chapter only when the following conditions are met:

(1) The airport is adequate for the proposed operation, considering such items as size, surface, obstructions, and lighting.

(2) For an airplane carrying passengers at night, the pilot may not take off from, or land at, an airport unless—

(i) The pilot has determined the wind direction from an illuminated wind direction indicator or local ground communications or, in the case of takeoff, that pilot's personal observations; and

(ii) The limits of the area to be used for landing or takeoff are clearly shown by boundary or runway marker lights. If the area to be used for takeoff or landing is marked by flare pots or lanterns, their use must be authorized by the Administrator.

(e) A commercial operator and a pilot used by the commercial operator in conducting a domestic type operation, flag type operation, or supplemental type operation may operate an airplane at an airport operated by the U.S. Government that is not certificated under part 139 of this chapter only if that airport meets the equivalent—

(1) Safety standards for airports certificated under part 139 of this chapter; and

(2) Airport classification requirements under part 139 of this chapter to serve the type airplane to be operated and the type of operation to be conducted.

(f) For the purpose of this section, the terms—

Domestic type operation means any domestic operation conducted with—

(1) An airplane designed for at least 31 passenger seats (as determined by the aircraft type certificate issued by a competent civil aviation authority) at any land airport in any State of the United States, the District of Columbia, or any territory or possession of the United States; or

(2) An airplane designed for more than 9 passenger seats but less than 31 passenger seats (as determined by the aircraft type certificate issued by a competent civil aviation authority) at any land airport in any State of the United States (except Alaska), the District of Columbia, or any territory or possession of the United States.

Flag type operation means any flag operation conducted with—

(1) An airplane designed for at least 31 passenger seats (as determined by the aircraft type certificate issued by a competent civil aviation authority) at any land airport in any State of the United States, the District of Columbia, or any territory or possession of the United States; or

(2) An airplane designed for more than 9 passenger seats but less than 31 passenger seats (as determined by the aircraft type certificate issued by a competent civil aviation authority) at any land airport in any State of the United States

(except Alaska), the District of Columbia, or any territory or possession of the United States.

Supplemental type operation means any supplemental operation (except an all-cargo operation) conducted with an airplane designed for at least 31 passenger seats (as determined by the aircraft type certificate issued by a competent civil aviation authority) at any land airport in any State of the United States, the District of Columbia, or any territory or possession of the United States.

United States means the States of the United States, the District of Columbia, and the territories and possessions of the United States.

Note: Special Statutory Requirement to Operate to or From a Part 139 Airport. Each air carrier that provides—in an aircraft (e.g., airplane, rotorcraft, etc.) designed for more than 9 passenger seats—regularly scheduled charter air transportation for which the public is provided in advance a schedule containing the departure location, departure time, and arrival location of the flight must operate to and from an airport certificated under part 139 of this chapter in accordance with 49 U.S.C. 41104(b). That statutory provision contains stand-alone requirements for such air carriers and special exceptions for operations in Alaska and outside the United States. Nothing in §121.590 exempts the air carriers described in this note from the requirements of 49 U.S.C. 41104(b). Certain operations by air carriers that conduct public charter operations under 14 CFR part 380 are covered by the statutory requirements to operate to and from part 139 airports. See 49 U.S.C. 41104(b).

[Docket No. FAA–2000–7479, 69 FR 6424, Feb. 10, 2004; Amdt. 121–304, 69 FR 31522, June 4, 2004]

Subpart U—Dispatching and Flight Release Rules

Source: Docket No. 6258, 29 FR 19222, December 31, 1964, unless otherwise noted.

§121.591 Applicability.

This subpart prescribes dispatching rules for domestic and flag operations and flight release rules for supplemental operations.

[Docket No. 28154, 61 FR 2614, Jan. 26, 1996]

§121.593 Dispatching authority: Domestic operations.

Except when an airplane lands at an intermediate airport specified in the original dispatch release and remains there for not more than one hour, no person may start a flight unless an aircraft dispatcher specifically authorizes that flight.

[Docket No. 6258, 29 FR 19222, Dec. 31, 1964; as amended by Amdt. 121–253, 61 FR 2614, Jan. 26, 1996]

§121.595 Dispatching authority: Flag operations.

(a) No person may start a flight unless an aircraft dispatcher specifically authorizes that flight.

(b) No person may continue a flight from an intermediate airport without redispatch if the airplane has been on the ground more than six hours.

[Docket No. 6258, 29 FR 19222, Dec. 31, 1964; as amended by Amdt. 121–253, 61 FR 2614, Jan. 26, 1996]

§121.597 Flight release authority: Supplemental operations.

(a) No person may start a flight under a flight following system without specific authority from the person authorized by the operator to exercise operational control over the flight.

(b) No person may start a flight unless the pilot in command or the person authorized by the operator to exercise operational control over the flight has executed a flight release setting forth the conditions under which the flights will be conducted. The pilot in command may sign the flight release only when he and the person authorized by the operator to exercise operational control believe that the flight can be made with safety.

(c) No person may continue a flight from an intermediate airport without a new flight release if the aircraft has been on the ground more than six hours.

[Docket No. 6258, 29 FR 19222, Dec. 31, 1964; as amended by Amdt. 121–3, 30 FR 3639, March 19, 1965; Amdt. 121–253, 61 FR 2614, Jan. 26, 1996]

§121.599 Familiarity with weather conditions.

(a) *Domestic and flag operations.* No aircraft dispatcher may release a flight unless he is thoroughly familiar with reported and forecast weather conditions on the route to be flown.

(b) *Supplemental operations.* No pilot in command may begin a flight unless he is thoroughly familiar with reported and forecast weather conditions on the route to be flown.

[Docket No. 6258, 29 FR 19222, Dec. 31, 1964; as amended by Amdt. 121–253, 61 FR 2614, Jan. 26, 1996]

§121.601 Aircraft dispatcher information to pilot in command: Domestic and flag operations.

(a) The aircraft dispatcher shall provide the pilot in command all available current reports or information on airport conditions and irregularities of navigation facilities that may affect the safety of the flight.

(b) Before beginning a flight, the aircraft dispatcher shall provide the pilot in command with all available weather reports and forecasts of weather phenomena that may affect the safety of flight, including adverse weather phenomena, such as clear air turbulence, thunderstorms, and low altitude wind shear, for each route to be flown and each airport to be used.

(c) During a flight, the aircraft dispatcher shall provide the pilot in command any additional available information of meteorological conditions (including adverse weather phenomena, such as clear air turbulence, thunderstorms, and low altitude wind shear), and irregularities of facilities and services that may affect the safety of the flight.

[Docket No. 6258, 29 FR 19222, Dec. 31, 1964; as amended by Amdt. 121–134, 42 FR 27573, May 31, 1977; Amdt. 121–144, 43 FR 22649, May 25, 1978; Amdt. 121–253, 61 FR 2614, Jan. 26, 1996]

§121.603 Facilities and services: Supplemental operations.

(a) Before beginning a flight, each pilot in command shall obtain all available current reports or information on airport conditions and irregularities of navigation facilities that may affect the safety of the flight.

(b) During a flight, the pilot in command shall obtain any additional available information of meteorological conditions and irregularities of facilities and services that may affect the safety of the flight.

[Docket No. 6258, 29 FR 19222, Dec. 31, 1964; as amended by Amdt. 121–253, 61 FR 2614, Jan. 26, 1996]

§121.605 Airplane equipment.

No person may dispatch or release an airplane unless it is airworthy and is equipped as prescribed in §121.303.

§121.607 Communication and navigation facilities: Domestic and flag operations.

(a) Except as provided in paragraph (b) of this section for a certificate holder conducting flag operations, no person may dispatch an airplane over an approved route or route segment unless the communication and navigation facilities required by §§121.99 and 121.103 for the approval of that route or segment are in satisfactory operating condition.

(b) If, because of technical reasons or other reasons beyond the control of a certificate holder conducting flag operations, the facilities required by §§121.99 and 121.103 are not available over a route or route segment outside the United States, the certificate holder may dispatch an airplane over that route or route segment if the pilot in command and dispatcher find that communication and navigation facilities equal to those required are available and are in satisfactory operating condition.

[Docket No. 6258, 29 FR 19222, Dec. 31, 1964; as amended by Amdt. 121–253, 61 FR 2614, Jan. 26, 1996]

§121.609 Communication and navigation facilities: Supplemental operations.

No person may release an aircraft over any route or route segment unless communication and navigation facilities equal to those required by §121.121 are in satisfactory operating condition.

[Docket No. 6258, 29 FR 19222, Dec. 31, 1964; as amended by Amdt. 121–253, 61 FR 2614, Jan. 26, 1996]

§121.611 Dispatch or flight release under VFR.

No person may dispatch or release an aircraft for VFR operation unless the ceiling and visibility en route, as indicated by available weather reports or forecasts, or any combination thereof, are and will remain at or above applicable VFR minimums until the aircraft arrives at the airport or airports specified in the dispatch or flight release.

§121.613 Dispatch or flight release under IFR or over the top.

Except as provided in §121.615, no person may dispatch or release an aircraft for operations under IFR or over-the-top, unless appropriate weather reports or forecasts, or any combination thereof, indicate that the weather conditions will be at or above the authorized minimums at the estimated time of arrival at the airport or airports to which dispatched or released.

[Docket No. 6258, 29 FR 19222, Dec. 31, 1964; as amended by Amdt. 121–33, 32 FR 13912, Oct. 6, 1967]

§121.615 Dispatch or flight release over water: Flag and supplemental operations.

(a) No person may dispatch or release an aircraft for a flight that involves extended overwater operations unless appropriate weather reports or forecasts or any combination thereof, indicate that the weather conditions will be at or above the authorized minimums at the estimated time of arrival at any airport to which dispatched or released or to any required alternate airport.

(b) Each certificate holder conducting a flag or supplemental operation or a domestic operation within the State of Alaska shall conduct extended overwater operations under IFR unless it shows that operating under IFR is not necessary for safety.

(c) Each certificate holder conducting a flag or supplemental operation or a domestic operation within the State of Alaska shall conduct other overwater operations under IFR if the Administrator determines that operation under IFR is necessary for safety.

(d) Each authorization to conduct extended overwater operations under VFR and each requirement to conduct other overwater operations under IFR will be specified in the certificate holder's operations specifications.

[Docket No. 6258, 29 FR 19222, Dec. 31, 1964; as amended by Amdt. 121–33, 32 FR 13912, Oct. 6, 1967; Amdt. 121–253, 61 FR 2614, Jan. 26, 1996]

§121.617 Alternate airport for departure.

(a) If the weather conditions at the airport of takeoff are below the landing minimums in the certificate holder's operations specifications for that airport, no person may dispatch or release an aircraft from that airport unless the dispatch or flight release specifies an alternate airport located within the following distances from the airport of takeoff:

(1) *Aircraft having two engines.* Not more than one hour from the departure airport at normal cruising speed in still air with one engine inoperative.

(2) *Aircraft having three or more engines.* Not more than two hours from the departure airport at normal cruising speed in still air with one engine inoperative.

(b) For the purpose of paragraph (a) of this section, the alternate airport weather conditions must meet the requirements of the certificate holder's operations specifications.

(c) No person may dispatch or release an aircraft from an airport unless he lists each required alternate airport in the dispatch or flight release.

§121.619 Alternate airport for destination: IFR or over-the-top: Domestic operations.

(a) No person may dispatch an airplane under IFR or over-the-top unless he lists at least one alternate airport for each destination airport in the dispatch release. When the weather conditions forecast for the destination and first alternate airport are marginal at least one additional alternate must be designated. However, no alternate airport is required if for at least 1 hour before and 1 hour after the estimated time of arrival at the destination airport the appropriate weather reports or forecasts, or any combination of them, indicate—

(1) The ceiling will be at least 2,000 feet above the airport elevation; and

(2) Visibility will be at least 3 miles.

(b) For the purposes of paragraph (a) of this section, the weather conditions at the alternate airport must meet the requirements of §121.625.

(c) No person may dispatch a flight unless he lists each required alternate airport in the dispatch release.

[Docket No. 6258, 29 FR 19222, Dec. 31, 1964; as amended by Amdt. 121–159, 45 FR 41594, June 19, 1980; Amdt. 121–253, 61 FR 2614, Jan. 26, 1996]

§121.621 Alternate airport for destination: Flag operations.

(a) No person may dispatch an airplane under IFR or over-the-top unless he lists at least one alternate airport for each destination airport in the dispatch release, unless—

(1) The flight is scheduled for not more than 6 hours and, for at least 1 hour before and 1 hour after the estimated time of arrival at the destination airport, the appropriate weather reports or forecasts, or any combination of them, indicate the ceiling will be:

(i) At least 1,500 feet above the lowest circling MDA, if a circling approach is required and authorized for that airport; or

(ii) At least 1,500 feet above the lowest published instrument approach minimum or 2,000 feet above the airport elevation, whichever is greater; and

(iii) The visibility at that airport will be at least 3 miles, or 2 miles more than the lowest applicable visibility minimums, whichever is greater, for the instrument approach procedures to be used at the destination airport; or

(2) The flight is over a route approved without an available alternate airport for a particular destination airport and the airplane has enough fuel to meet the requirements of §121.641(b) or §121.645(c).

(b) For the purposes of paragraph (a) of this section, the weather conditions at the alternate airport must meet the requirements of the certificate holder's operations specifications.

(c) No person may dispatch a flight unless he lists each required alternate airport in the dispatch release.

[Docket No. 6258, 29 FR 19222, Dec. 31, 1964; as amended by Amdt. 121–159, 45 FR 41594, June 19, 1980; Amdt. 121–253, 61 FR 2614, Jan. 26, 1996]

§121.623 Alternate airport for destination; IFR or over-the-top: Supplemental operations.

(a) Except as provided in paragraph (b) of this section, each person releasing an aircraft for operation under IFR or over-the-top shall list at least one alternate airport for each destination airport in the flight release.

(b) An alternate airport need not be designated for IFR or over-the-top operations where the aircraft carries enough fuel to meet the requirements of §§121.643 and 121.645 for flights outside the

48 contiguous States and the District of Columbia over routes without an available alternate airport for a particular airport of destination.

(c) For the purposes of paragraph (a) of this section, the weather requirements at the alternate airport must meet the requirements of the certificate holder's operations specifications.

(d) No person may release a flight unless he lists each required alternate airport in the flight release.

[Docket No. 6258, 29 FR 19222, Dec. 31, 1964; as amended by Amdt. 121–253, 61 FR 2614, Jan. 26, 1996]

§121.624 ETOPS Alternate Airports.

(a) No person may dispatch or release an airplane for an ETOPS flight unless enough ETOPS Alternate Airports are listed in the dispatch or flight release such that the airplane remains within the authorized ETOPS maximum diversion time. In selecting these ETOPS Alternate Airports, the certificate holder must consider all adequate airports within the authorized ETOPS diversion time for the flight that meet the standards of this part.

(b) No person may list an airport as an ETOPS Alternate Airport in a dispatch or flight release unless, when it might be used (from the earliest to the latest possible landing time)—

(1) The appropriate weather reports or forecasts, or any combination thereof, indicate that the weather conditions will be at or above the ETOPS Alternate Airport minima specified in the certificate holder's operations specifications; and

(2) The field condition reports indicate that a safe landing can be made.

(c) Once a flight is en route, the weather conditions at each ETOPS Alternate Airport must meet the requirements of §121.631(c).

(d) No person may list an airport as an ETOPS Alternate Airport in the dispatch or flight release unless that airport meets the public protection requirements of §121.97(b)(1)(ii).

[Docket No. FAA–2002–6717, 72 FR 1881, Jan. 16, 2007]

§121.625 Alternate airport weather minima.

Except as provided in §121.624 for ETOPS Alternate Airports, no person may list an airport as an alternate in the dispatch or flight release unless the appropriate weather reports or forecasts, or any combination thereof, indicate that the weather conditions will be at or above the alternate weather minima specified in the certificate holder's operations specifications for that airport when the flight arrives.

[Docket No. FAA–2002–6717, 72 FR 1881, Jan. 16, 2007]

§121.627 Continuing flight in unsafe conditions.

(a) No pilot in command may allow a flight to continue toward any airport to which it has been dispatched or released if, in the opinion of the pilot in command or dispatcher (domestic and flag operations only), the flight cannot be completed safely; unless, in the opinion of the pilot in command, there is no safer procedure. In that event, continuation toward that airport is an emergency situation as set forth in §121.557.

(b) If any instrument or item of equipment required under this chapter for the particular operation becomes inoperative en route, the pilot in command shall comply with the approved procedures for such an occurrence as specified in the certificate holder's manual.

[Docket No. 6258, 29 FR 1922, Dec. 31, 1964; as amended by Amdt. 121–222, 56 FR 12310, March 22, 1991; Amdt. 121–253, 61 FR 2615, Jan. 26, 1996]

§121.628 Inoperable instruments and equipment.

(a) No person may take off an airplane with inoperable instruments or equipment installed unless the following conditions are met:

(1) An approved Minimum Equipment List exists for that airplane.

(2) The certificate-holding district office has issued the certificate holder operations specifications authorizing operations in accordance with an approved Minimum Equipment List. The flight crew shall have direct access at all times prior to flight to all of the information contained in the approved Minimum Equipment List through printed or other means approved by the Administrator in the certificate holders operations specifications. An approved Minimum Equipment List, as authorized by the operations specifications, constitutes an approved change to the type design without requiring recertification.

(3) The approved Minimum Equipment List must:

(i) Be prepared in accordance with the limitations specified in paragraph (b) of this section.

(ii) Provide for the operation of the airplane with certain instruments and equipment in an inoperable condition.

(4) Records identifying the inoperable instruments and equipment and the information required by paragraph (a)(3)(ii) of this section must be available to the pilot.

(5) The airplane is operated under all applicable conditions and limitations contained in the Minimum Equipment List and the operations specifications authorizing use of the Minimum Equipment List.

(b) The following instruments and equipment may not be included in the Minimum Equipment List:

(1) Instruments and equipment that are either specifically or otherwise required by the airworthiness requirements under which the airplane is type certificated and which are essential for safe operations under all operating conditions.

(2) Instruments and equipment required by an airworthiness directive to be in operable condition unless the airworthiness directive provides otherwise.

(3) Instruments and equipment required for specific operations by this part.

(c) Notwithstanding paragraphs (b)(1) and (b)(3) of this section, an airplane with inoperable instruments or equipment may be operated under a special flight permit under §§21.197 and 21.199 of this chapter.

[Docket No. 25780, 56 FR 12310, March 22, 1991; as amended by Amdt. 121–222, 56 FR 14290, April 8, 1991; Amdt. 121–253, 61 FR 2615, Jan. 26, 1996]

§121.629 Operation in icing conditions.

(a) No person may dispatch or release an aircraft, continue to operate an aircraft en route, or land an aircraft when in the opinion of the pilot in command or aircraft dispatcher (domestic and flag operations only), icing conditions are expected or met that might adversely affect the safety of the flight.

(b) No person may take off an aircraft when frost, ice, or snow is adhering to the wings, control surfaces, propellers, engine inlets or other critical surfaces of the aircraft or when the takeoff would not be in compliance with paragraph (c) of this section. Takeoffs with frost under the wing in the area of the fuel tanks may be authorized by the Administrator.

(c) Except as provided in paragraph (d) of this section, no person may dispatch, release, or take off an aircraft any time conditions are such that frost, ice, or snow may reasonably be expected to adhere to the aircraft, unless the certificate holder has an approved ground deicing/anti-icing program in its operations specifications and unless the dispatch, release, and takeoff comply with that program. The approved ground deicing/anti-icing program must include at least the following items:

(1) A detailed description of—

(i) How the certificate holder determines that conditions are such that frost, ice, or snow may reasonably be expected to adhere to the aircraft and that ground deicing/anti-icing operational procedures must be in effect;

(ii) Who is responsible for deciding that ground deicing/anti-icing operational procedures must be in effect;

(iii) The procedures for implementing ground deicing/anti-icing operational procedures;

(iv) The specific duties and responsibilities of each operational position or group responsible for getting the aircraft safely airborne while ground deicing/anti-icing operational procedures are in effect.

(2) Initial and annual recurrent ground training and testing for flight crewmembers and qualification for all other affected personnel (e.g., aircraft dispatchers, ground crews, contract personnel) concerning the specific requirements of the approved program and each person's responsibilities and duties under the approved program, specifically covering the following areas:

(i) The use of holdover times.

(ii) Aircraft deicing/anti-icing procedures, including inspection and check procedures and responsibilities.

(iii) Communications procedures.

(iv) Aircraft surface contamination (i.e., adherence of frost, ice, or snow) and critical area identification, and how contamination adversely affects aircraft performance and flight characteristics.

(v) Types and characteristics of deicing/anti-icing fluids.

(vi) Cold weather preflight inspection procedures;

(vii) Techniques for recognizing contamination on the aircraft.

(3) The certificate holder's holdover time-tables and the procedures for the use of these tables by the certificate holder's personnel. Holdover time is the estimated time deicing/anti-icing fluid will prevent the formation of frost or ice and the accumulation of snow on the protected surfaces of an aircraft. Holdover time begins when the final application of deicing/anti-icing fluid commences and expires when the deicing/anti-icing fluid applied to the aircraft loses its effectiveness. The holdover times must be supported by data acceptable to the Administrator. The certificate holder's program must include procedures for flight crewmembers to increase or decrease the determined holdover time in changing conditions. The program must provide that takeoff after exceeding any maximum holdover time in the certificate holder's holdover timetable is permitted only when at least one of the following conditions exists:

(i) A pretakeoff contamination check, as defined in paragraph (c)(4) of this section, determines that the wings, control surfaces, and other critical surfaces, as defined in the certificate holder's program, are free of frost, ice, or snow.

(ii) It is otherwise determined by an alternate procedure approved by the Administrator in accordance with the certificate holder's approved program that the wings, control surfaces, and other critical surfaces, as defined in the certificate holder's program, are free of frost, ice, or snow.

§121.631

(iii) The wings, control surfaces, and other critical surfaces are redeiced and a new holdover time is determined.

(4) Aircraft deicing/anti-icing procedures and responsibilities, pretakeoff check procedures and responsibilities, and pretakeoff contamination check procedures and responsibilities. A pretakeoff check is a check of the aircraft's wings or representative aircraft surfaces for frost, ice, or snow within the aircraft's holdover time. A pretakeoff contamination check is a check to make sure the wings, control surfaces, and other critical surfaces, as defined in the certificate holder's program, are free of frost, ice, and snow. It must be conducted within five minutes prior to beginning take off. This check must be accomplished from outside the aircraft unless the program specifies otherwise.

(d) A certificate holder may continue to operate under this section without a program as required in paragraph (c) of this section, if it includes in its operations specifications a requirement that, any time conditions are such that frost, ice, or snow may reasonably be expected to adhere to the aircraft, no aircraft will take off unless it has been checked to ensure that the wings, control surfaces, and other critical surfaces are free of frost, ice and snow. The check must occur within five minutes prior to beginning takeoff. This check must be accomplished from outside the aircraft.

[Docket No. 6258, 29 FR 19222, Dec. 31, 1964; as amended by Amdt. 121–231, 57 FR 44942, Sept. 29, 1992; Amdt. 121–253, 61 FR 2615, Jan. 26, 1996]

§121.631 Original dispatch or flight release, redispatch or amendment of dispatch or flight release.

(a) A certificate holder may specify any regular, provisional, or refueling airport, authorized for the type of aircraft, as a destination for the purpose of original dispatch or release.

(b) No person may allow a flight to continue to an airport to which it has been dispatched or released unless the weather conditions at an alternate airport that was specified in the dispatch or flight release are forecast to be at or above the alternate minimums specified in the operations specifications for that airport at the time the aircraft would arrive at the alternate airport. However, the dispatch or flight release may be amended en route to include any alternate airport that is within the fuel range of the aircraft as specified in §§121.639 through 121.647.

(c) No person may allow a flight to continue beyond the ETOPS Entry Point unless—

(1) Except as provided in paragraph (d) of this section, the weather conditions at each ETOPS Alternate Airport required by §121.624 are forecast to be at or above the operating minima for that airport in the certificate holder's operations specifications when it might be used (from the earliest to the latest possible landing time); and

(2) All ETOPS Alternate Airports within the authorized ETOPS maximum diversion time are reviewed and the flight crew advised of any changes in conditions that have occurred since dispatch.

(d) If paragraph (c)(1) of this section cannot be met for a specific airport, the dispatch or flight release may be amended to add an ETOPS Alternate Airport within the maximum ETOPS diversion time that could be authorized for that flight with weather conditions at or above operating minima.

(e) Before the ETOPS Entry Point, the pilot in command for a supplemental operator or a dispatcher for a flag operator must use company communications to update the flight plan if needed because of a re-evaluation of aircraft system capabilities.

(f) No person may change an original destination or alternate airport that is specified in the original dispatch or flight release to another airport while the aircraft is en route unless the other airport is authorized for that type of aircraft and the appropriate requirements of §§121.593 through 121.661 and 121.173 are met at the time of redispatch or amendment of the flight release.

(g) Each person who amends a dispatch or flight release en route shall record that amendment.

[Docket No. 6258, 29 FR 19222, Dec. 31, 1964; as amended by Amdt. 121–65, 35 FR 12709, Aug. 11, 1970; Amdt. 121–329, 72 FR 1881, Jan. 16, 2007]

§121.633 Considering time-limited systems in planning ETOPS alternates.

(a) For ETOPS up to and including 180 minutes, no person may list an airport as an ETOPS Alternate Airport in a dispatch or flight release if the time needed to fly to that airport (at the approved one-engine inoperative cruise speed under standard conditions in still air) would exceed the approved time for the airplane's most limiting ETOPS Significant System (including the airplane's most limiting fire suppression system time for those cargo and baggage compartments required by regulation to have fire-suppression systems) minus 15 minutes.

(b) For ETOPS beyond 180 minutes, no person may list an airport as an ETOPS Alternate Airport in a dispatch or flight release if the time needed to fly to that airport:

(1) at the all engine operating cruise speed, corrected for wind and temperature, exceeds the airplane's most limiting fire suppression system time minus 15 minutes for those cargo and bag-

gage compartments required by regulation to have fire suppression systems (except as provided in paragraph (c) of this section), or

(2) at the one-engine-inoperative cruise speed, corrected for wind and temperature, exceeds the airplane's most limiting ETOPS Significant System time (other than the airplane's most limiting fire suppression system time minus 15 minutes for those cargo and baggage compartments required by regulation to have fire-suppression systems).

(c) For turbine-engine powered airplanes with more than two engines, the certificate holder need not meet paragraph (b)(1) of this section until February 15, 2013.

[Docket No. FAA–2002–6717, 72 FR 1882, Jan. 16, 2007]

§121.635 Dispatch to and from refueling or provisional airports: Domestic and flag operations.

No person may dispatch an airplane to or from a refueling or provisional airport except in accordance with the requirements of this part applicable to dispatch from regular airports and unless that airport meets the requirements of this part applicable to regular airports.

[Docket No. 16383, 43 FR 22649, May 25, 1978; as amended by Amdt. 121–253, 61 FR 2615, Jan. 26, 1996]

§121.637 Takeoffs from unlisted and alternate airports: Domestic and flag operations.

(a) No pilot may takeoff an airplane from an airport that is not listed in the operations specifications unless—

(1) The airport and related facilities are adequate for the operation of the airplane;

(2) He can comply with the applicable airplane operating limitations;

(3) The airplane has been dispatched according to dispatching rules applicable to operation from an approved airport; and

(4) The weather conditions at that airport are equal to or better than the following:

(i) *Airports in the United States.* The weather minimums for takeoff prescribed in part 97 of this chapter; or where minimums are not prescribed for the airport, 800-2, 900-1-1/2, or 1,000-1.

(ii) *Airports outside the United States.* The weather minimums for takeoff prescribed or approved by the government of the country in which the airport is located; or where minimums are not prescribed or approved for the airport, 800-2, 900-1-1/2, or 1,000-1.

(b) No pilot may take off from an alternate airport unless the weather conditions are at least equal to the minimums prescribed in the certificate holder's operations specifications for alternate airports.

[Docket No. 6258, 29 FR 19222, Dec. 31, 1964; as amended by Amdt. 121–33, 32 FR 13912, Oct. 6, 1967; Amdt. 121–253, 61 FR 2615, Jan. 26, 1996]

§121.639 Fuel supply: All domestic operations.

No person may dispatch or take off an airplane unless it has enough fuel—

(a) To fly to the airport to which it is dispatched;

(b) Thereafter, to fly to and land at the most distant alternate airport (where required) for the airport to which dispatched; and

(c) Thereafter, to fly for 45 minutes at normal cruising fuel consumption or, for certificate holders who are authorized to conduct day VFR operations in their operations specifications and who are operating nontransport category airplanes type certificated after December 31, 1964, to fly for 30 minutes at normal cruising fuel consumption for day VFR operations.

[Docket No. 6258, 29 FR 19222, Dec. 31, 1964; as amended by Amdt. 121–251, 60 FR 65935, Dec. 20, 1995]

§121.641 Fuel supply: nonturbine and turbo-propeller-powered airplanes: Flag operations.

(a) No person may dispatch or take off a nonturbine or turbo-propeller-powered airplane unless, considering the wind and other weather conditions expected, it has enough fuel—

(1) To fly to and land at the airport to which it is dispatched;

(2) Thereafter, to fly to and land at the most distant alternate airport specified in the dispatch release; and

(3) Thereafter, to fly for 30 minutes plus 15 percent of the total time required to fly at normal cruising fuel consumption to the airports specified in paragraphs (a)(1) and (2) of this section or to fly for 90 minutes at normal cruising fuel consumption, whichever is less.

(b) No person may dispatch a nonturbine or turbo-propeller-powered airplane to an airport for which an alternate is not specified under §121.621(a)(2), unless it has enough fuel, considering wind and forecast weather conditions, to fly to that airport and thereafter to fly for three hours at normal cruising fuel consumption.

[Docket No. 6258, 29 FR 19222, Dec. 31, 1964; as amended by Amdt. 121–253, 61 FR 2615, Jan. 26, 1996]

§121.643 Fuel supply: Nonturbine and turbo-propeller-powered airplanes: Supplemental operations.

(a) Except as provided in paragraph (b) of this section, no person may release for flight or takeoff a nonturbine or turbo-propeller-powered airplane unless, considering the wind and other weather conditions expected, it has enough fuel—

(1) To fly to and land at the airport to which it is released;

(2) Thereafter, to fly to and land at the most distant alternate airport specified in the flight release; and

(3) Thereafter, to fly for 45 minutes at normal cruising fuel consumption or, for certificate holders who are authorized to conduct day VFR operations in their operations specifications and who are operating nontransport category airplanes type certificated after December 31, 1964, to fly for 30 minutes at normal cruising fuel consumption for day VFR operations.

(b) If the airplane is released for any flight other than from one point in the contiguous United States to another point in the contiguous United States, it must carry enough fuel to meet the requirements of paragraphs (a)(1) and (2) of this section and thereafter fly for 30 minutes plus 15 percent of the total time required to fly at normal cruising fuel consumption to the airports specified in paragraphs (a)(1) and (2) of this section, or to fly for 90 minutes at normal cruising fuel consumption, whichever is less.

(c) No person may release a nonturbine or turbo-propeller-powered airplane to an airport for which an alternate is not specified under §121.623(b), unless it has enough fuel, considering wind and other weather conditions expected, to fly to that airport and thereafter to fly for three hours at normal cruising fuel consumption.

[Docket No. 6258, 29 FR 19222, Dec. 31, 1964; as amended by Amdt. 121–10, 30 FR 10025, Aug. 12, 1965; Amdt. 121–251, 60 FR 65935, Dec. 20, 1995; Amdt. 121–253, 61 FR 2615, Jan. 26, 1996]

§121.645 Fuel supply: Turbine-engine powered airplanes, other than turbo-propeller: Flag and supplemental operations.

(a) Any flag operation within the 48 contiguous United States and the District of Columbia may use the fuel requirements of §121.639.

(b) For any certificate holder conducting flag or supplemental operations outside the 48 contiguous United States and the District of Columbia, unless authorized by the Administrator in the operations specifications, no person may release for flight or takeoff a turbine-engine powered airplane (other than a turbo-propeller powered airplane) unless, considering wind and other weather conditions expected, it has enough fuel—

(1) To fly to and land at the airport to which it is released;

(2) After that, to fly for a period of 10 percent of the total time required to fly from the airport of departure to, and land at, the airport to which it was released;

(3) After that, to fly to and land at the most distant alternate airport specified in the flight release, if an alternate is required; and

(4) After that, to fly for 30 minutes at holding speed at 1,500 feet above the alternate airport (or the destination airport if no alternate is required) under standard temperature conditions.

(c) No person may release a turbine-engine powered airplane (other than a turbo-propeller airplane) to an airport for which an alternate is not specified under §121.621(a)(2) or §121.623(b) unless it has enough fuel, considering wind and other weather conditions expected, to fly to that airport and thereafter to fly for at least two hours at normal cruising fuel consumption.

(d) The Administrator may amend the operations specifications of a certificate holder conducting flag or supplemental operations to require more fuel than any of the minimums stated in paragraph (a) or (b) of this section if he finds that additional fuel is necessary on a particular route in the interest of safety.

(e) For a supplemental operation within the 48 contiguous States and the District of Columbia with a turbine engine powered airplane the fuel requirements of §121.643 apply.

[Docket No. 6258, 29 FR 19222, Dec. 31, 1964; as amended by Amdt. 121–10, 30 FR 10025, Aug. 12, 1965; Amdt. 121–144, 43 FR 22649, May 25, 1978. Amdt. 121–253, 61 FR 2615, Jan. 26, 1996]

§121.646 En-route fuel supply: Flag and supplemental operations.

(a) No person may dispatch or release for flight a turbine-engine powered airplane with more than two engines for a flight more than 90 minutes (with all engines operating at cruise power) from an Adequate Airport unless the following fuel supply requirements are met:

(1) The airplane has enough fuel to meet the requirements of §121.645(b);

(2) The airplane has enough fuel to fly to the Adequate Airport—

(i) Assuming a rapid decompression at the most critical point;

(ii) Assuming a descent to a safe altitude in compliance with the oxygen supply requirements of §121.333; and

(iii) Considering expected wind and other weather conditions.

Part 121: Air Carriers & Commercial Operators §121.649

(3) The airplane has enough fuel to hold for 15 minutes at 1500 feet above field elevation and conduct a normal approach and landing.

(b) No person may dispatch or release for flight an ETOPS flight unless, considering wind and other weather conditions expected, it has the fuel otherwise required by this part and enough fuel to satisfy each of the following requirements:

(1) Fuel to fly to an ETOPS Alternate Airport.

(i) Fuel to account for rapid decompression and engine failure. The airplane must carry the greater of the following amounts of fuel:

(A) Fuel sufficient to fly to an ETOPS Alternate Airport assuming a rapid decompression at the most critical point followed by descent to a safe altitude in compliance with the oxygen supply requirements of §121.333 of this chapter;

(B) Fuel sufficient to fly to an ETOPS Alternate Airport (at the one-engine-inoperative cruise speed) assuming a rapid decompression and a simultaneous engine failure at the most critical point followed by descent to a safe altitude in compliance with the oxygen requirements of §121.333 of this chapter; or

(C) Fuel sufficient to fly to an ETOPS Alternate Airport (at the one engine inoperative cruise speed) assuming an engine failure at the most critical point followed by descent to the one engine inoperative cruise altitude.

(ii) Fuel to account for errors in wind forecasting. In calculating the amount of fuel required by paragraph (b)(1)(i) of this section, the certificate holder must increase the actual forecast wind speed by 5% (resulting in an increase in headwind or a decrease in tailwind) to account for any potential errors in wind forecasting. If a certificate holder is not using the actual forecast wind based on a wind model accepted by the FAA, the airplane must carry additional fuel equal to 5% of the fuel required for paragraph (b)(1)(i) of this section, as reserve fuel to allow for errors in wind data.

(iii) Fuel to account for icing. In calculating the amount of fuel required by paragraph (b)(1)(i) of this section (after completing the wind calculation in paragraph (b)(1)(ii) of this section), the certificate holder must ensure that the airplane carries the greater of the following amounts of fuel in anticipation of possible icing during the diversion:

(A) Fuel that would be burned as a result of airframe icing during 10 percent of the time icing is forecast (including the fuel used by engine and wing anti-ice during this period).

(B) Fuel that would be used for engine anti-ice, and if appropriate wing anti-ice, for the entire time during which icing is forecast.

(iv) Fuel to account for engine deterioration. In calculating the amount of fuel required by paragraph (b)(1)(i) of this section (after completing the wind calculation in paragraph (b)(1)(ii) of this section), the airplane also carries fuel equal to 5% of the fuel specified above, to account for deterioration in cruise fuel burn performance unless the certificate holder has a program to monitor airplane in-service deterioration to cruise fuel burn performance.

(2) Fuel to account for holding, approach, and landing. In addition to the fuel required by paragraph (b)(1) of this section, the airplane must carry fuel sufficient to hold at 1500 feet above field elevation for 15 minutes upon reaching an ETOPS Alternate Airport and then conduct an instrument approach and land.

(3) Fuel to account for APU use. If an APU is a required power source, the certificate holder must account for its fuel consumption during the appropriate phases of flight.

[Docket No. FAA–2002–6717, 72 FR 1882, Jan. 16, 2007; as amended by Amdt. 121–348, 75 FR 12121, March 15, 2010]

§121.647 Factors for computing fuel required.

Each person computing fuel required for the purposes of this subpart shall consider the following:

(a) Wind and other weather conditions forecast.

(b) Anticipated traffic delays.

(c) One instrument approach and possible missed approach at destination.

(d) Any other conditions that may delay landing of the aircraft.

For the purposes of this section, required fuel is in addition to unusable fuel.

§121.649 Takeoff and landing weather minimums: VFR: Domestic operations.

(a) Except as provided in paragraph (b) of this section, regardless of any clearance from ATC, no pilot may takeoff or land an airplane under VFR when the reported ceiling or visibility is less than the following:

(1) For day operations—1,000-foot ceiling and one-mile visibility.

(2) For night operations—1,000-foot ceiling and two-mile visibility.

(b) Where a local surface restriction to visibility exists (e.g., smoke, dust, blowing snow or sand) the visibility for day and night operations may be reduced to 1/2 mile, if all turns after takeoff and prior to landing, and all flight beyond one mile from the airport boundary can be accomplished above or outside the area of local surface visibility restriction.

(c) The weather minimums in this section do not apply to the VFR operation of fixed-wing aircraft at any of the locations where the special weather minimums of §91.157 of this chapter are not applicable (See part 91, Appendix D, section

3 of this chapter). The basic VFR weather minimums of §91.155 of this chapter apply at those locations.

[Docket No. 6258, 29 FR 19222, Dec. 31, 1964; as amended by Amdt. 121–39, 33 FR 4097, March 2, 1968; Amdt. 121–206, 54 FR 34331, Aug. 18, 1989; Amdt. 121–226, 56 FR 65663, Dec. 17, 1991; Amdt. 121–253, 61 FR 2615, Jan. 26, 1996]

§121.651 Takeoff and landing weather minimums: IFR: All certificate holders.

(a) Notwithstanding any clearance from ATC, no pilot may begin a takeoff in an airplane under IFR when the weather conditions reported by the U.S. National Weather Service, a source approved by that Service, or a source approved by the Administrator, are less than those specified in—

(1) The certificate holder's operations specifications; or

(2) Parts 91 and 97 of this chapter, if the certificate holder's operations specifications do not specify takeoff minimums for the airport.

(b) Except as provided in paragraph (d) of this section, no pilot may continue an approach past the final approach fix, or where a final approach fix is not used, begin the final approach segment of an instrument approach procedure—

(1) At any airport, unless the U.S. National Weather Service, a source approved by that Service, or a source approved by the Administrator, issues a weather report for that airport; and

(2) At airports within the United States and its territories or at U.S. military airports, unless the latest weather report for that airport issued by the U.S. National Weather Service, a source approved by that Service, or a source approved by the Administrator, reports the visibility to be equal to or more than the visibility minimums prescribed for that procedure. For the purpose of this section, the term "U.S. military airports" means airports in foreign countries where flight operations are under the control of U.S. military authority.

(c) If a pilot has begun the final approach segment of an instrument approach procedure in accordance with paragraph (b) of this section, and after that receives a later weather report indicating below-minimum conditions, the pilot may continue the approach to DA/DH or MDA. Upon reaching DA/DH or at MDA, and at any time before the missed approach point, the pilot may continue the approach below DA/DH or MDA if either the requirements of §91.175(l) of this chapter, or the following requirements are met:

(1) The aircraft is continuously in a position from which a descent to a landing on the intended runway can be made at a normal rate of descent using normal maneuvers, and where that descent rate will allow touchdown to occur within the touchdown zone of the runway of intended landing;

(2) The flight visibility is not less than the visibility prescribed in the standard instrument approach procedure being used;

(3) Except for Category II or Category III approaches where any necessary visual reference requirements are specified by authorization of the Administrator, at least one of the following visual references for the intended runway is distinctly visible and identifiable to the pilot:

(i) The approach light system, except that the pilot may not descend below 100 feet above the touchdown zone elevation using the approach lights as a reference unless the red terminating bars or the red side row bars are also distinctly visible and identifiable.

(ii) The threshold.

(iii) The threshold markings.

(iv) The threshold lights.

(v) The runway end identifier lights.

(vi) The visual approach slope indicator.

(vii) The touchdown zone or touchdown zone markings.

(viii) The touchdown zone lights.

(ix) The runway or runway markings.

(x) The runway lights; and

(4) When the aircraft is on a straight-in nonprecision approach procedure which incorporates a visual descent point, the aircraft has reached the visual descent point, except where the aircraft is not equipped for or capable of establishing that point, or a descent to the runway cannot be made using normal procedures or rates of descent if descent is delayed until reaching that point.

(d) A pilot may begin the final approach segment of an instrument approach procedure other than a Category II or Category III procedure at an airport when the visibility is less than the visibility minimums prescribed for that procedure if that airport is served by an operative ILS and an operative PAR, and both are used by the pilot. However, no pilot may continue an approach below the authorized DA/DH unless the requirements of §91.175(l) of this chapter, or the following requirements are met:

(1) The aircraft is continuously in a position from which a descent to a landing on the intended runway can be made at a normal rate of descent using normal maneuvers and where such a descent rate will allow touchdown to occur within the touchdown zone of the runway of intended landing;

(2) The flight visibility is not less than the visibility prescribed in the standard instrument approach procedure being used; and

(3) Except for Category II or Category III approaches where any necessary visual reference requirements are specified by the authorization of the Administrator, at least one of the following

visual references for the intended runway is distinctly visible and identifiable to the pilot:

(i) The approach light system, except that the pilot may not descend below 100 feet above the touchdown zone elevation using the approach lights as a reference unless the red terminating bars or the red side row bars are also distinctly visible and identifiable.

(ii) The threshold.
(iii) The threshold markings.
(iv) The threshold lights.
(v) The runway end identifier lights.
(vi) The visual approach slope indicator.
(vii) The touchdown zone or touchdown zone markings.
(viii) The touchdown zone lights.
(ix) The runway or runway markings.
(x) The runway lights.

(e) For the purpose of this section, the final approach segment begins at the final approach fix or facility prescribed in the instrument approach procedure. When a final approach fix is not prescribed for a procedure that includes a procedure turn, the final approach segment begins at the point where the procedure turn is completed and the aircraft is established inbound toward the airport on the final approach course within the distance prescribed in the procedure.

(f) Unless otherwise authorized in the certificate holder's operations specifications, each pilot making an IFR takeoff, approach, or landing at a foreign airport shall comply with the applicable instrument approach procedures and weather minimums prescribed by the authority having jurisdiction over the airport.

[Docket No. 20060, 46 FR 2291, Jan. 8, 1981; as amended by Amdt. 121–303, 69 FR 1641, Jan. 9, 2004; Amdt. 121–333, 72 FR 31682, June 7, 2007]

§121.652 Landing weather minimums: IFR: All certificate holders.

(a) If the pilot in command of an airplane has not served 100 hours as pilot in command in operations under this part in the type of airplane he is operating, the MDA or DA/DH and visibility landing minimums in the certificate holder's operations specification for regular, provisional, or refueling airports are increased by 100 feet and one-half mile (or the RVR equivalent). The MDA or DA/DH and visibility minimums need not be increased above those applicable to the airport when used as an alternate airport, but in no event may the landing minimums be less than 300 and 1. However, a pilot in command employed by a certificate holder conducting operations in large aircraft under part 135 of this chapter, may credit flight time acquired in operations conducted for that operator under part 91 in the same type airplane for up to 50 percent of the 100 hours of pilot in command experience required by this paragraph.

(b) The 100 hours of pilot in command experience required by paragraph (a) of this section may be reduced (not to exceed 50 percent) by substituting one landing in operations under this part in the type of airplane for 1 required hour of pilot in command experience, if the pilot has at least 100 hours as pilot in command of another type airplane in operations under this part.

(c) Category II minimums and the sliding scale when authorized in the certificate holder's operations specifications do not apply until the pilot in command subject to paragraph (a) of this section meets the requirements of that paragraph in the type of airplane he is operating.

[Docket No. 7594, 33 FR 10843, July 31, 1968; as amended by Amdt. 121–143, 43 FR 22642, May 25, 1978; Amdt. 121–253, 61 FR 2615, Jan. 26, 1996; Amdt. 121–333, 72 FR 31682, June 7, 2007]

§121.653 [Reserved]

§121.655 Applicability of reported weather minimums.

In conducting operations under §§121.649 through 121.653, the ceiling and visibility values in the main body of the latest weather report control for VFR and IFR takeoffs and landings and for instrument approach procedures on all runways of an airport. However, if the latest weather report, including an oral report from the control tower, contains a visibility value specified as runway visibility or runway visual range for a particular runway of an airport, that specified value controls for VFR and IFR landings and takeoffs and straight-in instrument approaches for that runway.

§121.657 Flight altitude rules.

(a) *General.* Notwithstanding §91.119 or any rule applicable outside the United States, no person may operate an aircraft below the minimums set forth in paragraphs (b) and (c) of this section, except when necessary for takeoff or landing, or except when, after considering the character of the terrain, the quality and quantity of meteorological services, the navigational facilities available, and other flight conditions, the Administrator prescribes other minimums for any route or part of a route where he finds that the safe conduct of the flight requires other altitudes. Outside of the United States the minimums prescribed in this section are controlling unless higher minimums are prescribed in the certificate holder's operations specifications or by the foreign country over which the aircraft is operating.

(b) *Day VFR operations.* No certificate holder conducting domestic operations may operate a passenger-carrying aircraft and no certificate holder conducting flag or supplemental operations may operate any aircraft under VFR during the day at an altitude less than 1,000 feet above the surface or less than 1,000 feet from any mountain, hill, or other obstruction to flight.

(c) *Night VFR, IFR, and over-the-top operations.* No person may operate an aircraft under IFR including over-the-top or at night under VFR at an altitude less than 1,000 feet above the highest obstacle within a horizontal distance of five miles from the center of the intended course, or, in designated mountainous areas, less than 2,000 feet above the highest obstacle within a horizontal distance of five miles from the center of the intended course.

(d) *Day over-the-top operations below minimum en route altitudes.* A person may conduct day over-the-top operations in an airplane at flight altitudes lower than the minimum en route IFR altitudes if—

(1) The operation is conducted at least 1,000 feet above the top of lower broken or overcast cloud cover;

(2) The top of the lower cloud cover is generally uniform and level;

(3) Flight visibility is at least five miles; and

(4) The base of any higher broken or overcast cloud cover is generally uniform and level and is at least 1,000 feet above the minimum en route IFR altitude for that route segment.

[Docket No. 6258, 29 FR 19222, Dec. 31, 1964; as amended by Amdt. 121–144, 43 FR 22649, May 25, 1978; Amdt. 121–206, 54 FR 34331, Aug. 18, 1989; Amdt. 121–253, 61 FR 2615, Jan. 26, 1996]

§121.659 Initial approach altitude: Domestic and supplemental operations.

(a) Except as provided in paragraph (b) of this section, when making an initial approach to a radio navigation facility under IFR, no person may descend an aircraft below the pertinent minimum altitude for initial approach (as specified in the instrument approach procedure for that facility) until his arrival over that facility has been definitely established.

(b) When making an initial approach on a flight being conducted under §121.657(d), no pilot may commence an instrument approach until his arrival over the radio facility has definitely been established. In making an instrument approach under these circumstances no person may descend an aircraft lower than 1,000 feet above the top of the lower cloud or the minimum altitude determined by the Administrator for that part of the IFR approach, whichever is lower.

[Docket No. 6258, 29 FR 19222, Dec. 31, 1964; as amended by Amdt. 121–253, 61 FR 2615, Jan. 26, 1996]

§121.661 Initial approach altitude: Flag operations.

When making an initial approach to a radio navigation facility under IFR, no person may descend below the pertinent minimum altitude for initial approach (as specified in the instrument approach procedure for that facility) until his arrival over that facility has been definitely established.

[Docket No. 6258, 29 FR 19222, Dec. 31, 1964; as amended by Amdt. 121–253, 61 FR 2615, Jan. 26, 1996]

§121.663 Responsibility for dispatch release: Domestic and flag operations.

Each certificate holder conducting domestic or flag operations shall prepare a dispatch release for each flight between specified points, based on information furnished by an authorized aircraft dispatcher. The pilot in command and an authorized aircraft dispatcher shall sign the release only if they both believe that the flight can be made with safety. The aircraft dispatcher may delegate authority to sign a release for a particular flight, but he may not delegate his authority to dispatch.

[Docket No. 28154, 61 FR 2615, Jan. 26, 1996]

§121.665 Load manifest.

Each certificate holder is responsible for the preparation and accuracy of a load manifest form before each takeoff. The form must be prepared and signed for each flight by employees of the certificate holder who have the duty of supervising the loading of aircraft and preparing the load manifest forms or by other qualified persons authorized by the certificate holder.

§121.667 Flight plan: VFR and IFR: Supplemental operations.

(a) No person may take off an aircraft unless the pilot in command has filed a flight plan, containing the appropriate information required by part 91, with the nearest FAA communication station or appropriate military station or, when operating outside the United States, with other appropriate authority. However, if communications facilities are not readily available, the pilot in command shall file the flight plan as soon as practicable after the aircraft is airborne. A flight plan must continue in effect for all parts of the flight.

(b) When flights are operated into military airports, the arrival or completion notice required by §§91.153 and 91.169 may be filed with the appropriate airport control tower or aeronautical communication facility used for that airport.

[Docket No. 6258, 29 FR 19222, Dec. 31, 1964; as amended by Amdt. 121–206, 54 FR 34331, Aug. 18, 1989; Amdt. 121–253, 61 FR 2615, Jan. 26, 1996]

Subpart V— Records and Reports

Source: Docket No. 6258, 29 FR 19226, December 31, 1964, unless otherwise noted.

§121.681 Applicability.

This subpart prescribes requirements for the preparation and maintenance of records and reports for all certificate holders.

§121.683 Crewmember and dispatcher record.

(a) Each certificate holder shall—

(1) Maintain current records of each crewmember and each aircraft dispatcher (domestic and flag operations only) that show whether the crewmember or aircraft dispatcher complies with the applicable sections of this chapter, including, but not limited to, proficiency and route checks, airplane and route qualifications, training, any required physical examinations, flight, duty, and rest time records; and

(2) Record each action taken concerning the release from employment or physical or professional disqualification of any flight crewmember or aircraft dispatcher (domestic and flag operations only) and keep the record for at least six months thereafter.

(b) Each certificate holder conducting supplemental operations shall maintain the records required by paragraph (a) of this section at its principal base of operations, or at another location used by it and approved by the Administrator.

(c) Computer record systems approved by the Administrator may be used in complying with the requirements of paragraph (a) of this section.

[Docket No. 6258, 29 FR 19226, Dec. 31, 1964; as amended by Amdt. 121-144, 43 FR 22649, May 25, 1978; Amdt. 121-241, 59 FR 42993, Aug. 19, 1994; Amdt. 121-253, 61 FR 2615, Jan. 26, 1996]

§121.685 Aircraft record: Domestic and flag operations.

Each certificate holder conducting domestic or flag operations shall maintain a current list of each aircraft that it operates in scheduled air transportation and shall send a copy of the record and each change to the certificate-holding district office. Airplanes of another certificate holder operated under an interchange agreement may be incorporated by reference.

[Docket No. 28154, 61 FR 2615, Jan. 26, 1996]

§121.687 Dispatch release: Flag and domestic operations.

(a) The dispatch release may be in any form but must contain at least the following information concerning each flight:

(1) Identification number of the aircraft.
(2) Trip number.
(3) Departure airport, intermediate stops, destination airports, and alternate airports.
(4) A statement of the type of operation (e.g., IFR, VFR).
(5) Minimum fuel supply.
(6) For each flight dispatched as an ETOPS flight, the ETOPS diversion time for which the flight is dispatched.

(b) The dispatch release must contain, or have attached to it, weather reports, available weather forecasts, or a combination thereof, for the destination airport, intermediate stops, and alternate airports, that are the latest available at the time the release is signed by the pilot in command and dispatcher. It may include any additional available weather reports or forecasts that the pilot in command or the aircraft dispatcher considers necessary or desirable.

[Docket No. 6258, 29 FR 19222, Dec. 31, 1964; as amended by Amdt. 121-253, 61 FR 2615, Jan. 26, 1996; Amdt. 121-329, 72 FR 1883, Jan. 16, 2007]

§121.689 Flight release form: Supplemental operations.

(a) Except as provided in paragraph (c) of this section, the flight release may be in any form but must contain at least the following information concerning each flight:

(1) Company or organization name.
(2) Make, model, and registration number of the aircraft being used.
(3) Flight or trip number, and date of flight.
(4) Name of each flight crewmember, flight attendant, and pilot designated as pilot in command.
(5) Departure airport, destination airports, alternate airports, and route.
(6) Minimum fuel supply (in gallons or pounds).
(7) A statement of the type of operation (e.g., IFR, VFR).
(8) For each flight released as an ETOPS flight, the ETOPS diversion time for which the flight is released.

(b) The aircraft flight release must contain, or have attached to it, weather reports, available weather forecasts, or a combination thereof, for the destination airport, and alternate airports, that are the latest available at the time the release is signed. It may include any additional available weather reports or forecasts that the pilot in command considers necessary or desirable.

§121.693   **Federal Aviation Regulations**

(c) Each certificate holder conducting domestic or flag operations under the rules of this part applicable to supplemental operations shall comply with the dispatch or flight release forms required for scheduled operations under this subpart.

[Docket No. 6258, 29 FR 19222, Dec. 31, 1964; as amended by Amdt. 121–253, 61 FR 2615, Jan. 26, 1996; Amdt. 121–329, 72 FR 1883, Jan. 16, 2007]

§121.691 [Reserved]

§121.693 Load manifest: All certificate holders.

The load manifest must contain the following information concerning the loading of the airplane at takeoff time:

(a) The weight of the aircraft, fuel and oil, cargo and baggage, passengers and crewmembers.

(b) The maximum allowable weight for that flight that must not exceed the least of the following weights:

(1) Maximum allowable takeoff weight for the runway intended to be used (including corrections for altitude and gradient, and wind and temperature conditions existing at the takeoff time).

(2) Maximum takeoff weight considering anticipated fuel and oil consumption that allows compliance with applicable en route performance limitations.

(3) Maximum takeoff weight considering anticipated fuel and oil consumption that allows compliance with the maximum authorized design landing weight limitations on arrival at the destination airport.

(4) Maximum takeoff weight considering anticipated fuel and oil consumption that allows compliance with landing distance limitations on arrival at the destination and alternate airports.

(c) The total weight computed under approved procedures.

(d) Evidence that the aircraft is loaded according to an approved schedule that insures that the center of gravity is within approved limits.

(e) Names of passengers, unless such information is maintained by other means by the certificate holder.

[Docket No. 6258, 29 FR 19226, Dec. 31, 1964; as amended by Amdt. 121–159, 45 FR 41595, June 19, 1980; Amdt. 121–253, 61 FR, Jan. 26, 1996]

§121.695 Disposition of load manifest, dispatch release, and flight plans: Domestic and flag operations.

(a) The pilot in command of an airplane shall carry in the airplane to its destination—

(1) A copy of the completed load manifest (or information from it, except information concerning cargo and passenger distribution);

(2) A copy of the dispatch release; and

(3) A copy of the flight plan.

(b) The certificate holder shall keep copies of the records required in this section for at least three months.

[Docket No. 6258, 29 FR 19226, Dec. 31, 1964; as amended by Amdt. 121–178, 47 FR 13316, March 29, 1982; Amdt. 121–253, 61 FR 2616, Jan. 26, 1996]

§121.697 Disposition of load manifest, flight release, and flight plans: Supplemental operations.

(a) The pilot in command of an airplane shall carry in the airplane to its destination the original or a signed copy of the—

(1) Load manifest;
(2) Flight release;
(3) Airworthiness release;
(4) Pilot route certification; and
(5) Flight plan.

(b) If a flight originates at the certificate holder's principal base of operations, it shall retain at that base a signed copy of each document listed in paragraph (a) of this section.

(c) Except as provided in paragraph (d) of this section, if a flight originates at a place other than the certificate holder's principal base of operations, the pilot in command (or another person not aboard the airplane who is authorized by the certificate holder) shall, before or immediately after departure of the flight, mail signed copies of the documents listed in paragraph (a) of this section, to the principal base of operations.

(d) If a flight originates at a place other than the certificate holder's principal base of operations, and there is at that place a person to manage the flight departure for the certificate holder who does not himself or herself depart on the airplane, signed copies of the documents listed in paragraph (a) of this section may be retained at that place for not more than 30 days before being sent to the certificate holder's principal base of operations. However, the documents for a particular flight need not be further retained at that place or be sent to the principal base of operations, if the originals or other copies of them have been previously returned to the principal base of operations.

(e) The certificate holder conducting supplemental operations shall:

(1) Identify in its operations manual the person having custody of the copies of documents retained in accordance with paragraph (d) of this section; and

(2) Retain at its principal base of operations either an original or a copy of the records required by this section for at least three months.

[Docket No. 6258, 29 FR 19226, Dec. 31, 1964; as amended by Amdt. 121–123, 40 FR 44541, Sept. 29, 1975; Amdt. 121–143, 43 FR 22642, May 25, 1978; Amdt. 121–178, 47 FR 13316, March 29, 1982; Amdt. 121–253, 61 FR 2616, Jan. 26, 1996]

§121.698–121.699 [Reserved]

§121.701 Maintenance log: Aircraft.

(a) Each person who takes action in the case of a reported or observed failure or malfunction of an airframe, engine, propeller, or appliance that is critical to the safety of flight shall make, or have made, a record of that action in the airplane's maintenance log.

(b) Each certificate holder shall have an approved procedure for keeping adequate copies of the record required in paragraph (a) of this section in the airplane in a place readily accessible to each flight crewmember and shall put that procedure in the certificate holder's manual.

§121.703 Service difficulty reports.

(a) Each certificate holder shall report the occurrence or detection of each failure, malfunction, or defect concerning—

(1) Fires during flight and whether the related fire-warning system functioned properly;

(2) Fires during flight not protected by a related fire-warning system;

(3) False fire warning during flight;

(4) An engine exhaust system that causes damage during flight to the engine, adjacent structure, equipment, or components;

(5) An aircraft component that causes accumulation or circulation of smoke, vapor, or toxic or noxious fumes in the crew compartment or passenger cabin during flight;

(6) Engine shutdown during flight because of flameout;

(7) Engine shutdown during flight when external damage to the engine or airplane structure occurs;

(8) Engine shutdown during flight due to foreign object ingestion or icing;

(9) Engine shutdown during flight of more than one engine;

(10) A propeller feathering system or ability of the system to control overspeed during flight;

(11) A fuel or fuel-dumping system that affects fuel flow or causes hazardous leakage during flight;

(12) An unwanted landing gear extension or retraction, or an unwanted opening or closing of landing gear doors during flight;

(13) Brake system components that result in loss of brake actuating force when the airplane is in motion on the ground;

(14) Aircraft structure that requires major repair;

(15) Cracks, permanent deformation, or corrosion of aircraft structures, if more than the maximum acceptable to the manufacturer or the FAA;

(16) Aircraft components or systems that result in taking emergency actions during flight (except action to shut down an engine); and

(17) Emergency evacuation systems or components including all exit doors, passenger emergency evacuation lighting systems, or evacuation equipment that are found defective, or that fail to perform the intended functions during an actual emergency or during training, testing, maintenance, demonstrations, or inadvertent deployments.

(b) For the purpose of this section *during flight* means the period from the moment the aircraft leaves the surface of the earth on takeoff until it touches down on landing.

(c) In addition to the reports required by paragraph (a) of this section, each certificate holder shall report any other failure, malfunction, or defect in an aircraft that occurs or is detected at any time if, in its opinion, that failure, malfunction, or defect has endangered or may endanger the safe operation of an aircraft used by it.

(d) Each certificate holder shall submit each report required by this section, covering each 24-hour period beginning at 0900 local time of each day and ending at 0900 local time on the next day, to the FAA offices in Oklahoma City, Oklahoma. Each report of occurrences during a 24-hour period shall be submitted to the collection point within the next 96 hours. However, a report due on Saturday or Sunday may be submitted on the following Monday, and a report due on a holiday may be submitted on the next work day.

(e) The certificate holder shall submit the reports required by this section on a form or in another format acceptable to the Administrator. The reports shall include the following information:

(1) Type and identification number of the aircraft.

(2) The name of the operator.

(3) The date, flight number, and stage during which the incident occurred (e.g., preflight, takeoff, climb, cruise, descent landing, and inspection).

(4) The emergency procedure affected (e.g., unscheduled landing and emergency descent).

(5) The nature of the failure, malfunction, or defect.

(6) Identification of the part and system involved, including available information pertaining to type designation of the major component and time since overhaul.

(7) Apparent cause of the failure, malfunction, or defect (e.g., wear, crack, design deficiency, or personnel error).

(8) Whether the part was repaired, replaced, sent to the manufacturer, or other action taken.

(9) Whether the aircraft was grounded.

(10) Other pertinent information necessary for more complete identification, determination of seriousness, or corrective action.

(f) A certificate holder that is also the holder of a Type Certificate (including a Supplemental Type Certificate), a Parts Manufacturer Approval, or a Technical Standard Order Authorization, or that is the licensee of a type certificate holder, need not report a failure, malfunction, or defect under this section if the failure, malfunction, or defect has been reported by it under §21.3 of this chapter or under the accident reporting provisions of 14 CFR part 830.

(g) No person may withhold a report required by this section even though all information required in this section is not available.

(h) When certificate holder gets additional information, including information from the manufacturer or other agency, concerning a report required by this section, it shall expeditiously submit it as a supplement to the first report and reference the date and place of submission of the first report.

[Docket No. 6258, 29 FR 19226, Dec. 31, 1964, as amended by Docket No. 8084, 32 FR 5770, April 11, 1967; Amdt. 121–72, 35 FR 18188, Nov. 28, 1970; Amdt. 121–143, 43 FR 22642, May 25, 1978; Amdt. 121–178, 47 FR 13316, March 29, 1982; Amdt. 121–187, 50 FR 32375, Aug. 9, 1985; Amdt. 121–195, 53 FR 8728, March 16, 1988; Amdt. 121–251, 60 FR 65936, Dec. 20, 1995; Amdt. 121–319, 70 FR 76979, Dec. 29, 2005]

§121.705 Mechanical interruption summary report.

Each certificate holder shall submit to the Administrator, before the end of the 10th day of the following month, a summary report for the previous month of:

(a) Each interruption to a flight, unscheduled change of aircraft en route, or unscheduled stop or diversion from a route, caused by known or suspected mechanical difficulties or malfunctions that are not required to be reported under §121.703.

(b) The number of engines removed prematurely because of malfunction, failure or defect, listed by make and model and the aircraft type in which it was installed.

(c) The number of propeller featherings in flight, listed by type of propeller and engine and aircraft on which it was installed. Propeller featherings for training, demonstration, or flight check purposes need not be reported.

[Docket No. 6258, 29 FR 19226, Dec. 31, 1964, as amended by Amdt. 121–10, 30 FR 10025, Aug. 12, 1965; Amdt. 121–319, 70 FR 76979, Dec. 29, 2005]

§121.707 Alteration and repair reports.

(a) Each certificate holder shall, promptly upon its completion, prepare a report of each major alteration or major repair of an airframe, aircraft engine, propeller, or appliance of an aircraft operated by it.

(b) The certificate holder shall submit a copy of each report of a major alteration to, and shall keep a copy of each report of a major repair available for inspection by, the representative of the Administrator who is assigned to it.

§121.709 Airworthiness release or aircraft log entry.

(a) No certificate holder may operate an aircraft after maintenance, preventive maintenance or alterations are performed on the aircraft unless the certificate holder, or the person with whom the certificate holder arranges for the performance of the maintenance, preventive maintenance, or alterations, prepares or causes to be prepared—
 (1) An airworthiness release; or
 (2) An appropriate entry in the aircraft log.

(b) The airworthiness release or log entry required by paragraph (a) of this section must—
 (1) Be prepared in accordance with the procedures set forth in the certificate holder's manual;
 (2) Include a certification that—
  (i) The work was performed in accordance with the requirements of the certificate holder's manual;
  (ii) All items required to be inspected were inspected by an authorized person who determined that the work was satisfactorily completed;
  (iii) No known condition exists that would make the airplane unairworthy; and
  (iv) So far as the work performed is concerned, the aircraft is in condition for safe operation; and
 (3) Be signed by an authorized certificated mechanic or repairman except that a certificated repairman may sign the release or entry only for the work for which he is employed and certificated.

(c) Notwithstanding paragraph (b)(3) of this section, after maintenance, preventive maintenance, or alterations performed by a repair station that is located outside the United States, the airworthiness release or log entry required by paragraph (a) of this section may be signed by a person authorized by that repair station.

(d) When an airworthiness release form is prepared the certificate holder must give a copy to the pilot in command and must keep a record thereof for at least 2 months.

(e) Instead of restating each of the conditions of the certification required by paragraph (b) of this section, the air carrier may state in its manual that the signature of an authorized certificated mechanic or repairman constitutes that certification.

[Docket No. 6258, 29 FR 19226, Dec. 31, 1964; as amended by Amdt. 121–6, 30 FR 6432, May 8, 1965; Amdt. 121–21, 31 FR 10613, Aug. 9, 1966; Amdt. 121–286, 66 FR 41116, Aug. 6, 2001]

§121.711 Communication records: Domestic and flag operations.

(a) Each certificate holder conducting domestic or flag operations must record each en route communication between the certificate holder and its pilots using a communication system as required by §121.99 of this part.

(b) For purposes of this section the term en route means from the time the aircraft pushes back from the departing gate until the time the aircraft reaches the arrival gate at its destination.

(c) The record required in paragraph (a) of this section must contain at least the following information:

(1) The date and time of the contact;
(2) The flight number;
(3) Aircraft registration number;
(4) Approximate position of the aircraft during the contact;
(5) Call sign; and
(6) Narrative of the contact.

(d) The record required in paragraph (a) of this section must be kept for at least 30 days.

[Docket No. 28154, 61 FR 2616, Jan. 26, 1996; as amended by Amdt. 121–366, 78 FR 67841, Nov. 12, 2013]

§121.713 Retention of contracts and amendments: Commercial operators who conduct intrastate operations for compensation or hire.

(a) Each commercial operator who conducts intrastate operations for compensation or hire shall keep a copy of each written contract under which it provides services as a commercial operator for a period of at least 1 year after the date of execution of the contract. In the case of an oral contract, it shall keep a memorandum stating its elements, and of any amendments to it, for a period of at least one year after the execution of that contract or change.

(b) Each commercial operator who conducts intrastate operations for compensation or hire shall submit a financial report for the first 6 months of each fiscal year and another financial report for each complete fiscal year. If that person's operating certificate is suspended for more than 29 days, that person shall submit a financial report as of the last day of the month in which the suspension is terminated. The report required to be submitted by this section shall be submitted within 60 days of the last day of the period covered by the report and must include—

(1) A balance sheet that shows assets, liabilities, and net worth on the last day of the reporting period;

(2) The information required by §119.36(e)(2), (e)(7), and (e)(8) of this chapter.

(3) An itemization of claims in litigation against the applicant, if any, as of the last day of the period covered by the report;

(4) A profit and loss statement with the separation of items relating to the applicant's commercial operator activities from his other business activities, if any; and

(5) A list of each contract that gave rise to operating income on the profit and loss statement, including the names and addresses of the contracting parties and the nature, scope, date, and duration of each contract.

[Docket No. 28154, 60 FR 65936, Dec. 20, 1995; as amended by Amdt. 121–262, 62 FR 13257, March 19, 1997]

Subpart W— Crewmember Certificate: International

Source: Docket No. 28154, 61 FR 30435, June 14, 1996, unless otherwise noted.

§121.721 Applicability.

This section describes the certificates that were issued to United States citizens who were employed by air carriers at the time of issuance as flight crewmembers on United States registered aircraft engaged in international air commerce. The purpose of the certificate is to facilitate the entry and clearance of those crewmembers into ICAO contracting states. They were issued under Annex 9; as amended, to the Convention on International Civil Aviation.

§121.723 Surrender of international crewmember certificate.

The holder of a certificate issued under this section, or the air carrier by whom the holder is employed, shall surrender the certificate for cancellation at the nearest FAA Flight Standards District Office at the termination of the holder's employment with that air carrier.

Subpart X— Emergency Medical Equipment and Training

Source: Docket No. FAA–2000–7119, 66 FR 19028, April 12, 2001 unless otherwise noted.

§121.801 Applicability.

This subpart prescribes the emergency medical equipment and training requirements applicable to all certificate holders operating passenger-carrying airplanes under this part. Nothing in this subpart is intended to require certificate holders or its agents to provide emergency medical care or to establish a standard of care for the provision of emergency medical care.

§121.803 Emergency medical equipment.

(a) No person may operate a passenger-carrying airplane under this part unless it is equipped with the emergency medical equipment listed in this section.

(b) Each equipment item listed in this section—

(1) Must be inspected regularly in accordance with inspection periods established in the operations specifications to ensure its condition for continued serviceability and immediate readiness to perform its intended emergency purposes;

(2) Must be readily accessible to the crew and, with regard to equipment located in the passenger compartment, to passengers;

(3) Must be clearly identified and clearly marked to indicate its method of operation; and

(4) When carried in a compartment or container, must be carried in a compartment or container marked as to contents and the compartment or container, or the item itself, must be marked as to date of last inspection.

(c) For treatment of injuries, medical events, or minor accidents that might occur during flight time each airplane must have the following equipment that meets the specifications and requirements of appendix A of this part:

(1) Approved first-aid kits.

(2) In airplanes for which a flight attendant is required, an approved emergency medical kit.

(3) In airplanes for which a flight attendant is required, an approved emergency medical kit as modified effective April 12, 2004.

(4) In airplanes for which a flight attendant is required and with a maximum payload capacity of more than 7,500 pounds, an approved automated external defibrillator as of April 12, 2004.

§121.805 Crewmember training for in-flight medical events.

(a) Each training program must provide the instruction set forth in this section with respect to each airplane type, model, and configuration, each required crewmember, and each kind of operation conducted, insofar as appropriate for each crewmember and the certificate holder.

(b) Training must provide the following:

(1) Instruction in emergency medical event procedures, including coordination among crewmembers.

(2) Instruction in the location, function, and intended operation of emergency medical equipment.

(3) Instruction to familiarize crewmembers with the content of the emergency medical kit.

(4) Instruction to familiarize crewmembers with the content of the emergency medical kit as modified on April 12, 2004.

(5) For each flight attendant—

(i) Instruction, to include performance drills, in the proper use of automated external defibrillators.

(ii) Instruction, to include performance drills, in cardiopulmonary resuscitation.

(iii) Recurrent training, to include performance drills, in the proper use of an automated external defibrillators and in cardiopulmonary resuscitation at least once every 24 months.

(c) The crewmember instruction, performance drills, and recurrent training required under this section are not required to be equivalent to the expert level of proficiency attained by professional emergency medical personnel.

Subpart Y— Advanced Qualification Program

Source: Docket No. FAA–2005–20750, 70 FR 54815, September 16, 2005, unless otherwise noted.

§121.901 Purpose and eligibility.

(a) Contrary provisions of parts 61, 63, 65, 121, 135, and 142 of this chapter notwithstanding, this subpart provides for approval of an alternative method (known as "Advanced Qualification Program" or "AQP") for qualifying, training, certifying, and otherwise ensuring competency of crewmembers, aircraft dispatchers, other operations personnel, instructors, and evaluators who are required to be trained under parts 121 and 135 of this chapter.

(b) A certificate holder is eligible under this subpart if the certificate holder is required or elects to have an approved training program under §§121.401, 135.3(c), or 135.341 of this chapter.

(c) A certificate holder obtains approval of each proposed curriculum under this AQP as specified in §121.909.

§121.903 General requirements for Advanced Qualification Programs.

(a) A curriculum approved under an AQP may include elements of existing training programs under part 121 and part 135 of this chapter. Each curriculum must specify the make, model, series or variant of aircraft and each crewmember position or other positions to be covered by that curriculum. Positions to be covered by the AQP must include all flight crewmember positions, flight instructors, and evaluators and may include other positions, such as flight attendants, aircraft dispatchers, and other operations personnel.

(b) Each certificate holder that obtains approval of an AQP under this subpart must comply with all the requirements of the AQP and this subpart instead of the corresponding provisions of parts 61, 63, 65, 121, or 135 of this chapter. However, each applicable requirement of parts 61, 63, 65, 121, or 135 of this chapter, including but not limited to practical test requirements, that is not specifically addressed in the AQP continues to apply to the certificate holder and to the individuals being trained and qualified by the certificate holder. No person may be trained under an AQP unless that AQP has been approved by the FAA and the person complies with all the requirements of the AQP and this subpart.

(c) No certificate holder that conducts its training program under this subpart may use any person nor may any person serve in any duty position as a required crewmember, an aircraft dispatcher, an instructor, or an evaluator, unless that person has satisfactorily accomplished, in a training program approved under this subpart for the certificate holder, the training and evaluation of proficiency required by the AQP for that type airplane and duty position.

(d) All documentation and data required under this subpart must be submitted in a form and manner acceptable to the FAA.

(e) Any training or evaluation required under an AQP that is satisfactorily completed in the calendar month before or the calendar month after the calendar month in which it is due is considered to have been completed in the calendar month it was due.

§121.905 Confidential commercial information.

(a) Each certificate holder that claims that AQP information or data it is submitting to the FAA is entitled to confidential treatment under 5 U.S.C. 552(b)(4) because it constitutes confidential commercial information as described in 5 U.S.C. 552(b)(4), and should be withheld from public disclosure, must include its request for confidentiality with each submission.

(b) When requesting confidentiality for submitted information or data, the certificate holder must:

(1) If the information or data is transmitted electronically, embed the claim of confidentiality within the electronic record so the portions claimed to be confidential are readily apparent when received and reviewed.

(2) If the information or data is submitted in paper format, place the word "CONFIDENTIAL" on the top of each page containing information or data claimed to be confidential.

(3) Justify the basis for a claim of confidentiality under 5 U.S.C. 552(b)(4).

§121.907 Definitions.

The following definitions apply to this subpart:

Crew Resource Management (CRM) means the effective use of all the resources available to crewmembers, including each other, to achieve a safe and efficient flight.

Curriculum outline means a listing of each segment, module, lesson, and lesson element in a curriculum, or an equivalent listing acceptable to the FAA.

Evaluation of proficiency means a Line Operational Evaluation (LOE) or an equivalent evaluation under an AQP acceptable to the FAA.

Evaluator means a person who assesses or judges the performance of crewmembers, instructors, other evaluators, aircraft dispatchers, or other operations personnel.

First Look means the assessment of performance to determine proficiency on designated flight tasks before any briefing, training, or practice on those tasks is given in the training session for a continuing qualification curriculum. First Look is conducted during an AQP continuing qualification cycle to determine trends of degraded proficiency, if any, due in part to the length of the interval between training sessions.

Instructional systems development means a systematic methodology for developing or modifying qualification standards and associated curriculum content based on a documented analysis of the job tasks, skills, and knowledge required for job proficiency.

Job task listing means a listing of all tasks, subtasks, knowledge, and skills required for accomplishing the operational job.

Line Operational Evaluation (LOE) means a simulated line environment, the scenario content of which is designed to test integrating technical and CRM skills.

Line Operational Simulation (LOS) means a training or evaluation session, as applicable, that is conducted in a simulated line environment using equipment qualified and approved for its intended purpose in an AQP.

Planned hours means the estimated amount of time (as specified in a curriculum outline) that it takes a typical student to complete a segment of instruction (to include all instruction, demonstration, practice, and evaluation, as appropriate, to reach proficiency).

Qualification standard means a statement of a minimum required performance, applicable parameters, criteria, applicable flight conditions, evaluation strategy, evaluation media, and applicable document references.

Qualification standards document means a single document containing all the qualification standards for an AQP together with a prologue that provides a detailed description of all facets of the evaluation process.

Special tracking means assigning a person to an augmented schedule of training, checking, or both.

Training session means a contiguously scheduled period devoted to training activities at a facility approved by the FAA for that purpose.

Variant means a specifically configured aircraft for which the FAA has identified training and qualifications that are significantly different from those applicable to other aircraft of the same make, model, and series.

§121.909 Approval of Advanced Qualification Program.

(a) *Approval process.* Application for approval of an AQP curriculum under this subpart is made, through the FAA office responsible for approval of the certificate holder's operations specifications, to the Manager of the Advanced Qualification Program.

(b) *Approval criteria.* Each AQP must have separate curriculums for indoctrination, qualification, and continuing qualification (including upgrade, transition, and requalification), as specified in §§121.911, 121.913, and 121.915. All AQP curriculums must be based on an instructional systems development methodology. This methodology must incorporate a thorough analysis of the certificate holder's operations, aircraft, line environment and job functions. All AQP qualification and continuing qualification curriculums must integrate the training and evaluation of CRM and technical skills and knowledge. An application for approval of an AQP curriculum may be approved if the program meets the following requirements:

(1) The program must meet all the requirements of this subpart.

(2) Each indoctrination, qualification, and continuing qualification AQP, and derivatives must include the following documentation:

(i) Initial application for AQP.

(ii) Initial job task listing.

(iii) Instructional systems development methodology.

(iv) Qualification standards document.

(v) Curriculum outline.

(vi) Implementation and operations plan.

(3) Subject to approval by the FAA, certificate holders may elect, where appropriate, to consolidate information about multiple programs within any of the documents referenced in paragraph (b)(2) of this section.

(4) The Qualification Standards Document must indicate specifically the requirements of the parts 61, 63, 65, 121, or 135 of this chapter, as applicable, that would be replaced by an AQP curriculum. If a practical test requirement of parts 61, 63, 65, 121, or 135 of this chapter is replaced by an AQP curriculum, the certificate holder must establish an initial justification and a continuing process approved by the FAA to show how the AQP curriculum provides an equivalent level of safety for each requirement that is to be replaced.

(c) *Application and transition.* Each certificate holder that applies for one or more advanced qualification curriculums must include as part of its application a proposed transition plan (containing a calendar of events) for moving from its present approved training to the advanced qualification program training.

(d) *Advanced Qualification Program revisions or rescissions of approval.* If after a certificate holder begins training and qualification under an AQP, the FAA finds the certificate holder is not meeting the provisions of its approved AQP, the FAA may require the certificate holder, pursuant to §121.405(e), to make revisions. Or if otherwise warranted, the FAA may withdraw AQP approval and require the certificate holder to submit and obtain approval for a plan (containing a schedule of events) that the certificate holder must comply with and use to transition to an approved training program under subpart N of this part or under subpart H of part 135 of this chapter, as appropriate. The certificate holder may also voluntarily submit and obtain approval for a plan (containing a schedule of events) to transition to an approved training program under subpart N of this part or under subpart H of part 135 of this chapter, as appropriate.

(e) *Approval by the FAA.* Final approval of an AQP by the FAA indicates the FAA has accepted the justification provided under paragraph (b)(4) of this section and the applicant's initial justification and continuing process establish an equivalent level of safety for each requirement of parts 61, 63, 65, 121, and 135 of this chapter that is being replaced.

§121.911 Indoctrination curriculum.

Each indoctrination curriculum must include the following:

(a) *For newly hired persons being trained under an AQP:* The certificate holder's policies and operating practices and general operational knowledge.

(b) *For newly hired crewmembers and aircraft dispatchers:* General aeronautical knowledge appropriate to the duty position.

(c) *For instructors:* The fundamental principles of the teaching and learning process; methods and theories of instruction; and the knowledge necessary to use aircraft, flight training devices, flight simulators, and other training equipment in advanced qualification curriculums, as appropriate.

(d) *For evaluators:* General evaluation requirements of the AQP; methods of evaluating crewmembers and aircraft dispatchers and other operations personnel, as appropriate, and policies and practices used to conduct the kinds of evaluations particular to an AQP (e.g., LOE).

§121.913 Qualification curriculum.

Each qualification curriculum must contain training, evaluation, and certification activities, as applicable for specific positions subject to the AQP, as follows:

(a) The certificate holder's planned hours of training, evaluation, and supervised operating experience.

(b) *For crewmembers, aircraft dispatchers, and other operations personnel, the following:*

(1) Training, evaluation, and certification activities that are aircraft- and equipment-specific to qualify a person for a particular duty position on, or duties related to the operation of, a specific make, model, series, or variant aircraft.

(2) A list of and text describing the knowledge requirements, subject materials, job skills, and qualification standards of each proficiency objective to be trained and evaluated.

(3) The requirements of the certificate holder's approved AQP program that are in addition to or in place of, the requirements of parts 61, 63, 65, 121 or 135 of this chapter, including any applicable practical test requirements.

(4) A list of and text describing operating experience, evaluation/remediation strategies, provisions for special tracking, and how recency of experience requirements will be accomplished.

(c) *For flight crewmembers:* Initial operating experience and line check.

(d) *For instructors, the following as appropriate:*

(1) Training and evaluation activities to qualify a person to conduct instruction on how to operate, or on how to ensure the safe operation of a particular make, model, and series aircraft (or variant).

(2) A list of and text describing the knowledge requirements, subject materials, job skills, and qualification standards of each procedure and proficiency objective to be trained and evaluated.

(3) A list of and text describing evaluation/remediation strategies, standardization policies and recency requirements.

(e) *For evaluators:* The requirements of paragraph (d)(1) of this section plus the following, as appropriate:

(1) Training and evaluation activities that are aircraft and equipment specific to qualify a person to assess the performance of persons who operate or who ensure the safe operation of, a particular make, model, and series aircraft (or variant).

(2) A list of and text describing the knowledge requirements, subject materials, job skills, and qualification standards of each procedure and proficiency objective to be trained and evaluated.

(3) A list of and text describing evaluation/remediation strategies, standardization policies and recency requirements.

§121.915 Continuing qualification curriculum.

Each continuing qualification curriculum must contain training and evaluation activities, as applicable for specific positions subject to the AQP, as follows:

(a) *Continuing qualification cycle.* A continuing qualification cycle that ensures that during each cycle each person qualified under an AQP, including instructors and evaluators, will receive a mix that will ensure training and evaluation on all events and subjects necessary to ensure that each person maintains proficiency in knowledge, technical skills, and cognitive skills required for initial qualification in accordance with the approved continuing qualification AQP, evaluation/remediation strategies, and provisions for special tracking. Each continuing qualification cycle must include at least the following:

(1) *Evaluation period.* Initially the continuing qualification cycle is comprised of two or more evaluation periods of equal duration. Each person qualified under an AQP must receive ground training and flight training, as appropriate, and an evaluation of proficiency during each evaluation period at a training facility. The number and frequency of training sessions must be approved by the FAA.

(2) *Training.* Continuing qualification must include training in all tasks, procedures and subjects required in accordance with the approved program documentation, as follows:

(i) For pilots in command, seconds in command, and flight engineers, First Look in accordance with the certificate holder's FAA-approved program documentation.

(ii) For pilots in command, seconds in command, flight engineers, flight attendants, instructors and evaluators: Ground training including a general review of knowledge and skills covered in qualification training, updated information on newly developed procedures, and safety information.

(iii) For crewmembers, instructors, evaluators, and other operational personnel who conduct their duties in flight: Proficiency training in an aircraft, flight training device, flight simulator, or other equipment, as appropriate, on normal, abnormal, and emergency flight procedures and maneuvers.

(iv) For dispatchers and other operational personnel who do not conduct their duties in flight: ground training including a general review of knowledge and skills covered in qualification training, updated information on newly developed procedures, safety related information, and, if applicable, a line observation program.

(v) For instructors and evaluators: Proficiency training in the type flight training device or the type flight simulator, as appropriate, regarding training equipment operation. For instructors and evaluators who are limited to conducting their duties in flight simulators or flight training devices: Training in operational flight procedures and maneuvers (normal, abnormal, and emergency).

(b) *Evaluation of performance.* Continuing qualification must include evaluation of performance on a sample of those events and major subjects identified as diagnostic of competence and approved for that purpose by the FAA. The following evaluation requirements apply:

(1) *Evaluation of proficiency as follows:*

(i) For pilots in command, seconds in command, and flight engineers: An evaluation of proficiency, portions of which may be conducted in an aircraft, flight simulator, or flight training device as approved in the certificate holder's curriculum that must be completed during each evaluation period.

(ii) For any other persons covered by an AQP, a means to evaluate their proficiency in the performance of their duties in their assigned tasks in an operational setting.

(2) *Line checks as follows:*

(i) Except as provided in paragraph (b)(2)(ii) of this section, for pilots in command: A line check conducted in an aircraft during actual flight operations under part 121 or part 135 of this chapter or during operationally (line) oriented flights, such as ferry flights or proving flights. A line check must be completed in the calendar month at the midpoint of the evaluation period.

(ii) With the FAA's approval, a no-notice line check strategy may be used in lieu of the line check required by paragraph (b)(2)(i) of this section. The certificate holder who elects to exercise this option must ensure the "no-notice" line checks are administered so the flight crewmembers are not notified before the evaluation. In addition, the AQP certificate holder must ensure that each pilot in command receives at least one "no-notice" line check every 24 months. As a minimum, the number of "no-notice" line checks administered each calendar year must equal at least 50% of the certificate holder's pilot-in-command workforce in accordance with a strategy approved by the FAA for that purpose. In addition, the line checks to be conducted under this paragraph must be conducted over all geographic areas flown by the certificate holder in accordance with a sampling methodology approved by the FAA for that purpose.

(iii) During the line checks required under paragraph (b)(2)(i) and (ii) of this section, each person performing duties as a pilot in command, second in command, or flight engineer for that flight, must be individually evaluated to determine whether the person remains adequately trained and currently proficient with respect to the particular aircraft, crew position, and type of operation in which he or she serves; and the person has sufficient knowledge and skills to operate effectively as part of a crew. The evaluator must be a check airman, an APD, or an FAA inspector and must hold the certificates and ratings required of the pilot in command.

(c) *Recency of experience.* For pilots in command, seconds in command, flight engineers, aircraft dispatchers, instructors, evaluators, and flight attendants, approved recency of experience requirements appropriate to the duty position.

(d) *Duration of cycles and periods.* Initially, the continuing qualification cycle approved for an AQP must not exceed 24 calendar months in duration, and must include two or more evaluation periods of equal duration. After that, upon demonstration by a certificate holder that an extension is warranted, the FAA may approve an extension of the continuing qualification cycle to a maximum of 36 calendar months in duration.

(e) *Requalification.* Each continuing qualification curriculum must include a curriculum segment that covers the requirements for requalifying a crewmember, aircraft dispatcher, other operations personnel, instructor, or evaluator who has not maintained continuing qualification.

§121.917 Other requirements.

In addition to the requirements of §§121.913 and 121.915, each AQP qualification and continuing qualification curriculum must include the following requirements:

(a) Integrated Crew Resource Management (CRM) or Dispatcher Resource Management

(DRM) ground and if appropriate flight training applicable to each position for which training is provided under an AQP.

(b) Approved training on and evaluation of skills and proficiency of each person being trained under AQP to use his or her resource management skills and his or her technical (piloting or other) skills in an actual or simulated operations scenario. For flight crewmembers this training and evaluation must be conducted in an approved flight training device, flight simulator, or, if approved under this subpart, in an aircraft.

(c) Data collection and analysis processes acceptable to the FAA that will ensure the certificate holder provides performance information on its crewmembers, dispatchers, instructors, evaluators, and other operations personnel that will enable the certificate holder and the FAA to determine whether the form and content of training and evaluation activities are satisfactorily accomplishing the overall objectives of the curriculum.

§121.919 Certification.

A person subject to an AQP is eligible to receive a commercial or airline transport pilot, flight engineer, or aircraft dispatcher certificate or appropriate rating based on the successful completion of training and evaluation events accomplished under that program if the following requirements are met:

(a) Training and evaluation of required knowledge and skills under the AQP must meet minimum certification and rating criteria established by the FAA in parts 61, 63, or 65 of this chapter. The FAA may approve alternatives to the certification and rating criteria of parts 61, 63, or 65 of this chapter, including practical test requirements, if it can be demonstrated that the newly established criteria or requirements represent an equivalent or better measure of crewmember or dispatcher competence, operational proficiency, and safety.

(b) The applicant satisfactorily completes the appropriate qualification curriculum.

(c) The applicant shows competence in required technical knowledge and skills (e.g., piloting or other) and crew resource management (e.g., CRM or DRM) knowledge and skills in scenarios (i.e., LOE) that test both types of knowledge and skills together.

(d) The applicant is otherwise eligible under the applicable requirements of part 61, 63, or 65 of this chapter.

(e) The applicant has been trained to proficiency on the certificate holder's approved AQP Qualification Standards as witnessed by an instructor, check airman, or APD and has passed an LOE administered by an APD or the FAA.

§121.921 Training devices and simulators.

(a) Each flight training device or airplane simulator that will be used in an AQP for one of the following purposes must be evaluated by the FAA for assignment of a flight training device or flight simulator qualification level:

(1) Required evaluation of individual or crew proficiency.

(2) Training to proficiency or training activities that determine if an individual or crew is ready for an evaluation of proficiency.

(3) Activities used to meet recency of experience requirements.

(4) Line Operational Simulations (LOS).

(b) Approval of other training equipment.

(1) Any training equipment that is intended to be used in an AQP for purposes other than those set forth in paragraph (a) of this section must be approved by the FAA for its intended use.

(2) An applicant for approval of training equipment under this paragraph must identify the device by its nomenclature and describe its intended use.

(3) Each training device approved for use in an AQP must be part of a continuing program to provide for its serviceability and fitness to perform its intended function as approved by the FAA.

§121.923 Approval of training, qualification, or evaluation by a person who provides training by arrangement.

(a) A certificate holder operating under part 121 or part 135 of this chapter may arrange to have AQP training, qualification, evaluation, or certification functions performed by another person (a "training provider") if the following requirements are met:

(1) The training provider is certificated under part 119 or 142 of this chapter.

(2) The training provider's AQP training and qualification curriculums, curriculum segments, or portions of curriculum segments must be provisionally approved by the FAA. A training provider may apply for provisional approval independently or in conjunction with a certificate holder's application for AQP approval. Application for provisional approval must be made, through the FAA office directly responsible for oversight of the training provider, to the Manager of the Advanced Qualification Program.

(3) The specific use of provisionally approved curriculums, curriculum segments, or portions of curriculum segments in a certificate holder's AQP must be approved by the FAA as set forth in §121.909.

(b) An applicant for provisional approval of a curriculum, curriculum segment, or portion of a curriculum segment under this paragraph must show the following requirements are met:

(1) The applicant must have a curriculum for the qualification and continuing qualification of each instructor and evaluator used by the applicant.

(2) The applicant's facilities must be found by the FAA to be adequate for any planned training, qualification, or evaluation for a certificate holder operating under part 121 or part 135 of this chapter.

(3) Except for indoctrination curriculums, the curriculum, curriculum segment, or portion of a curriculum segment must identify the specific make, model, and series aircraft (or variant) and crewmember or other positions for which it is designed.

(c) A certificate holder who wants approval to use a training provider's provisionally approved curriculum, curriculum segment, or portion of a curriculum segment in its AQP, must show the following requirements are met:

(1) Each instructor or evaluator used by the training provider must meet all the qualification and continuing qualification requirements that apply to employees of the certificate holder that has arranged for the training, including knowledge of the certificate holder's operations.

(2) Each provisionally approved curriculum, curriculum segment, or portion of a curriculum segment must be approved by the FAA for use in the certificate holder's AQP. The FAA will either provide approval or require modifications to ensure that each curriculum, curriculum segment, or portion of a curriculum segment is applicable to the certificate holder's AQP.

§121.925 Recordkeeping requirements.

Each certificate holder conducting an approved AQP must establish and maintain records in sufficient detail to demonstrate the certificate holder is in compliance with all the requirements of the AQP and this subpart.

Subpart Z— Hazardous Materials Training Program

Source: Docket No. FAA–2003–15085, 70 FR 58823, October 7, 2005, unless otherwise noted.

§121.1001 Applicability and definitions.

(a) This subpart prescribes the requirements applicable to each certificate holder for training each crewmember and person performing or directly supervising any of the following job functions involving any item for transport on board an aircraft:

(1) Acceptance;
(2) Rejection;
(3) Handling;
(4) Storage incidental to transport;
(5) Packaging of company material; or
(6) Loading.

(b) *Definitions.* For purposes of this subpart, the following definitions apply:

(1) Company material (COMAT)—Material owned or used by a certificate holder.

(2) Initial hazardous materials training—The basic training required for each newly hired person, or each person changing job functions, who performs or directly supervises any of the job functions specified in paragraph (a) of this section.

(3) Recurrent hazardous materials training—The training required every 24 months for each person who has satisfactorily completed the certificate holder's approved initial hazardous materials training program and performs or directly supervises any of the job functions specified in paragraph (a) of this section.

§121.1003 Hazardous materials training: General.

(a) Each certificate holder must establish and implement a hazardous materials training program that:

(1) Satisfies the requirements of Appendix O of this part;

(2) Ensures that each person performing or directly supervising any of the job functions specified in §121.1001(a) is trained to comply with all applicable parts of 49 CFR parts 171 through 180 and the requirements of this subpart; and

(3) Enables the trained person to recognize items that contain, or may contain, hazardous materials regulated by 49 CFR parts 171 through 180.

(b) Each certificate holder must provide initial hazardous materials training and recurrent hazardous materials training to each crewmember and person performing or directly supervising any of the job functions specified in §121.1001(a).

(c) Each certificate holder's hazardous materials training program must be approved by the FAA prior to implementation.

§121.1005 Hazardous materials training required.

(a) *Training requirement.* Except as provided in paragraphs (b), (c) and (f) of this section, no certificate holder may use any crewmember or person to perform any of the job functions or direct supervisory responsibilities, and no person may perform any of the job functions or direct supervisory responsibilities, specified in §121.1001(a) unless that person has satisfactorily completed the certificate holder's FAA-approved initial or recurrent hazardous materials training program within the past 24 months.

(b) *New hire or new job function.* A person who is a new hire and has not yet satisfactorily completed the required initial hazardous materials training, or a person who is changing job functions and has not received initial or recurrent training for a job function involving storage incidental to transport, or loading of items for transport on an aircraft, may perform those job functions for not more than 30 days from the date of hire or a change in job function, if the person is under the direct visual supervision of a person who is authorized by the certificate holder to supervise that person and who has successfully completed the certificate holder's FAA-approved initial or recurrent training program within the past 24 months.

(c) *Persons who work for more than one certificate holder.* A certificate holder that uses or assigns a person to perform or directly supervise a job function specified in §121.1001(a), when that person also performs or directly supervises the same job function for another certificate holder, need only train that person in its own policies and procedures regarding those job functions, if all of the following are met:

(1) The certificate holder using this exception receives written verification from the person designated to hold the training records representing the other certificate holder that the person has satisfactorily completed hazardous materials training for the specific job function under the other certificate holder's FAA approved hazardous material training program under Appendix O of this part; and

(2) The certificate holder who trained the person has the same operations specifications regarding the acceptance, handling, and transport of hazardous materials as the certificate holder using this exception.

(d) *Recurrent hazardous materials training—Completion date.* A person who satisfactorily completes recurrent hazardous materials training in the calendar month before, or the calendar month after, the month in which the recurrent training is due, is considered to have taken that training during the month in which it is due. If the person completes this training earlier than the month before it is due, the month of the completion date becomes his or her new anniversary month.

(e) *Repair stations.* A certificate holder must ensure that each repair station performing work for, or on the certificate holder's behalf is notified in writing of the certificate holder's policies and operations specification authorization permitting or prohibition against the acceptance, rejection, handling, storage incidental to transport, and transportation of hazardous materials, including company material. This notification requirement applies only to repair stations that are regulated by 49 CFR parts 171 through 180.

(f) *Certificate holders operating at foreign locations.* This exception applies if a certificate holder operating at a foreign location where the country requires the certificate holder to use persons working in that country to load aircraft. In such a case, the certificate holder may use those persons even if they have not been trained in accordance with the certificate holder's FAA approved hazardous materials training program. Those persons, however, must be under the direct visual supervision of someone who has successfully completed the certificate holder's approved initial or recurrent hazardous materials training program in accordance with this part. This exception applies only to those persons who load aircraft.

§121.1007 Hazardous materials training records.

(a) *General requirement.* Each certificate holder must maintain a record of all training required by this part received within the preceding three years for each person who performs or directly supervises a job function specified in §121.1001(a). The record must be maintained during the time that the person performs or directly supervises any of those job functions, and for 90 days thereafter. These training records must be kept for direct employees of the certificate holder, as well as independent contractors, subcontractors, and any other person who performs or directly supervises these job functions for or on behalf of the certificate holder.

(b) *Location of records.* The certificate holder must retain the training records required by paragraph (a) of this section for all initial and recurrent training received within the preceding 3 years for all persons performing or directly supervising the job functions listed in Appendix O at a designated location. The records must be available upon request at the location where the trained person performs or directly supervises the job function specified in §121.1001(a). Records may be maintained electronically and provided on location electronically. When the person ceases to perform or directly supervise a hazardous materials job function, the certificate holder must retain the hazardous materials training records for an additional 90 days and make them available upon request at the last location where the person worked.

(c) *Content of records.* Each record must contain the following:
(1) The individual's name;
(2) The most recent training completion date;
(3) A description, copy or reference to training materials used to meet the training requirement;
(4) The name and address of the organization providing the training; and
(5) A copy of the certification issued when the individual was trained, which shows that a test has been completed satisfactorily.

(d) *New hire or new job function.* Each certificate holder using a person under the exception in §121.1005(b) must maintain a record for that person. The records must be available upon request at the location where the trained person performs or directly supervises the job function specified in §121.1001(a). Records may be maintained electronically and provided on location electronically. The record must include the following:
(1) A signed statement from an authorized representative of the certificate holder authorizing the use of the person in accordance with the exception;
(2) The date of hire or change in job function;
(3) The person's name and assigned job function;
(4) The name of the supervisor of the job function; and
(5) The date the person is to complete hazardous materials training in accordance with appendix O of this part.

Subpart AA— Continued Airworthiness and Safety Improvements

Source: Docket No. FAA–2004–18379, 72 FR 63411, November 8, 2007, unless otherwise noted.

§121.1101 Purpose and definition.

(a) This subpart requires persons holding an air carrier or operating certificate under part 119 of this chapter to support the continued airworthiness of each airplane. These requirements may include, but are not limited to, revising the maintenance program, incorporating design changes, and incorporating revisions to Instructions for Continued Airworthiness.

(b) For purposes of this subpart, the "FAA Oversight Office" is the aircraft certification office or office of the Transport Airplane Directorate with oversight responsibility for the relevant type certificate or supplemental type certificate, as determined by the Administrator.

§121.1103 [Reserved]

§121.1105 Aging airplane inspections and records reviews.

(a) *Applicability.* This section applies to all airplanes operated by a certificate holder under this part, except for those airplanes operated between any point within the State of Alaska and any other point within the State of Alaska.

(b) *Operation after inspection and records review.* After the dates specified in this paragraph, a certificate holder may not operate an airplane under this part unless the Administrator has notified the certificate holder that the Administrator has completed the aging airplane inspection and records review required by this section. During the inspection and records review, the certificate holder must demonstrate to the Administrator that the maintenance of age-sensitive parts and components of the airplane has been adequate and timely enough to ensure the highest degree of safety.
(1) Airplanes exceeding 24 years in service on December 8, 2003; initial and repetitive inspections and records reviews. For an airplane that has exceeded 24 years in service on December 8, 2003, no later than December 5, 2007, and thereafter at intervals not to exceed 7 years.
(2) Airplanes exceeding 14 years in service but not 24 years in service on December 8, 2003; initial and repetitive inspections and records reviews. For an airplane that has exceeded 14 years in service but not 24 years in service on December 8, 2003, no later than December 4, 2008, and thereafter at intervals not to exceed 7 years.
(3) Airplanes not exceeding 14 years in service on December 8, 2003; initial and repetitive inspections and records reviews. For an airplane that has not exceeded 14 years in service on December 8, 2003, no later than 5 years after the start of the airplane's 15th year in service and thereafter at intervals not to exceed 7 years.

(c) *Unforeseen schedule conflict.* In the event of an unforeseen scheduling conflict for a specific airplane, the Administrator may approve an extension of up to 90 days beyond an interval specified in paragraph (b) of this section.

(d) *Airplane and records availability.* The certificate holder must make available to the Administrator each airplane for which an inspection and records review is required under this section, in a condition for inspection specified by the Administrator, together with records containing the following information:
(1) Total years in service of the airplane;
(2) Total time in service of the airframe;
(3) Total flight cycles of the airframe;
(4) Date of the last inspection and records review required by this section;
(5) Current status of life-limited parts of the airframe;

(6) Time since the last overhaul of all structural components required to be overhauled on a specific time basis;

(7) Current inspection status of the airplane, including the time since the last inspection required by the inspection program under which the airplane is maintained;

(8) Current status of applicable airworthiness directives, including the date and methods of compliance, and if the airworthiness directive involves recurring action, the time and date when the next action is required;

(9) A list of major structural alterations; and

(10) A report of major structural repairs and the current inspection status for those repairs.

(e) *Notification to Administrator.* Each certificate holder must notify the Administrator at least 60 days before the date on which the airplane and airplane records will be made available for the inspection and records review.

§121.1107 Repairs assessment for pressurized fuselages.

(a) No certificate holder may operate an Airbus Model A300 (excluding the –600 series), British Aerospace Model BAC 1–11, Boeing Model 707, 720, 727, 737, or 747, McDonnell Douglas Model DC–8, DC–9/MD–80 or DC–10, Fokker Model F28, or Lockheed Model L–1011 airplane beyond the applicable flight cycle implementation time specified below, or May 25, 2001, whichever occurs later, unless operations specifications have been issued to reference repair assessment guidelines applicable to the fuselage pressure boundary (fuselage skin, door skin, and bulkhead webs), and those guidelines are incorporated in its maintenance program. The repair assessment guidelines must be approved by the FAA Aircraft Certification Office (ACO), or office of the Transport Airplane Directorate, having cognizance over the type certificate for the affected airplane.

(1) For the Airbus Model A300 (excluding the –600 series), the flight cycle implementation time is:

(i) Model B2: 36,000 flights.

(ii) Model B4–100 (including Model B4–2C): 30,000 flights above the window line, and 36,000 flights below the window line.

(iii) Model B4–200: 25,500 flights above the window line, and 34,000 flights below the window line.

(2) For all models of the British Aerospace BAC 1–11, the flight cycle implementation time is 60,000 flights.

(3) For all models of the Boeing 707, the flight cycle implementation time is 15,000 flights.

(4) For all models of the Boeing 720, the flight cycle implementation time is 23,000 flights.

(5) For all models of the Boeing 727, the flight cycle implementation time is 45,000 flights.

(6) For all models of the Boeing 737, the flight cycle implementation time is 60,000 flights.

(7) For all models of the Boeing 747, the flight cycle implementation time is 15,000 flights.

(8) For all models of the McDonnell Douglas DC–8, the flight cycle implementation time is 30,000 flights.

(9) For all models of the McDonnell Douglas DC–9/MD–80, the flight cycle implementation time is 60,000 flights.

(10) For all models of the McDonnell Douglas DC–10, the flight cycle implementation time is 30,000 flights.

(11) For all models of the Lockheed L–1011, the flight cycle implementation time is 27,000 flights.

(12) For the Fokker F–28 Mark 1000, 2000, 3000, and 4000, the flight cycle implementation time is 60,000 flights.

(b) [Reserved]

§121.1109 Supplemental inspections.

(a) *Applicability.* Except as specified in paragraph (b) of this section, this section applies to transport category, turbine powered airplanes with a type certificate issued after January 1, 1958, that as a result of original type certification or later increase in capacity have—

(1) A maximum type certificated passenger seating capacity of 30 or more; or

(2) A maximum payload capacity of 7,500 pounds or more.

(b) *Exception.* This section does not apply to an airplane operated by a certificate holder under this part between any point within the State of Alaska and any other point within the State of Alaska.

(c) *General requirements.* After December 20, 2010, a certificate holder may not operate an airplane under this part unless the following requirements have been met:

(1) *Baseline Structure.* The certificate holder's maintenance program for the airplane includes FAA-approved damage-tolerance-based inspections and procedures for airplane structure susceptible to fatigue cracking that could contribute to a catastrophic failure. For the purpose of this section, this structure is termed "fatigue critical structure."

(2) *Adverse effects of repairs, alterations, and modifications.* The maintenance program for the airplane includes a means for addressing the adverse effects repairs, alterations, and modifications may have on fatigue critical structure and on inspections required by paragraph (c)(1) of this section. The means for addressing these adverse effects must be approved by the FAA Oversight Office.

(3) *Changes to maintenance program.* The changes made to the maintenance program required by paragraphs (c)(1) and (c)(2) of this section, and any later revisions to these changes, must be submitted to the Principal Maintenance Inspector for review and approval.

[Docket No. FAA–2004–18379, 72 FR 63411, Nov. 8, 2007; as amended by Amdt. 121–337, 72 FR 70508, Dec. 12, 2007]

§121.1111 Electrical wiring interconnection systems (EWIS) maintenance program.

(a) Except as provided in paragraph (f) of this section, this section applies to transport category, turbine-powered airplanes with a type certificate issued after January 1, 1958, that, as a result of original type certification or later increase in capacity, have—

(1) A maximum type-certificated passenger capacity of 30 or more, or

(2) A maximum payload capacity of 7500 pounds or more.

(b) After March 10, 2011, no certificate holder may operate an airplane identified in paragraph (a) of this section unless the maintenance program for that airplane includes inspections and procedures for electrical wiring interconnection systems (EWIS).

(c) The proposed EWIS maintenance program changes must be based on EWIS Instructions for Continued Airworthiness (ICA) that have been developed in accordance with the provisions of Appendix H of part 25 of this chapter applicable to each affected airplane (including those ICA developed for supplemental type certificates installed on each airplane) and that have been approved by the FAA Oversight Office.

(1) For airplanes subject to §26.11 of this chapter, the EWIS ICA must comply with paragraphs H25.5(a)(1) and (b).

(2) For airplanes subject to §25.1729 of this chapter, the EWIS ICA must comply with paragraph H25.4 and all of paragraph H25.5.

(d) After March 10, 2011, before returning an airplane to service after any alterations for which EWIS ICA are developed, the certificate holder must include in the airplane's maintenance program inspections and procedures for EWIS based on those ICA.

(e) The EWIS maintenance program changes identified in paragraphs (c) and (d) of this section and any later EWIS revisions must be submitted to the Principal Inspector for review and approval.

(f) This section does not apply to the following airplane models:

(1) Lockheed L-188
(2) Bombardier CL-44
(3) Mitsubishi YS-11
(4) British Aerospace BAC 1-11
(5) Concorde
(6) deHavilland D.H. 106 Comet 4C
(7) VFW-Vereinigte Flugtechnische Werk VFW-614
(8) Illyushin Aviation IL 96T
(9) Bristol Aircraft Britannia 305
(10) Handley Page Herald Type 300
(11) Avions Marcel Dassault—Breguet Aviation Mercure 100C
(12) Airbus Caravelle
(13) Lockheed L-300

§121.1113 Fuel tank system maintenance program.

(a) Except as provided in paragraph (g) of this section, this section applies to transport category, turbine-powered airplanes with a type certificate issued after January 1, 1958, that, as a result of original type certification or later increase in capacity, have—

(1) A maximum type-certificated passenger capacity of 30 or more, or

(2) A maximum payload capacity of 7500 pounds or more.

(b) For each airplane on which an auxiliary fuel tank is installed under a field approval, before June 16, 2008, the certificate holder must submit to the FAA Oversight Office proposed maintenance instructions for the tank that meet the requirements of Special Federal Aviation Regulation No. 88 (SFAR 88) of this chapter.

(c) After December 16, 2008, no certificate holder may operate an airplane identified in paragraph (a) of this section unless the maintenance program for that airplane has been revised to include applicable inspections, procedures, and limitations for fuel tanks systems.

(d) The proposed fuel tank system maintenance program revisions must be based on fuel tank system Instructions for Continued Airworthiness (ICA) that have been developed in accordance with the applicable provisions of SFAR 88 of this chapter or §25.1529 and part 25, Appendix H, of this chapter, in effect on June 6, 2001 (including those developed for auxiliary fuel tanks, if any, installed under supplemental type certificates or other design approval) and that have been approved by the FAA Oversight Office.

(e) After December 16, 2008, before returning an aircraft to service after any alteration for which fuel tank ICA are developed under SFAR 88 or under §25.1529 in effect on June 6, 2001, the certificate holder must include in the maintenance program for the airplane inspections and procedures for the fuel tank system based on those ICA.

(f) The fuel tank system maintenance program changes identified in paragraphs (d) and (e) of this section and any later fuel tank system revisions must be submitted to the Principal Inspector for review and approval.

(g) This section does not apply to the following airplane models:
(1) Bombardier CL-44
(2) Concorde
(3) deHavilland D.H. 106 Comet 4C
(4) VFW-Vereinigte Flugtechnische Werk VFW-614
(5) Illyushin Aviation IL 96T
(6) Bristol Aircraft Britannia 305
(7) Handley Page Herald Type 300
(8) Avions Marcel Dassault—Breguet Aviation Mercure 100C
(9) Airbus Caravelle
(10) Lockheed L-300

§121.1115 Limit of validity.

(a) *Applicability.* This section applies to certificate holders operating any transport category, turbine-powered airplane with a maximum takeoff gross weight greater than 75,000 pounds and a type certificate issued after January 1, 1958, regardless of whether the maximum takeoff gross weight is a result of an original type certificate or a later design change. This section also applies to certificate holders operating any transport category, turbine-powered airplane with a type certificate issued after January 1, 1958, regardless of the maximum takeoff gross weight, for which a limit of validity of the engineering data that supports the structural maintenance program (hereafter referred to as LOV) is required in accordance with §25.571 or §26.21 of this chapter after January 14, 2011.

(b) *Limit of validity.* No certificate holder may operate an airplane identified in paragraph (a) of this section after the applicable date identified in Table 1 of this section unless an Airworthiness Limitations section approved under Appendix H to part 25 or §26.21 of this chapter is incorporated into its maintenance program. The ALS must—
(1) Include an LOV approved under §25.571 or §26.21 of this chapter, as applicable, except as provided in paragraph (f) of this section; and
(2) Be clearly distinguishable within its maintenance program.

(c) *Operation of airplanes excluded from §26.21.* No certificate holder may operate an airplane identified in §26.21(g) of this chapter after July 14, 2013, unless an Airworthiness Limitations section approved under Appendix H to Part 25 or §26.21 of this chapter is incorporated into its maintenance program. The ALS must—
(1) Include an LOV approved under §25.571 or §26.21 of this chapter, as applicable, except as provided in paragraph (f) of this section; and
(2) Be clearly distinguishable within its maintenance program.

(d) *Extended limit of validity.* No certificate holder may operate an airplane beyond the LOV, or extended LOV, specified in paragraph (b)(1), (c), (d), or (f) of this section, as applicable, unless the following conditions are met:
(1) An ALS must be incorporated into its maintenance program that—
(i) Includes an extended LOV and any widespread fatigue damage airworthiness limitation items approved under §26.23 of this chapter; and
(ii) Is approved under §26.23 of this chapter.
(2) The extended LOV and the airworthiness limitation items pertaining to widespread fatigue damage must be clearly distinguishable within its maintenance program.

(e) *Principal Maintenance Inspector Approval.* Certificate holders must submit the maintenance program revisions required by paragraphs (b), (c), and (d) of this section to the Principal Maintenance Inspector for review and approval.

(f) *Exception.* For any airplane for which an LOV has not been approved as of the applicable compliance date specified in paragraph (c) or Table 1 of this section, instead of including an approved LOV in the ALS, an operator must include the applicable default LOV specified in Table 1 or Table 2 of this section, as applicable, in the ALS.

§121.1115 Federal Aviation Regulations

TABLE 1 — AIRPLANES SUBJECT TO SECTION 26.1

Airplane model	Compliance date—months after January 14, 2011	Default LOV [flight cycles (FC) or flight hours (FH)]
Airbus—Existing[1] Models Only:		
A300 B2-1A, B2-1C, B2K-3C, B2-203	30	48,000 FC
A300 B4-2C, B4-103	30	40,000 FC
A300 B4-203	30	34,000 FC
A300-600 Series	60	30,000 FC/67,500 FH
A310-200 Series	60	40,000 FC/60,000 FH
A310-300 Series	60	35,000 FC/60,000 FH
A318 Series	60	48,000 FC/60,000 FH
A319 Series	60	48,000 FC/60,000 FH
A320-100 Series	60	48,000 FC/48,000 FH
A320-200 Series	60	48,000 FC/60,000 FH
A321 Series	60	48,000 FC/60,000 FH
A330-200, -300 Series (except WV050 family) (non enhanced)	60	40,000 FC/60,000 FH
A330-200, -300 Series WV050 family (enhanced)	60	33,000 FC/100,000 FH
A330-200 Freighter Series	60	*See* NOTE
A340-200, -300 Series (except WV027 and WV050 family) (non enhanced)	60	20,000 FC/80,000 FH
A340-200, -300 Series WV027 (non enhanced)	60	30,000 FC/60,000 FH
A340-300 Series WV050 family (enhanced)	60	20,000 FC/100,000 FH
A340-500, -600 Series	60	16,600 FC/100,000 FH
A380-800 Series	72	*See* NOTE
Boeing—Existing[1] Models Only:		
717	60	60,000 FC/60,000 FH
727 (all series)	30	60,000 FC
737 (Classics): 737-100, -200, -200C, -300, -400, -500	30	75,000 FC
737 (NG): 737-600, -700, -700C, -800, -900, -900ER	60	75,000 FC
747 (Classics): 747-100, -100B, -100B SUD, -200B, -200C, -200F, -300, 747SP, 747SR	30	20,000 FC
747-400: 747-400, -400D, -400F	60	20,000 FC
757	60	50,000 FC
767	60	50,000 FC
777-200, -300	60	40,000 FC
777-200LR, 777-300ER	72	40,000 FC
777F	72	11,000 FC
Bombardier—Existing[1] Models Only:		
CL-600: 2D15 (Regional Jet Series 705), 2D24 (Regional Jet Series 900)	72	60,000 FC
Embraer—Existing[1] Models Only:		
ERJ 170	72	*See* NOTE
ERJ 190	72	*See* NOTE
Fokker—Existing[1] Models Only:		
F.28 Mark 0070, Mark 0100	30	90,000 FC

Part 121: Air Carriers & Commercial Operators §121.1115

Airplane model	Compliance date—months after January 14, 2011	Default LOV [flight cycles (FC) or flight hours (FH)]
Lockheed—Existing[1] Models Only:		
L-1011	30	36,000 FC
188	30	26,600 FC
382 (all series)	30	20,000 FC/50,000 FH
McDonnell Douglas—Existing[1] Models Only:		
DC-8, -8F	30	50,000 FC/50,000 FH
DC-9 (except for MD-80 models)	30	100,000 FC/100,000 FH
MD-80 (DC-9-81, -82, -83, -87, MD-88)	30	50,000 FC/50,000 FH
MD-90	60	60,000 FC/90,000 FH
DC-10-10, -15	30	42,000 FC/60,000 FH
DC-10-30, -40, 10F, -30F, -40F	30	30,000 FC/60,000 FH
MD-10-10F	60	42,000 FC/60,000 FH
MD-10-30F	60	30,000 FC/60,000 FH
MD-11, MDD-11F	60	20,000 FC/60,000 FH
Maximum Takeoff Gross Weight Changes: All airplanes whose maximum takeoff gross weight has been decreased to 75,000 pounds or below after January 14, 2011 or increased to greater than 75,000 pounds at any time by an amended type certificate or supplemental type certificate.	30, or within 12 months after the LOV is approved, or before operating the airplane, whichever occurs latest.	Not applicable.
All Other Airplane Models (TCs and amended TCs) not Listed in Table 2	72, or within 12 months after the LOV is approved, or before operating the airplane, whichever occurs latest.	Not applicable.

[1] Type certificated as of January 14, 2011.

Note: Airplane operation limitation is stated in the Airworthiness Limitation section.

§121.1115

TABLE 2 — AIRPLANES EXCLUDED FROM SECTION 26.21

Airplane model	Default LOV [flight cycles (FC) or flight hours (FH)]
Airbus:	
Caravelle	15,000 FC/24,000 FH
Avions Marcel Dassault:	
Breguet Aviation Mercure 100C	20,000 FC/16,000 FH
Boeing:	
Boeing 707 (-100 Series and -200 Series)	20,000 FC
Boeing 707 (-300 Series and -400 Series)	20,000 FC
Boeing 720	30,000 FC
Bombardier:	
CL-44D4 and CL-44J	20,000 FC
BD-700	15,000 FH
Bristol Aeroplane Company:	
Britannia 305	10,000 FC
British Aerospace Airbus, Ltd.:	
BAC 1-11 (all models)	85,000 FC
British Aerospace (Commercial Aircraft) Ltd.:	
Armstrong Whitworth Argosy A.W. 650 Series 101	20,000 FC
BAE Systems (Operations) Ltd.:	
BAe 146-100A (all models)	50,000 FC
BAe 146-200-07	50,000 FC
BAe 146-200-07 Dev	50,000 FC
BAe 146-200-11	50,000 FC
BAe 146-200-07A	47,000 FC
BAe 146-200-11 Dev	43,000 FC
BAe 146-300 (all models)	40,000 FC
Avro 146-RJ70A (all models)	40,000 FC
Avro 146-RJ85A and 146-RJ100A (all models)	50,000 FC
D & R Nevada, LLC:	
Convair Model 22	1,000 FC/1,000 FH
Convair Model 23M	1,000 FC/1,000 FH
deHavilland Aircraft Company, Ltd.:	
D.H. 106 Comet 4C	8,000 FH
Gulfstream:	
GV	40,000 FH
GV-SP	40,000 FH
Ilyushin Aviation Complex:	
IL-96T	10,000 FC/30,000 FH
Lockheed:	
300-50A01 (USAF C 141A)	20,000 FC

[Docket No. FAA–2006–24281, 75 FR 69785, Nov. 15, 2010; as amended by Amdt. 121–360, 77 FR 30878, May 24, 2102; Amdt. 121–360A, 77 FR 55105, Sept. 7, 2012]

§121.1117 Flammability reduction means.

(a) *Applicability.* Except as provided in paragraph (o) of this section, this section applies to transport category, turbine-powered airplanes with a type certificate issued after January 1, 1958, that, as a result of original type certification or later increase in capacity have:

(1) A maximum type-certificated passenger capacity of 30 or more, or

(2) A maximum payload capacity of 7,500 pounds or more.

(b) *New Production Airplanes.* Except in accordance with §121.628, no certificate holder may operate an airplane identified in Table 1 of this section (including all-cargo airplanes) for which the State of Manufacture issued the original certificate of airworthiness or export airworthiness approval after December 27, 2010 unless an Ignition Mitigation Means (IMM) or Flammability Reduction Means (FRM) meeting the requirements of §26.33 of this chapter is operational.

TABLE 1

Model—Boeing	Model—Airbus
747 Series	A318, A319, A320, A321 Series
737 Series	A330, A340 Series
777 Series	
767 Series	

(c) *Auxiliary Fuel Tanks.* After the applicable date stated in paragraph (e) of this section, no certificate holder may operate any airplane subject to §26.33 of this chapter that has an Auxiliary Fuel Tank installed pursuant to a field approval, unless the following requirements are met:

(1) The certificate holder complies with 14 CFR 26.35 by the applicable date stated in that section.

(2) The certificate holder installs Flammability Impact Mitigation Means (FIMM), if applicable, that is approved by the FAA Oversight Office.

(3) Except in accordance with §121.628, the FIMM, if applicable, is operational.

(d) *Retrofit.* Except as provided in paragraphs (j), (k), and (l) of this section, after the dates specified in paragraph (e) of this section, no certificate holder may operate an airplane to which this section applies unless the requirements of paragraphs (d)(1) and (d)(2) of this section are met.

(1) IMM, FRM or FIMM, if required by §§26.33, 26.35, or 26.37 of this chapter, that are approved by the FAA Oversight Office, are installed within the compliance times specified in paragraph (e) of this section.

(2) Except in accordance with §121.628, the IMM, FRM or FIMM, as applicable, are operational.

(e) *Compliance Times.* Except as provided in paragraphs (k) and (l) of this section, the installations required by paragraph (d) of this section must be accomplished no later than the applicable dates specified in paragraph (e)(1), (e)(2), or (e)(3) of this section.

(1) Fifty percent of each certificate holder's fleet identified in paragraph (d)(1) of this section must be modified no later than December 26, 2014.

(2) One hundred percent of each certificate holder's fleet identified in paragraph (d)(1) of this section must be modified no later than December 26, 2017.

(3) For those certificate holders that have only one airplane of a model identified in Table 1 of this section, the airplane must be modified no later than December 26, 2017.

(f) *Compliance After Installation.* Except in accordance with §121.628, no certificate holder may—

(1) Operate an airplane on which IMM or FRM has been installed before the dates specified in paragraph (e) of this section unless the IMM or FRM is operational, or

(2) Deactivate or remove an IMM or FRM once installed unless it is replaced by a means that complies with paragraph (d) of this section.

(g) *Maintenance Program Revisions.* No certificate holder may operate an airplane for which airworthiness limitations have been approved by the FAA Oversight Office in accordance with §§26.33, 26.35, or 26.37 of this chapter after the airplane is modified in accordance with paragraph (d) of this section unless the maintenance program for that airplane is revised to include those applicable airworthiness limitations.

(h) After the maintenance program is revised as required by paragraph (g) of this section, before returning an airplane to service after any alteration for which airworthiness limitations are required by §§25.981, 26.33, or 26.37 of this chapter, the certificate holder must revise the maintenance program for the airplane to include those airworthiness limitations.

(i) The maintenance program changes identified in paragraphs (g) and (h) of this section must be submitted to the operator's Principal Maintenance Inspector responsible for review and approval prior to incorporation.

(j) The requirements of paragraph (d) of this section do not apply to airplanes operated in all-cargo service, but those airplanes are subject to paragraph (f) of this section.

(k) The compliance dates specified in paragraph (e) of this section may be extended by one year, provided that—

(1) No later than March 26, 2009, the certificate holder notifies its assigned Flight Standards Office or Principal Inspector that it intends to comply with this paragraph;

(2) No later than June 24, 2009, the certificate holder applies for an amendment to its opera-

tions specification in accordance with §119.51 of this chapter and revises the manual required by §121.133 to include a requirement for the airplane models specified in Table 2 of this section to use ground air conditioning systems for actual gate times of more than 30 minutes, when available at the gate and operational, whenever the ambient temperature exceeds 60 degrees Fahrenheit; and

(3) Thereafter, the certificate holder uses ground air conditioning systems as described in paragraph (k)(2) of this section on each airplane subject to the extension.

TABLE 2

Model—Boeing	Model—Airbus
747 Series	A318, A319, A320, A321 Series
737 Series	A300, A310 Series
777 Series	A330, A340 Series
767 Series	
757 Series	

(l) For any certificate holder for which the operating certificate is issued after December 26, 2008, the compliance date specified in paragraph (e) of this section may be extended by one year, provided that the certificate holder meets the requirements of paragraph (k)(2) of this section when its initial operations specifications are issued and, thereafter, uses ground air conditioning systems as described in paragraph (k)(2) of this section on each airplane subject to the extension.

(m) After the date by which any person is required by this section to modify 100 percent of the affected fleet, no certificate holder may operate in passenger service any airplane model specified in Table 2 of this section unless the airplane has been modified to comply with §26.33(c) of this chapter.

(n) No certificate holder may operate any airplane on which an auxiliary fuel tank is installed after December 26, 2017 unless the FAA has certified the tank as compliant with §25.981 of this chapter, in effect on December 26, 2008.

(o) *Exclusions.* The requirements of this section do not apply to the following airplane models:

(1) Convair CV–240, 340, 440, including turbine powered conversions.
(2) Lockheed L–188 Electra.
(3) Vickers VC–10.
(4) Douglas DC-3, including turbine powered conversions.
(5) Bombardier CL–44.
(6) Mitsubishi YS–11.
(7) BAC 1–11.
(8) Concorde.
(9) deHavilland D.H. 106 Comet 4C.
(10) VFW—Vereinigte Flugtechnische VFW–614.
(11) Illyushin Aviation IL 96T.
(12) Bristol Aircraft Britannia 305.
(13) Handley Page Herald Type 300.
(14) Avions Marcel Dassault—Breguet Aviation Mercure 100C.
(15) Airbus Caravelle.
(16) Fokker F–27/Fairchild Hiller FH–227.
(17) Lockheed L–300.

[Docket No. FAA–2005–22997, 73 FR 42501, July 21, 2008; as amended by Amdt. 121–345, 74 FR 31619, July 2, 2009]

Subpart BB—[Reserved]

§§121.1200–121.1399 [Reserved]

Subpart CC—[Reserved]

§§121.1400–121.1499 [Reserved]

Subpart DD— Special Federal Aviation Regulations

Source: Docket No. FAA-2011-0186, 76 FR 12555, Mar. 8, 2011 unless otherwise noted.

§121.1500 SFAR No. 111—Lavatory Oxygen Systems.

(a) *Applicability.* This SFAR applies to the following persons:

(1) All operators of transport category airplanes that are required to comply with AD 2012-11-09, but only for airplanes on which the actions required by that AD have not been accomplished.
(2) Applicants for airworthiness certificates.
(3) Holders of production certificates.
(4) Applicants for type certificates, including changes to type certificates.

(b) *Regulatory relief.* Except as noted in paragraph (d) of this section and contrary provisions of 14 CFR part 21, and 14 CFR §§25.1447, 119.51, 121.329, 121.333 and 129.13, notwithstanding, for the duration of this SFAR:

(1) A person described in paragraph (a) of this section may conduct flight operations and add airplanes to operations specifications with disabled lavatory oxygen systems, modified in accordance with FAA Airworthiness Directive 2011-04-09, subject to the following limitations:

(i) This relief is limited to regulatory compliance of lavatory oxygen systems.
(ii) Within 30 days of March 29, 2013, all oxygen masks must be removed from affected lavatories, and the mask stowage location must be reclosed.

(iii) Within 60 days of March 29, 2013 each affected operator must verify that crew emergency procedures specifically include a visual check of the lavatory as a priority when checking the cabin following any event where oxygen masks were deployed in the cabin.

(2) An applicant for an airworthiness certificate may obtain an airworthiness certificate for airplanes to be operated by a person described in paragraph (a) of this section, although the airplane lavatory oxygen system is disabled.

(3) A holder of a production certificate may apply for an airworthiness certificate or approval for airplanes to be operated by a person described in paragraph (a) of this section.

(4) An applicant for a type certificate or change to a type certificate may obtain a design approval without showing compliance with §25.1447(c)(1) of this chapter for lavatory oxygen systems, in accordance with this SFAR.

(5) Each person covered by paragraph (a) of this section may inform passengers that the lavatories are not equipped with supplemental oxygen.

(c) *Return to service documentation.* When a person described in paragraph (a) of this section has modified airplanes as required by Airworthiness Directive 2011-04-09, the affected airplanes must be returned to service with a note in the airplane maintenance records that the modification was done under the provisions of this SFAR.

(d) *Expiration.* This SFAR expires on September 10, 2015, except this SFAR will continue to apply to any airplane for which the FAA approves an extension of the AD compliance time for the duration of the extension.

[Docket No. FAA-2011-0186, 76 FR 12555, Mar. 8, 2011; as amended by Amdt. 121–362, 78 FR 5710, Jan. 28, 2013]

APPENDIX A TO PART 121
FIRST-AID KITS AND EMERGENCY MEDICAL KITS

FIRST-AID KITS

Approved first-aid kits, at least one approved emergency medical kit, and at least one approved automated external defibrillator required under §121.803 of this part must be readily accessible to the crew, stored securely, and kept free from dust, moisture, and damaging temperatures.

(1) The minimum number of first-aid kits required is set forth in the following table:

No. of passenger seats	No. of first-aid kits
0–50	1
51–150	2
151–250	3
More than 250	4

(2) Except as provided in paragraph (3), each approved first-aid kit must contain at least the following appropriately maintained contents in the specified quantities:

Contents	Quantity
Adhesive bandage compresses, 1-inch	16
Antiseptic swabs	20
Ammonia inhalants	10
Bandage compresses, 4-inch	8
Triangular bandage compresses, 40-inch	5
Arm splint, noninflatable	1
Leg splint, noninflatable	1
Roller bandage, 4-inch	4
Adhesive tape, 1-inch standard roll	2
Bandage scissors	1

(3) Arm and leg splints which do not fit within a first-aid kit may be stowed in a readily accessible location that is as near as practicable to the kit.

EMERGENCY MEDICAL KITS

(1) Until April 12, 2004, at least one approved emergency medical kit that must contain at least the following appropriately maintained contents in the specified quantities:

Contents	Quantity
Sphygmomanometer	1
Stethoscope	1
Airways, oropharyngeal (3 sizes)	3
Syringes (sizes necessary to administer required drugs)	4
Needles (sizes necessary to administer required drugs)	6
50% Dextrose injection, 50cc	1
Epinephrine 1:1000, single dose ampule or equivalent	2
Diphenhydramine HCl injection, single dose ampule or equivalent	2
Nitroglycerin tablets	10
Basic instructions for use of the drugs in the kit	1
Protective nonpermeable gloves or equivalent	1 pair

Appendix A to Part 121

(2) As of April 12, 2004, at least one approved emergency medical kit that must contain at least the following appropriately maintained contents in the specified quantities:

Contents	Quantity
Sphygmonanometer	1
Stethoscope	1
Airways, oropharyngeal (3 sizes): 1 pediatric, 1 small adult, 1 large adult or equivalent	3
Self-inflating manual resuscitation device with 3 masks (1 pediatric, 1 small adult, 1 large adult or equivalent)	1:3 masks
CPR mask (3 sizes), 1 pediatric, 1 small adult, 1 large adult, or equivalent	3
IV Admin Set: Tubing w/ 2 Y connectors	1
Alcohol sponges	2
Adhesive tape, 1-inch standard roll adhesive	1
Tape scissors	1 pair
Tourniquet	1
Saline solution, 500 cc	1
Protective nonpermeable gloves or equivalent	1 pair
Needles (2-18 ga., 2-20 ga., 2-22 ga., or sizes necessary to administer required medications)	6
Syringes (1-5 cc, 2-10 cc, or sizes necessary to administer required medications)	4
Analgesic, non-narcotic, tablets, 325 mg	4
Antihistamine tablets, 25 mg	4
Antihistamine injectable, 50 mg, (single dose ampule or equivalent)	2
Atropine, 0.5 mg, 5 cc (single dose ampule or equivalent)	2
Aspirin tablets, 325 mg	4
Bronchodilator, inhaled (metered dose inhaler or equivalent)	1
Dextrose, 50%/50 cc injectable, (single dose ampule or equivalent)	1
Epinephrine 1:1000, 1 cc, injectable, (single dose ampule or equivalent)	2
Epinephrine 1:10,000, 2 cc, injectable, (single dose ampule or equivalent)	2
Lidocaine, 5 cc, 20 mg/ml, injectable (single dose ampule or equivalent)	2
Nitroglycerin tablets, 0.4 mg	10
Basic instructions for use of the drugs in the kit	1

(3) If all of the above-listed items do not fit into one container, more than one container may be used.

AUTOMATED EXTERNAL DEFIBRILLATORS

At least one approved automated external defibrillator, legally marketed in the United States in accordance with Food and Drug Administration requirements, that must:

(1) Be stored in the passenger cabin.

(2) After April 30, 2005:

(a) Have a power source that meets FAA Technical Standard Order requirements for power sources for electronic devices used in aviation as approved by the Administrator; or

(b) Have a power source that was manufactured before July 30, 2004, and been found by the FAA to be equivalent to a power source that meets the Technical Standard Order requirements of paragraph (a) of this section.

(3) Be maintained in accordance with the manufacturer's specifications.

[Docket No. 12384, 38 FR 35234, Dec. 26, 1973; as amended by Amdt. 121–115, 40 FR 1039, Jan. 6, 1975; Amdt. 121–188, 51 FR 1223, Jan. 9, 1986; Amdt. 121–236, 59 FR 1781, Jan. 12, 1994; Amdt. 121–242, 59 FR 52642, October 18, 1994; Amdt. 121–243, 59 FR 62276, Dec. 2, 1994; Amdt. 121–281, 66 FR 19044, April 12, 2001; Amdt. 121–280, 69 FR 19762, April 14, 2004; Amdt. 121–309, 70 FR 15196, March 24, 2005]

Appendix B to Part 121
Airplane Flight Recorder Specifications

Parameters	Range	Accuracy sensor input to DFDR readout	Sampling interval (per second)	Resolution[4] readout
Time (GMT or Frame Counter) (range 0 to 4095, sampled 1 per frame)	24 Hrs	±0.125% per hour	0.25 (1 per 4 seconds)	1 sec.
Altitude	−1,000 ft to max certificated altitude of aircraft	±100 to ±700 ft (See Table 1, TSO-C51a)	1	5′ to 35′[1]
Airspeed	50 KIAS to V_{SO}, and V_{SO} to 1.2 V_D	±5%, ±3%	1	1 kt.
Heading	360°	±2°	1	0.5°
Normal Acceleration (Vertical)	−3g to +6g	±1% of max range excluding datum error of ±5%	8	0.01g
Pitch Attitude	±75°	±2°	1	0.5°
Roll Attitude	±180°	±2°	1	0.5°
Radio Transmitter Keying	On-Off (Discrete)	±2°	±2%	
Thrust/Power on Each Engine	Full Range Forward	±2°	1 (per engine)	0.2%[2]
Trailing Edge Flap or Cockpit Control Selection	Full Range or Each Discrete Position	±3° or as Pilot's Indicator	0.5	0.5%[2]
Leading Edge Flap or Cockpit Control Selection	Full Range or Each Discrete Position	±3° or as Pilot's Indicator	0.5	0.5%[2]
Thrust Reverser Position	Stowed, in Transit, and Reverse (Discrete)		1 (per 4 seconds per engine)	
Ground Spoiler Position/Speed Brake Selection	Full Range or Each Discrete Position	±2% Unless Higher Accuracy Uniquely Required	1	0.2%[2]
Marker Beacon Passage	Discrete		1	
Autopilot Engagement	Discrete		1	
Longitudinal Acceleration	±1g	±1.5% max range excluding datum error of ±5%	4	0.01g
Pilot Input and/or Surface Position—Primary Controls (Pitch, Roll, Yaw)[3]	Full Range	±2° Unless Higher Accuracy Uniquely Required	1	0.2%[2]
Lateral Acceleration	±1g	±1.5% max range excluding datum error of ±5%	4	0.01g
Pitch Trim Position	Full Range	±3% Unless Higher Accuracy Uniquely Required	1	0.3%[2]
Glideslope Deviation	±400 Microamps	±3%	1	0.3%[2]
Localizer Deviation	±400 Microamps	±3%	1	0.3%[2]
AFCS Mode and Engagement Status	Discrete		1	
Radio Altitude	−20 ft to 2,500 ft	±2 Ft or ±3% Whichever is Greater Below 500 Ft and ±5% Above 500 Ft	1	1 ft + 5%[2] above 500′
Master Warning	Discrete		1	
Main Gear Squat Switch Status	Discrete		1	
Angle of Attack (if recorded directly)	As installed	As installed	2	0.3%[2]
Outside Air Temperature or Total Air Temperature	−50°C to +90°C	±2°C	0.5	0.3°C or 0.5%[2]
Hydraulics, Each System Low Pressure	Discrete	Most Accurate Systems Installed (IMS Equipped Aircraft Only)	0.5	
Groundspeed	As installed		1	0.2%[2]

Appendix B to Part 121   **Federal Aviation Regulations**

APPENDIX B TO PART 121
AIRPLANE FLIGHT RECORDER SPECIFICATION (CONTINUED)

If additional recording capacity is available, recording of the following parameters is recommended. The parameters are listed in order of significance:

Parameters	Range	Accuracy sensor input to DFDR readout	Sampling interval (per second)	Resolution[4] readout
Drift Angle	When available, As installed	As installed	4	
Wind Speed and Direction	When available, As installed	As installed	4	
Latitude and Longitude	When available, As installed	As installed	4	
Brake pressure / Brake pedal position	As installed	As installed	1	
Additional engine parameters:				
EPR	As installed	As installed	1 (per engine)	
N1	As installed	As installed	1 (per engine)	
N2	As installed	As installed	1 (per engine)	
EGT	As installed	As installed	1 (per engine)	
Throttle Lever Position	As installed	As installed	1 (per engine)	
Fuel Flow	As installed	As installed	1 (per engine)	
TCAS:				
TA	As installed	As installed	1	
RA	As installed	As installed	1	
Sensitivity level (as selected by crew)	As installed	As installed	2	
GPWS (ground proximity warning system)	Discrete		1	
Landing gear or gear selector position	Discrete		0.25 (1 per 4 seconds)	
DME 1 and 2 Distance	0–200 NM	As installed	0.25	1 mi.
Nav 1 and 2 Frequency Selection	Full range	As installed	0.25	

[1] When altitude rate is recorded. Altitude rate must have sufficient resolution and sampling to permit the derivation of altitude to 5 feet.
[2] Percent of full range
[3] For airplanes that can demonstrate the capability of deriving either the control input on control movement (one from the other) for all modes of operation and flight regimes, the "or" applies. For airplanes with non-mechanical control systems (fly-by-wire) the "and" applies. In airplanes with split surfaces, suitable combination of inputs is acceptable in lieu of recording each surface separately.
[4] This column applies to aircraft manufactured after October 11, 1991.

[Docket No. 25530, 53 FR 26147, July 11, 1988; 53 FR 30906, August 16, 1988]

APPENDIX C TO PART 121
C-46 NONTRANSPORT CATEGORY AIRPLANES

CARGO OPERATIONS

1. Required engines.
(a) Except as provided in paragraph (b) of this section, the engines specified in subparagraphs (1) or (2) of this section must be installed in C-46 nontransport category airplanes operated at gross weights exceeding 45,000 pounds:

(1) Pratt and Whitney R2800-51-M1 or R2800-75-M1 engines (engines converted from basic model R2800-51 or R2800-75 engines in accordance with FAA approved data) that—

(i) Conform to Engine Specification 5E–8;

(ii) Conform to the applicable portions of the operator's manual;

(iii) Comply with all the applicable airworthiness directives; and

(iv) Are equipped with high capacity oil pump drive gears in accordance with FAA approved data.

(2) Other engines found acceptable by the FAA Regional Flight Standards Division having type certification responsibility for the C–46 airplane.

(b) Upon application by an operator conducting cargo operations with nontransport category C-46 airplanes between points within the State of Alaska, the appropriate FAA Flight Standards District Office, Alaskan Region, may authorize the operation of such airplanes, between points within the State of Alaska; without compliance with paragraph (a) of this section if the operator shows that, in its area of operation, installation of the modified engines is not necessary to provide adequate cooling for single-engine operations. Such authorization and any conditions or limitations therefor is made a part of the Operations Specifications of the operator.

2. Minimum acceptable means of complying with the special airworthiness requirements. Unless otherwise authorized under §121.213, the data set forth in sections 3 through 34 of this appendix, as correlated to the C-46 nontransport category airplane, is the minimum means of compliance with the special airworthiness requirements of §§121.215 through 121.281.

3. Susceptibility of material to fire. [Deleted as unnecessary]

4. Cabin interiors. C-46 crew compartments must meet all the requirements of §121.215, and, as required in §121.221, the door between the crew compartment and main cabin (cargo) compartment must be flame resistant.

5. Internal doors. Internal doors, including the crew to main cabin door, must meet all the requirements of §121.217.

6. Ventilation. Standard C-46 crew compartments meet the ventilation requirements of §121.219 if a means of ventilation for controlling the flow of air is available between the crew compartment and main cabin. The ventilation requirement may be met by use of a door between the crew compartment and main cabin. The door need not have louvers installed; however, if louvers are installed, they must be controllable.

7. Fire precautions. Compliance is required with all the provisions of §121.221.

(a) In establishing compliance with this section, the C-46 main cabin is considered as a Class A compartment if—

(1) The operator utilizes a standard system of cargo loading and tiedown that allows easy access in flight to all cargo in such compartment, and, such system is included in the appropriate portion of the operator's manual; and

(2) A cargo barrier is installed in the forward end of the main cabin cargo compartment. The barrier must—

(i) Establish the most forward location beyond which cargo cannot be carried;

(ii) Protect the components and systems of the airplane that are essential to its safe operation from cargo damage; and

(iii) Permit easy access, in flight, to cargo in the main cabin cargo compartment.

The barrier may be a cargo net or a network of steel cables or other means acceptable to the Administrator which would provide equivalent protection to that of a cargo net. The barrier need not meet crash load requirements of FAR §25.561; however, it must be attached to the cargo retention fittings and provide the degree of cargo retention that is required by the operators' standard system of cargo loading and tiedown.

(b) C-46 forward and aft baggage compartments must meet, as a minimum, Class B requirements of this section or be placarded in a manner to preclude their use as cargo or baggage compartments.

8. Proof of compliance. The demonstration of compliance required by §121.223 is not required for C-46 airplanes in which—

(1) The main cabin conforms to Class A cargo compartment requirements of §121.219; and

(2) Forward and aft baggage compartments conform to Class B requirements of §121.221, or are placarded to preclude their use as cargo or baggage compartments.

9. Propeller deicing fluid. No change from the requirements of §121.225. Isopropyl alcohol is a combustible fluid within the meaning of this section.

10. Pressure cross-feed arrangements, location of fuel tanks, and fuel system lines and fittings. C-46 fuel systems which conform to all applicable Curtiss design specifications and which comply with the FAA type certification requirements are in compliance with the provisions of §§121.227 through 121.231.

11. Fuel lines and fittings in designated fire zones. No change from the requirements of §121.233.

12. Fuel valves. Compliance is required with all the provisions of §121.235. Compliance can be established by showing that the fuel system conforms to all the applicable Curtiss design specifications, the FAA type certification requirements, and, in addition, has explosion-proof fuel booster pump electrical selector switches installed in lieu of the open contact type used originally.

13. Oil lines and fittings in designated fire zones. No change from the requirements of §121.237.

14. Oil valves. C-46 oil shutoff valves must conform to the requirements of §121.239. In addition, C-46 airplanes using Hamilton Standard propellers must provide, by use of stand pipes in the engine oil tanks or other approved means, a positive source of oil for feathering each propeller.

15. Oil system drains. The standard C-46 "Y" drains installed in the main oil inlet line for each engine meet the requirements of §121.241.

16. Engine breather line. The standard C-46 engine breather line installation meets the requirements of §121.243 if the lower breather lines actually extend to the trailing edge of the oil cooler air exit duct.

17. Firewalls and firewall construction. Compliance is required with all of the provisions of §§121.245 and 121.247. The following requirements must be met in showing compliance with these sections:

(a) *Engine compartment.* The engine firewalls of the C-46 airplane must—

(1) Conform to type design, and all applicable airworthiness directives;

(2) Be constructed of stainless steel or approved equivalent; and

(3) Have fireproof shields over the fairleads used for the engine control cables that pass through each firewall.

(b) *Combustion heater compartment.* C-46 airplanes must have a combustion heater fire extinguishing system which complies with AD-49-18-1 or an FAA approved equivalent.

18. Cowling. Standard C-46 engine cowling (cowling of aluminum construction employing stainless steel exhaust shrouds) which conforms to the type design and cowling configurations which conform to the C-46 transport category requirements meet the requirements of §121.249.

19. Engine accessory section diaphragm. C-46 engine nacelles which conform to the C-46 transport category requirements meet the requirements of §121.251. As provided for in that section, a means of equivalent protection which does not require provision of a diaphragm to isolate the engine power section and exhaust system from the engine accessory compartment is the designation of the entire engine compartment forward of and including the firewall as a designated fire zone, and the installation of adequate fire detection and fire extinguishing systems which meet the requirements of §121.263 and §121.273, respectively, in such zone.

20. Powerplant fire protection. C-46 engine compartments and combustion heater compartments are considered as designated fire zones within the meaning of §121.253.

21. Flammable fluids—

(a) *Engine compartment.* C-46 engine compartments which conform to the type design and which comply with all applicable airworthiness directives meet the requirements of §121.255.

(b) *Combustion heater compartment.* C-46 combustion heater compartments which conform to type design and which meet all the requirements of AD-49-18-1 or an FAA approved equivalent meet the requirements of §121.255.

22. Shutoff means—

(a) *Engine compartment.* C-46 engine compartments which comply with AD-62-10-2 or FAA approved equivalent meet the requirements of §121.257 applicable to engine compartments, if, in addition, a means satisfactory to the Administrator is provided to shut off the flow of hydraulic fluid to the cowl flap cylinder in each engine nacelle. The shutoff means must be located aft of the engine firewall. The operator's manual must include, in the emergency portion, adequate instructions for proper operation of the additional shutoff means to assure correct sequential positioning of engine cowl flaps under emergency conditions. In accordance with §121.315, this positioning must also be incorporated in the emergency section of the pilot's checklist.

(b) *Combustion heater compartment.* C-46 heater compartments which comply with paragraph (5) of AD-49-18-1 or FAA approved equivalent meet the requirements of §121.257 applicable to heater compartments if, in addition, a shutoff valve located above the main cabin floor level is installed in the alcohol supply line or lines between the alcohol supply tank and those alcohol pumps located under the main cabin floor. If all of the alcohol pumps are located above the main cabin floor, the alcohol shutoff valve need not be installed. In complying with paragraph (5) of AD-49-18-1, a fail-safe electric fuel shutoff valve may be used in lieu of the manually operated valve.

23. Lines and fittings—

(a) *Engine compartment.* C-46 engine compartments which comply with all applicable airworthiness directives, including AD-62-10-2, by using FAA approved fire-resistant lines, hoses, and end fittings, and engine compartments which meet the C-46 transport category requirements, meet the requirements of §121.259.

(b) *Combustion heater compartments.* All lines, hoses, and end fittings, and couplings which carry fuel to the heaters and heater controls, must be of FAA approved fire-resistant construction.

24. Vent and drain lines.

(a) *Engine compartment.* C-46 engine compartments meet the requirements of §121.261 if—

(1) The compartments conform to type design and comply with all applicable airworthiness directives or FAA approved equivalent; and

(2) Drain lines from supercharger case, engine-driven fuel pump, and engine-driven hydraulic pump reach into the scupper drain located in the lower cowling segment.

(b) *Combustion heater compartment.* C-46 heater compartments meet the requirements of §121.261 if they conform to AD-49-18-1 or FAA approved equivalent.

25. Fire-extinguishing system.

(a) To meet the requirements of §121.263, C-46 airplanes must have installed fire extinguishing systems to serve all designated fire zones. The fire-extinguishing systems, the quantity of extinguishing agent, and the rate of discharge shall be such as to provide a minimum of one adequate discharge for each designated fire zone. Compliance with this provision requires the installation of a separate fire extinguisher for each engine compartment. Insofar as the engine compartment is concerned, the system shall be capable of protecting the entire compartment against the various types of fires likely to occur in the compartment.

(b) Fire-extinguishing systems which conform to the C-46 transport category requirements meet the requirements set forth in paragraph (a). Furthermore, fire-extinguishing systems for combustion heater compartments which conform to the requirements of AD-49-18-1 or an FAA approved equivalent also meet the requirements in paragraph (a).

In addition, a fire-extinguishing system for C-46 airplanes meets the adequacy requirement of paragraph (a) if it provides the same or equivalent protection to that demonstrated by the CAA in tests conducted in 1941 and 1942, using a CW-20 type engine nacelle (without diaphragm). These tests were conducted at the Bureau of Standards facilities in Washington, DC, and copies of the test reports are available through the FAA Regional Engineering Offices. In this connection, the flow rates and distribution of extinguishing agent substantiated in American Airmotive Report No. 128-52-d, FAA approved February 9, 1953, provides protection equivalent to that demonstrated by the CAA in the CW-20 tests. In evaluating any C-46 fire-extinguishing system with respect to the aforementioned CW-20 tests, the Administration would require data in a narrative form, utilizing drawings or photographs to show at least the following:

Installation of containers; installation and routing of plumbing; type, number, and location of outlets or nozzles; type, total volume, and distribution of extinguishing agent; length of time required for discharging; means for thermal relief, including type and location of discharge indicators; means of discharging, e.g., mechanical cutterheads, electric cartridge, or other method; and whether a one- or two-shot system is used; and if the latter is used, means of cross-feeding or otherwise selecting distribution of extinguishing agent; and types of materials used in makeup of plumbing.

High rate discharge (HRD) systems using agents such as bromotrifluoromethane, dibrodifluoromethane and chlorobromomethane (CB), may also meet the requirements of paragraph (a).

26. Fire-extinguishing agents, Extinguishing agent container pressure relief, Extinguishing agent container compartment temperatures, and Fire-extinguishing system materials. No change from the requirements of §§121.265 through 121.271.

27. Fire-detector system. Compliance with the requirements of §121.273 requires that C-46 fire detector systems conform to:

(a) AD-62-10-2 or FAA approved equivalent for engine compartments; and

(b) AD-49-18-1 or FAA approved equivalent for combustion heater compartments

28. Fire detectors. No change from the requirements of §121.275.

29. Protection of other airplane components against fire. To meet the requirements of §121.277, C-46 airplanes must—

(a) Conform to the type design and all applicable airworthiness directives; and

(b) Be modified or have operational procedures established to provide additional fire protection for the wheel well door aft of each engine compartment. Modifications may consist of improvements in sealing of the main landing gear wheel well doors. An operational procedure which is acceptable to the Agency is one requiring the landing gear control to be placed in the up position in case of in-flight engine fire. In accordance with §121.315, such procedure must be set forth in the emergency portion of the operator's emergency checklist pertaining to in-flight engine fire.

30. Control of engine rotation. C-46 propeller feathering systems which conform to the type design and all applicable airworthiness directives meet the requirements of §121.279.

31. Fuel system independence. C-46 fuel systems which conform to the type design and all applicable airworthiness directives meet the requirements of §121.281.

Appendix C to Part 121

32. Induction system ice prevention. The C-46 carburetor anti-icing system which conforms to the type design and all applicable airworthiness directives meets the requirements of §121.283.

33. Carriage of cargo in passenger compartments. Section 121.285 is not applicable to non-transport category C-46 cargo airplanes.

34. Carriage of cargo in cargo compartments. A standard cargo loading and tiedown arrangement set forth in the operator's manual and found acceptable to the Administrator must be used in complying with §121.287.

35. Performance data. Performance data on Curtiss model C-46 airplane certificated for maximum weight of 45,000 and 48,000 pounds for cargo-only operations.

1. The following performance limitation data, applicable to the Curtiss model C-46 airplane for cargo-only operation, must be used in determining compliance with §§121.199 through 121.205. These data are presented in the tables and figures of this appendix.

TABLE 1 — TAKEOFF LIMITATIONS

(a) Curtiss C-46 certificated for maximum weight of 45,000 pounds.

(1) *Effective length* of runway required when effective length is determined in accordance with §121.171 (distance to accelerate to 93 knots TIAS and stop, with zero wind and zero gradient). (Factor=1.00)

[Distance in feet]

Standard altitude in feet	Airplane weight in pounds		
	39,000	42,000	45,000[1]
S.L.	4,110	4,290	4,570
1,000	4,250	4,440	4,720
2,000	4,400	4,600	4,880
3,000	4,650	4,880	5,190
4,000	4,910	5,170	5,500
5,000	5,160	5,450	5,810
6,000	5,420	5,730	6,120
7,000	5,680	6,000	6,440
8,000	5,940	6,280	([1])

[1] Ref. Fig. 1(a)(1) for weight and distance for altitudes above 7,000'.

(2) Actual length of runway required when *effective length*, considering obstacles, is not determined (distance to accelerate to 93 knots TIAS and stop, divided by the factor 0.85).

[Distance in feet]

Standard altitude in feet	Airplane weight in pounds		
	39,000	42,000	45,000[1]
S.L.	4,830	5,050	5,370
1,000	5,000	5,230	5,550
2,000	5,170	5,410	5,740
3,000	5,470	5,740	6,100
4,000	5,770	6,080	6,470
5,000	6,070	6,410	6,830
6,000	6,380	6,740	7,200
7,000	6,680	7,070	7,570
8,000	6,990	7,410	([1])

[1] Ref. Fig. 1(a)(2) for weight and distance for altitudes above 7,000'.

(b) Curtiss C-46 certificated for maximum weight 48,000 pounds.

(1) *Effective length* of runway required when effective length is determined in accordance with §121.171 (distance to accelerate to 93 knots TIAS and stop, with zero wind and zero gradient). (Factor=1.00)

[Distance in feet]

Standard altitude in feet	Airplane weight in pounds			
	39,000	42,000	45,000	48,000[1]
S.L.	4,110	4,290	4,570	4,950
1,000	4,250	4,440	4,720	5,130
2,000	4,400	4,600	4,880	5,300
3,000	4,650	4,880	5,190	5,670
4,000	4,910	5,170	5,500	6,050
5,000	5,160	5,450	5,810	6,420
6,000	5,420	5,730	6,120	6,800
7,000	5,680	6,000	6,440	([1])
8,000	5,940	6,280	6,750	([1])

[1] Ref. Fig. 1(b)(1) for weight and distance for altitudes above 6,000'.

(2) Actual length of runway required when *effective length*, considering obstacles, is not determined (distance to accelerate to 93 knots TIAS and stop, divided by the factor 0.85).

[Distance in feet]

Standard altitude in feet	Airplane weight in pounds			
	39,000	42,000	45,000	48,000[1]
S.L.	4,830	5,050	5,370	5,830
1,000	5,000	5,230	5,550	6,030
2,000	5,170	5,410	5,740	6,230
3,000	5,470	5,740	6,100	6,670
4,000	5,770	6,080	6,470	7,120
5,000	6,070	6,410	6,830	7,560
6,000	6,380	6,740	7,200	8,010
7,000	6,680	7,070	7,570	([1])
8,000	6,990	7,410	7,940	([1])

[1] Ref. Fig. 1(b)(2) for weight and distance for altitudes above 6,000'.

TABLE 2—EN ROUTE LIMITATIONS

(a) Curtiss model C-46 certificated for maximum weight of 45,000 pounds (based on a climb speed of 113 knots (TIAS)).

Weight (pounds)	Terrain clearance (feet)[1]	Blower setting
45,000	6,450	Low.
44,000	7,000	Do.
43,000	7,500	Do.
42,200	8,000	High.
41,000	9,600	Do.
40,000	11,000	Do.
39,000	12,300	Do.

[1] Highest altitude of terrain over which airplanes may be operated in compliance with §121.201.
Ref. Fig. 2(a).

(b) Curtiss model C-46 certificated for maximum weight of 48,000 pounds or with engine installation approved for 2,550 revolutions per minute (1,700 brake horsepower). Maximum continuous power in low blower (based on a climb speed of 113 knots (TIAS)).

Weight (pounds)	Terrain clearance (feet)[1]	Blower setting
48,000	5,850	Low.
47,000	6,300	Do.
46,000	6,700	Do.
45,000	7,200	Do.
44,500	7,450	Do.
44,250	8,000	High.
44,000	8,550	Do.
43,000	10,800	Do.
42,000	12,500	Do.
41,000	13,000	Do.

[1] Highest altitude of terrain over which airplanes may be operated in compliance with §121.201.
Ref. Fig. 2(b).

Appendix C to Part 121   **Federal Aviation Regulations**

TABLE 3—LANDING LIMITATIONS

(a) Intended Destination.
Effective length of runway required for intended destination when effective length is determined in accordance with §121.171 with zero wind and zero gradient.

(1) Curtiss model C-46 certificated for maximum weight of 45,000 pounds. (0.60 factor)

Distance in feet

Standard altitude in feet	Airplane weight in pounds and approach speeds[1] in knots									
	40,000	V_{50}	42,000	V_{50}	44,000	V_{50}	45,000	V_{50}
S.L.	4,320	86	4,500	88	4,700	90	4,800	91
1,000	4,440	86	4,620	88	4,830	90	4,930	91
2,000	4,550	86	4,750	88	4,960	90	5,050	91
3,000	4,670	86	4,880	88	5,090	90	5,190	91
4,000	4,800	86	5,000	88	5,220	90	5,320	91
5,000	4,920	86	5,140	88	5,360	90	5,460	91
6,000	5,040	86	5,270	88	5,550	90	5,600	91
7,000	5,170	86	5,410	88	5,650	90	5,750	91
8,000	5,310	86	5,550	88	5,800	90	5,900	91

[1] Steady approach speed through 50-foot height TIAS denoted by symbol V_{50}.
Ref. Fig. 3(a)(1).

(2) Curtiss model C-46 certificated for maximum weight of 48,000 pounds.[1] (0.60 factor)

Distance in feet

Standard altitude in feet	Airplane weight in pounds and approach speeds[2] in knots									
	42,000	V_{50}	44,000	V_{50}	46,000	V_{50}	43,000	V_{50}
S.L.	3,370	80	3,490	82	3,620	84	3,740	86
1,000	3,460	80	3,580	82	3,710	84	3,830	86
2,000	3,540	80	3,670	82	3,800	84	3,920	86
3,000	3,630	80	3,760	82	3,890	84	4,020	86
4,000	3,720	80	3,850	82	3,980	84	4,110	86
5,000	3,800	80	3,940	82	4,080	84	4,220	86
6,000	3,890	80	4,040	82	4,180	84	4,320	86
7,000	3,980	80	4,140	82	4,280	84	4,440	86
8,000	4,080	80	4,240	82	4,390	84	4,550	86

[1] For use with Curtiss model C-46 airplanes when approved for this weight.
[2] Steady approach speed through 50 height knots TIAS denoted by the symbol $V_{50}{}^3$.
Ref. Fig. 3(a)(2).

Part 121: Air Carriers & Commercial Operators **Appendix C to Part 121**

(b) Alternate Airports.
Effective length of runway required when effective length is determined in accordance with §121.171 with zero wind and zero gradient.
(1) Curtiss model C-46 certificated for maximum weight of 45,000 pounds. (0.70 factor.)

Distance in feet

Standard altitude in feet	Airplane weight in pounds and approach speeds[1] in knots								
	40,000	V_{50}	42,000	V_{50}	44,000	V_{50}	45,000	V_{50}
S.L.	3,700	86	3,860	88	4,030	90	4,110	91
1,000	3,800	86	3,960	88	4,140	90	4,220	91
2,000	3,900	86	4,070	88	4,250	90	4,340	91
3,000	4,000	86	4,180	88	4,360	90	4,450	91
4,000	4,110	86	4,290	88	4,470	90	4,560	91
5,000	4,210	86	4,400	88	4,590	90	4,680	91
6,000	4,330	86	4,510	88	4,710	90	4,800	91
7,000	4,430	86	4,630	88	4,840	90	4,930	91
8,000	4,550	86	4,750	88	4,970	90	5,060	91

[1] Steady approach speed through 50 foot-height-knots TIAS denoted by symbol V_{50}.
Ref. Fig. 3(b)(1).

(2) Curtiss model C-46 certificated for maximum weight of 48,000 pounds.[1] (0.70 factor.)

Distance in feet

Standard altitude in feet	Airplane weight in pounds and approach speeds[2] in knots								
	42,000	V_{50}	44,000	V_{50}	46,000	V_{50}	48,000	V_{50}
S.L.	2,890	80	3,000	82	3,110	84	3,220	86
1,000	2,960	80	3,070	82	3,180	84	3,280	86
2,000	3,040	80	3,150	82	3,260	84	3,360	86
3,000	3,110	80	3,220	82	3,340	84	3,440	86
4,000	3,180	80	3,300	82	3,410	84	3,520	86
5,000	3,260	80	3,380	82	3,500	84	3,610	86
6,000	3,330	80	3,460	82	3,580	84	3,700	86
7,000	3,420	80	3,540	82	3,670	84	3,800	86
8,000	3,500	80	3,630	82	3,760	84	3,900	86

[1] For use with Curtiss model C-46 airplanes when approved for this weight.
[2] Steady approach speed through 50 foot-height-knots TIAS denoted by the symbol V_{50}.
Ref. Fig. 3(b)(2).

Appendix C to Part 121 Federal Aviation Regulations

(c) Actual length of runway required when effective length, considering obstacles, is not determined in accordance with §121.171.

(1) Curtiss model C-46 certificated for maximum weight of 45,000 pounds. (0.55 factor.)

Distance in feet

Standard altitude in feet	Airplane weight in pounds and approach speeds[1] in knots								
	40,000	V_{50}	42,000	V_{50}	44,000	V_{50}	45,000	V_{50}
S.L.	4,710	86	4,910	88	5,130	90	5,230	91
1,000	4,840	86	5,050	88	5,270	90	5,370	91
2,000	4,960	86	5,180	88	5,410	90	5,510	91
3,000	5,090	86	5,320	88	5,550	90	5,660	91
4,000	5,230	86	5,460	88	5,700	90	5,810	91
5,000	5,360	86	5,600	88	5,850	90	5,960	91
6,000	5,500	86	5,740	88	6,000	90	6,110	91
7,000	5,640	86	5,900	88	6,170	90	6,280	91
8,000	5,790	86	6,050	88	6,340	90	6,450	91

[1] Steady approach speed through 50 foot-height-knots TIAS denoted by symbol V_{50}.
Ref. Fig. 3(c)(1).

(2) Curtiss C-46 certificated for maximum weight of 48,000 pounds.[1] (0.55 factor.)

Distance in feet

Standard altitude in feet	Airplane weight in pounds and approach speeds[2] in knots								
	42,000	V_{50}	44,000	V_{50}	46,000	V_{50}	48,000	V_{50}
S.L.	3,680	80	3,820	82	3,960	84	4,090	86
1,000	3,770	80	3,910	82	4,050	84	4,180	86
2,000	3,860	80	4,000	82	4,140	84	4,280	86
3,000	3,960	80	4,090	82	4,240	84	4,380	86
4,000	4,050	80	4,190	82	4,340	84	4,490	86
5,000	4,150	80	4,290	82	4,450	84	4,600	86
6,000	4,240	80	4,400	82	4,560	84	4,710	86
7,000	4,350	80	4,510	82	4,670	84	4,840	86
8,000	4,450	80	4,620	82	4,790	84	4,960	86

[1] For use with Curtiss model C-46 airplanes when approved for this weight.
[2] Steady approach speed through 50 foot-height-knots TIAS denoted by the symbol V_{50}.
Ref. Fig. 3(c)(2).

Part 121: Air Carriers & Commercial Operators **Appendix C to Part 121**

Curtiss C-46 Models
Certificated for max. weight of 45,000 lbs.

Takeoff limitation. Zero wind and zero gradient.
Based on effective takeoff length. (1.00 Factor) FAR 121.199

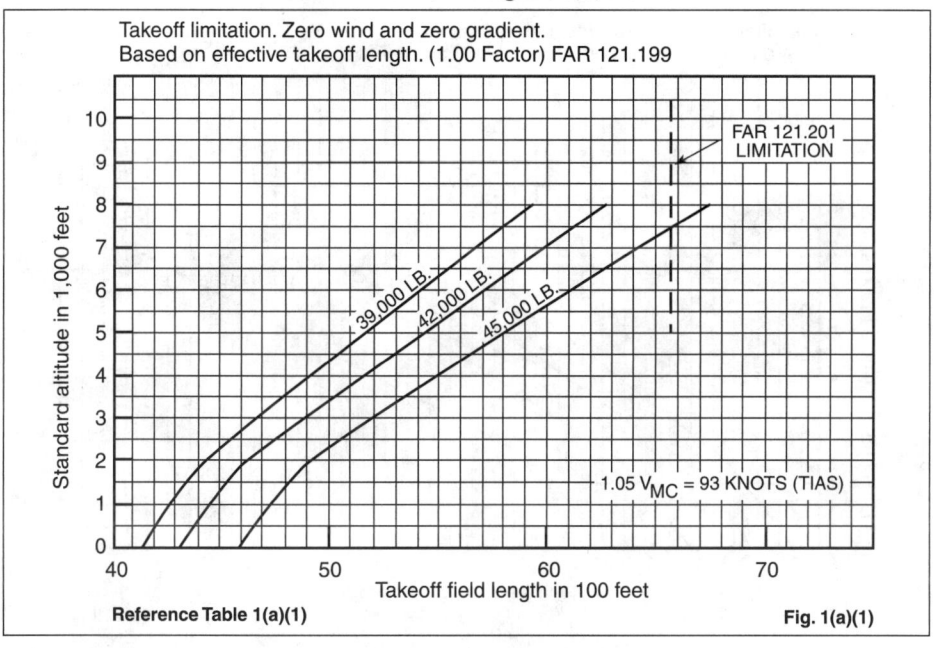

Reference Table 1(a)(1)

Fig. 1(a)(1)

Curtiss C-46 Models
Certificated for max. weight of 45,000 lbs.

Takeoff limitation. Zero wind and zero gradient
Based on actual takeoff length when effective length is not determined. (0.85 Factor)

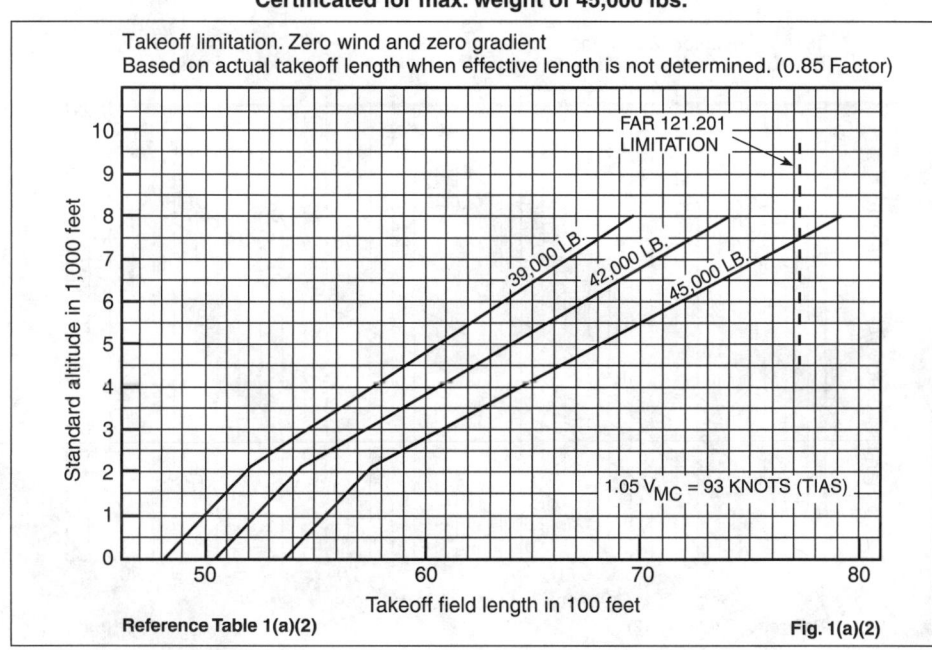

Reference Table 1(a)(2)

Fig. 1(a)(2)

Appendix C to Part 121   **Federal Aviation Regulations**

Curtiss C-46 Models
Certificated for max. weight of 48,000 lbs.

Takeoff limitation. Zero wind and zero gradient
Based on effective takeoff length. (1.00 Factor) FAR 121.199

FAR 121.201 LIMITATION

1.05 V_{MC} = 93 KNOTS (TIAS)

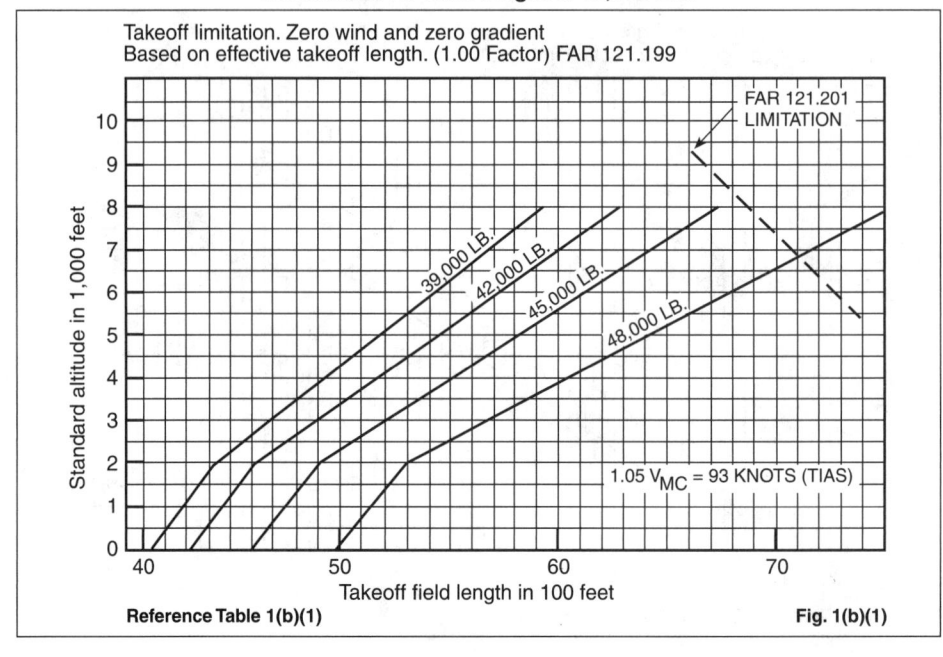

Reference Table 1(b)(1)   Fig. 1(b)(1)

Curtiss C-46 Models
Certificated for max. weight of 48,000 lbs.

Takeoff limitation. Zero wind and zero gradient
Based on actual takeoff length when effective length is not determined. (0.85 Factor)

FAR 121.201 LIMITATION

1.05 V_{MC} = 93 KNOTS (TIAS)

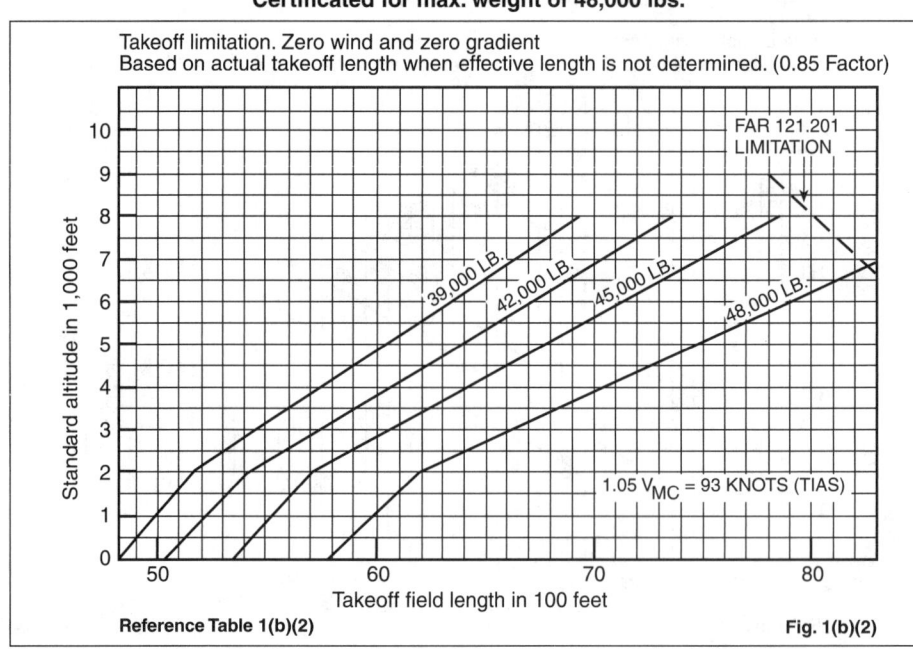

Reference Table 1(b)(2)   Fig. 1(b)(2)

Part 121: Air Carriers & Commercial Operators   **Appendix C to Part 121**

Runway Gradient Correction for Accelerate-Stop Distance

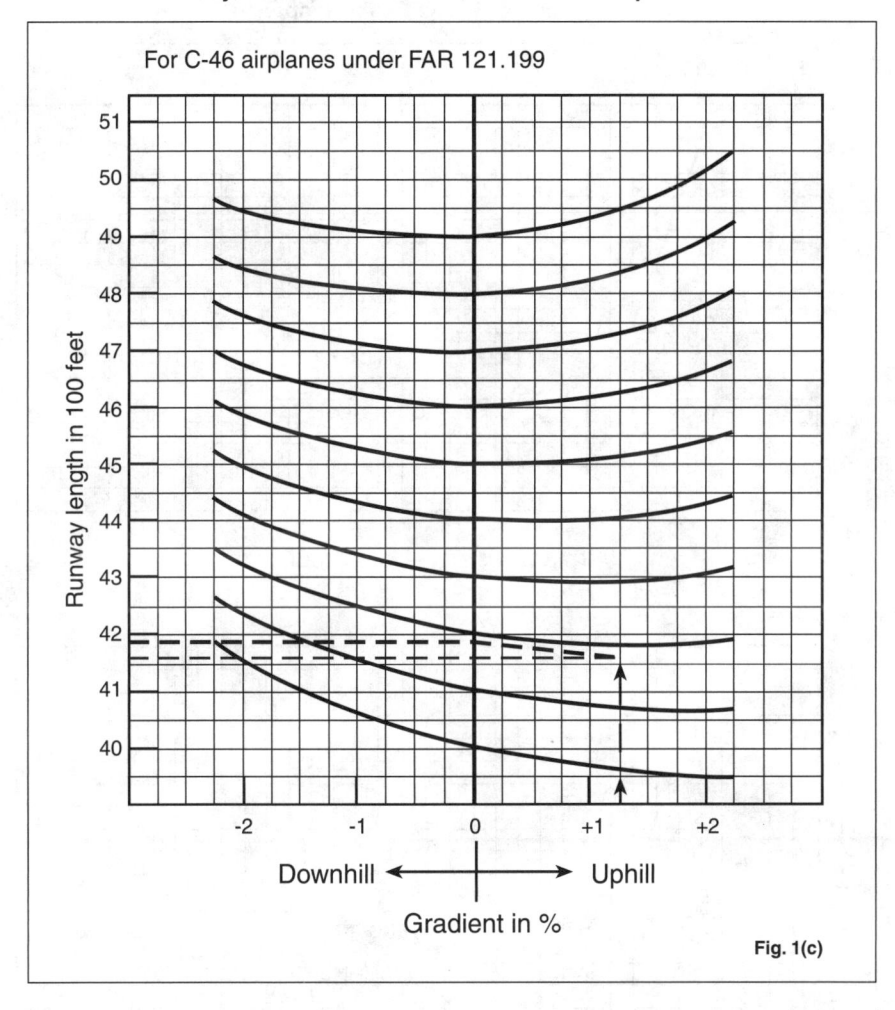

Fig. 1(c)

Appendix C to Part 121   **Federal Aviation Regulations**

Curtiss C-46 Models
Enroute Limitations – One Engine Inoperative

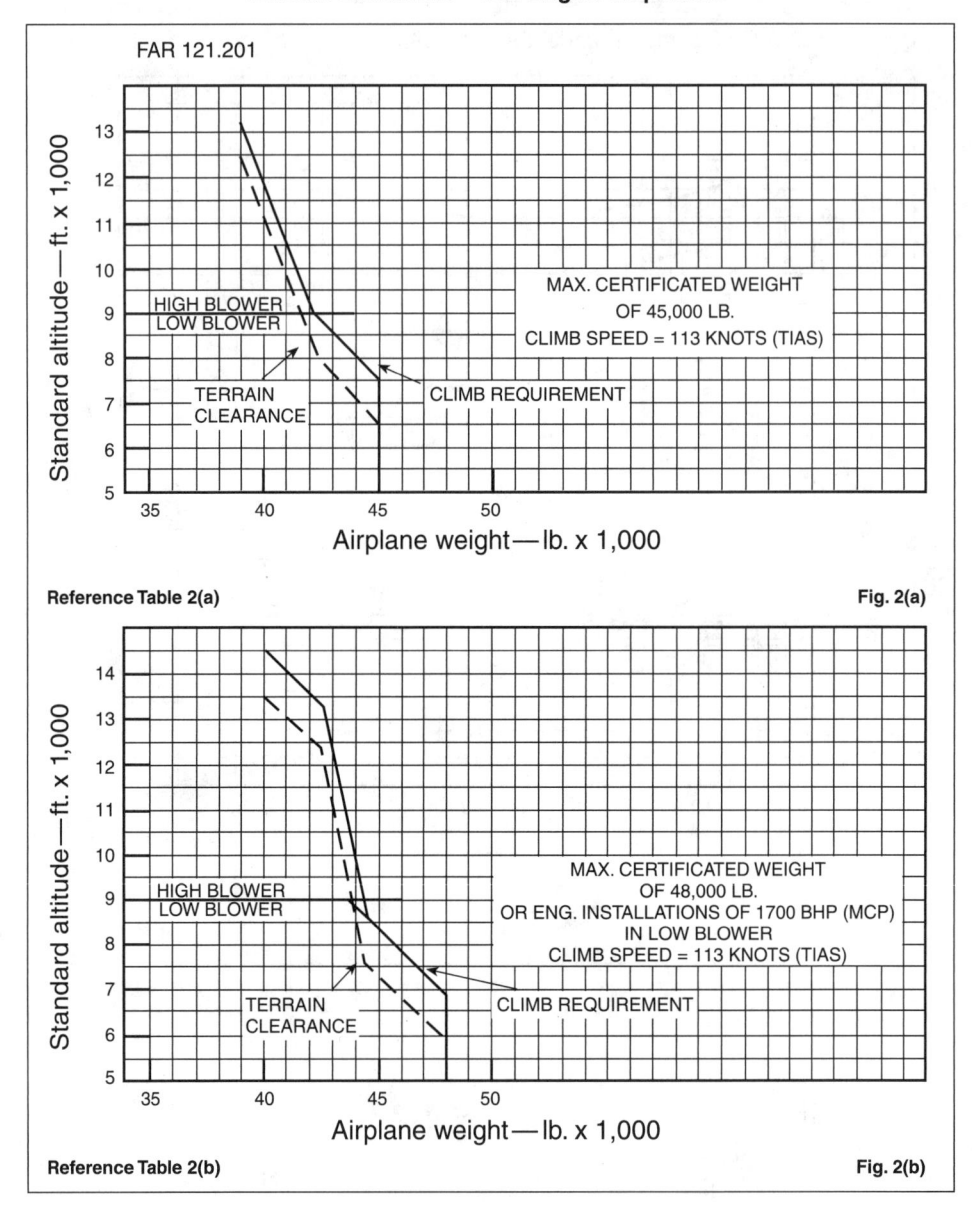

FAR 121.201

Reference Table 2(a)   Fig. 2(a)

Graph: Standard altitude—ft. x 1,000 vs. Airplane weight—lb. x 1,000. MAX. CERTIFICATED WEIGHT OF 45,000 LB. CLIMB SPEED = 113 KNOTS (TIAS). Curves labeled HIGH BLOWER, LOW BLOWER, TERRAIN CLEARANCE, CLIMB REQUIREMENT.

Reference Table 2(b)   Fig. 2(b)

Graph: Standard altitude—ft. x 1,000 vs. Airplane weight—lb. x 1,000. MAX. CERTIFICATED WEIGHT OF 48,000 LB. OR ENG. INSTALLATIONS OF 1700 BHP (MCP) IN LOW BLOWER. CLIMB SPEED = 113 KNOTS (TIAS). Curves labeled HIGH BLOWER, LOW BLOWER, TERRAIN CLEARANCE, CLIMB REQUIREMENT.

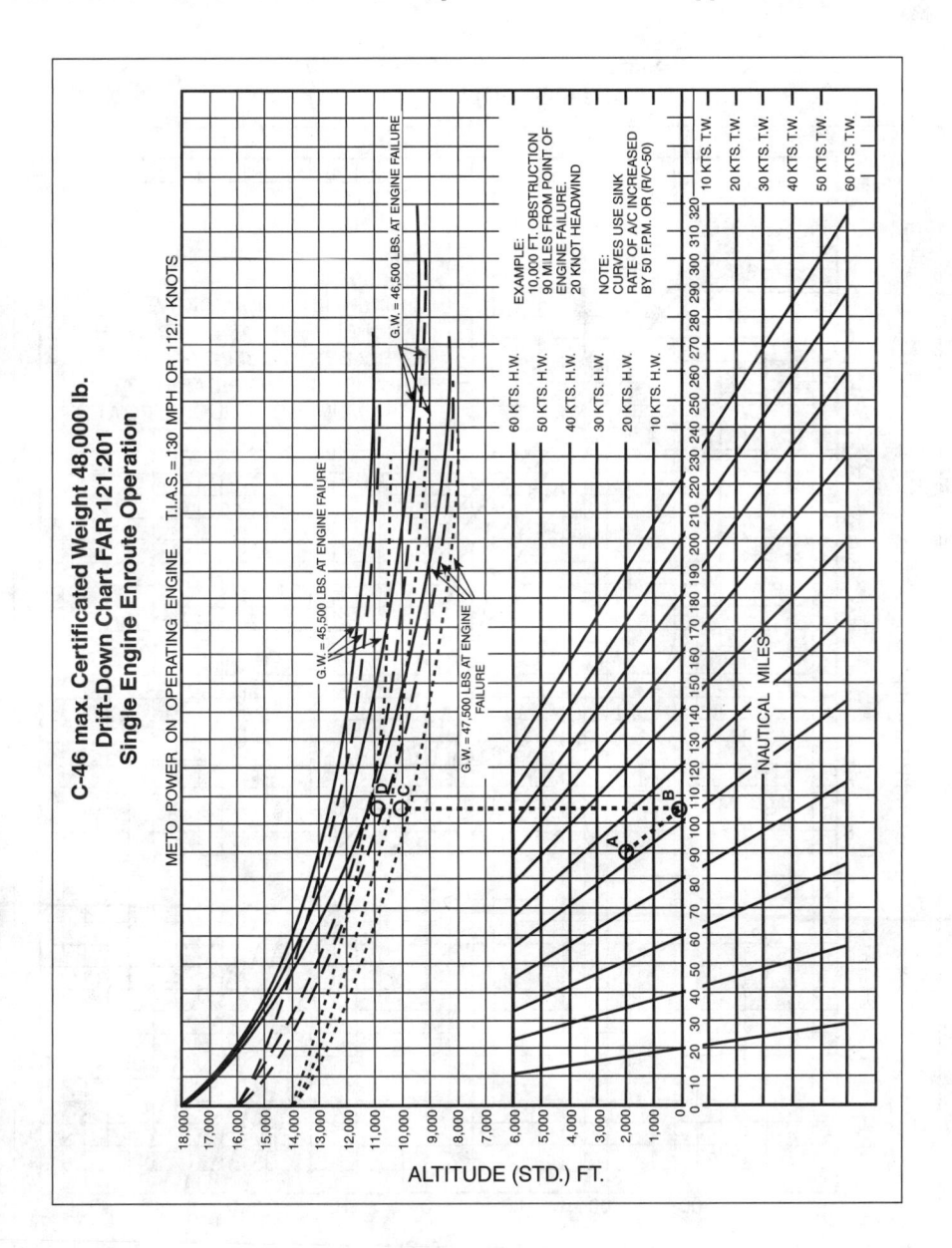

Part 121: Air Carriers & Commercial Operators **Appendix C to Part 121**

Appendix C to Part 121   **Federal Aviation Regulations**

C-46 max. Certificated Weight 48,000 lbs.
Enroute Climb Summary

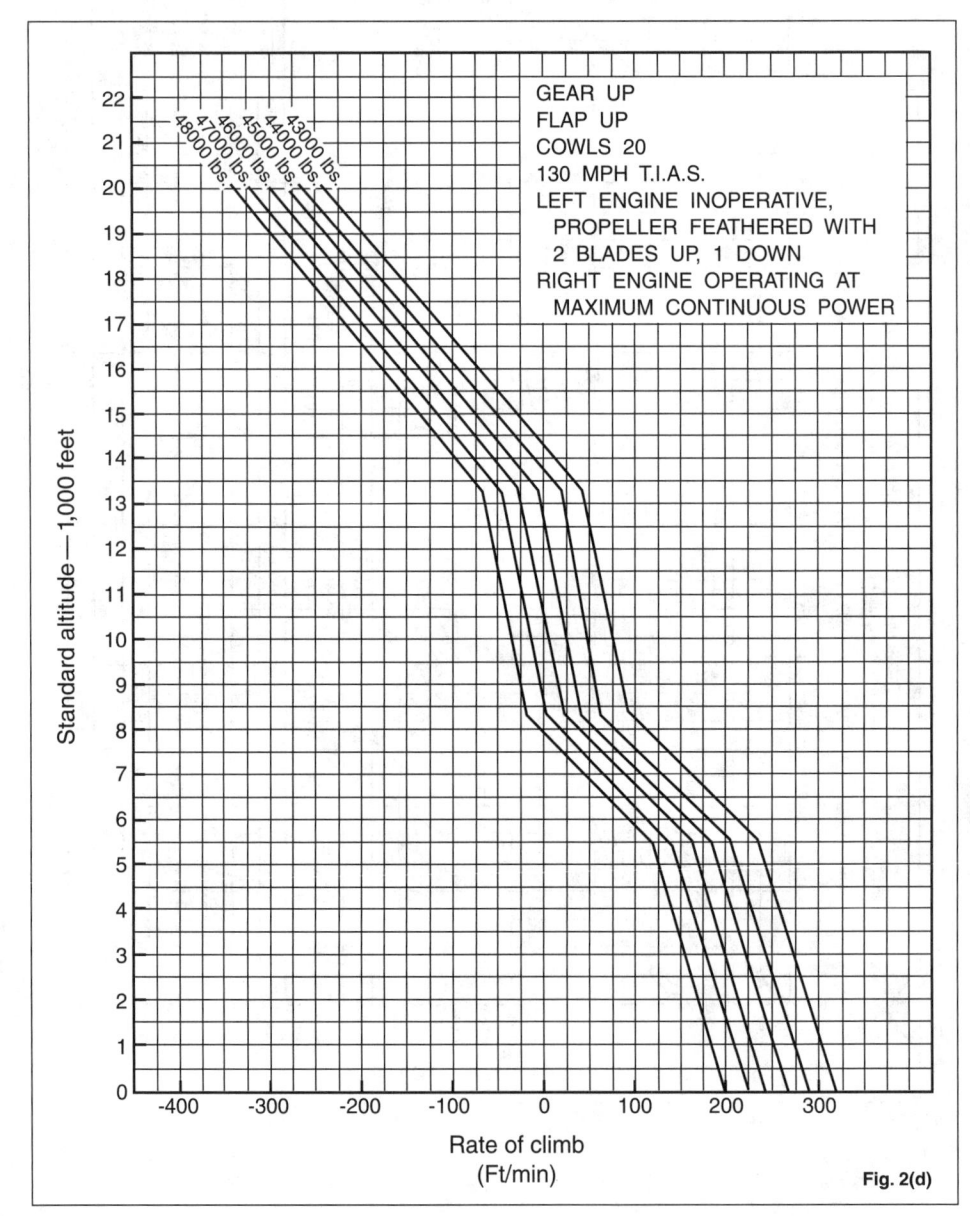

Fig. 2(d)

Part 121: Air Carriers & Commercial Operators **Appendix C to Part 121**

Curtiss C-46 Models
Certificated for max. weight of 45,000 lbs.

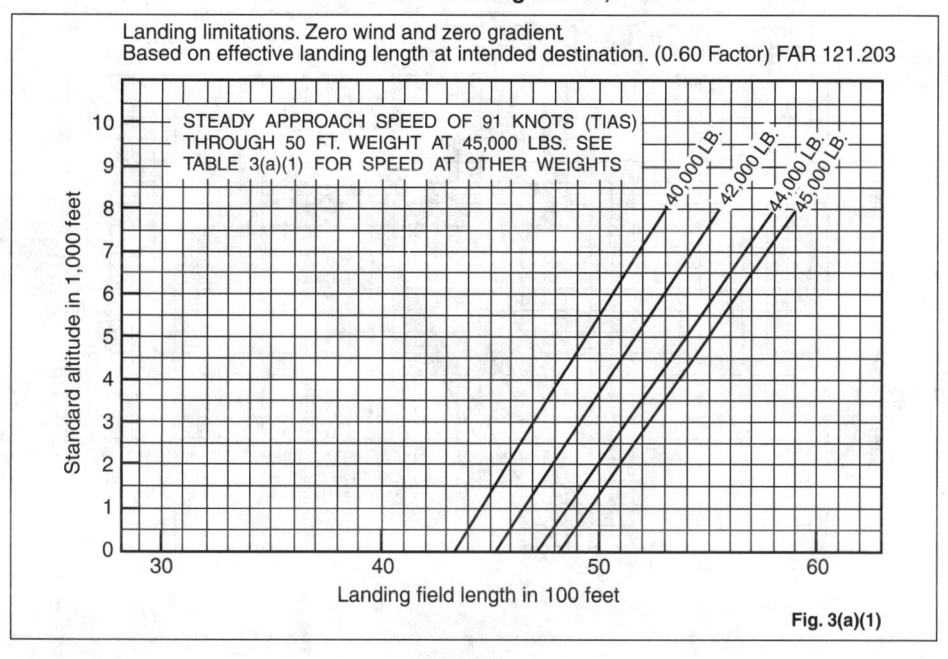

Landing limitations. Zero wind and zero gradient.
Based on effective landing length at intended destination. (0.60 Factor) FAR 121.203

STEADY APPROACH SPEED OF 91 KNOTS (TIAS) THROUGH 50 FT. WEIGHT AT 45,000 LBS. SEE TABLE 3(a)(1) FOR SPEED AT OTHER WEIGHTS

Fig. 3(a)(1)

Curtiss C-46 Models
Certificated for max. weight of 48,000 lbs.

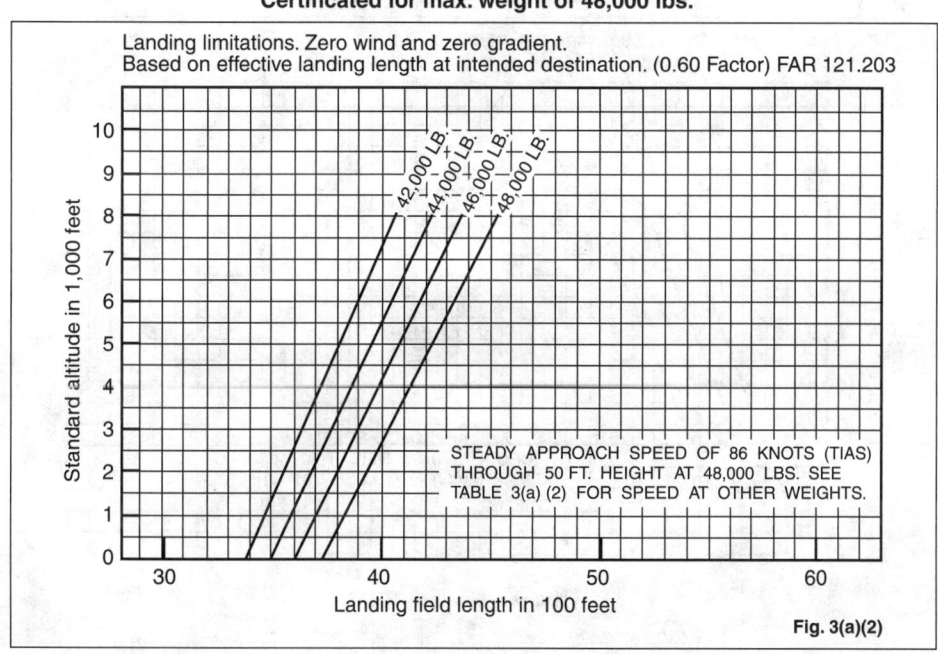

Landing limitations. Zero wind and zero gradient.
Based on effective landing length at intended destination. (0.60 Factor) FAR 121.203

STEADY APPROACH SPEED OF 86 KNOTS (TIAS) THROUGH 50 FT. HEIGHT AT 48,000 LBS. SEE TABLE 3(a)(2) FOR SPEED AT OTHER WEIGHTS.

Fig. 3(a)(2)

Appendix C to Part 121   **Federal Aviation Regulations**

Curtiss C-46 Models
Certificated for max. weight of 45,000 lbs.

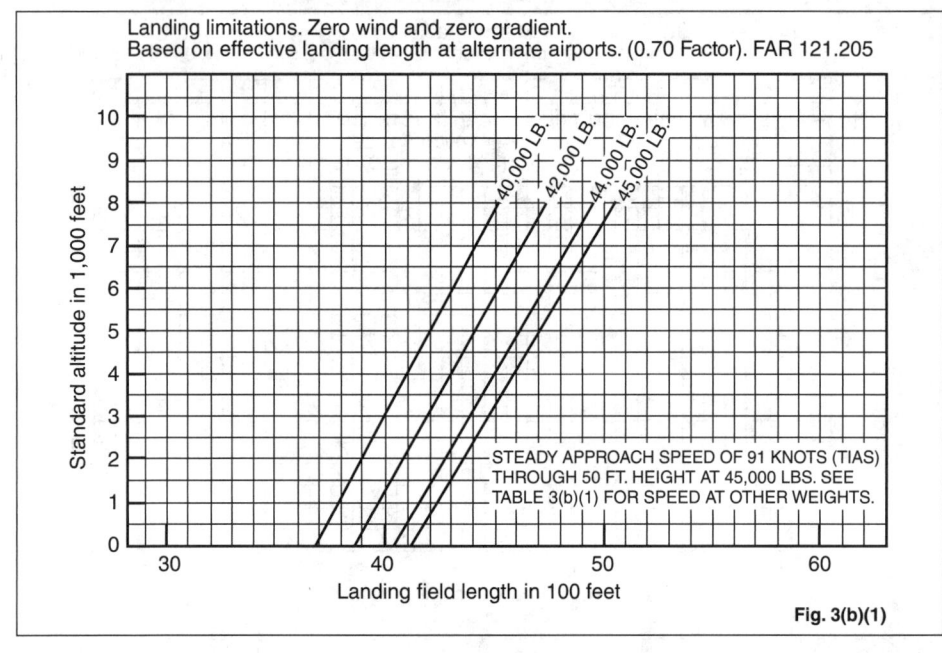

Landing limitations. Zero wind and zero gradient.
Based on effective landing length at alternate airports. (0.70 Factor). FAR 121.205

STEADY APPROACH SPEED OF 91 KNOTS (TIAS) THROUGH 50 FT. HEIGHT AT 45,000 LBS. SEE TABLE 3(b)(1) FOR SPEED AT OTHER WEIGHTS.

Fig. 3(b)(1)

Curtiss C-46 Models
Certificated for max. weight of 48,000 lbs.

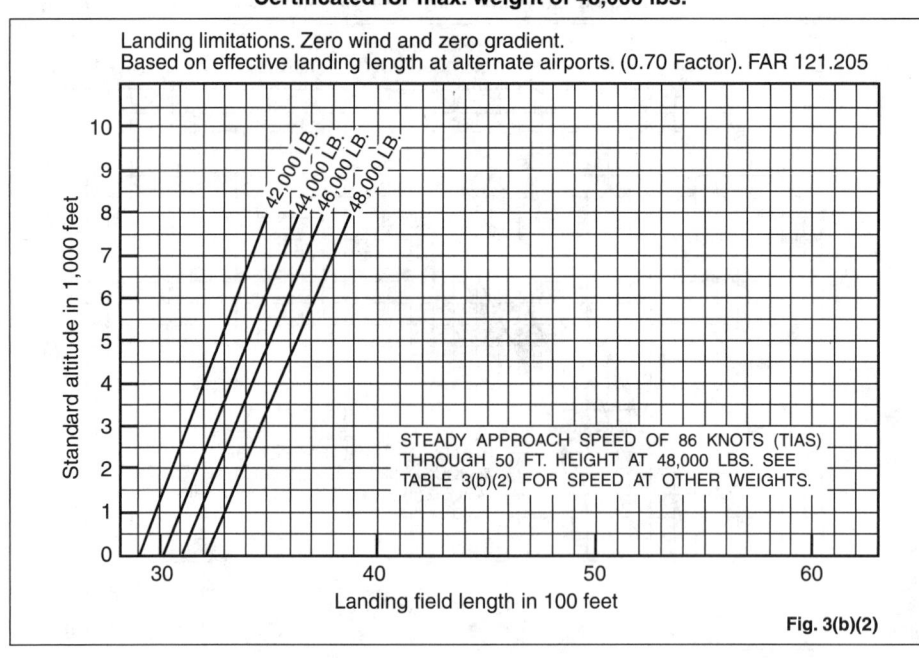

Landing limitations. Zero wind and zero gradient.
Based on effective landing length at alternate airports. (0.70 Factor). FAR 121.205

STEADY APPROACH SPEED OF 86 KNOTS (TIAS) THROUGH 50 FT. HEIGHT AT 48,000 LBS. SEE TABLE 3(b)(2) FOR SPEED AT OTHER WEIGHTS.

Fig. 3(b)(2)

Part 121: Air Carriers & Commercial Operators **Appendix C to Part 121**

Curtiss C-46 Models
Certificated for max. weight of 45,000 lbs.

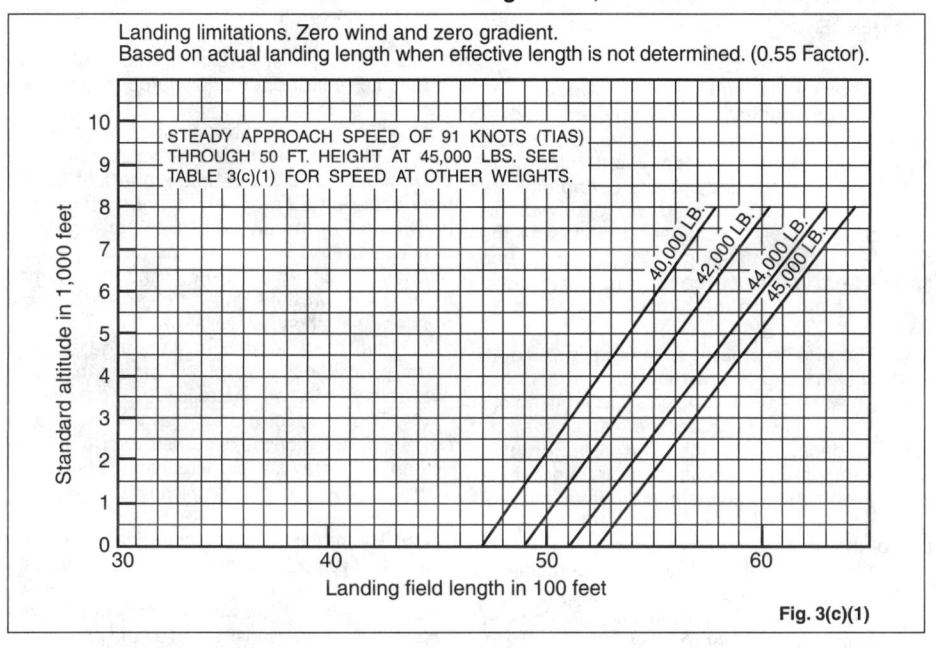

Landing limitations. Zero wind and zero gradient.
Based on actual landing length when effective length is not determined. (0.55 Factor).

STEADY APPROACH SPEED OF 91 KNOTS (TIAS) THROUGH 50 FT. HEIGHT AT 45,000 LBS. SEE TABLE 3(c)(1) FOR SPEED AT OTHER WEIGHTS.

Fig. 3(c)(1)

Curtiss C-46 Models
Certificated for max. weight of 48,000 lbs.

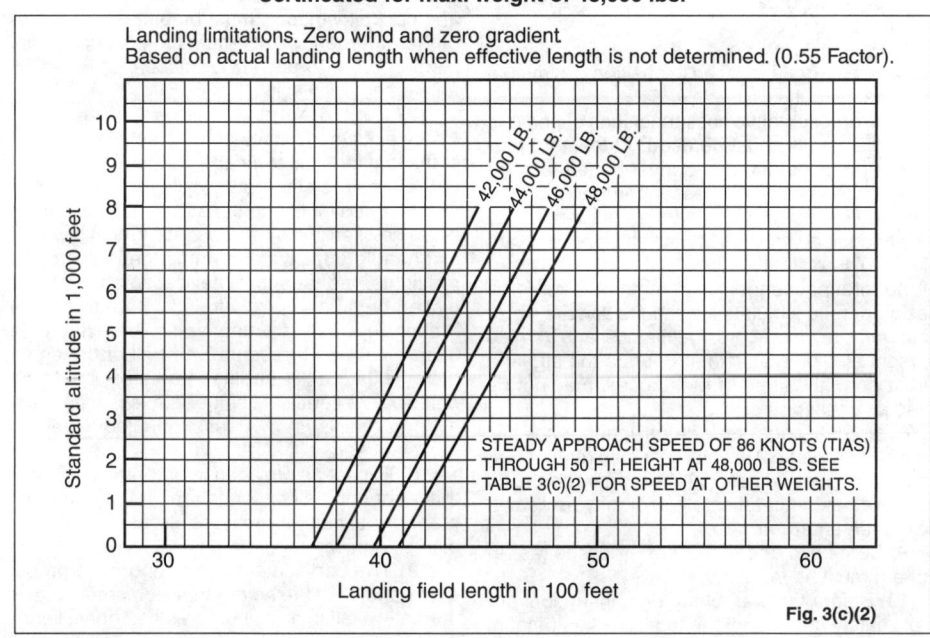

Landing limitations. Zero wind and zero gradient.
Based on actual landing length when effective length is not determined. (0.55 Factor).

STEADY APPROACH SPEED OF 86 KNOTS (TIAS) THROUGH 50 FT. HEIGHT AT 48,000 LBS. SEE TABLE 3(c)(2) FOR SPEED AT OTHER WEIGHTS.

Fig. 3(c)(2)

[Docket No. 4080, 30 FR 258, Jan. 3, 1965; 30 FR 481, Jan. 14, 1965; as amended by Amdt. 121–207, 54 FR 39293, Sept. 25, 1989]

APPENDIX D TO PART 121
CRITERIA FOR DEMONSTRATION OF EMERGENCY EVACUATION PROCEDURES UNDER §121.291

(a) *Aborted takeoff demonstration.*

(1) The demonstration must be conducted either during the dark of the night or during daylight with the dark of the night simulated. If the demonstration is conducted indoors during daylight hours, it must be conducted with each window covered and each door closed to minimize the daylight effect. Illumination on the floor or ground may be used, but it must be kept low and shielded against shining into the airplane's windows or doors.

(2) The airplane must be a normal ground attitude with landing gear extended.

(3) Unless the airplane is equipped with an off-wing descent means, stands or ramps may be used for descent from the wing to the ground. Safety equipment such as mats or inverted life rafts may be placed on the floor or ground to protect participants. No other equipment that is not part of the emergency evacuation equipment of the airplane may be used to aid the participants in reaching the ground.

(4) The airplane's normal electrical power sources must be deenergized.

(5) All emergency equipment for the type of passenger-carrying operation involved must be installed in accordance with the certificate holder's manual.

(6) Each external door and exit, and each internal door or curtain must be in position to simulate a normal takeoff.

(7) A representative passenger load of persons in normal health must be used. At least 40 percent of the passenger load must be females. At least 35 percent of the passenger load must be over 50 years of age. At least 15 percent of the passenger load must be female and over 50 years of age. Three life-size dolls, not included as part of the total passenger load, must be carried by passengers to simulate live infants 2 years old or younger. Crewmembers, mechanics, and training personnel, who maintain or operate the airplane in the normal course of their duties, may not be used as passengers.

(8) No passenger may be assigned a specific seat except as the Administrator may require. Except as required by item (12) of this paragraph, no employee of the certificate holder may be seated next to an emergency exit.

(9) Seat belts and shoulder harnesses (as required) must be fastened.

(10) Before the start of the demonstration, approximately one-half of the total average amount of carry-on baggage, blankets, pillows, and other similar articles must be distributed at several locations in the aisles and emergency exit access ways to create minor obstructions.

(11) The seating density and arrangement of the airplane must be representative of the highest capacity passenger version of that airplane the certificate holder operates or proposes to operate.

(12) Each crewmember must be a member of a regularly scheduled line crew, except that flight crewmembers need not be members of a regularly scheduled line crew, provided they have knowledge of the airplane. Each crewmember must be seated in the seat the crewmember is normally assigned for takeoff, and must remain in that seat until the signal for commencement of the demonstration is received.

(13) No crewmember or passenger may be given prior knowledge of the emergency exits available for the demonstration.

(14) The certificate holder may not practice, rehearse, or describe the demonstration for the participants nor may any participant have taken part in this type of demonstration within the preceding 6 months.

(15) The pretakeoff passenger briefing required by §121.571 may be given in accordance with the certificate holder's manual. The passengers may also be warned to follow directions of crewmembers, but may not be instructed on the procedures to be followed in the demonstration.

(16) If safety equipment as allowed by item (3) of this section is provided, either all passenger and cockpit windows must be blacked out or all of the emergency exits must have safety equipment in order to prevent disclosure of the available emergency exits.

(17) Not more than 50 percent of the emergency exits in the sides of the fuselage of an airplane that meet all of the requirements applicable to the required emergency exits for that airplane may be used for the demonstration. Exits that are not to be used in the demonstration must have the exit handle deactivated or must be indicated by red lights, red tape, or other acceptable means, placed outside the exits to indicate fire or other reason that they are unusable. The exits to be used must be representative of all of the emergency exits on the airplane and must be designated by the certificate holder, subject to approval by the Administrator. At least one floor level exit must be used.

(18) Except as provided in paragraph (a)(3) of this appendix, all evacuees must leave the airplane by a means provided as part of the airplane's equipment.

(19) The certificate holder's approved procedures and all of the emergency equipment that is normally available, including slides, ropes, lights, and megaphones, must be fully utilized during the demonstration, except that the flightcrew must

take no active role in assisting others inside the cabin during the demonstration.

(20) The evacuation time period is completed when the last occupant has evacuated the airplane and is on the ground. Evacuees using stands or ramps allowed by item (3) above are considered to be on the ground when they are on the stand or ramp: *Provided,* That the acceptance rate of the stand or ramp is no greater than the acceptance rate of the means available on the airplane for descent from the wing during an actual crash situation.

(b) *Ditching demonstration.* The demonstration must assume that daylight hours exist outside the airplane, and that all required crewmembers are available for the demonstration.

(1) If the certificate holder's manual requires the use of passengers to assist in the launching of liferafts, the needed passengers must be aboard the airplane and participate in the demonstration according to the manual.

(2) A stand must be placed at each emergency exit and wing, with the top of the platform at a height simulating the water level of the airplane following a ditching.

(3) After the ditching signal has been received, each evacuee must don a life vest according to the certificate holder's manual.

(4) Each liferaft must be launched and inflated, according to the certificate holder's manual, and all other required emergency equipment must be placed in rafts.

(5) Each evacuee must enter a liferaft, and the crewmembers assigned to each liferaft must indicate the location of emergency equipment aboard the raft and describe its use.

(6) Either the airplane, a mockup of the airplane or a floating device simulating a passenger compartment must be used.

(i) If a mockup of the airplane is used, it must be a life-size mockup of the interior and representative of the airplane currently used by or proposed to be used by the certificate holder, and must contain adequate seats for use of the evacuees. Operation of the emergency exits and the doors must closely simulate those on the airplane. Sufficient wing area must be installed outside the over-the-wing exits to demonstrate the evacuation.

(ii) If a floating device simulating a passenger compartment is used, it must be representative, to the extent possible, of the passenger compartment of the airplane used in operations. Operation of the emergency exits and the doors must closely simulate operation on that airplane. Sufficient wing area must be installed outside the over-the-wing exits to demonstrate the evacuation. The device must be equipped with the same survival equipment as is installed on the airplane, to accommodate all persons participating in the demonstration.

[Docket No. 2033, 30 FR 3206, March 9, 1965; as amended by Amdt. 121–30, 32 FR 13268, Sept. 20, 1967; Amdt. 121–41, 33 FR 9067, June 20, 1968; Amdt. 121–46, 34 FR 5545, March 22, 1969; Amdt. 121–47, 34 FR 11489, July 11, 1969; Amdt. 121–233, 58 FR 45230, Aug. 26, 1993]

Appendix E to Part 121
Flight Training Requirements

The maneuvers and procedures required by §121.424 of this part for pilot initial, transition, and upgrade flight training are set forth in the certificate holder's approved low-altitude windshear flight training program, §121.423 extended envelope training, and in this appendix. All required maneuvers and procedures must be performed inflight except that windshear and extended envelope training maneuvers and procedures must be performed in an airplane simulator in which the maneuvers and procedures are specifically authorized to be accomplished. Certain other maneuvers and procedures may be performed in an airplane simulator with a visual system (visual simulator), an airplane simulator without a visual system (nonvisual simulator), a training device, or a static airplane as indicated by the appropriate symbol in the respective column opposite the maneuver or procedure.

Whenever a maneuver or procedure is authorized to be performed in a nonvisual simulator, it may be performed in a visual simulator; when authorized in a training device, it may be performed in a visual or nonvisual simulator, and in some cases, a static airplane. Whenever the requirement may be performed in either a training device or a static airplane, the appropriate symbols are entered in the respective columns.

For the purpose of this appendix, the following symbols mean—

P = Pilot in Command (PIC).
S = Second in Command (SIC).
B = PIC and SIC.
F = Flight Engineer.
PJ = PIC transition Jet to Jet.
PP = PIC transition Prop. to Prop.
SJ = SIC transition Jet to Jet.
SP = SIC transition Prop. to Prop.
AT = All transition categories (PJ, PP, SJ, SP).
PS = SIC upgrading to PIC (same airplane).
SF = Flight Engineer upgrading to SIC (same airplane).
BU = Both SIC and Flight Engineer upgrading (same airplane).

Appendix E to Part 121 — **Federal Aviation Regulations**

FLIGHT TRAINING REQUIREMENTS

Maneuvers/Procedures	Initial training A/P Inflight	Initial training A/P Static	Initial training Simulator Visual simulator	Initial training Simulator Nonvisual simulator	Initial training Training device	Transition training A/P Inflight	Transition training A/P Static	Transition training Simulator Visual simulator	Transition training Simulator Nonvisual simulator	Transition training Training device	Upgrade training A/P Inflight	Upgrade training A/P Static	Upgrade training Simulator Visual simulator	Upgrade training Simulator Nonvisual simulator	Upgrade training Training device
As appropriate to the airplane and the operation involved, flight training for pilots must include the following maneuvers and procedures.															
I. Preflight															
(a) Visual inspection of the exterior and interior of the airplane, the location of each item to be inspected, and the purpose for inspecting it. If a flight engineer is a required crewmember for the particular type of airplane, the visual inspection may be replaced by using an approved pictorial means that realistically portrays the location and detail of preflight inspection items.		B					AT					BU			
(b) Use of the prestart check list, appropriate control system checks, starting procedures, radio and electronic equipment checks, and the selection of proper navigation and communications radio facilities and frequencies prior to flight.				B					AT					BU	
(c)(1) Before March 12, 2019, taxiing, sailing, and docking procedures in compliance with instructions issued by the appropriate Traffic Control Authority or by the person conducting the training.	B					AT					BU				
(c)(2) Taxiing. Beginning on March 12, 2019, this maneuver includes the following: (i) Taxiing, sailing, and docking procedures in compliance with instructions issued by the appropriate Traffic Control Authority or by the person conducting the training. (ii) Use of airport diagram (surface movement chart). (iii) Obtaining appropriate clearance before crossing or entering active runways. (iv) Observation of all surface movement guidance control markings and lighting.	B					AT					BU				
(d)(1) Before March 12, 2019, pre-takeoff checks that include power-plant checks.				B											
(d)(2) Beginning on March 12, 2019, pre-takeoff procedures that include power-plant checks, receipt of takeoff clearance and confirmation of aircraft location, and FMS entry (if appropriate), for departure runway prior to crossing hold short line for takeoff.			B					AT					BU		
II. Takeoffs:															
(a) Normal takeoffs which, for the purpose of this maneuver, begin when the airplane is taxied into position on the runway to be used.	B					AT					BU				
(b) Takeoffs with instrument conditions simulated at or before reaching an altitude of 100' above the airport elevation.			B					AT					BU		

Part 121: Air Carriers & Commercial Operators — Appendix E to Part 121

FLIGHT TRAINING REQUIREMENTS (CONTINUED)

Maneuvers/Procedures	Initial training — A/P Inflight	Initial training — A/P Static	Initial training — Simulator Visual simulator	Initial training — Simulator Nonvisual simulator	Initial training — Training device	Transition training — A/P Inflight	Transition training — A/P Static	Transition training — Simulator Visual simulator	Transition training — Simulator Nonvisual simulator	Transition training — Training device	Upgrade training — A/P Inflight	Upgrade training — A/P Static	Upgrade training — Simulator Visual simulator	Upgrade training — Simulator Nonvisual simulator	Upgrade training — Training device
(c)(1) Crosswind takeoffs	B					AT					BU				
(c)(2) Beginning on March 12, 2019, crosswind takeoffs including crosswind takeoffs with gusts if practicable under the existing meteorological, airport, and traffic conditions.	B					AT					BU				
(d) Takeoffs with a simulated failure of the most critical powerplant—			B					AT					BU		
(1) At a point after V_1 and before V_2 that in the judgment of the person conducting the training is appropriate to the airplane type under the prevailing conditions; or															
(2) At a point as close as possible after V_1 when V_1 and V_2 or V_1 and V_R are identical; or															
(3) At the appropriate speed for nontransport category airplanes.															
For transition training in an airplane group with engines mounted in similar positions, or from wing-mounted engines to aft fuselage-mounted engines, the maneuver may be performed in a nonvisual simulator.															
(e) Rejected takeoffs accomplished during a normal takeoff run after reaching a reasonable speed determined by giving due consideration to aircraft characteristics, runway length, surface conditions, wind directions and velocity, brake heat energy, and any other pertinent factors that may adversely affect safety of the airplane.				B					AT					BU	
Training in at least one of the above takeoffs must be accomplished at night. For transitioning pilots this requirement may be met during the operating experience required under §121.434 of this part by performing a normal takeoff at night when a check airman serving as pilot-in-command is occupying a pilot station.															
III. Flight Maneuvers and Procedures:															
(a) Turns with and without spoilers				B					AT					BU	
(b) Tuck and Mach buffet				B					AT					BU	
(c) Maximum endurance and maximum range procedures				B					AT					BU	
(d) Operation of systems and controls at the flight engineer station				B					AT					PS	
(e) Runaway and jammed stabilizer				B					AT					BU	
(f) Normal and abnormal or alternate operation of the following systems and procedures:															
(1) Pressurization					B					AT					BU

Appendix E to Part 121 — **Federal Aviation Regulations**

FLIGHT TRAINING REQUIREMENTS (CONTINUED)

Maneuvers/Procedures	Initial training A/P Inflight	Initial training A/P Static	Initial training Simulator Visual simulator	Initial training Simulator Nonvisual simulator	Initial training Training device	Transition training A/P Inflight	Transition training A/P Static	Transition training Simulator Visual simulator	Transition training Simulator Nonvisual simulator	Transition training Training device	Upgrade training A/P Inflight	Upgrade training A/P Static	Upgrade training Simulator Visual simulator	Upgrade training Simulator Nonvisual simulator	Upgrade training Training device
(2) Pneumatic					B					AT					BU
(3) Air conditioning					B					AT					BU
(4) Fuel and oil		B			B		AT			AT		BU			BU
(5) Electrical		B			B		AT			AT		BU			BU
(6) Hydraulic		B			B		AT			AT		BU			BU
(7) Flight control		B			B		AT					BU			BU
(8) Anti-icing and deicing				B					AT					BU	
(9) Auto-pilot				B					AT					BU	
(10) Automatic or other approach aids	B			B					AT		SF			BU	
(11) Stall warning devices, stall avoidance devices, and stability augmentation devices	B			B					AT		SF			BU	
(12) Airborne radar devices				B					AT					BU	
(13) Any other systems, devices, or aids available				B					AT					BU	
(14) Electrical, hydraulic, flight control, and flight instrument system malfunctioning or failure		B			B		AT			B		BU			BU
(15) Landing gear and flap systems failure or malfunction		B			B		AT			AT		BU			BU
(16) Failure of navigation or communications equipment				B					AT					BU	
(g) Flight emergency procedures that include at least the following:															
(1) Powerplant, heater, cargo compartment, cabin, flight deck, wing, and electrical fires		B			B		AT			AT		BU			BU
(2) Smoke control		B			B		AT			AT		BU			BU
(3) Powerplant failures				B			B			B		BU			BU
(4) Fuel jettisoning		B			B		AT					BU			BU
(5) Any other emergency procedures outlined in the appropriate flight manual				P					PJ					PS	

(h) Steep turns in each direction. Each steep turn must involve a bank angle of 45° with a heading change of at least 180° but not more than 360°.

334 ASA

FLIGHT TRAINING REQUIREMENTS (CONTINUED)

Maneuvers/Procedures	Initial A/P Inflight	Initial A/P Static	Initial Visual simulator	Initial Nonvisual simulator	Initial Training device	Transition A/P Inflight	Transition A/P Static	Transition Visual simulator	Transition Nonvisual simulator	Transition Training device	Upgrade A/P Inflight	Upgrade A/P Static	Upgrade Visual simulator	Upgrade Nonvisual simulator	Upgrade Training device
(i) Stall Prevention. For the purpose of this training the approved recovery procedure must be initiated at the first indication of an impending stall buffet, stick shaker, aural warning). Stall prevention training must be conducted in at least the following configurations:				B					AT					BU	
(1) Takeoff configuration (except where the airplane uses a zero-flap takeoff configuration.															
(2) Clean configuration.															
(3) Landing configuration.															
Training in at least one of the above configurations must be accomplished while in a turn with a bank angle between 15° and 30°.															
(j) Recovery from specific flight characteristics that are peculiar to the airplane type.				B					AT					BU	
(k) Instrument procedures that include the following:															
(1) Area departure and arrival				B					AT					BU	
(2) Use of navigation systems including adherence to assigned radials				B					AT					BU	
(3) Holding				B					AT					BU	
(l) ILS instrument approaches that include the following:															
(1) Normal ILS approaches	B					AT					BU				
(2) Manually controlled ILS approaches with a simulated failure of one powerplant which occurs before initiating the final approach course and continues to touchdown or through the missed approach procedure.	B							AT					BU		
(m) Instrument approaches and missed approaches other than ILS which include the following:															
(1) Nonprecision approaches that the trainee is likely to use.					B			AT							AT
(2) In addition to subparagraph (1) of this paragraph, at least one other nonprecision approach and missed approach procedure that the trainee is likely to use.			B					AT					BU		
In connection with paragraph III(k) and III(l), each instrument approach must be performed according to any procedures and limitations approved for the approach facility used. The instrument approach begins when the airplane is over the initial approach fix for the approach procedure being used (or turned over to the final approach controller in the case of GCA approach) and ends when the airplane touches down on runway or when transition to a missed approach configuration is completed.													BU		

Appendix E to Part 121   **Federal Aviation Regulations**

FLIGHT TRAINING REQUIREMENTS (CONTINUED)

Maneuvers/Procedures	Initial training A/P Inflight	Initial training A/P Static	Initial training Simulator Visual simulator	Initial training Simulator Nonvisual simulator	Initial training Training device	Transition training A/P Inflight	Transition training A/P Static	Transition training Simulator Visual simulator	Transition training Simulator Nonvisual simulator	Transition training Training device	Upgrade training A/P Inflight	Upgrade training A/P Static	Upgrade training Simulator Visual simulator	Upgrade training Simulator Nonvisual simulator	Upgrade training Training device
(n) Circling approaches which include the following:	B					AT					BU				
(1) That portion of the circling approach to the authorized minimum altitude for the procedure being used must be made under simulated instrument conditions.															
(2) The circling approach must be made to the authorized minimum circling approach altitude followed by a change in heading and the necessary maneuvering (by visual reference) to maintain a flight path that permits a normal landing on a runway at least 90° from the final approach course of the simulated instrument portion of the approach.															
(3) The circling approach must be performed without excessive maneuvering, and without exceeding the normal operating limits of the airplane. The angle of bank should not exceed 30°.															
Training in the circling approach maneuver is not required for a pilot employed by a certificate holder subject to the operating rules of Part 121 of this chapter if the certificate holder's manual prohibits a circling approach in weather conditions below 1000 – 3 (ceiling and visibility); for a SIC if the certificate holder's manual prohibits the SIC from performing a circling approach in operations under this part.															
(o) Zero-flap approaches. Training in this maneuver is not required for a particular airplane type if the Administrator has determined that the probability of flap extension failure on that type airplane is extremely remote due to system design. In making this determination, the Administrator determines whether training on slats only and partial flap approaches is necessary.	P							PP, PJ					PS		
(p) Missed approaches which include the following:															
(1) Missed approaches from ILS approaches			B					AT					BU		
(2) Other missed approaches					B					AT					BU
(3) Missed approaches that include a complete approved missed approach procedure					B					AT					BU
(4) Missed approaches that include a powerplant failure			B					AT					BU		

Part 121: Air Carriers & Commercial Operators **Appendix E to Part 121**

FLIGHT TRAINING REQUIREMENTS (CONTINUED)

Maneuvers/Procedures	Initial training					Transition training					Upgrade training				
		A/P		Simulator			A/P		Simulator			A/P		Simulator	
	Inflight	Static	Visual simulator	Nonvisual simulator	Training device	Inflight	Static	Visual simulator	Nonvisual simulator	Training device	Inflight	Static	Visual simulator	Nonvisual simulator	Training device
IV. Landings and Approaches to Landings:																
(a) Normal landings	B					AT					BU				
(b) Landing and go around with the horizontal stabilizer out of trim	P							PJ, PP							PS
(c) Landing in sequence from an ILS instrument approach	B					AT		AT			BU		BU		
(d)(1) Cross wind landing	B					AT					BU				
(d)(2) Beginning on March 12, 2019, crosswind landing, including crosswind landings with gusts if practicable under the existing meteorological, airport, and traffic conditions.															
(e) Maneuvering to a landing with simulated powerplant failure, as follows:															
(1) Except as provided in subparagraph (3) of this paragraph in the case of 3-engine airplanes, maneuvering to a landing with an approved procedure that approximates the loss of two powerplants (center and one outboard engine).	P								PJ, PP				PS		
(2) Except as provided in subparagraph (3) of this paragraph, in the case of other multiengine airplanes, maneuvering to a landing with a simulated failure of 50 percent of available powerplants with the simulated loss of power on one side of the airplane.	P							PJ, PP					PS		
(3) Notwithstanding the requirements of subparagraphs (1) and (2) of this paragraph, flight crewmembers who satisfy those requirements in a visual simulator must also:															
(i) Take inflight training in one-engine inoperative landings; and															
(ii) In the case of a second-in-command upgrading to a pilot-in-command and who has not previously performed the maneuvers required by this paragraph in flight, meet the requirements of this paragraph applicable to initial training for pilots-in-command.															
(4) In the case of flight crewmembers other than the pilot-in-command, perform the maneuver with the simulated loss of power of the most critical powerplant only.															
(f) Landing under simulated circling approach conditions (exceptions under III(n) applicable to this requirement.	B							AT			BU				
(g) Rejected landings that include a normal missed approach procedure after the landing is rejected. For the purpose of this maneuver the landing should be rejected at approximately 50 feet and approximately over the runway threshold.	B							AT			BU				

Appendix E to Part 121 — Federal Aviation Regulations

FLIGHT TRAINING REQUIREMENTS (CONTINUED)

Maneuvers/Procedures	Initial training					Transition training					Upgrade training				
	A/P		Simulator		Training device	A/P		Simulator		Training device	A/P		Simulator		Training device
	Inflight	Static	Visual simulator	Nonvisual simulator		Inflight	Static	Visual simulator	Nonvisual simulator		Inflight	Static	Visual simulator	Nonvisual simulator	
(h) Zero-flap landings if the Administrator finds that maneuver appropriate for training in the airplane.	P							PP, PJ					PS		
(i) Manual reversion (if appropriate)			B					AT					BU		
Training in landings and approaches to landings must include the types and conditions provided in IV(a) through (i) but more than one type may be combined where appropriate.															
Training in one of the above landings must be accomplished at night. For transitioning pilots, this requirement may be met during the operating experience required under §121.434 of this part by performing a normal landing when a check pilot serving as pilot-in-command is occupying a pilot station.	B						AT					BU			

[Docket No. 9509, 35 FR 97, Jan. 3, 1970; as amended by Amdt. 121–91, 37 FR 10730, May 27, 1972; Amdt. 121–108, 38 FR 35446, Dec. 28, 1973; Amdt. 121–159, 45 FR 41595, June 19, 1980; Amdt. 121–199, 53 FR 37697, Sept. 27, 1988; Amdt. 121–366, 78 FR 67841, Nov.12, 2013]

```
P  = Pilot in Command (PIC)
S  = Second in Command (SIC)
B  = PIC and SIC
F  = Flight Engineer
PJ = PIC transition Jet to Jet
PP = PIC transition Prop. to Prop
SJ = SIC transition Jet to Jet
SP = SIC transition Prop. to Prop
AT = All transition categories (PJ, PP, SJ, SP)
PS = SIC upgrading to PIC (same airplane)
SF = Flight Engineer upgrading to SIC (same airplane)
BU = Both SIC and Flight Engineer upgrading (same airplane)
```

Appendix F to Part 121

Proficiency Check Requirements

The maneuvers and procedures required by §121.441 for pilot proficiency checks are set forth in this appendix and must be performed inflight except to the extent that certain maneuvers and procedures may be performed in an airplane simulator with a visual system (visual simulator), an airplane simulator without a visual system (nonvisual simulator), or a training device as indicated by the appropriate symbol in the respective column opposite the maneuver or procedure.

Whenever a maneuver or procedure is authorized to be performed in a nonvisual simulator, it may also be performed in a visual simulator; when authorized in a training device, it may be performed in a visual or nonvisual simulator. For the purpose of this appendix, the following symbols mean—

P = Pilot in Command.
B = Both Pilot in Command and Second in Command.
* = A symbol and asterisk (B*) indicates that a particular condition is specified in the maneuvers and procedures column.
# = When a maneuver is preceded by this symbol it indicates the maneuver may be required in the airplane at the discretion of the person conducting the check.

Throughout the maneuvers prescribed in this appendix, good judgment commensurate with a high level of safety must be demonstrated. In determining whether such judgment has been shown, the person conducting the check considers adherence to approved procedures, actions based on analysis of situations for which there is no prescribed procedure or recommended practice, and qualities of prudence and care in selecting a course of action.

Maneuvers/Procedures	Required		Permitted			
	Simulated instrument conditions	Inflight	Visual simulator	Nonvisual simulator	Training device	Waiver provisions of §121.441(d)
The procedures and maneuvers set forth in this appendix must be performed in a manner that satisfactorily demonstrates knowledge and skill with respect to—						
(1) The airplane, its systems and components;						
(2) Proper control of airspeed, configuration, direction, altitude, and attitude in accordance with procedures and limitations contained in the approved Airplane Flight Manual, the certificate holder's operations Manual, check lists, or other approved material appropriate to the airplane type; and						
(3) Compliance with approach, ATC, or other applicable procedures.						
I. Preflight:						
(a) *Equipment examination (oral or written).* As part of the practical test, the equipment examination must be closely coordinated with, and related to, the flight maneuvers portion but may not be given during the flight maneuvers portion. The equipment examination must cover—					B	
(1) Subjects requiring a practical knowledge of the airplane, its powerplants, systems, components, operational and performance factors;						
(2) Normal, abnormal, and emergency procedures, and the operations and limitations relating thereto; and						
(3) The appropriate provisions of the approved Airplane Flight Manual.						
The person conducting the check may accept, as equal to this equipment test, an equipment test given to the pilot in the certificate holder's ground school within the preceding 6 calendar months.					B	B*
(b) *Preflight inspection.* The pilot must—						
(1) Conduct an actual visual inspection of the exterior and interior of the airplane, locating each item and explaining briefly the purpose for inspecting it; and						
(2) Demonstrate the use of the prestart check list, appropriate control system checks, starting procedures, radio and electronic equipment checks, and the selection of proper navigation and communications radio facilities and frequencies prior to flight.						

Appendix F to Part 121   **Federal Aviation Regulations**

Maneuvers/Procedures (continued)	Required		Permitted			
	Simulated instrument conditions	Inflight	Visual simulator	Nonvisual simulator	Training device	Waiver provisions of §121.441(d)
Except for flight checks required by §121.424(d)(1)(ii), an approved pictorial means that realistically portrays the location and detail of preflight inspection items and provides for the portrayal of abnormal conditions may be substituted for the preflight inspection. If a flight engineer is a required flight crewmember for the particular type airplane, the visual inspection may be waived under §121.441(d).						
(c)(1) *Taxiing.* Before March 12, 2019, this maneuver includes taxiing (in the case of a second in command proficiency check to the extent practical from the second in command crew position), sailing, or docking procedures in compliance with instructions issued by the appropriate traffic control authority or by the person conducting the checks.		B				
(c)(2) *Taxiing.* Beginning on March 12, 2019, this maneuver includes the following: (i) Taxiing (in the case of a second in command proficiency check to the extent practical from the second in command crew position), sailing, or docking procedures in compliance with instructions issued by the appropriate traffic control authority or by the person conducting the checks. (ii) Use of airport diagram (surface movement chart). (iii) Obtaining appropriate clearance before crossing or entering active runways. (iv) Observation of all surface movement guidance control markings and lighting.		B				
(d)(1) *Power-plant checks.* As appropriate to the airplane type.					B	
(d)(2) Beginning March 12, 2019, pre-takeoff procedures that include power-plant checks, receipt of takeoff clearance and confirmation of aircraft location, and FMS entry (if appropriate), for departure runway prior to crossing hold short line for takeoff.		B				
II. Takeoff:						
(a) *Normal.* One normal takeoff which, for the purpose of this maneuver, begins when the airplane is taxied into position on the runway to be used.						
(b) *Instrument.* One takeoff with instrument conditions simulated at or before reaching an altitude of 100′ above the airport elevation.	B		B*			
(c)(1) *Crosswind.* Before March 12, 2019, one crosswind takeoff, if practicable, under the existing meteorological, airport, and traffic conditions.		B*				
(c)(2) Beginning March 12, 2019, one crosswind takeoff with gusts, if practicable, under the existing meteorological, airport, and traffic conditions.		B*				
Requirements (a) and (c) may be combined, and requirements (a), (b), and (c) may be combined if (b) is performed inflight.						
(d) *Powerplant failure.* One takeoff with a simulated failure of the most critical powerplant—				B		
(1) At a point after V_1 and before V_2 that in the judgment of the person conducting the check is appropriate to the airplane type under the prevailing conditions;						
(2) At a point as close as possible after V_1 when V_1 and V_2 or V_1 and V_r are identical; or						
(3) At the appropriate speed for non-transport category airplanes.						
In an airplane group with aft fuselage-mounted engines, this maneuver may be performed in a non-visual simulator.						
(e) *Rejected.* A rejected takeoff may be performed in an airplane during a normal takeoff run after reaching a reasonable speed determined by giving due consideration to aircraft characteristics, runway length, surface conditions, wind direction and velocity, brake heat energy, and any other pertinent factors that may adversely affect safety or the airplane.				B*		B

Part 121: Air Carriers & Commercial Operators **Appendix F to Part 121**

Maneuvers/Procedures (continued)	Required		Permitted		
	Simulated instrument conditions	Inflight	Visual simulator	Nonvisual simulator	Training device	Waiver provisions of §121.441(d)
III. Instrument procedures:						
(a) *Area departure and area arrival.* During each of these maneuvers the applicant must—	B			B		B*
(1) Adhere to actual or simulated ATC clearances (including assigned radials); and						
(2) Properly use available navigation facilities.						
Either area arrival or area departure, but not both, may be waived under §121.441(d).						
(b) *Holding.* This maneuver includes entering, maintaining, and leaving holding patterns. It may be performed in connection with either area departure or area arrival.	B			B		B
(c) *ILS and other instrument approaches.* There must be the following:						
(1) At least one normal ILS approach.	B		B			
(2) At least one manually-controlled ILS approach with a simulated failure of one powerplant. The simulated failure should occur before initiating the final approach course and must continue to touchdown or through the missed approach procedure.	B					
(3) At least one nonprecision approach procedure that is representative of the nonprecision approach procedures that the certificate holder is likely to use.	B		B			
(4) Demonstration of at least one nonprecision approach procedure on a letdown aid other than the approach procedure performed under subparagraph (3) of this paragraph that the certificate holder is approved to use.	B				B	
Each instrument approach must be performed according to any procedures and limitations approved for the approach facility used. The instrument approach begins when the airplane is over the initial approach fix for the approach procedure being used (or turned over to the final approach controller in the case of GCA approach), and ends when the airplane touches down on the runway or when transition to a missed approach configuration is completed. Instrument conditions need not be simulated below 100' above touchdown zone elevation.						
(d) *Circling approaches.* If the certificate holder is approved for circling minimums below 1000–3, at least one circling approach must be made under the following conditions—			B*			B*
(1) The portion of the approach to the authorized minimum circling approach altitude must be made under simulated instrument conditions.	B					
(2) The approach must be made to the authorized minimum circling approach altitude followed by a change in heading and the necessary maneuvering (by visual reference) to maintain a flight path that permits a normal landing on a runway at least 90° from the final approach course of the simulated instrument portion of the approach.						
(3) The circling approach must be performed without excessive maneuvering, and without exceeding the normal operating limits of the airplane. The angle of bank should not exceed 30°.						
If local conditions beyond the control of the pilot prohibit the maneuver or prevent it from being performed as required, it may be waived as provided in §121.441(d): Provided, however, that the maneuver may not be waived under this provision for two successive proficiency checks. The circling approach maneuver is not required for a second-in-command if the certificate holder s manual prohibits a second-in-command from performing a circling approach in operations under this part.						
(e) *Missed approach.*						
(1) Each pilot must perform at least one missed approach from an ILS approach.			B*			
(2) Each pilot in command must perform at least one additional missed approach.			P*			
A complete approved missed approach procedure must be accomplished at least once. At the discretion of the person conducting the check, a simulated powerplant failure may be required during any of the missed approaches. These maneuvers may be performed either independently or in conjunction with maneuvers required under Sections III or V of this appendix. At least one missed approach must be performed in flight.						

Appendix F to Part 121

Federal Aviation Regulations

Maneuvers/Procedures *(continued)*	Required			Permitted		
	Simulated instrument conditions	Inflight	Visual simulator	Nonvisual simulator	Training device	Waiver provisions of §121.441(d)
IV. Inflight Maneuvers:						
(a) *Steep turns*. At least one steep turn in each direction must be performed. Each steep turn must involve a bank angle of 45° with a heading change of at least 180° but not more than 360°.		P		P		P
(b) *Stall Prevention*. For the purpose of this maneuver the approved recovery procedure must be initiated at the first indication of an impending stall (buffet, stick shaker, aural warning). Except as provided below there must be at least three stall prevention recoveries as follows:		B		B		B*
(1) One in the takeoff configuration (except where the airplane uses only a zero-flap takeoff configuration).						
(2) One in a clean configuration.						
(3) One in a landing configuration.						
At the discretion of the person conducting the check, one stall prevention recovery must be performed in one of the above configurations while in a turn with the bank angle between 15° and 30°. Two out of the three stall prevention recoveries required by this paragraph may be waived.						
If the certificate holder is authorized to dispatch or flight release the airplane with a stall warning device inoperative, the device may not be used during this maneuver.						
(c) *Specific flight characteristics*. Recovery from specific flight characteristics that are peculiar to the airplane type.				B		B
(d) *Powerplant failures*. In addition to specific requirements for maneuvers with simulated powerplant failures, the person conducting the check may require a simulated powerplant failure at any time during the check.				B		
V. Landings and Approaches to Landings:						
Notwithstanding the authorizations for combining and waiving maneuvers and for the use of a simulator, at least two actual landings (one to a full stop) must be made for all pilot-in-command and initial second-in-command proficiency checks.						
Landings and approaches to landings must include the types listed below, but more than one type may be combined where appropriate:						
(a) *Normal landing*.			B			
(b) Landing in sequence from an ILS instrument approach except that if circumstances beyond the control of the pilot prevent an actual landing, the person conducting the check may accept an approach to a point where in his judgment a landing to a full stop could have been made.			B*			
(c)(1) Crosswind landing, if practical under existing meteorological, airport, and traffic conditions.			B*			
(c)(2) Beginning March 12, 2019, crosswind landing with gusts, if practical under existing meteorological, airport, and traffic conditions.			B*			
(d) *Maneuvering to a landing with simulated powerplant failure as follows:*						
(1) In the case of 3-engine airplanes, maneuvering to a landing with an approved procedure that approximates the loss of two powerplants (center and one outboard engine); or				B*		
(2) In the case of other multiengine airplanes, maneuvering to a landing with a simulated failure of 50 percent of available powerplants, with the simulated loss of power on one side of the airplane.				B*		
Notwithstanding the requirements of subparagraphs (d)(1) and (2) of this paragraph, in a proficiency check for other than a pilot-in-command, the simulated loss of power may be only the most critical powerplant. However, if a pilot satisfies the requirements of subparagraphs (d)(1) or (2) of this paragraph in a visual simulator, he also must maneuver in flight to a landing with a simulated failure of the most critical powerplant. In addition, a pilot-in-command may omit the maneuver required by subparagraph (d)(1) or (d)(2) of this paragraph during a required proficiency check or simulator course of training if he satisfactorily performed that maneuver during the preceding proficiency check, or during the preceding approved simulator course of training under the observation of a check airman, whichever was completed later.						

Part 121: Air Carriers & Commercial Operators — Appendix F to Part 121

Maneuvers/Procedures *(continued)*	Required: Simulated instrument conditions	Required: Inflight	Permitted: Visual simulator	Permitted: Nonvisual simulator	Permitted: Training device	Waiver provisions of §121.441(d)
(e) Except as provided in paragraph (f) of this section, if the certificate holder is approved for circling minimums below 1000 – 3, a landing under simulated circling approach conditions. However, when performed in an airplane, if circumstances beyond the control of the pilot prevent a landing, the person conducting the check may accept an approach to a point where, in his judgment, a landing to a full stop could have been made.			B*			
(f) A rejected landing, including a normal missed approach procedure, that is rejected approximately 50′ over the runway and approximately over the runway threshold. This maneuver may be combined with instrument, circling, or missed approach procedures, but instrument conditions need not be simulated below 100 feet above the runway.			B			
VI. Normal and Abnormal Procedures:						
Each applicant must demonstrate the proper use of as many of the systems and devices listed below as the person conducting the check finds are necessary to determine that the person being checked has a practical knowledge of the use of the systems and devices appropriate to the airplane type:						
(a) Anti-icing and de-icing systems				B		
(b) Auto-pilot systems				B		
(c) Automatic or other approach aid systems				B		
(d) Stall warning devices, stall avoidance devices, and stability augmentation devices				B		
(e) Airborne radar devices				B		
(f) Any other systems, devices, or aids available				B		
(g) Hydraulic and electrical system failures and malfunctions					B	
(h) Landing gear and flap systems failure or malfunction					B	
(i) Failure of navigation or communications equipment				B		
VII. Emergency Procedures:						
Each applicant must demonstrate the proper emergency procedures for as many of the emergency situations listed below as the person conducting the check finds are necessary to determine that the person being checked has an adequate knowledge of, and ability to perform, such procedure:						
(a) Fire in flight				B		
(b) Smoke control				B		
(c) Rapid decompression				B		
(d) Emergency descent				B		
(e) Any other emergency procedures outlined in the appropriate approved Airplane Flight Manual.				B		

[Docket No. 9509, 35 FR 99, Jan. 3, 1970; as amended by Amdt. 121–80, 36 FR 19362, Oct. 5, 1971; Amdt. 121–91, 37 FR 10730, May 27, 1972; Amdt. 121–92, 37 FR 12717, June 28, 1972; Amdt. 121–108, 38 FR 35448, Dec. 28, 1973; Amdt. 121–136, 42 FR 43389, Aug. 29, 1977; Amdt. 121–366, 78 FR 67844, Nov. 12, 2013]

APPENDIX G TO PART 121
DOPPLER RADAR AND INERTIAL NAVIGATION SYSTEM (INS): REQUEST FOR EVALUATION; EQUIPMENT AND EQUIPMENT INSTALLATION; TRAINING PROGRAM; EQUIPMENT ACCURACY AND RELIABILITY; EVALUATION PROGRAM

1. Application authority.

(a) An applicant for authority to use a Doppler Radar or Inertial Navigation System must submit a request for evaluation of the system to the Flight Standards District Office or International Field Office charged with the overall inspection of its operations 30 days prior to the start of evaluation flights.

(b) The application must contain:

(1) A summary of experience with the system showing to the satisfaction of the Administrator a history of the accuracy and reliability of the system proposed to be used.

(2) A training program curriculum for initial approval under §121.405.

(3) A maintenance program for compliance with Subpart L of this part.

(4) A description of equipment installation.

(5) Proposed revisions to the Operations Manual outlining all normal and emergency procedures relative to use of the proposed system, including detailed methods for continuing the navigational function with partial or complete equipment failure, and methods for determining the most accurate system when an unusually large divergence between systems occurs. For the purpose of this appendix, a large divergence is a divergence that results in a track that falls beyond clearance limits.

(6) Any proposed revisions to the minimum equipment list with adequate justification therefor.

(7) A list of operations to be conducted using the system, containing an analysis of each with respect to length, magnetic compass reliability, availability of en route aids, and adequacy of gateway and terminal radio facilities to support the system. For the purpose of this appendix, a gateway is a specific navigational fix where use of long range navigation commences or terminates.

2. Equipment and equipment installation—Inertial Navigation Systems (INS) or Doppler Radar System.

(a) Inertial Navigation and Doppler Radar Systems must be installed in accordance with applicable airworthiness requirements.

(b) Cockpit arrangement must be visible and usable by either pilot seated at his duty station.

(c) The equipment must provide, by visual, mechanical, or electrical output signals, indications of the invalidity of output data upon the occurrence of probable failures or malfunctions within the system.

(d) A probable failure or malfunction within the system must not result in loss of the aircraft's required navigation capability.

(e) The alignment, updating, and navigation computer functions of the system must not be invalidated by normal aircraft power interruptions and transients.

(f) The system must not be the source of cause of objectionable radio frequency interference, and must not be adversely affected by radio frequency interference from other aircraft systems.

(g) The FAA-approved airplane flight manual, or supplement thereto, must include pertinent material as required to define the normal and emergency operating procedures and applicable operating limitations associated with INS and Doppler performance (such as maximum latitude at which ground alignment capability is provided, or deviations between systems).

3. Equipment and equipment installation—Inertial Navigation Systems (INS).

(a) If an applicant elects to use an Inertial Navigation System it must be at least a dual system (including navigational computers and reference units). At least two systems must be operational at takeoff. The dual system may consist of either two INS units, or one INS unit and one Doppler Radar unit.

(b) Each Inertial Navigation System must incorporate the following:

(1) Valid ground alignment capability at all latitudes appropriate for intended use of the installation.

(2) A display of alignment status or a ready to navigate light showing completed alignment to the flight crew.

(3) The present position of the airplane in suitable coordinates.

(4) Information relative to destinations or waypoint positions:

(i) The information needed to gain and maintain a desired track and to determine deviations from the desired track.

(ii) The information needed to determine distance and time to go to the next waypoint or destination.

(c) For INS installations that do not have memory or other inflight alignment means, a separate electrical power source (independent of the main propulsion system) must be provided which can supply, for at least 5 minutes, enough power (as shown by analysis or as demonstrated in the airplane) to maintain the INS in such condition that its full capability is restored upon the reactivation of the normal electrical supply.

(d) The equipment must provide such visual, mechanical, or electrical output signals as may be required to permit the flight crew to detect probable failures or malfunctions in the system.

4. Equipment and equipment installation—Doppler Radar Systems.

(a) If an applicant elects to use a Doppler Radar System it must be at least a dual system (including dual antennas or a combined antenna designed for multiple operation), except that:

(1) A single operating transmitter with a standby capable of operation may be used in lieu of two operating transmitters.

(2) Single heading source information to all installations may be utilized, provided a compass comparator system is installed and operational procedures call for frequent cross-checks of all compass heading indicators by crewmembers. The dual system may consist of either two Doppler Radar units or one Doppler Radar unit and one INS unit.

(b) At least two systems must be operational at takeoff.

(c) As determined by the Administrator and specified in the certificate holder's operations specifications, other navigational aids may be required to update the Doppler Radar for a particular operation. These may include Loran, Consol, DME, VOR, ADF, ground-based radar, and airborne weather radar. When these aids are required, the cockpit arrangement must be such that all controls are accessible to each pilot seated at his duty station.

5. Training programs. The initial training program for Doppler Radar and Inertial Navigation Systems must include the following:

(a) Duties and responsibilities of flight crewmembers, dispatchers, and maintenance personnel.

(b) For pilots, instruction in the following:

(1) Theory and procedures, limitations, detection of malfunctions, preflight and inflight testing, and cross-checking methods.

(2) The use of computers, an explanation of all systems, compass limitations at high latitudes, a review of navigation, flight planning, and applicable meteorology.

(3) The methods for updating by means of reliable fixes.

(4) The actual plotting of fixes.

(c) Abnormal and emergency procedures.

6. Equipment accuracy and reliability.

(a) Each Inertial Navigation System must meet the following accuracy requirements, as appropriate:

(1) For flights up to 10 hours' duration, no greater than 2 nautical miles per hour of circular error on 95 percent of system flights completed is permitted.

(2) For flights over 10 hours' duration, a tolerance of ±20 miles cross-track and ±25 miles along-track on 95 percent of system flights completed is permitted.

(b) Compass heading information to the Doppler Radar must be maintained to an accuracy of ±1° and total system deviations must not exceed 2. When free gyro techniques are used, procedures shall be utilized to ensure that an equivalent level of heading accuracy and total system deviation is attained.

(c) Each Doppler Radar System must meet accuracy requirements of ±20 miles cross-track and ±25 miles along-track for 95 percent of the system flights completed. Updating is permitted. A system that does not meet the requirements of this section will be considered a failed system.

7. Evaluation program.

(a) Approval by evaluation must be requested as a part of the application for operational approval of a Doppler Radar or Inertial Navigation System.

(b) The applicant must provide sufficient flights which show to the satisfaction of the Administrator the applicant's ability to use cockpit navigation in his operation.

(c) The Administrator bases his evaluation on the following:

(1) Adequacy of operational procedures.

(2) Operational accuracy and reliability of equipment and feasibility of the system with regard to proposed operations.

(3) Availability of terminal, gateway, area, and en route ground-based aids, if required, to support the self-contained system.

(4) Acceptability of cockpit workload.

(5) Adequacy of flight crew qualifications.

(6) Adequacy of maintenance training and availability of spare parts.

After successful completion of evaluation demonstrations, FAA approval is indicated by issuance of amended operations specifications and en route flight procedures defining the new operation. Approval is limited to those operations for which the adequacy of the equipment and the feasibility of cockpit navigation has been satisfactorily demonstrated.

[Dookot No. 10204, 37 FR 6464, March 30, 1972; as amended by Amdt. 121-207, 54 FR 39293, Sept. 25, 1989]

APPENDIX H TO PART 121
ADVANCED SIMULATION

This appendix provides guidelines and a means for achieving flightcrew training in advanced airplane simulators. The requirements in this appendix are in addition to the simulator approval requirements in §121.407. Each simulator used under this appendix must be approved as a Level B, C, or D simulator, as appropriate.

ADVANCED SIMULATION TRAINING PROGRAM

For an operator to conduct Level C or D training under this appendix all required simulator instruction and checks must be conducted under an advanced simulation training program approved by the Administrator for the operator. This program must also ensure that all instructors and check airmen used in appendix H training and checking are highly qualified to provide the training required in the training program. The advanced simulation training program must include the following:

1. The operator's initial, transition, upgrade, and recurrent simulator training programs and its procedures for re-establishing recency of experience in the simulator.

2. How the training program will integrate Level B, C, and D simulators with other simulators and training devices to maximize the total training, checking, and certification functions.

3. Documentation that each instructor and check airman has served for at least 1 year in that capacity in a certificate holder's approved program or has served for at least 1 year as a pilot in command or second in command in an airplane of the group in which that pilot is instructing or checking.

4. A procedure to ensure that each instructor and check airman actively participates in either an approved regularly scheduled line flying program as a flight crewmember or an approved line observation program in the same airplane type for which that person is instructing or checking.

5. A procedure to ensure that each instructor and check airman is given a minimum of 4 hours of training each year to become familiar with the operator's advanced simulation training program, or changes to it, and to emphasize their respective roles in the program. Training for simulator instructors and check airmen must include training policies and procedures, instruction methods and techniques, operation of simulator controls (including environmental and trouble panels), limitations of the simulator, and minimum equipment required for each course of training.

6. A special Line Oriented Flight Training (LOFT) program to facilitate the transition from the simulator to line flying. This LOFT program must consist of at least a 4-hour course of training for each flightcrew. It also must contain at least two representative flight segments of the operator's route. One of the flight segments must contain strictly normal operating procedures from push back at one airport to arrival at another. Another flight segment must contain training in appropriate abnormal and emergency flight operations. After March 12, 2019, the LOFT must provide an opportunity for the pilot to demonstrate workload management and pilot monitoring skills.

LEVEL B
TRAINING AND CHECKING PERMITTED

1. Recency of experience (§121.439).
2. Night takeoffs and landings (Part 121, Appendix E).
3. Landings in a proficiency check without the landing on the line requirements (§121.441).

LEVEL C
TRAINING AND CHECKING PERMITTED

1. For all pilots, transition training between airplanes in the same group, and for a pilot in command the certification check required by §61.153 of this chapter.

2. Upgrade to pilot-in-command training and the certification check when the pilot—
a. Has previously qualified as second in command in the equipment to which the pilot is upgrading;
b. Has at least 500 hours of actual flight time while serving as second in command in an airplane of the same group; and
c. Is currently serving as second in command in an airplane in this same group.

3. Initial pilot-in-command training and the certification check when the pilot—
a. Is currently serving as second in command in an airplane of the same group;
b. Has a minimum of 2,500 flight hours as second in command in an airplane of the same group; and
c. Has served as second in command on at least two airplanes of the same group.

4. For all second-in-command pilot applicants who meet the aeronautical experience requirements of §61.159 of this chapter in the airplane, the initial and upgrade training and checking required by this part, and the certification check requirements of §61.153 of this chapter.

5. For all pilots, the extended envelope training required by §121.423 of this part.

LEVEL D
TRAINING AND CHECKING PERMITTED

Except for the requirements listed in the next sentence, all pilot flight training and checking required by this part and the certification check requirements of §61.153(h) of this chapter. The line check required by §121.440, the static airplane requirements of appendix E of this part, and the operating experience requirements of §121.434 must still be performed in the airplane.

[Docket No. FAA–2002–12461, 71 FR 63640, Oct. 30, 2006; as amended by Amdt. 121–365, 78 FR 42379, July 15, 2013; Amdt. 121–366, 78 FR 67846, Nov. 12, 2013]

APPENDIX I TO PART 121—[RESERVED]

APPENDIX J TO PART 121—[RESERVED]

APPENDIX K TO PART 121
PERFORMANCE REQUIREMENTS FOR CERTAIN TURBOPROPELLER POWERED AIRPLANES

1. Applicability. This appendix specifies requirements for the following turbopropeller powered airplanes that must comply with the Airplane Performance Operating Limitations in §§121.189 through 121.197:

a. After December 20, 2010, each airplane manufactured before March 20, 1997, and type certificated in the:

  i. Normal category before July 1, 1970, and meets special conditions issued by the Administrator for airplanes intended for use in operations under part 135 of this chapter.

  ii. Normal category before July 19, 1970, and meets the additional airworthiness standards in SFAR No. 23 of 14 CFR part 23.

  iii. Normal category, and complies with the additional airworthiness standards in Appendix A of part 135 of this chapter.

  iv. Normal category, and complies with section 1.(a) or 1.(b) of SFAR No. 41 of 14 CFR part 21.

b. After March 20, 1997, each airplane:

  i. Type certificated prior to March 29, 1995, in the commuter category.

  ii. Manufactured on or after March 20, 1997, and that was type certificated in the normal category, and complies with the requirements described in paragraphs 1.a.i through iii of this appendix.

2. Background. Sections 121.157 and 121.173(b) require that the airplanes operated under this part and described in paragraph 1 of this appendix, comply with the Airplane Performance Operating Limitations in §§121.189 through 121.197. Airplanes described in §121.157(f) and paragraph 1.a of this appendix must comply on and after December 20, 2010. Airplanes described in §121.157(e) and paragraph 1.b of this appendix must comply on and after March 20, 1997. (Airplanes type certificated in the normal category, and in accordance with SFAR No. 41 of 14 CFR part 21, as described in paragraph 1.a.iv of this appendix, may not be produced after October 17, 1991.)

3. References. Unless otherwise specified, references in this appendix to sections of part 23 of this chapter are to those sections of 14 CFR part 23; as amended by Amendment No. 23–45 (August 6, 1993, 58 FR 42156).

PERFORMANCE

4. Interim Airplane Performance Operating Limitations.

a. Until December 20, 2010, airplanes described in paragraph 1.a of this appendix may continue to comply with the requirements in Subpart I of part 135 and §135.181(a)(2) of this chapter that apply to small, nontransport category airplanes.

b. Until March 20, 1997, airplanes described in paragraph 1.b.i of this appendix may continue to comply with the requirements in Subpart I of part 135 of this chapter that apply to commuter category airplanes.

5. Final Airplane Performance Operating Limitations.

a. Through an amended type certification program or a supplemental type certification program, each airplane described in paragraph 1.a and 1.b.ii of this appendix must be shown to comply with the commuter category performance requirements specified in this appendix, which are included in part 23 of this chapter. Each new revision to a current airplane performance operating limitation for an airplane that is or has been demonstrated to comply, must also be approved by the Administrator. An airplane approved to the requirements of section 1.(b) of SFAR No. 41 of 14 CFR part 21, as described in paragraph 1.a.iv of this appendix, and that has been demonstrated to comply with the additional requirements of section 4.(c) of SFAR No. 41 of 14 CFR part 21 and International Civil Aviation Organization Annex 8 (available from the FAA, 800 Independence Avenue SW, Washington, DC 20591), will be considered to be in compliance with the commuter category performance requirements.

b. Each turbopropeller powered airplane subject to this appendix must be demonstrated to comply with the airplane performance operating limitation requirements of this chapter specified as follows:
   i. Section 23.45 Performance General.
   ii. Section 23.51 Takeoff.
   iii. Section 23.53 Takeoff speeds.
   iv. Section 23.55 Accelerate stop distance.
   v. Section 23.57 Takeoff path.
   vi. Section 23.59 Takeoff distance and takeoff run.
   vii. Section 23.61 Takeoff flight path.
   viii. Section 23.65 Climb: All engines operating.
   ix. Section 23.67 Climb: one engine inoperative.
   x. Section 23.75 Landing.
   xi. Section 23.77 Balked landing.
   xii. Sections 23.1581 through 23.1589 Airplane flight manual and approved manual material.

6. Operation. After compliance with the final airplane performance operating limitations requirements has been demonstrated and added to the Airplane Flight Manual performance data of the affected airplane, that airplane must be operated in accordance with the performance limitations of §§121.189 through 121.197.

[Docket No. 28154, 60 FR 65936, Dec. 20, 1995]

APPENDIX L TO PART 121
TYPE CERTIFICATION REGULATIONS MADE PREVIOUSLY EFFECTIVE

Appendix L lists regulations in this part that require compliance with standards contained in superseded type certification regulations that continue to apply to certain transport category airplanes. The tables set out citations to current CFR section, applicable aircraft, superseded type certification regulation and applicable time periods, and the CFR edition and Federal Register documents where the regulation having prior effect is found. Copies of all superseded regulations may be obtained at the Federal Aviation Administration Law Library, Room 924, 800 Independence Avenue SW, Washington, D.C.

Editorial Note: See the following Table.

Part 121: Air Carriers & Commercial Operators — Appendix L to Part 121

Part 121 section	Applicable aircraft	Provisions: CFR/FR references
§121.312(a)(1)(i)	Transport category; or nontransport category type certificated before January 1, 1965; passenger capacity of 20 or more; manufactured prior to August 20, 1990.	Heat release rate testing. 14 CFR 25.853(d) in effect March 6, 1995: 14 CFR parts 1 to 59, Revised as of January 1, 1995, and amended by Amdt 25–83, 60 FR 6623, February 2, 1995. Formerly 14 CFR 25.853(a-1) in effect August 20, 1986: 14 CFR parts 1 to 59, Revised as of January 1, 1986.
§121.312(a)(1)(ii)	Transport category; or nontransport category type certificated before January 1, 1965; passenger capacity of 20 or more; manufactured after August 19, 1990.	Heat release rate and smoke testing. 14 CFR 25.853(d) in effect March 6, 1995: 14 CFR parts 1 to 59, Revised as of January 1, 1995, and amended by Amdt 25–83, 60 FR 6623, February 2, 1995. Formerly 14 CFR 25.853(a-1) in effect September 26, 1988: 14 CFR parts 1 to 59, Revised as of January 1, 1988, and amended by Amdt 25–66, 53 FR 32584, August 25, 1988.
§121.312(a)(2)(i)	Transport category; or nontransport category type certificate before January 1, 1965; application for type certificate filed prior to May 1, 1972; substantially complete replacement of cabin interior on or after May 1, 1972.	Provisions of 14 CFR 25.853 in effect on April 30, 1972: 14 CFR parts 1 to 59, Revised as of January 1, 1972.
§121.312(a)(3)(i)	Transport category type certificated after January 1, 1958; nontransport category type certificated after January 1, 1958, but before January 1, 1965; passenger capacity of 20 or more; substantially complete replacement of the cabin interior on or after March 6, 1995.	Heat release rate testing. 14 CFR 25.853(d) in effect March 6, 1995: 14 CFR parts 1 to 59, Revised as of January 1, 1995; and amended by Amdt 25–83, 60 FR 6623, February 2, 1995. Formerly 14 CFR 25.853(a-1) in effect August 20, 1986: 14 CFR parts 1 to 59, Revised as of January 1, 1986.
§121.312(a)(3)(ii)	Transport category type certificated after January 1, 1958; nontransport category type certificated after January 1, 1958, but before January 1, 1965; passenger capacity of 20 or more; substantially complete replacement of the cabin interior on or after August 20, 1990.	Heat release rate and smoke testing. 14 CFR 25.853(d) in effect March 6, 1995; 14 CFR parts 1 to 59, Revised as of January 1, 1995; and amended by Amdt 25–83, 60 FR 6623, February 2, 1995. Formerly 14 CFR 25.853(a-1) in effect September 26, 1988: CFR, Title 14, Parts 1 to 59, Revised as of January 1, 1988, and amended by Amdt 25–66, 53 FR 32584, August 25, 1988.
§121.312(b) (1) and (2)	Transport category airplane type certificated after January 1, 1958; Nontransport category airplane type certificated after December 31, 1964.	Seat cushions. 14 CFR 25.853(c) effective on November 26, 1984: 14 CFR parts 1 to 59, Revised as of January 1, 1984, and amended by Amdt 25–59, 49 FR 43188, October 26, 1984.
§121.312(c)	Airplane type certificated in accordance with SFAR No. 41; maximum certificated takeoff weight in excess of 12,500 pounds.	Compartment interior requirements. 14 CFR 25.853(a) in effect March 6, 1995: 14 CFR parts 1 to 59, Revised as of January 1, 1995, and amended by Amdt 25–83, 60 FR 6623, February 2, 1995. Formerly 14 CFR 25.853(a), (b-1), (b-2), and (b-3) in effect on September 26, 1978: 14 CFR parts 1 to 59, Revised as of January 1, 1978.
§121.314(a)	Transport category airplanes type certificated after January 1, 1958.	Class C or D cargo or baggage compartment definition, 14 CFR 25.857 in effect on June 16, 1986, 14 CFR parts 1 to 59, Revised 1/1/97, and amended by Amendment 25–60, 51 FR 18243, May 16, 1986.

[Docket No. 28154, 60 FR 65936, Dec. 20, 1995; as amended by Amdt. 121–269, 63 FR 8049, Feb. 17, 1998]

APPENDIX M TO PART 121
AIRPLANE FLIGHT RECORDER SPECIFICATIONS

The recorded values must meet the designated range, resolution and accuracy requirements during static and dynamic conditions. Dynamic condition means the parameter is experiencing change at the maximum rate attainable, including the maximum rate of reversal. All data recorded must be correlated in time to within one second.

Parameters	Range	Accuracy (sensor input)	Seconds per sampling interval	Resolution	Remarks
1. Time or Relative Times Counts[1]	24 Hrs, 0 to 4095	±0.125% Per Hour	4	1 sec	UTC time preferred when available. Count increments each 4 seconds of system operation.
2. Pressure Altitude	−1000 ft to max certificated altitude of aircraft. +5000 ft.	±100 to ±700 ft (see table, TSO C124a or TSO C51a)	1	5' to 35'	Data should be obtained from the air data computer when practicable.
3. Indicated airspeed or Calibrated airspeed	50 KIAS or minimum value to Max V_{SO} to 1.2 V_D	±5% and ±3%	1	1 kt	Data should be obtained from the air data computer when practicable.
4. Heading (Primary flight crew reference)	0–360° and Discrete "true" or "mag"	±2°	1	0.5°	When true or magnetic heading can be selected as the primary heading reference, a discrete indicating selection must be recorded.
5. Normal Acceleration (Vertical)[9]	−3g to +6g	±1% of max range excluding datum error of ±5%	0.125	0.004g	—
6. Pitch Attitude	±75°	±2°	1 or 0.25 for airplanes operated under §121.344(f)	0.5°	A sampling rate of 0.25 is recommended.
7. Roll Attitude 2	±180°	±2°	1 or 0.5 for airplanes operated under §121.344(f)	0.5°	A sampling rate of 0.5 is recommended.
8. Manual Radio Transmitter Keying or CVR/DFDR synchronization reference	On-Off (Discrete) None	—	1	—	Preferably each crewmember but one discrete acceptable for all transmission provided the CVR/FDR system complies with TSO C124a CVR synchronization requirements (paragraph 4.2.1 ED-55).
9. Thrust/Power on each engine—primary flight crew reference.	Full range forward	±2%	1 (per engine)	0.3% of full range	Sufficient parameters (e.g. EPR, N1 or Torque, NP) as appropriate to the particular engine being recorded to determine power in forward and reverse thrust, including potential overspeed conditions.
10. Autopilot Engagement	Discrete "on" or "off"	—	1	—	—
11. Longitudinal Acceleration	±1g	±1.5% max. range excluding datum error of ±5%	0.25	0.004g	—

APPENDIX M TO PART 121
AIRPLANE FLIGHT RECORDER SPECIFICATIONS (CONTINUED)

The recorded values must meet the designated range, resolution and accuracy requirements during static and dynamic conditions. Dynamic condition means the parameter is experiencing change at the maximum rate attainable, including the maximum rate of reversal. All data recorded must be correlated in time to within one second.

Parameters	Range	Accuracy (sensor input)	Seconds per sampling interval	Resolution	Remarks
12a. Pitch control(s) position (nonfly-by-wire systems)[18]	Full Range	±2° Unless Higher Accuracy Uniquely Required	0.5 or 0.25 for airplanes operated under §121.344(f)	0.5% of full range	For airplanes that have a flight control breakaway capability that allows either pilot to operate the controls independently, record both control inputs. The control inputs may be sampled alternately once per second to produce the sampling interval of 0.5 or 0.25, as applicable.
12b. Pitch Control(s) position (fly-by-wire systems)[3][18]	Full Range	±2° Unless Higher Accuracy Uniquely Required	0.5 or 0.25 for airplanes operated under §121.344(f)	0.2% of full range	—
13a. Lateral Control position(s) (nonfly-by-wire)[18]	Full Range	±2° Unless Higher Accuracy Uniquely Required	0.5 or 0.25 for airplanes operated under §121.344(f)	0.2% of full range	For airplanes that have a flight control breakaway capability that allows either pilot to operate the controls independently, record both control inputs. The control inputs may be sampled alternately once per second to produce the sampling interval of 0.5 or 0.25, as applicable.
13b. Lateral Control position(s) (fly-by-wire)[4][18]	Full Range	±2° Unless Higher Accuracy Uniquely Required	0.5 or 0.25 for airplanes operated under §121.344(f)	0.2% of full range	—
14a. Yaw control position(s) (nonfly-by-wire)[5][18]	Full Range	±2° Unless Higher Accuracy Uniquely Required	0.5	0.3% of full range	For airplanes that have a flight control breakaway capability that allows either pilot to operate the controls independently, record both control inputs. The control inputs may be sampled alternately once per second to produce the sampling interval of 0.5.
14b. Yaw Control position(s) (fly-by-wire)[18]	Full Range	±2° Unless Higher Accuracy Uniquely Required	0.5	0.2% of full range	—
15. Pitch Control Surface(s) Position[6][18]	Full Range	±2° Unless Higher Accuracy Uniquely Required	0.5 or 0.25 for airplanes operated under §121.344(f)	0.3% of full range	For airplanes fitted with multiple or split surfaces, a suitable combination of inputs is acceptable in lieu of recording each surface separately. The control surfaces may be sampled alternately to produce the sampling interval of 0.5 or 0.25.

Appendix M to Part 121   **Federal Aviation Regulations**

APPENDIX M TO PART 121
AIRPLANE FLIGHT RECORDER SPECIFICATIONS (*CONTINUED*)

The recorded values must meet the designated range, resolution and accuracy requirements during static and dynamic conditions. Dynamic condition means the parameter is experiencing change at the maximum rate attainable, including the maximum rate of reversal. All data recorded must be correlated in time to within one second.

Parameters	Range	Accuracy (sensor input)	Seconds per sampling interval	Resolution	Remarks
16. Lateral Control Surface(s) Position[7][18]	Full Range	±2° Unless Higher Accuracy Uniquely Required	0.5 or 0.25 for airplanes operated under §121.344(f)	0.3% of full range	A suitable combination of surface position sensors is acceptable in lieu of recording each surface separately. The control surfaces may be sampled alternately to produce the sampling interval of 0.5 or 0.25.
17. Yaw Control Surface(s) Position[8][18]	Full Range	±2° Unless Higher Accuracy Uniquely Required	0.5[8]	0.2% of full range	For airplanes with multiple or split surfaces, a suitable combination of surface position sensors is acceptable in lieu of recording each surface separately. The control surfaces may be sampled alternately to produce the sampling interval of 0.5.
18. Lateral Acceleration	±1g	±1.5% max. range excluding datum error of ±5%	0.25	0.004g	—
19. Pitch Trim Surface Position	Full Range	±3° Unless Higher Accuracy Uniquely Required	1	0.6% of full range	—
20. Trailing Edge Flap or Cockpit Control Selection[10]	Full Range or Each Position (discrete)	±3° or as Pilot's indicator	2	0.5% of full range	Flap position and cockpit control may each be sampled at 4 second intervals, to give a data point every 2 seconds.
21. Leading Edge Flap or Cockpit Control Selection[11]	Full Range or Each Discrete Position	±3° or as Pilot's indicator and sufficient to determine each discrete position	2	0.5% of full range	Left and right sides, or flap position and cockpit control may each be sampled at 4 second intervals, so as to give a data point every 2 seconds.
22. Each Thrust Reverser Position (or equivalent for propeller airplane)	Stowed, In Transit, and Reverse (Discrete)	—	1 (per engine)	—	Turbo-jet – 2 discretes enable the 3 states to be determined. Turbo-prop – discrete.
23. Ground Spoiler Position or Speed Brake Selection[12]	Full Range or Each Position (discrete)	±2° Unless Higher Accuracy Uniquely Required	1 or 0.5 for airplanes operated under §121.344(f)	0.5% of full range	—
24. Outside Air Temperature or Total Air Temperature[13]	−50°C to +90°C	±2°C	2	0.3°C	—
25. Autopilot/Auto-throttle/AFCS Mode and Engagement Status	A suitable combination of discretes	—	1	—	Discretes should show which systems are engaged and which primary modes are controlling the flight path and speed of the aircraft.

352   ASA

APPENDIX M TO PART 121
AIRPLANE FLIGHT RECORDER SPECIFICATIONS (CONTINUED)

The recorded values must meet the designated range, resolution and accuracy requirements during static and dynamic conditions.
Dynamic condition means the parameter is experiencing change at the maximum rate attainable, including the maximum rate of reversal.
All data recorded must be correlated in time to within one second.

Parameters	Range	Accuracy (sensor input)	Seconds per sampling interval	Resolution	Remarks
26. Radio Altitude[14]	–20 ft to 2,500 ft	±2 ft or ±3% whichever is greater below 500 ft and ±5% above 500 ft	1	1 ft + 5% above 500 ft	For autoland/category 3 operations. Each radio altimeter should be recorded, but arranged so that at least one is recorded each second.
27. Localizer Deviation, MLS Azimuth, or GPS Latitude Deviation	±400 Microamps or available sensor range as installed ±62°	As installed ±3% recommended	1	0.3% of full range	For autoland/category 3 operations. Each system should be recorded, but arranged so that at least one is recorded each second. It is not necessary to record ILS and MLS at the same time, only the approach aid in use need be recorded.
28. Glideslope Deviation, MLS Elevation, or GPS Vertical Deviation	±400 Microamps or available sensor range as installed 0.9 to +30°	As installed ±3% recommended	1	0.3% of full range	For autoland/category 3 operations. Each system should be recorded, but arranged so that at least one is recorded each second. It is not necessary to record ILS and MLS at the same time, only the approach aid in use need be recorded.
29. Marker Beacon Passage	Discrete "on" or "off"	—	1	—	A single discrete is acceptable for all markers.
30. Master Warning	Discrete	—	1	—	Record the master warning and record each "red" warning that cannot be determined from other parameters or from the cockpit voice recorder.
31. Air/ground sensor (primary airplane system reference nose or main gear)	Discrete "air" or "ground"	—	1 (0.25 recommended)	—	—
32. Angle of Attack (if measured directly)	As installed	As installed	2 or 0.5 for airplanes operated under §121.344(f)	0.3% of full range	If left and right sensors are available, each may be recorded at 4 or 1 second intervals, as appropriate, so as to give a data point at 2 seconds or 0.5 second, as required.
33. Hydraulic Pressure Low, Each System	Discrete or available sensor range, "low" or "normal"	±5%	2	0.5% of full range	—
34. Groundspeed	As installed	Most Accurate Systems Installed	1	0.2% of full range	—
35. GPWS (ground proximity warning system)	Discrete "warning" or "off"	—	1	—	A suitable combination of discretes unless recorder capacity is limited in which case a single discrete for all modes is acceptable.

Appendix M to Part 121

Airplane Flight Recorder Specifications (CONTINUED)

The recorded values must meet the designated range, resolution and accuracy requirements during static and dynamic conditions. Dynamic condition means the parameter is experiencing change at the maximum rate attainable, including the maximum rate of reversal. All data recorded must be correlated in time to within one second.

Parameters	Range	Accuracy (sensor input)	Seconds per sampling interval	Resolution	Remarks
36. Landing Gear Position or Landing gear cockpit control selection	Discrete	—	4	—	A suitable combination of discretes should be recorded.
37. Drift Angle[15]	As installed	As installed	4	0.1°	—
38. Wind Speed and Direction	As installed	As installed	4	1 knot, and 1.0°	—
39. Latitude and Longitude	As installed	As installed	4	0.002°, or as installed	Provided by the Primary Navigation System Reference. Where capacity permits Latitude/longitude resolution should be 0.0002°.
40. Stick shaker and pusher activation	Discrete(s) "on" or "off"	—	1	—	A suitable combination of discretes to determine activation.
41. Windshear Detection	Discrete "warning" or "off"	—	1	—	—
42. Throttle/power lever position[16]	Full Range	±2%	1 for each lever	2% of full range	For airplanes with non-mechanically linked cockpit engine controls.
43. Additional Engine Parameters	As installed	As installed	Each engine, each second	2% of full range	Where capacity permits, the preferred priority is indicated vibration level, N2, EGT, Fuel Flow, Fuel Cut-off lever position and N3, unless engine manufacturer recommends otherwise.
44. Traffic Alert and Collision Avoidance System (TCAS)	Discretes	As installed	1	—	A suitable combination of discretes should be recorded to determine the status of – Combined Control, Vertical Control, Up Advisory, and Down Advisory. (ref. ARINC Characteristic 735 Attachment 6E, TCAS VERTICAL RA DATA OUTPUT WORD.)
45. DME 1 and 2 Distance	0–200 NM	As installed	4	1 NM	1 mile
46. Nav 1 and 2 Selected Frequency	Full Range	As installed	4	—	Sufficient to determine selected frequency.
47. Selected barometric setting	Full Range	±5%	(1 per 64 sec.)	0.2% of full range	—
48. Selected Altitude	Full Range	±5%	1	100 ft	—
49. Selected speed	Full Range	±5%	1	1 knot	—

Appendix M to Part 121
Airplane Flight Recorder Specifications (CONTINUED)

The recorded values must meet the designated range, resolution and accuracy requirements during static and dynamic conditions. Dynamic condition means the parameter is experiencing change at the maximum rate attainable, including the maximum rate of reversal. All data recorded must be correlated in time to within one second.

Parameters	Range	Accuracy (sensor input)	Seconds per sampling interval	Resolution	Remarks
50. Selected Mach	Full Range	±5%	1	0.01	—
51. Selected vertical speed	Full Range	±5%	1	100 ft/min	—
52. Selected heading	Full Range	±5%	1	1°	—
53. Selected flight path	Full Range	±5%	1	1°	—
54. Selected decision height	Full Range	±5%	64	1 ft	—
55. EFIS display format	Discrete(s)	—	4	—	Discretes should show the display system status (e.g., off, normal, fail, composite, sector, plan, nav aids, weather radar, range, copy).
56. Multi-function/Engine Alerts Display format	Discrete(s)	—	4	—	Discretes should show the display system status (e.g., off, normal, fail, and the identity of display pages for emergency procedures, need not be recorded.)
57. Thrust command[17]	Full Range	±2%	2	2% of full range	—
58. Thrust target	Full Range	±2%	4	2% of full range	—
59. Fuel quantity in CG trim tank	Full Range	±5%	(1 per 64 sec.)	1% of full range	—
60. Primary Navigation System Reference	Discrete GPS, INS, VOR/DME, MLS, Loran C, Omega, Localizer Glideslope	—	4	—	A suitable combination of discretes to determine the Primary Navigation System reference.
61. Ice Detection	Discrete "ice" or "no ice"	—	4	—	—
62. Engine warning each engine vibration	Discrete	—	1	—	—
63. Engine warning each engine over temp	Discrete	—	1	—	—
64. Engine warning each engine oil pressure low	Discrete	—	1	—	—
65. Engine warning each engine over speed	Discrete	—	1	—	—

Appendix M to Part 121

Airplane Flight Recorder Specifications (CONTINUED)

The recorded values must meet the designated range, resolution and accuracy requirements during static and dynamic conditions. Dynamic condition means the parameter is experiencing change at the maximum rate attainable, including the maximum rate of reversal. All data recorded must be correlated in time to within one second.

Parameters	Range	Accuracy (sensor input)	Seconds per sampling interval	Resolution	Remarks
66. Yaw Trim Surface Position	Full Range	±3% Unless Higher Accuracy Uniquely Required	2	0.3% of full range	—
67. Roll Trim Surface Position	Full Range	±3% Unless Higher Accuracy Uniquely Required	2	0.3% of full range	—
68. Brake Pressure (left and right)	As installed	±5%	1	—	To determine braking effort applied by pilots or by autobrakes.
69. Brake Pedal Application (left and right)	Discrete or Analog "applied" or "off"	±5% (Analog)	1	—	To determine braking applied by pilots.
70. Yaw or sideslip angle	Full Range	±5%	1	0.5°	—
71. Engine bleed valve position	Discrete "open" or "closed"	—	4	—	—
72. Deicing or anti-icing system selection	Discrete "on" or "off"	—	4	—	—
73. Computed center of gravity	Full Range	±5%	(1 per 64 sec.)	1% of full range	—
74. AC electrical bus status	Discrete "power" or "off"	—	4	—	Each bus.
75. DC electrical bus status	Discrete "power" or "off"	—	4	—	Each bus.
76. APU bleed valve position	Discrete "open" or "closed"	—	4	—	—
77. Hydraulic Pressure (each system)	Full Range	±5%	2	100 psi	—
78. Loss of cabin pressure	Discrete "loss" or "normal"	—	1	—	—
79. Computer failure (critical flight and engine control systems)	Discrete "fail" or "normal"	—	4	—	—
80. Heads-up display (when an information source is installed)	Discrete(s) "on" or "off"	—	4	—	—
81. Para-visual display (when an information source is installed)	Discrete(s) "on" or "off"	—	—	—	—

Appendix M to Part 121
Airplane Flight Recorder Specifications (CONTINUED)

The recorded values must meet the designated range, resolution and accuracy requirements during static and dynamic conditions. Dynamic condition means the parameter is experiencing change at the maximum rate attainable, including the maximum rate of reversal. All data recorded must be correlated in time to within one second.

Parameters	Range	Accuracy (sensor input)	Seconds per sampling interval	Resolution	Remarks
82. Cockpit trim control input position – pitch	Full Range	±5%	1	0.2% of full range	Where mechanical means for control inputs are not available, cockpit display trim positions should be recorded.
83. Cockpit trim control input position – roll	Full Range	±5%	1	0.7% of full range	Where mechanical means for control inputs are not available, cockpit display trim position should be recorded.
84. Cockpit trim control input position – yaw	Full Range	±5%	1	0.3% of full range	Where mechanical means for control input are not available, cockpit display trim positions should be recorded.
85. Trailing edge flap and cockpit flap control position	Full Range	±5%	2	0.5% of full range	Trailing edge flaps and cockpit flap control position may each be sampled alternately at 4 second intervals to provide a sample each 0.5 second.
86. Leading edge flap and cockpit flap control position	Full Range or Discrete	±5%	1	0.5% of full range	—
87. Ground spoiler position and speed brake selection	Full Range or Discrete	±5%	0.5	0.3% of full range	—
88. All cockpit flight control input forces (control wheel, control column, rudder pedal)[18][19]	Full Range Control wheel ±70 lbs. Control column ±85 lbs. Rudder pedal ±165 lbs.	±5%	1	0.3% of full range	For fly-by-wire flight control systems, where flight control surface position is a function of the displacement of the control input device only, it is not necessary to record this parameter. For airplanes that have a flight control break away capability that allows either pilot to operate the control independently, record both control force inputs. The control force inputs may be sampled alternately once per 2 seconds to produce the sampling interval of 1.
89. Yaw damper status	Discrete (on/off)	—	0.5	—	—
90. Yaw damper command	Full range	As installed	0.5	1% of full range	—
91. Standby rudder valve status	Discrete	—	0.5	—	—

See Appendix M Footnotes on the next page.

Appendix M to Part 121   **Federal Aviation Regulations**

[1] For A300 B2/B4 airplanes, resolution = 6 seconds.
[2] For A330/A340 series airplanes, resolution = 0.703°.
[3] For A318/A319/A320/A321 series airplanes, resolution = 0.275% (0.088° > 0.064°).
For A330/A340 series airplanes, resolution = 2.20% (0.703° > 0.064°).
[4] For A318/A319/A320/A321 series airplanes, resolution = 0.22% (0.088° > 0.080°).
For A330/A340 series airplanes, resolution = 1.76% (0.703° > 0.080°).
[5] For A330/A340 series airplanes, resolution = 1.18% (0.703° > 0.120°).
For A330/A340 series airplanes, seconds per sampling interval = 1.
[6] For A330/A340 series airplanes, resolution = 0.783% (0.352° > 0.090°).
[7] For A330/A340 series airplanes, aileron resolution = 0.704% (0.352° > 0.100°).
For A330/A340 series airplanes, spoiler resolution = 1.406% (0.703° > 0.100°).
[8] For A330/A340 series airplanes, resolution = 0.30% (0.176° > 0.12°).
For A330/A340 series airplanes, seconds per sampling interval = 1.
[9] For B-717 series airplanes, resolution = .005g. For Dassault F900C/F900EX airplanes, resolution = .007g.
[10] For A330/A340 series airplanes, resolution = 1.05% (0.250° > 0.120°).
[11] For A330/A340 series airplanes, resolution = 1.05% (0.250° > 0.120°).
For A300 B2/B4 series airplanes, resolution = 0.92% (0.230° > 0.125°).
[12] For A330/A340 series airplanes, spoiler resolution = 1.406% (0.703° > 0.100°).
[13] For A330/A340 series airplanes, resolution = 0.5°C.
[14] For Dassault F900C/F900EX airplanes, Radio altitude resolution = 1.25 ft.
[15] For A330/A340 series airplanes, resolution = 0.352°.
[16] For A318/A319/A320/A321 series airplanes, resolution = 4.32%.
For A330/A340 series airplanes, resolution is 3.27% of full range for throttle lever angle (TLA); for reverse thrust, reverse throttle lever angle (RLA) resolution is nonlinear over the active reverse thrust range, which is 51.54° to 96.14°. The resolved element is 2.8° uniformly over the entire active reverse thrust range, or 2.9% of the full range value of 96.14°.
[17] For A318/A319/A320/A321 series airplanes, with IAE engines, resolution = 2.58%.
[18] For all aircraft manufactured on or after December 6, 2010, the seconds per sampling interval is 0.125. Each input must be recorded at this rate. Alternately sampling inputs (interleaving) to meet this sampling interval is prohibited.
[19] For 737 model airplanes manufactured between August 19, 2000 and April 6, 2010: the seconds per sampling interval is 0.5 per control input; the remarks regarding the sampling rate do not apply; a single control wheel force transducer installed on the left cable control is acceptable provided the left and right control wheel positions also are recorded.

[Docket No. 28109, 62 FR 38382, July 17, 1997; as amended by Amdt. 121–266, 62 FR 48135, Sept. 12, 1997; Amdt. 121–271, 64 FR 46120, Aug. 24, 1999; Amdt. 121–278, 65 FR 51745, Aug. 24, 2000; Amdt. 121–292, 67 FR 54322, Aug. 21, 2002; Amdt. 121–299, 68 FR 42936, July 18, 2003; Amdt. 121–288, 68 FR 50069, Aug. 20, 2003; Docket No. FAA–2003–15682, 70 FR 41134, July 18, 2005; Amdt. 121–338, 73 FR 12566, March 7, 2008; Amdt. 121–342, 73 FR 73178, Dec. 2, 2008; Amdt. 121–347, 75 FR 7356, Feb. 19, 2010; Amdt. 121–349, 75 FR 17046, April 5, 2010; Amdt. 121–364, 78 FR 39971, July 3, 2013]

APPENDIX N TO PART 121—
[RESERVED]

APPENDIX O TO PART 121
HAZARDOUS MATERIALS TRAINING REQUIREMENTS FOR CERTIFICATE HOLDERS

This appendix prescribes the requirements for hazardous materials training under part 121, subpart Z, and part 135, subpart K of this chapter. The training requirements for various categories of persons are defined by job function or responsibility. An "X" in a box under a category of persons indicates that the specified category must receive the noted training. All training requirements apply to direct supervisors as well as to persons actually performing the job function. Training requirements for certificate holders authorized in their operations specifications to transport hazardous materials (will-carry) are prescribed in Table 1. Those certificate holders with a prohibition in their operations specifications against carrying or handling hazardous materials (will-not-carry) must follow the curriculum prescribed in Table 2. The method of delivering the training will be determined by the certificate holder. The certificate holder is responsible for providing a method (may include email, telecommunication, etc.) to answer all questions prior to testing regardless of the method of instruction. The certificate holder must certify that a test has been completed satisfactorily to verify understanding of the regulations and requirements.

Editorial Note: See Tables 1 and 2 on the following pages.

Appendix O to Part 121 — Federal Aviation Regulations

TABLE 1. OPERATORS THAT TRANSPORT HAZARDOUS MATERIALS — WILL-CARRY CERTIFICATE HOLDERS

Aspects of transport of hazardous materials by air with which they must be familiar, as a minimum (See Note 1)	Shippers (See Note 2) Will-carry	Operators and ground-handling agent's staff accepting hazardous materials (See Note 3) Will-carry	Operators and ground-handling agent's staff responsible for the handling, storage, and loading of cargo and baggage Will-carry	Passenger-handling staff Will-carry	Flight crewmembers and load planners Will-carry	Crewmembers (other than flight crewmembers) Will-carry
General philosophy	X	X	X	X	X	X
Limitations	X	X	X	X	X	X
General requirements for shippers	X	X				
Classification	X	X				
List of hazardous materials	X	X			X	
General packing requirements	X	X				
Labeling and marking	X	X	X	X	X	X
Hazardous materials transport document and other relevant documentation	X	X				
Acceptance procedures		X				
Recognition of undeclared hazardous materials	X	X	X	X	X	X
Storage and loading procedures		X	X		X	
Pilots' notification		X	X		X	
Provisions for passengers and crew		X	X	X	X	X
Emergency procedures	X	X	X	X	X	X

Note 1: Depending on the responsibilities of the person, the aspects of training to be covered may vary from those shown in the table.

Note 2: When a person offers a consignment of hazmat, including COMAT, for or on behalf of the certificate holder, then the person must be trained in the certificate holder's training program and comply with shipper responsibilities and training. If offering goods on another certificate holder's equipment, the person must be trained in compliance with the training requirements in 49 CFR. All shippers of hazmat must be trained under 49 CFR. The shipper functions in 49 CFR mirror the training aspects that must be covered for any shipper offering hazmat for transport.

Note 3: When an operator, its subsidiary, or an agent of the operator is undertaking the responsibilities of acceptance staff, such as the passenger handling staff accepting small parcel cargo, the certificate holder, its subsidy, or the agent must be trained in the certificate holder's training program and comply with the acceptance staff training requirements.

Part 121: Air Carriers & Commercial Operators

Appendix O to Part 121

Table 2. Operators That Do Not Transport Hazardous Materials—Will-Not-Carry Certificate Holders

Aspects of transport of hazardous materials by air with which they must be familiar, as a minimum (See Note 1)	Shippers (See Note 2) Will-not-carry	Operators and ground-handling agent's staff accepting cargo other than hazardous materials (See Note 3) Will-not-carry	Operators and ground-handling agent's staff responsible for the handling, storage, and loading of cargo and baggage Will-not-carry	Passenger-handling staff Will-not-carry	Flight crewmembers and load planners Will-not-carry	Crewmembers (other than flight crewmembers) Will-not-carry
General philosophy	X	X	X	X	X	X
Limitations	X	X	X	X	X	X
General requirements for shippers	X					
Classification	X					
List of hazardous materials	X					
General packing requirements	X					
Labeling and marking	X	X	X	X	X	X
Hazardous materials transport document and other relevant documentation	X	X				
Acceptance procedures						
Recognition of undeclared hazardous materials	X	X	X	X	X	
Storage and loading procedures						
Pilots' notification						
Provisions for passengers and crew		X	X	X	X	X
Emergency procedures	X	X	X	X	X	X

Note 1: Depending on the responsibilities of the person, the aspects of training to be covered may vary from those shown in the table.

Note 2: When a person offers a consignment of hazmat, including COMAT, for air transport for or on behalf of the certificate holder, then that person must be properly trained. All shippers of hazmat must be trained under 49 CFR. The shipper functions in 49 CFR mirror the training aspects that must be covered for any shipper, including a will-not-carry certificate holder offering dangerous goods for transport, with the exception of recognition training. Recognition training is a separate FAA requirement in the certificate holder's training program.

Note 3: When an operator, its subsidiary, or an agent of the operator is undertaking the responsibilities of acceptance staff, such as the passenger handling staff accepting small parcel cargo, the certificate holder, its subsidiary, or the agent must be trained in the certificate holder's training program and comply with the acceptance staff training requirements.

[Docket No. FAA–2003–15085, 70 FR 58825, Oct. 7, 2005; as amended by Amdt. 121–318, 70 FR 75396, Dec. 20, 2005]

APPENDIX P TO PART 121
REQUIREMENTS FOR ETOPS AND POLAR OPERATIONS

Source: Docket No. FAA–2002–6717, 72 FR 1883, Jan. 16, 2007, unless otherwise noted.

The FAA approves ETOPS in accordance with the requirements and limitations in this appendix.

Section I. ETOPS Approvals: Airplanes with Two engines.

(a) *Propulsion system reliability for ETOPS.*

(1) Before the FAA grants ETOPS operational approval, the operator must be able to demonstrate the ability to achieve and maintain the level of propulsion system reliability, if any, that is required by §21.4(b)(2) of this chapter for the ETOPS-approved airplane–engine combination to be used.

(2) Following ETOPS operational approval, the operator must monitor the propulsion system reliability for the airplane–engine combination used in ETOPS, and take action as required by §121.374(i) for the specified IFSD rates.

(b) *75 Minutes ETOPS*—

(1) *Caribbean/Western Atlantic Area.* The FAA grants approvals to conduct ETOPS with maximum diversion times up to 75 minutes on Western Atlantic/Caribbean area routes as follows:

(i) The FAA reviews the airplane–engine combination to ensure the absence of factors that could prevent safe operations. The airplane–engine combination need not be type-design-approved for ETOPS; however, it must have sufficient favorable experience to demonstrate to the Administrator a level of reliability appropriate for 75-minute ETOPS.

(ii) The certificate holder must comply with the requirements of §121.633 for time-limited system planning.

(iii) The certificate holder must operate in accordance with the ETOPS authority as contained in its operations specifications.

(iv) The certificate holder must comply with the maintenance program requirements of §121.374, except that a pre-departure service check before departure of the return flight is not required.

(2) *Other Areas.* The FAA grants approvals to conduct ETOPS with maximum diversion times up to 75 minutes on other than Western Atlantic/Caribbean area routes as follows:

(i) The FAA reviews the airplane–engine combination to ensure the absence of factors that could prevent safe operations. The airplane–engine combination need not be type-design-approved for ETOPS; however, it must have sufficient favorable experience to demonstrate to the Administrator a level of reliability appropriate for 75-minute ETOPS.

(ii) The certificate holder must comply with the requirements of §121.633 for time-limited system planning.

(iii) The certificate holder must operate in accordance with the ETOPS authority as contained in its operations specifications.

(iv) The certificate holder must comply with the maintenance program requirements of §121.374.

(v) The certificate holder must comply with the MEL in its operations specifications for 120-minute ETOPS.

(c) *90-minutes ETOPS (Micronesia).* The FAA grants approvals to conduct ETOPS with maximum diversion times up to 90 minutes on Micronesian area routes as follows:

(1) The airplane–engine combination must be type-design approved for ETOPS of at least 120-minutes.

(2) The certificate holder must operate in accordance with the ETOPS authority as contained in its operations specifications.

(3) The certificate holder must comply with the maintenance program requirements of §121.374, except that a pre-departure service check before departure of the return flight is not required.

(4) The certificate holder must comply with the MEL requirements in its operations specifications for 120-minute ETOPS.

(d) *120-minute ETOPS.* The FAA grants approvals to conduct ETOPS with maximum diversion times up to 120 minutes as follows:

(1) The airplane–engine combination must be type-design-approved for ETOPS of at least 120 minutes.

(2) The certificate holder must operate in accordance with the ETOPS authority as contained in its operations specifications.

(3) The certificate holder must comply with the maintenance program requirements of §121.374.

(4) The certificate holder must comply with the MEL requirements for 120-minute ETOPS.

(e) *138-Minute ETOPS.* The FAA grants approval to conduct ETOPS with maximum diversion times up to 138 minutes as follows:

(1) Operators with 120-minute ETOPS approval. The FAA grants 138-minute ETOPS approval as an extension of an existing 120-minute ETOPS approval as follows:

(i) The authority may be exercised only for specific flights for which the 120-minute diversion time must be exceeded.

(ii) For these flight-by-flight exceptions, the airplane–engine combination must be type-design-approved for ETOPS up to at least 120 minutes. The capability of the airplane's time-limited systems may not be less than 138 minutes calculated in accordance with §121.633.

(iii) The certificate holder must operate in accordance with the ETOPS authority as contained in its operations specifications.

(iv) The certificate holder must comply with the maintenance program requirements of §121.374.

(v) The certificate holder must comply with minimum equipment list (MEL) requirements in its operations specifications for "beyond 120 minutes ETOPS." Operators without a "beyond 120-minute ETOPS" MEL may apply to AFS-200 through their certificate holding district office for a modified MEL which satisfies the master MEL policy for system/component relief in ETOPS beyond 120 minutes.

(vi) The certificate holder must conduct training for maintenance, dispatch, and flight crew personnel regarding differences between 138-minute ETOPS authority and its previously-approved 120-minute ETOPS authority.

(2) Operators with existing 180-minute ETOPS approval. The FAA grants approvals to conduct 138-minute ETOPS (without the limitation in paragraph (e)(1)(i) of section I of this appendix) to certificate holders with existing 180-minute ETOPS approval as follows:

(i) The airplane–engine combination must be type-design-approved for ETOPS of at least 180 minutes.

(ii) The certificate holder must operate in accordance with the ETOPS authority as contained in its operations specifications.

(iii) The certificate holder must comply with the maintenance program requirements of §121.374.

(iv) The certificate holder must comply with the MEL requirements for "beyond 120 minutes ETOPS."

(v) The certificate holder must conduct training for maintenance, dispatch and flight crew personnel for differences between 138-minute ETOPS diversion approval and its previously approved 180-minute ETOPS diversion authority.

(f) *180-minute ETOPS.* The FAA grants approval to conduct ETOPS with diversion times up to 180 minutes as follows:

(1) For these operations the airplane–engine combination must be type-design-approved for ETOPS of at least 180 minutes.

(2) The certificate holder must operate in accordance with the ETOPS authority as contained in its operations specifications.

(3) The certificate holder must comply with the maintenance program requirements of §121.374.

(4) The certificate holder must comply with the MEL requirements for "beyond 120 minutes ETOPS."

(g) *Greater than 180-minute ETOPS.* The FAA grants approval to conduct ETOPS greater than 180 minutes. The following are requirements for all operations greater than 180 minutes.

(1) The FAA grants approval only to certificate holders with existing 180-minute ETOPS operating authority for the airplane–engine combination to be operated.

(2) The certificate holder must have previous ETOPS experience satisfactory to the Administrator.

(3) In selecting ETOPS Alternate Airports, the operator must make every effort to plan ETOPS with maximum diversion distances of 180 minutes or less, if possible. If conditions necessitate using an ETOPS Alternate Airport beyond 180 minutes, the route may be flown only if the requirements for the specific operating area in paragraph (h) or (i) of section I of this appendix are met.

(4) The certificate holder must inform the flight crew each time an airplane is proposed for dispatch for greater than 180 minutes and tell them why the route was selected.

(5) In addition to the equipment specified in the certificate holder's MEL for 180-minute ETOPS, the following systems must be operational for dispatch:

(i) The fuel quantity indicating system.

(ii) The APU (including electrical and pneumatic supply and operating to the APU's designed capability).

(iii) The auto throttle system.

(iv) The communication system required by §121.99(d) or §121.122(c), as applicable.

(v) One-engine-inoperative auto-land capability, if flight planning is predicated on its use.

(6) The certificate holder must operate in accordance with the ETOPS authority as contained in its operations specifications.

(7) The certificate holder must comply with the maintenance program requirements of §121.374.

(h) *207-minute ETOPS in the North Pacific Area of Operations.*

(1) The FAA grants approval to conduct ETOPS with maximum diversion times up to 207 minutes in the North Pacific Area of Operations as an extension to 180-minute ETOPS authority to be used on an exception basis. This exception may be used only on a flight-by-flight basis when an ETOPS Alternate Airport is not available within 180 minutes for reasons such as political or military concerns; volcanic activity; temporary airport conditions; and airport weather below dispatch requirements or other weather related events.

(2) The nearest available ETOPS Alternate Airport within 207 minutes diversion time must be specified in the dispatch or flight release.

(3) In conducting such a flight the certificate holder must consider Air Traffic Service's preferred track.

(4) The airplane–engine combination must be type-design-approved for ETOPS of at least 180 minutes. The approved time for the airplane's most limiting ETOPS significant system and most limiting cargo-fire suppression time for those cargo and baggage compartments required by regulation to have fire-suppression systems must be at least 222 minutes.

(5) The certificate holder must track how many times 207-minute authority is used.

(i) *240-minute ETOPS in the North Polar Area, in the area north of the NOPAC, and in the Pacific Ocean north of the equator.*

(1) The FAA grants approval to conduct 240-minute ETOPS authority with maximum diversion times in the North Polar Area, in the area north of the NOPAC area, and the Pacific Ocean area north of the equator as an extension to 180-minute ETOPS authority to be used on an exception basis. This exception may be used only on a flight-by-flight basis when an ETOPS Alternate Airport is not available within 180 minutes. In that case, the nearest available ETOPS Alternate Airport within 240 minutes diversion time must be specified in the dispatch or flight release.

(2) This exception may be used in the North Polar Area and in the area north of NOPAC only in extreme conditions particular to these areas such as volcanic activity, extreme cold weather at en-route airports, airport weather below dispatch requirements, temporary airport conditions, and other weather related events. The criteria used by the certificate holder to decide that extreme weather precludes using an airport must be established by the certificate holder, accepted by the FAA, and published in the certificate holder's manual for the use of dispatchers and pilots.

(3) This exception may be used in the Pacific Ocean area north of the equator only for reasons such as political or military concern, volcanic activity, airport weather below dispatch requirements, temporary airport conditions and other weather related events.

(4) The airplane–engine combination must be type design approved for ETOPS greater than 180 minutes.

(j) *240-minute ETOPS in areas South of the equator.*

(1) The FAA grants approval to conduct ETOPS with maximum diversion times of up to 240 minutes in the following areas:

(i) Pacific oceanic areas between the U.S. West coast and Australia, New Zealand and Polynesia.

(ii) South Atlantic oceanic areas.

(iii) Indian Ocean areas.

(iv) Oceanic areas between Australia and South America.

(2) The operator must designate the nearest available ETOPS Alternate Airports along the planned route of flight.

(3) The airplane–engine combination must be type-design-approved for ETOPS greater than 180 minutes.

(k) *ETOPS beyond 240 minutes.*

(1) The FAA grants approval to conduct ETOPS with diversion times beyond 240 minutes for operations between specified city pairs on routes in the following areas:

(i) The Pacific oceanic areas between the U.S. west coast and Australia, New Zealand, and Polynesia;

(ii) The South Atlantic oceanic areas;

(iii) The Indian Oceanic areas; and

(iv) The oceanic areas between Australia and South America, and the South Polar Area.

(2) This approval is granted to certificate holders who have been operating under 180-minute or greater ETOPS authority for at least 24 consecutive months, of which at least 12 consecutive months must be under 240-minute ETOPS authority with the airplane–engine combination to be used.

(3) The operator must designate the nearest available ETOPS alternate or alternates along the planned route of flight.

(4) For these operations, the airplane–engine combination must be type-design-approved for ETOPS greater than 180 minutes.

Section II. ETOPS Approval: Passenger-carrying Airplanes With More Than Two Engines.

(a) The FAA grants approval to conduct ETOPS, as follows:

(1) Except as provided in §121.162, the airplane–engine combination must be type-design-approved for ETOPS.

(2) The operator must designate the nearest available ETOPS Alternate Airports within 240 minutes diversion time (at one-engine-inoperative cruise speed under standard conditions in still air). If an ETOPS alternate is not available within 240 minutes, the operator must designate the nearest available ETOPS Alternate Airports along the planned route of flight.

(3) The MEL limitations for the authorized ETOPS diversion time apply.

(i) The Fuel Quantity Indicating System must be operational.

(ii) The communications systems required by §121.99(d) or §121.122(c) must be operational.

(4) The certificate holder must operate in accordance with the ETOPS authority as contained in its operations specifications.

Section III. Approvals for operations whose airplane routes are planned to traverse either the North Polar or South Polar Areas.

(a) Except for intrastate operations within the State of Alaska, no certificate holder may operate an aircraft in the North Polar Area or South Polar Area, unless authorized by the FAA.

(b) In addition to any of the applicable requirements of sections I and II of this appendix, the certificate holder's operations specifications must contain the following:

(1) The designation of airports that may be used for en-route diversions and the requirements the airports must meet at the time of diversion.

(2) Except for supplemental all-cargo operations, a recovery plan for passengers at designated diversion airports.

(3) A fuel-freeze strategy and procedures for monitoring fuel freezing.

(4) A plan to ensure communication capability for these operations.

(5) An MEL for these operations.

(6) A training plan for operations in these areas.

(7) A plan for mitigating crew exposure to radiation during solar flare activity.

(8) A plan for providing at least two cold weather anti-exposure suits in the aircraft, to protect crewmembers during outside activity at a diversion airport with extreme climatic conditions. The FAA may relieve the certificate holder from this requirement if the season of the year makes the equipment unnecessary.

14 CFR • Subchapter G—Air Carriers and Operators for
Compensation or Hire: Certification and Operations

PART 135

OPERATING REQUIREMENTS: COMMUTER AND ON DEMAND OPERATIONS AND RULES GOVERNING PERSONS ON BOARD SUCH AIRCRAFT

SPECIAL FEDERAL AVIATION REGULATIONS
SFAR No. 50–2 [Note]
SFAR No. 97
SFAR No. 106 [Note]
SFAR No. 108 [Note]

Subpart A—General

Sec.
*135.1 Applicability.
135.2 Compliance schedule for operators that transition to part 121 of this chapter; certain new entrant operators
*135.3 Rules applicable to operations subject to this part.
135.4 Applicability of rules for eligible on-demand operations.
135.7 Applicability of rules to unauthorized operators.
135.12 Previously trained crewmembers.
135.19 Emergency operations.
135.21 Manual requirements.
135.23 Manual contents.
135.25 Aircraft requirements.
135.41 Carriage of narcotic drugs, marijuana, and depressant or stimulant drugs or substances.
135.43 Crewmember certificates: International operations.

Subpart B—Flight Operations

135.61 General.
135.63 Recordkeeping requirements.
135.64 Retention of contracts and amendments: Commercial operators who conduct intrastate operations for compensation or hire.
135.65 Reporting mechanical irregularities.
135.67 Reporting potentially hazardous meteorological conditions and irregularities of ground facilities or navigation aids.
135.69 Restriction or suspension of operations: Continuation of flight in an emergency.
135.71 Airworthiness check.
135.73 Inspections and tests.
135.75 Inspectors credentials: Admission to pilots' compartment: Forward observer's seat.
135.76 DOD Commercial Air Carrier Evaluator's Credentials: Admission to pilots compartment: Forward observer's seat.
135.77 Responsibility for operational control.
135.78 Instrument approach procedures and IFR landing minimums.
135.79 Flight locating requirements.
135.81 Informing personnel of operational information and appropriate changes.
135.83 Operating information required.
135.85 Carriage of persons without compliance with the passenger-carrying provisions of this part.
135.87 Carriage of cargo including carry-on baggage.
135.89 Pilot requirements: Use of oxygen.
135.91 Oxygen for medical use by passengers.
*135.93 Minimum altitudes for use of autopilot.
135.95 Airmen: Limitations on use of services.
135.97 Aircraft and facilities for recent flight experience.
135.98 Operations in the North Polar Area.
135.99 Composition of flight crew.
135.100 Flight crewmember duties.
135.101 Second in command required under IFR.
135.103 [Reserved]
135.105 Exception to second in command requirement: Approval for use of autopilot system.
135.107 Flight attendant crewmember requirement.
135.109 Pilot in command or second in command: Designation required.
135.111 Second in command required in Category II operations.
135.113 Passenger occupancy of pilot seat.
135.115 Manipulation of controls.
*135.117 Briefing of passengers before flight.
135.119 Prohibition against carriage of weapons.
135.120 Prohibition on interference with crewmembers.
135.121 Alcoholic beverages.
135.122 Stowage of food, beverage, and passenger service equipment during aircraft movement on the surface, takeoff, and landing.

ASA 367

135.123	Emergency and emergency evacuation duties.	135.178	Additional emergency equipment.
135.125	Aircraft security.	135.179	Inoperable instruments and equipment.
135.127	Passenger information requirements and smoking prohibitions.	135.180	Traffic Alert and Collision Avoidance System.
*135.128	**Use of safety belts and child restraint systems.**	135.181	Performance requirements: Aircraft operated over-the-top or in IFR conditions.
135.129	Exit seating.	135.183	Performance requirements: Land aircraft operated over water.

Subpart C—Aircraft and Equipment

		135.185	Empty weight and center of gravity: Currency requirement.
135.141	Applicability.		
135.143	General requirements.		
135.144	Portable electronic devices.		

Subpart D—
VFR/IFR Operating Limitations and Weather Requirements

135.145	Aircraft proving and validation tests.		
135.147	Dual controls required.	135.201	Applicability.
135.149	Equipment requirements: General.	135.203	VFR: Minimum altitudes.
135.150	Public address and crewmember interphone systems.	135.205	VFR: Visibility requirements.
135.151	Cockpit voice recorders.	135.207	VFR: Helicopter surface reference requirements.
135.152	Flight data recorders.	135.209	VFR: Fuel supply.
135.153	[Reserved]	135.211	VFR: Over-the-top carrying passengers: Operating limitations.
135.154	Terrain awareness and warning system.	135.213	Weather reports and forecasts.
135.155	Fire extinguishers: Passenger-carrying aircraft.	135.215	IFR: Operating limitations.
135.156	Flight data recorders: Filtered data.	135.217	IFR: Takeoff limitations.
135.157	Oxygen equipment requirements.	135.219	IFR: Destination airport weather minimums.
135.158	Pitot heat indication systems.	*135.221	**IFR: Alternate airport weather minimums.**
135.159	Equipment requirements: Carrying passengers under VFR at night or under VFR over-the-top conditions.	135.223	IFR: Alternate airport requirements.
*135.160	**Radio altimeters for rotorcraft operations.**	135.225	IFR: Takeoff, approach and landing minimums.
135.161	Communication and navigation equipment for aircraft operations under VFR over routes navigated by pilotage.	135.227	Icing conditions: Operating limitations.
135.163	Equipment requirements: Aircraft carrying passengers under IFR.	135.229	Airport requirements.

Subpart E—
Flight Crewmember Requirements

135.165	Communication and navigation equipment: Extended overwater or IFR operations.	135.241	Applicability.
135.167	Emergency equipment: Extended overwater operations.	135.243	Pilot in command qualifications.
		135.244	Operating experience.
*135.168	**Emergency equipment: Overwater rotorcraft operations.**	135.245	Second in command qualifications.
135.169	Additional airworthiness requirements.	135.247	Pilot qualifications: Recent experience.
135.170	Materials for compartment interiors.	135.249	[Reserved]
135.171	Shoulder harness installation at flight crewmember stations.	135.251	[Reserved]
		135.253	[Reserved]
135.173	Airborne thunderstorm detection equipment requirements.	135.255	[Reserved]

Subpart F—
Crewmember Flight Time and Duty Period Limitations and Rest Requirements

135.175	Airborne weather radar equipment requirements.	135.261	Applicability.
135.177	Emergency equipment requirements for aircraft having a passenger seating configuration of more than 19 passengers.	135.263	Flight time limitations and rest requirements: All certificate holders.

Part 135: Commuter & On Demand Operations

135.265 Flight time limitations and rest requirements: Scheduled operations.
135.267 Flight time limitations and rest requirements: Unscheduled one- and two-pilot crews.
135.269 Flight time limitations and rest requirements: Unscheduled three- and four-pilot crews.
135.271 Helicopter hospital emergency medical evacuation service (HEMES).
135.273 Duty period limitations and rest time requirements.

Subpart G—
Crewmember Testing Requirements

135.291 Applicability.
*135.293 Initial and recurrent pilot testing requirements.
135.295 Initial and recurrent flight attendant crewmember testing requirements.
*135.297 Pilot in command: Instrument proficiency check requirements.
135.299 Pilot in command: Line checks: Routes and airports.
135.301 Crewmember: Tests and checks, grace provisions, training to accepted standards.

Subpart H—Training

135.321 Applicability and terms used.
135.323 Training program: General.
135.324 Training program: Special rules.
135.325 Training program and revision: Initial and final approval.
135.327 Training program: Curriculum.
135.329 Crewmember training requirements.
135.330 Crew resource management training.
135.331 Crewmember emergency training.
135.335 Approval of aircraft simulators and other training devices.
*135.336 Airline transport pilot certification training program.
135.337 Qualifications: Check airmen (aircraft) and check airmen (simulator).
135.338 Qualifications: Flight instructors (aircraft) and flight instructors (simulator).
135.339 Initial and transition training and checking: Check airmen (aircraft), check airmen (simulator).
135.340 Initial and transition training and checking: Flight instructors (aircraft), flight instructors (simulator).
*135.341 Pilot and flight attendant crewmember training programs.

135.343 Crewmember initial and recurrent training requirements.
135.345 Pilots: Initial, transition, and upgrade ground training.
135.347 Pilots: Initial, transition, upgrade, and differences flight training.
135.349 Flight attendants: Initial and transition ground training.
135.351 Recurrent training.
135.353 [Reserved]

Subpart I—
Airplane Performance Operating Limitations

135.361 Applicability.
135.363 General.
135.364 Maximum flying time outside the United States.
135.365 Large transport category airplanes: Reciprocating engine powered: Weight limitations.
135.367 Large transport category airplanes: Reciprocating engine powered: Takeoff limitations.
135.369 Large transport category airplanes: Reciprocating engine powered: En route limitations: All engines operating.
135.371 Large transport category airplanes: Reciprocating engine powered: En route limitations: One engine inoperative.
135.373 Part 25 transport category airplanes with four or more engines: Reciprocating engine powered: En route limitations: Two engines inoperative.
135.375 Large transport category airplanes: Reciprocating engine powered: Landing limitations: Destination airports.
135.377 Large transport category airplanes: Reciprocating engine powered: Landing limitations: Alternate airports.
135.379 Large transport category airplanes: Turbine engine powered: Takeoff limitations.
135.381 Large transport category airplanes: Turbine engine powered: En route limitations: One engine inoperative.
135.383 Large transport category airplanes: Turbine engine powered: En route limitations: Two engines inoperative.
135.385 Large transport category airplanes: Turbine engine powered: Landing limitations: Destination airports.

135.387 Large transport category airplanes: Turbine engine powered: Landing limitations: Alternate airports.
135.389 Large nontransport category airplanes: Takeoff limitations.
135.391 Large nontransport category airplanes: En route limitations: One engine inoperative.
135.393 Large nontransport category airplanes: Landing limitations: Destination airports.
135.395 Large nontransport category airplanes: Landing limitations: Alternate airports.
135.397 Small transport category airplane performance operating limitations.
135.398 Commuter category airplanes performance operating limitations.
135.399 Small nontransport category airplane performance operating limitations.

Subpart J—Maintenance, Preventive Maintenance, and Alterations

135.411 Applicability.
135.413 Responsibility for airworthiness.
135.415 Service difficulty reports.
135.417 Mechanical interruption summary report.
135.419 Approved aircraft inspection program.
135.421 Additional maintenance requirements.
135.422 Aging airplane inspections and records reviews for multiengine airplanes certificated with nine or fewer passenger seats.
135.423 Maintenance, preventive maintenance, and alteration organization.
135.425 Maintenance, preventive maintenance, and alteration programs.
135.427 Manual requirements.
135.429 Required inspection personnel.
135.431 Continuing analysis and surveillance.
135.433 Maintenance and preventive maintenance training program.
135.435 Certificate requirements.
135.437 Authority to perform and approve maintenance, preventive maintenance, and alterations.
135.439 Maintenance recording requirements.
135.441 Transfer of maintenance records.
135.443 Airworthiness release or aircraft maintenance log entry.

Subpart K—Hazardous Materials Training Program

135.501 Applicability and definitions.
135.503 Hazardous materials training: General.
135.505 Hazardous materials training required.
135.507 Hazardous materials training records.

Subpart L—Helicopter Air Ambulance Equipment, Operations, and Training Requirements

*135.601 Applicability and definitions.
*135.603 Pilot-in-command instrument qualifications.
*135.605 Helicopter terrain awareness and warning system (HTAWS).
*135.607 Flight Data Monitoring System.
*135.609 VFR ceiling and visibility requirements for Class G airspace.
*135.611 IFR operations at locations without weather reporting.
*135.613 Approach/departure IFR transitions.
*135.615 VFR flight planning.
*135.617 Pre-flight risk analysis.
*135.619 Operations control centers.
*135.621 Briefing of medical personnel.

APPENDICES TO PART 135

Appendix A—Additional Airworthiness Standards for 10 or More Passenger Airplanes
Appendix B—Airplane Flight Recorder Specifications
Appendix C—Helicopter Flight Recorder Specifications
Appendix D—Airplane Flight Recorder Specifications
Appendix E—Helicopter Flight Recorder Specifications
Appendix F—Airplane Flight Recorder Specifications
Appendix G—Extended Operations (ETOPS)

Authority: 49 U.S.C. 106(f), 106(g), 41706, 44113, 44701–44702, 44705, 44709, 44711–44713, 44715–44717, 44722, 44730, 45101–45105; Pub. L. 112–95, 126 Stat. 58 (49 U.S.C. 44730).

Source: Docket No. 16097, 43 FR 46783, October 10, 1978, unless otherwise noted.

SPECIAL FEDERAL AVIATION REGULATIONS

SFAR No. 50–2 to Part 135
SPECIAL FLIGHT RULES IN THE VICINITY OF THE GRAND CANYON NATIONAL PARK, AZ

Editorial note: For the text of SFAR No. 50–2, see Part 121 of this chapter.

SFAR No. 97 to Part 135
SPECIAL OPERATING RULES FOR THE CONDUCT OF INSTRUMENT FLIGHT RULES (IFR) AREA NAVIGATION (RNAV) OPERATIONS USING GLOBAL POSITIONING SYSTEMS (GPS) IN ALASKA

Those persons identified in Section 1 may conduct IFR en route RNAV operations in the State of Alaska and its airspace on published air traffic routes using TSO C145a/C146a navigation systems as the only means of IFR navigation. Despite contrary provisions of parts 71, 91, 95, 121, 125, and 135 of this chapter, a person may operate aircraft in accordance with this SFAR if the following requirements are met.

1. *Purpose, use, and limitations*

(a) This SFAR permits TSO C145a/C146a GPS (RNAV) systems to be used for IFR en route operations in the United States airspace over and near Alaska (as set forth in paragraph c of this section) at Special Minimum En Route Altitudes (MEA) that are outside the operational service volume of ground-based navigation aids, if the aircraft operation also meets the requirements of sections 3 and 4 of this SFAR.

(b) Certificate holders and part 91 operators may operate aircraft under this SFAR provided that they comply with the requirements of this SFAR.

(c) Operations conducted under this SFAR are limited to United States Airspace within and near the State of Alaska as defined in the following area description:
From 62°00'00.000"N, Long. 141°00'00.00"W.;
to Lat. 59°47'54.11"N., Long. 135°28'38.34"W.;
to Lat. 56°00'04.11"N., Long. 130°00'07.80"W.;
to Lat. 54°43'00.00"N., Long. 130°37'00.00"W.;
to Lat. 51°24'00.00"N., Long. 167°49'00.00"W.;
to Lat. 50°08'00.00"N., Long. 176°34'00.00"W.;
to Lat. 45°42'00.00"N., Long. -162°55'00.00"E.;
to Lat. 50°05'00.00"N., Long. -159°00'00.00"E.;
to Lat. 54°00'00.00"N., Long. -169°00'00.00"E.;
to Lat. 60°00'00.00"N., Long. -180°00'00.00"E;
to Lat. 65°00'00.00"N., Long. 168°58'23.00"W.;
to Lat. 90°00'00.00"N., Long. 00°00'0.00"W.;
to Lat. 62°00'00.000"N, Long. 141°00'00.00"W.

(d) No person may operate an aircraft under IFR during the en route portion of flight below the standard MEA or at the special MEA unless the operation is conducted in accordance with sections 3 and 4 of this SFAR.

2. *Definitions and abbreviations*
For the purposes of this SFAR, the following definitions and abbreviations apply.

Area navigation (RNAV). RNAV is a method of navigation that permits aircraft operations on any desired flight path.

Area navigation (RNAV) route. RNAV route is a published route based on RNAV that can be used by suitably equipped aircraft.

Certificate holder. A certificate holder means a person holding a certificate issued under part 119 or part 125 of this chapter or holding operations specifications issued under part 129 of this chapter.

Global Navigation Satellite System (GNSS). GNSS is a world-wide position and time determination system that uses satellite ranging signals to determine user location. It encompasses all satellite ranging technologies, including GPS and additional satellites. Components of the GNSS include GPS, the Global Orbiting Navigation Satellite System, and WAAS satellites.

Global Positioning System (GPS). GPS is a satellite-based radio navigational, positioning, and time transfer system. The system provides highly accurate position and velocity information and precise time on a continuous global basis to properly equipped users.

Minimum crossing altitude (MCA). The minimum crossing altitude (MCA) applies to the operation of an aircraft proceeding to a higher minimum en route altitude when crossing specified fixes.

Required navigation system. Required navigation system means navigation equipment that meets the performance requirements of TSO C145a / C146a navigation systems certified for IFR en route operations.

Route segment. Route segment is a portion of a route bounded on each end by a fix or NAVAID.

Special MEA. Special MEA refers to the minimum en route altitudes, using required navigation systems, on published routes outside the operational service volume of ground-based navigation aids and are depicted on the published Low Altitude and High Altitude En Route Charts using the color blue and with the suffix "G." For example, a GPS MEA of 4000 feet MSL would be depicted using the color blue, as 4000G.

Standard MEA. Standard MEA refers to the minimum en route IFR altitude on published routes that uses ground-based navigation aids and are depicted on the published Low Altitude and High Altitude En Route Charts using the color black.

Station referenced. Station referenced refers to radio navigational aids or fixes that are referenced by ground based navigation facilities such as VOR facilities.

Wide Area Augmentation System (WAAS). WAAS is an augmentation to GPS that calculates GPS integrity and correction data on the ground and uses geo-stationary satellites to broadcast GPS integrity and correction data to GPS/WAAS users and to provide ranging signals. It is a safety critical system consisting of a ground network of reference and integrity monitor data processing sites to assess current GPS performance, as well as a space segment that broadcasts that assessment to GNSS users to support en route through precision approach navigation. Users of the system include all aircraft applying the WAAS data and ranging signal.

3. Operational Requirements

To operate an aircraft under this SFAR, the following requirements must be met:

(a) Training and qualification for operations and maintenance personnel on required navigation equipment used under this SFAR.

(b) Use authorized procedures for normal, abnormal, and emergency situations unique to these operations, including degraded navigation capabilities, and satellite system outages.

(c) For certificate holders, training of flight crewmembers and other personnel authorized to exercise operational control on the use of those procedures specified in paragraph b of this section.

(d) Part 129 operators must have approval from the State of the operator to conduct operations in accordance with this SFAR.

(e) In order to operate under this SFAR, a certificate holder must be authorized in operations specifications.

4. Equipment Requirements

(a) The certificate holder must have properly installed, certificated, and functional dual required navigation systems as defined in section 2 of this SFAR for the en route operations covered under this SFAR.

(b) When the aircraft is being operated under part 91, the aircraft must be equipped with at least one properly installed, certificated, and functional required navigation system as defined in section 2 of this SFAR for the en route operations covered under this SFAR.

5. Expiration date

This Special Federal Aviation Regulation will remain in effect until rescinded.

[Docket FAA–2003–14305, SFAR No. 97; 68 FR 14077, March 21, 2003]

SFAR No. 106 to Part 135
Rules for Use of Portable Oxygen Concentrator Systems On Board Aircraft

Editorial Note: For the text of SFAR No. 106, see Part 121 of this chapter.

SFAR No. 108 to Part 135
Mitsubishi MU–2B Series Airplane Special Training, Experience, and Operating Requirements

Editorial Note: For the text of SFAR No. 108, go to www.faa.gov

Subpart A—General

§135.1 Applicability.

(a) This part prescribes rules governing—

(1) The commuter or on-demand operations of each person who holds or is required to hold an Air Carrier Certificate or Operating Certificate under part 119 of this chapter.

(2) Each person employed or used by a certificate holder conducting operations under this part including the maintenance, preventative maintenance and alteration of an aircraft.

(3) The transportation of mail by aircraft conducted under a postal service contract awarded under 39 U.S.C. 5402c.

(4) Each person who applies for provisional approval of an Advanced Qualification Program curriculum, curriculum segment, or portion of a curriculum segment under Subpart Y of Part 121 of this chapter and each person employed or used by an air carrier or commercial operator under this part to perform training, qualification, or evaluation functions under an Advanced Qualification Program under Subpart Y of Part 121 of this chapter.

(5) Nonstop Commercial Air Tour flights conducted for compensation or hire in accordance with §119.1(e)(2) of this chapter that begin and end at the same airport and are conducted within a 25-statute-mile radius of that airport; provided further that these operations must comply only with the drug and alcohol testing requirements in §§120.31, 120.33, 120.35, 120.37, and 120.39 of this chapter; and with the provisions of part 136, subpart A, and §91.147 of this chapter by September 11, 2007.

(6) Each person who is on board an aircraft being operated under this part.

(7) Each person who is an applicant for an Air Carrier Certificate or an Operating Certificate un-

der 119 of this chapter, when conducting proving tests.

(8) Commercial Air tours conducted by holders of operations specifications issued under this part must comply with the provisions of part 136, Subpart A of this chapter by September 11, 2007.

(9) Helicopter air ambulance operations as defined in §135.601(b)(1).

(b) [Reserved]

(c) An operator who does not hold a part 119 certificate and who operates under the provisions of §91.147 of this chapter is permitted to use a person who is otherwise authorized to perform aircraft maintenance or preventive maintenance duties and who is not subject to anti-drug and alcohol misuse prevent programs to perform—

(1) Aircraft maintenance or preventive maintenance on the operator's aircraft if the operator would otherwise be required to transport the aircraft more than 50 nautical miles further than the repair point closest to operator's principal place of operation to obtain these services; or

(2) Emergency repairs on the operator's aircraft if the aircraft cannot be safely operated to a location where an employee subject to FAA-approved programs can perform the repairs.

[Docket No. 16097, 43 FR 46783, Oct. 10, 1978; as amended by Amdt. 135–5, 45 FR 43162, June 26, 1980; Amdt. 135–7, 45 FR 67235, Oct. 9, 1980; Amdt. 135–20, 51 FR 40709, Nov. 7, 1986; Amdt. 135–28, 53 FR 47060, Nov. 21, 1988; Amdt. 135–32, 54 FR 34332, Aug. 18, 1989; Amdt. 135–37, 55 FR 40278, Oct. 2, 1990; Amdt. 135–41, 56 FR 43976, Sept. 5, 1991; Amdt. 135–48, 59 FR 7396, Feb. 15, 1994; Amdt. 135–58, 60 FR 65938, Dec. 20, 1995; Amdt. 135–99, 70 FR 54819, Sept. 16, 2005; Amdt. 135–107, 72 FR 6912, Feb. 13, 2007; Amdt. 135–11774, FR 22668, May 14, 2009; Amdt. 135–117A, 75 FR 3154, Jan. 20, 2010; Amdt. 135–129, 79 FR 9973, Feb. 21, 2014]

§135.2 Compliance schedule for operators that transition to part 121 of this chapter; certain new entrant operators.

(a) *Applicability.* This section applies to the following:

(1) Each certificate holder that was issued an air carrier or operating certificate and operations specifications under the requirements of part 135 of this chapter or under SFAR No. 38–2 of 14 CFR part 121 before January 19, 1996, and that conducts scheduled passenger-carrying operations with:

(i) Nontransport category turbopropeller powered airplanes type certificated after December 31, 1964, that have a passenger seat configuration of 10–19 seats;

(ii) Transport category turbopropeller powered airplanes that have a passenger seat configuration of 20–30 seats; or

(iii) Turbojet engine powered airplanes having a passenger seat configuration of 1–30 seats.

(2) Each person who, after January 19, 1996, applies for or obtains an initial air carrier or operating certificate and operations specifications to conduct scheduled passenger-carrying operations in the kinds of airplanes described in paragraphs (a)(1)(i), (a)(1)(ii), or paragraph (a)(1)(iii) of this section.

(b) *Obtaining operations specifications.* A certificate holder described in paragraph (a)(1) of this section may not, after March 20, 1997, operate an airplane described in paragraphs (a)(1)(i), (a)(1)(ii), or (a)(1)(iii) of this section in scheduled passenger-carrying operations, unless it obtains operations specifications to conduct its scheduled operations under part 121 of this chapter on or before March 20, 1997.

(c) *Regular or accelerated compliance.* Except as provided in paragraphs (d) and (e) of this section, each certificate holder described in paragraphs (a)(1) of this section shall comply with each applicable requirement of part 121 of this chapter on and after March 20, 1997 or on and after the date on which the certificate holder is issued operations specifications under this part, whichever occurs first. Except as provided in paragraphs (d) and (e) of this section, each person described in paragraph (a)(2) of this section shall comply with each applicable requirement of part 121 of this chapter on and after the date on which that person is issued a certificate and operations specifications under part 121 of this chapter.

(d) *Delayed compliance dates.* Unless paragraph (e) of this section specifies an earlier compliance date, no certificate holder that is covered by paragraph (a) of this section may operate an airplane in 14 CFR part 121 operations on or after a date listed in this paragraph unless that airplane meets the applicable requirement of this paragraph:

(1) Nontransport category turbopropeller powered airplanes type certificated after December 31, 1964, that have a passenger seat configuration of 10–19 seats. No certificate holder may operate under this part an airplane that is described in paragraph (a)(1)(i) of this section on or after a date listed in paragraph (d)(1) of this section unless that airplane meets the applicable requirement listed in paragraph (d)(1) of this section:

(i) December 20, 1997:

(A) Section 121.289, Landing gear aural warning.

(B) Section 121.308, Lavatory fire protection.

(C) Section 121.310(e), Emergency exit handle illumination.

(D) Section 121.337(b)(8), Protective breathing equipment.

(E) Section 121.340, Emergency flotation means.

(ii) December 20, 1999: Section 121.342, Pitot heat indication system.

(iii) December 20, 2010:

(A) For airplanes described in §121.157(f), the Airplane Performance Operating Limitations in §§121.189 through 121.197.

(B) Section 121.161(b), Ditching approval.

(C) Section 121.305(j), Third attitude indicator.

(D) Section 121.312(c), Passenger seat cushion flammability.

(iv) March 12, 1999: Section 121.310(b)(1), Interior emergency exit locating sign.

(2) Transport category turbopropeller powered airplanes that have a passenger seat configuration of 20–30 seats. No certificate holder may operate under this part an airplane that is described in paragraph (a)(1)(ii) of this section on or after a date listed in paragraph (d)(2) of this section unless that airplane meets the applicable requirement listed in paragraph (d)(2) of this section:

(i) December 20, 1997:

(A) Section 121.308, Lavatory fire protection.

(B) Section 121.337(b)(8) and (9), Protective breathing equipment.

(C) Section 121.340, Emergency flotation means.

(ii) December 20, 2010: Section 121.305(j), Third attitude indicator.

(e) *Newly manufactured airplanes.* No certificate holder that is described in paragraph (a) of this section may operate under part 121 of this chapter an airplane manufactured on or after a date listed in this paragraph (e) unless that airplane meets the applicable requirement listed in this paragraph (e).

(1) For nontransport category turbopropeller powered airplanes type certificated after December 31, 1964, that have a passenger seat configuration of 10–19 seats:

(i) Manufactured on or after March 20, 1997:

(A) Section 121.305(j), Third attitude indicator.

(B) Section 121.311(f), Safety belts and shoulder harnesses.

(ii) Manufactured on or after December 20, 1997: Section 121.317(a), Fasten seat belt light.

(iii) Manufactured on or after December 20, 1999: Section 121.293, Takeoff warning system.

(iv) Manufactured on or after March 12, 1999: Section 121.310(b)(1), Interior emergency exit locating sign.

(2) For transport category turbopropeller powered airplanes that have a passenger seat configuration of 20–30 seats manufactured on or after March 20, 1997: Section 121.305(j), Third attitude indicator.

(f) *New type certification requirements.* No person may operate an airplane for which the application for a type certificate was filed after March 29, 1995, in 14 CFR part 121 operations unless that airplane is type certificated under part 25 of this chapter.

(g) *Transition plan.* Before March 19, 1996, each certificate holder described in paragraph (a)(1) of this section must submit to the FAA a transition plan (containing a calendar of events) for moving from conducting its scheduled operations under the commuter requirements of part 135 of this chapter to the requirements for domestic or flag operations under part 121 of this chapter. Each transition plan must contain details on the following:

(1) Plans for obtaining new operations specifications authorizing domestic or flag operations;

(2) Plans for being in compliance with the applicable requirements of part 121 of this chapter on or before March 20, 1997; and

(3) Plans for complying with the compliance date schedules contained in paragraphs (d) and (e) of this section.

[Docket No. 28154, 60 FR 65938, Dec. 20, 1995; as amended by Amdt. 135–65, 61 FR 30435, June 14, 1996; Amdt. 135–66, 62 FR 13257, March 19, 1997]

§135.3 Rules applicable to operations subject to this part.

(a) Each person operating an aircraft in operations under this part shall—

(1) While operating inside the United States, comply with the applicable rules of this chapter; and

(2) While operating outside the United States, comply with Annex 2, Rules of the Air, to the Convention on International Civil Aviation or the regulations of any foreign country, whichever applies, and with any rules of parts 61 and 91 of this chapter and this part that are more restrictive than that Annex or those regulations and that can be complied with without violating that Annex or those regulations. Annex 2 is incorporated by reference in §91.703(b) of this chapter.

(b) Each certificate holder that conducts commuter operations under this part with airplanes in which two pilots are required by the type certification rules of this chapter shall comply with subparts N and O of part 121 of this chapter instead of the requirements of subparts E, G, and H of this part. Notwithstanding the requirements of this paragraph, a pilot serving under this part as second in command in a commuter operation with airplanes in which two pilots are required by the type certification rules of this chapter may meet the requirements of §135.245 instead of the requirements of §121.436.

(c) If authorized by the Administrator upon application, each certificate holder that conducts operations under this part to which paragraph (b) of this section does not apply, may comply with the applicable sections of subparts N and O of part 121 instead of the requirements of subparts E, G, and H of this part, except that those authorized certificate holders may choose to comply with the operating experience requirements of §135.244, instead of the requirements of §121.434 of this chapter.

[Docket No. 27993, 60 FR 65949, Dec. 20, 1995; as amended by Amdt. 135–65, 61 FR 30435, June 14, 1996; Amdt. 135–127A, 78 FR 77574, Dec. 24, 2013]

§135.4 Applicability of rules for eligible on-demand operations.

(a) An "eligible on-demand operation" is an on-demand operation conducted under this part that meets the following requirements:

(1) *Two-pilot crew.* The flightcrew must consist of at least two qualified pilots employed or contracted by the certificate holder.

(2) *Flight crew experience.* The crewmembers must have met the applicable requirements of part 61 of this chapter and have the following experience and ratings:

(i) Total flight time for all pilots:

(A) Pilot in command—A minimum of 1,500 hours.

(B) Second in command—A minimum of 500 hours.

(ii) For multi-engine turbine-powered fixed-wing and powered-lift aircraft, the following FAA certification and ratings requirements:

(A) Pilot in command—Airline transport pilot and applicable type ratings.

(B) Second in command—Commercial pilot and instrument ratings.

(iii) For all other aircraft, the following FAA certification and rating requirements:

(A) Pilot in command—Commercial pilot and instrument ratings.

(B) Second in command—Commercial pilot and instrument ratings.

(3) *Pilot operating limitations.* If the second in command of a fixed-wing aircraft has fewer than 100 hours of flight time as second in command flying in the aircraft make and model and, if a type rating is required, in the type aircraft being flown, and the pilot in command is not an appropriately qualified check pilot, the pilot in command shall make all takeoffs and landings in any of the following situations:

(i) Landings at the destination airport when a Destination Airport Analysis is required by §135.385(f); and

(ii) In any of the following conditions:

(A) The prevailing visibility for the airport is at or below 3/4 mile.

(B) The runway visual range for the runway to be used is at or below 4,000 feet.

(C) The runway to be used has water, snow, slush, ice, or similar contamination that may adversely affect aircraft performance.

(D) The braking action on the runway to be used is reported to be less than "good."

(E) The crosswind component for the runway to be used is in excess of 15 knots.

(F) Windshear is reported in the vicinity of the airport.

(G) Any other condition in which the pilot in command determines it to be prudent to exercise the pilot in command's authority.

(4) *Crew pairing.* Either the pilot in command or the second in command must have at least 75 hours of flight time in that aircraft make or model and, if a type rating is required, for that type aircraft, either as pilot in command or second in command.

(b) The Administrator may authorize deviations from paragraphs (a)(2)(i) or (a)(4) of this section if the Flight Standards District Office that issued the certificate holder's operations specifications finds that the crewmember has comparable experience, and can effectively perform the functions associated with the position in accordance with the requirements of this chapter. The Administrator may, at any time, terminate any grant of deviation authority issued under this paragraph. Grants of deviation under this paragraph may be granted after consideration of the size and scope of the operation, the qualifications of the intended personnel and the following circumstances:

(1) A newly authorized certificate holder does not employ any pilots who meet the minimum requirements of paragraphs (a)(2)(i) or (a)(4) of this section.

(2) An existing certificate holder adds to its fleet a new category and class aircraft not used before in its operation.

(3) An existing certificate holder establishes a new base to which it assigns pilots who will be required to become qualified on the aircraft operated from that base.

(c) An eligible on-demand operation may comply with alternative requirements specified in §§135.225(b), 135.385(f), and 135.387(b) instead of the requirements that apply to other on-demand operations.

[Docket No. FAA–2001–10047, 68 FR 54585, Sept. 17, 2003]

§135.7 Applicability of rules to unauthorized operators.

The rules in this part which apply to a person certificated under part 119 of this chapter also apply to a person who engages in any operation governed by this part without an appropriate certificate and operations specifications required by part 119 of this chapter.

[Docket No. 16097, 43 FR 46783, Oct. 10, 1978; as amended by Amdt. 135–58, 60 FR 65939, Dec. 20, 1995]

§135.12 Previously trained crewmembers.

A certificate holder may use a crewmember who received the certificate holder's training in accordance with subparts E, G, and H of this part before March 19, 1997, without complying with initial training and qualification requirements of subparts N and O of part 121 of this chapter. The crewmember must comply with the applicable recurrent training requirements of part 121 of this chapter.

[Docket No. 27993, 60 FR 65950, Dec. 20, 1995]

§135.19 Emergency operations.

(a) In an emergency involving the safety of persons or property, the certificate holder may deviate from the rules of this part relating to aircraft and equipment and weather minimums to the extent required to meet that emergency.

(b) In an emergency involving the safety of persons or property, the pilot in command may deviate from the rules of this part to the extent required to meet that emergency.

(c) Each person who, under the authority of this section, deviates from a rule of this part shall, within 10 days, excluding Saturdays, Sundays, and Federal holidays, after the deviation, send to the FAA Flight Standards District Office charged with the overall inspection of the certificate holder a complete report of the aircraft operation involved, including a description of the deviation and reasons for it.

§135.21 Manual requirements.

(a) Each certificate holder, other than one who uses only one pilot in the certificate holder's operations, shall prepare and keep current a manual setting forth the certificate holder's procedures and policies acceptable to the Administrator. This manual must be used by the certificate holder's flight, ground, and maintenance personnel in conducting its operations. However, the Administrator may authorize a deviation from this paragraph if the Administrator finds that, because of the limited size of the operation, all or part of the manual is not necessary for guidance of flight, ground, or maintenance personnel.

(b) Each certificate holder shall maintain at least one copy of the manual at its principal base of operations.

(c) The manual must not be contrary to any applicable Federal regulations, foreign regulation applicable to the certificate holder's operations in foreign countries, or the certificate holder's operating certificate or operations specifications.

(d) A copy of the manual, or appropriate portions of the manual (and changes and additions) shall be made available to maintenance and ground operations personnel by the certificate holder and furnished to—

(1) Its flight crewmembers; and

(2) Representatives of the Administrator assigned to the certificate holder.

(e) Each employee of the certificate holder to whom a manual or appropriate portions of it are furnished under paragraph (d)(1) of this section shall keep it up to date with the changes and additions furnished to them.

(f) Except as provided in paragraph (h) of this section, each certificate holder must carry appropriate parts of the manual on each aircraft when away from the principal operations base. The appropriate parts must be available for use by ground or flight personnel.

(g) For the purpose of complying with paragraph (d) of this section, a certificate holder may furnish the persons listed therein with all or part of its manual in printed form or other form, acceptable to the Administrator, that is retrievable in the English language. If the certificate holder furnishes all or part of the manual in other than printed form, it must ensure there is a compatible reading device available to those persons that provides a legible image of the information and instructions, or a system that is able to retrieve the information and instructions in the English language.

(h) If a certificate holder conducts aircraft inspections or maintenance at specified stations where it keeps the approved inspection program manual, it is not required to carry the manual aboard the aircraft en route to those stations.

[Docket No. 16097, 43 FR 46783, Oct. 10, 1978; as amended by Amdt. 135–18, 47 FR 33396, Aug. 2, 1982; Amdt. 135–58, 60 FR 65939, Dec. 20, 1995; Amdt. 135–66, 62 FR 13257, March 19, 1997; Amdt. 135–91, 68 FR 54585, Sept. 17, 2003]

§135.23 Manual contents.

Each manual shall have the date of the last revision on each revised page. The manual must include—

(a) The name of each management person required under §119.69(a) of this chapter who is authorized to act for the certificate holder, the person's assigned area of responsibility, the person's duties, responsibilities, and authority, and the name and title of each person authorized to exercise operational control under §135.77;

(b) Procedures for ensuring compliance with aircraft weight and balance limitations and, for multiengine aircraft, for determining compliance with §135.185;

(c) Copies of the certificate holder's operations specifications or appropriate extracted informa-

Part 135: Commuter & On Demand Operations §135.23

tion, including area of operations authorized, category and class of aircraft authorized, crew complements, and types of operations authorized;

(d) Procedures for complying with accident notification requirements;

(e) Procedures for ensuring that the pilot in command knows that required airworthiness inspections have been made and that the aircraft has been approved for return to service in compliance with applicable maintenance requirements;

(f) Procedures for reporting and recording mechanical irregularities that come to the attention of the pilot in command before, during, and after completion of a flight;

(g) Procedures to be followed by the pilot in command for determining that mechanical irregularities or defects reported for previous flights have been corrected or that correction has been deferred;

(h) Procedures to be followed by the pilot in command to obtain maintenance, preventive maintenance, and servicing of the aircraft at a place where previous arrangements have not been made by the operator, when the pilot is authorized to so act for the operator;

(i) Procedures under §135.179 for the release for, or continuation of, flight if any item of equipment required for the particular type of operation becomes inoperative or unserviceable en route;

(j) Procedures for refueling aircraft, eliminating fuel contamination, protecting from fire (including electrostatic protection), and supervising and protecting passengers during refueling;

(k) Procedures to be followed by the pilot in command in the briefing under §135.117;

(l) Flight locating procedures, when applicable;

(m) Procedures for ensuring compliance with emergency procedures, including a list of the functions assigned each category of required crewmembers in connection with an emergency and emergency evacuation duties under §135.123;

(n) En route qualification procedures for pilots, when applicable;

(o) The approved aircraft inspection program, when applicable;

(p)(1) Procedures and information, as described in paragraph (p)(2) of this section, to assist each crewmember and person performing or directly supervising the following job functions involving items for transport on an aircraft:
 (i) Acceptance;
 (ii) Rejection;
 (iii) Handling;
 (iv) Storage incidental to transport;
 (v) Packaging of company material; or
 (vi) Loading.

(2) Ensure that the procedures and information described in this paragraph are sufficient to assist a person in identifying packages that are marked or labeled as containing hazardous materials or that show signs of containing undeclared hazardous materials. The procedures and information must include:

 (i) Procedures for rejecting packages that do not conform to the Hazardous Materials Regulations in 49 CFR parts 171 through 180 or that appear to contain undeclared hazardous materials;

 (ii) Procedures for complying with the hazardous materials incident reporting requirements of 49 CFR 171.15 and 171.16 and discrepancy reporting requirements of 49 CFR 175.31.

 (iii) The certificate holder's hazmat policies and whether the certificate holder is authorized to carry, or is prohibited from carrying, hazardous materials; and

 (iv) If the certificate holder's operations specifications permit the transport of hazardous materials, procedures and information to ensure the following:

 (A) That packages containing hazardous materials are properly offered and accepted in compliance with 49 CFR parts 171 through 180;

 (B) That packages containing hazardous materials are properly handled, stored, packaged, loaded and carried on board an aircraft in compliance with 49 CFR parts 171 through 180;

 (C) That the requirements for Notice to the Pilot in Command (49 CFR 175.33) are complied with; and

 (D) That aircraft replacement parts, consumable materials or other items regulated by 49 CFR parts 171 through 180 are properly handled, packaged, and transported.

(q) Procedures for the evacuation of persons who may need the assistance of another person to move expeditiously to an exit if an emergency occurs; and

(r) If required by §135.385, an approved Destination Airport Analysis establishing runway safety margins at destination airports, taking into account the following factors as supported by published aircraft performance data supplied by the aircraft manufacturer for the appropriate runway conditions—

 (1) Pilot qualifications and experience;
 (2) Aircraft performance data to include normal, abnormal and emergency procedures as supplied by the aircraft manufacturer;
 (3) Airport facilities and topography;
 (4) Runway conditions (including contamination);
 (5) Airport or area weather reporting;
 (6) Appropriate additional runway safety margins, if required;
 (7) Airplane inoperative equipment;
 (8) Environmental conditions; and
 (9) Other criteria affecting aircraft performance.

(s) Other procedures and policy instructions regarding the certificate holder's operations issued by the certificate holder.

[Docket No. 16097, 43 FR 46783, Oct. 10, 1978; as amended by Amdt. 135–20, 51 FR 40709, Nov. 7, 1986; Amdt. 135–58, 60 FR 65939, Dec. 20, 1995; Amdt. 135–91, 68 FR 54586, Sept. 17, 2003; Amdt. 135–101, 70 FR 58829, Oct. 7, 2005]

§135.25 Aircraft requirements.

(a) Except as provided in paragraph (d) of this section, no certificate holder may operate an aircraft under this part unless that aircraft—

(1) Is registered as a civil aircraft of the United States and carries an appropriate and current airworthiness certificate issued under this chapter; and

(2) Is in an airworthy condition and meets the applicable airworthiness requirements of this chapter, including those relating to identification and equipment.

(b) Each certificate holder must have the exclusive use of at least one aircraft that meets the requirements for at least one kind of operation authorized in the certificate holder's operations specifications. In addition, for each kind of operation for which the certificate holder does not have the exclusive use of an aircraft, the certificate holder must have available for use under a written agreement (including arrangements for performing required maintenance) at least one aircraft that meets the requirements for that kind of operation. However, this paragraph does not prohibit the operator from using or authorizing the use of the aircraft for other than operations under this part and does not require the certificate holder to have exclusive use of all aircraft that the certificate holder uses.

(c) For the purposes of paragraph (b) of this section, a person has exclusive use of an aircraft if that person has the sole possession, control, and use of it for flight, as owner, or has a written agreement (including arrangements for performing required maintenance), in effect when the aircraft is operated, giving the person that possession, control, and use for at least 6 consecutive months.

(d) A certificate holder may operate in common carriage, and for the carriage of mail, a civil aircraft which is leased or chartered to it without crew and is registered in a country which is a party to the Convention on International Civil Aviation if—

(1) The aircraft carries an appropriate airworthiness certificate issued by the country of registration and meets the registration and identification requirements of that country;

(2) The aircraft is of a type design which is approved under a U.S. type certificate and complies with all of the requirements of this chapter (14 CFR chapter 1) that would be applicable to that aircraft were it registered in the United States, including the requirements which must be met for issuance of a U.S. standard airworthiness certificate (including type design conformity, condition for safe operation, and the noise, fuel venting, and engine emission requirements of this chapter), except that a U.S. registration certificate and a U.S. standard airworthiness certificate will not be issued for the aircraft;

(3) The aircraft is operated by U.S.-certificated airmen employed by the certificate holder; and

(4) The certificate holder files a copy of the aircraft lease or charter agreement with the FAA Aircraft Registry, Department of Transportation, 6400 South MacArthur Boulevard, Oklahoma City, OK (Mailing address: P.O. Box 25504, Oklahoma City, OK 73125).

[Docket No. 16097, 43 FR 46783, Oct. 10, 1978; as amended by Amdt. 135–8, 45 FR 68649, Oct. 16, 1980; Amdt. 135–66, 62 FR 13257, March 19, 1997]

§135.41 Carriage of narcotic drugs, marijuana, and depressant or stimulant drugs or substances.

If the holder of a certificate operating under this part allows any aircraft owned or leased by that holder to be engaged in any operation that the certificate holder knows to be in violation of §91.19(a) of this chapter, that operation is a basis for suspending or revoking the certificate.

[Docket No. 28154, 60 FR 65939, Dec. 20, 1995]

§135.43 Crewmember certificates: International operations.

(a) This section describes the certificates that were issued to United States citizens who were employed by air carriers at the time of issuance as flight crewmembers on United States registered aircraft engaged in international air commerce. The purpose of the certificate is to facilitate the entry and clearance of those crewmembers into ICAO contracting states. They were issued under Annex 9, as amended, to the Convention on International Civil Aviation.

(b) The holder of a certificate issued under this section, or the air carrier by whom the holder is employed, shall surrender the certificate for cancellation at the nearest FAA Flight Standards District Office at the termination of the holder's employment with that air carrier.

[Docket No. 28154, 61 FR 30435, June 14, 1996]

Subpart B—
Flight Operations

§135.61 General.

This subpart prescribes rules, in addition to those in part 91 of this chapter, that apply to operations under this part.

§135.63 Recordkeeping requirements.

(a) Each certificate holder shall keep at its principal business office or at other places approved by the Administrator, and shall make available for inspection by the Administrator the following—

(1) The certificate holder's operating certificate;

(2) The certificate holder's operations specifications;

(3) A current list of the aircraft used or available for use in operations under this part and the operations for which each is equipped;

(4) An individual record of each pilot used in operations under this part, including the following information:

(i) The full name of the pilot.

(ii) The pilot certificate (by type and number) and ratings that the pilot holds.

(iii) The pilot's aeronautical experience in sufficient detail to determine the pilot's qualifications to pilot aircraft in operations under this part.

(iv) The pilot's current duties and the date of the pilot's assignment to those duties.

(v) The effective date and class of the medical certificate that the pilot holds.

(vi) The date and result of each of the initial and recurrent competency tests and proficiency and route checks required by this part and the type of aircraft flown during that test or check.

(vii) The pilot's flight time in sufficient detail to determine compliance with the flight time limitations of this part.

(viii) The pilot's check pilot authorization, if any.

(ix) Any action taken concerning the pilot's release from employment for physical or professional disqualification.

(x) The date of the completion of the initial phase and each recurrent phase of the training required by this part; and

(5) An individual record for each flight attendant who is required under this part, maintained in sufficient detail to determine compliance with the applicable portions of §135.273 of this part.

(b) Each certificate holder must keep each record required by paragraph (a)(3) of this section for at least 6 months, and must keep each record required by paragraphs (a)(4) and (a)(5) of this section for at least 12 months.

(c) For multiengine aircraft, each certificate holder is responsible for the preparation and accuracy of a load manifest in duplicate containing information concerning the loading of the aircraft. The manifest must be prepared before each takeoff and must include:

(1) The number of passengers;

(2) The total weight of the loaded aircraft;

(3) The maximum allowable takeoff weight for that flight;

(4) The center of gravity limits;

(5) The center of gravity of the loaded aircraft, except that the actual center of gravity need not be computed if the aircraft is loaded according to a loading schedule or other approved method that ensures that the center of gravity of the loaded aircraft is within approved limits. In those cases, an entry shall be made on the manifest indicating that the center of gravity is within limits according to a loading schedule or other approved method;

(6) The registration number of the aircraft or flight number;

(7) The origin and destination; and

(8) Identification of crew members and their crew position assignments.

(d) The pilot in command of an aircraft for which a load manifest must be prepared shall carry a copy of the completed load manifest in the aircraft to its destination. The certificate holder shall keep copies of completed load manifests for at least 30 days at its principal operations base, or at another location used by it and approved by the Administrator.

[Docket No. 16097, 43 FR 46783, Oct. 10, 1978; as amended by Amdt. 135–52, 59 FR 42993, Aug. 19, 1994]

§135.64 Retention of contracts and amendments: Commercial operators who conduct intrastate operations for compensation or hire.

Each commercial operator who conducts intrastate operations for compensation or hire shall keep a copy of each written contract under which it provides services as a commercial operator for a period of at least one year after the date of execution of the contract. In the case of an oral contract, it shall keep a memorandum stating its elements, and of any amendments to it, for a period of at least one year after the execution of that contract or change.

[Docket No. 28154, 60 FR 65939, Dec. 20, 1995; as amended by Amdt. 135–65, 61 FR 30435, June 14, 1996; Amdt. 135–66, 62 FR 13257, March 19, 1997]

§135.65 Reporting mechanical irregularities.

(a) Each certificate holder shall provide an aircraft maintenance log to be carried on board each aircraft for recording or deferring mechanical irregularities and their correction.

(b) The pilot in command shall enter or have entered in the aircraft maintenance log each me-

§135.67

chanical irregularity that comes to the pilot's attention during flight time. Before each flight, the pilot in command shall, if the pilot does not already know, determine the status of each irregularity entered in the maintenance log at the end of the preceding flight.

(c) Each person who takes corrective action or defers action concerning a reported or observed failure or malfunction of an airframe, powerplant, propeller, rotor, or appliance, shall record the action taken in the aircraft maintenance log under the applicable maintenance requirements of this chapter.

(d) Each certificate holder shall establish a procedure for keeping copies of the aircraft maintenance log required by this section in the aircraft for access by appropriate personnel and shall include that procedure in the manual required by §135.21.

§135.67 Reporting potentially hazardous meteorological conditions and irregularities of ground facilities or navigation aids.

Whenever a pilot encounters a potentially hazardous meteorological condition or an irregularity in a ground facility or navigation aid in flight, the knowledge of which the pilot considers essential to the safety of other flights, the pilot shall notify an appropriate ground radio station as soon as practicable.

[Docket No. 16097, 43 FR 46783, Oct. 1, 1978; as amended by Amdt. 135–1, 44 FR 26737, May 7, 1979; Amdt. 135–110, 72 FR 31684, June 7, 2007]

§135.69 Restriction or suspension of operations: Continuation of flight in an emergency.

(a) During operations under this part, if a certificate holder or pilot in command knows of conditions, including airport and runway conditions, that are a hazard to safe operations, the certificate holder or pilot in command, as the case may be, shall restrict or suspend operations as necessary until those conditions are corrected.

(b) No pilot in command may allow a flight to continue toward any airport of intended landing under the conditions set forth in paragraph (a) of this section, unless, in the opinion of the pilot in command, the conditions that are a hazard to safe operations may reasonably be expected to be corrected by the estimated time of arrival or, unless there is no safer procedure. In the latter event, the continuation toward that airport is an emergency situation under §135.19.

§135.71 Airworthiness check.

The pilot in command may not begin a flight unless the pilot determines that the airworthiness inspections required by §91.409 of this chapter, or §135.419, whichever is applicable, have been made.

[Docket No. 16097, 43 FR 46783, Oct. 10, 1978; as amended by Amdt. 135–32, 54 FR 34432, Aug. 18, 1989]

§135.73 Inspections and tests.

Each certificate holder and each person employed by the certificate holder shall allow the Administrator, at any time or place, to make inspections or tests (including en route inspections) to determine the holder's compliance with the Federal Aviation Act of 1958, applicable regulations, and the certificate holder's operating certificate, and operations specifications.

§135.75 Inspectors credentials: admission to pilots' compartment: Forward observer's seat.

(a) Whenever, in performing the duties of conducting an inspection, an FAA inspector presents an Aviation Safety Inspector credential, FAA Form 110A, to the pilot in command of an aircraft operated by the certificate holder, the inspector must be given free and uninterrupted access to the pilot compartment of that aircraft. However, this paragraph does not limit the emergency authority of the pilot in command to exclude any person from the pilot compartment in the interest of safety.

(b) A forward observer's seat on the flight deck, or forward passenger seat with headset or speaker must be provided for use by the Administrator while conducting en route inspections. The suitability of the location of the seat and the headset or speaker for use in conducting en route inspections is determined by the Administrator.

§135.76 DOD Commercial Air Carrier Evaluator's Credentials: Admission to pilots' compartment: Forward observer's seat.

(a) Whenever, in performing the duties of conducting an evaluation, a DOD commercial air carrier evaluator presents S&A Form 110B, "DOD Commercial Air Carrier Evaluator's Credential," to the pilot in command of an aircraft operated by the certificate holder, the evaluator must be given free and uninterrupted access to the pilot's compartment of that aircraft. However, this paragraph does not limit the emergency authority of the pilot in command to exclude any person from the pilot compartment in the interest of safety.

(b) A forward observer's seat on the flight deck or forward passenger seat with headset or speaker must be provided for use by the evaluator while conducting en route evaluations. The suitability of the location of the seat and the headset or speaker for use in conducting en route evaluations is determined by the FAA.

[Docket No. FAA–2003–15571, 68 FR 41218, July 10, 2003]

§135.77 Responsibility for operational control.

Each certificate holder is responsible for operational control and shall list, in the manual required by §135.21, the name and title of each person authorized by it to exercise operational control.

§135.78 Instrument approach procedures and IFR landing minimums.

No person may make an instrument approach at an airport except in accordance with IFR weather minimums and instrument approach procedures set forth in the certificate holder's operations specifications.

[Docket No. FAA–2002–14002, 72 FR 31684, June 7, 2007]

§135.79 Flight locating requirements.

(a) Each certificate holder must have procedures established for locating each flight, for which an FAA flight plan is not filed, that—

(1) Provide the certificate holder with at least the information required to be included in a VFR flight plan;

(2) Provide for timely notification of an FAA facility or search and rescue facility, if an aircraft is overdue or missing; and

(3) Provide the certificate holder with the location, date, and estimated time for reestablishing communications, if the flight will operate in an area where communications cannot be maintained.

(b) Flight locating information shall be retained at the certificate holder's principal place of business, or at other places designated by the certificate holder in the flight locating procedures, until the completion of the flight.

(c) Each certificate holder shall furnish the representative of the Administrator assigned to it with a copy of its flight locating procedures and any changes or additions, unless those procedures are included in a manual required under this part.

[Docket No. 16097, 43 FR 46783, Oct. 10, 1978; as amended by Amdt. 135–110, 72 FR 31684, June 7, 2007]

§135.81 Informing personnel of operational information and appropriate changes.

Each certificate holder shall inform each person in its employment of the operations specifications that apply to that person's duties and responsibilities and shall make available to each pilot in the certificate holder's employ the following materials in current form:

(a) Airman's Information Manual (Alaska Supplement in Alaska and Pacific Chart Supplement in Pacific-Asia Regions) or a commercial publication that contains the same information.

(b) This part and part 91 of this chapter.

(c) Aircraft Equipment Manuals, and Aircraft Flight Manual or equivalent.

(d) For foreign operations, the International Flight Information Manual or a commercial publication that contains the same information concerning the pertinent operational and entry requirements of the foreign country or countries involved.

§135.83 Operating information required.

(a) The operator of an aircraft must provide the following materials, in current and appropriate form, accessible to the pilot at the pilot station, and the pilot shall use them:

(1) A cockpit checklist.

(2) For multiengine aircraft or for aircraft with retractable landing gear, an emergency cockpit checklist containing the procedures required by paragraph (c) of this section, as appropriate.

(3) Pertinent aeronautical charts.

(4) For IFR operations, each pertinent navigational en route, terminal area, and approach and letdown chart.

(5) For multiengine aircraft, one-engine-inoperative climb performance data and if the aircraft is approved for use in IFR or over-the-top operations, that data must be sufficient to enable the pilot to determine compliance with §135.181(a)(2).

(b) Each cockpit checklist required by paragraph (a)(1) of this section must contain the following procedures:

(1) Before starting engines;
(2) Before takeoff;
(3) Cruise;
(4) Before landing;
(5) After landing;
(6) Stopping engines.

(c) Each emergency cockpit checklist required by paragraph (a)(2) of this section must contain the following procedures, as appropriate:

(1) Emergency operation of fuel, hydraulic, electrical, and mechanical systems.

(2) Emergency operation of instruments and controls.

(3) Engine inoperative procedures.
(4) Any other emergency procedures necessary for safety.

§135.85 Carriage of persons without compliance with the passenger-carrying provisions of this part.

The following persons may be carried aboard an aircraft without complying with the passenger-carrying requirements of this part:

(a) A crewmember or other employee of the certificate holder.

(b) A person necessary for the safe handling of animals on the aircraft.

(c) A person necessary for the safe handling of hazardous materials (as defined in subchapter C of title 49 CFR).

(d) A person performing duty as a security or honor guard accompanying a shipment made by or under the authority of the U.S. Government.

(e) A military courier or a military route supervisor carried by a military cargo contract air carrier or commercial operator in operations under a military cargo contract, if that carriage is specifically authorized by the appropriate military service.

(f) An authorized representative of the Administrator conducting an en route inspection.

(g) A person, authorized by the Administrator, who is performing a duty connected with a cargo operation of the certificate holder.

(h) A DOD commercial air carrier evaluator conducting an en route evaluation.

[Docket No. 16097, 43 FR 46783, Oct. 10, 1978; as amended by Amdt. 135–88, 68 FR 41368, July 10, 2003]

§135.87 Carriage of cargo including carry-on baggage.

No person may carry cargo, including carry-on baggage, in or on any aircraft unless—

(a) It is carried in an approved cargo rack, bin, or compartment installed in or on the aircraft;

(b) It is secured by an approved means; or

(c) It is carried in accordance with each of the following:

(1) For cargo, it is properly secured by a safety belt or other tie-down having enough strength to eliminate the possibility of shifting under all normally anticipated flight and ground conditions, or for carry-on baggage, it is restrained so as to prevent its movement during air turbulence.

(2) It is packaged or covered to avoid possible injury to occupants.

(3) It does not impose any load on seats or on the floor structure that exceeds the load limitation for those components.

(4) It is not located in a position that obstructs the access to, or use of, any required emergency or regular exit, or the use of the aisle between the crew and the passenger compartment, or located in a position that obscures any passenger's view of the "seat belt" sign, "no smoking" sign, or any required exit sign, unless an auxiliary sign or other approved means for proper notification of the passengers is provided.

(5) It is not carried directly above seated occupants.

(6) It is stowed in compliance with this section for takeoff and landing.

(7) For cargo only operations, paragraph (c)(4) of this section does not apply if the cargo is loaded so that at least one emergency or regular exit is available to provide all occupants of the aircraft a means of unobstructed exit from the aircraft if an emergency occurs.

(d) Each passenger seat under which baggage is stowed shall be fitted with a means to prevent articles of baggage stowed under it from sliding under crash impacts severe enough to induce the ultimate inertia forces specified in the emergency landing condition regulations under which the aircraft was type certificated.

(e) When cargo is carried in cargo compartments that are designed to require the physical entry of a crewmember to extinguish any fire that may occur during flight, the cargo must be loaded so as to allow a crewmember to effectively reach all parts of the compartment with the contents of a hand fire extinguisher.

§135.89 Pilot requirements: Use of oxygen.

(a) Unpressurized aircraft. Each pilot of an unpressurized aircraft shall use oxygen continuously when flying—

(1) At altitudes above 10,000 feet through 12,000 feet MSL for that part of the flight at those altitudes that is of more than 30 minutes duration; and

(2) Above 12,000 feet MSL.

(b) Pressurized aircraft.

(1) Whenever a pressurized aircraft is operated with the cabin pressure altitude more than 10,000 feet MSL, each pilot shall comply with paragraph (a) of this section.

(2) Whenever a pressurized aircraft is operated at altitudes above 25,000 feet through 35,000 feet MSL, unless each pilot has an approved quick-donning type oxygen mask—

(i) At least one pilot at the controls shall wear, secured and sealed, an oxygen mask that either supplies oxygen at all times or automatically supplies oxygen whenever the cabin pressure altitude exceeds 12,000 feet MSL; and

(ii) During that flight, each other pilot on flight deck duty shall have an oxygen mask, connected to an oxygen supply, located so as to allow immediate placing of the mask on the pilot's face sealed and secured for use.

(3) Whenever a pressurized aircraft is operated at altitudes above 35,000 feet MSL, at least one pilot at the controls shall wear, secured and sealed, an oxygen mask required by paragraph (b)(2)(i) of this section.

(4) If one pilot leaves a pilot duty station of an aircraft when operating at altitudes above 25,000 feet MSL, the remaining pilot at the controls shall put on and use an approved oxygen mask until the other pilot returns to the pilot duty station of the aircraft.

§135.91 Oxygen for medical use by passengers.

(a) Except as provided in paragraphs (d) and (e) of this section, no certificate holder may allow the carriage or operation of equipment for the storage, generation or dispensing of medical oxygen unless the unit to be carried is constructed so that all valves, fittings, and gauges are protected from damage during that carriage or operation and unless the following conditions are met—

(1) The equipment must be—

(i) Of an approved type or in conformity with the manufacturing, packaging, marking, labeling, and maintenance requirements of title 49 CFR parts 171, 172, and 173, except §173.24(a)(1);

(ii) When owned by the certificate holder, maintained under the certificate holder's approved maintenance program;

(iii) Free of flammable contaminants on all exterior surfaces; and

(iv) Appropriately secured.

(2) When the oxygen is stored in the form of a liquid, the equipment must have been under the certificate holder's approved maintenance program since its purchase new or since the storage container was last purged.

(3) When the oxygen is stored in the form of a compressed gas as defined in title 49 CFR 173.300(a)—

(i) When owned by the certificate holder, it must be maintained under its approved maintenance program; and

(ii) The pressure in any oxygen cylinder must not exceed the rated cylinder pressure.

(4) The pilot in command must be advised when the equipment is on board, and when it is intended to be used.

(5) The equipment must be stowed, and each person using the equipment must be seated, so as not to restrict access to or use of any required emergency or regular exit, or of the aisle in the passenger compartment.

(b) No person may smoke and no certificate holder may allow any person to smoke within 10 feet of oxygen storage and dispensing equipment carried under paragraph (a) of this section.

(c) No certificate holder may allow any person other than a person trained in the use of medical oxygen equipment to connect or disconnect oxygen bottles or any other ancillary component while any passenger is aboard the aircraft.

(d) Paragraph (a)(1)(i) of this section does not apply when that equipment is furnished by a professional or medical emergency service for use on board an aircraft in a medical emergency when no other practical means of transportation (including any other properly equipped certificate holder) is reasonably available and the person carried under the medical emergency is accompanied by a person trained in the use of medical oxygen.

(e) Each certificate holder who, under the authority of paragraph (d) of this section, deviates from paragraph (a)(1)(i) of this section under a medical emergency shall, within 10 days, excluding Saturdays, Sundays, and Federal holidays, after the deviation, send to the certificate-holding district office a complete report of the operation involved, including a description of the deviation and the reasons for it.

[Docket No. 16097, 43 FR 46783, Oct. 10, 1978; as amended by Amdt. 135–60, 61 FR 2616, Jan. 26, 1996]

§135.93 Minimum altitudes for use of autopilot.

(a) *Definitions.* For purpose of this section—

(1) Altitudes for takeoff/initial climb and go-around/missed approach are defined as above the airport elevation.

(2) Altitudes for enroute operations are defined as above terrain elevation.

(3) Altitudes for approach are defined as above the touchdown zone elevation (TDZE), unless the altitude is specifically in reference to DA (H) or MDA, in which case the altitude is defined by reference to the DA(H) or MDA itself.

(b) *Takeoff and initial climb.* No person may use an autopilot for takeoff or initial climb below the higher of 500 feet or an altitude that is no lower than twice the altitude loss specified in the Airplane Flight Manual (AFM), except as follows—

(1) At a minimum engagement altitude specified in the AFM; or

(2) At an altitude specified by the Administrator, whichever is greater.

(c) *Enroute.* No person may use an autopilot enroute, including climb and descent, below the following—

(1) 500 feet;

(2) At an altitude that is no lower than twice the altitude loss specified in the AFM for an autopilot malfunction in cruise conditions; or

(3) At an altitude specified by the Administrator, whichever is greater.

(d) Approach. No person may use an autopilot at an altitude lower than 50 feet below the DA(H) or MDA for the instrument procedure being flown, except as follows—

(1) For autopilots with an AFM specified altitude loss for approach operations—

(i) An altitude no lower than twice the specified altitude loss if higher than 50 feet below the MDA or DA(H);

(ii) An altitude no lower than 50 feet higher than the altitude loss specified in the AFM, when the following conditions are met—

(A) Reported weather conditions are less than the basic VFR weather conditions in §91.155 of this chapter;

(B) Suitable visual references specified in §91.175 of this chapter have been established on the instrument approach procedure; and

(C) The autopilot is coupled and receiving both lateral and vertical path references;

(iii) An altitude no lower than the higher of the altitude loss specified in the AFM or 50 feet above the TDZE, when the following conditions are met—

(A) Reported weather conditions are equal to or better than the basic VFR weather conditions in §91.155 of this chapter; and

(B) The autopilot is coupled and receiving both lateral and vertical path references; or

(iv) A greater altitude specified by the Administrator.

(2) For autopilots with AFM specified approach altitude limitations, the greater of—

(i) The minimum use altitude specified for the coupled approach mode selected;

(ii) 50 feet; or

(iii) An altitude specified by Administrator.

(3) For autopilots with an AFM specified negligible or zero altitude loss for an autopilot approach mode malfunction, the greater of—

(i) 50 feet; or

(ii) An altitude specified by Administrator.

(4) If executing an autopilot coupled go-around or missed approach using a certificated and functioning autopilot in accordance with paragraph (e) in this section.

(e) Go-Around/Missed Approach. No person may engage an autopilot during a go-around or missed approach below the minimum engagement altitude specified for takeoff and initial climb in paragraph (b) in this section. An autopilot minimum use altitude does not apply to a go-around/missed approach initiated with an engaged autopilot. Performing a go-around or missed approach with an engaged autopilot must not adversely affect safe obstacle clearance.

(f) Landing. Notwithstanding paragraph (d) of this section, autopilot minimum use altitudes do not apply to autopilot operations when an approved automatic landing system mode is being used for landing. Automatic landing systems must be authorized in an operations specification issued to the operator.

(g) This section does not apply to operations conducted in rotorcraft.

[Docket No. 16097, 43 FR 46783, Oct. 10, 1978; as amended by Amdt. 135–32, 54 FR 34332, Aug. 18, 1989; Amdt. 135–68, 62 FR 27923, May 21, 1997; Amdt. 135–128, 79 FR 6088, Feb. 3, 2014]

§135.95 Airmen: Limitations on use of services.

No certificate holder may use the services of any person as an airman unless the person performing those services—

(a) Holds an appropriate and current airman certificate; and

(b) Is qualified, under this chapter, for the operation for which the person is to be used.

§135.97 Aircraft and facilities for recent flight experience.

Each certificate holder shall provide aircraft and facilities to enable each of its pilots to maintain and demonstrate the pilot's ability to conduct all operations for which the pilot is authorized.

§135.98 Operations in the North Polar Area.

After August 13, 2008, no certificate holder may operate an aircraft in the region north of 78°N latitude ("North Polar Area"), other than intrastate operations wholly within the state of Alaska, unless authorized by the FAA. The certificate holder's operation specifications must include the following:

(a) The designation of airports that may be used for enroute diversions and the requirements the airports must meet at the time of diversion.

(b) Except for all-cargo operations, a recovery plan for passengers at designated diversion airports.

(c) A fuel-freeze strategy and procedures for monitoring fuel freezing for operations in the North Polar Area.

(d) A plan to ensure communication capability for operations in the North Polar Area.

(e) An MEL for operations in the North Polar Area.

(f) A training plan for operations in the North Polar Area.

(g) A plan for mitigating crew exposure to radiation during solar flare activity.

(h) A plan for providing at least two cold weather anti-exposure suits in the aircraft, to protect crewmembers during outside activity at a diversion airport with extreme climatic conditions. The FAA may relieve the certificate holder from this requirement if the season of the year makes the equipment unnecessary.

[Docket No. FAA-2002-6717, 72 FR 1884, Jan. 16, 2007; as amended by Amdt. 135-112, 73 FR 8798, Feb. 15, 2008]

§135.99 Composition of flight crew.

(a) No certificate holder may operate an aircraft with less than the minimum flight crew specified in the aircraft operating limitations or the Aircraft Flight Manual for that aircraft and required by this part for the kind of operation being conducted.

(b) No certificate holder may operate an aircraft without a second in command if that aircraft has a passenger seating configuration, excluding any pilot seat, of ten seats or more.

§135.100 Flight crewmember duties.

(a) No certificate holder shall require, nor may any flight crewmember perform, any duties during a critical phase of flight except those duties required for the safe operation of the aircraft. Duties such as company required calls made for such nonsafety related purposes as ordering galley supplies and confirming passenger connections, announcements made to passengers promoting the air carrier or pointing out sights of interest, and filling out company payroll and related records are not required for the safe operation of the aircraft.

(b) No flight crewmember may engage in, nor may any pilot in command permit, any activity during a critical phase of flight which could distract any flight crewmember from the performance of his or her duties or which could interfere in any way with the proper conduct of those duties. Activities such as eating meals, engaging in nonessential conversations within the cockpit and nonessential communications between the cabin and cockpit crews, and reading publications not related to the proper conduct of the flight are not required for the safe operation of the aircraft.

(c) For the purposes of this section, critical phases of flight includes all ground operations involving taxi, takeoff and landing, and all other flight operations conducted below 10,000 feet, except cruise flight.

Note: Taxi is defined as "movement of an airplane under its own power on the surface of an airport."

[Docket No. 20661, 46 FR 5502, Jan. 19, 1981]

§135.101 Second in command required under IFR.

Except as provided in §135.105, no person may operate an aircraft carrying passengers under IFR unless there is a second in command in the aircraft.

[Docket No. 28743, 62 FR 42374, Aug. 6, 1997]

§135.103 [Reserved]

§135.105 Exception to second in command requirement: Approval for use of autopilot system.

(a) Except as provided in §§135.99 and 135.111, unless two pilots are required by this chapter for operations under VFR, a person may operate an aircraft without a second in command, if it is equipped with an operative approved autopilot system and the use of that system is authorized by appropriate operations specifications. No certificate holder may use any person, nor may any person serve, as a pilot in command under this section of an aircraft operated in a commuter operation, as defined in part 119 of this chapter unless that person has at least 100 hours pilot in command flight time in the make and model of aircraft to be flown and has met all other applicable requirements of this part.

(b) The certificate holder may apply for an amendment of its operations specifications to authorize the use of an autopilot system in place of a second in command.

(c) The Administrator issues an amendment to the operations specifications authorizing the use of an autopilot system, in place of a second in command, if—

(1) The autopilot is capable of operating the aircraft controls to maintain flight and maneuver it about the three axes; and

(2) The certificate holder shows, to the satisfaction of the Administrator, that operations using the autopilot system can be conducted safely and in compliance with this part.

The amendment contains any conditions or limitations on the use of the autopilot system that the Administrator determines are needed in the interest of safety.

[Docket No. 16097, 43 FR 46783, Oct. 10, 1978; as amended by Amdt. 135-3, 45 FR 7542, Feb. 4, 1980; Amdt. 135-58, 60 FR 65939, Dec. 20, 1995]

§135.107 Flight attendant crewmember requirement.

No certificate holder may operate an aircraft that has a passenger seating configuration, excluding any pilot seat, of more than 19 unless there is a flight attendant crewmember on board the aircraft.

§135.109 Pilot in command or second in command: Designation required.

(a) Each certificate holder shall designate a—
(1) Pilot in command for each flight; and
(2) Second in command for each flight requiring two pilots.

§135.111

(b) The pilot in command, as designated by the certificate holder, shall remain the pilot in command at all times during that flight.

§135.111 Second in command required in Category II operations.

No person may operate an aircraft in a Category II operation unless there is a second in command of the aircraft.

§135.113 Passenger occupancy of pilot seat.

No certificate holder may operate an aircraft type certificated after October 15, 1971, that has a passenger seating configuration, excluding any pilot seat, of more than eight seats if any person other than the pilot in command, a second in command, a company check airman, or an authorized representative of the Administrator, the National Transportation Safety Board, or the United States Postal Service occupies a pilot seat.

§135.115 Manipulation of controls.

No pilot in command may allow any person to manipulate the flight controls of an aircraft during flight conducted under this part, nor may any person manipulate the controls during such flight unless that person is—

(a) A pilot employed by the certificate holder and qualified in the aircraft; or

(b) An authorized safety representative of the Administrator who has the permission of the pilot in command, is qualified in the aircraft, and is checking flight operations.

§135.117 Briefing of passengers before flight.

(a) Before each takeoff each pilot in command of an aircraft carrying passengers shall ensure that all passengers have been orally briefed on—

(1) *Smoking.* Each passenger shall be briefed on when, where, and under what conditions smoking is prohibited (including, but not limited to, any applicable requirements of part 252 of this title). This briefing shall include a statement that the Federal Aviation Regulations require passenger compliance with the lighted passenger information signs (if such signs are required), posted placards, areas designated for safety purposes as no smoking areas, and crewmember instructions with regard to these items. The briefing shall also include a statement (if the aircraft is equipped with a lavatory) that Federal law prohibits: tampering with, disabling, or destroying any smoke detector installed in an aircraft lavatory; smoking in lavatories; and when applicable, smoking in passenger compartments.

(2) *Use of safety belts, including instructions on how to fasten and unfasten the safety belts.* Each passenger shall be briefed on when, where and under what conditions the safety belt must be fastened about that passenger. This briefing shall include a statement that the Federal Aviation Regulations require passenger compliance with lighted passenger information signs and crewmember instructions concerning the use of safety belts.

(3) The placement of seat backs in an upright position before takeoff and landing;

(4) Location and means for opening the passenger entry door and emergency exits;

(5) Location of survival equipment;

(6) If the flight involves extended overwater operation, ditching procedures and the use of required flotation equipment;

(7) If the flight involves operations above 12,000 feet MSL, the normal and emergency use of oxygen; and

(8) Location and operation of fire extinguishers.

(9) If a rotorcraft operation involves flight beyond autorotational distance from the shoreline, as defined in §135.168(a), use of life preservers, ditching procedures and emergency exit from the rotorcraft in the event of a ditching; and the location and use of life rafts and other life preserver devices if applicable.

(b) Before each takeoff the pilot in command shall ensure that each person who may need the assistance of another person to move expeditiously to an exit if an emergency occurs and that person's attendant, if any, has received a briefing as to the procedures to be followed if an evacuation occurs. This paragraph does not apply to a person who has been given a briefing before a previous leg of a flight in the same aircraft.

(c) The oral briefing required by paragraph (a) of this section shall be given by the pilot in command or a crewmember.

(d) Notwithstanding the provisions of paragraph (c) of this section, for aircraft certificated to carry 19 passengers or less, the oral briefing required by paragraph (a) of this section shall be given by the pilot in command, a crewmember, or other qualified person designated by the certificate holder and approved by the Administrator.

(e) The oral briefing required by paragraph (a) of this section must be supplemented by printed cards which must be carried in the aircraft in locations convenient for the use of each passenger. The cards must—

(1) Be appropriate for the aircraft on which they are to be used;

(2) Contain a diagram of, and method of operating, the emergency exits;

(3) Contain other instructions necessary for the use of emergency equipment on board the aircraft; and

(4) No later than June 12, 2005, for scheduled Commuter passenger-carrying flights, include

the sentence, "Final assembly of this aircraft was completed in [INSERT NAME OF COUNTRY]."

(f) The briefing required by paragraph (a) may be delivered by means of an approved recording playback device that is audible to each passenger under normal noise levels.

[Docket No. 16097, 43 FR 46783, Oct. 10, 1978; as amended by Amdt. 135–9, 51 FR 40709, Nov. 7, 1986; Amdt. 135–25, 53 FR 12362, Apr. 13, 1988; Amdt. 135–44, 57 FR 42675, Sept. 15, 1992; 57 FR 43776, Sept. 22, 1992; Amdt. 135–98, 69 FR 39294, June 29, 2004; Amdt. 135–98, 70 FR 36020, June 22, 2005; Amdt. 135–129, 79 FR 9973, Feb. 21, 2014]

§135.119 Prohibition against carriage of weapons.

No person may, while on board an aircraft being operated by a certificate holder, carry on or about that person a deadly or dangerous weapon, either concealed or unconcealed. This section does not apply to—

(a) Officials or employees of a municipality or a State, or of the United States, who are authorized to carry arms; or

(b) Crewmembers and other persons authorized by the certificate holder to carry arms.

§135.120 Prohibition on interference with crewmembers.

No person may assault, threaten, intimidate, or interfere with a crewmember in the performance of the crewmember's duties aboard an aircraft being operated under this part.

[Docket No. 16097, 43 FR 46783, Oct. 10, 1978; as amended by Amdt. 135–73, 64 FR 1080, Jan. 7, 1999]

§135.121 Alcoholic beverages.

(a) No person may drink any alcoholic beverage aboard an aircraft unless the certificate holder operating the aircraft has served that beverage.

(b) No certificate holder may serve any alcoholic beverage to any person aboard its aircraft if that person appears to be intoxicated.

(c) No certificate holder may allow any person to board any of its aircraft if that person appears to be intoxicated.

§135.122 Stowage of food, beverage, and passenger service equipment during aircraft movement on the surface, takeoff, and landing.

(a) No certificate holder may move an aircraft on the surface, takeoff, or land when any food, beverage, or tableware furnished by the certificate holder is located at any passenger seat.

(b) No certificate holder may move an aircraft on the surface, takeoff, or land unless each food and beverage tray and seat back tray table is secured in its stowed position.

(c) No certificate holder may permit an aircraft to move on surface, takeoff or land unless each passenger serving cart is secured in its stowed position.

(d) Each passenger shall comply with instructions given by a crewmember with regard to compliance with this section.

[Docket No. 26142, 57 FR 42675, Sept. 15, 1992]

§135.123 Emergency and emergency evacuation duties.

(a) Each certificate holder shall assign to each required crewmember for each type of aircraft as appropriate, the necessary functions to be performed in an emergency or in a situation requiring emergency evacuation. The certificate holder shall ensure that those functions can be practicably accomplished, and will meet any reasonably anticipated emergency including incapacitation of individual crewmembers or their inability to reach the passenger cabin because of shifting cargo in combination cargo-passenger aircraft.

(b) The certificate holder shall describe in the manual required under §135.21 the functions of each category of required crewmembers assigned under paragraph (a) of this section.

§135.125 Aircraft security.

Certificate holders conducting operations under this part must comply with the applicable security requirements in 49 CFR chapter XII.

[Docket No. TSA–2002–11602, 67 FR 8350, Feb. 22, 2002]

§135.127 Passenger information requirements and smoking prohibitions.

(a) No person may conduct a scheduled flight on which smoking is prohibited by part 252 of this title unless the "No Smoking" passenger information signs are lighted during the entire flight, or one or more "No Smoking" placards meeting the requirements of §25.1541 of this chapter are posted during the entire flight. If both the lighted signs and the placards are used, the signs must remain lighted during the entire flight segment.

(b) No person may smoke while a "No Smoking" sign is lighted or while "No Smoking" placards are posted, except as follows:

(1) *On-demand operations.* The pilot in command of an aircraft engaged in an on-demand operation may authorize smoking on the flight deck (if it is physically separated from any passenger compartment), except in any of the following situations:

§135.127

(i) During aircraft movement on the surface or during takeoff or landing;

(ii) During scheduled passenger-carrying public charter operations conducted under part 380 of this title;

(iii) During on-demand operations conducted interstate that meet paragraph (2) of the definition "On-demand operation" in §110.2 of this chapter, unless permitted under paragraph (b)(2) of this section; or

(iv) During any operation where smoking is prohibited by part 252 of this title or by international agreement.

(2) *Certain intrastate commuter operations and certain intrastate on-demand operations.* Except during aircraft movement on the surface or during takeoff or landing, a pilot in command of an aircraft engaged in a commuter operation or an on-demand operation that meets paragraph (2) of the definition of "On-demand operation" in §110.2 of this chapter may authorize smoking on the flight deck (if it is physically separated from the passenger compartment, if any) if—

(i) Smoking on the flight deck is not otherwise prohibited by part 252 of this title;

(ii) The flight is conducted entirely within the same State of the United States (a flight from one place in Hawaii to another place in Hawaii through the airspace over a place outside Hawaii is not entirely within the same State); and

(iii) The aircraft is either not turbojet-powered or the aircraft is not capable of carrying at least 30 passengers.

(c) No person may smoke in any aircraft lavatory.

(d) No person may operate an aircraft with a lavatory equipped with a smoke detector unless there is in that lavatory a sign or placard which reads: "Federal law provides for a penalty of up to $2,000 for tampering with the smoke detector installed in this lavatory."

(e) No person may tamper with, disable, or destroy any smoke detector installed in any aircraft lavatory.

(f) On flight segments other than those described in paragraph (a) of this section, the "No Smoking" sign required by §135.177(a)(3) of this part must be turned on during any movement of the aircraft on the surface, for each takeoff or landing, and at any other time considered necessary by the pilot in command.

(g) The passenger information requirements prescribed in §91.517(b) and (d) of this chapter are in addition to the requirements prescribed in this section.

(h) Each passenger shall comply with instructions given him or her by crewmembers regarding compliance with paragraphs (b), (c), and (e) of this section.

[Docket No. 25590, 55 FR 8367, March 7, 1990; as amended by Amdt. 135–35, 55 FR 20135, May 15, 1990; Amdt. 135–44, 57 FR 42675, Sept. 15, 1992; Amdt. 135–60, 61 FR 2616, Jan. 26, 1996; Amdt. 135–76, 65 FR 36780, June 9, 2000; Amdt. 135–124, 76 FR 7491, Feb. 10, 2011]

§135.128 Use of safety belts and child restraint systems.

(a) Except as provided in this paragraph, each person on board an aircraft operated under this part shall occupy an approved seat or berth with a separate safety belt properly secured about him or her during movement on the surface, takeoff and landing. For seaplane and float equipped rotorcraft operations during movement on the surface, the person pushing off the seaplane or rotorcraft from the dock and the person mooring the seaplane or rotorcraft at the dock are excepted from the preceding seating and safety belt requirements. A safety belt provided for the occupant of a seat may not be used by more than one person who has reached his or her second birthday. Not withstanding the preceding requirements, a child may:

(1) Be held by an adult who is occupying an approved seat or berth, provided the child has not reached his or her second birthday and the child does not occupy or use any restraining device; or

(2) Notwithstanding any other requirement of this chapter, occupy an approved child restraint system furnished by the certificate holder or one of the persons described in paragraph (a)(2)(i) of this section, provided:

(i) The child is accompanied by a parent, guardian, or attendant designated by the child's parent or guardian to attend to the safety of the child during flight;

(ii) Except as provided in paragraph (a)(2)(ii)(D) of this section, the approved child restraint system bears one or more labels as follows:

(A) Seats manufactured to U.S. standards between January 1, 1981, and February 25, 1985, must bear the label: "This child restraint system conforms to all applicable Federal motor vehicle safety standards";

(B) Seats manufactured to U.S. standards on or after February 26, 1985, must bear two labels:

(1) "This child restraint system conforms to all applicable Federal motor vehicle safety standards"; and

(2) "THIS RESTRAINT IS CERTIFIED FOR USE IN MOTOR VEHICLES AND AIRCRAFT" in red lettering;

(C) Seats that do not qualify under paragraphs (a)(2)(ii)(A) and (a)(2)(ii)(B) of this section must bear a label or markings showing:

(1) That the seat was approved by a foreign government;

(2) That the seat was manufactured under the standards of the United Nations;

(3) That the seat or child restraint device furnished by the certificate holder was approved by the FAA through Type Certificate or Supplemental Type Certificate; or

(4) That the seat or child restraint device furnished by the certificate holder, or one of the persons described in paragraph (a)(2)(i) of this section, was approved by the FAA in accordance with §21.8(d) of this chapter or Technical Standard Order C-100b, or a later version. The child restraint device manufactured by AmSafe, Inc. (CARES, Part No. 4082) and approved by the FAA in accordance with §21.305(d) (2010 ed.) of this chapter may continue to bear a label or markings showing FAA approval in accordance with §21.305(d) (2010 ed.) of this chapter.

(D) Except as provided in §135.128 (a)(2)(ii)(C)(3) and §135.128(a)(2)(ii)(C)(4), booster-type child restraint systems (as defined in Federal Motor Vehicle Safety Standard No. 213 (49 CFR 571.213)), vest- and harness-type child restraint systems, and lap held child restraints are not approved for use in aircraft; and

(iii) The certificate holder complies with the following requirements:

(A) The restraint system must be properly secured to an approved forward-facing seat or berth;

(B) The child must be properly secured in the restraint system and must not exceed the specified weight limit for the restraint system; and

(C) The restraint system must bear the appropriate label(s).

(b) Except as provided in paragraph (b)(3) of this section, the following prohibitions apply to certificate holders:

(1) Except as provided in §135.128(a)(2)(ii)(C)(3) and §135.128(a)(2)(ii)(C)(4), no certificate holder may permit a child, in an aircraft, to occupy a booster-type child restraint system, a vest-type child restraint system, a harness-type child restraint system, or a lap held child restraint system during take off, landing, and movement on the surface.

(2) Except as required in paragraph (b)(1) of this section, no certificate holder may prohibit a child, if requested by the child's parent, guardian, or designated attendant, from occupying a child restraint system furnished by the child's parent, guardian, or designated attendant provided:

(i) The child holds a ticket for an approved seat or berth or such seat or berth is otherwise made available by the certificate holder for the child's use;

(ii) The requirements of paragraph (a)(2)(i) of this section are met;

(iii) The requirements of paragraph (a)(2)(iii) of this section are met; and

(iv) The child restraint system has one or more of the labels described in paragraphs (a)(2)(ii)(A) through (a)(2)(ii)(C) of this section.

(3) This section does not prohibit the certificate holder from providing child restraint systems authorized by this or, consistent with safe operating practices, determining the most appropriate passenger seat location for the child restraint system.

[Docket No. 26142, 57 FR 42676, Sept. 15, 1992; as amended by Amdt. 135–62, 61 FR 28422, June 4, 1996; Amdt. 135–100, 70 FR 50907, Aug. 26, 2005; Amdt. 135–106, 71 FR 59374, Oct. 10, 2006; Amdt. 135–130, 79 FR 28812, May 20, 2014]

§135.129 Exit seating.

(a)(1) *Applicability.* This section applies to all certificate holders operating under this part, except for on-demand operations with aircraft having 19 or fewer passenger seats and commuter operations with aircraft having 9 or fewer passenger seats.

(2) *Duty to make determination of suitability.* Each certificate holder shall determine, to the extent necessary to perform the applicable functions of paragraph (d) of this section, the suitability of each person it permits to occupy an exit seat. For the purpose of this section—

(i) Exit seat means—

(A) Each seat having direct access to an exit; and

(B) Each seat in a row of seats through which passengers would have to pass to gain access to an exit, from the first seat inboard of the exit to the first aisle inboard of the exit.

(ii) A passenger seat having *direct access* means a seat from which a passenger can proceed directly to the exit without entering an aisle or passing around an obstruction.

(3) *Persons designated to make determination.* Each certificate holder shall make the passenger exit seating determinations required by this paragraph in a non-discriminatory manner consistent with the requirements of this section, by persons designated in the certificate holder's required operations manual.

(4) *Submission of designation for approval.* Each certificate holder shall designate the exit seats for each passenger seating configuration in its fleet in accordance with the definitions in this paragraph and submit those designations for approval as part of the procedures required to be submitted for approval under paragraphs (n) and (p) of this section.

(b) No certificate holder may seat a person in a seat affected by this section if the certificate holder determines that it is likely that the person would be unable to perform one or more of the applicable functions listed in paragraph (d) of this section because—

(1) The person lacks sufficient mobility, strength, or dexterity in both arms and hands, and both legs:

(i) To reach upward, sideways, and downward to the location of emergency exit and exit-slide operating mechanisms;

(ii) To grasp and push, pull, turn, or otherwise manipulate those mechanisms;

(iii) To push, shove, pull, or otherwise open emergency exits;

(iv) To lift out, hold, deposit on nearby seats, or maneuver over the seatbacks to the next row objects the size and weight of over-wing window exit doors;

(v) To remove obstructions of size and weight similar over-wing exit doors;

(vi) To reach the emergency exit expeditiously;

(vii) To maintain balance while removing obstructions;

(viii) To exit expeditiously;

(ix) To stabilize an escape slide after deployment; or

(x) To assist others in getting off an escape slide;

(2) The person is less than 15 years of age or lacks the capacity to perform one or more of the applicable functions listed in paragraph (d) of this section without the assistance of an adult companion, parent, or other relative;

(3) The person lacks the ability to read and understand instructions required by this section and related to emergency evacuation provided by the certificate holder in printed or graphic form or the ability to understand oral crew commands.

(4) The person lacks sufficient visual capacity to perform one or more of the applicable functions in paragraph (d) of this section without the assistance of visual aids beyond contact lenses or eyeglasses;

(5) The person lacks sufficient aural capacity to hear and understand instructions shouted by flight attendants, without assistance beyond a hearing aid;

(6) The person lacks the ability adequately to impart information orally to other passengers; or,

(7) The person has:

(i) A condition or responsibilities, such as caring for small children, that might prevent the person from performing one or more of the applicable functions listed in paragraph (d) of this section; or

(ii) A condition that might cause the person harm if he or she performs one or more of the applicable functions listed in paragraph (d) of this section.

(c) Each passenger shall comply with instructions given by a crewmember or other authorized employee of the certificate holder implementing exit seating restrictions established in accordance with this section.

(d) Each certificate holder shall include on passenger information cards, presented in the languages in which briefings and oral commands are given by the crew, at each exit seat affected by this section, information that, in the event of an emergency in which a crewmember is not available to assist, a passenger occupying an exit row seat may use if called upon to perform the following functions:

(1) Locate the emergency exit;

(2) Recognize the emergency exit opening mechanism;

(3) Comprehend the instructions for operating the emergency exit;

(4) Operate the emergency exit;

(5) Assess whether opening the emergency exit will increase the hazards to which passengers may be exposed;

(6) Follow oral directions and hand signals given by a crewmember;

(7) Stow or secure the emergency exit door so that it will not impede use of the exit;

(8) Assess the condition of an escape slide, activate the slide, and stabilize the slide after deployment to assist others in getting off the slide;

(9) Pass expeditiously through the emergency exit; and

(10) Assess, select, and follow a safe path away from the emergency exit.

(e) Each certificate holder shall include on passenger information cards, at each exit seat—

(1) In the primary language in which emergency commands are given by the crew, the selection criteria set forth in paragraph (b) of this section, and a request that a passenger identify himself or herself to allow reseating if he or she—

(i) Cannot meet the selection criteria set forth in paragraph (b) of this section;

(ii) Has a nondiscernible condition that will prevent him or her from performing the applicable functions listed in paragraph (d) of this section;

(iii) May suffer bodily harm as the result of performing one or more of those functions; or,

(iv) Does not wish to perform those functions; and,

(2) In each language used by the certificate holder for passenger information cards, a request that a passenger identify himself or herself to allow reseating if he or she lacks the ability to read, speak, or understand the language or the graphic form in which instructions required by this section and related to emergency evacuation are provided by the certificate holder, or the ability to understand the specified language in which crew commands will be given in an emergency;

(3) May suffer bodily harm as the result of performing one or more of those functions; or,

(4) Does not wish to perform those functions.

A certificate holder shall not require the passenger to disclose his or her reason for needing reseating.

(f) Each certificate holder shall make available for inspection by the public at all passenger loading gates and ticket counters at each airport where it conducts passenger operations, written procedures established for making determinations in regard to exit row seating.

(g) No certificate holder may allow taxi or pushback unless at least one required crewmember has verified that no exit row seat is occupied by a person the crewmember determines is likely to be unable to perform the applicable functions listed in paragraph (d) of this section.

(h) Each certificate holder shall include in its passenger briefings a reference to the passenger information cards, required by paragraphs (d) and (e), the selection criteria set forth in paragraph (b), and the functions to be performed, set forth in paragraph (d) of this section.

(i) Each certificate holder shall include in its passenger briefings a request that a passenger identify himself or herself to allow reseating if he or she—

(1) Cannot meet the selection criteria set forth in paragraph (b) of this section;

(2) Has a nondiscernible condition that will prevent him or her from performing the applicable functions listed in paragraph (d) of this section;

(3) May suffer bodily harm as the result of performing one or more of those functions; or,

(4) Does not wish to perform those functions. A certificate holder shall not require the passenger to disclose his or her reason for needing reseating.

(j) [Reserved]

(k) In the event a certificate holder determines in accordance with this section that it is likely that a passenger assigned to an exit row seat would be unable to perform the functions listed in paragraph (d) of this section or a passenger requests a non-exit seat, the certificate holder shall expeditiously relocate the passenger to a non-exit seat.

(l) In the event of full booking in the non-exit seats, and if necessary to accommodate a passenger being relocated from an exit seat, the certificate holder shall move a passenger who is willing and able to assume the evacuation functions that may be required, to an exit seat.

(m) A certificate holder may deny transportation to any passenger under this section only because—

(1) The passenger refuses to comply with instructions given by a crewmember or other authorized employee of the certificate holder implementing exit seating restrictions established in accordance with this section, or

(2) The only seat that will physically accommodate the person's handicap is an exit seat.

(n) In order to comply with this section certificate holders shall—

(1) Establish procedures that address:

(i) The criteria listed in paragraph (b) of this section;

(ii) The functions listed in paragraph (d) of this section;

(iii) The requirements for airport information, passenger information cards, crewmember verification of appropriate seating in exit rows, passenger briefings, seat assignments, and denial of transportation as set forth in this section;

(iv) How to resolve disputes arising from implementation of this section, including identification of the certificate holder employee on the airport to whom complaints should be addressed for resolution; and,

(2) Submit their procedures for preliminary review and approval to the principal operations inspectors assigned to them at the certificate-holding district office.

(o) Certificate holders shall assign seats prior to boarding consistent with the criteria listed in paragraph (b) and the functions listed in paragraph (d) of this section, to the maximum extent feasible.

(p) The procedures required by paragraph (n) of this section will not become effective until final approval is granted by the Director, Flight Standards Service, Washington, DC. Approval will be based solely upon the safety aspects of the certificate holder's procedures.

[Docket No. 25821, 55 FR 8073, March 6, 1990; as amended by Amdt. 135–45, 57 FR 48664, Oct. 27, 1992; Amdt. 135–50, 59 FR 33603, June 29, 1994; Amdt. 135–60, 61 FR 2616, Jan. 26, 1996]

Subpart C— Aircraft and Equipment

§135.141 Applicability.

This subpart prescribes aircraft and equipment requirements for operations under this part. The requirements of this subpart are in addition to the aircraft and equipment requirements of part 91 of this chapter. However, this part does not require the duplication of any equipment required by this chapter.

§135.143 General requirements.

(a) No person may operate an aircraft under this part unless that aircraft and its equipment meet the applicable regulations of this chapter.

(b) Except as provided in §135.179, no person may operate an aircraft under this part unless the required instruments and equipment in it have been approved and are in an operable condition.

(c) ATC transponder equipment installed within the time periods indicated below must meet the performance and environmental requirements of the following TSOs:

(1) *Through January 1, 1992:*

(i) Any class of TSO-C74b or any class of TSO-C74c as appropriate, provided that the equipment was manufactured before January 1, 1990; or

(ii) The appropriate class of TSO-C112 (Mode S).

(2) *After January 1, 1992:* The appropriate class of TSO-C112 (Mode S). For purposes of paragraph (c)(2) of this section, "installation" does not include—

(i) Temporary installation of TSO-C74b or TSO-C74c substitute equipment, as appropriate, during maintenance of the permanent equipment;

(ii) Reinstallation of equipment after temporary removal for maintenance; or

(iii) For fleet operations, installation of equipment in a fleet aircraft after removal of the equipment for maintenance from another aircraft in the same operator's fleet.

[Docket No. 16097, 43 FR 46783, Oct. 10, 1978; as amended by Amdt. 135–22, 52 FR 3392, Feb. 3, 1987]

§135.144 Portable electronic devices.

(a) Except as provided in paragraph (b) of this section, no person may operate, nor may any operator or pilot in command of an aircraft allow the operation of, any portable electronic device on any of the following U.S.-registered civil aircraft operating under this part.

(b) Paragraph (a) of this section does not apply to—

(1) Portable voice recorders;

(2) Hearing aids;

(3) Heart pacemakers;

(4) Electric shavers; or

(5) Any other portable electronic device that the part 119 certificate holder has determined will not cause interference with the navigation or communication system of the aircraft on which it is to be used.

(c) The determination required by paragraph (b)(5) of this section shall be made by that part 119 certificate holder operating the aircraft on which the particular device is to be used.

[Docket No. 16097, 43 FR 46783, Oct. 10, 1978; as amended by Amdt. 135–73, 64 FR 1080, Jan. 7, 1999]

§135.145 Aircraft proving and validation tests.

(a) No certificate holder may operate an aircraft, other than a turbojet aircraft, for which two pilots are required by this chapter for operations under VFR, if it has not previously proved such an aircraft in operations under this part in at least 25 hours of proving tests acceptable to the Administrator including—

(1) Five hours of night time, if night flights are to be authorized;

(2) Five instrument approach procedures under simulated or actual conditions, if IFR flights are to be authorized; and

(3) Entry into a representative number of en route airports as determined by the Administrator.

(b) No certificate holder may operate a turbojet airplane if it has not previously proved a turbojet airplane in operations under this part in at least 25 hours of proving tests acceptable to the Administrator including—

(1) Five hours of night time, if night flights are to be authorized;

(2) Five instrument approach procedures under simulated or actual conditions, if IFR flights are to be authorized; and

(3) Entry into a representative number of en route airports as determined by the Administrator.

(c) No certificate holder may carry passengers in an aircraft during proving tests, except those needed to make the tests and those designated by the Administrator to observe the tests. However, pilot flight training may be conducted during the proving tests.

(d) Validation testing is required to determine that a certificate holder is capable of conducting operations safely and in compliance with applicable regulatory standards. Validation tests are required for the following authorizations:

(1) The addition of an aircraft for which two pilots are required for operations under VFR or a turbojet airplane, if that aircraft or an aircraft of the same make or similar design has not been previously proved or validated in operations under this part.

(2) Operations outside U.S. airspace.

(3) Class II navigation authorizations.

(4) Special performance or operational authorizations.

(e) Validation tests must be accomplished by test methods acceptable to the Administrator. Actual flights may not be required when an applicant can demonstrate competence and compliance with appropriate regulations without conducting a flight.

(f) Proving tests and validation tests may be conducted simultaneously when appropriate.

(g) The Administrator may authorize deviations from this section if the Administrator finds that special circumstances make full compliance with this section unnecessary.

[Docket No. FAA–2001–10047, 68 FR 54586, Sept. 17, 2003]

§135.147 Dual controls required.

No person may operate an aircraft in operations requiring two pilots unless it is equipped with functioning dual controls. However, if the aircraft type certification operating limitations do not require two pilots, a throwover control wheel may be used in place of two control wheels.

Part 135: Commuter & On Demand Operations §135.151

§135.149 Equipment requirements: General.

No person may operate an aircraft unless it is equipped with—

(a) A sensitive altimeter that is adjustable for barometric pressure;

(b) Heating or deicing equipment for each carburetor or, for a pressure carburetor, an alternate air source;

(c) For turbojet airplanes, in addition to two gyroscopic bank-and-pitch indicators (artificial horizons) for use at the pilot stations, a third indicator that is installed in accordance with the instrument requirements prescribed in §121.305(j) of this chapter.

(d) [Reserved]

(e) For turbine powered aircraft, any other equipment as the Administrator may require.

[Docket No. 16097, 43 FR 46783, Oct. 10, 1978; as amended by Amdt. 135–1, 44 FR 26537, May 7, 1979; Amdt. 135–34, 54 FR 43926, Oct. 27, 1989; Amdt. 135–38, 55 FR 43310, Oct. 26, 1990]

§135.150 Public address and crewmember interphone systems.

No person may operate an aircraft having a passenger seating configuration, excluding any pilot seat, of more than 19 unless it is equipped with—

(a) A public address system which—

(1) Is capable of operation independent of the crewmember interphone system required by paragraph (b) of this section, except for handsets, headsets, microphones, selector switches, and signaling devices;

(2) Is approved in accordance with §21.305 of this chapter;

(3) Is accessible for immediate use from each of two flight crewmember stations in the pilot compartment;

(4) For each required floor-level passenger emergency exit which has an adjacent flight attendant seat, has a microphone which is readily accessible to the seated flight attendant, except that one microphone may serve more than one exit, provided the proximity of the exits allows unassisted verbal communication between seated flight attendants;

(5) Is capable of operation within 10 seconds by a flight attendant at each of those stations in the passenger compartment from which its use is accessible;

(6) Is audible at all passenger seats, lavatories, and flight attendant seats and work stations; and

(7) For transport category airplanes manufactured on or after November 27, 1990, meets the requirements of §25.1423 of this chapter.

(b) A crewmember interphone system which—

(1) Is capable of operation independent of the public address system required by paragraph (a) of this section, except for handsets, headsets, microphones, selector switches, and signaling devices;

(2) Is approved in accordance with §21.305 of this chapter;

(3) Provides a means of two-way communication between the pilot compartment and—

(i) Each passenger compartment; and

(ii) Each galley located on other than the main passenger deck level;

(4) Is accessible for immediate use from each of two flight crewmember stations in the pilot compartment;

(5) Is accessible for use from at least one normal flight attendant station in each passenger compartment;

(6) Is capable of operation within 10 seconds by a flight attendant at each of those stations in each passenger compartment from which its use is accessible; and

(7) For large turbojet-powered airplanes—

(i) Is accessible for use at enough flight attendant stations so that all floor-level emergency exits (or entryways to those exits in the case of exits located within galleys) in each passenger compartment are observable from one or more of those stations so equipped;

(ii) Has an alerting system incorporating aural or visual signals for use by flight crewmembers to alert flight attendants and for use by flight attendants to alert flight crewmembers;

(iii) For the alerting system required by paragraph (b)(7)(ii) of this section, has a means for the recipient of a call to determine whether it is a normal call or an emergency call; and

(iv) When the airplane is on the ground, provides a means of two-way communication between ground personnel and either of at least two flight crewmembers in the pilot compartment. The interphone system station for use by ground personnel must be so located that personnel using the system may avoid visible detection from within the airplane.

[Docket No. 24995, 54 FR 43926, Oct. 27, 1989]

§135.151 Cockpit voice recorders.

(a) No person may operate a multiengine, turbine-powered airplane or rotorcraft having a passenger seating configuration of six or more and for which two pilots are required by certification or operating rules unless it is equipped with an approved cockpit voice recorder that:

(1) Is installed in compliance with §23.1457(a)(1) and (2), (b), (c), (d)(1)(i), (2) and (3), (e), (f), and (g); §25.1457(a)(1) and (2), (b), (c), (d)(1)(i), (2) and (3), (e), (f), and (g); §27.1457(a)(1) and (2), (b), (c), (d)(1)(i), (2) and (3), (e), (f), and (g);

§135.151

or §29.1457(a)(1) and (2), (b), (c), (d)(1)(i), (2) and (3), (e), (f), and (g) of this chapter, as applicable; and

(2) Is operated continuously from the use of the checklist before the flight to completion of the final checklist at the end of the flight.

(b) No person may operate a multiengine, turbine-powered airplane or rotorcraft having a passenger seating configuration of 20 or more seats unless it is equipped with an approved cockpit voice recorder that—

(1) Is installed in accordance with the requirements of §23.1457 (except paragraphs (a)(6), (d)(1)(ii), (4), and (5)); §25.1457 (except paragraphs (a)(6), (d)(1)(ii), (4), and (5)); §27.1457 (except paragraphs (a)(6), (d)(1)(ii), (4), and (5)); or §29.1457 (except paragraphs (a)(6), (d)(1)(ii), (4), and (5)) of this chapter, as applicable; and

(2) Is operated continuously from the use of the check list before the flight to completion of the final check list at the end of the flight.

(c) In the event of an accident, or occurrence requiring immediate notification of the National Transportation Safety Board which results in termination of the flight, the certificate holder shall keep the recorded information for at least 60 days or, if requested by the Administrator or the Board, for a longer period. Information obtained from the record may be used to assist in determining the cause of accidents or occurrences in connection with investigations. The Administrator does not use the record in any civil penalty or certificate action.

(d) For those aircraft equipped to record the uninterrupted audio signals received by a boom or a mask microphone the flight crewmembers are required to use the boom microphone below 18,000 feet mean sea level. No person may operate a large turbine engine powered airplane manufactured after October 11, 1991, or on which a cockpit voice recorder has been installed after October 11, 1991, unless it is equipped to record the uninterrupted audio signal received by a boom or mask microphone in accordance with §25.1457(c)(5) of this chapter.

(e) In complying with this section, an approved cockpit voice recorder having an erasure feature may be used, so that during the operation of the recorder, information:

(1) Recorded in accordance with paragraph (a) of this section and recorded more than 15 minutes earlier; or

(2) Recorded in accordance with paragraph (b) of this section and recorded more than 30 minutes earlier; may be erased or otherwise obliterated.

(f) By April 7, 2012, all airplanes subject to paragraph (a) or paragraph (b) of this section that are manufactured before April 7, 2010, and that are required to have a flight data recorder installed in accordance with §135.152, must have a cockpit voice recorder that also—

(1) Meets the requirements in §23.1457(d)(6) or §25.1457(d)(6) of this chapter, as applicable; and

(2) If transport category, meet the requirements in §25.1457(a)(3), (a)(4), and (a)(5) of this chapter.

(g)(1) No person may operate a multiengine, turbine-powered airplane or rotorcraft that is manufactured on or after April 7, 2010, that has a passenger seating configuration of six or more seats, for which two pilots are required by certification or operating rules, and that is required to have a flight data recorder under §135.152, unless it is equipped with an approved cockpit voice recorder that also—

(i) Is installed in accordance with the requirements of §23.1457 (except for paragraph (a)(6)); §25.1457 (except for paragraph (a)(6)); §27.1457 (except for paragraph (a)(6)); or §29.1457 (except for paragraph (a)(6)) of this chapter, as applicable; and

(ii) Is operated continuously from the use of the check list before the flight, to completion of the final check list at the end of the flight; and

(iii) Retains at least the last 2 hours of recorded information using a recorder that meets the standards of TSO-C123a, or later revision.

(iv) For all airplanes or rotorcraft manufactured on or after December 6, 2010, also meets the requirements of §23.1457(a)(6); §25.1457(a)(6); §27.1457(a)(6); or §29.1457(a)(6) of this chapter, as applicable.

(2) No person may operate a multiengine, turbine-powered airplane or rotorcraft that is manufactured on or after April 7, 2010, has a passenger seating configuration of 20 or more seats, and that is required to have a flight data recorder under §135.152, unless it is equipped with an approved cockpit voice recorder that also

(i) Is installed in accordance with the requirements of §23.1457 (except for paragraph (a)(6)); §25.1457 (except for paragraph (a)(6)); §27.1457 (except for paragraph (a)(6)); or §29.1457 (except for paragraph (a)(6)) of this chapter, as applicable; and

(ii) Is operated continuously from the use of the check list before the flight, to completion of the final check list at the end of the flight; and

(iii) Retains at least the last 2 hours of recorded information using a recorder that meets the standards of TSO-C123a, or later revision.

(iv) For all airplanes or rotorcraft manufactured on or after December 6, 2010, also meets the requirements of §23.1457(a)(6); §25.1457(a)(6); §27.1457(a)(6); or §29.1457(a)(6) of this chapter, as applicable.

(h) All airplanes or rotorcraft required by this part to have a cockpit voice recorder and a flight data recorder, that install datalink communication

Part 135: Commuter & On Demand Operations §135.152

equipment on or after December 6, 2010, must record all datalink messages as required by the certification rule applicable to the aircraft.

[Docket No. 16097, 43 FR 46783, Oct. 10, 1978; as amended by Amdt. 135–23, 52 FR 9637, March 25, 1987; Amdt. 135–26, 53 FR 26151, July 11, 1988; Amdt. 135–60, 61 FR 2616, Jan. 26, 1996; Amdt. 135–113, 73 FR 12570, March 7, 2008; Amdt. 135–113, 74 FR 32801, July 9, 2009; Amdt. 135–121, 75 FR 17346, April 5, 2010]

§135.152 Flight data recorders.

(a) Except as provided in paragraph (k) of this section, no person may operate under this part a multi-engine, turbine-engine powered airplane or rotorcraft having a passenger seating configuration, excluding any required crewmember seat, of 10 to 19 seats, that was either brought onto the U.S. register after, or was registered outside the United States and added to the operator's U.S. operations specifications after, October 11, 1991, unless it is equipped with one or more approved flight recorders that use a digital method of recording and storing data and a method of readily retrieving that data from the storage medium. The parameters specified in either Appendix B or C of this part, as applicable must be recorded within the range, accuracy, resolution, and recording intervals as specified. The recorder shall retain no less than 25 hours of aircraft operation.

(b) After October 11, 1991, no person may operate a multiengine, turbine-powered airplane having a passenger seating configuration of 20 to 30 seats or a multiengine, turbine-powered rotorcraft having a passenger seating configuration of 20 or more seats unless it is equipped with one or more approved flight recorders that utilize a digital method of recording and storing data, and a method of readily retrieving that data from the storage medium. The parameters in Appendix D or E of this part, as applicable, that are set forth below, must be recorded within the ranges, accuracies, resolutions, and sampling intervals as specified.

(1) Except as provided in paragraph (b)(3) of this section for aircraft type certificated before October 1, 1969, the following parameters must be recorded:
 (i) Time;
 (ii) Altitude;
 (iii) Airspeed;
 (iv) Vertical acceleration;
 (v) Heading;
 (vi) Time of each radio transmission to or from air traffic control;
 (vii) Pitch attitude;
 (viii) Roll attitude;
 (ix) Longitudinal acceleration;
 (x) Control column or pitch control surface position; and
 (xi) Thrust of each engine.

(2) Except as provided in paragraph (b)(3) of this section for aircraft type certificated after September 30, 1969, the following parameters must be recorded:
 (i) Time;
 (ii) Altitude;
 (iii) Airspeed;
 (iv) Vertical acceleration;
 (v) Heading;
 (vi) Time of each radio transmission either to or from air traffic control;
 (vii) Pitch attitude;
 (viii) Roll attitude;
 (ix) Longitudinal acceleration;
 (x) Pitch trim position;
 (xi) Control column or pitch control surface position;
 (xii) Control wheel or lateral control surface position;
 (xiii) Rudder pedal or yaw control surface position;
 (xiv) Thrust of each engine;
 (xv) Position of each thrust reverser;
 (xvi) Trailing edge flap or cockpit flap control position; and
 (xvii) Leading edge flap or cockpit flap control position.

(3) For aircraft manufactured after October 11, 1991, all of the parameters listed in Appendix D or E of this part, as applicable, must be recorded.

(c) Whenever a flight recorder required by this section is installed, it must be operated continuously from the instant the airplane begins the takeoff roll or the rotorcraft begins the lift-off until the airplane has completed the landing roll or the rotorcraft has landed at its destination.

(d) Except as provided in paragraph (c) of this section, and except for recorded data erased as authorized in this paragraph, each certificate holder shall keep the recorded data prescribed in paragraph (a) of this section until the aircraft has been operating for at least 25 hours of the operating time specified in paragraph (c) of this section. In addition, each certificate holder shall keep the recorded data prescribed in paragraph (b) of this section for an airplane until the airplane has been operating for at least 25 hours, and for a rotorcraft until the rotorcraft has been operating for at least 10 hours, of the operating time specified in paragraph (c) of this section. A total of 1 hour of recorded data may be erased for the purpose of testing the flight recorder or the flight recorder system. Any erasure made in accordance with this paragraph must be of the oldest recorded data accumulated at the time of testing. Except as provided in paragraph (c) of this section, no record need be kept more than 60 days.

(e) In the event of an accident or occurrence that requires the immediate notification of the National Transportation Safety Board under 49 CFR

§135.152

part 830 of its regulations and that results in termination of the flight, the certificate holder shall remove the recording media from the aircraft and keep the recorded data required by paragraphs (a) and (b) of this section for at least 60 days or for a longer period upon request of the Board or the Administrator.

(f)(1) For airplanes manufactured on or before August 18, 2000, and all other aircraft, each flight recorder required by this section must be installed in accordance with the requirements of §23.1459 (except paragraphs (a)(3)(ii) and (6)), §25.1459 (except paragraphs (a)(3)(ii) and (7)), §27.1459 (except paragraphs (a)(3)(ii) and (6)), or §29.1459 (except paragraphs (a)(3)(ii) and (6)), as appropriate, of this chapter. The correlation required by paragraph (c) of §§23.1459, 25.1459, 27.1459, or 29.1459 of this chapter, as appropriate, need be established only on one aircraft of a group of aircraft:

(i) That are of the same type;

(ii) On which the flight recorder models and their installations are the same; and

(iii) On which there are no differences in the type designs with respect to the installation of the first pilot's instruments associated with the flight recorder. The most recent instrument calibration, including the recording medium from which this calibration is derived, and the recorder correlation must be retained by the certificate holder.

(2) For airplanes manufactured after August 18, 2000, each flight data recorder system required by this section must be installed in accordance with the requirements of §23.1459(a) (except paragraphs (a)(3)(ii) and (6)), (b), (d) and (e), or §25.1459(a) (except paragraphs (a)(3)(ii) and (7)), (b), (d) and (e) of this chapter. A correlation must be established between the values recorded by the flight data recorder and the corresponding values being measured. The correlation must contain a sufficient number of correlation points to accurately establish the conversion from the recorded values to engineering units or discrete state over the full operating range of the parameter. Except for airplanes having separate altitude and airspeed sensors that are an integral part of the flight data recorder system, a single correlation may be established for any group of airplanes—

(i) That are of the same type;

(ii) On which the flight recorder system and its installation are the same; and

(iii) On which there is no difference in the type design with respect to the installation of those sensors associated with the flight data recorder system. Documentation sufficient to convert recorded data into the engineering units and discrete values specified in the applicable appendix must be maintained by the certificate holder.

(g) Each flight recorder required by this section that records the data specified in paragraphs (a) and (b) of this section must have an approved device to assist in locating that recorder under water.

(h) The operational parameters required to be recorded by digital flight data recorders required by paragraphs (i) and (j) of this section are as follows, the phrase "when an information source is installed" following a parameter indicates that recording of that parameter is not intended to require a change in installed equipment.

(1) Time;

(2) Pressure altitude;

(3) Indicated airspeed;

(4) Heading—primary flight crew reference (if selectable, record discrete, true or magnetic);

(5) Normal acceleration (Vertical);

(6) Pitch attitude;

(7) Roll attitude;

(8) Manual radio transmitter keying, or CVR/DFDR synchronization reference;

(9) Thrust/power of each engine—primary flight crew reference;

(10) Autopilot engagement status;

(11) Longitudinal acceleration;

(12) Pitch control input;

(13) Lateral control input;

(14) Rudder pedal input;

(15) Primary pitch control surface position;

(16) Primary lateral control surface position;

(17) Primary yaw control surface position;

(18) Lateral acceleration;

(19) Pitch trim surface position or parameters of paragraph (h)(82) of this section if currently recorded;

(20) Trailing edge flap or cockpit flap control selection (except when parameters of paragraph (h)(85) of this section apply);

(21) Leading edge flap or cockpit flap control selection (except when parameters of paragraph (h)(86) of this section apply);

(22) Each Thrust reverser position (or equivalent for propeller airplane);

(23) Ground spoiler position or speed brake selection (except when parameters of paragraph (h)(87) of this section apply);

(24) Outside or total air temperature;

(25) Automatic Flight Control System (AFCS) modes and engagement status, including autothrottle;

(26) Radio altitude (when an information source is installed);

(27) Localizer deviation, MLS Azimuth;

(28) Glideslope deviation, MLS Elevation;

(29) Marker beacon passage;

(30) Master warning;

(31) Air/ground sensor (primary airplane system reference nose or main gear);

Part 135: Commuter & On Demand Operations §135.152

(32) Angle of attack (when information source is installed);
(33) Hydraulic pressure low (each system);
(34) Ground speed (when an information source is installed);
(35) Ground proximity warning system;
(36) Landing gear position or landing gear cockpit control selection;
(37) Drift angle (when an information source is installed);
(38) Wind speed and direction (when an information source is installed);
(39) Latitude and longitude (when an information source is installed);
(40) Stick shaker/pusher (when an information source is installed);
(41) Windshear (when an information source is installed);
(42) Throttle/power lever position;
(43) Additional engine parameters (as designated in Appendix F of this part);
(44) Traffic alert and collision avoidance system;
(45) DME 1 and 2 distances;
(46) Nav 1 and 2 selected frequency;
(47) Selected barometric setting (when an information source is installed);
(48) Selected altitude (when an information source is installed);
(49) Selected speed (when an information source is installed);
(50) Selected mach (when an information source is installed);
(51) Selected vertical speed (when an information source is installed);
(52) Selected heading (when an information source is installed);
(53) Selected flight path (when an information source is installed);
(54) Selected decision height (when an information source is installed);
(55) EFIS display format;
(56) Multi-function/engine/alerts display format;
(57) Thrust command (when an information source is installed);
(58) Thrust target (when an information source is installed);
(59) Fuel quantity in CG trim tank (when an information source is installed);
(60) Primary Navigation System Reference;
(61) Icing (when an information source is installed);
(62) Engine warning each engine vibration (when an information source is installed);
(63) Engine warning each engine over temp. (when an information source is installed);
(64) Engine warning each engine oil pressure low (when an information source is installed);
(65) Engine warning each engine over speed (when an information source is installed;
(66) Yaw trim surface position;
(67) Roll trim surface position;
(68) Brake pressure (selected system);
(69) Brake pedal application (left and right);
(70) Yaw or sideslip angle (when an information source is installed);
(71) Engine bleed valve position (when an information source is installed);
(72) De-icing or anti-icing system selection (when an information source is installed);
(73) Computed center of gravity (when an information source is installed);
(74) AC electrical bus status;
(75) DC electrical bus status;
(76) APU bleed valve position (when an information source is installed);
(77) Hydraulic pressure (each system);
(78) Loss of cabin pressure;
(79) Computer failure;
(80) Heads-up display (when an information source is installed);
(81) Para-visual display (when an information source is installed);
(82) Cockpit trim control input position—pitch;
(83) Cockpit trim control input position—roll;
(84) Cockpit trim control input position—yaw;
(85) Trailing edge flap and cockpit flap control position;
(86) Leading edge flap and cockpit flap control position;
(87) Ground spoiler position and speed brake selection; and
(88) All cockpit flight control input forces (control wheel, control column, rudder pedal).

(i) For all turbine-engine powered airplanes with a seating configuration, excluding any required crewmember seat, of 10 to 30 passenger seats, manufactured after August 18, 2000—

(1) The parameters listed in paragraphs (h)(1) through (h)(57) of this section must be recorded within the ranges, accuracies, resolutions, and recording intervals specified in Appendix F of this part.

(2) Commensurate with the capacity of the recording system, all additional parameters for which information sources are installed and which are connected to the recording system must be recorded within the ranges, accuracies, resolutions, and sampling intervals specified in Appendix F of this part.

(j) For all turbine-engine-powered airplanes with a seating configuration, excluding any required crewmember seat, of 10 to 30 passenger seats, that are manufactured after August 19, 2002 the parameters listed in paragraph (a)(1) through (a)(88) of this section must be recorded within the ranges, accuracies, resolutions, and re-

§135.154

cording intervals specified in Appendix F of this part.

(k) For aircraft manufactured before August 18, 1997, the following aircraft types need not comply with this section: Bell 212, Bell 214ST, Bell 412, Bell 412SP, Boeing Chinook (BV-234), Boeing/Kawasaki Vertol 107 (BV/KV-107-II), deHavilland DHC-6, Eurocopter Puma 330J, Sikorsky 58, Sikorsky 61N, Sikorsky 76A.

(l) By April 7, 2012, all aircraft manufactured before April 7, 2010, must also meet the requirements in §23.1459(a)(7), §25.1459(a)(8), §27.1459(e), or §29.1459(e) of this chapter, as applicable.

(m) All aircraft manufactured on or after April 7, 2010, must have a flight data recorder installed that also—

(1) Meets the requirements of §23.1459(a)(3), (a)(6), and (a)(7), §25.1459(a)(3), (a)(7), and (a)(8), §27.1459(a)(3), (a)(6), and (e), or §29.1459(a)(3), (a)(6), and (e) of this chapter, as applicable; and

(2) Retains the 25 hours of recorded information required in paragraph (d) of this section using a recorder that meets the standards of TSO-C124a, or later revision.

[Docket No. 25530, 53 FR 26151, July 11, 1988; as amended by Amdt. 135–69, 62 FR 38396, July 17, 1997; Amdt. 135–69, 62 FR 48135, Sept. 12, 1997; Amdt. 135–84, 68 FR 42939, July 18, 2003; Amdt. 135–113, 73 FR 12570, March 7, 2008; Amdt. 135–113, 74 FR 32801, July 9, 2009]

§135.153 [Reserved]

§135.154 Terrain awareness and warning system.

(a) *Airplanes manufactured after March 29, 2002:*

(1) No person may operate a turbine-powered airplane configured with 10 or more passenger seats, excluding any pilot seat, unless that airplane is equipped with an approved terrain awareness and warning system that meets the requirements for Class A equipment in Technical Standard Order (TSO)–C151. The airplane must also include an approved terrain situational awareness display.

(2) No person may operate a turbine-powered airplane configured with 6 to 9 passenger seats, excluding any pilot seat, unless that airplane is equipped with an approved terrain awareness and warning system that meets as a minimum the requirements for Class B equipment in Technical Standard Order (TSO)–C151.

(b) *Airplanes manufactured on or before March 29, 2002:*

(1) No person may operate a turbine-powered airplane configured with 10 or more passenger seats, excluding any pilot seat, after March 29, 2005, unless that airplane is equipped with an approved terrain awareness and warning system that meets the requirements for Class A equipment in Technical Standard Order (TSO)–C151. The airplane must also include an approved terrain situational awareness display.

(2) No person may operate a turbine-powered airplane configured with 6 to 9 passenger seats, excluding any pilot seat, after March 29, 2005, unless that airplane is equipped with an approved terrain awareness and warning system that meets as a minimum the requirements for Class B equipment in Technical Standard Order (TSO)–C151.

(Approved by the Office of Management and Budget under control number 2120-0631)

(c) *Airplane Flight Manual.* The Airplane Flight Manual shall contain appropriate procedures for—

(1) The use of the terrain awareness and warning system; and

(2) Proper flight crew reaction in response to the terrain awareness and warning system audio and visual warnings.

[Docket No. 29312, 65 FR 16755, March 29, 2000]

§135.155 Fire extinguishers: Passenger-carrying aircraft.

No person may operate an aircraft carrying passengers unless it is equipped with hand fire extinguishers of an approved type for use in crew and passenger compartments as follows—

(a) The type and quantity of extinguishing agent must be suitable for the kinds of fires likely to occur;

(b) At least one hand fire extinguisher must be provided and conveniently located on the flight deck for use by the flight crew; and

(c) At least one hand fire extinguisher must be conveniently located in the passenger compartment of each aircraft having a passenger seating configuration, excluding any pilot seat, of at least 10 seats but less than 31 seats.

§135.156 Flight data recorders: Filtered data.

(a) A flight data signal is filtered when an original sensor signal has been changed in any way, other than changes necessary to:

(1) Accomplish analog to digital conversion of the signal;

(2) Format a digital signal to be DFDR compatible; or

(3) Eliminate a high frequency component of a signal that is outside the operational bandwidth of the sensor.

(b) An original sensor signal for any flight recorder parameter required to be recorded under §135.152 may be filtered only if the recorded signal value continues to meet the requirements of Appendix D or F of this part, as applicable.

(c) For a parameter described in §135.152(h)(12) through (17), (42), or (88), or the corresponding parameter in Appendix D of this part, if the recorded signal value is filtered and does not meet the requirements of Appendix D or F of this part, as applicable, the certificate holder must:

(1) Remove the filtering and ensure that the recorded signal value meets the requirements of Appendix D or F of this part, as applicable; or

(2) Demonstrate by test and analysis that the original sensor signal value can be reconstructed from the recorded data. This demonstration requires that:

(i) The FAA determine that the procedure and test results submitted by the certificate holder as its compliance with paragraph (c)(2) of this section are repeatable; and

(ii) The certificate holder maintains documentation of the procedure required to reconstruct the original sensor signal value. This documentation is also subject to the requirements of §135.152(e).

(d) *Compliance.* Compliance is required as follows:

(1) No later than October 20, 2011, each operator must determine, for each aircraft on its operations specifications, whether the aircraft's DFDR system is filtering any of the parameters listed in paragraph (c) of this section. The operator must create a record of this determination for each aircraft it operates, and maintain it as part of the correlation documentation required by §135.152(f)(1)(iii) or (f)(2)(iii) of this part as applicable.

(2) For aircraft that are not filtering any listed parameter, no further action is required unless the aircraft's DFDR system is modified in a manner that would cause it to meet the definition of filtering on any listed parameter.

(3) For aircraft found to be filtering a parameter listed in paragraph (c) of this section the operator must either:

(i) No later than April 21, 2014, remove the filtering; or

(ii) No later than April 22, 2013, submit the necessary procedure and test results required by paragraph (c)(2) of this section.

(4) After April 21, 2014, no aircraft flight data recording system may filter any parameter listed in paragraph (c) of this section that does not meet the requirements of Appendix D or F of this part, unless the certificate holder possesses test and analysis procedures and the test results that have been approved by the FAA. All records of tests, analysis and procedures used to comply with this section must be maintained as part of the correlation documentation required by §135.152(f)(1)(iii) or (f)(2)(iii) of this part as applicable.

[Docket No. FAA–2006–26135, 75 FR 7357, Feb. 19, 2010]

§135.157 Oxygen equipment requirements.

(a) *Unpressurized aircraft.* No person may operate an unpressurized aircraft at altitudes prescribed in this section unless it is equipped with enough oxygen dispensers and oxygen to supply the pilots under §135.89(a) and to supply, when flying—

(1) At altitudes above 10,000 feet through 15,000 feet MSL, oxygen to at least 10 percent of the occupants of the aircraft, other than the pilots, for that part of the flight at those altitudes that is of more than 30 minutes duration; and

(2) Above 15,000 feet MSL, oxygen to each occupant of the aircraft other than the pilots.

(b) *Pressurized aircraft.* No person may operate a pressurized aircraft—

(1) At altitudes above 25,000 feet MSL, unless at least a 10-minute supply of supplemental oxygen is available for each occupant of the aircraft, other than the pilots, for use when a descent is necessary due to loss of cabin pressurization; and

(2) Unless it is equipped with enough oxygen dispensers and oxygen to comply with paragraph (a) of this section whenever the cabin pressure altitude exceeds 10,000 feet MSL and, if the cabin pressurization fails, to comply with §135.89(a) or to provide a 2-hour supply for each pilot, whichever is greater, and to supply when flying—

(i) At altitudes above 10,000 feet through 15,000 feet MSL, oxygen to at least 10 percent of the occupants of the aircraft, other than the pilots, for that part of the flight at those altitudes that is of more than 30 minutes duration; and

(ii) Above 15,000 feet MSL, oxygen to each occupant of the aircraft, other than the pilots, for one hour unless, at all times during flight above that altitude, the aircraft can safely descend to 15,000 feet MSL within four minutes, in which case only a 30-minute supply is required.

(c) The equipment required by this section must have a means—

(1) To enable the pilots to readily determine, in flight, the amount of oxygen available in each source of supply and whether the oxygen is being delivered to the dispensing units; or

(2) In the case of individual dispensing units, to enable each user to make those determinations with respect to that person's oxygen supply and delivery; and

(3) To allow the pilots to use undiluted oxygen at their discretion at altitudes above 25,000 feet MSL.

§135.158 Pitot heat indication systems.

(a) Except as provided in paragraph (b) of this section, after April 12, 1981, no person may operate a transport category airplane equipped with a flight instrument pitot heating system unless the airplane is also equipped with an operable pitot heat indication system that complies with §25.1326 of this chapter in effect on April 12, 1978.

(b) A certificate holder may obtain an extension of the April 12, 1981, compliance date specified in paragraph (a) of this section, but not beyond April 12, 1983, from the Director, Flight Standards Service if the certificate holder—

(1) Shows that due to circumstances beyond its control it cannot comply by the specified compliance date; and

(2) Submits by the specified compliance date a schedule for compliance, acceptable to the Director, indicating that compliance will be achieved at the earliest practicable date.

[Docket No. 18094, Amdt. 135–17, 46 FR 48306, Aug. 31, 1981; as amended by Amdt. 135–33, 54 FR 39294, Sept. 25, 1989]

§135.159 Equipment requirements: Carrying passengers under VFR at night or under VFR over-the-top conditions.

No person may operate an aircraft carrying passengers under VFR at night or under VFR over-the-top, unless it is equipped with—

(a) A gyroscopic rate-of-turn indicator except on the following aircraft:

(1) Airplanes with a third attitude instrument system usable through flight attitudes of 360 degrees of pitch-and-roll and installed in accordance with the instrument requirements prescribed in §121.305(j) of this chapter.

(2) Helicopters with a third attitude instrument system usable through flight attitudes of ±80 degrees of pitch and ±120 degrees of roll and installed in accordance with §29.1303(g) of this chapter.

(3) Helicopters with a maximum certificated takeoff weight of 6,000 pounds or less.

(b) A slip skid indicator.

(c) A gyroscopic bank-and-pitch indicator.

(d) A gyroscopic direction indicator.

(e) A generator or generators able to supply all probable combinations of continuous in-flight electrical loads for required equipment and for recharging the battery.

(f) For night flights—

(1) An anticollision light system;

(2) Instrument lights to make all instruments, switches, and gauges easily readable, the direct rays of which are shielded from the pilots' eyes; and

(3) A flashlight having at least two size "D" cells or equivalent.

(g) For the purpose of paragraph (e) of this section, a continuous in-flight electrical load includes one that draws current continuously during flight, such as radio equipment and electrically driven instruments and lights, but does not include occasional intermittent loads.

(h) Notwithstanding provisions of paragraphs (b), (c), and (d), helicopters having a maximum certificated takeoff weight of 6,000 pounds or less may be operated until January 6, 1988, under visual flight rules at night without a slip skid indicator, a gyroscopic bank-and-pitch indicator, or a gyroscopic direction indicator.

[Docket No. 24550, 51 FR 40709, Nov. 7, 1986; as amended by Amdt. 135–38, 55 FR 43310, Oct. 26, 1990]

§135.160 Radio altimeters for rotorcraft operations.

(a) After April 24, 2017, no person may operate a rotorcraft unless that rotorcraft is equipped with an operable FAA-approved radio altimeter, or an FAA-approved device that incorporates a radio altimeter, unless otherwise authorized in the certificate holder's approved minimum equipment list.

(b) Deviation authority. The Administrator may authorize deviations from paragraph (a) of this section for rotorcraft that are unable to incorporate a radio altimeter. This deviation will be issued as a Letter of Deviation Authority. The deviation may be terminated or amended at any time by the Administrator. The request for deviation authority is applicable to rotorcraft with a maximum gross takeoff weight no greater than 2,950 pounds. The request for deviation authority must contain a complete statement of the circumstances and justification, and must be submitted to the nearest Flight Standards District Office, not less than 60 days prior to the date of intended operations.

[Docket No. FAA–2010–0982, 79 FR 9973, Feb. 21, 2014]

§135.161 Communication and navigation equipment for aircraft operations under VFR over routes navigated by pilotage.

(a) No person may operate an aircraft under VFR over routes that can be navigated by pilotage unless the aircraft is equipped with the two-way radio communication equipment necessary under normal operating conditions to fulfill the following:

(1) Communicate with at least one appropriate station from any point on the route, except in remote locations and areas of mountainous terrain where geographical constraints make such communication impossible.

(2) Communicate with appropriate air traffic control facilities from any point within Class B, Class C, or Class D airspace, or within a Class E surface area designated for an airport in which flights are intended; and

(3) Receive meteorological information from any point en route, except in remote locations and areas of mountainous terrain where geographical constraints make such communication impossible.

(b) No person may operate an aircraft at night under VFR over routes that can be navigated by pilotage unless that aircraft is equipped with—

(1) Two-way radio communication equipment necessary under normal operating conditions to fulfill the functions specified in paragraph (a) of this section; and

(2) Navigation equipment suitable for the route to be flown.

[Docket No. FAA–2002–14002, 72 FR 31684, June 7, 2007; as amended by Amdt. 135–116, 74 FR 20205, May 1, 2009]

§135.163 Equipment requirements: Aircraft carrying passengers under IFR.

No person may operate an aircraft under IFR, carrying passengers, unless it has—

(a) A vertical speed indicator;

(b) A free-air temperature indicator;

(c) A heated pitot tube for each airspeed indicator;

(d) A power failure warning device or vacuum indicator to show the power available for gyroscopic instruments from each power source;

(e) An alternate source of static pressure for the altimeter and the airspeed and vertical speed indicators;

(f) For a single-engine aircraft:

(1) Two independent electrical power generating sources each of which is able to supply all probable combinations of continuous inflight electrical loads for required instruments and equipment; or

(2) In addition to the primary electrical power generating source, a standby battery or an alternate source of electric power that is capable of supplying 150% of the electrical loads of all required instruments and equipment necessary for safe emergency operation of the aircraft for at least one hour;

(g) For multi-engine aircraft, at least two generators or alternators each of which is on a separate engine, of which any combination of one-half of the total number are rated sufficiently to supply the electrical loads of all required instruments and equipment necessary for safe emergency operation of the aircraft except that for multi-engine helicopters, the two required generators may be mounted on the main rotor drive train; and

(h) Two independent sources of energy (with means of selecting either) of which at least one is an engine-driven pump or generator, each of which is able to drive all required gyroscopic instruments powered by, or to be powered by, that particular source and installed so that failure of one instrument or source, does not interfere with the energy supply to the remaining instruments or the other energy source unless, for single-engine aircraft in all cargo operations only, the rate of turn indicator has a source of energy separate from the bank and pitch and direction indicators. For the purpose of this paragraph, for multi-engine aircraft, each engine-driven source of energy must be on a different engine.

(i) For the purpose of paragraph (f) of this section, a continuous inflight electrical load includes one that draws current continuously during flight, such as radio equipment, electrically driven instruments, and lights, but does not include occasional intermittent loads.

[Docket No. 16097, 43 FR 46783, Oct. 10, 1978; as amended by Amdt. 135–70, 62 FR 42374, Aug. 6, 1997; Amdt. 135–73, 63 FR 25573, May 8, 1998]

§135.165 Communication and navigation equipment: Extended overwater or IFR operations.

(a) *Aircraft navigation equipment requirements—General.* Except as provided in paragraph (g) of this section, no person may conduct operations under IFR or extended over-water unless—

(1) The en route navigation aids necessary for navigating the aircraft along the route (e.g., ATS routes, arrival and departure routes, and instrument approach procedures, including missed approach procedures if a missed approach routing is specified in the procedure) are available and suitable for use by the navigation systems required by this section:

(2) The aircraft used in extended over-water operations is equipped with at least two-approved independent navigation systems suitable for navigating the aircraft along the route to be flown within the degree of accuracy required for ATC.

(3) The aircraft used for IFR operations is equipped with at least—

(i) One marker beacon receiver providing visual and aural signals; and

(ii) One ILS receiver.

(4) Any RNAV system used to meet the navigation equipment requirements of this section is authorized in the certificate holder's operations specifications.

(b) *Use of a single independent navigation system for IFR operations.* The aircraft may be

§135.165

equipped with a single independent navigation system suitable for navigating the aircraft along the route to be flown within the degree of accuracy required for ATC if:

(1) It can be shown that the aircraft is equipped with at least one other independent navigation system suitable, in the event of loss of the navigation capability of the single independent navigation system permitted by this paragraph at any point along the route, for proceeding safely to a suitable airport and completing an instrument approach; and

(2) The aircraft has sufficient fuel so that the flight may proceed safely to a suitable airport by use of the remaining navigation system, and complete an instrument approach and land.

(c) *VOR navigation equipment.* Whenever VOR navigation equipment is required by paragraph (a) or (b) of this section, no person may operate an aircraft unless it is equipped with at least one approved DME or suitable RNAV system.

(d) *Airplane communication equipment requirements.* Except as permitted in paragraph (e) of this section, no person may operate a turbojet airplane having a passenger seat configuration, excluding any pilot seat, of 10 seats or more, or a multiengine airplane in a commuter operation, as defined in part 119 of this chapter, under IFR or in extended over-water operations unless the airplane is equipped with—

(1) At least two independent communication systems necessary under normal operating conditions to fulfill the functions specified in §121.347(a) of this chapter; and

(2) At least one of the communication systems required by paragraph (d)(1) of this section must have two-way voice communication capability.

(e) *IFR or extended over-water communications equipment requirements.* A person may operate an aircraft other than that specified in paragraph (d) of this section under IFR or in extended over-water operations if it meets all of the requirements of this section, with the exception that only one communication system transmitter is required for operations other than extended over-water operations.

(f) *Additional aircraft communication equipment requirements.* In addition to the requirements in paragraphs (d) and (e) of this section, no person may operate an aircraft under IFR or in extended over-water operations unless it is equipped with at least:

(1) Two microphones; and

(2) Two headsets or one headset and one speaker.

(g) *Extended over-water exceptions.* Notwithstanding the requirements of paragraphs (a), (d), and (e) of this section, installation and use of a single long-range navigation system and a single long-range communication system for extended over-water operations in certain geographic areas may be authorized by the Administrator and approved in the certificate holder's operations specifications. The following are among the operational factors the Administrator may consider in granting an authorization:

(1) The ability of the flight crew to navigate the airplane along the route within the degree of accuracy required for ATC;

(2) The length of the route being flown; and

(3) The duration of the very high frequency communications gap.

[Docket No. FAA–2002–14002, 72 FR 31684, June 7, 2007]

§135.167 Emergency equipment: Extended overwater operations.

(a) Except where the Administrator, by amending the operations specifications of the certificate holder, requires the carriage of all or any specific items of the equipment listed below for any overwater operation, or, upon application of the certificate holder, the Administrator allows deviation for a particular extended overwater operation, no person may operate an aircraft in extended overwater operations unless it carries, installed in conspicuously marked locations easily accessible to the occupants if a ditching occurs, the following equipment:

(1) An approved life preserver equipped with an approved survivor locator light for each occupant of the aircraft. The life preserver must be easily accessible to each seated occupant.

(2) Enough approved liferafts of a rated capacity and buoyancy to accommodate the occupants of the aircraft.

(b) Each liferaft required by paragraph (a) of this section must be equipped with or contain at least the following:

(1) One approved survivor locator light.
(2) One approved pyrotechnic signaling device.
(3) Either—
  (i) One survival kit, appropriately equipped for the route to be flown; or
  (ii) One canopy (for sail, sunshade, or rain catcher);
  (iii) One radar reflector;
  (iv) One liferaft repair kit;
  (v) One bailing bucket;
  (vi) One signaling mirror;
  (vii) One police whistle;
  (viii) One raft knife;
  (ix) One CO_2 bottle for emergency inflation;
  (x) One inflation pump;
  (xi) Two oars;
  (xii) One 75-foot retaining line;
  (xiii) One magnetic compass;
  (xiv) One dye marker;
  (xv) One flashlight having at least two size "D" cells or equivalent;

(xvi) A 2-day supply of emergency food rations supplying at least 1,000 calories per day for each person;
(xvii) For each two persons the raft is rated to carry, two pints of water or one sea water desalting kit;
(xviii) One fishing kit; and
(xix) One book on survival appropriate for the area in which the aircraft is operated.

(c) No person may operate an airplane in extended overwater operations unless there is attached to one of the life rafts required by paragraph (a) of this section, an approved survival type emergency locator transmitter. Batteries used in this transmitter must be replaced (or recharged, if the batteries are rechargeable) when the transmitter has been in use for more than 1 cumulative hour, or, when 50 percent of their useful life (or for rechargeable batteries, 50 percent of their useful life of charge) has expired, as established by the transmitter manufacturer under its approval. The new expiration date for replacing (or recharging) the battery must be legibly marked on the outside of the transmitter. The battery useful life (or useful life of charge) requirements of this paragraph do not apply to batteries (such as water-activated batteries) that are essentially unaffected during probable storage intervals.

[Docket No. 16097, 43 FR 46783, Oct. 10, 1978; as amended by Amdt. 135–4, 45 FR 38348, June 30, 1980; Amdt. 135–20, 51 FR 40710, Nov. 7, 1986; Amdt. 135–49, 59 FR 32058, June 21, 1994; Amdt. 135–91, 68 FR 54586, Sept. 17, 2003]

§135.168 Emergency equipment: Overwater rotorcraft operations.

(a) *Definitions.* For the purposes of this section, the following definitions apply—

Autorotational distance refers to the distance a rotorcraft can travel in autorotation as described by the manufacturer in the approved Rotorcraft Flight Manual.

Shoreline means that area of the land adjacent to the water of an ocean, sea, lake, pond, river, or tidal basin that is above the high-water mark at which a rotorcraft could be landed safely. This does not include land areas which are unsuitable for landing such as vertical cliffs or land intermittently under water.

(b) *Required equipment.* After April 24, 2017, except as provided for in paragraph (c), when authorized by the certificate holder's operations specifications, or when necessary only for take-off or landing, no person may operate a rotorcraft beyond autorotational distance from the shoreline unless it carries:

(1) An approved life preserver equipped with an approved survivor locator light for each occupant of the rotorcraft. The life preserver must be worn by each occupant while the rotorcraft is beyond autorotational distance from the shoreline, except for a patient transported during a helicopter air ambulance operation, as defined in §135.601(b)(1), when wearing a life preserver would be inadvisable for medical reasons; and

(2) An approved and installed 406 MHz emergency locator transmitter (ELT) with 121.5 MHz homing capability. Batteries used in ELTs must be maintained in accordance with the following—

(i) Non-rechargeable batteries must be replaced when the transmitter has been in use for more than 1 cumulative hour or when 50% of their useful lives have expired, as established by the transmitter manufacturer under its approval. The new expiration date for replacing the batteries must be legibly marked on the outside of the transmitter. The battery useful life requirements of this paragraph (b)(2) do not apply to batteries (such as water-activated batteries) that are essentially unaffected during probable storage intervals; or

(ii) Rechargeable batteries used in the transmitter must be recharged when the transmitter has been in use for more than 1 cumulative hour or when 50% of their useful-life-of-charge has expired, as established by the transmitter manufacturer under its approval. The new expiration date for recharging the batteries must be legibly marked on the outside of the transmitter. The battery useful-life-of-charge requirements of this paragraph (b)(2) do not apply to batteries (such as water-activated batteries) that are essentially unaffected during probable storage intervals.

(c) *Maintenance.* The equipment required by this section must be maintained in accordance with §135.419.

(d) *ELT standards.* The ELT required by paragraph (b)(2) of this section must meet the requirements in:

(1) TSO-C126, TSO-C126a, or TSO-C126b; and

(2) Section 2 of either RTCA DO-204 or RTCA DO-204A, as specified by the TSO complied with in paragraph (d)(1) of this section.

(e) *ELT alternative compliance.* Operators with an ELT required by paragraph (b)(2) of this section, or an ELT with an approved deviation under §21.618 of this chapter, are in compliance with this section.

(f) *Incorporation by reference.* The standards required in this section are incorporated by reference into this section with the approval of the Director of the Federal Register under 5 U.S.C. 552(a) and 1 CFR part 51. To enforce any edition other than that specified in this section, the FAA must publish notice of change in the Federal Register and the material must be available to the public. All approved material is available for inspection at the FAA's Office of Rulemaking

(ARM-1), 800 Independence Avenue SW., Washington, DC 20591 (telephone (202) 267-9677) and from the sources indicated below. It is also available for inspection at the National Archives and Records Administration (NARA). For information on the availability of this material at NARA, call (202) 741-6030 or go to **http://www.archives. gov/federal_register/code_of_federal_regulations/ibr_locations.html**.

(1) U.S. Department of Transportation, Subsequent Distribution Office, DOT Warehouse M30, Ardmore East Business Center, 3341 Q 75th Avenue, Landover, MD 20785; telephone (301) 322-5377. Copies are also available on the FAA's Web site. Use the following link and type the TSO number in the search box: **http://www.airweb. faa.gov/Regulatory_and_Guidance_Library/ rgTSO.nsf/Frameset?OpenPage**.

(i) TSO-C126, 406 MHz Emergency Locator Transmitter (ELT), Dec. 23, 1992;

(ii) TSO-C126a, 406 MHz Emergency Locator Transmitter (ELT), Dec. 17, 2008, and

(iii) TSO-C126b, 406 MHz Emergency Locator Transmitter (ELT), Nov. 26, 2012.

(2) RTCA, Inc., 1150 18th Street NW., Suite 910, Washington, DC 20036, telephone (202) 833-9339, and are also available on RTCA's Web site at **http://www.rtca.org/onlinecart/index. cfm**.

(i) RTCA DO-204, Minimum Operational Performance Standards (MOPS) 406 MHz Emergency Locator Transmitters (ELTs), Sept. 29, 1989, and

(ii) RTCA DO-204A, Minimum Operational Performance Standards (MOPS) 406 MHz Emergency Locator Transmitters (ELT), Dec. 6, 2007.

[Docket No. FAA–2010–0982, 79 FR 9973, Feb. 21, 2014]

§135.169 Additional airworthiness requirements.

(a) Except for commuter category airplanes, no person may operate a large airplane unless it meets the additional airworthiness requirements of §§121.213 through 121.283 and 121.307 of this chapter.

(b) No person may operate a reciprocating-engine or turbopropeller-powered small airplane that has a passenger seating configuration, excluding pilot seats, of 10 seats or more unless it is type certificated—

(1) In the transport category;

(2) Before July 1, 1970, in the normal category and meets special conditions issued by the Administrator for airplanes intended for use in operations under this part;

(3) Before July 19, 1970, in the normal category and meets the additional airworthiness standards in Special Federal Aviation Regulation No. 23;

(4) In the normal category and meets the additional airworthiness standards in Appendix A;

(5) In the normal category and complies with section 1.(a) of Special Federal Aviation Regulation No. 41;

(6) In the normal category and complies with section 1.(b) of Special Federal Aviation Regulation No. 41; or

(7) In the commuter category.

(c) No person may operate a small airplane with a passenger seating configuration, excluding any pilot seat, of 10 seats or more, with a seating configuration greater than the maximum seating configuration used in that type airplane in operations under this part before August 19, 1977. This paragraph does not apply to—

(1) An airplane that is type certificated in the transport category; or

(2) An airplane that complies with—

(i) Appendix A of this part provided that its passenger seating configuration, excluding pilot seats, does not exceed 19 seats; or

(ii) Special Federal Aviation Regulation No. 41.

(d) Cargo or baggage compartments:

(1) After March 20, 1991, each Class C or D compartment, as defined in §25.857 of part 25 of this chapter, greater than 200 cubic feet in volume in a transport category airplane type certificated after January 1, 1958, must have ceiling and sidewall panels which are constructed of:

(i) Glass fiber reinforced resin;

(ii) Materials which meet the test requirements of part 25, Appendix F, part III of this chapter; or

(iii) In the case of liner installations approved prior to March 20, 1989, aluminum.

(2) For compliance with this paragraph, the term "liner" includes any design feature, such as a joint or fastener, which would affect the capability of the liner to safely contain a fire.

[Docket No. 16097, 43 FR 46783, Oct. 10, 1978; as amended by Amdt. 135–2, 44 FR 53731, Sept. 17, 1979; Amdt. 135–21, 52 FR 1836, Jan. 15, 1987; 52 FR 34745, Sept. 14, 1987; Amdt. 135–31, 54 FR 7389, Feb. 17, 1989; Amdt. 135–55, 60 FR 6628, Feb. 2, 1995]

§135.170 Materials for compartment interiors.

(a) No person may operate an airplane that conforms to an amended or supplemental type certificate issued in accordance with SFAR No. 41 for a maximum certificated takeoff weight in excess of 12,500 pounds unless within one year after issuance of the initial airworthiness certificate under that SFAR, the airplane meets the compartment interior requirements set forth in §25.853(a) in effect March 6, 1995 (formerly §25.853(a), (b), (b-1), (b-2), and (b-3) of this chapter in effect on September 26, 1978).

(b) Except for commuter category airplanes and airplanes certificated under Special Federal

Part 135: Commuter & On Demand Operations §135.170

Aviation Regulation No. 41, no person may operate a large airplane unless it meets the following additional airworthiness requirements:

(1) Except for those materials covered by paragraph (b)(2) of this section, all materials in each compartment used by the crewmembers or passengers must meet the requirements of §25.853 of this chapter in effect as follows or later amendment thereto:

(i) Except as provided in paragraph (b)(1)(iv) of this section, each airplane with a passenger capacity of 20 or more and manufactured after August 19, 1988, but prior to August 20, 1990, must comply with the heat release rate testing provisions of §25.853(d) in effect March 6, 1995 (formerly §25.853(a-1) in effect on August 20, 1986), except that the total heat release over the first 2 minutes of sample exposure rate must not exceed 100 kilowatt minutes per square meter and the peak heat release rate must not exceed 100 kilowatts per square meter.

(ii) Each airplane with a passenger capacity of 20 or more and manufactured after August 19, 1990, must comply with the heat release rate and smoke testing provisions of §25.853(d) in effect March 6, 1995 (formerly §25.83(a-1) in effect on September 26, 1988).

(iii) Except as provided in paragraph (b)(1)(v) or (vi) of this section, each airplane for which the application for type certificate was filed prior to May 1, 1972, must comply with the provisions of §25.853 in effect on April 30, 1972, regardless of the passenger capacity, if there is a substantially complete replacement of the cabin interior after April 30, 1972.

(iv) Except as provided in paragraph (b)(1)(v) or (vi) of this section, each airplane for which the application for type certificate was filed after May 1, 1972, must comply with the material requirements under which the airplane was type certificated regardless of the passenger capacity if there is a substantially complete replacement of the cabin interior after that date.

(v) Except as provided in paragraph (b)(1)(vi) of this section, each airplane that was type certificated after January 1, 1958, must comply with the heat release testing provisions of §25.853(d) in effect March 6, 1995 (formerly §25.853(a-1) in effect on August 20, 1986), if there is a substantially complete replacement of the cabin interior components identified in that paragraph on or after that date, except that the total heat release over the first 2 minutes of sample exposure shall not exceed 100 kilowatt-minutes per square meter and the peak heat release rate shall not exceed 100 kilowatts per square meter.

(vi) Each airplane that was type certificated after January 1, 1958, must comply with the heat release rate and smoke testing provisions of §25.853(d) in effect March 6, 1995 (formerly §25.853(a-1) in effect on August 20, 1986), if there is a substantially complete replacement of the cabin interior components identified in that paragraph after August 19, 1990.

(vii) Contrary provisions of this section notwithstanding, the Manager of the Transport Airplane Directorate, Aircraft Certification Service, Federal Aviation Administration, may authorize deviation from the requirements of paragraph (b)(1)(i), (b)(1)(ii), (b)(1)(v), or (b)(1)(vi) of this section for specific components of the cabin interior that do not meet applicable flammability and smoke emission requirements, if the determination is made that special circumstances exist that make compliance impractical. Such grants of deviation will be limited to those airplanes manufactured within 1 year after the applicable date specified in this section and those airplanes in which the interior is replaced within 1 year of that date. A request for such grant of deviation must include a thorough and accurate analysis of each component subject to §25.853(d) in effect March 6, 1995 (formerly §25.853(a-1) in effect on August 20, 1986), the steps being taken to achieve compliance, and for the few components for which timely compliance will not be achieved, credible reasons for such noncompliance.

(viii) Contrary provisions of this section notwithstanding, galley carts and standard galley containers that do not meet the flammability and smoke emission requirements of §25.853(d) in effect March 6, 1995 (formerly §25.853(a-1) in effect on August 20, 1986), may be used in airplanes that must meet the requirements of paragraph (b)(1)(i), (b)(1)(ii), (b)(1)(iv) or (b)(1)(vi) of this section provided the galley carts or standard containers were manufactured prior to March 6, 1995.

(2) For airplanes type certificated after January 1, 1958, seat cushions, except those on flight crewmember seats, in any compartment occupied by crew or passengers must comply with the requirements pertaining to fire protection of seat cushions in §25.853(c) effective November 26, 1984.

(c) *Thermal/acoustic insulation materials.* For transport category airplanes type certificated after January 1, 1958:

(1) For airplanes manufactured before September 2, 2005, when thermal/acoustic insulation is installed in the fuselage as replacements after September 2, 2005, the insulation must meet the flame propagation requirements of §25.856 of this chapter, effective September 2, 2003, if it is:

(i) Of a blanket construction, or

(ii) Installed around air ducting.

(2) For airplanes manufactured after September 2, 2005, thermal/acoustic insulation materials installed in the fuselage must meet the flame

§135.171

propagation requirements of §25.856 of this chapter, effective September 2, 2003.

[Docket No. 26192, 60 FR 6628, Feb. 2, 1995; as amended by Amdt. 135–55, 60 FR 11194, March 1, 1995; Amdt. 135–56, 60 FR 13011, March 9, 1995: Amdt. 135–90, 68 FR 45084, July 31, 2003; Amdt. 135–103, 70 FR 77752, Dec. 30, 2005]

§135.171 Shoulder harness installation at flight crewmember stations.

(a) No person may operate a turbojet aircraft or an aircraft having a passenger seating configuration, excluding any pilot seat, of 10 seats or more unless it is equipped with an approved shoulder harness installed for each flight crewmember station.

(b) Each flight crewmember occupying a station equipped with a shoulder harness must fasten the shoulder harness during takeoff and landing, except that the shoulder harness may be unfastened if the crewmember cannot perform the required duties with the shoulder harness fastened.

§135.173 Airborne thunderstorm detection equipment requirements.

(a) No person may operate an aircraft that has a passenger seating configuration, excluding any pilot seat, of 10 seats or more in passenger-carrying operations, except a helicopter operating under day VFR conditions, unless the aircraft is equipped with either approved thunderstorm detection equipment or approved airborne weather radar equipment.

(b) No person may operate a helicopter that has a passenger seating configuration, excluding any pilot seat, of 10 seats or more in passenger-carrying operations, under night VFR when current weather reports indicate that thunderstorms or other potentially hazardous weather conditions that can be detected with airborne thunderstorm detection equipment may reasonably be expected along the route to be flown, unless the helicopter is equipped with either approved thunderstorm detection equipment or approved airborne weather radar equipment.

(c) No person may begin a flight under IFR or night VFR conditions when current weather reports indicate that thunderstorms or other potentially hazardous weather conditions that can be detected with airborne thunderstorm detection equipment, required by paragraph (a) or (b) of this section, may reasonably be expected along the route to be flown, unless the airborne thunderstorm detection equipment is in satisfactory operating condition.

(d) If the airborne thunderstorm detection equipment becomes inoperative en route, the aircraft must be operated under the instructions and

Federal Aviation Regulations

procedures specified for that event in the manual required by §135.21.

(e) This section does not apply to aircraft used solely within the State of Hawaii, within the State of Alaska, within that part of Canada west of longitude 130 degrees W, between latitude 70 degrees N, and latitude 53 degrees N, or during any training, test, or ferry flight.

(f) Without regard to any other provision of this part, an alternate electrical power supply is not required for airborne thunderstorm detection equipment.

[Docket No. 16097, 43 FR 46783, Oct. 10, 1978; as amended by Amdt. 135–20, 51 FR 40710, Nov. 7, 1986; Amdt. 135–60, 61 FR 2616, Jan. 26, 1996]

§135.175 Airborne weather radar equipment requirements.

(a) No person may operate a large, transport category aircraft in passenger-carrying operations unless approved airborne weather radar equipment is installed in the aircraft.

(b) No person may begin a flight under IFR or night VFR conditions when current weather reports indicate that thunderstorms, or other potentially hazardous weather conditions that can be detected with airborne weather radar equipment, may reasonably be expected along the route to be flown, unless the airborne weather radar equipment required by paragraph (a) of this section is in satisfactory operating condition.

(c) If the airborne weather radar equipment becomes inoperative en route, the aircraft must be operated under the instructions and procedures specified for that event in the manual required by §135.21.

(d) This section does not apply to aircraft used solely within the State of Hawaii, within the State of Alaska, within that part of Canada west of longitude 130 degrees W, between latitude 70 degrees N, and latitude 53 degrees N, or during any training, test, or ferry flight.

(e) Without regard to any other provision of this part, an alternate electrical power supply is not required for airborne weather radar equipment.

§135.177 Emergency equipment requirements for aircraft having a passenger seating configuration of more than 19 passengers.

(a) No person may operate an aircraft having a passenger seating configuration, excluding any pilot seat, of more than 19 seats unless it is equipped with the following emergency equipment:

(1) At least one approved first-aid kit for treatment of injuries likely to occur in flight or in a minor accident that must:

(i) Be readily accessible to crewmembers.
(ii) Be stored securely and kept free from dust, moisture, and damaging temperatures.
(iii) Contain at least the following appropriately maintained contents in the specified quantities:

Contents	Quantity
Adhesive bandage compresses, 1-inch	16
Antiseptic swabs	20
Ammonia inhalants	10
Bandage compresses, 4-inch	8
Triangular bandage compresses, 40-inch	5
Arm splint, noninflatable	1
Leg splint, noninflatable	1
Roller bandage, 4-inch	4
Adhesive tape, 1-inch standard roll	2
Bandage scissors	1
Protective nonpermeable gloves or equivalent	1 Pair

(2) A crash axe carried so as to be accessible to the crew but inaccessible to passengers during normal operations.

(3) Signs that are visible to all occupants to notify them when smoking is prohibited and when safety belts must be fastened. The signs must be constructed so that they can be turned on during any movement of the aircraft on the surface, for each takeoff or landing, and at other times considered necessary by the pilot in command. "No smoking" signs shall be turned on when required by §135.127.

(4) [Reserved]

(b) Each item of equipment must be inspected regularly under inspection periods established in the operations specifications to ensure its condition for continued serviceability and immediate readiness to perform its intended emergency purposes.

[Docket No. 16097, 43 FR 46783, Oct. 10, 1978; as amended by Amdt. 135–25, 53 FR 12362, April 13, 1988; Amdt. 135–43, 57 FR 19245, May 4, 1992; Amdt. 135–44, 57 FR 42676, Sept. 15, 1992; Amdt. 135–47, 59 FR 1781, Jan. 12, 1994; Amdt. 135–53, 59 FR 52643, Oct. 18, 1994, 59 FR 55208, Nov. 4, 1994; Amdt. 135–80, 66 FR 19045, April 12, 2001]

§135.178 Additional emergency equipment.

No person may operate an airplane having a passenger seating configuration of more than 19 seats, unless it has the additional emergency equipment specified in paragraphs (a) through (l) of this section.

(a) *Means for emergency evacuation.* Each passenger-carrying landplane emergency exit (other than over-the-wing) that is more than 6 feet from the ground, with the airplane on the ground and the landing gear extended, must have an approved means to assist the occupants in descending to the ground. The assisting means for a floor-level emergency exit must meet the requirements of §25.809(f)(1) of this chapter in effect on April 30, 1972, except that, for any airplane for which the application for the type certificate was filed after that date, it must meet the requirements under which the airplane was type certificated. An assisting means that deploys automatically must be armed during taxiing, takeoffs, and landings; however, the Administrator may grant a deviation from the requirement of automatic deployment if he finds that the design of the exit makes compliance impractical, if the assisting means automatically erects upon deployment and, with respect to required emergency exits, if an emergency evacuation demonstration is conducted in accordance with §121.291(a) of this chapter. This paragraph does not apply to the rear window emergency exit of Douglas DC-3 airplanes operated with fewer than 36 occupants, including crewmembers, and fewer than five exits authorized for passenger use.

(b) *Interior emergency exit marking.* The following must be complied with for each passenger-carrying airplane:

(1) Each passenger emergency exit, its means of access, and its means of opening must be conspicuously marked. The identity and locating of each passenger emergency exit must be recognizable from a distance equal to the width of the cabin. The location of each passenger emergency exit must be indicated by a sign visible to occupants approaching along the main passenger aisle. There must be a locating sign—

(i) Above the aisle near each over-the-wing passenger emergency exit, or at another ceiling location if it is more practical because of low headroom;

(ii) Next to each floor level passenger emergency exit, except that one sign may serve two such exits if they both can be seen readily from that sign; and

(iii) On each bulkhead or divider that prevents fore and aft vision along the passenger cabin, to indicate emergency exits beyond and obscured by it, except that if this is not possible, the sign may be placed at another appropriate location.

(2) Each passenger emergency exit marking and each locating sign must meet the following:

(i) For an airplane for which the application for the type certificate was filed prior to May 1, 1972, each passenger emergency exit marking and each locating sign must be manufactured to meet the requirements of §25.812(b) of this chapter in effect on April 30, 1972. On these airplanes, no sign may continue to be used if its luminescence (brightness) decreases to below 100 microlamberts. The colors may be reversed if it increases the emergency illumination of the passenger compartment. However, the Administrator may authorize deviation from the 2-inch background requirements if he finds that special circumstances exist that make compliance impractical and that the proposed deviation provides an equivalent level of safety.

(ii) For an airplane for which the application for the type certificate was filed on or after May 1, 1972, each passenger emergency exit marking and each locating sign must be manufactured to meet the interior emergency exit marking requirements under which the airplane was type certificated. On these airplanes, no sign may continue to be used if its luminescence (brightness) decreases to below 250 microlamberts.

(c) *Lighting for interior emergency exit markings.* Each passenger-carrying airplane must have an emergency lighting system, independent of the main lighting system; however, sources of general cabin illumination may be common to both the emergency and the main lighting systems if the power supply to the emergency lighting system is independent of the power supply to the main lighting system. The emergency lighting system must—

(1) Illuminate each passenger exit marking and locating sign;

(2) Provide enough general lighting in the passenger cabin so that the average illumination when measured at 40-inch intervals at seat armrest height, on the centerline of the main passenger aisle, is at least 0.05 foot-candles; and

(3) For airplanes type certificated after January 1, 1958, include floor proximity emergency escape path marking which meets the requirements of §25.812(e) of this chapter in effect on November 26, 1984.

(d) *Emergency light operation.* Except for lights forming part of emergency lighting subsystems provided in compliance with §25.812(h) of this chapter (as prescribed in paragraph (h) of this section) that serve no more than one assist means, are independent of the airplane's main emergency lighting systems, and are automatically activated when the assist means is deployed, each light required by paragraphs (c) and (h) of this section must:

(1) Be operable manually both from the flightcrew station and from a point in the passenger compartment that is readily accessible to a normal flight attendant seat;

(2) Have a means to prevent inadvertent operation of the manual controls;

(3) When armed or turned on at either station, remain lighted or become lighted upon interruption of the airplane's normal electric power;

(4) Be armed or turned on during taxiing, takeoff, and landing. In showing compliance with this paragraph, a transverse vertical separation of the fuselage need not be considered;

(5) Provide the required level of illumination for at least 10 minutes at the critical ambient conditions after emergency landing; and

(6) Have a cockpit control device that has an "on," "off," and "armed" position.

(e) *Emergency exit operating handles.*

(1) For a passenger-carrying airplane for which the application for the type certificate was filed prior to May 1, 1972, the location of each passenger emergency exit operating handle, and instructions for opening the exit, must be shown by a marking on or near the exit that is readable from a distance of 30 inches. In addition, for each Type I and Type II emergency exit with a locking mechanism released by rotary motion of the handle, the instructions for opening must be shown by—

(i) A red arrow with a shaft at least three-fourths inch wide and a head twice the width of the shaft, extending along at least 70° of arc at a radius approximately equal to three-fourths of the handle length; and

(ii) The word "open" in red letters 1 inch high placed horizontally near the head of the arrow.

(2) For a passenger-carrying airplane for which the application for the type certificate was filed on or after May 1, 1972, the location of each passenger emergency exit operating handle and instructions for opening the exit must be shown in accordance with the requirements under which the airplane was type certificated. On these airplanes, no operating handle or operating handle cover may continue to be used if its luminescence (brightness) decreases to below 100 microlamberts.

(f) *Emergency exit access.* Access to emergency exits must be provided as follows for each passenger-carrying airplane:

(1) Each passageway between individual passenger areas, or leading to a Type I or Type II emergency exit, must be unobstructed and at least 20 inches wide.

(2) There must be enough space next to each Type I or Type II emergency exit to allow a crewmember to assist in the evacuation of passengers without reducing the unobstructed width of the passageway below that required in paragraph (f)(1) of this section; however, the Administrator may authorize deviation from this requirement for an airplane certificated under the provisions of part 4b of the Civil Air Regulations in effect before December 20, 1951, if he finds that special circumstances exist that provide an equivalent level of safety.

(3) There must be access from the main aisle to each Type III and Type IV exit. The access from the aisle to these exits must not be obstructed by seats, berths, or other protrusions in a manner that would reduce the effectiveness of the exit. In addition, for a transport category airplane type certificated after January 1, 1958, there must be

Part 135: Commuter & On Demand Operations §135.178

placards installed in accordance with §25.813(c)(3) of this chapter for each Type III exit after December 3, 1992.

(4) If it is necessary to pass through a passageway between passenger compartments to reach any required emergency exit from any seat in the passenger cabin, the passageway must not be obstructed. Curtains may, however, be used if they allow free entry through the passageway.

(5) No door may be installed in any partition between passenger compartments.

(6) If it is necessary to pass through a doorway separating the passenger cabin from other areas to reach a required emergency exit from any passenger seat, the door must have a means to latch it in the open position, and the door must be latched open during each takeoff and landing. The latching means must be able to withstand the loads imposed upon it when the door is subjected to the ultimate inertia forces, relative to the surrounding structure, listed in §25.561(b) of this chapter.

(g) *Exterior exit markings.* Each passenger emergency exit and the means of opening that exit from the outside must be marked on the outside of the airplane. There must be a 2-inch colored band outlining each passenger emergency exit on the side of the fuselage. Each outside marking, including the band, must be readily distinguishable from the surrounding fuselage area by contrast in color. The markings must comply with the following:

(1) If the reflectance of the darker color is 15 percent or less, the reflectance of the lighter color must be at least 45 percent.

(2) If the reflectance of the darker color is greater than 15 percent, at least a 30 percent difference between its reflectance and the reflectance of the lighter color must be provided.

(3) Exits that are not in the side of the fuselage must have the external means of opening and applicable instructions marked conspicuously in red or, if red is inconspicuous against the background color, in bright chrome yellow and, when the opening means for such an exit is located on only one side of the fuselage, a conspicuous marking to that effect must be provided on the other side. "Reflectance" is the ratio of the luminous flux reflected by a body to the luminous flux it receives.

(h) *Exterior emergency lighting and escape route.*

(1) Each passenger-carrying airplane must be equipped with exterior lighting that meets the following requirements:

(i) For an airplane for which the application for the type certificate was filed prior to May 1, 1972, the requirements of §25.812(f) and (g) of this chapter in effect on April 30, 1972.

(ii) For an airplane for which the application for the type certificate was filed on or after May 1, 1972, the exterior emergency lighting requirements under which the airplane was type certificated.

(2) Each passenger-carrying airplane must be equipped with a slip-resistant escape route that meets the following requirements:

(i) For an airplane for which the application for the type certificate was filed prior to May 1, 1972, the requirements of §25.803(e) of this chapter in effect on April 30, 1972.

(ii) For an airplane for which the application for the type certificate was filed on or after May 1, 1972, the slip-resistant escape route requirements under which the airplane was type certificated.

(i) *Floor level exits.* Each floor level door or exit in the side of the fuselage (other than those leading into a cargo or baggage compartment that is not accessible from the passenger cabin) that is 44 or more inches high and 20 or more inches wide, but not wider than 46 inches, each passenger ventral exit (except the ventral exits on Martin 404 and Convair 240 airplanes), and each tail cone exit, must meet the requirements of this section for floor level emergency exits. However, the Administrator may grant a deviation from this paragraph if he finds that circumstances make full compliance impractical and that an acceptable level of safety has been achieved.

(j) *Additional emergency exits.* Approved emergency exits in the passenger compartments that are in excess of the minimum number of required emergency exits must meet all of the applicable provisions of this section, except paragraphs (f)(1), (2), and (3) of this section, and must be readily accessible.

(k) On each large passenger-carrying turbojet-powered airplane, each ventral exit and tailcone exit must be—

(1) Designed and constructed so that it cannot be opened during flight; and

(2) Marked with a placard readable from a distance of 30 inches and installed at a conspicuous location near the means of opening the exit, stating that the exit has been designed and constructed so that it cannot be opened during flight.

(l) *Portable lights.* No person may operate a passenger-carrying airplane unless it is equipped with flashlight stowage provisions accessible from each flight attendant seat.

[Docket No. 26530, 57 FR 19245, May 4, 1992; 57 FR 29120, June 30, 1992; as amended by 57 FR 34682, Aug. 6, 1992]

§135.179 Inoperable instruments and equipment.

(a) No person may take off an aircraft with inoperable instruments or equipment installed unless the following conditions are met:

(1) An approved Minimum Equipment List exists for that aircraft.

(2) The certificate-holding district office has issued the certificate holder operations specifications authorizing operations in accordance with an approved Minimum Equipment List. The flight crew shall have direct access at all times prior to flight to all of the information contained in the approved Minimum Equipment List through printed or other means approved by the Administrator in the certificate holder's operations specifications. An approved Minimum Equipment List, as authorized by the operations specifications, constitutes an approved change to the type design without requiring recertification.

(3) The approved Minimum Equipment List must:

(i) Be prepared in accordance with the limitations specified in paragraph (b) of this section.

(ii) Provide for the operation of the aircraft with certain instruments and equipment in an inoperable condition.

(4) Records identifying the inoperable instruments and equipment and the information required by (a)(3)(ii) of this section must be available to the pilot.

(5) The aircraft is operated under all applicable conditions and limitations contained in the Minimum Equipment List and the operations specifications authorizing use of the Minimum Equipment List.

(b) The following instruments and equipment may not be included in the Minimum Equipment List:

(1) Instruments and equipment that are either specifically or otherwise required by the airworthiness requirements under which the airplane is type certificated and which are essential for safe operations under all operating conditions.

(2) Instruments and equipment required by an airworthiness directive to be in operable condition unless the airworthiness directive provides otherwise.

(3) Instruments and equipment required for specific operations by this part.

(c) Notwithstanding paragraphs (b)(1) and (b)(3) of this section, an aircraft with inoperable instruments or equipment may be operated under a special flight permit under §§21.197 and 21.199 of this chapter.

[Docket No. 25780, 56 FR 12311, March 22, 1991; 56 FR 14920, April 8, 1991; as amended by Amdt. 135–60, 61 FR 2616, Jan. 26, 1996; Amdt. 135–91, 68 FR 54586, Sept. 17, 2003]

§135.180 Traffic Alert and Collision Avoidance System.

(a) Unless otherwise authorized by the Administrator, after December 31, 1995, no person may operate a turbine powered airplane that has a passenger seat configuration, excluding any pilot seat, of 10 to 30 seats unless it is equipped with an approved traffic alert and collision avoidance system. If a TCAS II system is installed, it must be capable of coordinating with TCAS units that meet TSO C-119.

(b) The airplane flight manual required by §135.21 of this part shall contain the following information on the TCAS I system required by this section:

(1) Appropriate procedures for—

(i) The use of the equipment; and

(ii) Proper flightcrew action with respect to the equipment operation.

(2) An outline of all input sources that must be operating for the TCAS to function properly.

[Docket No. 25355, 54 FR 951, Jan. 10, 1989; as amended by Amdt. 135–54, 59 FR 67587, Dec. 29, 1994]

§135.181 Performance requirements: Aircraft operated over-the-top or in IFR conditions.

(a) Except as provided in paragraphs (b) and (c) of this section, no person may—

(1) Operate a single-engine aircraft carrying passengers over-the-top; or

(2) Operate a multiengine aircraft carrying passengers over-the-top or in IFR conditions at a weight that will not allow it to climb, with the critical engine inoperative, at least 50 feet a minute when operating at the MEAs of the route to be flown or 5,000 feet MSL, whichever is higher.

(b) Notwithstanding the restrictions in paragraph (a)(2) of this section, multiengine helicopters carrying passengers offshore may conduct such operations in over-the-top or in IFR conditions at a weight that will allow the helicopter to climb at least 50 feet per minute with the critical engine inoperative when operating at the MEA of the route to be flown or 1,500 feet MSL, whichever is higher.

(c) Without regard to paragraph (a) of this section, if the latest weather reports or forecasts, or any combination of them, indicate that the weather along the planned route (including takeoff and landing) allows flight under VFR under the ceiling (if a ceiling exists) and that the weather is forecast to remain so until at least 1 hour after the estimated time of arrival at the destination, a person may operate an aircraft over-the-top.

(d) Without regard to paragraph (a) of this section, a person may operate an aircraft over-the-top under conditions allowing—

Part 135: Commuter & On Demand Operations §135.211

(1) For multiengine aircraft, descent or continuance of the flight under VFR if its critical engine fails; or

(2) For single-engine aircraft, descent under VFR if its engine fails.

[Docket No. 16097, 43 FR 46783, Oct. 10, 1978; as amended by Amdt. 135–20, 51 FR 40710, Nov. 7, 1986; Amdt. 135–70, 62 FR 42374, Aug. 6, 1997]

§135.183 Performance requirements: Land aircraft operated over water.

No person may operate a land aircraft carrying passengers over water unless—

(a) It is operated at an altitude that allows it to reach land in the case of engine failure;

(b) It is necessary for takeoff or landing;

(c) It is a multiengine aircraft operated at a weight that will allow it to climb, with the critical engine inoperative, at least 50 feet a minute, at an altitude of 1,000 feet above the surface; or

(d) It is a helicopter equipped with helicopter flotation devices.

§135.185 Empty weight and center of gravity: Currency requirement.

(a) No person may operate a multiengine aircraft unless the current empty weight and center of gravity are calculated from values established by actual weighing of the aircraft within the preceding 36 calendar months.

(b) Paragraph (a) of this section does not apply to—

(1) Aircraft issued an original airworthiness certificate within the preceding 36 calendar months; and

(2) Aircraft operated under a weight and balance system approved in the operations specifications of the certificate holder.

Subpart D—
VFR/IFR Operating Limitations and Weather Requirements

§135.201 Applicability.

This subpart prescribes the operating limitations for VFR/IFR flight operations and associated weather requirements for operations under this part.

§135.203 VFR: Minimum altitudes.

Except when necessary for takeoff and landing, no person may operate under VFR—

(a) An airplane—

(1) During the day, below 500 feet above the surface or less than 500 feet horizontally from any obstacle; or

(2) At night, at an altitude less than 1,000 feet above the highest obstacle within a horizontal distance of 5 miles from the course intended to be flown or, in designated mountainous terrain, less than 2,000 feet above the highest obstacle within a horizontal distance of 5 miles from the course intended to be flown; or

(b) A helicopter over a congested area at an altitude less than 300 feet above the surface.

§135.205 VFR: Visibility requirements.

(a) No person may operate an airplane under VFR in uncontrolled airspace when the ceiling is less than 1,000 feet unless flight visibility is at least 2 miles.

(b) No person may operate a helicopter under VFR in Class G airspace at an altitude of 1,200 feet or less above the surface or within the lateral boundaries of the surface areas of Class B, Class C, Class D, or Class E airspace designated for an airport unless the visibility is at least—

(1) During the day—1/2 mile; or

(2) At night—1 mile.

[Docket No. 16097, 43 FR 46783, Oct. 10, 1978; as amended by Amdt. 135–41, 56 FR 65663, Dec. 17, 1991]

§135.207 VFR: Helicopter surface reference requirements.

No person may operate a helicopter under VFR unless that person has visual surface reference or, at night, visual surface light reference, sufficient to safely control the helicopter.

§135.209 VFR: Fuel supply.

(a) No person may begin a flight operation in an airplane under VFR unless, considering wind and forecast weather conditions, it has enough fuel to fly to the first point of intended landing and, assuming normal cruising fuel consumption—

(1) During the day, to fly after that for at least 30 minutes; or

(2) At night, to fly after that for at least 45 minutes.

(b) No person may begin a flight operation in a helicopter under VFR unless, considering wind and forecast weather conditions, it has enough fuel to fly to the first point of intended landing and, assuming normal cruising fuel consumption, to fly after that for at least 20 minutes.

§135.211 VFR: Over-the-top carrying passengers: Operating limitations.

Subject to any additional limitations in §135.181, no person may operate an aircraft under VFR over-the-top carrying passengers, unless—

(a) Weather reports or forecasts, or any combination of them, indicate that the weather at the intended point of termination of over-the-top flight—

(1) Allows descent to beneath the ceiling under VFR and is forecast to remain so until at least 1 hour after the estimated time of arrival at that point; or

(2) Allows an IFR approach and landing with flight clear of the clouds until reaching the prescribed initial approach altitude over the final approach facility, unless the approach is made with the use of radar under §91.175(i) of this chapter; or

(b) It is operated under conditions allowing—

(1) For multiengine aircraft, descent or continuation of the flight under VFR if its critical engine fails; or

(2) For single-engine aircraft, descent under VFR if its engine fails.

[Docket No. 16097, 43 FR 46783, Oct. 10, 1978; as amended by Amdt. 135–32, 54 FR 34332, Aug. 18, 1989; 73 FR 20164, April 15, 2008]

§135.213 Weather reports and forecasts.

(a) Whenever a person operating an aircraft under this part is required to use a weather report or forecast, that person shall use that of the U.S. National Weather Service, a source approved by the U.S. National Weather Service, or a source approved by the Administrator. However, for operations under VFR, the pilot in command may, if such a report is not available, use weather information based on that pilot's own observations or on those of other persons competent to supply appropriate observations.

(b) For the purposes of paragraph (a) of this section, weather observations made and furnished to pilots to conduct IFR operations at an airport must be taken at the airport where those IFR operations are conducted, unless the Administrator issues operations specifications allowing the use of weather observations taken at a location not at the airport where the IFR operations are conducted. The Administrator issues such operations specifications when, after investigation by the U.S. National Weather Service and the certificate-holding district office, it is found that the standards of safety for that operation would allow the deviation from this paragraph for a particular operation for which an air carrier operating certificate or operating certificate has been issued.

[Docket No. 16097, 43 FR 46783, Oct. 10, 1978; as amended by Amdt. 135–60, 61 FR 2616, Jan. 26, 1996]

§135.215 IFR: Operating limitations.

(a) Except as provided in paragraphs (b), (c) and (d) of this section, no person may operate an aircraft under IFR outside of controlled airspace or at any airport that does not have an approved standard instrument approach procedure.

(b) The Administrator may issue operations specifications to the certificate holder to allow it to operate under IFR over routes outside controlled airspace if—

(1) The certificate holder shows the Administrator that the flight crew is able to navigate, without visual reference to the ground, over an intended track without deviating more than 5 degrees or 5 miles, whichever is less, from that track; and

(2) The Administrator determines that the proposed operations can be conducted safely.

(c) A person may operate an aircraft under IFR outside of controlled airspace if the certificate holder has been approved for the operations and that operation is necessary to—

(1) Conduct an instrument approach to an airport for which there is in use a current approved standard or special instrument approach procedure; or

(2) Climb into controlled airspace during an approved missed approach procedure; or

(3) Make an IFR departure from an airport having an approved instrument approach procedure.

(d) The Administrator may issue operations specifications to the certificate holder to allow it to depart at an airport that does not have an approved standard instrument approach procedure when the Administrator determines that it is necessary to make an IFR departure from that airport and that the proposed operations can be conducted safely. The approval to operate at that airport does not include an approval to make an IFR approach to that airport.

§135.217 IFR: Takeoff limitations.

No person may takeoff an aircraft under IFR from an airport where weather conditions are at or above takeoff minimums but are below authorized IFR landing minimums unless there is an alternate airport within 1 hour's flying time (at normal cruising speed, in still air) of the airport of departure.

§135.219 IFR: Destination airport weather minimums.

No person may take off an aircraft under IFR or begin an IFR or over-the-top operation unless the latest weather reports or forecasts, or any combination of them, indicate that weather conditions at the estimated time of arrival at the next airport of intended landing will be at or above authorized IFR landing minimums.

§135.221 IFR: Alternate airport weather minimums.

(a) *Aircraft other than rotorcraft.* No person may designate an alternate airport unless the weather reports or forecasts, or any combination of them, indicate that the weather conditions will be at or above authorized alternate airport landing minimums for that airport at the estimated time of arrival.

(b) *Rotorcraft.* Unless otherwise authorized by the Administrator, no person may include an alternate airport in an IFR flight plan unless appropriate weather reports or weather forecasts, or a combination of them, indicate that, at the estimated time of arrival at the alternate airport, the ceiling and visibility at that airport will be at or above the following weather minimums—

(1) If, for the alternate airport, an instrument approach procedure has been published in part 97 of this chapter or a special instrument approach procedure has been issued by the FAA to the certificate holder, the ceiling is 200 feet above the minimum for the approach to be flown, and visibility is at least 1 statute mile but never less than the minimum visibility for the approach to be flown.

(2) If, for the alternate airport, no instrument approach procedure has been published in part 97 of this chapter and no special instrument approach procedure has been issued by the FAA to the certificate holder, the ceiling and visibility minimums are those allowing descent from the minimum enroute altitude (MEA), approach, and landing under basic VFR.

[Docket No. 16097, 43 FR 46783, Oct. 10, 1978; as amended by Amdt. 135–129, 79 FR 9974, Feb. 21, 2014]

§135.223 IFR: Alternate airport requirements.

(a) Except as provided in paragraph (b) of this section, no person may operate an aircraft in IFR conditions unless it carries enough fuel (considering weather reports or forecasts or any combination of them) to—

(1) Complete the flight to the first airport of intended landing;

(2) Fly from that airport to the alternate airport; and

(3) Fly after that for 45 minutes at normal cruising speed or, for helicopters, fly after that for 30 minutes at normal cruising speed.

(b) Paragraph (a)(2) of this section does not apply if part 97 of this chapter prescribes a standard instrument approach procedure for the first airport of intended landing and, for at least one hour before and after the estimated time of arrival, the appropriate weather reports or forecasts, or any combination of them, indicate that—

(1) The ceiling will be at least 1,500 feet above the lowest circling approach MDA; or

(2) If a circling instrument approach is not authorized for the airport, the ceiling will be at least 1,500 feet above the lowest published minimum or 2,000 feet above the airport elevation, whichever is higher; and

(3) Visibility for that airport is forecast to be at least three miles, or two miles more than the lowest applicable visibility minimums, whichever is the greater, for the instrument approach procedure to be used at the destination airport.

[Docket No. 16097, 43 FR 46783, Oct. 10, 1978; as amended by Amdt. 135–20, 51 FR 40710, Nov. 7, 1986]

§135.225 IFR: Takeoff, approach and landing minimums.

(a) Except to the extent permitted by paragraph (b) of this section, no pilot may begin an instrument approach procedure to an airport unless—

(1) That airport has a weather reporting facility operated by the U.S. National Weather Service, a source approved by U.S. National Weather Service, or a source approved by the Administrator; and

(2) The latest weather report issued by that weather reporting facility indicates that weather conditions are at or above the authorized IFR landing minimums for that airport.

(b) A pilot conducting an eligible on-demand operation may begin an instrument approach procedure to an airport that does not have a weather reporting facility operated by the U.S. National Weather Service, a source approved by the U.S. National Weather Service, or a source approved by the Administrator if—

(1) The alternate airport has a weather reporting facility operated by the U.S. National Weather Service, a source approved by the U.S. National Weather Service, or a source approved by the Administrator; and

(2) The latest weather report issued by the weather reporting facility includes a current local altimeter setting for the destination airport. If no local altimeter setting for the destination airport is available, the pilot may use the current altimeter setting provided by the facility designated on the approach chart for the destination airport.

(c) If a pilot has begun the final approach segment of an instrument approach to an airport under paragraph (b) of this section, and the pilot receives a later weather report indicating that conditions have worsened to below the minimum requirements, then the pilot may continue the approach only if the requirements of §91.175(l) of this chapter, or both of the following conditions, are met—

(1) The later weather report is received when the aircraft is in one of the following approach phases:

§135.225

(i) The aircraft is on an ILS final approach and has passed the final approach fix;
(ii) The aircraft is on an ASR or PAR final approach and has been turned over to the final approach controller; or
(iii) The aircraft is on a nonprecision final approach and the aircraft—
(A) Has passed the appropriate facility or final approach fix; or
(B) Where a final approach fix is not specified, has completed the procedure turn and is established inbound toward the airport on the final approach course within the distance prescribed in the procedure; and
(2) The pilot in command finds, on reaching the authorized MDA or DA/DH, that the actual weather conditions are at or above the minimums prescribed for the procedure being used.

(d) If a pilot has begun the final approach segment of an instrument approach to an airport under paragraph (c) of this section and a later weather report indicating below minimum conditions is received after the aircraft is—
(1) On an ILS final approach and has passed the final approach fix;
(2) On an ASR or PAR final approach and has been turned over to the final approach controller; or
(3) On a final approach using a VOR, NDB, or comparable approach procedure; and the aircraft—
(i) Has passed the appropriate facility or final approach fix; or
(ii) Where a final approach fix is not specified, has completed the procedure turn and is established inbound toward the airport on the final approach course within the distance prescribed in the procedure; the approach may be continued and a landing made if the pilot finds, upon reaching the authorized MDA or DH, that actual weather conditions are at least equal to the minimums prescribed for the procedure.

(e) The MDA or DA/DH and visibility landing minimums prescribed in part 97 of this chapter or in the operator's operations specifications are increased by 100 feet and 1/2 mile respectively, but not to exceed the ceiling and visibility minimums for that airport when used as an alternate airport, for each pilot in command of a turbine-powered airplane who has not served at least 100 hours as pilot in command in that type of airplane.

(f) Each pilot making an IFR takeoff or approach and landing at a military or foreign airport shall comply with applicable instrument approach procedures and weather minimums prescribed by the authority having jurisdiction over that airport. In addition, unless authorized by the certificate holder's operations specifications, no pilot may, at that airport—

(1) Take off under IFR when the visibility is less than 1 mile; or
(2) Make an instrument approach when the visibility is less than 1/2 mile.

(g) If takeoff minimums are specified in part 97 of this chapter for the takeoff airport, no pilot may take off an aircraft under IFR when the weather conditions reported by the facility described in paragraph (a)(1) of this section are less than the takeoff minimums specified for the takeoff airport in part 97 or in the certificate holder's operations specifications.

(h) Except as provided in paragraph (i) of this section, if takeoff minimums are not prescribed in part 97 of this chapter for the takeoff airport, no pilot may takeoff an aircraft under IFR when the weather conditions reported by the facility described in paragraph (a)(1) of this section are less than that prescribed in part 91 of this chapter or in the certificate holder's operations specifications.

(i) At airports where straight-in instrument approach procedures are authorized, a pilot may take off an aircraft under IFR when the weather conditions reported by the facility described in paragraph (a)(1) of this section are equal to or better than the lowest straight-in landing minimums, unless otherwise restricted, if—
(1) The wind direction and velocity at the time of takeoff are such that a straight-in instrument approach can be made to the runway served by the instrument approach;
(2) The associated ground facilities upon which the landing minimums are predicated and the related airborne equipment are in normal operation; and
(3) The certificate holder has been approved for such operations.

[Docket No. 16097, 43 FR 46783, Oct. 10, 1978; as amended by Amdt. 135–91, 68 FR 54586, Sept. 17, 2003; Amdt. 135–93, 69 FR 1641, Jan. 9, 2004; Amdt. 135–110, 72 FR 31685, June 7, 2007; Amdt. 135–126, 77 FR 1632, Jan. 11, 2012]

§135.227 Icing conditions: Operating limitations.

(a) No pilot may take off an aircraft that has frost, ice, or snow adhering to any rotor blade, propeller, windshield, stabilizing or control surface; to a powerplant installation; or to an airspeed, altimeter, rate of climb, flight attitude instrument system, or wing, except that takeoffs may be made with frost under the wing in the area of the fuel tanks if authorized by the FAA.

(b) No certificate holder may authorize an airplane to take off and no pilot may take off an airplane any time conditions are such that frost, ice, or snow may reasonably be expected to adhere to the airplane unless the pilot has completed all applicable training as required by §135.341 and unless one of the following requirements is met:

(1) A pretakeoff contamination check, that has been established by the certificate holder and approved by the Administrator for the specific airplane type, has been completed within 5 minutes prior to beginning takeoff. A pretakeoff contamination check is a check to make sure the wings and control surfaces are free of frost, ice, or snow.

(2) The certificate holder has an approved alternative procedure and under that procedure the airplane is determined to be free of frost, ice, or snow.

(3) The certificate holder has an approved deicing/anti-icing program that complies with §121.629(c) of this chapter and the takeoff complies with that program.

(c) No pilot may fly under IFR into known or forecast light or moderate icing conditions or under VFR into known light or moderate icing conditions, unless—

(1) The aircraft has functioning deicing or anti-icing equipment protecting each rotor blade, propeller, windshield, wing, stabilizing or control surface, and each airspeed, altimeter, rate of climb, or flight attitude instrument system;

(2) The airplane has ice protection provisions that meet section 34 of appendix A of this part; or

(3) The airplane meets transport category airplane type certification provisions, including the requirements for certification for flight in icing conditions.

(d) No pilot may fly a helicopter under IFR into known or forecast icing conditions or under VFR into known icing conditions unless it has been type certificated and appropriately equipped for operations in icing conditions.

(e) Except for an airplane that has ice protection provisions that meet section 34 of Appendix A, or those for transport category airplane type certification, no pilot may fly an aircraft into known or forecast severe icing conditions.

(f) If current weather reports and briefing information relied upon by the pilot in command indicate that the forecast icing condition that would otherwise prohibit the flight will not be encountered during the flight because of changed weather conditions since the forecast, the restrictions in paragraphs (c), (d), and (e) of this section based on forecast conditions do not apply.

[Docket No. 16097, 43 FR 46783, Oct. 10, 1978; as amended by Amdt. 133–20, 51 FR 40710, Nov. 7, 1986; Amdt. 135–46, 58 FR 69629, Dec. 30, 1993; Amdt. 135–46, 58 FR 69629, Dec. 30, 1993; Amdt. 135–60, 61 FR, Jan. 26, 1996; Amdt. 135–119, 74 FR 62696, Dec. 1, 2009]

§135.229 Airport requirements.

(a) No certificate holder may use any airport unless it is adequate for the proposed operation, considering such items as size, surface, obstructions, and lighting.

(b) No pilot of an aircraft carrying passengers at night may take off from, or land on, an airport unless—

(1) That pilot has determined the wind direction from an illuminated wind direction indicator or local ground communications or, in the case of takeoff, that pilot's personal observations; and

(2) The limits of the area to be used for landing or takeoff are clearly shown—

(i) For airplanes, by boundary or runway marker lights;

(ii) For helicopters, by boundary or runway marker lights or reflective material.

(c) For the purpose of paragraph (b) of this section, if the area to be used for takeoff or landing is marked by flare pots or lanterns, their use must be approved by the Administrator.

Subpart E— Flight Crewmember Requirements

§135.241 Applicability.

Except as provided in §135.3, this subpart prescribes the flight crewmember requirements for operations under this part.

[Docket No. 16097, 43 FR 46783, Oct. 10, 1978; as amended by Amdt. 135–57, 60 FR 65950, Dec. 20, 1995]

§135.243 Pilot in command qualifications.

(a) No certificate holder may use a person, nor may any person serve, as pilot in command in passenger-carrying operations—

(1) Of a turbojet airplane, of an airplane having a passenger-seat configuration, excluding each crewmember seat, of 10 seats or more, or of a multiengine airplane in a commuter operation as defined in part 119 of this chapter, unless that person holds an airline transport pilot certificate with appropriate category and class ratings and, if required, an appropriate type rating for that airplane.

(2) Of a helicopter in a scheduled interstate air transportation operation by an air carrier within the 48 contiguous states unless that person holds an airline transport pilot certificate, appropriate type ratings, and an instrument rating.

(b) Except as provided in paragraph (a) of this section, no certificate holder may use a person, nor may any person serve, as pilot in command of an aircraft under VFR unless that person—

(1) Holds at least a commercial pilot certificate with appropriate category and class ratings and, if required, an appropriate type rating for that aircraft; and

§135.243

(2) Has had at least 500 hours of flight time as a pilot, including at least 100 hours of cross-country flight time, at least 25 hours of which were at night; and

(3) For an airplane, holds an instrument rating or an airline transport pilot certificate with an airplane category rating; or

(4) For helicopter operations conducted VFR over-the-top, holds a helicopter instrument rating, or an airline transport pilot certificate with a category and class rating for that aircraft, not limited to VFR.

(c) Except as provided in paragraph (a) of this section, no certificate holder may use a person, nor may any person serve, as pilot in command of an aircraft under IFR unless that person—

(1) Holds at least a commercial pilot certificate with appropriate category and class ratings and, if required, an appropriate type rating for that aircraft; and

(2) Has had at least 1,200 hours of flight time as a pilot, including 500 hours of cross country flight time, 100 hours of night flight time, and 75 hours of actual or simulated instrument time at least 50 hours of which were in actual flight; and

(3) For an airplane, holds an instrument rating or an airline transport pilot certificate with an airplane category rating; or

(4) For a helicopter, holds a helicopter instrument rating, or an airline transport pilot certificate with a category and class rating for that aircraft, not limited to VFR.

(d) Paragraph (b)(3) of this section does not apply when—

(1) The aircraft used is a single reciprocating-engine-powered airplane;

(2) The certificate holder does not conduct any operation pursuant to a published flight schedule which specifies five or more round trips a week between two or more points and places between which the round trips are performed, and does not transport mail by air under a contract or contracts with the United States Postal Service having total amount estimated at the beginning of any semiannual reporting period (January 1 – June 30; July 1 – December 31) to be in excess of $20,000 over the 12 months commencing with the beginning of the reporting period;

(3) The area, as specified in the certificate holder's operations specifications, is an isolated area, as determined by the Flight Standards district office, if it is shown that—

(i) The primary means of navigation in the area is by pilotage, since radio navigational aids are largely ineffective; and

(ii) The primary means of transportation in the area is by air;

(4) Each flight is conducted under day VFR with a ceiling of not less than 1,000 feet and visibility not less than 3 statute miles;

(5) Weather reports or forecasts, or any combination of them, indicate that for the period commencing with the planned departure and ending 30 minutes after the planned arrival at the destination the flight may be conducted under VFR with a ceiling of not less than 1,000 feet and visibility of not less than 3 statute miles, except that if weather reports and forecasts are not available, the pilot in command may use that pilot's observations or those of other persons competent to supply weather observations if those observations indicate the flight may be conducted under VFR with the ceiling and visibility required in this paragraph;

(6) The distance of each flight from the certificate holder's base of operation to destination does not exceed 250 nautical miles for a pilot who holds a commercial pilot certificate with an airplane rating without an instrument rating, provided the pilot's certificate does not contain any limitation to the contrary; and

(7) The areas to be flown are approved by the certificate-holding FAA Flight Standards district office and are listed in the certificate holder's operations specifications.

[Docket No. 16097, 43 FR 46783, Oct. 10, 1978; as amended by Amdt. 135–1, 43 FR 49975, Oct. 26, 1978; Amdt. 135–15, 46 FR 30971, June 11, 1981; Amdt. 135–58, 60 FR 65939, Dec. 20, 1995; 63 FR 53804, Oct. 7, 1998]

§135.244 Operating experience.

(a) No certificate holder may use any person, nor may any person serve, as a pilot in command of an aircraft operated in a commuter operation, as defined in part 119 of this chapter, unless that person has completed, prior to designation as pilot in command, on that make and basic model aircraft and in that crewmember position, the following operating experience in each make and basic model of aircraft to be flown:

(1) Aircraft, single engine—10 hours.

(2) Aircraft multiengine, reciprocating engine-powered—15 hours.

(3) Aircraft multiengine, turbine engine-powered—20 hours.

(4) Airplane, turbojet-powered—25 hours.

(b) In acquiring the operating experience, each person must comply with the following:

(1) The operating experience must be acquired after satisfactory completion of the appropriate ground and flight training for the aircraft and crewmember position. Approved provisions for the operating experience must be included in the certificate holder's training program.

(2) The experience must be acquired in flight during commuter passenger-carrying operations under this part. However, in the case of an aircraft not previously used by the certificate holder in operations under this part, operating experience ac-

quired in the aircraft during proving flights or ferry flights may be used to meet this requirement.

(3) Each person must acquire the operating experience while performing the duties of a pilot in command under the supervision of a qualified check pilot.

(4) The hours of operating experience may be reduced to not less than 50 percent of the hours required by this section by the substitution of one additional takeoff and landing for each hour of flight.

[Docket No. 20011, 45 FR 7541, Feb. 4, 1980; as amended by Amdt. 135–9, 45 FR 80461, Dec. 14, 1980; Amdt. 135–58, 60 FR 65940, Dec. 20, 1995]

§135.245 Second in command qualifications.

(a) Except as provided in paragraph (b), no certificate holder may use any person, nor may any person serve, as second in command of an aircraft unless that person holds at least a commercial pilot certificate with appropriate category and class ratings and an instrument rating. For flight under IFR, that person must meet the recent instrument experience requirements of part 61 of this chapter.

(b) A second in command of a helicopter operated under VFR, other than over-the-top, must have at least a commercial pilot certificate with an appropriate aircraft category and class rating.

[44 FR 26738, May 7, 1979]

§135.247 Pilot qualifications: Recent experience.

(a) No certificate holder may use any person, nor may any person serve, as pilot in command of an aircraft carrying passengers unless, within the preceding 90 days, that person has—

(1) Made three takeoffs and three landings as the sole manipulator of the flight controls in an aircraft of the same category and class and, if a type rating is required, of the same type in which that person is to serve; or

(2) For operation during the period beginning 1 hour after sunset and ending 1 hour before sunrise (as published in the Air Almanac), made three takeoffs and three landings during that period as the sole manipulator of the flight controls in an aircraft of the same category and class and, if a type rating is required, of the same type in which that person is to serve.

A person who complies with paragraph (a)(2) of this section need not comply with paragraph (a)(1) of this section.

(3) Paragraph (a)(2) of this section does not apply to a pilot in command of a turbine-powered airplane that is type certificated for more than one pilot crewmember, provided that pilot has complied with the requirements of paragraph (a)(3)(i) or (ii) of this section:

(i) The pilot in command must hold at least a commercial pilot certificate with the appropriate category, class, and type rating for each airplane that is type certificated for more than one pilot crewmember that the pilot seeks to operate under this alternative, and:

(A) That pilot must have logged at least 1,500 hours of aeronautical experience as a pilot;

(B) In each airplane that is type certificated for more than one pilot crewmember that the pilot seeks to operate under this alternative, that pilot must have accomplished and logged the daytime takeoff and landing recent flight experience of paragraph (a) of this section, as the sole manipulator of the flight controls;

(C) Within the preceding 90 days prior to the operation of that airplane that is type certificated for more than one pilot crewmember, the pilot must have accomplished and logged at least 15 hours of flight time in the type of airplane that the pilot seeks to operate under this alternative; and

(D) That pilot has accomplished and logged at least 3 takeoffs and 3 landings to a full stop, as the sole manipulator of the flight controls, in a turbine-powered airplane that requires more than one pilot crewmember. The pilot must have performed the takeoffs and landings during the period beginning 1 hour after sunset and ending 1 hour before sunrise within the preceding 6 months prior to the month of the flight.

(ii) The pilot in command must hold at least a commercial pilot certificate with the appropriate category, class, and type rating for each airplane that is type certificated for more than one pilot crewmember that the pilot seeks to operate under this alternative, and:

(A) That pilot must have logged at least 1,500 hours of aeronautical experience as a pilot;

(B) In each airplane that is type certificated for more than one pilot crewmember that the pilot seeks to operate under this alternative, that pilot must have accomplished and logged the daytime takeoff and landing recent flight experience of paragraph (a) of this section, as the sole manipulator of the flight controls;

(C) Within the preceding 90 days prior to the operation of that airplane that is type certificated for more than one pilot crewmember, the pilot must have accomplished and logged at least 15 hours of flight time in the type of airplane that the pilot seeks to operate under this alternative; and

(D) Within the preceding 12 months prior to the month of the flight, the pilot must have completed a training program that is approved under part 142 of this chapter. The approved training program must have required and the pilot must have performed, at least 6 takeoffs and 6 landings to a full stop as the sole manipulator of the

§135.261

controls in a flight simulator that is representative of a turbine-powered airplane that requires more than one pilot crewmember. The flight simulator's visual system must have been adjusted to represent the period beginning 1 hour after sunset and ending 1 hour before sunrise.

(b) For the purpose of paragraph (a) of this section, if the aircraft is a tailwheel airplane, each takeoff must be made in a tailwheel airplane and each landing must be made to a full stop in a tailwheel airplane.

[Docket No. 16097, 43 FR 46783, Oct. 10, 1978; as amended by Amdt. 135–91, 68 FR 54587, Sept. 17, 2003]

§135.249 [Reserved]

§135.251 [Reserved]

§135.253 [Reserved]

§135.255 [Reserved]

Subpart F— Crewmember Flight Time and Duty Period Limitations and Rest Requirements

Source: Docket No. 23634, 50 FR 29320, July 18, 1985, unless otherwise noted.

§135.261 Applicability.

Sections 135.263 through 135.273 of this part prescribe flight time limitations, duty period limitations, and rest requirements for operations conducted under this part as follows:

(a) Section 135.263 applies to all operations under this subpart.

(b) Section 135.265 applies to:

(1) Scheduled passenger-carrying operations except those conducted solely within the state of Alaska. "Scheduled passenger-carrying operations" means passenger-carrying operations that are conducted in accordance with a published schedule which covers at least five round trips per week on at least one route between two or more points, includes dates or times (or both), and is openly advertised or otherwise made readily available to the general public, and

(2) Any other operation under this part, if the operator elects to comply with §135.265 and obtains an appropriate operations specification amendment.

(c) Sections 135.267 and 135.269 apply to any operation that is not a scheduled passenger-carrying operation and to any operation conducted solely within the State of Alaska, unless the operator elects to comply with §135.265 as authorized under paragraph (b)(2) of this section.

(d) Section 135.271 contains special daily flight time limits for operations conducted under the helicopter emergency medical evacuation service (HEMES).

(e) Section 135.273 prescribes duty period limitations and rest requirements for flight attendants in all operations conducted under this part.

[Docket No. 23634, 50 FR 29320, July 18, 1985; as amended by Amdt. 135–52, 59 FR 42993, Aug. 19, 1994]

§135.263 Flight time limitations and rest requirements: All certificate holders.

(a) A certificate holder may assign a flight crewmember and a flight crewmember may accept an assignment for flight time only when the applicable requirements of §§135.263 through 135.271 are met.

(b) No certificate holder may assign any flight crewmember to any duty with the certificate holder during any required rest period.

(c) Time spent in transportation, not local in character, that a certificate holder requires of a flight crewmember and provides to transport the crewmember to an airport at which he is to serve on a flight as a crewmember, or from an airport at which he was relieved from duty to return to his home station, is not considered part of a rest period.

(d) A flight crewmember is not considered to be assigned flight time in excess of flight time limitations if the flights to which he is assigned normally terminate within the limitations, but due to circumstances beyond the control of the certificate holder or flight crewmember (such as adverse weather conditions), are not at the time of departure expected to reach their destination within the planned flight time.

§135.265 Flight time limitations and rest requirements: Scheduled operations.

(a) No certificate holder may schedule any flight crewmember, and no flight crewmember may accept an assignment, for flight time in scheduled operations or in other commercial flying if that crewmember's total flight time in all commercial flying will exceed—

(1) 1,200 hours in any calendar year.

(2) 120 hours in any calendar month.

(3) 34 hours in any 7 consecutive days.

(4) 8 hours during any 24 consecutive hours for a flight crew consisting of one pilot.

(5) 8 hours between required rest periods for a flight crew consisting of two pilots qualified under this part for the operation being conducted.

(b) Except as provided in paragraph (c) of this section, no certificate holder may schedule a flight crewmember, and no flight crewmember may accept an assignment, for flight time during the 24 consecutive hours preceding the scheduled completion of any flight segment without a scheduled rest period during that 24 hours of at least the following:

(1) 9 consecutive hours of rest for less than 8 hours of scheduled flight time.

(2) 10 consecutive hours of rest for 8 or more but less than 9 hours of scheduled flight time.

(3) 11 consecutive hours of rest for 9 or more hours of scheduled flight time.

(c) A certificate holder may schedule a flight crewmember for less than the rest required in paragraph (b) of this section or may reduce a scheduled rest under the following conditions:

(1) A rest required under paragraph (b)(1) of this section may be scheduled for or reduced to a minimum of 8 hours if the flight crewmember is given a rest period of at least 10 hours that must begin no later than 24 hours after the commencement of the reduced rest period.

(2) A rest required under paragraph (b)(2) of this section may be scheduled for or reduced to a minimum of 8 hours if the flight crewmember is given a rest period of at least 11 hours that must begin no later than 24 hours after the commencement of the reduced rest period.

(3) A rest required under paragraph (b)(3) of this section may be scheduled for or reduced to a minimum of 9 hours if the flight crewmember is given a rest period of at least 12 hours that must begin no later than 24 hours after the commencement of the reduced rest period.

(d) Each certificate holder shall relieve each flight crewmember engaged in scheduled air transportation from all further duty for at least 24 consecutive hours during any 7 consecutive days.

§135.267 Flight time limitations and rest requirements: Unscheduled one- and two-pilot crews.

(a) No certificate holder may assign any flight crewmember, and no flight crewmember may accept an assignment, for flight time as a member of a one- or two-pilot crew if that crewmember's total flight time in all commercial flying will exceed—

(1) 500 hours in any calendar quarter.

(2) 800 hours in any two consecutive calendar quarters.

(3) 1,400 hours in any calendar year.

(b) Except as provided in paragraph (c) of this section, during any 24 consecutive hours the total flight time of the assigned flight when added to any other commercial flying by that flight crewmember may not exceed—

(1) 8 hours for a flight crew consisting of one pilot; or

(2) 10 hours for a flight crew consisting of two pilots qualified under this part for the operation being conducted.

(c) A flight crewmember's flight time may exceed the flight time limits of paragraph (b) of this section if the assigned flight time occurs during a regularly assigned duty period of no more than 14 hours and—

(1) If this duty period is immediately preceded by and followed by a required rest period of at least 10 consecutive hours of rest;

(2) If flight time is assigned during this period, that total flight time when added to any other commercial flying by the flight crewmember may not exceed—

(i) 8 hours for a flight crew consisting of one pilot; or

(ii) 10 hours for a flight crew consisting of two pilots; and

(3) If the combined duty and rest periods equal 24 hours.

(d) Each assignment under paragraph (b) of this section must provide for at least 10 consecutive hours of rest during the 24-hour period that precedes the planned completion time of the assignment.

(e) When a flight crewmember has exceeded the daily flight time limitations in this section, because of circumstances beyond the control of the certificate holder or flight crewmember (such as adverse weather conditions), that flight crewmember must have a rest period before being assigned or accepting an assignment for flight time of at least—

(1) 11 consecutive hours of rest if the flight time limitation is exceeded by not more than 30 minutes;

(2) 12 consecutive hours of rest if the flight time limitation is exceeded by more than 30 minutes, but not more than 60 minutes; and

(3) 16 consecutive hours of rest if the flight time limitation is exceeded by more than 60 minutes.

(f) The certificate holder must provide each flight crewmember at least 13 rest periods of at least 24 consecutive hours each in each calendar quarter.

[Docket No. 23634, 50 FR 29320, July 18, 1085; as amended by Amdt. 135–33, 54 FR 39294, Sept. 25, 1989; Amdt. 135–60, 61 FR 2616, Jan. 26, 1996]

§135.269 Flight time limitations and rest requirements: Unscheduled three- and four-pilot crews.

(a) No certificate holder may assign any flight crewmember, and no flight crewmember may accept an assignment, for flight time as a member of a three- or four-pilot crew if that crewmember's total flight time in all commercial flying will exceed—

§135.271

(1) 500 hours in any calendar quarter.
(2) 800 hours in any two consecutive calendar quarters.
(3) 1,400 hours in any calendar year.
(b) No certificate holder may assign any pilot to a crew of three or four pilots, unless that assignment provides—
(1) At least 10 consecutive hours of rest immediately preceding the assignment;
(2) No more than 8 hours of flight deck duty in any 24 consecutive hours;
(3) No more than 18 duty hours for a three-pilot crew or 20 duty hours for a four-pilot crew in any 24 consecutive hours;
(4) No more than 12 hours aloft for a three-pilot crew or 16 hours aloft for a four-pilot crew during the maximum duty hours specified in paragraph (b)(3) of this section;
(5) Adequate sleeping facilities on the aircraft for the relief pilot;
(6) Upon completion of the assignment, a rest period of at least 12 hours;
(7) For a three-pilot crew, a crew which consists of at least the following:
(i) A pilot in command (PIC) who meets the applicable flight crewmember requirements of subpart E of part 135;
(ii) A PIC who meets the applicable flight crewmember requirements of subpart E of part 135, except those prescribed in §§135.244 and 135.247; and
(iii) A second in command (SIC) who meets the SIC qualifications of §135.245.
(8) For a four-pilot crew, at least three pilots who meet the conditions of paragraph (b)(7) of this section, plus a fourth pilot who meets the SIC qualifications of §135.245.
(c) When a flight crewmember has exceeded the daily flight deck duty limitation in this section by more than 60 minutes, because of circumstances beyond the control of the certificate holder or flight crewmember, that flight crewmember must have a rest period before the next duty period of at least 16 consecutive hours.
(d) A certificate holder must provide each flight crewmember at least 13 rest periods of at least 24 consecutive hours each in each calendar quarter.

§135.271 Helicopter hospital emergency medical evacuation service (HEMES).

(a) No certificate holder may assign any flight crewmember, and no flight crewmember may accept an assignment for flight time if that crewmember's total flight time in all commercial flight will exceed—
(1) 500 hours in any calendar quarter.
(2) 800 hours in any two consecutive calendar quarters.

(3) 1,400 hours in any calendar year.
(b) No certificate holder may assign a helicopter flight crewmember, and no flight crewmember may accept an assignment, for hospital emergency medical evacuation service helicopter operations unless that assignment provides for at least 10 consecutive hours of rest immediately preceding reporting to the hospital for availability for flight time.
(c) No flight crewmember may accrue more than 8 hours of flight time during any 24-consecutive hour period of a HEMES assignment, unless an emergency medical evacuation operation is prolonged. Each flight crewmember who exceeds the daily 8 hour flight time limitation in this paragraph must be relieved of the HEMES assignment immediately upon the completion of that emergency medical evacuation operation and must be given a rest period in compliance with paragraph (h) of this section.
(d) Each flight crewmember must receive at least 8 consecutive hours of rest during any 24 consecutive hour period of a HEMES assignment. A flight crewmember must be relieved of the HEMES assignment if he or she has not or cannot receive at least 8 consecutive hours of rest during any 24 consecutive hour period of a HEMES assignment.
(e) A HEMES assignment may not exceed 72 consecutive hours at the hospital.
(f) An adequate place of rest must be provided at, or in close proximity to, the hospital at which the HEMES assignment is being performed.
(g) No certificate holder may assign any other duties to a flight crewmember during a HEMES assignment.
(h) Each pilot must be given a rest period upon completion of the HEMES assignment and prior to being assigned any further duty with the certificate holder of—
(1) At least 12 consecutive hours for an assignment of less than 48 hours.
(2) At least 16 consecutive hours for an assignment of more than 48 hours.
(i) The certificate holder must provide each flight crewmember at least 13 rest periods of at least 24 consecutive hours each in each calendar quarter.

§135.273 Duty period limitations and rest time requirements.

(a) For purposes of this section—
Calendar day means the period of elapsed time, using Coordinated Universal Time or local time, that begins at midnight and ends 24 hours later at the next midnight.
Duty period means the period of elapsed time between reporting for an assignment involving flight time and release from that assignment by

the certificate holder. The time is calculated using either Coordinated Universal Time or local time to reflect the total elapsed time.

Flight attendant means an individual, other than a flight crewmember, who is assigned by the certificate holder, in accordance with the required minimum crew complement under the certificate holder's operations specifications or in addition to that minimum complement, to duty in an aircraft during flight time and whose duties include but are not necessarily limited to cabin-safety-related responsibilities.

Rest period means the period free of all responsibility for work or duty should the occasion arise.

(b) Except as provided in paragraph (c) of this section, a certificate holder may assign a duty period to a flight attendant only when the applicable duty period limitations and rest requirements of this paragraph are met.

(1) Except as provided in paragraphs (b)(4), (b)(5), and (b)(6) of this section, no certificate holder may assign a flight attendant to a scheduled duty period of more than 14 hours.

(2) Except as provided in paragraph (b)(3) of this section, a flight attendant scheduled to a duty period of 14 hours or less as provided under paragraph (b)(1) of this section must be given a scheduled rest period of at least 9 consecutive hours. This rest period must occur between the completion of the scheduled duty period and the commencement of the subsequent duty period.

(3) The rest period required under paragraph (b)(2) of this section may be scheduled or reduced to 8 consecutive hours if the flight attendant is provided a subsequent rest period of at least 10 consecutive hours; this subsequent rest period must be scheduled to begin no later than 24 hours after the beginning of the reduced rest period and must occur between the completion of the scheduled duty period and the commencement of the subsequent duty period.

(4) A certificate holder may assign a flight attendant to a scheduled duty period of more than 14 hours, but no more than 16 hours, if the certificate holder has assigned to the flight or flights in that duty period at least one flight attendant in addition to the minimum flight attendant complement required for the flight or flights in that duty period under the certificate holder's operations specifications.

(5) A certificate holder may assign a flight attendant to a scheduled duty period of more than 16 hours, but no more than 18 hours, if the certificate holder has assigned to the flight or flights in that duty period at least two flight attendants in addition to the minimum flight attendant complement required for the flight or flights in that duty period under the certificate holder's operations specifications.

(6) A certificate holder may assign a flight attendant to a scheduled duty period of more than 18 hours, but no more than 20 hours, if the scheduled duty period includes one or more flights that land or take off outside the 48 contiguous states and the District of Columbia, and if the certificate holder has assigned to the flight or flights in that duty period at least three flight attendants in addition to the minimum flight attendant complement required for the flight or flights in that duty period under the certificate holder's operations specifications.

(7) Except as provided in paragraph (b)(8) of this section, a flight attendant scheduled to a duty period of more than 14 hours but no more than 20 hours, as provided in paragraphs (b)(4), (b)(5), and (b)(6) of this section, must be given a scheduled rest period of at least 12 consecutive hours. This rest period must occur between the completion of the scheduled duty period and the commencement of the subsequent duty period.

(8) The rest period required under paragraph (b)(7) of this section may be scheduled or reduced to 10 consecutive hours if the flight attendant is provided a subsequent rest period of at least 14 consecutive hours; this subsequent rest period must be scheduled to begin no later than 24 hours after the beginning of the reduced rest period and must occur between the completion of the scheduled duty period and the commencement of the subsequent duty period.

(9) Notwithstanding paragraphs (b)(4), (b)(5), and (b)(6) of this section, if a certificate holder elects to reduce the rest period to 10 hours as authorized by paragraph (b)(8) of this section, the certificate holder may not schedule a flight attendant for a duty period of more than 14 hours during the 24-hour period commencing after the beginning of the reduced rest period.

(10) No certificate holder may assign a flight attendant any duty period with the certificate holder unless the flight attendant has had at least the minimum rest required under this section.

(11) No certificate holder may assign a flight attendant to perform any duty with the certificate holder during any required rest period.

(12) Time spent in transportation, not local in character, that a certificate holder requires of a flight attendant and provides to transport the flight attendant to an airport at which that flight attendant is to serve on a flight as a crewmember, or from an airport at which the flight attendant was relieved from duty to return to the flight attendant's home station, is not considered part of a rest period.

(13) Each certificate holder must relieve each flight attendant engaged in air transportation from all further duty for at least 24 consecutive hours during any 7 consecutive calendar days.

§135.273

(14) A flight attendant is not considered to be scheduled for duty in excess of duty period limitations if the flights to which the flight attendant is assigned are scheduled and normally terminate within the limitations but due to circumstances beyond the control of the certificate holder (such as adverse weather conditions) are not at the time of departure expected to reach their destination within the scheduled time.

(c) Notwithstanding paragraph (b) of this section, a certificate holder may apply the flight crewmember flight time and duty limitations and rest requirements of this part to flight attendants for all operations conducted under this part provided that—

(1) The certificate holder establishes written procedures that—

(i) Apply to all flight attendants used in the certificate holder's operation;

(ii) Include the flight crewmember requirements contained in subpart F of this part, as appropriate to the operation being conducted, except that rest facilities on board the aircraft are not required; and

(iii) Include provisions to add one flight attendant to the minimum flight attendant complement for each flight crewmember who is in excess of the minimum number required in the aircraft type certificate data sheet and who is assigned to the aircraft under the provisions of subpart F of this part, as applicable;

(iv) Are approved by the Administrator and described or referenced in the certificate holder's operations specifications; and

(2) Whenever the Administrator finds that revisions are necessary for the continued adequacy of duty period limitation and rest requirement procedures that are required by paragraph (c)(1) of this section and that had been granted final approval, the certificate holder must, after notification by the Administrator, make any changes in the procedures that are found necessary by the Administrator. Within 30 days after the certificate holder receives such notice, it may file a petition to reconsider the notice with the certificate-holding district office. The filing of a petition to reconsider stays the notice, pending decision by the Administrator. However, if the Administrator finds that there is an emergency that requires immediate action in the interest of safety, the Administrator may, upon a statement of the reasons, require a change effective without stay.

[Docket No. 23634, 50 FR 29320, July 18, 1985; as amended by Amdt. 135–52, 59 FR 42993, Aug. 19, 1994; Amdt. 135–60, 61 FR 2616, Jan. 26, 1996]

Subpart G—Crewmember Testing Requirements

§135.291 Applicability.

Except as provided in §135.3, this subpart—

(a) Prescribes the tests and checks required for pilot and flight attendant crewmembers and for the approval of check pilots in operations under this part; and

(b) Permits training center personnel authorized under part 142 of this chapter who meet the requirements of §§135.337 and 135.339 to conduct training, testing, and checking under contract or other arrangement to those persons subject to the requirements of this subpart.

[Docket No. 26933, 61 FR 34561, July 2, 1996; as amended by Amdt. 135–91, 68 FR 54587, Sept. 17, 2003]

§135.293 Initial and recurrent pilot testing requirements.

(a) No certificate holder may use a pilot, nor may any person serve as a pilot, unless, since the beginning of the 12th calendar month before that service, that pilot has passed a written or oral test, given by the Administrator or an authorized check pilot, on that pilot's knowledge in the following areas—

(1) The appropriate provisions of parts 61, 91, and 135 of this chapter and the operations specifications and the manual of the certificate holder;

(2) For each type of aircraft to be flown by the pilot, the aircraft powerplant, major components and systems, major appliances, performance and operating limitations, standard and emergency operating procedures, and the contents of the approved Aircraft Flight Manual or equivalent, as applicable;

(3) For each type of aircraft to be flown by the pilot, the method of determining compliance with weight and balance limitations for takeoff, landing and en route operations;

(4) Navigation and use of air navigation aids appropriate to the operation or pilot authorization, including, when applicable, instrument approach facilities and procedures;

(5) Air traffic control procedures, including IFR procedures when applicable;

(6) Meteorology in general, including the principles of frontal systems, icing, fog, thunderstorms, and windshear, and, if appropriate for the operation of the certificate holder, high altitude weather;

(7) Procedures for—

(i) Recognizing and avoiding severe weather situations;

(ii) Escaping from severe weather situations, in case of inadvertent encounters, including low-altitude windshear (except that rotorcraft pilots are not required to be tested on escaping from low-altitude windshear); and

(iii) Operating in or near thunderstorms (including best penetrating altitudes), turbulent air (including clear air turbulence), icing, hail, and other potentially hazardous meteorological conditions;

(8) New equipment, procedures, or techniques, as appropriate; and

(9) For rotorcraft pilots, procedures for aircraft handling in flat-light, whiteout, and brownout conditions, including methods for recognizing and avoiding those conditions.

(b) No certificate holder may use a pilot, nor may any person serve as a pilot, in any aircraft unless, since the beginning of the 12th calendar month before that service, that pilot has passed a competency check given by the Administrator or an authorized check pilot in that class of aircraft, if single-engine airplane other than turbojet, or that type of aircraft, if helicopter, multiengine airplane, or turbojet airplane, to determine the pilot's competence in practical skills and techniques in that aircraft or class of aircraft. The extent of the competency check shall be determined by the Administrator or authorized check pilot conducting the competency check. The competency check may include any of the maneuvers and procedures currently required for the original issuance of the particular pilot certificate required for the operations authorized and appropriate to the category, class and type of aircraft involved. For the purposes of this paragraph, type, as to an airplane, means any one of a group of airplanes determined by the Administrator to have a similar means of propulsion, the same manufacturer, and no significantly different handling or flight characteristics. For the purposes of this paragraph, type, as to a helicopter, means a basic make and model.

(c) Each competency check given in a rotorcraft must include a demonstration of the pilot's ability to maneuver the rotorcraft solely by reference to instruments. The check must determine the pilot's ability to safely maneuver the rotorcraft into visual meteorological conditions following an inadvertent encounter with instrument meteorological conditions. For competency checks in non-IFR-certified rotorcraft, the pilot must perform such maneuvers as are appropriate to the rotorcraft's installed equipment, the certificate holder's operations specifications, and the operating environment.

(d) The instrument proficiency check required by §135.297 may be substituted for the competency check required by this section for the type of aircraft used in the check.

(e) For the purpose of this part, competent performance of a procedure or maneuver by a person to be used as a pilot requires that the pilot be the obvious master of the aircraft, with the successful outcome of the maneuver never in doubt.

(f) The Administrator or authorized check pilot certifies the competency of each pilot who passes the knowledge or flight check in the certificate holder's pilot records.

(g) Portions of a required competency check may be given in an aircraft simulator or other appropriate training device, if approved by the Administrator.

(h) Rotorcraft pilots must be tested on the subjects in paragraph (a)(9) of this section when taking a written or oral knowledge test after April 22, 2015. Rotorcraft pilots must be checked on the maneuvers and procedures in paragraph (c) of this section when taking a competency check after April 22, 2015.

[Docket No. 16097, 43 FR 46783, Oct. 10, 1978; as amended by Amdt. 135–27, 53 FR 37697, Sept. 27, 1988; Amdt. 135–129, 79 FR 9974, Feb. 21, 2014; Amdt. 135–129, 79 FR 22012, Apr. 21, 2014]

§135.295 Initial and recurrent flight attendant crewmember testing requirements.

No certificate holder may use a flight attendant crewmember, nor may any person serve as a flight attendant crewmember unless, since the beginning of the 12th calendar month before that service, the certificate holder has determined by appropriate initial and recurrent testing that the person is knowledgeable and competent in the following areas as appropriate to assigned duties and responsibilities—

(a) Authority of the pilot in command;

(b) Passenger handling, including procedures to be followed in handling deranged persons or other persons whose conduct might jeopardize safety;

(c) Crewmember assignments, functions, and responsibilities during ditching and evacuation of persons who may need the assistance of another person to move expeditiously to an exit in an emergency;

(d) Briefing of passengers;

(e) Location and operation of portable fire extinguishers and other items of emergency equipment;

(f) Proper use of cabin equipment and controls;

(g) Location and operation of passenger oxygen equipment;

(h) Location and operation of all normal and emergency exits, including evacuation chutes and escape ropes; and

(i) Seating of persons who may need assistance of another person to move rapidly to an exit in an emergency as prescribed by the certificate holder's operations manual.

§135.297 Pilot in command: Instrument proficiency check requirements.

(a) No certificate holder may use a pilot, nor may any person serve, as a pilot in command of an aircraft under IFR unless, since the beginning of the 6th calendar month before that service, that pilot has passed an instrument proficiency check under this section administered by the Administrator or an authorized check pilot.

(b) No pilot may use any type of precision instrument approach procedure under IFR unless, since the beginning of the 6th calendar month before that use, the pilot satisfactorily demonstrated that type of approach procedure. No pilot may use any type of nonprecision approach procedure under IFR unless, since the beginning of the 6th calendar month before that use, the pilot has satisfactorily demonstrated either that type of approach procedure or any other two different types of nonprecision approach procedures. The instrument approach procedure or procedures must include at least one straight-in approach, one circling approach, and one missed approach. Each type of approach procedure demonstrated must be conducted to published minimums for that procedure.

(c) The instrument proficiency check required by paragraph (a) of this section consists of an oral or written equipment test and a flight check under simulated or actual IFR conditions. The equipment test includes questions on emergency procedures, engine operation, fuel and lubrication systems, power settings, stall speeds, best engine-out speed, propeller and supercharger operations, and hydraulic, mechanical, and electrical systems, as appropriate. The flight check includes navigation by instruments, recovery from simulated emergencies, and standard instrument approaches involving navigational facilities which that pilot is to be authorized to use. Each pilot taking the instrument proficiency check must show that standard of competence required by §135.293(e).

(1) The instrument proficiency check must—

(i) For a pilot in command of an airplane under §135.243(a), include the procedures and maneuvers for an airline transport pilot certificate in the particular type of airplane, if appropriate; and

(ii) For a pilot in command of an airplane or helicopter under §135.243(c), include the procedures and maneuvers for a commercial pilot certificate with an instrument rating and, if required, for the appropriate type rating.

(2) The instrument proficiency check must be given by an authorized check airman or by the Administrator.

(d) If the pilot in command is assigned to pilot only one type of aircraft, that pilot must take the instrument proficiency check required by paragraph (a) of this section in that type of aircraft.

(e) If the pilot in command is assigned to pilot more than one type of aircraft, that pilot must take the instrument proficiency check required by paragraph (a) of this section in each type of aircraft to which that pilot is assigned, in rotation, but not more than one flight check during each period described in paragraph (a) of this section.

(f) If the pilot in command is assigned to pilot both single-engine and multiengine aircraft, that pilot must initially take the instrument proficiency check required by paragraph (a) of this section in a multiengine aircraft, and each succeeding check alternately in single-engine and multiengine aircraft, but not more than one flight check during each period described in paragraph (a) of this section. Portions of a required flight check may be given in an aircraft simulator or other appropriate training device, if approved by the Administrator.

(g) If the pilot in command is authorized to use an autopilot system in place of a second in command, that pilot must show, during the required instrument proficiency check, that the pilot is able (without a second in command) both with and without using the autopilot to—

(1) Conduct instrument operations competently; and

(2) Properly conduct air-ground communications and comply with complex air traffic control instructions.

(3) Each pilot taking the autopilot check must show that, while using the autopilot, the airplane can be operated as proficiently as it would be if a second in command were present to handle air-ground communications and air traffic control instructions. The autopilot check need only be demonstrated once every 12 calendar months during the instrument proficiency check required under paragraph (a) of this section.

[Docket No. 16097, 43 FR 46783, Oct. 10, 1978; as amended by Amdt. 135–15, 46 FR 30971, June 11, 1981; Amdt. 135–129, 79 FR 9975, Feb. 21, 2014]

§135.299 Pilot in command: Line checks: Routes and airports.

(a) No certificate holder may use a pilot, nor may any person serve, as a pilot in command of a flight unless, since the beginning of the 12th calendar month before that service, that pilot has passed a flight check in one of the types of aircraft which that pilot is to fly. The flight check shall—

(1) Be given by an approved check pilot or by the Administrator;

(2) Consist of at least one flight over one route segment; and

(3) Include takeoffs and landings at one or more representative airports. In addition to the requirements of this paragraph, for a pilot authorized to conduct IFR operations, at least one flight

shall be flown over a civil airway, an approved off-airway route, or a portion of either of them.

(b) The pilot who conducts the check shall determine whether the pilot being checked satisfactorily performs the duties and responsibilities of a pilot in command in operations under this part, and shall so certify in the pilot training record.

(c) Each certificate holder shall establish in the manual required by §135.21 a procedure which will ensure that each pilot who has not flown over a route and into an airport within the preceding 90 days will, before beginning the flight, become familiar with all available information required for the safe operation of that flight.

§135.301 Crewmember: Tests and checks, grace provisions, training to accepted standards.

(a) If a crewmember who is required to take a test or a flight check under this part, completes the test or flight check in the calendar month before or after the calendar month in which it is required, that crewmember is considered to have completed the test or check in the calendar month in which it is required.

(b) If a pilot being checked under this subpart fails any of the required maneuvers, the person giving the check may give additional training to the pilot during the course of the check. In addition to repeating the maneuvers failed, the person giving the check may require the pilot being checked to repeat any other maneuvers that are necessary to determine the pilot's proficiency. If the pilot being checked is unable to demonstrate satisfactory performance to the person conducting the check, the certificate holder may not use the pilot, nor may the pilot serve, as a flight crewmember in operations under this part until the pilot has satisfactorily completed the check.

Subpart H—Training

§135.321 Applicability and terms used.

(a) Except as provided in §135.3, this subpart prescribes the requirements applicable to—

(1) A certificate holder under this part which contracts with, or otherwise arranges to use the services of a training center certificated under part 142 to perform training, testing, and checking functions;

(2) Each certificate holder for establishing and maintaining an approved training program for crewmembers, check airmen and instructors, and other operations personnel employed or used by that certificate holder; and

(3) Each certificate holder for the qualification, approval, and use of aircraft simulators and flight training devices in the conduct of the program.

(b) For the purposes of this subpart, the following terms and definitions apply:

(1) *Initial training.* The training required for crewmembers who have not qualified and served in the same capacity on an aircraft.

(2) *Transition training.* The training required for crewmembers who have qualified and served in the same capacity on another aircraft.

(3) *Upgrade training.* The training required for crewmembers who have qualified and served as second in command on a particular aircraft type, before they serve as pilot in command on that aircraft.

(4) *Differences training.* The training required for crewmembers who have qualified and served on a particular type aircraft, when the Administrator finds differences training is necessary before a crewmember serves in the same capacity on a particular variation of that aircraft.

(5) *Recurrent training.* The training required for crewmembers to remain adequately trained and currently proficient for each aircraft, crewmember position, and type of operation in which the crewmember serves.

(6) *In flight.* The maneuvers, procedures, or functions that must be conducted in the aircraft.

(7) *Training center.* An organization governed by the applicable requirements of part 142 of this chapter that conducts training, testing, and checking under contract or other arrangement to certificate holders subject to the requirements of this part.

(8) *Requalification training.* The training required for crewmembers previously trained and qualified, but who have become unqualified due to not having met within the required period the—

(i) Recurrent pilot testing requirements of §135.293;

(ii) Instrument proficiency check requirements of §135.297; or

(iii) Line checks required by §135.299.

[Docket No. 16097, 43 FR 46783, Oct. 10, 1978; as amended by Amdt. 135–57, 60 FR 65950, Dec. 20, 1995; Amdt. 135–63, 61 FR 34561, July 2, 1996; Amdt. 135–91, 68 FR 54588, Sept. 17, 2003]

§135.323 Training program: General.

(a) Each certificate holder required to have a training program under §135.341 shall:

(1) Establish and implement a training program that satisfies the requirements of this subpart and that ensures that each crewmember, aircraft dispatcher, flight instructor and check airman is adequately trained to perform his or her assigned duties. Prior to implementation, the certificate holder must obtain initial and final FAA approval of the training program.

(2) Provide adequate ground and flight training facilities and properly qualified ground instructors for the training required by this subpart.

§135.324

(3) Provide and keep current for each aircraft type used and, if applicable, the particular variations within the aircraft type, appropriate training material, examinations, forms, instructions, and procedures for use in conducting the training and checks required by this subpart.

(4) Provide enough flight instructors, check airmen, and simulator instructors to conduct required flight training and flight checks, and simulator training courses allowed under this subpart.

(b) Whenever a crewmember who is required to take recurrent training under this subpart completes the training in the calendar month before, or the calendar month after, the month in which that training is required, the crewmember is considered to have completed it in the calendar month in which it was required.

(c) Each instructor, supervisor, or check airman who is responsible for a particular ground training subject, segment of flight training, course of training, flight check, or competence check under this part shall certify as to the proficiency and knowledge of the crewmember, flight instructor, or check airman concerned upon completion of that training or check. That certification shall be made a part of the crewmember's record. When the certification required by this paragraph is made by an entry in a computerized recordkeeping system, the certifying instructor, supervisor, or check airman, must be identified with that entry. However, the signature of the certifying instructor, supervisor, or check airman, is not required for computerized entries.

(d) Training subjects that apply to more than one aircraft or crewmember position and that have been satisfactorily completed during previous training while employed by the certificate holder for another aircraft or another crewmember position, need not be repeated during subsequent training other than recurrent training.

(e) Aircraft simulators and other training devices may be used in the certificate holder's training program if approved by the Administrator.

[Docket No. 16097, 43 FR 46783, Oct. 10, 1978; as amended by Amdt. 135–101, 70 FR 58829, Oct. 7, 2005]

§135.324 Training program: Special rules.

(a) Other than the certificate holder, only another certificate holder certificated under this part or a training center certificated under part 142 of this chapter is eligible under this subpart to conduct training, testing, and checking under contract or other arrangement to those persons subject to the requirements of this subpart.

(b) A certificate holder may contract with, or otherwise arrange to use the services of, a training center certificated under part 142 of this chapter to conduct training, testing, and checking required by this part only if the training center—

(1) Holds applicable training specifications issued under part 142 of this chapter;

(2) Has facilities, training equipment, and course-ware meeting the applicable requirements of part 142 of this chapter;

(3) Has approved curriculums, curriculum segments, and portions of curriculum segments applicable for use in training courses required by this subpart; and

(4) Has sufficient instructor and check airmen qualified under the applicable requirements of §§135.337 through 135.340 to provide training, testing, and checking to persons subject to the requirements of this subpart.

[Docket No. 26933, 61 FR 34562, July 2, 1996; as amended by Amdt. 135–67, 62 FR 13791, March 21, 1997; Amdt. 135–91, 68 FR 54588, Sept. 17, 2003]

§135.325 Training program and revision: Initial and final approval.

(a) To obtain initial and final approval of a training program, or a revision to an approved training program, each certificate holder must submit to the Administrator—

(1) An outline of the proposed or revised curriculum, that provides enough information for a preliminary evaluation of the proposed training program or revision; and

(2) Additional relevant information that may be requested by the Administrator.

(b) If the proposed training program or revision complies with this subpart, the Administrator grants initial approval in writing after which the certificate holder may conduct the training under that program. The Administrator then evaluates the effectiveness of the training program and advises the certificate holder of deficiencies, if any, that must be corrected.

(c) The Administrator grants final approval of the proposed training program or revision if the certificate holder shows that the training conducted under the initial approval in paragraph (b) of this section ensures that each person who successfully completes the training is adequately trained to perform that person's assigned duties.

(d) Whenever the Administrator finds that revisions are necessary for the continued adequacy of a training program that has been granted final approval, the certificate holder shall, after notification by the Administrator, make any changes in the program that are found necessary by the Administrator. Within 30 days after the certificate holder receives the notice, it may file a petition to reconsider the notice with the Administrator. The filing of a petition to reconsider stays the notice pending a decision by the Administrator. However, if the Administrator finds that there is an emergency that requires immediate action in the interest of safety, the Administrator may, upon a statement of the reasons, require a change effective without stay.

§135.327 Training program: Curriculum.

(a) Each certificate holder must prepare and keep current a written training program curriculum for each type of aircraft for each crewmember required for that type aircraft. The curriculum must include ground and flight training required by this subpart.

(b) Each training program curriculum must include the following:

(1) A list of principal ground training subjects, including emergency training subjects, that are provided.

(2) A list of all the training devices, mockups, systems trainers, procedures trainers, or other training aids that the certificate holder will use.

(3) Detailed descriptions or pictorial displays of the approved normal, abnormal, and emergency maneuvers, procedures and functions that will be performed during each flight training phase or flight check, indicating those maneuvers, procedures and functions that are to be performed during the inflight portions of flight training and flight checks.

§135.329 Crewmember training requirements.

(a) Each certificate holder must include in its training program the following initial and transition ground training as appropriate to the particular assignment of the crewmember:

(1) Basic indoctrination ground training for newly hired crewmembers including instruction in at least the—

(i) Duties and responsibilities of crewmembers as applicable;

(ii) Appropriate provisions of this chapter;

(iii) Contents of the certificate holder's operating certificate and operations specifications (not required for flight attendants); and

(iv) Appropriate portions of the certificate holder's operating manual.

(2) The initial and transition ground training in §§135.345 and 135.349, as applicable.

(3) Emergency training in §135.331.

(4) Crew resource management training in §135.330.

(b) Each training program must provide the initial and transition flight training in §135.347, as applicable.

(c) Each training program must provide recurrent ground and flight training in §135.351.

(d) Upgrade training in §§135.345 and 135.347 for a particular type aircraft may be included in the training program for crewmembers who have qualified and served as second in command on that aircraft.

(e) In addition to initial, transition, upgrade and recurrent training, each training program must provide ground and flight training, instruction, and practice necessary to ensure that each crewmember—

(1) Remains adequately trained and currently proficient for each aircraft, crewmember position, and type of operation in which the crewmember serves; and

(2) Qualifies in new equipment, facilities, procedures, and techniques, including modifications to aircraft.

[Docket No. 16097, 43 FR 46783, October 10, 1978; as amended by Amdt. 135–122, 76 FR 3837, Jan. 21, 2011]

§135.330 Crew resource management training.

(a) Each certificate holder must have an approved crew resource management training program that includes initial and recurrent training. The training program must include at least the following:

(1) Authority of the pilot in command;

(2) Communication processes, decisions, and coordination, to include communication with Air Traffic Control, personnel performing flight locating and other operational functions, and passengers;

(3) Building and maintenance of a flight team;

(4) Workload and time management;

(5) Situational awareness;

(6) Effects of fatigue on performance, avoidance strategies and countermeasures;

(7) Effects of stress and stress reduction strategies; and

(8) Aeronautical decision-making and judgment training tailored to the operator's flight operations and aviation environment.

(b) After March 22, 2013, no certificate holder may use a person as a flightcrew member or flight attendant unless that person has completed approved crew resource management initial training with that certificate holder.

(c) For flightcrew members and flight attendants, the Administrator, at his or her discretion, may credit crew resource management training completed with that certificate holder before March 22, 2013, toward all or part of the initial CRM training required by this section.

(d) In granting credit for initial CRM training, the Administrator considers training aids, devices, methods and procedures used by the certificate holder in a voluntary CRM program included in a training program required by §§135.341, 135.345, or 135.349.

[Docket No. FAA–2009–0023, 76 FR 3837, Jan. 21, 2011]

§135.331 Crewmember emergency training.

(a) Each training program must provide emergency training under this section for each aircraft type, model, and configuration, each crewmember, and each kind of operation conducted, as appropriate for each crewmember and the certificate holder.

(b) Emergency training must provide the following:

(1) Instruction in emergency assignments and procedures, including coordination among crewmembers.

(2) Individual instruction in the location, function, and operation of emergency equipment including—

(i) Equipment used in ditching and evacuation;
(ii) First aid equipment and its proper use; and
(iii) Portable fire extinguishers, with emphasis on the type of extinguisher to be used on different classes of fires.

(3) Instruction in the handling of emergency situations including—

(i) Rapid decompression;
(ii) Fire in flight or on the surface and smoke control procedures with emphasis on electrical equipment and related circuit breakers found in cabin areas;
(iii) Ditching and evacuation;
(iv) Illness, injury, or other abnormal situations involving passengers or crewmembers; and
(v) Hijacking and other unusual situations.

(4) Review of the certificate holder's previous aircraft accidents and incidents involving actual emergency situations.

(c) Each crewmember must perform at least the following emergency drills, using the proper emergency equipment and procedures, unless the Administrator finds that, for a particular drill, the crewmember can be adequately trained by demonstration:

(1) Ditching, if applicable.
(2) Emergency evacuation.
(3) Fire extinguishing and smoke control.
(4) Operation and use of emergency exits, including deployment and use of evacuation chutes, if applicable.
(5) Use of crew and passenger oxygen.
(6) Removal of life rafts from the aircraft, inflation of the life rafts, use of life lines, and boarding of passengers and crew, if applicable.
(7) Donning and inflation of life vests and the use of other individual flotation devices, if applicable.

(d) Crewmembers who serve in operations above 25,000 feet must receive instruction in the following:

(1) Respiration.
(2) Hypoxia.
(3) Duration of consciousness without supplemental oxygen at altitude.
(4) Gas expansion.
(5) Gas bubble formation.
(6) Physical phenomena and incidents of decompression.

§135.335 Approval of aircraft simulators and other training devices.

(a) Training courses using aircraft simulators and other training devices may be included in the certificate holder's training program if approved by the Administrator.

(b) Each aircraft simulator and other training device that is used in a training course or in checks required under this subpart must meet the following requirements:

(1) It must be specifically approved for—
(i) The certificate holder; and
(ii) The particular maneuver, procedure, or crewmember function involved.

(2) It must maintain the performance, functional, and other characteristics that are required for approval.

(3) Additionally, for aircraft simulators, it must be—
(i) Approved for the type aircraft and, if applicable, the particular variation within type for which the training or check is being conducted; and
(ii) Modified to conform with any modification to the aircraft being simulated that changes the performance, functional, or other characteristics required for approval.

(c) A particular aircraft simulator or other training device may be used by more than one certificate holder.

(d) In granting initial and final approval of training programs or revisions to them, the Administrator considers the training devices, methods and procedures listed in the certificate holder's curriculum under §135.327.

[Docket No. 16907, 43 FR 46783, Oct. 10, 1978; as amended by Amdt. 135–1, 44 FR 26738, May 7, 1979]

§135.336 Airline transport pilot certification training program.

(a) A certificate holder may obtain approval to establish and implement a training program to satisfy the requirements of §61.156 of this chapter. The training program must be separate from the air carrier training program required by this part.

(b) No certificate holder may use a person nor may any person serve as an instructor in a training program approved to meet the requirements of §61.156 of this chapter unless the instructor:

(1) Holds an airline transport pilot certificate with an airplane category multiengine class rating;

(2) Has at least 2 years of experience as a pilot in command in operations conducted under §91.1053(a)(2)(i) of this chapter, §135.243(a)(1) of this part, or as a pilot in command or second in command in any operation conducted under part 121 of this chapter;

(3) Except for the holder of a flight instructor certificate, receives initial training on the following topics:

(i) The fundamental principles of the learning process;

(ii) Elements of effective teaching, instruction methods, and techniques;

(iii) Instructor duties, privileges, responsibilities, and limitations;

(iv) Training policies and procedures; and

(v) Evaluation.

(4) If providing training in a flight simulation training device, holds an aircraft type rating for the aircraft represented by the flight simulation training device utilized in the training program and have received training and evaluation within the preceding 12 months from the certificate holder on:

(i) Proper operation of flight simulator and flight training device controls and systems;

(ii) Proper operation of environmental and fault panels;

(iii) Data and motion limitations of simulation;

(iv) Minimum equipment requirements for each curriculum; and

(v) The maneuvers that will be demonstrated in the flight simulation training device.

(c) A certificate holder may not issue a graduation certificate to a student unless that student has completed all the curriculum requirements of the course.

(d) A certificate holder must conduct evaluations to ensure that training techniques, procedures, and standards are acceptable to the Administrator.

[Docket No. FAA–2010–0100, 78 FR 42379, July 15, 2013]

§135.337 Qualifications: Check airmen (aircraft) and check airmen (simulator).

(a) For the purposes of this section and §135.339:

(1) A check airman (aircraft) is a person who is qualified to conduct flight checks in an aircraft, in a flight simulator, or in a flight training device for a particular type aircraft.

(2) A check airman (simulator) is a person who is qualified to conduct flight checks, but only in a flight simulator, in a flight training device, or both, for a particular type aircraft.

(3) Check airmen (aircraft) and check airmen (simulator) are those check airmen who perform the functions described in §§135.321(a) and 135.323(a)(4) and (c).

(b) No certificate holder may use a person, nor may any person serve as a check airman (aircraft) in a training program established under this subpart unless, with respect to the aircraft type involved, that person—

(1) Holds the airman certificates and ratings required to serve as a pilot in command in operations under this part;

(2) Has satisfactorily completed the training phases for the aircraft, including recurrent training, that are required to serve as a pilot in command in operations under this part;

(3) Has satisfactorily completed the proficiency or competency checks that are required to serve as a pilot in command in operations under this part;

(4) Has satisfactorily completed the applicable training requirements of §135.339;

(5) Holds at least a Class III medical certificate unless serving as a required crewmember, in which case holds a Class I or Class II medical certificate as appropriate.

(6) Has satisfied the recency of experience requirements of §135.247; and

(7) Has been approved by the Administrator for the check airman duties involved.

(c) No certificate holder may use a person, nor may any person serve as a check airman (simulator) in a training program established under this subpart unless, with respect to the aircraft type involved, that person meets the provisions of paragraph (b) of this section, or—

(1) Holds the applicable airman certificates and ratings, except medical certificate, required to serve as a pilot in command in operations under this part;

(2) Has satisfactorily completed the appropriate training phases for the aircraft, including recurrent training, that are required to serve as a pilot in command in operations under this part;

(3) Has satisfactorily completed the appropriate proficiency or competency checks that are required to serve as a pilot in command in operations under this part;

(4) Has satisfactorily completed the applicable training requirements of §135.339; and

(5) Has been approved by the Administrator for the check airman (simulator) duties involved.

(d) Completion of the requirements in paragraphs (b)(2), (3), and (4) or (c)(2), (3), and (4) of this section, as applicable, shall be entered in the individual's training record maintained by the certificate holder.

(e) Check airmen who do not hold an appropriate medical certificate may function as check airmen (simulator), but may not serve as flightcrew members in operations under this part.

(f) A check airman (simulator) must accomplish the following—

(1) Fly at least two flight segments as a required crewmember for the type, class, or category aircraft involved within the 12-month preceding the performance of any check airman duty in a flight simulator; or

(2) Satisfactorily complete an approved line-observation program within the period prescribed by that program and that must precede the performance of any check airman duty in a flight simulator.

(g) The flight segments or line-observation program required in paragraph (f) of this section are considered to be completed in the month required if completed in the calendar month before or the calendar month after the month in which they are due.

[Docket No. 28471, 61 FR 30744, June 17, 1996]

§135.338 Qualifications: Flight instructors (aircraft) and flight instructors (simulator).

(a) For the purposes of this section and §135.340:

(1) A flight instructor (aircraft) is a person who is qualified to instruct in an aircraft, in a flight simulator, or in a flight training device for a particular type, class, or category aircraft.

(2) A flight instructor (simulator) is a person who is qualified to instruct in a flight simulator, in a flight training device, or in both, for a particular type, class, or category aircraft.

(3) Flight instructors (aircraft) and flight instructors (simulator) are those instructors who perform the functions described in §§135.321(a) and 135.323(a)(4) and (c).

(b) No certificate holder may use a person, nor may any person serve as a flight instructor (aircraft) in a training program established under this subpart unless, with respect to the type, class, or category aircraft involved, that person—

(1) Holds the airman certificates and ratings required to serve as a pilot in command in operations under this part;

(2) Has satisfactorily completed the training phases for the aircraft, including recurrent training, that are required to serve as a pilot in command in operations under this part;

(3) Has satisfactorily completed the proficiency or competency checks that are required to serve as a pilot in command in operations under this part;

(4) Has satisfactorily completed the applicable training requirements of §135.340;

(5) Holds at least a Class III medical certificate; and

(6) Has satisfied the recency of experience requirements of §135.247.

(c) No certificate holder may use a person, nor may any person serve as a flight instructor (simulator) in a training program established under this subpart, unless, with respect to the type, class, or category aircraft involved, that person meets the provisions of paragraph (b) of this section, or—

(1) Holds the airman certificates and ratings, except medical certificate, required to serve as a pilot in command in operations under this part except before March 19, 1997 that person need not hold a type rating for the type, class, or category of aircraft involved.

(2) Has satisfactorily completed the appropriate training phases for the aircraft, including recurrent training, that are required to serve as a pilot in command in operations under this part;

(3) Has satisfactorily completed the appropriate proficiency or competency checks that are required to serve as a pilot in command in operations under this part; and

(4) Has satisfactorily completed the applicable training requirements of §135.340.

(d) Completion of the requirements in paragraphs (b)(2), (3), and (4) or (c)(2), (3), and (4) of this section, as applicable, shall be entered in the individual's training record maintained by the certificate holder.

(e) An airman who does not hold a medical certificate may function as a flight instructor in an aircraft if functioning as a non-required crewmember, but may not serve as a flightcrew member in operations under this part.

(f) A flight instructor (simulator) must accomplish the following—

(1) Fly at least two flight segments as a required crewmember for the type, class, or category aircraft involved within the 12-month period preceding the performance of any flight instructor duty in a flight simulator; or

(2) Satisfactorily complete an approved line-observation program within the period prescribed by that program preceding the performance of any flight instructor duty in a flight simulator.

(g) The flight segments or line-observation program required in paragraph (f) of this section are considered completed in the month required if completed in the calendar month before, or in the calendar month after, the month in which they are due.

[Docket No. 28471, 61 FR 30744, June 17, 1996; as amended by Amdt. 135–64, 62 FR 3739, Jan. 24, 1997; Amdt. 121–355, 76 FR 35104, June 16, 2011]

§135.339 Initial and transition training and checking: Check airmen (aircraft), check airmen (simulator).

(a) No certificate holder may use a person nor may any person serve as a check airman unless—

(1) That person has satisfactorily completed initial or transition check airman training; and

(2) Within the preceding 24 calendar months, that person satisfactorily conducts a proficiency or competency check under the observation of an FAA inspector or an aircrew designated examiner employed by the operator. The observation check may be accomplished in part or in full in an aircraft, in a flight simulator, or in a flight training device. This paragraph applies after March 19, 1997.

(b) The observation check required by paragraph (a)(2) of this section is considered to have been completed in the month required if completed in the calendar month before or the calendar month after the month in which it is due.

(c) The initial ground training for check airmen must include the following:

(1) Check airman duties, functions, and responsibilities.

(2) The applicable Code of Federal Regulations and the certificate holder's policies and procedures.

(3) The applicable methods, procedures, and techniques for conducting the required checks.

(4) Proper evaluation of student performance including the detection of—

(i) Improper and insufficient training; and

(ii) Personal characteristics of an applicant that could adversely affect safety.

(5) The corrective action in the case of unsatisfactory checks.

(6) The approved methods, procedures, and limitations for performing the required normal, abnormal, and emergency procedures in the aircraft.

(d) The transition ground training for check airmen must include the approved methods, procedures, and limitations for performing the required normal, abnormal, and emergency procedures applicable to the aircraft to which the check airman is in transition.

(e) The initial and transition flight training for check airmen (aircraft) must include the following—

(1) The safety measures for emergency situations that are likely to develop during a check;

(2) The potential results of improper, untimely, or nonexecution of safety measures during a check;

(3) Training and practice in conducting flight checks from the left and right pilot seats in the required normal, abnormal, and emergency procedures to ensure competence to conduct the pilot flight checks required by this part; and

(4) The safety measures to be taken from either pilot seat for emergency situations that are likely to develop during checking.

(f) The requirements of paragraph (e) of this section may be accomplished in full or in part in flight, in a flight simulator, or in a flight training device, as appropriate.

(g) The initial and transition flight training for check airmen (simulator) must include the following:

(1) Training and practice in conducting flight checks in the required normal, abnormal, and emergency procedures to ensure competence to conduct the flight checks required by this part. This training and practice must be accomplished in a flight simulator or in a flight training device.

(2) Training in the operation of flight simulators, flight training devices, or both, to ensure competence to conduct the flight checks required by this part.

[Docket No. 28471, 61 FR 30745, June 17, 1996; as amended by Amdt. 135–64, 62 FR 3739, Jan. 24, 1997]

§135.340 Initial and transition training and checking: Flight instructors (aircraft), flight instructors (simulator).

(a) No certificate holder may use a person nor may any person serve as a flight instructor unless—

(1) That person has satisfactorily completed initial or transition flight instructor training; and

(2) Within the preceding 24 calendar months, that person satisfactorily conducts instruction under the observation of an FAA inspector, an operator check airman, or an aircrew designated examiner employed by the operator. The observation check may be accomplished in part or in full in an aircraft, in a flight simulator, or in a flight training device. This paragraph applies after March 19, 1997.

(b) The observation check required by paragraph (a)(2) of this section is considered to have been completed in the month required if completed In the calendar month before, or the calendar month after, the month in which it is due.

(c) The initial ground training for flight instructors must include the following:

(1) Flight instructor duties, functions, and responsibilities.

(2) The applicable Code of Federal Regulations and the certificate holder's policies and procedures.

(3) The applicable methods, procedures, and techniques for conducting flight instruction.

(4) Proper evaluation of student performance including the detection of—

§135.340

(i) Improper and insufficient training; and
(ii) Personal characteristics of an applicant that could adversely affect safety.

(5) The corrective action in the case of unsatisfactory training progress.

(6) The approved methods, procedures, and limitations for performing the required normal, abnormal, and emergency procedures in the aircraft.

(7) Except for holders of a flight instructor certificate—
(i) The fundamental principles of the teaching-learning process;
(ii) Teaching methods and procedures; and
(iii) The instructor-student relationship.

(d) The transition ground training for flight instructors must include the approved methods, procedures, and limitations for performing the required normal, abnormal, and emergency procedures applicable to the type, class, or category aircraft to which the flight instructor is in transition.

(e) The initial and transition flight training for flight instructors (aircraft) must include the following—
(1) The safety measures for emergency situations that are likely to develop during instruction;
(2) The potential results of improper or untimely safety measures during instruction;
(3) Training and practice from the left and right pilot seats in the required normal, abnormal, and emergency maneuvers to ensure competence to conduct the flight instruction required by this part; and
(4) The safety measures to be taken from either the left or right pilot seat for emergency situations that are likely to develop during instruction.

(f) The requirements of paragraph (e) of this section may be accomplished in full or in part in flight, in a flight simulator, or in a flight training device, as appropriate.

(g) The initial and transition flight training for a flight instructor (simulator) must include the following:
(1) Training and practice in the required normal, abnormal, and emergency procedures to ensure competence to conduct the flight instruction required by this part. These maneuvers and procedures must be accomplished in full or in part in a flight simulator or in a flight training device.
(2) Training in the operation of flight simulators, flight training devices, or both, to ensure competence to conduct the flight instruction required by this part.

[Docket No. 28471, 61 FR 30745, June 17, 1996; as amended by Amdt. 135–64, 62 FR 3739, Jan. 24, 1997]

§135.341 Pilot and flight attendant crewmember training programs.

(a) Each certificate holder, other than one who uses only one pilot in the certificate holder's operations, shall establish and maintain an approved pilot training program, and each certificate holder who uses a flight attendant crewmember shall establish and maintain an approved flight attendant training program, that is appropriate to the operations to which each pilot and flight attendant is to be assigned, and will ensure that they are adequately trained to meet the applicable knowledge and practical testing requirements of §§135.293 through 135.301. However, the Administrator may authorize a deviation from this section if the Administrator finds that, because of the limited size and scope of the operation, safety will allow a deviation from these requirements. This deviation authority does not extend to the training provided under §135.336.

(b) Each certificate holder required to have a training program by paragraph (a) of this section shall include in that program ground and flight training curriculums for—
(1) Initial training;
(2) Transition training;
(3) Upgrade training;
(4) Differences training; and
(5) Recurrent training.

(c) Each certificate holder required to have a training program by paragraph (a) of this section shall provide current and appropriate study materials for use by each required pilot and flight attendant.

(d) The certificate holder shall furnish copies of the pilot and flight attendant crewmember training program, and all changes and additions, to the assigned representative of the Administrator. If the certificate holder uses training facilities of other persons, a copy of those training programs or appropriate portions used for those facilities shall also be furnished. Curricula that follow FAA published curricula may be cited by reference in the copy of the training program furnished to the representative of the Administrator and need not be furnished with the program.

[Docket No. 16097, 43 FR 46783, Oct. 10, 1978; as amended by Amdt. 135–18, 47 FR 33396, Aug. 2, 1982; Amdt. 135–127, 78 FR 42379, July 15, 2013; Amdt. 135–127A, 78 FR 77574, Dec. 24, 2013]

§135.343 Crewmember initial and recurrent training requirements.

No certificate holder may use a person, nor may any person serve, as a crewmember in operations under this part unless that crewmember has completed the appropriate initial or recurrent training phase of the training program appropriate to the type of operation in which the crewmember is to serve since the beginning of the 12th calendar month before that service. This section does not apply to a certificate holder that uses only one pilot in the certificate holder's operations.

[Docket No. 16097, 43 FR 46783, Oct. 10, 1978; as amended by Amdt. 135–18, 47 FR 33396, Aug. 2, 1982]

§135.345 Pilots: Initial, transition, and upgrade ground training.

Initial, transition, and upgrade ground training for pilots must include instruction in at least the following, as applicable to their duties:

(a) General subjects—

(1) The certificate holder's flight locating procedures;

(2) Principles and methods for determining weight and balance, and runway limitations for takeoff and landing;

(3) Enough meteorology to ensure a practical knowledge of weather phenomena, including the principles of frontal systems, icing, fog, thunderstorms, windshear and, if appropriate, high altitude weather situations;

(4) Air traffic control systems, procedures, and phraseology;

(5) Navigation and the use of navigational aids, including instrument approach procedures;

(6) Normal and emergency communication procedures;

(7) Visual cues before and during descent below DA/DH or MDA;

(8) ETOPS, if applicable;

(9) After August 13, 2008, passenger recovery plan for any passenger-carrying operation (other than intrastate operations wholly within the state of Alaska) in the North Polar area; and

(10) Other instructions necessary to ensure the pilot's competence.

(b) For each aircraft type—

(1) A general description;

(2) Performance characteristics;

(3) Engines and propellers;

(4) Major components;

(5) Major aircraft systems (i.e., flight controls, electrical, and hydraulic), other systems, as appropriate, principles of normal, abnormal, and emergency operations, appropriate procedures and limitations;

(6) Knowledge and procedures for—

(i) Recognizing and avoiding severe weather situations;

(ii) Escaping from severe weather situations, in case of inadvertent encounters, including low-altitude windshear (except that rotorcraft pilots are not required to be trained in escaping from low-altitude windshear);

(iii) Operating in or near thunderstorms (including best penetrating altitudes), turbulent air (including clear air turbulence), icing, hail, and other potentially hazardous meteorological conditions; and

(iv) Operating airplanes during ground icing conditions, (i.e., any time conditions are such that frost, ice, or snow may reasonably be expected to adhere to the airplane), if the certificate holder expects to authorize takeoffs in ground icing conditions, including:

(A) The use of holdover times when using deicing/anti-icing fluids;

(B) Airplane deicing/anti-icing procedures, including inspection and check procedures and responsibilities;

(C) Communications;

(D) Airplane surface contamination (i.e., adherence of frost, ice, or snow) and critical area identification, and knowledge of how contamination adversely affects airplane performance and flight characteristics;

(E) Types and characteristics of deicing/anti-icing fluids, if used by the certificate holder;

(F) Cold weather preflight inspection procedures;

(G) Techniques for recognizing contamination on the airplane;

(7) Operating limitations;

(8) Fuel consumption and cruise control;

(9) Flight planning;

(10) Each normal and emergency procedure; and

(11) The approved Aircraft Flight Manual, or equivalent.

[Docket No. 16097, 43 FR 46783, Oct. 10, 1978; as amended by Amdt. 135–27, 53 FR 37697, Sept. 27, 1988; Amdt. 135–46, 58 FR 69630, Dec. 30, 1993; Amdt. 135–108, 72 FR 1885, Jan. 16, 2007; Amdt. 135–110, 72 FR 31685, June 7, 2007; Amdt. 135–112, 73 FR 8798, Feb. 15, 2008]

§135.347 Pilots: Initial, transition, upgrade, and differences flight training.

(a) Initial, transition, upgrade, and differences training for pilots must include flight and practice in each of the maneuvers and procedures in the approved training program curriculum.

(b) The maneuvers and procedures required by paragraph (a) of this section must be performed in flight, except to the extent that certain maneuvers and procedures may be performed in an aircraft simulator, or an appropriate training device, as allowed by this subpart.

(c) If the certificate holder's approved training program includes a course of training using an aircraft simulator or other training device, each pilot must successfully complete—

(1) Training and practice in the simulator or training device in at least the maneuvers and procedures in this subpart that are capable of being

performed in the aircraft simulator or training device; and

(2) A flight check in the aircraft or a check in the simulator or training device to the level of proficiency of a pilot in command or second in command, as applicable, in at least the maneuvers and procedures that are capable of being performed in an aircraft simulator or training device.

§135.349 Flight attendants: Initial and transition ground training.

Initial and transition ground training for flight attendants must include instruction in at least the following—

(a) General subjects—

(1) The authority of the pilot in command; and

(2) Passenger handling, including procedures to be followed in handling deranged persons or other persons whose conduct might jeopardize safety.

(b) For each aircraft type—

(1) A general description of the aircraft emphasizing physical characteristics that may have a bearing on ditching, evacuation, and inflight emergency procedures and on other related duties;

(2) The use of both the public address system and the means of communicating with other flight crewmembers, including emergency means in the case of attempted hijacking or other unusual situations; and

(3) Proper use of electrical galley equipment and the controls for cabin heat and ventilation.

§135.351 Recurrent training.

(a) Each certificate holder must ensure that each crewmember receives recurrent training and is adequately trained and currently proficient for the type aircraft and crewmember position involved.

(b) Recurrent ground training for crewmembers must include at least the following:

(1) A quiz or other review to determine the crewmember's knowledge of the aircraft and crewmember position involved.

(2) Instruction as necessary in the subjects required for initial ground training by this subpart, as appropriate, including low-altitude windshear training and training on operating during ground icing conditions as prescribed in §135.341 and described in §135.345, crew resource management training as prescribed in §135.330, and emergency training as prescribed in §135.331.

(c) Recurrent flight training for pilots must include, at least, flight training in the maneuvers or procedures in this subpart, except that satisfactory completion of the check required by §135.293 within the preceding 12 calendar months may be substituted for recurrent flight training.

[Docket No. 16097, 43 FR 46783, Oct. 10, 1978; as amended by Amdt. 135–27, 53 FR 37698, Sept. 27, 1988; Amdt. 135–46, 58 FR 69630, Dec. 30, 1993; Amdt. 135–122, 76 FR 3837, Jan. 21, 2011]

§135.353 [Reserved]

Subpart I—
Airplane Performance Operating Limitations

§135.361 Applicability.

(a) This subpart prescribes airplane performance operating limitations applicable to the operation of the categories of airplanes listed in §135.363 when operated under this part.

(b) For the purpose of this subpart, *effective length of the runway*, for landing means the distance from the point at which the obstruction clearance plane associated with the approach end of the runway intersects the centerline of the runway to the far end of the runway.

(c) For the purpose of this subpart, *obstruction clearance plane* means a plane sloping upward from the runway at a slope of 1:20 to the horizontal, and tangent to or clearing all obstructions within a specified area surrounding the runway as shown in a profile view of that area. In the plan view, the centerline of the specified area coincides with the centerline of the runway, beginning at the point where the obstruction clearance plane intersects the centerline of the runway and proceeding to a point at least 1,500 feet from the beginning point. After that the centerline coincides with the takeoff path over the ground for the runway (in the case of takeoffs) or with the instrument approach counterpart (for landings), or, where the applicable one of these paths has not been established, it proceeds consistent with turns of at least 4,000-foot radius until a point is reached beyond which the obstruction clearance plane clears all obstructions. This area extends laterally 200 feet on each side of the centerline at the point where the obstruction clearance plane intersects the runway and continues at this width to the end of the runway; then it increases uniformly to 500 feet on each side of the centerline at a point 1,500 feet from the intersection of the obstruction clearance plane with the runway; after that it extends laterally 500 feet on each side of the centerline.

§135.363 General.

(a) Each certificate holder operating a reciprocating engine powered large transport category airplane shall comply with §§135.365 through 135.377.

(b) Each certificate holder operating a turbine engine powered large transport category airplane shall comply with §§135.379 through 135.387, except that when it operates a turbopropeller-powered large transport category airplane certificated after August 29, 1959, but previously type certificated with the same number of reciprocating engines, it may comply with §§135.365 through 135.377.

(c) Each certificate holder operating a large nontransport category airplane shall comply with §§135.389 through 135.395 and any determination of compliance must be based only on approved performance data. For the purpose of this subpart, a large nontransport category airplane is an airplane that was type certificated before July 1, 1942.

(d) Each certificate holder operating a small transport category airplane shall comply with §135.397.

(e) Each certificate holder operating a small nontransport category airplane shall comply with §135.399.

(f) The performance data in the Airplane Flight Manual applies in determining compliance with §§135.365 through 135.387. Where conditions are different from those on which the performance data is based, compliance is determined by interpolation or by computing the effects of change in the specific variables, if the results of the interpolation or computations are substantially as accurate as the results of direct tests.

(g) No person may take off a reciprocating engine powered large transport category airplane at a weight that is more than the allowable weight for the runway being used (determined under the runway takeoff limitations of the transport category operating rules of this subpart) after taking into account the temperature operating correction factors in section 4a.749a-T or section 4b.117 of the Civil Air Regulations in effect on January 31, 1965, and in the applicable Airplane Flight Manual.

(h) The Administrator may authorize in the operations specifications deviations from this subpart if special circumstances make a literal observance of a requirement unnecessary for safety.

(i) The 10-mile width specified in §§135.369 through 135.373 may be reduced to 5 miles, for not more than 20 miles, when operating under VFR or where navigation facilities furnish reliable and accurate identification of high ground and obstructions located outside of 5 miles, but within 10 miles, on each side of the intended track.

(j) Each certificate holder operating a commuter category airplane shall comply with §135.398.

[Docket No. 16097, 43 FR 46783, Oct. 10, 1978; as amended by Amdt. 135-21, 52 FR 1836, Jan. 15, 1987]

§135.364 Maximum flying time outside the United States.

After August 13, 2008, no certificate holder may operate an airplane, other than an all-cargo airplane with more than two engines, on a planned route that exceeds 180 minutes flying time (at the one-engine-inoperative cruise speed under standard conditions in still air) from an Adequate Airport outside the continental United States unless the operation is approved by the FAA in accordance with Appendix G of this part, Extended Operations (ETOPS).

[Docket No. FAA–2002–6717, 72 FR 26541, May 10, 2007; as amended by Amdt. 135–112, 73 FR 8798, Feb. 15, 2008]

§135.365 Large transport category airplanes: Reciprocating engine powered: Weight limitations.

(a) No person may take off a reciprocating engine powered large transport category airplane from an airport located at an elevation outside of the range for which maximum takeoff weights have been determined for that airplane.

(b) No person may take off a reciprocating engine powered large transport category airplane for an airport of intended destination that is located at an elevation outside of the range for which maximum landing weights have been determined for that airplane.

(c) No person may specify, or have specified, an alternate airport that is located at an elevation outside of the range for which maximum landing weights have been determined for the reciprocating engine powered large transport category airplane concerned.

(d) No person may take off a reciprocating engine powered large transport category airplane at a weight more than the maximum authorized takeoff weight for the elevation of the airport.

(e) No person may take off a reciprocating engine powered large transport category airplane if its weight on arrival at the airport of destination will be more than the maximum authorized landing weight for the elevation of that airport, allowing for normal consumption of fuel and oil en route.

§135.367 Large transport category airplanes: Reciprocating engine powered: Takeoff limitations.

(a) No person operating a reciprocating engine powered large transport category airplane may take off that airplane unless it is possible—

(1) To stop the airplane safely on the runway, as shown by the accelerate-stop distance data, at any time during takeoff until reaching critical-engine failure speed;

§135.369

(2) If the critical engine fails at any time after the airplane reaches critical-engine failure speed V_1, to continue the takeoff and reach a height of 50 feet, as indicated by the takeoff path data, before passing over the end of the runway; and

(3) To clear all obstacles either by at least 50 feet vertically (as shown by the takeoff path data) or 200 feet horizontally within the airport boundaries and 300 feet horizontally beyond the boundaries, without banking before reaching a height of 50 feet (as shown by the takeoff path data) and after that without banking more than 15 degrees.

(b) In applying this section, corrections must be made for any runway gradient. To allow for wind effect, takeoff data based on still air may be corrected by taking into account not more than 50 percent of any reported headwind component and not less than 150 percent of any reported tailwind component.

§135.369 Large transport category airplanes: Reciprocating engine powered: En route limitations: All engines operating.

(a) No person operating a reciprocating engine powered large transport category airplane may take off that airplane at a weight, allowing for normal consumption of fuel and oil, that does not allow a rate of climb (in feet per minute), with all engines operating, of at least 6.90 V_{S0} (that is, the number of feet per minute obtained by multiplying the number of knots by 6.90) at an altitude of a least 1,000 feet above the highest ground or obstruction within ten miles of each side of the intended track.

(b) This section does not apply to large transport category airplanes certificated under part 4a of the Civil Air Regulations.

§135.371 Large transport category airplanes: Reciprocating engine powered: En route limitations: One engine inoperative.

(a) Except as provided in paragraph (b) of this section, no person operating a reciprocating engine powered large transport category airplane may take off that airplane at a weight, allowing for normal consumption of fuel and oil, that does not allow a rate of climb (in feet per minute), with one engine inoperative, of at least (0.079-0.106/N) V_{S0}^2 (where N is the number of engines installed and V_{S0} is expressed in knots) at an altitude of least 1,000 feet above the highest ground or obstruction within 10 miles of each side of the intended track. However, for the purposes of this paragraph the rate of climb for transport category airplanes certificated under part 4a of the Civil Air Regulations is 0.026 V_{S0}^2.

(b) In place of the requirements of paragraph (a) of this section, a person may, under an approved procedure, operate a reciprocating engine powered large transport category airplane at an all-engines-operating altitude that allows the airplane to continue, after an engine failure, to an alternate airport where a landing can be made under §135.377, allowing for normal consumption of fuel and oil. After the assumed failure, the flight path must clear the ground and any obstruction within five miles on each side of the intended track by at least 2,000 feet.

(c) If an approved procedure under paragraph (b) of this section is used, the certificate holder shall comply with the following:

(1) The rate of climb (as prescribed in the Airplane Flight Manual for the appropriate weight and altitude) used in calculating the airplane's flight path shall be diminished by an amount in feet per minute, equal to (0.079-0.106/N) V_{S0}^2 (when N is the number of engines installed and V_{S0} is expressed in knots) for airplanes certificated under part 25 of this chapter and by 0.026 V_{S0}^2 for airplanes certificated under part 4a of the Civil Air Regulations.

(2) The all-engines-operating altitude shall be sufficient so that in the event the critical engine becomes inoperative at any point along the route, the flight will be able to proceed to a predetermined alternate airport by use of this procedure. In determining the takeoff weight, the airplane is assumed to pass over the critical obstruction following engine failure at a point no closer to the critical obstruction than the nearest approved navigational fix, unless the Administrator approves a procedure established on a different basis upon finding that adequate operational safeguards exist.

(3) The airplane must meet the provisions of paragraph (a) of this section at 1,000 feet above the airport used as an alternate in this procedure.

(4) The procedure must include an approved method of accounting for winds and temperatures that would otherwise adversely affect the flight path.

(5) In complying with this procedure, fuel jettisoning is allowed if the certificate holder shows that it has an adequate training program, that proper instructions are given to the flight crew, and all other precautions are taken to ensure a safe procedure.

(6) The certificate holder and the pilot in command shall jointly elect an alternate airport for which the appropriate weather reports or forecasts, or any combination of them, indicate that weather conditions will be at or above the alternate weather minimum specified in the certificate holder's operations specifications for that airport when the flight arrives.

[Docket No. 16097, 43 FR 46783, Oct. 10, 1978; as amended by Amdt. 135–110, 72 FR 31685, June 7, 2007]

§135.373 Part 25 transport category airplanes with four or more engines: Reciprocating engine powered: En route limitations: Two engines inoperative.

(a) No person may operate an airplane certificated under part 25 and having four or more engines unless—

(1) There is no place along the intended track that is more than 90 minutes (with all engines operating at cruising power) from an airport that meets §135.377; or

(2) It is operated at a weight allowing the airplane, with the two critical engines inoperative, to climb at 0.013 V_{S0}^2 feet per minute (that is, the number of feet per minute obtained by multiplying the number of knots squared by 0.013) at an altitude of 1,000 feet above the highest ground or obstruction within 10 miles on each side of the intended track, or at an altitude of 5,000 feet, whichever is higher.

(b) For the purposes of paragraph (a)(2) of this section, it is assumed that—

(1) The two engines fail at the point that is most critical with respect to the takeoff weight;

(2) Consumption of fuel and oil is normal with all engines operating up to the point where the two engines fail with two engines operating beyond that point;

(3) Where the engines are assumed to fail at an altitude above the prescribed minimum altitude, compliance with the prescribed rate of climb at the prescribed minimum altitude need not be shown during the descent from the cruising altitude to the prescribed minimum altitude, if those requirements can be met once the prescribed minimum altitude is reached, and assuming descent to be along a net flight path and the rate of descent to be 0.013 V_{S0}^2 greater than the rate in the approved performance data; and

(4) If fuel jettisoning is provided, the airplane's weight at the point where the two engines fail is considered to be not less than that which would include enough fuel to proceed to an airport meeting §135.377 and to arrive at an altitude of at least 1,000 feet directly over that airport.

§135.375 Large transport category airplanes: Reciprocating engine powered: Landing limitations: Destination airports.

(a) Except as provided in paragraph (b) of this section, no person operating a reciprocating engine powered large transport category airplane may take off that airplane, unless its weight on arrival, allowing for normal consumption of fuel and oil in flight, would allow a full stop landing at the intended destination within 60 percent of the effective length of each runway described below from a point 50 feet directly above the intersection of the obstruction clearance plane and the runway. For the purposes of determining the allowable landing weight at the destination airport the following is assumed:

(1) The airplane is landed on the most favorable runway and in the most favorable direction in still air.

(2) The airplane is landed on the most suitable runway considering the probable wind velocity and direction (forecast for the expected time of arrival), the ground handling characteristics of the type of airplane, and other conditions such as landing aids and terrain, and allowing for the effect of the landing path and roll of not more than 50 percent of the headwind component or not less than 150 percent of the tailwind component.

(b) An airplane that would be prohibited from being taken off because it could not meet paragraph (a)(2) of this section may be taken off if an alternate airport is selected that meets all of this section except that the airplane can accomplish a full stop landing within 70 percent of the effective length of the runway.

§135.377 Large transport category airplanes: Reciprocating engine powered: Landing limitations: Alternate airports.

No person may list an airport as an alternate airport in a flight plan unless the airplane (at the weight anticipated at the time of arrival at the airport), based on the assumptions in §135.375(a)(1) and (2), can be brought to a full stop landing within 70 percent of the effective length of the runway.

§135.379 Large transport category airplanes: Turbine engine powered: Takeoff limitations.

(a) No person operating a turbine engine powered large transport category airplane may take off that airplane at a weight greater than that listed in the Airplane Flight Manual for the elevation of the airport and for the ambient temperature existing at take off.

(b) No person operating a turbine engine powered large transport category airplane certificated after August 26, 1957, but before August 30, 1959 (SR422, 422A), may take off that airplane at a weight greater than that listed in the Airplane Flight Manual for the minimum distance required for takeoff. In the case of an airplane certificated after September 30, 1958 (SR422A, 422B), the takeoff distance may include a clearway distance but the clearway distance included may not be greater than one-half of the takeoff run.

(c) No person operating a turbine engine powered large transport category airplane certificated after August 29, 1959 (SR422B), may take off that airplane at a weight greater than that listed in the Airplane Flight Manual at which compliance with the following may be shown:

(1) The accelerate-stop distance, as defined in §25.109 of this chapter, must not exceed the length of the runway plus the length of any stopway.

(2) The takeoff distance must not exceed the length of the runway plus the length of any clearway except that the length of any clearway included must not be greater than one-half the length of the runway.

(3) The takeoff run must not be greater than the length of the runway.

(d) No person operating a turbine engine powered large transport category airplane may take off that airplane at a weight greater than that listed in the Airplane Flight Manual—

(1) For an airplane certificated after August 26, 1957, but before October 1, 1958 (SR422), that allows a takeoff path that clears all obstacles either by at least (35+0.01 D) feet vertically (D is the distance along the intended flight path from the end of the runway in feet), or by at least 200 feet horizontally within the airport boundaries and by at least 300 feet horizontally after passing the boundaries; or

(2) For an airplane certificated after September 30, 1958 (SR422A, 422B), that allows a net takeoff flight path that clears all obstacles either by a height of at least 35 feet vertically, or by at least 200 feet horizontally within the airport boundaries and by at least 300 feet horizontally after passing the boundaries.

(e) In determining maximum weights, minimum distances, and flight paths under paragraphs (a) through (d) of this section, correction must be made for the runway to be used, the elevation of the airport, the effective runway gradient, the ambient temperature and wind component at the time of takeoff, and, if operating limitations exist for the minimum distances required for takeoff from wet runways, the runway surface condition (dry or wet). Wet runway distances associated with grooved or porous friction course runways, if provided in the Airplane Flight Manual, may be used only for runways that are grooved or treated with a porous friction course (PFC) overlay, and that the operator determines are designed, constructed, and maintained in a manner acceptable to the Administrator.

(f) For the purposes of this section, it is assumed that the airplane is not banked before reaching a height of 50 feet, as shown by the takeoff path or net takeoff flight path data (as appropriate) in the Airplane Flight Manual, and after that the maximum bank is not more than 15 degrees.

(g) For the purposes of this section, the terms, takeoff distance, takeoff run, net takeoff flight path, have the same meanings as set forth in the rules under which the airplane was certificated.

[Docket No. 16097, 43 FR 46783, Oct. 10, 1978; as amended by Amdt. 135–71, 63 FR 8321, Feb. 18, 1998]

§135.381 Large transport category airplanes: Turbine engine powered: En route limitations: One engine inoperative.

(a) No person operating a turbine engine powered large transport category airplane may take off that airplane at a weight, allowing for normal consumption of fuel and oil, that is greater than that which (under the approved, one engine inoperative, en route net flight path data in the Airplane Flight Manual for that airplane) will allow compliance with paragraph (a)(1) or (2) of this section, based on the ambient temperatures expected en route.

(1) There is a positive slope at an altitude of at least 1,000 feet above all terrain and obstructions within five statute miles on each side of the intended track, and, in addition, if that airplane was certificated after August 29, 1958 (SR422B), there is a positive slope at 1,500 feet above the airport where the airplane is assumed to land after an engine fails.

(2) The net flight path allows the airplane to continue flight from the cruising altitude to an airport where a landing can be made under §135.387 clearing all terrain and obstructions within five statute miles of the intended track by at least 2,000 feet vertically and with a positive slope at 1,000 feet above the airport where the airplane lands after an engine fails, or, if that airplane was certificated after September 30, 1958 (SR422A, 422B), with a positive slope at 1,500 feet above the airport where the airplane lands after an engine fails.

(b) For the purpose of paragraph (a)(2) of this section, it is assumed that—

(1) The engine fails at the most critical point en route;

(2) The airplane passes over the critical obstruction, after engine failure at a point that is no closer to the obstruction than the approved navigation fix, unless the Administrator authorizes a different procedure based on adequate operational safeguards;

(3) An approved method is used to allow for adverse winds;

(4) Fuel jettisoning will be allowed if the certificate holder shows that the crew is properly instructed, that the training program is adequate,

and that all other precautions are taken to ensure a safe procedure;

(5) The alternate airport is selected and meets the prescribed weather minimums; and

(6) The consumption of fuel and oil after engine failure is the same as the consumption that is allowed for in the approved net flight path data in the Airplane Flight Manual.

[Docket No. 16097, 43 FR 46783, Oct. 10, 1978; as amended by Amdt. 135–110, 72 FR 31685, June 7, 2007]

§135.383 Large transport category airplanes: Turbine engine powered: En route limitations: Two engines inoperative.

(a) Airplanes certificated after August 26, 1957, but before October 1, 1958 (SR422). No person may operate a turbine engine powered large transport category airplane along an intended route unless that person complies with either of the following:

(1) There is no place along the intended track that is more than 90 minutes (with all engines operating at cruising power) from an airport that meets §135.387.

(2) Its weight, according to the two-engine-inoperative, en route, net flight path data in the Airplane Flight Manual, allows the airplane to fly from the point where the two engines are assumed to fail simultaneously to an airport that meets §135.387, with a net flight path (considering the ambient temperature anticipated along the track) having a positive slope at an altitude of at least 1,000 feet above all terrain and obstructions within five statute miles on each side of the intended track, or at an altitude of 5,000 feet, whichever is higher.

For the purposes of paragraph (a)(2) of this section, it is assumed that the two engines fail at the most critical point en route, that if fuel jettisoning is provided, the airplane's weight at the point where the engines fail includes enough fuel to continue to the airport and to arrive at an altitude of at least 1,000 feet directly over the airport, and that the fuel and oil consumption after engine failure is the same as the consumption allowed for in the net flight path data in the Airplane Flight Manual.

(b) Airplanes certificated after September 30, 1958, but before August 30, 1959 (SR422A). No person may operate a turbine engine powered large transport category airplane along an intended route unless that person complies with either of the following:

(1) There is no place along the intended track that is more than 90 minutes (with all engines operating at cruising power) from an airport that meets §135.387.

(2) Its weight, according to the two-engine-inoperative, en route, net flight path data in the Airplane Flight Manual allows the airplane to fly from the point where the two engines are assumed to fail simultaneously to an airport that meets §135.387 with a net flight path (considering the ambient temperatures anticipated along the track) having a positive slope at an altitude of at least 1,000 feet above all terrain and obstructions within five statute miles on each side of the intended track, or at an altitude of 2,000 feet, whichever is higher.

For the purpose of paragraph (b)(2) of this section, it is assumed that the two engines fail at the most critical point en route, that the airplane's weight at the point where the engines fail includes enough fuel to continue to the airport, to arrive at an altitude of at least 1,500 feet directly over the airport, and after that to fly for 15 minutes at cruise power or thrust, or both, and that the consumption of fuel and oil after engine failure is the same as the consumption allowed for in the net flight path data in the Airplane Flight Manual.

(c) Aircraft certificated after August 29, 1959 (SR422B). No person may operate a turbine engine powered large transport category airplane along an intended route unless that person complies with either of the following:

(1) There is no place along the intended track that is more than 90 minutes (with all engines operating at cruising power) from an airport that meets §135.387.

(2) Its weight, according to the two-engine-inoperative, en route, net flight path data in the Airplane Flight Manual, allows the airplane to fly from the point where the two engines are assumed to fail simultaneously to an airport that meets §135.387, with the net flight path (considering the ambient temperatures anticipated along the track) clearing vertically by at least 2,000 feet all terrain and obstructions within five statute miles on each side of the intended track. For the purposes of this paragraph, it is assumed that—

(i) The two engines fail at the most critical point en route;

(ii) The net flight path has a positive slope at 1,500 feet above the airport where the landing is assumed to be made after the engines fail;

(iii) Fuel jettisoning will be approved if the certificate holder shows that the crew is properly instructed, that the training program is adequate, and that all other precautions are taken to ensure a safe procedure;

(iv) The airplane's weight at the point where the two engines are assumed to fail provides enough fuel to continue to the airport, to arrive at an altitude of at least 1,500 feet directly over the airport, and after that to fly for 15 minutes at cruise power or thrust, or both; and

(v) The consumption of fuel and oil after the engines fail is the same as the consumption that is allowed for in the net flight path data in the Airplane Flight Manual.

§135.385 Large transport category airplanes: Turbine engine powered: Landing limitations: Destination airports.

(a) No person operating a turbine engine powered large transport category airplane may take off that airplane at a weight that (allowing for normal consumption of fuel and oil in flight to the destination or alternate airport) the weight of the airplane on arrival would exceed the landing weight in the Airplane Flight Manual for the elevation of the destination or alternate airport and the ambient temperature anticipated at the time of landing.

(b) Except as provided in paragraph (c), (d), (e), or (f) of this section, no person operating a turbine engine powered large transport category airplane may take off that airplane unless its weight on arrival, allowing for normal consumption of fuel and oil in flight (in accordance with the landing distance in the Airplane Flight Manual for the elevation of the destination airport and the wind conditions expected there at the time of landing), would allow a full stop landing at the intended destination airport within 60 percent of the effective length of each runway described below from a point 50 feet above the intersection of the obstruction clearance plane and the runway. For the purpose of determining the allowable landing weight at the destination airport the following is assumed:

(1) The airplane is landed on the most favorable runway and in the most favorable direction, in still air.

(2) The airplane is landed on the most suitable runway considering the probable wind velocity and direction and the ground handling characteristics of the airplane, and considering other conditions such as landing aids and terrain.

(c) A turbopropeller powered airplane that would be prohibited from being taken off because it could not meet paragraph (b)(2) of this section, may be taken off if an alternate airport is selected that meets all of this section except that the airplane can accomplish a full stop landing within 70 percent of the effective length of the runway.

(d) Unless, based on a showing of actual operating landing techniques on wet runways, a shorter landing distance (but never less than that required by paragraph (b) of this section) has been approved for a specific type and model airplane and included in the Airplane Flight Manual, no person may take off a turbojet airplane when the appropriate weather reports or forecasts, or any combination of them, indicate that the runways at the destination airport may be wet or slippery at the estimated time of arrival unless the effective runway length at the destination airport is at least 115 percent of the runway length required under paragraph (b) of this section.

(e) A turbojet airplane that would be prohibited from being taken off because it could not meet paragraph (b)(2) of this section may be taken off if an alternate airport is selected that meets all of paragraph (b) of this section.

(f) An eligible on-demand operator may take off a turbine engine powered large transport category airplane on an on-demand flight if all of the following conditions exist:

(1) The operation is permitted by an approved Destination Airport Analysis in that person's operations manual.

(2) The airplane's weight on arrival, allowing for normal consumption of fuel and oil in flight (in accordance with the landing distance in the Airplane Flight Manual for the elevation of the destination airport and the wind conditions expected there at the time of landing), would allow a full stop landing at the intended destination airport within 80 percent of the effective length of each runway described below from a point 50 feet above the intersection of the obstruction clearance plane and the runway. For the purpose of determining the allowable landing weight at the destination airport, the following is assumed:

(i) The airplane is landed on the most favorable runway and in the most favorable direction, in still air.

(ii) The airplane is landed on the most suitable runway considering the probable wind velocity and direction and the ground handling characteristics of the airplane, and considering other conditions such as landing aids and terrain.

(3) The operation is authorized by operations specifications.

[Docket No. 16097, 43 FR 46783, Oct. 10, 1978; as amended by Amdt. 135–91, 68 FR 54588, Sept. 17, 2003]

§135.387 Large transport category airplanes: Turbine engine powered: Landing limitations: Alternate airports.

(a) Except as provided in paragraph (b) of this section, no person may select an airport as an alternate airport for a turbine engine powered large transport category airplane unless (based on the assumptions in §135.385(b)) that airplane, at the weight expected at the time of arrival, can be brought to a full stop landing within 70 percent of the effective length of the runway for turbo-propeller-powered airplanes and 60 percent of the effective length of the runway for turbojet airplanes, from a point 50 feet above the intersection of the obstruction clearance plane and the runway.

(b) Eligible on-demand operators may select an airport as an alternate airport for a turbine engine powered large transport category airplane if (based on the assumptions in §135.385(f)) that airplane, at the weight expected at the time of arrival, can be brought to a full stop landing within 80 percent of the effective length of the runway from a point 50 feet above the intersection of the obstruction clearance plane and the runway.

[Docket No. FAA–2001–10047, 68 FR 54588, Sept. 17, 2003]

§135.389 Large nontransport category airplanes: Takeoff limitations.

(a) No person operating a large nontransport category airplane may take off that airplane at a weight greater than the weight that would allow the airplane to be brought to a safe stop within the effective length of the runway, from any point during the takeoff before reaching 105 percent of minimum control speed (the minimum speed at which an airplane can be safely controlled in flight after an engine becomes inoperative) or 115 percent of the power off stalling speed in the takeoff configuration, whichever is greater.

(b) For the purposes of this section—
(1) It may be assumed that takeoff power is used on all engines during the acceleration;
(2) Not more than 50 percent of the reported headwind component, or not less than 150 percent of the reported tailwind component, may be taken into account;
(3) The average runway gradient (the difference between the elevations of the endpoints of the runway divided by the total length) must be considered if it is more than one-half of one percent;
(4) It is assumed that the airplane is operating in standard atmosphere; and
(5) For takeoff, *effective length of the runway* means the distance from the end of the runway at which the takeoff is started to a point at which the obstruction clearance plane associated with the other end of the runway intersects the runway centerline.

§135.391 Large nontransport category airplanes: En route limitations: One engine inoperative.

(a) Except as provided in paragraph (b) of this section, no person operating a large nontransport category airplane may take off that airplane at a weight that does not allow a rate of climb of at least 50 feet a minute, with the critical engine inoperative, at an altitude of at least 1,000 feet above the highest obstruction within five miles on each side of the intended track, or 5,000 feet, whichever is higher.

(b) Without regard to paragraph (a) of this section, if the Administrator finds that safe operations are not impaired, a person may operate the airplane at an altitude that allows the airplane, in case of engine failure, to clear all obstructions within five miles on each side of the intended track by 1,000 feet. If this procedure is used, the rate of descent for the appropriate weight and altitude is assumed to be 50 feet a minute greater than the rate in the approved performance data. Before approving such a procedure, the Administrator considers the following for the route, route segment, or area concerned:
(1) The reliability of wind and weather forecasting.
(2) The location and kinds of navigation aids.
(3) The prevailing weather conditions, particularly the frequency and amount of turbulence normally encountered.
(4) Terrain features.
(5) Air traffic problems.
(6) Any other operational factors that affect the operations.

(c) For the purposes of this section, it is assumed that—
(1) The critical engine is inoperative;
(2) The propeller of the inoperative engine is in the minimum drag position;
(3) The wing flaps and landing gear are in the most favorable position;
(4) The operating engines are operating at the maximum continuous power available;
(5) The airplane is operating in standard atmosphere; and
(6) The weight of the airplane is progressively reduced by the anticipated consumption of fuel and oil.

§135.393 Large nontransport category airplanes: Landing limitations: Destination airports.

(a) No person operating a large nontransport category airplane may take off that airplane at a weight that—
(1) Allowing for anticipated consumption of fuel and oil, is greater than the weight that would allow a full stop landing within 60 percent of the effective length of the most suitable runway at the destination airport; and
(2) Is greater than the weight allowable if the landing is to be made on the runway—
(i) With the greatest effective length in still air; and
(ii) Required by the probable wind, taking into account not more than 50 percent of the headwind component or not less than 150 percent of the tailwind component.

(b) For the purpose of this section, it is assumed that—

§135.395

(1) The airplane passes directly over the intersection of the obstruction clearance plane and the runway at a height of 50 feet in a steady gliding approach at a true indicated airspeed of at least 1.3 V_{S0};

(2) The landing does not require exceptional pilot skill; and

(3) The airplane is operating in standard atmosphere.

§135.395 Large nontransport category airplanes: Landing limitations: Alternate airports.

No person may select an airport as an alternate airport for a large nontransport category airplane unless that airplane (at the weight anticipated at the time of arrival), based on the assumptions in §135.393(b), can be brought to a full stop landing within 70 percent of the effective length of the runway.

§135.397 Small transport category airplane performance operating limitations.

(a) No person may operate a reciprocating engine powered small transport category airplane unless that person complies with the weight limitations in §135.365, the takeoff limitations in §135.367 (except paragraph (a)(3)), and the landing limitations in §§135.375 and 135.377.

(b) No person may operate a turbine engine powered small transport category airplane unless that person complies with the takeoff limitations in §135.379 (except paragraphs (d) and (f)) and the landing limitations in §§135.385 and 135.387.

§135.398 Commuter category airplanes performance operating limitations.

(a) No person may operate a commuter category airplane unless that person complies with the takeoff weight limitations in the approved Airplane Flight Manual.

(b) No person may take off an airplane type certificated in the commuter category at a weight greater than that listed in the Airplane Flight Manual that allows a net takeoff flight path that clears all obstacles either by a height of at least 35 feet vertically, or at least 200 feet horizontally within the airport boundaries and by at least 300 feet horizontally after passing the boundaries.

(c) No person may operate a commuter category airplane unless that person complies with the landing limitations prescribed in §§135.385 and 135.387 of this part. For purposes of this paragraph, §§135.385 and 135.387 are applicable to all commuter category airplanes notwithstanding their stated applicability to turbine-engine-powered large transport category airplanes.

(d) In determining maximum weights, minimum distances and flight paths under paragraphs (a) through (c) of this section, correction must be made for the runway to be used, the elevation of the airport, the effective runway gradient, and ambient temperature, and wind component at the time of takeoff.

(e) For the purposes of this section, the assumption is that the airplane is not banked before reaching a height of 50 feet as shown by the net takeoff flight path data in the Airplane Flight Manual and thereafter the maximum bank is not more than 15 degrees.

[Docket No. 23516, 52 FR 1836, Jan. 15, 1987]

§135.399 Small nontransport category airplane performance operating limitations.

(a) No person may operate a reciprocating engine or turbopropeller-powered small airplane that is certificated under §135.169(b)(2), (3), (4), (5), or (6) unless that person complies with the takeoff weight limitations in the approved Airplane Flight Manual or equivalent for operations under this part, and, if the airplane is certificated under §135.169(b)(4) or (5) with the landing weight limitations in the Approved Airplane Flight Manual or equivalent for operations under this part.

(b) No person may operate an airplane that is certificated under §135.169(b)(6) unless that person complies with the landing limitations prescribed in §§135.385 and 135.387 of this part. For purposes of this paragraph, §§135.385 and 135.387 are applicable to reciprocating and turbo-propeller-powered small airplanes notwithstanding their stated applicability to turbine engine powered large transport category airplanes.

[44 FR 53731, Sept. 17, 1979]

Subpart J—Maintenance, Preventive Maintenance, and Alterations

§135.411 Applicability.

(a) This subpart prescribes rules in addition to those in other parts of this chapter for the maintenance, preventive maintenance, and alterations for each certificate holder as follows:

(1) Aircraft that are type certificated for a passenger seating configuration, excluding any pilot seat, of nine seats or less, shall be maintained under parts 91 and 43 of this chapter and §§135.415, 135.417, 135.421 and 135.422. An approved aircraft inspection program may be used under §135.419.

(2) Aircraft that are type certificated for a passenger seating configuration, excluding any pilot

seat, of ten seats or more, shall be maintained under a maintenance program in §§135.415, 135.417, 135.423 through 135.443.

(b) A certificate holder who is not otherwise required, may elect to maintain its aircraft under paragraph (a)(2) of this section.

(c) Single engine aircraft used in passenger-carrying IFR operations shall also be maintained in accordance with §135.421(c), (d), and (e).

(d) A certificate holder who elects to operate in accordance with §135.364 must maintain its aircraft under paragraph (a)(2) of this section and the additional requirements of Appendix G of this part.

[Docket No. 16097, 43 FR 46783, Oct. 10, 1978; as amended by Amdt. 135–70, 62 FR 42374, Aug. 6, 1997; Amdt. 135–78, 65 FR 60556, Oct. 11, 2000; Amdt. 135–92, 68 FR 69308, Dec. 12, 2003; Amdt. 135–81, 70 FR 5533, Feb. 2, 2005; Amdt. 135–108, 72 FR 1885, Jan. 16, 2007; amended at 72 FR 53114, Sept. 18, 2007]

§135.413 Responsibility for airworthiness.

(a) Each certificate holder is primarily responsible for the airworthiness of its aircraft, including airframes, aircraft engines, propellers, rotors, appliances, and parts, and shall have its aircraft maintained under this chapter, and shall have defects repaired between required maintenance under part 43 of this chapter.

(b) Each certificate holder who maintains its aircraft under §135.411(a)(2) shall—

(1) Perform the maintenance, preventive maintenance, and alteration of its aircraft, including airframe, aircraft engines, propellers, rotors, appliances, emergency equipment and parts, under its manual and this chapter; or

(2) Make arrangements with another person for the performance of maintenance, preventive maintenance, or alteration. However, the certificate holder shall ensure that any maintenance, preventive maintenance, or alteration that is performed by another person is performed under the certificate holder's manual and this chapter.

§135.415 Service difficulty reports.

(a) Each certificate holder shall report the occurrence or detection of each failure, malfunction, or defect in an aircraft concerning—

(1) Fires during flight and whether the related fire-warning system functioned properly;

(2) Fires during flight not protected by related fire-warning system;

(3) False fire-warning during flight;

(4) An exhaust system that causes damage during flight to the engine, adjacent structure, equipment, or components;

(5) An aircraft component that causes accumulation or circulation of smoke, vapor, or toxic or noxious fumes in the crew compartment or passenger cabin during flight;

(6) Engine shutdown during flight because of flameout;

(7) Engine shutdown during flight when external damage to the engine or aircraft structure occurs;

(8) Engine shutdown during flight due to foreign object ingestion or icing;

(9) Shutdown of more than one engine during flight;

(10) A propeller feathering system or ability of the system to control overspeed during flight;

(11) A fuel or fuel-dumping system that affects fuel flow or causes hazardous leakage during flight;

(12) An unwanted landing gear extension or retraction or opening or closing of landing gear doors during flight;

(13) Brake system components that result in loss of brake actuating force when the aircraft is in motion on the ground;

(14) Aircraft structure that requires major repair;

(15) Cracks, permanent deformation, or corrosion of aircraft structures, if more than the maximum acceptable to the manufacturer or the FAA; and

(16) Aircraft components or systems that result in taking emergency actions during flight (except action to shut-down an engine).

(b) For the purpose of this section, during flight means the period from the moment the aircraft leaves the surface of the earth on takeoff until it touches down on landing.

(c) In addition to the reports required by paragraph (a) of this section, each certificate holder shall report any other failure, malfunction, or defect in an aircraft that occurs or is detected at any time if, in its opinion, the failure, malfunction, or defect has endangered or may endanger the safe operation of the aircraft.

(d) Each certificate holder shall submit each report required by this section, covering each 24-hour period beginning at 0900 local time of each day and ending at 0900 local time on the next day, to the FAA offices in Oklahoma City, Oklahoma. Each report of occurrences during a 24-hour period shall be submitted to the collection point within the next 96 hours. However, a report due on Saturday or Sunday may be submitted on the following Monday, and a report due on a holiday may be submitted on the next workday.

(e) The certificate holder shall transmit the reports required by this section on a form and in a manner prescribed by the Administrator, and shall include as much of the following as is available:

(1) The type and identification number of the aircraft.

§135.417

(2) The name of the operator.
(3) The date.
(4) The nature of the failure, malfunction, or defect.
(5) Identification of the part and system involved, including available information pertaining to type designation of the major component and time since last overhaul, if known.
(6) Apparent cause of the failure, malfunction or defect (e.g., wear, crack, design deficiency, or personnel error).
(7) Other pertinent information necessary for more complete identification, determination of seriousness, or corrective action.

(f) A certificate holder that is also the holder of a type certificate (including a supplemental type certificate), a Parts Manufacturer Approval, or a Technical Standard Order Authorization, or that is the licensee of a type certificate need not report a failure, malfunction, or defect under this section if the failure, malfunction, or defect has been reported by it under §21.3 or §37.17 of this chapter or under the accident reporting provisions of part 830 of the regulations of the National Transportation Safety Board.

(g) No person may withhold a report required by this section even though all information required by this section is not available.

(h) When the certificate holder gets additional information, including information from the manufacturer or other agency, concerning a report required by this section, it shall expeditiously submit it as a supplement to the first report and reference the date and place of submission of the first report.

[Docket No. 16097, 43 FR 46783, Oct. 10, 1978; as amended by Docket No. 28293, 65 FR 56201, Sept. 15, 2000; Amdt. 135–81, 66 FR 21626, April 30, 2001; Docket FAA–2000–7952, 66 FR 58912, Nov. 23, 2001; FAA–2000–7952, 67 FR 78970, Dec. 27, 2002; Docket No. FAA–2000–7952, 68 FR 75116, Dec. 30, 2003; Amdt. 135–102, 70 FR 76979, Dec. 29, 2005]

§135.417 Mechanical interruption summary report.

Each certificate holder shall mail or deliver, before the end of the 10th day of the following month, a summary report of the following occurrences in multiengine aircraft for the preceding month to the certificate-holding district office:

(a) Each interruption to a flight, unscheduled change of aircraft en route, or unscheduled stop or diversion from a route, caused by known or suspected mechanical difficulties or malfunctions that are not required to be reported under §135.415.

(b) The number of propeller featherings in flight, listed by type of propeller and engine and aircraft on which it was installed. Propeller featherings for training, demonstration, or flight check purposes need not be reported.

[Docket No. 16097, 43 FR 46783, Oct. 10, 1978; as amended by Docket No. 28293, 65 FR 56206, Sept. 15, 2000; Amdt. 135–81, 66 FR 21626, April 30, 2001; Docket FAA–2000–7952, 66 FR 58912, Nov. 23, 2001; FAA–2000–7952, 67 FR 78970, Dec. 27, 2002; Docket No. FAA–2000–7952, 68 FR 75116, Dec. 30, 2003; Amdt. 135–102, 70 FR 76979, Dec. 29, 2005]

§135.419 Approved aircraft inspection program.

(a) Whenever the Administrator finds that the aircraft inspections required or allowed under part 91 of this chapter are not adequate to meet this part, or upon application by a certificate holder, the Administrator may amend the certificate holder's operations specifications under §119.51, to require or allow an approved aircraft inspection program for any make and model aircraft of which the certificate holder has the exclusive use of at least one aircraft (as defined in §135.25(b)).

(b) A certificate holder who applies for an amendment of its operations specifications to allow an approved aircraft inspection program must submit that program with its application for approval by the Administrator.

(c) Each certificate holder who is required by its operations specifications to have an approved aircraft inspection program shall submit a program for approval by the Administrator within 30 days of the amendment of its operations specifications or within any other period that the Administrator may prescribe in the operations specifications.

(d) The aircraft inspection program submitted for approval by the Administrator must contain the following:

(1) Instructions and procedures for the conduct of aircraft inspections (which must include necessary tests and checks), setting forth in detail the parts and areas of the airframe, engines, propellers, rotors, and appliances, including emergency equipment, that must be inspected.

(2) A schedule for the performance of the aircraft inspections under paragraph (d)(1) of this section expressed in terms of the time in service, calendar time, number of system operations, or any combination of these.

(3) Instructions and procedures for recording discrepancies found during inspections and correction or deferral of discrepancies including form and disposition of records.

(e) After approval, the certificate holder shall include the approved aircraft inspection program in the manual required by §135.21.

(f) Whenever the Administrator finds that revisions to an approved aircraft inspection program are necessary for the continued adequacy of the program, the certificate holder shall, after notification by the Administrator, make any changes in the program found by the Administrator to be necessary. The certificate holder may petition the Administrator to reconsider the notice to make any changes in a program. The petition must be filed with the representatives of the Administrator assigned to it within 30 days after the certificate holder receives the notice. Except in the case of an emergency requiring immediate action in the interest of safety, the filing of the petition stays the notice pending a decision by the Administrator.

(g) Each certificate holder who has an approved aircraft inspection program shall have each aircraft that is subject to the program inspected in accordance with the program.

(h) The registration number of each aircraft that is subject to an approved aircraft inspection program must be included in the operations specifications of the certificate holder.

[Docket No. 16097, 43 FR 46783, Oct. 10, 1978; as amended by Amdt. 135–104, 71 FR 536, Jan. 4, 2006]

§135.421 Additional maintenance requirements.

(a) Each certificate holder who operates an aircraft type certificated for a passenger seating configuration, excluding any pilot seat, of nine seats or less, must comply with the manufacturer's recommended maintenance programs, or a program approved by the Administrator, for each aircraft engine, propeller, rotor, and each item of emergency equipment required by this chapter.

(b) For the purpose of this section, a manufacturer's maintenance program is one which is contained in the maintenance manual or maintenance instructions set forth by the manufacturer as required by this chapter for the aircraft, aircraft engine, propeller, rotor or item of emergency equipment.

(c) For each single engine aircraft to be used in passenger-carrying IFR operations, each certificate holder must incorporate into its maintenance program either:

(1) the manufacturer's recommended engine trend monitoring program, which includes an oil analysis, if appropriate, or

(2) an FAA approved engine trend monitoring program that includes an oil analysis at each 100 hour interval or at the manufacturer's suggested interval, whichever is more frequent.

(d) For single engine aircraft to be used in passenger-carrying IFR operations, written maintenance instructions containing the methods, techniques, and practices necessary to maintain the equipment specified in §§135.105, and 135.163 (f) and (h) are required.

(e) No certificate holder may operate a single engine aircraft under IFR, carrying passengers, unless the certificate holder records and maintains in the engine maintenance records the results of each test, observation, and inspection required by the applicable engine trend monitoring program specified in (c)(1) and (c)(2) of this section.

[Docket No. 16097, 43 FR 46783, Oct. 10, 1978; as amended by Amdt. 135–70, 62 FR 42374, Aug. 6, 1997]

§135.422 Aging airplane inspections and records reviews for multiengine airplanes certificated with nine or fewer passenger seats.

(a) *Applicability.* This section applies to multiengine airplanes certificated with nine or fewer passenger seats, operated by a certificate holder in a scheduled operation under this part, except for those airplanes operated by a certificate holder in a scheduled operation between any point within the State of Alaska and any other point within the State of Alaska.

(b) *Operation after inspections and records review.* After the dates specified in this paragraph, a certificate holder may not operate a multiengine airplane in a scheduled operation under this part unless the Administrator has notified the certificate holder that the Administrator has completed the aging airplane inspection and records review required by this section. During the inspection and records review, the certificate holder must demonstrate to the Administrator that the maintenance of age-sensitive parts and components of the airplane has been adequate and timely enough to ensure the highest degree of safety.

(1) Airplanes exceeding 24 years in service on December 8, 2003; initial and repetitive inspections and records reviews. For an airplane that has exceeded 24 years in service on December 8, 2003, no later than December 5, 2007, and thereafter at intervals not to exceed 7 years.

(2) Airplanes exceeding 14 years in service but not 24 years in service on December 8, 2003; initial and repetitive inspections and records reviews. For an airplane that has exceeded 14 years in service, but not 24 years in service, on December 8, 2003, no later than December 4, 2008, and thereafter at intervals not to exceed 7 years.

(3) Airplanes not exceeding 14 years in service on December 8, 2003; initial and repetitive inspections and records reviews. For an airplane that has not exceeded 14 years in service on December 8, 2003, no later than 5 years after the start of the airplane's 15th year in service and thereafter at intervals not to exceed 7 years.

(c) *Unforeseen schedule conflict.* In the event of an unforeseen scheduling conflict for a specific airplane, the Administrator may approve an extension of up to 90 days beyond an interval specified in paragraph (b) of this section.

(d) Airplane and records availability. The certificate holder must make available to the Administrator each airplane for which an inspection and records review is required under this section, in a condition for inspection specified by the Administrator, together with the records containing the following information:

(1) Total years in service of the airplane;
(2) Total time in service of the airframe;
(3) Date of the last inspection and records review required by this section;
(4) Current status of life-limited parts of the airframe;
(5) Time since the last overhaul of all structural components required to be overhauled on a specific time basis;
(6) Current inspection status of the airplane, including the time since the last inspection required by the inspection program under which the airplane is maintained;
(7) Current status of applicable airworthiness directives, including the date and methods of compliance, and, if the airworthiness directive involves recurring action, the time and date when the next action is required;
(8) A list of major structural alterations; and
(9) A report of major structural repairs and the current inspection status for these repairs.

(e) Notification to the Administrator. Each certificate holder must notify the Administrator at least 60 days before the date on which the airplane and airplane records will be made available for the inspection and records review.

[Docket No. FAA–1999–5401, 70 FR 5533, Feb. 2, 2005]

§135.423 Maintenance, preventive maintenance, and alteration organization.

(a) Each certificate holder that performs any of its maintenance (other than required inspections), preventive maintenance, or alterations, and each person with whom it arranges for the performance of that work, must have an organization adequate to perform the work.

(b) Each certificate holder that performs any inspections required by its manual under §135.427(b)(2) or (3), (in this subpart referred to as required inspections), and each person with whom it arranges for the performance of that work, must have an organization adequate to perform that work.

(c) Each person performing required inspections in addition to other maintenance, preventive maintenance, or alterations, shall organize the performance of those functions so as to separate the required inspection functions from the other maintenance, preventive maintenance, and alteration functions. The separation shall be below the level of administrative control at which overall responsibility for the required inspection functions and other maintenance, preventive maintenance, and alteration functions is exercised.

[Docket No. FAA–1999–5401, 70 FR 5533, Feb. 2, 2005]

§135.425 Maintenance, preventive maintenance, and alteration programs.

Each certificate holder shall have an inspection program and a program covering other maintenance, preventive maintenance, and alterations, that ensures that—

(a) Maintenance, preventive maintenance, and alterations performed by it, or by other persons, are performed under the certificate holder's manual;

(b) Competent personnel and adequate facilities and equipment are provided for the proper performance of maintenance, preventive maintenance, and alterations; and

(c) Each aircraft released to service is airworthy and has been properly maintained for operation under this part.

§135.427 Manual requirements.

(a) Each certificate holder shall put in its manual the chart or description of the certificate holder's organization required by §135.423 and a list of persons with whom it has arranged for the performance of any of its required inspections, other maintenance, preventive maintenance, or alterations, including a general description of that work.

(b) Each certificate holder shall put in its manual the programs required by §135.425 that must be followed in performing maintenance, preventive maintenance, and alterations of that certificate holder's aircraft, including airframes, aircraft engines, propellers, rotors, appliances, emergency equipment, and parts, and must include at least the following:

(1) The method of performing routine and nonroutine maintenance (other than required inspections), preventive maintenance, and alterations.
(2) A designation of the items of maintenance and alteration that must be inspected (required inspections) including at least those that could result in a failure, malfunction, or defect endangering the safe operation of the aircraft, if not performed properly or if improper parts or materials are used.
(3) The method of performing required inspections and a designation by occupational title of personnel authorized to perform each required inspection.
(4) Procedures for the reinspection of work performed under previous required inspection findings (*buy-back procedures*).
(5) Procedures, standards, and limits necessary for required inspections and acceptance or

rejection of the items required to be inspected and for periodic inspection and calibration of precision tools, measuring devices, and test equipment.

(6) Procedures to ensure that all required inspections are performed.

(7) Instructions to prevent any person who performs any item of work from performing any required inspection of that work.

(8) Instructions and procedures to prevent any decision of an inspector regarding any required inspection from being countermanded by persons other than supervisory personnel of the inspection unit, or a person at the level of administrative control that has overall responsibility for the management of both the required inspection functions and the other maintenance, preventive maintenance, and alterations functions.

(9) Procedures to ensure that required inspections, other maintenance, preventive maintenance, and alterations that are not completed as a result of work interruptions are properly completed before the aircraft is released to service.

(c) Each certificate holder shall put in its manual a suitable system (which may include a coded system) that provides for the retention of the following information—

(1) A description (or reference to data acceptable to the Administrator) of the work performed;

(2) The name of the person performing the work if the work is performed by a person outside the organization of the certificate holder; and

(3) The name or other positive identification of the individual approving the work.

(d) For the purposes of this part, the certificate holder must prepare that part of its manual containing maintenance information and instructions, in whole or in part, in printed form or other form, acceptable to the Administrator, that is retrievable in the English language.

[Docket No. 16097, 43 FR 46783, Oct. 10, 1978; as amended by Amdt. 135–66, 62 FR 13257, March 19, 1997; Docket No. FAA–2004–17119, 69 FR 18472, April 8, 2004; Amdt. 135–118, 74 FR 38522, Aug. 4, 2009]

§135.429 Required inspection personnel.

(a) No person may use any person to perform required inspections unless the person performing the inspection is appropriately certificated, properly trained, qualified, and authorized to do so.

(b) No person may allow any person to perform a required inspection unless, at the time, the person performing that inspection is under the supervision and control of an inspection unit.

(c) No person may perform a required inspection if that person performed the item of work required to be inspected.

(d) In the case of rotorcraft that operate in remote areas or sites, the Administrator may approve procedures for the performance of required inspection items by a pilot when no other qualified person is available, provided—

(1) The pilot is employed by the certificate holder;

(2) It can be shown to the satisfaction of the Administrator that each pilot authorized to perform required inspections is properly trained and qualified;

(3) The required inspection is a result of a mechanical interruption and is not a part of a certificate holder's continuous airworthiness maintenance program;

(4) Each item is inspected after each flight until the item has been inspected by an appropriately certificated mechanic other than the one who originally performed the item of work; and

(5) Each item of work that is a required inspection item that is part of the flight control system shall be flight tested and reinspected before the aircraft is approved for return to service.

(e) Each certificate holder shall maintain, or shall determine that each person with whom it arranges to perform its required inspections maintains, a current listing of persons who have been trained, qualified, and authorized to conduct required inspections. The persons must be identified by name, occupational title and the inspections that they are authorized to perform. The certificate holder (or person with whom it arranges to perform its required inspections) shall give written information to each person so authorized, describing the extent of that person's responsibilities, authorities, and inspectional limitations. The list shall be made available for inspection by the Administrator upon request.

[Docket No. 16097, 43 FR 46783, Oct. 10, 1978; as amended by Amdt. 135–20, 51 FR 40710, Nov. 7, 1986]

§135.431 Continuing analysis and surveillance.

(a) Each certificate holder shall establish and maintain a system for the continuing analysis and surveillance of the performance and effectiveness of its inspection program and the program covering other maintenance, preventive maintenance, and alterations and for the correction of any deficiency in those programs, regardless of whether those programs are carried out by the certificate holder or by another person.

(b) Whenever the Administrator finds that either or both of the programs described in paragraph (a) of this section does not contain adequate procedures and standards to meet this part, the certificate holder shall, after notification by the Administrator, make changes in those programs requested by the Administrator.

§135.433 **Federal Aviation Regulations**

(c) A certificate holder may petition the Administrator to reconsider the notice to make a change in a program. The petition must be filed with the certificate-holding district office within 30 days after the certificate holder receives the notice. Except in the case of an emergency requiring immediate action in the interest of safety, the filing of the petition stays the notice pending a decision by the Administrator.

[Docket No. 16097, 43 FR 46783, Oct. 10, 1978; as amended by Amdt. 135–60, 61 FR 2617, Jan. 26, 1996]

§135.433 Maintenance and preventive maintenance training program.

Each certificate holder or a person performing maintenance or preventive maintenance functions for it shall have a training program to ensure that each person (including inspection personnel) who determines the adequacy of work done is fully informed about procedures and techniques and new equipment in use and is competent to perform that person's duties.

§135.435 Certificate requirements.

(a) Except for maintenance, preventive maintenance, alterations, and required inspections performed by a certificated repair station that is located outside the United States, each person who is directly in charge of maintenance, preventive maintenance, or alterations, and each person performing required inspections must hold an appropriate airman certificate.

(b) For the purpose of this section, a person *directly in charge* is each person assigned to a position in which that person is responsible for the work of a shop or station that performs maintenance, preventive maintenance, alterations, or other functions affecting airworthiness. A person who is *directly in charge* need not physically observe and direct each worker constantly but must be available for consultation and decision on matters requiring instruction or decision from higher authority than that of the person performing the work.

[Docket No. 16097, 43 FR 46783, Oct. 10, 1978; as amended by Amdt. 135–82, 66 FR 41117, Aug. 6, 2001]

§135.437 Authority to perform and approve maintenance, preventive maintenance, and alterations.

(a) A certificate holder may perform or make arrangements with other persons to perform maintenance, preventive maintenance, and alterations as provided in its maintenance manual. In addition, a certificate holder may perform these functions for another certificate holder as provided in the maintenance manual of the other certificate holder.

(b) A certificate holder may approve any airframe, aircraft engine, propeller, rotor, or appliance for return to service after maintenance, preventive maintenance, or alterations that are performed under paragraph (a) of this section. However, in the case of a major repair or alteration, the work must have been done in accordance with technical data approved by the Administrator.

§135.439 Maintenance recording requirements.

(a) Each certificate holder shall keep (using the system specified in the manual required in §135.427) the following records for the periods specified in paragraph (b) of this section:

(1) All the records necessary to show that all requirements for the issuance of an airworthiness release under §135.443 have been met.

(2) Records containing the following information:

(i) The total time in service of the airframe, engine, propeller, and rotor.

(ii) The current status of life-limited parts of each airframe, engine, propeller, rotor, and appliance.

(iii) The time since last overhaul of each item installed on the aircraft which are required to be overhauled on a specified time basis.

(iv) The identification of the current inspection status of the aircraft, including the time since the last inspections required by the inspection program under which the aircraft and its appliances are maintained.

(v) The current status of applicable airworthiness directives, including the date and methods of compliance, and, if the airworthiness directive involves recurring action, the time and date when the next action is required.

(vi) A list of current major alterations and repairs to each airframe, engine, propeller, rotor, and appliance.

(b) Each certificate holder shall retain the records required to be kept by this section for the following periods:

(1) Except for the records of the last complete overhaul of each airframe, engine, propeller, rotor, and appliance the records specified in paragraph (a)(1) of this section shall be retained until the work is repeated or superseded by other work or for one year after the work is performed.

(2) The records of the last complete overhaul of each airframe, engine, propeller, rotor, and appliance shall be retained until the work is superseded by work of equivalent scope and detail.

(3) The records specified in paragraph (a)(2) of this section shall be retained and transferred with the aircraft at the time the aircraft is sold.

(c) The certificate holder shall make all maintenance records required to be kept by this section available for inspection by the Administrator or any representative of the National Transportation Safety Board.

[Docket No. 16097, 43 FR 46783, Oct. 10, 1978; 43 FR 49975, Oct. 26, 1978]

§135.441 Transfer of maintenance records.

Each certificate holder who sells a United States registered aircraft shall transfer to the purchaser, at the time of the sale, the following records of that aircraft, in plain language form or in coded form which provides for the preservation and retrieval of information in a manner acceptable to the Administrator:

(a) The records specified in §135.439(a)(2).

(b) The records specified in §135.439(a)(1) which are not included in the records covered by paragraph (a) of this section, except that the purchaser may allow the seller to keep physical custody of such records. However, custody of records by the seller does not relieve the purchaser of its responsibility under §135.439(c) to make the records available for inspection by the Administrator or any representative of the National Transportation Safety Board.

§135.443 Airworthiness release or aircraft maintenance log entry.

(a) No certificate holder may operate an aircraft after maintenance, preventive maintenance, or alterations are performed on the aircraft unless the certificate holder prepares, or causes the person with whom the certificate holder arranges for the performance of the maintenance, preventive maintenance, or alterations, to prepare—

(1) An airworthiness release; or

(2) An appropriate entry in the aircraft maintenance log.

(b) The airworthiness release or log entry required by paragraph (a) of this section must—

(1) Be prepared in accordance with the procedure in the certificate holder's manual;

(2) Include a certification that—

(i) The work was performed in accordance with the requirements of the certificate holder's manual;

(ii) All items required to be inspected were inspected by an authorized person who determined that the work was satisfactorily completed;

(iii) No known condition exists that would make the aircraft unairworthy; and

(iv) So far as the work performed is concerned, the aircraft is in condition for safe operation; and

(3) Be signed by an authorized certificated mechanic or repairman, except that a certificated repairman may sign the release or entry only for the work for which that person is employed and for which that person is certificated.

(c) Notwithstanding paragraph (b)(3) of this section, after maintenance, preventive maintenance, or alterations performed by a repair station located outside the United States, the airworthiness release or log entry required by paragraph (a) of this section may be signed by a person authorized by that repair station.

(d) Instead of restating each of the conditions of the certification required by paragraph (b) of this section, the certificate holder may state in its manual that the signature of an authorized certificated mechanic or repairman constitutes that certification.

[Docket No. 16097, 43 FR 46783, Oct. 10, 1978; as amended by Amdt. 135–29, 53 FR 47375, Nov. 22, 1988; Amdt. 135–82, 66 FR 41117, Aug. 6, 2001]

Subpart K—Hazardous Materials Training Program

Source: Docket No. FAA–2003–15085, 70 FR 58829, October 7, 2005, unless otherwise noted.

§135.501 Applicability and definitions.

(a) This subpart prescribes the requirements applicable to each certificate holder for training each crewmember and person performing or directly supervising any of the following job functions involving any item for transport on board an aircraft:

(1) Acceptance;
(2) Rejection;
(3) Handling;
(4) Storage incidental to transport;
(5) Packaging of company material; or
(6) Loading.

(b) *Definitions.* For purposes of this subpart, the following definitions apply:

(1) Company material (COMAT)—Material owned or used by a certificate holder.

(2) Initial hazardous materials training—The basic training required for each newly hired person, or each person changing job functions, who performs or directly supervises any of the job functions specified in paragraph (a) of this section.

(3) Recurrent hazardous materials training—The training required every 24 months for each person who has satisfactorily completed the certificate holder's approved initial hazardous materials training program and performs or directly supervises any of the job functions specified in paragraph (a) of this section.

§135.503 Hazardous materials training: General.

(a) Each certificate holder must establish and implement a hazardous materials training program that:

(1) Satisfies the requirements of Appendix O of part 121 of this part;

(2) Ensures that each person performing or directly supervising any of the job functions specified in §135.501(a) is trained to comply with all applicable parts of 49 CFR parts 171 through 180 and the requirements of this subpart; and

(3) Enables the trained person to recognize items that contain, or may contain, hazardous materials regulated by 49 CFR parts 171 through 180.

(b) Each certificate holder must provide initial hazardous materials training and recurrent hazardous materials training to each crewmember and person performing or directly supervising any of the job functions specified in §135.501(a).

(c) Each certificate holder's hazardous materials training program must be approved by the FAA prior to implementation.

§135.505 Hazardous materials training required.

(a) *Training requirement.* Except as provided in paragraphs (b), (c) and (f) of this section, no certificate holder may use any crewmember or person to perform any of the job functions or direct supervisory responsibilities, and no person may perform any of the job functions or direct supervisory responsibilities, specified in §135.501(a) unless that person has satisfactorily completed the certificate holder's FAA-approved initial or recurrent hazardous materials training program within the past 24 months.

(b) *New hire or new job function.* A person who is a new hire and has not yet satisfactorily completed the required initial hazardous materials training, or a person who is changing job functions and has not received initial or recurrent training for a job function involving storage incidental to transport, or loading of items for transport on an aircraft, may perform those job functions for not more than 30 days from the date of hire or a change in job function, if the person is under the direct visual supervision of a person who is authorized by the certificate holder to supervise that person and who has successfully completed the certificate holder's FAA-approved initial or recurrent training program within the past 24 months.

(c) *Persons who work for more than one certificate holder.* A certificate holder that uses or assigns a person to perform or directly supervise a job function specified in §135.501(a), when that person also performs or directly supervises the same job function for another certificate holder, need only train that person in its own policies and procedures regarding those job functions, if all of the following are met:

(1) The certificate holder using this exception receives written verification from the person designated to hold the training records representing the other certificate holder that the person has satisfactorily completed hazardous materials training for the specific job function under the other certificate holder's FAA approved hazardous material training program under appendix O of part 121 of this chapter; and

(2) The certificate holder who trained the person has the same operations specifications regarding the acceptance, handling, and transport of hazardous materials as the certificate holder using this exception.

(d) *Recurrent hazardous materials training—Completion date.* A person who satisfactorily completes recurrent hazardous materials training in the calendar month before, or the calendar month after, the month in which the recurrent training is due, is considered to have taken that training during the month in which it is due. If the person completes this training earlier than the month before it is due, the month of the completion date becomes his or her new anniversary month.

(e) *Repair stations.* A certificate holder must ensure that each repair station performing work for, or on the certificate holder's behalf is notified in writing of the certificate holder's policies and operations specification authorization permitting or prohibition against the acceptance, rejection, handling, storage incidental to transport, and transportation of hazardous materials, including company material. This notification requirement applies only to repair stations that are regulated by 49 CFR parts 171 through 180.

(f) *Certificate holders operating at foreign locations.* This exception applies if a certificate holder operating at a foreign location where the country requires the certificate holder to use persons working in that country to load aircraft. In such a case, the certificate holder may use those persons even if they have not been trained in accordance with the certificate holder's FAA approved hazardous materials training program. Those persons, however, must be under the direct visual supervision of someone who has successfully completed the certificate holder's approved initial or recurrent hazardous materials training program in accordance with this part. This exception applies only to those persons who load aircraft.

§135.507 Hazardous materials training records.

(a) *General requirement.* Each certificate holder must maintain a record of all training required by this part received within the preceding three years for each person who performs or directly supervises a job function specified in §135.501(a). The record must be maintained during the time that the person performs or directly supervises any of those job functions, and for 90 days thereafter. These training records must be kept for direct employees of the certificate holder, as well as independent contractors, subcontractors, and any other person who performs or directly supervises these job functions for the certificate holder.

(b) *Location of records.* The certificate holder must retain the training records required by paragraph (a) of this section for all initial and recurrent training received within the preceding 3 years for all persons performing or directly supervising the job functions listed in Appendix O of part 121 of this chapter at a designated location. The records must be available upon request at the location where the trained person performs or directly supervises the job function specified in §135.501(a). Records may be maintained electronically and provided on location electronically. When the person ceases to perform or directly supervise a hazardous materials job function, the certificate holder must retain the hazardous materials training records for an additional 90 days and make them available upon request at the last location where the person worked.

(c) *Content of records.* Each record must contain the following:

(1) The individual's name;

(2) The most recent training completion date;

(3) A description, copy or reference to training materials used to meet the training requirement;

(4) The name and address of the organization providing the training; and

(5) A copy of the certification issued when the individual was trained, which shows that a test has been completed satisfactorily.

(d) *New hire or new job function.* Each certificate holder using a person under the exception in §135.505(b) must maintain a record for that person. The records must be available upon request at the location where the trained person performs or directly supervises the job function specified in §135.501(a). Records may be maintained electronically and provided on location electronically. The record must include the following:

(1) A signed statement from an authorized representative of the certificate holder authorizing the use of the person in accordance with the exception;

(2) The date of hire or change in job function;

(3) The person's name and assigned job function;

(4) The name of the supervisor of the job function; and

(5) The date the person is to complete hazardous materials training in accordance with Appendix O of part 121 of this chapter.

Subpart L—Helicopter Air Ambulance Equipment, Operations, and Training Requirements

Source: Docket No. FAA–2010–0982, 79 FR 9975, February 21, 2014, unless otherwise noted.

§135.601 Applicability and definitions.

(a) *Applicability.* This subpart prescribes the requirements applicable to each certificate holder conducting helicopter air ambulance operations.

(b) *Definitions.* For purposes of this subpart, the following definitions apply:

(1) *Helicopter air ambulance operation* means a flight, or sequence of flights, with a patient or medical personnel on board, for the purpose of medical transportation, by a part 135 certificate holder authorized by the Administrator to conduct helicopter air ambulance operations. A helicopter air ambulance operation includes, but is not limited to—

(i) Flights conducted to position the helicopter at the site at which a patient or donor organ will be picked up.

(ii) Flights conducted to reposition the helicopter after completing the patient, or donor organ transport.

(iii) Flights initiated for the transport of a patient or donor organ that are terminated due to weather or other reasons.

(2) *Medical personnel* means a person or persons with medical training, including but not limited to flight physicians, flight nurses, or flight paramedics, who are carried aboard a helicopter during helicopter air ambulance operations in order to provide medical care.

(3) *Mountainous* means designated mountainous areas as listed in part 95 of this chapter.

(4) *Nonmountainous* means areas other than mountainous areas as listed in part 95 of this chapter.

§135.603 Pilot-in-command instrument qualifications.

After April 24, 2017, no certificate holder may use, nor may any person serve as, a pilot in command of a helicopter air ambulance operation unless that person meets the requirements of §135.243 and holds a helicopter instrument rat-

§135.605 Helicopter terrain awareness and warning system (HTAWS).

(a) After April 24, 2017, no person may operate a helicopter in helicopter air ambulance operations unless that helicopter is equipped with a helicopter terrain awareness and warning system (HTAWS) that meets the requirements in TSO-C194 and Section 2 of RTCA DO-309.

(b) The certificate holder's Rotorcraft Flight Manual must contain appropriate procedures for—

(1) The use of the HTAWS; and
(2) Proper flight crew response to HTAWS audio and visual warnings.

(c) Certificate holders with HTAWS required by this section with an approved deviation under §21.618 of this chapter are in compliance with this section.

(d) The standards required in this section are incorporated by reference into this section with the approval of the Director of the Federal Register under 5 U.S.C. 552(a) and 1 CFR part 51. To enforce any edition other than that specified in this section, the FAA must publish notice of change in the Federal Register and the material must be available to the public. All approved material is available for inspection at the FAA's Office of Rulemaking (ARM-1), 800 Independence Avenue SW., Washington, DC 20591 (telephone (202) 267-9677) and from the sources indicated below. It is also available for inspection at the National Archives and Records Administration (NARA). For information on the availability of this material at NARA, call (202) 741-6030 or go to http://www.archives.gov/federal_register/code_of_federal_regulations/ibr_locations.html.

(1) U.S. Department of Transportation, Subsequent Distribution Office, DOT Warehouse M30, Ardmore East Business Center, 3341 Q 75th Avenue, Landover, MD 20785; telephone (301) 322-5377. Copies are also available on the FAA's Web site. Use the following link and type the TSO number in the search box: http://rgl.faa.gov/Regulatory_and_Guidance_Library/rgTSO.nsf/Frameset?OpenPage.

(i) TSO C-194, Helicopter Terrain Awareness and Warning System (HTAWS), Dec. 17, 2008.
(ii) [Reserved]

(2) RTCA, Inc., 1150 18th Street NW., Suite 910, Washington, DC 20036, telephone (202) 833-9339, and are also available on RTCA's Web site at http://www.rtca.org/onlinecart/index.cfm.

(i) RTCA DO-309, Minimum Operational Performance Standards (MOPS) for Helicopter Terrain Awareness and Warning System (HTAWS) Airborne Equipment, Mar. 13, 2008.
(ii) [Reserved]

§135.607 Flight Data Monitoring System.

After April 23, 2018, no person may operate a helicopter in air ambulance operations unless it is equipped with an approved flight data monitoring system capable of recording flight performance data. This system must:

(a) Receive electrical power from the bus that provides the maximum reliability for operation without jeopardizing service to essential or emergency loads, and

(b) Be operated from the application of electrical power before takeoff until the removal of electrical power after termination of flight.

§135.609 VFR ceiling and visibility requirements for Class G airspace.

(a) Unless otherwise specified in the certificate holder's operations specifications, when conducting helicopter air ambulance operations in Class G airspace, the weather minimums in the following table apply:

Location	Day Ceiling	Day Flight Visibility	Night Ceiling	Night Flight Visibility	Night using an Approved NVIS or HTAWS Ceiling	Night using an Approved NVIS or HTAWS Flight Visibility
Nonmountainous local flying areas	800 feet	2 statute miles	1,000 feet	3 statute miles	800 feet	3 statute miles
Nonmountainous non-local flying areas	800 feet	3 statute miles	1,000 feet	5 statute miles	1,000 feet	3 statute miles
Mountainous local flying areas	800 feet	3 statute miles	1,500 feet	3 statute miles	1,000 feet	3 statute miles
Mountainous non-local flying areas	1,000 feet	3 statute miles	1,500 feet	5 statute miles	1,000 feet	5 statute miles

Part 135: Commuter & On Demand Operations §135.615

(b) A certificate holder may designate local flying areas in a manner acceptable to the Administrator, that must—

(1) Not exceed 50 nautical miles in any direction from each designated location;

(2) Take into account obstacles and terrain features that are easily identifiable by the pilot in command and from which the pilot in command may visually determine a position; and

(3) Take into account the operating environment and capabilities of the certificate holder's helicopters.

(c) A pilot must demonstrate a level of familiarity with the local flying area by passing an examination given by the certificate holder within the 12 calendar months prior to using the local flying area.

§135.611 IFR operations at locations without weather reporting.

(a) If a certificate holder is authorized to conduct helicopter IFR operations, the Administrator may authorize the certificate holder to conduct IFR helicopter air ambulance operations at airports with an instrument approach procedure and at which a weather report is not available from the U.S. National Weather Service (NWS), a source approved by the NWS, or a source approved by the FAA, subject to the following limitations:

(1) The certificate holder must obtain a weather report from a weather reporting facility operated by the NWS, a source approved by the NWS, or a source approved by the FAA, that is located within 15 nautical miles of the airport. If a weather report is not available, the certificate holder may obtain the area forecast from the NWS, a source approved by the NWS, or a source approved by the FAA, for information regarding the weather observed in the vicinity of the airport;

(2) Flight planning for IFR flights conducted under this paragraph must include selection of an alternate airport that meets the requirements of §§135.221 and 135.223;

(3) In Class G airspace, IFR departures are authorized only after the pilot in command determines that the weather conditions at the departure point are at or above VFR minimums in accordance with §135.609; and

(4) All approaches must be conducted at Category A approach speeds as established in part 97 or those required for the type of approach being used.

(b) Each helicopter air ambulance operated under this section must be equipped with functioning severe weather detection equipment.

(c) Pilots conducting operations pursuant to this section may use the weather information obtained in paragraph (a) to satisfy the weather report and forecast requirements of §135.213 and §135.225(a).

(d) After completing a landing at the airport at which a weather report is not available, the pilot in command is authorized to determine if the weather meets the takeoff requirements of part 97 of this chapter or the certificate holder's operations specification, as applicable.

§135.613 Approach/departure IFR transitions.

(a) *Approaches.* When conducting an authorized instrument approach and transitioning from IFR to VFR flight, upon transitioning to VFR flight the following weather minimums apply—

(1) For Point-in-Space (PinS) Copter Instrument approaches annotated with a "Proceed VFR" segment, if the distance from the missed approach point to the landing area is 1 NM or less, flight visibility must be at least 1 statute mile and the ceiling on the approach chart applies;

(2) For all instrument approaches, including PinS when paragraph (a)(1) of this section does not apply, if the distance from the missed approach point to the landing area is 3 NM or less, the applicable VFR weather minimums are—

(i) For Day Operations: No less than a 600-foot ceiling and 2 statute miles flight visibility;

(ii) For Night Operations: No less than a 600-foot ceiling and 3 statute miles flight visibility; or

(3) For all instrument approaches, including PinS, if the distance from the missed approach point to the landing area is greater than 3 NM, the VFR weather minimums required by the class of airspace.

(b) *Departures.* For transitions from VFR to IFR upon departure—

(1) The VFR weather minimums of paragraph (a) of this section apply if—

(i) An FAA-approved obstacle departure procedure is followed; and

(ii) An IFR clearance is obtained on or before reaching a predetermined location that is not more than 3 NM from the departure location.

(2) If the departure does not meet the requirements of paragraph (b)(1) of this section, the VFR weather minimums required by the class of airspace apply.

§135.615 VFR flight planning.

(a) *Pre-flight.* Prior to conducting VFR operations, the pilot in command must—

(1) Determine the minimum safe cruise altitude by evaluating the terrain and obstacles along the planned route of flight;

(2) Identify and document the highest obstacle along the planned route of flight; and

(3) Using the minimum safe cruise altitudes in paragraphs (b)(1)–(2) of this section, determine

ASA 453

the minimum required ceiling and visibility to conduct the planned flight by applying the weather minimums appropriate to the class of airspace for the planned flight.

(b) *Enroute.* While conducting VFR operations, the pilot in command must ensure that all terrain and obstacles along the route of flight are cleared vertically by no less than the following:

(1) 300 feet for day operations.

(2) 500 feet for night operations.

(c) *Rerouting the planned flight path.* A pilot in command may deviate from the planned flight path for reasons such as weather conditions or operational considerations. Such deviations do not relieve the pilot in command of the weather requirements or the requirements for terrain and obstacle clearance contained in this part and in part 91 of this chapter. Rerouting, change in destination, or other changes to the planned flight that occur while the helicopter is on the ground at an intermediate stop require evaluation of the new route in accordance with paragraph (a) of this section.

(d) *Operations manual.* Each certificate holder must document its VFR flight planning procedures in its operations manual.

§135.617 Pre-flight risk analysis.

(a) Each certificate holder conducting helicopter air ambulance operations must establish, and document in its operations manual, an FAA-approved preflight risk analysis that includes at least the following—

(1) Flight considerations, to include obstacles and terrain along the planned route of flight, landing zone conditions, and fuel requirements;

(2) Human factors, such as crew fatigue, life events, and other stressors;

(3) Weather, including departure, en route, destination, and forecasted;

(4) A procedure for determining whether another helicopter air ambulance operator has refused or rejected a flight request; and

(5) Strategies and procedures for mitigating identified risks, including procedures for obtaining and documenting approval of the certificate holder's management personnel to release a flight when a risk exceeds a level predetermined by the certificate holder.

(b) Each certificate holder must develop a preflight risk analysis worksheet to include, at a minimum, the items in paragraph (a) of this section.

(c) Prior to the first leg of each helicopter air ambulance operation, the pilot in command must conduct a preflight risk analysis and complete the preflight risk analysis worksheet in accordance with the certificate holder's FAA-approved procedures. The pilot in command must sign the preflight risk analysis worksheet and specify the date and time it was completed.

(d) The certificate holder must retain the original or a copy of each completed preflight risk analysis worksheet at a location specified in its operations manual for at least 90 days from the date of the operation.

§135.619 Operations control centers.

(a) *Operations control center.* After April 22, 2016, certificate holders authorized to conduct helicopter air ambulance operations, with 10 or more helicopter air ambulances assigned to the certificate holder's operations specifications, must have an operations control center. The operations control center must be staffed by operations control specialists who, at a minimum—

(1) Provide two-way communications with pilots;

(2) Provide pilots with weather briefings, to include current and forecasted weather along the planned route of flight;

(3) Monitor the progress of the flight; and

(4) Participate in the preflight risk analysis required under §135.617 to include the following:

(i) Ensure the pilot has completed all required items on the preflight risk analysis worksheet;

(ii) Confirm and verify all entries on the preflight risk analysis worksheet;

(iii) Assist the pilot in mitigating any identified risk prior to takeoff; and

(iv) Acknowledge in writing, specifying the date and time, that the preflight risk analysis worksheet has been accurately completed and that, according to their professional judgment, the flight can be conducted safely.

(b) *Operations control center staffing.* Each certificate holder conducting helicopter air ambulance operations must provide enough operations control specialists at each operations control center to ensure the certificate holder maintains operational control of each flight.

(c) *Documentation of duties and responsibilities.* Each certificate holder must describe in its operations manual the duties and responsibilities of operations control specialists, including preflight risk mitigation strategies and control measures, shift change checklist, and training and testing procedures to hold the position, including procedures for retesting.

(d) *Training requirements.* No certificate holder may use, nor may any person perform the duties of, an operations control specialist unless the operations control specialist has satisfactorily completed the training requirements of this paragraph.

(1) *Initial training.* Before performing the duties of an operations control specialist, each person must satisfactorily complete the certificate holder's FAA-approved operations control specialist initial training program and pass an FAA-approved knowledge and practical test given by

Part 135: Commuter & On Demand Operations §135.619

the certificate holder. Initial training must include a minimum of 80 hours of training on the topics listed in paragraph (f) of this section. A certificate holder may reduce the number of hours of initial training to a minimum of 40 hours for persons who have obtained, at the time of beginning initial training, a total of at least 2 years of experience during the last 5 years in any one or in any combination of the following areas—

　(i) In military aircraft operations as a pilot, flight navigator, or meteorologist;

　(ii) In air carrier operations as a pilot, flight engineer, certified aircraft dispatcher, or meteorologist; or

　(iii) In aircraft operations as an air traffic controller or a flight service specialist.

　(2) *Recurrent training.* Every 12 months after satisfactory completion of the initial training, each operations control specialist must complete a minimum of 40 hours of recurrent training on the topics listed in paragraph (f) of this section and pass an FAA-approved knowledge and practical test given by the certificate holder on those topics.

　(e) *Training records.* The certificate holder must maintain a training record for each operations control specialist employed by the certificate holder for the duration of that individual's employment and for 90 days thereafter. The training record must include a chronological log for each training course, including the number of training hours and the examination dates and results.

　(f) *Training topics.* Each certificate holder must have an FAA-approved operations control specialist training program that covers at least the following topics—

　(1) Aviation weather, including:
　(i) General meteorology;
　(ii) Prevailing weather;
　(iii) Adverse and deteriorating weather;
　(iv) Windshear;
　(v) Icing conditions;
　(vi) Use of aviation weather products;
　(vii) Available sources of information; and
　(viii) Weather minimums;

　(2) Navigation, including:
　(i) Navigation aids;
　(ii) Instrument approach procedures;
　(iii) Navigational publications; and
　(iv) Navigation techniques;

　(3) Flight monitoring, including:
　(i) Available flight-monitoring procedures; and
　(ii) Alternate flight-monitoring procedures;

　(4) Air traffic control, including:
　(i) Airspace;
　(ii) Air traffic control procedures;
　(iii) Aeronautical charts; and
　(iv) Aeronautical data sources;

　(5) Aviation communication, including:
　(i) Available aircraft communications systems;
　(ii) Normal communication procedures;
　(iii) Abnormal communication procedures; and
　(iv) Emergency communication procedures;

　(6) Aircraft systems, including:
　(i) Communications systems;
　(ii) Navigation systems;
　(iii) Surveillance systems;
　(iv) Fueling systems;
　(v) Specialized systems;
　(vi) General maintenance requirements; and
　(vii) Minimum equipment lists;

　(7) Aircraft limitations and performance, including:
　(i) Aircraft operational limitations;
　(ii) Aircraft performance;
　(iii) Weight and balance procedures and limitations; and
　(iv) Landing zone and landing facility requirements;

　(8) Aviation policy and regulations, including:
　(i) 14 CFR Parts 1, 27, 29, 61, 71, 91, and 135;
　(ii) 49 CFR Part 830;
　(iii) Company operations specifications;
　(iv) Company general operations policies;
　(v) Enhanced operational control policies;
　(vi) Aeronautical decision making and risk management;
　(vii) Lost aircraft procedures; and
　(viii) Emergency and search and rescue procedures, including plotting coordinates in degrees, minutes, seconds format, and degrees, decimal minutes format;

　(9) Crew resource management, including:
　(i) Concepts and practical application;
　(ii) Risk management and risk mitigation; and
　(iii) Pre-flight risk analysis procedures required under §135.617;

　(10) Local flying area orientation, including:
　(i) Terrain features;
　(ii) Obstructions;
　(iii) Weather phenomena for local area;
　(iv) Airspace and air traffic control facilities;
　(v) Heliports, airports, landing zones, and fuel facilities;
　(vi) Instrument approaches;
　(vii) Predominant air traffic flow;
　(viii) Landmarks and cultural features, including areas prone to flat-light, whiteout, and brownout conditions; and
　(ix) Local aviation and safety resources and contact information; and

　(11) Any other requirements as determined by the Administrator to ensure safe operations.

　(g) *Operations control specialist duty time limitations.*

(1) Each certificate holder must establish the daily duty period for an operations control specialist so that it begins at a time that allows that person to become thoroughly familiar with operational considerations, including existing and anticipated weather conditions in the area of operations, helicopter operations in progress, and helicopter maintenance status, before performing duties associated with any helicopter air ambulance operation. The operations control specialist must remain on duty until relieved by another qualified operations control specialist or until each helicopter air ambulance monitored by that person has completed its flight or gone beyond that person's jurisdiction.

(2) Except in cases where circumstances or emergency conditions beyond the control of the certificate holder require otherwise—

(i) No certificate holder may schedule an operations control specialist for more than 10 consecutive hours of duty;

(ii) If an operations control specialist is scheduled for more than 10 hours of duty in 24 consecutive hours, the certificate holder must provide that person a rest period of at least 8 hours at or before the end of 10 hours of duty;

(iii) If an operations control specialist is on duty for more than 10 consecutive hours, the certificate holder must provide that person a rest period of at least 8 hours before that person's next duty period;

(iv) Each operations control specialist must be relieved of all duty with the certificate holder for at least 24 consecutive hours during any 7 consecutive days.

(h) *Drug and alcohol testing.* Operations control specialists must be tested for drugs and alcohol according to the certificate holder's Drug and Alcohol Testing Program administered under part 120 of this chapter.

§135.621 Briefing of medical personnel.

(a) Except as provided in paragraph (b) of this section, prior to each helicopter air ambulance operation, each pilot in command, or other flight crewmember designated by the certificate holder, must ensure that all medical personnel have been briefed on the following—

(1) Passenger briefing requirements in §135.117(a) and (b); and
(2) Physiological aspects of flight;
(3) Patient loading and unloading;
(4) Safety in and around the helicopter;
(5) In-flight emergency procedures;
(6) Emergency landing procedures;
(7) Emergency evacuation procedures;
(8) Efficient and safe communications with the pilot; and
(9) Operational differences between day and night operations, if appropriate.

(b) The briefing required in paragraphs (a)(2) through (9) of this section may be omitted if all medical personnel on board have satisfactorily completed the certificate holder's FAA-approved medical personnel training program within the preceding 24 calendar months. Each training program must include a minimum of 4 hours of ground training, and 4 hours of training in and around an air ambulance helicopter, on the topics set forth in paragraph (a)(2) of this section.

(c) Each certificate holder must maintain a record for each person trained under this section that—

(1) Contains the individual's name, the most recent training completion date, and a description, copy, or reference to training materials used to meet the training requirement.

(2) Is maintained for 24 calendar months following the individual's completion of training.

APPENDIX A TO PART 135
ADDITIONAL AIRWORTHINESS STANDARDS FOR 10 OR MORE PASSENGER AIRPLANES

APPLICABILITY

1. *Applicability.* This appendix prescribes the additional airworthiness standards required by §135.169.

2. *References.* Unless otherwise provided, references in this appendix to specific sections of part 23 of the Federal Aviation Regulations (FAR part 23) are to those sections of part 23 in effect on March 30, 1967.

FLIGHT REQUIREMENTS

3. *General.* Compliance must be shown with the applicable requirements of subpart B of FAR part 23, as supplemented or modified in §§4 through 10.

PERFORMANCE

4. *General.*

(a) Unless otherwise prescribed in this appendix, compliance with each applicable performance requirement in sections 4 through 7 must be shown for ambient atmospheric conditions and still air.

(b) The performance must correspond to the propulsive thrust available under the particular ambient atmospheric conditions and the particular flight condition. The available propulsive thrust must correspond to engine power or thrust, not exceeding the approved power or thrust less—

(1) Installation losses; and
(2) The power or equivalent thrust absorbed by the accessories and services appropriate to the particular ambient atmospheric conditions and the particular flight condition.

(c) Unless otherwise prescribed in this appendix, the applicant must select the takeoff, en route, and landing configurations for the airplane.

(d) The airplane configuration may vary with weight, altitude, and temperature, to the extent they are compatible with the operating procedures required by paragraph (e) of this section.

(e) Unless otherwise prescribed in this appendix, in determining the critical engine inoperative takeoff performance, the accelerate-stop distance, takeoff distance, changes in the airplane's configuration, speed, power, and thrust must be made under procedures established by the applicant for operation in service.

(f) Procedures for the execution of balked landings must be established by the applicant and included in the Airplane Flight Manual.

(g) The procedures established under paragraphs (e) and (f) of this section must—

(1) Be able to be consistently executed in service by a crew of average skill;

(2) Use methods or devices that are safe and reliable; and

(3) Include allowance for any time delays in the execution of the procedures, that may reasonably be expected in service.

5. Takeoff—

(a) *General.* Takeoff speeds the accelerate-stop distance, the takeoff distance, and the one-engine-inoperative takeoff flight path data (described in paragraphs (b), (c), (d), and (f) of this section), must be determined for—

(1) Each weight, altitude, and ambient temperature within the operational limits selected by the applicant;

(2) The selected configuration for takeoff;

(3) The center of gravity in the most unfavorable position;

(4) The operating engine within approved operating limitations; and

(5) Takeoff data based on smooth, dry, hard-surface runway.

(b) *Takeoff speeds.*

(1) The decision speed V_1 is the calibrated airspeed on the ground at which, as a result of engine failure or other reasons, the pilot is assumed to have made a decision to continue or discontinue the takeoff. The speed V_1 must be selected by the applicant but may not be less than—

(i) 1.10 V_{S1};

(ii) 1.10 V_{MC};

(iii) A speed that allows acceleration to V_1 and stop under paragraph (c) of this section; or

(iv) A speed at which the airplane can be rotated for takeoff and shown to be adequate to safely continue the takeoff, using normal piloting skill, when the critical engine is suddenly made inoperative.

(2) The initial climb out speed V_2 in terms of calibrated airspeed, must be selected by the applicant so as to allow the gradient of climb required in section 6(b)(2), but it must not be less than V_1 or less than 1.2 V_{S1}.

(3) Other essential take off speeds necessary for safe operation of the airplane.

(c) *Accelerate-stop distance.*

(1) The accelerate-stop distance is the sum of the distances necessary to—

(i) Accelerate the airplane from a standing start to V_1; and

(ii) Come to a full stop from the point at which V_1 is reached assuming that in the case of engine failure, failure of the critical engine is recognized by the pilot at the speed V_1.

(2) Means other than wheel brakes may be used to determine the accelerate-stop distance if that means is available with the critical engine inoperative and—

(i) Is safe and reliable;

(ii) Is used so that consistent results can be expected under normal operating conditions; and

(iii) Is such that exceptional skill is not required to control the airplane.

(d) *All engines operating takeoff distance.* The all engine operating takeoff distance is the horizontal distance required to takeoff and climb to a height of 50 feet above the takeoff surface under the procedures in FAR 23.51(a).

(e) *One-engine-inoperative takeoff.* Determine the weight for each altitude and temperature within the operational limits established for the airplane, at which the airplane has the capability, after failure of the critical engine at V_1 determined under paragraph (b) of this section, to take off and climb at not less than V_2, to a height 1,000 feet above the takeoff surface and attain the speed and configuration at which compliance is shown with the en route one engine-inoperative gradient of climb specified in section 6(c).

(f) *One-engine-inoperative takeoff flight path data.* The one-engine-inoperative takeoff flight path data consist of takeoff flight paths extending from a standing start to a point in the takeoff at which the airplane reaches a height 1,000 feet above the takeoff surface under paragraph (e) of this section.

6. Climb—

(a) *Landing climb: All-engines operating.* The maximum weight must be determined with the airplane in the landing configuration, for each altitude, and ambient temperature within the operational limits established for the airplane, with the most unfavorable center of gravity, and out-of-ground effect in free air, at which the steady gradient of climb will not be less than 3.3 percent, with:

(1) The engines at the power that is available 8 seconds after initiation of movement of the power or thrust controls from the minimum flight idle to the takeoff position.

Appendix A to Part 135   **Federal Aviation Regulations**

(2) A climb speed not greater than the approach speed established under section 7 and not less than the greater of 1.05 V_{MC} or 1.10 V_{S1}.

(b) *Takeoff climb: one-engine-inoperative.* The maximum weight at which the airplane meets the minimum climb performance specified in paragraphs (1) and (2) of this paragraph must be determined for each altitude and ambient temperature within the operational limits established for the airplane, out of ground effect in free air, with the airplane in the takeoff configuration, with the most unfavorable center of gravity, the critical engine inoperative, the remaining engines at the maximum takeoff power or thrust, and the propeller of the inoperative engine windmilling with the propeller controls in the normal position except that, if an approved automatic feathering system is installed, the propellers may be in the feathered position:

(1) Takeoff: landing gear extended. The minimum steady gradient of climb must be measurably positive at the speed V_1.

(2) Takeoff: landing gear retracted. The minimum steady gradient of climb may not be less than 2 percent at speed V_2. For airplanes with fixed landing gear this requirement must be met with the landing gear extended.

(c) *En route climb: one-engine-inoperative.* The maximum weight must be determined for each altitude and ambient temperature within the operational limits established for the airplane, at which the steady gradient of climb is not less 1.2 percent at an altitude 1,000 feet above the takeoff surface, with the airplane in the en route configuration, the critical engine inoperative, the remaining engine at the maximum continuous power or thrust, and the most unfavorable center of gravity.

7. Landing.

(a) The landing field length described in paragraph (b) of this section must be determined for standard atmosphere at each weight and altitude within the operational limits established by the applicant.

(b) The landing field length is equal to the landing distance determined under FAR 23.75(a) divided by a factor of 0.6 for the destination airport and 0.7 for the alternate airport. Instead of the gliding approach specified in FAR 23.75(a)(1), the landing may be preceded by a steady approach down to the 50-foot height at a gradient of descent not greater than 5.2 percent (3°) at a calibrated airspeed not less than 1.3 V_{S1}.

Trim

8. Trim

(a) *Lateral and directional trim.* The airplane must maintain lateral and directional trim in level flight at a speed of V_H or V_{MO}/M_{MO}, whichever is lower, with landing gear and wing flaps retracted.

(b) *Longitudinal trim.* The airplane must maintain longitudinal trim during the following conditions, except that it need not maintain trim at a speed greater than V_{MO}/M_{MO}.

(1) In the approach conditions specified in FAR 23.161(c)(3) through (5), except that instead of the speeds specified in those paragraphs, trim must be maintained with a stick force of not more than 10 pounds down to a speed used in showing compliance with section 7 or 1.4 V_{S1} whichever is lower.

(2) In level flight at any speed from V_H or V_{MO}/M_{MO}, whichever is lower, to either V_X or 1.4 V_{S1}, with the landing gear and wing flaps retracted.

Stability

9. Static longitudinal stability.

(a) In showing compliance with FAR 23.175(b) and with paragraph (b) of this section, the airspeed must return to within ±7-1/2 percent of the trim speed.

(b) *Cruise stability.* The stick force curve must have a stable slope for a speed range of ±50 knots from the trim speed except that the speeds need not exceed V_{FC}/M_{FC} or be less than 1.4 V_{S1}. This speed range will be considered to begin at the outer extremes of the friction band and the stick force may not exceed 50 pounds with—

(1) Landing gear retracted;

(2) Wing flaps retracted;

(3) The maximum cruising power as selected by the applicant as an operating limitation for turbine engines or 75 percent of maximum continuous power for reciprocating engines except that the power need not exceed that required at V_{MO}/M_{MO};

(4) Maximum takeoff weight; and

(5) The airplane trimmed for level flight with the power specified in paragraph (3) of this paragraph.

V_{FC}/M_{FC} may not be less than a speed midway between V_{MO}/M_{MO} and V_{DF}/M_{DF}, except that, for altitudes where Mach number is the limiting factor, M_{FC} need not exceed the Mach number at which effective speed warning occurs.

(c) *Climb stability (turbopropeller powered airplanes only).* In showing compliance with FAR 23.175(a), an applicant must, instead of the power specified in FAR 23.175(a)(4), use the maximum power or thrust selected by the applicant as an operating limitation for use during climb at the best rate of climb speed, except that the speed need not be less than 1.4 V_{S1}.

Stalls

10. Stall warning. If artificial stall warning is required to comply with FAR 23.207, the warning device must give clearly distinguishable indications under expected conditions of flight. The use of a visual warning device that requires the attention of the crew within the cockpit is not acceptable by itself.

CONTROL SYSTEMS

11. Electric trim tabs. The airplane must meet FAR 23.677 and in addition it must be shown that the airplane is safely controllable and that a pilot can perform all the maneuvers and operations necessary to effect a safe landing following any probable electric trim tab runaway which might be reasonably expected in service allowing for appropriate time delay after pilot recognition of the runaway. This demonstration must be conducted at the critical airplane weights and center of gravity positions.

INSTRUMENTS: INSTALLATION

12. Arrangement and visibility. Each instrument must meet FAR 23.1321 and in addition:

(a) Each flight, navigation, and powerplant instrument for use by any pilot must be plainly visible to the pilot from the pilot's station with the minimum practicable deviation from the pilot's normal position and line of vision when the pilot is looking forward along the flight path.

(b) The flight instruments required by FAR 23.1303 and by the applicable operating rules must be grouped on the instrument panel and centered as nearly as practicable about the vertical plane of each pilot's forward vision. In addition—

(1) The instrument that most effectively indicates the attitude must be in the panel in the top center position;

(2) The instrument that most effectively indicates the airspeed must be on the panel directly to the left of the instrument in the top center position;

(3) The instrument that most effectively indicates altitude must be adjacent to and directly to the right of the instrument in the top center position; and

(4) The instrument that most effectively indicates direction of flight must be adjacent to and directly below the instrument in the top center position.

13. Airspeed indicating system. Each airspeed indicating system must meet FAR 23.1323 and in addition:

(a) Airspeed indicating instruments must be of an approved type and must be calibrated to indicate true airspeed at sea level in the standard atmosphere with a minimum practicable instrument calibration error when the corresponding pitot and static pressures are supplied to the instruments.

(b) The airspeed indicating system must be calibrated to determine the system error, i.e., the relation between IAS and CAS, in flight and during the accelerate-takeoff ground run. The ground run calibration must be obtained between 0.8 of the minimum value of V_1 and 1.2 times the maximum value of V_1, considering the approved ranges of altitude and weight. The ground run calibration is determined assuming an engine failure at the minimum value of V_1.

(c) The airspeed error of the installation excluding the instrument calibration error, must not exceed 3 percent or 5 knots whichever is greater, throughout the speed range from V_{MO} to 1.3 V_{S1} with flaps retracted and from 1.3 V_{S0} to V_{FE} with flaps in the landing position.

(d) Information showing the relationship between IAS and CAS must be shown in the Airplane Flight manual.

14. Static air vent system. The static air vent system must meet FAR 23.1325. The altimeter system calibration must be determined and shown in the Airplane Flight Manual.

OPERATING LIMITATIONS AND INFORMATION

15. Maximum operating limit speed V_{MO}/M_{MO}. Instead of establishing operating limitations based on V_{NE} and V_{NO}. the applicant must establish a maximum operating limit speed V_{MO}/M_{MO} as follows:

(a) The maximum operating limit speed must not exceed the design cruising speed V_C and must be sufficiently below V_D/M_D or V_{DF}/M_{DF} to make it highly improbable that the latter speeds will be inadvertently exceeded in flight.

(b) The speed V_{MO} must not exceed 0.8 V_D/M_D or 0.8 V_{DF}/M_{DF} unless flight demonstrations involving upsets as specified by the Administrator indicates a lower speed margin will not result in speeds exceeding V_D/M_D or V_{DF}. Atmospheric variations, horizontal gusts, system and equipment errors, and airframe production variations are taken into account.

16. Minimum flight crew. In addition to meeting FAR 23.1523, the applicant must establish the minimum number and type of qualified flight crew personnel sufficient for safe operation of the airplane considering—

(a) Each kind of operation for which the applicant desires approval;

(b) The workload on each crewmember considering the following:

(1) Flight path control.
(2) Collision avoidance.
(3) Navigation.
(4) Communications.
(5) Operation and monitoring of all essential aircraft systems.
(6) Command decisions; and

(c) The accessibility and ease of operation of necessary controls by the appropriate crewmember during all normal and emergency operations when at the crewmember flight station.

Appendix A to Part 135

17. *Airspeed indicator.* The airspeed indicator must meet FAR 23.1545 except that, the airspeed notations and markings in terms of V_{NO} and V_{NH} must be replaced by the V_{MO}/M_{MO} notations. The airspeed indicator markings must be easily read and understood by the pilot. A placard adjacent to the airspeed indicator is an acceptable means of showing compliance with FAR 23.1545(c).

Airplane Flight Manual

18. *General.* The Airplane Flight Manual must be prepared under FARs 23.1583 and 23.1587, and in addition the operating limitations and performance information in sections 19 and 20 must be included.

19. *Operating limitations.* The Airplane Flight Manual must include the following limitations—

(a) *Airspeed limitations.*

(1) The maximum operating limit speed V_{MO}/M_{MO} and a statement that this speed limit may not be deliberately exceeded in any regime of flight (climb. cruise, or descent) unless a higher speed is authorized for flight test or pilot training;

(2) If an airspeed limitation is based upon compressibility effects, a statement to this effect and information as to any symptoms the probable behavior of the airplane, and the recommended recovery procedures; and

(3) The airspeed limits, shown in terms of V_{MO}/M_{MO} instead of V_{NO} and V_{NE}.

(b) *Takeoff weight limitations.* The maximum takeoff weight for each airport elevation, ambient temperature, and available takeoff runway length within the range selected by the applicant may not exceed the weight at which—

(1) The all-engine-operating takeoff distance determined under section 5(b) or the accelerate-stop distance determined under section 5(c), whichever is greater, is equal to the available runway length;

(2) The airplane complies with the one-engine-inoperative takeoff requirements specified in section 5(e); and

(3) The airplane complies with the one-engine-inoperative takeoff and en route climb requirements specified in sections 6 (b) and (c).

(c) *Landing weight limitations.* The maximum landing weight for each airport elevation (standard temperature) and available landing runway length, within the range selected by the applicant. This weight may not exceed the weight at which the landing field length determined under section 7(b) is equal to the available runway length. In showing compliance with this operating limitation, it is acceptable to assume that the landing weight at the destination will be equal to the takeoff weight reduced by the normal consumption of fuel and oil en route.

20. *Performance information.* The Airplane Flight Manual must contain the performance information determined under the performance requirements of this appendix. The information must include the following:

(a) Sufficient information so that the takeoff weight limits specified in section 19(b) can be determined for all temperatures and altitudes within the operation limitations selected by the applicant.

(b) The conditions under which the performance information was obtained, including the airspeed at the 50-foot height used to determine landing distances.

(c) The performance information (determined by extrapolation and computed for the range of weights between the maximum landing and takeoff weights) for—

(1) Climb in the landing configuration; and

(2) Landing distance.

(d) Procedure established under section 4 related to the limitations and information required by this section in the form of guidance material including any relevant limitations or information.

(e) An explanation of significant or unusual flight or ground handling characteristics of the airplane.

(f) Airspeeds, as indicated airspeeds, corresponding to those determined for takeoff under section 5(b).

21. *Maximum operating altitudes.* The maximum operating altitude to which operation is allowed, as limited by flight, structural, powerplant, functional, or equipment characteristics, must be specified in the Airplane Flight Manual.

22. *Stowage provision for airplane flight manual.* Provision must be made for stowing the Airplane Flight Manual in a suitable fixed container which is readily accessible to the pilot.

23. *Operating procedures.* Procedures for restarting turbine engines in flight (including the effects of altitude) must be set forth in the Airplane Flight Manual.

Airframe Requirements
Flight Loads

24. *Engine torque.*

(a) Each turbopropeller engine mount and its supporting structure must be designed for the torque effects of:

(1) The conditions in FAR 23.361(a).

(2) The limit engine torque corresponding to takeoff power and propeller speed multiplied by a factor accounting for propeller control system malfunction, including quick feathering action, simultaneously with 1g level flight loads. In the absence of a rational analysis, a factor of 1.6 must be used.

(b) The limit torque is obtained by multiplying the mean torque by a factor of 1.25.

Part 135: Commuter & On Demand Operations   **Appendix A to Part 135**

25. Turbine engine gyroscopic loads. Each turbopropeller engine mount and its supporting structure must be designed for the gyroscopic loads that result, with the engines at maximum continuous r.p.m., under either—
(a) The conditions in FARs 23.351 and 23.423; or
(b) All possible combinations of the following:
(1) A yaw velocity of 2.5 radians per second.
(2) A pitch velocity of 1.0 radians per second.
(3) A normal load factor of 2.5.
(4) Maximum continuous thrust.

26. Unsymmetrical loads due to engine failure.
(a) Turbopropeller powered airplanes must be designed for the unsymmetrical loads resulting from the failure of the critical engine including the following conditions in combination with a single malfunction of the propeller drag limiting system, considering the probable pilot corrective action on the flight controls:
(1) At speeds between V_{MO} and V_D, the loads resulting from power failure because of fuel flow interruption are considered to be limit loads.
(2) At speeds between V_{MO} and V_C, the loads resulting from the disconnection of the engine compressor from the turbine or from loss of the turbine blades are considered to be ultimate loads.
(3) The time history of the thrust decay and drag buildup occurring as a result of the prescribed engine failures must be substantiated by test or other data applicable to the particular engine-propeller combination.
(4) The timing and magnitude of the probable pilot corrective action must be conservatively estimated, considering the characteristics of the particular engine-propeller-airplane combination.
(b) Pilot corrective action may be assumed to be initiated at the time maximum yawing velocity is reached, but not earlier than 2 seconds after the engine failure. The magnitude of the corrective action may be based on the control forces in FAR 23.397 except that lower forces may be assumed where it is shown by analysis or test that these forces can control the yaw and roll resulting from the prescribed engine failure conditions.

Ground Loads

27. Dual wheel landing gear units. Each dual wheel landing gear unit and its supporting structure must be shown to comply with the following:
(a) *Pivoting.* The airplane must be assumed to pivot about one side of the main gear with the brakes on that side locked. The limit vertical load factor must be 1.0 and the coefficient of friction 0.8. This condition need apply only to the main gear and its supporting structure.
(b) *Unequal tire inflation.* A 60–40 percent distribution of the loads established under FAR 23.471 through FAR 23.483 must be applied to the dual wheels.
(c) *Flat tire.*
(1) Sixty percent of the loads in FAR 23.471 through FAR 23.483 must be applied to either wheel in a unit.
(2) Sixty percent of the limit drag and side loads and 100 percent of the limit vertical load established under FARs 23.493 and 23.485 must be applied to either wheel in a unit except that the vertical load need not exceed the maximum vertical load in paragraph (c)(1) of this section.

Fatigue Evaluation

28. Fatigue evaluation of wing and associated structure. Unless it is shown that the structure, operating stress levels, materials and expected use are comparable from a fatigue standpoint to a similar design which has had substantial satisfactory service experience, the strength, detail design, and the fabrication of those parts of the wing, wing carry through, and attaching structure whose failure would be catastrophic must be evaluated under either—
(a) A fatigue strength investigation in which the structure is shown by analysis, tests, or both to be able to withstand the repeated loads of variable magnitude expected in service, or
(b) A fail-safe strength investigation in which it is shown by analysis, tests, or both that catastrophic failure of the structure is not probable after fatigue, or obvious partial failure, of a principal structural element, and that the remaining structure is able to withstand a static ultimate load factor of 75 percent of the critical limit load factor at V_C. These loads must be multiplied by a factor of 1.15 unless the dynamic effects of failure under static load are otherwise considered.

Design and Construction

29. Flutter. For multiengine turbopropeller powered airplanes, a dynamic evaluation must be made and must include—
(a) The significant elastic, inertia, and aerodynamic forces associated with the rotations and displacements of the plane of the propeller; and
(b) Engine-propeller-nacelle stiffness and damping variations appropriate to the particular configuration.

Landing Gear

30. Flap operated landing gear warning device. Airplanes having retractable landing gear and wing flaps must be equipped with a warning device that functions continuously when the wing flaps are extended to a flap position that activates the warning device to give adequate warning before landing, using normal landing procedures, if the landing gear is not fully extended and locked.

There may not be a manual shut off for this warning device. The flap position sensing unit may be installed at any suitable location. The system for this device may use any part of the system (including the aural warning device) provided for other landing gear warning devices.

PERSONNEL AND CARGO ACCOMMODATIONS

31. Cargo and baggage compartments. Cargo and baggage compartments must be designed to meet FAR 23.787 (a) and (b), and in addition means must be provided to protect passengers from injury by the contents of any cargo or baggage compartment when the ultimate forward inertia force is 9g.

32. Doors and exits. The airplane must meet FAR 23.783 and FAR 23.807 (a)(3), (b), and (c), and in addition:

(a) There must be a means to lock and safeguard each external door and exit against opening in flight either inadvertently by persons, or as a result of mechanical failure. Each external door must be operable from both the inside and the outside.

(b) There must be means for direct visual inspection of the locking mechanism by crewmembers to determine whether external doors and exits, for which the initial opening movement is outward, are fully locked. In addition, there must be a visual means to signal to crewmembers when normally used external doors are closed and fully locked.

(c) The passenger entrance door must qualify as a floor level emergency exit. Each additional required emergency exit except floor level exits must be located over the wing or must be provided with acceptable means to assist the occupants in descending to the ground. In addition to the passenger entrance door:

(1) For a total seating capacity of 15 or less, an emergency exit as defined in FAR 23.807(b) is required on each side of the cabin.

(2) For a total seating capacity of 16 through 23, three emergency exits as defined in FAR 23.807(b) are required with one on the same side as the door and two on the side opposite the door.

(d) An evacuation demonstration must be conducted utilizing the maximum number of occupants for which certification is desired. It must be conducted under simulated night conditions utilizing only the emergency exits on the most critical side of the aircraft. The participants must be representative of average airline passengers with no previous practice or rehearsal for the demonstration. Evacuation must be completed within 90 seconds.

(e) Each emergency exit must be marked with the word "Exit" by a sign which has white letters 1 inch high on a red background 2 inches high, be self-illuminated or independently internally electrically illuminated, and have a minimum luminescence (brightness) of at least 160 microlamberts.

The colors may be reversed if the passenger compartment illumination is essentially the same.

(f) Access to window type emergency exits must not be obstructed by seats or seat backs.

(g) The width of the main passenger aisle at any point between seats must equal or exceed the values in the following table:

Total seating capacity	Minimum main passenger aisle width	
	Less than 25 inches from floor	25 inches and more from floor
10 through 23	9 inches	15 inches

MISCELLANEOUS

33. Lightning strike protection. Parts that are electrically insulated from the basic airframe must be connected to it through lightning arrestors unless a lightning strike on the insulated part—

(a) Is improbable because of shielding by other parts; or

(b) Is not hazardous.

34. Ice protection. If certification with ice protection provisions is desired, compliance with the following must be shown:

(a) The recommended procedures for the use of the ice protection equipment must be set forth in the Airplane Flight Manual.

(b) An analysis must be performed to establish, on the basis of the airplane's operational needs, the adequacy of the ice protection system for the various components of the airplane. In addition, tests of the ice protection system must be conducted to demonstrate that the airplane is capable of operating safely in continuous maximum and intermittent maximum icing conditions as described in Appendix C of part 25 of this chapter.

(c) Compliance with all or portions of this section may be accomplished by reference, where applicable because of similarity of the designs, to analysis and tests performed by the applicant for a type certificated model.

35. Maintenance information. The applicant must make available to the owner at the time of delivery of the airplane the information the applicant considers essential for the proper maintenance of the airplane. That information must include the following:

(a) Description of systems, including electrical, hydraulic, and fuel controls.

(b) Lubrication instructions setting forth the frequency and the lubricants and fluids which are to be used in the various systems.

(c) Pressures and electrical loads applicable to the various systems.

(d) Tolerances and adjustments necessary for proper functioning.

(e) Methods of leveling, raising, and towing.

(f) Methods of balancing control surfaces.

(g) Identification of primary and secondary structures.
(h) Frequency and extent of inspections necessary to the proper operation of the airplane.
(i) Special repair methods applicable to the airplane.
(j) Special inspection techniques, such as X-ray, ultrasonic, and magnetic particle inspection.
(k) List of special tools.

PROPULSION

GENERAL

36. Vibration characteristics. For turbopropeller powered airplanes, the engine installation must not result in vibration characteristics of the engine exceeding those established during the type certification of the engine.

37. In flight restarting of engine. If the engine on turbopropeller powered airplanes cannot be restarted at the maximum cruise altitude, a determination must be made of the altitude below which restarts can be consistently accomplished. Restart information must be provided in the Airplane Flight Manual.

38. Engines.
(a) *For turbopropeller powered airplanes.* The engine installation must comply with the following:
(1) *Engine isolation.* The powerplants must be arranged and isolated from each other to allow operation, in at least one configuration, so that the failure or malfunction of any engine, or of any system that can affect the engine, will not—
(i) Prevent the continued safe operation of the remaining engines; or
(ii) Require immediate action by any crewmember for continued safe operation.
(2) *Control of engine rotation.* There must be a means to individually stop and restart the rotation of any engine in flight except that engine rotation need not be stopped if continued rotation could not jeopardize the safety of the airplane. Each component of the stopping and restarting system on the engine side of the firewall, and that might be exposed to fire, must be at least fire resistant. If hydraulic propeller feathering systems are used for this purpose, the feathering lines must be at least fire resistant under the operating conditions that may be expected to exist during feathering.
(3) *Engine speed and gas temperature control devices.* The powerplant systems associated with engine control devices, systems, and instrumentation must provide reasonable assurance that those engine operating limitations that adversely affect turbine rotor structural integrity will not be exceeded in service.
(b) *For reciprocating engine powered airplanes.* To provide engine isolation, the powerplants must be arranged and isolated from each other to allow operation, in at least one configuration, so that the failure or malfunction of any engine, or of any system that can affect that engine, will not—
(1) Prevent the continued safe operation of the remaining engines: or
(2) Require immediate action by any crewmember for continued safe operation.

39. Turbopropeller reversing systems.
(a) Turbopropeller reversing systems intended for ground operation must be designed so that no single failure or malfunction of the system will result in unwanted reverse thrust under any expected operating condition. Failure of structural elements need not be considered if the probability of this kind of failure is extremely remote.
(b) Turbopropeller reversing systems intended for in flight use must be designed so that no unsafe condition will result during normal operation of the system, or from any failure (or reasonably likely combination of failures) of the reversing system, under any anticipated condition of operation of the airplane. Failure of structural elements need not be considered if the probability of this kind of failure is extremely remote.
(c) Compliance with this section may be shown by failure analysis, testing, or both for propeller systems that allow propeller blades to move from the flight low-pitch position to a position that is substantially less than that at the normal flight low-pitch stop position. The analysis may include or be supported by the analysis made to show compliance with the type certification of the propeller and associated installation components. Credit will be given for pertinent analysis and testing completed by the engine and propeller manufacturers.

40. Turbopropeller drag-limiting systems. Turbopropeller drag-limiting systems must be designed so that no single failure or malfunction of any of the systems during normal or emergency operation results in propeller drag in excess of that for which the airplane was designed. Failure of structural elements of the drag-limiting systems need not be considered if the probability of this kind of failure is extremely remote.

41. Turbine engine powerplant operating characteristics. For turbopropeller powered airplanes, the turbine engine powerplant operating characteristics must be investigated in flight to determine that no adverse characteristics (such as stall, surge, or flameout) are present to a hazardous degree, during normal and emergency operation within the range of operating limitations of the airplane and of the engine.

42. Fuel flow.
(a) For turbopropeller powered airplanes—
(1) The fuel system must provide for continuous supply of fuel to the engines for normal operation without interruption due to depletion of fuel in any tank other than the main tank; and

Appendix A to Part 135 — **Federal Aviation Regulations**

(2) The fuel flow rate for turbopropeller engine fuel pump systems must not be less than 125 percent of the fuel flow required to develop the standard sea level atmospheric conditions takeoff power selected and included as an operating limitation in the Airplane Flight Manual.

(b) For reciprocating engine powered airplanes, it is acceptable for the fuel flow rate for each pump system (main and reserve supply) to be 125 percent of the takeoff fuel consumption of the engine.

FUEL SYSTEM COMPONENTS

43. Fuel pumps. For turbopropeller powered airplanes, a reliable and independent power source must be provided for each pump used with turbine engines which do not have provisions for mechanically driving the main pumps. It must be demonstrated that the pump installations provide a reliability and durability equivalent to that in FAR 23.991(a).

44. Fuel strainer or filter. For turbopropeller powered airplanes, the following apply:

(a) There must be a fuel strainer or filter between the tank outlet and the fuel metering device of the engine. In addition, the fuel strainer or filter must be —

(1) Between the tank outlet and the engine-driven positive displacement pump inlet, if there is an engine-driven positive displacement pump;

(2) Accessible for drainage and cleaning and, for the strainer screen, easily removable; and

(3) Mounted so that its weight is not supported by the connecting lines or by the inlet or outlet connections of the strainer or filter itself.

(b) Unless there are means in the fuel system to prevent the accumulation of ice on the filter, there must be means to automatically maintain the fuel-flow if ice-clogging of the filter occurs; and

(c) The fuel strainer or filter must be of adequate capacity (for operating limitations established to ensure proper service) and of appropriate mesh to insure proper engine operation, with the fuel contaminated to a degree (for particle size and density) that can be reasonably expected in service. The degree of fuel filtering may not be less than that established for the engine type certification.

45. Lightning strike protection. Protection must be provided against the ignition of flammable vapors in the fuel vent system due to lightning strikes.

COOLING

46. Cooling test procedures for turbopropeller powered airplanes.

(a) Turbopropeller powered airplanes must be shown to comply with FAR 23.1041 during takeoff, climb, en route, and landing stages of flight that correspond to the applicable performance requirements. The cooling tests must be conducted with the airplane in the configuration, and operating under the conditions that are critical relative to cooling during each stage of flight. For the cooling tests a temperature is "stabilized" when its rate of change is less than 2°F per minute.

(b) Temperatures must be stabilized under the conditions from which entry is made into each stage of flight being investigated unless the entry condition is not one during which component and engine fluid temperatures would stabilize, in which case, operation through the full entry condition must be conducted before entry into the stage of flight being investigated to allow temperatures to reach their natural levels at the time of entry. The takeoff cooling test must be preceded by a period during which the powerplant component and engine fluid temperatures are stabilized with the engines at ground idle.

(c) Cooling tests for each stage of flight must be continued until—

(1) The component and engine fluid temperatures stabilize;

(2) The stage of flight is completed; or

(3) An operating limitation is reached.

Induction System

47. Air induction. For turbopropeller powered airplanes —

(a) There must be means to prevent hazardous quantities of fuel leakage or overflow from drains, vents, or other components of flammable fluid systems from entering the engine intake systems; and

(b) The air inlet ducts must be located or protected so as to minimize the ingestion of foreign matter during takeoff, landing, and taxiing.

48. Induction system icing protection. For turbopropeller powered airplanes, each turbine engine must be able to operate throughout its flight power range without adverse effect on engine operation or serious loss of power or thrust, under the icing conditions specified in Appendix C of part 25 of this chapter. In addition, there must be means to indicate to appropriate flight crewmembers the functioning of the powerplant ice protection system.

49. Turbine engine bleed air systems. Turbine engine bleed air systems of turbopropeller powered airplanes must be investigated to determine —

(a) That no hazard to the airplane will result if a duct rupture occurs. This condition must consider that a failure of the duct can occur anywhere between the engine port and the airplane bleed service; and

(b) That, if the bleed air system is used for direct cabin pressurization, it is not possible for hazardous contamination of the cabin air system to occur in event of lubrication system failure.

EXHAUST SYSTEM

50. Exhaust system drains. Turbopropeller engine exhaust systems having low spots or pockets must incorporate drains at those locations. These drains must discharge clear of the airplane in normal and ground attitudes to prevent the accumulation of fuel after the failure of an attempted engine start.

POWERPLANT CONTROLS AND ACCESSORIES

51. Engine controls. If throttles or power levers for turbopropeller powered airplanes are such that any position of these controls will reduce the fuel flow to the engine(s) below that necessary for satisfactory and safe idle operation of the engine while the airplane is in flight, a means must be provided to prevent inadvertent movement of the control into this position. The means provided must incorporate a positive lock or stop at this idle position and must require a separate and distinct operation by the crew to displace the control from the normal engine operating range.

52. Reverse thrust controls. For turbopropeller powered airplanes, the propeller reverse thrust controls must have a means to prevent their inadvertent operation. The means must have a positive lock or stop at the idle position and must require a separate and distinct operation by the crew to displace the control from the flight regime.

53. Engine ignition systems. Each turbopropeller airplane ignition system must be considered an essential electrical load.

54. Powerplant accessories. The powerplant accessories must meet FAR 23.1163, and if the continued rotation of any accessory remotely driven by the engine is hazardous when malfunctioning occurs, there must be means to prevent rotation without interfering with the continued operation of the engine.

POWERPLANT FIRE PROTECTION

55. Fire detector system. For turbopropeller powered airplanes, the following apply:

(a) There must be a means that ensures prompt detection of fire in the engine compartment. An overtemperature switch in each engine cooling air exit is an acceptable method of meeting this requirement.

(b) Each fire detector must be constructed and installed to withstand the vibration, inertia, and other loads to which it may be subjected in operation.

(c) No fire detector may be affected by any oil, water, other fluids, or fumes that might be present.

(d) There must be means to allow the flight crew to check, in flight, the functioning of each fire detector electric circuit.

(e) Wiring and other components of each fire detector system in a fire zone must be at least fire resistant.

56. Fire protection, cowling and nacelle skin. For reciprocating engine powered airplanes, the engine cowling must be designed and constructed so that no fire originating in the engine compartment can enter either through openings or by burn through, any other region where it would create additional hazards.

57. Flammable fluid fire protection. If flammable fluids or vapors might be liberated by the leakage of fluid systems in areas other than engine compartments, there must be means to—

(a) Prevent the ignition of those fluids or vapors by any other equipment; or

(b) Control any fire resulting from that ignition.

EQUIPMENT

58. Powerplant instruments.

(a) The following are required for turbopropeller airplanes:

(1) The instruments required by FAR 23.1305 (a)(1) through (4), (b)(2) and (4).

(2) A gas temperature indicator for each engine.

(3) Free air temperature indicator.

(4) A fuel flowmeter indicator for each engine.

(5) Oil pressure warning means for each engine.

(6) A torque indicator or adequate means for indicating power output for each engine.

(7) Fire warning indicator for each engine.

(8) A means to indicate when the propeller blade angle is below the low-pitch position corresponding to idle operation in flight.

(9) A means to indicate the functioning of the ice protection system for each engine.

(b) For turbopropeller powered airplanes, the turbopropeller blade position indicator must begin indicating when the blade has moved below the flight low-pitch position.

(c) The following instruments are required for reciprocating engine powered airplanes:

(1) The instruments required by FAR 23.1305.

(2) A cylinder head temperature indicator for each engine.

(3) A manifold pressure indicator for each engine.

SYSTEMS AND EQUIPMENT
GENERAL

59. Function and installation. The systems and equipment of the airplane must meet FAR 23.1301, and the following:

(a) Each item of additional installed equipment must—

(1) Be of a kind and design appropriate to its intended function;

(2) Be labeled as to its identification, function, or operating limitations, or any applicable combination of these factors, unless misuse or inadvertent actuation cannot create a hazard

(3) Be installed according to limitations specified for that equipment; and

(4) Function properly when installed.

(b) Systems and installations must be designed to safeguard against hazards to the aircraft in the event of their malfunction or failure.

(c) Where an installation, the functioning of which is necessary in showing compliance with the applicable requirements, requires a power supply, that installation must be considered an essential load on the power supply, and the power sources and the distribution system must be capable of supplying the following power loads in probable operation combinations and for probable durations:

(1) All essential loads after failure of any prime mover, power converter, or energy storage device.

(2) All essential loads after failure of any one engine on two-engine airplanes.

(3) In determining the probable operating combinations and durations of essential loads for the power failure conditions described in paragraphs (1) and (2) of this paragraph, it is permissible to assume that the power loads are reduced in accordance with a monitoring procedure which is consistent with safety in the types of operations authorized.

60. Ventilation. The ventilation system of the airplane must meet FAR 23.831, and in addition, for pressurized aircraft, the ventilating air in flight crew and passenger compartments must be free of harmful or hazardous concentrations of gases and vapors in normal operation and in the event of reasonably probable failures or malfunctioning of the ventilating, heating, pressurization, or other systems, and equipment. If accumulation of hazardous quantities of smoke in the cockpit area is reasonably probable, smoke evacuation must be readily accomplished.

ELECTRICAL SYSTEMS AND EQUIPMENT

61. General. The electrical systems and equipment of the airplane must meet FAR 23.1351, and the following:

(a) *Electrical system capacity.* The required generating capacity, and number and kinds of power sources must—

(1) Be determined by an electrical load analysis; and

(2) Meet FAR 23.1301.

(b) *Generating system.* The generating system includes electrical power sources, main power busses, transmission cables, and associated control, regulation and protective devices. It must be designed so that—

(1) The system voltage and frequency (as applicable) at the terminals of all essential load equipment can be maintained within the limits for which the equipment is designed, during any probable operating conditions;

(2) System transients due to switching, fault clearing, or other causes do not make essential loads inoperative, and do not cause a smoke or fire hazard;

(3) There are means, accessible in flight to appropriate crewmembers, for the individual and collective disconnection of the electrical power sources from the system; and

(4) There are means to indicate to appropriate crewmembers the generating system quantities essential for the safe operation of the system, including the voltage and current supplied by each generator.

62. Electrical equipment and installation. Electrical equipment, controls, and wiring must be installed so that operation of any one unit or system of units will not adversely affect the simultaneous operation of any other electrical unit or system essential to the safe operation.

63. Distribution system.

(a) For the purpose of complying with this section, the distribution system includes the distribution busses, their associated feeders, and each control and protective device.

(b) Each system must be designed so that essential load circuits can be supplied in the event of reasonably probable faults or open circuits, including faults in heavy current carrying cables.

(c) If two independent sources of electrical power for particular equipment or systems are required under this appendix, their electrical energy supply must be ensured by means such as duplicate electrical equipment, throwover switching, or multichannel or loop circuits separately routed.

64. Circuit protective devices. The circuit protective devices for the electrical circuits of the airplane must meet FAR 23.1357, and in addition circuits for loads which are essential to safe operation must have individual and exclusive circuit protection.

APPENDIX B TO PART 135
AIRPLANE FLIGHT RECORDER SPECIFICATIONS

Parameters	Range	Installed system[1] minimum accuracy (to recovered data)	Sampling interval (per second)	Resolution[4] readout
Relative time (from recorded on prior to takeoff)	25 hr minimum	±0.125% per hour	1	1 sec.
Indicated airspeed	V_{S0} to V_D (KIAS)	±5% or ±10 knots, whichever is greater. Resolution 2 knots below 175 KIAS	1	1%[3]
Altitude	−1,000 feet to max cert. alt of A/C	±100 to ±700 feet (see Table 1, TSO C51-a)	1	25 to 150
Magnetic heading	360°	±5°	1	1°
Vertical acceleration	−3g to +6g	±0.2g in addition to ±0.3g maximum datum	4 (or 1 per second where peaks, ref. to 1g are recorded)	0.03g
Longitudinal acceleration	±1.0g	±1.5% max. range excluding datum error of ±5%	2	0.01g
Pitch attitude	100% of usable	±2°	1	0.8°
Roll attitude	±60° or 100% of usable range, whichever is greater	±2°	1	0.8°
Stabilizer trim position Or	Full range	±3% unless higher uniquely required	1	1%[3]
Pitch control position	Full range	±3% unless higher uniquely required	1	1%[3]
Engine Power, Each Engine				
Fan or N_1 speed or EPR or cockpit indications used for aircraft certification Or	Maximum range	±5%	1	1%[3]
Prop. speed and torque (sample once/sec as close together as practicable)			1 (prop speed), 1 (torque)	
Altitude rate[2] (need depends on altitude resolution)	±8,000 fpm	±10%. Resolution 250 fpm below 12,000 feet indicated	1	250 fpm below 12,000
Angle of attack[2] (need depends on altitude resolution)	−20° to 40° or of usable range	±2°	1	0.8%[3]
Radio transmitter keying (discrete)	On/off		1	
TE flaps (discrete or analog)	Each discrete position (U, D, T/O, AAP) Or Analog 0–100% range	±3°	1 1	1%[3]
LE flaps (discrete or analog)	Each discrete position (U, D, T/O, AAP) Or Analog 0–100% range	±3°	1 1	1%[3]
Thrust reverser, each engine (discrete)	Stowed or full reverse		1	
Spoiler/speedbrake (discrete)	Stowed or out		1	
Autopilot engaged (discrete)	Engaged or disengaged		1	

[1] When data sources are aircraft instruments (except altimeters) of acceptable quality to fly the aircraft the recording system excluding these sensors (but including all other characteristics of the recording system) shall contribute no more than half of the values in this column.
[2] If data from the altitude encoding altimeter (100 ft. resolution) is used, then either one of these parameters should also be recorded. If however, altitude is recorded at a minimum resolution of 25 feet, then these two parameters can be omitted.
[3] Percent of full range.
[4] This column applies to aircraft manufacturing after October 11, 1991.

[Docket No. 25530, 53 FR 26152, July 11, 1988; 53 FR 30906, Aug. 16, 1988; as amended by Amdt. 135-69, 62 FR 38397, July 17, 1997]

Appendix C to Part 135
Helicopter Flight Recorder Specifications

Parameters	Range	Installed system[1] minimum accuracy (to recovered data)	Sampling interval (per second)	Resolution[3] readout
Relative time (from recorded on prior to takeoff)	25 hr minimum	±0.125% per hour	1	1 sec.
Indicated airspeed	V_{MIN} to V_D (KIAS) (minimum airspeed signal attainable with installed pitot-static system)	±5% or ±10 kts, whichever is greater	1	1 kt.
Altitude	–1,000 feet to 20,000 ft pressure altitude	±100 to ±700 ft (see Table 1, TSO C51-a)	1	25 to 150 ft.
Magnetic heading	360°	±5°	1	1°
Vertical acceleration	–3g to + 6g	±0.2g in addition to ±0.3g maximum datum	4 (or 1 per second where peaks, ref. to 1g are recorded)	0.05g
Longitudinal acceleration	±1.0g	±1.5% max. range excluding datum error of ±5%	2	0.03g
Pitch attitude	100% of usable range	±2°	1	0.8°
Roll attitude	+60° or 100% of usable range, whichever is greater	±2°	1	0.8°
Altitude rate	±8,000 fpm	±10%. Resolution 250 fpm below 12,000 ft indicated	1	250 fpm below 12,000
Engine Power, Each Engine				
Main rotor speed	Maximum range	±5%	1	1%[2]
Free or power turbine	Maximum range	±5%	1	1%[2]
Engine torque	Maximum range	±5%	1	1%[2]
Flight Control— Hydraulic Pressure				
Primary (discrete)	High/low		1	
Secondary— if applicable (discrete)	High/low		1	
Radio transmitter keying (discrete)	On/off		1	
Autopilot engaged (discrete)	Engaged or disengaged			
SAS status—engaged (discrete)	Engaged / disengaged			
SAS fault status (discrete)	Fault / OK		1	
Flight Controls				
Collective[4]	Full range	±3%	2	1%[2]
Pedal position[4]	Full range	±3%	2	1%[2]
Lat. cyclic[4]	Full range	±3%	2	1%[2]
Long. cyclic[4]	Full range	±3%	2	1%[2]
Controllable stabilator position[4]	Full range	±3%	2	1%[2]

[1] When data sources are aircraft instruments (except altimeters) of acceptable quality to fly the aircraft the recording system excluding these sensors (but including all other characteristics of the recording system) shall contribute no more than half of the values in this column.

[2] Percent of full range.

[3] This column applies to aircraft manufactured after October 11, 1991.

[4] For all aircraft manufactured on or after December 6, 2010, the sampling interval per second is 4.

[Docket No. 25530, 53 FR 26152, July 11, 1988; 53 FR 30906, Aug. 16, 1988; as amended by Amdt. 135-69, 62 FR 38397, July 17, 1997; Amdt. 135–113, 73 FR 12570, March 7, 2008; Amdt. 135–121, 75 FR 17047, April 5, 2010]

Appendix D to Part 135
Airplane Flight Recorder Specifications

Parameters	Range	Accuracy sensor input to DFDR readout	Sampling interval (per second)	Resolution[4] readout
Time (GMT or Frame Counter) (range 0 to 4,095, sampled 1 per frame)	24 Hrs	±0.125% per hour	0.25 (1 per 4 seconds)	1 sec.
Altitude	–1,000 ft to max certificated altitude of aircraft	±100 to ±700 ft (See Table 1, TSO–C51a)	1	5' to 35'[1]
Airspeed	50 KIAS to V_{SO}, and V_{SO} to 1.2 V_D	±5%, ±3%	1	1 kt.
Heading	360°	±2°	1	0.5°
Normal Acceleration (Vertical)	–3g to +6g	±1% of max range excluding datum error of ±5%	8	0.01g
Pitch Attitude	±75°	±2°	1	0.5°
Roll Attitude	±180°	±2°	1	0.5°
Radio Transmitter Keying	On-Off (Discrete)		1	
Thrust / Power on Each Engine	Full range forward	±2°	1 (per engine)	0.2%[2]
Trailing Edge Flap or Cockpit Control Section	Full range or each discrete position	±3° or as pilot's indicator	0.5	0.5%[2]
Leading Edge Flap or Cockpit Control Selection	Full range or each discrete position	±3° or as pilot's indicator	0.5	0.5%[2]
Thrust Reverser Position	Stowed, in transit, and reverse (discretion)		1 (per 4 seconds per engine)	
Ground Spoiler Position / Speed Brake Selection	Full range or each discrete position	±2% unless higher accuracy uniquely required	1	0.2%[2]
Marker Beacon Passage	Discrete		1	
Autopilot Engagement	Discrete		1	
Longitudinal Acceleration	±1g	±1.5% max range excluding datum error of ±5%	4	0.01g
Pilot Input and/or Surface Position—Primary Controls (Pitch, Roll, Yaw)[3]	Full Range	±2° unless higher accuracy uniquely required	1	0.2%[2]
Lateral Acceleration	±1g	±1.5% max range excluding datum error of ±5%	4	0.01g
Pitch Trim Position	Full Range	±3% unless higher accuracy uniquely required	1	0.3%[2]
Glideslope Deviation	±400 Microamps	±3%	1	0.3%[2]
Localizer Deviation	±400 Microamps	±3%	1	0.3%[2]
AFCS Mode and Engagement Status	Discrete		1	
Radio Altitude	–20 ft to 2,500 ft	±2 Ft or ±3% whichever is greater below 500 ft and ±5% above 500 ft	1	1 ft + 5%[2] above 500'
Master Warning	Discrete		1	
Main Gear Squat Switch Status	Discrete		1	
Angle of Attack (if recorded directly)	As installed	As installed	2	0.3%[2]
Outside Air Temperature or Total Air Temperature	–50°C to +90°C	±2°C	0.5	0.3°C
Hydraulics, Each System Low Pressure	Discrete		0.5	or 0.5%[2]
Groundspeed	As installed	Most accurate systems installed (IMS equipped aircraft only)	1	0.2%[2]

Appendix D to Part 135   **Federal Aviation Regulations**

APPENDIX D TO PART 135
AIRPLANE FLIGHT RECORDER SPECIFICATIONS (CONTINUED)

If additional recording capacity is available, recording of the following parameters is recommended. The parameters are listed in order of significance:

Parameters	Range	Accuracy sensor input to DFDR readout	Sampling interval (per second)	Resolution[4] readout
Drift Angle	When available, As installed	As installed	4	
Wind Speed and Direction	When available, As installed	As installed	4	
Latitude and Longitude	When available, As installed	As installed	4	
Brake pressure / Brake pedal position	As installed	As installed	1	
Additional engine parameters:				
EPR	As installed	As installed	1 (per engine)	
N^1	As installed	As installed	1 (per engine)	
N^2	As installed	As installed	1 (per engine)	
EGT	As installed	As installed	1 (per engine)	
Throttle Lever Position	As installed	As installed	1 (per engine)	
Fuel Flow	As installed	As installed	1 (per engine)	
TCAS:				
TA	As installed	As installed	1	
RA	As installed	As installed	1	
Sensitivity level (as selected by crew)	As installed	As installed	2	
GPWS (ground proximity warning system)	Discrete		1	
Landing gear or gear selector position	Discrete		0.25 (1 per 4 seconds)	
DME 1 and 2 Distance	0–200 NM	As installed	0.25	1 mi.
Nav 1 and 2 Frequency Selection	Full range	As installed	0.25	

[1] When altitude rate is recorded. Altitude rate must have sufficient resolution and sampling to permit the derivation of altitude to 5 feet.
[2] Percent of full range
[3] For airplanes that can demonstrate the capability of deriving either the control input on control movement (one from the other) for all modes of operation and flight regimes, the "or" applies. For airplanes with non-mechanical control systems (fly-by-wire) the "and" applies. In airplanes with split surfaces, suitable combination of inputs is acceptable in lieu of recording each surface separately.
[4] This column applies to aircraft manufactured after October 11, 1991.

[Docket No. 25530, 53 FR 26153, July 11, 1988; 53 FR 30906, Aug. 16, 1988]

Appendix E to Part 135
Helicopter Flight Recorder Specifications

Parameters	Range	Installed system[1] minimum accuracy (to recovered data)	Sampling interval (per second)	Resolution[2] read out
Time (GMT)	24 Hrs	±0.125% per hour	0.25 (1 per 4 seconds)	1 sec
Altitude	−1,000 ft to max certificated altitude of aircraft	±100 to ±700 ft (see Table 1. TSO C51-a)	1	5' to 30'
Airspeed	As the installed measuring system	±3%	1	1 kt
Heading	360°	±2°	1	0.5°
Normal Acceleration (vertical)	−3g to +6g	±1% of max range excluding datum error of ±5%	8	0.01g
Pitch Attitude	±75°	±2°	2	0.5°
Roll Attitude	±180°	±2°	2	0.5°
Radio Transmitter Keying	On-Off (Discrete)		1	0.25 sec
Power in Each Engine: Free Power Turbine Speed *and* Engine Torque	0–130% (power Turbine Speed) Full range (Torque)	±2%	1 speed 1 torque (per engine)	0.2%[1] to 0.4%[1]
Main Rotor Speed	0–130%	±2%	2	0.3%[1]
Altitude Rate	±6,000 ft/min	As installed	2	0.2%[1]
Pilot input—Primary Controls (Collective, Longitudinal Cyclic, Lateral Cyclic, Pedal)[3]	Full Range	±3%	2	0.5%[1]
Flight Control Hydraulic Pressure Low	Discrete, each circuit		1	
Flight Control Hydraulic Pressure Selector Switch Position, 1st and 2nd stage	Discrete		1	
AFCS Mode and Engagement Status	Discrete (5 bits necessary)		1	
Stability Augmentation System Engage	Discrete		1	
SAS Fault Status	Discrete		0.25	
Main Gearbox Temperature Low	As installed	As installed	0.25	0.5%[1]
Main Gearbox Temperature High	As installed	As installed	0.5	0.5%[1]
Controllable Stabilator Position	Full range ±3%		2	0.4%[1]
Longitudinal Acceleration	±1g	±1.5% max range excluding datum of ±5%	4	0.01g
Lateral Acceleration	±1g	±1.5% max range excluding datum of ±5%		0.01g
Master Warning	Discrete		1	
Nav 1 and 2 Frequency Selection	Full range	As installed	0.25	
Outside Air Temperature	−50°C to +90°C	±2°C	0.5	0.3°C

[1] Percent of full range.
[2] This column applies to aircraft manufactured after October 11, 1991.
[3] For all aircraft manufactured on or after December 6, 2010, the sampling interval per second is 4.

[Docket No. 25530, 53 FR 26154, July 11, 1988; 53 FR 30906, Aug. 16, 1988; as amended by Amdt. 135–113, 73 FR 12571, March 7, 2008; Amdt. 135–121, 75 FR 17047, April 5, 2010]

Appendix F to Part 135
Airplane Flight Recorder Specifications

The recorded values must meet the designated range, resolution, and accuracy requirements during static and dynamic conditions. Dynamic condition means the parameter is experiencing change at the maximum rate attainable, including the maximum rate of reversal. All data recorded must be correlated in time to within one second.

Parameters	Range	Accuracy (sensor input)	Seconds per sampling interval	Resolution	Remarks
1. Time or Relative Time Counts[1]	24 Hrs, 0 to 4095	±0.125% Per Hour	4	1 sec	UTC time preferred when available. Counter increments each 4 seconds of system operation.
2. Pressure Altitude	−1000 ft to max certificated altitude of aircraft. +5000 ft.	±100 to ±700 ft (see table, TSO C124a or TSO C51a)	1	5' to 35'	Data should be obtained from the air data computer when practicable.
3. Indicated airspeed or Calibrated airspeed	50 KIAS or minimum value to Max V_{SO} to 1.2 V_D	±5% and ±3%	1	1 kt	Data should be obtained from the air data computer when practicable.
4. Heading (Primary flight crew reference)	0–360° and Discrete "true" or "mag"	±2°	1	0.5°	When true or magnetic heading can be selected as the primary heading reference, a discrete indicating selection must be recorded.
5. Normal Acceleration (Vertical)[9]	−3 g to +6 g	±1% of max range excluding datum error of ±5%	0.125	0.004g	—
6. Pitch Attitude	±75°	±2°	1 or 0.25 for airplanes operated under §135.152(j)	0.5°	A sampling rate of 0.25 is recommended.
7. Roll Attitude[2]	±180°	±2°	1 or 0.5 for airplanes operated under §135.152(j)	0.5°	A sampling rate of 0.5 is recommended.
8. Manual Radio Transmitter Keying or CVR/DFDR sychronization reference	On-Off (Discrete) None	—	1	—	Preferably each crewmember but one discrete acceptable for all transmission provided the CVR/FDR system complies with TSO C124a CVR synchronization requirements (paragraph 4.2.1 ED-55).
9. Thrust/Power on Each Engine—primary flight crew reference	Full Range Forward	±2%	1 (per engine)	0.3% of full range	Sufficient parameters (e.g. EPR, N1 or Torque, NP) as appropriate for the particular engine be recorded to determine power in forward and reverse thrust, including potential overspeed conditions.
10. Autopilot Engagement	Discrete "on" or "off"	—	1	—	—
11. Longitudinal Acceleration	±1g	±1.5% max. range excluding datum error of ±5%	0.25	0.004g	—

APPENDIX F TO PART 135
AIRPLANE FLIGHT RECORDER SPECIFICATIONS (CONTINUED)

The recorded values must meet the designated range, resolution, and accuracy requirements during static and dynamic conditions. Dynamic condition means the parameter is experiencing change at the maximum rate attainable, including the maximum rate of reversal. All data recorded must be correlated in time to within one second.

Parameters	Range	Accuracy (sensor input)	Seconds per sampling interval	Resolution	Remarks
12a. Pitch Control(s) position (nonfly-by-wire systems)[18]	Full Range	±2° Unless Higher Accuracy Uniquely Required	0.5 or 0.25 for airplanes operated under §135.152(j)	0.5% of full range	For airplanes that have a flight control break away capability that allows either pilot to operate the controls independently, record both control inputs. The control inputs may be sampled alternately once per second to produce the sampling interval of 0.5 or 0.25, as applicable.
12b. Pitch Control(s) position (fly-by-wire systems)[3][18]	Full Range	±2° Unless Higher Accuracy Uniquely Required	0.5 or 0.25 for airplanes operated under §135.152(j)	0.2% of full range	—
13a. Lateral Control position(s) (nonfly-by-wire)[18]	Full Range	±2° Unless Higher Accuracy Uniquely Required	0.5 or 0.25 for airplanes operated under §135.152(j)	0.2% of full range	For airplanes that have a flight control break away capability that allows either pilot to operate the controls independently, record both control inputs. The control inputs may be sampled alternately once per second to produce the sampling interval of 0.5 or 0.25, as applicable.
13b. Lateral Control position(s) (fly-by-wire)[4][18]	Full Range	±2° Unless Higher Accuracy Uniquely Required	0.5 or 0.25 for airplanes operated under §135.152(j)	0.2% of full range	—
14a. Yaw Control position(s) (nonfly-by-wire)[5][18]	Full Range	±2° Unless Higher Accuracy Uniquely Required	0.5	0.3% of full range	For airplanes that have a flight control breakaway capability that allows either pilot to operate the controls independently, record both control inputs. The control inputs may be sampled alternately once per second to produce the sampling of 0.5 or 0.25, as applicable.
14b. Yaw Control position(s) (fly-by-wire)[18]	Full Range	±2° Unless Higher Accuracy Uniquely Required	0.5	0.2% of full range	—
15. Pitch Control Surface(s) Position [6][18]	Full Range	±2° Unless Higher Accuracy Uniquely Required	0.5 or 0.25 for airplanes operated under §135.152(j)	0.3% of full range	For airplanes fitted with multiple or split surfaces, a suitable combination of inputs is acceptable in lieu of recording each surface separately. The control surfaces may be sampled alternately to produce the sampling interval of 0.5 or 0.25.

Appendix F to Part 135   **Federal Aviation Regulations**

APPENDIX F TO PART 135
AIRPLANE FLIGHT RECORDER SPECIFICATIONS (*CONTINUED*)

The recorded values must meet the designated range, resolution, and accuracy requirements during static and dynamic conditions. Dynamic condition means the parameter is experiencing change at the maximum rate attainable, including the maximum rate of reversal. All data recorded must be correlated in time to within one second.

Parameters	Range	Accuracy (sensor input)	Seconds per sampling interval	Resolution	Remarks
16. Lateral Control Surface(s) Position [7,18]	Full Range	±2° Unless Higher Accuracy Uniquely Required	0.5 or 0.25 for airplanes operated under §135.152(j)	0.2% of full range	A suitable combination of surface position sensors is acceptable in lieu of recording each surface separately. The control surfaces may be sampled alternately to produce the sampling interval of 0.5 or 0.25, as applicable.
17. Yaw Control Surface(s) Position [8,18]	Full Range	±2° Unless Higher Accuracy Uniquely Required	0.5	0.2% of full range	For airplanes with multiple or split surfaces, a suitable combination of surface position sensors is acceptable in lieu of recording each surface separately. The control surfaces may be sampled alternately to produce the sampling interval of 0.5.
18. Lateral Acceleration	±1g	±1.5% max. range excluding datum error of ±5%	0.25	0.004g	—
19. Pitch Trim Surface Position	Full Range	±3° Unless Higher Accuracy Uniquely Required	1	0.6% of full range	—
20. Trailing Edge Flap or Cockpit Control Selection [10]	Full Range or Each Position (discrete)	±3° or as Pilot's indicator	2	0.5% of full range	Flap position and cockpit control may each be sampled alternately at 4 second intervals, to give a data point every 2 seconds.
21. Leading Edge Flap or Cockpit Control Selection [11]	Full Range or Each Discrete Position	±3° or as Pilot's indicator and sufficient to determine each discrete position	2	0.5% of full range	Left and right sides of flap position and cockpit control may each be sampled at 4 second intervals, so as to give a data point every 2 seconds.
22. Each Thrust Reverser Position (or equivalent for propeller airplane)	Stowed, In Transit, and Reverse (Discrete)	—	1 (per engine)	—	Turbo-jet – 2 discretes enable the 3 states to be determined. Turbo-prop – 1 discrete.
23. Ground Spoiler Position or Speed Brake Selection [12]	Full Range or Each Position (discrete)	±2° Unless Higher Accuracy Uniquely Required	1 or 0.5 for airplanes operated under §135.152(j)	0.5% of full range	—
24. Outside Air Temperature or Total Air Temperature [13]	−50°C to +90°C	±2°C	2	0.3°C	—
25. Autopilot/Autothrottle/AFCS Mode and Engagement Status	A suitable combination of discretes	—	1	—	Discretes should show which systems are engaged and which primary modes are controlling the flight path and speed of the aircraft.

474   ASA

Appendix F to Part 135
Airplane Flight Recorder Specifications (Continued)

The recorded values must meet the designated range, resolution, and accuracy requirements during static and dynamic conditions. Dynamic condition means the parameter is experiencing change at the maximum rate attainable, including the maximum rate of reversal. All data recorded must be correlated in time to within one second.

Parameters	Range	Accuracy (sensor input)	Seconds per sampling interval	Resolution	Remarks
26. Radio Altitude[14]	–20 ft to 2,500 ft	±2 ft or ±3% Whichever is Greater Below 500 ft and ±5% Above 500 ft	1	1 ft + 5% above 500 ft	For autoland/category 3 operations. Each radio altimeter should be recorded, but arranged so that at least one is recorded each second.
27. Localizer Deviation, MLS Azimuth, or GPS Lateral Deviation	±400 Microamps or available sensor range as installed ±62°	As installed ±3% recommended	1	0.3% of full range	For autoland/category 3 operations. Each system should be recorded, but arranged so that at least one is recorded each second. It is not necessary to record ILS and MLS at the same time, only the approach aid in use need be recorded.
28. Glideslope Deviation, MLS Elevation, or GPS Vertical Deviation	±400 Microamps or available sensor range as installed 0.9 to +30°	As installed ±3% recommended	1	0.3% of full range	For autoland/category 3 operations. Each system should be recorded, but arranged so that at least one is recorded each second. It is not necessary to record ILS and MLS at the same time, only the approach aid in use need be recorded.
29. Marker Beacon Passage	Discrete "on" or "off"	—	1	—	A single discrete is acceptable for all markers.
30. Master Warning	Discrete	—	1	—	Record the master warning and record each "red" warning that cannot be determined from other parameters or from the cockpit voice recorder.
31. Air/ground sensor (primary airplane system reference nose or main gear)	Discrete "air" or "ground"	—	1 (0.25 recommended)	—	—
32. Angle of Attack (if measured directly)	As installed	As installed	2 or 0.5 for airplanes operated under §135.152(j)	0.3% of full range	If left and right sensors are available, each may be recorded at 4 or 1 second intervals, as appropriate, so as to give a data point at 2 seconds or 0.5 second, as required.
33. Hydraulic Pressure Low, Each System	Discrete or available sensor range, "low" or "normal"	±5%	2	0.5% of full range	—
34. Groundspeed	As installed	Most Accurate Systems Installed	1	0.2% of full range	—
35. GPWS (ground proximity warning system)	Discrete "warning" or "off"	—	1	—	A suitable combination of discretes unless recorder capacity is limited in which case a single discrete for all modes is acceptable.

Appendix F to Part 135

APPENDIX F TO PART 135
AIRPLANE FLIGHT RECORDER SPECIFICATIONS (CONTINUED)

The recorded values must meet the designated range, resolution, and accuracy requirements during static and dynamic conditions. Dynamic condition means the parameter is experiencing change at the maximum rate attainable, including the maximum rate of reversal. All data recorded must be correlated in time to within one second.

Parameters	Range	Accuracy (sensor input)	Seconds per sampling interval	Resolution	Remarks
36. Landing Gear Position or Landing gear cockpit control selection	Discrete	—	4	—	A suitable combination of discretes should be recorded.
37. Drift Angle[15]	As installed	As installed	4	0.1°	—
38. Wind Speed and Direction	As installed	As installed	4	1 knot, and 1.0°	—
39. Latitude and Longitude	As installed	As installed	4	0.002°, or as installed	Provided by the Primary Navigation System Reference. Where capacity permits latitude/longitude resolution should be 0.0002°.
40. Stick shaker and pusher activation	Discrete(s) "on" or "off"	—	1	—	A suitable combination of discretes to determine activation.
41. Windshear Detection	Discrete "warning" or "off"	—	1	—	—
42. Throttle/power lever position[16]	Full Range	±2%	1 for each lever	2% of full range	For airplanes with non-mechanically linked cockpit engine controls.
43. Additional Engine Parameters	As installed	As installed	Each engine, each second	2% of full range	Where capacity permits, the preferred priority is indicated vibration level, N2, EGT, Fuel Flow, Fuel Cut-off lever position and N3, unless engine manufacturer recommends otherwise.
44. Traffic Alert and Collision Avoidance System (TCAS)	Discretes	As installed	1	—	A suitable combination of discretes should be recorded to determine the status of – Combined Control, Vertical Control, Up Advisory, and Down Advisory. (ref. ARINC Characteristic 735 Attachment 6E, TCAS VERTICAL RA DATA OUTPUT WORD.)
45. DME 1 and 2 Distance	0–200 NM	As installed	4	1 NM	1 mile
46. Nav 1 and 2 Selected Frequency	Full Range	As installed	4	—	Sufficient to determine selected frequency.
47. Selected barometric setting	Full Range	±5%	(1 per 64 sec.)	0.2% of full range	—
48. Selected altitude	Full Range	±5%	1	100 ft	—

Appendix F to Part 135
Airplane Flight Recorder Specifications (Continued)

The recorded values must meet the designated range, resolution, and accuracy requirements during static and dynamic conditions. Dynamic condition means the parameter is experiencing change at the maximum rate attainable, including the maximum rate of reversal. All data recorded must be correlated in time to within one second.

Parameters	Range	Accuracy (sensor input)	Seconds per sampling interval	Resolution	Remarks
49. Selected speed	Full Range	±5%	1	1 knot	—
50. Selected Mach	Full Range	±5%	1	.01	—
51. Selected vertical speed	Full Range	±5%	1	100 ft/min	—
52. Selected heading	Full Range	±5%	1	1°	—
53. Selected flight path	Full Range	±5%	1	1°	—
54. Selected decision height	Full Range	±5%	64	1 ft	—
55. EFIS display format	Discrete(s)	—	4	—	Discretes should show the display system status (e.g., off, normal, fail, composite, sector, plan, nav aids, weather radar, range, copy).
56. Multi-function/Engine Alerts Display format	Discrete(s)	—	4	—	Discretes should show the display system status (e.g., off, normal, fail, and the identity of display pages for emergency procedures, need not be recorded.)
57. Thrust command [17]	Full Range	±2%	2	2% of full range	—
58. Thrust target	Full Range	±2%	4	2% of full range	—
59. Fuel quantity in CG trim tank	Full Range	±2%	(1 per 64 sec.)	1% of full range	—
60. Primary Navigation System Reference	Discrete GPS, INS, VOR/DME, MLS, Loran C, Omega, Localizer Glideslope	—	4	—	A suitable combination of discretes to determine the Primary Navigation System reference.
61. Ice Detection	Discrete "ice" or "no ice"	—	4	—	—
62. Engine warning each engine vibration	Discrete	—	1	—	—
63. Engine warning each engine over temp	Discrete	—	1	—	—

Appendix F to Part 135
Airplane Flight Recorder Specifications (Continued)

The recorded values must meet the designated range, resolution, and accuracy requirements during static and dynamic conditions. Dynamic condition means the parameter is experiencing change at the maximum rate attainable, including the maximum rate of reversal. All data recorded must be correlated in time to within one second.

Parameters	Range	Accuracy (sensor input)	Seconds per sampling interval	Resolution	Remarks
64. Engine warning each engine oil pressure low	Discrete	—	1	—	—
65. Engine warning each engine over speed	Discrete	—	1	—	—
66. Yaw Trim Surface Position	Full Range	±3% Unless Higher Accuracy Uniquely Required	2	0.3% of full range	—
67. Roll Trim Surface Position	Full Range	±3% Unless Higher Accuracy Uniquely Required	2	0.3% of full range	—
68. Brake Pressure (left and right)	As installed	±5%	1	—	To determine braking effort applied by pilots or by autobrakes.
69. Brake Pedal Application (left and right)	Discrete or Analog "applied" or "off"	±5% (Analog)	1	—	To determine braking applied by pilots.
70. Yaw or sideslip angle	Full Range	±5%	1	0.5°	—
71. Engine bleed valve position	Discrete "open" or "closed"	—	4	—	—
72. De-icing or anti-icing system selection	Discrete "on" or "off"	—	4	—	—
73. Computed center of gravity	Full Range	±5%	(1 per 64 sec.)	1% of full range	—
74. AC electrical bus status	Discrete "power" or "off"	—	4	—	Each bus.
75. DC electrical bus status	Discrete "power" or "off"	—	4	—	Each bus.
76. APU bleed valve position	Discrete "open" or "closed"	—	4	—	—
77. Hydraulic Pressure (each system)	Full Range	±5%	2	100 psi	—
78. Loss of cabin pressure	Discrete "loss" or "normal"	—	1	—	—
79. Computer failure (critical flight and engine control systems)	Discrete "fail" or "normal"	—	4	—	—
80. Heads-up display (when an information source is installed)	Discrete(s) "on" or "off"	—	4	—	—

Part 135: Commuter & On Demand Operations   **Appendix F to Part 135**

APPENDIX F TO PART 135
AIRPLANE FLIGHT RECORDER SPECIFICATIONS (*CONTINUED*)

The recorded values must meet the designated range, resolution, and accuracy requirements during static and dynamic conditions. Dynamic condition means the parameter is experiencing change at the maximum rate attainable, including the maximum rate of reversal. All data recorded must be correlated in time to within one second.

Parameters	Range	Accuracy (sensor input)	Seconds per sampling interval	Resolution	Remarks
81. Para-visual display (when an information source is installed)	Discrete(s) "on" or "off"	—	1	—	—
82. Cockpit trim control input position – pitch	Full Range	±5%	1	0.2% of full range	Where mechanical means for control inputs are not available, cockpit display trim positions should be recorded.
83. Cockpit trim control input position – roll	Full Range	±5%	1	0.7% of full range	Where mechanical means for control inputs are not available, cockpit display trim position should be recorded.
84. Cockpit trim control input position – yaw	Full Range	±5%	1	0.3% of full range	Where mechanical means for control input are not available, cockpit display trim positions should be recorded.
85. Trailing edge flap and cockpit flap control position	Full Range	±5%	2	0.5% of full range	Trailing edge flaps and cockpit flap control position may each be sampled alternately at 4 second intervals to provide a sample each 0.5 second.
86. Leading edge flap and cockpit flap control position	Full Range or Discrete	±5%	1	0.5% of full range	—
87. Ground spoiler position and speed brake selection	Full Range or Discrete	±5%	0.5	0.3% of full range	—
88. All cockpit flight control input forces (control wheel, control column, rudder pedal)[18]	Full Range Control wheel ±70 lbs Control column ± 85 lbs Rudder pedal ±165 lbs	±5%	1	0.3% of full range	For fly-by-wire flight control systems, where flight control surface position is a function of the displacement of the control input device only, it is not necessary to record this parameter. For airplanes that have a flight control breakaway capability that allows either pilot to operate the control independently, record both control force inputs. The control force inputs may be sampled alternately once per 2 seconds to produce the sampling interval of 1.

See Appendix F footnotes on the next page.

Appendix F to Part 135

[1] For A300 B2/B4 airplanes, resolution = 6 seconds.
[2] For A330/A340 series airplanes, resolution = 0.703°.
[3] For A318/A319/A320/A321 series airplanes, resolution = 0.275% (0.088°>0.064°).
   For A330/A340 series airplanes, resolution = 2.20% (0.703°>0.064°).
[4] For A318/A319/A320/A321 series airplanes, resolution = 0.22% (0.088°>0.080°).
   For A330/A340 series airplanes, resolution = 1.76% (0.703°>0.080°).
[5] For A330/A340 series airplanes, resolution = 1.18% (0.703°>0.120°).
[6] For A330/A340 series airplanes, resolution = 0.783% (0.352°>0.090°).
[7] For A330/A340 series airplanes, aileron resolution = 0.704% (0.352°>0.100°).
   For A330/A340 series airplanes, spoiler resolution = 1.406% (0.703°>0.100°).
[8] For A330/A340 series airplanes, resolution = 0.30% (0.176°>0.12°).
   For A330/A340 series airplanes, seconds per sampling interval = 1.
[9] For B-717 series airplanes, resolution = .005g.
   For Dassault F900C/F900EX airplanes, resolution = .007g.
[10] For A330/A340 series airplanes, resolution = 1.05% (0.250°>0.120°).
[11] For A330/A340 series airplanes, resolution = 1.05% (0.250°>0.120°).
   For A300 B2/B4 series airplanes, resolution = 0.92% (0.230°>0.125°).
[12] For A330/A340 series airplanes, spoiler resolution = 1.406% (0.703°>0.100°).
[13] For A330/A340 series airplanes, resolution = 0.5° C.
[14] For Dassault F900C/F900EX airplanes, Radio Altitude resolution = 1.25 ft.
[15] For A330/A340 series airplanes, resolution = 0.352 degrees.
[16] For A318/A319/A320/A321 series airplanes, resolution = 4.32%.
   For A330/A340 series airplanes, resolution is 3.27% of full range for throttle lever angle (TLA); for reverse thrust, reverse throttle lever angle (RLA) resolution is nonlinear over the active reverse thrust range, which is 51.54 degrees to 96.14 degrees. The resolved element is 2.8 degrees uniformly over the entire active reverse thrust range, or 2.9% of the full range value of 96.14 degrees.
[17] For A318/A319/A320/A321 series airplanes, with IAE engines, resolution = 2.58%.
[18] For all aircraft manufactured on or after December 6, 2010, the seconds per sampling interval is 0.125. Each input must be recorded at this rate. Alternately sampling inputs (interleaving) to meet this sampling interval is prohibited.

[Docket No. 28109, 62 FR 38396, July 17, 1997; as amended by Amdt. 135–69, 62 FR 48135, Sept. 12, 1997; Amdt. 135–85, 67 FR 54323, Aug. 21, 2002; Amdt. 135–84, 68 FR 42939, July 18, 2003; Amdt. 135–84, 68 FR 50069, Aug. 20, 2003; Amdt. 135–113, 73 FR 12571, March 7, 2008; Amdt. 135–120, 75 FR 7345, Feb. 19, 2010; Amdt. 135–121, 75 FR 17047, April 5, 2010]

APPENDIX G TO PART 135
EXTENDED OPERATIONS (ETOPS)

G135.1 DEFINITIONS.

G135.1.1 Adequate Airport means an airport that an airplane operator may list with approval from the FAA because that airport meets the landing limitations of §135.385 or is a military airport that is active and operational.

G135.1.2 ETOPS Alternate Airport means an adequate airport that is designated in a dispatch or flight release for use in the event of a diversion during ETOPS. This definition applies to flight planning and does not in any way limit the authority of the pilot in command during flight.

G135.1.3 ETOPS Entry Point means the first point on the route of an ETOPS flight, determined using a one-engine inoperative cruise speed under standard conditions in still air, that is more than 180 minutes from an adequate airport.

G135.1.4 ETOPS Qualified Person means a person, performing maintenance for the certificate holder, who has satisfactorily completed the certificate holder's ETOPS training program.

G135.2 REQUIREMENTS.

G135.2.1 General. After August 13, 2008, no certificate holder may operate an airplane, other than an all-cargo airplane with more than two engines, outside the continental United States more than 180 minutes flying time (at the one engine inoperative cruise speed under standard conditions in still air) from an airport described in §135.364 unless—

(a) The certificate holder receives ETOPS approval from the FAA;

(b) The operation is conducted in a multi-engine transport category turbine-powered airplane;

(c) The operation is planned to be no more than 240 minutes flying time (at the one engine inoperative cruise speed under standard conditions in still air) from an airport described in §135.364; and

(d) The certificate holder meets the requirements of this appendix.

G135.2.2 Required certificate holder experience prior to conducting ETOPS.

Before applying for ETOPS approval, the certificate holder must have at least 12 months experience conducting international operations (excluding Canada and Mexico) with multi-engine transport category turbine-engine powered airplanes. The certificate holder may consider the following experience as international operations:

(a) Operations to or from the State of Hawaii.

(b) For certificate holders granted approval to operate under part 135 or part 121 before February 15, 2007, up to 6 months of domestic operating experience and operations in Canada and Mexico in multi-engine transport category turbojet-powered airplanes may be credited as part of the required 12 months of international experience required by paragraph G135.2.2(a) of this appendix.

(c) ETOPS experience with other aircraft types to the extent authorized by the FAA.

G135.2.3 Airplane requirements. No certificate holder may conduct ETOPS in an airplane that was manufactured after February 17, 2015 unless the airplane meets the standards of §25.1535.

G135.2.4 Crew information requirements. The certificate holder must ensure that flight crews have in-flight access to current weather and operational information needed to comply with §135.83, §135.225, and §135.229. This includes information on all ETOPS Alternate Airports, all destination alternates, and the destination airport proposed for each ETOPS flight.

G135.2.5 Operational Requirements.

(a) No person may allow a flight to continue beyond its ETOPS Entry Point unless—

(1) The weather conditions at each ETOPS Alternate Airport are forecast to be at or above the operating minima in the certificate holder's operations specifications for that airport when it might be used (from the earliest to the latest possible landing time), and

(2) All ETOPS Alternate Airports within the authorized ETOPS maximum diversion time are reviewed for any changes in conditions that have occurred since dispatch.

(b) In the event that an operator cannot comply with paragraph G135.2.5(a)(1) of this appendix for a specific airport, another ETOPS Alternate Airport must be substituted within the maximum ETOPS diversion time that could be authorized for that flight with weather conditions at or above operating minima.

(c) Pilots must plan and conduct ETOPS under instrument flight rules.

(d) Time-Limited Systems.

(1) Except as provided in paragraph G135.2.5(d)(3) of this appendix, the time required to fly the distance to each ETOPS Alternate Airport (at the all-engines-operating cruise speed, corrected for wind and temperature) may not exceed the time specified in the Airplane Flight Manual for the airplane's most limiting fire suppression system time required by regulation for any cargo or baggage compartments (if installed), minus 15 minutes.

(2) Except as provided in G135.2.5(d)(3) of this appendix, the time required to fly the distance to each ETOPS Alternate Airport (at the approved one-engine-inoperative cruise speed, corrected for wind and temperature) may not exceed the time specified in the Airplane Flight Manual for the airplane's most time limited system time

Appendix G to Part 135 — Federal Aviation Regulations

(other than the airplane's most limiting fire suppression system time required by regulation for any cargo or baggage compartments), minus 15 minutes.

(3) A certificate holder operating an airplane without the Airplane Flight Manual information needed to comply with paragraphs G135.2.5(d)(1) and (d)(2) of this appendix, may continue ETOPS with that airplane until February 17, 2015.

G135.2.6 Communications Requirements.

(a) No person may conduct an ETOPS flight unless the following communications equipment, appropriate to the route to be flown, is installed and operational:

(1) Two independent communication transmitters, at least one of which allows voice communication.

(2) Two independent communication receivers, at least one of which allows voice communication.

(3) Two headsets, or one headset and one speaker.

(b) In areas where voice communication facilities are not available, or are of such poor quality that voice communication is not possible, communication using an alternative system must be substituted.

G135.2.7 Fuel Requirements.

No person may dispatch or release for flight an ETOPS flight unless, considering wind and other weather conditions expected, it has the fuel otherwise required by this part and enough fuel to satisfy each of the following requirements:

(a) Fuel to fly to an ETOPS Alternate Airport.

(1) Fuel to account for rapid decompression and engine failure. The airplane must carry the greater of the following amounts of fuel:

(i) Fuel sufficient to fly to an ETOPS Alternate Airport assuming a rapid decompression at the most critical point followed by descent to a safe altitude in compliance with the oxygen supply requirements of §135.157;

(ii) Fuel sufficient to fly to an ETOPS Alternate Airport (at the one-engine-inoperative cruise speed under standard conditions in still air) assuming a rapid decompression and a simultaneous engine failure at the most critical point followed by descent to a safe altitude in compliance with the oxygen requirements of §135.157; or

(iii) Fuel sufficient to fly to an ETOPS Alternate Airport (at the one-engine-inoperative cruise speed under standard conditions in still air) assuming an engine failure at the most critical point followed by descent to the one engine inoperative cruise altitude.

(2) Fuel to account for errors in wind forecasting. In calculating the amount of fuel required by paragraph G135.2.7(a)(1) of this appendix, the certificate holder must increase the actual forecast wind speed by 5% (resulting in an increase in headwind or a decrease in tailwind) to account for any potential errors in wind forecasting. If a certificate holder is not using the actual forecast wind based on a wind model accepted by the FAA, the airplane must carry additional fuel equal to 5% of the fuel required by paragraph G135.2.7(a) of this appendix, as reserve fuel to allow for errors in wind data.

(3) Fuel to account for icing. In calculating the amount of fuel required by paragraph G135.2.7(a)(1) of this appendix, (after completing the wind calculation in G135.2.7(a)(2) of this appendix), the certificate holder must ensure that the airplane carries the greater of the following amounts of fuel in anticipation of possible icing during the diversion:

(i) Fuel that would be burned as a result of airframe icing during 10 percent of the time icing is forecast (including the fuel used by engine and wing anti-ice during this period).

(ii) Fuel that would be used for engine anti-ice, and if appropriate wing anti-ice, for the entire time during which icing is forecast.

(4) Fuel to account for engine deterioration. In calculating the amount of fuel required by paragraph G135.2.7(a)(1) of this appendix (after completing the wind calculation in paragraph G135.2.7(a)(2) of this appendix), the certificate holder must ensure the airplane also carries fuel equal to 5% of the fuel specified above, to account for deterioration in cruise fuel burn performance unless the certificate holder has a program to monitor airplane in-service deterioration to cruise fuel burn performance.

(b) Fuel to account for holding, approach, and landing. In addition to the fuel required by paragraph G135.2.7 (a) of this appendix, the airplane must carry fuel sufficient to hold at 1,500 feet above field elevation for 15 minutes upon reaching the ETOPS Alternate Airport and then conduct an instrument approach and land.

(c) Fuel to account for APU use. If an APU is a required power source, the certificate holder must account for its fuel consumption during the appropriate phases of flight.

G135.2.8 Maintenance Program Requirements.

In order to conduct an ETOPS flight under §135.364, each certificate holder must develop and comply with the ETOPS maintenance program as authorized in the certificate holder's operations specifications for each two-engine airplane-engine combination used in ETOPS. This provision does not apply to operations using an airplane with more than two engines. The certificate holder must develop this ETOPS maintenance program to supplement the maintenance program currently approved for the operator. This ETOPS maintenance program must include the following elements:

(a) *ETOPS maintenance document.* The certificate holder must have an ETOPS maintenance document for use by each person involved in ETOPS. The document must—

(1) List each ETOPS Significant System;

(2) Refer to or include all of the ETOPS maintenance elements in this section;

(3) Refer to or include all supportive programs and procedures;

(4) Refer to or include all duties and responsibilities, and

(5) Clearly state where referenced material is located in the certificate holder's document system.

(b) *ETOPS pre-departure service check.* The certificate holder must develop a pre-departure check tailored to their specific operation.

(1) The certificate holder must complete a pre-departure service check immediately before each ETOPS flight.

(2) At a minimum, this check must:

(i) Verify the condition of all ETOPS Significant Systems;

(ii) Verify the overall status of the airplane by reviewing applicable maintenance records; and

(iii) Include an interior and exterior inspection to include a determination of engine and APU oil levels and consumption rates.

(3) An appropriately trained maintenance person, who is ETOPS qualified must accomplish and certify by signature ETOPS specific tasks. Before an ETOPS flight may commence, an ETOPS pre-departure service check (PDSC) Signatory Person, who has been authorized by the certificate holder, must certify by signature, that the ETOPS PDSC has been completed.

(4) For the purposes of this paragraph (b) only, the following definitions apply:

(i) *ETOPS qualified person:* A person is ETOPS qualified when that person satisfactorily completes the operator's ETOPS training program and is authorized by the certificate holder.

(ii) *ETOPS PDSC Signatory Person:* A person is an ETOPS PDSC Signatory Person when that person is ETOPS Qualified and that person:

(A) When certifying the completion of the ETOPS PDSC in the United States:

(1) Works for an operator authorized to engage in part 135 or 121 operation or works for a part 145 repair station; and

(2) Holds a U.S. Mechanic's Certificate with airframe and powerplant ratings.

(B) When certifying the completion of the ETOPS PDSC outside of the U.S. holds a certificate in accordance with §43.17(c)(1) of this chapter; or

(C) When certifying the completion of the ETOPS PDSC outside the U.S. holds the certificates needed or has the requisite experience or training to return aircraft to service on behalf of an ETOPS maintenance entity.

(iii) *ETOPS maintenance entity:* An entity authorized to perform ETOPS maintenance and complete ETOPS pre-departure service checks and that entity is:

(A) Certificated to engage in part 135 or 121 operations;

(B) Repair station certificated under part 145 of this title; or

(C) Entity authorized pursuant to §43.17(c)(2) of this chapter.

(c) *Limitations on dual maintenance.*

(1) Except as specified in paragraph G135.2.8(c)(2) of this appendix, the certificate holder may not perform scheduled or unscheduled dual maintenance during the same maintenance visit on the same or a substantially similar ETOPS Significant System listed in the ETOPS maintenance document, if the improper maintenance could result in the failure of an ETOPS Significant System.

(2) In the event dual maintenance as defined in paragraph G135.2.8(c)(1) of this appendix cannot be avoided, the certificate holder may perform maintenance provided:

(i) The maintenance action on each affected ETOPS Significant System is performed by a different technician, or

(ii) The maintenance action on each affected ETOPS Significant System is performed by the same technician under the direct supervision of a second qualified individual; and

(iii) For either paragraph G135.2.8(c)(2)(i) or (ii) of this appendix, a qualified individual conducts a ground verification test and any in-flight verification test required under the program developed pursuant to paragraph G135.2.8(d) of this appendix.

(d) *Verification program.* The certificate holder must develop a program for the resolution of discrepancies that will ensure the effectiveness of maintenance actions taken on ETOPS Significant Systems. The verification program must identify potential problems and verify satisfactory corrective action. The verification program must include ground verification and in-flight verification policy and procedures. The certificate holder must establish procedures to clearly indicate who is going to initiate the verification action and what action is necessary. The verification action may be performed on an ETOPS revenue flight provided the verification action is documented as satisfactorily completed upon reaching the ETOPS entry point.

(e) *Task identification.* The certificate holder must identify all ETOPS-specific tasks. An ETOPS qualified person must accomplish and certify by signature that the ETOPS-specific task has been completed.

(f) *Centralized maintenance control procedures.* The certificate holder must develop procedures for centralized maintenance control for ETOPS.

(g) *ETOPS parts control program.* The certificate holder must develop an ETOPS parts control program to ensure the proper identification of parts used to maintain the configuration of airplanes used in ETOPS.

(h) *Enhanced Continuing Analysis and Surveillance System (E-CASS) program.* A certificate holder's existing CASS must be enhanced to include all elements of the ETOPS maintenance program. In addition to the reporting requirements of §135.415 and §135.417, the program includes reporting procedures, in the form specified in §135.415(e), for the following significant events detrimental to ETOPS within 96 hours of the occurrence to the certificate holding district office (CHDO):

(1) IFSDs, except planned IFSDs performed for flight training.

(2) Diversions and turnbacks for failures, malfunctions, or defects associated with any airplane or engine system.

(3) Uncommanded power or thrust changes or surges.

(4) Inability to control the engine or obtain desired power or thrust.

(5) Inadvertent fuel loss or unavailability, or uncorrectable fuel imbalance in flight.

(6) Failures, malfunctions or defects associated with ETOPS Significant Systems.

(7) Any event that would jeopardize the safe flight and landing of the airplane on an ETOPS flight.

(i) *Propulsion system monitoring.* The certificate holder, in coordination with the CHDO, must—

(1) Establish criteria as to what action is to be taken when adverse trends in propulsion system conditions are detected, and

(2) Investigate common cause effects or systemic errors and submit the findings to the CHDO within 30 days.

(j) *Engine condition monitoring.*

(1) The certificate holder must establish an engine-condition monitoring program to detect deterioration at an early stage and to allow for corrective action before safe operation is affected.

(2) This program must describe the parameters to be monitored, the method of data collection, the method of analyzing data, and the process for taking corrective action.

(3) The program must ensure that engine limit margins are maintained so that a prolonged engine-inoperative diversion may be conducted at approved power levels and in all expected environmental conditions without exceeding approved engine limits. This includes approved limits for items such as rotor speeds and exhaust gas temperatures.

(k) *Oil consumption monitoring.* The certificate holder must develop an engine oil consumption monitoring program to ensure that there is enough oil to complete each ETOPS flight. APU oil consumption must be included if an APU is required for ETOPS. The operator's consumption limit may not exceed the manufacturer's recommendation. Monitoring must be continuous and include oil added at each ETOPS departure point. The program must compare the amount of oil added at each ETOPS departure point with the running average consumption to identify sudden increases.

(l) *APU in-flight start program.* If an APU is required for ETOPS, but is not required to run during the ETOPS portion of the flight, the certificate holder must have a program acceptable to the FAA for cold soak in-flight start and run reliability.

(m) *Maintenance training.* For each airplane-engine combination, the certificate holder must develop a maintenance training program to ensure that it provides training adequate to support ETOPS. It must include ETOPS specific training for all persons involved in ETOPS maintenance that focuses on the special nature of ETOPS. This training must be in addition to the operator's maintenance training program used to qualify individuals for specific airplanes and engines.

(n) *Configuration, maintenance, and procedures (CMP) document.* The certificate holder must use a system to ensure compliance with the minimum requirements set forth in the current version of the CMP document for each airplane-engine combination that has a CMP.

(o) *Reporting.* The certificate holder must report quarterly to the CHDO and the airplane and engine manufacturer for each airplane authorized for ETOPS. The report must provide the operating hours and cycles for each airplane.

G135.2.9 *Delayed compliance date for all airplanes.* A certificate holder need not comply with this appendix for any airplane until August 13, 2008.

[Docket No. FAA–2002–6717, 72 FR 1885, Jan. 16, 2007; as amended by Amdt. 135–108, 72 FR 7348, Feb. 15, 2007; Amdt. 135–108, 72 FR 26541, May 10, 2007; Amdt. 135–112, 73 FR 8798, Feb. 15, 2008; Amdt. 135–115, 73 FR 33882, June 16, 2008]

49 CFR PART 175
HAZARDOUS MATERIALS: CARRIAGE BY AIRCRAFT

Subpart A— General Information and Regulations

Sec.
175.1 Purpose, scope and applicability.
175.3 Unacceptable hazardous materials shipments.
175.8 Exceptions for operator equipment and items of replacement.
175.9 Special aircraft operations.
*175.10 Exceptions for passengers, crewmembers, and air operators.
175.20 Compliance and training.
*175.25 Notification at air passenger facilities of hazardous materials restrictions.
175.26 Notification at cargo facilities of hazardous materials requirements.
175.30 Inspecting shipments.
175.31 Reports of discrepancies.
175.33 Shipping paper and notification of pilot-in-command.
*175.34 Exceptions for cylinders of compressed oxygen or other oxidizing gases transported within the state of Alaska.

Subpart B— Loading, Unloading and Handling

*175.75 Quantity limitations and cargo location.
175.78 Stowage compatibility of cargo.
175.88 Inspection, orientation and securing packages of hazardous materials.
175.90 Damaged shipments.

Subpart C— Specific Regulations Applicable According to Classification of Material

175.310 Transportation of flammable liquid fuel; aircraft only means of transportation
175.501 Special requirements for oxidizers and compressed oxygen.
175.630 Special requirements for Division 6.1 (poisonous) material and Division 6.2 (infectious substances) materials.
175.700 Special limitations and requirements for Class 7 materials.
175.701 Separation distance requirements for packages containing Class 7 (radioactive) materials in passenger-carrying aircraft.
175.702 Separation distance requirements for packages containing Class 7 (radioactive) materials in cargo aircraft.
175.703 Other special requirements for the acceptance and carriage of packages containing Class 7 materials.
175.704 Plutonium shipments.
175.705 Radioactive contamination.
175.706 Separation distances for undeveloped film from packages containing Class 7 (radioactive) materials.
175.900 Handling requirements for carbon dioxide, solid (dry ice).

Authority: 49 U.S.C. 5101–5128, 44701; 49 CFR 1.81 and 1.97.

Source: Docket No. RSPA–02–11654 (HM-228), 71 FR 14604, March 22, 2006, unless otherwise noted.

Subpart A— General Information and Regulations

§175.1 Purpose, scope and applicability.

(a) This part prescribes requirements that apply to the transportation of hazardous materials in commerce aboard (including attached to or suspended from) aircraft. The requirements in this part are in addition to other requirements contained in parts 171, 172, 173, 178, and 180 of this subchapter.

(b) This part applies to the offering, acceptance, and transportation of hazardous materials in commerce by aircraft to, from, or within the United States, and to any aircraft of United States registry anywhere in air commerce. This subchapter applies to any person who performs, attempts to perform, or is required to perform any function subject to this subchapter, including—

(1) Air carriers, indirect air carriers, and freight forwarders and their flight and non-flight employees, agents, subsidiary and contract personnel (including cargo, passenger and baggage acceptance, handling, loading and unloading personnel); and

(2) Air passengers that carry any hazardous material on their person or in their carry-on or checked baggage.

(c) This part does not apply to aircraft of United States registry under lease to and operated by foreign nationals outside the United States if:

§175.3

(1) Hazardous materials forbidden aboard aircraft by §172.101 of this subchapter are not carried on the aircraft; and

(2) Other hazardous materials are carried in accordance with the regulations of the State (nation) of the aircraft operator.

§175.3 Unacceptable hazardous materials shipments.

A hazardous material that is not prepared for shipment in accordance with this subchapter may not be offered or accepted for transportation or transported aboard an aircraft.

§175.8 Exceptions for operator equipment and items of replacement.

(a) *Operator equipment.* This subchapter does not apply to—

(1) Aviation fuel and oil in tanks that are in compliance with the installation provisions of 14 CFR, chapter 1.

(2) Hazardous materials required aboard an aircraft in accordance with the applicable airworthiness requirements and operating regulations. Items of replacement for such materials must be transported in accordance with paragraph (a)(3) of this section.

(3) Items of replacement (company material (COMAT)) for hazardous materials described in paragraph (a)(2) of this section must be transported in accordance with this subchapter. When an operator transports its own replacement items described in paragraph (a)(2), the following exceptions apply:

(i) In place of required packagings, packagings specifically designed for the items of replacement may be used, provided such packagings provide at least an equivalent level of protection to those that would be required by this subchapter.

(ii) Aircraft batteries are not subject to quantity limitations such as those provided in §172.101 or §175.75(c) of this subchapter.

(b) *Other operator exceptions.* This subchapter does not apply to—

(1) Oxygen, or any hazardous material used for the generation of oxygen, for medical use by a passenger, which is furnished by the aircraft operator in accordance with 14 CFR 121.574 or 135.91. For the purposes of this paragraph, an aircraft operator that does not hold a certificate under 14 CFR parts 121 or 135 may apply this exception in conformance with 14 CFR 121.574 or 135.91 in the same manner as required for a certificate holder. See §175.501 for additional requirements applicable to the stowage of oxygen.

(2) Dry ice (carbon dioxide, solid) intended for use by the operator in food and beverage service aboard the aircraft.

(3) Aerosols of Division 2.2 only (for dispensing of food products), alcoholic beverages, colognes, liquefied gas lighters, perfumes, and portable electronic devices containing lithium cells or batteries that meet the requirements of §175.10(a)(18) carried aboard a passenger-carrying aircraft by the operator for use or sale on that specific aircraft. A liquefied gas lighter design must be examined and successfully tested by a person or agency authorized by the Associate Administrator.

(4) A tire assembly with a serviceable tire, provided the tire is not inflated to a gauge pressure exceeding the maximum rated pressure for that tire, and the tire (including valve assemblies) is protected from damage during transport. A tire or tire assembly which is unserviceable or damaged is forbidden from air transport; however, a damaged tire is not subject to the requirements of this subchapter if it contains no material meeting the definition of a hazardous material (e.g., Division 2.2).

[Docket No. RSPA–02–11654 (HM-228), 71 FR 14604, March 22, 2006; as amended at 72 FR 55693, Oct. 1, 2007; Docket No. PHMSA–2009–0126 (HM–215K), 76 FR 3381, Jan. 19, 2011; Docket No. PHMSA–2012–0027 (HM–215L), 78 FR 1092, Jan. 7, 2013]

§175.9 Special aircraft operations.

(a) This subchapter applies to rotorcraft external load operations transporting hazardous material on board, attached to, or suspended from an aircraft. Operators must have all applicable requirements prescribed in 14 CFR Part 133 approved by the FAA Administrator prior to accepting or transporting hazardous material. In addition, rotorcraft external load operations must be approved by the Associate Administrator prior to the initiation of such operations.

(b) *Exceptions.* This subchapter does not apply to the following materials used for special aircraft operations when applicable FAA operator requirements have been met, including training operator personnel on the proper handling and stowage of the hazardous materials carried:

(1) Hazardous materials loaded and carried in hoppers or tanks of aircraft certificated for use in aerial seeding, dusting spraying, fertilizing, crop improvement, or pest control, to be dispensed during such an operation.

(2) Parachute activation devices, lighting equipment, oxygen cylinders, flotation devices, smoke grenades, flares, or similar devices carried during a parachute operation.

(3) Smoke grenades, flares, and pyrotechnic devices affixed to aircraft during any flight conducted as part of a scheduled air show or exhibition of aeronautical skill. The aircraft may not carry any persons other than required flight crewmembers. The affixed installation accommodating the smoke grenades, flares, or pyrotechnic

devices on the aircraft must be approved for its intended use by the FAA Flight Standards District Office having responsibility for that aircraft.

(4) Hazardous materials are carried and used during dedicated air ambulance, fire fighting, or search and rescue operations.

(5) A transport incubator unit necessary to protect life or an organ preservation unit necessary to protect human organs, carried in the aircraft cabin, provided:

(i) The compressed gas used to operate the unit is in an authorized DOT specification cylinder and is marked, labeled, filled, and maintained as prescribed by this subchapter;

(ii) Each battery used is of the nonspillable type;

(iii) The unit is constructed so that valves, fittings, and gauges are protected from damage;

(iv) The pilot-in-command is advised when the unit is on board, and when it is intended for use;

(v) The unit is accompanied by a person qualified to operate it;

(vi) The unit is secured in the aircraft in a manner that does not restrict access to or use of any required emergency or regular exit or of the aisle in the passenger compartment; and,

(vii) Smoking within 3 m (10 feet) of the unit is prohibited.

(6) Hazardous materials that are loaded and carried on or in cargo only aircraft, and that are to be dispensed or expended during flight for weather control, environmental restoration or protection, forest preservation and protection, fire fighting and prevention, flood control, or avalanche control purposes, when the following requirements are met:

(i) Operations may not be conducted over densely populated areas, in a congested airway, or near any airport where carrier passenger operations are conducted.

(ii) Each operator must prepare and keep current a manual containing operational guidelines and handling procedures, for the use and guidance of flight, maintenance, and ground personnel concerned in the dispensing or expending of hazardous materials. The manual must be approved by the FAA Principal Operations Inspector assigned to the operator.

(iii) No person other than a required flight crewmember, FAA inspector, or person necessary for handling or dispensing the hazardous material may be carried on the aircraft.

(iv) The operator of the aircraft must have advance permission from the owner of any airport to be used for the dispensing or expending operation.

(v) When Division 1.1, 1.2, and 1.3 materials (except detonators and detonator assemblies) and detonators or detonator assemblies are carried for avalanche control flights, the explosives must be handled by, and at all times be under the control of, a qualified blaster. When required by a State or local authority, the blaster must be licensed and the State or local authority must be identified in writing to the FAA Principal Operations Inspector assigned to the operator.

[Docket No. PHMSA–2009–0126 (HM–215K), 76 FR 3381, Jan. 19, 2011]

§175.10 Exceptions for passengers, crewmembers, and air operators.

(a) This subchapter does not apply to the following hazardous materials when carried by aircraft passengers or crewmembers provided the requirements of §§171.15 and 171.16 (see paragraph (c) of this section) and the requirements of this section are met:

(1) (i) Non-radioactive medicinal and toilet articles for personal use (including aerosols) carried in carry-on and checked baggage. Release devices on aerosols must be protected by a cap or other suitable means to prevent inadvertent release.

(ii) Other aerosols in Div. 2.2 (nonflammable gas) with no subsidiary risk carried in checked baggage only. Release devices on aerosols must be protected by a cap or other suitable means to prevent inadvertent release; and

(iii) The aggregate quantity of these hazardous materials carried by each person may not exceed 2 kg (70 ounces) by mass or 2 L (68 fluid ounces) by volume and the capacity of each container may not exceed 0.5 kg (18 ounces) by mass or 500 ml (17 fluid ounces) by volume.

(2) One packet of safety matches or a lighter intended for use by an individual when carried on one's person or in carry-on baggage only. Lighter fuel, lighter refills, and lighters containing unabsorbed liquid fuel (other than liquefied gas) are not permitted on one's person or in carry-on or checked baggage.

(3) Implanted medical devices in humans or animals that contain hazardous materials, such as a heart pacemaker containing Class 7 (radioactive) material or lithium batteries; and radiopharmaceuticals that have been injected or ingested.

(4) Alcoholic beverages containing:
(i) Not more than 24% alcohol by volume; or
(ii) More than 24% and not more than 70% alcohol by volume when in unopened retail packagings not exceeding 5 liters (1.3 gallons) carried in carry-on or checked baggage, with a total net quantity per person of 5 liters (1.3) gallons for such beverages.

(5) Perfumes and colognes purchased through duty-free sales and carried on one's person or in carry-on baggage.

(6) Hair curlers (curling irons) containing a hydrocarbon gas such as butane, no more than one

§175.10 — Federal Aviation Regulations

per person, in carry-on or checked baggage. The safety cover must be securely fitted over the heating element. Gas refills for such curlers are not permitted in carry-on or checked baggage.

(7) A small medical or clinical mercury thermometer for personal use, when carried in a protective case in carry-on or checked baggage.

(8) Small arms ammunition for personal use carried by a crewmember or passenger in checked baggage only, if securely packed in boxes or other packagings specifically designed to carry small amounts of ammunition. Ammunition clips and magazines must also be securely boxed. This paragraph does not apply to persons traveling under the provisions of 49 CFR 1544.219.

(9) One self-defense spray (see §171.8 of this subchapter), not exceeding 118 mL (4 fluid ounces) by volume, that incorporates a positive means to prevent accidental discharge may be carried in checked baggage only.

(10) Dry ice (carbon dioxide, solid), with the approval of the operator:

(i) Quantities may not exceed 2.5 kg (5.5 pounds) per person when used to pack perishables not subject to the HMR. The package must permit the release of carbon dioxide gas; and

(ii) When carried in checked baggage, each package is marked "DRY ICE" or "CARBON DIOXIDE, SOLID," and marked with the net weight of dry ice or an indication the net weight is 2.5 kg (5.5 pounds) or less.

(11) A self-inflating life jacket fitted with no more than two small gas cartridges (containing no hazardous material other than a Div. 2.2 gas) for inflation purposes plus no more than two spare cartridges. The lifejacket and spare cartridges may be carried in carry-on or checked baggage, with the approval of the aircraft operator.

(12) Small compressed gas cylinders of Division 2.2 (containing no hazardous material other than a Division 2.2 gas) worn by the passenger for the operation of mechanical limbs and, in carry-on and checked baggage, spare cylinders of a similar size for the same purpose in sufficient quantities to ensure an adequate supply for the duration of the journey.

(13) A mercury barometer or thermometer carried as carry-on baggage, by a representative of a government weather bureau or similar official agency, provided that individual advises the operator of the presence of the barometer or thermometer in his baggage. The barometer or thermometer must be packaged in a strong packaging having a sealed inner liner or bag of strong, leak proof and puncture-resistant material impervious to mercury, which will prevent the escape of mercury from the package in any position.

(14) Electrically powered heat-producing articles (e.g., battery-operated equipment such as diving lamps and soldering equipment) as checked or carry-on baggage only and with the approval of the operator of the aircraft. The heat-producing component, the energy source, or other component (e.g., fuse) must be removed to prevent unintentional functioning during transport. Any battery that is removed must be protected against short circuit by placement in original retail packaging or by otherwise insulating terminals (e.g., by taping over exposed terminals or placing each battery in a separate plastic bag or protective pouch).

(15) A wheelchair or other battery-powered mobility aid equipped with a nonspillable battery or a dry sealed battery when carried as checked baggage, provided—

(i) The battery conforms to the requirements of §173.159a(d) of this subchapter for non-spillable batteries;

(ii) The battery conforms to the requirements of §172.102(c)(1), Special provision 130 of this subchapter for dry sealed batteries, as applicable;

(iii) Visual inspection including removal of the battery, where necessary, reveals no obvious defects (removal of the battery from the housing should be performed by qualified airline personnel only);

(iv) The battery is disconnected and the battery terminals are protected to prevent short circuits, unless the wheelchair or mobility aid design provides an effective means of preventing unintentional activation, and

(v) The battery is—

(A) Securely attached to the wheelchair or mobility aid;

(B) Is removed and placed in a strong, rigid packaging marked "NONSPILLABLE BATTERY" (unless fully enclosed in a rigid housing that is properly marked);

(C) Is removed and placed in a strong, rigid packaging marked with the words "not restricted" in accordance with paragraph (c)(2) of §172.102, Special provision 130, of this subchapter; or

(D) Is handled in accordance with paragraph (a)(16)(iv) of this section.

(16) A wheelchair or other battery-powered mobility aid equipped with a spillable battery, when carried as checked baggage, provided—

(i) Visual inspection including removal of the battery, where necessary, reveals no obvious defects (however, removal of the battery from the housing should be performed by qualified airline personnel only);

(ii) The battery is disconnected and terminals are insulated to prevent short circuits;

(iii) The pilot-in-command is advised, either orally or in writing, prior to departure, as to the location of the battery aboard the aircraft; and

(iv) The wheelchair or mobility aid is loaded, stowed, secured and unloaded in an upright position, or the battery is removed, and carried in a strong, rigid packaging under the following conditions:

(A) The packaging must be leak-tight and impervious to battery fluid. An inner liner may be used to satisfy this requirement if there is absorbent material placed inside of the liner and the liner has a leakproof closure;

(B) The battery must be protected against short circuits, secured upright in the packaging, and be packaged with enough compatible absorbent material to completely absorb liquid contents in the event of rupture of the battery; and

(C) The packaging must be labeled with a CORROSIVE label, marked to indicate proper orientation, and marked with the words "Battery, wet, with wheelchair."

(17) A wheelchair or other mobility aid equipped with a lithium ion battery, when carried as checked baggage, provided—

(i) The lithium ion battery must be of a type that successfully passed each test in the UN Manual of Tests and Criteria (IBR; see §171.7 of this subchapter), as specified in §173.185 of this subchapter, unless approved by the Associate Administrator;

(ii) The operator must verify that:

(A) Visual inspection of the wheelchair or other mobility aid reveals no obvious defects;

(B) Battery terminals are protected from short circuits (e.g., enclosed within a battery housing);

(C) The battery must be securely attached to the mobility aid; and

(D) Electrical circuits are isolated;

(iii) The wheelchair or other mobility aid must be loaded and stowed in such a manner to prevent its unintentional activation and its battery must be protected from short circuiting;

(iv) The wheelchair or other mobility aid must be protected from damage by the movement of baggage, mail, service items, or other cargo;

(v) Where a lithium ion batterypowered wheelchair or other mobility aid is specifically designed to allow its battery to be removed by the user (e.g., collapsible):

(A) The battery must be removed from the wheelchair or other mobility aid according to instructions provided by the wheelchair or other mobility aid owner or its manufacturer;

(B) The battery must be carried in carry-on baggage only;

(C) Battery terminals must be protected from short circuits (by placement in original retail packaging or otherwise insulating the terminal e.g. by taping over exposed terminals or placing each battery in a separate plastic bag or protective pouch);

(D) The battery must not exceed 25 grams aggregate equivalent lithium content; and

(E) A maximum of one spare battery not exceeding 25 grams aggregate equivalent lithium content or two spares not exceeding 13.5 grams aggregate equivalent lithium content each may be carried;

(vi) The pilot-in-command is advised either orally or in writing, prior to departure, as to the location of the lithium ion battery or batteries aboard the aircraft.

(18) Except as provided in §173.21 of this subchapter, portable electronic devices (for example, watches, calculating machines, cameras, cellular phones, lap-top and notebook computers, camcorders, etc.) containing cells or batteries (including lithium cells or batteries) and spare batteries and cells for these devices, when carried by passengers or crew members for personal use. Each spare battery must be individually protected so as to prevent short circuits (by placement in original retail packaging or by otherwise insulating terminals, e.g., by taping over exposed terminals or placing each battery in a separate plastic bag or protective pouch) and carried in carry-on baggage only. In addition, each installed or spare battery must comply with the following:

(i) For a lithium metal battery, a lithium content of not more than 2 grams per battery; or

(ii) For a lithium-ion battery, an aggregate equivalent lithium content of not more than 8 grams per battery, except that up to two batteries with an aggregate equivalent lithium content of more than 8 grams but not more than 25 grams may be carried.

(iii) For a non-spillable battery, the battery and equipment must conform to §173.159(d). Each battery must not exceed a voltage greater than 12 volts and a watt-hour rating of not more than 100 Wh. No more than two individually protected spare batteries may be carried. Such equipment and spare batteries must be carried in checked or carry-on baggage.

(19) Fuel cells used to power portable electronic devices (e.g., cameras, cellular phones, laptop computers and camcorders) and spare fuel cell cartridges when transported personal use under the following conditions:

(i) Fuel cells and fuel cell cartridges may contain only Division 2.1 liquefied flammable gas, or hydrogen in a metal hydride, Class 3 flammable liquid (including methanol), Division 4.3 water-reactive material, or Class 8 corrosive material;

(ii) The quantity of fuel in any fuel cell or fuel cell cartridge may not exceed:

(A) 200 mL (6.76 ounces) for liquids;

(B) 120 mL (4 fluid ounces) for liquefied gases in non-metallic fuel cell cartridges, or 200 mL (6.76 ounces) for liquefied gases in metal fuel cell cartridges;

(C) 200 g (7 ounces) for solids; or

§175.10

(D) For hydrogen in metal hydride, the fuel cell cartridges must have a water capacity of 120 mL (4 fluid ounces) or less;

(iii) No more than two spare fuel cell cartridges may be carried by a passenger or crew member as follows:

(A) Fuel cell cartridges containing Class 3 flammable liquid (including methanol) and Class 8 corrosive material in carry-on or checked baggage; and

(B) Division 2.1 liquefied flammable gas or hydrogen in a metal hydride and Division 4.3 water-reactive material in carry-on baggage only;

(iv) Fuel cells containing fuel are permitted in carry-on baggage only;

(v) Fuel cell cartridges containing hydrogen in a metal hydride must meet the requirements in §173.230(d) of this subchapter;

(vi) Refueling of a fuel cell aboard an aircraft is not permitted except that the installation of a spare cartridge is allowed;

(vii) Each fuel cell and fuel cell cartridge must conform to IEC 62282-6-100 and IEC 62282-6-100 Amend. 1 (IBR, see §171.7 of this subchapter) and must be marked with a manufacturer's certification that it conforms to the specification. In addition, each fuel cell cartridge must be marked with the maximum quantity and type of fuel in the cartridge;

(viii) Interaction between fuel cells and integrated batteries in a device must conform to IEC 62282-6-100 and IEC 62282-6-100 Amend. 1 (IBR, see §171.7 of this subchapter). Fuel cells whose sole function is to charge a battery in the device are not permitted; and

(ix) Fuel cells must be of a type that will not charge batteries when the consumer electronic device is not in use and must be durably marked by the manufacturer with the wording: "APPROVED FOR CARRIAGE IN AIRCRAFT CABIN ONLY" to indicate that the fuel cell meets this requirement.

(20) Permeation devices for calibrating air quality monitoring equipment when carried in checked baggage provided the devices are constructed and packaged in accordance with §173.175.

(21) An internal combustion or fuel cell engine or a machine or apparatus containing an internal combustion or fuel cell engine when carried as checked baggage, provided—

(i) The engine contains no liquid or gaseous fuel. An engine may be considered as not containing fuel when the engine components and any fuel lines have been completed drained, sufficiently cleaned of residue, and purged of vapors to remove any potential hazard and the engine when held in any orientation will not release any liquid fuel;

Federal Aviation Regulations

(ii) The fuel tank contains no liquid or gaseous fuel. A fuel tank may be considered as not containing fuel when the fuel tank and the fuel lines have been completed drained, sufficiently cleaned of residue, and purged of vapors to remove any potential hazard;

(iii) It is not equipped with a wet battery (including a non-spillable battery), a sodium battery or a lithium battery; and

(iv) It contains no other hazardous materials subject to the requirements of this subchapter.

(22) Non-infectious specimens transported in accordance with §173.4b(b).

(23) Insulated packagings containing refrigerated liquid nitrogen when carried in checked or carry-on baggage in accordance with the ICAO Technical Instructions (IBR, see §171.7 of this subchapter), Packing Instruction 202, the packaging specifications in part 6, chapter 5, and special provision A152.

(24) Small cartridges fitted into devices with no more than four small cylinders of carbon dioxide or other suitable gas in in Division 2.2. The water capacity of each cylinder must not exceed 50 mL (equivalent to a 28 g carbon dioxide cartridge), with the approval of the operator.

(b) The exceptions provided in paragraph (a) of this section also apply to aircraft operators when transporting passenger or crewmember baggage that has been separated from the passenger or crewmember, including transfer to another carrier for transport to its final destination.

(c) The requirements to submit incident reports as required under §§171.15 and 171.16 of this subchapter apply to the air carrier.

[Docket No. RSPA–02–11654 (HM-228), 71 FR 14604, March 22, 2006; as amended at 71 FR 78634, Dec. 29, 2006; 72 FR 44950, Aug. 9, 2007; 73 FR 4719, Jan. 28, 2008; 73 FR 23367, April 30, 2008; Docket Nos. PHMSA–2007–0065 (HM-224D) and PHMSA–2008–0005 (HM-215J), 74 FR 2266, Jan. 14, 2009; Docket Nos. PHMSA–2007–0065 (HM-224D) and PHMSA–2008–0005 (HM-215J), 75 FR 73, Jan. 4, 2010; Docket No. PHMSA–2009–0126 (HM-215K), 76 FR 3382, Jan. 19, 2011; Docket No. PHMSA–2009–0126 (HM-215K), 76 FR 82178, Dec. 30, 2011; Docket No. PHMSA–2012–0027 (HM-215L), 78 FR 1092, Jan. 7, 2013; Docket No. PHMSA–2009–0126 (HM-215K), 78 FR 1117, Jan. 7, 2013; Docket No. PHMSA–2013–0041; 78 FR 65485, Oct. 31, 2013]

§175.20 Compliance and training.

An air carrier may not transport a hazardous material by aircraft unless each of its hazmat employees involved in that transportation is trained as required by subpart H of part 172 of this subchapter. In addition, air carriers must comply with all applicable hazardous materials training requirements in 14 CFR Part 121 and 135.

§175.25 Notification at air passenger facilities of hazardous materials restrictions.

(a) *Notices of requirements.* Each person who engages in for-hire air transportation of passengers must display notices of the requirements applicable to the carriage of hazardous materials aboard aircraft, and the penalties for failure to comply with those requirements in accordance with this section. Each notice must be legible, and be prominently displayed so it can be seen by passengers in locations where the aircraft operator issues tickets, checks baggage, and maintains aircraft boarding areas. At a minimum, each notice must communicate the following information:

(1) Federal law forbids the carriage of hazardous materials aboard aircraft in your luggage or on your person. A violation can result in five years' imprisonment and penalties of $250,000 or more (49 U.S.C. 5124). Hazardous materials include explosives, compressed gases, flammable liquids and solids, oxidizers, poisons, corrosives and radioactive materials. Examples: Paints, lighter fluid, fireworks, tear gases, oxygen bottles, and radio-pharmaceuticals.

(2) There are special exceptions for small quantities (up to 70 ounces total) of medicinal and toilet articles carried in your luggage and certain smoking materials carried on your person. For further information contact your airline representative.

(b) *Ticket purchase.* During the ticket purchase process, regardless if the process is completed remotely (e.g., via the Internet or phone) or when completed at the airport, with or without assistance from another person (e.g., automated check-in facility), the aircraft operator must ensure that information on the types of hazardous materials a passenger is forbidden to transport aboard an aircraft is provided to passengers. Information may be in text or in pictorial form and, effective January 1, 2015, must be such that the final ticket purchase cannot be completed until the passenger or a person acting on the passenger's behalf has indicated that it understands the restrictions on hazardous materials in baggage.

(c) *Check-in.* Effective January 1, 2015, when the flight check-in process is conducted remotely (e.g., via the Internet or phone) or when completed at the airport, without assistance from another person (e.g., automated check-in kiosk), the aircraft operator must ensure that information on the types of hazardous materials a passenger is forbidden to transport aboard an aircraft is provided to passengers. Information may be in text or in pictorial form and should be such that the check in process cannot be completed until the passenger or a person acting on the passenger's behalf has indicated that it understands the restrictions on hazardous materials in baggage.

(d) *Signage.* When the check in process is not conducted remotely (e.g., at the airport with the assistance of an airline representative), passenger notification of permitted and forbidden hazardous materials may be completed through signage (electronic or otherwise), provided it is legible and prominently displayed.

[Docket No. PHMSA–2009–0126 (HM–215K), 76 FR 3382, Jan. 19, 2011; as amended by Docket No. PHMSA–2009–0126 (HM–215K), 78 FR 1117, Jan. 7, 2013; Docket No. PHMSA–2013–0041 78 FR 65486, Oct. 31, 2013]

§175.26 Notification at cargo facilities of hazardous materials requirements.

(a) Each person who engages in the acceptance or transport of cargo for transportation by aircraft shall display notices to persons offering such cargo of the requirements applicable to the carriage of hazardous materials aboard aircraft, and the penalties for failure to comply with those requirements, at each facility where cargo is accepted. Each notice must be legible, and be prominently displayed so it can be seen. At a minimum, each notice must communicate the following information:

(1) Cargo containing hazardous materials (dangerous goods) for transportation by aircraft must be offered in accordance with the Federal Hazardous Materials Regulations (49 CFR parts 171 through 180).

(2) A violation can result in five years' imprisonment and penalties of $250,000 or more (49 U.S.C. 5124).

(3) Hazardous materials (dangerous goods) include explosives, compressed gases, flammable liquids and solids, oxidizers, poisons, corrosives and radioactive materials.

(b) The information contained in paragraph (a) of this section must be printed:

(1) Legibly in English, and, where cargo is accepted outside of the United States, in the language of the host country; and

(2) On a background of contrasting color.

(c) Size and color of the notice are optional. Additional information, examples, or illustrations, if not inconsistent with required information, may be included.

(d) *Exceptions.* Display of a notice required by paragraph (a) of this section is not required at:

(1) An unattended location (e.g., a drop box) provided a general notice advising customers of a prohibition on shipments of hazardous materials through that location is prominently displayed; or

(2) A customer's facility where hazardous materials packages are accepted by a carrier.

§175.30 Inspecting shipments.

(a) No person may accept a hazardous material for transportation aboard an aircraft unless the aircraft operator ensures the hazardous material is:

(1) Authorized, and is within the quantity limitations specified for carriage aboard aircraft according to §172.101 of this subchapter or as otherwise specifically provided by this subchapter.

(2) Described and certified on a shipping paper prepared in duplicate in accordance with part 172 of this subchapter or as authorized by subpart C of part 171 of this subchapter. See §175.33 for shipping paper retention requirements;

(3) Marked and labeled in accordance with subparts D and E of part 172 or as authorized by subpart C of part 171 of this subchapter, and placarded (when required) in accordance with subpart F of part 172 of this subchapter; and

(4) Labeled with a "CARGO AIRCRAFT ONLY" label (see §172.448 of this subchapter) if the material as presented is not permitted aboard passenger-carrying aircraft.

(b) Except as provided in paragraph (d) of this section, no person may carry a hazardous material in a package, outside container, or overpack aboard an aircraft unless the package, outside container, or overpack is inspected by the operator of the aircraft immediately before placing it:

(1) Aboard the aircraft; or

(2) In a unit load device or on a pallet prior to loading aboard the aircraft.

(c) A hazardous material may be carried aboard an aircraft only if, based on the inspection by the operator, the package, outside container, or overpack containing the hazardous material:

(1) Has no holes, leakage or other indication that its integrity has been compromised; and

(2) For Class 7 (radioactive) materials, does not have a broken seal, except packages contained in overpacks need not be inspected for seal integrity.

(d) The requirements of paragraphs (b) and (c) of this section do not apply to Dry ice (carbon dioxide, solid).

(e) An overpack containing packages of hazardous materials may be accepted only if the operator has taken all reasonable steps to establish that:

(1) The overpack does not contain a package bearing the "CARGO AIRCRAFT ONLY" label unless—

(i) The overpack affords clear visibility of and easy access to the package;

(ii) The package contains a material which may be carried inaccessibly under the provisions of §175.75(e); or

(iii) Not more than one package is overpacked.

(2) The proper shipping names, identification numbers, labels and special handling instructions appearing on the inside packages are clearly visible or reproduced on the outside of the overpack, and

(3) The word "OVERPACK" appears on the outside of the overpack when specification packagings are required.

[Docket No. RSPA–02–11654 (HM-228), 71 FR 14604, March 22, 2006; as amended at 72 FR 25177, May 3, 2007; Docket No. PHMSA–2008–0227 (HM-244A), 73 FR 57006, Oct. 1, 2008; Docket No. PHMSA–2009–0126 (HM-215K), 76 FR 3383, Jan. 19, 2011]

§175.31 Reports of discrepancies.

(a) Each person who discovers a discrepancy, as defined in paragraph (b) of this section, relative to the shipment of a hazardous material following its acceptance for transportation aboard an aircraft shall, as soon as practicable, notify the nearest FAA Regional or Field Security Office by telephone or electronically, and shall provide the following information:

(1) Name and telephone number of the person reporting the discrepancy.

(2) Name of the aircraft operator.

(3) Specific location of the shipment concerned.

(4) Name of the shipper.

(5) Nature of discrepancy.

(6) Address of the shipper or person responsible for the discrepancy, if known, by the air carrier.

(b) Discrepancies which must be reported under paragraph (a) of this section are those involving hazardous materials which are improperly described, certified, labeled, marked, or packaged, in a manner not ascertainable when accepted under the provisions of §175.30(a) of this subchapter including packages or baggage which are found to contain hazardous materials subsequent to their being offered and accepted as other than hazardous materials.

§175.33 Shipping paper and notification of pilot-in-command.

(a) When a hazardous material subject to the provisions of this subchapter is carried in an aircraft, a copy of the shipping paper required by §175.30(a)(2) must accompany the shipment it covers during transportation aboard the aircraft, and the operator of the aircraft must provide the pilot-in-command with accurate and legible written information as early as practicable before departure of the aircraft, which specifies at least the following:

(1) The proper shipping name, hazard class and identification number of the material, including any remaining aboard from prior stops, as specified in §172.101 of this subchapter or the ICAO Technical Instructions. In the case of

Class 1 materials, the compatibility group letter also must be shown. If a hazardous material is described by the proper shipping name, hazard class, and identification number appearing in:

(i) Section 172.101 of this subchapter. Except for the requirement to indicate the type of package, any additional description requirements provided in §§172.202, and 172.203 of this subchapter must also be shown on the notification.

(ii) The ICAO Technical Instructions (IBR, see §171.7 of this subchapter), any additional information required to be shown on shipping papers by subpart C of part 171 of this subchapter must also be shown in the notification.

(2) The total number of packages;

(3) The net quantity or gross weight, as applicable, for each package except those containing Class 7 (radioactive) materials. For a shipment consisting of multiple packages containing hazardous materials bearing the same proper shipping name and identification number, only the total quantity and an indication of the quantity of the largest and smallest package at each loading location need to be provided;

(4) The location of the packages aboard the aircraft;

(5) Confirmation that no damaged or leaking packages have been loaded on the aircraft;

(6) For Class 7 (radioactive) materials, the number of packages, overpacks or freight containers, their category, transport index (if applicable), and their location aboard the aircraft;

(7) The date of the flight;

(8) The telephone number of a person not aboard the aircraft from whom the information contained in the notification of pilot-in-command can be obtained. The aircraft operator must ensure the telephone number is monitored at all times the aircraft is in flight. The telephone number is not required to be placed on the notification of pilot-in-command if the phone number is in a location in the cockpit available and known to the flight crew.

(9) Confirmation that the package must be carried only on cargo aircraft if its transportation aboard passenger-carrying aircraft is forbidden; and

(10) An indication, when applicable, that a hazardous material is being carried under terms of a special permit.

(11) For UN1845, Carbon dioxide, solid (dry ice), only the UN number, proper shipping name, hazard class, total quantity in each hold aboard the aircraft, and the airport at which the package(s) is to be unloaded must be provided.

(b) A copy of the written notification to pilot-in-command shall be readily available to the pilot-in-command during flight. Emergency response information required by subpart G of part 172 of this subchapter must be maintained in the same manner as the written notification to pilot-in-command during transport of the hazardous material aboard the aircraft.

(c) The aircraft operator must—

(1) Retain a copy of the shipping paper required by §175.30(a)(2) or an electronic image thereof, that is accessible at or through its principal place of business and must make the shipping paper available, upon request, to an authorized official of a federal, state, or local government agency at reasonable times and locations. For a hazardous waste, each shipping paper copy must be retained for three years after the material is accepted by the initial carrier. For all other hazardous materials, each shipping paper copy must be retained by the operator for one year after the material is accepted by the initial carrier. Each shipping paper copy must include the date of acceptance by the carrier. The date on the shipping paper may be the date a shipper notifies the air carrier that a shipment is ready for transportation, as indicated on the air bill or bill of lading, as an alternative to the date the shipment is picked up or accepted by the carrier. Only an initial carrier must receive and retain a copy of the shipper's certification, as required by §172.204 of this subchapter.

(2) Retain a copy of each notification of pilot-in-command, an electronic image thereof, or the information contained therein for 90 days at the airport of departure or the operator's principal place of business.

(3) Have the information required to be retained under this paragraph readily accessible at the airport of departure and the intended airport of arrival for the duration of the flight leg.

(4) Make available, upon request, to an authorized official of a Federal, State, or local government agency (including an emergency responder(s)) at reasonable times and locations, the documents or information required to be retained by this paragraph. In the event of a reportable incident, as defined in §171.15 of this subchapter, make immediately available to an authorized official of a Federal, State, or local government agency (including an emergency responders), the documents or information required to be retained by this paragraph.

(d) The documents required by paragraphs (a) and (b) this section may be combined into one document if it is given to the pilot-in-command before departure of the aircraft.

[Docket No. RSPA–02–11654 (HM-228), 71 FR 14604, March 22, 2006; as amended at 72 FR 25177, May 3, 2007; Docket No. PHMSA–2008–0227 (HM-244A), 73 FR 57006, Oct. 1, 2008; Docket Nos. PHMSA–2007–0065 (HM-224D) and PHMSA–2008–0005 (HM-215J), 74 FR 2267, Jan. 14, 2009]

§175.34 Exceptions for cylinders of compressed oxygen or other oxidizing gases transported within the State of Alaska.

(a) *Exceptions.* When transported in the State of Alaska, cylinders of compressed oxygen or other oxidizing gases aboard aircraft are excepted from all the requirements of §§173.302(f)(3) through (5) and 173.304(f)(3) through (5) of this subchapter subject to the following conditions:

(1) Transportation of the cylinders by a ground-based or water-based mode of transportation is unavailable and transportation by aircraft is the only practical means for transporting the cylinders to their destination;

(2) Each cylinder is fully covered with a fire or flame resistant blanket that is secured in place; and

(3) The operator of the aircraft complies with the applicable notification procedures under §175.33.

(b) *Aircraft restrictions.* This exception only applies to the following types of aircraft:

(1) Cargo-only aircraft transporting the cylinders to a delivery destination that receives cargo-only service at least once a week.

(2) Passenger and cargo-only aircraft transporting the cylinders to a delivery destination that does not receive cargo only service once a week.

[Docket No. PHMSA–2011–0158 (HM-233C), 79 FR 15046, Mar. 18, 2014]

Subpart B—Loading, Unloading and Handling

§175.75 Quantity limitations and cargo location.

(a) No person may carry on an aircraft a hazardous material except as permitted by this subchapter.

(b) Except as otherwise provided in this subchapter, no person may carry a hazardous material in the cabin of a passenger-carrying aircraft or on the flight deck of any aircraft, and the hazardous material must be located in a place that is inaccessible to persons other than crew members. Hazardous materials may be carried in a main deck cargo compartment of a passenger aircraft provided that the compartment is inaccessible to passengers and that it meets all certification requirements for a Class B aircraft cargo compartment in 14 CFR §25.857(b) or for a Class C aircraft cargo compartment in 14 CFR §25.857(c). A package bearing a "KEEP AWAY FROM HEAT" handling marking must be protected from direct sunshine and stored in a cool and ventilated place, away from sources of heat.

(c) For each package containing a hazardous material acceptable for carriage aboard passenger-carrying aircraft, no more than 25 kg (55 pounds) net weight of hazardous material may be loaded in an inaccessible manner. In addition to the 25 kg limitation, an additional 75 kg (165 pounds) net weight of Division 2.2 (non-flammable compressed gas) may be loaded in an inaccessible manner. The requirements of this paragraph do not apply to Class 9, articles of Identification Numbers UN0012, UN0014, or UN0055 also meeting the requirements of §173.63(b), and Limited or Excepted Quantity material.

(d) For the purposes of this section—

(1) *Accessible* means, on passenger-carrying or cargo-only aircraft that each package is loaded where a crew member or other authorized person can access, handle, and, when size and weight permit, separate such packages from other cargo during flight, including a freight container in an accessible cargo compartment when packages are loaded in an accessible manner. Additionally, a package is considered accessible when transported on a cargo-only aircraft if it is:

(i) In a cargo compartment certified by FAA as a Class C aircraft cargo compartment as defined in 14 CFR §25.857(c); or

(ii) In an FAA-certified freight container that has an approved fire or smoke detection system and fire suppression system equivalent to that required by the certification requirements for a Class C aircraft cargo compartment.

(2) *Inaccessible* means all other configurations to include packages loaded where a crew member or other authorized person cannot access, handle, and, when size and weight permit, separate such packages from other cargo during flight, including a freight container in an accessible cargo compartment when packages are loaded in an inaccessible manner.

(e) For transport aboard cargo-only aircraft, the requirements of paragraphs (c) and (d) of this section do not apply to the following hazardous materials:

(1) Class 3, PG III (unless the substance is also labeled CORROSIVE), Class 6.1 (unless the substance is also labeled for any hazard class or division except FLAMMABLE LIQUID), Division 6.2, Class 7 (unless the hazardous material meets the definition of another hazard class), Class 9, articles of Identification Numbers UN0012, UN0014, or UN0055 also meeting the requirements of §173.63(b), and those marked as a Limited Quantity or Excepted Quantity material.

(2) Packages of hazardous materials transported aboard a cargo aircraft, when other means of transportation are impracticable or not available, in accordance with procedures approved in

Part 175: Hazardous Materials §175.78

writing by the FAA Regional or Field Security Office in the region where the operator is located.

(3) Packages of hazardous materials carried on small, single pilot, cargo aircraft if:

(i) No person is carried on the aircraft other than the pilot, an FAA inspector, the shipper or consignee of the material, a representative of the shipper or consignee so designated in writing, or a person necessary for handling the material;

(ii) The pilot is provided with written instructions on the characteristics and proper handling of the materials; and

(iii) Whenever a change of pilots occurs while the material is on board, the new pilot is briefed under a hand-to-hand signature service provided by the operator of the aircraft.

(f) At a minimum, quantity limits and loading instructions in the following quantity and loading table must be followed to maintain acceptable quantity and loading between packages containing hazardous materials. The quantity and loading table is as follows:

QUANTITY AND LOADING TABLE

Applicability	Forbidden	Quantity Limitation: 25 kg net weight of hazardous material plus 75 kg net weight of Division 2.2 (non-flammable compressed gas) per cargo compartment	No limit
Passenger-carrying aircraft	Cargo Aircraft Only labeled packages	Inaccessible	Accessible
Cargo-only aircraft—Packages authorized aboard a passenger-carrying aircraft	Not applicable	Inaccessible (*see* Note 1)	Accessible (*see* Note 2)
Cargo-only aircraft—Packages not authorized aboard a passenger-carrying aircraft and displaying a Cargo Aircraft Only label	Inaccessible (*see* Note 1)	Not applicable	Accessible (*see* Note 2)

Note 1: The following materials are not subject to this loading restriction—
 a. Class 3, PG III (unless the substance is also labeled CORROSIVE).
 b. Division 6.1 (unless the substance is also labeled for any hazard class or division except FLAMMABLE LIQUID).
 c. Class 7 (unless the hazardous material meets the definition of another hazard class).
 d. Class 9, Limited Quantity or Excepted Quantity material.
 e. Articles of Identification Numbers UN0012, UN0014, or UN0055 also meeting the requirements of §173.63(b).

Note 2: Aboard cargo-only aircraft, packages required to be loaded in a position that is considered to be accessible include those loaded in a Class C cargo compartment.

[Docket No. RSPA–02–11654 (HM-228), 71 FR 14604, March 22, 2006; as amended at 71 FR 54395, Sept. 14, 2006; 72 FR 55693, Oct. 1, 2007; Docket Nos. PHMSA–2007–0065 (HM-224D) and PHMSA–2008–0005 (HM-215J), 74 FR 2267, Jan. 14, 2009; Docket No. PHMSA–2009–0126 (HM–215K), 76 FR 3383, Jan. 19, 2011; Docket No. PHMSA–2009–0126 (HM-215K), 76 FR 82178, Dec. 30, 2011; Docket No. PHMSA–2013–0041, 78 FR 65486, Oct. 31, 2013]

§175.78 Stowage compatibility of cargo.

(a) For stowage on an aircraft, in a cargo facility, or in any other area at an airport designated for the stowage of hazardous materials, packages containing hazardous materials which might react dangerously with one another may not be placed next to each other or in a position that would allow a dangerous interaction in the event of leakage.

(b) At a minimum, the segregation instructions prescribed in the following Segregation Table must be followed to maintain acceptable segregation between packages containing hazardous materials with different hazards. The Segregation Table instructions apply whether or not the class or division is the primary or subsidiary risk. The Segregation Table follows:

§175.78

SEGREGATION TABLE

Hazard label	Class or division								
	1	2	3	4.2	4.3	5.1	5.2	8
1	Note 1	Note 2	Note 2	Note 2	Note 2	Note 2	Note 2	Note 2
2	Note 2							
3	Note 2					X		
4.2	Note 2					X		
4.3	Note 2							X
5.1	Note 2			X	X			
5.2	Note 2							
8	Note 2				X			

(c) Instructions for using the Segregation Table are as follows:

(1) Hazard labels, classes or divisions not shown in the table are not subject to segregation requirements.

(2) Dots at the intersection of a row and column indicate that no restrictions apply.

(3) The letter "X" at the intersection of a row and column indicates that packages containing these classes of hazardous materials may not be stowed next to or in contact with each other, or in a position which would allow interaction in the event of leakage of the contents.

(4) Note 1. "Note 1" at the intersection of a row and column means the following:

(i) Only Division 1.4, Compatibility Group S, explosives are permitted to be transported aboard a passenger aircraft. Only certain Division 1.3, Compatibility Groups C and G, and Division 1.4, Compatibility Groups B, C, D, E, G and S, explosives may be transported aboard a cargo aircraft.

(ii) Division 1.4 explosives in Compatibility Group S may be stowed with Division 1.3 and 1.4 explosives in compatibility groups as permitted aboard aircraft under paragraph (c)(4)(i) above.

(iii) Except for Division 1.4B explosives and as otherwise provided in this Note, explosives of different compatibility groups may be stowed together whether or not they belong to the same division. Division 1.4B explosives must not be stowed together with any other explosive permitted aboard aircraft except Division 1.4S, unless segregated as prescribed in paragraph (c)(4)(iv) of this section ("Note 1").

(iv) Division 1.4B and Division 1.3 explosives may not be stowed together. Division 1.4B explosives must be loaded into separate unit load devices and, when stowed aboard the aircraft, the unit load devices must be separated by other cargo with a minimum separation of 2 m (6.5 feet). When not loaded in unit load devices, Division 1.4B and Division 1.3 explosives must be loaded into different, non-adjacent loading positions and separated by other cargo with a minimum separation of 2 m (6.5 feet).

(5) Note 2. "Note 2" at the intersection of a row and column means that other than explosives of Division 1.4, Compatibility Group S, explosives may not be stowed together with that class.

(6) Packages containing hazardous materials with multiple hazards in the class or divisions, which require segregation in accordance with the Segregation Table, need not be segregated from other packages bearing the same UN number.

(7) A package labeled "BLASTING AGENT" may not be stowed next to or in a position that will allow contact with a package of special fireworks or railway torpedoes.

[Docket No. RSPA–02–11654 (HM-228), 71 FR 14604, March 22, 2006; as amended at 71 FR 54395, Sept. 14, 2006; 71 FR 78634, Dec. 29, 2006; Docket No. PHMSA–2009–0126 (HM-215K), 76 FR 3384, Jan. 19, 2011]

§175.88 Inspection, orientation and securing packages of hazardous materials.

(a) A unit load device may not be loaded on an aircraft unless the device has been inspected and found to be free from any evidence of leakage from, or damage to, any package containing hazardous materials.

(b) A package containing hazardous materials marked "THIS SIDE UP" or "THIS END UP", or with arrows to indicate the proper orientation of the package, must be stored and loaded aboard an aircraft in accordance with such markings. A package without orientation markings containing liquid hazardous materials must be stored and loaded with top closure facing upward.

(c) Packages containing hazardous materials must be secured in an aircraft in a manner that will prevent any shifting or any change in the orientation of the packages. Packages containing Class 7 (radioactive) materials must be secured in a manner that ensures that the separation requirements of §§175.701 and 175.702 will be maintained at all times during flight.

[Docket No. RSPA–02–11654 (HM-228), 71 FR 14604, March 22, 2006; as amended by Docket Nos. PHMSA–2007–0065 (HM-224D) and PHMSA–2008–0005 (HM-215J), 74 FR 2268, Jan. 14, 2009]

§175.90 Damaged shipments.

(a) Packages or overpacks containing hazardous materials must be inspected for damage or leakage after being unloaded from an aircraft. When packages or overpacks containing hazardous materials have been transported in a unit load device, the area where the unit load device was stowed must be inspected for evidence of leakage or contamination immediately upon removal of the unit load device from the aircraft, and the packages or overpacks must be inspected for evidence of damage or leakage when the unit load device is unloaded. In the event of leakage or suspected leakage, the compartment in which the package, overpack, or unit load device was carried must be inspected for contamination and decontaminated, if applicable.

(b) Except as provided in §175.700, the operator of an aircraft must remove from the aircraft any package, baggage or cargo that appears to be leaking or contaminated by a hazardous material. In the case of a package, baggage or cargo that appears to be leaking, the operator must ensure that other packages, baggage or cargo in the same shipment are in proper condition for transport aboard the aircraft and that no other package, baggage or cargo has been contaminated or is leaking. If an operator becomes aware that a package, baggage or cargo not identified as containing a hazardous material has been contaminated, or the operator has cause to believe that a hazardous material may be the cause of the contamination, the operator must take reasonable steps to identify the nature and source of contamination before proceeding with the loading of the contaminated baggage or cargo. If the contaminating substance is found or suspected to be hazardous material, the operator must isolate the package, baggage or cargo and take appropriate steps to eliminate any identified hazard before continuing the transportation of the item by aircraft.

(c) No person may place aboard an aircraft a package, baggage or cargo that is contaminated with a hazardous material or appears to be leaking.

(d) If a package containing a material in Division 6.2 (infectious substance) is found to be damaged or leaking, the person finding the package must:

(1) Avoid handling the package or keep handling to a minimum;

(2) Inspect packages adjacent to the leaking package for contamination and withhold from further transportation any contaminated packages until it is ascertained that they can be safely transported;

(3) Comply with the reporting requirement of §§171.15 and 175.31 of this subchapter; and

(4) Notify the consignor or consignee.

Subpart C— Specific Regulations Applicable According to Classification of Material

§175.310 Transportation of flammable liquid fuel; aircraft only means of transportation.

(a) When other means of transportation are impracticable, flammable liquid fuels may be carried on certain passenger and cargo aircraft as provided in this section, without regard to the packaging references and quantity limits listed in Columns 7, 8 and 9 of the §172.101 Hazardous Materials Table. All requirements of this subchapter that are not specifically covered in this section continue to apply to shipments made under the provisions of this section. For purposes of this section "impracticable" means transportation is not physically possible or cannot be performed by routine and frequent means of other transportation, due to extenuating circumstances. Extenuating circumstances include: conditions precluding highway or water transportation, such as a frozen vessel route; road closures due to catastrophic weather or volcanic activity; or a declared state of emergency. The desire for expedience of a shipper, carrier, or consignor, is not relevant in determining whether other means of transportation are impracticable. The stowage requirements of §175.75(a) do not apply to a person operating an aircraft under the provisions of this section which, because of its size and configuration, makes it impossible to comply.

(b) A small passenger-carrying aircraft operated entirely within the State of Alaska or into a remote area, in other than scheduled passenger operations, may carry up to 76 L (20 gallons) of flammable liquid fuel (in Packing Group II or Packing Group III), when:

(1) The flight is necessary to meet the needs of a passenger; and

(2) The fuel is carried in one of the following types of containers:

(i) Strong tight metal containers of not more than 20 L (5.3 gallons) capacity, each packed inside a UN 4G fiberboard box, at the Packing Group II performance level, or each packed inside a UN 4C1 wooden box, at the Packing Group II performance level;

§175.310

(ii) Airtight, leakproof, inside containers of not more than 40 L (11 gallons) capacity and of at least 28-gauge metal, each packed inside a UN 4C1 wooden box, at the Packing Group II performance level;

(iii) UN 1A1 steel drums, at the Packing Group I or II performance level, of not more than 20 L (5.3 gallons) capacity; or

(iv) In fuel tanks attached to flammable liquid fuel powered equipment under the following conditions:

(A) Each piece of equipment is secured in an upright position;

(B) Each fuel tank is filled in a manner that will preclude spillage of fuel during loading, unloading, and transportation; and

(C) Fueling and refueling of the equipment is prohibited in or on the aircraft.

(3) In the case of a passenger-carrying helicopter, the fuel or fueled equipment must be carried on external cargo racks or slings.

(c) Flammable liquid fuels may be carried on a cargo aircraft, subject to the following conditions:

(1)(i) The flammable liquid fuel is in Packing Group II or Packing Group III except as indicated in paragraph (c)(1)(iv) of this section;

(ii) The fuel is carried in packagings authorized in paragraph (b) of this section;

(iii) The fuel is carried in metal drums (UN 1A1, 1B1, 1N1) authorized for Packing Group I or Packing Group II liquid hazardous materials and having rated capacities of 220 L (58 gallons) or less. These single packagings may not be transported in the same aircraft with Class 1, Class 5, or Class 8 materials.

(iv) Combustible and flammable liquid fuels (including those in Packing Group I) may be carried in installed aircraft tanks each having a capacity of more than 450 L (118.9 gallons), subject to the following additional conditions:

(A) The tanks and their associated piping and equipment and the installation thereof must have been approved for the material to be transported by the appropriate FAA Flight Standards District Office.

(B) In the case of an aircraft being operated by a certificate holder, the operator shall list the aircraft and the approval information in its operating specifications. If the aircraft is being operated by other than a certificate holder, a copy of the FAA Flight Standards District Office approval required by this section must be carried on the aircraft.

(C) The crew of the aircraft must be thoroughly briefed on the operation of the particular bulk tank system being used.

(D) During loading and unloading and thereafter until any remaining fumes within the aircraft are dissipated:

(1) Only those electrically operated bulk tank shutoff valves that have been approved under a supplemental type certificate may be electrically operated.

(2) No engine or electrical equipment, avionic equipment, or auxiliary power units may be operated, except position lights in the steady position and equipment required by approved loading or unloading procedures, as set forth in the operator's operations manual, or for operators that are not certificate holders, as set forth in a written statement.

(3) Static ground wires must be connected between the storage tank or fueler and the aircraft, and between the aircraft and a positive ground device.

(2) [Reserved]

(d) The following restrictions apply to loading, handling, or carrying fuel under the provisions of this section:

(1) During loading and unloading, no person may smoke, carry a lighted cigarette, cigar, or pipe, or operate any device capable of causing an open flame or spark within 15 m (50 feet) of the aircraft.

(2) No person may fill a container, other than an approved bulk tank, with a Class 3 material or combustible liquid or discharge a Class 3 material or combustible liquid from a container, other than an approved bulk tank, while that container is inside or within 15 m (50 feet) of the aircraft.

(3) When filling an approved bulk tank by hose from inside the aircraft, the doors and hatches of the aircraft must be fully open to insure proper ventilation.

(4) Each area or compartment in which the fuel is loaded is suitably ventilated to prevent the accumulation of fuel vapors.

(5) Fuel is transferred to the aircraft fuel tanks only while the aircraft is on the ground.

(6) Before each flight, the pilot-in-command:

(i) Prohibits smoking, lighting matches, the carrying of any lighted cigar, pipe, cigarette or flame, and the use of anything that might cause an open flame or spark, while in flight; and

(ii) For passenger aircraft, informs each passenger of the location of the fuel and the hazards involved.

(e) Operators must comply with the following:

(1) If the aircraft is being operated by a holder of a certificate issued under 14 CFR part 121 or part 135, operations must be conducted in accordance with conditions and limitations specified in the certificate holder's operations specifications or operations manual accepted by the FAA. If the aircraft is being operated under 14 CFR part 91, operations must be conducted in accordance with an operations plan accepted and acknowledged in writing by the FAA Principal Operations Inspector assigned to the operator.

(2) The aircraft and the loading arrangement to be used must be approved for the safe carriage

of the particular materials concerned by the FAA Principal Operations Inspector assigned to the operator.

§175.501 Special requirements for oxidizers and compressed oxygen.

(a) Compressed oxygen, when properly labeled Oxidizer or Oxygen, may be loaded and transported as provided in this section. Except for Oxygen, compressed, no person may load or transport a hazardous material for which an OXIDIZER label is required under this subchapter in an inaccessible cargo compartment that does not have a fire or smoke detection system and a fire suppression system.

(b) In addition to the quantity limitations prescribed in §175.75, no more than a combined total of six cylinders of compressed oxygen may be stowed on an aircraft in the inaccessible aircraft cargo compartment(s) that do not have fire or smoke detection systems and fire suppression systems.

(c) When loaded into a passenger-carrying aircraft or in an inaccessible cargo location on a cargo-only aircraft, cylinders of compressed oxygen must be stowed horizontally on the floor or as close as practicable to the floor of the cargo compartment or unit load device. This provision does not apply to cylinders stowed in the cabin of the aircraft in accordance with paragraph (e) of this section.

(d) When transported in a Class B aircraft cargo compartment (see 14 CFR 25.857(b)) or its equivalent (i.e., an accessible cargo compartment equipped with a fire or smoke detection system, but not a fire suppression system), cylinders of compressed oxygen must be loaded in a manner that a crew member can see, handle and, when size and weight permit, separate the cylinders from other cargo during flight. No more than six cylinders of compressed oxygen and, in addition, one cylinder of medical-use compressed oxygen per passenger needing oxygen at destination—with a rated capacity of 1000 L (34 cubic feet) or less of oxygen—may be carried in a Class B aircraft cargo compartment or its equivalent.

(e) A cylinder containing medical-use compressed oxygen, owned or leased by an aircraft operator or offered for transportation by a passenger needing it for personal medical use at destination, may be carried in the cabin of a passenger-carrying aircraft in accordance with the following provisions:

(1) No more than six cylinders belonging to the aircraft operator and, in addition, no more than one cylinder per passenger needing the oxygen at destination, may be transported in the cabin of the aircraft under the provisions of this paragraph (e);

(2) The rated capacity of each cylinder may not exceed 1,000 L (34 cubic feet);

(3) Each cylinder must conform to the provisions of this subchapter and be placed in:

(i) An outer packaging that conforms to the performance criteria of Air Transport Association (ATA) Specification 300 for a Category I Shipping Container; or

(ii) A metal, plastic or wood outer packaging that conforms to a UN standard at the Packing Group I or II performance level.

(4) The aircraft operator shall securely stow the cylinder in its overpack or outer packaging in the cabin of the aircraft and shall notify the pilot-in-command as specified in §175.33 of this part; and

(5) Shipments under this paragraph (e) are not subject to—

(i) Sections 173.302(f) and 173.304(f) of this subchapter, subpart C of part 172 of this subchapter, and, for passengers only, subpart H of part 172 of this subchapter;

(ii) Section 173.25(a)(4) of this subchapter; and

(iii) Paragraph (b) of this section.

[Docket No. RSPA-02-11654 (HM-228), 71 FR 14604, March 22, 2006; as amended at 72 FR 4456, Jan. 31 2007; 72 FR 55099, Sept. 28, 2007]

§175.630 Special requirements for Division 6.1 (poisonous) material and Division 6.2 (infectious substances) materials.

(a) A package required to bear a POISON, POISON INHALATION HAZARD, or INFECTIOUS SUBSTANCE label may not be carried in the same compartment of an aircraft with material which is marked as or known to be a foodstuff, feed, or any other edible material intended for consumption by humans or animals unless:

(1) The Division 6.1 or Division 6.2 material and the foodstuff, feed, or other edible material are loaded in separate unit load devices which, when stowed on the aircraft, are not adjacent to each other; or

(2) The Division 6.1 or Division 6.2 material are loaded in one closed unit load device and the foodstuff, feed or other material is loaded in another closed unit load device.

(b) No person may operate an aircraft that has been used to transport any package required to bear a POISON or POISON INHALATION HAZARD label unless, upon removal of such package, the area in the aircraft in which it was carried is visually inspected for evidence of leakage, spillage, or other contamination. All contamination discovered must be either isolated or removed from the aircraft. The operation of an aircraft contaminated with such Division 6.1 materials is considered to be the carriage of poisonous materials under paragraph (a) of this section.

§175.700

(c) When unloaded from the aircraft, each package, overpack, pallet, or unit load device containing a Division 6.2 material must be inspected for signs of leakage. If evidence of leakage is found, the cargo compartment in which the package, overpack, or unit load device was transported must be disinfected. Disinfection may be by any means that will make the material released ineffective at transmitting disease.

[Docket No. RSPA–02–11654 (HM-228), 71 FR 14604, March 22, 2006; as amended at 71 FR 32263, June 2, 2006]

§175.700 Special limitations and requirements for Class 7 materials.

(a) Except as provided in §§173.4a, 173.422 and 173.423 of this subchapter, no person may carry any Class 7 materials aboard a passenger-carrying aircraft unless that material is intended for use in, or incident to research (See §171.8 of this subchapter), medical diagnosis or treatment. Regardless of its intended use, no person may carry a Type B(M) package aboard a passenger-carrying aircraft, a vented Type B(M) package aboard any aircraft, or a liquid pyrophoric Class 7 material aboard any aircraft.

(b) Limits for transport index and criticality safety index. A person may carry the following Class 7 (radioactive) materials aboard an aircraft only when—

(1) On a passenger-carrying aircraft—
 (i) Each single package on the aircraft has a transport index no greater than 3.0;
 (ii) The combined transport index and the combined criticality index of all the packages on the aircraft are each no greater than 50.

(2) On a cargo aircraft—
 (i) Each single package on the aircraft has a transport index no greater than 10.0.
 (ii) The combined transport index of all the packages on the aircraft is no greater than 200, and the combined criticality index of all the packages on the aircraft is no greater than—
  (A) 50 on a non-exclusive use cargo aircraft, or
  (B) 100 on an aircraft assigned for the exclusive use of the shipper [offeror] for the specific shipment of fissile Class 7 material. Instructions for the exclusive use must be developed by the shipper [offeror] and carrier, and the instructions must accompany the shipping papers.

(3) The combined transport index and combined criticality index are determined by adding together the transport index and criticality index numbers, respectively, shown on the labels of the individual packages.

(c) No person may carry in a passenger-carrying aircraft any package required to be labeled RADIOACTIVE YELLOW–II or RADIOACTIVE YELLOW–III label unless the package is carried on the floor of the cargo compartment or freight container.

[Docket No. RSPA–02–11654 (HM-228), 71 FR 14604, March 22, 2006; as amended by Docket Nos. PHMSA–2007–0065 (HM-224D) and PHMSA–2008–0005 (HM-215J), 74 FR 2268, Jan. 14, 2009]

§175.701 Separation distance requirements for packages containing Class 7 (radioactive) materials in passenger-carrying aircraft.

(a) The following table prescribes the minimum separation distances that must be maintained in a passenger-carrying aircraft between Class 7 (radioactive) materials labeled RADIOACTIVE YELLOW–II or RADIOACTIVE YELLOW–III and passengers and crew:

Transport index or sum of transport indexes of all packages in the aircraft or predesignated area	Minimum separation distances	
	Centimeters	Inches
0.1 to 1.0	30	12
1.1 to 2.0	50	20
2.1 to 3.0	70	28
3.1 to 4.0	85	34
4.1 to 5.0	100	40
5.1 to 6.0	115	46
6.1 to 7.0	130	52
7.1 to 8.0	145	57
8.1 to 9.0	155	61
9.1 to 10.0	165	65
10.1 to 11.0	175	69
11.1 to 12.0	185	73
12.1 to 13.0	195	77
13.1 to 14.0	205	81
14.1 to 15.0	215	85
15.1 to 16.0	225	89
16.1 to 17.0	235	93
17.1 to 18.0	245	97
18.1 to 20.0	260	102
20.1 to 25.0	290	114
25.1 to 30.0	320	126
30.1 to 35.0	350	138
35.1 to 40.0	375	148
40.1 to 45.0	400	157
45.1 to 50.0	425	167

(b) When transported aboard passenger-carrying aircraft packages, overpacks or freight containers labeled Radioactive Yellow–II or Radioactive Yellow–III must be separated from live animals by a distance of at least 0.5 m (20 inches) for journeys not exceeding 24 hours, and by a distance of at least 1.0 m (39 inches) for journeys longer than 24 hours.

(c) Except as provided in paragraph (d) of this section, the minimum separation distances prescribed in paragraphs (a) and (b) of this section are determined by measuring the shortest distance between the surfaces of the Class 7 (radioactive) materials package and the surfaces bounding the space occupied by passengers or animals. If more than one package of Class 7 (radioactive) materials is placed in a passenger-carrying aircraft, the minimum separation distance for these packages shall be determined in accordance with paragraphs (a) and (b) of this section on the basis of the sum of the transport index numbers of the individual packages or overpacks.

(d) Predesignated areas. A package labeled RADIOACTIVE YELLOW–II or RADIOACTIVE YELLOW–III may be carried in a passenger-carrying aircraft in accordance with a system of predesignated areas established by the aircraft operator. Each aircraft operator that elects to use a system of predesignated areas shall submit a detailed description of the proposed system to the Associate Administrator for approval prior to implementation of the system. A proposed system of predesignated areas is approved if the Associate Administrator determines that it is designed to assure that:

(1) The packages can be placed in each predesignated area in accordance with the minimum separation distances prescribed in paragraph (a) of this section; and

(2) The predesignated areas are separated from each other by minimum distance equal to at least four times the distances required by paragraphs (a) and (b) of this section for the predesignated area containing packages with the largest sum of transport indexes.

§175.702 Separation distance requirements for packages containing Class 7 (radioactive) materials in cargo aircraft.

(a) No person may carry in a cargo aircraft any package required by §172.403 of this subchapter to be labeled Radioactive Yellow–II or Radioactive Yellow–III unless:

(1) The total transport index for all packages does not exceed 50.0 and the packages are carried in accordance with §175.701(a); or

(2) The total transport index for all packages exceeds 50.0; and

(i) The separation distance between the surfaces of the radioactive materials packages, overpacks or freight containers and any space occupied by live animals is at least 0.5 m (20 inches) for journeys not exceeding 24 hours and at least 1.0 m (39 inches) for journeys longer than 24 hours; and

(ii) The minimum separation distances between the radioactive material and any areas occupied by persons that are specified in the following table are maintained:

Transport index or sum of transport indexes of all packages in the aircraft or predesignated area	Minimum separation distances	
	Centimeters	Inches
50.1 to 60.0	465	183
60.1 to 70.0	505	199
70.1 to 80.0	545	215
80.1 to 90.0	580	228
90.1 to 100.0	610	240
100.1 to 110.0	645	254
110.1 to 120.0	670	264
120.1 to 130.0	700	276
130.1 to 140.0	730	287
140.1 to 150.0	755	297
150.1 to 160.0	780	307
160.1 to 170.0	805	317
170.1 to 180.0	830	327
180.1 to 190.0	855	337
190.1 to 200.0	875	344

(b) The criticality safety index of any single group of packages must not exceed 50.0 (as used in this section, the term "group of packages" means packages that are separated from each other in an aircraft by a distance of 6 m (20 feet) or less); and

(c) Each group of packages must be separated from every other group in the aircraft by not less than 6 m (20 feet), measured from the outer surface of each group.

[Docket No. RSPA–02–11654 (HM–228), 71 FR 14604, March 22, 2006; as amended at 71 FR 54395, Sept. 14, 2006; 77 FR 60943, Oct. 5, 2012]

§175.703 Other special requirements for the acceptance and carriage of packages containing Class 7 materials.

(a) No person may accept for carriage in an aircraft packages of Class 7 materials, other than limited quantities, contained in a rigid or non-rigid overpack, including a fiberboard box or plastic bag, unless they have been prepared for shipment in accordance with §172.403(h) of this subchapter.

(b) Each shipment of fissile material packages must conform to the requirements of §§173.457 and 173.459 of this subchapter.

§175.704

(c) No person shall offer or accept for transportation, or transport, by air—

(1) Vented Type B(M) packages, packages which require external cooling by an ancillary cooling system or packages subject to operational controls during transport; or

(2) Liquid pyrophoric Class 7 (radioactive) materials.

(d) Packages with radiation levels at the package surface or a transport index in excess of the limits specified in §173.441(a) of this subchapter may not be transported by aircraft except under special arrangements approved by the Associate Administrator.

§175.704 Plutonium shipments.

Shipments of plutonium which are subject to 10 CFR 71.88(a)(4) must comply with the following:

(a) Each package containing plutonium must be secured and restrained to prevent shifting under normal conditions.

(b) A package of plutonium having a gross mass less than 40 kg (88 pounds) and both its height and diameter less than 50 cm (19.5 inches)—

(1) May not be transported aboard an aircraft carrying other cargo required to bear a Division 1.1 label; and

(2) Must be stowed aboard the aircraft on the main deck or the lower cargo compartment in the aft-most location that is possible for cargo of its size and weight, and no other cargo may be stowed aft of packages containing plutonium.

(c) A package of plutonium exceeding the size and weight limitations in paragraph (b) of this section—

(1) May not be transported aboard an aircraft carrying other cargo required to bear any of the following labels: Class 1 (all Divisions), Class 2 (all Divisions), Class 3, Class 4 (all Divisions), Class 5 (all Divisions), or Class 8; and

(2) Must be securely cradled and tied down to the main deck of the aircraft in a manner that restrains the package against the following internal forces acting separately relative to the deck of the aircraft; Upward, 2g; Forward, 9g; Sideward, 1.5g; Downward, 4.5g.

§175.705 Radioactive contamination.

(a) A carrier shall take care to avoid possible inhalation, ingestion, or contact by any person with Class 7 (radioactive) materials that may have been released from their packagings.

(b) When contamination is present or suspected, the package containing a Class 7 material, any loose Class 7 material, associated packaging material, and any other materials that have been contaminated must be segregated as far as practicable from personnel contact until radiological advice or assistance is obtained from the U.S. Department of Energy or appropriate State or local radiological authorities.

(c) An aircraft in which Class 7 material has been released must be taken out of service and may not be returned to service or routinely occupied until the aircraft is checked for radioactive contamination and it is determined in accordance with §173.443 of this subchapter that the dose rate at every accessible surface is less than 0.005 mSv per hour (0.5 mrem per hour) and there is no significant removable surface contamination.

(d) Each aircraft used routinely for transporting Class 7 materials shall be periodically checked for radioactive contamination, and an aircraft must be taken out of service if contamination exceeds the level specified in paragraph (c). The frequency of these checks shall be related to the likelihood of contamination and the extent to which Class 7 materials are transported.

(e) In addition to the reporting requirements of §§171.15 and 171.16 of this subchapter and §175.31 of this part, an aircraft operator shall notify the offeror at the earliest practicable moment following any incident in which there has been breakage, spillage, or suspected radioactive contamination involving Class 7 (radioactive) materials shipments.

§175.706 Separation distances for undeveloped film from packages containing Class 7 (radioactive) materials.

No person may carry in an aircraft any package of Class 7 (radioactive) materials required by §172.403 of this subchapter to be labeled Radioactive Yellow–II or Radioactive Yellow–III closer than the distances shown in the table below to any package marked as containing underdeveloped film.

Part 175: Hazardous Materials §175.900

| Transport index | Minimum separation distance to nearest undeveloped film for various times in transit ||||||||||
| | Up to 2 hours || 2 to 4 hours || 4 to 8 hours || 8 to 12 hours || Over 12 hours ||
	Meters	Feet	Meters	Feet	Meters	Feet	Meters	Feet	Meters	Feet
0.1 to 1.0	0.3	1	0.6	2	0.9	3	1.2	4	1.5	5
1.1 to 5.0	0.9	3	1.2	4	1.8	6	2.4	8	3.3	11
5.1 to 10.0	1.2	4	1.8	6	2.7	9	3.3	11	4.5	15
10.1 to 20.0	1.5	5	2.4	8	3.6	12	4.8	16	6.6	22
20.1 to 30.0	2.1	7	3	10	4.5	15	6	20	8.7	29
30.1 to 40.0	2.4	8	3.3	11	5.1	17	6.6	22	9.9	33
40.1 to 50.0	2.7	9	3.6	12	5.7	19	7.2	24	10.8	36

§175.900 Handling requirements for carbon dioxide, solid (dry ice).

Carbon dioxide, solid (dry ice) when shipped by itself or when used as a refrigerant for other commodities, may be carried only if the operator has made suitable arrangements based on the aircraft type, the aircraft ventilation rates, the method of packing and stowing, whether animals will be carried on the same flight and other factors. The operator must ensure that the ground staff is informed that the dry ice is being loaded or is on board the aircraft. For arrangements between the shipper and operator, see §173.217 of this subchapter. Where dry ice is contained in a unit load device (ULD) or other type of pallet prepared by a single shipper in accordance with §173.217 and the operator after the acceptance adds additional dry ice, the operator must ensure that the information provided to the Pilot-in-Command and the marking on the ULD when used as a packaging reflects that revised quantity of dry ice.

[Docket No. PHMSA-05-21812 (HM-218D), 73 FR 4719, Jan. 28, 2008]

49 CFR • Subchapter C—Civil Aviation Security

49 CFR Part 1544
AIRCRAFT OPERATOR SECURITY: AIR CARRIERS AND COMMERCIAL OPERATORS

Subpart A—General
Sec.
1544.1 Applicability of this part.
1544.3 TSA inspection authority.

Subpart B—Security Program
1544.101 Adoption and implementation.
1544.103 Form, content, and availability.
1544.105 Approval and amendments.

Subpart C—Operations
1544.201 Acceptance and screening of individuals and accessible property.
1544.202 Persons and property onboard an all-cargo aircraft.
1544.203 Acceptance and screening of checked baggage.
1544.205 Acceptance and screening of cargo.
1544.207 Screening of individuals and property.
1544.209 Use of metal detection devices.
1544.211 Use of X-ray systems.
1544.213 Use of explosives detection systems.
1544.215 Security coordinators.
1544.217 Law enforcement personnel.
1544.219 Carriage of accessible weapons.
1544.221 Carriage of prisoners under the control of armed law enforcement officers.
1544.223 Transportation of Federal Air Marshals.
1544.225 Security of aircraft and facilities.
1544.227 Exclusive area agreement.
1544.228 Access to cargo and cargo screening: Security threat assessments for cargo personnel in the United States.
1544.229 Fingerprint-based criminal history records checks (CHRC): Unescorted access authority, authority to perform screening functions, and authority to perform checked baggage or cargo functions.
1544.230 Fingerprint-based criminal history records checks (CHRC): Flightcrew members.
1544.231 Airport-approved and exclusive area personnel identification systems.
1544.233 Security coordinators and crewmembers, training.
1544.235 Training and knowledge for individuals with security-related duties.
1544.237 Flight deck privileges.
1544.239 Known shipper program.

Subpart D—Threat and Threat Response
1544.301 Contingency plan.
1544.303 Bomb or air piracy threats.
1544.305 Security Directives and Information Circulars.

Subpart E—Screener Qualifications When the Aircraft Operator Performs Screening
1544.401 Applicability of this subpart.
1544.403 [Reserved]
1544.405 Qualifications of screening personnel.
1544.407 Training, testing, and knowledge of individuals who perform screening functions.
1544.409 Integrity of screener tests.
1544.411 Continuing qualifications of screening personnel.

Authority: 49 U.S.C. 114, 5103, 40113, 44901–44905, 44907, 44913–44914, 44916–44918, 44932, 44935–44936, 44942, 46105.

Source: 67 FR 8364, Feb. 22, 2002, unless otherwise noted.

Subpart A—General

§1544.1 Applicability of this part.

(a) This part prescribes aviation security rules governing the following:

(1) The operations of aircraft operators holding operating certificates under 14 CFR part 119 for scheduled passenger operations, public charter passenger operations, private charter passenger operations; the operations of aircraft operators holding operating certificates under 14 CFR part 119 operating aircraft with a maximum certificated takeoff weight of 12,500 pounds or more; and other aircraft operators adopting and obtaining approval of an aircraft operator security program.

(2) Each law enforcement officer flying armed aboard an aircraft operated by an aircraft operator described in paragraph (a)(1) of this section.

(3) Each aircraft operator that receives a Security Directive or Information Circular and each person who receives information from a Security Directive or Information Circular issued by TSA.

(b) As used in this part, "aircraft operator" means an aircraft operator subject to this part as described in §1544.101.

[67 FR 8364, Feb. 22, 2002, as amended at 67 FR 8209, Feb. 22, 2002]

§1544.3 TSA inspection authority.

(a) Each aircraft operator must allow TSA, at any time or place, to make any inspections or tests, including copying records, to determine compliance of an airport operator, aircraft operator, foreign air carrier, indirect air carrier, or other airport tenants with—

(1) This subchapter and any security program under this subchapter, and part 1520 of this chapter; and

(2) 49 U.S.C. Subtitle VII, as amended.

(b) At the request of TSA, each aircraft operator must provide evidence of compliance with this part and its security program, including copies of records.

(c) TSA may enter and be present within secured areas, AOAs, SIDAs, and other areas where security measures required by TSA are carried out, without access media or identification media issued or approved by an airport operator or aircraft operator, in order to inspect or test compliance, or perform other such duties as TSA may direct.

(d) At the request of TSA and the completion of SIDA training as required in a security program, each aircraft operator must promptly issue to TSA personnel access and identification media to provide TSA personnel with unescorted access to, and movement within, areas controlled by the aircraft operator under an exclusive area agreement.

[67 FR 8364, Feb. 22, 2002, as amended at 71 FR 30510, May 26, 2006]

Subpart B— Security Program

§1544.101 Adoption and implementation.

(a) *Full program.* Each aircraft operator must carry out subparts C, D, and E of this part and must adopt and carry out a security program that meets the requirements of §1544.103 for each of the following operations:

(1) A scheduled passenger or public charter passenger operation with an aircraft having a passenger seating configuration of 61 or more seats.

(2) A scheduled passenger or public charter passenger operation with an aircraft having a passenger seating configuration of 60 or fewer seats when passengers are enplaned from or deplaned into a sterile area.

(b) *Partial program—adoption.* Each aircraft operator must carry out the requirements specified in paragraph (c) of this section for each of the following operations:

(1) A scheduled passenger or public charter passenger operation with an aircraft having a passenger-seating configuration of 31 or more but 60 or fewer seats that does not enplane from or deplane into a sterile area.

(2) A scheduled passenger or public charter passenger operation with an aircraft having a passenger-seating configuration of 60 or fewer seats engaged in operations to, from, or outside the United States that does not enplane from or deplane into a sterile area.

(c) *Partial program-content:* For operations described in paragraph (b) of this section, the aircraft operator must carry out the following, and must adopt and carry out a security program that meets the applicable requirements in §1544.103(c):

(1) The requirements of §§1544.215, 1544.217, 1544.219, 1544.223, 1544.230, 1544.235, 1544.237, 1544.301, 1544.303, and 1544.305.

(2) Other provisions of subparts C, D, and E of this part that TSA has approved upon request.

(3) The remaining requirements of subparts C, D, and E when TSA notifies the aircraft operator in writing that a security threat exists concerning that operation.

(d) *Twelve-five program-adoption:* Each aircraft operator must carry out the requirements of

paragraph (e) of this section for each operation that meets all of the following—
(1) Is an aircraft with a maximum certificated takeoff weight of more than 12,500 pounds;
(2) Is in scheduled or charter service;
(3) Is carrying passengers or cargo or both; and
(4) Is not under a full program, partial program, or full all-cargo program under paragraph (a), (b), or (h) of this section.

(e) *Twelve-five program-contents:* For each operation described in paragraph (d) of this section, the aircraft operator must carry out the following, and must adopt and carry out a security program that meets the applicable requirements of §1544.103(c):
(1) The requirements of §§1544.215, 1544.217, 1544.219, 1544.223, 1544.230, 1544.235, 1544.237, 1544.301(a) and (b), 1544.303, and 1544.305; and in addition, for all-cargo operations of §§1544.202, 1544.205(a), (b), (d), and (f).
(2) Other provisions of subparts C, D, and E that TSA has approved upon request.
(3) The remaining requirements of subparts C, D, and E when TSA notifies the aircraft operator in writing that a security threat exists concerning that operation.

(f) *Private charter program.* In addition to paragraph (d) of this section, if applicable, each aircraft operator must carry out §§1544.201, 1544.207, 1544.209, 1544.211, 1544.215, 1544.217, 1544.219, 1544.225, 1544.229, 1544.230, 1544.233, 1544.235, 1544.303, 1544.305, and subpart E of this part and—
(1) Must adopt and carry out a security program that meets the applicable requirements of §1544.103 for each private charter passenger operation in which—
(i) The passengers are enplaned from or deplaned into a sterile area; or
(ii) The aircraft has a maximum certificated takeoff weight greater than 45,500 kg (100,309.3 pounds), or a passenger-seating configuration of 61 or more, and is not a government charter under paragraph (2) of the definition of private charter in §1540.5 of this chapter.
(2) The Administrator may authorize alternate procedures under paragraph (f)(1) of this section as appropriate.

(g) Limited program: In addition to paragraph (d) of this section, if applicable, TSA may approve a security program after receiving a request by an aircraft operator holding a certificate under 14 CFR part 119, other than one identified in paragraph (a), (b), (d), or (f) of this section. The aircraft operator must—
(1) Carry out selected provisions of subparts C, D, and E;
(2) Carry out the provisions of §1544.305, as specified in its security program; and

(3) Adopt and carry out a security program that meets the applicable requirements of §1544.103(c).

(h) *Full all-cargo program—adoption:* Each aircraft operator must carry out the requirements of paragraph (i) of this section for each operation that is—
(1) In an aircraft with a maximum certificated takeoff weight of more than 45,500 kg (100,309.3 pounds); and
(2) Carrying cargo and authorized persons and no passengers.

(i) *Full all-cargo program—contents:* For each operation described in paragraph (h) of this section, the aircraft operator must carry out the following, and must adopt and carry out a security program that meets the applicable requirements of §1544.103(c):
(1) The requirements of §§1544.202, 1544.205, 1544.207, 1544.209, 1544.211, 1544.215, 1544.217, 1544.219, 1544.225, 1544.227, 1544.228, 1544.229, 1544.230, 1544.231, 1544.233, 1544.235, 1544.237, 1544.301, 1544.303, and 1544.305.
(2) Other provisions of subpart C of this part that TSA has approved upon request.
(3) The remaining requirements of subpart C of this part when TSA notifies the aircraft operator in writing that a security threat exists concerning that operation.

[67 FR 8364, Feb. 22, 2002, as amended at 67 FR 8209, Feb. 22, 2002; 67 FR 41639, June 19, 2002; 67 FR 79887, Dec. 31, 2002; 71 FR 30510, May 26, 2006]

§1544.103 Form, content, and availability.

(a) *General requirements.* Each security program must:
(1) Provide for the safety of persons and property traveling on flights provided by the aircraft operator against acts of criminal violence and air piracy, and the introduction of explosives, incendiaries, or weapons aboard an aircraft.
(2) Be in writing and signed by the aircraft operator or any person delegated authority in this matter.
(3) Be approved by TSA.

(b) *Availability.* Each aircraft operator having a security program must:
(1) Maintain an original copy of the security program at its corporate office.
(2) Have accessible a complete copy, or the pertinent portions of its security program, or appropriate implementing instructions, at each airport served. An electronic version of the program is adequate.
(3) Make a copy of the security program available for inspection upon request of TSA.

§1544.103

(4) Restrict the distribution, disclosure, and availability of information contained in the security program to persons with a need-to-know as described in part 1520 of this chapter.

(5) Refer requests for such information by other persons to TSA.

(c) *Content.* The security program must include, as specified for that aircraft operator in §1544.101, the following:

(1) The procedures and description of the facilities and equipment used to comply with the requirements of §1544.201 regarding the acceptance and screening of individuals and their accessible property, including, if applicable, the carriage weapons as part of State-required emergency equipment.

(2) The procedures and description of the facilities and equipment used to comply with the requirements of §1544.203 regarding the acceptance and screening of checked baggage.

(3) The procedures and description of the facilities and equipment used to comply with the requirements of §1544.205 regarding the acceptance and screening of cargo.

(4) The procedures and description of the facilities and equipment used to comply with the requirements of §1544.207 regarding the screening of individuals and property.

(5) The procedures and description of the facilities and equipment used to comply with the requirements of §1544.209 regarding the use of metal detection devices.

(6) The procedures and description of the facilities and equipment used to comply with the requirements of §1544.211 regarding the use of x-ray systems.

(7) The procedures and description of the facilities and equipment used to comply with the requirements of §1544.213 regarding the use of explosives detection systems.

(8) The procedures used to comply with the requirements of §1544.215 regarding the responsibilities of security coordinators. The names of the Aircraft Operator Security Coordinator (AOSC) and any alternate, and the means for contacting the AOSC(s) on a 24-hour basis, as provided in §1544.215.

(9) The procedures used to comply with the requirements of §1544.217 regarding the requirements for law enforcement personnel.

(10) The procedures used to comply with the requirements of §1544.219 regarding carriage of accessible weapons.

(11) The procedures used to comply with the requirements of §1544.221 regarding carriage of prisoners under the control of armed law enforcement officers.

(12) The procedures used to comply with the requirements of §1544.223 regarding transportation of Federal Air Marshals.

(13) The procedures and description of the facilities and equipment used to perform the aircraft and facilities control function specified in §1544.225.

(14) The specific locations where the air carrier has entered into an exclusive area agreement under §1544.227.

(15) The procedures used to comply with the applicable requirements of §§1544.229 and 1544.230 regarding fingerprint-based criminal history records checks.

(16) The procedures used to comply with the requirements of §1544.231 regarding personnel identification systems.

(17) The procedures and syllabi used to accomplish the training required under §1544.233.

(18) The procedures and syllabi used to accomplish the training required under §1544.235.

(19) An aviation security contingency plan as specified under §1544.301.

(20) The procedures used to comply with the requirements of §1544.303 regarding bomb and air piracy threats.

(21) The procedures used to comply with §1544.237 regarding flight deck privileges.

(22) The Aircraft Operator Implementation Plan (AOIP) as required under 49 CFR 1560.109.

[67 FR 8364, Feb. 22, 2002, as amended at 67 FR 8209, Feb. 22, 2002; 73 FR 64061, Oct. 28, 2008]

§1544.105 Approval and amendments.

(a) *Initial approval of security program.* Unless otherwise authorized by TSA, each aircraft operator required to have a security program under this part must submit its proposed security program to the designated official for approval at least 90 days before the intended date of operations. The proposed security program must meet the requirements applicable to its operation as described in §1544.101. Such requests will be processed as follows:

(1) The designated official, within 30 days after receiving the proposed aircraft operator security program, will either approve the program or give the aircraft operator written notice to modify the program to comply with the applicable requirements of this part.

(2) The aircraft operator may either submit a modified security program to the designated official for approval, or petition the Administrator to reconsider the notice to modify within 30 days of receiving a notice to modify. A petition for reconsideration must be filed with the designated official.

(3) The designated official, upon receipt of a petition for reconsideration, either amends or withdraws the notice, or transmits the petition, together with any pertinent information, to the Administrator for reconsideration. The Administrator

disposes of the petition within 30 days of receipt by either directing the designated official to withdraw or amend the notice to modify, or by affirming the notice to modify.

(b) *Amendment requested by an aircraft operator.* An aircraft operator may submit a request to TSA to amend its security program as follows:

(1) The request for an amendment must be filed with the designated official at least 45 days before the date it proposes for the amendment to become effective, unless a shorter period is allowed by the designated official.

(2) Within 30 days after receiving a proposed amendment, the designated official, in writing, either approves or denies the request to amend.

(3) An amendment to an aircraft operator security program may be approved if the designated official determines that safety and the public interest will allow it, and the proposed amendment provides the level of security required under this part.

(4) Within 30 days after receiving a denial, the aircraft operator may petition the Administrator to reconsider the denial. A petition for reconsideration must be filed with the designated official.

(5) Upon receipt of a petition for reconsideration, the designated official either approves the request to amend or transmits the petition, together with any pertinent information, to the Administrator for reconsideration. The Administrator disposes of the petition within 30 days of receipt by either directing the designated official to approve the amendment, or affirming the denial.

(6) Any aircraft operator may submit a group proposal for an amendment that is on behalf of it and other aircraft operators that co-sign the proposal.

(c) *Amendment by TSA.* If safety and the public interest require an amendment, TSA may amend a security program as follows:

(1) The designated official notifies the aircraft operator, in writing, of the proposed amendment, fixing a period of not less than 30 days within which the aircraft operator may submit written information, views, and arguments on the amendment.

(2) After considering all relevant material, the designated official notifies the aircraft operator of any amendment adopted or rescinds the notice. If the amendment is adopted, it becomes effective not less than 30 days after the aircraft operator receives the notice of amendment, unless the aircraft operator petitions the Administrator to reconsider no later than 15 days before the effective date of the amendment. The aircraft operator must send the petition for reconsideration to the designated official. A timely petition for reconsideration stays the effective date of the amendment.

(3) Upon receipt of a petition for reconsideration, the designated official either amends or withdraws the notice or transmits the petition, together with any pertinent information, to the Administrator for reconsideration. The Administrator disposes of the petition within 30 days of receipt by either directing the designated official to withdraw or amend the amendment, or by affirming the amendment.

(d) *Emergency amendments.* If the designated official finds that there is an emergency requiring immediate action with respect to safety in air transportation or in air commerce that makes procedures in this section contrary to the public interest, the designated official may issue an amendment, without the prior notice and comment procedures in paragraph (c) of this section, effective without stay on the date the aircraft operator receives notice of it. In such a case, the designated official will incorporate in the notice a brief statement of the reasons and findings for the amendment to be adopted. The aircraft operator may file a petition for reconsideration under paragraph (c) of this section; however, this does not stay the effective date of the emergency amendment.

[67 FR 8364, Feb. 22, 2002, as amended by Amdt. 1544–10, 76 FR 51867, Aug. 18, 2011]

Subpart C—Operations

§1544.201 Acceptance and screening of individuals and accessible property.

(a) *Preventing or deterring the carriage of any explosive, incendiary, or deadly or dangerous weapon.* Each aircraft operator must use the measures in its security program to prevent or deter the carriage of any weapon, explosive, or incendiary on or about each individual's person or accessible property before boarding an aircraft or entering a sterile area.

(b) *Screening of individuals and accessible property.* Except as provided in its security program, each aircraft operator must ensure that each individual entering a sterile area at each preboard screening checkpoint for which it is responsible, and all accessible property under that individual's control, are inspected for weapons, explosives, and incendiaries as provided in §1544.207.

(c) *Refusal to transport.* Each aircraft operator must deny entry into a sterile area and must refuse to transport—

(1) Any individual who does not consent to a search or inspection of his or her person in accordance with the system prescribed in this part; and

§1544.202

(2) Any property of any individual or other person who does not consent to a search or inspection of that property in accordance with the system prescribed by this part.

(d) *Prohibitions on carrying a weapon, explosive, or incendiary.* Except as provided in §§1544.219, 1544.221, and 1544.223, no aircraft operator may permit any individual to have a weapon, explosive, or incendiary, on or about the individual's person or accessible property when onboard an aircraft.

(e) *Staffing.* Each aircraft operator must staff its security screening checkpoints with supervisory and non-supervisory personnel in accordance with the standards specified in its security program.

§1544.202 Persons and property onboard an all-cargo aircraft.

Each aircraft operator operating under a full all-cargo program, or a twelve-five program in an all-cargo operation, must apply the security measures in its security program for persons who board the aircraft for transportation, and for their property, to prevent or deter the carriage of any unauthorized persons, and any unauthorized weapons, explosives, incendiaries, and other destructive devices, items, or substances.

[71 FR 30510, May 26, 2006]

§1544.203 Acceptance and screening of checked baggage.

(a) *Preventing or deterring the carriage of any explosive or incendiary.* Each aircraft operator must use the procedures, facilities, and equipment described in its security program to prevent or deter the carriage of any unauthorized explosive or incendiary onboard aircraft in checked baggage.

(b) *Acceptance.* Each aircraft operator must ensure that checked baggage carried in the aircraft is received by its authorized aircraft operator representative.

(c) *Screening of checked baggage.* Except as provided in its security program, each aircraft operator must ensure that all checked baggage is inspected for explosives and incendiaries before loading it on its aircraft, in accordance with §1544.207.

(d) *Control.* Each aircraft operator must use the procedures in its security program to control checked baggage that it accepts for transport on an aircraft, in a manner that:

(1) Prevents the unauthorized carriage of any explosive or incendiary aboard the aircraft.

(2) Prevents access by persons other than an aircraft operator employee or its agent.

(e) *Refusal to transport.* Each aircraft operator must refuse to transport any individual's checked baggage or property if the individual does not consent to a search or inspection of that checked baggage or property in accordance with the system prescribed by this part.

(f) *Firearms in checked baggage.* No aircraft operator may knowingly permit any person to transport in checked baggage:

(1) Any loaded firearm(s).

(2) Any unloaded firearm(s) unless—

(i) The passenger declares to the aircraft operator, either orally or in writing before checking the baggage that any firearm carried in the baggage is unloaded;

(ii) The firearm is carried in a hard-sided container;

(iii) The container in which it is carried is locked, and only the individual checking the baggage retains the key or combination; and

(iv) The checked baggage containing the firearm is carried in an area that is inaccessible to passengers, and is not carried in the flightcrew compartment.

(3) Any unauthorized explosive or incendiary.

(g) *Ammunition.* This section does not prohibit the carriage of ammunition in checked baggage or in the same container as a firearm. Title 49 CFR part 175 provides additional requirements governing carriage of ammunition on aircraft.

§1544.205 Acceptance and screening of cargo.

(a) *Preventing or deterring the carriage of any explosive or incendiary.* Each aircraft operator operating under a full program, a full all-cargo program, or a twelve-five program in an all-cargo operation, must use the procedures, facilities, and equipment described in its security program to prevent or deter the carriage of any unauthorized persons, and any unauthorized explosives, incendiaries, and other destructive substances or items in cargo onboard an aircraft.

(b) *Screening and inspection of cargo.* Each aircraft operator operating under a full program or a full all-cargo program, or a twelve-five program in an all-cargo operation, must ensure that cargo is screened and inspected for any unauthorized person, and any unauthorized explosive, incendiary, and other destructive substance or item as provided in the aircraft operator's security program and §1544.207, and as provided in §1544.239 for operations under a full program, before loading it on its aircraft.

(c) *Control.* Each aircraft operator operating under a full program or a full all-cargo program must use the procedures in its security program to control cargo that it accepts for transport on an aircraft in a manner that:

(1) Prevents the carriage of any unauthorized person, and any unauthorized explosive, incen-

diary, and other destructive substance or item in cargo onboard an aircraft.

(2) Prevents unescorted access by persons other than an authorized aircraft operator employee or agent, or persons authorized by the airport operator or host government.

(d) *Refusal to transport.* Except as otherwise provided in its program, each aircraft operator operating under a full program, a full all-cargo program, or a twelve-five program in an all-cargo operation, must refuse to transport any cargo if the shipper does not consent to a search or inspection of that cargo in accordance with the system prescribed by this part.

(e) *Acceptance of cargo only from specified persons.* Each aircraft operator operating under a full program or a full all-cargo program may accept cargo to be loaded in the United States for air transportation only from the shipper, an aircraft operator, foreign air carrier, or indirect air carrier operating under a security program under this chapter with a comparable cargo security program, or, in the case of an operator under a full program, from a certified cargo screening facility, as provided in its security program.

(f) *Acceptance and screening of cargo outside the United States.* For cargo to be loaded on its aircraft outside the United States, each aircraft operator must carry out the requirements of its security program.

(g) *Screening of cargo loaded inside the United States by a full program operator.* For cargo to be loaded in the United States, each operator under a full program in §1544.101(a) must ensure that all cargo is screened in the United States as follows:

(1) *Amount screened.*

(i) Not later than February 3, 2009, each operator under a full program must ensure that at least 50 percent of its cargo is screened prior to transport on a passenger aircraft.

(ii) Not later than August 3, 2010, each operator under a full program must ensure that 100 percent of its cargo is screened prior to transport on a passenger aircraft.

(2) *Methods of screening.* For the purposes of this paragraph (g), the aircraft operator must ensure that cargo is screened using a physical examination or non-intrusive method of assessing whether cargo poses a threat to transportation security, as provided in its security program. Such methods may include TSA-approved x-ray systems, explosives detection systems, explosives trace detection, explosives detection canine teams certified by TSA, or a physical search together with manifest verification, or other method approved by TSA.

(3) *Limitation on who may conduct screening.* Screening must be conducted by the aircraft operator, by another aircraft operator or foreign air carrier operating under a security program under this chapter with a comparable cargo security program, by a certified cargo screening facility in accordance with 49 CFR part 1549, or by TSA.

(4) *Verification.* The aircraft operator must verify that the chain of custody measures for the screened cargo are intact prior to loading such cargo on aircraft, or must ensure that the cargo is re-screened in accordance with this chapter.

[71 FR 30510, May 26, 2006; as amended by Amdt. 1544–9, 74 FR 47703, Sept. 16, 2009; Amdt. 1544–10, 76 FR 51867, Aug. 18, 2011; Amdt. 1544–10, 76 FR 53080, Aug. 25, 2011]

§1544.207 Screening of individuals and property.

(a) *Applicability of this section.* This section applies to the inspection of individuals, accessible property, checked baggage, and cargo as required under this part.

(b) *Locations within the United States at which TSA conducts screening.* Each aircraft operator must ensure that the individuals or property have been inspected by TSA before boarding or loading on its aircraft. This paragraph applies when TSA is conducting screening using TSA employees or when using companies under contract with TSA.

(c) *Aircraft operator conducting screening.* Each aircraft operator must use the measures in its security program and in subpart E of this part to inspect the individual or property. This paragraph does not apply at locations identified in paragraphs (b) and (d) of this section.

(d) *Locations outside the United States at which the foreign government conducts screening.* Each aircraft operator must ensure that all individuals and property have been inspected by the foreign government. This paragraph applies when the host government is conducting screening using government employees or when using companies under contract with the government.

§1544.209 Use of metal detection devices.

(a) No aircraft operator may use a metal detection device within the United States or under the aircraft operator's operational control outside the United States to inspect persons, unless specifically authorized under a security program under this part. No aircraft operator may use such a device contrary to its security program.

(b) Metal detection devices must meet the calibration standards established by TSA.

§1544.211 Use of X-ray systems.

(a) *TSA authorization required.* No aircraft operator may use any X-ray system within the United States or under the aircraft operator's operational control outside the United States to inspect accessible property or checked baggage, unless specifically authorized under its security program. No aircraft operator may use such a system in a manner contrary to its security program. TSA authorizes aircraft operators to use X-ray systems for inspecting accessible property or checked baggage under a security program if the aircraft operator shows that—

(1) The system meets the standards for cabinet X-ray systems primarily for the inspection of baggage issued by the Food and Drug Administration (FDA) and published in 21 CFR 1020.40;

(2) A program for initial and recurrent training of operators of the system is established, which includes training in radiation safety, the efficient use of X-ray systems, and the identification of weapons, explosives, and incendiaries; and

(3) The system meets the imaging requirements set forth in its security program using the step wedge specified in American Society for Testing Materials (ASTM) Standard F792-88 (Reapproved 1993). This standard is incorporated by reference in paragraph (g) of this section.

(b) *Annual radiation survey.* No aircraft operator may use any X-ray system unless, within the preceding 12 calendar months, a radiation survey is conducted that shows that the system meets the applicable performance standards in 21 CFR 1020.40.

(c) *Radiation survey after installation or moving.* No aircraft operator may use any X-ray system after the system has been installed at a screening point or after the system has been moved unless a radiation survey is conducted which shows that the system meets the applicable performance standards in 21 CFR 1020.40. A radiation survey is not required for an X-ray system that is designed and constructed as a mobile unit and the aircraft operator shows that it can be moved without altering its performance.

(d) *Defect notice or modification order.* No aircraft operator may use any X-ray system that is not in full compliance with any defect notice or modification order issued for that system by the FDA, unless the FDA has advised TSA that the defect or failure to comply does not create a significant risk of injury, including genetic injury, to any person.

(e) *Signs and inspection of photographic equipment and film.*

(1) At locations at which an aircraft operator uses an X-ray system to inspect accessible property the aircraft operator must ensure that a sign is posted in a conspicuous place at the screening checkpoint. At locations outside the United States at which a foreign government uses an X-ray system to inspect accessible property the aircraft operator must ensure that a sign is posted in a conspicuous place at the screening checkpoint.

(2) At locations at which an aircraft operator or TSA uses an X-ray system to inspect checked baggage the aircraft operator must ensure that a sign is posted in a conspicuous place where the aircraft operator accepts checked baggage.

(3) The signs required under this paragraph (e) must notify individuals that such items are being inspected by an X-ray and advise them to remove all X-ray, scientific, and high-speed film from accessible property and checked baggage before inspection. This sign must also advise individuals that they may request that an inspection be made of their photographic equipment and film packages without exposure to an X-ray system. If the X-ray system exposes any accessible property or checked baggage to more than one milliroentgen during the inspection, the sign must advise individuals to remove film of all kinds from their articles before inspection.

(4) If requested by individuals, their photographic equipment and film packages must be inspected without exposure to an X-ray system.

(f) *Radiation survey verification after installation or moving.* Each aircraft operator must maintain at least one copy of the results of the most recent radiation survey conducted under paragraph (b) or (c) of this section and must make it available for inspection upon request by TSA at each of the following locations—

(1) The aircraft operator's principal business office; and

(2) The place where the X-ray system is in operation.

(g) *Incorporation by reference.* The American Society for Testing and Materials (ASTM) Standard F792-88 (Reapproved 1993), "Standard Practice for Design and Use of Ionizing Radiation Equipment for the Detection of Items Prohibited in Controlled Access Areas," is approved for incorporation by reference by the Director of the Federal Register pursuant to 5 U.S.C. 552(a) and I CFR part 51. ASTM Standard F792-88 may be examined at the Department of Transportation (DOT) Docket, 400 Seventh Street SW, Room Plaza 401, Washington, DC 20590, or on DOT's Docket Management System (DMS) web page at http://dms.dot.gov/search (under docket number FAA-2001-8725). Copies of the standard may be examined also at the National Archives and Records Administration (NARA). For information on the availability of this material at NARA, call 202-741-6030, or go to:

http://www.archives.gov/federal_register/code_of_federal_regulations/ibr_locations.html

In addition, ASTM Standard F792-88 (Reapproved 1993) may be obtained from the American Society for Testing and Materials, 100 Barr Harbor Drive, West Conshohocken, PA 19428-2959.

(h) *Duty time limitations.* Each aircraft operator must comply with the X-ray operator duty time limitations specified in its security program.

[67 FR 8364, Feb. 22, 2002, as amended at 69 FR 18803, Apr. 0, 2004]

§1544.213 Use of explosives detection systems.

(a) *Use of explosive detection equipment.* If TSA so requires by an amendment to an aircraft operator's security program, each aircraft operator required to conduct screening under a security program must use an explosives detection system approved by TSA to screen checked baggage on international flights.

(b) *Signs and inspection of photographic equipment and film.*

(1) At locations at which an aircraft operator or TSA uses an explosives detection system that uses X-ray technology to inspect checked baggage the aircraft operator must ensure that a sign is posted in a conspicuous place where the aircraft operator accepts checked baggage. The sign must notify individuals that such items are being inspected by an explosives detection system and advise them to remove all X-ray, scientific, and high-speed film from checked baggage before inspection. This sign must also advise individuals that they may request that an inspection be made of their photographic equipment and film packages without exposure to an explosives detection system.

(2) If the explosives detection system exposes any checked baggage to more than one milliroentgen during the inspection the aircraft operator must post a sign which advises individuals to remove film of all kinds from their articles before inspection. If requested by individuals, their photographic equipment and film packages must be inspected without exposure to an explosives detection system.

§1544.215 Security coordinators.

(a) *Aircraft Operator Security Coordinator.* Each aircraft operator must designate and use an Aircraft Operator Security Coordinator (AOSC). The AOSC and any alternates must be appointed at the corporate level and must serve as the aircraft operator's primary contact for security-related activities and communications with TSA, as set forth in the security program. Either the AOSC, or an alternate AOSC, must be available on a 24-hour basis.

(b) *Ground Security Coordinator.* Each aircraft operator must designate and use a Ground Security Coordinator for each domestic and international flight departure to carry out the Ground Security Coordinator duties specified in the aircraft operator's security program. The Ground Security Coordinator at each airport must conduct the following daily:

(1) A review of all security-related functions for which the aircraft operator is responsible, for effectiveness and compliance with this part, the aircraft operator's security program, and applicable Security Directives.

(2) Immediate initiation of corrective action for each instance of noncompliance with this part, the aircraft operator's security program, and applicable Security Directives. At foreign airports where such security measures are provided by an agency or contractor of a host government, the aircraft operator must notify TSA for assistance in resolving noncompliance issues.

(c) *In-flight Security Coordinator.* Each aircraft operator must designate and use the pilot in command as the In-flight Security Coordinator for each domestic and international flight to perform duties specified in the aircraft operator's security program.

§1544.217 Law enforcement personnel.

(a) The following applies to operations at airports within the United States that are not required to hold a security program under part 1542 of this chapter.

(1) For operations described in §1544.101(a) each aircraft operator must provide for law enforcement personnel meeting the qualifications and standards specified in §§1542.215 and 1542.217 of this chapter.

(2) For operations under a partial program under §1544.101(b) and (c), a twelve-five program under §1544.101(d) and (e), a private charter program under §1544.101(f), or a full all-cargo program under §1544.101(h) and (i), each aircraft operator must—

(i) Arrange for law enforcement personnel meeting the qualifications and standards specified in §1542.217 of this chapter to be available to respond to an incident; and

(ii) Provide its employees, including crewmembers, current information regarding procedures for obtaining law enforcement assistance at that airport.

(b) The following applies to operations at airports required to hold security programs under part 1542 of this chapter. For operations under a partial program under §1544.101(b) and (c), a twelve-five program under §1544.101 (d) and (e), a private charter program under §1544.101(f), or a full all-cargo program under §1544.101 (h) and (i), each aircraft operator must—

(1) Arrange with TSA and the airport operator, as appropriate, for law enforcement personnel

meeting the qualifications and standards specified in §1542.217 of this chapter to be available to respond to incidents, and

(2) Provide its employees, including crewmembers, current information regarding procedures for obtaining law enforcement assistance at that airport.

[67 FR 8364, Feb. 22, 2002, as amended at 71 FR 30510, May 26, 2006]

§1544.219 Carriage of accessible weapons.

(a) *Flights for which screening is conducted.* The provisions of §1544.201(d), with respect to accessible weapons, do not apply to a law enforcement officer (LEO) aboard a flight for which screening is required if the requirements of this section are met. Paragraph (a) of this section does not apply to a Federal Air Marshal on duty status under §1544.223.

(1) Unless otherwise authorized by TSA, the armed LEO must meet the following requirements:

(i) Be a Federal law enforcement officer or a full-time municipal, county, or state law enforcement officer who is a direct employee of a government agency.

(ii) Be sworn and commissioned to enforce criminal statutes or immigration statutes.

(iii) Be authorized by the employing agency to have the weapon in connection with assigned duties.

(iv) Has completed the training program "Law Enforcement Officers Flying Armed."

(2) In addition to the requirements of paragraph (a)(1) of this section, the armed LEO must have a need to have the weapon accessible from the time he or she would otherwise check the weapon until the time it would be claimed after deplaning. The need to have the weapon accessible must be determined by the employing agency, department, or service and be based on one of the following:

(i) The provision of protective duty, for instance, assigned to a principal or advance team, or on travel required to be prepared to engage in a protective function.

(ii) The conduct of a hazardous surveillance operation.

(iii) On official travel required to report to another location, armed and prepared for duty.

(iv) Employed as a Federal LEO, whether or not on official travel, and armed in accordance with an agency-wide policy governing that type of travel established by the employing agency by directive or policy statement.

(v) Control of a prisoner, in accordance with §1544.221, or an armed LEO on a round trip ticket returning from escorting, or traveling to pick up, a prisoner.

(vi) TSA Federal Air Marshal on duty status.

(3) The armed LEO must comply with the following notification requirements:

(i) All armed LEOs must notify the aircraft operator of the flight(s) on which he or she needs to have the weapon accessible at least 1 hour, or in an emergency as soon as practicable, before departure.

(ii) Identify himself or herself to the aircraft operator by presenting credentials that include a clear full-face picture, the signature of the armed LEO, and the signature of the authorizing official of the agency, service, or department or the official seal of the agency, service, or department. A badge, shield, or similar device may not be used, or accepted, as the sole means of identification.

(iii) If the armed LEO is a State, county, or municipal law enforcement officer, he or she must present an original letter of authority, signed by an authorizing official from his or her employing agency, service or department, confirming the need to travel armed and detailing the itinerary of the travel while armed.

(iv) If the armed LEO is an escort for a foreign official then this paragraph (a)(3) may be satisfied by a State Department notification.

(4) The aircraft operator must do the following:

(i) Obtain information or documentation required in paragraphs (a)(3)(ii), (iii), and (iv) of this section.

(ii) Advise the armed LEO, before boarding, of the aircraft operator's procedures for carrying out this section.

(iii) Have the LEO confirm he/she has completed the training program "Law Enforcement Officers Flying Armed" as required by TSA, unless otherwise authorized by TSA.

(iv) Ensure that the identity of the armed LEO is known to the appropriate personnel who are responsible for security during the boarding of the aircraft.

(v) Notify the pilot in command and other appropriate crewmembers, of the location of each armed LEO aboard the aircraft. Notify any other armed LEO of the location of each armed LEO, including FAMs. Under circumstances described in the security program, the aircraft operator must not close the doors until the notification is complete.

(vi) Ensure that the information required in paragraphs (a)(3)(i) and (ii) of this section is furnished to the flight crew of each additional connecting flight by the Ground Security Coordinator or other designated agent at each location.

(b) *Flights for which screening is not conducted.* The provisions of §1544.201(d), with respect to accessible weapons, do not apply to a LEO aboard a flight for which screening is not required if the requirements of paragraphs (a)(1), (3), and (4) of this section are met.

(c) *Alcohol.*

(1) No aircraft operator may serve any alcoholic beverage to an armed LEO.

(2) No armed LEO may:

(i) Consume any alcoholic beverage while aboard an aircraft operated by an aircraft operator.

(ii) Board an aircraft armed if they have consumed an alcoholic beverage within the previous 8 hours.

(d) *Location of weapon.*

(1) Any individual traveling aboard an aircraft while armed must at all times keep their weapon:

(i) Concealed and out of view, either on their person or in immediate reach, if the armed LEO is not in uniform.

(ii) On their person, if the armed LEO is in uniform.

(2) No individual may place a weapon in an overhead storage bin.

§1544.221 Carriage of prisoners under the control of armed law enforcement officers.

(a) This section applies as follows:

(1) This section applies to the transport of prisoners under the escort of an armed law enforcement officer.

(2) This section does not apply to the carriage of passengers under voluntary protective escort.

(3) This section does not apply to the escort of non-violent detainees of the Immigration and Naturalization Service. This section does not apply to individuals who may be traveling with a prisoner and armed escort, such as the family of a deportee who is under armed escort.

(b) For the purpose of this section:

(1) "High risk prisoner" means a prisoner who is an exceptional escape risk, as determined by the law enforcement agency, and charged with, or convicted of, a violent crime.

(2) "Low risk prisoner" means any prisoner who has not been designated as "high risk."

(c) No aircraft operator may carry a prisoner in the custody of an armed law enforcement officer aboard an aircraft for which screening is required unless, in addition to the requirements in §1544.219, the following requirements are met:

(1) The agency responsible for control of the prisoner has determined whether the prisoner is considered a high risk or a low risk.

(2) Unless otherwise authorized by TSA, no more than one high risk prisoner may be carried on the aircraft.

(d) No aircraft operator may carry a prisoner in the custody of an armed law enforcement officer aboard an aircraft for which screening is required unless the following staffing requirements are met:

(1) A minimum of one armed law enforcement officer must control a low risk prisoner on a flight that is scheduled for 4 hours or less. One armed law enforcement officer may control no more than two low risk prisoners.

(2) A minimum of two armed law enforcement officers must control a low risk prisoner on a flight that is scheduled for more than 4 hours. Two armed law enforcement officers may control no more than two low risk prisoners.

(3) For high-risk prisoners:

(i) For one high-risk prisoner on a flight: A minimum of two armed law enforcement officers must control a high risk prisoner. No other prisoners may be under the control of those two armed law enforcement officers.

(ii) If TSA has authorized more than one high-risk prisoner to be on the flight under paragraph (c)(2) of this section, a minimum of one armed law enforcement officer for each prisoner and one additional armed law enforcement officer must control the prisoners. No other prisoners may be under the control of those armed law enforcement officers.

(e) An armed law enforcement officer who is escorting a prisoner—

(1) Must notify the aircraft operator at least 24 hours before the scheduled departure, or, if that is not possible as far in advance as possible of the following—

(i) The identity of the prisoner to be carried and the flight on which it is proposed to carry the prisoner; and

(ii) Whether or not the prisoner is considered to be a high risk or a low risk.

(2) Must arrive at the check-in counter at least 1 hour before to the scheduled departure.

(3) Must assure the aircraft operator, before departure, that each prisoner under the control of the officer(s) has been searched and does not have on or about his or her person or property anything that can be used as a weapon.

(4) Must be seated between the prisoner and any aisle.

(5) Must accompany the prisoner at all times, and keep the prisoner under control while aboard the aircraft.

(f) No aircraft operator may carry a prisoner in the custody of an armed law enforcement officer aboard an aircraft unless the following are met:

(1) When practicable, the prisoner must be boarded before any other boarding passengers and deplaned after all other deplaning passengers.

(2) The prisoner must be seated in a seat that is neither located in any passenger lounge area nor located next to or directly across from any exit and, when practicable, the aircraft operator

should seat the prisoner in the rearmost seat of the passenger cabin.

(g) Each armed law enforcement officer escorting a prisoner and each aircraft operator must ensure that the prisoner is restrained from full use of his or her hands by an appropriate device that provides for minimum movement of the prisoner's hands, and must ensure that leg irons are not used.

(h) No aircraft operator may provide a prisoner under the control of a law enforcement officer—

(1) With food or beverage or metal eating utensils unless authorized to do so by the armed law enforcement officer.

(2) With any alcoholic beverage.

§1544.223 Transportation of Federal Air Marshals.

(a) A Federal Air Marshal on duty status may have a weapon accessible while aboard an aircraft for which screening is required.

(b) Each aircraft operator must carry Federal Air Marshals, in the number and manner specified by TSA, on each scheduled passenger operation, and public charter passenger operation designated by TSA.

(c) Each Federal Air Marshal must be carried on a first priority basis and without charge while on duty, including positioning and repositioning flights. When a Federal Air Marshal is assigned to a scheduled flight that is canceled for any reason, the aircraft operator must carry that Federal Air Marshal without charge on another flight as designated by TSA.

(d) Each aircraft operator must assign the specific seat requested by a Federal Air Marshal who is on duty status. If another LEO is assigned to that seat or requests that seat, the aircraft operator must inform the Federal Air Marshal. The Federal Air Marshal will coordinate seat assignments with the other LEO.

(e) The Federal Air Marshal identifies himself or herself to the aircraft operator by presenting credentials that include a clear, full-face picture, the signature of the Federal Air Marshal, and the signature of the FAA Administrator. A badge, shield, or similar device may not be used or accepted as the sole means of identification.

(f) The requirements of §1544.219(a) do not apply for a Federal Air Marshal on duty status.

(g) Each aircraft operator must restrict any information concerning the presence, seating, names, and purpose of Federal Air Marshals at any station or on any flight to those persons with an operational need to know.

(h) Law enforcement officers authorized to carry a weapon during a flight will be contacted directly by a Federal Air Marshal who is on that same flight.

§1544.225 Security of aircraft and facilities.

Each aircraft operator must use the procedures included, and the facilities and equipment described, in its security program to perform the following control functions with respect to each aircraft operation:

(a) Prevent unauthorized access to areas controlled by the aircraft operator under an exclusive area agreement in accordance with §1542.111 of this chapter.

(b) Prevent unauthorized access to each aircraft.

(c) Conduct a security inspection of each aircraft before placing it into passenger operations if access has not been controlled in accordance with the aircraft operator security program and as otherwise required in the security program.

(d) When operating under a full program or a full all-cargo program, prevent unauthorized access to the operational area of the aircraft while loading or unloading cargo.

[67 FR 8364, Feb. 22, 2002, as amended at 71 FR 30510, May 26, 2006]

§1544.227 Exclusive area agreement.

(a) An aircraft operator that has entered into an exclusive area agreement with an airport operator, under §1542.111 of this chapter must carry out that exclusive area agreement.

(b) The aircraft operator must list in its security program the locations at which it has entered into exclusive area agreements with an airport operator.

(c) The aircraft operator must provide the exclusive area agreement to TSA upon request.

(d) Any exclusive area agreements in effect on November 14, 2001, must meet the requirements of this section and §1542.111 of this chapter no later than November 14, 2002.

§1544.228 Access to cargo and cargo screening: Security threat assessments for cargo personnel in the United States.

This section applies in the United States to each aircraft operator operating under a full program under §1544.101(a) or a full all-cargo program under §1544.101(h).

(a) Before an aircraft operator authorizes and before an individual performs a function described in paragraph (b) of this section—

(1) Each individual must successfully complete a security threat assessment or comparable security threat assessment described in part 1540 subpart C of this chapter; and

(2) Each aircraft operator must complete the requirements in part 1540 subpart C.

(b) The security threat assessment required in paragraph (a) of this section applies to the following:

(1) Each individual who has unescorted access to cargo and access to information that such cargo will be transported on a passenger aircraft; or who has unescorted access to cargo that has been screened for transport on a passenger aircraft; or who performs certain functions related to the transportation, dispatch, or security of cargo for transport on a passenger aircraft or all-cargo aircraft, as specified in the aircraft operator's security program; from the time—

(i) The cargo reaches a location where an aircraft operator with a full all-cargo program consolidates or inspects it pursuant to security program requirements until the cargo enters an airport Security Identification Display Area or is transferred to another TSA-regulated aircraft operator, foreign air carrier, or indirect air carrier; or

(ii) An aircraft operator with a full program accepts the cargo until the cargo—

(A) Enters an airport Security Identification Display Area;

(B) Is removed from the destination airport; or

(C) Is transferred to another TSA-regulated aircraft operator, foreign air carrier, or indirect air carrier.

(2) Each individual the aircraft operator authorizes to screen cargo or to supervise the screening of cargo under §1544.205.

[Docket No. TSA–2009–0018, 74 FR 47704, Sept. 16, 2009]

§1544.229 Fingerprint-based criminal history records checks (CHRC): Unescorted access authority, authority to perform screening functions, and authority to perform checked baggage or cargo functions.

This section applies to each aircraft operator operating under a full program, a private charter program, or a full all-cargo program.

(a) *Scope.* The following individuals are within the scope of this section. Unescorted access authority, authority to perform screening functions, and authority to perform checked baggage or cargo functions, are collectively referred to as "covered functions."

(1) New unescorted access authority or authority to perform screening functions.

(i) Each employee or contract employee covered under a certification made to an airport operator on or after December 6, 2001, pursuant to 14 CFR 107.209(n) in effect prior to November 14, 2001 (see 14 CFR Parts 60 to 139 revised as of January 1, 2001) or §1542.209(n) of this chapter.

(ii) Each individual issued on or after December 6, 2001, an aircraft operator identification media that one or more airports accepts as airport-approved media for unescorted access authority within a security identification display area (SIDA), as described in §1542.205 of this chapter (referred to as "unescorted access authority").

(iii) Each individual granted authority to perform the following screening functions at locations within the United States (referred to as "authority to perform screening functions"):

(A) Screening passengers or property that will be carried in a cabin of an aircraft of an aircraft operator required to screen passengers under this part.

(B) Serving as an immediate supervisor (checkpoint security supervisor (CSS)), and the next supervisory level (shift or site supervisor), to those individuals described in paragraphs (a)(1)(iii)(A) or (a)(1)(iii)(C) of this section.

(C) Screening cargo that will be carried on an aircraft of an aircraft operator with a full all-cargo program.

(2) Current unescorted access authority or authority to perform screening functions.

(i) Each employee or contract employee covered under a certification made to an airport operator pursuant to 14 CFR 107.31(n) in effect prior to November 14, 2001 (see 14 CFR Parts 60 to 139 revised as of January 1, 2001), or pursuant to 14 CFR 107.209(n) in effect prior to December 6, 2001 (see 14 CFR Parts 60 to 139 revised as of January 1, 2001).

(ii) Each individual who holds on December 6, 2001, an aircraft operator identification media that one or more airports accepts as airport-approved media for unescorted access authority within a security identification display area (SIDA), as described in §1542.205 of this chapter.

(iii) Each individual who is performing on December 6, 2001, a screening function identified in paragraph (a)(1)(iii) of this section.

(3) New authority to perform checked baggage or cargo functions. Each individual who, on and after February 17, 2002, is granted the authority to perform the following checked baggage and cargo functions (referred to as "authority to perform checked baggage or cargo functions"), except for individuals described in paragraph (a)(1) of this section:

(i) Screening of checked baggage or cargo of an aircraft operator required to screen passengers under this part, or serving as an immediate supervisor of such an individual.

(ii) Accepting checked baggage for transport on behalf of an aircraft operator required to screen passengers under this part.

(4) Current authority to perform checked baggage or cargo functions. Each individual who holds on February 17, 2002, authority to perform checked baggage or cargo functions, except for

§1544.229

individuals described in paragraph (a)(1) or (2) of this section.

(b) *Individuals seeking unescorted access authority, authority to perform screening functions, or authority to perform checked baggage or cargo functions.* Each aircraft operator must ensure that each individual identified in paragraph (a)(1) or (3) of this section has undergone a fingerprint-based CHRC that does not disclose that he or she has a disqualifying criminal offense, as described in paragraph (d) of this section, before—

(1) Making a certification to an airport operator regarding that individual;

(2) Issuing an aircraft operator identification medium to that individual;

(3) Authorizing that individual to perform screening functions; or

(4) Authorizing that individual to perform checked baggage or cargo functions.

(c) *Individuals who have not had a CHRC—*

(1) Deadline for conducting a CHRC. Each aircraft operator must ensure that, on and after December 6, 2002:

(i) No individual retains unescorted access authority, whether obtained as a result of a certification to an airport operator under 14 CFR 107.31(n) in effect prior to November 14, 2001 (see 14 CFR parts 60 to 139 revised as of January 1, 2001), or under 14 CFR 107.209(n) in effect prior to December 6, 2001 (see 14 CFR Parts 60 to 139 revised as of January 1, 2001), or obtained as a result of the issuance of an aircraft operator's identification media, unless the individual has been subject to a fingerprint-based CHRC for unescorted access authority under this part.

(ii) No individual continues to have authority to perform screening functions described in paragraph (a)(1)(iii) of this section, unless the individual has been subject to a fingerprint-based CHRC under this part.

(iii) No individual continues to have authority to perform checked baggage or cargo functions described in paragraph (a)(3) of this section, unless the individual has been subject to a fingerprint-based CHRC under this part.

(2) Lookback for individuals with unescorted access authority or authority to perform screening functions. When a CHRC discloses a disqualifying criminal offense for which the conviction or finding was on or after December 6, 1991, the aircraft operator must immediately suspend that individual's unescorted access authority or authority to perform screening functions.

(3) Lookback for individuals with authority to perform checked baggage or cargo functions. When a CHRC discloses a disqualifying criminal offense for which the conviction or finding was on or after February 17, 1992, the aircraft operator must immediately suspend that individual's

authority to perform checked baggage or cargo functions.

(d) *Disqualifying criminal offenses.* An individual has a disqualifying criminal offense if the individual has been convicted, or found not guilty by reason of insanity, of any of the disqualifying crimes listed in this paragraph in any jurisdiction during the 10 years before the date of the individual's application for authority to perform covered functions, or while the individual has authority to perform covered functions. The disqualifying criminal offenses are as follows:

(1) Forgery of certificates, false marking of aircraft, and other aircraft registration violation; 49 U.S.C. 46306.

(2) Interference with air navigation; 49 U.S.C. 46308.

(3) Improper transportation of a hazardous material; 49 U.S.C. 46312.

(4) Aircraft piracy; 49 U.S.C. 46502.

(5) Interference with flight crew members or flight attendants; 49 U.S.C. 46504.

(6) Commission of certain crimes aboard aircraft in flight; 49 U.S.C. 46506.

(7) Carrying a weapon or explosive aboard aircraft; 49 U.S.C. 46505.

(8) Conveying false information and threats; 49 U.S.C. 46507.

(9) Aircraft piracy outside the special aircraft jurisdiction of the United States; 49 U.S.C. 46502(b).

(10) Lighting violations involving transporting controlled substances; 49 U.S.C. 46315.

(11) Unlawful entry into an aircraft or airport area that serves air carriers or foreign air carriers contrary to established security requirements; 49 U.S.C. 46314.

(12) Destruction of an aircraft or aircraft facility; 18 U.S.C. 32.

(13) Murder.

(14) Assault with intent to murder.

(15) Espionage.

(16) Sedition.

(17) Kidnapping or hostage taking.

(18) Treason.

(19) Rape or aggravated sexual abuse.

(20) Unlawful possession, use, sale, distribution, or manufacture of an explosive or weapon.

(21) Extortion.

(22) Armed or felony unarmed robbery.

(23) Distribution of, or intent to distribute, a controlled substance.

(24) Felony arson.

(25) Felony involving a threat.

(26) Felony involving—

(i) Willful destruction of property;

(ii) Importation or manufacture of a controlled substance;

(iii) Burglary;

(iv) Theft;

Part 1544: Security: Air Carriers & Commercial Operators §1544.229

(v) Dishonesty, fraud, or misrepresentation;
(vi) Possession or distribution of stolen property;
(vii) Aggravated assault;
(viii) Bribery; or
(ix) Illegal possession of a controlled substance punishable by a maximum term of imprisonment of more than 1 year.
(27) Violence at international airports; 18 U.S.C. 37.
(28) Conspiracy or attempt to commit any of the criminal acts listed in this paragraph (d).

(e) *Fingerprint application and processing.*
(1) At the time of fingerprinting, the aircraft operator must provide the individual to be fingerprinted a fingerprint application that includes only the following—
(i) The disqualifying criminal offenses described in paragraph (d) of this section.
(ii) A statement that the individual signing the application does not have a disqualifying criminal offense.
(iii) A statement informing the individual that Federal regulations under 49 CFR 1544.229 impose a continuing obligation to disclose to the aircraft operator within 24 hours if he or she is convicted of any disqualifying criminal offense that occurs while he or she has authority to perform a covered function.
(iv) A statement reading, "The information I have provided on this application is true, complete, and correct to the best of my knowledge and belief and is provided in good faith. I understand that a knowing and willful false statement on this application can be punished by fine or imprisonment or both. (See section 1001 of Title 18 United States Code.)"
(v) A line for the printed name of the individual.
(vi) A line for the individual's signature and date of signature.
(2) Each individual must complete and sign the application prior to submitting his or her fingerprints.
(3) The aircraft operator must verify the identity of the individual through two forms of identification prior to fingerprinting, and ensure that the printed name on the fingerprint application is legible. At least one of the two forms of identification must have been issued by a government authority, and at least one must include a photo.
(4) The aircraft operator must:
(i) Advise the individual that a copy of the criminal record received from the FBI will be provided to the individual, if requested by the individual in writing; and
(ii) Identify a point of contact if the individual has questions about the results of the CHRC.
(5) The aircraft operator must collect, control, and process one set of legible and classifiable fingerprints under direct observation by the aircraft operator or a law enforcement officer.

(6) Fingerprints may be obtained and processed electronically, or recorded on fingerprint cards approved by the FBI and distributed by TSA for that purpose.
(7) The fingerprint submission must be forwarded to TSA in the manner specified by TSA.

(f) *Fingerprinting fees.* Aircraft operators must pay for all fingerprints in a form and manner approved by TSA. The payment must be made at the designated rate (available from the local TSA security office) for each set of fingerprints submitted. Information about payment options is available though the designated TSA headquarters point of contact. Individual personal checks are not acceptable.

(g) *Determination of arrest status.*
(1) When a CHRC on an individual described in paragraph (a)(1) or (3) of this section discloses an arrest for any disqualifying criminal offense listed in paragraph (d) of this section without indicating a disposition, the aircraft operator must determine, after investigation, that the arrest did not result in a disqualifying offense before granting authority to perform a covered function. If there is no disposition, or if the disposition did not result in a conviction or in a finding of not guilty by reason of insanity of one of the offenses listed in paragraph (d) of this section, the individual is not disqualified under this section.
(2) When a CHRC on an individual described in paragraph (a)(2) or (4) of this section discloses an arrest for any disqualifying criminal offense without indicating a disposition, the aircraft operator must suspend the individual's authority to perform a covered function not later than 45 days after obtaining the CHRC unless the aircraft operator determines, after investigation, that the arrest did not result in a disqualifying criminal offense. If there is no disposition, or if the disposition did not result in a conviction or in a finding of not guilty by reason of insanity of one of the offenses listed in paragraph (d) of this section, the individual is not disqualified under this section.
(3) The aircraft operator may only make the determinations required in paragraphs (g)(1) and (g)(2) of this section for individuals for whom it is issuing, or has issued, authority to perform a covered function; and individuals who are covered by a certification from an aircraft operator under §1542.209(n) of this chapter. The aircraft operator may not make determinations for individuals described in §1542.209(a) of this chapter.

(h) *Correction of FBI records and notification of disqualification.*
(1) Before making a final decision to deny authority to an individual described in paragraph (a)(1) or (3) of this section, the aircraft operator must advise him or her that the FBI criminal record discloses information that would disqualify him or her from receiving or retaining authority to perform a

§1544.229

covered function and provide the individual with a copy of the FBI record if he or she requests it.

(2) The aircraft operator must notify an individual that a final decision has been made to grant or deny authority to perform a covered function.

(3) Immediately following the suspension of authority to perform a covered function, the aircraft operator must advise the individual that the FBI criminal record discloses information that disqualifies him or her from retaining his or her authority, and provide the individual with a copy of the FBI record if he or she requests it.

(i) *Corrective action by the individual.* The individual may contact the local jurisdiction responsible for the information and the FBI to complete or correct the information contained in his or her record, subject to the following conditions—

(1) For an individual seeking unescorted access authority or authority to perform screening functions on or after December 6, 2001; or an individual seeking authority to perform checked baggage or cargo functions on or after February 17, 2002; the following applies:

(i) Within 30 days after being advised that the criminal record received from the FBI discloses a disqualifying criminal offense, the individual must notify the aircraft operator in writing of his or her intent to correct any information he or she believes to be inaccurate. The aircraft operator must obtain a copy, or accept a copy from the individual, of the revised FBI record or a certified true copy of the information from the appropriate court, prior to authority to perform a covered function.

(ii) If no notification, as described in paragraph (h)(1) of this section, is received within 30 days, the aircraft operator may make a final determination to deny authority to perform a covered function.

(2) For an individual with unescorted access authority or authority to perform screening functions before December 6, 2001; or an individual with authority to perform checked baggage or cargo functions before February 17, 2002; the following applies: Within 30 days after being advised of suspension because the criminal record received from the FBI discloses a disqualifying criminal offense, the individual must notify the aircraft operator in writing of his or her intent to correct any information he or she believes to be inaccurate. The aircraft operator must obtain a copy, or accept a copy from the individual, of the revised FBI record, or a certified true copy of the information from the appropriate court, prior to reinstating authority to perform a covered function.

(j) *Limits on dissemination of results.* Criminal record information provided by the FBI may be used only to carry out this section and §1542.209 of this chapter. No person may disseminate the results of a CHRC to anyone other than:

Federal Aviation Regulations

(1) The individual to whom the record pertains, or that individual's authorized representative.

(2) Officials of airport operators who are determining whether to grant unescorted access to the individual under part 1542 of this chapter when the determination is not based on the aircraft operator's certification under §1542.209(n) of this chapter.

(3) Other aircraft operators who are determining whether to grant authority to perform a covered function under this part.

(4) Others designated by TSA.

(k) *Recordkeeping.* The aircraft operator must maintain the following information.

(1) *Investigation conducted before December 6, 2001.* The aircraft operator must maintain and control the access or employment history investigation files, including the criminal history records results portion, for investigations conducted before December 6, 2001.

(2) *Fingerprint application process on or after December 6, 2001.* The aircraft operator must physically maintain, control, and, as appropriate, destroy the fingerprint application and the criminal record. Only direct aircraft operator employees may carry out the responsibility for maintaining, controlling, and destroying criminal records.

(3) *Protection of records—all investigations.* The records required by this section must be maintained in a manner that is acceptable to TSA and in a manner that protects the confidentiality of the individual.

(4) *Duration—all investigations.* The records identified in this section with regard to an individual must be maintained until 180 days after the termination of the individual's authority to perform a covered function. When files are no longer maintained, the criminal record must be destroyed.

(l) *Continuing responsibilities.*

(1) Each individual with unescorted access authority or the authority to perform screening functions on December 6, 2001, who had a disqualifying criminal offense in paragraph (d) of this section on or after December 6, 1991, must, by January 7, 2002, report the conviction to the aircraft operator and surrender the SIDA access medium to the issuer and cease performing screening functions, as applicable.

(2) Each individual with authority to perform a covered function who has a disqualifying criminal offense must report the offense to the aircraft operator and surrender the SIDA access medium to the issuer within 24 hours of the conviction or the finding of not guilty by reason of insanity.

(3) If information becomes available to the aircraft operator indicating that an individual with authority to perform a covered function has a possible conviction for any disqualifying criminal offense in paragraph (d) of this section, the air-

craft operator must determine the status of the conviction. If a disqualifying criminal offense is confirmed the aircraft operator must immediately revoke any authority to perform a covered function.

(4) Each individual with authority to perform checked baggage or cargo functions on February 17, 2002, who had a disqualifying criminal offense in paragraph (d) of this section on or after February 17, 1992, must, by March 25 2002, report the conviction to the aircraft operator and cease performing check baggage or cargo functions.

(m) *Aircraft operator responsibility.* The aircraft operator must—

(1) Designate an individual(s) to be responsible for maintaining and controlling the employment history investigations for those whom the aircraft operator has made a certification to an airport operator under 14 CFR 107.209(n) in effect prior to November 14, 2001 (see 14 CFR Parts 60 to 139 revised as of January 1, 2001), and for those whom the aircraft operator has issued identification media that are airport-accepted. The aircraft operator must designate a direct employee to maintain, control, and, as appropriate, destroy criminal records.

(2) Designate an individual(s) to maintain the employment history investigations of individuals with authority to perform screening functions whose files must be maintained at the location or station where the screener is performing his or her duties.

(3) Designate an individual(s) at appropriate locations to serve as the contact to receive notification from individuals seeking authority to perform covered functions of their intent to seek correction of their FBI criminal record.

(4) Audit the employment history investigations performed in accordance with this section and 14 CFR 108.33 in effect prior to November 14, 2001 (see 14 CFR Parts 60 to 139 revised as of January 1, 2001). The aircraft operator must set forth the audit procedures in its security program.

[67 FR 8364, Feb. 22, 2002, as amended at 71 FR 30511, May 26, 2006]

§1544.230 Fingerprint-based criminal history records checks (CHRC): Flightcrew members.

(a) *Scope.* This section applies to each flightcrew member for each aircraft operator, except that this section does not apply to flightcrew members who are subject to §1544.229.

(b) *CHRC required.* Each aircraft operator must ensure that each flightcrew member has undergone a fingerprint-based CHRC that does not disclose that he or she has a disqualifying criminal offense, as described in §1544.229(d), before allowing that individual to serve as a flightcrew member.

(c) *Application and fees.* Each aircraft operator must ensure that each flightcrew member's fingerprints are obtained and submitted as described in §1544.229 (e) and (f).

(d) *Determination of arrest status.*

(1) When a CHRC on an individual described in paragraph (a) of this section discloses an arrest for any disqualifying criminal offense listed in §1544.229(d) without indicating a disposition, the aircraft operator must determine, after investigation, that the arrest did not result in a disqualifying offense before the individual may serve as a flightcrew member. If there is no disposition, or if the disposition did not result in a conviction or in a finding of not guilty by reason of insanity of one of the offenses listed in §1544.229(d), the flight crewmember is not disqualified under this section.

(2) When a CHRC on an individual described in paragraph (a) of this section discloses an arrest for any disqualifying criminal offense listed in §1544.229(d) without indicating a disposition, the aircraft operator must suspend the individual's flightcrew member privileges not later than 45 days after obtaining a CHRC, unless the aircraft operator determines, after investigation, that the arrest did not result in a disqualifying criminal offense. If there is no disposition, or if the disposition did not result in a conviction or in a finding of not guilty by reason of insanity of one of the offenses listed in §1544.229(d), the flight crewmember is not disqualified under this section.

(3) The aircraft operator may only make the determinations required in paragraphs (d)(1) and (d)(2) of this section for individuals whom it is using, or will use, as a flightcrew member. The aircraft operator may not make determinations for individuals described in §1542.209(a) of this chapter.

(e) *Correction of FBI records and notification of disqualification.*

(1) Before making a final decision to deny the individual the ability to serve as a flightcrew member, the aircraft operator must advise the individual that the FBI criminal record discloses information that would disqualify the individual from serving as a flightcrew member and provide the individual with a copy of the FBI record if the individual requests it.

(2) The aircraft operator must notify the individual that a final decision has been made to allow or deny the individual flightcrew member status.

(3) Immediately following the denial of flightcrew member status, the aircraft operator must advise the individual that the FBI criminal record discloses information that disqualifies him or her from retaining his or her flightcrew member status, and provide the individual with a copy of the FBI record if he or she requests it.

(f) *Corrective action by the individual.* The individual may contact the local jurisdiction responsible for the information and the FBI to complete or correct the information contained in his or her record, subject to the following conditions—

(1) Within 30 days after being advised that the criminal record received from the FBI discloses a disqualifying criminal offense, the individual must notify the aircraft operator in writing of his or her intent to correct any information he or she believes to be inaccurate. The aircraft operator must obtain a copy, or accept a copy from the individual, of the revised FBI record or a certified true copy of the information from the appropriate court, prior to allowing the individual to serve as a flightcrew member.

(2) If no notification, as described in paragraph (f)(1) of this section, is received within 30 days, the aircraft operator may make a final determination to deny the individual flightcrew member status.

(g) *Limits on the dissemination of results.* Criminal record information provided by the FBI may be used only to carry out this section. No person may disseminate the results of a CHRC to anyone other than—

(1) The individual to whom the record pertains, or that individual's authorized representative.

(2) Others designated by TSA.

(h) *Recordkeeping.*

(1) *Fingerprint application process.* The aircraft operator must physically maintain, control, and, as appropriate, destroy the fingerprint application and the criminal record. Only direct aircraft operator employees may carry out the responsibility for maintaining, controlling, and destroying criminal records.

(2) *Protection of records.* The records required by this section must be maintained by the aircraft operator in a manner that is acceptable to TSA that protects the confidentiality of the individual.

(3) *Duration.* The records identified in this section with regard to an individual must be made available upon request by TSA, and maintained by the aircraft operator until 180 days after the termination of the individual's privileges to perform flightcrew member duties with the aircraft operator. When files are no longer maintained, the aircraft operator must destroy the CHRC results.

(i) *Continuing responsibilities.*

(1) Each flightcrew member identified in paragraph (a) of this section who has a disqualifying criminal offense must report the offense to the aircraft operator within 24 hours of the conviction or the finding of not guilty by reason of insanity.

(2) If information becomes available to the aircraft operator indicating that a flightcrew member identified in paragraph (a) of this section has a possible conviction for any disqualifying criminal offense in §1544.229(d), the aircraft operator must determine the status of the conviction. If a disqualifying criminal offense is confirmed, the aircraft operator may not assign that individual to flightcrew duties in operations identified in paragraph (a).

(j) *Aircraft operator responsibility.* The aircraft operator must—

(1) Designate a direct employee to maintain, control, and, as appropriate, destroy criminal records.

(2) Designate an individual(s) to maintain the CHRC results.

(3) Designate an individual(s) at appropriate locations to receive notification from individuals of their intent to seek correction of their FBI criminal record.

(k) *Compliance date.* Each aircraft operator must comply with this section for each flightcrew member described in paragraph (a) of this section not later than December 6, 2002.

[67 FR 8209, Feb. 22, 2002]

§1544.231 Airport-approved and exclusive area personnel identification systems.

(a) Each aircraft operator must establish and carry out a personnel identification system for identification media that are airport-approved, or identification media that are issued for use in an exclusive area. The system must include the following:

(1) Personnel identification media that—

(i) Convey a full face image, full name, employer, and identification number of the individual to whom the identification medium is issued;

(ii) Indicate clearly the scope of the individual's access and movement privileges;

(iii) Indicate clearly an expiration date; and

(iv) Are of sufficient size and appearance as to be readily observable for challenge purposes.

(2) Procedures to ensure that each individual in the secured area or SIDA continuously displays the identification medium issued to that individual on the outermost garment above waist level, or is under escort.

(3) Procedures to ensure accountability through the following:

(i) Retrieving expired identification media.

(ii) Reporting lost or stolen identification media.

(iii) Securing unissued identification media stock and supplies.

(iv) Auditing the system at a minimum of once a year, or sooner, as necessary to ensure the integrity and accountability of all identification media.

(v) As specified in the aircraft operator security program, revalidate the identification system or reissue identification media if a portion of all issued, unexpired identification media are lost, stolen, or unretrieved, including identification media that are combined with access media.

(vi) Ensure that only one identification medium is issued to an individual at a time. A replacement identification medium may only be issued if an individual declares in writing that the medium has been lost or stolen.

(b) The aircraft operator may request approval of a temporary identification media system that meets the standards in §1542.211(b) of this chapter, or may arrange with the airport to use temporary airport identification media in accordance with that section.

(c) Each aircraft operator must submit a plan to carry out this section to TSA no later than May 13, 2002. Each aircraft operator must fully implement its plan no later than November 14, 2003.

§1544.233 Security coordinators and crewmembers, training.

(a) No aircraft operator may use any individual as a Ground Security Coordinator unless, within the preceding 12-calendar months, that individual has satisfactorily completed the security training as specified in the aircraft operator's security program.

(b) No aircraft operator may use any individual as an in-flight security coordinator or crewmember on any domestic or international flight unless, within the preceding 12-calendar months or within the time period specified in an Advanced Qualifications Program approved under SFAR 58 in 14 CFR part 121, that individual has satisfactorily completed the security training required by 14 CFR 121.417(b)(3)(v) or 135.331(b)(3)(v), and as specified in the aircraft operator's security program.

(c) With respect to training conducted under this section, whenever an individual completes recurrent training within one calendar month earlier, or one calendar month after the date it was required, that individual is considered to have completed the training in the calendar month in which it was required.

§1544.235 Training and knowledge for individuals with security-related duties.

(a) No aircraft operator may use any direct or contractor employee to perform any security-related duties to meet the requirements of its security program unless that individual has received training as specified in its security program including their individual responsibilities in §1540.105 of this chapter.

(b) Each aircraft operator must ensure that individuals performing security-related duties for the aircraft operator have knowledge of the provisions of this part, applicable Security Directives and Information Circulars, the approved airport security program applicable to their location, and the aircraft operator's security program to the extent that such individuals need to know in order to perform their duties.

§1544.237 Flight deck privileges.

(a) For each aircraft that has a door to the flight deck, each aircraft operator must restrict access to the flight deck as provided in its security program.

(b) This section does not restrict access for an FAA air carrier inspector, an authorized representative of the National Transportation Safety Board, or for an Agent of the United States Secret Service, under 14 CFR parts 121, 125, or 135. This section does not restrict access for a Federal Air Marshal under this part.

[67 FR 8210, Feb. 22, 2002]

§1544.239 Known shipper program.

This section applies to each aircraft operator operating under a full program under §1544.101 (a) of this part and to each aircraft operator with a TSA security program approved for transfer of cargo to an aircraft operator with a full program or a foreign air carrier under paragraphs §1546.101 (a) or (b) of this chapter.

(a) For cargo to be loaded on its aircraft in the United States, each aircraft operator must have and carry out a known shipper program in accordance with its security program. The program must—

(1) Determine the shipper's validity and integrity as provided in the security program;

(2) Provide that the aircraft operator will separate known shipper cargo from unknown shipper cargo; and

(3) Provide for the aircraft operator to ensure that cargo is screened or inspected as set forth in its security program.

(b) When required by TSA, each aircraft operator must submit in a form and manner acceptable to TSA—

(1) Information identified in its security program regarding a known shipper, or an applicant for that status; and

(2) Corrections and updates of this information upon learning of a change to the information specified in paragraph (b)(1) of this section.

[71 FR 30511, May 26, 2006]

Subpart D—Threat and Threat Response

§1544.301 Contingency plan.

Each aircraft operator must adopt a contingency plan and must:

(a) Implement its contingency plan when directed by TSA.

(b) Ensure that all information contained in the plan is updated annually and that appropriate persons are notified of any changes.

(c) Participate in an airport-sponsored exercise of the airport contingency plan or its equivalent, as provided in its security program.

§1544.303 Bomb or air piracy threats.

(a) *Flight: Notification.* Upon receipt of a specific and credible threat to the security of a flight, the aircraft operator must—

(1) Immediately notify the ground and in-flight security coordinators of the threat, any evaluation thereof, and any measures to be applied; and

(2) Ensure that the in-flight security coordinator notifies all crewmembers of the threat, any evaluation thereof, and any measures to be applied; and

(3) Immediately notify the appropriate airport operator.

(b) *Flight: Inspection.* Upon receipt of a specific and credible threat to the security of a flight, each aircraft operator must attempt to determine whether or not any explosive or incendiary is present by doing the following:

(1) Conduct a security inspection on the ground before the next flight or, if the aircraft is in flight, immediately after its next landing.

(2) If the aircraft is on the ground, immediately deplane all passengers and submit that aircraft to a security search.

(3) If the aircraft is in flight, immediately advise the pilot in command of all pertinent information available so that necessary emergency action can be taken.

(c) *Ground facility.* Upon receipt of a specific and credible threat to a specific ground facility at the airport, the aircraft operator must:

(1) Immediately notify the appropriate airport operator.

(2) Inform all other aircraft operators and foreign air carriers at the threatened facility.

(3) Conduct a security inspection.

(d) *Notification.* Upon receipt of any bomb threat against the security of a flight or facility, or upon receiving information that an act or suspected act of air piracy has been committed, the aircraft operator also must notify TSA. If the aircraft is in airspace under other than U.S. jurisdiction, the aircraft operator must also notify the appropriate authorities of the State in whose territory the aircraft is located and, if the aircraft is in flight, the appropriate authorities of the State in whose territory the aircraft is to land. Notification of the appropriate air traffic controlling authority is sufficient action to meet this requirement.

§1544.305 Security Directives and Information Circulars.

(a) TSA may issue an Information Circular to notify aircraft operators of security concerns. When TSA determines that additional security measures are necessary to respond to a threat assessment or to a specific threat against civil aviation, TSA issues a Security Directive setting forth mandatory measures.

(b) Each aircraft operator required to have an approved aircraft operator security program must comply with each Security Directive issued to the aircraft operator by TSA, within the time prescribed in the Security Directive for compliance.

(c) Each aircraft operator that receives a Security Directive must—

(1) Within the time prescribed in the Security Directive, verbally acknowledge receipt of the Security Directive to TSA.

(2) Within the time prescribed in the Security Directive, specify the method by which the measures in the Security Directive have been implemented (or will be implemented, if the Security Directive is not yet effective).

(d) In the event that the aircraft operator is unable to implement the measures in the Security Directive, the aircraft operator must submit proposed alternative measures and the basis for submitting the alternative measures to TSA for approval. The aircraft operator must submit the proposed alternative measures within the time prescribed in the Security Directive. The aircraft operator must implement any alternative measures approved by TSA.

(e) Each aircraft operator that receives a Security Directive may comment on the Security Directive by submitting data, views, or arguments in writing to TSA. TSA may amend the Security Directive based on comments received. Submission of a comment does not delay the effective date of the Security Directive.

(f) Each aircraft operator that receives a Security Directive or Information Circular and each person who receives information from a Security Directive or Information Circular must:

(1) Restrict the availability of the Security Directive or Information Circular, and information contained in either document, to those persons with an operational need-to-know.

(2) Refuse to release the Security Directive or Information Circular, and information contained in either document, to persons other than those with an operational need-to-know without the prior written consent of TSA.

Subpart E— Screener Qualifications When the Aircraft Operator Performs Screening

§1544.401 Applicability of this subpart.

This subpart applies when the aircraft operator is conducting inspections as provided in §1544.207.

[Docket No. TSA–2009–0018, 74 FR 47704, Sept. 16, 2009]

§1544.403 [Reserved]

§1544.405 Qualifications of screening personnel.

(a) No individual subject to this subpart may perform a screening function unless that individual has the qualifications described in §§1544.405 through 1544.411. No aircraft operator may use such an individual to perform a screening function unless that person complies with the requirements of §§1544.405 through 1544.411.

(b) A screener must have a satisfactory or better score on a screener selection test administered by TSA.

(c) A screener must be a citizen of the United States.

(d) A screener must have a high school diploma, a General Equivalency Diploma, or a combination of education and experience that the TSA has determined to be sufficient for the individual to perform the duties of the position.

(e) A screener must have basic aptitudes and physical abilities including color perception, visual and aural acuity, physical coordination, and motor skills to the following standards:

(1) Screeners operating screening equipment must be able to distinguish on the screening equipment monitor the appropriate imaging standard specified in the aircraft operator's security program.

(2) Screeners operating any screening equipment must be able to distinguish each color displayed on every type of screening equipment and explain what each color signifies.

(3) Screeners must be able to hear and respond to the spoken voice and to audible alarms generated by screening equipment at an active screening location.

(4) Screeners who perform physical searches or other related operations must be able to efficiently and thoroughly manipulate and handle such baggage, containers, cargo, and other objects subject to screening.

(5) Screeners who perform pat-downs or hand-held metal detector searches of individuals must have sufficient dexterity and capability to thoroughly conduct those procedures over an individual's entire body.

(f) A screener must have the ability to read, speak, and write English well enough to—

(1) Carry out written and oral instructions regarding the proper performance of screening duties;

(2) Read English language identification media, credentials, airline tickets, documents, air waybills, invoices, and labels on items normally encountered in the screening process;

(3) Provide direction to and understand and answer questions from English-speaking individuals undergoing screening; and

(4) Write incident reports and statements and log entries into security records in the English language.

(g) At locations outside the United States where the aircraft operator has operational control over a screening function, the aircraft operator may use screeners who do not meet the requirements of paragraph (f) of this section, provided that at least one representative of the aircraft operator who has the ability to functionally read and speak English is present while the aircraft operator's passengers are undergoing security screening. At such locations the aircraft operator may use screeners who are not United States citizens.

§1544.407 Training, testing, and knowledge of individuals who perform screening functions.

(a) *Training required.* Before performing screening functions, an individual must have completed initial, recurrent, and appropriate specialized training as specified in this section and the aircraft operator's security program. No aircraft operator may use any screener, screener in charge, or checkpoint security supervisor unless that individual has satisfactorily completed the required training. This paragraph does not prohibit the performance of screening functions during on-the-job training as provided in §1544.409(b).

(b) *Use of training programs.* Training for screeners must be conducted under programs provided by TSA. Training programs for screeners-in-charge and checkpoint security supervisors must be conducted in accordance with the aircraft operator's security program.

(c) *Citizenship.* A screener must be a citizen or national of the United States.

(d) *Screener readiness test.* Before beginning on-the-job training, a screener trainee must pass the screener readiness test prescribed by TSA.

(e) *On-the-job training and testing.* Each screener must complete at least 60 hours of on-the-job training and must pass an on-the-job training test prescribed by TSA. No aircraft operator may permit a screener trainee to exercise independent judgment as a screener, until the individual passes an on-the-job training test prescribed by TSA.

(f) *Knowledge requirements.* Each aircraft operator must ensure that individuals performing as screeners, screeners-in-charge, and checkpoint security supervisors for the aircraft operator have knowledge of the provisions of this part, the aircraft operator's security program, and applicable Security Directives and Information Circulars to the extent necessary to perform their duties.

(g) *Disclosure of sensitive security information during training.* The aircraft operator may not permit a trainee to have access to sensitive security information during screener training unless a criminal history records check has successfully been completed for that individual in accordance with §1544.229, and the individual has no disqualifying criminal offense.

[67 FR 8364, Feb. 22, 2002; as amended by Amdt. 1544–9, 74 FR 47703, Sept. 16, 2009]

§1544.409 Integrity of screener tests.

(a) *Cheating or other unauthorized conduct.*
(1) Except as authorized by the TSA, no person may—

(i) Copy or intentionally remove a test under this part;

(ii) Give to another or receive from another any part or copy of that test;

(iii) Give help on that test to or receive help on that test from any person during the period that the test is being given; or

(iv) Use any material or aid during the period that the test is being given.

(2) No person may take any part of that test on behalf of another person.

(3) No person may cause, assist, or participate intentionally in any act prohibited by this paragraph (a).

(b) *Administering and monitoring screener tests.*
(1) Each aircraft operator must notify TSA of the time and location at which it will administer each screener readiness test required under §1544.405(d).

(2) Either TSA or the aircraft operator must administer and monitor the screener readiness test. Where more than one aircraft operator or foreign air carrier uses a screening location, TSA may authorize an employee of one or more of the aircraft operators or foreign air carriers to monitor the test for a trainee who will screen at that location.

(3) If TSA or a representative of TSA is not available to administer and monitor a screener readiness test, the aircraft operator must provide a direct employee to administer and monitor the screener readiness test.

(4) An aircraft operator employee who administers and monitors a screener readiness test must not be an instructor, screener, screener-in-charge, checkpoint security supervisor, or other screening supervisor. The employee must be familiar with the procedures for administering and monitoring the test and must be capable of observing whether the trainee or others are engaging in cheating or other unauthorized conduct.

§1544.411 Continuing qualifications of screening personnel.

(a) *Impairment.* No individual may perform a screening function if he or she shows evidence of impairment, such as impairment due to illegal drugs, sleep deprivation, medication, or alcohol.

(b) *Training not complete.* An individual who has not completed the training required by §1544.405 may be deployed during the on-the-job portion of training to perform security functions provided that the individual—

(1) Is closely supervised; and

(2) Does not make independent judgments as to whether individuals or property may enter a sterile area or aircraft without further inspection.

(c) *Failure of operational test.* No aircraft operator may use an individual to perform a screening function after that individual has failed an operational test related to that function, until that individual has successfully completed the remedial training specified in the aircraft operator's security program.

(d) *Annual proficiency review.* Each individual assigned screening duties shall receive an annual evaluation. The aircraft operator must ensure that a Ground Security Coordinator conducts and documents an annual evaluation of each individual who performs screening functions. An individual who performs screening functions may not continue to perform such functions unless the evaluation demonstrates that the individual—

(1) Continues to meet all qualifications and standards required to perform a screening function;

(2) Has a satisfactory record of performance and attention to duty based on the standards and requirements in the aircraft operator's security program; and

(3) Demonstrates the current knowledge and skills necessary to courteously, vigilantly, and effectively perform screening functions.

Please submit terms you think should be added to the index, including the FAR section number to:
asa@asa2fly.com   ~Thank you!

A

abbreviations and symbols §1.2 12
accessory (appliance), defined §1.1............................ 1
administrator, defined §1.1 1
Advanced Qualification Program
   (AQP) §121.901–121.925...................... 292–298
aerodynamic coefficients, defined §1.1 1
aging airplane
   inspection & review §121.1105, 135.422 ..... 300, 445
air ambulance
   helicopter §135.601–135.621................................ 451
air carrier
   defined §1.1 1
   foreign, defined §1.1 5
air carrier and for hire operators, definitions
   Part 110.. 91–93
air commerce, defined §1.1 1
aircraft
   defined §1.1 1
   equipment requirements, and §135.141 391
   large aircraft, defined §1.1 6
   proving tests §135.145... 392
   small aircraft, defined §1.1 10
aircraft dispatcher, Part 121
   qualifications, duty time
      §121.461–121.465 251–252
aircraft dispatchers
   certificate required §65.51 40
   certification course
      content, hours §65.61.. 41
      facilities §65.65.. 42
      general §65.63... 41
   courses Part 65 App.A 50
   eligibility §65.53... 40
   experience required §65.57 40
   knowledge required §65.55 40
   personnel requirements §65.67 42
   skill required §65.59.. 41
   student records §65.70 42
   training required §65.57.. 40
aircraft engine, defined §1.1.. 1
aircraft performance
   operating limitations §135.361 434
aircraft requirements
   Part 135 operations §135.25................................ 378
aircraft requirements (Part 121 operations)
   certification and equipment §121.157.................. 168
   general §121.153.. 167
   limitations §121.161... 169
   proving tests §121.163... 170
   single-engine prohibition §121.159 169
aircraft simulators and other training
   devices §135.335 428
airframe, defined §1.1.. 1
airman and crewmember requirements
   domestic, flag, and supplemental
      operations §121.381–121.397............... 224–227
   Part 121 operations
      crewmember requirements
         at stops §121.393 226
      emergency, crewmember duties §121.397...... 227
      flight attendants §121.391, 121.394 .... 225, 226
      flight engineer §121.387.................................. 224
      flight navigator and specialized
         equipment §121.389................................. 224
      limitations, airman services §121.383............. 224
airmen
   limitations on use of services §121.383,
      135.95 .... 224, 384
airmen, other than flight crewmembers
   application for certificate §65.11 35
   temporary certificate §65.13 36
airplane
   defined §1.1 1
   evacuation capability §121.570............................ 265
   security §121.538... 261
   years in service §121.1105, 135.422 .... 300, 445
airplane components
   fire protection §121.277 182
airplane flight manual
   supplemental operations §121.141 167
airplane flight recorder
   specifications Part 121 App.B, App.M.......... 311, 350
airplane performance
   operating limitations §135.361–135.399 434–442
airplane performance operating limitations
   cargo service airplanes §121.198....................... 176
   domestic, flag, and supplemental
      §121.171–121.207................................. 170–178
   general, Part 121 operations §121.173................ 170
   nontransport category
      enroute limitations, one engine
         inoperative §121.201 177
      landing limitations, alternate §121.205............ 178
      landing limitations, destination §121.203......... 177
      takeoff limitations §121.199 177
   provisionally certificated airplanes §121.207........ 178
   reciprocating engine-powered
      enroute limitations, all engines §121.179 172
      enroute limitations,
         one engine inoperative §121.181.............. 172
      enroute limitations,
         two engines inoperative §121.183............ 172
      landing limitations, alternate §121.187............ 173
      landing limitations, destination §121.185......... 173
      takeoff limitations §121.177 171
      weight limitations §121.175 171
   turbine engine-powered
      enroute limitations, destination §121.195......... 175
      enroute limitations,
         one engine inoperative §121.191............... 174
      enroute limitations,
         two engines inoperative §121.193............ 175
      landing limitations, alternate §121.197............ 176
      takeoff limitations §121.189 173
airport
   defined §1.1 1
   requirements §135.229... 415
   use of certificated §121.590................................. 274
airship, defined §1.1 1
air taxi, commercial operators §135.1...................... 372
air taxi operators
   manual requirements §135.21 376
air traffic clearance, defined §1.1................................... 1

air traffic control, defined §1.1 1
air traffic control tower operators
 currency §65.50 40
 drugs and alcohol §120.17–120.21 121–122
 duties §65.45 39
 eligibility, knowledge, skill and other
  requirements for certificate
  §65.31–65.43 38–39
 facility ratings §65.39, 65.41 .... 38, 39
 facility ratings, exchange of §65.43 39
 maximum hours on duty §65.47 39
 operating positions §65.37 38
 operating rules §65.49 39
air traffic, defined §1.1 1
air traffic service (ATS) routes, defined §1.1 1
air transportation, defined §1.1 1
airworthiness
 check, pilot-in-command §135.71 380
 release, maintenance performed §135.443 449
 requirements §135.169 404
 responsibility for §135.413 443
alcohol
 and drug testing program Part 120 119–143
 handling of test results §120.219 137
 misuse of §120.19, 120.37 .... 122, 123
 testing, covered employees §120.215 134
 testing for §120.21, 120.39 .... 122, 124
 testing procedures §120.203 133
 testing program
  definitions §120.7 120
  implementation §120.225 140
  requirements §120.201–120.227 133–143
 test, refusal to submit to §63.12a,
  120.11–120.15 .... 17, 121
 tests required §120.217 134
alcoholic beverages §135.121 387
alcohol or drugs §63.12, 65.12 .... 17, 36
alcohol-related conduct §120.221 138
alert area, defined §1.1 1
all-cargo operation, defined §110.0 91
alternate airport
 defined §1.1 1
 weather minima §121.625 278
altitude engine, defined §1.1 1
altitude, minimum VFR §135.203 411
amateur rocket, defined §1.1 1
appliance, defined §1.1 1
application
 falsification, reproduction, or alteration §63.20 19
approved aircraft inspection program §135.419 444
approved, defined §1.1 1
AQP, Advanced Qualification Program
  §121.901–121.925 292–298
AQP approval process §121.909 294
AQP certification §121.919 297
area navigation (RNAV)
 defined §1.1 2
 route, defined §1.1 2
areas and routes, approval of
 for supplemental operations §121.111,
  121.113, 121.115 .... 162, 163
armed forces, defined §1.1 2
aural warning device §121.289 184
authority to refuse transportation §121.586 272

autopilot, use of §135.93, 135.105 .... 383, 385
autorotation, defined §1.1 2
auxiliary rotor, defined §1.1 2
aviation maintenance technician schools
 students from certificated schools §65.80 43

B

balloon, defined §1.1 2
brake horsepower, defined §1.1 2
briefing passengers, before flight §135.117 386
business names, use of §119.9 105

C

cabin interiors §121.215 178
cabin ozone concentration §121.578 267
calendar day, defined §135.273 420
calibrated airspeed, defined §1.1 2
canard configuration, defined §1.1 2
canard, defined §1.1 2
cargo, carriage of
 in cargo compartments §121.287 184
 in passenger compartments §121.285 183
carriage of cargo, carry-on baggage and
  mail §135.87 382
carry-on baggage §121.589 273
Category A, defined §1.1 2
Category B, defined §1.1 2
category, defined §1.1 2
Category III operations, defined §1.1 2
Category II operations, defined §1.1 2
CAT II, second-in-command §135.111 386
ceiling, defined §1.1 2
certificate
 amending §119.41 109
 application and issue §63.11 16
 change of address §63.21, 65.21 .... 19, 37
 change of name, replacement of lost
  §63.16, 65.16 .... 18, 36
 display of §65.89, 65.105 .... 44, 46
 duration of §63.15, 65.15 .... 17, 36
 falsification, reproduction, or alteration §63.20 19
 issuing or denying §119.39 109
 lost or destroyed §63.16, 65.16 .... 18, 36
 requirements, maintenance §135.435 448
 special purpose §63.23 19
 surrender of §119.61 114
 temporary §63.13 17
 under Part 119 §119.35, 119.36 107
certificate-holding district office, defined §110.2 91
certificates and ratings
 airmen other than flight crewmembers §65.1 35
 required §63.3 16
certification
 foreign airmen other than flight
  crewmembers §65.3 35
 foreign flight crewmembers
  other than pilots §63.2 16
change of address §119.47 109
check airmen
 qualifications §135.337 429
 training of §135.339 431
checklist
 required, Part 135 operations §135.83 381

Send additional terms to asa@asa2fly.com

civil aircraft, defined §1.1 2
class, defined §1.1 2
clearway, defined §1.1 2
climbout speed, defined §1.1 3
CMP document, defined §1.1 3
cockpit voice recorder §121.359 217
   required §135.151 393
collision avoidance system §121.356 215
commercial air tour §119.1,
   121.1, 135.1 .... 104, 156, 373
   defined §110.2 91
commercial operations
   carriage of narcotic drugs, marijuana,
      depressant or stimulant drugs or
      substances §135.41 378
   manual contents §135.23 376
   manual requirements §135.21 376
commercial operator §135.1 372
   defined §1.1 3
communication and navigation equipment
   extended overwater operations §121.351 214
   requirements §135.161 400
   VFR operation over routes navigated by
      pilotage §121.347 212
   VFR operations over routes not navigated by
      pilotage, or IFR operations, or over-the-
      top §121.349 213
commuter operation, defined §110.2 91
commuter or on-demand operations §135.1 372
compartment interiors
   materials allowed §135.170 404
   materials for §121.312 193
compressed oxygen
   transportation of (on aircraft) §175.501 499
consensus standard, defined §1.1 3
continued airworthiness and safety
   improvements §121.1101–121.1117 300–308
continuous airworthiness maintenance program
   (CAMP) §91.1411–91.1443, 121.374 ... 84–89, 220
contracts, retention of §135.64 379
controlled airspace, defined §1.1 3
controlled firing area, defined §1.1 3
cowling §121.249 181
crew
   pairing §135.4 375
   PIC designation required §135.109 385
   qualifications §135.243–135.247 415–418
   requirements, Part 135 operations §135.99 385
crewmember qualifications
   domestic, flag, and supplemental
      operations §121.431–121.453 243–250
   Part 121 operations
      experience, consolidation of knowledge and
         skills §121.434 245
      flight engineer §121.453 250
      general §121.432 244
      information required for
         pilot-in-command §121.443 250
      line checks §121.440 248
      pilot certificates §121.436 247
      pilot operating limitations, pairing
         requirements §121.438 247
      pilot, recent experience §121.439 248
      proficiency checks §121.441 249
      training required §121.433 244

crewmember(s)
   certificate, international §121.721–121.723 291
   defined §1.1 3
   duties §135.100 385
   emergency training §135.331 428
   flight time limitations, rest required §135.261 418
   initial and recurrent training
      requirements §135.343 432
   medical event training §121.805 292
   previously trained §135.12 376
   testing requirements §135.291 422
   tests and checks, grace provisions, training to
      accepted standards §135.301 425
   training requirements §135.329 427
Crew Resource Management (CRM) §121.907 293
critical altitude, defined §1.1 3
critical engine, defined §1.1 3
CRM, Crew Resource Management §121.907 293
currency requirements
   Part 135 operations §135.247 417

D

damage-tolerance-based inspections §121.1109 301
decision altitude (DA), defined §1.1 3
decision height (DH), defined §1.1 3
destination airport analysis §91.1037, 135.4 ...... 65, 375
deviation authority
   for an emergency operation §119.57 113
   for operations under U.S. military
      contract §119.55 113
digital flight recorders
   for 10-19 seat airplanes §121.344a 210
   for transport category airplanes §121.344 207
direct air carrier
   certificate, application requirements §119.35 107
   certificate, contents of §119.37 108
   defined §110.2 91
   instrastate common carriage §119.21 105
   requirements §119.33 107
dispatcher
   domestic and flag operations §121.395 227
dispatching and flight release rules
   domestic, flag, and supplemental
      operations §121.591–121.667 275–286
dispatching, flight release
   alternate airport §121.617 277
   alternate airport, destination, IFR or over-the-top
      domestic operations §121.619 277
      flag operations §121.621 277
      supplemental operations §121.623 277
   authority §121.593–121.597 275
   communications,
      navigation §121.607, 121.609 276
   continuing flight, unsafe conditions §121.627 278
   domestic and flag operations
      dispatch responsibility §121.663 286
      refueling or provisional airports §121.635 281
      takeoffs, unlisted and alternate
         airports §121.637 281
   domestic, flag, supplemental operations
      initial approach altitude §121.659 286
      takeoff and landing minimums,
         various §121.649–121.652 283–284
   facilities, services in supplemental
      operations §121.603 276

familiarity with weather conditions §121.599........275
flag operations
   initial approach altitude §121.661...................286
flight altitude rules §121.657.................................285
fuel supply §121.639–121.645....................281–282
icing conditions §121.629..279
IFR or over-the-top §121.613..................................276
information to pilot-in-command §121.601...........275
inoperable instruments and
   equipment §121.628.....................................278
load manifest §121.665..286
original, redispatch, or
   amendment of §121.631................................280
over water §121.615..276
supplemental operations
   VFR, IFR flight plan §121.667..........................286
VFR conditions §121.611..276
DOD commercial air carrier evaluator §121.548a.....263
   admission to pilots' compartment §135.76...........380
   defined §110.2...91
domestic and flag operations
   approval of routes §121.91–121.107............159–162
   communication facilities §121.99.........................161
   dispatch §121.107..162
   en route navigation facilities §121.103..................161
   required data, airports §121.97............................160
   route width §121.95...160
   servicing, maintenance §121.105.........................162
   weather reporting §121.101..................................161
domestic, flag, and supplemental operations
   aircraft requirements §121.151–121.163.....167–170
   applicability of rules §121.1..................................156
   carriage of narcotic drugs §121.15.......................159
   compliance schedule §121.2.................................157
   in foreign country §121.11....................................159
   manual requirements §121.131–121.141....165–167
domestic operation, defined §110.2............................91
doors, internal §121.217..179
Doppler radar and Inertial Navigation System
   (INS) Part 121 App.G...344
drug and alcohol testing program Part 120.......119–143
drugs
   carriage of narcotics §121.15................................159
   testing for prohibited §120.35..............................123
   testing program
      definitions §120.7..120
      use of prohibited §120.17, 120.33................121, 122
drug testing
   refusal to submit to §120.11–120.15....................121
   types required §120.109......................................125
drug testing program §120.101–120.125..........124–133
   implementation §120.117....................................130
dry-lease aircraft exchange §91.1001........................56
dual controls requirement §135.147........................392
duty period
   defined §135.273...420
   limitations and rest requirements §117.11–
      117.29, 135.273...............................97–101, 420

E

early ETOPS, defined §1.1..3
electrical wiring interconnection systems (EWIS)
   maintenance program §121.1111.....................302
eligible on-demand operation §135.4........................375
emergency
   continuation of flight in §135.69..........................380
   domestic and flag operations §121.557................263
   equipment
      §135.167, 135.177, 135.178..........402, 406, 407
      extended overwater operations §135.167.......402
   evacuation, crewmember duties §121.397..........227
   evacuation duties §135.123..................................387
   evacuation procedures,
      demonstration §121.291................................184
   evacuation procedures Part 121 App.D...............330
   medical equipment §121.801–121.805.................292
   medical, first aid kits Part 121 App.A...................309
   medical training §121.801–121.805......................292
   operations §135.19..376
      obtaining deviation authority §119.57...............113
   supplemental operations §121.559......................264
   training for crewmembers §135.331.....................428
emergency equipment
   rotorcraft, overwater §135.168.............................403
emergency medical evacuation service (HEMES)
   crew rest required §135.271................................420
Employee Assistance Program (EAP) §120.115......129
empty weight and center of gravity
   currency requirement §135.185...........................411
empty weight, defined §110.2......................................91
engine
   accessory section diaphragm §121.251...............181
   breather lines §121.243..181
   rotation §121.279...182
engine failure, reports required §135.417.................444
enhanced flight visibility (EFV), defined §1.1................3
enhanced flight vision system (EFVS),
   defined §1.1...3
en route inspections §135.75....................................380
equipment
   emergency, operations over uninhabited
      terrain areas §121.353...................................214
   operations using specialized means of
      navigation §121.355.......................................215
equipment interchange
   domestic and flag operations §121.569................265
equipment requirements
   carrying passengers, under IFR §135.163...........401
   commuter and on-demand
      operations §135.141–135.180..............391–411
   extended overwater or
      IFR operations §135.165...............................401
   rotorcraft, radio altimeters §135.160....................400
equivalent airspeed, defined §1.1.................................3
ETOPS
   alternate airport §121.99, 121.106, 121.122,
      121.624..................................161, 162, 164, 278
   defined §121.7...158
   and polar operations, requirements Part 121,
      App.P...362
   area of operation, defined §121.7........................158
   entry point §121.631..280
      defined §121.7..158
   significant system §121.374................................220
   type design approval §121.162.............................169

Send additional terms to asa@asa2fly.com

ETOPS significant system, defined §1.1........................ 4
EWIS maintenance program §121.1111.................... 302
exit row seating §135.129.. 389
exit seating §121.585... 270
extended operations (ETOPS) Part 135, App.G 481
    defined §1.1.. 4
extended over-water operation, defined §1.1.................. 4
external-load attaching, defined §1.1............................... 4
external load, defined §1.1 4

F

failure, mechanical, reports required §121.703,
    135.415 .... 289, 443
falsification, reproduction, or alteration
    of applications, certificates, logbooks,
        reports §63.20, 65.20, 121.9........... 19, 37, 159
fatigue risk management system
    (FRMS) §117.3, 117.7................................... 96, 97
Federal Air Marshal §1544.223................................... 516
final approach fix (FAF), defined §1.1............................... 4
final takeoff speed, defined §1.1...................................... 4
fingerprint-based criminal history records
    checks §1544.229, 1544.230 .... 517, 521
fire-detector systems §121.273, 121.275 182
fire extinguishers, requirements §135.155................ 398
fire-extinguishing
    agent container compartment
        temperature §121.269............................. 182
    agent container pressure relief §121.267............. 182
    agents §121.265 182
    system materials §121.271 182
    systems §121.263 182
fire, precautions §121.221 179
fireproof, defined §1.1.. 4
fire resistant, defined §1.1 4
fire walls §121.245, 121.247.. 181
flag operation, defined §110.2.. 92
flame resistant, defined §1.1.. 4
Flammability Reduction Means §121.1117................ 307
flammable
    defined §1.1.. 4
    fluids §121.225, 121.255............................. 180, 181
flammable liquid fuel
    transportation of (on aircraft) §175.310................ 497
flap extended speed, defined §1.1................................... 4
flash resistant, defined §1.1... 4
flight and duty limitations and rest requirements,
    flightcrew Part 117....................................... 95–101
flight attendant
    crewmember requirement §135.107 385
    crewmember testing requirements §135.295 423
    defined §135.273 421
    duty period limitations, rest requirements,
        Part 121 operations §121.467....................... 252
    initial and transition ground training §135.349 434
    requirements §121.391 225
    requirements §121.392 225
flight crew
    airman and crewmember requirements
        Part 121 operation
            flight crew composition §121.385................ 224
    at stops where passengers remain on
        board §121.393 226
    composition of §135.99 385
    minimum composition §121.385 224

flight crewmember
    at controls §121.543... 261
    defined §1.1.. 4
    duties §121.542, 135.100............................ 261, 385
    fitness for duty §117.5... 97
    flight and duty limitations and rest
        requirements Part 117........................... 95–101
    requirements §135.241 415
flight cycle implementation time §121.1107.............. 301
flight data recorders §91.609
    filtered data §121.346, 135.156 .... 212, 398
    required §135.152... 395
flight duty period (FDP) §117.3...................................... 96
flight engineer
    aeronautical experience required §63.37............... 21
    aircraft ratings §63.33 20
    and flight navigator special-purpose
        certificates §63.23....................................... 19
    courses §63.43... 22
    eligibility §63.31... 20
    knowledge requirements §63.35............................ 20
    requirements
        §63.31–63.43, 121.387 .... 20–22, 224
    skill required §63.31 22
    training course requirements Part 63 App.C 29
flight instructor
    qualifications §135.338 430
    training of §135.340 431
flight level, defined §1.1... 4
flight locating requirements §135.79........................... 381
flight navigators
    courses §63.61... 24
    eligibility §63.51... 23
    experience §63.55... 23
    knowledge required §63.53................................... 23
    requirements
        §63.51–63.61, 121.389 .... 23–24, 224
    skill required §63.57 23
    test requirements for certificate Part 63 App.A 24
    training course requirements Part 63 App.B 27
flight operations
    pilot monitoring §121.544................................... 262
flight operations §125.531–121.590,
    135.61–135.129 .... 260–275, 379–391
    admission to flight deck §121.547........................ 262
    airports, use of §121.590 274
    alcoholic beverages §121.575............................. 267
    all certificate holders §121.531–121.590 260–275
    aviation safety inspector's credentials,
        admission to pilot compartment §121.548.... 263
    briefing passengers before takeoff
        §121.571, 121.573 .... 265, 266
    carry-on baggage §121.589 273
    crew compartment door §121.587 273
    discreet notification of flightcrew §121.582.......... 269
    enroute inspections §121.581 269
    exit seating §121.585.. 270
    flightdeck door §121.584.................................... 270
    flying equipment §121.549................................. 263
    manipulation of controls §121.545 262
    minimum altitudes, autopilot use §121.579 268
    reporting engine inoperative landings §121.565 .. 264
    reporting mechanical irregularities §121.563......... 264
    reporting potential hazards §121.561 264
flight plan
    defined §1.1.. 4
    VFR and IFR, supplemental
        operations §121.667..................................... 286

flight simulation training
  device (FSTD), defined §1.1.................4
flight time
  defined §1.1................................4
  limitations for flag operations §121.480–
    121.493..............................255–257
  limitations for supplemental operations
    §121.500–121.525...................257–259
    flight engineers §121.511................258
    other airman and crewmembers
      §121.515–121.525..................258–259
    overseas, international §121.513.........258
    pilots §121.503–121.509.............257–258
  limitations, rest requirements for domestic
    operations §121.470, 121.471...........254
flight time limitations §135.263..............418
  and rest requirements §117.11–117.29,
    135.261–135.269.............97–101, 418–420
  scheduled operations §135.265.............418
  unscheduled 1-2 pilot crews §135.267......419
  unscheduled 3-4 pilot crews §135.269......419
flight time requirements
  Part 135 operations §135.243..............416
flight training
  requirements Part 121 App.E...............331
flight training devices
  defined §1.1...............................5
flight visibility, defined §1.1................5
foreign air carrier, defined §1.1..............5
foreign air commerce, defined §1.1.............5
foreign air transportation, defined §1.1.......5
former FAA employees §91.1050................68
former FAA employees §119.73................118
forward wing, defined §1.1....................5
fractional ownership operations
  §91.1001–91.1443........................56–89
  additional equipment §91.1045.............67
  aircraft maintenance §91.1109.............83
  CAMP, certificate requirements §91.1435...88
  CAMP (continuous airworthiness maintenance
    program) §91.1411–91.1443............84–89
  compliance date §91.1002..................57
  crewmember experience §91.1053............69
  crewmember testing and training
    requirements §91.1067–91.1087........74–78
  crew qualifications §91.1089–91.1101.....78–82
  defined §91.1001..........................56
  flight duty and rest time
    §91.1057–91.1062.....................70–73
  flight scheduling §91.1029................64
  IFR minimums §91.1039.....................66
  internal safety reporting §91.1021.........61
  management contract §91.1003..............57
  operating manual §91.1025.................62
  operational control §91.1009–91.1013......58
  passengers §91.1035.......................64
  pilot testing and training §91.1063.......72
  program management §91.1014,
    91.1443..............................59–89
  recordkeeping §91.1027....................63
  required operating information §91.1033...64
  tests and inspections §91.1019............61
  turbine-powered large transport category
    airplanes §91.1037......................65
  validation tests §91.1041.................66
fuel
  factors for computing, required §121.647..283

fuel requirements
  Part 135 operations §135.209..............411
fuel system
  independence §121.281....................183
  lines and fittings §121.231..............180
fuel tanks, location of §121.229............180
fuel tank system maintenance program §121.1113..302
full flight simulator (FFS), defined §1.1.....5
fuselage pressure boundary §121.1107........301

G

glider, defined §1.1..........................5
go-around power or thrust setting, defined §1.1...5
ground visibility, defined §1.1...............5
gyrodyne, defined §1.1........................5
gyroplane, defined §1.1.......................5

H

hazardous materials
  carriage by aircraft 49 CFR Part 175...485–503
  training requirements Part 121. App.O,
    §135.505..........................359, 450
  "will carry" operators Part 121 App.O....360
  "will-not-carry" operators Part 121 App.O....361
hazardous materials training
  program §121.1001–121.1007,
    §135.501–135.507...............298–300, 449
hazardous materials transportation
  exceptions for passengers, crewmembers and
    air operators §175.10..................487
  general information and regulations
    §175.1–175.33......................485–494
  handling §175.75–175.90.............494–497
  inspecting shipments §175.30.............492
  material classification §175.310–175.706....497–503
hazmat employees, training of §175.20.......490
helicopter
  defined §1.1..............................5
  minimum visibility,
    Part 135 operations §135.207..........411
  surface reference requirements,
    Part 135 operations §135.207..........411
helicopter air ambulance
  IFR operations §135.611, 135.613.........453
  operations control centers §135.619......454
helicopter air ambulance equipment, operations,
  and training requirements §135.601–
    135.621............................451–456
helicopter (HEMES) crew rest required §135.271....420
helicopter terrain awareness and warning system
  (HTAWS) §135.605.........................452
helioport, defined §1.1.......................5

I

icing, operations in §121.321................198
idle thrust, defined §1.1.....................5
IFR
  alternate airport requirements §135.223..413
  conditions, defined §1.1..................5
  equipment requirements §135.163..........401
  landing minimums, instrument approach
    procedures §121.567, 135.78......265, 381
  operating limitations §135.215...........412
  operations, equipment required §135.165..401

Send additional terms to asa@asa2fly.com

Part 135 operations §135.181 410
   second-in-command required §135.101 385
   takeoff limitations §135.217 412
   weather minimums
      alternate airport §135.221 413
      destination airport §135.219 412
IFR over-the-top, defined §1.1 5
indicated airspeed, defined §1.1 5
induction system, ice prevention §121.283 183
Inertial Navigation System (INS)
   and Doppler radar Part 121 App.G 344
in-flight shutdown (IFSD), defined §1.1 5
inoperable instruments and equipment
   §135.179 410
inspection and review
   aging airplane §121.1105, 135.422 .... 300, 445
inspection authorization
   application, requirements, eligibility
      §65.91–65.95 44–45
inspection program(s)
   required §135.419 444
inspections §91.409
   continuing analysis and surveillance §135.431 447
   damage-tolerance-based §121.1109 301
   supplemental §121.1109 301
inspectors
   admission to pilots' compartment §135.75 380
instrument and equipment requirements
   §135.149, 135.159 .... 393, 400
   domestic, flag, and supplemental
      operations §121.301–121.360 185–218
   Part 121 operations
      airborne weather radar §121.357 216
      airplane §121.303 185
      cargo, baggage compartments §121.314 196
      cockpit checks §121.315 196
      collision avoidance systems §121.356 215
      compartment interiors,
         materials for §121.312 193
      emergency equipment
         §121.309, 121.310 .... 187, 188
      emergency equipment, for extended
         over-water §121.339, 121.340 204
      engine §121.307 186
      flight and navigational §121.305 186
      flight data recorders §121.343 205
      flight data recorders, digital §121.344 207
      for icing conditions §121.341 205
      for IFR over-the-top §121.325 199
      for night operations §121.323 199
      fuel tanks §121.316 196
      interphone system §121.319 198
      lavatory fire protection §121.308 187
      miscellaneous equipment §121.313 195
      oxygen equipment standards §121.335 203
      passenger information §121.317 196
      pitot heat indication §121.342 205
      protective breathing equipment §121.337 203
      public address system §121.318 197
      seats, safety belts, shoulder
         harnesses §121.311 191
      supplemental oxygen
         §121.327–121.333 199–202
instrument approach procedure (IAP), defined §1.1 6
instrument, defined §1.1 6
international crewmember certificate
   surrender of §121.723 291

interstate air commerce, defined §1.1 6
interstate air transportation, defined §1.1 6
intrastate air transportation, defined §1.1 6
intrastate operations
   retention of contracts §135.64 379

J

justifiable aircraft equipment, defined §110.2 92

K

kind of operation, defined §110.2 92
kite, defined §1.1 6
knowledge tests
   cheating or other unauthorized conduct
      §63.18, 65.18 .... 18, 37

L

landing gear
   aural warning device §121.289 184
landing gear extended speed, defined §1.1 6
landing gear operating speed, defined §1.1 6
large nontransport category airplanes
   en route limitations §135.391 441
   landing limitations, alternate §135.395 442
   landing limitations, destination §135.393 441
   takeoff limitations §135.389 441
large transport category airplanes
   en route limitations §135.369 436
   landing limitations, alternate §135.377 437
   landing limitations, destination §135.375 437
   takeoff limitations §135.367 435
   turbine, en route limitations §135.381 438
   turbine, landing limitations
      alternate §135.387 440
      destination §135.385 440
   turbine, takeoff limitations §135.379 437
   weight limitations §135.365 435
lighter-than-air aircraft, defined §1.1 6
light-sport aircraft §65.85 44
   consensus standard, defined §1.1 3
   defined §1.1 6
   powered parachute, defined §1.1 8
   repairmen certificate for §65.107 47
   weight-shift-control aircraft, defined §1.1 11
line checks §135.299 424
lines and fittings
   fuel and other, requirements §121.231,
      121.233, 121.237, 121.259 .... 180, 181
load factor, defined §1.1 6
logbook, falsification, reproduction, or
   alteration §63.20 19
long-call reserve §117.21 99
long-range communication system, defined §1.1 6
long-range navigation system, defined §1.1 6

M

mach number, defined §1.1 7
mail, transportation of §135.1 372
main rotor, defined §1.1 7
maintenance
   authority to perform §135.437 448
   defined §1.1 7
   manual requirements §135.427 446

ASA 533

records, requirements §135.439 448
required inspection personnel §135.429 447
maintenance and preventive maintenance
   training program §135.433 448
maintenance, preventive maintenance,
   alterations, and required inspections,
   certificates required §135.435 448
maintenance, preventive maintenance, and alterations
   airworthiness release, or aircraft log
      entry §135.443 449
   authority to perform and approve §135.437 448
   domestic, flag, and supplemental
      operations §121.361–121.380a 218–223
   organization for §135.423 446
   Part 121 operations
      airworthiness responsibility §121.363 218
      analysis and surveillance §121.373 219
      authority to perform and approve §121.379 222
      certificate requirements §121.378 222
      duty time limitations §121.377 222
      inspection personnel §121.371 219
      manual requirements §121.369 219
      organization §121.365 218
      programs §121.367, 121.375 .... 218, 222
      records §121.380, 121.380a 223
   programs for §135.425 446
   rules for §135.411 442
maintenance program(s)
   fuel tank system §121.1113 302
maintenance requirements, additional §135.421 445
major alteration, defined §1.1 7
major repair, defined §1.1 7
malfunction(s), reports §121.703, 135.415 .... 289, 443
management personnel
   qualifications §119.67, 119.71 .... 115, 116
   required §119.65, 119.69 .... 114, 116
manifest
   recordkeeping requirements §135.63 379
manifold pressure, defined §1.1 7
manual contents, Part 135 operations §135.23 376
manual requirements
   domestic, flag, and supplemental
      operations §121.131–121.141 165–167
manual(s)
   availability §121.137 166
   contents §121.135 165
   distribution and availability §121.137 166
   preparation §121.133 165
   required aboard aircraft, supplemental
      operations §121.139 167
   requirements, for maintenance §135.427 446
   requirements, Part 121 maintenance §121.369 ... 219
   requirements, Part 135 operations §135.21 376
master parachute rigger
   certificate requirements §65.119 49
maximum continuous augmented
   thrust, defined §1.1 9
maximum continuous power, defined §1.1 9
maximum continuous thrust, defined §1.1 9
maximum engine overtorque, defined §1.1 7
maximum payload capacity, defined §110.2 92
maximum speed for stability characteristics,
   V_{FC}/M_{FC}, defined §1.1 7
maximum zero fuel weight, defined §110.2 92

mechanical interruption summary
   report §135.417 444
mechanical irregularities, reporting §135.65 379
mechanics
   airframe rating §65.85 44
   eligibility requirements §65.71 42
   experience requirements §65.77 43
   inspection authorization §65.91 44
      duration §65.92 44
      privileges and limitations §65.95 45
      renewal §65.93 45
   knowledge requirements §65.75 43
   powerplant rating §65.87 44
   privileges and limitations §65.81 43
   ratings §65.73 42
   recent experience requirements §65.83 43
   skill requirements §65.79 43
medical certificate
   defined §1.1 7
   physical deficiency §63.19 18
medical event training §121.805 292
military operations area (MOA), defined §1.1 7
military parachute riggers (or former)
   special certification rule §65.117 49
minimum altitudes
   use of autopilot §135.93 383
minimum descent altitude (MDA), defined §1.1 7
minimum equipment list §121.628, 135.179 ..... 278, 410
minor alteration, defined §1.1 7
minor repair, defined §1.1 7
multiengine aircraft
   Part 135 operations §135.181 410

N

national defense airspace, defined §1.1 7
navigable airspace, defined §1.1 7
navigation equipment, specialized §121.389 224
night currency requirements §135.247 417
night, defined §1.1 7
night operations
   (or VFR over-the-top), equipment required
      under Part 135 §135.159 400
noncommon carriage, defined §110.2 92
nonprecision approach procedure, defined §1.1 7
nonstop commercial air tours
   §119.1, 121.1, 135.1 .... 104, 156, 372
nontransport category airplanes
   C-46 cargo operations Part 121 App.C 313
   Part 121 operations
      enroute limitations §121.201 177
      landing limitations §121.203, 121.205 ..... 177, 178
      takeoff limitations §121.199 177
   special airworthiness requirements §121.293 185

O

OEI power, definitions §1.1 9
oil system drains §121.241 181
on-demand operations
   crew pairing §135.4 375
   defined §110.2 92
   eligible §135.4 375
   flight time §135.4 375

Send additional terms to asa@asa2fly.com

operate, defined §1.1 7
operating
    information required, checklists §135.83 381
    operating experience §135.244 416
operating limitations
    aircraft performance §135.361 434
    commuter category airplanes §135.398 442
    on-demand operations §135.4 375
    small nontransport category
        airplanes §135.399 442
    small transport category airplanes §135.397 442
    VFR over-the-top carrying
        passengers §135.211 411
operating requirements
    icing §121.321 198
operational control, defined §1.1 7
operational control, responsibility
    domestic operations §121.533 260
    flag operations §121.535 260
    supplementary operations §121.537 260
operations
    aircraft requirements §135.25 378
    alternate airport requirements §135.223 413
    autopilot, minimum altitudes for use §135.93 383
    commercial, air taxi §135.1 372
    commercial air tours §135.1 373
    continuation of flight
        in an emergency §135.69 380
    during physical deficiency §63.19 18
    equipment requirements, night or
        VFR over-the-top §135.159 400
    flight time limitations,
        rest requirements §135.263 418
    IFR, takeoff, approach, landing
        minimums §135.225 413
    in critical phases of flight §135.100 385
    limitations, icing conditions §135.227 414
operations in icing §121.321 198
operations, restriction or suspension of
    domestic and flag §121.551 263
    supplemental §121.553 263
operations schedules
    domestic and flag §121.541 261
operations specifications
    amending §119.51 111
    contents §119.49 110
    duty to maintain §119.43 109
    manual contents §135.23 376
    manual requirements §135.21 376
    recordkeeping requirements §135.63 379
overseas air commerce, defined §1.1 7
overseas air transportation, defined §1.1 7
over-the-top, defined §1.1 8
over water operations §135.183 411
oxygen
    compressed §175.501 499
    equipment requirements §135.157 399
    medical use by passengers §135.91 383
    use of by pilot §135.89 382
oxygen, portable systems on board aircraft
    SFAR 106 to Part 121 155–156
oxygen systems, lavatory §121.1500 308

P

parachute, defined §1.1 8
parachute riggers
    certificate privileges §65.125 49
    certification required §65.111 48
    eligibility §65.113 48
    facilities and equipment §65.127 50
    master certificate requirements §65.119 49
    military or former military, special certification
        rule §65.117 49
    performance standards §65.129 50
    records §65.131 50
    seal §65.133 50
    senior parachute rigger certificate §65.115 48
    type ratings §65.121, 65.123 49
passenger-carrying operation, defined §110.2 93
passenger information
    seat belt requirements §121.317 196
    smoking §121.317, 135.127 .... 196, 387
passengers
    and crew compartments §121.576 267
    briefing §121.571 265
    briefing, extended overwater
        operations §121.573 266
    oxygen for medical use §121.574 266
    service equipment, stowage of food,
        beverages §121.577 267
    signs and information, required §135.127 387
performance requirements
    aircraft operated over-the-top or in IFR
        conditions §135.181 410
person, defined §1.1 8
pilot
    operating limitations, pairing
        requirements §121.438 247
    reporting hazards §135.67 380
    requirements, use of oxygen §135.89 382
    routes and airports information required
        for §121.443, 121.445 250
pilotage, defined §1.1 8
pilot-in-command
    airworthiness check §135.71 380
    defined §1.1 8
    designation required §135.109 385
    instrument proficiency check
        requirements §135.297 424
    line checks, routes and airports §135.299 424
    qualifications §135.243 415
pilot qualifications
    recent experience §135.247 417
pilot seat
    passenger occupancy of §135.113 386
pilot testing requirements §135.293 422
pitch setting, defined §1.1 8
pitot heat indication systems
    for transport aircraft §135.158 400
plutonium §175.704 502
positive control, defined §1.1 8
powered-lift, defined §1.1 8
powered parachute, defined §1.1 8
powerplant fire protection §121.253 181
precision approach procedure, defined §1.1 8
pressure cross-fed §121.227 180

preventive maintenance, defined §1.1 8
principal base of operations, defined §110.2 93
proficiency check
   requirements Part 121 App.F 339
prohibited area, defined §1.1 8
proof of compliance
   with section 121.221 §121.223 180
propeller
   deicing fluid §121.225 180
propeller, defined §1.1 8
provisional airport, defined §110.2 93
public address, crewmember interphone systems
   required §135.150 393
public aircraft, defined §1.1 8

Q

qualifications
   flight instructors §135.338, 135.340 .... 430, 431
   second-in-command §135.245 417

R

radar
   weather avoidance equipment
     requirements §135.173 406
   weather radar requirements §135.175 406
radioactive contamination §175.705 502
radio equipment
   Part 121 operations §121.345 211
ratings
   requirements §135.243 415
recency of operation, under Part 119 §119.63 114
reciprocating engine-powered airplanes
   Part 121 operations
     enroute limitations §121.179–121.183 172–173
     landing limitations, alternate §121.187 173
     landing limitations, destination §121.185 173
     takeoff limitations §121.177 171
     weight limitations §121.175 171
   supplemental oxygen
     for pressurized cabin §121.331 201
     general §121.327 199
records, reports
   aircraft log entry §121.709 290
   aircraft records, domestic and flag §121.685 287
   airworthiness release §121.709 290
   alteration, repair §121.707 290
   communications records §121.711 291
   crewmember, dispatcher records §121.683 287
   dispatch release, domestic and flag §121.687 287
   disposition of, domestic and flag §121.695 288
   disposition of, supplemental §121.697 288
   domestic, flag, and supplemental
     operations §121.681–121.713 287–291
   flight release, supplemental §121.689 287
   load manifest §121.693 288
   maintenance log §121.701 289
   mechanical interruption summary §121.705 290
   recordkeeping requirements §135.63 379
   retention of contracts §121.713 291
recurrent training §135.351 434
reference landing speed, defined §1.1 10
regular airport, defined §110.2 93
repair assessment
   for pressurized fuselages §121.1107 301

repairmen
   eligibility, certificate §65.101 46
   experimental aircraft builder §65.104 46
   privileges, limitations §65.103 46
reporting points, defined §1.1 10
reports
   falsification, reproduction, or alteration §63.20 19
   mechanical irregularities §135.65 379
   of emergency operations §135.19 376
   potentially hazardous meteorological
     conditions, irregularities of ground
     facilities, navigation §135.67 380
rest period, defined §135.273 421
restricted areas, defined §1.1 10
risk analysis
   helicopter air ambulance, preflight §135.617 454
rocket, defined §1.1 10
rotorcraft, defined §1.1 10
rotorcraft-load combination, defined §1.1 10
rotorcraft operations
   emergency equipment for overwater §135.168 403
   radio altimeters for §135.160 400
rotorcraft operations, direct air carriers and
   commercial operators §119.25 106
routes and limitations, compliance with
   domestic and flag operations §121.555 263
routes, approval of
   domestic and flag operations
     §121.91–121.107 159–162
route segment, defined §1.1 10
rules of construction, defined §1.3 14
rules, Part 135 operations §135.3 374

S

safety belts
   child restraint systems, use of §135.128 388
scheduled operation, defined §110.2 93
sea level engine, defined §1.1 10
second-in-command
   CAT II operations §135.111 386
   defined §1.1 10
   required under IFR §135.101 385
Secret Service agents
   admission to flight deck §121.550 263
security
   aircraft and facilities §1544.225 516
   aircraft operator screening
     §1544.401–1544.11 525–526
   carriage of prisoners §1544.221 515
   coordinators §1544.215 513
   disqualification §63.14, 65.14 .... 17, 36
   known shipper program §1544.239 523
   operations §1544.201–1544.239 509–523
   screener training §1544.407–1544.411 525–526
   screening §1544.201–1544.213 509–513
   threat response §1544.301–1544.305 524
   training §1544.233, 1544.235 523
security, aircraft, air carrier and commercial
   operators 49 CFR Part 1544 505–526
senior parachute rigger certificate
   experience, knowledge, and skill
     requirements §65.115 48
service difficulty reports §121.703, 135.415 ..... 289, 443
short-call reserve §117.21 99

shoulder harness
    installation at crewmember stations §135.171 406
show, defined §1.1 10
shutoff means, engine §121.257 181
simulation, advanced Part 121 App.H 346
special airworthiness requirements
    Part 121 operations §121.211–121.293 178–185
special VFR conditions, defined §1.1 10
special VFR operations, defined §1.1 10
standard atmosphere, defined §1.1 10
stopway, defined §1.1 10
suitable RNAV system, defined §1.1 10
superseded type certification Part 121 App.L 348
supplemental inspections §121.1109 301
supplemental operations
    airplane flight manual §121.141 167
    approval of areas and routes §121.111–121.127 162
    defined §110.2 93
    en route facilities §121.121 163
    flight following §121.125, 121.127 .... 164, 165
    required data, airports §121.117 163
    servicing, maintenance §121.123 164
    weather reporting §121.119 163
synthetic vision, defined §1.1 10
synthetic vision system, defined §1.1 10

T

takeoff augmented thrust, defined §1.1 9
takeoff limitations, large aircraft §135.367 435
takeoff power, defined §1.1 .... 9, 10
takeoff safety speed, defined §1.1 11
takeoffs and landings experience §135.247 417
takeoff thrust, defined §1.1 11
tandem wing configuration, defined §1.1 11
TCAS. See traffic alert and collision avoidance system
TCAS I, defined §1.1 11
TCAS II, defined §1.1 11
TCAS III, defined §1.1 11
Technical Standard Order
    (TSO)-C151 §121.354, 135.154 .... 214, 398
terrain awareness and warning system
    §121.354, 135.154 .... 214, 398
test requirements
    flight navigator certificate Part 63 App.A 24
tests
    cheating §63.18, 65.18 .... 18, 37
    failure, additional training after §135.301 425
    flight line checks §135.299 424
    general §63.17, 65.17 .... 18, 37
    initial and recurrent pilot, flight attendant
        testing §135.293, 135.295 .... 422, 423
    instrument proficiency checks §135.297 424
    retesting after failure §65.19 37
threat assessment
    initial notification of §63.14, 65.14 .... 17, 36
thunderstorm detection equipment,
    requirements §135.173 406
time in service, defined §1.1 11
traffic alert and collision avoidance system
    (TCAS) §135.180 410
    requirements, large turbine-powered
        aircraft §135.180 410
traffic pattern, defined §1.1 11

training
    aircraft simulators and other training
        devices §135.335 428
    course requirements
        flight engineer Part 63 App.C 29
        flight navigator Part 63 App.B 27
    definitions of terms §135.321 425
    flight attendants, initial and transition
        ground §135.349 434
    for emergencies §135.331 428
    initial and recurrent for
        crewmembers §135.343 432
    initial, transition, and upgrade
        for pilots §135.345 433
    medical events §121.805 292
    of check airmen §135.339 431
    pilots, initial, transition, upgrade, and
        differences flight training §135.347 433
    recurrent §135.351 434
training program
    ATP certification §121.410, 135.336 .... 232, 428
    check airmen qualifications §135.337 429
    curriculum §135.327 427
    domestic, flag, and supplemental operations
        requirements §121.400–121.427 227–243
    maintenance or preventive
        maintenance §135.433 448
    Part 121 operations
        aircraft dispatcher, ground training
            §121.422 240
        airplane simulators and other training
            devices §121.409 231
        check airmen, initial and transition
            training §121.413 234
        check airmen qualifications §121.411 232
        compliance, crewmember resource
            management training §121.404 229
        crewmember, dispatcher training §121.415 236
        curriculum §121.403 229
        definitions §121.400 227
        differences training §121.418 238
        emergency training §121.417 237
        flight attendants, ground training §121.421 240
        flight engineers, flight training §121.425 242
        flight instructor qualifications §121.412 233
        flight instructors, initial and transition
            training §121.414 235
        general guidelines §121.401 228
        initial and final approval §121.405 229
        pilots and flight engineers, ground
            training §121.419 239
        pilots, flight training §121.424 241
        previous CRM/DRM training §121.406 230
        recurrent training §121.427 242
        simulators, approval of §121.407 230
        special rules §121.402 228
    pilot and flight attendant
        crewmember §135.341 432
    requirements §135.323 425
    revision of §135.325 426
    special rules §135.324 426
transfer of maintenance records at time of
    sale §135.441 449
Transportation Security Administration
    (TSA) §63.14, 65.14 .... 17, 36

true airspeed, defined *§1.1* 11
TSA inspection authority *§1544.3* 506
turbine engine-powered airplanes
   Part 121 operations
      enroute limitations *§121.191, 121.193* 174, 175
      landing limitations, alternate *§121.197* 176
      landing limitations, destination *§121.195* 175
      takeoff limitations *§121.189* 173
   supplemental oxygen, emergency descent
      and first aid §121.333 201
   supplemental oxygen, general *§121.329* 200
turbopropeller-powered airplanes
   performance requirements *Part 121 App.K* 347
type certfication
   superseded, provisions in CFR/FR
      references *Part 121 App.L* 349
type certification
   regulations made previously effective
      (superseded) *Part 121 App.L* 348
   superseded, applicable aircraft *Part 121 App.L* ... 349
type, defined *§1.1* 11

U

unauthorized operators
   applicability of Part 121 rules to *§121.4* 158
   applicability of rules to *§135.7* 375
United States air carrier, defined *§1.1* 11
United States, defined *§1.1* 11

V

valves
   fuel and oil, requirements *§121.235, 121.239,*
      121.257 .... 180, 181
vent and drain lines *§121.261* 182
ventilation *§121.219* 179
VFR
   fuel supply *§135.209* 411
   minimum altitudes *§135.203* 411
   over-the-top, defined *§1.1* 11
   visibility requirements *§135.205* 411
visibility requirements *§135.205* 411
V-speeds, defined *§1.2* 13

W

warning areas, defined *§1.1* 11
weapons
   prohibition against carriage of *§135.119* 387
weather radar
   equipment requirements *§121.357* 216
weather reports, forecasts *§135.213* 412
weight and balance
   multiengine aircraft *§135.185* 411
weight limitations, large aircraft *§135.365* 435
weight-shift-control aircraft, defined *§1.1* 11
wet lease, defined *§110.2* 93
wet leasing of aircraft, other arrangements for air
   transportation *§119.53* 112
windshear system equipment
   low-altitude, requirements *§121.358* 216
winglet or tip fin, defined *§1.1* 11
written (or, knowledge) tests
   cheating or other unauthorized
      conduct *§63.18, 65.18* 18, 37

Y

years in service, defined *§110.2* 93

How do you like to study?

Preparation is an aviator's most valuable asset. At ASA it's what we do. Our test prep products have been helping aspiring pilots achieve flight since 1947. In print or on the go — **Test Prep for all your study needs.**

Test Prep Books
The leading resource for FAA Knowledge Exam preparation. Also available in eBook PDF format.

Prepware Software
Comprehensive preparation test tool for your PC or Mac. Includes online access.

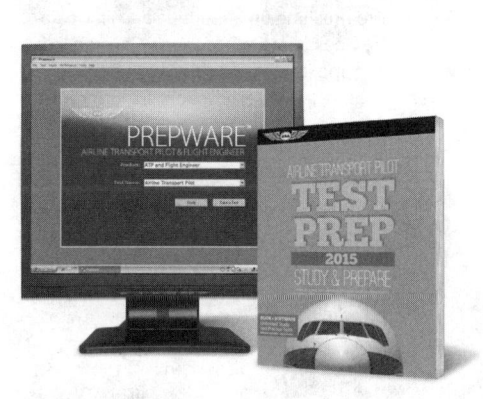

Test Prep Bundles
Combines Test Prep book, Prepware Software Download and online access for study flexibility and savings.

Prepware Apps
The ultimate mobile-learning solution available for Apple, Android, and Windows devices.

Training Starts Here.

AVIATION SUPPLIES & ACADEMICS, INC.
Quality & Service You Can Depend On

See our complete line of study aids, textbooks, pilot supplies and more at your local airport and in bookstores nationwide.
www.asa2fly.com | 800-ASA-2-FLY

Jump-start your career.

Professional Pilot
By John Lowery

This book takes you right up front with discussions on the details all career aviators must understand. Pilots will learn operational rules-of-thumb for day-to-day, real-world flying and gain a full indoctrination into the topics that matter when flying heavy, high, and fast. Also available as an eBook!

Fly the Wing
By Jim Webb and Billy Walker

A comprehensive textbook and companion CD-ROM for commercial and airline transport pilots operating transport-category airplanes. Includes coverage of modern cockpit automation, provides valuable tools and proven techniques for all flight operations. Pilots planning a career in aviation will find important insights not taught anywhere else.

Air Carrier Operations
By Mark J. Holt and Phillip J. Poynor

Ideal for Air Carrier Flight Operations or Airline Operations courses, this book examines the regulations governing Part 121 air carriers. Includes Part 119 and relevant portions of Parts 135, 91 and 61 with emphasis on IFR operations.

The Pilot's Guide to the Airline Cockpit
By Stephen M. Casner

Essential reading for anyone who wants to fly for an airline, this book takes you step-by-step through a challenging IFR line flight in the captain's seat. Learn how to use the autoflight system to help guide you along the route you have built with the flight management computer. Teaches how to deal with vectors, holds, diversions, intercepts, traffic, terrain, and cockpit automation. Also available as an eBook!

The Turbine Pilot's Flight Manual
By Greg Brown and Mark Holt

Whether you are a piston pilot preparing for turbine ground school, a military pilot transitioning to a corporate or airline job, or an old pro brushing up on turbine aircraft operations, this book is designed for you. Covers all major turboprop and jet systems, CRM, high-altitude weather, high-speed aerodynamics, and more. Also available as an eBook!

Practical Aviation Law
By J. Scott Hamilton

A must-read for anyone involved in aviation at any level. This bestselling book not only tells you how to avoid aviation lawyers, but also when it's in your best interest to call one. *Practical Aviation Law* provides the basic knowledge and perspective to understand how the legal system works in relation to aviation. Also available as an eBook!

Training Starts Here.

AVIATION SUPPLIES & ACADEMICS, INC.
Quality & Service You Can Depend On

See our complete line of study aids, textbooks, pilot supplies and more at your local airport and in bookstores nationwide.
www.asa2fly.com | 800-ASA-2-FLY

Professional aviation.

Written by the industry experts, these books provide insight for career pilots. Rely on them for advice on how to get your foot in the door at the airlines, hone your interview skills, and operate effectively as a professional aviator.

Checklist for Success
By Cheryl Cage
Takes aspiring professional pilots step-by-step from preparing their resume and application, through to the interview itself. A must-have reference for all job seekers. Includes interactive multi-media presentation.

Reporting Clear?
By Cheryl Cage
An easy to use, informative guide to conducting your own background check. Addresses, phone numbers, agencies and website info. A simple way to preflight your future.

Your Job Search Partner
By Cheryl Cage
An extensive, positive guide to marketing yourself more effectively while uncovering hidden talents and strengths.

Air Traffic Control Career Prep
By Dr. Patrick R. Mattson, CTO
A comprehensive guide to one of the best-paying Federal government careers, including test preparation for the initial Air Traffic Control exams. Includes software suite!

Mental Math for Pilots
By Ronald McElroy
Sharpen your math skills for the interview as well as for the cockpit with these great tips for figuring math problems in your head without paper or calculator—everything from fuel planning to temperature conversions to crosswind components.

Airline Pilot Technical Interviews
By Ronald McElroy
Prepares you for the airlines' technical side of the interview process with real-world exercises. Aspiring professional pilots will be prepared to display their flying skills during the simulator ride, as well as their aeronautical knowledge during the face-to-face oral questioning.

Job Hunting for Pilots
By Greg Brown
Covers all aspects of the job-hunting process and specifically focuses on how to get a resume hand-carried into flight departments. Not just another airline interview book—the author offers tips and techniques for job-seeking pilots at all levels of the industry, from commuter, corporate and airline pilots, to new CFIs and those flying helicopters. Second edition.

AVIATION SUPPLIES & ACADEMICS, INC.
Quality & Service You Can Depend On

Training Starts Here.
See our complete line of study aids, textbooks, pilot supplies and more at your local airport and in bookstores nationwide.
www.asa2fly.com | 800-ASA-2-FLY

Oral exam essentials.

Airline Transport Pilot Oral Exam Guide

By popular demand, author Michael Hayes wrote an Oral Exam Guide for pilots training for the Airline Transport Pilot certificate. This book is also beneficial to pilots transitioning from reciprocating to turbine aircraft, or to pilots preparing for airline ground school. Written in a question-and-answer format that simulates the oral portion of the checkride, the book lists the questions examiners are most likely to ask, and provides comprehensive yet quickly grasped responses. Also available as an eBook and App!

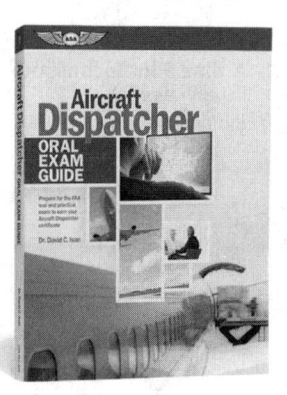

Aircraft Dispatcher Oral Exam Guide

Dispatchers are experts at utilizing all available resources to develop efficient, specific plans for aircraft crews worldwide. Now, dispatcher applicants can use this same methodology as they strive for their certification.

- Comprehensive oral exam preparation and certification process resources
- Great review for current dispatchers
- Excellent for aspiring airline pilots seeking a better understanding of dispatch flight operations

Also available as an eBook.

Versatile recordkeeping.

Flight Crew Logbook

Created with the input of airline pilots and instructors, these shirt-pocket-size logbooks are designed for long lasting and comprehensive recordkeeping on the road. Options are provided for tracking flight time, currency requirements, expenses, duty times, layovers and much more.

AVIATION SUPPLIES & ACADEMICS, INC.
Quality & Service You Can Depend On

Training Starts Here.
See our complete line of study aids, textbooks, pilot supplies and more at your local airport and in bookstores nationwide.
www.asa2fly.com | 800-ASA-2-FLY

Free app, free ebooks, free yourself...

The ASA Reader App
Aviation's Premier eLearning Solution

With access to over 80 titles and the flexibility to accommodate ebooks from other publishers, the ASA Reader puts your aviation library in the palm of your hand. Download for FREE at the App store or learn more at www.asa2fly.com/ASAReader.

Training Starts Here.
www.asa2fly.com | 800-ASA-2-FLY

UNIVERSITY AVIATION PRESS

Aviation Experts Wanted

University Aviation Press (UAP) supplies eBooks by respected subject experts to the worldwide aviation community. UAP provides a platform for invited educators, university professors, and flight training experts to publish and sell their ASA-vetted works to readers and students alike via desktop computer, smartphone and mobile tablet devices, including copyright and digital rights management (DRM) to protect their content. UAP eBooks can be read on any device or application compatible with an Adobe ID—including the free ASA Reader app.

Authors and educators are encouraged to visit the UAP website at **www.universityaviationpress.com** to explore the available titles and consider how they might benefit from using this platform to publish and distribute their own completed works.

www.universityaviationpress.com

A DIVISION OF AVIATION SUPPLIES & ACADEMICS, INC.